The Teacher's Calendar

School Year 2001-2002

The Day-by-Day Directory to Holidays, Historic Events, Birthdays and Special Days, Weeks and Months

Compiled by Sandy Whiteley

With Kathryn A. Keil and Sally M. Walker

Contemporary Books

Chicago New York San Francisco Lisbon London Madrid Mexico City Milan New Delhi San Juan Seoul Singapore Sydney Toronto

Library of Congress Cataloging-in-Publication Data

Whiteley, Sandra, 1943–
The teacher's calendar, 2001–2002 : the day-to-day directory to holidays, special days, weeks and months, festivals, historic events, and birthdays / compiled by Sandy Whiteley with Kathryn Keil and Sally M. Walker.
p. cm.
Includes bibliographical references and index.
ISBN 0-8092-9442-7
1. Holidays. 2. Birthdays. 3. Anniversaries. 4. Festivals. 5. Schedules, School. I. Keil, Kathryn. II. Walker, Sally M. M. III. Title. IV. Title: Teacher's calendar

LB3525.W55 2000
371.2'3—dc21 99-13240
ISSN 1533-0362 CIP

Contemporary Books
A Division of The ***McGraw-Hill*** *Companies*

1 2 3 4 5 6 7 8 9 0 MAL 0 9 8 7 6 5 4 3 2 1

ISBN 0-8092-9442-7

This book was set in Stone Print
Printed and bound by Malloy Lithographers

Cover design by Jeanette Wojtyla
Cover and interior illustrations by Dan Krovatin

NOTICE
Events listed herein are not necessarily endorsed by the editors or publisher. Every effort has been made to assure the correctness of all entries, but neither the authors nor the publisher can warrant their accuracy. IT IS IMPERATIVE, IF FINANCIAL PLANS ARE TO BE MADE IN CONNECTION WITH DATES OR EVENTS LISTED HEREIN, THAT PRINCIPALS BE CONSULTED FOR FINAL INFORMATION.

This book is printed on acid-free paper.

☆ *The Teacher's Calendar, 2001–2002* ☆

TABLE OF CONTENTS

How to Use This Book . . . . Inside front cover

Welcome to *The Teacher's Calendar* iv

Calendar of Events: Aug 1, 2001–July 31, 2002 1–237

National Education Goals 238

Calendar Information for 2001 239

Calendar Information for 2002 240

Perpetual Calendar 241–244

Selected Special Years 245

Chinese Calendar 245

Looking Forward 245

Some Facts About the States 246

State, Territory and Province Abbreviations 247

Some Facts About Canada 248

Some Facts About the Presidents 248–249

2001 American Library Association Awards for Children's Books 250

Resources 251

State Governors/US Senators/US Supreme Court 252

Alphabetical Index 253–284

★ in text indicates Presidential Proclamations

☆ *The Teacher's Calendar, 2001–2002* ☆

WELCOME TO *THE TEACHER'S CALENDAR*

Welcome to The Teacher's Calendar

This edition of *The Teacher's Calendar* contains more than 4,500 events that you can use in planning the school calendar, creating bulletin boards and developing lesson plans. Some of the entries were taken from the 2001 edition of *Chase's Calendar of Events*, a reference book which for 44 years has provided librarians and the media with events arranged day-by-day. Hundreds of entries were written especially for *The Teacher's Calendar*. For example, among the Birthdays Today entries are birthdays for authors of children's books. We've also added the dates of national professional meetings for teachers, children's book conferences and other events of interest to professional educators.

Types of Events

Presidential Proclamations: We have included in the day-by-day chronology proclamations that have continuing authority with a formula for calculating the dates of observance and those that have been issued consistently since 1995. The president issues proclamations only a few days before the actual event so it is possible that some dates may vary slightly for 2001–2002. The most recent proclamations can be found on the World Wide Web at the Federal Register Online: www.access.gpo.gov.

National holidays and State Days: Public holidays of other nations are gleaned from United Nations documents and from information from tourism agencies. Technically, the United States has no national holidays. Those holidays proclaimed by the president apply only to federal employees and to the District of Columbia. Governors of the states proclaim holidays for their states. In practice, federal holidays are usually proclaimed as state holidays as well. Some governors also proclaim holidays unique to their state but not all state holidays are commemorated with the closing of schools and offices.

Religious Observances: Principal observances of the Christian, Jewish and Muslim faiths are presented with background information from their respective calendars. We use anticipated dates for Muslim holidays. There is no single Hindu calendar and different Hindu sects define the Hindu lunar month differently. There is no single lunar calendar that serves as a model for all Buddhists either. Therefore, we are able to provide only a limited number of religious holidays for these faiths.

Historic Events and Birth Anniversaries: Dates for these entries have been gathered from a wide range of reference books. Most birthdays here are for people who are deceased. Birthdays of living people are usually listed under Birthdays Today.

Astronomical Phenomena: Information about eclipses, equinoxes and solstices, and moon phases is calculated from the annual publication, *Astronomical Phenomena*, from the US Naval Observatory. Dates for these events in *Astronomical Phenomena* are given in Universal Time (i.e., Greenwich Mean Time). We convert these dates and times into Eastern Standard or Eastern Daylight Time.

Sponsored Events: We obtain information on these events directly from their sponsors and provide contact information for the sponsoring organization.

Other Special Days, Weeks and Months: Information on these events is also obtained from their sponsors.

Process for Declaring Special Observances

How do special days, weeks and months get created? The president of the United States has the authority to declare a commemorative event by proclamation, but this is done infrequently. In 2000, for example, the president issued about 100 proclamations. Many of these, such as Mother's Day and Bill of Rights Week, were proclamations for which there was legislation giving continuing authority for a proclamation to be issued each year.

Until 1995, Congress was active in seeing that special observances were commemorated. Members of the Senate and House could introduce legislation for a special observance to commemorate people, events and other activities they thought worthy of national recognition. Because these bills took up a lot of time on the part of members of Congress, when Congress met in January 1995 to reform its rules and procedures, it was decided to discontinue this practice. Today, the Senate passes resolutions commemorating special days, weeks and months but these resolutions do not have the force of law.

It is not necessary to have the president or a senator declare a special day, week or month; many of the events in *The Teacher's Calendar* have been declared only by their sponsoring organizations.

Websites

Web addresses have been provided when relevant. These URLs were checked the first week in December 2000. Although we have tried to select sites maintained by the government, universities and other stable organizations, some of these sites undoubtedly will have disappeared by the time you try and look at them.

Curriculum Connections

These sidebars were written by Sally M. Walker, an author of children's books and a children's literature consultant, to give teachers ideas for integrating some of the events in *The Teacher's Calendar* into the classroom.

Acknowledgements

Thanks to the staff at the Evanston and Skokie public libraries who helped in the process of compiling *The Teacher's Calendar*. Special thanks to our colleagues at Contemporary Books: Martha Best, Denise Duffy-Fieldman, Gigi Grajdura, Richard Spears, Terry Stone and Jeanette Wojtyla. And now Associate Editor Kathy Keil and I invite you to join us in the celebration of the coming school year.

January 2001 — Sandy Whiteley, MLS, Editor

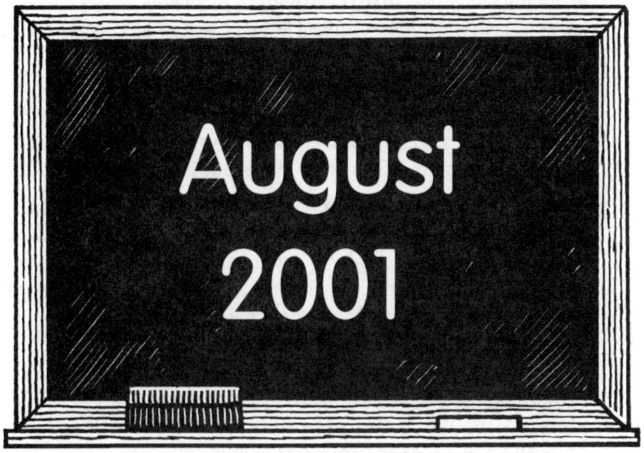

AUGUST 1 — WEDNESDAY

Day 213 — 152 Remaining

AMERICAN HISTORY ESSAY CONTEST. Aug 1–Dec 15. American History Committee activities are promoted throughout the year with the essay contest conducted in grades 5–8 beginning in August. Essays are submitted for judging by Dec 15, with the winners announced in April at the Daughters of the American Revolution Continental Congress. Events vary, but include programs, displays, spot announcements and recognition of essay writers. Essay topic can be obtained from DAR Headquarters. For info: Natl Soc Daughters of the American Revolution, Office of the Historian-General, Admin Bldg, 1776 D St NW, Washington, DC 20006-5392. Phone: (202) 628-1776.

BENIN, PEOPLE'S REPUBLIC OF: NATIONAL DAY. Aug 1. Public holiday. Commemorates independence from France in 1960. Benin at that time was known as Dahomey.

BURK, MARTHA (CALAMITY JANE): DEATH ANNIVERSARY. Aug 1, 1903. Known as a frontierswoman and companion to Wild Bill Hickock, Calamity Jane Burk was born Martha Jane Canary at Princeton, MO, in May 1852. As a young girl living in Montana, she became an excellent markswoman. She went to the Black Hills of South Dakota as a scout for a geological expedition in 1875. Several opposing traditions account for her nickname, one springing from her kindness to the less fortunate, while another attributes it to the harsh warnings she would give men who offended her. She died Aug 1, 1903, at Terry, SD, and was buried at Deadwood, SD, next to Wild Bill Hickock.

CHILDREN'S VISION AND LEARNING MONTH. Aug 1–31. A monthlong campaign encouraging parents to have their children's vision examined by an eye-care professional prior to the start of the new school year. For info: Mike Smith, Exec Dir, American Foundation for Vision Awareness (AFVA), 243 N Lindbergh Blvd, St. Louis, MO 63141. Phone: (800) 927-AFVA. Fax: (314) 991-4101. E-mail: afva@aol.com. Web: www.afva.org.

CHILDREN'S LITERATURE NEW ENGLAND INSTITUTE. Aug 1–4. Victoria University, Toronto, Canada. (Conference begins July 29.) Fifteenth annual conference, with the theme "Considering Boundaries." For info: Martha Walke, PO Box 1422, Pepperell, MA 01463. Phone: (978) 433-1911.

AUGUST 1–31
NATIONAL INVENTOR'S MONTH

Some inventions have changed the course of science history. One amazing invention was made in the 1590s when Zacharias Janssen, a Dutchman, put together the first microscope. Prior to that, people had known about the magnifying power of glass lenses; eyeglasses had been worn since the 1200–1300s. But Janssen's invention allowed human eyes to view extremely small objects clearly.

Anton van Leeuwenhoek invented a stronger single lens microscope in the 1670s that could magnify objects 270 times their actual size. In 1674, van Leeuwenhoek concluded that the tiny moving objects he saw with his lens were animals—a startling new thought to the scientific community of his time!

In 1931, Ernst Ruska and other scientists from Germany built the first electron microscope. This amazingly powerful microscope has let scientists examine particles that otherwise would be beyond our understanding.

If you don't have a microscope in your classroom, see if you can borrow one for a few days from another school—possibly the high school. There are a number of objects such as hair, paper, soil, vegetables and flowers that are fascinating to see and observe.

The Microscope Book, by Shar Levine & Leslie Johnstone (Sterling, 0-8069-4898-1, $19.95 Gr. 5 & up), is an excellent step-by-step guide for classroom microscope use. It contains numerous experiments and activities, all with an eye toward inquiry-based learning and discovery.

Encourage students to make detailed drawings of what they see through the microscope. Color the pictures and hang them around the classroom as a display of scientific art.

There are several books that will further extend student interest and involvement in the microscopic world. *Out of Sight*, by Seymour Simon (North Star, 1-5871-7011-6, $15.95 Gr. 2 & up), will grab student interest immediately. Simon goes beyond images taken through microscopes and also uses photos taken via stop action and satellite imagery. *Yikes! Your Body Up Close*, by Mike Janulewicz (Simon & Schuster, 0-689-81520-4, $15 Gr. 2–7), and *Yuck!*, by Robert Snedden (Simon & Schuster, 0-689-80676-0, $16 Gr. 2–7), explore objects that are fascinating and gross. *Sea Soup: Zooplankton*, by Mary Cerullo (Tilbury, 0-8844-8219-7, $16.95 Gr. 3 & up), has wonderful photomicrographs of the tiny creatures which form the base of the oceanic food chain. A teacher's guide is available as a separate purchase.

As a corollary to microscopes, some students might want to further research the development of lenses for eyeglasses and contact lenses. If they do, they will encounter Benjamin Franklin, who developed bifocal glasses.

COLORADO: ADMISSION DAY: 125th ANNIVERSARY. Aug 1, 1876. Colorado became the 38th state. Observed on the first Monday in August in Colorado (Aug 6 in 2001).

DIARY OF ANNE FRANK: THE LAST ENTRY: ANNIVERSARY. Aug 1, 1944. To escape deportation to concentration camps, the Jewish family of Otto Frank hid for two years in the warehouse of his food products business at Amsterdam. Gentile friends smuggled in food and other supplies during their confinement. Thirteen-year-old Anne Frank, who kept a journal during the time of their hiding, penned her last entry in the diary Aug 1, 1944: "[I] keep on trying to find a way of becoming what I would like to be, and what I could be, if . . . there weren't any other people living in the world." Three days later (Aug 4, 1944) Grüne Polizei raided the "Secret Annex" where the Frank family was hidden. Anne and her sister were sent to Bergen-Belsen concentration camp where Anne died at age 15, two months before the liberation of Holland. Young Anne's diary, later found in the family's hiding place, has been translated into 30 languages and has become a symbol of the indomitable strength of the human spirit. See also: "Frank, Anne: Birth Anniversary" (June 12). For more info: www.annefrank.com.

EMANCIPATION OF 500: ANNIVERSARY. Aug 1, 1791. Virginia planter Robert Carter III confounded his family and friends by filing a deed of emancipation for his 500 slaves. One of the wealthiest men in the state, Carter owned 60,000 acres over 18 plantations. The deed included the following words: "I have for some time past been convinced that to retain them in Slavery is contrary to the true principles of Religion and Justice and therefore it is my duty to manumit them." The document established a schedule by which 15 slaves would be freed each Jan 1, over a 21-year period, plus slave children would be freed at age 18 for females and 21 for males. It is believed this was the largest act of emancipation in US history and predated the Emancipation Proclamation by 70 years.

FIRST US CENSUS: ANNIVERSARY. Aug 1, 1790. The first census revealed that there were 3,939,326 citizens in the 16 states and the Ohio Territory. The US has taken a census every 10 years since 1790. The most recent one was taken in April 2000. For the population of the US today, calculated to the minute, go to www.census.gov/main/www/popclock.html.

KEY, FRANCIS SCOTT: BIRTH ANNIVERSARY. Aug 1, 1779. American attorney, social worker, poet and author of the US national anthem. While on a legal mission during the War of 1812, Key was detained on shipboard off Baltimore, during the British bombardment of Fort McHenry on the night of Sept 13–14, 1814. Thrilled to see the American flag still flying over the fort at daybreak, Key wrote the poem "The Star Spangled Banner." Printed in the *Baltimore American*, Sept 21, 1814, it was soon popularly sung to the music of an old English tune, "Anacreon in Heaven." It did not become the official US national anthem until 117 years later when, Mar 3, 1931, President Herbert Hoover signed into law an act for that purpose. Key was born at Frederick County, MD, and died at Baltimore, MD, Jan 11, 1843.

MITCHELL, MARIA: BIRTH ANNIVERSARY. Aug 1, 1818. An interest in her father's hobby and an ability for mathematics resulted in Maria Mitchell's becoming the first female professional astronomer. In 1847, while assisting her father in a survey of the sky for the US Coast Guard, Mitchell discovered a new comet and determined its orbit. She received many honors because of this, including being elected to the American Academy of Arts and Sciences—its first woman. Mitchell joined the staff at Vassar Female College in 1865—the first US female professor of astronomy—and in 1873 was a cofounder of the Association for the Advancement of Women. Born at Nantucket, MA, Mitchell died June 28, 1889, at Lynn, MA. For more info: *Maria's Comet*, by Deborah Hopkinson (Simon & Schuster, 0-689-81501-8, $16 Gr. K–3).

August 2001

S	M	T	W	T	F	S
			1	2	3	4
5	6	7	8	9	10	11
12	13	14	15	16	17	18
19	20	21	22	23	24	25
26	27	28	29	30	31	

NATIONAL BACK-TO-SCHOOL MONTH. Aug 1–31. Grassroots community activities such as free shopping sprees for kids to help impoverished children prepare mentally, emotionally and physically for the upcoming school year. A key component of the Back-To-School program is insuring that children have the proper clothes and supplies they need to feel good about going to school. To find out activities happening in your community call: Donna Strout, Operation Blessings Intl, 977 Centerville Turnpike, Virginia Beach, VA 23463. Phone: (757) 226-2443. Fax: (757) 226-6183. E-mail: donna.strout@OB.ORG.

NATIONAL COUNCIL FOR GEOGRAPHIC EDUCATION MEETING. Aug 1–4. Vancouver, BC, Canada. For info: Natl Council for Geographic Education, 16A Leonard Hall, Indiana Univ of PA, Indiana, PA 15705. Phone: (412) 357-6290. Web: www.ncge.org.

NATIONAL INVENTORS' MONTH. Aug 1–31. To educate the American public about the value of creativity and inventiveness and the importance of inventions and inventors to the quality of our lives. This will be accomplished through the placement of media stories about living inventors in most of the top national, local and trade publications, as well as through the electronic media. Sponsored by the United Inventors Association of the USA (UIA-USA), the Academy of Applied Science and *Inventors' Digest*. For info: Joanne Hayes-Rines, Inventors' Digest. Phone: (617) 367-4540. Fax: (617) 723-6988. E-mail: inventorsd@aol.com. Web: www.inventorsdigest.com. *See* Curriculum Connection.

OAK RIDGE ATOMIC PLANT BEGUN: ANNIVERSARY. Aug 1, 1943. Ground was broken at Oak Ridge, TN, for the first plant built to manufacture the uranium 235 needed to build an atomic bomb. The plant was largely completed by July of 1944 at a final cost of $280 million. By August 1945 the total cost for development of the A-bomb ran to $1 billion.

PRESIDENT'S ENVIRONMENTAL YOUTH AWARD NATIONAL COMPETITION. Aug 1–July 31, 2002. Young people in all 50 states are invited to participate in the President's Environmental Youth Award program, which offers them, individually and collectively, an opportunity to be recognized for environmental efforts in their community. The program encourages individuals, school classes, schools, summer camps and youth organizations to promote local environmental awareness and positive community involvement. For info: Doris Gillispie, Environmental Education Coord, US Environmental Protection Agency, 401 M St, #1707, Washington, DC 20460. Phone: (202) 260-8749. Fax: (202) 260-0790.

SCOTLAND: ABERDEEN INTERNATIONAL YOUTH FESTIVAL. Aug 1–11. Aberdeen, Scotland. Talented young people from all areas of the performing arts come from around the world to participate in this festival. Est attendance: 30,000. For info: Nicola Wallis, 3 Nutborn House, Clifton Rd, London, England SW19 4QT. Phone: (44) (20) 8946 2995. Fax: (44) (20) 8944 6507. E-mail: info@aberdeen-youth-fest.org.

SWITZERLAND: NATIONAL DAY. Aug 1. Anniversary of the founding of the Swiss Confederation. Commemorates a pact made in 1291. Parades, patriotic gatherings, bonfires and fireworks. Young citizens' coming-of-age ceremonies. Observed since 600th anniversary of Swiss Confederation was celebrated in 1891.

TRINIDAD AND TOBAGO: EMANCIPATION DAY. Aug 1. Public holiday.

UNITED NATIONS: INTERNATIONAL YEAR OF VOLUNTEERS. Aug 1–Dec 31, 2001. A year (which began Jan 1, 2001) to enhance the recognition, facilitation, networking and promotion of volunteer service in order to encourage service from an expanded number of individuals. The United Nations Volunteer Program is the focal point for the year. Info from: United Nations, Dept of Public Info, New York, NY 10017. Web: www.iyv2001.org.

UNITED NATIONS: YEAR OF DIALOGUE AMONG CIVILIZATIONS. Aug 1–Dec 31. The General Assembly (Res 53/22) invites governments, international organizations and non-governmental organizations to implement cultural, educational and social programs to promote the concept of dialogue among civilizations, including organizing conferences and seminars and disseminating information on the subject. For more info: United Nations, Dept of Public Info, New York, NY 10017.

WORLD WIDE WEB: ANNIVERSARY. Aug 1, 1990. The creation of what would become the World Wide Web was suggested this month by Tim Berners-Lee at CERN, the European Laboratory for Particle Physics at Switzerland. By October, he had designed a prototype Web browser. By early 1993, there were 50 Web servers worldwide.

BIRTHDAYS TODAY

Gail Gibbons, 57, author and illustrator (*Fire! Fire!*), born Oak Park, IL, Aug 1, 1944.

Edgerrin James, 23, football player, born Immokalee, FL, Aug 1, 1978.

AUGUST 2 — THURSDAY

Day 214 — 151 Remaining

ALBERT EINSTEIN'S ATOMIC BOMB LETTER: ANNIVERSARY. Aug 2, 1939. Albert Einstein, world-famous scientist, a refugee from Nazi Germany, wrote a letter to US President Franklin D. Roosevelt, first mentioning a possible "new phenomenon . . . chain reactions . . . vast amounts of power" and "the construction of bombs." "A single bomb of this type," he wrote, "carried by boat and exploded in a port, might very well destroy the whole port together with some of the surrounding territory." An historic letter that marked the beginning of atomic weaponry. Six years and four days later, Aug 6, 1945, the Japanese port of Hiroshima was destroyed by the first atomic bombing of a populated place.

COSTA RICA: FEAST OF OUR LADY OF THE ANGELS. Aug 2. National holiday. In honor of Costa Rica's patron saint.

DECLARATION OF INDEPENDENCE: OFFICIAL SIGNING: 225th ANNIVERSARY. Aug 2, 1776. Contrary to widespread misconceptions, the 56 signers did not sign as a group and did not do so July 4, 1776. John Hancock and Charles Thomson signed only draft copies that day, the official day the Declaration was adopted by Congress. The signing of the official declaration occurred Aug 2, 1776, when 50 men probably took part. George Washington, Patrick Henry and several others were not in Philadelphia and thus were unable to sign. Later that year, five more signed separately and one added his name in a subsequent year. (From "Signers of the Declaration . . ." US Dept of the Interior, 1975.) See also: "Declaration of Independence: Approval and Signing" (July 4). For more info: *Give Me Liberty! The Story of the Declaration of Independence*, by Russell Freedman (Holiday House, 0-8234-1448-5, $24.95 Gr. 5 & up).

DISABILITY DAY IN KENTUCKY. Aug 2.

HOLLING, HOLLING C.: BIRTH ANNIVERSARY. Aug 2, 1900. Author and illustrator (*Paddle-to-the-Sea*), born Holling Allison Clancy at Holling Corners, MI. Died Sept 7, 1973.

L'ENFANT, PIERRE CHARLES: BIRTH ANNIVERSARY. Aug 2, 1754. The architect, engineer and Revolutionary War officer who designed the plan for the city of Washington, DC, Pierre Charles L'Enfant was born at Paris, France. He died at Prince Georges County, MD, June 14, 1825.

MACEDONIA, FORMER YUGOSLAV REPUBLIC OF: NATIONAL DAY. Aug 2. Commemorates the nationalist uprising against the Ottoman Empire in 1903. Also known as St. Elias Day, the most sacred and celebrated day of the Macedonian people.

VIRGIN ISLANDS NATIONAL PARK ESTABLISHED: ANNIVERSARY. Aug 2, 1956. The Virgin Islands, including areas on St. John and St. Thomas, were established as a national park and preserve. On Oct 5, 1962, it was established that Virgin Islands National Park be enlarged to include offshore areas, including coral reefs, shorelines and sea grass beds. For more info: www.nps.gov/viis/index.htm.

BIRTHDAYS TODAY

Hallie Kate Eisenberg, 9, actress (*Beautiful, The Miracle Worker*), born East Brunswick, NJ, Aug 2, 1992.

James Howe, 55, author (the Bunnicula series), born Oneida, NY, Aug 2, 1946.

AUGUST 3 — FRIDAY

Day 215 — 150 Remaining

COLUMBUS SAILS FOR THE NEW WORLD: ANNIVERSARY. Aug 3, 1492. Christopher Columbus, "Admiral of the Ocean Sea," set sail half an hour before sunrise from Palos, Spain. With three ships, the *Niña*, the *Pinta* and the *Santa Maria*, and a crew of 90, he sailed "for Cathay" but found instead a New World of the Americas, first landing at Guanahani (San Salvador Island in the Bahamas) Oct 12. See also: "Columbus Day (Traditional)" (Oct 12).

EQUATORIAL GUINEA: ARMED FORCES DAY. Aug 3. National holiday.

GUINEA-BISSAU: COLONIZATION MARTYR'S DAY. Aug 3. National holiday is observed.

NIGER: INDEPENDENCE DAY. Aug 3. Commemorates the independence of this West African nation from France on this date in 1960.

OHIO STATE FAIR. Aug 3–19. Columbus, OH. Family fun, amusement rides, games, food booths, parades, entertainment, rodeos, circus, auto thrill show and tractor pulls. Est attendance: 900,000. For info: Ohio State Fair, 717 E 17th Ave, Columbus, OH 43211. Phone: (614) 644-4000. Fax: (614) 644-4031. Web: www.ohiostatefair.com.

SCOPES, JOHN T.: BIRTH ANNIVERSARY. Aug 3, 1900. Central figure in a cause célèbre (the "Scopes Trial" or the "Monkey Trial"), John Thomas Scopes was born at Paducah, KY. An obscure 24-year-old schoolteacher at the Dayton, TN, high school in 1925, he became the focus of world attention. Scopes never uttered a word at his trial, which was a contest between two of America's best-known lawyers (William Jennings Bryan and Clarence Darrow). The trial, July 10–21, 1925, resulted in Scopes's conviction "for teaching evolution" in Tennessee. He was fined $100. The verdict was upset on a technicality and the statute he was accused of breaching was repealed in 1967. Scopes died at Shreveport, LA, Oct 21, 1970. For more info: *The Scopes Monkey Trial: A Headline Court Case*, by Freya Ottem Hanson (Enslow, 0-7660-1388-X, $19.95 Gr. 8 & up) or www.umkc.edu/famoustrials.

SUSSEX COUNTY FARM AND HORSE SHOW/NEW JERSEY STATE FAIR. Aug 3–12. Augusta, NJ. The state's largest livestock and horse show also includes educational exhibits, amusements, commercial exhibits and entertainment. Gate opens 1 PM Friday and closes 7 PM Sunday. Est attendance: 220,000. For info: Howard Worts, Mgr, Sussex County Farm & Horse Show, PO Box 2456, Branchville, NJ 07826. Phone: (973) 948-5500. Fax: (973) 948-0147. E-mail: thefair@ptd.net. Web: www.newjerseystatefair.org.

WISCONSIN STATE FAIR. Aug 3–13. State Fair Park, Milwaukee, WI. Wisconsin celebrates its rural heritage at the state's most popular and most historic annual event. Features giant midway, 26 free stages, livestock, food and flower judging and top-name entertainment. [Call 24-hour recorded information line at 1-800-884-FAIR for performance times and dates.] Est attendance: 910,000. For info: PR Dept, Wisconsin State Fair Park, PO Box 14990, West Allis, WI 53214-0990. Fax: (414) 266-7007. E-mail: wsfp@sfp.state.wi.us. Web: www.wistatefair.com.

BIRTHDAYS TODAY

Mary Calhoun, 75, author (*High-Wire Henry*), born Keokuk, IA, Aug 3, 1926.

AUGUST 4 — SATURDAY

Day 216 — 149 Remaining

BURKINA FASO: REVOLUTION DAY. Aug 4. National holiday. Commemorates a 1983 coup.

COAST GUARD DAY. Aug 4. Celebrates anniversary of founding of the US Coast Guard in 1790.

MANDELA, NELSON: ARREST ANNIVERSARY. Aug 4, 1962. Nelson Rolihlahla Mandela, charismatic black South African leader, was born in 1918, the son of the Tembu tribal chief, at Umtata, Transkei territory of South Africa. A lawyer and political activist, Mandela, who in 1952 established the first black law partnership in South Africa, had been in conflict with the white government there much of his life. Acquitted of a treason charge after a trial that lasted from 1956 to 1961, he was apprehended again by security police, Aug 4, 1962. The subsequent trial, widely viewed as an indictment of white domination, resulted in Mandela's being sentenced to five years in prison. In 1963 he was taken from the Pretoria prison to face a new trial—for sabotage, high treason and conspiracy to overthrow the government—and in June 1964 he was sentenced to life in prison. See also: "Mandela, Nelson: Prison Release: Anniversary" (Feb 11).

NATIONAL MUSTARD DAY. Aug 4. Mustard lovers across the nation pay tribute to the king of condiments by slathering their favorite mustard on hot dogs, pretzels, licorice and even ice cream (an acquired taste)! The Mount Horeb Mustard Museum contains the world's largest collection of prepared mustards and mustard memorabilia. Celebration festivities include free hot dogs, mustard games and mustard squirting. Annually, the first Saturday in August. Est attendance: 1,000. For info: Barry M. Levenson, Curator, The Mount Horeb Mustard Museum, 109 E Main St, Mount Horeb, WI 53572. Phone: (608) 437-3986. Fax: (608) 437-4018. E-mail: curator@mustardmuseum.com. Web: www.mustardmuseum.com.

RICHARD, MAURICE ("ROCKET"): BIRTH ANNIVERSARY. Aug 4, 1921. Hockey Hall of Fame right wing, born at Montreal, QC, Canada. Died May 25, 2000, at Montreal.

SCHUMAN, WILLIAM HOWARD: BIRTH ANNIVERSARY. Aug 4, 1910. American composer who won the first Pulitzer Prize for composition and founded the Juilliard School of Music, was born at New York. His compositions include *American Festival Overture*, the baseball opera *The Mighty Casey* and *On Freedom's Ground*, written for the centennial of the Statue of Liberty in 1986. He was instrumental in the conception of the Lincoln Center for the Performing Arts and served as its first president. In 1985 he was awarded a special Pulitzer Prize. He also received a National Medal of Arts in 1985 and a Kennedy Center Honor in 1989. Schuman died at New York City, Feb 15, 1992.

BIRTHDAYS TODAY

Yasser Arafat, 72, president of the Palestinian National Authority, born Jerusalem, Aug 4, 1929.

Nancy White Carlstrom, 53, author (*Jesse Bear, What Will You Wear?; Does God Know How to Tie Shoes?*), born Washington, PA, Aug 4, 1948.

Roger Clemens, 39, baseball player, born Dayton, OH, Aug 4, 1962.

Jeff Gordon, 30, race car driver, born Pittsboro, IN, Aug 4, 1971.

AUGUST 5 — SUNDAY

Day 217 — 148 Remaining

AMERICAN FAMILY DAY IN ARIZONA. Aug 5. Commemorated on the first Sunday in August.

BATTLE OF MOBILE BAY: ANNIVERSARY. Aug 5, 1864. A Union fleet under Admiral David Farragut attempted to run past three Confederate forts into Mobile Bay, AL. After coming under fire, the Union fleet headed into a maze of underwater mines, known at that time as torpedos. The ironclad *Tecumseh* was sunk by a torpedo, after which Farragut is said to have exclaimed, "Damn the torpedos, full steam ahead." The Union fleet was successful and Mobile Bay was secured.

BURKINA FASO: REPUBLIC DAY. Aug 5. Burkina Faso (formerly Upper Volta) gained autonomy from France in 1960.

CROATIA: HOMELAND THANKSGIVING DAY. Aug 5. National holiday.

ELIOT, JOHN: BIRTH ANNIVERSARY. Aug 5, 1604. American "Apostle to the Indians," translator of the Bible into an Indian

August 2001

S	M	T	W	T	F	S
			1	2	3	4
5	6	7	8	9	10	11
12	13	14	15	16	17	18
19	20	21	22	23	24	25
26	27	28	29	30	31	

tongue (the first Bible to be printed in America), was born at Hertfordshire, England. He died at Roxbury, MA, May 21, 1690.

FIRST ENGLISH COLONY IN NORTH AMERICA: FOUNDING ANNIVERSARY. Aug 5, 1583. Sir Humphrey Gilbert, English navigator and explorer, aboard his sailing ship, the *Squirrel*, sighted the Newfoundland coast and took possession of the area around St. John's harbor in the name of the Queen, thus establishing the first English colony in North America. Gilbert was lost at sea, in a storm off the Azores, on his return trip to England.

LYNCH, THOMAS: BIRTH ANNIVERSARY. Aug 5, 1749. Signer, Declaration of Independence, born Prince George's Parish, SC. Died 1779 (lost at sea, exact date of death unknown).

SISTERS' DAY. Aug 5. Celebrating the spirit of sisterhood—sisters nationwide show appreciation and give recognition to one another for the special relationship they share. Send a card, make a phone call, share memories, photos, flowers, candy, etc. Sisters may include biological sisters, sisterly friends, etc. Annually, the first Sunday in August each year. For info: Tricia Eleogram, 666 Hawthorne, Memphis, TN 38107. Phone: (901) 725-5190 or (901) 755-0751. Fax: (901) 754-9923. E-mail: sistersday@aol.com.

WALLENBERG, RAOUL: BIRTH ANNIVERSARY. Aug 5, 1912. Swedish architect Raoul Gustaf Wallenberg was born at Stockholm, Sweden. He was the second person in history (Winston Churchill was the first) to be voted honorary American citizenship (US House of Representatives 396–2, Sept 22, 1981). He is credited with saving 100,000 Hungarian Jews from almost certain death at the hands of the Nazis during WWII. Wallenberg was arrested by Soviet troops at Budapest, Hungary, Jan 17, 1945, and, according to the official Soviet press agency Tass, died in prison at Moscow, July 17, 1947.

BIRTHDAYS TODAY

Neil Alden Armstrong, 71, former astronaut (first man to walk on moon), born Wapakoneta, OH, Aug 5, 1930.

Brendon Ryan Barrett, 15, actor (*Casper*), born Roseville, CA, Aug 5, 1986.

Patrick Aloysius Ewing, 39, basketball player, born Kingston, Jamaica, Aug 5, 1962.

AUGUST 6 — MONDAY

Day 218 — 147 Remaining

ANTIGUA AND BARBUDA: AUGUST MONDAY. Aug 6–7. The first Monday in August and the day following form the August Monday public holiday in this Caribbean nation.

ATOMIC BOMB DROPPED ON HIROSHIMA: ANNIVERSARY. Aug 6, 1945. At 8:15 AM, local time, an American B-29 bomber, the *Enola Gay*, dropped an atomic bomb named "Little Boy" over the center of the city of Hiroshima, Japan. The bomb exploded about 1,800 ft above the ground, killing more than 105,000 civilians and destroying the city. It is estimated that another 100,000 persons were injured and died subsequently as a direct result of the bomb and the radiation it produced. This was the first time in history that such a devastating weapon had been used by any nation.

AUSTRALIA: PICNIC DAY. Aug 6. The first Monday in August is a bank holiday in New South Wales and Picnic Day in Northern Territory, Australia.

BAHAMAS: EMANCIPATION DAY. Aug 6. Public holiday in Bahamas. Annually, the first Monday in August. Commemorates the emancipation of slaves by the British in 1834.

BOLIVIA: INDEPENDENCE DAY: ANNIVERSARY. Aug 6. National holiday. Gained freedom from Spain in 1825. Named after Simon Bolivar.

CANADA: CIVIC HOLIDAY. Aug 6. The first Monday in August is observed as a holiday in seven of Canada's 10 provinces. Civic Holiday in Manitoba, Northwest Territories, Ontario and Saskatchewan, British Columbia Day in British Columbia, New Brunswick Day in New Brunswick, Natal Day in Nova Scotia and Heritage Day in Alberta.

COLORADO: ADMISSION DAY: OBSERVED. Aug 6. Colorado. Annually, the first Monday in August. Commemorates Admission Day when Colorado became the 38th state, Aug 1, 1876.

AUGUST 6
BARBARA COONEY'S BIRTHDAY

Born on August 6, 1917, in Brooklyn, New York, Barbara Cooney is one of America's best-loved children's book illustrators. The clean, clear lines of her artwork bring a beauty, grace, and often humor which always perfectly complement the accompanying storyline. She won her first Caldecott Medal, for excellence in illustration, in 1959 for *Chanticleer and the Fox* and received the award a second time, in 1980, for *Ox-Cart Man*, written by Donald Hall.

You can incorporate her artwork and stories into the curriculum in many ways. Cooney's *Ox-Cart Man* illustrations are rendered in the style of Early American art. She chose this style deliberately to reflect the culture of early 19th century New England. Look at several other books illustrated by Cooney, *Tortillitas para Mama*, by Margot Griego, *Island Boy* (written by Cooney), and *Spirit Child*, retold by John Bierhorst, for example. Ask children to compare the illustrations and discuss how they reflect the cultures they depict. What items or articles of clothing can they find that reflect the story's culture?

Group Cooney's books according to art media used. (Copyright pages often list what materials were used to produce the illustrations.) Have children decide how using different media changes the viewers response to the story. What emotions are evoked?

Miss Rumphius is one of Cooney's loveliest books. Children will enjoy meeting Miss Rumphius and appreciate the strong bond between Miss Rumphius and her father. Planting flower seeds around the schoolyard or in classroom window boxes is a nice activity with a science application for units on seeds. In language arts, children could write their own stories of things they can do to make their world more beautiful. For geography, map Miss Rumphius' voyages.

Meet Eleanor Roosevelt in *Eleanor*, Cooney's picture book biography. Young Eleanor's mother was displeased because her daughter was born homely. Children will relate to Eleanor's hurt feelings and will be gratified to learn that Eleanor later became one of the world's most loved and honored ladies. Students may wish to seek further information about Eleanor Roosevelt. Talk about how Cooney's pictures depict Eleanor when she is sad and lonely, happy, brave, and finally as a mature, confident woman.

A delightful and imaginative art project could be centered around *Roxaboxen*, by Alice McLerran and illustrated by Cooney. Children can draw their own imaginary villages or even create them as three dimensional sculpture.

Barbara Cooney died in Portland, Maine on March 14, 2000.

COONEY, BARBARA: BIRTH ANNIVERSARY. Aug 6, 1917. Children's author and illustrator, born at Brooklyn, NY. Cooney won Caldecott Medals for *Ox-Cart Man* and *Chanticleer and the Fox*. Her 1982 publication *Miss Rumphius* received the National Book Award for 1983. She died at Portland, ME, Mar 14, 2000. *See* Curriculum Connection.

FARBER, NORMA: BIRTH ANNIVERSARY. Aug 6, 1909. Poet (*How the Hibernators Came to Bethlehem*), born at Boston, MA. Died Mar 21, 1984, at Boston.

FIRST WOMAN SWIMS THE ENGLISH CHANNEL: 75th ANNIVERSARY. Aug 6, 1926. The first woman to swim the English Channel was 19-year-old Gertrude Ederle of New York, NY. Her swim was completed in 14 hours and 31 minutes.

FLEMING, ALEXANDER: BIRTH ANNIVERSARY. Aug 6, 1881. Sir Alexander Fleming, Scottish bacteriologist, discoverer of penicillin and 1954 Nobel Prize recipient, was born at Lochfield, Scotland. He died at London, England, Mar 11, 1955.

"GREAT DEBATE": ANNIVERSARY. Aug 6–Sept 10, 1787. The Constitutional Convention engaged in the "Great Debate" over the draft constitution, during which it determined that Congress should have the right to regulate foreign trade and interstate commerce, established a four-year term of office for the president and appointed a five-man committee to prepare a final draft of the Constitution.

GRENADA: EMANCIPATION DAY. Aug 6. Grenada observes public holiday annually on the first Monday in August. Commemorates the emancipation of slaves by the British in 1834.

HALFWAY POINT OF SUMMER. Aug 6. On this day, 47 days will have elapsed and the equivalent will remain before Sept 22, 2001, the autumnal equinox and the beginning of autumn.

HIROSHIMA DAY: ANNIVERSARY. Aug 6. There are memorial observances in many places for victims of the first atomic bombing of a populated place, which occurred at Hiroshima, Japan, in 1945, when an American B-29 bomber dropped an atomic bomb over the center of the city. More than 205,000 civilians died either immediately in the explosion or subsequently of radiation. A peace festival is held annually at Peace Memorial Park at Hiroshima in memory of the victims of the bombing.

ICELAND: SHOP AND OFFICE WORKERS' HOLIDAY. Aug 6. In Iceland an annual holiday for shop and office workers is observed on the first Monday in August.

ICELAND: AUGUST HOLIDAY. Aug 6. National holiday. Commemorates the constitution of 1874.

JAMAICA: INDEPENDENCE DAY OBSERVED. Aug 6. National holiday observing achievement of Jamaican independence from Britain Aug 6, 1962. Annually, the first Monday in August.

August 2001

S	M	T	W	T	F	S
			1	2	3	4
5	6	7	8	9	10	11
12	13	14	15	16	17	18
19	20	21	22	23	24	25
26	27	28	29	30	31	

JAMAICA: INDEPENDENCE ACHIEVED: ANNIVERSARY. Aug 6, 1962. Jamaica attained its independence this date after centuries of British rule. Independence Day is observed on the first Monday in August.

NATIONAL SMILE WEEK. Aug 6–12. "Share a smile and it will come back to you, bringing happiness to you and the giver." Annually, the first Monday in August through the following Sunday. For info: Heloise, Newspaper Columnist, Box 795000, San Antonio, TX 78279. Fax: (210) 435-6473. E-mail: heloise@compuserve.com. Web: www.heloise.com.

ROOSEVELT, EDITH KERMIT CAROW: BIRTH ANNIVERSARY. Aug 6, 1861. Second wife of Theodore Roosevelt, 26th president of the US, whom she married in 1886. Born at Norwich, CT, she died at Long Island, NY, Sept 30, 1948.

VOTING RIGHTS ACT OF 1965 SIGNED: ANNIVERSARY. Aug 6, 1965. Signed into law by President Lyndon Johnson, the Voting Rights Act of 1965 was designed to thwart attempts to discriminate against minorities at the polls. The act suspended literacy and other disqualifying tests, authorized appointment of federal voting examiners and provided for judicial relief on the federal level to bar discriminatory poll taxes. Congress voted to extend the Act in 1975, 1984 and 1991.

ZAMBIA: YOUTH DAY. Aug 6. National holiday. Focal point is Lusaka's Independence Stadium. Annually, the first Monday in August.

BIRTHDAYS TODAY

Frank Asch, 55, author and illustrator (*Mooncake*), born Somerville, NJ, Aug 6, 1946.

Catherine Hicks, 50, actress ("7th Heaven"), born Scottsdale, AZ, Aug 6, 1951.

David Robinson, 36, basketball player, born Key West, FL, Aug 6, 1965.

AUGUST 7 — TUESDAY

Day 219 — 146 Remaining

BUNCHE, RALPH JOHNSON: BIRTH ANNIVERSARY. Aug 7, 1904. American statesman, UN official, Nobel Peace Prize recipient (the first black to win the award), born at Detroit, MI. Died Dec 9, 1971, at New York, NY. For more info: *Ralph J. Bunch: Peacemaker*, by Patricia and Fredrick McKissack (Enslow, 0-8949-0300-4, $14.95 Gr. K–3).

COLOMBIA: BATTLE OF BOYACÁ DAY. Aug 7. National holiday. Commemorates 1819 victory over Spanish forces.

CÔTE D'IVOIRE: NATIONAL DAY. Aug 7. Commemorates the independence of the Ivory Coast from France in 1960.

DESERT SHIELD: ANNIVERSARY. Aug 7, 1990. Five days after the Iraqi invasion of Kuwait, US President George Bush ordered the military buildup that would become known as Desert Shield, to prevent further Iraqi advances. In January 1991, this would lead to the Persian Gulf War or Desert Storm.

FIRST PICTURE OF EARTH FROM SPACE: ANNIVERSARY. Aug 7, 1959. US satellite *Explorer VI* transmitted the first picture of Earth from space. For the first time we had a likeness of our planet based on more than projections and conjectures. For a current view of Earth from a satellite, visit Earth Viewer: www.fourmilab.to/earthview.

NATIONAL NIGHT OUT. Aug 7. Designed to heighten crime prevention awareness and to promote police-community partnerships. Annually, the first Tuesday in August. For info: Matt A. Peskin, Dir, Natl Assn of Town Watch, PO Box 303, Wynnewood, PA 19096. Phone: (610) 649-7055 or (800) 648-3688. Web: www.natw.org.

PURPLE HEART: ANNIVERSARY. Aug 7, 1782. At Newburgh, NY, General George Washington ordered the creation of a Badge of Military Merit. The badge consisted of a purple cloth heart with silver braided edge. Only three are known to have been awarded during the Revolutionary War. The award was reinstituted on the bicentennial of Washington's birth, Feb 22, 1932, and recognizes those wounded in action.

US WAR DEPARTMENT ESTABLISHED: ANNIVERSARY. Aug 7, 1789. The second presidential cabinet department, the War Department, was established by Congress. In 1947 it became part of the Department of Defense. See also: "US Department of Defense Established" (July 26).

BIRTHDAYS TODAY

Betsy Byars, 73, author (*The Summer of the Swans*, the Bingo Brown series), born Charlotte, NC, Aug 7, 1928.

Joy Cowley, 65, author (*Red-Eyed Tree Frog*), born New Zealand, Aug 7, 1936.

Maia Wojciechowska, 74, author (*Shadow of a Bull*), born Warsaw, Poland, Aug 7, 1927.

AUGUST 8 — WEDNESDAY

Day 220 — 145 Remaining

BHUTAN: NATIONAL DAY. Aug 8. National holiday observed commemorating independence from India in 1949.

BONZA BOTTLER DAY™. Aug 8. To celebrate when the number of the day is the same as the number of the month. Bonza Bottler Day™ is an excuse to have a party at least once a month. For info: Gail M. Berger, 109 Matthew Ave, Poca, WV 25159. Phone: (304) 776-7746. E-mail: gberger5@aol.com.

HENSON, MATTHEW A.: BIRTH ANNIVERSARY. Aug 8, 1866. American black explorer, born at Charles County, MD. He met Robert E. Peary while working in a Washington, DC, store in 1888 and was hired to be Peary's valet. He accompanied Peary on his seven subsequent Arctic expeditions. During the successful 1908–09 expedition to the North Pole, Henson and two of the four Eskimo guides reached their destination on Apr 6, 1909. Peary arrived minutes later and verified the location. Henson's account of the expedition, *A Negro Explorer at the North Pole*, was published in 1912. In addition to the Congressional medal awarded all members of the North Pole expedition, Henson received the Gold Medal of the Geographical Society of Chicago and, at 81, was made an honorary member of the Explorers Club at New York, NY. Died Mar 9, 1955, at New York, NY. For more info: *Matthew Henson and the North Pole Expedition*, by Ann Graham Gaines (Child's World, 1-56766-743-0, $25.64 Gr. 4–6).

INDIANA STATE FAIR. Aug 8–19. Indiana State Fairgrounds Event Center, Indianapolis, IN. Top-rated livestock exhibition, world-class harness racing, top country music, giant midway and Pioneer Village. Est attendance: 725,000. For info: Jeff Fites, Media Relations Dir, Indiana State Fair, 1202 E 38th St, Indianapolis, IN 46205-2869. Phone: (317) 927-7500. Fax: (317) 927-7578. Web: www.iquest.net/statefair.

ODIE: BIRTHDAY. Aug 8, 1978. Commemorates the birthday of Odie, Garfield's sidekick, who first appeared in the Garfield comic strip in 1978. For info: Kim Campbell, Paws, Inc, 5440 E Co Rd, 450 N, Albany, IN 47320. Web: www.garfield.com.

RAWLINGS, MARJORIE KINNAN: BIRTH ANNIVERSARY. Aug 8, 1896. American short-story writer and novelist (*The Yearling*), born at Washington, DC. Rawlings died at St. Augustine, FL, Dec 14, 1953. For a study guide to *The Yearling*: glencoe.com/sec/literature/litlibrary.

TANZANIA: FARMERS' DAY. Aug 8. National holiday. Also called "Nane Nane" or "8-8."

BIRTHDAYS TODAY

JC Chasez, 25, singer ('N Sync), born Joshua Scott, Washington, DC, Aug 8, 1976.

Jane Dee Hull, 66, Governor of Arizona (R), born Kansas City, MO, Aug 8, 1935.

AUGUST 9 — THURSDAY

Day 221 — 144 Remaining

ATOMIC BOMB DROPPED ON NAGASAKI: ANNIVERSARY. Aug 9, 1945. Three days after the atomic bombing of Hiroshima, an American B-29 bomber named *Bock's Car* left its base on Tinian Island carrying a plutonium bomb nicknamed "Fat Man." Its target was the Japanese city of Kokura, but because of clouds and poor visibility the bomber headed for a secondary target, Nagasaki, where at 11:02 AM, local time, it dropped the bomb, killing an estimated 70,000 persons and destroying about half the city. The next day the Japanese government surrendered, bringing WWII to an end.

COCHRAN, JACQUELINE: DEATH ANNIVERSARY. Aug 9, 1980. American pilot Jacqueline Cochran was born at Pensacola, FL, in 1910. She began flying in 1932 and by the time of her death she had set more distance, speed and altitude records than any other pilot, male or female. She was founder and head of the WASPs (Women's Air Force Service Pilots) during WWII. She also won the Distinguished Service Medal in 1945 and the US Air Force Distinguished Flying Cross in 1969. She died at Indio, CA.

IOWA STATE FAIR. Aug 9–19. Iowa State Fairgrounds, Des Moines, IA. One of America's oldest and largest state fairs with one of the world's largest livestock shows. Ten-acre carnival, superstar grandstand stage shows, track events, spectacular free entertainment. 160-acre campgrounds. Est attendance: 970,000. For info: Kathie Swift, Mktg Dir, Iowa State Fair, Statehouse, 400 E 14th St, Des Moines, IA 50319. Phone: (515) 262-3111. Fax: (515) 262-6906. Web: iowastatefair.org.

LASSEN VOLCANIC NATIONAL PARK ESTABLISHED: 85th ANNIVERSARY. Aug 9, 1916. California's Lassen Peak and Cinder Cone National Monument, proclaimed May 6, 1907, and other wilderness land were combined and established as a national park. For more info: www.nps.gov/lavo/index.htm.

MISSOURI STATE FAIR. Aug 9–19. Sedalia, MO. Livestock shows, commercial and competitive exhibits, horse show, car races, tractor pulls, carnival and headline musical entertainment.

Economical family entertainment. Est attendance: 350,000. For info: Kimberly Allen, PR Dir, Missouri State Fair, 2503 W 16th, Sedalia, MO 65301. Phone: (816) 530-5600. Fax: (816) 530-5609. Web: www.mostatefair.com.

NIXON RESIGNS: ANNIVERSARY. Aug 9, 1974. Richard Milhous Nixon's resignation from the presidency of the US, which he had announced in a speech to the American people on Thursday evening, Aug 8, became effective at noon. Nixon, under threat of impeachment as a result of the Watergate scandal, became the first person to resign the presidency. He was succeeded by Vice President Gerald Rudolph Ford, the first person to serve as vice president and president without having been elected to either office. Ford granted Nixon a "full, free and absolute pardon" Sept 8, 1974. Although Nixon was the first US president to resign, two vice presidents had resigned: John C. Calhoun, Dec 18, 1832, and Spiro T. Agnew, Oct 10, 1973.

PERSEID METEOR SHOWERS. Aug 9–13. Among the best-known and most spectacular meteor showers are the Perseids, peaking about Aug 10–12. As many as 50–100 may be seen in a single night. Wish upon a "falling star"!

PIAGET, JEAN: BIRTH ANNIVERSARY. Aug 9, 1896. Born at Neuchâtel, Switzerland, Piaget is the major figure in developmental psychology. His theory of cognitive development still influences educators today. Piaget died at Geneva, Switzerland, Sept 16, 1980.

SINGAPORE: NATIONAL DAY. Aug 9, 1965. Most festivals in Singapore are Chinese, Indian or Malay, but celebration of national day is shared by all to commemorate the withdrawal of Singapore from Malaysia and its becoming an independent state in 1965. Music, parades, dancing.

SOUTH AFRICA: NATIONAL WOMEN'S DAY: 45th ANNIVERSARY. Aug 9. National holiday. Commemorates the march of women in Pretoria to protest the pass laws in 1956.

TRAVERS, P.L.: BIRTH ANNIVERSARY. Aug 9, 1899. Famous for her Mary Poppins series, P.L. Travers was born at Maryborough, Queensland, Australia. *Mary Poppins* was made into a movie by Disney in 1964. Travers died at London, England, Apr 23, 1996.

UNITED NATIONS: INTERNATIONAL DAY OF THE WORLD'S INDIGENOUS PEOPLE. Aug 9. On Dec 23, 1994, the General Assembly decided that the International Day of the World's Indigenous People shall be observed every year during the International Decade of the World's Indigenous People (1994–2004) (Res 49/214). The date marks the anniversary of the first day of the meeting in 1992 of the Working Group on Indigenous Populations of the Subcommission on Prevention of Discrimination and Protection of Minorities. For info: United Nations, Dept of Public Info, Public Inquiries Unit, RM GA-57, New York, NY 10017. Phone: (212) 963-4475. Fax: (212) 963-0071. E-mail: inquiries@un.org.

August 2001

S	M	T	W	T	F	S
			1	2	3	4
5	6	7	8	9	10	11
12	13	14	15	16	17	18
19	20	21	22	23	24	25
26	27	28	29	30	31	

VEEP DAY. Aug 9. Commemorates the day in 1974 when Richard Nixon's resignation let Gerald Ford succeed to the presidency of the US. This was the first time the new Constitutional provisions for presidential succession in the Twenty-Fifth Amendment of 1967 were used. For info: c/o Bob Birch, The Puns Corps, PO Box 2364, Falls Church, VA 22042-0364. Phone: (703) 533-3668.

WEBSTER-ASHBURTON TREATY SIGNED: ANNIVERSARY. Aug 9, 1842. The treaty delimiting the eastern section of the Canadian-American border was negotiated by the US Secretary of State, Daniel Webster, and Alexander Baring, president of the British Board of Trade. The treaty established the boundaries between the St. Croix and Connecticut rivers, between Lake Superior and the Lake of the Woods and between Lakes Huron and Superior. The treaty was signed at Washington, DC.

BIRTHDAYS TODAY

William Daley, 53, former US Secretary of Commerce (Clinton administration), born Chicago, IL, Aug 9, 1948.

Chamique Holdsclaw, 24, basketball player, born Flushing, NY, Aug 9, 1977.

Whitney Houston, 38, singer ("And I Will Always Love You"), actress (*Waiting to Exhale*), born Newark, NJ, Aug 9, 1963.

Brett Hull, 37, hockey player, born Belleville, ON, Canada, Aug 9, 1964.

Hazel Hutchins, 49, author (*One Duck*), born Calgary, AB, Canada, Aug 9, 1952.

Ashley Johnson, 18, actress ("Growing Pains," voice of Gretchen on "Recess"), born Camarillo, CA, Aug 9, 1983.

Patricia McKissack, 57, author, with her husband Fredrick (*Christmas in the Big House*), born Nashville, TN, Aug 9, 1944.

Deion Sanders, 34, football and baseball player, born Ft Meyers, FL, Aug 9, 1967.

Seymour Simon, 70, author (*Earthquakes, The Universe*), born New York, NY, Aug 9, 1931.

AUGUST 10 — FRIDAY

Day 222 — 143 Remaining

ECUADOR: INDEPENDENCE DAY. Aug 10. National holiday. Celebrates declaration of independence in 1809. Freedom from Spain attained May 24, 1822.

HOOVER, HERBERT CLARK: BIRTH ANNIVERSARY. Aug 10, 1874. The 31st president (Mar 4, 1929–Mar 3, 1933) of the US was born at West Branch, IA. Hoover was the first president born west of the Mississippi River and the first to have a telephone on his desk (installed Mar 27, 1929). "Older men declare war. But it is youth that must fight and die," he said at Chicago, IL, at the Republican National Convention, June 27, 1944. Hoover died at New York, NY, Oct 20, 1964. The Sunday nearest Aug 10th is observed in Iowa as Herbert Hoover Day (Aug 12 in 2001). For info: www.ipl.org/ref/POTUS.

ILLINOIS STATE FAIR. Aug 10–19. Springfield, IL. Amusement rides, food booths, parade, various types of entertainment, rodeos and tractor pulls. For info: Joe Saputo, Illinois State Fair, PO Box 19427, Springfield, IL 62794. Phone: (217) 782-6661. Fax: (217) 782-9115. Web: www.state.il.us/fair.

JAPAN'S UNCONDITIONAL SURRENDER: ANNIVERSARY. Aug 10, 1945. A gathering to discuss surrender terms took place in Emperor Hirohito's bomb shelter; the participants were stalemated. Hirohito settled the question, believing continuation of the war would only result in further loss of Japanese lives. A message was transmitted to Japanese ambassadors in Switzerland and Sweden to accept the terms issued at Potsdam, July 26, 1945, except that the Japanese emperor's sovereignty must be maintained. The Allies devised a plan under which the emperor and the Japanese government would administer under the rule of the Supreme Commander of the Allied Powers and the Japanese surrendered.

MISSOURI: ADMISSION DAY: ANNIVERSARY. Aug 10. Became 24th state in 1821.

SMITHSONIAN INSTITUTION FOUNDED: ANNIVERSARY. Aug 10, 1846. Founding of the Smithsonian Institution at Washington, DC, designed to hold the many scientifc, historical and cultural collections that belong to the US. The National Museum of Natural History, the National Zoo, the National Museum of American Art, the National Air and Space Museum and the National Gallery of Art are among the museums in the Smithsonian Institution. For info for teachers from the Smithsonian: educate.si.edu. For info: Smithsonian Institution, 900 Jefferson Dr SW, Washington, DC 20560. Phone: (202) 357-2700.

BIRTHDAYS TODAY

Thomas J. Dygard, 70, author of sports books (*Game Plan*), born Little Rock, AR, Aug 10, 1931.

AUGUST 11 — SATURDAY

Day 223 — 142 Remaining

ATCHISON, DAVID R.: BIRTH ANNIVERSARY. Aug 11, 1807. Missouri legislator who was president of the US for one day. Born at Frogtown, KY, Atchison's strong pro-slavery opinions made his name prominent in legislative debates. He served as president pro tempore of the Senate a number of times, and he became president of the US for one day—Sunday, Mar 4, 1849—pending the swearing in of President-elect Zachary Taylor, Mar 5, 1849. The city of Atchison, KS, and the county of Atchison, MO, are named for him. He died at Gower, MO, Jan 26, 1886.

BUD BILLIKEN PARADE. Aug 11. Chicago, IL. A parade especially for children begun in 1929 by Robert S. Abbott. The second largest parade in the US, it features bands, floats, drill teams and celebrities. Annually, the second Saturday in August. For info: Michael Brown, PR Dir, Chicago Defender Charities, 2400 S Michigan, Chicago, IL 60616. Phone: (312) 225-2400. Fax: (312) 255-9231.

CHAD: INDEPENDENCE DAY. Aug 11. National holiday. Commemorates independence from France in 1960.

FREDERICK DOUGLASS SPEAKS: ANNIVERSARY. Aug 11, 1841. Having escaped from slavery only three years earlier, Frederick Douglass was legally a fugitive when he first spoke before an audience. At an antislavery convention on Nantucket Island, Douglass spoke simply but eloquently about his life as a slave. His words were so moving that he was asked to become a full-time lecturer for the Massachusetts Anti-Slavery Society. Douglass became a brilliant orator, writer and abolitionist who championed the rights of blacks as well as the rights of all humankind.

FREEMAN, DON: BIRTH ANNIVERSARY. Aug 11, 1908. Author and illustrator (*Corduroy*), born at San Diego, CA. Died Feb 1, 1978.

HALEY, ALEX PALMER: 80th BIRTH ANNIVERSARY. Aug 11, 1921. Born at Ithaca, NY, Alex Haley was raised by his grandmother at Henning, TN. In 1939 he entered the US Coast Guard and served as a cook, but eventually he became a writer and college professor. His first book, *The Autobiography of Malcolm X*, sold six million copies and was translated into eight languages. *Roots*, his Pulitzer Prize–winning book published in 1976, sold millions, was translated into 37 languages and was made into an eight-part TV miniseries in 1977. The story generated an enormous interest in family ancestry. Haley died at Seattle, WA, Feb 13, 1992.

MONTANAFAIR. Aug 11–18. MetraPark, Billings, MT. Montana's biggest event featuring exhibits, livestock events, carnival, rodeo and entertainment. Est attendance: 240,000. For info: MetraPark, PO Box 2514, Billings, MT 59103. Phone: (406) 256-2400.

"RUGRATS" TV PREMIERE: ANNIVERSARY. Aug 11, 1991. This animated cartoon features the toddler children of a trio of suburban families. One-year-old Tommy Pickles and his dog Spike play with 15-month-old twins Phil and Lil DeVille. Other characters include Tommy's three-year-old cousin Angelica, two-year-old Chuckie and Tommy's new brother Dil. Created by the animators of "The Simpsons." *The Rugrats Movie* was released in 1998 and *The Rugrats in Paris* in 2000.

SAINT CLARE OF ASSISI: FEAST DAY. Aug 11, 1253. Chiara Favorone di Offreduccio, a religious leader inspired by St. Francis of Assisi, was the first woman to write her own religious order rule. Born at Assisi, Italy, July 16, 1194, she died there Aug 11, 1253. A "Privilege of Poverty" freed her order from any constraint to accept material security, making the "Poor Clares" totally dependent on God.

WYOMING STATE FAIR. Aug 11–18. Douglas, WY. Recognizing the products, achievements and cultural heritage of the people of Wyoming. Bringing together rural and urban citizens for an inexpensive, entertaining and educational experience. Features Livestock show for beef, swine, sheep and horses, Junior Livestock show for beef, swine, sheep, horses, dogs and rabbits, competitions and displays for culinary arts, needlework, visual arts and floriculture, 4-H and FFA County Chapters State qualifications competitions, Youth Talent Show, Demo Derby, live entertainment, midway, PRCA Rodeo and an All Girl Rodeo (rough stock). Est attendance: 82,000. For info: Wyoming State Fair, Drawer 10, Douglas, WY 82633. Phone: (307) 358-2398. Fax: (307) 358-6030. E-mail: wystfair@coffey.com.

ZIMBABWE: HEROES' DAY. Aug 11. National holiday. Followed by Defense Forces Day on Aug 12.

BIRTHDAYS TODAY

Joanna Cole, 57, author (the Magic School Bus series), born Newark, NJ, Aug 11, 1944.

Will Friedle, 25, actor ("Boy Meets World"), born Hartford, CT, Aug 11, 1976.

Hulk Hogan, 48, wrestler, actor, born Terry Gene Bollea, Augusta, GA, Aug 11, 1953.

Tim Hutchinson, 52, US Senator (R, Arkansas), born Gravette, AR, Aug 11, 1949.

Stephen Wozniak, 51, Apple computer cofounder, born Sunnyvale, CA, Aug 11, 1950.

AUGUST 12 — SUNDAY

Day 224 — 141 Remaining

KING PHILIP ASSASSINATION: 325th ANNIVERSARY. Aug 12, 1676. Philip, son of Massasoit, chief of the Wampanog tribe, was killed near Mt Hope, RI, by a renegade Indian of his own tribe, bringing to an end the first and bloodiest war between American Indians and white settlers of New England, a war that had raged for nearly two years and was known as King Philip's War.

MOON PHASE: LAST QUARTER. Aug 12. Moon enters Last Quarter phase at 3:53 PM, EDT.

SPACE MILESTONE: *ECHO I* (US): ANNIVERSARY. Aug 12, 1960. First successful communications satellite in Earth's orbit launched, used to relay voice and TV signals from one ground station to another.

THAILAND: BIRTHDAY OF THE QUEEN. Aug 12. The entire kingdom of Thailand celebrates the birthday of Queen Sirikit.

BIRTHDAYS TODAY

Ruth Stiles Gannett, 78, author (*My Father's Dragon, Elmer and the Dragon*), born New York, NY, Aug 12, 1923.

Mary Ann Hoberman, 71, author (*One of Each*), born Stamford, CT, Aug 12, 1930.

Ann Martin, 46, author (The Baby-Sitters Club series), born Princeton, NJ, Aug 12, 1955.

Fredrick McKissack, 62, author, with his wife Patricia (*Christmas in the Big House*), born Nashville, TN, Aug 12, 1939.

Walter Dean Myers, 64, author (*Slam!, Harlem: A Poem*), born Martinsburg, WV, Aug 12, 1937.

Kyla Pratt, 13, actress (*Dr. Dolittle*, "The Baby-Sitters Club"), born North Kansas City, MO, Aug 12, 1988.

Pete Sampras, 30, tennis player, born Washington, DC, Aug 12, 1971.

Antoine Walker, 25, basketball player, born Chicago, IL, Aug 12, 1976.

AUGUST 13 — MONDAY

Day 225 — 140 Remaining

BERLIN WALL ERECTED: 40th ANNIVERSARY. Aug 13, 1961. Early in the morning, the East German government closed the border between the east and west sectors of Berlin with barbed wire fence to discourage further population movement to the west. Telephone and postal services were interrupted, and, later in the week, a concrete wall was built to strengthen the barrier between official crossing points. The dismantling of the wall began Nov 9, 1989. See also: "Berlin Wall Opened: Anniversary" (Nov 9). For more info: *The Berlin Wall*, by R.G. Grant (Raintree, 0-8172-5017-4, $28.55 Gr. 5–7).

CANADA: YUKON DISCOVERY DAY. Aug 13. In the Klondike region of the Yukon, at Bonanza Creek (formerly known as Rabbit Creek), George Washington Carmack discovered gold Aug 16 or 17, 1896. During the following year more than 30,000 people joined the gold rush to the area. Anniversary is celebrated as a holiday (Discovery Day) in the Yukon, on nearest Monday.

CAXTON, WILLIAM: BIRTH ANNIVERSARY. Aug 13, 1422. First English printer, born at Kent, England. Died at London, England, 1491. Caxton produced the first book printed in English (while working for a printer at Bruges, Belgium), the *Recuyell of the Histories of Troy*, in 1476, and in the autumn of 1476 set up a print shop at Westminster, becoming the first printer in England.

CENTRAL AFRICAN REPUBLIC: INDEPENDENCE DAY. Aug 13. Commemorates Proclamation of Independence from France of the Central African Republic in 1960.

OAKLEY, ANNIE: BIRTH ANNIVERSARY. Aug 13, 1860. Annie Oakley was born at Darke County, OH. She developed an eye as a markswoman early as a child, becoming so proficient that she was able to pay off the mortgage on her family farm by selling the game she killed. A few years after defeating vaudeville marksman Frank Butler in a shooting match, she married him and they toured as a team until joining Buffalo Bill's Wild West Show in 1885. She was one of the star attractions for 17 years. She died Nov 3, 1926, at Greenville, OH.

STONE, LUCY: BIRTH ANNIVERSARY. Aug 13, 1818. American women's rights pioneer, born near West Brookfield, MA, Lucy Stone dedicated her life to the abolition of slavery and the emancipation of women. A graduate of Oberlin College, she had to finance her education by teaching for nine years because her father did not favor college education for women. An eloquent speaker for her causes, she headed the list of 89 men and women who signed the call to the first national Woman's Rights Convention, held at Worcester, MA, October 1850. On May 1, 1855, she married Henry Blackwell. She and her husband aided in the founding of the American Suffrage Association, taking part in numerous referendum campaigns to win suffrage amendments to state constitutions. She died Oct 18, 1893, at Dorchester, MA.

TUNISIA: WOMEN'S DAY. Aug 13. General holiday. Celebration of independence of women.

BIRTHDAYS TODAY

Fidel Castro, 74, President of Cuba, born Mayari, Cuba, Aug 13, 1927.

AUGUST 14 — TUESDAY

Day 226 — 139 Remaining

ATLANTIC CHARTER SIGNING: 60th ANNIVERSARY. Aug 14, 1941. The charter grew out of a three-day conference aboard ship in the Atlantic Ocean, off the Newfoundland coast, and stated policies and goals for the postwar world. The eight-point agreement was signed by US President Franklin D. Roosevelt and British Prime Minister Winston S. Churchill.

SOCIAL SECURITY ACT: ANNIVERSARY. Aug 14, 1935. The Congress approved the Social Security Act, which contained provisions for the establishment of a Social Security Board to administer federal old-age and survivors' insurance in the US. By signing the bill into law, President Franklin D. Roosevelt was fulfilling a 1932 campaign promise. For more info: www.ssa.gov.

V-J (VICTORY OVER JAPAN) DAY: 55th ANNIVERSARY. Aug 14, 1945. Anniversary of President Truman's announcement that Japan had surrendered to the Allies, setting off celebrations across the nation. Official ratification of surrender occurred aboard the USS *Missouri* at Tokyo Bay, Sept 2 (Far Eastern time).

BIRTHDAYS TODAY

Lynne Cheney, 60, Second Lady, wife of Richard Cheney, 46th vice president of US, born Casper, WY, Aug 14, 1941.

Earvin (Magic) Johnson, Jr, 42, former basketball player, born Lansing, MI, Aug 14, 1959.

Gary Larson, 51, cartoonist ("The Far Side"), born Tacoma, WA, Aug 14, 1950.

August 2001

S	M	T	W	T	F	S
			1	2	3	4
5	6	7	8	9	10	11
12	13	14	15	16	17	18
19	20	21	22	23	24	25
26	27	28	29	30	31	

Alice Provensen, 83, author and illustrator, with her husband Martin (Caldecott for *The Glorious Flight: Across the Channel with Louis Bleriot*), born Chicago, IL, Aug 14, 1918.

AUGUST 15 — WEDNESDAY

Day 227 — 138 Remaining

ASSUMPTION OF THE VIRGIN MARY. Aug 15. Greek and Roman Catholic churches celebrate Mary's ascent to Heaven.

BONAPARTE, NAPOLEON: BIRTH ANNIVERSARY. Aug 15, 1769. Anniversary of birth of French emperor Napoleon Bonaparte on the island of Corsica. He died in exile May 5, 1821, on the island of St. Helena. Public holiday at Corsica, France.

CHAUVIN DAY. Aug 15. A day named for Nicholas Chauvin, French soldier from Rochefort, France, who idolized Napoleon and who eventually became a subject of ridicule because of his blind loyalty and dedication to anything French. Originally referring to bellicose patriotism, chauvinism has come to mean blind or absurdly intense attachment to any cause. Observed on Napoleon's birth anniversary because Chauvin's birth date is unknown.

CONGO (BRAZZAVILLE): NATIONAL HOLIDAY. Aug 15. National day of the People's Republic of the Congo. Commemorates independence from France in 1960.

EQUATORIAL GUINEA: CONSTITUTION DAY. Aug 15. National holiday. Commemorates a 1982 revision of the constitution.

HARDING, FLORENCE KLING DeWOLFE: BIRTH ANNIVERSARY. Aug 15. Wife of Warren Gamaliel Harding, 29th president of the US, born at Marion, OH, Aug 15, 1860. Died at Marion, OH, Nov 21, 1924.

INDIA: INDEPENDENCE DAY. Aug 15. National holiday. Anniversary of Indian independence from Britain in 1947.

KOREA: LIBERATION DAY. Aug 15. National holiday commemorates acceptance by Japan of Allied terms of surrender in 1945, thereby freeing Korea from 36 years of Japanese domination. Also marks formal proclamation of the Republic of Korea in 1948. Military parades and ceremonies throughout country.

LIECHTENSTEIN: NATIONAL DAY. Aug 15. Public holiday.

NESBIT, E. (EDITH): BIRTH ANNIVERSARY. Aug 15, 1858. Born in London on Aug 15, 1858 (some sources say Aug 19, 1858), Edith Nesbit wrote enduring works of fiction for children in several genres. Her realistic fiction included stories about the Bastable children (*The Wouldbegoods, The Story of the Treasure Seekers*) as well as stand-alone novels like *The Railway Children*. Some of her most famous fantasy novels included *The Enchanted Castle, The Five Children and It,* and *The Phoenix and the Carpet*. She died at New Romney, Kent, England on May 4, 1924.

TRANSCONTINENTAL US RAILWAY COMPLETION: ANNIVERSARY. Aug 15, 1870. The Golden Spike ceremony at Promontory Point, UT, May 10, 1869, was long regarded as the final link in a transcontinental railroad track reaching from an Atlantic port to a Pacific port. In fact, that link occurred unceremoniously on another date in another state. Diaries of engineers working at the site establish "the completion of a transcontinental track at a point 928 feet east of today's milepost 602, or 3,812 feet east of the present Union Pacific depot building at Strasburg (formerly Comanche)," CO. The final link was made at 2:53 PM, Aug 15, 1870. Annual celebration at Strasburg, CO, on a weekend in August. See also: "Golden Spike Driving: Anniversary" (May 10).

BIRTHDAYS TODAY

Ben Affleck, 29, actor (*Good Will Hunting*), born Berkeley, CA, Aug 15, 1972.

Stephen G. Breyer, 63, Associate Justice of the Supreme Court, born San Francisco, CA, Aug 15, 1938.

Linda Ellerbee, 57, journalist, host of "Nick News," born Bryan, TX, Aug 15, 1944.

AUGUST 16 — THURSDAY

Day 228 — 137 Remaining

BENNINGTON BATTLE DAY: ANNIVERSARY. Aug 16, 1777. Anniversary of this Revolutionary War battle is a legal holiday in Vermont.

CHRISTOPHER, MATT: BIRTH ANNIVERSARY. Aug 16, 1917. Children's author known for his sports-related fiction and athlete biographies, he was born at Bath, PA. He died in 1997 at Charlotte, NC.

DOMINICAN REPUBLIC: RESTORATION OF THE REPUBLIC. Aug 16. The anniversary of the Restoration of the Republic in 1863 is celebrated as an official public holiday.

INTERNATIONAL FEDERATION OF LIBRARY ASSOCIATIONS ANNUAL CONFERENCE. Aug 16–25. Boston, MA. "Libraries and Librarians: Making a Difference in the Knowledge Age." The 67th annual conference. For info: Intl Federation of Library Associations, The Royal Library, PO Box 95312, The Hague, Netherlands. Web: www.ifla2001.org.

KENTUCKY STATE FAIR (WITH WORLD CHAMPIONSHIP HORSE SHOW). Aug 16–26. Kentucky Fair and Expo Center, Louisville, KY. Midway, concerts by nationally known artists and the World's Championship Horse Show. Est attendance: 700,000. For info: Marketing Dept, KY Fair and Expo Center, Box 37130, Louisville, KY 40233. Phone: (502) 367-5000 or (502) 367-5291. Web: www.kyfairexpo.og.

LAWRENCE (OF ARABIA), T.E.: BIRTH ANNIVERSARY. Aug 16, 1888. British soldier, archaeologist and writer, born at Tremadoc, North Wales. During WWI, led the Arab revolt against the Turks and served as a spy for the British. His book, *Seven Pillars of Wisdom*, is a personal account of the Arab revolt. He was killed in a motorcycle accident at Dorset, England, May 19, 1935.

SCHENK de REGNIERS, BEATRICE: BIRTH ANNIVERSARY. Aug 16, 1914. Author who perfectly captured the emotions of the young, she was born at Lafayette, IN. Her books included *May I Bring a Friend?* and *A Little House of Your Own*, and she edited the poetry collection *Sing a Song of Popcorn*. Died at Washington, DC, Mar 1, 2000.

BIRTHDAYS TODAY

Diana Wynne Jones, 67, author (*Dark Lord of Derkholm*), born London, England, Aug 16, 1934.

LL Cool J, 33, rap singer, born James Todd Smith, Queens, NY, Aug 16, 1968.

Reginald VelJohnson, 49, actor ("Family Matters"), born Raleigh, NC, Aug 16, 1952.

AUGUST 17 — FRIDAY

Day 229 — 136 Remaining

ARGENTINA: DEATH ANNIVERSARY OF SAN MARTÍN. Aug 17. National holiday. Commemorates the death in 1850 of the hero of the struggle for independence from Spain.

BALLOON CROSSING OF ATLANTIC OCEAN: ANNIVERSARY. Aug 17, 1978. Three Americans—Maxie Anderson, 44, Ben Abruzzo, 48, and Larry Newman, 31—all of Albuquerque, NM, became the first people to complete a transatlantic trip in a balloon. Starting from Presque Isle, ME, Aug 11, they traveled some 3,200 miles in 137 hours, 18 minutes, landing at Miserey, France (about 60 miles west of Paris), in their craft, named the *Double Eagle II*.

CALIFORNIA STATE FAIR. Aug 17–Sept 3. Sacramento, CA. Top-name entertainment, fireworks, California counties exhibits, livestock nursery, culinary delights, carnival rides, demolition derbies and award-winning wines and microbrews. For info: Cal Expo, PO Box 15649, Sacramento, CA 95852. Phone: (916) 263-3000. E-mail: SallyCSF@aol.com.

COLORADO STATE FAIR. Aug 17–Sept 2. State Fairgrounds, Pueblo, CO. One of the nation's oldest western fairs, it is also Colorado's largest single event, drawing more than a million visitors. Family fun, top-name entertainment, lots of food and festivities. For info: Colorado State Fair, Jerry Robbe, Pres/Genl Mgr, Pueblo, CO 81004. Phone: (719) 561-8484.

CROCKETT, DAVID "DAVY": BIRTH ANNIVERSARY. Aug 17, 1786. American frontiersman, adventurer and soldier, born at Hawkins County, TN. Died during final heroic defense of the Alamo, Mar 6, 1836, at San Antonio, TX. In his *Autobiography* (1834), Crockett wrote, "I leave this rule for others when I'm dead, Be always sure you're right—then go ahead."

FORT SUMTER SHELLED BY NORTHERN FORCES: ANNIVERSARY. Aug 17, 1863. In what would become a long siege, Union forces began shelling Fort Sumter at Charleston, SC. The site of the first shots fired during the Civil War, Sumter endured the siege for a year and a half before being returned to Union hands. For more info: *The Firing on Fort Sumter: A Splintered Nation Goes to War*, by Nancy Colbert (Morgan Reynolds, 1-883846-51-X, $19.95 Gr. 6 & up).

FULTON SAILS STEAMBOAT: ANNIVERSARY. Aug 17, 1807. Robert Fulton began the first American steamboat trip between Albany and New York, NY, on a boat later called the *Clermont*. After years of promoting submarine warfare, Fulton engaged in a partnership with Robert R. Livingston, the US minister to France, allowing Fulton to design and construct a steamboat. His first success came in August 1803 when he launched a steam-powered vessel on the Seine. That same year the US Congress granted Livingston and Fulton exclusive rights to operate steamboats on New York waters during the next 20 years. The first Albany-to-New York trip took 32 hours to travel the 150-mile course. Although his efforts were labeled "Fulton's Folly" by his detractors, his success allowed the partnership to begin commercial service the next year, Sept 4, 1808.

GABON: NATIONAL DAY. Aug 17. National holiday. Commemorates independence from France in 1960.

August 2001

S	M	T	W	T	F	S
			1	2	3	4
5	6	7	8	9	10	11
12	13	14	15	16	17	18
19	20	21	22	23	24	25
26	27	28	29	30	31	

GINZA HOLIDAY: JAPANESE CULTURAL FESTIVAL. Aug 17–19. Midwest Buddhist Temple, Chicago, IL. Experience the Waza (National Treasures tradition) by viewing 300 years of Edo craft tradition and seeing it come alive as master craftsmen from Tokyo demonstrate their arts. Japanese folk and classical dancing, martial arts, taiko (drums), flower arrangements and cultural displays. Chicken teriyaki, sushi, udon, shaved ice, corn on the cob and refreshments. Annually, the third weekend in August. Est attendance: 5,000. For info: Office Secretary, Midwest Buddhist Temple, 435 W Menomonee St, Chicago, IL 60614. Phone: (312) 943-7801. Fax: (312) 943-8069.

INDONESIA: INDEPENDENCE DAY. Aug 17. National holiday. Republic proclaimed in 1945. It was only after several years of fighting, however, that Indonesia was formally granted its independence by the Netherlands, Dec 27, 1949.

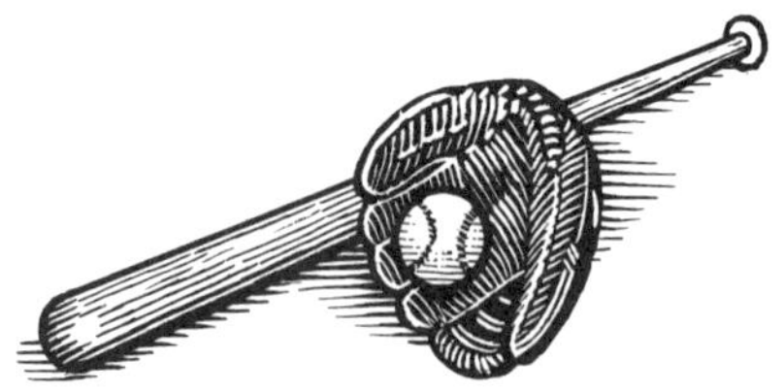

LITTLE LEAGUE BASEBALL WORLD SERIES. Aug 17–25. Williamsport, PA. Sixteen teams from the US and foreign countries compete for the World Championship. Est attendance: 200,000. For info: Little League Baseball HQ, Box 3485, Williamsport, PA 17701. Phone: (570) 326-1921. Web: www.littleleague.org.

TURKISH EARTHQUAKE: ANNIVERSARY. Aug 17, 1999. An earthquake with a magnitude of 7.4 struck northwestern Turkey where 45 percent of the population lives. More than 17,000 people died and thousands more remained missing. Many of the deaths were due to the shoddy construction of apartment buildings. On Nov 12, 1999, a magnitude 7.2 earthquake struck Turkey, killing more than 800 people. Also in 1999 there were earthquakes in Greece (139 dead) and Taiwan (2,200 dead). For more info go to the National Earthquake Information Center: wwwneic.cr.usgus.gov.

BIRTHDAYS TODAY

Christian Laettner, 32, NBA forward, member of the Dream Team in the 1992 Olympics, born Angola, NY, Aug 17, 1969.

Myra Cohn Livingston, 75, poet (*Sky Songs, Space Songs*), born Omaha, NE, Aug 17, 1926.

AUGUST 18 — SATURDAY

Day 230 — 135 Remaining

CLEMENTE, ROBERTO: BIRTH ANNIVERSARY. Aug 18, 1934. National League baseball player, born at Carolina, Puerto Rico. Drafted by the Pittsburgh Pirates in 1954, he played his entire major league career with them. Clemente died in a plane crash Dec 31, 1972, while on a mission of mercy to Nicaragua to deliver supplies he had collected for survivors of an earthquake. He was elected to the Baseball Hall of Fame in 1973.

DARE, VIRGINIA: BIRTH ANNIVERSARY. Aug 18, 1587. Virginia Dare, the first child of English parents to be born in the New World, was born to Ellinor and Ananias Dare, at Roanoke Island, NC. When a ship arrived to replenish their supplies in 1591, the settlers (including Virginia Dare) had vanished, without leaving a trace of the settlement.

LEWIS, MERIWETHER: BIRTH ANNIVERSARY. Aug 18, 1774. American explorer (of Lewis and Clark expedition), born at Albemarle County, VA. Died Oct 11, 1809, near Nashville, TN. For info: *How We Crossed the West: The Adventures of Lewis & Clark*, by Rosalyn Schanzer (National Geographic, 0-79-223738-2, $18 Gr. 3–7).

MAIL-ORDER CATALOG: ANNIVERSARY. Aug 18, 1872. The first mail-order catalog was published by Montgomery Ward. It was only a single sheet of paper. By 1904, the Montgomery Ward catalog weighed four pounds. In 1985, Montgomery Ward closed its catalog business; in 2000, it announced it was closing its retail stores.

MOON PHASE: NEW MOON. Aug 18. Moon enters New Moon phase at 10:55 PM, EDT.

NINETEENTH AMENDMENT TO US CONSTITUTION RATIFIED: VOTES FOR WOMEN: ANNIVERSARY. Aug 18, 1920. The 19th Amendment extended the right to vote to women.

PERIGEAN SPRING TIDES. Aug 18. Spring tides, the highest possible tides, occur when New Moon or Full Moon falls within 24 hours of the moment the Moon is nearest Earth (perigee) in its monthly orbit at 11 PM, EDT. These tides are not named for the season of spring but for the German word *springen*, "to rise up."

BIRTHDAYS TODAY

Rosalynn (Eleanor) Smith Carter, 74, former First Lady, wife of President Jimmy Carter, 39th president of the US, born Plains, GA, Aug 18, 1927.

Paula Danziger, 57, author (*The Cat Ate My Gymsuit, Amber Brown Is Not a Crayon*), born Washington, DC, Aug 18, 1944.

Mike Johanns, 51, Governor of Nebraska (R), born Osage, IA, Aug 18, 1950.

Shannon Johnson, 27, basketball player, born Hartsville, SC, Aug 18, 1974.

Martin Mull, 58, actor ("Sabrina, the Teenage Witch"), born Chicago, IL, Aug 18, 1943.

AUGUST 19 — SUNDAY

Day 231 — 134 Remaining

AFGHANISTAN: INDEPENDENCE DAY. Aug 19. National day. Commemorates independence from British control over foreign affairs in 1919.

CLINTON, WILLIAM JEFFERSON (BILL): 55th BIRTHDAY. Aug 19, 1946. The 42nd US president (1993–2001), born at Hope, AR. For info: www.ipl.org/ref/POTUS.

JCC MACCABI YOUTH GAMES. Aug 19–24. Philadelphia, Miami, Atlanta. Open to Jewish teens 13–16. More than 1,200 athletes will compete. For info: Phone: (215) 446-3022. Web: www.phillymaccabi.com.

★ **NATIONAL AVIATION DAY.** Aug 19. Presidential Proclamation 2343, of July 25, 1939, covers all succeeding years. Always Aug 19 of each year since 1939. Observed annually on anniversary of birth of Orville Wright, who piloted "first self-powered flight in history," Dec 17, 1903. First proclaimed by President Franklin D. Roosevelt.

SPACE MILESTONE: *SPUTNIK 5* (USSR): ANNIVERSARY. Aug 19, 1960. Space menagerie satellite with dogs Belka and Strelka, mice, rats, houseflies and plants launched. These passengers became first living organisms recovered from orbit when the satellite returned safely to Earth the next day.

WRIGHT, ORVILLE: BIRTH ANNIVERSARY. Aug 19, 1871. Aviation pioneer (with his brother Wilbur), born at Dayton, OH, Aug 19, 1871, and died there Jan 30, 1948.

BIRTHDAYS TODAY

Victor Ambrus, 66, author (*The Three Poor Tailors*), born Budapest, Hungary, Aug 19, 1935.

William Jefferson (Bill) Clinton, 55, 42nd president of the US, born Hope, AR, Aug 19, 1946.

John Stamos, 38, actor ("Full House"), born Cypress, CA, Aug 19, 1963.

Fred Thompson, 59, US Senator (R, Tennessee), actor (*In the Line of Fire*), born Sheffield, AL, Aug 19, 1942.

AUGUST 20 — MONDAY

Day 232 — 133 Remaining

HARRISON, BENJAMIN: BIRTH ANNIVERSARY. Aug 20, 1833. The 23rd president of the US, born at North Bend, OH. He was the grandson of William Henry Harrison, 9th president of the US. His term of office, Mar 4, 1889–Mar 3, 1893, was preceded and followed by the presidential terms of Grover Cleveland (who thus became the 22nd and 24th president of the US). Harrison died at Indianapolis, IN, Mar 13, 1901. For info: www.ipl.org/ref/POTUS.

HUNGARY: ST. STEPHEN'S DAY. Aug 20. National holiday. Commemorates the canonization of St. Stephen in 1083. Under the Communists celebrated as Constitution Day.

O'HIGGINS, BERNARDO: BIRTH ANNIVERSARY. Aug 20, 1778. First ruler of Chile after its declaration of independence. Called the "Liberator of Chile." Born at Chillan, Chile. Died at Lima, Peru, Oct 24, 1842.

SPACE MILESTONE: *VOYAGER 2* (US). Aug 20, 1977. This unmanned spacecraft journeyed past Jupiter in 1979, Saturn in 1981, Uranus in 1986 and Neptune in 1989, sending photographs and data back to scientists on Earth.

BIRTHDAYS TODAY

Tara Dakides, 26, snowboarder, born Mission Viejo, CA, Aug 20, 1975.

Al Roker, 47, TV meteorologist ("Today Show"), born Brooklyn, NY, Aug 20, 1954.

AUGUST 21 — TUESDAY

Day 233 — 132 Remaining

CHAMBERLAIN, WILT: BIRTH ANNIVERSARY. Aug 21, 1936. Basketball Hall of Fame center, born at Philadelphia, PA. Died Oct 12, 1999, at Los Angeles, CA.

HAWAII: ADMISSION DAY: ANNIVERSARY. Aug 21, 1959. President Dwight Eisenhower signed a proclamation admitting Hawaii to the Union. The statehood bill had passed the previous March with a stipulation that statehood should be approved by a vote of Hawaiian residents. The referendum passed by a huge margin in June and Eisenhower proclaimed Hawaii the 50th state Aug 21. The third Friday in August is observed as a state holiday in Hawaii, commemorating statehood (Aug 17 in 2001).

MICHIGAN STATE FAIR. Aug 21–Sept 3. State Fairgrounds, Detroit, MI. Est attendance: 400,000. For info: State of Michigan, Dept of Agriculture, 1120 W State Fair Ave, Detroit, MI 48203. Phone: (313) 369-8250.

BIRTHDAYS TODAY

Steve Case, 43, president, America Online, born Honolulu, HI, Aug 21, 1958.
Akili Smith, 26, football player, born San Diego, CA, Aug 21, 1975.
Arthur Yorinks, 48, author (*Hey, Al*), born Roslyn, NY, Aug 21, 1953.

AUGUST 22 — WEDNESDAY

Day 234 — 131 Remaining

BE AN ANGEL DAY. Aug 22. A day to do "one small act of service for someone. Be a blessing in someone's life." Annually, Aug 22. For info: Angel Heights Healing Center, Rev Jayne M. Howard, PO Box 95, Upperco, MD 21155. Phone: (410) 833-6912. Fax: (410) 429-4077. E-mail: blessing@erols.com. Web: drwnet.com/angel.

CAMEROON: VOLCANIC ERUPTION: 15th ANNIVERSARY. Aug 22, 1986. Deadly fumes from a presumed volcanic eruption under Lake Nios at Cameroon killed more than 1,500 persons. A similar occurrence two years earlier had killed 37 persons. For more info visit Volcano World: volcano.und.nodak.edu.

DEBUSSY, CLAUDE: BIRTH ANNIVERSARY. Aug 22, 1862. (Achille) Claude Debussy, French musician and composer, especially remembered for his impressionistic "tone poems," was born at St. Germain-en-Laye, France. He died at Paris, France, Mar 25, 1918.

NEVADA STATE FAIR. Aug 22–26. Reno Livestock Events Center, Reno, NV. State entertainment and carnival, with home arts, agriculture and commercial exhibits. Est attendance: 73,000. For info: Gary Lubra, CEO, Nevada State Fair, 1350-A N Wells Ave, Reno, NV 89512. Phone: (775) 688-5767. Fax: (775) 688-5763. E-mail: nvstatefair@inetworld.com. Web: www.nevadastatefair.org.

VIETNAM CONFLICT BEGINS: ANNIVERSARY. Aug 22, 1945. Less than a week after the Japanese surrender ended WWII, a team of Free French parachuted into southern Indochina in response to a successful coup by a Communist guerrilla named Ho Chi Minh in the French colony.

BIRTHDAYS TODAY

Ray Bradbury, 81, author (*The Toynbee Convector, Fahrenheit 451*), born Waukegan, IL, Aug 22, 1920.
Howie Dorough, 28, singer (Backstreet Boys), born Orlando, FL, Aug 22, 1973.
Will Hobbs, 54, author (*Downriver, Far North*), born Pittsburgh, PA, Aug 22, 1947.
Paul Molitor, 45, former baseball player, born St. Paul, MN, Aug 22, 1956.

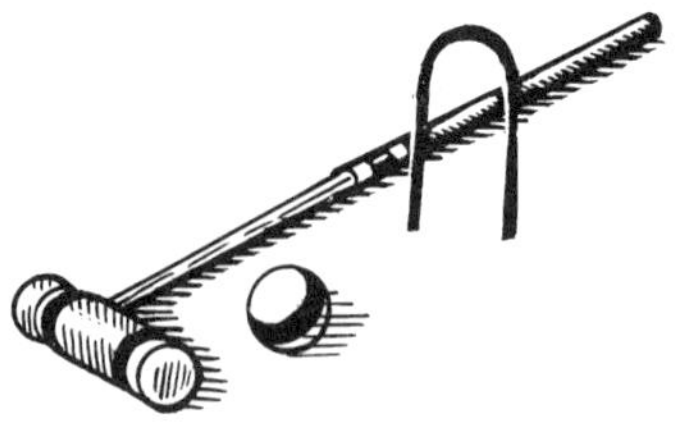

August 2001

S	M	T	W	T	F	S
			1	2	3	4
5	6	7	8	9	10	11
12	13	14	15	16	17	18
19	20	21	22	23	24	25
26	27	28	29	30	31	

AUGUST 23 — THURSDAY

Day 235 — 130 Remaining

FIRST MAN-POWERED FLIGHT: ANNIVERSARY. Aug 23, 1977. At Schafter, CA, Bryan Allen pedaled the 70-lb *Gossamer Condor* for a mile at a "minimal altitude of two pylons" in a flight certified by the Royal Aeronautical Society of Britain, winning a £50,000 prize offered by British industrialist Henry Kremer.

MINNESOTA STATE FAIR. Aug 23–Sept 3. St. Paul, MN. Major entertainers, agricultural displays, arts, crafts, food, carnival rides, animal judging and performances. Est attendance: 1,700,000. For info: Minnesota State Fair, 1265 Snelling Ave N, St. Paul, MN 55108-3099. Phone: (651) 642-2200. E-mail: fairinfo@mnstate fair.org.

NEW YORK STATE FAIR. Aug 23–Sept 3. Empire Expo Center, Syracuse, NY. Agricultural and livestock competitions, top-name entertainment, the International Horse Show, business and industrial exhibits, the midway and ethnic presentations. Est attendance: 900,000. For info: Joseph LaGuardia, Dir of Mktg, NY State Fair, Empire Expo Center, Syracuse, NY 13209. Phone: (315) 487-7711. Fax: (315) 487-9260.

OREGON STATE FAIR. Aug 23–Sept 3. Salem, OR. Exhibits, products and displays illustrate Oregon's role as one of the nation's major agricultural and recreational states. Floral gardens, carnival, big-name entertainment, horse show and food. Annually, 12 days ending on Labor Day. Est attendance: 700,000. For info: Oregon State Fair, 2330 17th St NE, Salem, OR 97303-3201. Phone: (503) 378-3247.

PERRY, OLIVER HAZARD: BIRTH ANNIVERSARY. Aug 23, 1785. American naval hero, born at South Kingston, RI. Died Aug 23, 1819, at sea. Best remembered is his announcement of victory at the Battle of Lake Erie, Sept 10, 1813 during the War of 1812: "We have met the enemy, and they are ours."

VIRGO, THE VIRGIN. Aug 23–Sept 22. In the astronomical/astrological zodiac, which divides the sun's apparent orbit into 12 segments, the period Aug 23–Sept 22 is identified, traditionally, as the sun sign of Virgo, the Virgin. The ruling planet is Mercury.

BIRTHDAYS TODAY

Kobe Bryant, 23, basketball player, born Philadelphia, PA, Aug 23, 1978.
Rik Smits, 35, former basketball player, born Eindhoven, The Netherlands, Aug 23, 1966.

AUGUST 24 — FRIDAY

Day 236 — 129 Remaining

ALASKA STATE FAIR. Aug 24–Sept 3. Palmer, AK. Cows and critters, music and dancing, rides, excitement and family fun at the state's largest summer extravaganza. See 100-lb cabbages, native art and more than 500 events including demonstrations, high-caliber entertainment, rodeos, horse shows, crafts and agricultural exhibits. Est attendance: 280,000. For info: Alaska State Fair, Inc, 2075 Glenn Hwy, Palmer, AK 99645. Phone: (907) 745-4827 or (800) 850-FAIR. Fax: (907) 746-2699. Web: www.alaskastate fair.org.

ITALY: VESUVIUS DAY. Aug 24, AD 79. Anniversary of the eruption of Vesuvius, an active volcano in southern Italy, which destroyed the cities of Pompeii, Stabiae and Herculaneum. For more info: *In Search of Pompeii* (Peter Bedrick, 0-87226-545-5, $18.95 Gr. 5 & up) or visit Volcano World: volcano.und.nodak .edu. *See* Curriculum Connection.

AUGUST 24
ERUPTION OF MOUNT VESUVIUS

When Mount Vesuvius erupted in AD 79, Pliny the Younger, a Roman teenager at the time, wrote a letter to the historian Tacitus. In his letter, Pliny describes the eruption of this huge volcano and how it affected the area. He was one of the fortunate people who escaped the fiery hot cloud that engulfed the city of Pompeii. Many inhabitants were suffocated and killed by poisonous gas and gritty ash in the air. The nearby city of Herculaneum was buried by lava flows and mud as deep as 100 feet.

Over the years the cities have been excavated numerous times. Some of the excavators were robbers, who stole valuable artifacts. These cities are now protected by the Italian government which allows responsible archaeological excavations to be conducted. The television show "NOVA" has produced a video entitled "Deadly Shadow of Vesuvius" (visit www.pbs.org/nova/vesuvius) and the National Geographic Society has one entitled "In the Shadow of Vesuvius." Check your public library for a copy.

An interesting science project would be to divide the students into three groups of Volcano Investigators. One group will discover information about pyroclastic flows. These are the deadly, rapidly moving flows of ash. More than 28,000 people were killed by a pyroclastic flow from Mount Pelee, in Martinique in 1902. The website Volcano World at volcano.und.nodak.edu has excellent information.

The second group can discover information about two lavas called pahoehoe and aa. These are the slow moving lava flows found in Hawaii.

The third group should find information about lahars. These are devastating mud flows that are triggered by volcanic eruptions. A lahar was caused when Nevado del Ruíz erupted in Colombia in 1985, buried the town of Armero and killed more than 25,000 people.

Each group can present its findings so the class can compare and contrast the three various flows. Many students are surprised to learn volcanoes aren't just lava flows. Discuss the hazards associated with each flow and whether evacuation plans for threatened cities are realistic in terms of implementation.

Nonfiction books about volcanoes include: *Why Do Volcanoes Blow Their Tops?*, by Melvin Berger and Gilda Berger (Scholastic, 0-439-09580-8, $14.95 Gr. 2–4); *Shaping the Earth*, by Dorothy Hinshaw Patent (Houghton Mifflin, 0-395-85691-4, $18 Gr. 5 & up); and *Volcanoes: Earth's Inner Fire*, by Sally M. Walker (Carolrhoda, 0-8761-4812-7, $15.95 Gr. 4–7).

Books about Mount Vesuvius include: *Pompeii...Buried Alive*, by Edith Kunhardt (Random House, 0-394-88866-9, $3.99 Gr. K–3); *In Search of Pompeii*, by Giovanni Caselli (Peter Bedrick, 0-87226-545-5, $18.95 Gr. 5 & up); and *The Buried City of Pompeii*, by Shelley Tanaka (Hyperion, 0-7868-0285-5, $16.95 Gr. 3–7). Mary Pope Osborne's novel *Vacation Under the Volcano* (Random House, 0-679-89050-5, $3.99 Gr. 2–5) is one of the Magic Tree House adventures for younger readers.

Novels featuring other volcanoes include: *Rage of Fire*, by Gloria Skurzynski (National Geographic, 0-7922-7035-5, $15.95 Gr. 4–8), which takes place in Hawaii, and *The Volcano Disaster*, by Peg Kehret (Pocket, 0-671-00968-0, $3.99 Gr. 4–7), which is a Mount St. Helens time-travel adventure.

LIBERIA: FLAG DAY. Aug 24. National holiday.

MARYLAND STATE FAIR. Aug 24–Sept 3. Timonium, MD. Home arts, agricultural and livestock presentations, midway rides, live entertainment and thoroughbred horse racing. Est attendance: 500,000. For info: Max Mosner, State Fairgrounds, PO Box 188, Timonium, MD 21094. Phone: (410) 252-0200.

NEBRASKA STATE FAIR. Aug 24–Sept 3. Lincoln, NE. Book fair, food booths, variety of entertainment, rodeos, amusement rides and tractor pulls. For info: Nebraska State Fair, PO Box 81223, Lincoln, NE 68501. Phone: (402) 473-4110. Fax: (402) 473-4114. E-mail: nestatefair@statefair.org.

UKRAINE: INDEPENDENCE DAY: 10th ANNIVERSARY. Aug 24. National day. Commemorates independence from the former Soviet Union in 1991.

WARNER WEATHER QUOTATION: ANNIVERSARY. Aug 24, 1897. Charles Dudley Warner, American newspaper editor for the *Hartford Courant*, published this now-famous and oft-quoted sentence, "Everybody talks about the weather, but nobody does anything about it." The quotation is often mistakenly attributed to his friend and colleague Mark Twain. Warner and Twain were part of the most notable American literary circle during the late 19th century. Warner was a journalist, essayist, novelist, biographer and author who collaborated with Mark Twain in writing *The Gilded Age* in 1873.

WASHINGTON, DC: INVASION ANNIVERSARY. Aug 24–25, 1814. During the War of 1812, British forces briefly invaded and raided Washington, DC, burning the Capitol, the president's house and most other public buildings. President James Madison and other high US government officials fled to safety until British troops (not knowing the strength of their position) departed the city two days later.

BIRTHDAYS TODAY

Max Cleland, 59, US Senator (D, Georgia), born Atlanta, GA, Aug 24, 1942.

Bob Holden, 52, Governor of Missouri (D), born Kansas City, MO, Aug 24, 1949.

Mike Huckabee, 46, Governor of Arkansas (R), born Hope, AR, Aug 24, 1955.

Reginald (Reggie) Miller, 36, basketball player, born Riverside, CA, Aug 24, 1965.

Kenny Quinn, 65, Governor of Nevada (R), born Garland, AR, Aug 24, 1936.

Calvin Edward (Cal) Ripken, Jr, 41, baseball player, born Havre de Grace, MD, Aug 24, 1960.

Merlin Tuttle, 60, scientist who works with bats, author (*Bats for Kids*), born Honolulu, HI, Aug 24, 1941.

AUGUST 25 — SATURDAY

Day 237 — 128 Remaining

BE KIND TO HUMANKIND WEEK. Aug 25–31. All of the negative news that you read about in the paper each day and hear on your local news station is disheartening—but the truth is the "positive" stories outweigh the negative stories by a long shot! We just don't hear about them as often. Take heart . . . most people are caring individuals. Show you care by being kind. For info: Lorraine Jara, PO Box 586, Island Heights, NJ 08732-0586. Web: www.bkhk.org.

BERNSTEIN, LEONARD: BIRTH ANNIVERSARY. Aug 25, 1918. American conductor and composer, born at Lawrence, MA. One of the greatest conductors in American music history, he first conducted the New York Philharmonic Orchestra at age 25 and was its director from 1959 to 1969. His musicals include *West Side Story* and *On the Town*, and his operas and operettas include *Candide*. He died five days after his retirement Oct 14, 1990, at New York, NY.

CHILDREN'S DAY. Aug 25. Woodstock, VT. Traditional farm activities from corn shelling to sawing firewood—19th-century games, traditional spelling bee, ice cream and butter making, wagon rides. Children ages 12 and under and accompanied by an adult are admitted free. For info: Billings Farm Museum, PO Box 489, Woodstock, VT 05091. Phone: (802) 457-2355. Fax: (802) 457-4663. E-mail: billings.farm@valley.net.

KELLY, WALT: BIRTH ANNIVERSARY. Aug 25, 1913. American cartoonist and creator of the comic strip "Pogo" was born at Philadelphia, PA. It was Kelly's character Pogo who paraphrased Oliver Hazard Perry to say, "We has met the enemy, and it is us." Kelly died at Hollywood, CA, Oct 18, 1973. See also: "Perry, Oliver Hazard: Birth Anniversary" (Aug 23).

MOON PHASE: FIRST QUARTER. Aug 25. Moon enters First Quarter phase at 3:55 PM, EDT.

PARIS LIBERATED: ANNIVERSARY. Aug 25, 1944. As dawn broke, the men of the 2nd French Armored Division entered Paris, ending the long German occupation of the City of Light. That afternoon General Charles de Gaulle led a parade down the Champs Elysées. Though Hitler had ordered the destruction of Paris, German occupying-officer General Dietrich von Choltitz refused that order and instead surrendered to French Major General Jacques Le Clerc.

SMITH, SAMANTHA: DEATH ANNIVERSARY. Aug 25, 1985. American schoolgirl whose interest in world peace drew praise and affection from people around the world. In 1982, the 10-year-old wrote a letter to Soviet leader Yuri Andropov asking him, "Why do you want to conquer the whole world, or at least our country?" The letter was widely publicized in the USSR and Andropov replied personally to her. Samantha Smith was invited to visit and tour the Soviet Union. On Aug 25, 1985, the airplane on which she was riding crashed at Maine, killing all aboard, including Samantha and her father. In 1986, minor planet No 3147, an asteroid between Mars and Jupiter, was named Samantha Smith in her memory.

URUGUAY: INDEPENDENCE DAY. Aug 25. National holiday. Gained independence from Brazil in 1828.

***THE WIZARD OF OZ* FIRST RELEASED: ANNIVERSARY.** Aug 25, 1939. This motion-picture classic featured Dorothy and her dog Toto. The two were swept into a tornado and landed in a fictional place called Munchkinland. To get home she must go and see the Wizard of Oz and on the way meets the Scarecrow, the Tin Man and the Cowardly Lion. The cast included Judy Garland as Dorothy, Frank Morgan as the Wizard, Ray Bolger as Scarecrow, Bert Lahr as the Lion, Jack Haley as Tin Man and Margaret Hamilton as the Wicked Witch of the West.

August 2001

S	M	T	W	T	F	S
			1	2	3	4
5	6	7	8	9	10	11
12	13	14	15	16	17	18
19	20	21	22	23	24	25
26	27	28	29	30	31	

BIRTHDAYS TODAY

Albert Belle, 35, baseball player, born Shreveport, LA, Aug 25, 1966.
Tim Burton, 43, producer (*The Nightmare Before Christmas*), born Burbank, CA, Aug 25, 1958.
Sean Connery, 71, actor (James Bond movies; *The Man Who Would Be King*), born Edinburgh, Scotland, Aug 25, 1930.
Kel Mitchell, 23, actor ("All That," "Kenan & Kel"), born Chicago, IL, Aug 25, 1978.
Lane Smith, 42, author, illustrator (Caldecott honor for *The Stinky Cheese Man; The Happy Hocky Family*), born Tulsa, OK, Aug 25, 1959.

AUGUST 26 — SUNDAY

Day 238 — 127 Remaining

BELGIUM: WEDDING OF THE GIANTS. Aug 26. Traditional cultural observance. Annually, the fourth Sunday in August.

De FOREST, LEE: BIRTH ANNIVERSARY. Aug 26, 1873. American inventor of the electron tube, radio knife for surgery and the photoelectric cell and a pioneer in the creation of talking pictures and television. Born at Council Bluffs, IA, De Forest was holder of hundreds of patents but perhaps best remembered by the moniker he gave himself in the title of his autobiography, *Father of Radio*, published in 1950. So unbelievable was the idea of wireless radio broadcasting that De Forest was accused of fraud and arrested for selling stock to underwrite the invention that later was to become an essential part of daily life. De Forest died at Hollywood, CA, June 30, 1961.

FIRST BASEBALL GAMES TELEVISED: ANNIVERSARY. Aug 26, 1939. WXBS television, at New York City, broadcast the first major league baseball games—a doubleheader between the Cincinnati Reds and the Brooklyn Dodgers at Ebbets Field. Announcer Red Barber interviewed Leo Durocher, manager of the Dodgers, and William McKechnie, manager of the Reds, between games.

KRAKATOA ERUPTION: ANNIVERSARY. Aug 26, 1883. Anniversary of the biggest explosion in historic times. The eruption of the Indonesian volcanic island, Krakatoa (Krakatau) was heard 3,000 miles away, created tidal waves 120 ft high (killing 36,000 persons), hurled five cubic miles of earth fragments into the air (some to a height of 50 miles) and affected the oceans and the atmosphere for years.

MONTGOLFIER, JOSEPH MICHEL: BIRTH ANNIVERSARY. Aug 26, 1740. French merchant and inventor, born at Vidalonlez-Annonay, France, who, with his brother Jacques Etienne in November 1782, conducted experiments with paper and fabric bags filled with smoke and hot air which led to the invention of the hot-air balloon and man's first flight. Died at Balaruc-les-Bains, France, June 26, 1810. See also: "Montgolfier, Jacques Etienne: Birth Anniversary" (Jan 7), "First Balloon Flight: Anniversary" (June 5) and "Aviation History Month" (Nov 1).

NAMIBIA: HEROES' DAY. Aug 26. National holiday. Commemorates the beginning of the struggle for independence in 1966.

PHILIPPINES: NATIONAL HEROES' DAY. Aug 26. National holiday. Commemorates the 1896 start of the revolution for independence from Spain.

SABIN, ALBERT BRUCE: BIRTH ANNIVERSARY. Aug 26, 1906. American medical researcher, born at Bialystok, Poland. He is most noted for his oral vaccine for polio, which replaced Jonas Salk's injected vaccine because Sabin's provided lifetime protection. He was awarded the US National Medal of Science in 1971. Sabin died Mar 3, 1993, at Washington, DC.

★ **WOMEN'S EQUALITY DAY.** Aug 26. Presidential Proclamation issued in 1973 and 1974 at request and since 1975 without request.

WOMEN'S EQUALITY DAY. Aug 26. Anniversary of certification as part of US Constitution, in 1920, of the 19th Amendment, prohibiting discrimination on the basis of sex with regard to voting. Congresswoman Bella Abzug's bill to designate Aug 26 of each year as "Women's Equality Day" in August 1974 became Public Law 93–382.

BIRTHDAYS TODAY

Patricia Beatty, 79, author (*Charley Skedaddle*), born Portland, OR, Aug 26, 1922.

Macaulay Culkin, 21, actor (*Home Alone, My Girl*), born New York, NY, Aug 26, 1980.

Thomas J. Ridge, 56, Governor of Pennsylvania (R), born Munhall, PA, Aug 26, 1945.

Robert G. Torricelli, 50, US Senator (D, New Jersey), born Paterson, NJ, Aug 26, 1951.

AUGUST 27 — MONDAY

Day 239 — 126 Remaining

DAWES, CHARLES GATES: BIRTH ANNIVERSARY. Aug 27, 1865. The 30th vice president of the US (1925–1929), born at Marietta, OH. Won the Nobel Peace Prize in 1925 for the "Dawes Plan" for German reparations. Died at Evanston, IL, Apr 23, 1951.

FIRST COMMERCIAL OIL WELL: ANNIVERSARY. Aug 27, 1859. W.A. "Uncle Billy" Smith discovered oil in a shaft being sunk by Colonel E.L. Drake at Titusville, in western Pennsylvania. Drilling had reached 69 feet, 6 inches when Smith saw a dark film floating on the water below the derrick floor. Soon 20 barrels of crude were being pumped each day. At first, oil was refined into kerosene and used for lighting, in place of whale oil. Only later was it refined into gasoline for cars. The first gas station opened in 1907.

FIRST PLAY PRESENTED IN NORTH AMERICAN COLONIES: ANNIVERSARY. Aug 27, 1655. Acomac, VA, was the site of the first play presented in the North American colonies. The play was *Ye Bare and Ye Cubb*, by Phillip Alexander Bruce. Three local residents were arrested and fined for acting in the play. At the time, most colonies had laws prohibiting public performances; Virginia, however, had no such ordinance.

HAMLIN, HANNIBAL: BIRTH ANNIVERSARY. Aug 27, 1809. The 15th vice president of the US (1861–1865) born at Paris, ME. Died at Bangor, ME, July 4, 1891.

HONG KONG: LIBERATION DAY. Aug 27. Public holiday to celebrate liberation from the Japanese in 1945. Annually, the last Monday in August.

JOHNSON, LYNDON BAINES: BIRTH ANNIVERSARY. Aug 27, 1908. The 36th president of the US succeeded to the presidency following the assassination of John F. Kennedy and then was elected to one term on his own. Johnson's term of office: Nov 22, 1963–Jan 20, 1969. In 1964, he said: "The challenge of the next half-century is whether we have the wisdom to use [our] wealth to enrich and elevate our national life—and to advance the quality of American civilization." Johnson was born near

AUGUST 27
MOCK NEWBERY—MAKE LITERATURE A SCHOOL YEAR HABIT

Get the school year off to a rousing start by focusing on the best of recently published children's literature. Do this by holding a Mock Newbery Award competition in your classroom. This activity must be started during the first few weeks of school. Students will need the following three months to read the list of Mock Newbery candidate books.

John Newbery (1731–1767), an Englishman, is a famous historical figure in children's literature. The owner of a London bookstore, Newbery was the first person to publish and sell books for children. The Newbery Medal is sponsored each year by the Association for Library Service to Children division of the American Library Association. Announced in January or February, the annual medal is given to the author of the book that a selection committee deems the most distinguished contribution to children's literature published during the preceding year. Only authors who are US citizens or residents are eligible for the Newbery Medal, which was established in 1922.

The best way to establish a Mock Newbery list is to contact the children's literature specialist in a local bookstore or the Youth Services Librarian at your public library. He or she should be very up to date on new book titles. Each book you look at for this year's Mock Newbery should have a 2001 copyright date. Work with your contact to develop a list of 10 to 15 books, more if you're really energetic. (Some bookstores may already have a Mock Newbery partnership—and a ready list—with local schools. See if there's one in your area.) Include one or two nonfiction titles and a poetry book. Approach your learning center director, principal or PTO for funds to buy at least one copy of each book. They can all be added to the school's collection by mid-January.

To get the award selection process underway, book talk each title with the students. Perhaps the bookstore representative would be willing to do this. Or, ask willing students to read and booktalk the titles to their classmates. Then, let students sign out and read the books. Every student will have a vote; the only rule is that they must read at least a certain number of the books on the list (you decide: seven to ten of the offered books—or more?). Students who have read the same book can get together, discuss it and decide if they want it to go on to the next round. They should focus on plot, theme, use of language, character development, etc. When a group decides to support a book, they must pitch its merits to their classmates during the next selection committee meeting (whole class, always). Plan on holding several selection committee meetings. At the end of each meeting, take a vote. Books with the lowest votes are off the list. Your goal is to gradually whittle the list down to two or three books in December. Then, the supporters of those books must really work to get others to read their book, so a final winner can be chosen. Select one medal recipient and two honor books. Hang signs in the hallway announcing your results.

Enthusiastic students might be persuaded to give a short commercial for the winners at a school assembly.

Compare your finalists to those chosen by the American Library Association selection committee. They are listed on ALA's website at www.ala.org/alsc/newbery.html. Do your students concur with the committee's choice of medal winner and honor books?

Stonewall, TX, and died at San Antonio, TX, Jan 22, 1973. His birthday is observed as a holiday in Texas. For info: www.ipl.org/ref/POTUS.

MOLDOVA: INDEPENDENCE DAY: 10th ANNIVERSARY. Aug 27. Republic of Moldova declared its independence from the Soviet Union in 1991.

MOTHER TERESA: BIRTH ANNIVERSARY. Aug 27, 1910. Albanian Roman Catholic nun, born Agnes Gonxha Bojaxhiu at Skopje, Macedonia. She founded the Order of the Missionaries of Charity, which cared for the destitute of Calcutta, India. She won the Nobel Peace Prize in 1979. She died at Calcutta, Sept 5, 1997.

SWEDISH LANGUAGE AND CULTURE DAY CAMP. Aug 27–31. West Riverside Historic Site, Cambridge, MN. Children learn to speak Swedish and understand Swedish culture through songs, games, language classes and craft classes. Families see what their children have learned at a program at the end of the week. Annually, the last full week in August. For info: Valerie Arrowsmith, Isanti County Historical Soc, PO Box 525, Cambridge, MN 55008. Phone: (612) 689-4229. Fax: (612) 689-5134.

BIRTHDAYS TODAY

Suzy Kline, 58, author (the Horrible Harry series), born Berkeley, CA, Aug 27, 1943.

Carlos Moya, 25, tennis player, born Palma de Mallorca, Aug 27, 1976.

Ann Rinaldi, 67, author (*Time Enough for Drums, A Stitch in Time*), born New York, NY, Aug 27, 1934.

Paul Rubens (Pee-Wee Herman), 49, actor, writer ("Pee-Wee's Playhouse," *Pee-Wee's Big Adventure*), born Peekskill, NY, Aug 27, 1952.

Suzanne Fisher Staples, 56, author (*Shabanu: Daughter of the Wind, Haveli*), born Philadelphia, PA, Aug 27, 1945.

Sarah Stewart, 63, author (*The Library, The Gardener*), born Corpus Christi, TX, Aug 27, 1938.

AUGUST 28 — TUESDAY

Day 240 — 125 Remaining

DUVOISIN, ROGER: BIRTH ANNIVERSARY. Aug 28, 1904. Author and illustrator (*Hide and Seek Fog*), born at Geneva, Switzerland. Died June 30, 1980.

FEAST OF SAINT AUGUSTINE. Aug 28. Bishop of Hippo, author of *Confessions* and *The City of God*, born Nov 13, 354, at Tagaste, in what is now Algeria. Died Aug 28, 430, at Hippo, also in North Africa.

HAYES, LUCY WARE WEBB: BIRTH ANNIVERSARY. Aug 28, 1831. Wife of Rutherford Birchard Hayes, 19th president of the US, born at Chillicothe, OH. Died at Fremont, OH, June 25, 1889. She was nicknamed "Lemonade Lucy" because she and the president, both abstainers, served no alcoholic beverages at White House receptions.

MARCH ON WASHINGTON: ANNIVERSARY. Aug 28, 1963. More than 250,000 people attended this Civil Rights rally at Washington, DC, at which Reverend Dr. Martin Luther King, Jr, made his famous "I have a dream" speech. For the text of his speech: *I Have a Dream*, by Dr. Martin Luther King, Jr (Scholastic, 0-590-20516-1, $16.95 All ages). An audio version of Dr. King's speech is available at www.historychannel.com/speech/index.html.

August 2001

S	M	T	W	T	F	S
			1	2	3	4
5	6	7	8	9	10	11
12	13	14	15	16	17	18
19	20	21	22	23	24	25
26	27	28	29	30	31	

PETERSON, ROGER TORY: BIRTH ANNIVERSARY. Aug 28, 1908. Naturalist, author of *A Field Guide to Birds*, born at Jamestown, NY. Peterson died at Old Lyme, CT, July 28, 1996.

RADIO COMMERCIALS: ANNIVERSARY. Aug 28, 1922. Broadcasters realized radio could earn profits from the sale of advertising time. WEAF in New York ran a commercial "spot," which was sponsored by the Queensboro Realty Corporation of Jackson Heights to promote Hawthorne Court, a group of apartment buildings at Queens. The commercial rate was $100 for 10 minutes.

SETON, ELIZABETH ANN BAYLEY: BIRTH ANNIVERSARY. Aug 28, 1774. First American-born saint was born at New York, NY. Seton died Jan 4, 1821, at Emmitsburg, MD. The founder of the American Sisters of Charity, the first American order of Roman Catholic nuns, she was canonized in 1975.

BIRTHDAYS TODAY

William S. Cohen, 61, former US Secretary of Defense (Clinton administration), born Bangor, ME, Aug 28, 1940.

Michael Galeota, 17, actor (*Can't Be Heaven, Clubhouse Detectives*), born Long Island, NY, Aug 28, 1984.

Scott Hamilton, 43, Olympic gold medal figure skater, born Toledo, OH, Aug 28, 1958.

J. Brian Pinkney, 40, illustrator (*Duke Ellington: The Piano Prince and His Orchestra*), born Boston, MA, Aug 28, 1961.

LeAnn Rimes, 19, singer, born Jackson, MS, Aug 28, 1982.

Allen Say, 64, illustrator and author (Caldecott for *Grandfather's Journey*), born Yokohama, Japan, Aug 28, 1937.

Tasha Tudor, 86, illustrator (*A Little Princess, A Child's Garden of Verses*), author (*Corgiville Fair*), born Starling Burgess at Boston MA, Aug 28, 1915.

AUGUST 29 — WEDNESDAY

Day 241 — 124 Remaining

"ACCORDING TO HOYLE" DAY (EDMOND HOYLE DEATH ANNIVERSARY). Aug 29, 1769. A day to remember Edmond Hoyle and a day for fun and games *according to the rules*. He is believed to have studied law. For many years he lived at London, England, and gave instructions in the playing of games. His "Short Treatise" on the game of whist (published in 1742) became a model guide to the rules of the game. Hoyle's name became synonymous with the idea of correct play according to the rules, and the phrase "according to Hoyle" became a part of the English language. Hoyle was born about 1672, at London and died there.

***AMISTAD* SEIZED: ANNIVERSARY.** Aug 29, 1839. In January 1839, 53 Africans were seized near modern-day Sierra Leone, taken to Cuba and sold as slaves. While being transferred to another part of the island on the ship *Amistad*, led by the African, Cinque, they seized control of the ship, telling the crew to take them back to Africa. However, the crew secretly changed course and the ship landed at Long Island, NY, where it and its "cargo" were seized as salvage. The *Amistad* was towed to New Haven, CT, where the Africans were imprisoned and a lengthy legal battle began to determine if they were property to be returned to Cuba or free men. John Quincy Adams took their case all the way to the Supreme Court, where on Mar 9, 1841, it was determined that they were free and could return to Africa. For more info: *Amistad: A Long Road to Freedom*, by Walter Dean Myers (Dutton, 0-525-45970-7, $16.99 Gr. 7 and up) or *Freedom's Sons: The True Story of the Amistad Mutiny*, by Suzanne Jurmain (Lothrop, 0-688-11072-X, $15 Gr. 4–8). A replica of the *Amistad* was built at the Mystic

Seaport Museum, Mystic, CT (amistad.mysticseaport.org). For more info on the trial: www.umkc.edu/FamousTrials.

PARKER, CHARLIE: BIRTH ANNIVERSARY. Aug 29, 1920. Jazz saxophonist Charlie Parker was born at Kansas City, KS. He earned the nickname "Yardbird" (later "Bird") from his habit of sitting in the backyard of speakeasies, fingering his saxophone. His career as a jazz saxophonist took him from jam sessions in Kansas City to New York, where he met Dizzy Gillespie and others who were creating a style of music that would become known as bop or bebop. He died at Rochester, NY, Mar 12, 1955, at the age of 34. For more info: *Charlie Parker Played Be Bop*, by Chris Raschka (Orchard, 0-531-05999-3, $15.95 Gr. K–1).

SHAYS REBELLION: ANNIVERSARY. Aug 29, 1786. Daniel Shays, veteran of the battles of Lexington, Bunker Hill, Ticonderoga and Saratoga, was one of the leaders of more than 1,000 rebels who sought redress of grievances during the depression days of 1786–87. They prevented general court sessions and they prevented Supreme Court sessions at Springfield, MA, Sept 26. On Jan 25, 1787, they attacked the federal arsenal at Springfield; Feb 2, Shays's troops were routed and fled. Shays was sentenced to death but pardoned June 13, 1788. Later he received a small pension for services in the American Revolution.

SLOVAKIA: NATIONAL UPRISING DAY. Aug 29. National holiday. Commemorates the beginning of the 1944 resistance to Nazi occupation.

SOVIET COMMUNIST PARTY SUSPENDED: 10th ANNIVERSARY. Aug 29, 1991. The Supreme Soviet, the parliament of the USSR, suspended all activities of the Communist Party, seizing its property and bringing to an end the institution that ruled the Soviet Union for nearly 75 years. The action followed an unsuccessful coup Aug 19–21 that sought to overthrow the government of Soviet President Mikhail Gorbachev but instead prompted a sweeping wave of democratic change. Gorbachev quit as party leader Aug 24.

BIRTHDAYS TODAY

Karen Hesse, 49, author (Newbery for *Out of the Dust*), born Baltimore, MD, Aug 29, 1952.

Michael Jackson, 43, singer, songwriter ("We Are the World," *Bad, Thriller, Beat It*), born Gary, IN, Aug 29, 1958.

John Sidney McCain III, 65, US Senator (R, Arizona), born Panama Canal Zone, Aug 29, 1936.

AUGUST 30 — THURSDAY

Day 242 — 123 Remaining

ARTHUR, ELLEN LEWIS HERNDON: BIRTH ANNIVERSARY. Aug 30, 1837. Wife of Chester Alan Arthur, 21st president of the US, born at Fredericksburg, VA. Died at New York, NY, Jan 12, 1880.

BURTON, VIRGINIA LEE: BIRTH ANNIVERSARY. Aug 30, 1909. Author and illustrator, born at Newton Centre, MA. Her book *The Little House* won the Caldecott Medal in 1942. Other works include *Choo, Choo* and *Mike Mulligan and His Steam Shovel.* Burton died at Boston, MA, Oct 15, 1968.

FIRST WHITE HOUSE PRESIDENTIAL BABY: BIRTH ANNIVERSARY. Aug 30, 1893. Frances Folsom Cleveland (Mrs Grover Cleveland) was the first presidential wife to have a baby at the White House when she gave birth to a baby girl (Esther). The first child ever born in the White House was a granddaughter to Thomas Jefferson in 1806.

MacMURRAY, FRED: BIRTH ANNIVERSARY. Aug 30, 1908. Born at Kankakee, IL, MacMurray's film and television career included a wide variety of roles, ranging from comedy (*The Absent-Minded Professor, Son of Flubber, The Shaggy Dog*) to serious drama (*The Caine Mutiny, Double Indemnity*). During 1960–72 he portrayed the father on "My Three Sons," which was second only to "Ozzie and Harriet" as network TV's longest running family sitcom. He died Nov 5, 1991, at Santa Monica, CA.

PERU: SAINT ROSE OF LIMA DAY. Aug 30. Saint Rose of Lima was the first saint of the western hemisphere. She lived at the time of the colonization by Spain in the 16th century. Patron saint of the Americas and the Philippines. Public holiday in Peru.

RUTHERFORD, ERNEST: BIRTH ANNIVERSARY. Aug 30, 1871. Physicist, born at Nelson, New Zealand. He established the nuclear nature of the atom, the electrical structure of matter and achieved the transmutation of elements, research which later resulted in the atomic bomb. Rutherford died at Cambridge, England, Oct 19, 1937.

SHELLEY, MARY WOLLSTONECRAFT: BIRTH ANNIVERSARY. Aug 30, 1797. English novelist Mary Shelley, daughter of the philosopher William Godwin and the feminist Mary Wollstonecraft and wife of the poet Percy Bysshe Shelley, was born at London and died there Feb 1, 1851. In addition to being the author of the famous novel *Frankenstein*, Shelley is important in literary history for her work in the editing and publishing of her husband's unpublished work after his early death.

SPACE MILESTONE: *DISCOVERY* (US). Aug 30, 1984. Space shuttle *Discovery* was launched from Kennedy Space Center, FL, for its maiden flight with a six-member crew. During the flight the crew deployed three satellites and used a robot arm before landing at Edwards Air Force Base, CA, Sept 5.

TURKEY: VICTORY DAY. Aug 30. Commemorates victory in War of Independence in 1922. Military parades, performing of the Mehtar band (the world's oldest military band), fireworks.

WILKINS, ROY: 100th BIRTH ANNIVERSARY. Aug 30, 1901. Roy Wilkins, grandson of a Mississippi slave, civil rights leader, active in the National Association for the Advancement of Colored People (NAACP), retired as its executive director in 1977. Born at St. Louis, MO, he died at New York, NY, Sept 8, 1981.

BIRTHDAYS TODAY

Helen Craig, 67, illustrator (the Angelina Ballerina series, *This Is the Bear*), born London, England, Aug 30, 1934.

Donald Crews, 63, author, illustrator (*Bigmama's, Freight Train*), born Newark, NJ, Aug 30, 1938.

Ted Williams, 83, baseball Hall of Fame outfielder, born San Diego, CA, Aug 30, 1918.

AUGUST 31 — FRIDAY

Day 243 — 122 Remaining

CANADA: KLONDIKE ELDORADO GOLD DISCOVERY: ANNIVERSARY. Aug 31, 1896. Two weeks after the Rabbit/Bonanza Creek claim was filed, gold was discovered on Eldorado Creek, a tributary of Bonanza. More than $30 million worth of gold (worth some $600–$700 million in today's dollars) was mined from the Eldorado Claim in 1896.

KAZAKHSTAN: CONSTITUTION DAY. Aug 31. National holiday. Commemorates the constitution of 1995.

KYRGYZSTAN: INDEPENDENCE DAY: 10th ANNIVERSARY. Aug 31. National holiday. Commemorates independence from the former Soviet Union in 1991.

MALAYSIA: FREEDOM DAY: ANNIVERSARY. Aug 31. National holiday. Merdeka (Freedom) Day commemorates independence from Britain in 1957.

MOLDOVA: NATIONAL LANGUAGE DAY. Aug 31. National holiday. Commemorates the 1991 replacement of the Cyrillic alphabet with the Roman alphabet.

MONTESSORI, MARIA: BIRTH ANNIVERSARY. Aug 31, 1870. Italian physician and educator, born at Chiaraville, Italy. Founder of the Montessori method of teaching children. She believed that children need to work at tasks that interest them and if given the right materials and tasks, they learn best through individual attention. Montessori died at Noordwijk, Holland, May 6, 1952.

POLAND: SOLIDARITY FOUNDED: ANNIVERSARY. Aug 31, 1980. The Polish trade union Solidarity was formed at the Baltic Sea port of Gdansk, Poland. Outlawed by the government, many of its leaders were arrested. Led by Lech Walesa, Solidarity persisted in its opposition to the Communist-controlled government, and on Aug 19, 1989, Polish president Wojcieck Jaruzelski astonished the world by nominating for the post of prime minister Tadeusz Mazowiecki, a deputy in the Polish Assembly, 1961–72, and editor-in-chief of Solidarity's weekly newspaper, bringing to an end 42 years of Communist Party domination.

TRINIDAD AND TOBAGO: INDEPENDENCE DAY. Aug 31. National holiday. Became Commonwealth nation in 1962.

VERMONT STATE FAIR. Aug 31–Sept 9. Fairgrounds, Rutland, VT. Annually, the Friday before Labor Day to the weekend after Labor Day. Est attendance: 100,000. For info: Vermont State Fair, 175 S Main St, Rutland, VT 05701. Phone: (802) 775-5200.

BIRTHDAYS TODAY

Jennifer Azzi, 33, basketball player, born Oak Ridge, TN, Aug 31, 1968.

Edwin Corley Moses, 46, Olympic gold medal track athlete, born Dayton, OH, Aug 31, 1955.

Hideo Nomo, 33, baseball player, born Osaka, Japan, Aug 31, 1968.

SEPTEMBER 1 — SATURDAY

Day 244 — 121 Remaining

BABY SAFETY MONTH. Sept 1–30. The Juvenile Products Manufacturers Association, Inc (JPMA), a national trade organization of juvenile product manufacturers devoted to helping parents keep baby safe, is disseminating information to parents, grandparents and other child caregivers about baby safety. The information from JPMA pertains to safe selection of juvenile products through the Association's Safety Certification Program and tips on correct use of products such as cribs, car seats, infant carriers and decorative accessories. For a free copy of JPMA's brochure "Safe and Sound for Baby," write to the address below and mark ATTN: JPMA Safety Brochure. Enclose a self-addressed stamped envelope and specify whether you want the brochure in English or Spanish. For info: JPMA, PR Dept, 236 Rte 38-W, Ste 100, Moorestown, NJ 08057.

BACK-TO-SCHOOL HEAD LICE PREVENTION CAMPAIGN. Sept 1–30. Time for an "All Out Comb Out." This 17th annual campaign stresses the four steps for lice prevention. The aim is to reach parents before outbreaks occur. For info: Natl Pediculosis Assn, PO Box 610189, Newton, MA 02461. Phone: (781) 449-NITS. Fax: (781) 449-8129. E-mail: npa@headlice.org. Web: www.headlice.org.

BRAZIL: INDEPENDENCE WEEK. Sept 1–7. The independence of Brazil from Portugal in 1822 is commemorated with civic and cultural ceremonies promoted by federal, state and municipal authorities. On Sept 7, a grand military parade takes place and the National Defense League organizes the Running Race in Honor of the Symbolic Torch of the Brazilian Nation.

BURROUGHS, EDGAR RICE: BIRTH ANNIVERSARY. Sept 1, 1875. US novelist (*Tarzan of the Apes*), born at Chicago, IL. Correspondent for the *Los Angeles Times*, he died at Encino, CA, Mar 19, 1950. For more info: *Edgar Rice Burroughs: Creator of Tarzan*, by William J. Boerst (Morgan Reynolds, 1-883846-56-0, $19.95 Gr. 5–8).

CARTIER, JACQUES: DEATH ANNIVERSARY. Sept 1, 1557. French navigator and explorer who sailed from St. Malo, France, Apr 20, 1534, in search of a northwest passage to the Orient. Instead, he discovered the St. Lawrence River, explored Canada's coastal regions and took possession of the country for France. Cartier was born at St. Malo, about 1491 (exact date unknown) and died there.

CHILDREN'S EYE HEALTH AND SAFETY MONTH. Sept 1–30. Prevent Blindness America® directs its educational efforts to common causes of eye injuries and common eye problems among children. Materials that can easily be posted or distributed to the community will be provided. For info: Prevent Blindness America®, 500 E Remington Rd, Schaumburg, IL 60173. Phone: (800) 331-2020. Fax: (847) 843-8458. Web: www.preventblindness.org.

CHILDREN'S GOOD MANNERS MONTH. Sept 1–30. Starts the school year with a national program of teachers and parents encouraging good manners in children. The yearlong program includes monthly objectives that work in conjunction with a reinforcing home program. For info: "Dr. Manners," Fleming Allaire, PhD, 35 Eastfield St, Manchester, CT 06040. Phone: (860) 643-0051.

CHILE: NATIONAL MONTH. Sept 1–30. A month of special significance in Chile: arrival of spring, Independence of Chile anniversary (proclaimed Sept 18, 1810), anniversary of the armed forces rising of Sept 11, 1973, to overthrow the government and celebration of the 1980 Constitution and Army Day, Sept 19.

D.A.R.E. LAUNCHED: ANNIVERSARY. Sept 1, 1983. D.A.R.E. (Drug Abuse Resistance Education) is a police officer-led series of classroom lessons that teaches students how to resist peer pressure and lead productive drug- and violence-free lives. The program, which was developed jointly by the Los Angeles Police Department and the Los Angeles Unified School District, initially

SEPTEMBER 1–30
NATIONAL SCHOOL SUCCESS MONTH—SETTING CLASSROOM GOALS

Get your school year off on the right track. National School Success Month focuses on helping students and parents be aware of the importance of academic work. Observing this theme can serve a two-fold purpose: First, it can be used to create a sense of cohesion among new classmates; secondly, it can help provide a yardstick by which students can measure social and academic progress.

After beginning of the year introductions are out of the way, ask students to help you list the pluses and minuses they experienced in class *as a class* last year. What actions and/or emotions were productive and created a sense of unity in their respective rooms? What detracted from this?

For homework, ask students to talk with family members and friends about their experiences in school. Have each student write a list of five helpful and five detrimental actions for achieving a classroom that functions successfully. Make two lists that include all comments. Form groups of four or five students and brainstorm ways that helpful actions can be implemented in the classroom. This divides the class initially, but some students will speak more freely when they are not intimidated by the large group. Come back together as a class and discuss the suggestions. Together, make a general list of five classroom goals for academic and social success in your classroom. An example might be "study buddies," students who quiz each other on multiplication facts or language usage. A sign up sheet entitled "I Could Use a Helping Hand" could be posted. After a student signs up, a student proficient in the task could offer to help out by quizzing or discussion. A necessary corollary to this is removing any social stigma in admitting the need for some extra help. The eye should always be focused on attaining classroom success.

Highlight goals with a student generated bulletin board for the first few weeks of school. Hold a weekly goal assessment meeting for the first two months. After that, make it a monthly task if all seems to be flowing smoothly.

focused on elementary school children but has now been expanded to include middle and high school students. D.A.R.E. has been implemented in 75 percent of US school districts and in 44 other countries. For info: D.A.R.E. America, PO Box 512090, Los Angeles, CA 90051-0090. Phone: (800) 223-DARE. Web: www.dare-america.com.

EMMA M. NUTT DAY. Sept 1. A day to honor the first woman telephone operator, Emma M. Nutt, who reportedly began her professional career at Boston, MA, Sept 1, 1878, and continued working as a telephone operator for some 33 years.

LIBRARY CARD SIGN-UP MONTH. Sept 1–30. National effort to sign up every child for a library card. Annually, the month of September. For info: American Library Assn, Public Information Office, 50 E Huron St, Chicago, IL 60611. Phone: (312) 280-5043 or (312) 280-5042. E-mail: pio@ala.org. Web: www.ala.org.

LIBYA: REVOLUTION DAY. Sept 1. Commemorates the revolution in 1969 when King Idris I was overthrown by Colonel Qaddafi. National holiday.

MEXICO: PRESIDENT'S STATE OF THE UNION ADDRESS. Sept 1. National holiday.

NATIONAL CHILDHOOD INJURY PREVENTION WEEK. Sept 1–7. To stress the importance of community involvement in protecting the nation's children from harm. Safety By Design® sponsors this week, providing a full week of opportunities to raise awareness of the problem of unintentional injury to children and highlight the roles members of the community play in reducing injury rates. Information and materials are available. For info: Safety By Design® Ltd, PO Box 4312, Great Neck, NY 11023. Phone and Fax: (516) 482-1475.

NATIONAL HISTORY DAY. Sept 1, 2001–June 2002. This year-long project begins in September when curriculum and contest materials are distributed to coordinators and teachers around the country. District History Day contests are usually held in February or March and state contests in late April or early May. The national contest is held in June at the University of Maryland. There are two divisions of the competition: junior (Gr. 6–8) and senior (Gr. 9–12). Some states also sponsor a contest for students in grades 4 and 5. Students can enter the contest with a paper, an individual or group exhibit, an individual or group performance or individual or group media. Visit the website for the theme for 2001–2002. For info: National History Day, 0119 Cecil Hall, Univ of Maryland, College Park, MD 20742. Phone: (301) 314-9739. E-mail: hstryday@aol.com. Web: www.thehistorynet.com/NationalHistoryDay.

September 2001

S	M	T	W	T	F	S
						1
2	3	4	5	6	7	8
9	10	11	12	13	14	15
16	17	18	19	20	21	22
23	24	25	26	27	28	29
30						

NATIONAL HONEY MONTH. Sept 1–30. To honor the US's 211,600 beekeepers and 2.63 million colonies of honey bees, which produce more than 220 million pounds of honey each year. For info: Gretchen Lichtenwalner, Natl Honey Board, 390 Lashley St, Longmont, CO 80501-6045. Phone: (303) 776-2337. Web: www.honey.com.

NATIONAL PIANO MONTH. Sept 1–30. Recognizes America's most popular instrument and its more than 20 million players; also encourages piano study by people of all ages. For info: Donald W. Dillon, Exec Dir, Natl Piano Foundation, 4020 McEwen, Ste 105, Dallas, TX 75244-5019. Phone: (972) 233-9107. Fax: (972) 490-4219. E-mail: don@dondillon.com. Web: www.pianonet.com.

NATIONAL SCHOOL SUCCESS MONTH. Sept 1–30. Today's young people have many distractions from school and are sometimes overwhelmed when it comes to academics. Parents are often unskilled at effectively redirecting the attention of their children, especially their teenagers. This observance is to recognize parents who want to support and encourage their children to succeed in school and to explore ways to do that. Annually, the month of September. For info send SASE to: Teresa Langston, Dir, Parenting Without Pressure, 1330 Boyer St, Longwood, FL 32750-6311. Phone: (407) 767-2524. *See* Curriculum Connection.

NATIONAL STORYTELLER OF THE YEAR CONTEST. Sept 1. Millersport, OH. Official Storyteller of the Year named at this event. Sponsored by the Creative Arts Institute, Inc, *Adventures in Storytelling* magazine and the Ohio Arts Council. Annually, the Saturday before Labor Day. Est attendance: 500. For info: Donna Foster, Creative Arts, 8021 Kennedy Rd, Blacklick, OH 43004. Phone: (614) 759-9407. Fax: (614) 759-8480. E-mail: dfoster@freenet.columbus.oh.us.

SEA CADET MONTH. Sept 1–30. Nationwide year-round youth program for boys and girls 11–17 teaches leadership and self-discipline with emphasis on nautically-oriented training without military obligation. Est attendance: 9,000. For info: US Naval Sea Cadet Corps, 2300 Wilson Blvd, Arlington, VA 22201. Phone: (703) 243-6910. Fax: (703) 243-3985. E-mail: mford@NAVYLEAGUE.org. Web: www.seacadets.org.

SLOVAKIA: NATIONAL DAY. Sept 1. Anniversary of the adoption of the Constitution of the Slovak Republic in 1992.

TAIWAN: CHENG CHENG KUNG BIRTH ANNIVERSARY. Sept 1. Joyous celebration of birth of Cheng Cheng Kung (Koxinga), born at Hirado, Japan, the Ming Dynasty loyalist who ousted the Dutch colonists from Taiwan in 1661. Dutch landing is commemorated annually Apr 29, but Cheng's birthday is honored on the 14th day of the seventh moon according to the Chinese lunar calendar. Cheng Cheng Kung died June 23, 1662, at Taiwan. See also: "Taiwan: Cheng Cheng Kung Landing Day" (Apr 29).

UZBEKISTAN: INDEPENDENCE DAY: 10th ANNIVERSARY. Sept 1. National holiday. Commemorates independence from the Soviet Union in 1991.

BIRTHDAYS TODAY

Jim Arnosky, 55, author and illustrator (*Watching Water Birds*), born New York, NY, Sept 1, 1946.

Rosa Guy, 73, author (*Billy the Great*), born Trinidad, West Indies, Sept 1, 1928.

Tim Hardaway, 35, basketball player, born Chicago, IL, Sept 1, 1966.

SEPTEMBER 2 — SUNDAY

Day 245 — 120 Remaining

CALENDAR ADJUSTMENT DAY: ANNIVERSARY. Sept 2, 1752. Pursuant to the British Calendar Act of 1751, Britain (and the American colonies) made the "Gregorian Correction" in 1752. The Act proclaimed that the day following Wednesday, Sept 2, should become Thursday, Sept 14, 1752. There was rioting in the streets by those who felt cheated and who demanded the eleven days back. The Act also provided that New Year's Day (and the change of year number) should fall Jan 1 (instead of Mar 25) in 1752 and every year thereafter. See also: "Gregorian Calendar Adjustment: Anniversary" (Feb 24, Oct 4).

CHINA: FESTIVAL OF HUNGRY GHOSTS. Sept 2. Important Chinese festival, also known as Ghosts Month. According to Chinese legend, during the seventh lunar month the souls of the dead are released from purgatory to roam the Earth. Joss sticks are burnt in homes; prayers, food and "ghost money" are offered to appease the ghosts. Market stallholders combine to hold celebrations to ensure that their businesses will prosper in the coming year. Wayang (Chinese street opera) and puppet shows are performed, and fruit and Chinese delicacies are offered to the spirits of the dead. Chung Yuan (All Souls' Day) is observed on the 15th day of the seventh lunar month.

DAYS OF MARATHON: ANNIVERSARY. Sept 2–9, 490 BC. Anniversary of the event during the Persian Wars from which the marathon race is derived. Phidippides, "an Athenian and by profession and practice a trained runner," according to Herodotus, was dispatched from Marathon to Sparta (26 miles), Sept 2 to seek help in repelling the invading Persian army. Help being unavailable by religious law until after the next full moon, Phidippides ran the 26 miles back to Marathon Sept 4. Without Spartan aid, the Athenians defeated the Persians at the Battle of Marathon Sept 9. According to legend Phidippides carried the news of the battle to Athens and died as he spoke the words, "Rejoice, we are victorious." The marathon race was revived at the 1896 Olympic Games in Athens. Course distance, since 1924, is 26 miles, 385 yards.

ENGLAND: GREAT FIRE OF LONDON: ANNIVERSARY. Sept 2–5, 1666. The fire generally credited with bringing about our system of fire insurance started Sept 2, 1666, in the wooden house of a baker named Farryner, at London's Pudding Lane, near the Tower. During the ensuing three days more than 13,000 houses were destroyed, though it is believed that only six lives were lost in the fire.

FORTEN, JAMES: BIRTH ANNIVERSARY. Sept 2, 1766. James Forten was born of free black parents at Philadelphia, PA. As a powder boy on an American Revolutionary warship, he escaped being sold as a slave when his ship was captured due to the intervention of the British commander's son. While in England he became involved with abolitionists. On his return to Philadelphia, he became an apprentice to a sailmaker and eventually purchased the company for which he worked. He was active in the abolition movement, and in 1816, his support was sought by the American Colonization Society for the plan to settle American blacks at Liberia. He rejected their ideas and their plans to make him the ruler of the colony. From the large profits of his successful sailmaking company, he contributed heavily to the abolitionist movement and was a supporter of William Lloyd Garrison's anti-slavery journal, *The Liberator*. Died at Philadelphia, PA, Mar 4, 1842.

ITALY: HISTORICAL REGATTA. Sept 2. Venice. Traditional competition among two-oar racing gondolas, preceded by a procession of Venetian ceremonial boats of the epoch of the Venetian Republic. Annually, the first Sunday in September.

McAULIFFE, CHRISTA: BIRTH ANNIVERSARY. Sept 2, 1948. Christa McAuliffe, a 37-year-old Concord, NH, high school teacher, was to have been the first "ordinary citizen" in space. Born Sharon Christa Corrigan at Boston, MA, she perished with six crew members in the Space Shuttle *Challenger* explosion Jan 28, 1986. See also: "*Challenger* Space Shuttle Explosion: Anniversary" (Jan 28).

MOON PHASE: FULL MOON. Sept 2. Moon enters Full Moon phase at 5:43 PM, EDT.

SHERMAN ENTERS ATLANTA: ANNIVERSARY. Sept 2, 1864. After a four-week siege, Union General William Tecumseh Sherman entered Atlanta, GA. The city had been evacuated on the previous day by Confederate troops under General John B. Hood. Hood had mistakenly assumed Sherman was ending the siege Aug 27, when actually Sherman was beginning the final stages of his attack. Hood then sent troops to attack the Union forces at Jonesboro. Hood's troops were defeated, opening the way for the capture of Atlanta.

US TREASURY DEPARTMENT: ANNIVERSARY. Sept 2, 1789. The third presidential cabinet department, the Treasury Department, was established by Congress.

V-J (VICTORY OVER JAPAN) DAY: ANNIVERSARY. Sept 2, 1945. Official ratification of Japanese surrender to the Allies occurred aboard the USS *Missouri* at Tokyo Bay Sept 2 (Far Eastern time) in 1945, thus prompting President Truman's declaration of this day as Victory-over-Japan Day. Japan's initial, informal agreement of surrender was announced by Truman and celebrated in the US Aug 14.

VIETNAM: INDEPENDENCE DAY. Sept 2. Ho Chi Minh formally proclaimed the independence of Vietnam from France and the establishment of the Democratic Republic of Vietnam in 1945. National holiday.

BIRTHDAYS TODAY

John Bierhorst, 65, author (*The Woman Who Fell from the Sky*), born Boston, MA, Sept 2, 1936.

Demi, 59, author (*One Grain of Rice*), born Charlotte Dumaresque Hunt, Cambridge, MA, Sept 2, 1942.

Elizabeth Borton de Trevino, 97, author (*I, Juan de Pareja*), born Bakersfield, CA, Sept 2, 1904.

Barbara Dillon, 74, author (*The Teddy Bear Tree*), born Montclair, NJ, Sept 2, 1927.

Bernard Most, 64, author and illustrator (*Where to Look for a Dinosaur*), born New York, NY, Sept 2, 1937.

Carlos Valderrama, 40, soccer player, born Santa Marta, Colombia, Sept 2, 1961.

SEPTEMBER 3 — MONDAY

Day 246 — 119 Remaining

★**AMERICA GOES BACK TO SCHOOL.** Sept 3–9 (tentative).

CANADA: LABOR DAY. Sept 3. Annually, the first Monday in September.

DOUGLASS ESCAPES TO FREEDOM: ANNIVERSARY. Sept 3, 1838. Dressed as a sailor and carrying identification papers borrowed from a retired merchant seaman, Frederick Douglass boarded a train at Baltimore, MD, a slave state, and rode to Wilmington, DE, where he caught a steamboat to the free city of Philadelphia. He then transferred to a train headed for New York City where he entered the protection of the Underground Railway network. Douglass later became a great orator and one of the leaders of the antislavery struggle.

ITALY SURRENDERS: ANNIVERSARY. Sept 3, 1943. General Giuseppe Castellano signed three copies of the "short armistice," effectively surrendering unconditionally for the Italian government in World War II. That same day the British Eighth Army, commanded by General Bernard Montgomery, invaded the Italian mainland.

LABOR DAY. Sept 3. Legal public holiday. Public Law 90–363 sets Labor Day on the first Monday in September. Observed in all states. First observance believed to have been a parade at 10 AM, Tuesday, Sept 5, 1882, at New York, NY, probably organized by Peter J. McGuire, a Carpenters and Joiners Union secretary. In 1883, a union resolution declared "the first Monday in September of each year a Labor Day." By 1893, more than half of the states were observing Labor Day on one or another day, and a bill to establish Labor Day as a federal holiday was introduced in Congress. On June 28, 1894, President Grover Cleveland signed into law an act making the first Monday in September a legal holiday for federal employees and the District of Columbia. Canada also celebrates Labor Day on the first Monday in September. In most other countries, Labor Day is observed May 1. For links to Labor Day websites, go to: deil.lang.uiuc.edu/web.pages/holidays/labor.html.

QATAR: INDEPENDENCE DAY: 30th ANNIVERSARY. Sept 3. National holiday. Commemorates the severing in 1971 of the treaty with Britain, which had handled Qatar's foreign relations.

SAN MARINO: NATIONAL DAY. Sept 3. Public holiday. Honors St. Marinus, the traditional founder of San Marino.

September 2001

S	M	T	W	T	F	S
						1
2	3	4	5	6	7	8
9	10	11	12	13	14	15
16	17	18	19	20	21	22
23	24	25	26	27	28	29
30						

TREATY OF PARIS ENDS AMERICAN REVOLUTION: ANNIVERSARY. Sept 3, 1783. Treaty between Britain and the US, ending the Revolutionary War, signed at Paris, France. American signatories: John Adams, Benjamin Franklin and John Jay.

BIRTHDAYS TODAY

Aliki, 72, Aliki Liacouras Brandenberg, author and illustrator (*Three Gold Pieces*), born Wildwood Crest, NJ, Sept 3, 1929.

Damon Stoudamire, 28, basketball player, born Portland, OR, Sept 3, 1973.

SEPTEMBER 4 — TUESDAY

Day 247 — 118 Remaining

FIRST ELECTRIC LIGHTING: ANNIVERSARY. Sept 4, 1882. Four hundred electric lights came on in offices on Spruce, Wall, Nassau and Pearl streets in lower Manhattan as Thomas Edison hooked up light bulbs to an underground cable carrying direct current electrical power. Edison had demonstrated his first incandescent light bulb in 1879. See also: "Incandescent Lamp Demonstrated: Anniversary" (Oct 21).

JASON XIII PROJECT. Sept 4. A year-round scientific experiment designed to engage students through the study of sea and space in geography, science and technology. For grades 4–9. Teacher training available. For info: JASON Foundation for Education, 395 Totten Pond Rd, Waltham, MA 02451. Phone: 888-527-6600. Web: www.jason.org.

LOS ANGELES, CALIFORNIA FOUNDED: ANNIVERSARY. Sept 4, 1781. Los Angeles founded by decree and called "El Pueblo de Nuestra Senora La Reina de Los Angeles de Porciuncula." For more info: *City of Angeles: In and Around Los Angeles*, by Julie Jaskol and Brian Lewis (Dutton, 0-525-46214-7, $16.99 All ages).

NEWSPAPER CARRIER DAY. Sept 4. Anniversary of the hiring of the first "newsboy" in the US, 10-year-old Barney Flaherty, who is said to have answered the following classified advertisement which appeared in *The New York Sun*, in 1833: "To the Unemployed—a number of steady men can find employment by vending this paper. A liberal discount is allowed to those who buy to sell again."

POLK, SARAH CHILDRESS: BIRTH ANNIVERSARY. Sept 4, 1803. Wife of James Knox Polk, 11th president of the US. Born at Murfreesboro, TN, and died at Nashville, TN, Aug 14, 1891.

WRIGHT, RICHARD: BIRTH ANNIVERSARY. Sept 4, 1908. African American novelist and short story writer whose works included *Native Son, Uncle Tom's Children* and *Black Boy*. Born at Natchez, MS, Wright died at Paris, France, Nov 28, 1960. For more info: *Richard Wright and the Library Card*, by William Miller (Lee & Low, 1-88000-57-1, $6.95 Gr. 1–4).

BIRTHDAYS TODAY

Joan Aiken, 77, author (*The Wolves of Willoughby Chase, Cold Shoulder Road)*, born Rye, Sussex, England, Sept 4, 1924.

Jason David Frank, 28, actor (*Turbo: A Power Rangers Movie*, "Power Rangers Turbo"), born Covina, CA, Sept 4, 1973.

Syd Hoff, 89, author (*Corn Is Maize: The Gift of the Indians; Danny and the Dinosaur*), born New York, NY, Sept 4, 1912.

Mike Piazza, 33, baseball player, born Norristown, PA, Sept 4, 1968.

SEPTEMBER 5 — WEDNESDAY

Day 248 — 117 Remaining

BE LATE FOR SOMETHING DAY. Sept 5. To create a release from the stresses and strains resulting from a consistent need to be on time. For info: Les Waas, Pres, Procrastinators' Club of America, Inc, Box 712, Bryn Athyn, PA 19009. Phone: (215) 947-9020. Fax: (215) 947-7007.

FIRST CONTINENTAL CONGRESS ASSEMBLY: ANNIVERSARY. Sept 5, 1774. The first assembly of this forerunner of the US Congress took place at Philadelphia, PA. All 13 colonies were represented except Georgia. Peyton Randolph, delegate from Virginia, was elected president. The second Continental Congress met beginning May 10, 1775, also at Philadelphia.

JAMES, JESSE: BIRTH ANNIVERSARY. Sept 5, 1847. Western legend and bandit Jesse Woodson James was born at Centerville (now Kearney), MO. His criminal exploits were glorified and romanticized by writers for Eastern readers looking for stories of Western adventure and heroism. After the Civil War, James and his brother, Frank, formed a group of eight outlaws who robbed banks, stagecoaches and stores. In 1873, the James gang began holding up trains. The original James gang was put out of business Sept 7, 1876, while attempting to rob a bank at Northfield, MN. Every member of the gang except for the James brothers was killed or captured. The brothers formed a new gang and resumed their criminal careers in 1879. Two years later, the governor of Missouri offered a $10,000 reward for their capture, dead or alive. On Apr 3, 1882 at St. Joseph, MO, Robert Ford, a member of the gang, shot 34-year-old Jesse in the back of the head and claimed the reward.

NIELSEN, ARTHUR CHARLES: BIRTH ANNIVERSARY. Sept 5, 1897. Marketing research engineer, founder of A.C. Nielsen Company, in 1923, known for radio and TV audience surveys and ratings, was born at Chicago, IL, and died there June 1, 1980.

SPACE MILESTONE: *VOYAGER 1* (US). Sept 5, 1977. Twin of *Voyager 2* which was launched Aug 20. On Feb 18, 1998, *Voyager 1* set a new distance record when after more than 20 years in space it reached 6.5 billion miles from Earth.

BIRTHDAYS TODAY

Paul Fleischman, 49, author, poet (Newbery for *Joyful Noise: Poems for Two Voices*), born Monterey, CA, Sept 5, 1952.

Roxie Munro, 56, author (*The Inside-Outside Book of Libraries*), born Mineral Wells, TX, Sept 5, 1945.

SEPTEMBER 6 — THURSDAY

Day 249 — 116 Remaining

ADDAMS, JANE: BIRTH ANNIVERSARY. Sept 6, 1860. American worker for peace, social welfare and the rights of women. The founder of Chicago's Hull House settlement house, she was co-winner of the Nobel Peace Prize in 1931. Born at Cedarville, IL, she died May 21, 1935, at Chicago, IL.

BALTIC STATES' INDEPENDENCE RECOGNIZED: 10th ANNIVERSARY. Sept 6, 1991. The Soviet government recognized the independence of the Baltic states—Latvia, Estonia and Lithuania. The action came 51 years after the Baltic states were annexed by the Soviet Union. All three Baltic states had earlier declared their independence, and many nations had already recognized them diplomatically, including the US, Sept 2, 1991.

BULGARIA: UNIFICATION DAY. Sept 6. National holiday. Commemorates the 1885 reunification of the South and the rest of Bulgaria.

LAFAYETTE, MARQUIS DE: BIRTH ANNIVERSARY. Sept 6, 1757. French general and aristocrat, Lafayette, whose full name was Marie-Joseph-Paul-Yves-Roch-Gilbert du Motier, came to America to assist in the revolutionary cause. He was awarded a major-generalship and began a lasting friendship with the American commander-in-chief, George Washington. After an alliance was signed with France, he returned to his native country and persuaded Louis XVI to send a 6,000-man force to assist the Americans. On his return, he was given command of an army at Virginia and was instrumental in forcing the surrender of Lord Cornwallis at Yorktown, leading to the end of the war and American independence. He was hailed as "The Hero of Two Worlds" and was appointed a brigadier general on his return to France in 1782. He became a leader of the liberal aristocrats during the early days of the French revolution, presenting to the National Assembly his draft of "A Declaration of the Rights of Man and of the Citizen." As the commander of the newly formed national guard of Paris, he rescued Louis XVI and Marie-Antoinette from a crowd that stormed Versailles Oct 6, 1789, returning them to Paris where they became hostages of the revolution. His popularity waned after his guards opened fire on angry demonstrators demanding abdication of the king in 1791. He fled to Austria with the overthrow of the monarchy in 1792, returning when Napoleon Bonaparte came to power. Born at Chavaniac, he died at Paris, May 20, 1834. For more info: *Why Not, Lafayette?*, by Jean Fritz (Putnam, 0-399-23411-X, $16.99 Gr. 3–7).

SAINT PETERSBURG NAME RESTORED: 10th ANNIVERSARY. Sept 6, 1991. Russian legislators voted to restore the name Saint Petersburg to the nation's second largest city. The city had been known as Leningrad for 67 years in honor of the Soviet Union's founder, Vladimir I. Lenin. The city, founded in 1703 by Peter the Great, has had three names in the 20th century with Russian leaders changing its German-sounding name to Petrograd at the beginning of WWI in 1914 and Soviet Communist leaders changing its name to Leningrad in 1924 following their leader's death.

SWAZILAND: INDEPENDENCE DAY. Sept 6. Commemorates attainment of independence from Britain in 1968. National holiday.

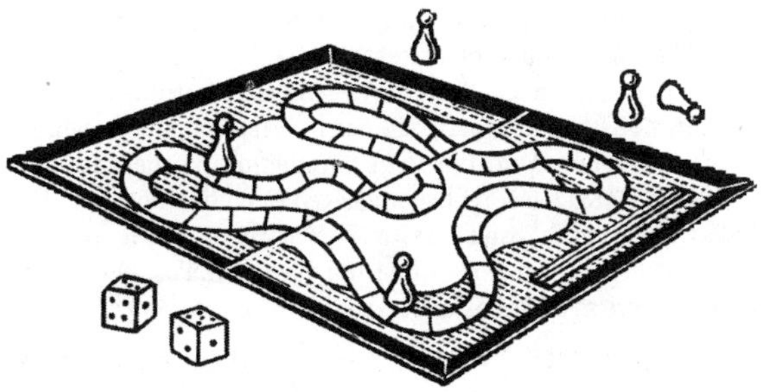

UTAH STATE FAIR. Sept 6–16. Salt Lake City, UT. Est attendance: 360,000. For info: Utah State Fair Park, 155 N 1000 W, Salt Lake City, UT 84116. Phone: (801) 538-8440. Fax: (801) 538-8455. E-mail: donna@fiber.net.

BIRTHDAYS TODAY

Chad Scott, 27, football player, born Washington, DC, Sept 6, 1974.

SEPTEMBER 7 — FRIDAY

Day 250 — 115 Remaining

BRAZIL: INDEPENDENCE DAY. Sept 7. Declared independence from Portugal in 1822. National holiday.

ELIZABETH I: BIRTH ANNIVERSARY. Sept 7, 1533. Queen of England, after whom the "Elizabethan Age" was named, born at Greenwich Palace, daughter of Henry VIII and Anne Boleyn. She succeeded to the throne in 1558 and ruled England until her death on May 24, 1603. Her reign was one of the most dynamic in English history and she was held in great affection by her people. The British defeated the Spanish Armada and England became a world power during her reign. For more info: *Good Queen Bess: The Story of Elizabeth I of England*, by Diane Stanley and Peter Vennema (Morrow, out-of-print).

GRANDMA MOSES DAY. Sept 7. Anna Mary Robertson Moses, modern primitive American painter, born at Greenwich, NY, Sept 7, 1860. She started painting at the age of 78. Her 100th birthday was proclaimed Grandma Moses Day in New York state. Died at Hoosick Falls, NY, Dec 13, 1961. For info: *Grandma Moses*, by Zibby O'Neal (Puffin, 0-14-032220-5, $4.99 Gr. 4–8).

KANSAS STATE FAIR. Sept 7–16. Hutchinson, KS. Commercial and competitive exhibits, entertainment, carnival, car racing and other special attractions. Annually, beginning the first Friday after Labor Day. Est attendance: 400,000. For info: Bill Ogg, Gen Mgr, Kansas State Fair, 2000 N Poplar, Hutchinson, KS 67502. Phone: (316) 669-3600. E-mail: ksfair@southwind.net. Web: www.kansasstatefair.com.

LAWRENCE, JACOB: BIRTH ANNIVERSARY. Sept 7, 1917. African American painter, born at Atlantic City, NJ. Lawrence was best known for his series of historical paintings on John Brown and on the migration of African Americans out of the South. He also illustrated children's books. A recipient of the NAACP's Spingarn Medal, he won many other awards during his lifetime. Lawrence died June 9, 2000, in Seattle, WA. For more info: *Story Painter: The Life of Jacob Lawrence*, by John Duggleby (Chronicle, $16.95, 0-8118-2082-3 Gr. 4–7) and *The Great Migration: An American Story*, by Jacob Lawrence (Harper Trophy, $8.95, 0-06-443428-1 Gr. 4–7).

NEITHER SNOW NOR RAIN DAY. Sept 7. Anniversary of the opening to the public, on Labor Day, 1914, of the New York Post Office Building at Eighth Avenue between 31st and 33rd Streets. On the front of this building was an inscription supplied by William M. Kendall of the architectural firm that planned the building. The inscription, a free translation from Herodotus, reads: "Neither snow nor rain nor heat nor gloom of night stays these couriers from the swift completion of their appointed rounds." This has long been believed to be the motto of the US Post Office and Postal Service. They have, in fact, no motto . . . but the legend remains. [Info from: New York Post Office, Public Info Office and US Postal Service.]

NEW MEXICO STATE FAIR. Sept 7–23. Albuquerque, NM. Fireworks, blues, country, gospel, pop and rock entertainment. Rodeos, circus, auto thrill show, tractor pulls, horse racing and free grandstand shows. For info: New Mexico State Fair, PO Box 8546, Albuquerque, NM 87198. Phone: (505) 265-1791. Fax: (505) 266-7784.

TENNESSEE STATE FAIR. Sept 7–16. Nashville, TN. A huge variety of exhibits, carnival midway, animal and variety shows, live stage presentations, livestock, agricultural and craft competitions and food and game booths. Est attendance: 350,000. For info: Tennessee Fair Office, PO Box 40208, Melrose Station, Nashville, TN 37204. Phone: (615) 862-8980. Fax: (615) 862-8992. Web: www.tennesseestatefair.org.

BIRTHDAYS TODAY

Alexandra Day, 60, author and illustrator (*The Teddy Bears' Picnic*), born Cincinnati, OH, Sept 7, 1941.
Eric Hill, 74, author (*Where's Spot?; Spot Goes to School; Spot Visits His Grandparents;* etc.), born London, England, Sept 7, 1927.
Daniel Ken Inouye, 77, US Senator (D, Hawaii), born Honolulu, HI, Sept 7, 1924.

SEPTEMBER 8 — SATURDAY

Day 251 — 114 Remaining

ANDORRA: NATIONAL HOLIDAY. Sept 8. Honors our Lady of Meritxell.

★**FEDERAL LANDS CLEANUP DAY.** Sept 8. Presidential Proclamation 5521, of Sept 5, 1986, covers all succeeding years. The first Saturday after Labor Day. (PL99–402 of Aug 27, 1986.)

GALVESTON HURRICANE: ANNIVERSARY. Sept 8, 1900. The worst national disaster in US history in terms of lives lost. More than 6,000 people were killed when a hurricane struck Galveston, TX. For more info about hurricanes: www.fema.gov/kids/hurr.htm.

KID'RIFIC. Sept 8–9. Hartford, CT. A two-day children's festival on Constitution Plaza in downtown Hartford, produced by the Hartford Downtown Council. Kid'rific will feature hands-on art and science activities, storytelling, master teaching artists' workshops, continuous stage entertainment, a petting zoo with a 13' tall giraffe and lots more. Annually, the first weekend after Labor Day. Est attendance: 50,000. For info: Steven A. Lazaroff, Dir for Events Programming, Hartford Downtown Council, 250 Constitution Plaza, Hartford, CT 06103. Phone: (860) 728-3089. Fax: (860) 527-9696. Web: www.hartford-hdc.com.

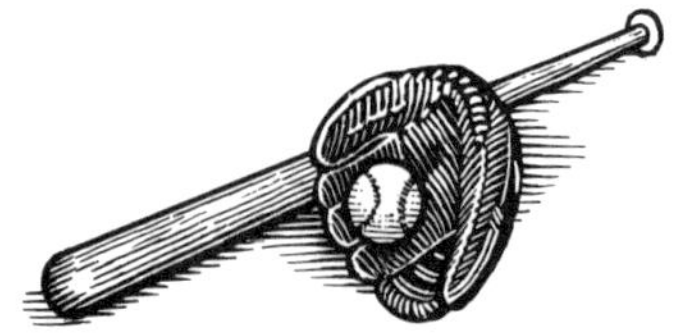

McGWIRE HITS 62nd HOME RUN: ANNIVERSARY. Sept 8, 1998. Mark McGwire of the St. Louis Cardinals hit his 62nd home run, breaking Roger Maris's 1961 record for the most home runs in a single season. McGwire hit his homer against pitcher Steve Trachsel of the Chicago Cubs at Busch Stadium at St. Louis as the Cardinals won, 6–3. A few days later, Sept 13, 1998, Sammy Sosa of the Chicago Cubs hit his 62nd homer. McGwire ended the season with a total of 70 home runs; Sosa with a total of 66.

NORTHERN PACIFIC RAILROAD COMPLETED: ANNIVERSARY. Sept 8, 1883. After 19 years of construction, the Northern Pacific Railroad became the second railroad to link the two coasts. The Union Pacific and Central Pacific lines met at Utah in 1869.

September 2001

S	M	T	W	T	F	S
						1
2	3	4	5	6	7	8
9	10	11	12	13	14	15
16	17	18	19	20	21	22
23	24	25	26	27	28	29
30						

PUBLIC LANDS DAY. Sept 8. To involve citizen volunteers in cleaning and maintaining public lands. Annually, the Saturday after Labor Day. Est attendance: 1,000,000. For info: Keep America Beautiful, Inc, Washington Square, 1010 Washington Blvd, Stamford, CT 06901. E-mail: keepamerbe@aol.com.

"STAR TREK" TV PREMIERE: 35th ANNIVERSARY. Sept 8, 1966. The first of 79 episodes of the TV series "Star Trek" was aired on the NBC network. Although the science fiction show set in the future only lasted a few seasons, it has remained enormously popular through syndication reruns. It has been given new life through six motion pictures, a cartoon TV series and the very popular TV series "Star Trek: The Next Generation," "Star Trek: Deep Space Nine" and "Star Trek: Voyager." It has consistently ranked among the biggest titles in the motion picture, television, home video and licensing divisions of Paramount Pictures.

UNITED NATIONS: INTERNATIONAL LITERACY DAY. Sept 8. An international day observed by the organizations of the United Nations system. Info from: United Nations, Dept of Public Info, New York, NY 10017.

BIRTHDAYS TODAY

Michael Hague, 53, illustrator (*The Children's Book of Virtues, The Wind in the Willows, The Hobbit*), born Los Angeles, CA, Sept 8, 1948.

Jack Prelutsky, 61, poet (*The New Kid on the Block*), born Brooklyn, NY, Sept 8, 1940.

Jon Scieszka, 47, author (*The Stinky Cheese Man and Other Fairly Stupid Tales, Math Curse*), born Flint, MI, Sept 8, 1954.

Latrell Sprewell, 31, basketball player, born Milwaukee, WI, Sept 8, 1970.

Jonathan Taylor Thomas, 20, actor ("Home Improvement," voice of Simba in *The Lion King*), born Bethlehem, PA, Sept 8, 1981.

SEPTEMBER 9 — SUNDAY

Day 252 — 113 Remaining

BONZA BOTTLER DAY™. Sept 9. To celebrate when the number of the day is the same as the number of the month. Bonza Bottler Day™ is an excuse to have a party at least once a month. For info: Gail M. Berger, 109 Matthew Ave, Poca, WV 25159. Phone: (304) 776-7746. E-mail: gberger5@aol.com.

CALIFORNIA: ADMISSION DAY: ANNIVERSARY. Sept 9. Became 31st state in 1850.

COLONIES BECOME UNITED STATES: ANNIVERSARY. Sept 9, 1776. The Continental Congress resolved that the name United States was to replace United Colonies.

ENGLAND: BATTLE OF BRITAIN WEEK. Sept 9–15. Annually, the third week of September—the week containing Battle of Britain Day (Sept 15).

"FAT ALBERT AND THE COSBY KIDS" TV PREMIERE: ANNIVERSARY. Sept 9, 1972. This cartoon series was hosted by Bill Cosby, with characters based on his childhood friends at Philadelphia. Its central characters—Fat Albert, Weird Harold, Mush Mouth and Donald—were weird-looking but very human. The show sent messages of tolerance and harmony. In 1979 the show was renamed "The New Fat Albert Show."

IRISH FAMINE BEGINS: ANNIVERSARY. Sept 9, 1845. On this day, *The Dublin Evening Post* reported the partial failure of the potato crop in Ireland. A blight caused by a fungus destroyed 30 percent of the crop; in 1846, 1848 and 1849 nearly the entire potato crop failed. More than 1.6 million people died in the resulting famine or emigrated to the US, Canada and Australia. The 1850 US census showed that more than 40 percent of the country's foreign-born population was Irish.

KOREA, DEMOCRATIC PEOPLE'S REPUBLIC OF: NATIONAL DAY. Sept 9. National holiday in the Democratic People's Republic of [North] Korea.

LUXEMBOURG: ANNIVERSARY LIBERATION CEREMONY. Sept 9. Petange. Commemoration of liberation of Grand-Duchy by the Allied forces in 1944. Ceremony at monument of the American soldier.

NATIONAL 5-A-DAY WEEK. Sept 9–15. To encourage all Americans to increase the amount of fruits and vegetables they eat to five or more servings per day, to better their health and reduce their risk of cancer and other chronic diseases. For information on the US Department of Agriculture's Food Pyramid, go to www.nal.usda.gov/fnic/Fpyr/pyramid.html. For more info: *The Edible Pyramid: Good Eating Every Day*, by Loreen Leedy (Holiday House, 0-8234-1126-5, $15.95 Gr. 5–7) and *The Food Pyramid*, by Joan Kalbacken (Children's Press, 0-516-20756-3, $21 Gr. 2–4). For info: Produce for Better Health Foundation, 5301 Limestone Rd, Ste 101, Wilmington, DE 19808. Web: www.5aday.com.

★ **NATIONAL GRANDPARENTS' DAY.** Sept 9. Presidential Proclamation 4679, of Sept 6, 1979, covers all succeeding years. First Sunday in September following Labor Day (PL96–62 of Sept 6, 1979). First issued in 1978 (Proc 4580 of Aug 3, 1978), requested by Public Law 325 of July 28, 1978.

SUBSTITUTE TEACHER APPRECIATION WEEK. Sept 9–15. Although substitute teachers get no sick days or respect, they teach when the regular teacher cannot and continually adjust to different classroom situations. Annually, the second week of September. For info: Dorothy Zjawin, 61 W Colfax Ave, Roselle Park, NJ 07204. Phone: (908) 241-6241. Fax: (908) 241-6241.

TAJIKISTAN: INDEPENDENCE DAY: 10th ANNIVERSARY. Sept 9. National holiday commemorating independence from the Soviet Union in 1991.

WILLIAM, THE CONQUEROR: DEATH ANNIVERSARY. Sept 9, 1087. William I, The Conqueror, King of England and Duke of Normandy, whose image is portrayed in the Bayeux Tapestry, was born about 1028 at Falaise, Normandy. Victorious over Harold at the Battle of Hastings (the Norman Conquest) in 1066, William was crowned King of England at Westminster Abbey on Christmas Day of that year. Later, while waging war in France, William met his death at Rouen, Sept 9, 1087.

BIRTHDAYS TODAY

Benjamin Roy (BJ) Armstrong, 34, basketball player, born Detroit, MI, Sept 9, 1967.

Kimberly Willis Holt, 41, author (*When Zachary Beaver Came to Town*) born Pensacola, FL, Sept 9, 1960.

Adam Sandler, 35, actor (*The Waterboy, Billy Madison*), born Brooklyn, NY, Sept 9, 1966.

Mildred Pitts Walter, 79, author (*Justin and the Best Biscuits in the World*), born De Ridder, LA, Sept 9, 1922.

SEPTEMBER 10 — MONDAY

Day 253 — 112 Remaining

BELIZE: SAINT GEORGE'S CAYE DAY. Sept 10. Public holiday celebrated in honor of the battle between the European Baymen Settlers and the Spaniards for the territory of Belize.

BRAXTON, CARTER: BIRTH ANNIVERSARY. Sept 10, 1736. American revolutionary statesman and signer of the Declaration of Independence. Born at Newington, VA, he died Oct 10, 1797, at Richmond, VA.

KEIKO RETURNS TO ICELAND: ANNIVERSARY. Sept 10, 1998. Keiko, the killer whale or orca who starred in the 1993 film *Free Willy*, was returned to his home in waters off Iceland after spending 19 years in captivity. Keiko was to be kept in a specially-built cage in the ocean until it was determined if he could return to the wild. For more info: *Keiko's Story: A Killer Whale Goes Home*, by Linda Moore Kurth (Millbrook, 0-7613-1500-4, $23.90 Gr. 4–8).

MARIS, ROGER: BIRTH ANNIVERSARY. Sept 10, 1934. Baseball player born Roger Eugene Maris at Hibbing, MN. In 1961, Maris broke one of baseball's sacred records, hitting 61 home runs to surpass the mark set by Babe Ruth in 1927. This record wasn't broken until 1998. He won the American League MVP award in 1960 and 1961 and finished his career with the St. Louis Cardinals. Died at Houston, TX, Dec 14, 1985.

MOON PHASE: LAST QUARTER. Sept 10. Moon enters Last Quarter phase at 2:59 PM, EDT.

BIRTHDAYS TODAY

Babette Cole, 52, author (*Dr. Dog, Princess Smartypants*), born Jersey, Channel Islands, UK, Sept 10, 1949.

Matt Geiger, 32, baseball player, born Salem, MA, Sept 10, 1969.

Randy Johnson, 38, baseball player, born Walnut Creek, CA, Sept 10, 1963.

SEPTEMBER 11 — TUESDAY

Day 254 — 111 Remaining

BATTLE OF BRANDYWINE: ANNIVERSARY. Sept 11, 1777. The largest engagement of the American Revolution, between the Continental Army led by General George Washington and British forces led by General William Howe. Howe was marching to take Philadelphia when Washington chose an area on the Brandywine Creek near Chadds Ford, PA to stop the advance. The American forces were defeated here and the British went on to take Philadelphia Sept 26. They spent the winter in the city while Washington's troops suffered in their encampment at Valley Forge, PA. For more info, visit the Independence Hall Association website at www.ushistory.org/brandywine/index.html.

ETHIOPIA: NEW YEAR'S DAY. Sept 11. Public holiday. This day in 2001 begins the year 1995 on the Ethiopian calendar. This is also the beginning of the year 1718 on the Coptic calendar.

"LITTLE HOUSE ON THE PRAIRIE" TV PREMIERE: ANNIVERSARY. Sept 11, 1974. This hour-long family drama was based on the books by Laura Ingalls Wilder. It focused on the Ingalls family and their neighbors living at Walnut Grove, MN: Michael Landon as Charles (Pa), Karen Grassle as Caroline (Ma), Melissa Sue Anderson as daughter Mary, Melissa Gilbert as daughter Laura, from whose point of view the stories were told, Lindsay and Sidney Greenbush as daughter Carrie and Wendi and Brenda Turnbaugh as daughter Grace. The series spent one season at Winoka, Dakota. In its last season (1982), the show's name was changed to "Little House: A New Beginning." Landon appeared less often and the show centered around Laura and her husband.

911 DAY. Sept 11. To foster the implementation of a universal emergency telephone number system. For info: Sonya Carius, Publications Mgr, Natl Emergency Number Assn, 47849 Papermill Rd, Coshocton, OH 43812. Phone: (614) 622-8911. Fax: (614) 622-2090. Web: www.nena9-1-1.org.

PAKISTAN: FOUNDER'S DEATH ANNIVERSARY. Sept 11. Pakistan observes the death anniversary in 1948 of Qaid-i-Azam Mohammed Ali Jinnah (founder of Pakistan) as a national holiday.

SPACE MILESTONE: *MARS GLOBAL SURVEYOR* (US). Sept 11, 1997. Launched Nov 7, 1996, this unmanned vehicle was put in orbit around Mars. It is designed to compile global maps of Mars by taking high resolution photos. This mission inaugurated a new series of Mars expeditions in which NASA will launch pairs of orbiters and landers to Mars every 26 months into the next decade. *Mars Global Surveyor* was paired with the lander *Mars Pathfinder*. More than 20,000 images of Mars taken by the spacecraft can be seen at www.msss.com/moc-gallery/index.html. See also: "Space Milestone: *Mars Pathfinder*" (July 4).

BIRTHDAYS TODAY

Daniel Akaka, 77, US Senator (D, Hawaii), born Honolulu, HI, Sept 11, 1924.

Anthony Browne, 55, author (*Voices in the Park*), born Sheffield, England, Sept 11, 1946.

SEPTEMBER 12 — WEDNESDAY

Day 255 — 110 Remaining

DEFENDERS DAY. Sept 12. Maryland. Public holiday. Annual reenactment of bombardment of Fort McHenry in 1814 which inspired Francis Scott Key to write the "Star-Spangled Banner."

"FRAGGLE ROCK" TV PREMIERE: ANNIVERSARY. Sept 12, 1987. This children's show was a cartoon version of the live Jim Henson puppet production on HBO. It was set in the rock underneath a scientist's house and featured characters such as the Fraggles, the Doozers and the Gorgs.

HIGHLIGHTS® FOUNDATION WRITER'S WORKSHOP. Sept 12–16. Honesdale, PA. Workshops offered several times during the year for authors and illustrators of children's books. For info: Highlights Foundation, 803 Church St, Honesdale, PA 18431. Phone: (570) 253-1080. Fax: (570) 253-0179.

"LASSIE" TV PREMIERE: ANNIVERSARY. Sept 12, 1954. This long-running series was originally about a boy and his courageous and intelligent dog, Lassie (played by more than six different dogs, all male). For the first few seasons, Lassie lived on the Miller farm. The family included Jeff (Tommy Rettig), his widowed mother Ellen (Jan Clayton) and George Cleveland as Gramps. Throughout the 22 years the show was on the air there were many format and cast changes, as Lassie was exchanged from one family to another in order to have a variety of new perils and escapades. Other featured performers over the years include Cloris Leachman, June Lockhart and Larry Wilcox.

September 2001

S	M	T	W	T	F	S
						1
2	3	4	5	6	7	8
9	10	11	12	13	14	15
16	17	18	19	20	21	22
23	24	25	26	27	28	29
30						

SEPTEMBER 12
JESSE OWENS' BIRTHDAY

Jesse Owens' parents were sharecroppers and he was born on a farm in Alabama, in 1913. His name was James Cleveland and his family called him J.C. He had seven brothers and sisters. J.C. became known as Jesse after the family moved to Cleveland, Ohio. When a teacher asked his name, Jesse replied "J.C." His teacher, unused to hearing a southern accent, mistakenly thought he said "Jesse." Too shy to correct her, J.C. simply became "Jesse." He grew up with little material wealth, but his life was rich with love and the many activities his family enjoyed doing together. One activity Jesse's dad enjoyed was the foot race often held after church on Sunday; he was the fastest man in the area. Little did he know that some day his son would become the fastest man in the world and win four gold medals in the 1936 Olympic Games at Berlin, Germany.

After his track career ended, Jesse Owens traveled all over the world, giving speeches and talking about his athletic accomplishments. Jesse was elected to the Track and Field Hall of Fame in 1974 and in 1979, President Jimmy Carter awarded him the Living Legends Award. Jesse died of cancer on March 31, 1980.

Why not honor Jesse's memory with a class 100-meter dash and long jump contest during physical education? Before holding the event, let one or two students go to the learning center and find out Jesse's Olympic and world record times and lengths. Outdoors, measure off 100 meters and in a sandy area (or grassy spot) make a line for a takeoff point for long jumps. If your space is limited, hold a 50-meter dash and halve Jesse's 100-meter time.

Since gym time is limited, divide the class into thirds and let everyone participate in a qualifying heat. Borrow a stopwatch from the gym teacher and time the top six winners individually (two winners from each heat).

Let interested students compete in the long jump. Nonjumpers can serve as takeoff board monitors, measurers, the cheering crowd, etc.

In math class, compare the class results with Jesse's. How many times faster/farther did he run or jump?

Older students can check newspaper sports sections from papers dated September 25–30, 2000, and compare Michael Johnson's race speeds and gold medal totals at the Sydney Olympics with those Jesse earned in 1936.

Lutz Long was Germany's champion long jumper. He went against Adolf Hitler's racist policies by offering tips and the hand of friendship to African American Jesse Owens. Older students could discuss how difficult and brave it was for Lutz to disregard an unfair policy and be a "good neighbor." Students might discuss ways they could extend a hand of friendship to students of all ethnic and religious backgrounds.

Biographies about Owens include: *Jesse Owens*, by Jane Sutcliffe (Lerner, 1-57505-487-6, $5.95 Gr. K–3); *Jesse Owens: Olympic Star*, by Patricia and Frederick McKissack (Enslow, 0-8949-0312-8, $14.95 Gr. 1–4); and *Jesse Owens: Track and Field Legend*, by Judith Pinkerton Josephson (Enslow, 0-8949-0812-X, $19.95 Gr. 7 & up).

OWENS, JESSE: BIRTH ANNIVERSARY. Sept 12, 1913. James Cleveland (Jesse) Owens, American athlete, winner of four gold medals at the 1936 Olympic Games at Berlin, Germany, was born at Oakville, AL. Owens set 11 world records in track and field. During one track meet, at Ann Arbor, MI, May 23, 1935, Owens, representing Ohio State University, broke five world records and tied a sixth in the space of 45 minutes. Died at Tucson, AZ, Mar 31, 1980. For more info: *Jesse Owens*, by Tom Streissguth (Lerner, 0-8225-4940-9, $25.26 Gr. 4–6). *See* Curriculum Connection.

SPACE MILESTONE: *LUNA 2* (USSR). Sept 12, 1959. First spacecraft to land on moon was launched.

VIDEO GAMES DAY. Sept 12. A day for kids who love video games to celebrate the fun they have playing them and to thank their parents for all the cartridges and quarters they have provided to indulge this hobby.

BIRTHDAYS TODAY

Sam Brownback, 45, US Senator (R, Kansas), born Garnett, KS, Sept 12, 1956.

Peter Scolari, 47, actor ("Honey I Shrunk the Kids: The TV Show"), born Rochelle, IL, Sept 12, 1954.

Valerie Tripp, 50, author (the Molly, Felicity, Samantha and Josefina series in the American Girls collection), born Mt Kisco, NY, Sept 12, 1951.

SEPTEMBER 13 — THURSDAY

Day 256 — 109 Remaining

BARRY, JOHN: DEATH ANNIVERSARY. Sept 13, 1803. Revolutionary War hero John Barry, first American to hold the rank of commodore, died at Philadelphia, PA. He was born at Tacumshane, County Wexford, Ireland, in 1745. He has been called the "Father of the American Navy."

CORN ISLAND STORYTELLING FESTIVAL. Sept 13–16. Louisville, KY. More than 50 storytellers. Festival includes an "olio," mixture of tales, "Fest of Storytelling" and "ghost tales" told at Long Run Park. Est attendance: 16,000. For info: Joy Pennington, Intl Order of EARS, Inc, 12019 Donohue Ave, Louisville, KY 40243. Phone: (502) 245-0643. Fax: (502) 254-7542. E-mail: l-jpenn@prodigy.net.

DAHL, ROALD: 85th BIRTH ANNIVERSARY. Sept 13, 1916. Author (*Charlie and the Chocolate Factory, James and the Giant Peach, Matilda*), born at Llandaff, South Wales, Great Britain. Died Nov 23, 1990, at Oxford, England.

"THE MUPPET SHOW" TV PREMIERE: 25th ANNIVERSARY. Sept 13, 1976. This comedy variety show was hosted by Kermit the Frog from "Sesame Street." Other Jim Henson puppet characters included Miss Piggy, Fozzie the Bear and The Great Gonzo. Many celebrities made guest appearances on the show, which was broadcast in more than 100 countries. "Muppet Babies" was a Saturday morning cartoon spin-off that aired from 1984 to 1992. *The Muppet Movie* (1979) was the first of five films based on "The Muppet Show."

REED, WALTER: 150th BIRTH ANNIVERSARY. Sept 13, 1851. American army physician especially known for his Yellow Fever research. Born at Gloucester County, VA, he served as an army surgeon for more than 20 years and as a professor at the Army Medical College. He died at Washington, DC, Nov 22, 1902. The US Army's general hospital at Washington, DC, is named in his honor.

SCHUMANN, CLARA: BIRTH ANNIVERSARY. Sept 13, 1819. Pianist and composer, wife of composer Robert Schumann. Born at Leipzig, Germany, she died May 20, 1896, at Frankfurt, Germany. For info: *Clara Schumann: Piano Virtuoso*, by Susanna Reich (Clarion, 0-395-89119-1, $18 Gr. 5 & up) and *Her Piano Sang: A Story About Clara Schumann*, by Barbara Allman (Carolrhoda, 1-57505-012-9, $15.95 Gr. 3–6).

"STAR-SPANGLED BANNER" INSPIRED: ANNIVERSARY. Sept 13–14, 1814. During the War of 1812, on the night of Sept 13, Francis Scott Key was aboard a ship that was delayed in Baltimore harbor by the British attack there on Fort McHenry. Key had no choice but to anxiously watch the battle. That experience and seeing the American flag still flying over the fort the next morning inspired him to pen the verses that, coupled with the tune of a popular drinking song, became our official national anthem in 1931, 117 years after the words were written.

US CAPITAL ESTABLISHED AT NEW YORK CITY: ANNIVERSARY. Sept 13, 1789. Congress picked New York, NY, as the location of the new US government in place of Philadelphia, which had served as the capital up until this time. In 1790 the capital moved back to Philadelphia, and in 1800 moved permanently to Washington, DC.

BIRTHDAYS TODAY

William Janklow, 62, Governor of South Dakota (R), born Chicago, IL, Sept 13, 1939.

Else Holmelund Minarik, 81, author (the Little Bear series), born Aarhus, Denmark, Sept 13, 1920.

Ben Savage, 21, actor ("Boy Meets World"), born Chicago, IL, Sept 13, 1980.

Mildred Taylor, 58, author (Newbery for *Roll of Thunder, Hear My Cry*), born Jackson, MS, Sept 13, 1943.

September 2001

S	M	T	W	T	F	S
						1
2	3	4	5	6	7	8
9	10	11	12	13	14	15
16	17	18	19	20	21	22
23	24	25	26	27	28	29
30						

SEPTEMBER 14 — FRIDAY

Day 257 — 108 Remaining

ARMSTRONG, WILLIAM H.: BIRTH ANNIVERSARY. Sept 14, 1914. Newbery Award-winning author (*Sounder*). Born at Lexington, VA, he died Apr 11, 1999, at Kent, CT.

THE BIG E. Sept 14–30. West Springfield, MA. New England's fall classic and one of the nation's largest fairs. Each September, The Big E features all free entertainment including top-name talent, a big-top circus and horse show. Also children's attractions, daily parade, historic village, Avenue of States, Better Living Center and much more. Annually, beginning the second Friday after Labor Day. Est attendance: 1,000,000. For info: Eastern States Exposition, 1305 Memorial Ave, West Springfield, MA 01089. Phone: (413) 737-2443. Fax: (413) 787-0127. E-mail: info@thebige.com. Web: www.thebige.com.

NORTHERN APPALACHIAN STORYTELLING FESTIVAL. Sept 14–16. Straughn Hall, Mansfield University, Mansfield, PA. Showcases the talent of the nation's top storytellers who share through their performances a sense of roots and cultural diversity. There are performances Saturday afternoon and Friday and Saturday evening, plus a ghost story session late Friday night. In addition, there are storytelling master classes Saturday morning and a workshop on Thursday and Friday. Est attendance: 3,000. For info: Dr. Priscilla M Travis, N Appalachian Storytelling Fest, PO Box 434, Mansfield, PA 16933. Phone: (717) 662-4785. Fax: (717) 662-4112. E-mail: ptravis@mnsfld.edu. Web: wso.net/story fest.

SOLO TRANSATLANTIC BALLOON CROSSING: ANNIVERSARY. Sept 14–18, 1984. Joe W. Kittinger, 56-year-old balloonist, left Caribou, ME, in a 10-story-tall helium-filled balloon named *Rosie O'Grady's Balloon of Peace* Sept 14, 1984, crossed the Atlantic Ocean and reached the French coast, above the town of Capbreton, in bad weather Sept 17 at 4:29 PM, EDT. He crash-landed amid wind and rain near Savone, Italy, at 8:08 AM, EDT, Sept 18. His nearly 84-hour flight, covering about 3,535 miles, was the first solo balloon crossing of the Atlantic Ocean.

STATE FAIR OF OKLAHOMA. Sept 14–30. Fairgrounds, Oklahoma City, Oklahoma. Third largest fair in North America includes seven buildings of commercial exhibits; Walt Disney's World on Ice, the State Fair Super Circus, PRCA championship rodeo, livestock competitions, top-name concerts and motorsports events. Annually, second Friday after Labor Day. Est attendance: 1,300,000. For info: State Fair of Oklahoma, PO Box 74943, Oklahoma City, OK 73107. Phone: (405) 948-6700. Fax: (405) 948-6828. E-mail: oklafair@oklafair.org. Web: www.oklafair.org.

WILSON, JAMES: BIRTH ANNIVERSARY. Sept 14, 1742. Signer of the Declaration of Independence and one of the first associate justices of the US Supreme Court. Born at Fifeshire, Scotland, he died Aug 21, 1798, at Edenton, NC.

BIRTHDAYS TODAY

Diane Goode, 52, author (*Diane Goode's Book of Scary Stories and Songs*,), illustrator (*When I Was Young in the Mountains, Diane Goode's Book of Giants and Little People*), born Brooklyn, NY, Sept 14, 1949.

John Steptoe, 51, author and illustrator (*Mufaro's Beautiful Daughters: An African Tale*), born Brooklyn, NY, Sept 14, 1950.

Elizabeth Winthrop, 53, author (*The Castle in the Attic, The Battle for the Castle*), born Washington, DC, Sept 14, 1948.

SEPTEMBER 15 — SATURDAY

Day 258 — 107 Remaining

COOPER, JAMES FENIMORE: BIRTH ANNIVERSARY. Sept 15, 1789. American novelist, historian and social critic, born at Burlington, NJ, Cooper was one of the earliest American writers to develop a native American literary tradition. His most popular works are the five novels comprising *The Leatherstocking Tales,* featuring the exploits of one of the truly unique American fictional characters, Natty Bumppo. These novels, *The Deerslayer, The Last of the Mohicans, The Pathfinder, The Pioneers* and *The Prairie,* chronicle Natty Bumppo's continuing flight away from the rapid settlement of America. Cooper died Sept 14, 1851, at Cooperstown, NY, the town founded by his father.

COSTA RICA: INDEPENDENCE DAY. Sept 15. National holiday. Gained independence from Spain in 1821.

EL SALVADOR: INDEPENDENCE DAY. Sept 15. National holiday. Gained independence from Spain in 1821.

ENGLAND: BATTLE OF BRITAIN DAY. Sept 15. Commemorates end of biggest daylight bombing raid of Britain by German Luftwaffe, in 1940. Said to have been the turning point against Hitler's siege of Britain in WWII.

FIRST NATIONAL CONVENTION FOR BLACKS: ANNIVERSARY. Sept 15, 1830. The first national convention for blacks was held at Bethel Church, Philadelphia, PA. The convention was called to find ways to better the condition of black people and was attended by delegates from seven states. Bishop Richard Allen was elected as the first convention president.

GUATEMALA: INDEPENDENCE DAY. Sept 15. National holiday. Gained independence from Spain in 1821.

HONDURAS: INDEPENDENCE DAY. Sept 15. National holiday. Gained independence from Spain in 1821.

INTERNATIONAL CHILDREN'S FESTIVAL. Sept 15–16. Wolf Trap Farm Park, Vienna, VA. Performers from around the world come to celebrate children. Simultaneous performances by student performers on several stages as well as hands-on workshops. The Craft Workshop will feature crafts from many countries. The Arts/Technology Pavilion allows visitors to experience state-of-the-art technology. For info: Arts Council of Fairfax County, 4022 Hummer Rd, Annandale, VA 22003-2403. Phone: (703) 642-0862. Web: www.allnva.com/partners/acfc/icf.html.

JAPAN: OLD PEOPLE'S DAY OR RESPECT FOR THE AGED DAY. Sept 15. National holiday.

KIRSTEN, SAMANTHA AND MOLLY DEBUT: ANNIVERSARY. Sept 15, 1986. The first three American Girl dolls representing different historical periods debuted. They were joined in later years by Addy, Felicity, Josefina and Kit. More than 4 million dolls and 48 million books about them have been sold. For more info: www.americangirl.com.

LAURA INGALLS WILDER FESTIVAL. Sept 15. Mansfield, MO. Laura Wilder lived in Mansfield on the farm she and her husband Almanzo built when she wrote the "Little House" series of books. The Laura Ingalls Wilder museum and home will be open for tours. There will be activities for the whole family—contests, parades, music, arts and crafts, food, games, an outdoor musical and more. For info: Chamber of Commerce, PO Box 322, Mansfield, MO 65704. Phone: (417) 924-3525.

LAURA INGALLS WILDER FESTIVAL. Sept 15–16. Pepin, WI. 10th annual. Experience life in the mid-1800s with demonstrations of blacksmithing, woodworking, ironworking, weaving, quilting and wool-spinning by individuals dressed in period costumes. Stories and songs cited in Little House books are also performed and there's a Laura Ingalls look-alike contest. Additional attractions include a traveling exhibit of Wilder's written materials, sanctioned horse-pull, Civil War encampment, children's games from the period, parade, crafts and antiques at Laura Ingalls Wilder Memorial Park. For info: Wisconsin Dept of Tourism, Laura Ingalls Festival, PO Box 7976, Madison, WI 53707. Phone: (715) 442-2461 or (715) 442-2147. E-mail: tourinfo@tourism.state.wi.us. Web: travelwisconsin.com.

"THE LONE RANGER" TV PREMIERE: ANNIVERSARY. Sept 15, 1949. This character was created for a radio serial in 1933 by George W. Trendle. The famous masked man was the alter ego of John Reid, a Texas Ranger who was the only survivor of an ambush. He was nursed back to health by his Native American friend, Tonto. Both men traveled around the West on their trusty steeds, Silver and Scout, fighting injustice. On TV Clayton Moore played the Lone Ranger/John Reid and Jay Silverheels costarred as Tonto. The theme music was Rossini's "William Tell Overture."

★ **NATIONAL HISPANIC HERITAGE MONTH.** Sept 15–Oct 15. Presidential Proclamation. Beginning in 1989, always issued for Sept 15–Oct 15 of each year (PL 100–402 of Aug 17, 1988). Previously issued each year for the week including Sept 15 and 16 since 1968 at request (PL90–498 of Sept 17, 1968). For info: *The New York Public Library Amazing Hispanic American History: A Book of Answers for Kids,* by George Ochoa (Wiley, 0-471-19204-X, $12.95 Gr. 4 & up) and *Big Spanish Heritage Activity Book,* by Walter Yoder (Sunstone Press, 0-86534-239-3, $8.95 Gr. 3–9).

NATIONAL KIDSDAY®. Sept 15. A national holiday to recognize the value, dignity and inherent worth of children everywhere (also known as National Children's Day™). Supervised and licensed by KidsPeace®, The National Center for Kids Overcoming Crisis, a private, not-for-profit organization that has been providing hope and healing to kids in crisis since 1882. KidsPeace offers the country's widest array of children's critical care services available under a "single roof" and crisis education to families across the US. Annually, the third Saturday in September. For info: Paula Knouse, KidsPeace, 5300 KidsPeace Dr, Orefield, PA 18069-9101. Phone: (610) 799-8325.

NICARAGUA: INDEPENDENCE DAY. Sept 15. National holiday. Gained independence from Spain in 1821.

PIPER, WATTY: BIRTH ANNIVERSARY. Sept 15, 1870. Born Mabel Caroline Bragg at Milford, MA. Piper is best-known for her classic tale *The Little Engine That Could.* She died Apr 25, 1945.

TAFT, WILLIAM HOWARD: BIRTH ANNIVERSARY. Sept 15, 1857. The 27th president of the US was born at Cincinnati, OH. His term of office was Mar 4, 1909–Mar 3, 1913. Following his presidency he became a law professor at Yale University until his appointment as Chief Justice of the US Supreme Court in 1921. Died at Washington, DC, Mar 8, 1930, and was buried at Arlington National Cemetery. For info: www.ipl.org/ref/POTUS.

BIRTHDAYS TODAY

Tomie DePaola, 67, illustrator and author (*Strega Nona*), born Thomas De Paola, Meriden, CT, Sept 15, 1934.

Prince Harry, 17, Henry Charles Albert David, son of Prince Charles and Princess Diana, born London, England, Sept 15, 1984.

Robert McCloskey, 87, illustrator and author (Caldecott Awards for *Time of Wonder, Make Way for Ducklings*), born Hamilton, OH, Sept 15, 1914.

SEPTEMBER 16 — SUNDAY

Day 259 — 106 Remaining

CHEROKEE STRIP DAY: ANNIVERSARY. Sept 16, 1893. Optional school holiday, Oklahoma. Greatest "run" for Oklahoma land in 1893.

GENERAL MOTORS: FOUNDING ANNIVERSARY. Sept 16, 1908. The giant automobile manufacturing company was founded by William Crapo "Billy" Durant, a Flint, MI, entrepreneur.

MAYFLOWER DAY: ANNIVERSARY. Sept 16, 1620. Anniversary of the departure of the *Mayflower* from Plymouth, England with 102 passengers and a small crew. Vicious storms were encountered en route which caused serious doubt about the wisdom of continuing, but she reached Provincetown, MA, Nov 21, and discharged the Pilgrims at Plymouth, MA, Dec 26, 1620.

MEXICO: INDEPENDENCE DAY. Sept 16. National Day. The official celebration begins at 11 PM, Sept 15 and continues through Sept 16. On the night of the 15th, the President of Mexico steps onto the balcony of the National Palace at Mexico City and voices the same "El Grito" (Cry for Freedom) that Father Hidalgo gave on the night of Sept 15, 1810, which began Mexico's rebellion from Spain.

NATIONAL CONSTITUTION CENTER CONSTITUTION WEEK. Sept 16–22. To celebrate and commemorate the signing of the US Constitution Sept 17, 1787, the National Constitution Center sponsors ceremonial signings of the Constitution nationwide. Everyone is invited to participate and receive educational materials about the world's oldest working Constitution. For info: Natl Constitution Center, The Bourse, 111 S Independence Mall East, Ste 560, Philadelphia, PA 19106. Phone: (215) 923-0004. Fax: (215) 923-1749. Web: www.constitutioncenter.org.

NATIONAL FARM ANIMALS AWARENESS WEEK. Sept 16–22. A week to promote awareness of farm animals and their natural behaviors. Each day of the week is dedicated to learning about a specific group of farm animals and to appreciating their many interesting and unique qualities. Annually, the third full week in September. For info: David Kuemmerle, Program Mgr, The Humane Soc of the US, Farm Animal Section, 2100 L St NW, Washington, DC 20037. Phone: (202) 452-1100. E-mail: dave hsus@ix.netcom.com.

★ **NATIONAL FARM SAFETY AND HEALTH WEEK.** Sept 16–22. Presidential Proclamation issued since 1982 for the third week in September. Previously, from 1944, for one of the last two weeks in July.

★ **NATIONAL HISTORICALLY BLACK COLLEGES AND UNIVERSITIES WEEK.** Sept 16–22.

September 2001

S	M	T	W	T	F	S
						1
2	3	4	5	6	7	8
9	10	11	12	13	14	15
16	17	18	19	20	21	22
23	24	25	26	27	28	29
30						

NATIONAL PLAY-DOH® DAY. Sept 16. To commemorate the introduction of Play-Doh. Joe McVicker of Cincinnati sent some non-toxic wallpaper cleaner to his sister-in-law, a nursery school teacher. She found it to be an excellent replacement for modeling clay. In 1955, McVicker took the product to an educational convention and by 1956 Play-Doh was being sold commercially.

PAPUA NEW GUINEA: INDEPENDENCE DAY. Sept 16. National holiday. Commemorates independence from Australian administration in 1975.

REY, H.A.: BIRTH ANNIVERSARY. Sept 16, 1898. Born Hans Augusto Rey at Hamburg, Germany. Rey illustrated the Curious George series, while his wife, Margaret Rey, wrote the stories. He died at Cambridge, MA, Aug 26, 1977.

UNITED NATIONS: INTERNATIONAL DAY FOR THE PRESERVATION OF THE OZONE LAYER. Sept 16. On Dec 19, 1994, the General Assembly proclaimed this day to commemorate the date in 1987 on which Montreal Protocol on Substances that Deplete the Ozone Layer was signed (Res 49/114). States are invited to devote the Day to promote, at the national level, activities in accordance with the objectives of the Protocol. The ozone layer filters sunlight and prevents the adverse effects of ultraviolet radiation from reaching the Earth's surface, thereby preserving life on the planet. For info: United Nations, Dept of Public Info, Public Inquiries Unit, Rm GA-57, New York, NY 10017. Phone: (212) 963-4475. Fax: (212) 963-0071. E-mail: inquiries@un.org.

BIRTHDAYS TODAY

David Copperfield, 45, magician, illusionist, born Metuchen, NJ, Sept 16, 1956.

Robin Yount, 46, Baseball Hall of Fame player, born Danville, IL, Sept 16, 1955.

SEPTEMBER 17 — MONDAY

Day 260 — 105 Remaining

BATTLE OF ANTIETAM: ANNIVERSARY. Sept 17, 1862. This date has been called America's bloodiest day in recognition of the high casualties suffered in the Civil War battle between General Robert E. Lee's Confederate forces and General George McClellan's Union army. Estimates vary, but more than 25,000 Union and Confederate soldiers were killed or wounded in this battle on the banks of the Potomac River at Maryland.

BURGER, WARREN E.: BIRTH ANNIVERSARY. Sept 17, 1907. Former Chief Justice of the US, Warren E. Burger was born at St. Paul, MN. A conservative on criminal matters, but a progressive on social issues, he had the longest tenure (1969–86) of any chief justice in this century. Appointed by President Nixon, he voted in the majority on *Roe v Wade* (1973), which upheld a woman's right to an abortion, and on *US v Nixon* (1974), which forced Nixon to surrender audiotapes to the Watergate special prosecutor. He died June 25, 1995, at Washington, DC.

★ **CITIZENSHIP DAY.** Sept 17. Presidential Proclamation always issued for Sept 17 at request (PL82-261 of Feb 29, 1952). Customarily issued as "Citizenship Day and Constitution Week." Replaces Constitution Day.

CONSTITUTION OF THE US: ANNIVERSARY. Sept 17, 1787. Delegations from 12 states at the Constitutional Convention at Philadelphia, PA, voted unanimously to approve the proposed document. Thirty-nine of the 42 delegates present signed it and the Convention adjourned, after drafting a letter of transmittal to the Congress. The proposed constitution stipulated that it would take effect when ratified by nine states. This day is a legal holiday in Arizona and Florida. For activities and lesson plans on the Constitution, visit the National Archives website at www.nara.gov/education/teaching/constitution/home.html.

★ **CONSTITUTION WEEK.** Sept 17–23. Presidential Proclamation always issued for the period of Sept 17–23 each year since 1955 (PL 84–915 of Aug 2, 1956).

FOSTER, ANDREW "RUBE": BIRTH ANNIVERSARY. Sept 17, 1879. Rube Foster's efforts in baseball earned him the title of "The Father of Negro Baseball." He was a manager and star pitcher, pitching 51 victories in one year. In 1919, he called a meeting of black baseball owners and organized the first black baseball league, the Negro National League. He served as its president until his death in 1930. Foster was born at Calvert, TX, the son of a minister. He died Dec 9, 1930, at Kankakee, IL.

HENDRICKS, THOMAS ANDREWS: BIRTH ANNIVERSARY. Sept 17, 1819. The 21st vice president of the US (1885), born at Muskingum County, OH. Died at Indianapolis, IN, Nov 25, 1885.

"HOME IMPROVEMENT" TV PREMIERE: ANNIVERSARY. Sept 17, 1991. This comedy centered around the Taylors. Tim Taylor, played by Tim Allen, was a TV host on the popular fix-it show "Tool Time." Jill, played by Patricia Richardson, was a housewife and mother going back to school to get a degree in psychology. The couple's three sons were played by Zachery Ty Bryan, Jonathan Taylor Thomas and Taran Noah Smith. Other cast members included Richard Karn, Earl Hindman, Debbe Dunning and Pamela Anderson. The last episode aired May 25, 1999.

MOON PHASE: NEW MOON. Sept 17. Moon enters New Moon phase at 6:27 AM, EDT.

NATIONAL CONSTITUTION CENTER GROUNDBREAKING: ANNIVERSARY. Sept 17, 2000. Established by an act of Congress, the National Constitution Center is being constructed on Independence Mall at Philadelphia. It will open in 2003. It was established to increase awareness and understanding of the US Constitution, its history and relevance to our daily lives. For more info, including teacher resources: www.constitutioncenter.org.

NATIONAL FOOTBALL LEAGUE FORMED: ANNIVERSARY. Sept 17, 1920. The National Football League was formed at Canton, OH.

PERIGEAN SPRING TIDES. Sept 17. Spring tides, the highest possible tides, occur when New Moon or Full Moon falls within 24 hours of the moment the Moon is nearest Earth (perigee) in its monthly orbit at 4 AM, EDT. The word *spring* refers not to the season but comes from the German word *springen*, "to rise up."

ROSH HASHANAH BEGINS AT SUNDOWN. Sept 17. Jewish New Year. See "Rosh Hashanah" (Sept 18).

SPACE MILESTONE: *PEGASUS 1* (US). Sept 17, 1978. This 23,000-pound research satellite broke up over Africa and fell to Earth. Major pieces are believed to have fallen into Atlantic Ocean off the coast of Angola. The satellite had been orbiting Earth for more than 13 years since being launched Feb 16, 1965.

VON STEUBEN, BARON FRIEDRICH: BIRTH ANNIVERSARY. Sept 17, 1730. Prussian-born general, born at Magdeburg, Prussia, who served in the American Revolution. He died at Remsen, NY, Nov 28, 1794.

BIRTHDAYS TODAY

Bjorn Berg, 78, illustrator (*Old Mrs Pepperpot*), born Munich, Germany, Sept 17, 1923.

Paul Goble, 68, author and illustrator (Caldecott for *The Girl Who Loved Wild Horses*), born Surrey, England, Sept 17, 1933.

Charles Ernest Grassley, 68, US Senator (R, Iowa), born New Hartford, IA, Sept 17, 1933.

Philip D. (Phil) Jackson, 56, basketball coach, former player, born Deer Lodge, MT, Sept 17, 1945.

Gail Carson Levine, 54, author (*Ella Enchanted*), born New York, NY, Sept 17, 1947.

David H. Souter, 62, Associate Justice of the US Supreme Court, born Melrose, MA, Sept 17, 1939.

SEPTEMBER 18 — TUESDAY

Day 261 — 104 Remaining

"THE ADDAMS FAMILY" TV PREMIERE: ANNIVERSARY. Sept 18, 1964. Charles Addams' quirky *New Yorker* cartoon creations were brought to life in this ABC sitcom about a family full of oddballs. John Astin played lawyer Gomez Addams, with Carolyn Jones as his morbid wife Morticia, Ken Weatherwax as son Pugsley, Lisa Loring as daughter Wednesday, Jackie Coogan as Uncle Fester, Ted Cassidy as both Lurch, the butler, and Thing, a disembodied hand, Blossom Rock as Grandmama and Felix Silla as Cousin Itt. *The Addams Family* movie was released in 1991, starring Angelica Huston as Morticia, Raul Julia as Gomez, Christopher Lloyd as Uncle Fester, Jimmy Workman as Pugsley and Christina Ricci as Wednesday. *Addams Family Values* was released in 1993.

CHILE: INDEPENDENCE DAY. Sept 18. National holiday. Gained independence from Spain in 1810.

DIEFENBAKER, JOHN: BIRTH ANNIVERSARY. Sept 18, 1895. Canadian lawyer, statesman and Conservative prime minister (1957–63). Born at Normandy Township, Ontario, Canada, he died at Ottawa, Ontario, Aug 16, 1979. Diefenbaker was a member of the Canadian Parliament from 1940 until his death.

IRON HORSE OUTRACED BY HORSE: ANNIVERSARY. Sept 18, 1830. In a widely celebrated race, the first locomotive built in America, the Tom Thumb, lost to a horse. Mechanical difficulties plagued the steam engine over the nine-mile course between Riley's Tavern and Baltimore, MD, and a boiler leak prevented the locomotive from finishing the race. In the early days of trains, engines were nicknamed "Iron Horses."

NETHERLANDS: PRINSJESDAG. Sept 18. Official opening of parliament at The Hague. The queen of the Netherlands, by tradition, rides in a golden coach to the hall of knights for the annual opening of parliament. Annually, on the third Tuesday in September.

READ, GEORGE: BIRTH ANNIVERSARY. Sept 18, 1733. Lawyer and signer of the Declaration of Independence, born at Cecil County, MD. Died Sept 21, 1798, at New Castle, DE.

ROSH HASHANAH or JEWISH NEW YEAR. Sept 18–19. Jewish holy day; observed on following day also. Hebrew calendar date: Tishri 1, 5762. Rosh Hashanah (literally "Head of the Year") is the beginning of 10 days of repentance and spiritual renewal. (Began at sundown of previous day.)

STORY, JOSEPH: BIRTH ANNIVERSARY. Sept 18, 1779. Associate justice of the US Supreme Court (1811–45) was born at Marblehead, MA. "It is astonishing," he wrote a few months before his death, "how easily men satisfy themselves that the Constitution is exactly what they wish it to be." Story died Sept 10, 1845, at Cambridge, MA, having served 33 years on the Supreme Court bench.

UNITED NATIONS: INTERNATIONAL DAY OF PEACE/OPENING DAY OF GENERAL ASSEMBLY. Sept 18. The United Nations General Assembly, Nov 30, 1981, declared "the third Tuesday of September, the opening day of the regular sessions of the General Assembly, shall be officially proclaimed and observed as International Day of Peace and shall be devoted to commemorating and strengthening the ideals of peace both within and among all nations and peoples."

US AIR FORCE ESTABLISHED: ANNIVERSARY. Sept 18, 1947. Although its heritage dates back to 1907 when the Army first established military aviation, the US Air Force became a separate military service on this date.

US CAPITOL CORNERSTONE LAID: ANNIVERSARY. Sept 18, 1793. President George Washington laid the Capitol cornerstone at Washington, DC, in a Masonic ceremony. That event was the first and last recorded occasion at which the stone with its engraved silver plate was seen. In 1958, during the extension of the east front of the Capitol, an unsuccessful effort was made to find it. For a virtual tour of the capitol: www.senate.gov/vtour/welcome.htm.

BIRTHDAYS TODAY

Lance Armstrong, 30, cyclist, winner of the Tour de France, born Plano, TX, Sept 18, 1971.

Robert F. Bennett, 68, US Senator (R, Utah), born Salt Lake City, UT, Sept 18, 1933.

Ticha Penichiero, 27, basketball player, born Figueira da Foz, Portugal, Sept 18, 1974.

SEPTEMBER 19 — WEDNESDAY

Day 262 — 103 Remaining

CARROLL, CHARLES: BIRTH ANNIVERSARY. Sept 19, 1737. American Revolutionary leader and signer of the Declaration of Independence, born at Annapolis, MD. The last surviving signer of the Declaration, he died Nov 14, 1832, at Baltimore, MD.

MEXICO CITY EARTHQUAKE: ANNIVERSARY. Sept 19–20, 1985. Nearly 10,000 persons perished in the earthquakes (8.1 and 7.5 respectively, on the Richter Scale) that devastated Mexico City. Damage to buildings was estimated at more than $1 billion, and 100,000 homes were destroyed or severely damaged. For more info go to the National Earthquake Information Center: wwwneic.cr.usgs.gov.

POWELL, LEWIS F., JR: BIRTH ANNIVERSARY. Sept 19, 1907. Former associate justice of the Supreme Court of the US, nominated by President Nixon Oct 21, 1971. (Took office Jan 7, 1972.) Justice Powell was born at Suffolk, VA. In 1987, he announced his retirement from the Court. He died Aug 25, 1998, at Richmond, VA. For more info: oyez.northwestern.edu/justices/justices.cgi.

SAINT CHRISTOPHER (SAINT KITTS) AND NEVIS: INDEPENDENCE DAY. Sept 19. National holiday. Commemorates the independence of these Caribbean islands from Britain in 1983.

SAINT JANUARIUS (GENNARO): FEAST DAY. Sept 19. Fourth-century bishop of Benevento, martyred near Naples, Italy, whose relics in the Naples Cathedral are particularly famous because on his feast days the blood in a glass vial is said to liquefy in response to prayers of the faithful. This phenomenon is said to occur also on the first Saturday in May (May 5 in 2001).

BIRTHDAYS TODAY

James Haskins, 60, author (*Bayard Rustin: Behind the Scenes of the Civil Rights Movement*), born Montgomery, AL, Sept 19, 1941.

Kevin Zegers, 17, actor (*Air Bud*), born St. Mary's, Ontario, Canada, Sept 19, 1984.

SEPTEMBER 20 — THURSDAY

Day 263 — 102 Remaining

"THE COSBY SHOW" TV PREMIERE: ANNIVERSARY. Sept 20, 1984. Comedian Bill Cosby starred as Dr. Cliff Huxtable in this sitcom about an upper-middle class black family living in Brooklyn. Phylicia Rashad played his wife Claire, an attorney. Their five children were played by Sabrina LeBeauf, Lisa Bonet, Malcolm-Jamal Warner, Tempestt Bledsoe and Keshia Knight Pulliam. "A Different World" was a spin-off, with daughter Denise (Lisa Bonet) attending her parents' alma mater, Hillman College.

FAST OF GEDALYA. Sept 20. Jewish holiday. Hebrew calendar date: Tishri 3, 5762. Tzom Gedalya begins at first light of day and commemorates the 6th-century BC assassination of Gedalya Ben Achikam.

NATIONAL STUDENT DAY™. Sept 20. Created to recognize all students from preschool through postgraduate, this is the perfect day to show the students in our lives how proud we are of them, to recognize their hard work and to show support for their efforts. For info: Ralph E. Williams, Exec Dir, Natl Assn of College Students, PO Box 655, Lincolnshire, IL 60069. Phone: (800) 500-4255 or (941) 489-1530. Fax: (941) 489-1142. E-mail: nacs@collegeknowledge.com. Web: www.collegeknowledge.com.

BIRTHDAYS TODAY

Arthur Geisert, 60, author and illustrator (*Roman Numerals I to M*), born Dallas, TX, Sept 20, 1941.

Tony Tallarico, 68, author, illustrator (*I Can Draw Everything, Drawing & Cartooning Sci Fi*), born Brooklyn, NY, Sept 20, 1933.

September 2001

S	M	T	W	T	F	S
						1
2	3	4	5	6	7	8
9	10	11	12	13	14	15
16	17	18	19	20	21	22
23	24	25	26	27	28	29
30						

SEPTEMBER 21 — FRIDAY

Day 264 — 101 Remaining

ARMENIA: NATIONAL DAY: 10th ANNIVERSARY. Sept 21. Public holiday. Commemorates independence from the Soviet Union in 1991.

BELIZE: INDEPENDENCE DAY: 20th ANNIVERSARY. Sept 21. National holiday. Commemorates independence of the former British Honduras from Britain in 1981.

HOPKINSON, FRANCIS: BIRTH ANNIVERSARY. Sept 21, 1737. Signer of the Declaration of Independence. Born at Philadelphia, PA, he died there May 9, 1791.

HURRICANE HUGO HITS AMERICAN COAST: ANNIVERSARY. Sept 21, 1989. After ravaging the Virgin Islands, Hurricane Hugo hit the American coast at Charleston, SC. In its wake, Hugo left destruction totaling at least $8 billion. For more info about hurricanes: www.fema.gov/kids/hurr.htm.

JOSEPH, CHIEF: DEATH ANNIVERSARY. Sept 21, 1904. Nez Percé chief, whose Indian name was In-Mut-Too-Yah-Lat-Lat, was born about 1840 at Wallowa Valley, Oregon Territory, and died on the Colville Reservation at Washington State. Faced with war or resettlement to a reservation, Chief Joseph led a dramatic attempt to escape to Canada. After three months and more than 1,000 miles, he and his people were surrounded 40 miles from Canada and sent to a reservation at Oklahoma. Though the few survivors were later allowed to relocate to another reservation at Washington, they never regained their ancestral lands.

MALTA: INDEPENDENCE DAY. Sept 21. National Day. Commemorates independence from Britain in 1964.

NATIVE AMERICAN DAY IN MASSACHUSETTS. Sept 21. Proclaimed annually by the governor for the third Friday in September.

TAYLOR, MARGARET SMITH: BIRTH ANNIVERSARY. Sept 21, 1788. Wife of Zachary Taylor, 12th president of the US, born at Calvert County, MD. Died Aug 18, 1852.

BIRTHDAYS TODAY

Stephen King, 54, author (*Pet Sematary, The Shining, Misery*), born Portland, ME, Sept 21, 1947.

Bill Murray, 51, comedian ("Saturday Night Live"), actor (*Ghostbusters, Groundhog Day*), born Evanston, IL, Sept 21, 1950.

SEPTEMBER 22 — SATURDAY

Day 265 — 100 Remaining

AUTUMN. Sept 22–Dec 21. In the Northern Hemisphere, autumn begins today with the autumnal equinox, at 7:04 PM, EDT. Note that in the Southern Hemisphere today is the beginning of spring. Everywhere on Earth (except near the poles) the sun rises due east and sets due west and daylight length is nearly identical—about 12 hours, 8 minutes. *See* Curriculum Connection.

BANNED BOOKS WEEK—CELEBRATING THE FREEDOM TO READ. Sept 22–29. Brings to the attention of the general public the importance of the freedom to read and the harm censorship causes to our society. Sponsors: American Library Association, American Booksellers Association, American Booksellers Association for Free Expression, American Society of Journalists and Authors, Association of American Publishers, National Association of College Stores. For lists of frequently challenged books, visit the following websites: www.ala.org/bbooks/index.html and www.cs.cmu.edu/People/spok/most-banned.html. For info: Judith F. Krug, American Library Assn, Office for Intellectual Freedom, 50 E Huron St, Chicago, IL 60611. Phone: (312) 280-4223. Fax: (312) 280-4227. E-mail: oif@ala.org. Web: www.ala.org/bbooks.

ELEPHANT APPRECIATION DAY. Sept 22. Celebrate the earth's largest, most interesting and most noble endangered land animal. Free info kit from: Wayne Hepburn, WildHeart Productions, PO Box 50095, Sarasota, FL 34232. Phone: (941) 365-7787. Fax: (941) 363-0273. E-mail: elefunt@gte.net. Web: www.wildheart.com.

EMANCIPATION PROCLAMATION: ANNIVERSARY. Sept 22, 1862. One of the most important presidential proclamations of American history is that of Sept 22, 1862, in which Abraham Lincoln, by executive proclamation, freed the slaves in the rebelling states. (Four slave states had not seceded from the Union.) "That on . . . [Jan 1, 1863] . . . all persons held as slaves within any state or designated part of a state, the people whereof

SEPTEMBER 22
AUTUMN EQUINOX

This year September 22 is the first day of autumn in the northern hemisphere. The word "equinox" is derived from two Latin words that mean "equal night." On this day, which is either September 22 or 23, the daylight hours are nearly equal to the number of hours of nighttime all over the earth. That's because the sun is positioned directly above the equator. In the northern hemisphere, this heralds the arrival of autumn and signals that winter is approaching. In the southern hemisphere, it's the arrival of spring.

In science class, focus on prediction. Scientists make predictions based on their observations and experiences. Ask students to think about what occurrences they have observed in the past as autumn approached. Now zero in on your community. If there are trees on the school grounds, let students predict what colors the leaves on each tree will turn and the dates they think certain trees will lose their leaves (say 90 percent or more). Predict the day/night the first frost will occur. Have students make a chart that lists their predictions and see which ones prove most accurate. Draw conclusions about tree species, color and leaf loss.

Ask them to notice any signs of animal behavior that signal autumn is approaching. Two common signs are V-shaped formations of bird flocks and squirrels burying nuts.

Younger children will enjoy leaf-related science activities found in *Red Leaf, Yellow Leaf*, by Lois Ehlert (Harcourt, 0-15-266197-2, $16 Gr. PreK–3), and the art projects in Morteza Sohi's *Look What I Did With a Leaf* (Walker, 0-08027-7440-7, $5.95 Gr. PreK–3).

Fall Leaves Fall!, by Zoe Hall (Scholastic, 0-590-10079-3, $15.95 Gr. PreK–1), is a good book for preschoolers and primary students. *Autumn Leaves*, by Ken Robbins (Scholastic, 0-590-29879-8, $15.95 Gr. 2 & up), is a beautiful photo book of leaves.

The autumn equinox is also an opportunity to focus on the harvest season. *The Autumn Equinox: Celebrating the Harvest*, by Ellen Jackson (Millbrook, 0-7613-1354-0, $22.90 Gr. PreK–3), provides a wealth of information about the equinox and the many ways that cultures celebrate the harvest season. A collection of art and culinary activities are included at the end of the book. One of them, in keeping with the thanksgiving theme often associated with harvest, is a lovely variation on the fortune cookie. It uses crescent rolls and penciled notes of thanksgiving.

shall then be in rebellion against the United States, shall be then, thenceforward, and forever, free. . . ." For more info go to Ben's Guide to US Government for Kids: bensguide.gpo.gov. See also: "13th Amendment: Anniversary" (Dec 18) for abolition of slavery in all states.

ICE CREAM CONE: BIRTHDAY. Sept 22, 1903. Italo Marchiony emigrated from Italy in the late 1800s and soon thereafter went into business at New York, NY, with a pushcart dispensing lemon ice. Success soon led to a small fleet of pushcarts, and the inventive Marchiony was inspired to develop a cone, first made of paper, later of pastry, to hold the tasty delicacy. On Sept 22, 1903, his application for a patent for his new mold was filed, and US Patent No 746971 was issued to him Dec 15, 1903.

JAPAN: AUTUMNAL EQUINOX DAY. Sept 22. National holiday.

KIWANIS KIDS' DAY. Sept 22. To honor and assist youth—our greatest resource. Annually, the fourth Saturday in September. For info: Kiwanis Intl, Program Dvmt Dept, 3636 Woodview Trace, Indianapolis, IN 46268. E-mail: kiwanismail@kiwanis.org. Web: www.kiwanis.org.

MALI: INDEPENDENCE DAY. Sept 22. National holiday commemorating independence from France in 1960. Mali, in West Africa, was known as French Sudan while a colony.

★ **NATIONAL HUNTING AND FISHING DAY.** Sept 22. Presidential Proclamation 4682, of Sept 11, 1979, covers all succeeding years. Annually, the fourth Saturday of September.

US POSTMASTER GENERAL ESTABLISHED: ANNIVERSARY. Sept 22, 1789. Congress established the office of postmaster general, following the departments of state, war and treasury.

BIRTHDAYS TODAY

Bonnie Hunt, 37, actress (*Beethoven, Beethoven's 2nd*), born Chicago, IL, Sept 22, 1964.

Ronaldo, 25, Brazilian soccer star, born Ronaldo Luiz Nazario de Lima, Rio de Janeiro, Brazil, Sept 22, 1976.

Esphyr Slobodkina, 93, author and illustrator (*Caps for Sale: A Tale of a Peddler, Some Monkeys and Their Monkey Business*), born Cheliabinsk, Siberia, Sept 22, 1908.

SEPTEMBER 23 — SUNDAY

Day 266 — 99 Remaining

DEAF AWARENESS WEEK. Sept 23–29. Nationwide celebration to promote deaf culture, American Sign Language and deaf heritage. Activities include library displays, interpreted story hours, Open Houses in residential schools and mainstream programs, exhibit booths in shopping malls with "Five Minute Sign Language Lessons," material distribution. Annually, the last full week of September. For info: Natl Assn of the Deaf, 814 Thayer Ave, Silver Spring, MD 20910-4500. Fax: (301) 587-1791. E-mail: nad info@nad.org. Web: www.nad.org.

"THE JETSONS" TV PREMIERE: ANNIVERSARY. Sept 23, 1962. "Meet George Jetson. His boy Elroy. Daughter Judy. Jane, his wife. . . . " These words introduced us to the Jetsons, a cartoon family living in the twenty-first century, the Flintstones of the Space Age. We followed the exploits of George and his family, as well as his unstable work relationship with his greedy, ruthless boss Cosmo Spacely. Voices were provided by George O'Hanlon as George, Penny Singleton as Jane, Janet Waldo as Judy, Daws Butler as Elroy, Don Messick as Astro, the family dog and Mel Blanc as Spacely. New episodes were created in 1985 which introduced a new pet, Orbity.

September 2001

S	M	T	W	T	F	S
						1
2	3	4	5	6	7	8
9	10	11	12	13	14	15
16	17	18	19	20	21	22
23	24	25	26	27	28	29
30						

LIBRA, THE BALANCE. Sept 23–Oct 22. In the astronomical/astrological zodiac that divides the sun's apparent orbit into 12 segments, the period Sept 23–Oct 22 is identified traditionally as the sun sign of Libra, the Balance. The ruling planet is Venus.

"LITTLE ROCK NINE": ANNIVERSARY. Sept 23, 1957. Nine African American students entered Central High School in Little Rock, AR. They had tried to begin school Sept 4 but were denied entrance by National Guard troops called out by Governor Orval Faubus to resist integration. President Dwight Eisenhower responded by sending federal troops to protect the students. Eight of the nine students completed the school year, showing America that black students could endure the hatred directed at them.

McGUFFEY, WILLIAM HOLMES: BIRTH ANNIVERSARY. Sept 23, 1800. American educator and author of the famous *McGuffey Readers*, born at Washington County, PA. Probably no other textbooks have had a greater influence on American life. More than 120 million copies were sold. McGuffey died at Charlottesville, VA, May 4, 1873.

★ **MINORITY ENTERPRISE DEVELOPMENT WEEK.** Sept 23–29 (tentative). Presidential Proclamation issued without request since 1983 for the first full week in October except in 1991 when issued for Sept 22–28, in 1992 for Sept 27–Oct 3, to coincide with the National Conference, in 1997 for Sept 21–27, in 1999 for Sept 19–25 and in 2000 for Sept 24–30.

NATIONAL DOG WEEK. Sept 23–29. To promote the relationship of dogs to mankind and emphasize the need for the proper care and treatment of dogs. Annually, the last full week in September. For info: Morris Raskin, Secy, Dogs on Stamps Study Unit (DOSSU), 202 A Newport Rd, Cranbury, NJ 08512. Phone: (609) 655-7411.

PLANET NEPTUNE DISCOVERY: ANNIVERSARY. Sept 23, 1846. Neptune is 2,796,700,000 miles from the sun (about 30 times as far from the sun as Earth). Eighth planet from the sun, Neptune takes 164.8 years to revolve around the sun. Diameter is about 31,000 miles compared to Earth at 7,927 miles. Discovered by German astronomer Johann Galle. For more info: *Uranus, Neptune, and Pluto*, by Robin Kerrod (Lerner, 0-8225-3908-X, $21.27 Gr. 4–6) or go to Nine Planets: Multimedia Tour of the Solar System at www.seds.org/billa/tnp.

SAUDI ARABIA: ANNIVERSARY KINGDOM UNIFICATION. Sept 23. National holiday. Commemorates unification in 1932.

BIRTHDAYS TODAY

Bruce Brooks, 51, author (*What Hearts, The Moves Make the Man*), born Washington, DC, Sept 23, 1950.

Sila María Calderón, 59, Governor of Puerto Rico, born San Juan, PR, Sept 23, 1942.

Eric Scott Montross, 30, basketball player, born Indianapolis, IN, Sept 23, 1971.

SEPTEMBER 24 — MONDAY

Day 267 — 98 Remaining

BEHN, HARRY: BIRTH ANNIVERSARY. Sept 24, 1898. Author, best remembered for his children's books, *Trees* and *Crickets and Bullfrogs and Whispers of Thunder*. Born at McCabe, CT, Behn died Sept 5, 1973.

CAMBODIA: CONSTITUTIONAL DECLARATION DAY. Sept 24. National holiday. Commemorates the constitution of 1993.

GUINEA-BISSAU: INDEPENDENCE DAY. Sept 24. National holiday. Commemorates independence from Portugal in 1974.

HENSON, JIM: 65th BIRTH ANNIVERSARY. Sept 24, 1936. Puppeteer, born at Greenville, MS. Jim Henson created a unique brand of puppetry known as the Muppets. Kermit the Frog, Big Bird, Rowlf, Bert and Ernie, Gonzo, Animal, Miss Piggy and Oscar the Grouch are a few of the puppets that captured the hearts of children and adults alike in television and film productions including "Sesame Street," "The Jimmy Dean Show," "The Muppet Show," *The Muppet Movie, The Muppets Take Manhattan, The Great Muppet Caper* and *The Dark Crystal*. Henson began his career in 1954 as producer of the TV show "Sam and Friends" at Washington, DC. He introduced the Muppets in 1956. His creativity was rewarded with 18 Emmy Awards, seven Grammy Awards, four Peabody Awards and five ACE Awards from the National Cable Television Association. Henson died unexpectedly May 16, 1990, at New York, NY. For more info: *Jim Henson: Young Puppeteer*, by Leslie Gourse (Aladdin, 0-68-983398-9, $4.99 Gr. 4–7).

MARSHALL, JOHN: BIRTH ANNIVERSARY. Sept 24, 1755. Fourth Chief Justice of Supreme Court, born at Germantown, VA. Served in House of Representatives and as secretary of state under John Adams. Appointed by President Adams to the position of chief justice in January 1801, he became known as "The Great Chief Justice." Marshall's court was largely responsible for defining the role of the Supreme Court and basic organizing principles of government in the early years after adoption of the Constitution in such cases as *Marbury v Madison, McCulloch v Maryland, Cohens v Virginia* and *Gibbons v Ogden*. He died at Philadelphia, PA, July 6, 1835. For more info: oyez.northwestern.edu/justices/justice.cgi.

MOON PHASE: FIRST QUARTER. Sept 24. Moon enters First Quarter phase at 5:31 AM, EDT.

MOZAMBIQUE: ARMED FORCES DAY. Sept 24. National holiday. Commemorates the beginning of the 1964 war for independence.

RAWLS, WILSON: BIRTH ANNIVERSARY. Sept 24, 1913. Author (*Where the Red Fern Grows*), born at Scraper, OK. Died Dec 16, 1984. For a study guide to *Where the Red Fern Grows*: glencoe.com/sec/literature/litlibrary.

SOUTH AFRICA: HERITAGE DAY. Sept 24. A celebration of South African nationhood, commemorating the multicultural heritage of this rainbow nation.

TAKE CHARGE OF YOUR TV WEEK. Sept 24–28. To help families make more informed television viewing choices. Co-sponsored by the National PTA, Cable in the Classroom and the National Cable Television Association. For info: Natl PTA, 330 N Wabash, Ste 2100, Chicago, IL 60611. Phone: (312) 670-6782. E-mail: info@pta.org. Web: www.pta.org.

BIRTHDAYS TODAY

Eddie George, 28, football player, born Philadelphia, PA, Sept 24, 1973.

Kevin Sorbo, 43, actor ("Hercules"), born Mound, MN, Sept 24, 1958.

SEPTEMBER 25 — TUESDAY

Day 268 — 97 Remaining

FIRST AMERICAN NEWSPAPER PUBLISHED: ANNIVERSARY. Sept 25, 1690. The first (and only) edition of *Publick Occurrences Both Foreign and Domestick* was published by Benjamin Harris, at the London-Coffee-House, Boston, MA. Authorities considered this first newspaper published in the US offensive and ordered immediate suppression.

FIRST WOMAN SUPREME COURT JUSTICE: 20th ANNIVERSARY. Sept 25, 1981. Sandra Day O'Connor was sworn in as the first woman associate justice of the US Supreme Court on this date. She had been nominated by President Ronald Reagan in July 1981. For more info: oyez.northwestern.edu/justices/justices.cgi.

GREENWICH MEAN TIME BEGINS: ANNIVERSARY. Sept 25, 1676. On this day two very accurate clocks were set in motion at the Royal Observatory at Greenwich, England. Greenwich Mean Time (now called Universal Time) became standard for England; in 1884 it became standard for the world.

MAJOR LEAGUE BASEBALL'S FIRST DOUBLEHEADER: ANNIVERSARY. Sept 25, 1882. The first major league baseball doubleheader was played between the Providence, RI and Worcester, MA teams.

PACIFIC OCEAN DISCOVERED: ANNIVERSARY. Sept 25, 1513. Vasco Núñez de Balboa, a Spanish conquistador, stood high atop a peak in the Darien, in present-day Panama, becoming the first European to look upon the Pacific Ocean, claiming it as the South Sea in the name of the King of Spain.

"THE PARTRIDGE FAMILY" TV PREMIERE: ANNIVERSARY. Sept 25, 1970. A fatherless family of five kids form a rock band with their mother Shirley (played by Shirley Jones), and go on the road. Son Keith was played by David Cassidy (who became a real-life rock star), daughter Laurie was played by Susan Dey, Danny Bonaduce played son Danny, youngest son Chris was played by Jeremy Gelbwaks and Brian Forster and youngest daughter Tracy by Suzanne Crough. Reuben Kincaid, the family's agent, was played by Dave Madden. The TV family recorded several albums, and songs such as "I Think I Love You" and "Cherish" went on to be hits.

RWANDA: REPUBLIC DAY. Sept 25. National holiday. Commemorates the 1961 referendum that abolished the monarchy.

SEQUOIA AND KINGS CANYON NATIONAL PARKS ESTABLISHED: ANNIVERSARY. Sept 25, 1890. Area in central California established as a national park. For more info:

www.nps.gov/seki/index.htm. For more park info: Sequoia Natl Park, Three Rivers, CA 93271.

BIRTHDAYS TODAY

Cooper Edens, 56, author (*If You're Afraid of the Dark, Remember the Night Rainbow; Santa Cows*), born Washington, DC, Sept 25, 1945.

Jim Murphy, 54, author of nonfiction (*The Great Fire*), born Newark, NJ, Sept 25, 1947.

Andrea Davis Pinkney, 38, author (*Dear Benjamin Banneker, I Smell Honey, Duke Ellington*), born Sept 25, 1963.

Scottie Pippen, 36, basketball player, born Hamburg, AR, Sept 25, 1965.

James Ransome, 40, illustrator (*Sweet Clara and the Freedom Quilt*), born Rich Square, NC, Sept 25, 1961.

Christopher Reeve, 49, actor (*Superman*), born New York, NY, Sept 25, 1952.

Will Smith, 33, rapper, actor ("The Fresh Prince of Bel Air," *Men in Black*), born Philadelphia, PA, Sept 25, 1968.

Barbara Walters, 70, journalist, interviewer, TV host ("20/20"), born Boston, MA, Sept 25, 1931.

SEPTEMBER 26 — WEDNESDAY

Day 269 — 96 Remaining

APPLESEED, JOHNNY: BIRTH ANNIVERSARY. Sept 26, 1774. John Chapman, better known as Johnny Appleseed, believed to have been born at Leominster, MA. Died at Allen County, IN, Mar 11, 1845. Planter of orchards and friend of wild animals, he was regarded as a great medicine man by the Indians. *See* Curriculum Connection.

"THE BRADY BUNCH" TV PREMIERE: ANNIVERSARY. Sept 26, 1969. This sitcom, which spawned a whole industry, starred Robert Reed as widower Mike Brady, who has three sons and is married to Carol (played by Florence Henderson), who has three daughters. Nutty housekeeper Alice was played by Ann B. Davis. Sons Greg (Barry Williams), Peter (Christopher Knight) and Bobby (Mike Lookinland) and daughters Marcia (Maureen McCormick), Jan (Eve Plumb) and Cindy (Susan Olsen) experienced the typical crises of youth. The show steered clear of social issues, portraying childhood as a time of innocence. This is probably why it has remained popular in reruns in the after-school time slot. "The Brady Kids" (1972–74) was a Sunday morning cartoon show. On "The Brady Bunch Hour" (1976–77) the family hosted a variety show. "The Brady Brides" (1981) was a sitcom about the two older girls adjusting to marriage. *A Very Brady Christmas* (1988) was CBS's highest-rated special for the season. *The Brady Bunch Movie*, released in 1995, appealed to fans who had watched the show 25 years before.

FIRST TELEVISED PRESIDENTIAL DEBATE: ANNIVERSARY. Sept 26, 1960. The debate between presidential candidates John F. Kennedy and Richard Nixon was televised from a Chicago TV studio.

GERSHWIN, GEORGE: BIRTH ANNIVERSARY. Sept 26, 1898. American composer remembered for his many enduring songs and melodies, including "The Man I Love," "Strike Up the Band," "Funny Face," "I Got Rhythm" and the opera *Porgy and Bess*. Many of his works were in collaboration with his brother, Ira. Born at Brooklyn, NY, he died of a brain tumor at Beverly Hills, CA, July 11, 1937. See also: "Gershwin, Ira: Birth Anniversary" (Dec 6). For more info: *George Gershwin: American Composer*, by Catherine Reef (Morgan Reynolds, 1-883846-58-7, $19.95 Gr. 5–8).

NATIONAL YOUTH OF THE YEAR. Sept 26. Washington, DC. Each year a Boys and Girls Club member is selected by a panel of judges from among five regional finalists to be the National Youth of the Year and spokesperson for Boys and Girls Clubs of America. This selection is open to Boys and Girls Club members only—ages 18 and under. Finalists are selected based on leadership qualities and service exhibited to home and family, spiritual values, service to community and Club, excellence in school and obstacles overcome. Winners are presented at a Congressional breakfast and to the president at the White House. For info: Kevin

September 2001

S	M	T	W	T	F	S
						1
2	3	4	5	6	7	8
9	10	11	12	13	14	15
16	17	18	19	20	21	22
23	24	25	26	27	28	29
30						

SEPTEMBER 26
JOHN CHAPMAN'S BIRTHDAY

John Chapman, better known as Johnny Appleseed, was born on September 26, 1774, in Leominster, Massachusetts. When he was in his 20s, John began a lifelong apple planting mission along the American Frontier (Ohio and Indiana) that later catapulted him into folk legend fame. He earned the name "Johnny Appleseed" as a result of his widespread orchard plantings. Chapman died in 1845.

September is the perfect time to celebrate an apple grower's life. One activity might be to hold a classroom apple tasting. This could be patterned on a blind wine tasting event. Buy several varieties of apples from your local supermarket and make a list of them. Keep the varieties separated from one another. Set up apple "orchards" in numbered stations around the room. Leave one apple of each variety whole. Cut the rest into small pieces, enough to let each student have a taste.

Before students visit each "orchard," have them make a comparison grid, listing taste, crunchiness, color, size, etc. across the top. List orchard numbers down the side of the paper. At each station, students can evaluate the apple they see and taste. Young students might want to draw a picture on the back of their graph.

After everyone has sampled and observed, graph student findings as a whole and see if their observations can help them correctly name each apple variety. (You will need to have a list of characteristics of each variety on hand.)

Other activities might include having children bring a favorite apple recipe from home. Compile them and make a classroom book, which can be distributed to each student. Artsy apple posters featuring the slogan "An apple a day keeps the doctor away," or other apple-oriented slogans the students can invent, will liven up bulletin boards. The whole apples from each station can be cut in half and used to make apple print gift wrapping. Students can plant the seeds in containers and monitor their growth. Plant seedlings at the end of the year.

Books to complement the activities include: *Johnny Appleseed*, by Patricia Demuth (Putnam, 0-448-41130-X, $3.99 Gr. PreK–1); *Johnny Appleseed*, by Reeve Lindbergh (Little, Brown, 0-316-52634-7, $6.95 Gr. PreK–3); *The Real Johnny Appleseed*, by Laurie Lawlor (Albert Whitman, 0-8075-6909-7, $13.95 Gr. 4–7); *Apples, Apples, Apples*, by Nancy Elizabeth Wallace (Winslow, 1-8908-1719-8, $15.95 Gr. K–3); *The Life and Times of the Apple*, by Charles Micucci (Orchard, 0-531-07067-0, $5.95 Gr. 2–5); and *Apples*, by Gail Gibbons (Holiday House, 0-8234-1497-3, $16.95 Gr. 3–6). There are many others available.

W. Davis, Dir of Program Services, Boys and Girls Clubs of America, 1230 W Peachtree St NW, Atlanta, GA 30309. Web: www.bgca.org

POPE PAUL VI: BIRTH ANNIVERSARY. Sept 26, 1897. Giovanni Battista Montini, 262nd pope of the Roman Catholic Church, born at Concesio, Italy. Elected pope June 21, 1963. Died at Castel Gandolfo, near Rome, Italy, Aug 6, 1978.

SHAMU'S BIRTHDAY. Sept 26. Shamu was born at Sea World at Orlando, FL, Sept 26, 1985, and is the first killer whale born in captivity to survive. Shamu is now living at Sea World's Texas park. For more info: www.seaworld.org/killer_whale/killerwhales.html.

YOM KIPPUR BEGINS AT SUNDOWN. Sept 26. Jewish Day of Atonement. See "Yom Kippur" (Sept 27).

BIRTHDAYS TODAY

Christine T. Whitman, 55, Administrator of the Environmental Protection Agency, former Governor of New Jersey (R), born New York, NY, Sept 26, 1946.

Serena Williams, 20, tennis player, born Saginaw, MI, Sept 26, 1981.

SEPTEMBER 27 — THURSDAY

Day 270 — 95 Remaining

ADAMS, SAMUEL: BIRTH ANNIVERSARY. Sept 27, 1722. Revolutionary leader and Massachusetts state politician Samuel Adams, cousin to President John Adams, was born at Boston. He died there Oct 2, 1803. As a delegate to the First and Second Continental Congresses, Adams urged a vigorous stand against England. He signed the Declaration of Independence and the Articles of Confederation and supported the war for independence. Adams served as lieutenant governor of Massachusetts under John Hancock from 1789 to 1793 and then as governor until 1797.

ANCESTOR APPRECIATION DAY. Sept 27. A day to learn about and appreciate one's forebears. For info: W.D. Chase, A.A.D. Assn, PO Box 3, Montague, MI 49437-0003.

ETHIOPIA: CROSS DAY. Sept 27. National holiday. Commemorates the finding of the true cross (*Maskal*). Also a holiday in Eritrea.

McGWIRE HITS 70th HOME RUN: ANNIVERSARY. Sept 27, 1998. Mark McGwire of the St. Louis Cardinals made baseball history by hitting his 70th home run of the season. On Sept 8, 1998, he had broken the previous record of 61 homers set by Roger Maris in 1961.

SAINT VINCENT DE PAUL: FEAST DAY. Sept 27. French priest, patron of charitable organizations, and founder of the Vincentian Order and cofounder of the Sisters of Charity. Canonized 1737 (lived 1581?–1660).

STATE FAIR OF VIRGINIA ON STRAWBERRY HILL. Sept 27–Oct 7. Richmond, VA. The pride of Virginia's industry of agriculture can be seen in more than 3,000 exhibitions, competitions and shows. Virginia's greatest annual educational and entertainment event. Est attendance: 600,000. For info: Keith T. Hessey, Genl Mgr, PO Box 26805, Richmond, VA 23261-6805. Phone: (804) 569-3200. Fax: (804) 569-3252. Web: www.statefair.com.

YOM KIPPUR or DAY OF ATONEMENT. Sept 27. Holiest Jewish observance. A day for fasting, repentance and seeking forgiveness. Hebrew calendar date: Tishri 10, 5762.

BIRTHDAYS TODAY

Martin Handford, 45, author and illustrator (*Where's Waldo?*), born London, England, Sept 27, 1956.

Stephen Douglas (Steve) Kerr, 36, basketball player, born Beirut, Lebanon, Sept 27, 1965.

Mike Schmidt, 52, Baseball Hall of Fame third baseman, born Dayton, OH, Sept 27, 1949.

Gerhard Schröder, 51, Chancellor of Germany, born Mossenberg, Germany, Sept 27, 1950.

Bernard Waber, 77, author (*Ira Sleeps Over*), born Philadelphia, PA, Sept 27, 1924.

SEPTEMBER 28 — FRIDAY

Day 271 — 94 Remaining

CABRILLO DAY: ANNIVERSARY OF DISCOVERY OF CALIFORNIA. Sept 28, 1542. California. Commemorates discovery of California by Portuguese navigator Juan Rodriguez Cabrillo who reached San Diego Bay. Cabrillo died at San Miguel Island, CA, Jan 3, 1543. His birth date is unknown. The Cabrillo National Monument marks his landfall and Cabrillo Day is still observed in California (in some areas on the Saturday nearest Sept 28, Sept 29 in 2001).

POKÉMON DEBUTS: ANNIVERSARY. Sept 28, 1998. This wildly popular Game Boy game, featuring Mewtwo, Pikachu, Meowth and Giovanni, first debuted in Japan on Feb 27, 1996. The goal of the game is to find, capture and train all 151 Pokémons (pocket monsters). Trading cards also proved popular with US kids. The Pokémon animated TV show debuted in 1998 and *Pokémon the First Movie: Mewtwo Strikes Back* was released Nov 10, 1999.

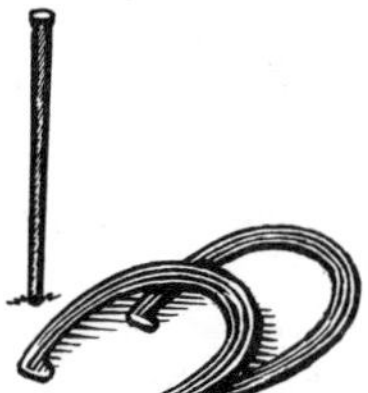

STATE FAIR OF TEXAS. Sept 28–Oct 21. Fair Park, Dallas, TX. Features a Broadway musical, college football games, new car show, concerts, livestock shows and traditional events and entertainment including exhibits, creative arts and parades. Est attendance: 3,200,000. For info: Nancy Wiley, State Fair of Texas, PO Box 150009, Dallas, TX 75315. Phone: (214) 421-8716. Fax: (214) 421-8710. E-mail: pr@greatstatefair.com. Web: www.bigtex.com.

TAIWAN: CONFUCIUS'S BIRTHDAY AND TEACHERS' DAY. Sept 28. National holiday, designated as Teachers' Day. Confucius is the Latinized name of Kung-futzu, born at Shantung province on the 27th day of the tenth moon (lunar calendar) in the 22nd year of Kuke Hsiang of Lu (551 BC). He died at age 72, having spent some 40 years as a teacher. Teachers' Day is observed annually on Sept 28.

WIGGIN, KATE DOUGLAS: BIRTH ANNIVERSARY. Sept 28, 1856. Kate Wiggin was born Kate Douglas Smith at Philadelphia, PA. She helped organize the first free kindergarten on the West Coast in 1878 at San Francisco and in 1880 she and her sister established the California Kindergarten Training School. After moving back to the East Coast she devoted herself to writing, producing a number of children's books including *The Birds' Christmas Carol, Polly Oliver's Problem* and *Rebecca of Sunnybrook Farm.* She died at Harrow, England, Aug 24, 1923.

WILLARD, FRANCES ELIZABETH CAROLINE: BIRTH ANNIVERSARY. Sept 28, 1839. American educator and reformer, president of the Women's Christian Temperance Union, 1879–98 and women's suffrage leader, born at Churchville, NY. Died at New York, NY, Feb 18, 1898.

BIRTHDAYS TODAY

Se Ri Pak, 24, golfer, born Daejeon, South Korea, Sept 28, 1977.

Gwyneth Paltrow, 28, actress (*Hook, Emma*), born Los Angeles, CA, Sept 28, 1973.

SEPTEMBER 29 — SATURDAY

Day 272 — 93 Remaining

ENGLAND: SCOTLAND YARD: FIRST APPEARANCE ANNIVERSARY. Sept 29, 1829. The first public appearance of Greater London's Metropolitan Police occurred amid jeering and abuse from disapproving political opponents. Public sentiment turned to confidence and respect in the ensuing years. The Metropolitan Police had been established by an act of Parliament in June 1829, at the request of Home Secretary Sir Robert Peel, after whom the London police officers became more affectionately known as "bobbies." Scotland Yard, the site of their first headquarters near Charing Cross, soon became the official name of the force.

FERMI, ENRICO: 100th BIRTH ANNIVERSARY. Sept 29, 1901. Nuclear physicist, born at Rome, Italy. Played a prominent role in the splitting of the atom and in the construction of the first American nuclear reactor. Died at Chicago, IL, Nov 16, 1954.

MICHAELMAS. Sept 29. The feast of St. Michael and All Angels in the Greek and Roman Catholic Churches.

PARAGUAY: BOQUERÓN DAY. Sept 29. National holiday. Commemorates a battle during the Chaco War in 1932.

SPACE MILESTONE: *DISCOVERY* (US). Sept 29, 1988. Space Shuttle *Discovery*, after numerous reschedulings, launched from Kennedy Space Center, FL, with a five-member crew on board, and landed Oct 3 at Edwards Air Force Base, CA. It marked the first American manned flight since the Challenger tragedy in 1986. See also: "*Challenger* Space Shuttle Explosion: Anniversary" (Jan 28).

BIRTHDAYS TODAY

Stan Berenstain, 78, author and illustrator, with his wife Jan (the Berenstain Bears series), born Philadelphia, PA, Sept 29, 1923.

Bryant Gumbel, 53, TV host ("Today," "The Public Eye"), sportscaster, born New Orleans, LA, Sept 29, 1948.

Donald Hall, 73, poet and author (*The Ox-Cart Man, When Willard Met Babe Ruth*), born New Haven, CT, Sept 29, 1928.

Bill Nelson, 59, US Senator (D, Florida), born Miami, FL, Sept 29, 1942.

Lech Walesa, 58, Poland labor leader, Solidarity founder, born Popowo, Poland, Sept 29, 1943.

September 2001

S	M	T	W	T	F	S
						1
2	3	4	5	6	7	8
9	10	11	12	13	14	15
16	17	18	19	20	21	22
23	24	25	26	27	28	29
30						

SEPTEMBER 30 — SUNDAY

Day 273 — 92 Remaining

BABE SETS HOME RUN RECORD: ANNIVERSARY. Sept 30, 1927. George Herman "Babe" Ruth hit his 60th home run of the season off Tom Zachary of the Washington Senators. Ruth's record for the most homers in a single season stood for 34 years—until Roger Maris hit 61 in 1961. Maris's record was broken in 1998, first by Mark McGwire of the St. Louis Cardinals and then by Sammy Sosa of the Chicago Cubs.

BOTSWANA: INDEPENDENCE DAY: 35th ANNIVERSARY. Sept 30. National holiday. The former Bechuanaland Protectorate (British Colony) became the independent Republic of Botswana in 1966.

D'AULAIRE, EDGAR PARIN: BIRTH ANNIVERSARY. Sept 30, 1898. Author, with his wife Ingri (*Norse Gods and Giants*), born at Munich, Germany. Died May 1, 1986.

FEAST OF SAINT JEROME. Sept 30. Patron saint of scholars and librarians.

"THE FLINTSTONES" TV PREMIERE: ANNIVERSARY. Sept 30, 1960. This Hanna Barbera cartoon comedy was set in prehistoric times. Characters included two Stone Age families, Fred and Wilma Flintstone and their neighbors Barney and Betty Rubble. In 1994 *The Flintstones* film was released, starring John Goodman, Rick Moranis, Elizabeth Perkins and Rosie O'Donnell.

★ **GOLD STAR MOTHER'S DAY.** Sept 30. Presidential Proclamation always for last Sunday of each September since 1936. Proclamation 2424 of Sept 14, 1940, covers all succeeding years.

GUADALUPE MOUNTAINS NATIONAL PARK ESTABLISHED: ANNIVERSARY. Sept 30, 1972. Area in western Texas along Texas–New Mexico border, originally authorized Oct 15, 1966, was established as a national park. For more info: www.nps.gov/gumo/index.htm.

HALEAKALA NATIONAL PARK ESTABLISHED: 85th ANNIVERSARY. Sept 30, 1960. Summit of a volcano on Maui in the Hawaiian Islands was authorized as a part of Hawaii National Park on Aug 1, 1916. In 1960 Haleakala was established as a separate national park. The park was expanded in 1969 to include the Kipahulu Valley. For more info: www.nps.gov/hale/index.htm.

MEREDITH ENROLLS AT OLE MISS: ANNIVERSARY. Sept 30, 1962. Rioting broke out when James Meredith became the first black to enroll in the all-white University of Mississippi. President Kennedy sent US troops to the area to force compliance with the law. Three people died in the fighting and 50 were injured. On June 6, 1966, Meredith was shot while participating in a civil rights march at Mississippi. On June 25 Meredith, barely recovered, rejoined the marchers near Jackson, MS.

BIRTHDAYS TODAY

Mike Damus, 22, actor ("Teen Angel"), born New York, NY, Sept 30, 1979.

Carol Fenner, 72, author (*Yolonda's Genius*), born New York, NY, Sept 30, 1929.

Martina Hingis, 21, tennis player, born Kosice, Slovakia, Sept 30, 1980.

Blanche Lambert Lincoln, 41, US Senator (D, Arkansas), born Helena, MT, Sept 30, 1960.

Dominique Moceanu, 20, gymnast, born Hollywood, CA, Sept 30, 1981.

OCTOBER 1 — MONDAY

Day 274 — 91 Remaining

ADOPT-A-SHELTER DOG MONTH. Oct 1–31. To promote the adoption of dogs from local shelters, the ASPCA sponsors this important observance. For info: ASPCA Public Affairs Dept, 424 E 92nd St, New York, NY 10128. Phone: (212) 876-7700. E-mail: press@aspca.org. Web: www.aspca.org.

BOOK IT! READING INCENTIVE PROGRAM. Oct 1, 2001–Mar 29, 2002. This is a five-month program for students in grades K–6 sponsored by Pizza Hut. Teachers set monthly reading goals for students. When a monthly reading goal is met, the child receives a certificate for a free pizza. If the whole class meets its goal, a pizza party is provided for the class. For info: Book It!, PO Box 2999, Wichita, KS 67201. Phone: (800) 4-BOOK IT. Fax: (316) 687-8937. Web: www.bookitprogram.com.

CAMPAIGN FOR HEALTHIER BABIES MONTH. Oct 1–31. A month-long concentrated effort to focus attention on the March of Dimes Birth Defects Foundation and its community health programs, public awareness messages, advocacy and fundraising efforts. This month is designated to raise awareness of how to prevent birth defects and infant mortality. For info: March of Dimes Birth Resource Center, 1275 Mamaroneck Ave, White Plains, NY 10605. Phone: (914) 997-4600. E-mail: rc@modimes.org. Web: www.modimes.org.

CARTER, JIMMY: BIRTHDAY. Oct 1, 1924. The 39th president (Jan 20, 1977–Jan 20, 1981) of the US, born James Earl Carter at Plains, GA. For info: www.ipl.org/ref/POTUS.

CD PLAYER DEBUTS: ANNIVERSARY. Oct 1, 1982. The first compact disc player, jointly developed by Sony, Philips and Polygram, went on sale. It cost $625 (more than $1,000 in current dollars).

CHILD HEALTH MONTH. Oct 1–31. Sponsored since 1992 by the American Academy of Pediatrics to promote child health messages on nutrition, immunizations, violence prevention, injury prevention and substance abuse prevention. Local AAP chapters may choose to commemorate this on another date. For info: American Academy of Pediatrics, 141 Northwest Point Blvd, Elk Grove Village, IL 60007. Phone: (847) 228-5005. Web: www.aap.org.

★**CHILD HEALTH DAY.** Oct 1. Presidential Proclamation always issued for the first Monday of October. Proclamation has been issued since 1928. In 1959 Congress changed celebration day from May 1 to the present observance (Pub Res No. 46 of May 18, 1928, and PL86–352 of Sept 22, 1959).

OCTOBER 1–31
INTERNATIONAL DINOSAUR MONTH

In recent years the study of dinosaurs has often been first section news in some of the world's largest newspapers. Much of this focus has been in two areas: the theory that birds are the living descendants of dinosaurs; and exciting studies about the internal organs of dinosaurs—or "guts" if you want to grab a student's attention.

Digging for Bird Dinosaurs, by Nic Bishop (Houghton Mifflin, 0-395-96056-8, $16 Gr. 5–8), is an engrossing nonfiction book that discusses the work of paleontologist Cathy Forster and her quest for fossils of a primitive reptilian bird, *Rahonavis*. Readers accompany Forster on her fossil dig in Madagascar and become virtual paleontologists involved in all aspects of excavation, preservation and the laboratory reconstruction of the bones she finds. This is a great inside peek for students who are interested in becoming paleontologists. *Feathered Dinosaurs*, by Christopher Sloan (National Geographic, 0-7922-7219-6, $17.95 Gr. 5 & up), examines, in depth, the most recent information about the connection between birds and dinosaurs. Skeletal comparisons, scale and feather developments, interesting photographs of feathered fossils, and imaginative paintings of feathered dinosaurs make this a helpful tool for history of life units. Examining a feather visually and then comparing the naked eye observations with those found while examining the same feather with a microscope will amaze students.

The subject of dinosaur metabolism and whether they were cold-blooded or warm-blooded has raged for more than a decade. New scanning equipment used for medical diagnoses, plus some startling fossil finds, are opening up a whole new area of dinosaur study. *Outside and Inside Dinosaurs*, by Sandra Markle (Simon & Schuster, 0-689-82300-2, $16 Gr. 2–5), is a good general introduction to the internal physiology of dinosaurs. *Dinosaur Eggs*, by Jennifer Dussling (Grosset, 0-448-42093-7, $3.99 Gr. 1–4), is good for younger readers who want to learn more about what paleontologists have discovered about juvenile dinosaurs from studies done on fossilized dinosaur eggs.

One recent, startling discovery by Dr. Andrew Kuzmitz was that of a dinosaur heart. Dr. Kuzmitz used computerized tomography to scan a 66-million-year-old dinosaur fossil. He was surprised to find two large, oval chambers inside the rib cage area, which give every appearance of being the dinosaur's heart. For more information about this discovery see the April 21, 2000, issue of *Science* magazine, pages 416 and 503. Kuzmitz and his coworkers have found that the structure of this heart is closer to the structure of bird and mammal hearts than it is to reptilian hearts. This has fanned the flames on the bird/dinosaur connection. Students from middle school and up might want to research the issue and hold a scientific debate to discuss pro- and anti-bird arguments.

Dr. Paul Sereno of the University of Chicago is one of today's most famous paleontologists. Visit his website at dinosaur.uchicago.edu for a treasure trove of information about Sereno and his work. Several videos are listed and also references that will lead you to his articles about bird evolution.

For a look at several paleontologists and other dinosaur finds, see *Graveyards of the Dinosaurs*, by Shelley Tanaka (Hyperion, 0-7868-0375-4, $16.95 Gr. 3–7).

CHINA: MID-AUTUMN FESTIVAL. Oct 1. To worship the moon god. According to folk legend this day is also the birthday of the earth god T'u-ti Kung. The festival indicates the year's hard work in the fields will soon end with the harvest. People express gratitude to heaven as represented by the moon and earth as symbolized by the earth god for all good things from the preceding year. 15th day of eighth month of Chinese lunar calendar.

CHINA: NATIONAL DAY. Oct 1. Commemorates the founding of the People's Republic of China in 1949.

COMPUTER LEARNING MONTH. Oct 1–31. A monthlong focus of events and activities for learning new uses of computers and software, sharing ideas and helping others gain the benefits of computers and software. National contests are held to recognize students, educators and parents for their innovative ideas; computers and software are awarded to winning entries. Annually, the month of October. For info: Computer Learning Foundation, Dept CHS, PO Box 60007, Palo Alto, CA 94306-0007. Phone: (408) 720-8898. Fax: (408) 720-8777. E-mail: clf@computerlearning.org. Web: www.computerlearning.org.

CYPRUS: INDEPENDENCE DAY. Oct 1. National holiday. Commemorates independence from Britain in 1960.

DISNEY WORLD OPENED: 30th ANNIVERSARY. Oct 1, 1971. Disney's second theme park opened at Orlando, FL. See also "Disneyland Opened: Anniversary" (July 17).

DIVERSITY AWARENESS MONTH. Oct 1–31. Celebrating, promoting and appreciating the diversity of our society. Also, a month to foster and further our understanding of the inherent value of all races, genders, nationalities, age groups, religions, sexual orientations, classes and disabilities. Annually, in October. For info: Carole Copeland Thomas, C. Thomas & Assoc, 400 W Cummings Park, Ste 1725-154, Woburn, MA 01801. Phone: (800) 801-6599 or (617) 361-2044. Fax: (617) 361-1355. E-mail: Carole@TellCarole.com. Web: www.TellCarole.com. For info: *Our Family, Our Friends, Our World: An Annotated Guide to Significant Multicultural Books for Children and Teenagers*, by Lyn Miller-Lachmann (Bowker, 0-8352-3025-2, $49.95) and *This Land is Our Land: A Guide to Multicultural Literature for Children and Young Adults*, by Althea K. Helbig and Agnes Regan Perkins (Greenwood, 0-313-28742-2, $49.95).

DOMESTIC VIOLENCE AWARENESS MONTH. Oct 1–31. Commemorated since 1987, this month attempts to raise awareness of efforts to end violence against women and their children. The Domestic Violence Awareness Month Project is a collaborative effort of the National Resource Center on Domestic Violence, Family Violence Prevention Fund, National Coalition Against Domestic Violence, National Domestic Violence Hotline and the National Network to End Domestic Violence. For info: Natl Resource Center on Domestic Violence, 6400 Flank Dr, Ste 1300, Harrisburg, PA 17112-2778. Phone: (800) 537-2238.

FAMILY HEALTH MONTH. Oct 1–31. For info: American Academy of Family Physicians, 11400 Tomahawk Creek Pkwy, Leawood, KS 66211-2672. Phone: (800) 274-2237. Web: www.familyhealthmonth.org.

FIREPUP'S BIRTHDAY. Oct 1. Firepup spends his time teaching fire safety awareness to children in a fun-filled and non-threatening manner. The US Fire Administration's site at www.usfa.fema.gov/kids/ has materials to help kids learn fire safety. For info: Natl Fire Safety Council, Inc, PO Box 378, Michigan Center, MI 49254-0378. Phone: (517) 764-2811.

HARRISON, CAROLINE LAVINIA SCOTT: BIRTH ANNIVERSARY. Oct 1, 1832. First wife of Benjamin Harrison, 23rd president of the US, born at Oxford, OH. Died at Washington, DC, Oct 25, 1892. She was the second first lady to die in the White House.

INTERNATIONAL DINOSAUR MONTH. Oct 1–31. Devoted to the study of dinosaurs and the protection and preservation of their fossils. Also in appreciation of the contributions to human knowledge of paleontologists, dino-artists and dino-educators. For info: Dinosaurs Intl, Planetarium Station, Box 502 IDM00, New York, NY 10024-0502. Web: www.dinosaur.org. *See* Curriculum Connection.

JAPAN: NEWSPAPER WEEK. Oct 1–7. During this week newspapers make an extensive effort to acquaint the public with their functions and the role of a newspaper in a free society. Annually, the first week in October.

KIDS LOVE A MYSTERY MONTH. Oct 1–31. A month of celebration of mysteries for children. For info: Joan Lowery Nixon, 657 Shenandoah Trail, Elgin, IL 60123. Phone: (847) 695-9781.

KOREA: CHUSOK. Oct 1. Gala celebration by Koreans everywhere. Autumn harvest thanksgiving moon festival. Observed on 15th day of eighth lunar month (eighth full moon of lunar calendar) each year. Koreans pay homage to ancestors and express gratitude to guarding spirits for another year of rich crops. A time to visit tombs, leave food and prepare for coming winter season. Traditional food is "moon cake," made on eve of Chusok, with rice, chestnuts and jujube fruits. Games, dancing and gift exchanges. Observed since Silla Dynasty (beginning of first millennium).

LIONS CLUBS INTERNATIONAL PEACE POSTER CONTEST. Oct 1. Contest for children ages 11–13. All entries must be sponsored by a local Lions Club. Today is the deadline to request contest kits from the International Headquarters. Posters due to sponsoring Lions Club by Nov 15, 2001. Finalist judging held on February 1, 2002. For info: Public Relations Dept, Intl Assn of Lions Clubs, 300 22nd St, Oak Brook, IL 60523-8842. Phone: (630) 571-5466. Web: www.lionsclub.org.

MARIS HITS 61st HOME RUN: 40th ANNIVERSARY. Oct 1, 1961. Roger Maris of the New York Yankees hit his 61st home run, breaking Babe Ruth's record for the most home runs in a season. Maris hit his homer against pitcher Tracy Stallard of the Boston Red Sox as the Yankees won, 1–0. Controversy over the record arose because the American League had adopted a 162-game schedule in 1961, and Maris played in 161 games. In 1927, when Ruth set his record, the schedule called for 154 games, and Ruth played in 151. On Sept 8, 1998, Mark McGwire of the St. Louis Cardinals hit his 62nd home run, breaking Maris's record, and a few days later, Sept 13, 1998, Sammy Sosa of the Chicago Cubs also hit his 62nd.

MONTH OF THE YOUNG ADOLESCENT. Oct 1–31. Youth between the ages of 10–15 undergo more extensive physical, mental, social and emotional changes than at any other time of life, with the exception of infancy. Initiated by the National Middle School Association and endorsed by 29 other national organizations focusing on youth, this month is designed to bring attention to the importance of this age in a person's development. For info: Natl Middle School Assn, 4151 Executive Pkwy, Ste 300, Westerville, OH 43081. Phone: (800) 528-NMSA. E-mail: info@nmsa.org. Web: www.nmsa.org.

October 2001

S	M	T	W	T	F	S
	1	2	3	4	5	6
7	8	9	10	11	12	13
14	15	16	17	18	19	20
21	22	23	24	25	26	27
28	29	30	31			

OCTOBER 1–31
NATIONAL PASTA MONTH

October is National Pasta Month. The wide variety of pasta shapes and the many cultures that eat it make pasta a fun and informative classroom topic. The word pasta comes from an Italian word that means dough. As pasta has become trendy, its shape has gotten fancier, including wagon wheels and letters. The addition of all kinds of vegetables has given us a rainbow assortment to choose from.

The song "On Top of Spaghetti," an old camp favorite, taught us that meatballs grow on trees. Well, pasta grows in fields. See *From Wheat to Pasta*, by Robert Evans (Children's Press, 0-516-26069-3, $6.95 Gr. 2–5), for the details on its "growth."*Pasta Factory*, by Hana Machotka (Houghton, 0-395-60197-5, $14.95 Gr. 1–4), shows how pasta is made. Teacher Created Materials has published *Pasta and Pizza: Thematic Units*, by Larry Bauer (1-5769-0374-5, $9.95), for use with primary students.

The obvious first choice for a pasta activity is to incorporate it into the art curriculum. Students have been creating pasta art for decades. Instead of the traditional pictures children usually make, why not use pasta to teach texture and line? The flat, smooth sides of linguine and lasagna noodles contrast nicely with the ridgy sides of rigatoni. Lasagna noodles have lovely, wavy edges that direct the viewer's eye in a different direction than spaghetti or elbow noodles do. Another project is creating pasta mosaics. Let students find mosaic patterns and geometric designs from several cultures. Turkish and Italian tile murals and American Indian or Australian Aboriginal geometric designs provide good examples. Use tiny pasta, or even couscous, to create the pictures.

Many cultures flavor pasta in a number of different ways. Three books, *Everybody Cooks Rice, Everybody Bakes Bread* and *Everybody Serves Soup*, by Norah Dooley (Lerner, 0-8761-4591-8, $6.95; 0-8761-4895X, $6.95; and 1-5750-5422-1, $15.95 Gr. K–3), would serve as good models for your own classroom book about pasta. Each child can bring in a favorite pasta recipe from home. Encourage them to use traditional recipes that may have been handed down from grandparents or relatives from countries other than the United States. If your student population lacks cultural diversity, let students choose a culture and seek recipes from books. Libraries usually have cookbook sections that feature ethnic cuisines. October is also Vegetarian Awareness Month. Pasta can be used to make many yummy meatless dishes.

In science, you might want to call attention to the nutritional information found on the side of pasta boxes. Enriched pasta is a source of B vitamins and is high in carbohydrates, a good source for quick energy. (Many school athletic teams hold a pasta supper the night before a game.) You might wish to discuss the food pyramid and where pasta belongs on it.

Some schools hold spaghetti dinners as beginning of the year get-togethers and even as fund-raisers. If your school wants to try one, October is the perfect month. Sharing an informal meal is a good way to welcome new families to the school and provides the opportunity for old friends to reconnect. And since it's a family activity, no one has to worry about babysitters or door-to-door selling.

Don't forget how silly pasta can be. Most children like to suck in spaghetti. For a silly story about pasta, read Tomie de Paola's *Strega Nona* (Simon & Schuster, 0-671-66606-1, $6.95 Gr. PreK–3) and other books in the series. Children love Big Anthony's overflowing pasta pot.

MONTH OF THE DINOSAUR. Oct 1–31. Promoting scientific awareness and educating everyone about our environment both present and past. Special on-line forums and activities as well as educational materials available to educators. For info: Ellen Sue Blakey, Big Horn Basin Foundation, PO Box 71, Thermopolis, WY 82443.

MOON FESTIVAL or MID-AUTUMN FESTIVAL. Oct 1. This festival, observed on the 15th day of the eighth moon of the lunar calendar year, is called by different names in different places, but is widely recognized throughout the Far East, including People's Republic of China, Taiwan, Korea, Singapore and Hong Kong. An important harvest festival at the time the moon is brightest, it is also a time for homage to ancestors. Special harvest foods are eaten, especially "moon cakes."

NATIONAL CRIME PREVENTION MONTH. Oct 1–31. During Crime Prevention Month, individuals can commit to working on at least one of three levels—family, neighborhood or community—to drive violence and drugs from our world. It is also a time to honor individuals who have accepted personal responsibility for their neighborhoods and groups who work for the community's common good. Annually, every October. For info: Natl Crime Prevention Council, 1700 K St, Second Floor, Washington, DC, 2006-1356. Phone: (202) 466-6272. Fax: (202) 296-1356. Web: www.weprevent.org or www.ncpc.org.

NATIONAL DENTAL HYGIENE MONTH. Oct 1–31. To increase public awareness of the importance of preventive oral health care and the dental hygienist's role as the preventive professional. Annually, during the month of October. For info: Public Relations, American Dental Hygienists' Assn, 444 N Michigan Ave, Ste 3400, Chicago, IL 60611. Phone: (312) 440-8900. Fax: (312) 440-6780. Web: www.adha.org.

★**NATIONAL DISABILITY EMPLOYMENT AWARENESS MONTH.** Oct 1–31. Presidential Proclamation issued for the month of October (PL100–630, Title III, Sec 301a of Nov 7, 1988). Previously issued as "National Employ the Handicapped Week" for a week beginning during the first week in October since 1945.

★**NATIONAL DOMESTIC VIOLENCE AWARENESS MONTH.** Oct 1–31.

NATIONAL FAMILY SEXUALITY EDUCATION MONTH. Oct 1–31. A national coalition effort to support parents as the first and primary sexuality educators of their children by providing information for parents and young people. For info: Planned Parenthood Federation of America, Education Dept, 810 Seventh Ave, New York, NY 10019. Phone: (800) 829-7732. Fax: (212) 247-6269. E-mail: education@ppfa.org. Web: www.plannedparenthood.org.

NATIONAL ORTHODONTIC HEALTH MONTH. Oct 1–31. A beautiful, healthy smile is only the most obvious benefit of orthodontic treatment. National Orthodontic Health Month spotlights the important role of orthodontic care in overall physical health and emotional well-being. The observance is sponsored by the American Association of Orthodontists (AAO), which supports research and education leading to quality patient care and promotes increased public awareness of the need for and benefits of orthodontic treatment. For info: Bill Beggs, Media Relations Mgr, The Hughes Group, 130 S Bemiston, St. Louis, MO 63105.

NATIONAL PASTA MONTH. Oct 1–31. To promote the nutritional value of pasta while educating the public about healthy, easy ways to prepare it. Annually, the month of October. For info: Emily A. Holt or Robert Davis. Phone: (703) 841-0818. Web: www.ilovepasta.org. *See* Curriculum Connection.

NATIONAL POPCORN POPPIN' MONTH. Oct 1–31. To celebrate the wholesome, economical, natural food value of popcorn, America's native snack. For info: The Popcorn Board, 401 N Michigan Ave, Chicago, IL 60611-4267. Phone: (312) 644-6610. Fax: (312) 245-1083. Web: www.popcorn.org.

NATIONAL ROLLER SKATING MONTH. Oct 1–31. A month-long celebration recognizing the health benefits and recreational enjoyment of this long-loved pastime. Also includes in-line skating and an emphasis on Safe Skating. For info: Roller Skating Assn, 6905 Corporate Dr, Indianapolis, IN 46278. Phone: (317) 347-2626. Fax: (317) 347-2636. E-mail: rsa@rollerskating.org. Web: www.rollerskating.com.

NATIONAL STAMP COLLECTING MONTH. Oct 1–31. Sponsored by the US Postal Service, which also sponsors STAMPERS, a program to introduce a new generation to the exciting world of stamp collecting. By calling the toll-free number 1-888-STAMP-FUN, children can receive free mailings which include magazines, posters and other educational items to help them start their own stamp collection. For info: Stamp Services, US Postal Service, 475 L'Enfant Plaza SW, Rm 4474-EB, Washington, DC 20260. Web: www.usps.gov.

NATIONAL WALK OUR CHILDREN TO SCHOOL WEEK. Oct 1–5. Parents and other caregivers are encouraged to walk children to school to demonstrate the healthful effects of walking, to teach children safe pedestrian behaviors and to help select safe routes to school. For info: Walking Magazine, 45 Bromfield St, 8th Floor, Boston, MA 02108. Phone: (617) 574-0076. Fax: (617) 338-7433.

NIGERIA: INDEPENDENCE DAY. Oct 1. National holiday. This West African nation became independent of Great Britain in 1960 and a republic in 1963.

PEDIATRIC CANCER AWARENESS MONTH. Oct 1–31. Cancer is the chief cause of death by disease in children. More than 1,000 children in the US die of cancer every year. For info: Bear Necessities Pediatric Cancer Foundation, 85 W Algonquin Rd, Ste 165, Arlington Heights, IL 60005. Phone: (847) 952-9164.

POLISH AMERICAN HERITAGE MONTH. Oct 1–31. A national celebration of Polish history, culture and pride, in cooperation with the Polish American Congress and Polonia Across America. For info: Michael Blichasz, Chair, Polish American Cultural Center, Natl HQ, 308 Walnut St, Philadelphia, PA 19106. Phone: (215) 922-1700. Fax: (215) 922-1518. Web: www.polishamericancenter.org.

STOCKTON, RICHARD: BIRTH ANNIVERSARY. Oct 1, 1730. Lawyer and signer of the Declaration of Independence, born at Princeton, NJ. Died there, Feb 8, 1781.

October 2001

S	M	T	W	T	F	S
	1	2	3	4	5	6
7	8	9	10	11	12	13
14	15	16	17	18	19	20
21	22	23	24	25	26	27
28	29	30	31			

SUKKOT BEGINS AT SUNDOWN. Oct 1. Jewish Feast of Tabernacles. See "Sukkot" (Oct 2).

SUPER MARIO BROTHERS RELEASED: ANNIVERSARY. Oct 1, 1985. In 1985 the Nintendo Entertainment System (NES) for home use was introduced and the popular game for the NES, Super Mario Brothers, was released on this date. In 1989 Nintendo introduced Game Boy, the first hand-held game system with interchangeable game cartridges. For more info: www.nintendo.com.

SUPREME COURT 2001–2002 TERM BEGINS. Oct 1. Traditionally, the Supreme Court's annual term begins on the first Monday in October and continues with seven two-week sessions of oral arguments. Between the sessions are six recesses during which the opinions are written by the Justices. Ordinarily, all cases are decided by the following June or July. For a database of cases, biographies of the justices past and present and a virtual tour of the Supreme Court building on the Web: oyez.northwestern.edu.

TUVALU: NATIONAL HOLIDAY. Oct 1. Commemorates independence from Great Britain in 1978.

UNITED NATIONS: INTERNATIONAL DAY OF OLDER PERSONS. Oct 1. On Dec 14, 1990, the General Assembly designated Oct 1 as the International Day for the Elderly. It appealed for contributions to the Trust Fund for Aging (which supports projects in developing countries in implementation of the Vienna International Plan of Action on Aging adopted at the 1982 World Assembly on Aging) and endorsed an action program on aging for 1992 and beyond as outlined by the Secretary-General (Res 45/106). On Dec 21, 1995, the Assembly changed the name from "for the Elderly" to "of Older Persons" to conform with the 1991 UN Principles for Older Persons. Info from: United Nations, Dept of Public Info, Public Inquiries Unit, Rm GA-57, New York, NY 10017. Phone: (212) 963-4475. Fax: (212) 963-0071. E-mail: inquiries@un.org.

UNITED NATIONS: WORLD HABITAT DAY. Oct 1. The United Nations General Assembly, by a resolution of Dec 17, 1985, has designated the first Monday of October each year as World Habitat Day. The first observance of this day, Oct 5, 1986, marked the 10th anniversary of the first international conference on the subject. (Habitat: United Nations Conference on Human Settlements, Vancouver, Canada, 1976.) Info from: United Nations, Dept of Public Info, Public Inquiries Unit, Rm GA-57, New York, NY 10017. Phone: (212) 963-4475. Fax: (212) 963-0071. E-mail: inquiries@un.org.

UNIVERSAL CHILDREN'S WEEK. Oct 1–7. To disseminate throughout the world info on the needs of children and to distribute copies of the Declaration of the Rights of the Child. For complete info, send $4 to cover expense of printing, handling and postage. Annually, the first seven days of October. For info: Dr. Stanley Drake, Pres, Intl Soc of Friendship and Good Will, 8592 Roswell Rd, Ste 434, Atlanta, GA 30350-1870.

UNMASKING HALLOWEEN DANGERS. Oct 1–31. Children should be encouraged to use makeup instead of masks, which obscure vision. Costume props should be carefully selected so that Halloween will be fun and safe. For info: Prevent Blindness America®, 500 E Remington Rd, Schaumburg, IL 60173. Phone: (800) 331-2020. Fax: (847) 843-8458. Web: www.preventblindness.org.

US 2002 FEDERAL FISCAL YEAR BEGINS. Oct 1, 2001–Sept 30, 2002.

VEGETARIAN AWARENESS MONTH. Oct 1–31. This educational event advances awareness of the many surprising ethical, environmental, economic, health, humanitarian and other benefits of the increasingly popular vegetarian lifestyle. Each year in the US about one million more people become vegetarians. This event promotes personal and planetary healing with respect for all life. For info: Vegetarian Awareness Network, Communications Center, PO Box 321, Knoxville, TN 37901-0321. Phone: (800) USA-VEGE.

WORLD VEGETARIAN DAY. Oct 1. Celebration of vegetarianism's benefits to humans, animals and our planet. In addition to individuals, participants include libraries, schools, colleges, restaurants, food services, health-care centers, health food stores, workplaces and many more. For info: North American Vegetarian Soc, Box 72, Dolgeville, NY 13329. Phone: (518) 568-7970. Fax: (518) 568-7979. E-mail: navs@telenet.net. Web: navs-online.com.

YOSEMITE NATIONAL PARK ESTABLISHED: ANNIVERSARY. Oct 1, 1890. Yosemite Valley and Mariposa Big Tree Grove, granted to the State of California June 30, 1864, were combined and established as a national park. For more park info: Yosemite Natl Park, PO Box 577, Yosemite Natl Park, CA 95389. Web: www.nps.gov/yose.

BIRTHDAYS TODAY

Jimmy Carter, 77, 39th president of the US, born James Earl Carter, Jr, Plains, GA, Oct 1, 1924.

Stephen Collins, 54, actor ("7th Heaven"), born Des Moines, IA, Oct 1, 1947.

Julie Andrews Edwards, 66, actress (*The Sound of Music, Mary Poppins*), author (*Mandy, The Last of the Really Great Whangdoodles, Dumpy the Dump Truck*), born Walton-on-Thames, Surrey, England, Oct 1, 1935.

Mark McGwire, 38, baseball player, born Pomona, CA, Oct 1, 1963.

Ann Morris, 71, author (*Bread, Bread, Bread; Houses and Homes*), born New York, NY, Oct 1, 1930.

Elizabeth Partridge, 50, author (*Restless Spirit: The Life and Work of Dorothea Lange*), born Berkeley, CA, Oct 1, 1951.

William Hubbs Rehnquist, 77, Chief Justice of the US Supreme Court, born Milwaukee, WI, Oct 1, 1924.

OCTOBER 2 — TUESDAY

Day 275 — 90 Remaining

GANDHI, MOHANDAS KARAMCHAND (MAHATMA): BIRTH ANNIVERSARY. Oct 2, 1869. Indian political and spiritual leader who achieved world honor and fame for his advocacy of nonviolent resistance as a weapon against tyranny was born at Porbandar, India. He was assassinated in the garden of his home at New Delhi, Jan 30, 1948. On the anniversary of Gandhi's birth (Gandhi Jayanti) thousands gather at the park on the Jumna River at Delhi where Gandhi's body was cremated. Hymns are sung, verses from the Gita, the Koran and the Bible are recited and cotton thread is spun on small spinning wheels (one of Gandhi's favorite activities). Other observances held at his birthplace and throughout India on this public holiday. For more info: www.mahatma.org.in.

GUINEA: INDEPENDENCE DAY. Oct 2. National Day. Guinea gained independence from France in 1958.

HARVEST MOON. Oct 2. So called because the full moon nearest the autumnal equinox extends the hours of light into the evening and helps the harvester with his long day's work. Moon enters Full Moon phase at 9:49 AM, EDT.

MOON PHASE: FULL MOON. Oct 2. Moon enters Full Moon phase at 9:49 AM, EDT.

NATIONAL CUSTODIAL WORKERS DAY. Oct 2. A day to honor custodial workers—those who clean up after us. For info: Bette Tadajewski, Saint John the Baptist Church, 2425 Frederick, Alpena, MI 49707. Phone: (517) 354-3019.

NORTH CASCADES NATIONAL PARK ESTABLISHED: ANNIVERSARY. Oct 2, 1968. Located in the state of Washington. For more info: www.nps.gov/noca/index.htm.

***PEANUTS* DEBUTS: ANNIVERSARY.** Oct 2, 1950. This comic strip by Charles M. Schulz featured Charlie Brown, his sister Sally, Lucy, Linus and Charlie's dog Snoopy. The last daily *Peanuts* strip was published Jan 3, 2000 and the last Sunday strip was published Feb 13, 2000.

REDWOOD NATIONAL PARK ESTABLISHED: ANNIVERSARY. Oct 2, 1968. California's Redwood National Park was established. For more info: www.nps.gov/redw/index.html. For more park info: Redwood Natl Park, 1111 Second St, Crescent City, CA 95531.

SUKKOT, SUCCOTH or FEAST OF TABERNACLES, FIRST DAY. Oct 2. Hebrew calendar date: Tishri 15, 5762, begins nine-day festival in commemoration of Jewish people's 40 years of wandering in the desert and thanksgiving for the fall harvest. This high holiday season closes with Shemini Atzeret (see entry on Oct 9) and Simchat Torah (see entry on Oct 10).

BIRTHDAYS TODAY

Jennifer Owings Dewey, 60, author (*Stories on Stone*), born Chicago, IL, Oct 2, 1941.

Thomas Muster, 34, tennis player, born Leibnitz, Austria, Oct 2, 1967.

OCTOBER 3 — WEDNESDAY

Day 276 — 89 Remaining

"THE ANDY GRIFFITH SHOW" TV PREMIERE: ANNIVERSARY. Oct 3, 1960. Marks the airing of the first episode of this popular show set at Mayberry, NC. Andy Griffith starred as Sheriff Andy Taylor, Ron Howard was his son Opie, Frances Bavier was Aunt Bee Taylor and Don Knotts played Deputy Barney Fife. The 12,000+ members of "The Andy Griffith Show" Rerun Watchers Club and others celebrate this day with festivities every year.

"CAPTAIN KANGAROO" TV PREMIERE: ANNIVERSARY. Oct 3, 1955. On the air until 1985, this was the longest-running children's TV show until it was surpassed by "Sesame Street." Starring Bob Keeshan as Captain Kangaroo, it was broadcast on CBS and PBS. Other characters included Mr Green Jeans, Grandfather Clock, Bunny Rabbit, Mr Moose and Dancing Bear. Keeshan was an advocate for excellence in children's programming and even supervised which commercials would appear on the program. In 1997 "The All New Captain Kangaroo" debuted, starring John McDonough.

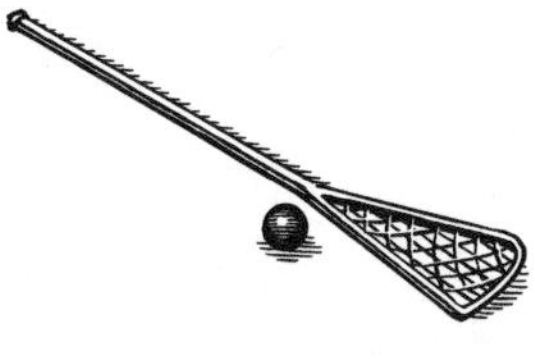

GERMAN REUNIFICATION: ANNIVERSARY. Oct 3, 1990. After 45 years of division, East and West Germany reunited, just four days short of East Germany's 41st founding anniversary (Oct 7, 1949). The new united Germany took the name the Federal Republic of Germany, the formal name of the former West Germany and adopted the constitution of the former West Germany. Today is a national holiday in Germany.

HONDURAS: FRANCISCO MORAZAN HOLIDAY. Oct 3. Public holiday in honor of Francisco Morazan, national hero, who was born in 1799.

KOREA: NATIONAL FOUNDATION DAY. Oct 3. National holiday also called Tangun Day, as it commemorates the day when legendary founder of the Korean nation, Tangun, established his kingdom of Chosun in 2333 BC.

"MICKEY MOUSE CLUB" TV PREMIERE: ANNIVERSARY. Oct 3, 1955. This afternoon show for children was on ABC. Among its young cast members were Mouseketeers Annette Funicello and Shelley Fabares. The show was revived in 1977 and 1989. Christina Aguilera, Keri Russell and Britney Spears were cast members.

MISSISSIPPI STATE FAIR. Oct 3–14. Jackson, MS. Features nightly professional entertainment, livestock show, midway carnival, domestic art exhibits. Est attendance: 620,000. For info: Mississippi Fair Commission, PO Box 892, Jackson, MS 39205. Phone: (601) 961-4000. Fax: (601) 354-6545.

NATIONAL WALK OUR CHILDREN TO SCHOOL DAY. Oct 3 (tentative). This day was established to encourage adults and children to walk together to raise awareness about three things: the exercise value of walking, the importance of teaching children safe walking behaviors and the need for more walkable communities. In 1998 children from 775 elementary schools in 27 states and 5 Canadian provinces took part. Sponsored by the Partnership for a Walkable America, a national alliance of public and private organizations committed to making walking safer, easier and more enjoyable. Annually, the Wednesday of the first full week in October. For info: Natl Walk Our Children to School Day, Natl Safety Council, 1121 Spring Lake Dr, Itasca, IL 60143-3201. Phone: (800) 621-7615, ext 2383. Fax: (630) 775-2185. E-mail: thompsoh@nsc.org. Web: www.walktoschool-usa.org.

ROBINSON NAMED BASEBALL'S FIRST BLACK MAJOR LEAGUE MANAGER: ANNIVERSARY. Oct 3, 1974. The only major league player selected most valuable player in both the American and National Leagues, Frank Robinson was hired by the Cleveland Indians as baseball's first black major league manager. During his playing career Robinson represented the American League in four World Series playing for the Baltimore Orioles, led the Cincinnati Reds to a National League pennant and hit 586 home runs in 21 years of play.

BIRTHDAYS TODAY

Jeff Bingaman, 58, US Senator (D, New Mexico), born El Paso, TX, Oct 3, 1943.

Molly Cone, 83, author (*Mishmash, The Story of Shabbat*), born Tacoma, WA, Oct 3, 1918.

Kevin Richardson, 29, singer (Backstreet Boys), born Lexington, KY, Oct 3, 1972.

October 2001

S	M	T	W	T	F	S
	1	2	3	4	5	6
7	8	9	10	11	12	13
14	15	16	17	18	19	20
21	22	23	24	25	26	27
28	29	30	31			

OCTOBER 4 — THURSDAY

Day 277 — 88 Remaining

"THE ALVIN SHOW" TV PREMIERE: 40th ANNIVERSARY. Oct 4, 1961. This prime-time cartoon was based on Ross Bagdasarian's novelty group called The Chipmunks, which had begun as recordings with speeded-up vocals. In the series, the three chipmunks, Alvin, Simon and Theodore, sang and had adventures along with their songwriter-manager David Seville. Bagdasarian supplied the voices. Part of the show featured the adventures of inventor Clyde Crashcup. "Alvin" was more successful as a Saturday morning cartoon. It returned in reruns in 1979 and also prompted a sequel, called "Alvin and the Chipmunks," in 1983.

GREGORIAN CALENDAR ADJUSTMENT: ANNIVERSARY. Oct 4, 1582. Pope Gregory XIII issued a bulletin that decreed that the day following Thursday, Oct 4, 1582, should be Friday, Oct 15, 1582, thus correcting the Julian Calendar, then 10 days out of date relative to the seasons. This reform was effective in most Catholic countries, though the Julian Calendar continued in use in Britain and the American colonies until 1752, in Japan until 1873, in China until 1912, in Russia until 1918, in Greece until 1923 and in Turkey until 1927. See also: "Gregorian Calendar Day: Anniversary" (Feb 24) and "Calendar Adjustment Day: Anniversary" (Sept 2).

HAYES, RUTHERFORD BIRCHARD: BIRTH ANNIVERSARY. Oct 4, 1822. The 19th president of the US (Mar 4, 1877–Mar 3, 1881), born at Delaware, OH. In his inaugural address, Hayes said: "He serves his party best who serves the country best." He died at Fremont, OH, Jan 17, 1893. For info: www.ipl.org/ref/POTUS.

JOHNSON, ELIZA McCARDLE: BIRTH ANNIVERSARY. Oct 4, 1810. Wife of Andrew Johnson, 17th president of the US, born at Leesburg, TN. Died at Greeneville, TN, Jan 15, 1876.

LAWSON, ROBERT: BIRTH ANNIVERSARY. Oct 4, 1892. Author and illustrator (*Rabbit Hill, Ben & Me*), born at New York, NY. Died May 26, 1957.

"LEAVE IT TO BEAVER" TV PREMIERE: ANNIVERSARY. Oct 4, 1957. This family sitcom was a stereotypical portrayal of American family life. It focused on Theodore "Beaver" Cleaver (Jerry Mathers), his misadventures and his family: his patient, understanding, all-knowing and firm father, Ward (Hugh Beaumont), impeccably dressed housewife and mother June (Barbara Billingsley) and Wally (Tony Dow), Beaver's good-natured all-American brother. The "perfectness" of the Cleaver family was balanced by other, less than perfect characters. "Leave It to Beaver" has remained popular in reruns.

LESOTHO: NATIONAL DAY: 35th ANNIVERSARY. Oct 4. National holiday. Commemorates independence from Britain in 1966.

SAINT FRANCIS OF ASSISI: FEAST DAY. Oct 4. Giovanni Francesco Bernardone, religious leader, founder of the Friars Minor (Franciscan Order), born at Assisi, Umbria, Italy, in 1181. Died at Porziuncula, Oct 3, 1226. One of the best-loved saints of all time. For more info: *Brother Sun, Sister Moon: The Life and Stories of St. Francis*, by Margaret Mayo (Little, Brown, 0-316-56466-4, $16.95 Gr. 3–6).

SOUTH CAROLINA STATE FAIR. Oct 4–14. Columbia, SC. Conklin Shows, rides, musical entertainment, food booths and children's activities. Est attendance: 576,000. For info: South Carolina State Fair, PO Box 393, Columbia, SC 29202. Phone: (803) 799-3387. Fax: (803) 799-1760. E-mail: geninfo@scsn.net.

SPACE MILESTONE: *SPUTNIK* (USSR). Oct 4, 1957. Anniversary of launching of first successful man-made earth satellite. *Sputnik I* ("satellite") weighing 184 lbs was fired into orbit from the USSR's Tyuratam launch site. Transmitted radio signal for 21 days, decayed Jan 4, 1958. The beginning of the Space Age and man's exploration beyond Earth. This first-in-space triumph by the Soviets resulted in a stepped-up emphasis on the teaching of science in American classrooms.

STRATEMEYER, EDWARD L.: BIRTH ANNIVERSARY. Oct 4, 1862. American author of children's books, Stratemeyer was born at Elizabeth, NJ. He created numerous series of popular children's books including "The Bobbsey Twins," "The Hardy Boys," "Nancy Drew" and "Tom Swift." He and his Stratemeyer Syndicate, using 60 or more pen names, produced more than 800 books. More than four million copies were in print in 1987. Stratemeyer died at Newark, NJ, May 10, 1930.

BIRTHDAYS TODAY

Vicky Bullett, 34, basketball player, born Martinsburg, WV, Oct 4, 1967

Rachel Leigh Cook, 22, actress (*She's All That*, "The Baby-Sitters Club"), born Minneapolis, MN, Oct 4, 1979.

Karen Cushman, 60, author (*Catherine, Called Birdy*; Newbery for *The Midwife's Apprentice*), born Chicago, IL, Oct 4, 1941.

Chuck Hagel, 55, US Senator (R, Nebraska), born North Platte, NE, Oct 4, 1946.

Susan Meddaugh, 57, author, illustrator (*Martha Speaks*), born Montclair, NJ, Oct 4, 1944.

Alicia Silverstone, 25, actress (*Batman & Robin*), born San Francisco, CA, Oct 4, 1976.

Donald Sobol, 77, author (Encyclopedia Brown series), born New York, NY, Oct 4, 1924.

OCTOBER 5 — FRIDAY

Day 278 — 87 Remaining

ALABAMA NATIONAL FAIR. Oct 5–14. Garrett Coliseum/Fairgrounds, Montgomery, AL. A midway filled with exciting rides and games, arts and crafts, exhibits, livestock shows, racing pigs, a circus, a petting zoo, food and entertainment. Est attendance: 227,000. For info: Hazel Ashmore, PO Box 3304, Montgomery, AL 36109-0304. Phone: (334) 272-6831. Fax: (334) 272-6835.

ARKANSAS STATE FAIR AND LIVESTOCK SHOW. Oct 5–13. Barton Coliseum and State Fairground, Little Rock, AR. Est attendance: 400,000. For info: Arkansas State Fair, PO Box 166660, Little Rock, AR 72216. Phone: (501) 372-8341. Fax: (501) 372-4197. Web: www.arkfairgrounds.com.

ARTHUR, CHESTER ALAN: BIRTH ANNIVERSARY. Oct 5, 1829. The 21st president of the US, born at Fairfield, VT, succeeded to the presidency following the death of James A. Garfield. Term of office: Sept 20, 1881–Mar 3, 1885. Arthur was not successful in obtaining the Republican party's nomination for the following term. He died at New York, NY, Nov 18, 1886. For info: www.ipl.org/ref/POTUS.

BASKETBALL HALL OF FAME ENSHRINEMENT CEREMONIES. Oct 5. Springfield, MA. New electees are enshrined into the Basketball Hall of Fame. Est attendance: 1,500. For info: Public Relations & Publishing, Basketball Hall of Fame, 1150 W Columbus Ave, PO Box 179, Springfield, MA 01101-0179. Phone: (413) 781-6500. Web: www.hoophall.com.

CHIEF JOSEPH SURRENDER: ANNIVERSARY. Oct 5, 1877. After a 1,700-mile retreat, Chief Joseph and the Nez Perce Indians surrendered to US Cavalry troops at Bear's Paw near Chinook, MT, Oct 5, 1877. Chief Joseph made his famous speech of surrender, "From where the sun now stands, I will fight no more forever."

FITZHUGH, LOUISE: BIRTH ANNIVERSARY. Oct 5, 1928. Author (*Harriet the Spy*), born at Memphis, TN. Died Nov 19, 1974.

GEORGIA NATIONAL FAIR. Oct 5–14. Georgia National Fairgrounds, Perry, GA. Traditional state agricultural fair features thousands of entries in horse, livestock, horticultural, youth, home and fine arts categories. Family entertainment, education and fun. Sponsored by the State of Georgia. Annually, beginning the fifth Friday after Labor Day. Est attendance: 352,000. For info: John P. Webb, Jr, CFE, Georgia Natl Fair, PO Box 1367, 401 Larry Walker Pkwy, Perry, GA 31069. Phone: (912) 987-3247. Fax: (912) 987-7218. E-mail: webb1@alltell.net. Web: www.gnfa.com.

GODDARD, ROBERT HUTCHINGS: BIRTH ANNIVERSARY. Oct 5, 1882. The "father of the Space Age," born at Worcester, MA. Largely ignored or ridiculed during his lifetime because of his dreams of rocket travel, including travel to other planets. Launched a liquid-fuel-powered rocket Mar 16, 1926, at Auburn, MA. Died Aug 10, 1945, at Baltimore, MD. See also: "Goddard Day" (Mar 16).

NATIONAL STORYTELLING FESTIVAL. Oct 5–7. Jonesborough, TN. Tennessee's oldest town plays host to the most dynamic storytelling event dedicated to the oral tradition. This three-day celebration showcases storytellers, stories and traditions from across America and around the world. Annually, the first full weekend in October. Est attendance: 10,000. For info: Storytelling Foundation Intl (SFI), 116 W Main, Jonesborough, TN 37659. Phone: (800) 952-8392. Fax: (423) 913-8219. Web: www.storytellingfestival.net.

PORTUGAL: REPUBLIC DAY. Oct 5. National holiday. Commemorates the founding of the republic in 1910.

STONE, THOMAS: DEATH ANNIVERSARY. Oct 5, 1787. Signer of the Declaration of Independence, born 1743 (exact date unknown) at Charles County, MD. Died at Alexandria, VA.

TECUMSEH: DEATH ANNIVERSARY. Oct 5, 1813. Shawnee Indian chief and orator, born at Old Piqua near Springfield, OH, in March 1768. Tecumseh is regarded as one of the greatest of American Indians. He came to prominence between the years 1799 and 1804 as a powerful orator, defending his people against whites. He denounced as invalid all treaties by which Indians ceded their lands and condemned the chieftains who had entered into such agreements. With his brother Tenskwatawa, the Prophet, he established a town on the Tippecanoe River near Lafayette, IN, and then embarked on a mission to organize an Indian confederation to stop white encroachment. Although he advocated peaceful methods and negotiation, he did not rule out war as a last resort as he visited tribes throughout the country. While he was away, William Henry Harrison defeated the Prophet at the Battle of Tippecanoe Nov 7, 1811, and burned the town. Tecumseh organized a large force of Indian warriors and assisted the British in the War of 1812. Tecumseh was defeated and killed at the Battle of the Thames, Oct 5, 1813.

ZION, GENE: BIRTH ANNIVERSARY. Oct 5, 1913. Author, best known for *Harry the Dirty Dog*, born at New York, NY. Zion died Dec 5, 1975.

BIRTHDAYS TODAY

Grant Hill, 29, basketball player, born Dallas, TX, Oct 5, 1972.

Bil Keane, 79, cartoonist ("Family Circus"), born Philadelphia, PA, Oct 5, 1922.

Mario Lemieux, 36, Hall of Fame hockey player, born Montreal, QC, Canada, Oct 5, 1965.

Patrick Roy, 36, hockey player, born Quebec City, QC, Canada, Oct 5, 1965.

David Shannon, 42, author and illustrator (*No, David!*), born Washington, DC, Oct 5, 1959.

Kate Winslet, 26, actress (*Titanic*), born Reading, England, Oct 5, 1975.

OCTOBER 6 — SATURDAY

Day 279 — 86 Remaining

EGYPT: ARMED FORCES DAY. Oct 6. The Egyptian Army celebrates crossing into Sinai in 1973. For info: Egyptian Tourist Authority, 645 N Michigan Ave, Ste 829, Chicago, IL 60611. Phone: (312) 280-4666. Fax: (312) 280-4788.

★ **GERMAN-AMERICAN DAY.** Oct 6. Celebration of German heritage and contributions German Americans have made to the building of the nation. A Presidential Proclamation has been issued each year since 1987. Annually, Oct 6.

INTERNATIONAL FRUGAL FUN DAY. Oct 6. A day to celebrate that having fun doesn't have to be costly. Do at least one fun thing for yourself and/or your family that is free of cost or under $5 a person: a concert or play, a hike, a meal out, a picnic, an art gallery or museum tour, a day trip, a boat ride. Annually, the first Saturday in October. For info: Shel Horowitz, PO Box 1164, Northampton, MA 01061-1164. Phone: (413) 586-2388. Fax: (617) 249-0153. E-mail: info@frugalfun.com. Web: www.frugalfun.com/frugalfundayideas.html.

VINING, ELIZABETH GRAY: BIRTH ANNIVERSARY. Oct 6, 1902. Author of *Adam of the Road* under the name Elizabeth Gray, born at Philadelphia, PA. Won Newbery Medal (1943). Died Nov 27, 1999, at Kennett Square, PA.

YOM KIPPUR WAR: ANNIVERSARY. Oct 6–25, 1973. A surprise attack by Egypt and Syria pushed Israeli forces several miles behind the 1967 cease-fire lines. Israel was caught off guard, partly because the attack came on the holiest Jewish religious day. After 18 days of fighting, hostilities were halted by the UN Oct 25. Israel partially recovered from the initial setback but failed to regain all the land lost in the fighting.

BIRTHDAYS TODAY

James Gilmore III, 52, Governor of Virginia (R), born Richmond, VA, Oct 6, 1949.

Betsy Hearne, 59, author (*Seven Brave Women*), born Wilsonville, AL, Oct 6, 1942.

Rebecca Lobo, 28, basketball player, born Southwick, MA, Oct 6, 1973.

Jeanette Winter, 62, author and illustrator (*My Name Is Georgia*), born Chicago, IL, Oct 6, 1939.

October 2001

S	M	T	W	T	F	S
	1	2	3	4	5	6
7	8	9	10	11	12	13
14	15	16	17	18	19	20
21	22	23	24	25	26	27
28	29	30	31			

OCTOBER 7 — SUNDAY

Day 280 — 85 Remaining

"ARTHUR" TV PREMIERE: ANNIVERSARY. Oct 7, 1996. This animated show, based on Marc Brown's popular series of books, features the aardvark Arthur, his sister D.W. and a host of friends from their elementary school.

CABBAGE PATCH® KIDS DEBUTED: ANNIVERSARY. Oct 7, 1983. These popular dolls come with their own birth certificates and adoption papers. More than 3 million of the dolls were sold for the holiday season in 1983. Today, there are several varieties of Cabbage Patch® Kids.

FIRE PREVENTION WEEK. Oct 7–13. To increase awareness of the dangers of fire and to educate the public on how to stay safe from fire. The theme this year is "Fire Drills: The Great Escape!" For info: Public Affairs Office, Natl Fire Protection Assn, One Batterymarch Park, Quincy, MA 02269. Phone: (617) 770-3000. Web: www.nfpa.org. and www.sparky.org.

★ **FIRE PREVENTION WEEK.** Oct 7–13. Presidential Proclamation issued annually for the first or second week in October since 1925. For many years prior to 1925, National Fire Prevention Day was observed in October. Annually, the Sunday through Saturday period during which Oct 9 falls.

GET ORGANIZED WEEK. Oct 7–13. This is an opportunity to streamline your life, create more time, lower your stress and increase your profit. Simplify your situation and make it more manageable by taking advantage of this time to get organized. Annually, the first full week in October. For info: Natl Assn of Professional Organizers, PO Box 140647, Austin, TX 78714-0647. Web: www.napo.net.

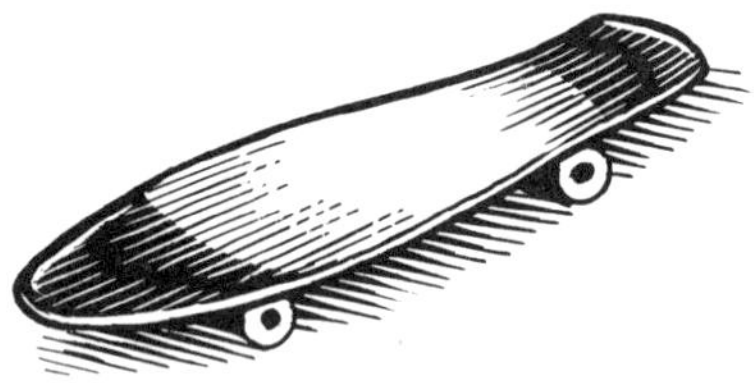

NATIONAL METRIC WEEK. Oct 7–13. To maintain an awareness of the importance of the metric system as the primary system of measurement for the US. Annually, the week of the tenth month containing the tenth day of the month. For info: US Metric Assn, 10245 Andasol Ave, Northridge, CA 91325-1504. Phone: (813) 363-5606. Web: lamar.colostate.edu/~hillger.

RODNEY, CAESAR: BIRTH ANNIVERSARY. Oct 7, 1728. Signer of the Declaration of Independence who cast a tie-breaking vote. Born near Dover, DE, he died at Dover, June 29, 1784.

WALLACE, HENRY AGARD: BIRTH ANNIVERSARY. Oct 7, 1888. The 33rd vice president of the US (1941–45), born at Adair County, IA. Died at Danbury, CT, Nov 18, 1965.

WORLD COMMUNION SUNDAY. Oct 7. Communion is celebrated by Christians all over the world. Annually, the first Sunday in October.

BIRTHDAYS TODAY

Diane Ackerman, 53, author (*The Moon of Light*), born Waukegan, IL, Oct 7, 1948.

Vladimir Putin, 49, Russian president, born St. Petersburg, Russia, Oct 7, 1952.

Desmond Tutu, 70, South African archbishop, Nobel Peace Prize winner, born Klerksdrop, South Africa, Oct 7, 1931.

OCTOBER 8 — MONDAY

Day 281 — 84 Remaining

AMERICAN INDIAN HERITAGE DAY (ALABAMA). Oct 8. First declared in 2000, this state holiday will also be observed as Columbus Day in Alabama. Annually, the second Monday in October.

CANADA: THANKSGIVING DAY. Oct 8. Observed on second Monday in October each year.

COLUMBUS DAY OBSERVANCE. Oct 8. Public Law 90–363 sets observance of Columbus Day on the second Monday in October. Applicable to federal employees and to the District of Columbia, but also observed in most states. Commemorates the landfall of Columbus in the New World, Oct 12, 1492. See also: "Columbus Day (Traditional)" (Oct 12). For links to Columbus Day websites, go to: deil.lang.uiuc.edu/web.pages/holidays/columbus.html.

★ **COLUMBUS DAY.** Oct 8. Presidential Proclamation, always the second Monday in October. Observed Oct 12 from 1934 to 1970 (Pub Res No 21 of Apr 30, 1934). PL90–363 of June 28, 1968, required that beginning in 1971 it would be observed on the second Monday in October.

FIJI: INDEPENDENCE DAY. Oct 8. National holiday on the 2nd Monday in October. Commemorates independence from Britain in 1970.

GREAT CHICAGO FIRE: ANNIVERSARY. Oct 8, 1871. Great fire of Chicago began, according to legend, when Mrs O'Leary's cow kicked over the lantern in her barn on DeKoven Street. The fire leveled 3½ sq miles, destroying 17,450 buildings and leaving 98,500 people homeless and about 250 people dead. Financially, the loss was $200 million. On the same day a fire destroyed the entire town of Peshtigo, WI, killing more than 1,100 people. For more info: *The Great Fire*, by Jim Murphy (Scholastic, 0-59-047267-4, $16.95 Gr. 3–7) or www.chicagohistory.org/fire.

JAPAN: HEALTH-SPORTS DAY. Oct 8. National holiday to encourage physical activity for building sound body and mind. Created in 1966 to commemorate the day of the opening of the 18th Olympic Games at Tokyo, Oct 10, 1964. Celebrated on the second Monday in October.

NATIONAL PET PEEVE WEEK. Oct 8–12. A chance for people to make others aware of all the little things in life they find so annoying, in the hope of changing some of them. Annually, the second full week of October. When requesting info, please send SASE. For info: Ad-America, Pine Tree Center Indust Park, 2215 29th St SE, Ste B-7, Grand Rapids, MI 49508. Phone: (616) 247-3797. Fax: (616) 247-3798. E-mail: adamerica@aol.com.

NATIVE AMERICANS DAY IN SOUTH DAKOTA. Oct 8. Observed as a legal holiday, dedicated to the remembrance of the great Native American leaders who contributed so much to the history of South Dakota. Annually, the second Monday in October.

PERU: DAY OF THE NAVY. Oct 8. Public holiday in Peru, commemorating Combat of Angamos.

PESHTIGO FOREST FIRE: ANNIVERSARY. Oct 8, 1871. One of the most disastrous forest fires in history began at Peshtigo, WI, the same day the Great Chicago Fire began. The Wisconsin fire burned across six counties, killing more than 1,100 persons.

US VIRGIN ISLANDS–PUERTO RICO FRIENDSHIP DAY. Oct 8. Columbus Day (second Monday in October) also celebrates historical friendship between peoples of the Virgin Islands and Puerto Rico.

YORKTOWN VICTORY DAY. Oct 8. Observed as a holiday in Virginia. Annually, the second Monday in October. See "Yorktown Day: Anniversary" (Oct 19).

BIRTHDAYS TODAY

Chevy Chase, 58, comedian, actor (*Christmas Vacation, Vegas Vacation*), born Cornelius Crane, New York, NY, Oct 8, 1943.

Matt Damon, 31, actor (*Saving Private Ryan*), born Cambridge, MA, Oct 8, 1970.

Barthe DeClements, 81, author (*Nothing's Fair in Fifth Grade*), born Seattle, WA, Oct 8, 1920.

Jesse Jackson, 60, clergyman, civil rights leader ("I am somebody," "Keep hope alive"), born Greenville, NC, Oct 8, 1941.

Faith Ringgold, 71, artist, author (*Tar Beach, My Dream of Martin Luther King*), born New York, NY, Oct 8, 1930.

Rashaan Salaam, 27, football player, born San Diego, CA, Oct 8, 1974.

R.L. Stine, 58, author (the Goosebumps series), born Columbus, OH, Oct 8, 1943.

OCTOBER 9 — TUESDAY

Day 282 — 83 Remaining

ICELAND: LEIF ERIKSON DAY. Oct 9. Celebrates the discovery of North America in the year 1000 by the Norse explorer.

KOREA: ALPHABET DAY (HANGUL). Oct 9. Celebrates anniversary of promulgation of Hangul (24-letter phonetic alphabet) by King Sejong of the Yi Dynasty, in 1446.

★ **LEIF ERIKSON DAY.** Oct 9. Presidential Proclamation always issued for Oct 9 since 1964 (PL88–566 of Sept 2, 1964) at request. Honors the Norse explorer who is widely believed to have been the first European to visit the American continent.

PERU: DAY OF NATIONAL HONOR. Oct 9. National holiday. Commemorates the 1968 nationalization of the oil fields.

SHEMINI ATZERET. Oct 9. Hebrew calendar date: Tishri 22, 5762. The eighth day of Solemn Assembly, part of the Sukkot Festival (see entry on Oct 2), with memorial services and cycle of Biblical readings in the synagogue.

UGANDA: INDEPENDENCE DAY. Oct 9. National holiday commemorating achievement of autonomy from Britain in 1962.

UNITED NATIONS: WORLD POST DAY. Oct 9. An annual special observance of Postal Administrations of the Universal Postal Union (UPU). For info: United Nations, Dept of Public Info, Public Inquiries Unit, Rm GA-57, New York, NY 10017. Phone: (212) 963-4475. Fax: (212) 963-0071. E-mail: inquiries@un.org.

"WISHBONE" TV PREMIERE: ANNIVERSARY. Oct 9, 1995. The first episode of this popular series that retells classic stories with a dog named Wishbone who imagines himself as a character in signature scenes premiered on PBS. It was the first of a two-part series titled "Tail in Twain," based on Mark Twain's *The Adventures of Tom Sawyer*. Other episodes have been based on stories by Ovid, Goethe, Jane Austen, Washington Irving, Edgar Allen Poe and others. For more info: www.pbs.org/wishbone.

BIRTHDAYS TODAY

Zachery Ty Bryan, 20, actor ("Home Improvement"), born Aurora, CO, Oct 9, 1981.

Steven Burns, 28, TV host ("Blue's Clues"), born Boyertown, PA, Oct 9, 1973.

Johanna Hurwitz, 64, author (*Busybody Nora*), born New York, NY, Oct 9, 1937.

Trent Lott, 60, US Senator (R, Mississippi), born Duck Hill, MS, Oct 9, 1941.
Mike Singletary, 43, Hall of Fame football player, born Houston, TX, Oct 9, 1958.
Annika Sorenstam, 31, golfer, born Stockholm, Sweden, Oct 9, 1970.

OCTOBER 10 — WEDNESDAY

Day 283 — 82 Remaining

BONZA BOTTLER DAY™. Oct 10. To celebrate when the number of the day is the same as the number of the month. Bonza Bottler Day™ is an excuse to have a party at least once a month. For info: Gail M. Berger, 109 Matthew Ave, Poca, WV 25159. Phone: (304) 776-7746. E-mail: gberger5@aol.com.

CUBA: BEGINNING OF INDEPENDENCE WARS DAY. Oct 10. National holiday. Commemorates the beginning of the struggle against Spain in 1868.

DOUBLE TENTH DAY: 90th ANNIVERSARY. Oct 10. Tenth day of 10th month, Double Tenth Day, is observed by many Chinese as the anniversary of the outbreak of the revolution against the imperial Manchu dynasty, Oct 10, 1911. Sun Yat-Sen and Huan Hsing were among the revolutionary leaders.

MARSHALL, JAMES: BIRTH ANNIVERSARY. Oct 10, 1942. Illustrator, born at San Antonio, TX. Marshall is best known for his George and Martha series of books. He illustrated more than 70 children's books including *The Owl and the Pussycat.* Died at New York, NY, Oct 13, 1992.

MOON PHASE: LAST QUARTER. Oct 10. Moon enters Last Quarter phase at 12:20 AM, EDT.

SIMCHAT TORAH. Oct 10. Hebrew calendar date: Tishri 23, 5762. Rejoicing in the Torah concludes the nine-day Sukkot Festival (see entry on Oct 2). Public reading of the Pentateuch is completed and begun again, symbolizing the need for ever-continuing study.

UNITED NATIONS: INTERNATIONAL DAY FOR NATURAL DISASTER REDUCTION. Oct 10. The General Assembly made this designation for the second Wednesday of October each year as part of its efforts to foster international cooperation in reducing the loss of life, property damage and social and economic disruption caused by natural disasters. For info: United Nations, Dept of Public Info, New York, NY 10017.

US NAVAL ACADEMY FOUNDED: ANNIVERSARY. Oct 10, 1845. A college to train officers for the navy was founded at Annapolis, MD. Women were admitted in 1976. The Academy's motto is "Honor, Courage, Commitment." For more info: www.usna.edu.

BIRTHDAYS TODAY

Nancy Carlson, 48, author (*I Like Me!; Louanne Pig in the Talent Show; Arnie and the New Kid*), born Minneapolis, MN, Oct 10, 1953.
Brett Favre, 32, quarterback, born Gulfport, MS, Oct 10, 1969.
Mario Lopez, 28, actor ("Saved by the Bell," "Pacific Blue"), born San Diego, CA, Oct 10, 1973.
Robert D. San Souci, 55, author (*Short & Shivery, The Faithful Friend, Young Merlin*), born San Francisco, CA, Oct 10, 1946.

October 2001

S	M	T	W	T	F	S
	1	2	3	4	5	6
7	8	9	10	11	12	13
14	15	16	17	18	19	20
21	22	23	24	25	26	27
28	29	30	31			

OCTOBER 11 — THURSDAY

Day 284 — 81 Remaining

CHICAGO INTERNATIONAL CHILDREN'S FILM FESTIVAL. Oct 11–21 (tentative). Cannes for Kids! Children's films from around the world plus workshops with directors, animators and movie makeup artists. For info: Chicago Intl Children's Film Festival, Facets Multimedia, 1517 W Fullerton Ave, Chicago, IL 60614. Phone: (773) 281-9075. E-mail: kidsfest@facets.org.

★**GENERAL PULASKI MEMORIAL DAY.** Oct 11. Presidential Proclamation always issued for Oct 11 since 1929. Requested by Congressional Resolution each year from 1929–1946. (Since 1947 has been issued by custom.) Note: Proclamation 4869, of Oct 5, 1981, covers all succeeding years.

ROBINSON, ROSCOE, JR: BIRTH ANNIVERSARY. Oct 11, 1928. The first black American to achieve the Army rank of four-star general. Born at St. Louis, MO, and died at Washington, DC, July 22, 1993.

ROOSEVELT, ANNA ELEANOR: BIRTH ANNIVERSARY. Oct 11, 1884. Wife of Franklin Delano Roosevelt, 32nd president of the US, was born at New York, NY. She led an active and independent life and was the first wife of a president to give her own news conference in the White House (1933). Widely known throughout the world, she was affectionately called "the first lady of the world." She served as US delegate to the United Nations General Assembly for a number of years before her death at New York, NY, Nov 7, 1962. A prolific writer, she wrote in *This Is My Story*, "No one can make you feel inferior without your consent." For more info: *Eleanor*, by Barbara Cooney (Viking, 0-670-86159-6, $15.99 Gr. K–3).

SPACE MILESTONE: 100th SHUTTLE FLIGHT: *DISCOVERY STS-92*. Oct 11, 2000. The Space Shuttle *Discovery* was launched on its 28th flight. This marked the shuttle program's 100th mission. On this flight, *Discovery* was headed to the International Space Station, where it docked successfully on Oct 13. On earlier flights, the shuttles *Columbia, Challenger, Endeavour, Atlantis* and *Discovery* had launched the Hubble Space Telescope and Chandra X-Ray Observatory, docked with the *Mir* space station, and supported scientific research. The first shuttle flight took place in 1981. Since the first mission, space shuttles have carried 261 individuals and nearly 3 million pounds of payload, and logged an estimated 350 million miles. See: "Space Milestone: *Columbia STS-1*" (Apr 12). For more info: *The Space Shuttle*, by Allison Lassieur (Children's Press, 0-516-22003-9, $22 Gr. 2–4).

STONE, HARLAN FISKE: BIRTH ANNIVERSARY. Oct 11, 1872. Former associate justice and later chief justice of the US Supreme Court who wrote more than 600 opinions and dissents for that court, Stone was born at Chesterfield, NH. He served on the Supreme Court from 1925 until his death, at Washington, DC, Apr 22, 1946.

VATICAN COUNCIL II: ANNIVERSARY. Oct 11, 1962. The 21st ecumenical council of the Roman Catholic Church was convened by Pope John XXIII. It met in four annual sessions, concluding Dec 8, 1965. It dealt with the renewal of the Church and introduced sweeping changes, such as the use of the vernacular rather than Latin in the Mass.

BIRTHDAYS TODAY

Russell Freedman, 72, author (Newbery for *Lincoln: A Photobiography*), born San Francisco, CA, Oct 11, 1929.

Orlando Hernandez, 32, baseball player, known as "El Duque," born Villa Clara, Cuba, Oct 11, 1969.

Patty Murray, 51, US Senator (D, Washington), born Seattle, WA, Oct 11, 1950.

Michelle Trachtenberg, 16, actress (*Harriet the Spy, Inspector Gadget*), born New York, NY, Oct 11, 1985.

Jon Steven (Steve) Young, 40, football player, born Salt Lake City, UT, Oct 11, 1961.

OCTOBER 12 — FRIDAY

Day 285 — 80 Remaining

BAHAMAS: DISCOVERY DAY. Oct 12. Commemorates the landing of Columbus in the Bahamas in 1492.

BELIZE: COLUMBUS DAY. Oct 12. Public holiday.

BOER WAR: ANNIVERSARY. Oct 12, 1899. The Boers of the Transvaal and Orange Free State in southern Africa declared war on the British. The Boer states were annexed by Britain in 1900 but guerrilla warfare on the part of the Boers caused the war to drag on. It was finally ended May 31, 1902 by the Treaty of Vereeniging.

COLUMBUS DAY (TRADITIONAL). Oct 12. Public holiday in most countries in the Americas and in most Spanish-speaking countries. Observed under different names (Dia de la Raza or Day of the Race) and on different dates (most often, as in US, on the second Monday in October). Anniversary of Christopher Columbus's arrival, Oct 12, 1492, after a dangerous voyage across "shoreless Seas," at the Bahamas (probably the island of Guanahani), which he renamed El Salvador and claimed in the name of the Spanish crown. In his *Journal*, he wrote: "As I saw that they (the natives) were friendly to us, and perceived that they could be much more easily converted to our holy faith by gentle means than by force, I presented them with some red caps, and strings of beads to wear upon the neck, and many other trifles of small value, wherewith they were much delighted, and becamed wonderfully attached to us." See also: "Columbus Day Observance" (Oct 8).

DAY OF THE SIX BILLION: ANNIVERSARY. Oct 12, 1999. According to the United Nations, the population of the world reached six billion on this date. More than one-third of the world's people live in China and India. It wasn't until 1804 that the world's population reached one billion; now a billion people are added to the population about every 12 years. See also: "Day of the Five Billion: Anniversary" (July 11).

EQUATORIAL GUINEA: INDEPENDENCE DAY. Oct 12. National holiday. The former Spanish Guinea gained independence from Spain in 1968.

MEXICO: DIA DE LA RAZA. Oct 12. Columbus Day is observed as the "Day of the Race," a fiesta time to commemorate the discovery of America as well as the common interests and cultural heritage of the Spanish and Indian peoples and the Hispanic nations.

NATIONAL SCHOOL CELEBRATION. Oct 12. "Pledge Across America"—a synchronized recitation of the Pledge of Allegiance coast to coast, 8 AM Hawaiian time to 2 PM Eastern time. The National School Celebration will provide a high-profile celebration uniting our nation's youth during regular school hours for a patriotic observance. Every school in the nation is invited to participate. This event perpetuates the original spirit of the 1892 National School Celebration declared by President Benjamin Harrison, for which the first Pledge of Allegiance was written. Free resources available from Farmers Insurance and Celebration USA, including a CD with musical renditions of the Pledge, Constitution, Bill of Rights and other selections. Annually, the second Friday in October. For info: Paula Burton, Pres, Celebration USA, 17853 Santiago Blvd, Ste 107, Villa Park, CA 92667. Phone: (714) 283-1892. Web: www.americanpromise.com.

NOVELLO FESTIVAL OF READING. Oct 12–26. Various locations, Charlotte, NC. An annual event that celebrates the enjoyment of reading and literature. For one to two weeks each October, the library hosts more than twenty children's authors and illustrators as well as adult fiction and non-fiction authors. The Novello Festival consists of evening author presentations, school-based activities, a storytelling festival, a luncheon for the business community, a street festival for families, literary contests and more. Est attendance: 50,000. For info: Jessica Walter, Program Dir, Public Library of Charlotte & Mecklenburg County, 310 North Tryon St, Charlotte, NC 28202. Phone: (704) 336-2020. Fax: (704) 336-2677. E-mail: jwalter@plcmc.lib.nc.us. Web: www.novellofestival.net.

SOUTHERN FESTIVAL OF BOOKS: A CELEBRATION OF THE WRITTEN WORD. Oct 12–14. War Memorial Plaza, Nashville, TN. To promote reading, writing, the literary arts and a broader understanding of the language and culture of the South, this annual festival will feature readings, talks and panel discussions by more than 200 authors, exhibit booths of publishing companies and bookstores, autographing sessions, a comprehensive children's program and the Cafe Stage, which is a performance corner for authors, storytellers and musicians. Est attendance: 30,000. For info: Galyn Martin, Coord, Southern Festival of Books, Tennessee Humanities Council, 1003 18th Ave S, Nashville, TN 37212. Phone: 6153207001 ext 15. Fax: (615) 321-4586. E-mail: galyn@tn-humanities.org. Web: www.tn-humanities.org.

SPAIN: NATIONAL HOLIDAY. Oct 12.

BIRTHDAYS TODAY

Kirk Cameron, 31, actor ("Growing Pains"), born Panorama City, CA, Oct 12, 1970.

Alice Childress, 81, author (*A Hero Ain't Nothin' But a Sandwich*), born Charlestown, SC, Oct 12, 1920.

John Engler, 53, Governor of Michigan (R), born Mt Pleasant, MI, Oct 12, 1948.

Marion Jones, 26, track runner, born Los Angeles, CA, Oct 12, 1975.

OCTOBER 13 — SATURDAY

Day 286 — 79 Remaining

BROWN, JESSE LEROY: BIRTH ANNIVERSARY. Oct 13, 1926. Jesse Leroy Brown was the first black American naval aviator and also the first black naval officer to lose his life in combat when he was shot down over Korea, Dec 4, 1950. On Mar 18, 1972, USS *Jesse L. Brown* was launched as the first ship to be named in honor of a black naval officer. Brown was born at Hattiesburg, MS.

BURUNDI: ASSASSINATION OF THE HERO OF THE NATION DAY. Oct 13. National holiday. Commemorates assassination of Prince Louis Rwagasore in 1961.

HONG KONG: BIRTHDAY OF CONFUCIUS. Oct 13. Religious observances are held by the Confucian Society at Confucius Temple at Causeway Bay. Observed on the 27th day of the eighth lunar month.

LOS ANGELES LATINO BOOK & FAMILY FESTIVAL. Oct 13–14. Los Angeles Convention Center. To expose children and adults to a wide range of English and Spanish-language books. Author readings, arts and crafts, health, career and travel information, entertainment. Est attendance: 26,000. For info: Los Angeles Latino Book & Family Festival, 3980 Cazador St., Los Angeles, CA 92008-2856. E-mail: kathy@latinobookfestival.com. Web: www.latinobookfestival.com.

PITCHER, MOLLY: BIRTH ANNIVERSARY. Oct 13, 1754. "Molly Pitcher," heroine of the American Revolution, was a water carrier at the Battle of Monmouth (Sunday, June 28, 1778) where she distinguished herself by loading and firing a cannon after her husband, John Hays, was wounded. Affectionately known as "Sergeant Molly" after General Washington issued her a warrant as a noncommissioned officer. Her real name was Mary Hays McCauley (née Ludwig). Born near Trenton, NJ, she died at Carlisle, PA, Jan 22, 1832.

RICHTER, CONRAD: BIRTH ANNIVERSARY. Oct 13, 1890. Author of books for children and adults, born at Pine Grove, PA. His book *The Light in the Forest* was made into a Disney film in 1958. *The Fields* won the Pulitzer Prize for fiction in 1951. Other works include *The Trees* and *The Town*. Richter died at Pottsville, PA, Oct 30, 1968.

US NAVY: AUTHORIZATION ANNIVERSARY. Oct 13, 1775. Commemorates legislation passed by Second Continental Congress authorizing the acquisition of ships and establishment of a navy.

WHITE HOUSE CORNERSTONE LAID: ANNIVERSARY. Oct 13, 1792. The cornerstone for the presidential residence at 1600 Pennsylvania Ave NW, Washington, DC, designed by James Hoban, was laid. The first presidential family to occupy it was that of John Adams, in November 1800. With three stories and more than 100 rooms, the White House is the oldest building at Washington. First described as the "presidential palace," it acquired the name "White House" about 10 years after construction was completed. Burned by British troops in 1814, it was reconstructed, refurbished and reoccupied by 1817. For more info: *The White House*, by Nathan Aaseng (Lucent, 1-56006-708-X, $19.96 Gr. 7–10). Take a virtual tour of the White House at www.whitehouse.gov. Young children can visit the White House for Kids site at www.whitehouse.gov/WH/kids/html/home.html.

BIRTHDAYS TODAY

Maria Cantwell, 43, US Senator (D, Washington), born Indianapolis, IN, Oct 13, 1958.

Jerry Rice, 39, football player, born Starkville, MS, Oct 13, 1962.

Summer Sanders, 29, Olympic gold medal swimmer, host ("Figure It Out"), born Roseville, CA, Oct 13, 1972.

Paul Simon, 60, singer/songwriter, born Newark, NJ, Oct 13, 1941.

October 2001

S	M	T	W	T	F	S
	1	2	3	4	5	6
7	8	9	10	11	12	13
14	15	16	17	18	19	20
21	22	23	24	25	26	27
28	29	30	31			

OCTOBER 14 — SUNDAY

Day 287 — 78 Remaining

ALASKA DAY CELEBRATION. Oct 14–18. Sitka, AK. Celebration of the transfer ceremony in which the Russian flag was lowered and the Stars and Stripes raised, formally transferring the ownership of Alaska to the US, Oct 18, 1867. Annually, Oct 14–18. For info: Sitka Conv and Visitors Bureau, Box 1226, Sitka, AK 99835. Phone: (907) 747-5940.

AMERICAN SAMOA: WHITE SUNDAY. Oct 14. Second Sunday in October is "children's day" on the island. Children perform skits, prayers, songs and special presentations for parents, friends and relatives. A feast is prepared by the parents and served to the children.

AMERICA'S SAFE SCHOOLS WEEK. Oct 14–20. To motivate key education and law enforcement policymakers, as well as parents, students and community residents, to vigorously advocate schools that are safe and free of violence, weapons and drugs. Annually, the third week in October, from Sunday–Saturday. For info: Natl School Safety Center, 141 Duesenberg Dr, Ste 11, Westlake Village, CA 91362. Phone: (805) 373-9977. Web: www.nssc1.org.

EISENHOWER, DWIGHT DAVID: BIRTH ANNIVERSARY. Oct 14, 1890. The 34th president of the US, born at Denison, TX. Served two terms as president, Jan 20, 1953–Jan 20, 1961. Nicknamed "Ike," he held the rank of five-star general of the army (resigned in 1952, and restored by act of Congress in 1961). He served as supreme commander of the Allied forces in western Europe during WWII. In his Farewell Address (Jan 17, 1961), speaking about the "conjunction of an immense military establishment and a large arms industry," he warned: "In the councils of government, we must guard against the acquisition of unwarranted influence, whether sought or unsought, by the military-industrial complex. The potential of the disastrous rise of misplaced power exists and will persist." An American hero, Eisenhower died at Washington, DC, Mar 28, 1969. For info: www.ipl.org/ref/POTUS.

GRANDMOTHER'S DAY IN FLORIDA AND KENTUCKY. Oct 14. A ceremonial day on the second Sunday in October.

ISRA AL MI'RAJ: ASCENT OF THE PROPHET MUHAMMAD. Oct 14. Islamic calendar date: Rajab 27, 1422. Commemorates the journey of the Prophet Muhammad from Mecca to Jerusalem, his ascension into the Seven Heavens and his return on the same night. Muslims believe that on that night Muhammad prayed together with Abraham, Moses and Jesus in the area of the Al-Aqsa Mosque at Jerusalem. The rock from which he is believed to have ascended to heaven to speak with God is the one inside The Dome of the Rock. Different methods for "anticipating" the visibility of the new moon crescent at Mecca are used by different Muslim groups. US date may vary.

KING WINS NOBEL PEACE PRIZE: ANNIVERSARY. Oct 14, 1964. Martin Luther King, Jr, became the youngest recipient of the Nobel Peace Prize when awarded the honor. Dr. King donated the entire $54,000 prize money to furthering the causes of the civil rights movement.

LEE, FRANCIS LIGHTFOOT: BIRTH ANNIVERSARY. Oct 14, 1734. Signer of the Declaration of Independence. Born at Westmoreland County, VA, he died Jan 11, 1797, at Richmond County, VA.

LENSKI, LOIS: BIRTH ANNIVERSARY. Oct 14, 1893. Children's author and illustrator, born at Springfield, OH. She wrote *Cotton In My Sack* and *Strawberry Girl*, which was awarded the Newbery Medal in 1946. Lenski died at Tarpon Springs, FL, Sept 11, 1974.

★**NATIONAL CHARACTER COUNTS WEEK.** Oct 14–20 (tentative).

★**NATIONAL CHILDREN'S DAY.** Oct 14.

★**NATIONAL SCHOOL LUNCH WEEK.** Oct 14–20. Presidential Proclamation issued for the week beginning with the second Sunday in October since 1962 (PL87–780 of Oct 9, 1962). Note: Not issued in 1981.

PENN, WILLIAM: BIRTH ANNIVERSARY. Oct 14, 1644. Founder of Pennsylvania, born at London, England. Penn died July 30, 1718, at Buckinghamshire, England. Presidential Proclamation 5284 of Nov 28, 1984, conferred honorary citizenship of the USA upon William Penn and his second wife, Hannah Callowhill Penn. They were the third and fourth persons to receive honorary US citizenship (following Winston Churchill and Raoul Wallenberg). For more info: *William Penn: Founder of Pennsylvania*, by Steven Kroll (Holiday, 0-8234-1439-6, $16.96 Gr. 3–5).

SAMOA: WHITE SUNDAY. Oct 14. The second Sunday in October. For the children of Samoa, this is the biggest day of the year. Traditional roles are reversed, as children lead church services, are served special foods and receive gifts of new church clothes and other special items. All the children dress in white. The following Monday is an official holiday.

SOUND BARRIER BROKEN: ANNIVERSARY. Oct 14, 1947. Flying a Bell X-1 at Muroc Dry Lake Bed, CA, Air Force pilot Chuck Yeager flew faster than the speed of sound, ushering in the era of supersonic flight.

TEEN READ WEEK. Oct 14–20. The teen years are a time when many kids reject reading as being just another dreary assignment. The goal of Teen Read Week is to encourage young adults to read for sheer pleasure as well as learning. Also to remind parents, teachers and others that reading for fun is important for teens as well as young children and to increase awareness of the resources available at libraries. For info: Young Adult Library Services Assn, American Library Assn, 50 E Huron St, Chicago, IL 60611. Phone: (800) 545-2433, ext 4390. E-mail: yalsa@ala.org. Web: www.ala.org/teenread.

WORLD RAINFOREST WEEK. Oct 14–21. Rainforest activists from 140 worldwide action groups will sponsor events to increase public awareness of rainforest destruction and motivate people to protect the Earth's rainforest and support the rights of their inhabitants. The global rate of destruction of rainforests is 2.4 acres per second—equivalent to two US football fields. For info: M. Holmgren, Grassroots Coord, Rainforest Action Network, 221 Pine St, 5th Floor, San Francisco, CA 94104. Phone: (415) 398-4404. E-mail: rainforest@ran.org. Web: www.ran.org.

BIRTHDAYS TODAY

Jordan Brower, 20, actor ("Teen Angel"), born Vandenberg, CA, Oct 14, 1981.

Elisa Kleven, 43, author (*The Puddle Pail*), born Los Angeles, CA, Oct 14, 1958.

OCTOBER 15 — MONDAY

Day 288 — 77 Remaining

CROW RESERVATION OPENED FOR SETTLEMENT: ANNIVERSARY. Oct 15, 1892. By Presidential Proclamation 1.8 million acres of Crow Indian reservation were opened to settlers. The government had induced the Crow to give up a portion of their land in the mountainous western area in the state of Montana, for which they received 50 cents per acre.

FIRST MANNED FLIGHT: ANNIVERSARY. Oct 15, 1783. Jean Francois Pilatre de Rozier and Francois Laurent, Marquis d'Arlandes, became the first people to fly when they ascended in a Montgolfier hot-air balloon at Paris, France, less than three months after the first public balloon flight demonstration (June 5, 1783), and only a year after the first experiments with small paper and fabric balloons by the Montgolfier brothers, Joseph and Jacques, in November 1782. The first manned free flight lasted about 4 minutes and carried the passengers at a height of about 84 feet. On Nov 21, 1783, they soared 3,000 feet over Paris for 25 minutes.

"I LOVE LUCY" TV PREMIERE: 50th ANNIVERSARY. Oct 15, 1951. This enormously popular sitcom, TV's first smash hit, starred the real-life husband and wife team of Cuban actor/bandleader Desi Arnaz and talented redheaded actress/comedienne Lucille Ball. They played Ricky and Lucy Ricardo, a New York bandleader and his aspiring actress/homemaker wife who was always scheming to get on stage. Costarring were William Frawley and Vivian Vance as Fred and Ethel Mertz, the Ricardos' landlords and good friends. This was the first sitcom to be filmed live before a studio audience and it did extremely well in the ratings both the first time around and in reruns.

INTERNATIONAL SCHOOL LIBRARY DAY. Oct 15. Annually, the third Monday in October. For info: Intl Assn of School Librarians, Ste 300, PO Box 34069, Seattle, WA 98124-1069. Fax: (604) 925-0566. E-mail: iasl@rockland.com. Web: www.hi.is/~anne/sldindex.html.

JAMAICA: NATIONAL HEROES DAY. Oct 15. National holiday established in 1969. Always observed on the third Monday of October.

MY MOM IS A STUDENT DAY. Oct 15. Kids can show their support to their moms by treating them with new pens, paper clips and other little school supplies. They can also fix mom a school lunch with a supportive note inside. Annually, Oct 15. For info: Patti Veld, c/o Davenport College Library, 8200 Georgia St, Merrillville, IN 46410.

NATIONAL GROUCH DAY. Oct 15. Honor a grouch. All grouches deserve a day to be recognized. Annually, Oct 15. For info: Alan R. Miller, Carter Middle School, 300 Upland Dr, Room 207, Clio, MI 48420. Phone: (810) 591-0503.

NATIONAL HEALTH EDUCATION WEEK. Oct 15–21. Annually, the third week in October. For info: Lynne Whitt, Natl Center for Health Education, 72 Spring St, Ste 208, New York, NY 10012. Phone: (212) 334-9470.

NATIONAL SCHOOL LUNCH WEEK. Oct 15–19. To celebrate good nutrition and healthy, low-cost school lunches. Annually, the second full week in October. For info: Communications Dept, American School Food Service Assn, 1600 Duke St, 7th Fl, Alexandria, VA 22314-3436. Phone: (703) 739-3900 x133.

SPACE MILESTONE: *CASSINI* (US). Oct 15, 1997. This plutonium-powered spacecraft is to arrive at Saturn in July 2004. It will orbit the planet, take pictures of its 18 known moons and dispatch a probe to Titan, the largest of these moons.

VIRGIN ISLANDS: HURRICANE THANKSGIVING DAY. Oct 15. Third Monday of October is a legal holiday celebrating the end of hurricane season.

★ **WHITE CANE SAFETY DAY.** Oct 15. Presidential Proclamation always issued for Oct 15 since 1964 (PL88–628 of Oct 6, 1964).

WILSON, EDITH BOLLING GALT: BIRTH ANNIVERSARY. Oct 15, 1872. Second wife of Woodrow Wilson, 28th president of the US, born at Wytheville, VA. She died at Washington, DC, Dec 28, 1961.

BIRTHDAYS TODAY

Barry Moser, 61, illustrator (*The Bird House*), born Chattanooga, TN, Oct 15, 1940.

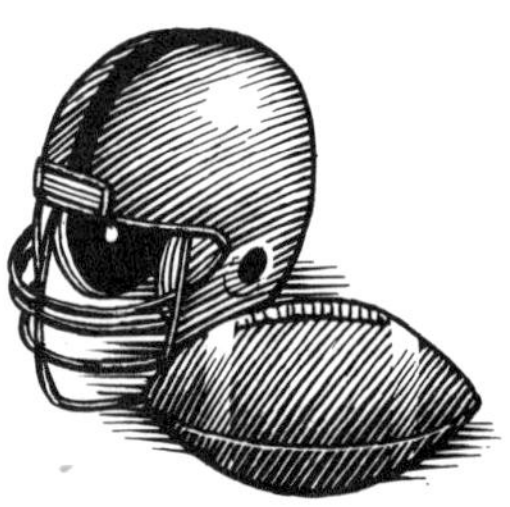

OCTOBER 16 — TUESDAY

Day 289 — 76 Remaining

AMERICA'S FIRST DEPARTMENT STORE: ANNIVERSARY. Oct 16, 1868. Salt Lake City, UT. America's first department store, "ZCMI" (Zion's Co-Operative Mercantile Institution), is still operating at Salt Lake City. It was founded under the direction of Brigham Young. For info: Museum of Church History and Art, 45 North West Temple, Salt Lake City, UT 84150. Phone: (801) 240-4604.

BEN-GURION, DAVID: BIRTH ANNIVERSARY. Oct 16, 1886. First prime minister of the state of Israel. Born at Plonsk, Poland, he died at Tel Aviv, Israel, Dec 1, 1973.

DICTIONARY DAY. Oct 16. The birthday of Noah Webster, American teacher and lexicographer, is occasion to encourage every person to acquire at least one dictionary—and to use it regularly. *See* Curriculum Connection.

DOUGLAS, WILLIAM ORVILLE: BIRTH ANNIVERSARY. Oct 16, 1898. American jurist, world traveler, conservationist, outdoorsman and author. Born at Maine, MN, he served as justice of the US Supreme Court longer than any other justice (36 years). Died at Washington, DC, Jan 19, 1980.

GRANT PUT IN CHARGE OF THE MISSISSIPPI REGION: ANNIVERSARY. Oct 16, 1863. After his impressive success taking Vicksburg, MS, Ulysses S. Grant, a brigadier general of the militia, was appointed a general in the regular army and, with the subsequent reorganization of the departments of war at Ohio, Cumberland and Tennessee, was placed in charge of the newly formed Military Division of the Mississippi. Grant's first priority was to save the besieged and starving Union troops at Chattanooga, TN.

October 2001

S	M	T	W	T	F	S
	1	2	3	4	5	6
7	8	9	10	11	12	13
14	15	16	17	18	19	20
21	22	23	24	25	26	27
28	29	30	31			

OCTOBER 16
DICTIONARY DAY AND NOAH WEBSTER'S BIRTHDAY

Noah Webster, born in 1758, compiled the first dictionary of American English. He must have been a person who loved words. Enjoying words—their look, sound and meanings—makes reading and writing pleasurable.

Students can have fun with words in many ways. *The Pig in the Spigot*, by Richard Wilbur (Harcourt, 0-15-202019-5, $16 Gr. 3 & up), is a delightful model for a classroom exercise that could be entitled Two Words at Once. Each of the words featured in this book becomes the core of a poem that connects the larger parent word to a smaller word contained within. For example: "*Sea* is in *nausea*, which seems strange to me/since *nausea* comes of tossing in the *sea*." Students can have fun searching the dictionary for other words that have smaller words in them. Publish your own classroom book. One suggestion: work on a poem about a rat, featuring the word separate. It's a helpful way to remember how to spell separate correctly.

Another book that provides a great model for a classroom book of word definitions is *Serendipity*, by Tobi Tobias (Simon & Schuster, 0-689-83373-3, $12 All ages). Tobias defines the word serendipity by creating fun examples and illustrations to define the essence of the word. They help students remember what the word means and understand how to use it. They also highlight the pleasure of saying a lovely word that flows off one's tongue. Two examples from the book include: "Serendipity is when the big boys need another player on their team, and you happen to be carrying your mitt" and "Serendipity is a hole in the sweater you've always hated." Let students write and illustrate definitions for interesting words they find—delicious or problematical, for example.

Go Hang a Salami! I'm a Lasagna Hog! And Other Palindromes, by Jon Agee (Farrar, 0-374-33473-0, $14.50 Gr. 5 & up), is a humorous look at groups of words that read the same backwards and forwards. Agee has written similar books on anagrams and oxymorons.

The Secret Lives of Words, by Paul West (Harcourt, 0-15-100466-8, $24 Gr. 9 & up), is a good resource for the history of selected words. Sometimes wry, often sarcastic, West has chosen an entertaining collection of words. Teachers of high school English classes will find this book useful.

JOHN BROWN'S RAID: ANNIVERSARY. Oct 16, 1859. Abolitionist John Brown, with a band of about 20 men, seized the US Arsenal at Harpers Ferry, WV. Brown was captured and the insurrection put down by Oct 19. Brown was hanged at Charles Town, VA (now WV), Dec 2, 1859. For more info: *The John Brown Slavery Revolt*, by David DeVillers (Enslow, 0-7660-1385-5, $20.95 Gr. 6 & up).

LITERATURE FESTIVAL. Oct 16. University of Kansas Union, Lawrence, KS. Festival of children's literature. For info: The Writing Conference, Inc, PO Box 664, Ottawa, KS 66067. Fax: (785) 242-0407. E-mail: jbushman@writingconference.com. Web: www.writingconference.com.

MILLION MAN MARCH: ANNIVERSARY. Oct 16, 1995. Hundreds of thousands of black men met at Washington, DC, for a "holy day of atonement and reconciliation" organized by Louis Farrakhan, leader of the Nation of Islam. Marchers pledged to take responsibility for themselves, their families and their communities.

MOON PHASE: NEW MOON. Oct 16. Moon enters New Moon phase at 3:23 PM, EDT.

UNITED NATIONS: WORLD FOOD DAY. Oct 16. Annual observance to heighten public awareness of the world food problem and to strengthen solidarity in the struggle against hunger, malnutrition and poverty. Date of observance is anniversary of the founding of the Food and Agriculture Organization (FAO), Oct 16, 1945, at Quebec, Canada. For info: United Nations, Dept of Public Info, New York, NY 10017.

WEBSTER, NOAH: BIRTH ANNIVERSARY. Oct 16, 1758. American teacher and journalist whose name became synonymous with the word "dictionary" after his compilations of the earliest American dictionaries of the English language. Born at West Hartford, CT, he died at New Haven, CT, May 28, 1843.

WORLD FOOD DAY. Oct 16. To increase awareness, understanding and informed action on hunger. Annually, on the founding date of the UN Food and Agriculture Organization. For info: Patricia Young, US Natl Committee for World Food Day, 2175 K St NW, Washington, DC 20437. Phone: (202) 653-2404. Web: www.gsu.edu/~wwwwfd.

BIRTHDAYS TODAY

Joseph Bruchac, 59, author (*Thirteen Moons on Turtle's Back, The Boy Who Lived with Bears and Other Iroquois Stories*), born Saratoga Springs, NY, Oct 16, 1942.

Paul Kariya, 27, hockey player, born Vancouver, BC, Canada, Oct 16, 1974.

Kordell Stewart, 29, football player, born New Orleans, LA, Oct 16, 1972.

OCTOBER 17 — WEDNESDAY

Day 290 — 75 Remaining

BLACK POETRY DAY. Oct 17 (tentative). To recognize the contribution of black poets to American life and culture and to honor Jupiter Hammon, the first black in America to publish his own verse. Jupiter Hammon of Huntington, Long Island, NY, was born Oct 17, 1711. For info: Alexis Levitin, Black Poetry Day Committee, Dept of English, SUNY-Plattsburgh, Plattsburgh, NY 12901-2681. Phone: (518) 564-2426. Fax: (518) 564-2140. E-mail: levitia@splava.cc.plattsburgh.edu.

HAMMON, JUPITER: BIRTH ANNIVERSARY. Oct 17, 1711. America's first published black poet, whose birth anniversary is celebrated annually as Black Poetry Day, was born into slavery, probably at Long Island, NY. He was taught to read, however, and as a trusted servant was allowed to use his master's library. With the publication on Christmas Day, 1760, of the 88-line broadside poem 'An Evening Thought,' Jupiter Hammon, then 49, became the first black in America to publish poetry. Hammon died in 1790. The exact date and place of his death are unknown.

JOHNSON, RICHARD MENTOR: BIRTH ANNIVERSARY. Oct 17, 1780. Ninth vice president of the US (1837–41). Born at Floyd's Station, KY, he died at Frankfort, KY, Nov 19, 1850.

MISSOURI DAY. Oct 17. Observed by teachers and pupils of schools with appropriate exercises throughout the state of Missouri. Annually, the third Wednesday of October.

POPE JOHN PAUL I: BIRTH ANNIVERSARY. Oct 17, 1912. Albino Luciani, 263rd pope of the Roman Catholic Church. Born at Forno di Canale, Italy, he was elected pope Aug 26, 1978. Died at Rome, 34 days after his election, Sept 28, 1978. Shortest papacy since Pope Leo XI (Apr 1–27, 1605).

SAN FRANCISCO 1989 EARTHQUAKE: ANNIVERSARY. Oct 17, 1989. The San Francisco Bay area was rocked by an earthquake registering 7.1 on the Richter scale at 5:04 PM, EDT, just as the nation's baseball fans settled in to watch the 1989 World Series. A large audience was tuned in to the pregame coverage when the quake hit and knocked the broadcast off the air. The quake caused damage estimated at $10 billion and killed 67 people, many of whom were caught in the collapse of the double-decked Interstate 80, at Oakland, CA. For more: *The San Francisco Earthquake, 1989*, by Victoria Sherrow (Enslow, 0-7660-1060-0, $18.95 Gr. 4–8) or go the National Earthquake Information Center: wwwneic.cr.usgs.gov.

UNITED NATIONS: INTERNATIONAL DAY FOR THE ERADICATION OF POVERTY. Oct 17. The General Assembly proclaimed this observance (Res 47/196) to promote public awareness of the need to eradicate poverty and destitution in all countries, particularly the developing nations. For more info, go to the UN's website for children at www.un.org/Pubs/Cyber SchoolBus/. Annually on Oct 17.

BIRTHDAYS TODAY

Brandon Call, 25, actor ("Step By Step"), born Torrance, CA, Oct 17, 1976.

Judith Caseley, 50, author (*When Grandpa Came to Stay*), born Rahway, NJ, Oct 17, 1951.

Alan Garner, 67, author (*The Stone Book*), born Congleton, England, Oct 17, 1934.

Mae Jemison, 45, scientist, astronaut, host ("Susan B. Anthony Slept Here"), born Decatur, AL, Oct 17, 1956.

Chris Kirkpatrick, 30, singer ('N Sync), born Pittsburgh, PA, Oct 17, 1971.

OCTOBER 18 — THURSDAY

Day 291 — 74 Remaining

ALASKA DAY. Oct 18. Alaska. Anniversary of transfer of Alaska from Russia to the US, which became official on Sitka's Castle Hill in 1867. This is a holiday in Alaska; when it falls on a weekend it is observed on the following Monday.

SAINT LUKE: FEAST DAY. Oct 18. Patron saint of doctors and artists, himself a physician and painter, authorship of the third Gospel and Acts of the Apostles is attributed to him. Died about AD 68. Legend says that he painted portraits of Mary and Jesus.

SCHOOLTECH EXPO AND CONFERENCE. Oct 18–20. Chicago, IL. Sponsored by *Technology & Learning* magazine, the conference features training workshops and technology exhibits. Est attendance: 3,000. For info: Miller Freeman Inc, 600 Harrison St, San Francisco, CA 94109. Phone: (888) 857-6883. Web: www.schooltechexpo.com.

SILVERSTEIN, SHEL: BIRTH ANNIVERSARY. Oct 18, 1932. Cartoonist and children's author, best remembered for his poetry that included *A Light in the Attic* and *The Giving Tree*. Silverstein won the Michigan Young Reader's Award for *Where The Sidewalk Ends*. Also a songwriter, he wrote "The Unicorn Song" and "A Boy Named Sue" for Johnny Cash. Born at Chicago, IL, he died at Key West, FL, May 9, 1999.

WATER POLLUTION CONTROL ACT: ANNIVERSARY. Oct 18, 1972. Overriding President Nixon's veto, Congress passed a $25 billion Water Pollution Control Act.

BIRTHDAYS TODAY

Joyce Hansen, 59, author (*I Thought My Soul Would Rise and Fly: The Diary of Patsy, a Freed Girl*), born New York, NY, Oct 18, 1942.

Jesse Helms, 80, US Senator (R, North Carolina), born Monroe, NC, Oct 18, 1921.

Wynton Marsalis, 40, classical and jazz musician, born New Orleans, LA, Oct 18, 1961.

OCTOBER 19 — FRIDAY

Day 292 — 73 Remaining

JEFFERSON, MARTHA WAYLES SKELTON: BIRTH ANNIVERSARY. Oct 19, 1748. Wife of Thomas Jefferson, third president of the US. Born at Charles City County, VA, she died at Monticello, VA, Sept 6, 1782.

STATE FAIR OF LOUISIANA. Oct 19–Nov 4. Fairgrounds, Shreveport, LA. Educational, agricultural, commercial exhibits, entertainment. Est attendance: 250,000. For info: Sam Giordano, Pres/General Mgr, Louisiana State Fairgrounds, PO Box 38327, Shreveport, LA 71133. Phone: (318) 635-1361. Fax: (318) 631-4909.

YORKTOWN DAY: "AMERICA'S REAL INDEPENDENCE DAY." Oct 19. Yorktown, VA. Representatives of the US, France and other nations involved in the American Revolution gather to celebrate the anniversary of the victory (Oct 19, 1781) that assured American independence. Parade and commemorative ceremonies. Annually, Oct 19. Est attendance: 2,000. For info: Public Affairs Officer, Colonial Natl Historical Park, Box 210, Yorktown, VA 23690. Phone: (757) 898-2410. Web: www.nps.gov/colo.

YORKTOWN DAY: ANNIVERSARY. Oct 19, 1781. More than 7,000 English and Hessian troops, led by British General Lord Cornwallis, surrendered to General George Washington at Yorktown, VA, effectively ending the war between Britain and her American colonies. There were no more major battles, but the provisional treaty of peace was not signed until Nov 30, 1782, and the final Treaty of Paris, Sept 3, 1783.

BIRTHDAYS TODAY

Ed Emberley, 70, author, illustrator (*Go Away, Big Green Monster; Ed Emberley's Great Thumbprint Drawing Book; Drummer Hoff*), born Malden, MA, Oct 19, 1931.

Dan Gutman, 46, author (*Honus and Me, The Kid Who Ran for President*), born New York, NY, Oct 19, 1955.

John Lithgow, 56, actor ("Third Rock from the Sun"), author (*The Remarkable Farkle McBride*), born Rochester, NY, Oct 19, 1945.

Bernard Lodge, 68, author (*There Was an Old Woman Who Lived in a Glove, Prince Ivan and the Firebird*), born Chalfont, St. Peter, Buckinghamshire, England, Oct 19, 1933.

Philip Pullman, 55, author (*The Golden Compass, The Subtle Knife*), born Norwich, England, Oct 19, 1946.

October 2001

S	M	T	W	T	F	S
	1	2	3	4	5	6
7	8	9	10	11	12	13
14	15	16	17	18	19	20
21	22	23	24	25	26	27
28	29	30	31			

OCTOBER 20 — SATURDAY

Day 293 — 72 Remaining

DEWEY, JOHN: BIRTH ANNIVERSARY. Oct 20, 1859. Philosopher of education, born near Burlington, VT. A professor at the University of Chicago and Columbia University, Dewey was committed to child-centered education, learning by doing and integrating schools with the outside world. He died at New York, NY, June 2, 1952.

DISCOVERY YOUNG SCIENTIST CHALLENGE. Oct 20–25 (tentative). Washington, DC. Students in grades 5–8 compete in Science Service-affiliated fairs in the spring. Forty finalists are selected to compete for scholarship money at the Smithsonian Institution the following October. Three winners are selected. For info: Science Service, 1719 N St NW, Washington, DC 20036. Phone: (202) 785-2255. Web: www.sciserv.org/dysc or school .discovery.com/sciencefaircentral/dysc/index.html.

GUATEMALA: REVOLUTION DAY. Oct 20. Public holiday in Guatemala.

JOHNSON, CROCKETT: BIRTH ANNIVERSARY. Oct 20, 1906. Author (*Harold and the Purple Crayon*), cartoonist, born David Leisk at New York, NY. Died July 11, 1975. For more info: www.ksu.edu/english/nelp/purple/index.html.

KENYA: KENYATTA DAY. Oct 20. Observed as a public holiday. Honors Jomo Kenyatta, first president of Kenya.

MacARTHUR RETURNS TO THE PHILIPPINES: ANNIVERSARY. Oct 20, 1944. In mid-September of 1944 American military leaders made the decision to begin the invasion of the Philippines on Leyte, a small island north of the Surigao Strait. With General Douglas MacArthur in overall command, US aircraft dropped hundreds of tons of bombs in the area of Dulag. Four divisions landed on the east coast, and after a few hours General MacArthur set foot on Philippine soil for the first time since he was ordered to Australia Mar 11, 1942, thus fulfilling his promise, "I shall return."

MANTLE, MICKEY: 70th BIRTH ANNIVERSARY. Oct 20, 1931. Baseball Hall of Famer, born at Spavinaw, OK. Died Aug 13, 1995, at Dallas, TX.

BIRTHDAYS TODAY

Peter Fitzgerald, 41, US Senator (R, Illinois), born Elgin, IL, Oct 20, 1960.

Nikki Grimes, 51, poet and author (*Meet Danitra Brown*), also writes as Naomi McMillen, born New York, NY, Oct 20, 1950.

Eddie Jones, 30, basketball player, born Pompano Beach, FL, Oct 20, 1971.

OCTOBER 21 — SUNDAY

Day 294 — 71 Remaining

ARIZONA STATE FAIR. Oct 21–Nov 7. Phoenix, AZ. Festival, concerts, flea markets, entertainment and food. For info: Mktg Dept, Arizona State Fair, PO Box 6728, Phoenix, AZ 85005. Phone: (602) 252-6771. Fax: (602) 495-1302.

THE DAY OF NATIONAL CONCERN ABOUT YOUNG PEOPLE AND GUN VIOLENCE. Oct 21. Students are encouraged on this day to sign a pledge that they will never carry a gun to school or resolve a dispute with a gun and they will urge their friends to do the same. More than 1,000,000 middle and high school students have signed the Pledge Against Gun Violence. For info: Student Pledge Against Gun Violence, 112 Nevada St, Northfield, MN 55057. Phone: (507) 645-5378. Web: www.pledge.org.

FILLMORE, CAROLINE CARMICHAEL McINTOSH: BIRTH ANNIVERSARY. Oct 21, 1813. Second wife of Millard Fillmore, 13th president of the US, born at Morristown, NJ. Died at New York, NY, Aug 11, 1881.

INCANDESCENT LAMP DEMONSTRATED: ANNIVERSARY. Oct 21, 1879. Thomas A. Edison demonstrated the first incandescent lamp that could be used economically for domestic purposes. This prototype, developed at his Menlo Park, NJ, laboratory, could burn for 13½ hours.

★**NATIONAL DAY OF CONCERN ABOUT YOUNG PEOPLE AND GUN VIOLENCE.** Oct 21. Students are asked to voluntarily sign a "Student Pledge Against Gun Violence," a promise never to bring a gun to school, never to use a gun to settle a dispute and to discourage their friends from using guns.

★**NATIONAL FOREST PRODUCTS WEEK.** Oct 21–27. Presidential Proclamation always issued for the week beginning with the third Sunday in October since 1960 (PL86–753 of Sept 13, 1960).

NATIONAL SCHOOL BUS SAFETY WEEK. Oct 21–27. This week is set aside to focus attention on school bus safety—from the standpoint of the bus drivers, students and the motoring public. Annually, the third full week of October, starting on Sunday. For info: Natl School Bus Safety Week Committee, 625 Slaters Ln, Ste 205, Alexandria, VA 22314.

NOBEL, ALFRED BERNHARD: BIRTH ANNIVERSARY. Oct 21, 1833. Swedish chemist and engineer who invented dynamite was born at Stockholm, Sweden, and died at San Remo, Italy, Dec 10, 1896. His will established the Nobel Prize. See also "Nobel Prize Awards Ceremonies" (Dec 10). For more info: www.nobel.se.

SOMALIA: NATIONAL DAY. Oct 21. National holiday. Anniversary of the revolution.

TAIWAN: OVERSEAS CHINESE DAY. Oct 21. Thousands of overseas Chinese come to Taiwan for this and other occasions that make October a particularly memorable month.

YWCA WEEK WITHOUT VIOLENCE. Oct 21–27. Third full week in October. For info: YWCA of the USA, Empire State Bldg, Ste 301, 350 Fifth Ave, New York, NY 10118. Phone: (212) 273-7800. Web: www.ywca.org.

BIRTHDAYS TODAY

Janet Ahlberg, 57, illustrator (*The Jolly Postman*), born Croydon, England, Oct 21, 1944.

Nakia Burrise, 27, actress (*Turbo: A Power Rangers Movie,* "Power Rangers Turbo"), born San Diego, CA, Oct 21, 1974.

Ann Cameron, 58, author (*The Most Beautiful Place in the World*), born Rice Lake, WI, Oct 21, 1943.

Ursula K. Le Guin, 72, author of science fiction (*The Tombs of Atuan*), born Berkeley, CA, Oct 21, 1929.

Jeremy Miller, 25, actor ("Growing Pains"), born West Covina, CA, Oct 21, 1976.

OCTOBER 22 — MONDAY

Day 295 — 70 Remaining

FOXX, JIMMIE: BIRTH ANNIVERSARY. Oct 22, 1907. Baseball Hall of Fame first baseman, born at Sudlersville, MD. Died at Miami, FL, July 21, 1967.

HOLY SEE: NATIONAL HOLIDAY. Oct 22. The state of Vatican City and the Holy See observe Oct 22 as a national holiday.

INTERNATIONAL STUTTERING AWARENESS DAY. Oct 22. For info: National Stuttering Assn, 5100 E La Palma, Ste 208, Anaheim, CA 92807. Phone: (800) 364-1677. Fax: (714) 693-7554. Web: www.nsastutter.org or www.stutteringhomepage.com.

LISZT, FRANZ: BIRTH ANNIVERSARY. Oct 22, 1811. Hungarian pianist and composer (*Hungarian Rhapsodies*). Born at Raiding, Hungary, he died July 31, 1886, at Bayreuth, Germany. *See* Curriculum Connection.

NEW ZEALAND: LABOR DAY. Oct 22. National holiday. The fourth Monday in October.

RANDOLPH, PEYTON: DEATH ANNIVERSARY. Oct 22, 1775. First president of the Continental Congress, died at Philadelphia, PA. Born about 1721 (exact date unknown), at Williamsburg, VA.

ZAMBIA: INDEPENDENCE DAY. Oct 22. National holiday commemorates independence of what was then Northern Rhodesia from Britain in 1964. Celebrations in all cities, but main parades of military, labor and youth organizations are at capital, Lusaka. The fourth Monday in October.

OCTOBER 22
FRANZ LISZT'S BIRTHDAY

Franz Liszt was one of the most popular pianists of the 19th century. He was born in the town of Raiding, Hungary, which is now part of Austria. Liszt was a child prodigy and by the time he was 12 years old, he had performed piano recitals in Hungary, Germany, and Austria.

Franz's father, an amateur musician, taught young Franz how to play the piano, but it soon became apparent that Franz's talent and affinity for music needed more scope than his father could provide. Franz began his formal music education, in 1823, when he traveled to Paris to attend music school to learn composition and music theory.

Everywhere he played, Liszt astounded people with his keyboard virtuosity. His skill at improvising, plus his engaging personality made him a crowd favorite. He began his career as a composer in 1848.

There is a wide variety of music composed by Liszt readily available in library collections and music stores. He composed many solo pieces for the piano, as well as ballads and waltzes. One of his compositions, *Hungarian Rhapsody no. 2*, is a musical classic that every child should learn to appreciate and recognize. (If you hear a recording of this piece, you will immediately recognize the music even if the name is unfamiliar!) The first half of *Rhapsody no. 2* opens with a slow, introductory section dominated by the stringed instruments. It represents the anguish and hardships suffered by Hungary's gypsies as they wandered throughout the countryside. Short clarinet solos periodically reflect this somber theme during the piece. A whimsical, light-hearted, and capricious tone takes over the second half of the piece. Students will immediately feel like dancing and many may say, "This sounds like a circus," or "I've heard this before!" (And they're right. *Hungarian Rhapsody no. 2* was used as background music for loads of cartoons.)

Say "Happy Birthday, Franz!" by playing the *Hungarian Rhapsody no. 2*. Children can respond to it by drawing pictures that reflect their own mood and how it changes as the music and tempo build. Older students can write prose or poetry to reflect their moods. Perhaps they could discuss what the music tells the listener about a gypsy's life.

Or you could just listen and appreciate the music. Your students will love it and probably ask for an encore.

BIRTHDAYS TODAY

Brian Anthony Boitano, 38, Olympic gold medal figure skater, born Mountain View, CA, Oct 22, 1963.

Jeff Goldblum, 49, actor (*The Lost World: Jurassic Park*), born Pittsburgh, PA, Oct 22, 1952.

Zachary Walker Hanson, 16, singer (Hanson), born Arlington, VA, Oct 22, 1985.

Jonathan Lipnicki, 11, actor (*Jerry Maguire, The Little Vampire*), born Westlake Village, CA, Oct 22, 1990.

Bill Owens, 51, Governor of Colorado (R), born Fort Worth, TX, Oct 22, 1950.

OCTOBER 23 — TUESDAY

Day 296 — 69 Remaining

APPERT, NICOLAS: BIRTH ANNIVERSARY. Oct 23, 1752. Also known as "Canning Day," this is the anniversary of the birth of French chef, chemist, confectioner, inventor and author Nicolas Appert, at Chalons-Sur-Marne. Appert, who also invented the bouillon tablet, is best remembered for devising a system of heating foods and sealing them in airtight containers. Known as the "father of canning," Appert won a prize of 12,000 francs from the French government in 1809, and the title "Benefactor of Humanity" in 1812, for his inventions which revolutionized our previously seasonal diet. Appert died at Massy, France, June 3, 1841.

CAMBODIA: PEACE TREATY DAY. Oct 23. National holiday. Commemorates 1991 peace treaty.

EAGER, EDWARD: DEATH ANNIVERSARY. Oct 23, 1964. Born in Toledo, OH in 1911, Eager wrote children's fantasy novels in the style of his favorite author, E. Nesbit. Like Nesbit, he wrote about ordinary children caught up in magical adventures. Some of his more popular books are *Half Magic* and *Magic By the Lake*. He died in Connecticut on Oct 23, 1964.

EDERLE, GERTRUDE: BIRTH ANNIVERSARY. Oct 23, 1906. American swimming champion, born at New York City. Gertrude Ederle was the first woman to swim the English channel (from Cape Griz-nez, France, to Dover, England). On Aug 6, 1926, at age 19, she broke the previous world record by swimming the 35-mile distance in $14\frac{1}{2}$ hours, two hours faster than any man had done. She was also a gold medal winner at the 1924 Olympic Games. For more info: *America's Champion Swimmer: Gertrude Ederle*, by David A. Adler (Harcourt/Gulliver, 0-15-201969-3, $16 Gr. K–3).

HUNGARY: 45th ANNIVERSARY OF 1956 REVOLUTION. Oct 23. National holiday.

HUNGARY DECLARED INDEPENDENT: ANNIVERSARY. Oct 23, 1989. Hungary declared itself an independent republic, 33 years after Russian troops crushed a popular revolt against Soviet rule. The announcement followed a week-long purge by Parliament of the Stalinist elements from Hungary's 1949 constitution, which defined the country as a socialist people's republic. Acting head of state Matyas Szuros made the declaration in front of tens of thousands of Hungarians at Parliament Square, speaking from the same balcony from which Imre Nagy addressed rebels 33 years earlier. Nagy was hanged for treason after Soviet intervention. Free elections held in March 1990 removed the Communist party to the ranks of the opposition for the first time in four decades.

October 2001

S	M	T	W	T	F	S
	1	2	3	4	5	6
7	8	9	10	11	12	13
14	15	16	17	18	19	20
21	22	23	24	25	26	27
28	29	30	31			

MOON PHASE: FIRST QUARTER. Oct 23. Moon enters First Quarter phase at 10:58 PM, EDT.

SCORPIO, THE SCORPION. Oct 23–Nov 22. In the astronomical/astrological zodiac that divides the sun's apparent orbit into 12 segments, the period Oct 23–Nov 22 is identified, traditionally, as the sun sign of Scorpio, the Scorpion. The ruling planet is Pluto or Mars.

STEVENSON, ADLAI EWING: BIRTH ANNIVERSARY. Oct 23, 1835. The 23rd vice president of the US (1893–97) born at Christian County, KY. Died at Chicago, IL, June 14, 1914. He was grandfather of Adlai E. Stevenson, the Democratic candidate for president in 1952 and 1956.

THAILAND: CHULALONGKORN DAY. Oct 23. Annual commemoration of the death of King Chulalongkorn the Great, who died Oct 23, 1910, after a 42-year reign. King Chulalongkorn abolished slavery in Thailand. Special ceremonies with floral tributes and incense at the foot of his equestrian statue in front of Bangkok's National Assembly Hall.

BIRTHDAYS TODAY

Laurie Halse Anderson, 40, author (*Speak*), born Potsdam, NY, Oct 23, 1961.

Jim Bunning, 70, US Senator (R, Kentucky), born Southgate, KY, Oct 23, 1931.

Gordon Korman, 38, author (*The Toilet Paper Tigers, The Twinkie Squad*), born Montreal, QC, Canada, Oct 23, 1963.

Melquiades (Mel) R. Martinez, 55, US Secretary of Housing and Urban Development (George W. Bush administration), born Sagua la Grande, Cuba, Oct 23, 1946.

Pele, 61, former soccer player, born Edson Arantes do Nascimento, Tres Coracoes, Brazil, Oct 23, 1940.

Keith Van Horn, 26, basketball player, born Fullerton, CA, Oct 23, 1975.

"Weird Al" Yankovic, 42, singer, satirist ("The Weird Al Show"), born Lynwood, CA, Oct 23, 1959.

OCTOBER 24 — WEDNESDAY

Day 297 — 68 Remaining

NATIONAL FFA CONVENTION. Oct 24–27. Kentucky Fair & Exposition Center, Louisville, KY. This 74th annual convention is an opportunity for recognition, business, elections and celebration. Delegates from each state discuss topics affecting the national agriculture education organization and elect a new team of national officers. Students compete in final rounds of leadership and career events and learn about education and career opportunities in a 300-exhibitor career show. Est attendance: 45,000. For info: Natl FFA Organization, 1410 King St, Ste 400, Alexandria, VA 22314. Phone: (800) 772-0939 or (703) 838-5889. E-mail: aboutffa@ffa.org. Web: www.ffa.org.

SHERMAN, JAMES SCHOOLCRAFT: BIRTH ANNIVERSARY. Oct 24, 1855. The 27th vice president of the US (1909–12), born at Utica, NY. Died there Oct 30, 1912.

★ **UNITED NATIONS DAY.** Oct 24. Presidential Proclamation. Always issued for Oct 24 since 1948. (By unanimous request of the UN General Assembly.)

UNITED NATIONS DAY: ANNIVERSARY OF FOUNDING. Oct 24, 1945. Official United Nations holiday commemorates founding of the United Nations and effective date of the United Nations Charter. In 1971 the General Assembly recommended this day be observed as a public holiday by UN Member States

(Res 2782/xxvi). For more info, visit the UN's website for children at www.un.org/Pubs/CyberSchoolBus/.

UNITED NATIONS: DISARMAMENT WEEK. Oct 24–30. In 1978, the General Assembly called on member states to highlight the danger of the arms race, propogate the need for its cessation and increase public understanding of the urgent task of disarmament. Observed annually, beginning on the anniversary of the founding of the UN.

UNITED NATIONS: WORLD DEVELOPMENT INFORMATION DAY. Oct 24. Anniversary of adoption by United Nations General Assembly, in 1970, of the International Development Strategy for the Second United Nations Development Decade. Object is to "draw the attention of the world public opinion each year to development problems and the necessity of strengthening international cooperation to solve them." For info: United Nations, Dept of Public Info, New York, NY 10017.

BIRTHDAYS TODAY

Kweisi Mfume, 53, NAACP president, born Baltimore, MD, Oct 24, 1948.
Monica, 21, singer, born Monica Arnold, Atlanta, GA, Oct 24, 1980.
Catherine Sutherland, 27, actress (*Turbo: A Power Rangers Movie*, "Power Rangers Turbo"), born Sydney, Australia, Oct 24, 1974.

OCTOBER 25 — THURSDAY

Day 298 — 67 Remaining

HONG KONG: CHUNG YEUNG FESTIVAL. Oct 25. This festival relates to the old story of the Han Dynasty, when a soothsayer advised a man to take his family to a high place on the ninth day of the ninth moon for 24 hours in order to avoid disaster. The man obeyed and found, on returning home, that all living things had died a sudden death in his absence. Part of the celebration is climbing to high places.

KAZAKHSTAN: INDEPENDENCE DAY. Oct 25. National holiday. Commemorates 1991 declaration of independence from the USSR.

PICASSO, PABLO RUIZ: BIRTH ANNIVERSARY. Oct 25, 1881. Called by many the greatest artist of the 20th century, Pablo Picasso excelled as a painter, sculptor and engraver. He is said to have commented once: "I am only a public entertainer who has understood his time." Born at Malaga, Spain, he died Apr 9, 1973, at Mougins, France. For more info: *Picasso*, by Stefano Loria (Peter Bedrick, 0-87226-318-5, $22.50 Gr. 4–7).

STATE CONSTITUTION DAY IN MASSACHUSETTS. Oct 25. Proclaimed annually by the governor to commemorate the adoption of the state constitution in 1780.

TAIWAN: RETROCESSION DAY. Oct 25. Commemorates restoration of Taiwan to Chinese rule in 1945, after half a century of Japanese occupation.

BIRTHDAYS TODAY

Brad Gilchrist, 42, cartoonist ("Nancy"), works with his brother Guy Gilchrist, born Torrington, CT, Oct 25, 1959.
Benjamin Gould, 21, actor ("Saved by the Bell: The New Class"), born Sacramento, CA, Oct 25, 1980.
Fred Marcellino, 62, illustrator, author (*I, Crocodile; The Story of Little Babaji; A Rat's Tale*), born New York, NY, Oct 25, 1939.
Pedro Martinez, 30, baseball player, born Manoguyabo, Dominican Republic, Oct 25, 1971.
Midori, 30, violinist, born Osaka, Japan, Oct 25, 1971.

OCTOBER 26 — FRIDAY

Day 299 — 66 Remaining

AUSTRIA: NATIONAL DAY. Oct 26. Also called Flag Day. Commemorates the withdrawal of Soviet troops in 1955.

ERIE CANAL: ANNIVERSARY. Oct 26, 1825. The Erie Canal, first US major man-made waterway, was opened, providing a water route from Lake Erie to the Hudson River. Construction started July 4, 1817, and the canal cost $7,602,000. Cannons fired and celebrations were held all along the route for the opening. For more info: *The Amazing, Impossible Erie Canal*, by Cheryl Harness (S&S, 0-02-742641-6, $16 Gr. 3–8) or the New York State Canal System's website at www.canals.state.ny.us/.

MULE DAY. Oct 26. Anniversary of the first importation of Spanish jacks to the US, a gift from King Charles III of Spain. Mules are said to have been bred first in this country by George Washington from a pair delivered at Boston, Oct 26, 1785.

BIRTHDAYS TODAY

Hillary Rodham Clinton, 54, US Senator (D, New York), former First Lady, born Park Ridge, IL, Oct 26, 1947.
Steven Kellogg, 60, author and illustrator (*Can I Keep Him?, Chicken Little*), born Norwalk, CT, Oct 26, 1941.
Natalie Merchant, 38, singer, born Jamestown, NY, Oct 26, 1963.
Eric Rohmann, 44, author and illustrator (*Time Flies, The Cinder-Eyed Cats*), born Riverside, IL, Oct 26, 1957.

OCTOBER 27 — SATURDAY

Day 300 — 65 Remaining

BAGNOLD, ENID: BIRTH ANNIVERSARY. Oct 27, 1889. Novelist and playwright (*National Velvet*), born at Rochester, Kent, England. She died at London, England, Mar 31, 1981.

CHILDREN'S LITERATURE FESTIVAL. Oct 27. Keene State College, Keene, NH. Twenty-fifth anniversary in 2001. To promote the reading, studying and use of children's literature. Speakers for the festival include Tomie dePaola, Trina Schart Hyman, Jane Yolen, Patricia and Fredrick McKissack, Patricia MacLachlan, and David Shannon. For info: Dr. David E. White, Festival Dir, Keene State College, 229 Main St, Keene, NH 03435. Phone: (603) 358-2302. E-mail: dwhite@keene.edu. Web: www.keene.edu/clf/clfnews.htm.

COOK, JAMES: BIRTH ANNIVERSARY. Oct 27, 1728. English sea captain and explorer who discovered the Hawaiian Islands and brought Australia and New Zealand into the British Empire. The US space shuttle *Endeavour* is named after his ship. Born at Marton-in-Cleveland, Yorkshire, England and was killed Feb 14, 1779, at Hawaii.

HURRICANE MITCH: ANNIVERSARY. Oct 27, 1998. More than 6,000 people were killed in Honduras by flooding caused by Hurricane Mitch. Several thousand more were killed in other Central American countries, especially Nicaragua. On Sept 21, 1974, more than 8,000 people had been killed in Honduras by flooding caused by a hurricane. For info about hurricanes: www.fema.gov/kids/hurr.htm.

MAKE A DIFFERENCE DAY. Oct 27. This national day of community service is sponsored by *USA WEEKEND* (a Sunday magazine delivered in more than 500 newspapers). Volunteer projects completed are judged by well-known celebrities. More than $2.5 million in donations are awarded to charity. Key projects are honored in April during National Volunteer Week at a special Make A Difference Day awards luncheon and at the White House. The Points of Light Foundation is a partner. Nearly two million people nationwide participate. For info: Make a Difference Day, *USA WEEKEND*, 1000 Wilson Blvd, Arlington, VA 22229-0012. Phone: (800) 416-3824. Web: www.makeadifferenceday.com.

NAVY DAY. Oct 27. Observed since 1922.

NEW YORK CITY SUBWAY: ANNIVERSARY. Oct 27, 1904. Running from City Hall to West 145th Street, the New York City subway began operation. It was privately operated by the Interborough Rapid Transit Company and later became part of the system operated by the New York City Transit Authority.

ROOSEVELT, THEODORE: BIRTH ANNIVERSARY. Oct 27, 1858. The 26th president of the US, succeeded to the presidency on the assassination of William McKinley. He was the youngest man to have ever served as president of the US. His term of office: Sept 14, 1901–Mar 3, 1909. Roosevelt was the first president to ride in an automobile (1902), to submerge in a submarine (1905) and to fly in an airplane (1910). Although his best remembered quote is, "Speak softly and carry a big stick," he also said, "The first requisite of a good citizen in this Republic of ours is that he shall be able and willing to pull his weight." Born at New York, NY, Roosevelt died at Oyster Bay, NY, Jan 6, 1919. For more info: *Bully for You, Teddy Roosevelt!*, by Jean Fritz (Putnam, 0-399-21769-X, $15.99 Gr. 7–9) and *Young Teddy Roosevelt*, by Cheryl Harness (National Geographic, 0-7922-7094-0, $17.95 Gr. 2–5) or www.ipl.org/ref/POTUS.

SAINT VINCENT AND THE GRENADINES: INDEPENDENCE DAY. Oct 27. National Day.

TURKMENISTAN: INDEPENDENCE DAY: 10th ANNIVERSARY. Oct 27. National holiday. Commemorates independence from the Soviet Union in 1991.

VIRGINIA CHILDREN'S FESTIVAL. Oct 27. Town Point Park, Norfolk, VA. An all-day family program hosted by nationally famous children's entertainers, costumed characters and five stages of entertainment. Also, magic, giant puppets, creative dance and many other activities for a day of fantasy and fun. Est attendance: 45,000. For info: Norfolk Festevents, Ltd, 120 W Main St, Norfolk, VA 23510. Phone: (757) 441-2345. Fax: (757) 441-5198. Web: www.festeventsva.org.

"WALT DISNEY" TV PREMIERE: ANNIVERSARY. Oct 27, 1954. This highly successful and long-running show appeared on different networks under different names but was essentially the same show. It was the first ABC series to break the Nielsen Top Twenty and the first prime-time anthology series for kids. "Walt Disney" was originally titled "Disneyland" to promote the park and upcoming Disney releases. Later the title was changed to "Walt Disney Presents." When it switched networks, it was called "Walt Disney's Wonderful World of Color" to highlight its being broadcast in color. Future titles included "The Wonderful World of Disney," "Disney's Wonderful World," "The Disney Sunday Movie" and "The Magical World of Disney." Presentations included edited versions of previously released Disney films and original productions (including natural history documentaries, behind-the-scenes at Disney shows and dramatic shows, including the popular Davy Crockett segments that were the first TV miniseries). The show went off the air in December 1980 after 25 years, making it the longest-running series in prime-time TV history.

October 2001

S	M	T	W	T	F	S
	1	2	3	4	5	6
7	8	9	10	11	12	13
14	15	16	17	18	19	20
21	22	23	24	25	26	27
28	29	30	31			

BIRTHDAYS TODAY

Brad Radke, 29, baseball player, born Eau Claire, WI, Oct 27, 1972.

OCTOBER 28 — SUNDAY

Day 301 — 64 Remaining

CZECH REPUBLIC: FOUNDATION OF THE REPUBLIC. Oct 28, 1918. National Day, anniversary of the bloodless revolution in Prague, after which the Czechs and Slovaks united to form Czechoslovakia (a union they dissolved without bloodshed in 1993).

CZECH REPUBLIC: INDEPENDENCE DAY. Oct 28. National holiday. Commemorates independence from the Austro-Hungarian Empire in 1918.

DAYLIGHT SAVING TIME ENDS; STANDARD TIME RESUMES. Oct 28–Apr 7, 2002. Standard Time resumes at 2 AM on the last Sunday in October in each time zone, as provided by the Uniform Time Act of 1966 (as amended in 1986 by Public Law 99–359). Many use the popular rule: "spring forward, fall back" to remember which way to turn their clocks.

GREECE: "OCHI DAY." Oct 28. National holiday commemorating Greek resistance and refusal to open her borders when Mussolini's Italian troops attacked Greece in 1940. "Ochi" means no! Celebrated with military parades, especially at Athens and Thessaloniki.

SAINT JUDE'S DAY. Oct 28. St. Jude, the saint of hopeless causes, was martyred along with St. Simon at Persia, and their feast is celebrated jointly. St. Jude was supposedly the brother of Jesus, and, like his brother, a carpenter by trade. He is most popular with those who attempt the impossible and with students, who often ask for his help on exams.

SALK, JONAS: BIRTH ANNIVERSARY. Oct 28, 1914. Dr. Jonas Salk, developer of the Salk polio vaccine, was born at New York, NY. Salk announced his development of a successful vaccine in 1953, the year after a polio epidemic claimed some 3,300 lives in the US. Polio deaths were reduced by 95 percent after the introduction of the vaccine. Salk spent the last 10 years of his life doing AIDS research. He died June 23, 1995, at La Jolla, CA.

SPACE MILESTONE: INTERNATIONAL SPACE RESCUE AGREEMENT: ANNIVERSARY. Oct 28, 1970. US and USSR officials agreed upon space rescue cooperation.

STATUE OF LIBERTY: DEDICATION ANNIVERSARY. Oct 28, 1886. Frederic Auguste Bartholdi's famous sculpture, the statue of *Liberty Enlightening the World*, on Bedloe's Island at New York Harbor, was dedicated. Ground breaking for the structure was in April 1883. A sonnet by Emma Lazarus, inside the pedestal of the statue, contains the words: "Give me your tired, your poor, your huddled masses yearning to breathe free, the wretched refuse of your teeming shore. Send these, the homeless, tempest-tost to me, I lift my lamp beside the golden door!" For more info: *Liberty*, by Lynn Curlee (Atheneum, 0-68-982823-3, $18 Gr. 2–7) or visit the National Parks Service website at www.nps.gov/stli/index.htm. The Sept 2001 issue of *Appleseeds* magazine (for grades 2–4) is devoted to the Statue of Liberty.

BIRTHDAYS TODAY

Carolyn Coman, 50, author (*What Jamie Saw, Many Stones*), born Evanston, IL, Oct 28, 1951.

Terrell Davis, 29, football player, born San Diego, CA, Oct 28, 1972.

Bill Gates, 46, computer software executive (Microsoft), born Seattle, WA, Oct 28, 1955.

OCTOBER 29 — MONDAY

Day 302 — 63 Remaining

EMMETT, DANIEL DECATUR: BIRTH ANNIVERSARY. Oct 29, 1815. Creator of words and music for the song "Dixie," which became a fighting song for Confederate troops and the unofficial "national anthem" of the South. Emmett was born at Mount Vernon, OH, and died there June 28, 1904.

INTERNET CREATED: ANNIVERSARY. Oct 29, 1969. The first connection on what would become the Internet was made on this day when bits of data flowed between computers at UCLA and the Stanford Research Institute. This was the beginning of Arpanet, the precurser to the Internet developed by the Department of Defense. By the end of 1969, four sites were connected: UCLA, the Stanford Research Institute, the University of California, Santa Barbara and the University of Utah. By the next year there were 10 sites and soon there were applications like e-mail and file transfer utilities. The @ symbol was adopted in 1972 and a year later 75 percent of Arpanet traffic was e-mail. Arpanet was decommissioned in 1990 and the National Science Foundation's NSFnet took over the role of backbone of the Internet.

RALEIGH, SIR WALTER: DEATH ANNIVERSARY. Oct 29, 1618. Soldier, colonizer and writer born about 1552 at Hayes Barton, South Devon, England. After 1581 he spelled his name Ralegh. A favorite of Queen Elizabeth I, he sent colonists to North Carolina who brought back tobacco and the potato, which he popularized in Britain. In 1595 and 1617, he went to South America and gathered stories about gold mines. He fell out of favor with Elizabeth's successor, James I, and was beheaded in 1618. For info: *Sir Walter Ralegh and the Quest for El Dorado*, by Marc Aronson (Houghton, 0-395-84827-X, $20 Gr. 7 & up).

SPACE MILESTONE: *DISCOVERY* (US): OLDEST MAN IN SPACE. Oct 29, 1998. Former astronaut and senator John Glenn became the oldest man in space when he traveled on the shuttle *Discovery* at the age of 77. In 1962 on *Friendship 7* he had been the first American to orbit Earth. See "Space Milestone: *Friendship 7*" (Feb 20). For more info: *John Glenn's Return to Space*, by Greg Vogt (Twenty-First Century, 0-7613-1614-0, $22.90 Gr. 4–7).

STOCK MARKET CRASH: ANNIVERSARY. Oct 29, 1929. Prices on the New York Stock Exchange plummeted and virtually collapsed four days after President Herbert Hoover had declared,

OCTOBER 29
FABULOUS, FRIGHTENING FANGS

"I vant to suck your blood" is the classic vampire line. Of course, there aren't any human vampires. The truth about vampire animals is: they don't suck out blood. (They also don't kill their victims.) The vampire bat uses its fangs to nip a small piece of flesh from its victim. Then it uses its tongue. The vampire bat has an unusual tongue with grooves along its sides and on the bottom. When the bat sticks its tongue into the victim's wound, blood runs into the grooves. Capillary action pulls it upward into the bat's mouth. By this point, you may be saying "Yuck, that's disgusting!" So will children—but they'll be paying really close attention and wanting to hear more. As Halloween approaches, introduce Focusing on Frightening Fangs as a theme.

Many animals have sharp fangs which are great for grabbing and stabbing prey. Fangs may be defensive weapons to use against predators. Animals have different types of fangs. Divide students into pairs or small groups. In their group, students can brainstorm reasons why fangs may have evolved. If students go to the learning center, ask them to see what information they can find about fangs in general. For example, some fangs are used to inject venom. Others are used for ripping or shredding flesh. This is a good time to introduce specific tooth names such as incisors and canines.

Create four larger student groups named Fish, Mammals, Reptiles and the Ancient Ones. Before researching, children should list animals with frightening fangs that belong in their group. Suggestions include:

Fish: Sharks, viperfish and other deep-sea fishes, barracudas and piranhas.

Mammals: lions, tigers, bears and shrews (they have venom glands).

Reptiles: Mambas, rattlesnakes, alligators, crocodiles and Gila monsters (venom, again).

Ancient Ones: Carnivorous dinosaurs, saber-toothed tigers and other fossil finds.

Prior to any research, ask the students to list what information they know about each animal. Then, let the groups go on a Fun Fang Fact-Finding Foray. After they collect information, ask each group to create a myth vs. reality fact sheet about one (or more) of their animals. Students who enjoy art projects can supply drawings, paintings and/or collages of their group's animals. Close-ups featuring what the fangs look like will give the room an appropriately scary atmosphere. Perhaps they would want to make masks featuring certain animals. If you speak with the learning center director in advance, you may be able to arrange for all the books located in one research period to be checked out as a group loan to your classroom. That way the books could be used as classroom decoration and free-time browsing stops during the length of the focus on fangs.

Some books that will interest students are: *Bats*, by Gail Gibbons (Holiday House, 0-8234-1457-4, $16.95 Gr. K–3); *Bats!: Strange and Wonderful*, by Laurence Pringle (Boyds Mills, 1-56397-327-8, $15.95 Gr. 1–3); *All About Rattlesnakes*, by Jim Arnosky (Scholastic, 0-590-46794-8, $15.95 Gr. 2–6); *Shark Attack!*, by Cathy East Dubowski (Dorling Kindersley, 0-7894-3440-7, $3.95 Gr. 1–3); *Outside and Inside Alligators*, by Sandra Markle (Atheneum, 0-689-81457-7, $16 Gr. 3 & up); *Vampire Bats*, by Laurence Pringle (Out of print, but available in libraries, Gr. 5 & up); *Ferocious Fangs*, by Sally Fleming (NorthWord Press, 1-55971-587-1, $7.95 Gr. 2 & up).

The fundamental business of the country . . . is on a sound and prosperous basis." More than 16 million shares were dumped and billions of dollars were lost. The boom was over and the nation faced nearly a decade of depression. Some analysts had warned that the buying spree, with prices 15 to 150 times above earnings, had to stop at some point. Frightened investors ordered their brokers to sell at whatever price. The resulting Great Depression, which lasted till about 1939, involved North America, Europe and other industrialized countries. In 1932 one out of four US workers was unemployed.

TURKEY: REPUBLIC DAY. Oct 29. Anniversary of the founding of the republic in 1923.

BIRTHDAYS TODAY

Rhonda Gowler Greene, 46, author (*Barnyard Song*), born Salem, IL, Oct 29, 1955.

Dirk Kempthorne, 50, Governor of Idaho (R), born San Diego, CA, Oct 29, 1951.

OCTOBER 30 — TUESDAY

Day 303 — 62 Remaining

ADAMS, JOHN: BIRTH ANNIVERSARY. Oct 30, 1735. First vice-president and second president of the US (Mar 4, 1797–Mar 3, 1801), born at Braintree, MA. Adams had been George Washington's vice president. He once wrote in a letter to Thomas Jefferson: "You and I ought not to die before we have explained ourselves to each other." John Adams and Thomas Jefferson died on the same day, July 4, 1826, the 50th anniversary of adoption of the Declaration of Independence. Adams's last words: "Thomas Jefferson still survives." Jefferson's last words: "Is it the fourth?" Adams was the father of John Quincy Adams (sixth president of the US). For info: www.ipl.org/ref/POTUS.

DEVIL'S NIGHT. Oct 30. Formerly a "Mischief Night" on the evening before Halloween and an occasion for harmless pranks, chiefly observed by children. However, in some areas of the US, the destruction of property and endangering of lives has led to the imposition of dusk-to-dawn curfews during the last two or three days of October. Not to be confused with "Trick or Treat" or "Beggar's Night," usually observed on Halloween. See also: "Hallowe'en" (Oct 31).

POST, EMILY: BIRTH ANNIVERSARY. Oct 30, 1872. Emily Post was born at Baltimore, MD. Published in 1922, her book *Etiquette: The Blue Book of Social Usage* instantly became the American bible of manners and social behavior and established Post as the household name in matters of etiquette. It was in its 10th edition at the time of her death Sept 25, 1960, at New York, NY. *Etiquette* inspired a great many letters asking Post for advice on manners in specific situations. She used these letters as the basis for her radio show and for her syndicated newspaper column, which eventually appeared in more than 200 papers.

BIRTHDAYS TODAY

Eric A. Kimmel, 55, author (*Hershel and the Hanukkah Goblins, Anansi and the Talking Melon*), born Brooklyn, NY, Oct 30, 1946.

October 2001

S	M	T	W	T	F	S
	1	2	3	4	5	6
7	8	9	10	11	12	13
14	15	16	17	18	19	20
21	22	23	24	25	26	27
28	29	30	31			

Diego Maradona, 41, former soccer player, born Lanus, Argentina, Oct 30, 1960.

Henry Winkler, 56, producer, actor ("The Fonz" on "Happy Days"), born New York, NY, Oct 30, 1945.

OCTOBER 31 — WEDNESDAY

Day 304 — 61 Remaining

FIRST BLACK PLAYS IN NBA GAME: ANNIVERSARY. Oct 31, 1950. Earl Lloyd became the first black ever to play in an NBA game when he took the floor for the Washington Capitols at Rochester, NY. Lloyd was actually one of three blacks to become NBA players in the 1950 season, the others being Nat "Sweetwater" Clifton, who was signed by the New York Knicks, and Chuck Cooper, who was drafted by the Boston Celtics (and debuted the night after Lloyd).

HALLOWE'EN or ALL HALLOW'S EVE. Oct 31. An ancient celebration combining Druid autumn festival and Christian customs. Hallowe'en (All Hallow's Eve) is the beginning of Hallowtide, a season that embraces the Feast of All Saints (Nov 1) and the Feast of All Souls (Nov 2). The observance, dating from the sixth or seventh centuries, has long been associated with thoughts of the dead, spirits, witches, ghosts and devils. In fact, the ancient Celtic Feast of Samhain, the festival that marked the beginning of winter and of the New Year, was observed Nov 1. See also: "Trick or Treat or Beggar's Night" (Oct 31). For more info: *Halloween Program Sourcebook*, edited by Sue Ellen Thompson (Omnigraphics, 0-7808-0388-4, $48 All ages). For links to sites about Halloween on the web go to: deil.lang.uiuc.edu/web.pages/holidays/halloween.html.

LOW, JULIET GORDON: BIRTH ANNIVERSARY. Oct 31, 1860. Founded Girl Scouts of the USA Mar 12, 1912, at Savannah, GA. Born at Savannah, she died there Jan 17, 1927.

MOUNT RUSHMORE COMPLETION: 60th ANNIVERSARY. Oct 31, 1941. The Mount Rushmore National Memorial was completed after 14 years of work. First suggested by Jonah Robinson of the South Dakota State Historical Society, the memorial was dedicated in 1925, and work began in 1927. The memorial contains sculptures of the heads of Presidents George Washington, Thomas Jefferson, Abraham Lincoln and Theodore Roosevelt. The 60-foot-tall sculptures represent, respectively, the nation's founding, political philosophy, preservation, expansion and conservation. For more info: www.nps.gov/moru.

NATIONAL MAGIC DAY. Oct 31. Traditionally observed on the anniversary of the death of Harry Houdini in 1926.

★ **NATIONAL UNICEF DAY.** Oct 31. Presidential Proclamation 3817, of Oct 27, 1967, covers all succeeding years. Annually, Oct 31. For more info: www.unicef.org.

NEVADA: ADMISSION DAY: ANNIVERSARY. Oct 31. Became 36th state in 1864. Observed as a holiday in Nevada.

PACA, WILLIAM: BIRTH ANNIVERSARY. Oct 31, 1740. Signer of the Declaration of Independence. Born at Abingdon, MD, he died Oct 13, 1799, at Talbot County, MD.

REFORMATION DAY: ANNIVERSARY. Oct 31, 1517. Anniversary of the day on which Martin Luther nailed his 95 theses to the door of Wittenberg's Palace church, denouncing the selling of papal indulgences—the beginning of the Reformation in Germany. Observed by many Protestant churches as Reformation Sunday, on this day if it is a Sunday or on the Sunday before Oct 31 (Oct 28 in 2001).

TAIWAN: CHIANG KAI-SHEK DAY. Oct 31. National holiday to honor memory of Generalissimo Chiang Kai-Shek, the first constitutional president of the Republic of China, born on this day in 1887.

TAYLOR, SYDNEY: BIRTH ANNIVERSARY. Oct 31, 1904. Author (*All-of-a-Kind Family*), born at New York, NY. Died Feb 12, 1978.

TRICK OR TREAT or BEGGAR'S NIGHT. Oct 31. A popular custom on Hallowe'en, in which children wearing costumes visit neighbors' homes, calling out "Trick or Treat" and "begging" for candies or gifts to place in their beggars' bags. Some children Trick or Treat for UNICEF, collecting money for this organization. For more info, go to www.unicef.org. In recent years there has been increased participation by adults, often parading in elaborate or outrageous costumes and also requesting candy.

BIRTHDAYS TODAY

Katherine Paterson, 69, author (Newbery for *The Bridge to Terabithia, Jacob Have I Loved*), born Qing Jiang, China, Oct 31, 1932.

Jane Pauley, 51, TV journalist ("Dateline"), born Indianapolis, IN, Oct 31, 1950.

Dan Rather, 70, journalist (coanchor "CBS Evening News"), born Wharton, TX, Oct 31, 1931.

Adrienne Richard, 80, author (*Pistol*), born Evanston, IL, Oct 31, 1921.

NOVEMBER 1 — THURSDAY

Day 305 — 60 Remaining

ALGERIA: REVOLUTION ANNIVERSARY. Nov 1. National holiday commemorating the revolution against France in 1954.

ALL HALLOWS or ALL SAINTS' DAY. Nov 1. Roman Catholic Holy Day of Obligation. Commemorates the blessed, especially those who have no special feast days. Observed Nov 1 since Pope Gregory IV set the date of recognition in 835. All Saints' Day is a legal holiday in Louisiana. Halloween is the evening before All Hallows Day.

ANTIGUA AND BARBUDA: NATIONAL HOLIDAY: 20th ANNIVERSARY. Nov 1. Commemorates independence from Britain in 1981.

AVIATION HISTORY MONTH. Nov 1–30. Anniversary of aeronautical experiments in November 1782 (exact dates unknown), by Joseph Michel Montgolfier and Jacques Etienne Montgolfier, brothers living at Annonay, France. Inspired by Joseph Priestley's book *Experiments Relating to the Different Kinds of Air*, the brothers experimented with filling paper and fabric bags with smoke and hot air, leading to the invention of the hot-air balloon, man's first flight and the entire science of aviation and flight.

DAVID McCORD CHILDREN'S LITERATURE FESTIVAL. Nov 1. Framingham State College, Framingham, MA. For info: Joan Claflin, 121 Mechanic St, Upton, MA 01568. Phone: (508) 529-3367.

GUATEMALA: KITE FESTIVAL OF SANTIAGO SACATEPEQUEZ. Nov 1. Long ago, when evil spirits disturbed the good spirits in the local cemetery, a magician told the townspeople a secret way to get rid of the evil spirits—by flying kites (because the evil spirits were frightened by the noise of wind against paper). Since then, the kite festival has been held at the cemetery each year Nov 1 or Nov 2, and it is said that "to this day no one knows of bad spirits roaming the streets or the cemetery of Santiago Sacatepequez," a village about 20 miles from Guatemala City. Nowadays, the youth of the village work for many weeks to make the elaborate and giant kites to fly on All Saints' Day (Nov 1) or All Souls' Day (Nov 2).

November 2001

S	M	T	W	T	F	S
				1	2	3
4	5	6	7	8	9	10
11	12	13	14	15	16	17
18	19	20	21	22	23	24
25	26	27	28	29	30	

NOVEMBER 1–30
NATIONAL AMERICAN INDIAN HERITAGE MONTH

By Presidential Proclamation, November has been declared National American Indian Heritage Month. Each day, feature an American Indian who has figured prominently in history. Or, you might want to choose a specific aspect of Indian culture. One way to grab children's attention and create a sense of anticipation is by making a "Fact of the Day" box.

Use a cardboard box the size of those used to package reams of copier paper. Duct tape the lid to the box. Cut a hole about five inches by five inches in the top. Paint the outside of the box and decorate it with art motifs found in American Indian cultures; for example, patterns used to decorate Pueblo Indian pottery. See *Children of Clay*, by Rina Swentzell (Lerner, 0-8225-9627-X, $6.95 Gr. 3–7).

On 20 to 30 blank index cards (or comparable size poster board) write several sentences that tell an American Indian fact. You might describe famous Indians leaders such as Sitting Bull, Cochise, Geronimo, and Wilma Mankiller (see entry under November 18). One card could feature the anniversary of the Little Bighorn, which is on November 25. Some cards could include information about writers whose heritage is American Indian. Joseph Bruchac, Michael Dorris, Gayle Ross and Louise Erdrich have written many books for young readers. Include and booktalk a title for each author. Don't forget sports figures such as Jim Thorpe. There are several famous monuments dedicated to Indians as well. The monument to Crazy Horse is one of them.

Glue or tape a heavy metal washer or several large paper clips to the back of each card. Put all the cards into the decorated box. Get a stick about 12 inches long—dowel rods come in many diameters and are cheap. Tie a string about 18 inches long to one end of the stick and a magnet to the other end to create a fact-finding fishing rod.

Set aside a few minutes at the beginning of each day for thinking about the heritage of American Indians and their contributions to the history of the United States. Let each student have a turn to fish through the hole for an index card. After the student reads the card aloud, post it on the board for the day and let students read it as the opportunity presents itself. The fun of fishing makes everyone look forward to his or her turn. (You may have to do two facts on certain days in order for everyone to have a turn.) The mystery of what interesting fact will come next heightens student interest and anticipation.

New literature to connect with this month's theme includes: *Crazy Horse's Vision*, by Joseph Bruchac (Publisher's Group West, 1-88-000094-6, $16.95 Gr. 1–4); *Indian School*, by Michael Cooper (Clarion, 0-395-92084-1, $15 Gr. 5 & up); *The Long March*, by Mary Louise Fitzpatrick (Tricycle Press, 1-8836-7291-0, $14.95 Gr. 2–5); *Sitting Bull and His World*, by Albert Marrin (Knopf, 0-525-45944-8, $27.50 Gr. 7 & up); *An Algonquian Year*, by Michael McCurdy (Houghton Mifflin, 0-618-00705-9, $15 Gr. 2–4); and *A Braid of Lives*, edited by Neil Philip (Clarion, 0-395-64528-X, $20 Gr. 6 & up). Websites with information about today's Native Americans include www.indiancountry.com and www.indians.org. For a history of Indians in the United States military, go to history.navy.mil/faqs/faq61-1.html.

NOVEMBER 1–30
INTERNATIONAL DRUM MONTH

Most people respond to the beat of drums. Their rhythmic patterns seem to reach deep inside listeners and connect in an elemental way. It's almost impossible to avoid tapping a finger or toes or nodding one's head in response to a drum. There are many different forms of international drums. During International Drum Month, you might wish to focus on different regions and the styles and drums found there.

One of the catchy new trends is a growing admiration for steel drum bands. Steel pans originated in Trinidad in the years after World War II. The pans, which range from short-sided, higher-pitched lead pans to deep bass pans, are made from empty oil drums left behind in Trinidad at the war's end. People created notes by hammering indentations in the flat portion of the can. Traditional songs reflect the Caribbean heritage; however, a growing number of bands are exploring the diversity and new sound that steel pans bring to classical pieces and modern compositions. Liam Teague is an outstanding pan player. Teague, a soft-spoken, highly talented young musician from Trinidad, has taken the concert stage by storm and is bringing worldwide attention to the versatility and fun of this unique drum. You can visit his website at liamsteelpan.homestead.com. His CDs *Hands Like Lightning* and *Emotions of Steel* are truly inspired.

Japanese taiko drums are huge and deeply resonant. They require enormous energy to play and it's very exciting to watch a group of musicians perform taiko compositions. Two excellent websites are: Tqjunior.thinkquest.org/5997/ and www.Taikodojo.org/play-taiko.html. The first site is geared specifically to children and has a lot of information about the drums' history and playing. Photos feature young players. The second site is sponsored by San Francisco Taiko Dojo, the only US taiko company. The videos and sound samples of each type of taiko drum will captivate students. CDs of San Francisco Taiko Dojo music are available. A fun literature connection is the picture book *The Drums of Noto Hanto*, by J. Alison James (Dorling Kindersley, 0-7894-2574-2, $16.95 All ages.).

Hand drums are found in many cultures. Latin American music often features bongos and congas. Tabla are pot-shaped Indian hand drums, played while sitting cross-legged on the floor. Ireland's bodhran, often accompanied by a fiddle, is played with the hands or with a short beater stick. Drums are important in African culture. Babatunde Olatunji's CD, *Drums of Passion*, is a good example of African drumming.

Timpani, the kettledrums used in orchestras, are tunable drums capable of low murmurs or thunderous rumblings.

You can also connect Drum Month with poetry. Both require an underlying rhythmic pattern, so they complement each other well. Older students might try writing short poems that reflect specific drum rhythms.

If you have a percussion student in your class, she or he might be willing to conduct a short drum lesson. Wooden chopsticks or unsharpened pencils make adequate substitute drumsticks for a whole class participation in drumming rudiments and rolls.

Also, students might enjoy discovering the joys of tap dancing, which is actually foot drumming of a sort. Savion Glover is a hot young performer who is dazzling kids with his footwork and his focus and commitment to excellence. *Savion! My Life in Tap*, by Savion Glover and Bruce Weber (Morrow, 0-688-15329-0, $19.95 Gr. 5 & up), is for all those pencil tappers in your room. The rhythms in this book, spelled out in large, colorful letters, are fun to chant aloud.

HOCKEY MASK INVENTED: ANNIVERSARY. Nov 1, 1959. Tired of stopping hockey pucks with his face, Montreal Canadiens goalie Jacques Plante, having received another wound, reemerged from the locker room with seven new stitches—and a plastic face mask he had made from fiberglass and resin. Although Cliff Benedict had tried a leather mask back in the '20s, the idea didn't catch on but after Plante wore his, goalies throughout the NHL began wearing protective plastic face shields.

HUNTER'S MOON. Nov 1. The full moon following Harvest Moon. So called because the moon's light in the evening extends the day's length for hunters. Moon enters Full Moon phase at 12:41 AM, EST.

INTERNATIONAL DRUM MONTH. Nov 1–30. To celebrate the worldwide popularity of all types of drums. Annually, the month of November. For info: David Levine, Full Circle Management, Percussion Mktg Council, 12665 Kling St, Studio City, CA 91604. Phone: (818) 753-1310. Fax: (818) 753-1313. E-mail: drums360@earthlink.net. *See* Curriculum Connection.

LIBERIA: THANKSGIVING DAY. Nov 1. National holiday on the first Thursday in November.

MATHCOUNTS. Nov 1. Registration deadline for this national math coaching and competition program for 7th and 8th grade students. At the beginning of each year, the MATHCOUNTS Foundation distributes its free school handbook. Teachers and volunteers use these materials to coach "mathletes." Participating schools select four students to compete individually and as a team in written and oral competitions in one of more than 500 local meets in February. Winners progress to state contests in March. State winners go to the national finals in Washington, DC in May. Est attendance: 500,000. For info: MATHCOUNTS Foundation, 1420 King St, Alexandria, VA 22314. Phone: (703) 684-2828. E-mail: mathcounts@nspe.org. Web: www.mathcounts.org.

MEDICAL SCHOOL FOR WOMEN OPENED AT BOSTON: ANNIVERSARY. Nov 1, 1848. Founded by Samuel Gregory, a pioneer in medical education for women, the Boston Female Medical School opened as the first medical school exclusively for women. The original enrollment was 12 students. In 1874, the school merged with the Boston University School of Medicine and formed one of the first coed medical schools in the world.

MERLIN'S SNUG HUGS FOR KIDS. Nov 1–Dec 19. Nationwide. Each community is encouraged to provide new winter outerwear for foster and needy children. Event runs for six weeks, and includes Kids Helping Kids, scout participation and the Crochet and Knit-A-Thon, and on the final day (Dec 19), Merlin's caravan collects the new winter clothes and delivers them to Children's Home & Aid Society. Sponsor: Merlin's Muffler & Brake. Annually, the first week of November through the third week of December. For info: Kathleen Quinn, ProQuest/2020, PO Box 2373, Glenview, IL 60025-2373. Phone: (847) 998-9950. Fax: (847) 998-9945. E-mail: SHFK2000@aol.com. Web: www.merlins.com.

MEXICO: DAY OF THE DEAD. Nov 1–2. Observance begins during last days of October when "Dead Men's Bread" is sold in bakeries—round loaves, decorated with sugar skulls. Departed souls are remembered not with mourning but with a spirit of friendliness and good humor. Cemeteries are visited and graves are decorated.

MOON PHASE: FULL MOON. Nov 1. Moon enters Full Moon phase at 12:41 AM, EST.

★**NATIONAL ADOPTION MONTH.** Nov 1–30.

★**NATIONAL AMERICAN INDIAN HERITAGE MONTH.** Nov 1–30. *See* Curriculum Connection.

NATIONAL AUTHORS' DAY. Nov 1. This observance was adopted by the General Federation of Women's Clubs in 1929 and in 1949 was given a place on the list of special days, weeks and months prepared by the US Dept of Commerce. The resolution states: "by celebrating an Authors' Day as a nation, we would not only show patriotism, loyalty, and appreciation of the men and women who have made American literature possible, but would also encourage and inspire others to give of themselves in making a better America. . . ." It was also resolved "that we commemorate an Authors' Day to be observed on November First each year."

NATIONAL FAMILY LITERACY DAY®. Nov 1. Celebrated all over the country with special activities and events that showcase the importance of family literacy programs. Family literacy programs bring parents and children together in the classroom to learn and support each other in efforts to further their education and improve their life skills. Sponsored by the National Center for Family Literacy and Toyota. Annually, Nov 1. For info: Natl Center for Family Literacy, 325 W Main St, Ste 200, Louisville, KY 40202. Phone: (502) 584-1133. Fax: (502) 584-0172. E-mail: ncfl@famlit.org. Web: www.famlit.org.

NATIONAL HEALTHY SKIN MONTH. Nov 1–30. For info: American Academy of Dermatology, 930 N Meacham Rd., Schaumburg, IL 60173. Phone: (847) 330-0230 or 888-462-DERM. Web: www.aad.org.

NATIONAL MIDDLE SCHOOL ASSOCIATION ANNUAL CONFERENCE. Nov 1–3. Washington, DC. For info: Natl Middle School Assn, 2600 Corporate Exchange Dr, Ste 370, Columbus, OH 43231. Phone: (614) 895-4730 or (800) 528-NMSA. Web: www.nmsa.org.

PEANUT BUTTER LOVERS' MONTH. Nov 1–30. Celebration of America's favorite food and #1 sandwich. For info: Peanut Advisory Board, 50 Hurt Plaza, Ste 1220, Atlanta, GA 30303. Web: www.peanutbutterlovers.com.

PRESIDENT FIRST OCCUPIES THE WHITE HOUSE: ANNIVERSARY. Nov 1, 1800. The federal government had been located at Philadelphia from 1790 until 1800. On Nov 1, 1800, President John Adams and his family moved into the newly-completed White House at Washington, DC, the nation's new capital. To take a virtual tour of the White House, go to: www.whitehouse.gov.

PRIME MERIDIAN SET: ANNIVERSARY. Nov 1, 1884. Delegates from 25 nations met in October, 1884, at Washington, DC at the International Meridian Conference to set up time zones for the world. On this day the treaty adopted by the Conference took effect, making Greenwich, England the Prime Meridian (i.e., zero longitude) and setting the International Date Line at 180° longitude in the Pacific. Every 15° of longitude equals one hour and there are 24 meridians. While some countries do not strictly observe this system (for example, while China stretches over five time zones, it is the same time everywhere in China), it has brought predictability and logic to time throughout the world.

US VIRGIN ISLANDS: LIBERTY DAY. Nov 1. Officially "D. Hamilton Jackson Memorial Day," commemorating establishment of the first press in the Virgin Islands in 1915.

November 2001

S	M	T	W	T	F	S
				1	2	3
4	5	6	7	8	9	10
11	12	13	14	15	16	17
18	19	20	21	22	23	24
25	26	27	28	29	30	

WORLD COMMUNICATION WEEK. Nov 1–7. To stress the importance of communication among the more than five billion human beings in the world who speak more than 3,000 languages and to promote communication by means of the international language Esperanto. For complete info, send $4 to cover expense of printing, handling and postage. Annually, the first seven days of November. For info: Dr. Stanley Drake, Pres, Intl Society of Friendship and Goodwill, 8592 Roswell Rd, Ste 434, Atlanta, GA 30350-1870.

BIRTHDAYS TODAY

Hilary Knight, 75, illustrator (Eloise series), born Hempstead, Long Island, NY, Nov 1, 1926.

Nicholasa Mohr, 63, author (*The Magic Shell/El Regalo Mágico, Nilda*), born New York, NY, Nov 1, 1938.

Fernando Anguamea Valenzuela, 41, former baseball player, born Navojoa, Sonora, Mexico, Nov 1, 1960.

NOVEMBER 2 — FRIDAY

Day 306 — 59 Remaining

ALL SOULS' DAY. Nov 2. Commemorates the faithful departed. Catholic observance.

BACKYARD NATIONAL CHILDREN'S FILM FESTIVAL. Nov 2–3 (tentative). Los Angeles, CA. A festival of films made by kids 9 to 18 years old. For info: Backyard Natl Children's Film Festival, Los Angeles, CA. Phone: (877) KID-FILM or (310) 476-5975. E-mail: info@backyardfilm.org. Web: childrensfilmfest.org.

BOONE, DANIEL: BIRTH ANNIVERSARY. Nov 2, 1734. American frontiersman, explorer and militia officer, born at Berks County, near Reading, PA. In February 1778, he was captured at Blue Licks, KY, by Shawnee Indians, under Chief Blackfish, who adopted Boone when he was inducted into the tribe as "Big Turtle." Boone escaped after five months, and in 1781 was captured briefly by the British. He experienced a series of personal and financial disasters during his life but continued a rugged existence, hunting until his 80s. Boone died at St. Charles County, MO, Sept 26, 1820. The bodies of Daniel Boone and his wife, Rebecca, were moved to Frankfort, KY, in 1845.

FIRST SCHEDULED RADIO BROADCAST: ANNIVERSARY. Nov 2, 1920. Station KDKA at Pittsburgh, PA broadcast the results of the presidential election. The station received its license to broadcast Nov 7, 1921. By 1922 there were about 400 licensed radio stations in the US.

HARDING, WARREN GAMALIEL: BIRTH ANNIVERSARY. Nov 2, 1865. The 29th president of the US was born at Corsica, OH. His term of office: Mar 4, 1921–Aug 2, 1923 (died in office). His undistinguished administration was tainted by the Teapot Dome scandal, and his sudden death while on a western speaking tour (San Francisco, CA, Aug 2, 1923) prompted many rumors. For info: www.ipl.org/ref/POTUS.

NOVEMBER 2
INTERNATIONAL SPACE STATION

The grand opening of the multinational space station was November 2, 2000. This installation, orbiting 230 miles above the Earth, is a permanent one that will be occupied by crew members from many different nations. It is being built in stages through the cooperation of 16 nations, and will be completed in 2006. William Shepherd is the station's first commander with a crew of Russian astronauts, Yuri Gidzenko and Sergei Krikalev. Their two-day flight took them to the space station for a three-month-long stay (November 2000 through February 2001), after which they will be replaced by other astronauts.

The space station is expected to serve as a study center for the next 15 years. Orbiting the Earth at about 17,500 miles per hour, the space station will become one of the most brightly visible objects in the night sky over time as more stages are added.

Suggest that students search the Internet for updates on the space station's construction and current crew members. The NASA site at spaceflight.nasa.gov/station should be a first stop. On newspaper websites, keyword search on "international space station." If possible, organize a star-watching night and see if you can spot the station. The Real Time Station Data section of NASA's Website has information on when the station can be best be seen from your location. *Sky & Telescope*, the astronomy magazine, also has information on its website to help find the station at www.skypub.com. Look at the Sights/Satellite Observing section. Newspapers and local planetariums should also have this information.

As a writing project, students could write what they think life on a space station would be like. You might wish to send letters to NASA, asking for information. Information from a "NOVA" TV special is available on the Web at www.pbs.org/spacestation. The Discovery Channel also has information on its site at www.discovery.com/schooladventures/spacestation/index.html.

In art, ask students to design their idea of a perfect space station. Compare them with the real thing. How are they similar and different? See "NASA Ames Space Settlement Contest" (March 31) for a space station design competition for students in grades 6–12.

Two books elementary students will find interesting are: *Floating in Space*, by Franklyn Branley (HarperCollins, 0-06-445142-9, $4.95 Gr. K–3), and *The International Space Station*, by Franklyn Branley (HarperCollins, 0-06-445209-3, $5.95, Gr. K–4). For danger and drama see *Space Station: Accident on Mir*, by Angela Royston (Dorling Kindersley, 0-7894-6686-4, $3.95 Gr. 2–4).

The International Space Station heralds a new era in space exploration. If you were excited by Neil Armstrong's small steps, don't miss out on the excitement happening now.

NORTH DAKOTA: ADMISSION DAY: ANNIVERSARY. Nov 2. Became 39th state in 1889.

POLK, JAMES KNOX: BIRTH ANNIVERSARY. Nov 2, 1795. The 11th president of the US (Mar 4, 1845–Mar 3, 1849) was born at Mecklenburg County, NC. A compromise candidate at the 1844 Democratic Party convention, Polk was awarded the nomination on the ninth ballot. He declined to be a candidate for a second term and declared himself to be "exceedingly relieved" at the completion of his presidency. He died shortly thereafter at Nashville, TN, June 15, 1849. For info: www.ipl.org/ref/POTUS.

SOUTH DAKOTA: ADMISSION DAY: ANNIVERSARY. Nov 2. Became 40th state in 1889.

SPACE MILESTONE: INTERNATIONAL SPACE STATION INHABITED. Nov 2, 2000. On Oct 31, 2000, a *Soyuz* shuttle left with the first crew to live in the International Space Station, American commander Bill Shepherd and two Russians, Yuri Gidzenko and Sergei Krikalev. The flight left from the same site in Central Asia where *Sputnik* was launched in 1957, beginning the Space Age. The astronauts were to stay on board the International Space Station (ISS) until February of 2001, when they would be replaced by a crew that arrived on the shuttle *Discovery*. The ISS has no formal name but has been nicknamed *Alpha* by its crew. It orbits the Earth every 90 minutes at an altitude of 230 miles. Sixteen nations are participating in the ISS project. The construction of the station will be complete in 2006. See also: "Space Milestones: International Space Station Launch" (Dec 4). *See* Curriculum Connection.

TEXAS BOOK FESTIVAL. Nov 2–4. Austin, TX. For info: Texas Book Festival, PO Box 13143, Austin, TX 78711. Phone: (512) 477-4055. Fax: (512) 322-0722. Web: www.austin360.com/entertainment/books/features/bookfest/

BIRTHDAYS TODAY

Jeannie Baker, 51, author and illustrator (*Where the Forest Meets the Sea*), born Nov 2, 1950.
Danny Cooksey, 26, actor ("Pepper Ann," *The Little Mermaid*), born Moore, OK, Nov 2, 1975.
Adam Luke Springfield, 19, actor ("Wishbone"), born Santa Barbara, CA, Nov 2, 1982.

NOVEMBER 3 — SATURDAY

Day 307 — 58 Remaining

AUSTIN, STEPHEN FULLER: BIRTH ANNIVERSARY. Nov 3, 1793. A principal founder of Texas, for whom its capital city was named, Austin was born at Wythe County, VA. He first visited Texas in 1821 and established a settlement there the following year, continuing a colonization project started by his father, Moses Austin. Thrown in prison when he advocated formation of a separate state (Texas still belonged to Mexico), he was freed in 1835, lost a campaign for the presidency (of the Republic of Texas) to Sam Houston in 1836, and died (while serving as Texas secretary of state) at Austin, TX, Dec 27, 1836.

DOMINICA: NATIONAL DAY. Nov 3. National holiday. Commemorates the independence of this Caribbean island from Britain on this day in 1978.

FESTIVAL OF BOOKS FOR YOUNG PEOPLE. Nov 3. Iowa Memorial Union, Iowa City, IA. Annual festival will feature talks by children's authors, booktalk sessions and exhibits of new books for young people. For info: School of Library and Information Science, Univ of Iowa, Iowa City, IA 52242-1420. Phone: (319) 335-5707. E-mail: ethel-bloesch@uiowa.edu.

JAPAN: CULTURE DAY. Nov 3. National holiday.

MICRONESIA: INDEPENDENCE DAY: 15th ANNIVERSARY. Nov 3. National holiday commemorating independence from the US in 1986.

PANAMA: INDEPENDENCE DAY. Nov 3. Panama declared itself independent of Colombia in 1903.

PUBLIC TELEVISION DEBUTS: ANNIVERSARY. Nov 3, 1969. A string of local educational TV channels united on this day under the Public Broadcasting System banner. Today there are 348 PBS stations.

SADIE HAWKINS DAY. Nov 3. Widely observed in US, usually on the first Saturday in November. Tradition established in "Li'l Abner" comic strip in 1930s by cartoonist Al Capp. A popular occasion when women and girls are encouraged to take the initiative in inviting the man or boy of their choice for a date. A similar tradition is associated with Feb 29 in leap years.

SANDWICH DAY: BIRTH ANNIVERSARY OF JOHN MONTAGUE. Nov 3, 1718. A day to recognize the inventor of the sandwich, John Montague, Fourth Earl of Sandwich, born at London, England. He was England's first lord of the admiralty, secretary of state for the northern department, postmaster general and the man after whom Captain Cook named the Sandwich Islands in 1778. A rake and a gambler, he is said to have invented the sandwich as a time-saving nourishment while engaged in a 24-hour-long gambling session in 1762. He died at London, England, Apr 30, 1792.

SPACE MILESTONE: *SPUTNIK 2* (USSR). Nov 3, 1957. A dog named Laika became the first animal sent into space. Total weight of craft and dog was 1,121 lbs. The satellite was not capable of returning the dog to Earth and she died when her air supply was gone. Nicknamed "Muttnik" by the American press.

SWEDEN: ALL SAINTS' DAY. Nov 3. Honors the memory of deceased friends and relatives. Annually, the Saturday following Oct 30.

WHITE, EDWARD DOUGLASS: BIRTH ANNIVERSARY. Nov 3, 1845. Ninth Chief Justice of the Supreme Court, born at La Fourche Parish, LA. During the Civil War, he served in the Confederate Army after which he returned to New Orleans to practice law. Elected to the US Senate in 1891, he was appointed to the Supreme Court by Grover Cleveland in 1894. He became Chief Justice under President William Taft in 1910 and served until 1921. He died at Washington, DC, May 19, 1921. For more info: oyez.northwestern.edu/justices/justices.cgi.

BIRTHDAYS TODAY

Brent Ashabranner, 80, author (*Our Beckoning Borders: Illegal Immigration to America*), born Shawnee, OK, Nov 3, 1921.

Janell Cannon, 44, author, illustrator (*Stellaluna, Crickwing*), born St. Paul, MN, Nov 3, 1957.

Roseanne, 48, comedienne, actress ("Roseanne," *She-Devil*), born Roseanne Barr, Salt Lake City, UT, Nov 3, 1953.

NOVEMBER 4 — SUNDAY

Day 308 — 57 Remaining

CIRCLE K INTERNATIONAL SERVICE WEEK. Nov 4–10. This week is set aside for all Circle K clubs worldwide to perform a campus and community service project to benefit children ages 6–13. Circle K is a college student service organization sponsored by Kiwanis. For info: Circle K Intl, 3636 Woodview Trace, Indianapolis, IN 46268-3196. Phone: (317) 875-8755 or (317) 875-8755. Fax: (317) 879-0204. E-mail: cki@kiwanis.org. Web: www.kiwanis.org.

ITALY: VICTORY DAY. Nov 4. Commemorates the signing of a WWI treaty by Austria in 1918 which resulted in the transfer of Trentino and Trieste from Austria to Italy.

November 2001

S	M	T	W	T	F	S
				1	2	3
4	5	6	7	8	9	10
11	12	13	14	15	16	17
18	19	20	21	22	23	24
25	26	27	28	29	30	

NOVEMBER 4
THE DISCOVERY OF KING TUT'S TOMB

The beautiful gold mask that covered King Tutankhamen's mummy is one of the most famous of all Egyptian antiquities. But the mask was only one of the amazing treasures found in the boy-king's tomb. Children will especially relate to the everyday objects, such as ship models, games and a trumpet that can still be blown. Children also relate to King Tut because he was only about nine years old when he became pharaoh, in 1361 BC. He died at the age of 18 or 19. Tutankhamen's short reign was undistinguished in Egypt's history. His more famous relatives include Akhenaton, the heretic pharaoh, who may have been his brother or father (scholars are not in agreement), and Akhenaton's queen Nefertiti. Young readers will love *Tut's Mummy*, by Judy Donnelly (Random House, 0-394-89189-9, $3.99 Gr. K–3). Middle school students will enjoy the photos in *DK Discoveries: Tutankhamun: Life and Death of a Pharaoh*, by David Murdoch (DK, 0-7894-3420-2, $16.96 Gr. 3–7). For young adults & up see *Tutankhamen: Life and Death of a Boy-King*, by Christine El Mahdy (St. Martins, 0-312-26241-8, $24.95). Many books for adults about Tutankhamen have pictures that children will enjoy. The 1923 edition of *National Geographic*, which reported on the find, is on the Web at www.nationalgeographic.com/egypt.

Many people, including children, are fascinated by the exotic allure of ancient Egypt. A marvelous idea for an art perspective would be to compare and contrast the difference in the style of art found in traditional wall and tomb reliefs with the freer, more natural, style found in art of the Amarna Period (Akhenaton's reign.)

Children love experimenting with hieroglyphics—ancient Egyptian writing. The pictures represent sounds. A bit of research into sound/picture equivalents may allow students to transcribe their names into hieroglyphics. Older students could compare and contrast the nature of hieroglyphics with the writing systems of other civilizations. Good books for young readers include *Seeker of Knowledge: The Man Who Deciphered Egyptian Hieroglyphics*, by James Rumford (Houghton Mifflin, 0-395-97934-X, $15.95 Gr. 2–6); *The Shipwrecked Sailor*, by Tamara Bower (Atheneum, 0-689-83046-7, $17 Gr. 2 & up), a translation of a story from an ancient papyrus scroll that includes phrases in hieroglyphics.

The science of mummification has tremendous classroom appeal. There are many books available about mummies. You might want to let students research mummies from different cultures. Here are a few books to get your students started: *Secrets of the Mummies*, by Shelley Tanaka (Hyperion, 0-7868-0473-4, $16.99 Gr. 3–7); *Mummies and Their Mysteries*, by Charlotte Wilcox (Lerner, 0-8761-4643-4, $7.95 Gr. 3–7); *Mummies, Bones, & Body Parts*, by Charlotte Wilcox (Carolrhoda, 1-57505-428-0, $25.26 Gr. 4–7); *Cat Mummies*, by Kelly Trumble (Houghton Mifflin, 0-395-96891-7, $5.95 Gr. 3–6); *Bodies From the Bog*, by James M. Deem (Houghton Mifflin, 0-395-85784-8, $16 Gr. 3–7); *Ice Mummy: Discovery of a 5,000 Year Old Man*, by M. & C. Dubowski (Random House, 0-679-85647-1, $3.99 Gr. 3 & up); *Discovering the Inca Ice Maiden*, by Johan Reinhard (National Geographic, 0-7922-7142-4, $17.95 Gr. 4 & up). Reinhard found three more Incan mummies in 1999. See the article in the *Chicago Tribune* (April 7, 1999, sec. 1, page 4) for more information.

KING TUT TOMB DISCOVERY: ANNIVERSARY. Nov 4, 1922. In 1922, one of the most important archaeological discoveries of modern times occurred at Luxor, Egypt. It was the tomb of Egypt's child-king, Tutankhamen, who became pharaoh at the age of nine and died, probably in the year 1352 BC, when he was 19. Perhaps the only ancient Egyptian royal tomb to have escaped plundering by grave robbers, it was discovered more than 3,000 years after Tutankhamen's death by English archaeologist Howard Carter, leader of an expedition financed by Lord Carnarvon. The entrance to the tomb was found on this day but the tomb was not entered until later in the month. The priceless relics yielded by King Tut's tomb were placed in Egypt's National Museum at Cairo. *See* Curriculum Connection.

MISCHIEF NIGHT. Nov 4. Observed in England, Australia and New Zealand. Nov 4, the eve of Guy Fawkes Day, is occasion for bonfires and firecrackers to commemorate failure of the plot to blow up the Houses of Parliament Nov 5, 1605. See also: "England: Guy Fawkes Day" (Nov 5).

NATIONAL CHEMISTRY WEEK. Nov 4–10. To celebrate the contributions of chemistry to modern life and to help the public understand that chemistry affects every part of our lives. Activities include an array of outreach programs such as open houses, contests, workshops, exhibits and classroom visits. 10 million participants nationwide. For info: Natl Chemistry Week Office, American Chemical Soc, 1155 16th St NW, Washington, DC 20036. Phone: (202) 872-6078. Fax: (202) 833-7722. E-mail: ncw@acs.org. Web: www.acs.org/ncw.

NATIONAL SPLIT PEA SOUP WEEK. Nov 4–10. To promote the use and enjoyment of split pea soup. For info: Peter Klaiber, USA Dry Pea and Lentil Council, 2780 W Pullman Rd, Moscow, ID 83843-4024. Phone: (208) 882-3023. Fax: (208) 882-6406. E-mail: pulse@pea-lentil.com.

NORTH, STERLING: BIRTH ANNIVERSARY. Nov 4, 1906. Author (*Rascal*), born at Edgerton, WI. Died Dec 21, 1974.

PANAMA: FLAG DAY. Nov 4. Public holiday.

UNESCO: 55th ANNIVERSARY. Nov 4, 1946. The United Nations Educational, Scientific and Cultural Organization was formed. For more info: www.unesco.org.

BIRTHDAYS TODAY

Laura Bush, 55, First Lady, wife of George W. Bush, 43d president of the US, born Laura Welch, Midland, TX, Nov 4, 1946.

Gail E. Haley, 62, author and illustrator (Caldecott for *A Story, A Story*), born Charlotte, NC, Nov 4, 1939.

Ralph Macchio, 39, actor ("Eight Is Enough," *The Karate Kid*), born Huntington, NY, Nov 4, 1962.

Andrea McArdle, 38, singer, actress (Broadway's original *Annie*), born Philadelphia, PA, Nov 4, 1963.

NOVEMBER 5 — MONDAY

Day 309 — 56 Remaining

AUSTRALIA: RECREATION DAY. Nov 5. The first Monday in November is observed as Recreation Day at Northern Tasmania, Australia.

EL SALVADOR: DAY OF THE FIRST SHOUT FOR INDEPENDENCE. Nov 5. National holiday. Commemorates the first Central American battle for independence from Spain in 1811.

ENGLAND: GUY FAWKES DAY. Nov 5. United Kingdom. Anniversary of the "Gunpowder Plot." Conspirators planned to blow up the Houses of Parliament and King James I in 1605. Twenty barrels of gunpowder, which they had secreted in a cellar under Parliament, were discovered on the night of Nov 4, the very eve of the intended explosion, and the conspirators were arrested. They were tried and convicted, and Jan 31, 1606, eight (including Guy Fawkes) were beheaded and their heads displayed on pikes at London Bridge. Though there were at least 11 conspirators, Guy Fawkes is most remembered. In 1606, the Parliament, which was to have been annihilated, enacted a law establishing Nov 5 as a day of public thanksgiving. It is still observed, and on the night of Nov 5, the whole country lights up with bonfires and celebration. "Guys" are burned in effigy and the old verses repeated: "Remember, remember the fifth of November/Gunpowder treason and plot;/I see no reason why Gunpowder Treason/Should ever be forgot." For more info: www.worldbook.com/fun/holidays/html/fawkes.htm.

KIDS' GOALS EDUCATION WEEK. Nov 5–9. Encourage parents to foster goal-setting habits in their children's lives so that their children can make their dreams come true. For info: Gary Ryan Blair, The GoalsGuy, 911 East Klosterman Rd, Tarpon Springs, FL 34689. Phone: (877) GOALSGUY. Fax: (800) 731-GOALS. E-mail: kgew@goalsguy.com. Web: www.goalsguy.com.

ROGERS, ROY: BIRTH ANNIVERSARY. Nov 5, 1912. Known as the "King of the Cowboys," Rogers was born Leonard Slye at Cincinnati, OH. His many songs included "Don't Fence Me In" and "Happy Trails to You." He made his acting debut in *Under Western Stars* in 1935 and later hosted his own show, "The Roy Rogers Show," in 1951. Rogers died at Apple Valley, CA, July 6, 1998. See also: "The Roy Rogers Show" TV Premiere: Anniversary (Dec 30).

BIRTHDAYS TODAY

Tatum O'Neal, 38, actress (Oscar for *Paper Moon*; *Bad News Bears*), born Los Angeles, CA, Nov 5, 1963.

Marcia Sewall, 66, author (*The Pilgrims of Plimoth*), born Providence, RI, Nov 5, 1935.

Jerry Stackhouse, 27, basketball player, born Kinston, NC, Nov 5, 1974.

NOVEMBER 6 — TUESDAY

Day 310 — 55 Remaining

ELECTION DAY. Nov 6. Annually, the first Tuesday after the first Monday in November. Many state and local government elections are held on this day, as well as presidential and congressional elections. All US House seats and one-third of US Senate seats are up for election in even-numbered years. Presidential elections are held in even-numbered years that can be divided by four. This day is a holiday in 12 states.

"GOOD MORNING AMERICA" TV PREMIERE: ANNIVERSARY. Nov 6, 1975. This ABC morning program, set in a living room, is a mixture of news reports, features and interviews with newsmakers and people of interest. It was the first program to compete with NBC's "Today" show and initially aired as "A.M. America." Hosts have included David Hartman, Nancy Dussault, Sandy Hill, Charles Gibson, Joan Lunden, Lisa McRee and Kevin Newman.

HALFWAY POINT OF AUTUMN. Nov 6. On this day, 45 days of autumn will have elapsed and the equivalent will remain before Dec 21, 2001, which is the winter solstice and the beginning of winter.

NAISMITH, JAMES: BIRTH ANNIVERSARY. Nov 6, 1861. Inventor of the game of basketball was born at Almonte, Ontario, Canada. Died at Lawrence, KS, Nov 28, 1939. Basketball became an Olympic sport in 1936.

SAXOPHONE DAY (ADOLPHE SAX BIRTH ANNIVERSARY). Nov 6. A day to recognize the birth anniversary of Adolphe Sax, Belgian musician and inventor of the saxophone and the saxotromba. Born at Dinant, Belgium in 1814, Antoine Joseph Sax, later known as Adolphe, was the eldest of 11 children of a musical instrument builder. Sax contributed an entire family of brass wind instruments for band and orchestra use. He was accorded fame and great wealth, but business misfortunes led to bankruptcy. Sax died in poverty at Paris, Feb 7, 1894.

SOUSA, JOHN PHILIP: BIRTH ANNIVERSARY. Nov 6, 1854. American composer and band conductor, remembered for stirring marches such as "The Stars and Stripes Forever," "Semper Fidelis," and "El Capitan," born at Washington, DC. Died at Reading, PA, Mar 6, 1932. See also: "The Stars and Stripes Forever: Anniversary" (May 14).

SWEDEN: GUSTAVUS ADOLPHUS DAY. Nov 6. Honors Sweden's King and military leader killed in 1632.

BIRTHDAYS TODAY

Sally Field, 55, actress (Oscars for *Norma Rae, Places in the Heart; Mrs Doubtfire*), born Pasadena, CA, Nov 6, 1946.

Ethan Hawke, 31, actor (*Dead Poets Society, Reality Bites*), born Austin, TX, Nov 6, 1970.

Maria Shriver, 46, broadcast journalist ("Dateline NBC"), author (*What's Heaven?*), born Chicago, IL, Nov 6, 1955.

NOVEMBER 7 — WEDNESDAY

Day 311 — 54 Remaining

ASSOCIATION FOR EDUCATIONAL COMMUNICATIONS AND TECHNOLOGY CONFERENCE. Nov 7–10. Atlanta, GA. For info: Assn for Educational Communications & Technology, 1800 N Stonelake Dr, Ste 2, Bloomington, IN 47404. Phone: (877) 677-AECT. Fax: (812) 335-7678. E-mail: aect@aect.org. Web: www.aect.org.

BANGLADESH: SOLIDARITY DAY. Nov 7. National holiday. Commemorates a 1975 coup.

CANADIAN PACIFIC RAILWAY: TRANSCONTINENTAL COMPLETION ANNIVERSARY. Nov 7, 1885. At 9:30 AM the last spike was driven at Craigellachie, British Columbia, completing the Canadian Pacific Railway's 2,980-mile transcontinental railroad track between Montreal, Quebec, in the east and Port Moody, British Columbia, in the west.

November 2001

S	M	T	W	T	F	S
				1	2	3
4	5	6	7	8	9	10
11	12	13	14	15	16	17
18	19	20	21	22	23	24
25	26	27	28	29	30	

CURIE, MARIE SKLODOWSKA: BIRTH ANNIVERSARY. Nov 7, 1867. Polish chemist and physicist, born at Warsaw, Poland. In 1903 she was awarded, with her husband Pierre, the Nobel Prize for physics for their discovery of the element radium. Died near Sallanches, France, July 4, 1934. For more info: *Marie Curie*, by Leonard Everett Fisher (Macmillan, 0-02-735375-3, $14.95 Gr. 3–6).

FIRST BLACK GOVERNOR ELECTED: ANNIVERSARY. Nov 7, 1989. L. Douglas Wilder was elected governor of Virginia, becoming the first elected black governor in US history. Wilder had previously served as lieutenant governor of Virginia.

GREAT OCTOBER SOCIALIST REVOLUTION: ANNIVERSARY. Nov 7, 1917. This holiday in the old Soviet Union was observed for two days with parades, military displays and appearances by Soviet leaders. According to the old Russian calendar, the revolution took place Oct 25, 1917. Soviet calendar reform causes observance to fall Nov 7 (Gregorian). The Bolshevik Revolution began at Petrograd, Russia, on the evening of Nov 6 (Gregorian), 1917. A new government headed by Nikolai Lenin took office the following day under the name Council of People's Commissars. Leon Trotsky was commissar for foreign affairs and Josef Stalin became commissar of national minorities. In the mid-1990s, President Yeltsin issued a decree renaming this holiday the "Day of National Reconciliation and Agreement."

NATIONAL ASSOCIATION FOR GIFTED CHILDREN CONVENTION. Nov 7–11. Cincinnati, OH. Educational sessions for administrators, counselors, coordinators, teachers and parents. Est attendance: 3,000. For info: Natl Assn for Gifted Children, 1707 L St NW, Ste 550, Washington, DC 20036. Phone: (202) 785-4268.

REPUBLICAN SYMBOL: ANNIVERSARY. Nov 7, 1874. Thomas Nast used an elephant to represent the Republican Party in a satirical cartoon in *Harper's Weekly*. Today the elephant is still a well-recognized symbol for the Republican Party in political cartoons.

ROOSEVELT ELECTED TO FOURTH TERM: ANNIVERSARY. Nov 7, 1944. Defeating Thomas Dewey, Franklin D. Roosevelt became the first, and only, person elected to four terms as President of the US. Roosevelt was inaugurated the following Jan 20 but died in office Apr 12, 1945, serving only 53 days of the fourth term.

RUSSIA: OCTOBER REVOLUTION. Nov 7. National holiday in Russia and Ukraine. Commemorates the Great Socialist Revolution which occurred in October 1917 under the Old Style calendar. In the mid-1990s, President Yeltsin issued a decree renaming the holiday the "Day of National Reconciliation and Agreement."

TECHNOLOGY + LEARNING CONFERENCE. Nov 7 – 10. Atlanta, GA. The annual conference will bring together 3,000 K–12 educators to see what's new, share experiences and find out what's working in every area of education technology. Sponsored by the National School Board Assocation and cosponsored by 25 education organizations. Workshops, roundtables, exhibits and more. The 2002 conference will take place in Anaheim, CA on

Nov 12–15, 2002. For info: Natl School Boards Assn, 1680 Duke St, Alexandria, VA 22314. Phone: (703) 838-6722. E-mail: info@nsba.org. Web: www.nsba.org.

BIRTHDAYS TODAY

Mary Travers, 64, composer, singer (Peter, Paul and Mary, "Puff, the Magic Dragon"), born Louisville, KY, Nov 7, 1937.

NOVEMBER 8 — THURSDAY

Day 312 — 53 Remaining

CORTÉS CONQUERS MEXICO: ANNIVERSARY. Nov 8, 1519. After landing on the Yucatan peninsula in April, Spaniard Hernan Cortés and his troops marched into the interior of Mexico to the Aztec capital and took the Aztec emperor Montezuma hostage.

HALLEY, EDMUND: BIRTH ANNIVERSARY. Nov 8, 1656. Astronomer and mathematician, born at London, England. Astronomer Royal, 1721–42. Died at Greenwich, England, Jan 14, 1742. He observed the great comet of 1682 (now named for him), first conceived its periodicity and wrote in his *Synopsis of Comet Astronomy*: ". . . I may venture to foretell that this Comet will return again in the year 1758." It did, and Edmund Halley's memory is kept alive by the once-every-generation appearance of Halley's Comet. There have been 28 recorded appearances of this comet since 240 BC. Average time between appearances is 76 years. Halley's Comet is next expected to be visible in 2061.

MONTANA: ADMISSION DAY: ANNIVERSARY. Nov 8. Became 41st state in 1889.

MOON PHASE: LAST QUARTER. Nov 8. Moon enters Last Quarter phase at 7:21 AM, EST.

X-RAY DISCOVERY DAY: ANNIVERSARY. Nov 8, 1895. Physicist Wilhelm Conrad Röntgen discovered X-rays, beginning a new era in physics and medicine. Although X-rays had been observed previously, it was Röntgen, a professor at the University of Wurzburg (Germany), who successfully repeated X-ray experimentation and who is credited with the discovery. For more info: *The Mysterious Rays of Dr. Röntgen*, by Beverly Gherman (Atheneum, 0-689-31839-1, $14.95 Gr. 2–5).

BIRTHDAYS TODAY

Alfre Woodard, 48, actress (*Cross Creek, Miss Evers' Boys*), born Tulsa, OK, Nov 8, 1953.

NOVEMBER 9 — FRIDAY

Day 313 — 52 Remaining

AGNEW, SPIRO THEODORE: BIRTH ANNIVERSARY. Nov 9, 1918. The 39th vice president of the US, born at Baltimore, MD. Twice elected vice president (1968 and 1972), Agnew became the second person to resign that office, on Oct 10, 1973. Agnew entered a plea of no contest to a charge of income tax evasion (on contract kickbacks received while he was governor of Maryland and after he became vice president). He died Sept 17, 1996, at Berlin, MD. See also: "Calhoun, John Caldwell: Birth Anniversary" (Mar 18).

BANNEKER, BENJAMIN: BIRTH ANNIVERSARY. Nov 9, 1731. American astronomer, mathematician, clockmaker, surveyor and almanac author, called "first black man of science." Took part in original survey of city of Washington. Banneker's *Almanac* was published 1792–97. Born at Elliott's Mills, MD, he died at Baltimore, MD, Oct 9, 1806. A fire that started during his funeral destroyed his home, library, notebooks, almanac calculations, clocks and virtually all belongings and documents related to his life. For more info: *Dear Benjamin Banneker*, by Andrea Davis Pinkney (Harcourt, 0-15-200417-3, $14.95 Gr. 2–4).

BERLIN WALL OPENED: ANNIVERSARY. Nov 9, 1989. After 28 years as a symbol of the Cold War, the Berlin Wall was opened. East Germany opened checkpoints along its border with West Germany after a troubled month that saw many citizens flee to the West through other countries. Coming amidst the celebration of East Germany's 40-year anniversary, the pro-democracy demonstrations led to the resignation of Erich Honecker, East Germany's head of state and party chief, who had supervised the construction of the Wall. He was replaced by Egon Krenz, who promised open political debate and a lessening of restrictions on travel in attempts to stem the flow of East Germans to the West. By opening the Berlin Wall, East Germany began a course that led to the de facto reunification of the two Germanys by summer 1990. The Berlin Wall was constructed Aug 13, 1961. Berlin was at the center of a superpower crisis as US President Kennedy increased troop strength in response to the blockade of West Berlin by the Soviets. Honecker started construction, with Soviet leader Krushchev's blessing, of the 27.9-mile wall across the city. Many attempts to scale or breech the wall ensued throughout the years. But on the evening of Nov 9, 1989, citizens of both sides walked freely through the barrier as others danced atop the structure to celebrate the end of an era.

CAMBODIA: INDEPENDENCE DAY. Nov 9. National Day. Commemorates independence from France in 1949.

EAST COAST BLACKOUT: ANNIVERSARY. Nov 9, 1965. Massive electric power failure starting in western New York state at 5:16 PM, cut electric power to much of northeastern US and Ontario and Quebec in Canada. More than 30 million persons in an area of 80,000 square miles were affected. The experience provoked studies of the vulnerability of 20th-century technology.

KRISTALLNACHT (CRYSTAL NIGHT): ANNIVERSARY. Nov 9–10, 1938. During the evening of Nov 9 and into the morning of Nov 10, 1938, mobs in Germany destroyed thousands of shops and homes carrying out a pogrom against Jews. Synagogues were burned down or demolished. There were bonfires in every Jewish neighborhood, fueled by Jewish prayer books, Torah scrolls and volumes of philosophy, history and poetry. More than 30,000 Jews were arrested and 91 killed. The night got its name from the smashing of glass store windows. For more info on the Holocaust: www.ushmm.org/outreach.

NATIONAL CHILD SAFETY COUNCIL: FOUNDING ANNIVERSARY. Nov 9, 1955. National Child Safety Council (NCSC) at Jackson, MI. NCSC is the oldest and largest nonprofit organization in the US dedicated solely to the personal safety and well-being of young children. For info: Barbara Handley Huggett, Dir Research and Development, NCSC, Box 1368, Jackson, MI 49204-1368. Phone: (517) 764-6070.

THOMPSON, KAY: BIRTH ANNIVERSARY. Nov 9, 1908. Born at St. Louis, MO, Thompson wrote the Eloise series of children's books. Eloise was a spoiled, mischievous six-year-old who lives in New York's Plaza Hotel. Books include *Eloise in Paris, Eloise in Moscow* and *Eloise at Christmastime*. In 1999, Simon and Schuster released a new version called *The Absolutely Essential Eloise*. Thompson died at New York, NY, July 2, 1998.

BIRTHDAYS TODAY

Pat Cummings, 51, author (*Talking with Adventurers*), born Chicago, IL, Nov 9, 1950.

Lois Ehlert, 67, author and illustrator (*Planting a Rainbow, Eating the Alphabet*), born Beaver Dam, WI, Nov 9, 1934.

Lou Ferrigno, 50, actor (*Pumping Iron*, "The Incredible Hulk"), former bodybuilder, born Brooklyn, NY, Nov 9, 1951.

Robert Graham, 65, US Senator (D, Florida), born Dade County, FL, Nov 9, 1936.

Lynn Hall, 64, author (the Dragon series), born Lombard, IL, Nov 9, 1937.

NOVEMBER 10 — SATURDAY

Day 314 — 51 Remaining

AREA CODES INTRODUCED: 50th ANNIVERSARY. Nov 10, 1951. The North American Numbering Plan which provided area codes for Canada, the US, and many Caribbean nations was devised in 1947 by AT&T and Bell Labs. However, all long-distance calls were operator-assisted. On this date, the mayor of Englewood, NJ (area code 201) direct-dialed the mayor of Alameda, CA. By 1960 all telephone customers could dial long-distance calls. Because of the proliferation of faxes, modems and cell phones, the US could run out of area codes as early as 2007.

BADLANDS NATIONAL PARK ESTABLISHED: ANNIVERSARY. Nov 10, 1978. South Dakota's Badlands National Monument, authorized Mar 4, 1929, was established as a national park and preserve. For more info: www.nps.gov/badl/index.htm.

***EDMUND FITZGERALD* SINKING: ANNIVERSARY.** Nov 10, 1975. The ore carrier *Edmund Fitzgerald* broke in two during a heavy storm in Lake Superior (near Whitefish Point). There were no survivors of this, the worst Great Lakes ship disaster of the decade, which took the lives of 29 crew members.

JEWISH BOOK MONTH. Nov 10–Dec 10. To promote interest in Jewish books. For info: Carolyn Starman Hessel, Jewish Book Council, 15 E 26th St, New York, NY 10010. Phone: (212) 532-4949. Fax: (212) 481-4174. E-mail: JBC@jewishbooks.org. Web: www.avotaynu.com/jbc.html.

MARINE CORPS BIRTHDAY: ANNIVERSARY. Nov 10. Commemorates the Marine Corps' establishment in 1775. Originally part of the navy, it became a separate unit July 11, 1789.

MAZZA COLLECTION INSTITUTE. Nov 10. University of Findlay, Findlay, OH. The Mazza Collection is the largest teaching gallery in the world specializing in art from picture books. Meet and learn from internationally recognized illustrators and authors of children's books. For info: Benjamin Sapp, Mazza Collection Galleria, University of Findlay, 1000 N Main St, Findlay, OH 45840. Phone: (419) 424-5343. Fax: (419) 424-6480. E-mail: sapp@river.findlay.edu. Web: www.findlay.edu/academic/mazza/index.html.

MICROSOFT RELEASES WINDOWS: ANNIVERSARY. Nov 10, 1983. In 1980, Microsoft signed a contract with IBM to design an operating system, MS-DOS, for a personal computer that IBM was developing. On this date Microsoft released Windows, an extension of MS-DOS with a graphical user interface.

PANAMA: FIRST SHOUT OF INDEPENDENCE. Nov 10. National holiday. Commemorates Panama's first battle for independence from Spain in 1821.

"SESAME STREET" TV PREMIERE: ANNIVERSARY. Nov 10, 1969. An important, successful long-running children's show, "Sesame Street" educates children while they have fun. It takes place along a city street, featuring a diverse cast of humans and puppets. Through singing, puppetry, film clips and skits, kids are taught letters, numbers, concepts and other lessons. Shows are "sponsored" by letters and numbers. Human cast members have included: Loretta Long, Matt Robinson, Roscoe Orman, Bob McGrath, Linda Bove, Buffy Sainte-Marie, Ruth Buzzi, Will Lee, Northern J. Calloway, Emilio Delgado and Sonia Manzano. Favorite Jim Henson Muppets include Ernie, Bert, Grover, Oscar the Grouch, Kermit the Frog, Cookie Monster, life-sized Big Bird and Mr Snuffleupagus. Variations on "Sesame Street" are aired in 78 countries. For more info: www.pbs.org/kids/sesame.

SPACE MILESTONE: *LUNA 17* (USSR): ANNIVERSARY. Nov 10, 1970. This unmanned spacecraft landed and released *Lunakhod 1* (8-wheel, radio-controlled vehicle) on Moon's Sea of Rains Nov 17, which explored the lunar surface, sending data back to Earth.

BIRTHDAYS TODAY

Sal Barracca, 54, author, with wife Debra (*The Adventures of Taxi Dog*), born Brooklyn, NY, Nov 10, 1947.

Sinbad, 45, actor (*Unnecessary Roughness*, "A Different World"), born David Adkins, Benton Harbor, MI, Nov 10, 1956.

NOVEMBER 11 — SUNDAY

Day 315 — 50 Remaining

★ **AMERICAN EDUCATION WEEK.** Nov 11–17. Presidential Proclamation 5403, of Oct 30, 1985, covers all succeeding years. Always the first full week preceding the fourth Thursday in November. Issued from 1921–25 and in 1936, sometimes for a week in December and sometimes as National Education Week. After an absence of a number of years, this proclamation was issued each year from 1955–82 (issued in 1955 as a prelude to the White House Conference on Education). Previously, Proclamation 4967, of Sept 13, 1982, covered all succeeding years as the second week in November.

AMERICAN EDUCATION WEEK. Nov 11–17. Focuses attention on the importance of education and all that it stands for. Annually, the week preceding the week of Thanksgiving. For info: Natl Education Assn (NEA), 1201 16th St NW, Washington, DC 20036. Phone: (202) 833-4000. Web: www.nea.org.

ANGOLA: INDEPENDENCE DAY: ANNIVERSARY. Nov 11. National holiday. The West African state of Angola gained its independence from Portugal in 1975.

BONZA BOTTLER DAY™. Nov 11. To celebrate when the number of the day is the same as the number of the month. Bonza Bottler Day™ is an excuse to have a party at least once a month. For info: Gail M. Berger, 109 Matthew Ave, Poca, WV 25159. Phone: (304) 776-7746. E-mail: gberger5@aol.com.

CANADA: REMEMBRANCE DAY. Nov 11. Public holiday.

COLOMBIA: CARTAGENA INDEPENDENCE DAY. Nov 11. National holiday. Commemorates the declaration of independence of the city in 1811.

FRENCH WEST INDIES: CONCORDIA DAY. Nov 11. St. Martin. Public holiday. Parades and joint ceremony by French and Dutch officials at the obelisk Border Monument commemorating the long-standing peaceful coexistence of both countries. For info: Ms Michel Coutosiev, Mktg Challenges Int'l, 10 E 21st St, New York, NY 10010. Phone: (212) 529-9069.

"GOD BLESS AMERICA" FIRST PERFORMED: ANNIVERSARY. Nov 11, 1938. Irving Berlin wrote this song especially for Kate Smith. She first sang it during her regular radio broad-

November 2001

S	M	T	W	T	F	S
				1	2	3
4	5	6	7	8	9	10
11	12	13	14	15	16	17
18	19	20	21	22	23	24
25	26	27	28	29	30	

cast. It quickly became a great patriotic favorite of the nation and one of Smith's most requested songs.

MARTINMAS. Nov 11. The Feast Day of St. Martin of Tours, who lived about AD 316–397. A bishop, he became one of the most popular saints of the Middle Ages. The period of warm weather often occurring about the time of his feast day is sometimes called St. Martin's Summer (especially in England).

NATIONAL GEOGRAPHY AWARENESS WEEK. Nov 11–17. To focus public awareness on the importance of the knowledge of geography. For information and classroom activities, visit the National Geographic Society's website at www.nationalgeographic.com/gaw and the US Geological Survey's site at www.usgs.gov/education/learnweb/index.html.

POLAND: INDEPENDENCE DAY. Nov 11. Poland regained independence in 1918, after having been partitioned among Austria, Prussia and Russia for more than 120 years.

RANDOM ACTS OF KINDNESS WEEK. Nov 11–17. The 6th annual RAK week has been changed from its usual February time frame to November to coincide with the 1st annual World Kindness Day, Nov 13. RAK Week is a global grass roots awareness campaign and celebration of the power of Random Acts of Kindness as a counterbalance to random acts of violence. Anyone can join in during this week and the Random Acts of Kindness Foundation can help you with ideas on how to promote this wonderful celebration! Call for a Community Coordinator Kit or a Teacher's Kit. For info: Random Acts of Kindness Foundation. Phone: (800) 660-2811. Web: www.actsofkindness.org.

SPACE MILESTONE: *GEMINI 12* (US): 35th ANNIVERSARY. Nov 11, 1966. Last Project Gemini manned Earth orbit launched. Buzz Aldrin spent five hours on a space walk, setting a new record.

SWEDEN: SAINT MARTIN'S DAY. Nov 11. Originally in memory of St. Martin of Tours; also associated with Martin Luther, who is celebrated the day before. Marks the end of the autumn's work and the beginning of winter activities.

VETERANS DAY. Nov 11. Veterans Day was observed Nov 11 from 1919 through 1970. Public Law 90–363, the "Monday Holiday Law," provided that, beginning in 1971, Veterans Day would be observed on "the fourth Monday in October." This movable observance date, which separated Veterans Day from the Nov 11 anniversary of WWI Armistice, proved unpopular. State after state moved its observance back to the traditional Nov 11 date, and finally Public Law 94–97 of Sept 18, 1975, required that, effective Jan 1, 1978, the observance of Veterans Day revert to Nov 11. See also: "Armistice Day" (Nov 11). For more info about Veterans Day, go to the website of the US Department of Veterans Affairs at www.va.gov/pubaff/vetsday or the Veterans of Foreign Wars at www.vfw.org/amesm/origins.shtml.

★ **VETERANS DAY.** Nov 11. Presidential Proclamation. Formerly called "Armistice Day" and proclaimed each year since 1926 for Nov 11. PL83–380 of June 1, 1954, changed the name to "Veterans Day." PL90–363 of June 28, 1968, required that beginning in 1971 it would be observed the fourth Monday in October. PL 94–97 of Sept 18, 1975, required that effective Jan 1, 1978, the observance would revert to Nov 11.

WASHINGTON: ADMISSION DAY: ANNIVERSARY. Nov 11. Became 42nd state in 1889.

WEST POINT BICENTENNIAL ENGINEERING DESIGN CONTEST. Nov 11. The qualifying round for this bridge-building contest for students in grades K–12 begins Nov 11, 2001, when contestants download the West Point Bridge Designer from the Web. On Feb 28, 2002, the top ten teams will be selected to advance to the semi-final round held Mar 16, 2002. The final round will be held at West Point on April 26–28, 2002. Scholarship money will be awarded to winners. For more info: bridgecontest.usma.edu.

WORLD WAR I ARMISTICE: ANNIVERSARY. Nov 11, 1918. Anniversary of armistice between Allied and Central Powers ending WWI, signed at 5 AM, Nov 11, 1918, in Marshal Foch's railway car in the Forest of Compiegne, France. Hostilities ceased at 11 AM. Recognized in many countries as Armistice Day, Remembrance Day, Veterans Day, Victory Day or World War I Memorial Day. Many places observe a silent memorial at the 11th hour of the 11th day of the 11th month each year. See also: "Veterans Day" (Nov 11).

BIRTHDAYS TODAY

Barbara Boxer, 61, US Senator (D, California), born Brooklyn, NY, Nov 11, 1940.

Leonardo DiCaprio, 26, actor (*What's Eating Gilbert Grape?, Titanic*), born Ridgewood, NJ, Nov 11, 1975.

Peg Kehret, 65, author (*Horror at the Haunted House*), born LaCrosse, WI, Nov 11, 1936.

Kurt Vonnegut, Jr, 79, novelist (*Slaughterhouse Five, Cat's Cradle*), born Indianapolis, IN, Nov 11, 1922.

NOVEMBER 12 — MONDAY

Day 316 — 49 Remaining

ARCHES NATIONAL PARK ESTABLISHED: 30th ANNIVERSARY. Nov 12, 1971. Area of natural wind-eroded formations in eastern Utah, originally proclaimed a national monument Apr 12, 1929, was established as a national park. For info: www.nps.gov/arch/index.htm.

BLACKMUN, HARRY A.: BIRTH ANNIVERSARY. Nov 12, 1908. Former associate justice of the Supreme Court of the US, nominated by President Nixon Apr 14, 1970. Justice Blackmun was born at Nashville, IL, Nov 12, 1908. He retired from the Court Aug 3, 1994, and died Mar 4, 1999, at Arlington, VA.

NATIONAL CHILDREN'S BOOK WEEK. Nov 12–18. To encourage the enjoyment of reading for young people. Each year, the week has a theme. For the 82nd annual celebration, the theme is "Get Carried Away. . .Read." For info: The Children's Book Council, Inc, 12 W 37th St, 2nd flr, New York, NY 10018-2073. Phone: (212) 966-1990. Fax: (212) 966-2073. E-mail: staff@cbcbooks.org. Web: www.cbcbooks.org.

STANTON, ELIZABETH CADY: BIRTH ANNIVERSARY. Nov 12, 1815. American woman suffragist and reformer, Elizabeth Cady Stanton was born at Johnstown, NY. "We hold these truths to be self-evident," she said at the first Women's Rights Convention, in 1848, "that all men and women are created equal." She died at New York, NY, Oct 26, 1902. For more info: *You Want Women to Vote, Lizzie Stanton?*, by Jean Fritz (Putnam, 0-399-22786-

5, $16.99 Gr. 5–9) or www.nps.gov/wori/ecs.htm. The March 2000 issue of *Cobblestone* magazine is devoted to Stanton.

SUN YAT-SEN: BIRTH ANNIVERSARY (TRADITIONAL). Nov 12. Although his actual birth date in 1866 is not known, Dr. Sun Yat-Sen's traditional birthday commemoration is held Nov 12. Heroic leader of China's 1911 revolution, he died at Peking, Mar 12, 1925. The death anniversary is also widely observed. See also: "Sun Yat-Sen: Death Anniversary" (Mar 12).

TYLER, LETITIA CHRISTIAN: BIRTH ANNIVERSARY. Nov 12, 1790. First wife of John Tyler, 10th president of the US, born at New Kent County, VA. Died at Washington, DC, Sept 10, 1842.

VETERANS DAY OBSERVED. Nov 12. For federal employees, when a holiday falls on a Sunday, it is observed on the following Monday.

YOUTH APPRECIATION WEEK. Nov 12–18. Annually, the second full week of November, Monday–Sunday. For info: Optimist Intl, 4494 Lindell Blvd, St. Louis, MO 63108. Phone: (314) 371-6000 or your local Optimist club.

BIRTHDAYS TODAY

Norman Mineta, 70, US Secretary of Transportation (George W. Bush administration), former Commerce secretary (Clinton administration), born San Jose, CA, Nov 12, 1931.

Jack Reed, 52, US Senator (D, Rhode Island), born Providence, RI, Nov 12, 1949.

Sammy Sosa, 33, baseball player, born San Pedro de Macoris, Dominican Republic, Nov 12, 1968.

NOVEMBER 13 — TUESDAY

Day 317 — 48 Remaining

BRANDEIS, LOUIS DEMBITZ: BIRTH ANNIVERSARY. Nov 13, 1856. American jurist, associate justice of US Supreme Court (1916–39), born at Louisville, KY. Died at Washington, DC, Oct 5, 1941.

***JOBARIA* EXHIBITED: ANNIVERSARY.** Nov 13, 1999. The dinosaur *Jobaria tiguidensis* was first exhibited at the National Geographic Society at Washington, DC, on this date. The 135-million-year-old sauropod was discovered in the African country of Niger in 1997. It is 15 feet high at the hip and 70 feet long. A mold of the plant-eating dinosaur is being exhibited since the actual skeleton is too heavy. The original skeleton is being returned to Niger. For more info: www.jobaria.org.

NATIONAL COMMUNITY EDUCATION DAY. Nov 13. To recognize and promote strong relationships between public schools and the communities they serve and to help schools develop new relationships with parents, community members, local organizations and agencies. Annually, the Tuesday of American Education Week. For info: Natl Community Education Assn, 3929 Old Lee Hway, Ste 91-A, Fairfax, VA 22030-2401. Phone: (703) 359-8973. Fax: (703) 359-0972. E-mail: ncea@ncea.com. Web: www.ncea.com.

STEVENSON, ROBERT LOUIS: BIRTH ANNIVERSARY. Nov 13, 1850. Scottish author, born at Edinburgh, Scotland, known for his *Child's Garden of Verses* and novels such as *Treasure Island* and *Kidnapped*. Died at Samoa, Dec 3, 1894.

STOKES BECOMES FIRST BLACK MAYOR IN US: ANNIVERSARY. Nov 13, 1967. Carl Burton Stokes became the first black in the US elected mayor when he won the Cleveland, OH, mayoral election. Died Apr 3, 1996.

BIRTHDAYS TODAY

Jez Alborough, 42, author and illustrator (*Where's My Teddy?*), born Surrey, England, Nov 13, 1959.

Whoopi Goldberg, 52, comedienne, actress (*Ghost, Sister Act, The Color Purple*), born New York, NY, Nov 13, 1949.

Randy Moss, 24, football player, born Rand, WV, Nov 13, 1977.

Vincent (Vinny) Testaverde, 38, football player, born New York, NY, Nov 13, 1963.

NOVEMBER 14 — WEDNESDAY

Day 318 — 47 Remaining

AMERICAN ASSOCIATION OF SCHOOL LIBRARIANS CONFERENCE. Nov 14–18. Indianapolis, IN. Eleventh national conference. For info: American Assn of School Librarians, 50 E. Huron St, Chicago, IL 60611. Phone: (800) 545-2433. Web: www.ala.org/aasl.

AROUND THE WORLD IN 72 DAYS: ANNIVERSARY. Nov 14, 1889. Newspaper reporter Nellie Bly (pen name used by Elizabeth Cochrane Seaman) set off in 1889, to attempt to break Jules Verne's imaginary hero Phileas Fogg's record of voyaging around the world in 80 days. She did beat Fogg's record, taking 72 days, 6 hours, 11 minutes and 14 seconds to make the trip.

BLOOD TRANSFUSION: ANNIVERSARY. Nov 14, 1666. Samuel Pepys, diarist and Fellow of the Royal Society, wrote in his diary for Nov 14, 1666: "Dr. Croone told me. . .there was a pretty experiment of the blood of one dog let out, till he died, into the body of another on one side, while all his own run out on the other side. The first died upon the place, and the other very well and likely to do well. This did give occasion to many pretty wishes, as of the blood of a Quaker to be let into an Archbishop, and such like; but, as Dr. Croone says, may, if it takes, be of mighty use to man's health, for the amending of bad blood by borrowing from a better body."

COPLAND, AARON: BIRTH ANNIVERSARY. Nov 14, 1900. American composer, born at Brooklyn, NY. Incorporating American folk music, he strove to create an American music style that was both popular and artistic. He composed ballets, film scores and orchestral works, including *Fanfare for the Common Man* (1942), *Appalachian Spring* (1944) (for which he won the Pulitzer Prize) and the score for *The Heiress* (1948) (for which he won an Oscar). He died Dec 2, 1990, at North Tarrytown, NY. *See* Curriculum Connection.

EISENHOWER, MAMIE DOUD: BIRTH ANNIVERSARY. Nov 14, 1896. Wife of Dwight David Eisenhower, 34th president of the US, born at Boone, IA. Died Nov 1, 1979, at Gettysburg, PA.

GUINEA-BISSAU: RE-ADJUSTMENT MOVEMENT'S DAY. Nov 14. National holiday.

INDIA: CHILDREN'S DAY. Nov 14. Holiday observed throughout India.

INDIA: DIWALI (DEEPAVALI). Nov 14. Diwali (or Divali), the five-day festival of lights, is the prettiest of all Indian festivals. It celebrates the victory of Lord Rama over the demon king Ravana. Thousands of flickering lights illuminate houses and transform

November 2001

S	M	T	W	T	F	S
				1	2	3
4	5	6	7	8	9	10
11	12	13	14	15	16	17
18	19	20	21	22	23	24
25	26	27	28	29	30	

NOVEMBER 14
AARON COPLAND'S BIRTHDAY

Aaron Copland was one of the greatest American composers. His music—filled with interesting rhythms, syncopation and many musical themes that are great for humming— celebrates American life. He incorporated elements of jazz and folk songs.

Copland was born in Brooklyn, New York, November 14, 1900, to parents who immigrated from Lithuania. Copland's father ran a dry goods (department) store and the family's living quarters were above it.

Many of his compositions are ones that young listeners will enjoy. *Billy the Kid* (1938), *Rodeo* (1942) and *Appalachian Spring* (1944) are three ballets that are particularly appealing. The first two epitomize the spirit of the American West. Use selections from them to add musical depth to units on westward expansion. *Appalachian Spring* celebrates the building of a new farmhouse in a rural Pennsylvania farming community during the early 1800s. The repeated theme from the Shaker hymn "Simple Gifts" is very stirring and develops into an emotional fullness that echoes the richness found in the lives of the people and the soil that supports their farms. Every child should be introduced to this piece, for which Copland won the 1945 Pulitzer Prize for Music.

All of the above music is easy to find. If you are willing to dig deeper, try to locate *Lincoln Portrait*, which features a narrator reading aloud writings by Abraham Lincoln. There are several different recordings—Carl Sandburg and Melvyn Douglas are narrators on two of them. *El Salón México* is another composition worth hunting for. It features Mexican folk music themes.

Before sharing these works with children, you might want to summarize the story of the ballets. Prior to playing a dance selection, it may help to include a comment to start student imaginations rolling. For example: "Can you imagine horse-drawn wagons rolling down a dirt-covered Main Street," before playing "Street in a Frontier Town," from *Billy the Kid*. Or "Imagine the fun these dancers are having. How would you move around if you were one of them?" before playing "Hoe-Down" from *Rodeo*. When playing *Appalachian Spring*, identify the musical theme of "Simple Gifts" and ask children to notice how it changes as the ballet continues.

The best way to celebrate Copland is by playing his music. However, some children may want additional information about the composer. Steer younger readers toward Mike Venezia's *Aaron Copland* (Grolier, 0-516-44538-3, $6.95 Gr. 4–7). High school students may enjoy browsing the in-depth, adult biography, *Aaron Copland: The Life and Work of an Uncommon Man*, by Howard Pollack (Univ of Illinois Press, 0-252-06900-5 $24.95).

the drab urban landscape of cities and towns while fireworks add color and noise. The goddess of wealth, Lakshmi, is worshipped in Hindu homes on Diwali. Houses are white-washed and cleaned and elaborate designs drawn on thresholds with colored powder to welcome the fastidious goddess. Because there is no one universally accepted Hindu calendar, this holiday may be celebrated on a different date in some parts of India but it always falls in the months of October or November. For more info: *Divali*, by Dilip Kadodwala (Raintree, 0-8172-4616-9, $22.11 Gr. 4–6).

JORDAN: KING HUSSEIN: BIRTH ANNIVERSARY. Nov 14. H.M. King Hussein is honored each year on the anniversary of his birth in 1935 at Amman, Jordan. He died there Feb 7, 1999.

MILES, MISKA: BIRTH ANNIVERSARY. Nov 14, 1899. Author (*Annie and the Old One*), whose real name was Patricia Miles Martin, born at Cherokee, KS. Died Jan 1, 1986.

MONET, CLAUDE: BIRTH ANNIVERSARY. Nov 14, 1840. French Impressionist painter (*Water Lillies*), born at Paris. Died at Giverny, France, Dec 5, 1926.

NATIONAL AMERICAN TEDDY BEAR DAY. Nov 14. The Vermont Teddy Bear Company® celebrates the birth of America's most beloved companion, the Teddy bear, annually on Nov 14. The legend goes that President Theodore Roosevelt spared the life of a bear cub while on a big game hunt in Mississippi in 1902. Clifford Berryman, political cartoonist, recorded the incident. Thus America's love affair with the Teddy bear began. For info: The Vermont Teddy Bear Company®, 6655 Shelburne Rd, Shelburne, VT 05482. Web: VermontTeddyBear.com.

NATIONAL EDUCATIONAL SUPPORT PERSONNEL DAY. Nov 14. A mandate of the delegates to the 1987 National Education Association Representative Assembly called for a special day during American Education Week to honor the contributions of school support employees. Local associations and school districts salute support staff on this 14th annual observance, the Wednesday of American Education Week. For info: Connie Morris, Natl Education Assn (NEA), 1201 16th St NW, Washington, DC 20036. Phone: (202) 822-7262. Fax: (202) 822-7292. Web: www.nea.org.

NATIONAL YOUNG READER'S DAY. Nov 14. Pizza Hut and the Center for the Book in the Library of Congress established National Young Reader's Day to remind Americans of the joys and importance of reading for young people. Schools, libraries, families and communities nationwide use this day to celebrate youth reading in a variety of creative and educational ways. Ideas on ways you can celebrate this special day are available. For info: Shelley Morehead, The BOOK IT! Program, PO Box 2999, Wichita, KS 67201. Phone: (800) 426-6548. Fax: (316) 685-0977. E-mail: read@bookitprogram.com. Web: www.bookitprogram.com.

NEHRU, JAWAHARLAL: BIRTH ANNIVERSARY. Nov 14, 1889. Indian leader and first prime minister after independence. Born at Allahabad, India, he died May 27, 1964, at New Delhi.

BIRTHDAYS TODAY

Ben Cayetano, 62, Governor of Hawaii (D), born Honolulu, HI, Nov 14, 1939.

Prince Charles, 53, Prince of Wales, heir to the British throne, born London, England, Nov 14, 1948.

Astrid Lindgren, 94, children's author (*Pippi Longstocking, The Brothers Lionheart*), born Vimmerby, Sweden, Nov 14, 1907.

Condoleezza Rice, 47, US National Security Adviser, born Birmingham, Al, Nov 14, 1954.

Curt Schilling, 35, baseball player, born Anchorage, AK, Nov 14, 1966.

William Steig, 94, cartoonist, illustrator and author (*Pete's a Pizza*, Caldecott for *Sylvester and the Magic Pebble*), born New York, NY, Nov 14, 1907.

NOVEMBER 15 — THURSDAY

Day 319 — 46 Remaining

★**AMERICA RECYCLES DAY.** Nov 15.

AMERICAN SPEECH–LANGUAGE–HEARING ASSOCIATION CONVENTION. Nov 15–18. New Orleans, LA. Scientific sessions held on language, speech disorders, hearing science and hearing disorders and matters of professional interest to speech-language pathologists and audiologists. Est attendance: 10,000. For info: Cheryl Russell, Conv Dir, American Speech–Language–Hearing Assn, 10801 Rockville Pike, Rockville, MD 20852-3279. Phone: (301) 897-5700. Web: www.asha.org.

BRAZIL: REPUBLIC DAY. Nov 15. Commemorates the Proclamation of the Republic in 1889.

GREAT AMERICAN SMOKEOUT. Nov 15. A day observed to celebrate smoke-free environments. Annually, the third Thursday in November. For info: PR Dept, American Cancer Soc, 1599 Clifton Rd NE, Atlanta, GA 30329. Phone: (404) 329-5735. Web: www.2cancer.org/gas/index.cfm

JAPAN: SHICHI-GO-SAN. Nov 15. Annual children's festival. The *Shichi-Go-San* (Seven-Five-Three) rite, observed Nov 15, is "the most picturesque event in the autumn season." Parents take their three-year-old children of either sex, five-year-old boys and seven-year-old girls to the parish shrines dressed in their best clothes. There the guardian spirits are thanked for the healthy growth of the children and prayers are offered for their further development.

MOON PHASE: NEW MOON. Nov 15. Moon enters New Moon phase at 1:40 AM, EST.

NATIONAL COUNCIL OF TEACHERS OF ENGLISH ANNUAL CONVENTION. Nov 15–18. Baltimore, MD. Conference theme: "Re-Creating the Classroom." For info: Natl Council of Teachers of English, 1111 W Kenyon Rd, Urbana, IL 61801-1096. Phone: (800) 369-6283 or (217) 328-3870. Web: www.ncte.org.

★**NATIONAL GREAT AMERICAN SMOKEOUT DAY.** Nov 15.

O'KEEFFE, GEORGIA: BIRTH ANNIVERSARY. Nov 15, 1887. Described as one of the greatest American artists of the 20th century, O'Keeffe painted desert landscapes and flower studies. Born at Sun Prairie, WI, she was married to the famous photographer Alfred Stieglitz. She died at Santa Fe, NM, Mar 6, 1986. For more info: *My Name is Georgia: A Portrait*, by Jeanette Winter (Harcourt, 0-15-201649-X, $16 Gr. 2–4).

BIRTHDAYS TODAY

Daniel Manus Pinkwater, 60, author (*Lizard Music, Snarkout Boys and the Avocado of Death*), born Memphis, TN, Nov 15, 1941.

November 2001

S	M	T	W	T	F	S
				1	2	3
4	5	6	7	8	9	10
11	12	13	14	15	16	17
18	19	20	21	22	23	24
25	26	27	28	29	30	

NOVEMBER 16 — FRIDAY

Day 320 — 45 Remaining

AMERICAN COUNCIL ON THE TEACHING OF FOREIGN LANGUAGES ANNUAL CONFERENCE. Nov 16–18. Washington, DC. For info: American Council on the Teaching of Foreign Languages, 6 Executive Plaza, Yonkers, NY 10701-6801. Phone: (914) 963-8830. Web: www.actfl.org.

ESTONIA: DAY OF NATIONAL REBIRTH. Nov 16. National holiday. Commemorates the 1988 Declaration of Sovereignty.

NATIONAL COUNCIL FOR THE SOCIAL STUDIES ANNUAL MEETING. Nov 16–18. Washington, DC. 81st annual meeting. For info: Natl Council for the Social Studies, 3501 Newark St NW, Washington, DC 20016. Phone: (202) 966-7840. Web: www.ncss.org.

★**NATIONAL FARM-CITY WEEK.** Nov 16–22. Presidential Proclamation issued for a week in November since 1956, customarily for the week ending with Thanksgiving Day. Requested by congressional resolutions from 1956–1958; since 1959 issued annually without request.

OKLAHOMA: ADMISSION DAY: ANNIVERSARY. Nov 16. Became 46th state in 1907.

RAMADAN: THE ISLAMIC MONTH OF FASTING. Nov 16–Dec 15. Begins on Islamic lunar calendar date Ramadan 1, 1422. Ramadan, the ninth month of the Islamic calendar, is holy because it was during this month that the Holy Qur'an [Koran] was revealed. All adults of sound body and mind fast from dawn (before sunrise) until sunset to achieve spiritual and physical purification and self-discipline, abstaining from food, drink and intimate relations. It is a time for feeling a common bond with the poor and needy, a time of piety and prayer. Different methods for "anticipating" the visibility of the new moon crescent at Mecca are used by different Muslim groups. US date may vary. For links to Ramadan sites on the web, go to: deil.lang.uiuc.edu/web.pages/holidays/ramadan.html or holidays.net/ramadan/.

RIEL, LOUIS: HANGING ANNIVERSARY. Nov 16, 1885. Born at St. Boniface, Manitoba, Canada, Oct 23, 1844, Louis Riel, leader of the Metis (French/Indian mixed ancestry), was elected to Canada's House of Commons in 1873 and 1874, but never seated. Confined to asylums for madness (feigned or falsely charged, some said), Riel became a US citizen in 1883. In 1885 he returned to western Canada to lead the North West Rebellion. Defeated, he surrendered and was tried for treason, convicted and hanged, at Regina, Northwest Territory, Canada. Seen as a patriot and protector of French culture in Canada, Riel's life and death became a legend and a symbol of the problems between French and English Canadians.

ROMAN CATHOLICS ISSUE NEW CATECHISM: ANNIVERSARY. Nov 16, 1992. For the first time since 1563, the Roman Catholic Church issued a new universal catechism, which addressed modern-day issues.

SAINT EUSTATIUS, WEST INDIES: STATIA AND AMERICA DAY: 225th ANNIVERSARY. Nov 16. St. Eustatius, Leeward Islands. To commemorate the first salute to an American flag by a foreign government, from Fort Oranje in 1776. Festivities include sports events and dancing. During the American Revolution St. Eustatius was an important trading center and a supply base for the colonies.

SPACE MILESTONE: *VENERA 3* (USSR). Nov 16, 1965. This unmanned space probe crashed into Venus, Mar 1, 1966. First manmade object on another planet.

TEXAS PTA CONVENTION. Nov 16–18. Dallas, TX. The annual business meeting of the Texas PTA. General business meeting includes adoption of legislative positions and resolutions. More than 40 workshops are presented on parenting and parent involvement issues. Est attendance: 2,000. For info: Joan Thurman, Texas PTA, 408 W 11th St, Austin, TX 78701-2199. Phone: (512) 476-6769 or (800) TALK-PTA. Fax: (512) 476-8152. E-mail: info@txpta.org. Web: www.txpta.org.

UNITED NATIONS: INTERNATIONAL DAY FOR TOLERANCE. Nov 16. On Dec 12, 1996, the General Assembly established the International Day for Tolerance, to commemorate the adoption by UNESCO member states of the Declaration of Principles on Tolerance Nov 16, 1995. For info: United Nations, Dept of Public Info, New York, NY 10017.

BIRTHDAYS TODAY

Oksana Baiul, 24, Olympic figure skater, born Dniepropetrovsk, Ukraine, Nov 16, 1977.

Victoria Chess, 62, illustrator (*King Long Shanks*), born Chicago, IL, Nov 16, 1939.

Jean Fritz, 86, author (Laura Ingalls Wilder Medal for *The Cabin Faced West;* Newberry Honor for *Homesick: My Own Story*), born Hankow, China, Nov 16, 1915.

Dwight Eugene Gooden, 37, baseball player, born Tampa, FL, Nov 16, 1964.

Robin McKinley, 49, author (Newbery for *The Hero and the Crown*), born Jennifer Carolyn Robin McKinley, Warren, OH, Nov 16, 1952.

Carolyn Reeder, 64, author (*Shades of Gray*), born Washington, DC, Nov 16, 1937.

NOVEMBER 17 — SATURDAY

Day 321 — 44 Remaining

NATIONAL COMMUNITY EDUCATION ASSOCIATION CONFERENCE. Nov 17–20. Charleston Place, Charleston, SC. 36th annual. Largest national gathering for community educators and others interested in promoting parent-community involvement in education, forming community partnerships to address community needs and expanding lifelong learning opportunities for all community residents. Est attendance: 700. For info: Ursula Ellis, Dir of Communications, Natl Community Education Assn, 3929 Old Lee Hwy, Ste 91-A, Fairfax, VA 22030-2401. Phone: (703) 359-8973. Fax: (703) 359-0972. E-mail: ncea@ncea.com. Web: www.ncea.com.

THAILAND: ELEPHANT ROUND-UP AT SURIN. Nov 17. Elephant demonstrations in morning, elephant races and tug-of-war between 100 men and one elephant. Observed since 1961 on third Saturday in November. Special trains from Bangkok on previous day.

WORLD PEACE DAY. Nov 17. World Peace Day was created to give the common person a way to demonstrate his or her desire for peace. To do this, people pray for peace all day, drive with their headlights on, wear a white ribbon for peace (everyday) and sign the petition for peace (available on the web page listed below) or print a petition for peace and have 20 people sign it. Annually, Nov 17. For info: Don Morris, PO Box 565245, Miami, FL 33256-5245. Phone: (305) 270-8890. E-mail: peaceguy@peaceday.org. Web: www.peaceday.org.

BIRTHDAYS TODAY

Justin Cooper, 13, actor (*Liar, Liar;* "Brother's Keeper"), born Los Angeles, CA, Nov 17, 1988.

Howard Dean, 53, Governor of Vermont (D), born East Hampton, NY, Nov 17, 1948.

Danny DeVito, 57, actor (*Twins, Matilda*), born Neptune, NJ, Nov 17, 1944.

(Clarke) Isaac Hanson, 21, singer (Hanson), born Tulsa, OK, Nov 17, 1980.

James M. Inhofe, 67, US Senator (R, Oklahoma), born Des Moines, IA, Nov 17, 1934.

NOVEMBER 18 — SUNDAY

Day 322 — 43 Remaining

DAGUERRE, LOUIS JACQUES MANDE: BIRTH ANNIVERSARY. Nov 18, 1789. French tax collector, theater scene-painter, physicist and inventor, was born at Cormeilles-en-Parisis, France. He is remembered for his invention of the daguerreotype photographic process—one of the earliest to permit a photographic image to be chemically fixed to provide a permanent picture. The process was presented to the French Academy of Science Jan 7, 1839. Daguerre died near Paris, France, July 10, 1851.

GERMANY: VOLKSTRAUERTAG. Nov 18. Memorial Day and national day of mourning in all German states.

LATVIA: INDEPENDENCE DAY. Nov 18. National holiday. Commemorates the declaration of an independent Latvia in 1918.

MICKEY MOUSE'S BIRTHDAY. Nov 18. The comical activities of squeaky-voiced Mickey Mouse first appeared in 1928, on the screen of the Colony Theatre at New York City. The film, Walt Disney's *Steamboat Willie,* was the first animated cartoon talking picture. For more info: disney.go.com.

NATIONAL ADOPTION WEEK. Nov 18–24. To commemorate the success of three kinds of adoption—infant, special needs and intercountry—through a variety of special events. Annually, the week of Thanksgiving. Est attendance: 15,000. For info: Natl Council for Adoption, 1930 17th St NW, Washington, DC 20009-6207. Phone: (202) 328-1200. Fax: (202) 332-0935.

NATIONAL BIBLE WEEK. Nov 18–25. An interfaith campaign to promote reading and study of the Bible. Resource packets available. Governors and mayors across the country proclaim National Bible Week observance in their constituencies. Annually, from the Sunday preceding Thanksgiving to the following Sunday. For info: Thomas R. May, Exec Dir, Natl Bible Assn, 1865 Broadway, 7th Floor, New York, NY 10023. Phone: (212) 408-1390.

★**NATIONAL FAMILY WEEK.** Nov 18–24.

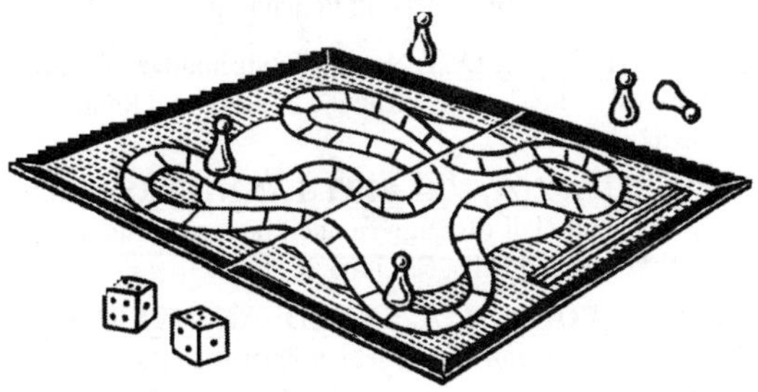

NATIONAL GAME AND PUZZLE WEEK. Nov 18–24. To increase appreciation of games and puzzles while preserving the tradition of investing time with family and friends. Annually, the Sunday through Saturday of Thanksgiving week. For info: Frank Beres, Patch Products, PO Box 268, Beloit, WI 53512-0268. Phone: (608) 362-6896. Fax: (608) 362-8178. E-mail: patch@patchproducts.com. Web: www.patchproducts.com.

OMAN: NATIONAL HOLIDAY. Nov 18. Sultanate of Oman celebrates its national day.

SHEPARD, ALAN: BIRTH ANNIVERSARY. Nov 18, 1923. Astronaut, born at East Derry, NH. Shepard was the first American in space when he flew *Freedom 7* in 1961, just 23 days after Russian Yuri Gargarin was the first person in space. Shepard died July 21, 1998, near Monterey, CA.

SOUTH AFRICA ADOPTS NEW CONSTITUTION: ANNIVERSARY. Nov 18, 1993. After more than 300 years of white majority rule, basic civil rights were finally granted to blacks in South Africa. The constitution providing such rights was approved by representatives of the ruling party, as well as members of 20 other political parties.

TEDDY BEAR: ANNIVERSARY. Nov 18, 1902. The *Washington Evening Star* published a cartoon on this day showing President Teddy Roosevelt refusing to shoot a mother bear while he was on a hunting trip in Mississippi. Candy store operator Morris Michtom and his wife of Brooklyn, NY, obtained the president's permission to use his name on their brown plush toy bear. While stuffed bears had been available for many years, this was the first to be called a teddy bear.

US UNIFORM TIME ZONE PLAN: ANNIVERSARY. Nov 18, 1883. Charles Ferdinand Dowd, a Connecticut school teacher and one of the early advocates of uniform time, proposed a time zone plan of the US (four zones of 15 degrees), which he and others persuaded the railroads to adopt and place in operation. Info from National Bureau of Standards Monograph 155. See also: "US Standard Time Act: Anniversary" (Mar 19).

BIRTHDAYS TODAY

Dante Bichette, 38, baseball player, born West Palm Beach, FL, Nov 18, 1963.

Raghib (Rocket) Ismail, 32, football player, born Elizabeth, NJ, Nov 18, 1969.

Wilma Mankiller, 56, Chief of the Cherokee Nation 1985–95, born Tahlequah, OK, Nov 18, 1945.

Warren Moon, 45, football player, born Los Angeles, CA, Nov 18, 1956.

Ted Stevens, 78, US Senator (R, Alaska), born Indianapolis, IN, Nov 18, 1923.

Nancy Van Laan, 62, author (*So Say the Little Monkeys*), born Baton Rouge, LA, Nov 18, 1939.

NOVEMBER 19 — MONDAY

Day 323 — 42 Remaining

BELIZE: GARIFUNA DAY. Nov 19. Public holiday celebrating the first arrival of Black Caribs from St. Vincent and Rotan to southern Belize in 1823.

CAMPANELLA, ROY: 80th BIRTH ANNIVERSARY. Nov 19, 1921. Baseball Hall of Fame catcher, born at Philadelphia, PA. Died at Woodland Hills, CA, June 26, 1993.

COLD WAR FORMALLY ENDED: ANNIVERSARY. Nov 19–21, 1990. A summit was held at Paris with the leaders of the Conference on Security and Cooperation in Europe (CSCE) Nov 19–21, 1990. The highlight of the summit was the signing of a treaty to dramatically reduce conventional weapons in Europe, thereby ending the Cold War.

FINLAND: INTERNATIONAL CHILDREN'S FILM FESTIVAL. Nov 19–25. Oulu. This one-week event gives festival visitors an opportunity to view several dozen feature-length films. Est attendance: 10,000. For info: Finnish Tourist Board, 655 Third Ave, New York, NY 10017. Phone: (212) 885-9700 or (358) (8) 881-1293. Fax: (358) (8) 8811290. Web: www.ouka.fi/oekeng.htm.

FIRST AUTOMATIC TOLL COLLECTION MACHINE: ANNIVERSARY. Nov 19, 1954. At the Union Toll Plaza on New Jersey's Garden State Parkway motorists dropped 25 ¢ into a wire mesh hopper and a green light would flash. The first modern toll road was the Pennsylvania Turnpike, which opened in 1940.

GARFIELD, JAMES ABRAM: BIRTH ANNIVERSARY. Nov 19, 1831. The 20th president of the US was born at Orange, OH and was the first left-handed president. Term of office: Mar 4–Sept 19, 1881. While walking into the Washington, DC, railway station on the morning of July 2, 1881, Garfield was shot by disappointed office seeker Charles J. Guiteau. He survived, in very weak condition, until Sept 19, 1881, when he succumbed to blood poisoning at Elberon, NJ (where he had been taken for recuperation). Guiteau was tried, convicted and hanged at the jail at Washington, June 30, 1882. For info: www.ipl.org/ref/POTUS.

LINCOLN'S GETTYSBURG ADDRESS: ANNIVERSARY. Nov 19, 1863. Seventeen acres of the Civil War battlefield at Gettysburg, PA, were dedicated as a national cemetery. Noted orator Edward Everett spoke for two hours; the address that Lincoln delivered in less than two minutes was later recognized as one of the most eloquent of the English language. Five manuscript copies in Lincoln's hand survive, including the rough draft begun in ink at the executive mansion at Washington and concluded in pencil at Gettysburg on the morning of the dedication (kept at the Library of Congress). For more info: *The Gettysburg Address* (Houghton Mifflin, 0-395-69824-3, $14.95 Gr. 3–5) or *Abraham Lincoln's Gettysburg Address: Four Score and More*, by Barbara Silberdick Feinberg (Twenty-First Century, 0-7613-1410-8, $24.40 Gr. 4–8) or go to Ben's Guide to US Government for Kids: bens guide.gpo.gov.

MONACO: NATIONAL HOLIDAY. Nov 19.

PUERTO RICO: DISCOVERY DAY. Nov 19. Public holiday. Columbus discovered Puerto Rico in 1493 on his second voyage to the New World.

RETIRED TEACHER'S DAY IN FLORIDA. Nov 19. A ceremonial day to honor the retired teachers of the state.

"ROCKY AND HIS FRIENDS" TV PREMIERE: ANNIVERSARY. Nov 19, 1959. This popular cartoon featured the adventures of a talking squirrel, Rocky (Rocket J. Squirrel), and his friend Bullwinkle, a flaky moose. The tongue-in-cheek dialogue contrasted with the simple plots in which Rocky and Bull-

November 2001

S	M	T	W	T	F	S
				1	2	3
4	5	6	7	8	9	10
11	12	13	14	15	16	17
18	19	20	21	22	23	24
25	26	27	28	29	30	

winkle tangled with Russian bad guys Boris Badenov and Natasha (who worked for Mr Big). Other popular segments on the show included the adventures of Sherman and Mr Peabody (an intelligent talking dog). In 1961 the show was renamed "The Bullwinkle Show," but the cast of characters remained the same.

SCHAEFER, JACK: BIRTH ANNIVERSARY. Nov 19, 1907. Author of the bestseller *Shane*, which was later made into an award-winning film. Born at Cleveland, OH, Schaefer died Jan 24, 1991, at Santa Fe, NM.

ZION NATIONAL PARK ESTABLISHED: ANNIVERSARY. Nov 19, 1919. Utah's Mukuntuweap National Monument, proclaimed July 31, 1909, and later incorporated in Zion National Monument by proclamation Mar 18, 1918, was established as Zion National Park in 1919. For more park info: Zion Natl Park, Springdale, UT 84767-1099. Web: www.nps.gov/zion.

BIRTHDAYS TODAY

Eileen Collins, 45, first female shuttle commander, Lieutenant Colonel USAF, born Elmira, NY, Nov 19, 1956.

Gail Devers, 35, Olympic gold medal sprinter, born Seattle, WA, Nov 19, 1966.

Jodie Foster, 39, actress (*Little Man Tate, Nell*), director (*Home for the Holidays*), born Los Angeles, CA, Nov 19, 1962.

Thomas R. Harkin, 62, US Senator (D, Iowa), born Cumming, IA, Nov 19, 1939.

Jim Hodges, 45, Governor of South Carolina (D), born Lancaster, SC, Nov 19, 1956.

Ahmad Rashad, 52, sportscaster, former football player, born Bobby Moore, Portland, OR, Nov 19, 1949.

Meg Ryan, 40, actress (*Sleepless in Seattle*), born Fairfield, CT, Nov 19, 1961.

Kerri Strug, 24, Olympic gymnast, born Tucson, AZ, Nov 19, 1977.

Tommy G. Thompson, 60, Secretary, US Department of Health and Human Services (George W. Bush administration), former governor of Wisconsin (R), born Elroy, WI, Nov 19, 1941.

Ted Turner, 63, baseball, basketball and cable TV executive, born Cincinnati, OH, Nov 19, 1938.

NOVEMBER 20 — TUESDAY

Day 324 — 41 Remaining

BILL OF RIGHTS: ANNIVERSARY OF FIRST STATE RATIFICATION. Nov 20, 1789. New Jersey became the first state to ratify 10 of the 12 amendments to the US Constitution proposed by Congress Sept 25. These 10 amendments came to be known as the Bill of Rights.

KENNEDY, ROBERT FRANCIS: BIRTH ANNIVERSARY. Nov 20, 1925. US Senator and younger brother of John F. Kennedy (35th president), born at Brookline, MA. An assassin shot him at Los Angeles, CA, June 5, 1968, while he was campaigning for the presidential nomination. He died the next day. Sirhan Sirhan was convicted of his murder.

LAURIER, SIR WILFRED: BIRTH ANNIVERSARY. Nov 20, 1841. Canadian statesman (premier, 1896–1911), born at St. Lin, Quebec. Died Feb 17, 1919, at Ottawa, Ontario.

MEXICO: REVOLUTION DAY. Nov 20. Anniversary of the social revolution launched by Francisco I. Madero in 1910. National holiday.

NATIONAL ASSOCIATION FOR THE EDUCATION OF YOUNG CHILDREN CONFERENCE. Nov 20–23. New York, NY. For info: Natl Assn for the Education of Young Children, 1509 16th St NW, Washington, DC 20036. Phone: (202) 232-8777. Fax: (202) 328-1846. E-mail: naeyc@naeyc.org. Web: www.naeyc.org.

UNITED NATIONS: UNIVERSAL CHILDREN'S DAY. Nov 20. Designated by the United Nations General Assembly as Universal Children's Day. First observance was in 1953. A time to honor children with special ceremonies and festivals and to make children's needs known to governments. Observed on different days in more than 120 nations; Nov 20 marks the day in 1959 when the General Assembly adopted the Declaration of the Rights of the Child.

WOLCOTT, OLIVER: 275th BIRTH ANNIVERSARY. Nov 20, 1726. Signer of the Declaration of Independence, Governor of Connecticut, born at Windsor, CT. Died Dec 1, 1797, at Litchfield, CT.

BIRTHDAYS TODAY

Marion Dane Bauer, 63, author (*On My Honor*), born Oglesby, IL, Nov 20, 1938.

Joseph Robinette Biden, Jr, 59, US Senator (D, Delaware), born Scranton, PA, Nov 20, 1942.

Robert C. Byrd, 84, US Senator (D, West Virginia), born North Wilkesboro, NC, Nov 20, 1917.

Donald T. DiFrancesco, 57, Governor of New Jersey (R), born Trenton, New Jersey, Nov 20, 1944.

NOVEMBER 21 — WEDNESDAY

Day 325 — 40 Remaining

CONGRESS FIRST MEETS IN WASHINGTON: ANNIVERSARY. Nov 21, 1800. Congress met at Philadelphia from 1790 to 1800, when the north wing of the new Capitol at Washington, DC was completed. The House and Senate were scheduled to meet in the new building Nov 17, 1800 but a quorum wasn't achieved until Nov 21. To take a virtual tour of the Capitol, go to: www.senate.gov/vtour.

GERMANY: BUSS UND BETTAG. Nov 21. Buss und Bettag (Repentance Day) is observed on the Wednesday before the last Sunday of the church year. A legal public holiday in all German states except Bavaria (where it is observed only in communities with predominantly Protestant populations).

NORTH CAROLINA RATIFIES CONSTITUTION: ANNIVERSARY. Nov 21. Became 12th state to ratify Constitution in 1789.

SPEARE, ELIZABETH GEORGE: BIRTH ANNIVERSARY. Nov 21, 1908. Author (Newbery for *The Bronze Bow, The Witch of Blackbird Pond*), born at Melrose, MA. Died at Tucson, AZ, Nov 15, 1994. For a study guide to *The Witch of Blackbird Pond*: glencoe.com/sec/literature/litlibrary.

UNITED NATIONS: WORLD TELEVISION DAY:5th ANNIVERSARY. Nov 21. On Dec 17, 1996, the General Assembly proclaimed this day as World Television Day, commemorating the date in 1996 on which the first World Television Forum was held at the UN. Info from: United Nations, Dept of Public Info, New York, NY 10017.

"WHAT DO YOU LOVE ABOUT AMERICA" DAY. Nov 21. One day to talk about what's great about our country and its people. In the midst of cynicism, let's talk to each other about what we love. Annually, the day before Thanksgiving. For info: Chuck Sutherland, 6906 Waggoner Pl, Dallas, TX 75230. Phone: (214) 696-9214. Fax: (214) 696-6742. E-mail: sutherla@swbell.net.

WORLD HELLO DAY. Nov 21. Everyone who participates greets 10 people. People in 180 countries have participated in this annual activity for advancing peace through personal communication. Heads of state of 114 countries have expressed approval of the event. 29th annual observance. For info: Michael McCormack, The McCormack Brothers, Box 993, Omaha, NE 68101. Web: www.worldhelloday.org.

BIRTHDAYS TODAY

Troy Aikman, 35, football player, born West Covina, CA, Nov 21, 1966.

Richard J. Durbin, 57, US Senator (D, Illinois), born East St. Louis, IL, Nov 21, 1944.

George Kenneth (Ken) Griffey, Jr, 32, baseball player, born Donora, PA, Nov 21, 1969.

Stanley (Stan the Man) Musial, 81, Baseball Hall of Fame outfielder and first baseman, born Donora, PA, Nov 21, 1920.

Harold Ramis, 57, actor (*Ghostbusters, Ghostbusters II*), born Chicago, IL, Nov 21, 1944.

Marlo Thomas, 63, actress ("That Girl"), author (*Free to Be . . . You and Me*), born Detroit, MI, Nov 21, 1938.

Megan Whalen Turner, 36, author (*The Thief*), born Fort Sill, OK, Nov 21, 1965.

NOVEMBER 22 — THURSDAY

Day 326 — 39 Remaining

ADAMS, ABIGAIL SMITH: BIRTH ANNIVERSARY. Nov 22, 1744. Wife of John Adams, second president of the US, born at Weymouth, MA. Died Oct 28, 1818, at Quincy, MA.

AMERICA'S THANKSGIVING PARADE. Nov 22. Woodward Ave, Detroit, MI. The annual parade kicks off the holiday season with nearly 100 units marching. Annually, on Thanksgiving morning. Est attendance: 1,300,000. For info: Dennis Carnovale, The Parade Co, 9600 Mt Elliott, Detroit, MI 48211. Phone: (313) 923-7400. Fax: (313) 923-2920.

GARNER, JOHN NANCE: BIRTH ANNIVERSARY. Nov 22, 1868. The 32nd vice president of US (1933–41) born at Red River County, TX. Died at Uvalde, TX, Nov 7, 1967.

LEBANON: INDEPENDENCE DAY. Nov 22. National Day. Gained independence from France in 1943.

MACY'S THANKSGIVING DAY PARADE. Nov 22. New York, NY. Starts at 9 AM, EST, in Central Park West. A part of everyone's Thanksgiving, the parade grows bigger and better each year. Featuring floats, giant balloons, marching bands and famous stars, the parade is televised for the whole country. 73rd annual parade. For info: New York CVB, 810 Seventh Ave, New York, NY 10019. Phone: (212) 484-1222. Web: www.nycvisit.com.

MOON PHASE: FIRST QUARTER. Nov 22. Moon enters First Quarter phase at 6:21 PM, EST.

NATIONAL STOP THE VIOLENCE DAY. Nov 22. Radio and television stations across the nation are encouraged to promote "Peace on the Streets" and help put an end to gang (and other) violence through Stop the Violence Day. Participating stations unite to call for a one-day cease fire, the idea being, "If we can stop the violence for one day, we can stop the violence everyday, one day at a time." Stations also encourage listeners/viewers to wear and display white ribbons that day and drive with their headlights on as a show of peace. Many stations hold peace rallies with local community leaders and also conduct a moment of silence on the air in honor of the year's victims of violence. Begun in 1990. Annually, on the anniversary of President John F. Kennedy's assassination. For info: Cliff Berkowitz, Pres, Lost Coast Communications, Inc, PO Box 25, Ferndale, CA 95536. Phone: (707) 786-5104. Fax: (707) 786-5100.

★**THANKSGIVING DAY.** Nov 22. Presidential Proclamation. Always issued for the fourth Thursday in November. See also: "First US Holiday by Presidential Proclamation: Anniversary" (Nov 26).

THANKSGIVING DAY. Nov 22. Legal public holiday (Public Law 90–363 sets Thanksgiving Day on the fourth Thursday in November). Observed in all states. In most states, the Friday after Thanksgiving is also a holiday; in Nevada it is called Family Day. For more info: *Let's Celebrate Thanksgiving*, by Peter and Connie Roop (Millbrook, 0-7613-0973-X, $19.90 Gr. PreK–3). For links to sites about Thanksgiving on the web, go to: deil.lang.uiuc.edu/web.pages/holidays/thanksgiving.html.

BIRTHDAYS TODAY

Boris Becker, 34, tennis player, born Leimen, Germany, Nov 22, 1967.

Guion S. Bluford, Jr, 59, first black astronaut in space, born Philadelphia, PA, Nov 22, 1942.

Jamie Lee Curtis, 43, actress, author (*Today I Feel Silly and Other Moods That Make My Day*), born Los Angeles, CA, Nov 22, 1958.

Keyshawn Johnson, 29, football player, born Los Angeles, CA, Nov 22, 1972.

NOVEMBER 23 — FRIDAY

Day 327 — 38 Remaining

BLACK FRIDAY. Nov 23. The traditional beginning of the Christmas shopping season on the Friday after Thanksgiving.

BUY NOTHING DAY. Nov 23. A 24-hour moratorium on consumer spending, a celebration of simplicity, about getting our runaway consumer culture back onto a sustainable path. Annually, on the first shopping day after Thanksgiving. For info: The Media Foundation, 1243 W. 7th Ave, Vancouver, BC, Canada V6H 1B7. Phone: (800) 663-1243. Fax: (604) 737-6021. E-mail: buynothingday@adbusters.org.

FAMILY DAY IN NEVADA. Nov 23. Observed annually on the Friday following the fourth Thursday in November.

JAPAN: LABOR THANKSGIVING DAY. Nov 23. National holiday.

PIERCE, FRANKLIN: BIRTH ANNIVERSARY. Nov 23, 1804. The 14th president of the US (Mar 4, 1853–Mar 3, 1857) was born at Hillsboro, NH. Not nominated until the 49th ballot at the Democratic party convention in 1852, he was refused his party's nomination in 1856 for a second term. Pierce died at Concord, NH, Oct 8, 1869. For info: www.ipl.org/ref/POTUS.

November 2001

S	M	T	W	T	F	S
				1	2	3
4	5	6	7	8	9	10
11	12	13	14	15	16	17
18	19	20	21	22	23	24
25	26	27	28	29	30	

RUTLEDGE, EDWARD: BIRTH ANNIVERSARY. Nov 23, 1749. Signer of the Declaration of Independence, governor of South Carolina, born at Charleston, SC. Died there Jan 23, 1800.

SAGITTARIUS, THE ARCHER. Nov 23–Dec 21. In the astronomical/astrological zodiac that divides the sun's apparent orbit into 12 segments, the period Nov 22–Dec 21 is identified, traditionally, as the sun-sign of Sagittarius, the Archer. The ruling planet is Jupiter.

BIRTHDAYS TODAY

Vin Baker, 30, basketball player, born Lake Wales, FL, Nov 23, 1971.

Mary L. Landrieu, 46, US Senator (D, Louisiana), born Arlington, VA, Nov 23, 1955.

Charles E. Schumer, 51, US Senator (D, New York), born Brooklyn, NY, Nov 23, 1950.

Gloria Whelan, 78, author (National Book Award for *Homeless Bird; Once on This Island, The Indian School,*), born Detroit, MI, Nov 23, 1923.

NOVEMBER 24 — SATURDAY

Day 328 — 37 Remaining

BARKLEY, ALBEN WILLIAM: BIRTH ANNIVERSARY. Nov 24, 1877. The 35th vice president of the US (1949–53), born at Graves County, KY. Died at Lexington, VA, Apr 30, 1956.

BURNETT, FRANCES HODGSON: BIRTH ANNIVERSARY. Nov 24, 1849. Children's author, noted for the classics *Little Lord Fauntleroy, The Secret Garden* and *A Little Princess*. Born at Manchester, England, she died at Long Island, NY, Oct 29, 1924.

MEXICO: GUADALAJARA INTERNATIONAL BOOK FAIR. Nov 24–Dec 2. Mexico's largest book fair with exhibitors from all over the Spanish-speaking world. Est attendance: 275,000. For info: David Unger, Guadalajara Book Fair–US Office, Div of Hum, NAC 6293, City College, New York, NY 10031. Phone: (212) 650-7925. Fax: (212) 650-7912. E-mail: daucc@cunyvm.cuny.edu.

TAYLOR, ZACHARY: BIRTH ANNIVERSARY. Nov 24, 1784. The soldier who became 12th president of the US (Mar 4, 1849–July 9, 1850) was born at Orange County, VA. He was nominated at the Whig party convention in 1848, but, the story goes, he did not accept the letter notifying him of his nomination because it had postage due. He cast his first vote in 1846, when he was 62 years old. Becoming ill July 4, 1850, he died at the White House, July 9. For info: www.ipl.org/ref/POTUS.

UCHIDA, YOSHIKO: BIRTH ANNIVERSARY. Nov 24, 1921. Author of *Journey to Topaz: A Story of the Japanese-American Evacuation*, born at Alameda, CA. Died in 1992. For a study guide to *Picture Bride*: glencoe.com/sec/literature/litlibrary.

BIRTHDAYS TODAY

Sylvia Louise Engdahl, 68, author (*Enchantress from the Stars*), born Los Angeles, CA, Nov 24, 1933.

Mordicai Gerstein, 66, author (*The Wild Boy*), born Los Angeles, CA, Nov 24, 1935.

Dan Glickman, 57, former US Secretary of Agriculture, born Wichita, KS, Nov 24, 1944.

Meredith Henderson, 18, actress ("The Adventures of Shirley Holmes: Detective"), born Ottawa, ON, Canada, Nov 24, 1983.

Ruth Sanderson, 50, author, illustrator (*The Twelve Dancing Princesses, Papa Gatto*), born Ware, MA, Nov 24, 1951.

NOVEMBER 25 — SUNDAY

Day 329 — 36 Remaining

AUTOMOBILE SPEED REDUCTION: ANNIVERSARY. Nov 25, 1973. Anniversary of the presidential order requiring a cutback from the 70 mph speed limit due to the energy crisis. The 55 mph National Maximum Speed Limit (NMSL) was established by Congress in January 1974. The National Highway Traffic Administration reported that "the 55 mph NMSL forestalled 48,310 fatalities through 1980. There were also reductions in crash-related injuries and property damage." Motor fuel savings were estimated at 2.4 billion gallons per year. Notwithstanding, in 1987 Congress permitted states to increase speed limits on rural interstate highways to 65 mph.

BOSNIA AND HERZEGOVINA: NATIONAL DAY. Nov 25. National holiday. Commemorates the 1943 declaration of statehood within the Yugoslav Federation.

CARNEGIE, ANDREW: BIRTH ANNIVERSARY. Nov 25, 1835. American financier, philanthropist and benefactor of more than 2,500 libraries, was born at Dunfermline, Scotland. Carnegie Hall, Carnegie Foundation and the Carnegie Endowment for International Peace are among his gifts. Carnegie wrote in 1889, "Surplus wealth is a sacred trust which its possessor is bound to administer in his lifetime for the good of the community. . . . The man who dies . . . rich dies disgraced." Carnegie died at his summer estate, "Shadowbrook," MA, Aug 11, 1919. For more info: www.pbs.org/wgbh/amex/carnegie.

DiMAGGIO, JOSEPH PAUL (JOE): BIRTH ANNIVERSARY. Nov 25, 1914. Baseball Hall of Fame outfielder, born at Martinez, CA. In 1941 he was on "the streak," getting a hit in 56 consecutive games. He was the American League MVP for three years, was the batting champion in 1939 and led the league in RBIs in both 1941 and 1948. DiMaggio died at Harbour Island, FL, Mar 8, 1999. For more info: www.pbs.org/wgbh/amex/dimaggio.

EASTMAN, P.D.: BIRTH ANNIVERSARY. Nov 25, 1909. Philip Dey Eastman was born at Amherst, MA. His *Are You My Mother?* and *Go, Dog, Go!* rank among the bestselling children's books of all time. He died Jan 7, 1986.

JOHN F. KENNEDY DAY IN MASSACHUSETTS. Nov 25. Proclaimed annually by the governor for the last Sunday in November.

PASADENA DOO DAH PARADE. Nov 25. Pasadena, CA. No theme, no judging, no prizes, no order of march, no motorized vehicles and no animals. Annually, the Sunday following Thanksgiving Day.

POPE JOHN XXIII: BIRTH ANNIVERSARY. Nov 25, 1881. Angelo Roncalli, 261st pope of the Roman Catholic Church, born at Sotte il Monte, Italy. Elected pope, Oct 28, 1958. Died June 3, 1963, at Rome, Italy.

SHOPPING REMINDER DAY. Nov 25. One month before Christmas, a reminder to shoppers that there are only 28 more shopping days (excluding Christmas Eve) after today until Christmas, and that one month from today a new countdown will begin for Christmas 2002.

SURINAME: INDEPENDENCE DAY. Nov 25. Holiday. Gained independence from the Netherlands in 1975.

BIRTHDAYS TODAY

Marc Brown, 55, author and illustrator (the Arthur series), born Erie, PA, Nov 25, 1946.

Cris Carter, 36, football player, born Troy, OH, Nov 25, 1965.

Shirley Climo, 73, author (*The Egyptian Cinderella, The Irish Cinderlad*), born Cleveland, OH, Nov 25, 1928.
Crescent Dragonwagon, 49, author (*Half a Moon and One Whole Star*), born Ellen Zolotow, New York, NY, Nov 25, 1952.
Donovan McNabb, 25, football player, born Dolton, IL, Nov 25, 1976.
Andrea Stinson, 34, basketball player, born Mooresville, NC, Nov 25, 1967.

NOVEMBER 26 — MONDAY

Day 330 — 35 Remaining

ALICE IN WONDERLAND PUBLISHED: ANNIVERSARY. Nov 26, 1865. Lewis Carroll's novel was published on this date. *Through the Looking Glass* followed in 1871.

CUSTER BATTLEFIELD BECOMES LITTLE BIGHORN BATTLEFIELD: ANNIVERSARY. Nov 26, 1991. The US Congress approved a bill renaming Custer Battlefield National Monument as Little Bighorn Battlefield National Monument. The bill also authorized the construction of a memorial to the Native Americans who fought and died at the battle known as Custer's Last Stand. Introduced by then Representative Ben Nighthorse Campbell, the only Native American in Congress, the bill was signed into law by President George Bush. For more info: www.nps.gov/libi/index.htm.

FIRST US HOLIDAY BY PRESIDENTIAL PROCLAMATION: ANNIVERSARY. Nov 26, 1789. President George Washington proclaimed Nov 26, 1789, to be Thanksgiving Day. Both Houses of Congress, by their joint committee, had requested him to recommend "a day of public thanksgiving and prayer, to be observed by acknowledging with grateful hearts the many and signal favors of Almighty God, especially by affording them an opportunity to peaceably establish a form of government for their safety and happiness." Proclamation issued Oct 3, 1789.

MONGOLIA: REPUBLIC DAY. Nov 26. National day. Commemorates declaration of the republic in 1924.

SCHULZ, CHARLES: BIRTH ANNIVERSARY. Nov 26, 1922. Cartoonist, born at Minneapolis, MN. Created the "Peanuts" comic strip that debuted on Oct 2, 1950. The strip included Charlie Brown, his sister Sally, his dog Snoopy, friends Linus and Lucy and a variety of other characters. Stricken with colon cancer, Schulz's last daily strip was published Jan 3, 2000, and his last Sunday strip was published Feb 13, 2000, the day after he died. The strip ran in more than 2,500 newspapers in many different countries. Schulz won the Reuben Award in both 1955 and 1964 and was named International Cartoonist of the Year in 1978. Several TV specials were spin-offs of the strip including "It's the Great Pumpkin Charlie Brown" and "You're a Good Man Charlie Brown." Schulz died at Santa Rosa, CA Feb 12, 2000. See also "Peanuts Debuts: Anniversary" (Oct 2).

SLINKY® INTRODUCED: ANNIVERSARY. Nov 26, 1945. In 1943 engineer Richard James was working in a Philadelphia shipyard trying to find a way to stabilize a piece of equipment on a ship in heavy seas. One idea was to suspend it on springs. One day a spring tumbled off his desk, giving him the idea for a toy. The accidental plaything was introduced by James and his wife in a Philadelphia department store during the 1945 Christmas season. Today more than 250,000,000 Slinkys have been sold. For more info: www.slinkytoys.com.

TRUTH, SOJOURNER: DEATH ANNIVERSARY. Nov 26, 1883. A former slave who had been sold four different times, Sojourner Truth became an evangelist who argued for abolition and women's rights. After a troubled early life, she began her evangelical career in 1843, traveling through New England until she discovered the utopian colony called the Northampton Association of Education and Industry. It was there she was exposed to, and became an advocate for, the cause of abolition, working with Frederick Douglass, Wendell Phillips, William Lloyd Garrison and others. In 1850 she befriended Lucretia Mott, Elizabeth Cady Stanton and other feminist leaders and actively began supporting calls for women's rights. In 1870 she attempted to petition Congress to create a "Negro State" on public lands in the West. Born at Ulster County, NY, about 1790, with the name Isabella Van Wagener, she died Nov 26, 1883, at Battle Creek, MI. For more info: *Sojourner Truth: A Voice for Freedom*, by Patricia and Fredrick McKissack (Enslow, 0-8949-0313-6, $14.95 Gr. K–3) or *Sojourner Truth: Ain' I a Woman?* by Patricia and Fredrick McKissack (Scholastic, 0-59-044691-6, $4.50 Gr. 3–7) or www.sojournertruth.org.

BIRTHDAYS TODAY

Jessica Bowman, 21, actress ("Dr. Quinn, Medicine Woman"), born Walnut Creek, CA, Nov 26, 1980.
Shannon Dunn, 29, Olympic snowboarder, born Arlington Heights, IL, Nov 26, 1972.
Shawn Kemp, 32, NBA forward, member of Dream Team II, born Elkhart, IN, Nov 26, 1969.
Laurence Pringle, 66, science writer (*An Extraordinary Life: The Story of a Monarch Butterfly*), born Rochester, NY, Nov 26, 1935.

NOVEMBER 27 — TUESDAY

Day 331 — 34 Remaining

LIVINGSTON, ROBERT R.: BIRTH ANNIVERSARY. Nov 27, 1746. Member of the Continental Congress, farmer, diplomat and jurist, born at New York, NY. It was Livingston who administered the oath of office to President George Washington in 1789. He died at Clermont, NY, Feb 26, 1813.

WEIZMANN, CHAIM: BIRTH ANNIVERSARY. Nov 27, 1874. Israeli statesman, born near Pinsk, Byelorussia. He played an important role in bringing about the British government's Balfour Declaration, calling for the establishment of a national home for Jews at Palestine. He died at Tel Aviv, Israel, Nov 9, 1952.

BIRTHDAYS TODAY

Kevin Henkes, 41, author and illustrator (*Lilly's Purple Plastic Purse*), born Racine, WI, Nov 27, 1960.
Bill Nye, 46, host ("Bill Nye, the Science Guy"), born Washington, DC, Nov 27, 1955.
Nick Van Exel, 30, basketball player, born Kenosha, WI, Nov 27, 1971.
Jaleel White, 25, actor ("Family Matters"), born Los Angeles, CA, Nov 27, 1976.

November 2001

S	M	T	W	T	F	S
				1	2	3
4	5	6	7	8	9	10
11	12	13	14	15	16	17
18	19	20	21	22	23	24
25	26	27	28	29	30	

NOVEMBER 28 — WEDNESDAY

Day 332 — 33 Remaining

ALBANIA: INDEPENDENCE DAY. Nov 28. National holiday. Commemorates independence from the Ottoman Empire in 1912.

CHAD: REPUBLIC DAY. Nov 28. National holiday. Commemorates the proclamation of the republic in 1958.

CHRISTMAS TREE AT ROCKEFELLER CENTER. Nov 28 (tentative). New York, NY. Lighting of the huge Christmas tree in Rockefeller Plaza signals the opening of the holiday season at New York City. Date approximate; usually a weekday during the week after Thanksgiving.

MAURITANIA: INDEPENDENCE DAY. Nov 28. National holiday. This country in the northwest part of Africa attained sovereignty from France on this day in 1960.

PANAMA: INDEPENDENCE FROM SPAIN. Nov 28. Public holiday. Commemorates the independence of Panama (which at the time was part of Colombia) from Spain in 1821.

BIRTHDAYS TODAY

Stephanie Calmenson, 49, author (*Dinner at the Panda Palace, The Gator Girls*), born Brooklyn, NY, Nov 28, 1952.

Ed Harris, 51, actor (*The Right Stuff*), born Englewood, NJ, Nov 28, 1950.

Mary Lyons, 54, author of biographies (*Catching the Fire: Philip Simmons, Blacksmith*), born Macon, GA, Nov 28, 1947.

Ed Young, 70, author and illustrator (Caldecott for *Lon Po Po: A Red Riding Hood Story from China*), born Tientsin, China, Nov 28, 1931.

NOVEMBER 29 — THURSDAY

Day 333 — 32 Remaining

ALCOTT, LOUISA MAY: BIRTH ANNIVERSARY. Nov 29, 1832. American author, born at Philadelphia, PA. Died at Boston, MA, Mar 6, 1888. Her most famous novel was *Little Women*, the classic story of Meg, Jo, Beth and Amy. For info: www.alcottweb.com and www.louisamayalcott.org.

CZECHOSLOVAKIA ENDS COMMUNIST RULE: ANNIVERSARY. Nov 29, 1989. Czechoslovakia ended 41 years of one-party communist rule when the Czechoslovak parliament voted unanimously to repeal the constitutional clauses giving the Communist Party a guaranteed leading role in the country and promoting Marxism-Leninism as the state ideology. The vote came at the end of a 12-day revolution sparked by the beating of protestors Nov 17. Although the Communist party remained in power, the tide of reform led to its ouster by the Civic Forum, headed by playwright Vaclav Havel. The Civic Forum demanded free elections with equal rights for all parties, a mixed economy and support for foreign investment. In the first free elections in Czechoslovakia since WWII, Vaclav Havel was elected president.

"KUKLA, FRAN AND OLLIE" TV PREMIERE: ANNIVERSARY. Nov 29, 1948. This popular children's show featured puppets created and handled by Burr Tillstrom and was equally popular with adults. Fran Allison was the only human on the show. Tillstrom's lively and eclectic cast of characters, called the "Kuklapolitans," included the bald, high-voiced Kukla, the big-toothed Oliver J. Dragon (Ollie), Fletcher Rabbit, Cecil Bill, Beulah the Witch, Colonel Crackie, Madame Ooglepuss and Dolores Dragon. Most shows were performed without scripts.

LEWIS, C.S. (CLIVE STAPLES): BIRTH ANNIVERSARY. Nov 29, 1898. British scholar, novelist and author (*The Screwtape Letters, Chronicles of Narnia*), born at Belfast, Ireland. *The Lion, the Witch and the Wardrobe*, the first volume in the seven-volume Chronicles of Narnia series, was published in 1950. Died at Oxford, England, Nov 22, 1963.

WAITE, MORRISON R.: BIRTH ANNIVERSARY. Nov 29, 1816. Seventh Chief Justice of the Supreme Court, born at Lyme, CT. Appointed Chief Justice by President Ulysses S. Grant Jan 19, 1874. The Waite Court is remembered for its controversial rulings that did much to rehabilitate the idea of states' rights after the Civil War and early Reconstruction years. Waite died at Washington, DC, Mar 23, 1888.

BIRTHDAYS TODAY

Helga Aichinger, 64, illustrator (*The Shepherd*), born Traun, Austria, Nov 29, 1937.

Eric Beddows, 50, illustrator (*Joyful Noise*), born Ontario, Canada, Nov 29, 1951.

Jacques Rene Chirac, 69, President of France, born Paris, France, Nov 29, 1932.

Madeleine L'Engle, 83, author (Newbery for *A Wrinkle in Time*), born New York, NY, Nov 29, 1918.

Howie Mandel, 46, actor, producer ("Bobby's World"), born Toronto, ON, Canada, Nov 29, 1955.

Andrew McCarthy, 39, actor (*Pretty in Pink, Weekend at Bernie's*), born Westfield, NJ, Nov 29, 1962.

Mariano Rivera, 32, baseball player, born Panama City, Panama, Nov 29, 1969.

Adam Zolotin, 18, actor (*Jack*), born Long Island, NY, Nov 29, 1983.

NOVEMBER 30 — FRIDAY

Day 334 — 31 Remaining

BARBADOS: INDEPENDENCE DAY: 35th ANNIVERSARY. Nov 30. National holiday. Gained independence from Great Britain in 1966.

BLUE MOON. Nov 30. When two full moons fall within the same month, the second is called a "Blue Moon."

MONTGOMERY, LUCY MAUD: BIRTH ANNIVERSARY. Nov 30, 1874. Author, known for her classic Anne of Green Gables series of books. Her first, *Anne of Green Gables*, was published in 1908. Born at New London, Prince Edward Island, Canada, Montgomery died at Toronto, Canada, Apr 24, 1952.

MOON PHASE: FULL MOON. Nov 30. Moon enters Full Moon phase at 3:49 PM, EST. This is the second full moon this month and is called a Blue Moon.

NATIONAL GEOGRAPHY BEE, SCHOOL LEVEL. Nov 30–Jan 11, 2002. Principals must register their schools by Oct 15, 2000. Nationwide contest involving millions of students at the school level. The Bee is designed to encourage the teaching and study of geography. There are three levels of competition. A student must win a school-level Bee in order to win the right to take a written exam. The written test determines the top 100 students in each state who are eligible to go on to the state level. National Geographic brings the state winner and his/her teacher to Washington for the national level in May. Alex Trebek moderates the national level. For info: Natl Geography Bee, Natl Geographic Soc, 1145 17th St NW, Washington, DC 20036. Phone: (202) 857-7001. Web: www.nationalgeographic.com.

PHILIPPINES: BONIFACIO DAY. Nov 30. Also known as National Heroes' Day. Commemorates birth in 1863 of Andres Bonifacio, leader of the 1896 revolt against Spain.

SAINT ANDREW'S DAY. Nov 30. Feast day of the apostle and martyr, Andrew, who died about AD 60. Patron saint of Scotland.

TWAIN, MARK: BIRTH ANNIVERSARY. Nov 30, 1835. Celebrated American author, born Samuel Langhorne Clemens, whose books include: *The Adventures of Tom Sawyer, The Adventures of Huckleberry Finn* and *The Prince and the Pauper*. Born at Florida, MO, Twain is quoted as saying, "I came in with Halley's Comet in 1835. It is coming again next year, and I expect to go out with it." He did. Twain died at Redding, CT, Apr 21, 1910 (just one day after Halley's Comet perihelion).

ZEMACH, MARGOT: BIRTH ANNIVERSARY. Nov 30, 1931. Illustrator (Caldecott for *Duffy and the Devil*), born at Los Angeles, CA. Died May 21, 1989.

BIRTHDAYS TODAY

Joan Ganz Cooney, 72, founder of the Children's Television Workshop and creator of "Sesame Street," born Nov 30, 1929.

Des'ree, 31, singer (*I Ain't Movin'*), born London, England, Nov 30, 1970.

Mandy Patinkin, 49, actor (Tony for *Evita; Sunday in the Park with George*, "Chicago Hope"), born Chicago, IL, Nov 30, 1952.

Ivan Rodriguez, 30, baseball player, born Vega Baja, Puerto Rico, Nov 30, 1971.

Paul Stookey, 64, singer, songwriter (Peter, Paul and Mary), born Baltimore, MD, Nov 30, 1937.

Lawrence Summers, 47, former US Secretary of the Treasury (Clinton administration), born New Haven, CT, Nov 30, 1954.

Natalie Williams, 31, basketball player, born Long Beach, CA, Nov 30, 1970.

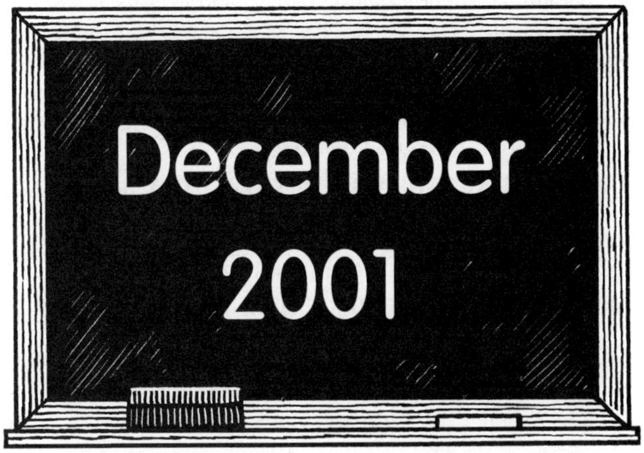

DECEMBER 1 — SATURDAY

Day 335 — 30 Remaining

ANTARCTICA MADE A SCIENTIFIC PRESERVE: ANNIVERSARY. Dec 1, 1959. Representatives of 12 nations, including the US and the Soviet Union, signed a treaty at Washington, DC, setting aside Antarctica as a scientific preserve, free from military activity. Antarctica is equal in area to the US and Europe combined. For more info: quest.arc.nasa.gov/antarctica2/main/s_index.html.

BASKETBALL CREATED: ANNIVERSARY. Dec 1, 1891. James Naismith was a teacher of physical education at the International YMCA Training College at Springfield, MA. In order to create an indoor sport that could be played during the winter months, he nailed up peach baskets at opposite ends of the gym and gave students soccer balls to toss into them. Thus was born the game of basketball.

HUG-A-WEEK FOR THE HEARING IMPAIRED. Dec 1–31. Give a hug to someone who doesn't hear so well, each week until the end of the year. As we approach the holiday season, start with a weekly hug and find out how you might proactively include people with hearing loss in the season's festivities. A little extra time and a few special moments may help someone who can't hear so well be included and more able to share throughout the season. Annually, the month of December. For info: Carol MacKenzie, Communicate with Care, 12 Kayla Cir, Plymouth, MA 02362. Phone: (508) 224-3640. E-mail: commwcare@aol.com.

PORTUGAL: INDEPENDENCE DAY. Dec 1. Public holiday. Became independent of Spain in 1640.

ROMANIA: NATIONAL DAY. Dec 1. National holiday. Commemorates unification of Romania and Transylvania in 1918.

ROSA PARKS DAY: ANNIVERSARY OF ARREST. Dec 1, 1955. Anniversary of the arrest of Rosa Parks, at Montgomery, AL, for refusing to give up her seat and move to the back of a municipal bus. Her arrest triggered a yearlong boycott of the city bus system and led to legal actions which ended racial segregation on municipal buses throughout the southern US. The event has been called the birth of the modern civil rights movement. Rosa McCauley Parks was born at Tuskegee, AL, Feb 4, 1913. For more info: *If a Bus Could Talk: The Story of Rosa Parks*, by Faith Ringgold (S&S, 0-68-981892-0, $16 Gr. K–3).

SAFE TOYS AND GIFTS MONTH. Dec 1–31. What toys are dangerous to children's eyesight? Tips on how to choose age-appropriate toys will be distributed. For info: Prevent Blindness America®, 500 E Remington Rd, Schaumburg, IL 60173. Phone: (800) 331-2020. Fax: (847) 843-8458. Web: www.preventblindness.org.

SAN BERNARDINO LATINO BOOK & FAMILY FESTIVAL. Dec 1–2. National Orange Show, San Bernardino, CA. Produced along with actor James Olmos, this festival is a celebration of books, careers, culture, education, health, recreation, travel and more. It is the largest Latino consumer trade show in the US. Attendees will enjoy hundreds of booths and activities including book signings, storytelling, poetry readings, food, entertainment and workshops. For info: Latino Book & Family Festivals, 3980 Cazador St., Los Angeles, CA 90065. E-mail: kathy@latinobookfestival.com. Web: www.latinobookfestival.com.

UNITED NATIONS: WORLD AIDS DAY. Dec 1. In 1988 the World Health Organization of the United Nations declared Dec 1 as World AIDS Day, an international day of awareness and education about AIDS. The WHO is the leader in global direction and coordination of AIDS prevention, control, research and education. A program called UN-AIDS was created to bring together the skills and expertise of the World Bank, UNDP, UNESCO, UNICEF, UNFPA and the WHO to strengthen and expand national capacities to respond to the pandemic. Also see the World AIDS Day entry (Dec 1) for information address in US.

UNIVERSAL HUMAN RIGHTS MONTH. Dec 1–31. To disseminate throughout the world information about human rights and distribute copies of the Universal Declaration of Human Rights in English and other languages. Please send $4 to cover expense of printing, handling and postage. Annually, the month of December. For info: Dr. Stanley Drake, Pres, Intl Soc of Friendship & Good Will, 8592 Roswell Rd, Ste 434, Atlanta, GA 30350-1870

WORLD AIDS DAY. Dec 1. US observance of UN day to focus world attention on the fight against HIV/AIDS. For info: American Assn for World Health, World AIDS Day, 1825 K St NW, Ste 1208, Washington, DC 20006. Phone: (202) 466-5883. Fax: (202) 466-5896. E-mail: aawhstaff@aol.com. Web: www.aawhworldhealth.org.

★ **WORLD AIDS DAY.** Dec 1.

BIRTHDAYS TODAY

Jan Brett, 52, author and illustrator (*Trouble with Trolls, The Mitten*), born Hingham, MA, Dec 1, 1949.

Larry Walker, 35, baseball player, born Maple Ridge, BC, Canada, Dec 1, 1966.

Tisha Waller, 31, track and field athlete, born Atlanta, GA, Dec 1, 1970.

DECEMBER 2 — SUNDAY

Day 336 — 29 Remaining

ADVENT, FIRST SUNDAY. Dec 2. Advent includes the four Sundays before Christmas: Dec 2, Dec 9, Dec 16 and Dec 23 in 2001.

ARTIFICIAL HEART TRANSPLANT: ANNIVERSARY. Dec 2, 1982. Barney C. Clark, 61, became the first recipient of a permanent artificial heart. The operation was performed at the University of Utah Medical Center at Salt Lake City. Near death at the time of the operation, Clark survived almost 112 days after the implantation. He died Mar 23, 1983.

CLERC-GALLAUDET WEEK. Dec 2–8. Week in which to celebrate the birth anniversaries of Laurent Clerc (Dec 26, 1785) and Thomas Hopkins Gallaudet (Dec 10, 1787). Clerc and Gallaudet pioneered education for the deaf in the US. Library activities will include a lecture on Clerc and Gallaudet and their contemporaries, storytelling for all ages and a display of books, videotapes, magazines, newspapers and posters. For info: Library for Deaf Action, 2930 Craiglawn Rd, Silver Spring, MD 20904-1816. Phone: (301) 572-5168 (TTY). Fax: (301) 572-4134. E-mail: alhagemeyer@juno.com. Web: www.LibraryDeaf.com.

FIRST SELF-SUSTAINING NUCLEAR CHAIN REACTION: ANNIVERSARY. Dec 2, 1942. Physicist Enrico Fermi led a team of scientists at the University of Chicago in producing the first controlled, self-sustaining nuclear chain reaction. As part of the "Manhattan Project," their first simple nuclear reactor was built under the stands of the University's football stadium. This work led to the development of the atomic bomb, first tested on July 16, 1945, at Alamogordo, NM.

GATES OF THE ARCTIC NATIONAL PARK AND PRESERVE ESTABLISHED: ANNIVERSARY. Dec 2, 1980. Alaska's Gates of the Arctic National Monument, proclaimed Dec 1, 1978, was established as a national park and preserve. For more info: www.nps.gov/gaar/index.htm.

GLACIER BAY NATIONAL PARK AND PRESERVE ESTABLISHED: ANNIVERSARY. Dec 2, 1980. Alaska's Glacier Bay National Monument, proclaimed Feb 25, 1925, was established as a national park and preserve. For more info: www.nps.gov/glba/index.htm.

KATAMI NATIONAL PARK AND PRESERVE ESTABLISHED: ANNIVERSARY. Dec 2, 1980. Alaska's Katmai National Monument, proclaimed Sept 24, 1918, was established as a national park and preserve. For more info: www.nps.gov/kata/index.htm.

KENAI FJORDS NATIONAL PARK ESTABLISHED: ANNIVERSARY. Dec 2, 1980. Alaska's Kenai Fjords National Monument, proclaimed Dec 1, 1978, was established as a national park. For more info: www.nps.gov/kefj/index.htm.

KOBUK VALLEY NATIONAL PARK ESTABLISHED: ANNIVERSARY. Dec 2, 1980. Alaska's Kobuk Valley National Monument, proclaimed Dec 1, 1978, was established as a national park. For more info: www.nps.gov/kova/index.htm.

LAKE CLARK NATIONAL PARK AND PRESERVE ESTABLISHED: ANNIVERSARY. Dec 2, 1980. Alaska's Lake Clark National Monument, proclaimed Dec 1, 1978, was established as a national park and preserve. For more info: www.nps.gov/laca/index.htm.

LAOS: NATIONAL DAY. Dec 2. National holiday commemorating proclamation of Lao People's Democratic Republic in 1975.

MONROE DOCTRINE: ANNIVERSARY. Dec 2, 1823. President James Monroe, in his annual message to Congress, enunciated the doctrine that bears his name and that was long hailed as a statement of US policy. ." . . In the wars of the European powers in matters relating to themselves we have never taken any part . . . we should consider any attempt on their part to extend their system to any portion of this hemi-sphere as dangerous to our peace and safety. . . ."

★ **PAN AMERICAN HEALTH DAY.** Dec 2. Presidential Proclamation 2447, of Nov 23, 1940, covers all succeeding years. Annually, Dec 2. The 1940 Pan American Conference of National Directors of Health adopted a resolution recommending that a "Health Day" be held annually in the countries of the Pan American Union.

SEURAT, GEORGES: BIRTH ANNIVERSARY. Dec 2, 1859. French Neo-Impressionist painter, born at Paris, France. Died there Mar 29, 1891. Seurat is known for his style of painting with small dots of color called "pointillism."

UNITED ARAB EMIRATES: NATIONAL DAY: 30th ANNIVERSARY OF INDEPENDENCE. Dec 2. Anniversary of the day in 1971 when a federation of seven sheikdoms declared independence and became known as the United Arab Emirates.

WRANGELL–SAINT ELIAS NATIONAL PARK AND PRESERVE ESTABLISHED: ANNIVERSARY. Dec 2, 1980. Alaska's Wrangell–St. Elias National Monument, proclaimed Dec 1, 1978, was established as a national park and preserve. For more info: www.nps.gov/wrst/index.htm.

BIRTHDAYS TODAY

Wayne Allard, 58, US Senator (R, Colorado), born Fort Collins, CO, Dec 2, 1943.

Randy Gardner, 43, figure skater, born Marina del Rey, CA, Dec 2, 1958.

David Macaulay, 55, illustrator and author (*The New Way Things Work*, Caldecott for *Black and White*), born Burton-on-Trent, England, Dec 2, 1946.

Stone Phillips, 47, anchor ("Dateline," "20/20"), born Texas City, TX, Dec 2, 1954.

Harry Reid, 62, US Senator (D, Nevada), born Searchlight, NV, Dec 2, 1939.

Monica Seles, 28, tennis player, born Novi Sad, Yugoslavia, Dec 2, 1973.

Britney Spears, 20, singer, born Kentwood, LA, Dec 2, 1981.

William Wegman, 58, artist/photographer (of dogs), born Holyoke, MA, Dec 2, 1943.

DECEMBER 3 — MONDAY

Day 337 — 28 Remaining

CENTRAL AFRICAN REPUBLIC: NATIONAL DAY OBSERVED. Dec 3. Commemorates Proclamation of the Republic Dec 1, 1958. On this date, the country called Ubangi-Shari changed its name to Central African Republic. In 1960 it gained its independence from France. Usually observed on the first Monday in December.

ILLINOIS: ADMISSION DAY: ANNIVERSARY. Dec 3. Became 21st state in 1818.

SNOW DAY FOR SOUTHERN STUDENTS. Dec 3. All states south of a line from Ohio through New Jersey. Why should only students in northern states enjoy the fun of staying home because of snow? Now we can all share in the joy of a snow day! For info: Benjamin Rich, Baldwin Wallace College, Rm 101, Berea, OH 44017. Phone: (440) 260-4272. E-mail: btrich@bw.edu.

UNITED NATIONS: INTERNATIONAL DAY OF DISABLED PERSONS. Dec 3. On Oct 14, 1992 (Res 47/3), at the end of the Decade of Disabled Persons, the General Assembly proclaimed Dec 3 to be an annual observance to promote the continuation of integrating the disabled into general society.

BIRTHDAYS TODAY

Francesca Lia Block, 39, author (*Weetzie Bat, Violet & Claire*), born Los Angeles, CA, Dec 3, 1962.

Brian Bonsall, 20, actor (*Blank Check*, "Family Ties"), born Torrance, CA, Dec 3, 1981.

December 2001

S	M	T	W	T	F	S
						1
2	3	4	5	6	7	8
9	10	11	12	13	14	15
16	17	18	19	20	21	22
23	24	25	26	27	28	29
30	31					

Anna Chlumsky, 21, actress (*My Girl, My Girl 2*), born Chicago, IL, Dec 3, 1980.
Sheree Fitch, 45, author (*Toes in My Nose, Sleeping Dragons All Around*), born Ottawa, ON, Canada, Dec 3, 1956.
Brendan Fraser, 33, actor (*George of the Jungle*), born Indianapolis, IN, Dec 3, 1968.
Katarina Witt, 36, Olympic figure skater, born Karl-Marx-Stadt, East Germany, Dec 3, 1965.

DECEMBER 4 — TUESDAY

Day 338 — 27 Remaining

LEAF, MUNRO: BIRTH ANNIVERSARY. Dec 4, 1905. Born at Hamilton, MD. Leaf authored and illustrated the children's book *The Story of Ferdinand*. He died at Garrett Park, MD, Dec 21, 1976.

SPACE MILESTONE: INTERNATIONAL SPACE STATION LAUNCH (US). Dec 4, 1998. The shuttle *Endeavour* took a US component of the space station named *Unity* into orbit 220 miles from Earth where spacewalking astronauts fastened it to a component launched by the Russians on Nov 20, 1998. It will take a total of 45 US and Russian launches over the next five years before the space station is complete. When completed, it will be 356 feet across and 290 feet long and will support a crew of up to seven. For more info: *The International Space Station*, by Franklyn M. Branley (HarperCollins, 0-06-028702-0, $16.89 Gr. K–3). See also: "Space Milestones: International Space Station Inhabited" (Nov 2).

BIRTHDAYS TODAY

George Ancona, 72, author (*Pablo Remembers: The Fiesta of the Day of the Dead*), born New York, NY, Dec 4, 1929.
Tyra Banks, 28, model, author (*Tyra's Beauty Inside & Out*), born Los Angeles, CA, Dec 4, 1973.
Jeff Blake, 31, football player, born Sanford, FL, Dec 4, 1970.
Paul O'Neill, 66, US Secretary of the Treasury (George W. Bush administration), born St. Louis, MO, Dec 4, 1935.

DECEMBER 5 — WEDNESDAY

Day 339 — 26 Remaining

"THE ABBOTT AND COSTELLO SHOW" TV PREMIERE: ANNIVERSARY. Dec 5, 1952. Bud Abbott and Lou Costello made 52 half-hour films for television incorporating many of their best burlesque routines. The show ran for two seasons, until 1954. In 1966 Hanna-Barbera Productions produced an animated cartoon based on the characters of Abbott and Costello. Abbott supplied his own voice while Stan Irwin imitated Costello. Bud Abbott was born at Asbury Park, NJ, Oct 2, 1895 and died at Woodland Hills, CA, Apr 24, 1974. Lou Costello was born at Paterson, NJ, Mar 6, 1906 and died at East Los Angeles, CA, Mar 3, 1959.

AFL-CIO FOUNDED: ANNIVERSARY. Dec 5. The American Federation of Labor and the Congress of Industrial Organizations joined together in 1955, following 20 years of rivalry, to become the nation's leading advocate for trade unions.

DISNEY, WALT: 100th BIRTH ANNIVERSARY. Dec 5, 1901. Animator, filmmaker, born at Chicago, IL. Disney died at Los Angeles, CA, Dec 15, 1966. For more info: *The Man Behind the Magic: The Story of Walt Disney*, by Katherine Greene and Richard Greene (Viking, 0-67-088476-6, $14.99 Gr. 4–7).

HAITI: DISCOVERY DAY: ANNIVERSARY. Dec 5. Commemorates the discovery of Haiti by Christopher Columbus in 1492. Public holiday.

MONTGOMERY BUS BOYCOTT BEGINS: ANNIVERSARY. Dec 5, 1955. Rosa Parks was arrested at Montgomery, AL, Dec 1, 1955, for refusing to give up her seat on a bus to a white man. In support of Parks, and to protest the arrest, the black com-

DECEMBER 5
BILL PICKETT'S BIRTHDAY

Born in Texas on December 5, 1870, Bill Pickett grew up to become one of the most famous African American cowboys. Almost every child dreams of becoming a cowboy, or cowgirl, at one time in his or her life. There's something so exotic and alluring about life on the trail, not to mention the derring-do of steer wrestling, roping and horseback riding.

Bill Pickett was the second of thirteen children born to Thomas Jefferson Pickett and his wife, Mary. By the time he was 11, Bill was hired out as a ranch hand. Over the next several years, he perfected skills in riding, roping and "bulldogging." By the time Bill was 16, he was known nationally. Later, he performed in international rodeos.

Pickett died on April 2, 1932 of a fractured skull, the result of being kicked by a horse. In 1971, he was the first African American cowboy to be admitted to the National Rodeo Hall of Fame. Biographies about Pickett include: *Bill Pickett: Rodeo-Ridin' Cowboy*, by Andrea Pinkney (Harcourt, 0-15-202103-5, $6 Gr. PreK–3), and *Guts: Legendary Black Rodeo Cowboy Bill Pickett*, by Cecil Johnson (Summit, 1-5653-0162-5, $19.95 Ages YA & up).

Because cowboys are so popular with elementary students, you might want to consider developing a cowboy unit. Two books that may help are: *Black Cowboys*, by Gina De Angelis (Chelsea House, 1-7910-2590-X, $9.95 Gr. 5 & up), and *Cowboys*, by Martin Sandler (HarperCollins, 0-06-446745-7, $10.95 Gr. 5 & up).

Social studies projects could include identifying other famous cowboys. Bob Lemmons and George Mcjunkin are two well-known African American cowboys. Students can research and describe life on a working ranch in the late 1800s. They could also map specific routes that cowboys frequently used while driving herds. Discuss how the advent of railroads altered the cowboy's way of life. Try *Black Frontiers*, by Lillian Schlissel (Simon & Schuster, 0-689-80285-4, $18 Gr. 3–7), for a look at African Americans in the West. Girls may want to research the role of women wranglers and present their findings to the class.

Have fun in language arts with *The Cowboy ABC*, by Chris Demarest (DK Ink, 0-7894-2509-2, $15.95 Gr. PreK–1), and *Home on the Range: Cowboy Poetry*, by Paul Janeczko (Dial, 0-8037-1910-8, $15.99 Gr. K–4). Young adult audiences may enjoy Baxter Black's poetry, including *Coyote Cowboy Poetry* (out-of-print, but may be available in libraries). Tony Johnston's fairy tale *The Cowboy and the Black-Eyed Pea* (Putnam, 0-698-11356-X, $4.95) will delight students of all ages.

Regardless of whether you incorporate cowboys as a unit or as individual studies of people such as Bill Pickett, at this time of year students' minds are starting to go into holiday shutdown. Dusty trails, chuck wagons and some roughriders may be just what's needed to hold their attention.

munity of Montgomery organized a boycott of the bus system. The boycott lasted from Dec 5, 1955, to Dec 20, 1956, when a US Supreme Court ruling was implemented at Montgomery, integrating the public transportation system.

NETHERLANDS: SINTERKLAAS. Dec 5. Traditionally on the eve of St. Nicholas Day (Dec 6), Sinterklaas brings gifts to Dutch children, accompanied by his Moorish helper, "Black Pete." However, the number of people celebrating this holiday has dropped, as more Dutch families exchange gifts on Dec 25 instead.

PICKETT, BILL: BIRTH ANNIVERSARY. Dec 5, 1870. African American cowboy, born at Jenks-Branch, TX. A star rodeo performer, Pickett died Apr 2, 1932 at Ponca City, OK. *See* Curriculum Connection.

THAILAND: KING'S BIRTHDAY AND NATIONAL DAY. Dec 5. Celebrated throughout the kingdom with colorful pageantry. Stores and houses decorated with spectacular illuminations at night. Public holiday.

TWENTY-FIRST AMENDMENT TO THE US CONSTITUTION RATIFIED: ANNIVERSARY. Dec 5, 1933. Prohibition ended with the repeal of the Eighteenth Amendment by the Twenty-First Amendment.

UNITED NATIONS: INTERNATIONAL VOLUNTEER DAY FOR ECONOMIC AND SOCIAL DEVELOPMENT. Dec 5. In a resolution of Dec 17, 1985, the United Nations General Assembly recognized the desirability of encouraging the work of all volunteers. It invited governments to observe, annually Dec 5, the "International Volunteer Day for Economic and Social Development, urging them to take measures to heighten awareness of the important contribution of volunteer service." A day commemorating the establishment in December 1970 of the UN Volunteers program and inviting world recognition of volunteerism in the international development movement. For info: United Nations, Dept of Public Info, Public Inquiries Unit, Rm GA-57, New York, NY 10017. Phone: (212) 963-4475. Fax: (212) 963-0071. E-mail: inquiries@un.org.

VAN BUREN, MARTIN: BIRTH ANNIVERSARY. Dec 5, 1782. The eighth president of the US (Mar 4, 1837–Mar 3, 1841), Van Buren was the first to have been born a citizen of the US. He had served as vice-president under Andrew Jackson. He was a widower for nearly two decades before he entered the White House. His daughter-in-law, Angelica, served as White House hostess during an administration troubled by bank and business failures, depression and unemployment. Van Buren was born at Kinderhook, NY, and died there July 24, 1862. For info: www.ipl.org/ref/POTUS.

WHEATLEY, PHILLIS: DEATH ANNIVERSARY. Dec 5, 1784. Born at Senegal, West Africa about 1753, Phillis Wheatley was brought to the US in 1761 and purchased as a slave by a Boston tailor named John Wheatley. She was allotted unusual privileges for a slave, including being allowed to learn to read and write. She wrote her first poetry at age 14, and her first work was published in 1770. Wheatley's fame as a poet spread throughout Europe as well as the US after her *Poems on Various Subjects, Religious and Moral* was published at England in 1773. She was invited to visit George Washington's army headquarters after he read a poem she had written about him in 1776. Phillis Wheatley died at about age 30 at Boston, MA. For more info: *Hang a Thousand Trees with Ribbons: The Story of Phillis Wheatley*, by Ann Rinaldi (Harcourt, 0-15-200876-4, $12 Gr. 4–9).

December 2001

S	M	T	W	T	F	S
						1
2	3	4	5	6	7	8
9	10	11	12	13	14	15
16	17	18	19	20	21	22
23	24	25	26	27	28	29
30	31					

BIRTHDAYS TODAY

Frankie Muniz, 16, actor ("Malcolm in the Middle," *My Dog Skip*), born Ridgewood, NJ, Dec 5, 1985.

Strom Thurmond, 99, US Senator (R, South Carolina), born Edgefield, SC, Dec 5, 1902.

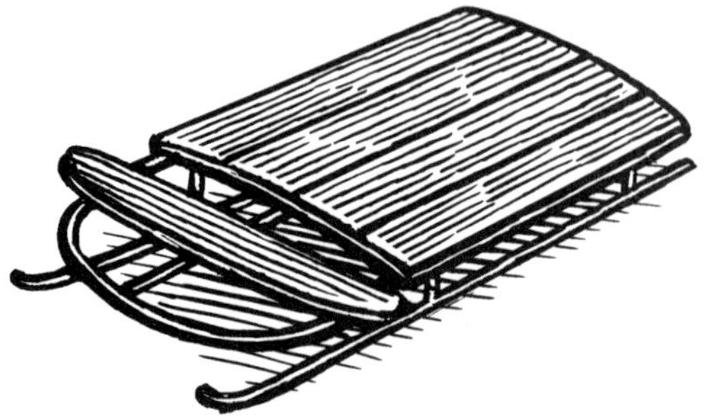

DECEMBER 6 — THURSDAY

Day 340 — 25 Remaining

ECUADOR: DAY OF QUITO. Dec 6. Commemorates founding of city of Quito by Spaniards in 1534.

EVERGLADES NATIONAL PARK ESTABLISHED: ANNIVERSARY. Dec 6, 1947. Part of vast marshland area on the southern Florida peninsula, originally authorized May 30, 1934, was established as a national park. For more info: www.nps.gov/ever/index.htm.

FINLAND: INDEPENDENCE DAY. Dec 6. National holiday. Declaration of independence from Russia in 1917.

GERALD FORD SWORN IN AS VICE PRESIDENT: ANNIVERSARY. Dec 6, 1973. Gerald Ford was sworn in as vice president under Richard Nixon, following the resignation of Spiro Agnew who pled no contest to a charge of income tax evasion. See also "Agnew, Spiro Theodore: Birth Anniversary" (Nov 9).

GERSHWIN, IRA: BIRTH ANNIVERSARY. Dec 6, 1896. Pulitzer Prize–winning American lyricist and author who collaborated with his brother, George, and with many other composers. Among his Broadway successes: *Lady Be Good, Funny Face, Strike Up the Band* and such songs as "The Man I Love," "Someone to Watch Over Me," "I Got Rhythm" and hundreds of others. Born at New York, NY, he died at Beverly Hills, CA, Aug 17, 1983. See also: "Gershwin, George: Birth Anniversary" (Sept 26).

HALIFAX, NOVA SCOTIA, DESTROYED: ANNIVERSARY. Dec 6, 1917. More than 1,650 people were killed at Halifax when the Norwegian ship *Imo* plowed into the French munitions ship *Mont Blanc. Mont Blanc* was loaded with 4,000 tons of TNT, 2,300 tons of picric acid, 61 tons of other explosives and a deck of highly flammable benzene, which ignited and touched off an explosion. In addition to those killed, 1,028 were injured. A tidal wave, caused by the explosion, washed much of the city out to sea.

LAILAT UL QADR: THE NIGHT OF POWER. Dec 6 (also Dec 8, 10, 12 or 14). "The Night of Power" falls on one of the last 10 days of Ramadan on an odd-numbered day (Islamic calendar dates: Ramadan 21, 23, 25, 27 or 29, 1421). The Holy Qur'an states that praying on this night is better than praying 1,000 months. Since it is not known which day it is, Muslims feel it is best to pray on each of the possible nights. Different methods for "anticipating" the visibility of the new moon crescent at Mecca are used by different Muslim sects or groups. US date may vary.

MISSOURI EARTHQUAKES: ANNIVERSARY. Dec 6, 1811. The most violent and prolonged series of earthquakes in US history occurred not in California, but in the Midwest at New Madrid, MO. They lasted until Feb 12, 1812. There were few deaths because of the sparse population. For more info go to the National Earthquake Information Center: wwwneic.cr.usgs.gov.

SAINT NICHOLAS DAY. Dec 6. One of the most venerated saints of both eastern and western Christian churches, of whose life little is known, except that he was Bishop of Myra in what is now Turkey in the fourth century, and that from early times he has been one of the most often pictured saints, especially noted for his charity. Santa Claus and the presentation of gifts is said to derive from Saint Nicholas. For more info: *Saint Nicholas*, by Ann Tompert (Boyds Mills Press, 1-56397-844-X, $15.95 Gr. 1 & up).

SPAIN: CONSTITUTION DAY. Dec 6. National holiday. Commemorates the approval of the new constitution in 1978.

THIRTEENTH AMENDMENT TO THE US CONSTITUTION RATIFIED: ANNIVERSARY. Dec 6, 1865. The Thirteenth Amendment to the Constitution was ratified, abolishing slavery in the US. "Neither slavery nor involuntary servitude, save as a punishment for crime whereof the party shall have been duly convicted, shall exist within the United States, or any place subject to their jurisdiction." This amendment was proclaimed Dec 18, 1865. The Thirteenth, Fourteenth and Fifteenth amendments are considered the Civil War Amendments. See also: "Emancipation Proclamation: Anniversary" (Jan 1) for Lincoln's proclamation freeing slaves in the rebelling states.

BIRTHDAYS TODAY

Andrew Cuomo, 44, former US Secretary of Housing and Urban Development (Clinton administration), born Queens, NY, Dec 6, 1957.

John Reynolds Gardiner, 57, author (*Stone Fox, Top Secret*), born at Los Angeles, CA, Dec 6, 1944.

Don Nickles, 53, US Senator (R, Oklahoma), born Ponca City, OK, Dec 6, 1948.

DECEMBER 7 — FRIDAY

Day 341 — 24 Remaining

CÔTE D'IVOIRE: DEATH OF THE FIRST PRESIDENT. Dec 7. National holiday. Commemorates the death of Félix Boigny in 1993.

DELAWARE RATIFIES CONSTITUTION: ANNIVERSARY. Dec 7, 1787. Delaware became the first state to ratify the proposed Constitution. It did so by unanimous vote.

MOON PHASE: LAST QUARTER. Dec 7. Moon enters Last Quarter phase at 2:52 PM, EST.

★**NATIONAL PEARL HARBOR REMEMBRANCE DAY.** Dec 7.

PEARL HARBOR DAY: 60th ANNIVERSARY. Dec 7, 1941. At 7:55 AM (local time), "a date that will live in infamy," nearly 200 Japanese aircraft attacked Pearl Harbor, HI, long considered the US "Gibraltar of the Pacific." The raid, which lasted little more than one hour, left nearly 3,000 dead. Nearly the entire US Pacific Fleet was at anchor there, and few ships escaped damage. Several were sunk or disabled, while 200 US aircraft on the ground were destroyed. The attack on Pearl Harbor brought about immediate US entry into WWII, a Declaration of War being requested by President Franklin D. Roosevelt and approved by the Congress Dec 8, 1941.

SPACE MILESTONE: *GALILEO* (US): ANNIVERSARY. Dec 7, 1995. Launched Oct 18, 1989 by the space shuttle *Atlantis*, the spacecraft *Galileo* entered the orbit of Jupiter on this date after a six-year journey. It orbited Jupiter for two years, sending out probes to study three of its moons. Organic compounds, the ingredients of life, were found on them. For more info: galileo.jpl .nasa.gov.

TUNIS, JOHN: BIRTH ANNIVERSARY. Dec 7, 1889. Author of sports books (*The Kid Comes Back, Iron Duke*), born at Boston, MA. Died Feb 4, 1975.

UNITED NATIONS: INTERNATIONAL CIVIL AVIATION DAY. Dec 7. On Dec 6, 1996, the General Assembly proclaimed Dec 7 as International Civil Aviation Day. On Dec 7, 1944, the convention on International Civil Aviation, which established the International Civil Aviation Organization, was signed. Info from: United Nations, Dept of Public Info, New York, NY 10017.

BIRTHDAYS TODAY

Larry Bird, 45, basketball coach, former player, born West Baden, IN, Dec 7, 1956.

Aaron Carter, 14, singer ("Shake It"), born Tampa, FL, Dec 7, 1987.

Thad Cochran, 64, US Senator (R, Mississippi), born Pontotoc, MS, Dec 7, 1937.

Susan M. Collins, 49, US Senator (R, Maine), born Caribou, ME, Dec 7, 1952.

Anne Fine, 54, author (*The Tulip Touch, Alias Madame Doubtfire*), born County Durham, England, Dec 7, 1947.

Steve Parker, 49, author (*The Body Atlas, Brain Surgery for Beginners*), born Warrington, England, Dec 7, 1952.

DECEMBER 8 — SATURDAY

Day 342 — 23 Remaining

AMERICAN FEDERATION OF LABOR (AFL) FOUNDED: ANNIVERSARY. Dec 8, 1886. Originally founded at Pittsburgh, PA, as the Federation of Organized Trades and Labor Unions of the United States and Canada in 1881, the union was reorganized in 1886 under the name American Federation of Labor (AFL). The AFL was dissolved as a separate entity in 1955 when it merged with the Congress of Industrial Organizations to form the AFL-CIO. See also: "AFL-CIO Founded: Anniversary (Dec 5)."

CAN YOU TELL ME HOW TO GET TO SESAME STREET?. Dec 8–Aug 25, 2002. Missouri Historical Society, St. Louis, MO. This exhibit allows visitors literally to step into "Sesame Street." The interactive exhibit will allow children to explore and participate in activities on the themes of literacy, numeracy and diversity. There will also be information for adults on why and how the innovative children's program emerged and developed into a successful educational medium. For info: Missouri Historical Society, PO Box 11940, St. Louis, MO 63112-0040. Phone: (314) 367-8877.

CHICAGO LATINO BOOK & FAMILY FESTIVAL. Dec 8–9. McCormick Place, Chicago, IL. Produced along with actor Edward James Olmos, this festival is a celebration of books, careers, culture, education, health, recreation, travel and more. It is the largest Latino consumer trade show in the US. Attendees will enjoy hundreds of booths and activities including book signings, storytelling, poetry readings, food, entertainment and workshops. For info: Latino Book & Family Festivals, 3980 Cazador St., Los Angeles, CA 90065. E-mail: kathy@latinobookfestival.com. Web: www.latinobookfestival.com.

CHILDREN'S FESTIVAL OF FUN. Dec 8–9. Tempe, AZ. Games, entertainment, activities. For info: Total Experience Productions. Phone: (480) 250-7098. E-mail: info@childrensfestivaloffun.com. Web: childrensfestivaloffun.com.

CHINESE NATIONALISTS MOVE TO FORMOSA: ANNIVERSARY. Dec 8, 1949. The government of Chiang Kai–Shek moved to Formosa (Taiwan) after being driven out of mainland China by the Communists led by Mao Tse–Tung.

CIVIL RIGHTS WEEK IN MASSACHUSETTS. Dec 8–14. Proclaimed annually by the governor.

FEAST OF THE IMMACULATE CONCEPTION. Dec 8. Roman Catholic Holy Day of Obligation.

FIRST STEP TOWARD A NUCLEAR-FREE WORLD: ANNIVERSARY. Dec 8, 1987. The former Soviet Union and the US signed a treaty at Washington eliminating medium-range and shorter-range missiles. This was the first treaty completely doing away with two entire classes of nuclear arms. These missiles, with a range of 500 to 5,500 kilometers, were to be scrapped under strict supervision within three years of the signing.

GUAM: LADY OF CAMARIN DAY HOLIDAY. Dec 8. Declared a legal holiday by Guam legislature, Mar 2, 1971.

NAFTA SIGNED: ANNIVERSARY. Dec 8, 1993. President Clinton signed the North American Free Trade Agreement which cut tariffs and eliminated other trade barriers between the US, Canada and Mexico. The Agreement went into effect Jan 1, 1994.

SEGAR, ELZIE CRISLER: BIRTH ANNIVERSARY. Dec 8, 1894. Creator of *Thimble Theater,* the comic strip that came to be known as *Popeye*. Centered on the Oyl family, especially daughter Olive, the strip introduced a new central character in 1929. A one-eyed sailor with bulging muscles, Popeye became the strip's star attraction almost immediately. Popeye made it to the silver screen in animated form and in 1980 became a movie with Robin Williams playing the lead. Segar was born at Chester, IL. He died Oct 13, 1938, at Santa Monica, CA.

SOVIET UNION DISSOLVED: 10th ANNIVERSARY. Dec 8, 1991. The Union of Soviet Socialist Republics ceased to exist, as the republics of Russia, Byelorussia and Ukraine signed an agreement at Minsk, Byelorussia, creating the Commonwealth of Independent States. The remaining republics, with the exception of Georgia, joined in the new Commonwealth as it began the slow and arduous process of removing the yoke of Communism and dealing with strong separatist and nationalistic movements within the various republics.

THURBER, JAMES: BIRTH ANNIVERSARY. Dec 8, 1894. Author for adults and children (*The Thirteen Clocks*), born at Columbus, OH. Died at New York, NY, Nov 2, 1961.

December 2001	S	M	T	W	T	F	S
							1
	2	3	4	5	6	7	8
	9	10	11	12	13	14	15
	16	17	18	19	20	21	22
	23	24	25	26	27	28	29
	30	31					

BIRTHDAYS TODAY

Mary Azarian, 61, illustrator (Caldecott for *Snowflake Bentley*), born Washington, DC, Dec 8, 1940.

Kim Basinger, 48, actress (*Batman, My Stepmother Is an Alien*), born Athens, GA, Dec 8, 1953.

Teri Hatcher, 37, actress ("Lois & Clark"), born Sunnyvale, CA, Dec 8, 1964.

Teresa Weatherspoon, 36, basketball player, US Olympic Basketball Team, born Jasper, TX, Dec 8, 1965.

DECEMBER 9 — SUNDAY

Day 343 — 22 Remaining

BIRDSEYE, CLARENCE: BIRTH ANNIVERSARY. Dec 9, 1886. American industrialist who developed a way of deep-freezing foods. He was marketing frozen fish by 1925 and was one of the founders of General Foods Corporation. Born at Brooklyn, NY, he died at New York, NY, Oct 7, 1956.

BRUNHOFF, JEAN DE: BIRTH ANNIVERSARY. Dec 9, 1899. Author and illustrator of *The Story of Babar* and *The Little Elephant.* Born at Paris, France, Brunhoff died at Switzerland, Oct 16, 1937. In later years, the Babar series was continued by his son Laurent.

COMPUTER MOUSE DEVELOPED: ANNIVERSARY. Dec 9, 1968. Designed as a pointing device to help users interact with their computers, the mouse was first developed in 1968 but its use didn't become widespread until 1984 when Apple attached it to its Macintosh computer.

HARRIS, JOEL CHANDLER: BIRTH ANNIVERSARY. Dec 9, 1848. American author, creator of the Uncle Remus stories, born at Eatonton, GA. Died July 3, 1908, at Atlanta, GA.

INTERNATIONAL CHILDREN'S DAY OF BROADCASTING. Dec 9. A celebration of the enormous energy and creative potential of children. More than 2,000 broadcasters around the world produce special programs for and about children. Annually, the second Sunday in December. For more info: UNICEF, United Nations, New York, NY 10017. Web: www.unicef.org/icdb.

INTERNATIONAL SHAREWARE DAY. Dec 9. A day to take the time to reward the efforts of thousands of computer programmers who trust that if we try their programs and like them, we will pay for them. Unfortunately, very few payments are received, thus stifling the programmers' efforts. This observance is meant to prompt each of us to inventory our PCs and Macs, see if we are using any shareware, and then take the time in the holiday spirit to write payment checks to the authors. Hopefully this will keep shareware coming. Annually, the second Sunday in December. For info: David Lawrence, Host, Online Today, PO Box 32320, Baltimore, MD 21282. Phone: (800) 396-6546. E-mail: david@online-today.com. Web: online-today.com.

McGRAW, ELOISE JARVIS: BIRTH ANNIVERSARY. Dec 9, 1915. Award-winning author of fantasy and historical novels for children, she was born at Houston, TX. She received the Newbery Honor Award three times, in 1953 for *Moccasin Trail,* in 1962 for *The Golden Goblet,* and in 1997 for *The Moorchild*. She died at Portland, OR, Nov 30, 2000.

NATIONAL CHILDREN'S MEMORIAL DAY. Dec 9. A day to remember the more than 79,000 young people who die in the US every year. Annually, the second Sunday in December. For info: The Compassionate Friends, Inc, PO Box 3696, Oak Brook, IL 60522-3696. Phone: (630) 990-0010. E-mail: tcf_national@prodigy.com. Web: www.compassionatefriends.com.

PETRIFIED FOREST NATIONAL PARK ESTABLISHED: ANNIVERSARY. Dec 9, 1962. Arizona's Petrified Forest National Monument, proclaimed Dec 8, 1906, was established as a national park. For more info: www.nps.gov/pefo/index.htm.

TANZANIA: INDEPENDENCE AND REPUBLIC DAY: 40th ANNIVERSARY. Dec 9. Tanganyika became independent of Britain on this day in 1961. The republics of Tanganyika and Zanzibar joined to become one state (Apr 27, 1964) renamed (Oct 29, 1964) the United Republic of Tanzania.

BIRTHDAYS TODAY

Joan W. Blos, 73, author (Newbery for *A Gathering of Days: A New England Girl's Journal, 1830–1832*), born New York, NY, Dec 9, 1928.

Thomas Andrew Daschle, 54, US Senator (D, South Dakota), born Aberdeen, SD, Dec 9, 1947.

Mary Downing Hahn, 64, author (*Time for Andrew, The Doll in the Garden*), born Washington, DC, Dec 9, 1937.

Donny Osmond, 44, actor, singer ("Donny and Marie"; stage: *Joseph and the Amazing Technicolor Dreamcoat*), born Ogden, UT, Dec 9, 1957.

DECEMBER 10 — MONDAY

Day 344 — 21 Remaining

CHANUKAH. Dec 10–17. Feast of Lights or Feast of Dedication. This festival lasting eight days commemorates the victory of Maccabees over Syrians (165 BC) and rededication of the Temple of Jerusalem. Begins on Hebrew calendar date Kislev 25, 5762. For more info: *A Hanukkah Treasury*, edited by Eric A. Kimmel (Holt, 0-8050-5293-3, $19.95 All ages).

DEWEY, MELVIL: 150th BIRTH ANNIVERSARY. Dec 10, 1851. American librarian and inventor of the Dewey decimal book classification system was born at Adams Center, NY. Born Melville Louis Kossuth Dewey, he was an advocate of spelling reform, urged use of the metric system and was interested in many other education reforms. Dewey died at Highlands County, FL, Dec 26, 1931.

DICKINSON, EMILY: BIRTH ANNIVERSARY. Dec 10, 1830. One of America's greatest poets, Emily Dickinson was born at Amherst, MA. She was reclusive and frail in health. She died May 15, 1886, at Amherst. Seven of her poems were published during her life, but after her death her sister, Lavinia, discovered almost 2,000 more poems locked in her bureau. They were published gradually, over 50 years, beginning in 1890. The little-known Emily Dickinson who was born, lived and died at Amherst is now recognized as one of the most original poets of the English-speaking world.

FIRST US SCIENTIST RECEIVES NOBEL PRIZE: ANNIVERSARY. Dec 10, 1907. University of Chicago professor Albert Michelson, eminent physicist known for his research on the speed of light and optics, became the first US scientist to receive the Nobel Prize.

GALLAUDET, THOMAS HOPKINS: BIRTH ANNIVERSARY. Dec 10, 1787. A hearing educator who, with Laurent Clerc, founded the first public school for deaf people, Connecticut Asylum for the Education and Instruction of Deaf and Dumb Persons (now the American School for the Deaf), at Hartford, CT, Apr 15, 1817. Gallaudet was born at Philadelphia, PA, and died Sept 9, 1851, at Hartford, CT.

GODDEN, RUMER: BIRTH ANNIVERSARY. Dec 10, 1907. Author of the popular children's tales *The Mousewife* and *The Story of Holly & Ivy*. Born at Sussex, England, Godden died at Thornhill, Scotland, Nov 8, 1998.

★**HUMAN RIGHTS DAY.** Dec 10. Presidential Proclamation 2866, of Dec 6, 1949, covers all succeeding years. Customarily issued as "Bill of Rights Day, Human Rights Day and Week."

★**HUMAN RIGHTS WEEK.** Dec 10–16. Presidential Proclamation issued since 1958 for the week of Dec 10–16, except in 1986. See also: "Human Rights Day" (Dec 10) and "Bill of Rights Day" (Dec 15).

"THE MIGHTY MOUSE PLAYHOUSE" TV PREMIERE: ANNIVERSARY. Dec 10, 1955. An all-time favorite of the Saturday-morning crowd (including adults). CBS had a hit with their pint-sized cartoon character Mighty Mouse, who was a tongue-in-cheek version of Superman. The show had other feature cartoons such as "The Adventures of Gandy Goose" and "Heckle and Jeckle."

DECEMBER 10
MARY NORTON'S BIRTHDAY

Mary Norton, author of the children's literature classic, *The Borrowers*, was born on December 10, 1903, in London, England. Not much is known about her life; however, her books are world famous. Encourage your students to read and discuss them. A biography about her works and life written for adults is entitled *Mary Norton*, by Jon Stott (Macmillan, 0-8057-7054-2, $22.95).

The Borrowers (Harcourt, 0-15-209990-5, $6 Gr. 3–7), published in 1953, is the first of Norton's five books that chronicle the adventures of Pod, Homily and Arriety Clock, a family of tiny people who live between the walls in an English home. This fantasy family must use discarded and borrowed materials from the large house to create their own comfortable home. Their ingenuity is totally charming and often laugh-out-loud funny. The other four books in the series are: *The Borrowers Afield, The Borrowers Afloat, The Borrowers Aloft*, and *The Borrowers Avenged*. All are readily available in school and public libraries and in paperback in bookstores.

As is usually the case with fantasy involving tiny people, normal-sized humans pose the greatest threat to the continued existence of the little people. This issue is one children relate to, perhaps because they themselves are trying to make their own way through a world inhabited by larger people.

A fun way to enjoy and explore the themes and situations found in the Borrowers series is to have children read them (as part of a fantasy genre unit, perhaps) and also the excellent Mennym series, by Sylvia Waugh. The Mennyms are a family of life-sized rag dolls who live in a house in England. *The Mennyms* (Morrow, 0-380-72528-2, $4.99 Gr. 4–8) is the first book of the series and is followed by four more. Set in modern times, the Mennyms have many exciting adventures as they foray into the world of humans. There are sufficient similarities and plenty of differences to make them a good example of how literature can be compared and contrasted.

As a writing project, children might enjoy writing about where the Borrowers would live in their house, if they were to move in. What kinds of things would pose a threat (pets?), and what items would they be likely to borrow?

MISSISSIPPI: ADMISSION DAY: ANNIVERSARY. Dec 10. Became 20th state in 1817.

NOBEL PRIZE AWARDS CEREMONIES: 100th ANNIVERSARY. Dec 10. Oslo, Norway and Stockholm, Sweden. Alfred Nobel, Swedish chemist and inventor of dynamite, who died in 1896, provided in his will that income from his $9 million estate should be used for annual prizes to be awarded to people who are judged to have made the most valuable contributions to the good of humanity. The Nobel Peace Prize is awarded by a committee of the Norwegian parliament and the presentation is made at the Oslo City Hall. Five other prizes, for physics, chemistry, medicine, literature and economics, are presented in a ceremony at Stockholm, Sweden. Both ceremonies traditionally are held on the anniversary of the death of Alfred Nobel. First awarded in 1901, the current value of each prize is about $1,000,000. See also "Nobel, Alfred Bernhard: Birth Anniversary" (Oct 21). For more info: www.nobel.se.

NORTON, MARY: BIRTH ANNIVERSARY. Dec 10, 1903. British children's writer known for The Borrowers series, for which she received the Carnegie Medal. Her book *Bed-Knob and Broomstick* was made into a movie by Disney in 1971. Born at London, England, she died at Hartland, Devon, England, Aug 29, 1992. *See* Curriculum Connection.

RALPH BUNCHE AWARDED NOBEL PEACE PRIZE: ANNIVERSARY. Dec 10, 1950. Dr. Ralph Johnson Bunche became the first black man awarded the Nobel Peace Prize. Bunche was awarded the prize for his efforts in mediation between Israel and neighboring Arab states in 1949.

RED CLOUD: DEATH ANNIVERSARY. Dec 10, 1909. Sioux Indian chief Red Cloud was born in 1822 (exact date unknown), near North Platte, NE. A courageous leader and defender of Indian rights, Red Cloud was the son of Lone Man and Walks as She Thinks. His unrelenting determination caused US abandonment of the Bozeman trail and of three forts that interfered with Indian hunting grounds. Red Cloud died at Pine Ridge, SD.

THAILAND: CONSTITUTION DAY. Dec 10. A public holiday throughout Thailand.

TREATY OF PARIS ENDS SPANISH-AMERICAN WAR: ANNIVERSARY. Dec 10, 1898. Following the conclusion of the Spanish-American War in 1898, American and Spanish ambassadors met at Paris, France, to negotiate a treaty. Under the terms of this treaty, Spain granted the US the Philippine Islands and the islands of Guam and Puerto Rico, and agreed to withdraw from Cuba. Senatorial debate over the treaty centered on the US's move toward imperialism by acquiring the Philippines. A vote was taken Feb 6, 1899 and the treaty passed by a one-vote margin. President William McKinley signed the treaty Feb 10, 1899.

UNITED NATIONS: HUMAN RIGHTS DAY. Dec 10. Official United Nations observance day. Date is the anniversary of adoption of the "Universal Declaration of Human Rights" in 1948. The Declaration sets forth basic rights and fundamental freedoms to which all men and women everywhere in the world are entitled. For more info, go to the UN's website for children at www.un.org/Pubs/CyberSchoolBus/.

December 2001

S	M	T	W	T	F	S
						1
2	3	4	5	6	7	8
9	10	11	12	13	14	15
16	17	18	19	20	21	22
23	24	25	26	27	28	29
30	31					

UNITED NATIONS: THIRD DECADE TO COMBAT RACISM AND RACIAL DISCRIMINATION: YEAR EIGHT. Dec 10. In 1973 the United Nations General Assembly proclaimed the years 1973–83, beginning Dec 10, UN Human Rights Day, as the Decade to Combat Racism and Racial Discrimination. Renewing its efforts, the UN designated the years 1983–93 as the Second Decade to Combat Racism and Racial Discrimination. The adopted Program of Action states the decade's goals and outlines the measures to be taken at the regional, national and international levels to achieve them. In Res 47/77 of Dec 16, 1992, the Assembly called upon the international community to provide resources for the program to be carried out during a third decade (1993–2003), particularly for the monitoring of the transition from apartheid in South Africa. Info from: United Nations, Dept of Public Info, New York, NY 10017.

UZBEKISTAN: CONSTITUTION DAY. Dec 10. National holiday. Commemorates the constitution of 1991.

BIRTHDAYS TODAY

Raven Symone, 16, actress ("The Cosby Show," *Doctor Dolittle*), born Atlanta, GA, Dec 10, 1985.

DECEMBER 11 — TUESDAY

Day 345 — 20 Remaining

BURKINA FASO: NATIONAL DAY. Dec 11. Gained independence within the French community, 1958.

INDIANA: ADMISSION DAY: ANNIVERSARY. Dec 11. Became 19th state in 1816.

SPACE MILESTONE: *MARS CLIMATE ORBITER* (US). Dec 11, 1998. This unmanned rocket was to track the movement of water vapor over Mars, which it was scheduled to reach in September 1999. However, it flew too close to Mars and is presumed destroyed. On Jan 3, 1999, *Mars Polar Lander* was launched. It was to burrow into the ground and analyze the soil of Mars. However, on Dec 3, 1999, as it was landing, communications with the robot craft were lost.

UNITED NATIONS: UNICEF: 55th ANNIVERSARY. Dec 11, 1946. Anniversary of the establishment by the United Nations General Assembly of the United Nations International Children's Emergency Fund (UNICEF). For info: United Nations, Dept of Public Info, New York, NY 10017. Web: www.unicef.org.

BIRTHDAYS TODAY

Max Baucus, 60, US Senator (D, Montana), born Helena, MT, Dec 11, 1941.

Jermaine Jackson, 47, singer, musician (Jackson 5, "Daddy's Home," "Let's Get Serious"), born Gary, IN, Dec 11, 1954.

William Joyce, 44, author and illustrator (*Bently and Egg*), born Shreveport, LA, Dec 11, 1957.

John F. Kerry, 58, US Senator (D, Massachusetts), born Denver, CO, Dec 11, 1943.

Rider Strong, 22, actor ("Boy Meets World"), born San Francisco, CA, Dec 11, 1979.

DECEMBER 12 — WEDNESDAY

Day 346 — 19 Remaining

BONZA BOTTLER DAY™. Dec 12. To celebrate when the number of the day is the same as the number of the month. Bonza Bottler Day™ is an excuse to have a party at least once a month. For info: Gail M. Berger, 109 Matthew Ave, Poca, WV 25159. Phone: (304) 776-7746. E-mail: gberger5@aol.com.

DAY OF OUR LADY OF GUADALUPE. Dec 12. The legend of Guadalupe tells how in December 1531, an Indian, Juan Diego, saw the Virgin Mother on a hill near Mexico City, who instructed him to go to the bishop and have him build a shrine to her on the site of the vision. After his request was initially rebuffed, the Virgin Mother appeared to Juan Diego three days later. She instructed him to pick roses growing on a stony and barren hillside nearby and take them to the bishop as proof. Although flowers do not normally bloom in December, Juan Diego found the roses and took them to the bishop. As he opened his mantle to drop the roses on the floor, an image of the Virgin Mary appeared among them. The bishop built the sanctuary as instructed. Our Lady of Guadalupe became the patroness of Mexico City and by 1746 was the patron saint of all New Spain and by 1910 of all Latin America.

FIRST BLACK SERVES IN US HOUSE OF REPRESENTATIVES: ANNIVERSARY. Dec 12, 1870. Joseph Hayne Rainey of Georgetown, SC, was sworn in as the first black to serve in the US House of Representatives. Rainey filled the seat of Benjamin Franklin Whittemore, which had been declared vacant by the House. He served until Mar 3, 1879.

JAY, JOHN: BIRTH ANNIVERSARY. Dec 12, 1745. American statesman, diplomat and first chief justice of the US Supreme Court (1789–95), coauthor (with Alexander Hamilton and James Madison) of the influential *Federalist* papers, was born at New York, NY. Jay died at Bedford, NY, May 17, 1829.

KENYA: JAMHURI DAY. Dec 12. Jamhuri Day (Independence Day) is Kenya's official National Day, commemorating proclamation of the republic and independence from the UK in 1963.

MEXICO: GUADALUPE DAY. Dec 12. One of Mexico's major celebrations. Honors the "Dark Virgin of Guadalupe," the republic's patron saint. Parties and pilgrimages, with special ceremonies at the Shrine of Our Lady of Guadalupe, at Mexico City.

PENNSYLVANIA RATIFIES CONSTITUTION: ANNIVERSARY. Dec 12, 1787. Pennsylvania became the second state to ratify the US Constitution, by a vote of 46 to 23.

POINSETTIA DAY (JOEL ROBERTS POINSETT: DEATH ANNIVERSARY). Dec 12. A day to enjoy poinsettias and to honor Dr. Joel Roberts Poinsett, the American diplomat who introduced the Central American plant that is named for him into the US. Poinsett was born at Charleston, SC, Mar 2, 1799. He also served as a member of Congress and as secretary of war. He died near Statesburg, SC, Dec 12, 1851. The poinsettia has become a favorite Christmas season plant.

RUSSIA: CONSTITUTION DAY. Dec 12. National holiday commemorating the adoption of the new constitution in 1993.

SUPREME COURT RULES FOR BUSH: ANNIVERSARY. Dec 12, 2000. The Supreme Court effectively handed the 2000 presidential election to George W. Bush, ruling by a vote of 5 to 4 that there could be no further counting of Florida's disputed presidential votes. After five weeks of conflict over the vote count in Florida, Democratic candidate Al Gore conceded the election to Bush. While Bush won the electoral vote to become the nation's 43rd president, Gore won the popular vote. Bush was only the fourth president in American history to be elected without winning the popular vote.

TURKMENISTAN: NEUTRALITY DAY. Dec 12. National holiday. Commemorates the UN's recognition of neutrality in 1995.

BIRTHDAYS TODAY

Tracy Austin, 39, former tennis player, born Rolling Hills Estates, CA, Dec 12, 1962.

Mayim Bialik, 26, actress ("Blossom"), born San Diego, CA, Dec 12, 1975.

DECEMBER 13 — THURSDAY

Day 347 — 18 Remaining

LINCOLN, MARY TODD: BIRTH ANNIVERSARY. Dec 13, 1818. Wife of Abraham Lincoln, 16th president of the US, born at Lexington, KY. Died at Springfield, IL, July 16, 1882.

MALTA: REPUBLIC DAY. Dec 13. National holiday. Malta became a republic in 1974.

NEW ZEALAND FIRST SIGHTED BY EUROPEANS: ANNIVERSARY. Dec 13, 1642. Captain Abel Tasman of the Dutch East India Company first sighted New Zealand but was kept from landing by Maori warriors. In 1769 Captain James Cook landed and claimed formal possession for Great Britain.

NORTH AND SOUTH KOREA END WAR: 10th ANNIVERSARY. Dec 13, 1991. North and South Korea signed a treaty of reconciliation and nonaggression, formally ending the Korean War—38 years after fighting ceased in 1953. This agreement was not hailed as a peace treaty, and the armistice that was signed July 27, 1953, between the UN and North Korea, was to remain in effect until it could be transformed into a formal peace.

SWEDEN: SANTA LUCIA DAY. Dec 13. Nationwide celebration of festival of light, honoring St. Lucia. Many hotels have their own Lucia, a young girl attired in a long, flowing white gown with a wreath of candles in her hair, who serves guests coffee and lussekatter (saffron buns) in the early morning.

BIRTHDAYS TODAY

Sergei Federov, 32, hockey player, born Pskov, Russia, Dec 13, 1969.

Tamora Pierce, 47, author (*In the Realms of the Gods*, the Magic Circle series), born Connellsville, PA, Dec 13, 1954.

Johan Reinhard, 58, author (*Discovering the Inca Ice Maiden, My Adventures on Ampato*), born Joliet, IL, Dec 13, 1943.

Dick Van Dyke, 76, actor, comedian (*Mary Poppins*, "The Dick Van Dyke Show"), born West Plains, MO, Dec 13, 1925.

Tom Vilsack, 51, Governor of Iowa (D), born Pittsburgh, PA, Dec 13, 1950.

DECEMBER 14 — FRIDAY

Day 348 — 17 Remaining

ALABAMA: ADMISSION DAY: ANNIVERSARY. Dec 14. Became the 22nd state in 1819.

HALCYON DAYS. Dec 14–28. Traditionally, the seven days before and the seven days after the winter solstice. To the ancients a time when a fabled bird (called the halcyon–pronounced hal-cee-on) calmed the wind and waves—a time of calm and tranquility.

MOON PHASE: NEW MOON. Dec 14. Moon enters New Moon phase at 3:47 PM, EST.

SOLAR ECLIPSE. Dec 14. Annular eclipse of the sun. Eclipse begins at 1:03 PM, EST, reaches greatest eclipse at 3:44 PM and ends at 6:40 PM. Visible in Pacific Ocean, NW South America, Central America, USA, western and southern parts of Canada.

SOUTH POLE DISCOVERY: 90th ANNIVERSARY. Dec 14, 1911. The elusive object of many expeditions dating from the 7th century, the South Pole was located and visited by Roald Amundsen with four companions and 52 sled dogs. All five men and 12 of the dogs returned to base camp safely. Next to visit the South Pole, Jan 17, 1912, was a party of five led by Captain Robert F. Scott, all of whom perished during the return trip. A search party found their frozen bodies 11 months later. See also: "Amundsen, Roald: Birth Anniversary" (July 16).

SUTCLIFFE, ROSEMARY: BIRTH ANNIVERSARY. Dec 14, 1920. Author of historical novels for children (*The Lantern Bearers, Eagle of the Ninth*), born at East Clanden, England. Died July 23, 1992.

BIRTHDAYS TODAY

Craig Biggio, 36, baseball player, born Smithtown, NY, Dec 14, 1965.

Rhoda Blumberg, 84, author (*Full Steam Ahead: The Race to Build a Transcontinental Railroad*), born New York, NY, Dec 14, 1917.

Patty Duke, 55, actress (Oscar for *The Miracle Worker*; Emmy for *My Sweet Charlie*), born New York, NY, Dec 14, 1946.

John Neufeld, 63, author (*Lisa, Bright and Dark; Edgar Allen*), born Chicago, IL, Dec 14, 1938.

DECEMBER 15 — SATURDAY

Day 349 — 16 Remaining

★**BILL OF RIGHTS DAY.** Dec 15. Presidential Proclamation. Has been proclaimed each year since 1962, but was omitted in 1967 and 1968. (Issued in 1941 and 1946 at Congressional request and in 1947 without request.) Since 1968 has been included in Human Rights Day and Week Proclamation.

BILL OF RIGHTS: ANNIVERSARY. Dec 15, 1791. The first 10 amendments to the US Constitution, known as the Bill of Rights, became effective following ratification by Virginia. The anniversary of ratification and of effect is observed as Bill of Rights Day and is proclaimed annually by the President. For more info: *A Kids' Guide to America's Bill of Rights: Curfews, Censorship, and the 100-Pound Giant*, by Kathleen Krull (Avon/Camelot, 0-380-97497-5, $16 Gr. 5–8) or go to Ben's Guide to US Government for Kids: bensguide.gpo.gov.

December 2001

S	M	T	W	T	F	S
						1
2	3	4	5	6	7	8
9	10	11	12	13	14	15
16	17	18	19	20	21	22
23	24	25	26	27	28	29
30	31					

DECEMBER 15
SITTING BULL'S DEATH ANNIVERSARY

Sitting Bull, also known by his native name, Tatan´ka Iyota´ke, was a famous and highly revered Hunkpapa Lakota warrior and leader. He was a *wichasha wakan*, the Lakota words for a holy man or seer. One of his prophetic visions was of "soldiers falling into camp," which many believed foretold the results of the Battle of the Little Bighorn.

He was born about 1831, the son of Her Holy Door and Sitting Bull (his father's name). At the baby's naming ceremony, his father named him Jumping Badger, but the young boy soon received the nickname "Slow." Slow was known as a keen observer and a quick learner. He spent a lot of time with horses and was an excellent horseman. When he was about 14 years old, Slow went on his first war party, against Crow Indians. This was when he scored his first coup—he whacked a Crow warrior with his coup stick. That caused the Crow warrior to miss his shot and earned great honor for Slow. Later, when the war party recounted their victory, Slow received his adult name. His father acknowledged his son's bravery by giving his most valuable possession—his own name to his son. From then on, Slow was known as Sitting Bull. Sitting Bull drew many pictures that depicted his deeds. He represented his presence in a scene with a drawing of a sitting buffalo bull. A brave warrior, Sitting Bull had a reputation for upholding strict moral principals and obeying the tribe's rules.

Sitting Bull was one of the Indian leaders at the Battle of the Little Big Horn, on June 25, 1876. The 7th Cavalry, commanded by George Armstrong Custer, was defeated by the Indian warriors.

Inflamed by the defeat, the army became determined to conquer and capture Sitting Bull. His belief and request, often repeated, that Native Americans be free to choose their own way of life was ignored. A series of wars broke out. Finally, Sitting Bull fled to Canada, where he remained until 1881. Faced with starvation after two brutal winters, Sitting Bull was forced to return to the United States.

In the summer of 1885, Sitting Bull accompanied Wild Bill Cody and his Wild West Show and appeared in New York, Philadelphia and Washington, D.C. He led parades and greeted visitors to the show in his lodge. After one season, Sitting Bull returned to South Dakota to live on the Standing Rock Reservation. While there, he supported the Ghost Dance. Whites saw this as a threat and attempt to renew the Indian wars. Sitting Bull was shot and killed on December 15, 1890, when Indian police officers attempted to arrest him.

Books for young readers include: *A Boy Called Slow*, by Joseph Bruchac (Putnam, 0-698-11616-X, $6.99 Gr. K–3), and *Sitting Bull and His World*, by Albert Marrin (Dutton, 0-525-45944-8, $27.50 Gr. 6 & up). Marrin's book is a comprehensive biography that includes information about the Lakota and how changes brought by the expansion of white culture affected them. He presents all issues with perspectives from both sides, making this an excellent choice for class discussion. Some moments in this book will bring tears to your eyes. Most of all, your students will understand and respect Sitting Bull, a unique and charismatic leader.

CURAÇAO: KINGDOM DAY AND ANTILLEAN FLAG DAY. Dec 15. This day commemorates the Charter of Kingdom, signed at the Knight's Hall at The Hague in 1954, granting the Netherlands Antilles complete autonomy. The Antillean Flag was hoisted for the first time Dec 15, 1959.

"DAVY CROCKETT" TV PREMIERE: ANNIVERSARY. Dec 15, 1954. This show, a series of five segments, can be considered TV's first miniseries. Shown on Walt Disney's "Disneyland" show, it starred Fess Parker as American western hero Davy Crockett and was immensely popular. The show spawned Crockett paraphernalia, including the famous coonskin cap (even after we found out that Boone never wore a coonskin cap).

EIFFEL, ALEXANDRE GUSTAVE: BIRTH ANNIVERSARY. Dec 15, 1832. Eiffel, the French engineer who designed the 1,000 ft-high, million-dollar, open-lattice wrought iron Eiffel Tower, and who participated in designing the Statue of Liberty, was born at Dijon, France. The Eiffel Tower, weighing more than 7,000 tons, was built for the Paris International Exposition of 1889. Eiffel died at Paris, France, Dec 23, 1923.

PUERTO RICO: NAVIDADES. Dec 15–Jan 6. Traditional Christmas season begins mid-December and ends on Three Kings Day. Elaborate nativity scenes, carolers, special Christmas foods and trees from Canada and US. Gifts on Christmas Day and on Three Kings Day.

SITTING BULL: DEATH ANNIVERSARY. Dec 15, 1890. Famous Sioux Indian leader, medicine man and warrior of the Hunkpapa Teton band. Known also by his native name, Tatanka-yatanka, Sitting Bull was born on the Grand River, SD. He first accompanied his father on the warpath at the age of 14 against the Crow and thereafter rapidly gained influence within his tribe. In 1886 he led a raid on Fort Buford. His steadfast refusal to go to a reservation led General Phillip Sheridan to initiate a campaign against him which led to the massacre of Lieutenant Colonel George Custer's men at Little Bighorn, after which Sitting Bull fled to Canada, remaining there until 1881. Although many in his tribe surrendered on their return, Sitting Bull remained hostile until his death in a skirmish with the US soldiers along the Grand River. For more info: *Sitting Bull and His World*, by Albert Marrin (Dutton, 0-525-45944-8, $25 Gr. 6–12). *See* Curriculum Connection.

SMITH, BETTY: BIRTH ANNIVERSARY. Dec 15, 1904. Author, born at New York, NY. Her books include *A Tree Grows in Brooklyn*, *Tomorrow Will Be Better* and *Joy in the Morning*. Smith died at Shelton, CT, Jan 17, 1972.

BIRTHDAYS TODAY

Alexandra Stevenson, 21, tennis player, born San Diego, CA, Dec 15, 1980.

Garrett Wang, 33, actor ("Star Trek: Voyager"), born Riverside, CA, Dec 15, 1968.

DECEMBER 16 — SUNDAY

Day 350 — 15 Remaining

BAHRAIN: INDEPENDENCE DAY: 30th ANNIVERSARY. Dec 16. National holiday. Commemorates independence from British protection in 1971.

BANGLADESH: VICTORY DAY: 30th ANNIVERSARY. Dec 16. National holiday. Commemorates victory over Pakistan in 1971. The former East Pakistan became Bangladesh.

BATTLE OF THE BULGE: ANNIVERSARY. Dec 16, 1944. By late 1944 the German Army was in retreat and Allied forces were on German soil. But a surprise German offensive was launched in the Belgian Ardennes Forest on this date. The Nazi commanders, hoping to minimize any aerial counterattack by the Allies, chose a time when foggy, rainy weather prevailed and the initial attack by eight armored divisions along a 75-mile front took the Allies by surprise, the 5th Panzer Army penetrating to within 20 miles of crossings on the Meuse River. US troops were able to hold fast at bottlenecks in the Ardennes, but by the end of December the German push had penetrated 65 miles into the Allied lines (though their line had narrowed from the initial 75 miles to 20 miles). By that time the Allies began to respond and the Germans were stopped by Montgomery on the Meuse and by Patton at Bastogne. The weather cleared and Allied aircraft began to bomb the German forces and supply lines by Dec 26. The German Army withdrew from the Ardennes, Jan 21, 1945, having lost 120,000 men.

BEETHOVEN, LUDWIG VAN: BIRTH ANNIVERSARY. Dec 16, 1770. Regarded by many as the greatest orchestral composer of all time, Ludwig van Beethoven was born at Bonn, Germany. Impairment of his hearing began before he was 30, but even total deafness did not halt his composing and conducting. His last appearance on the concert stage was to conduct the premiere of his *Ninth Symphony*, at Vienna, May 7, 1824. He was unable to hear either the orchestra or the applause. Of a stormy temperament, he is said to have died during a violent thunderstorm Mar 26, 1827, at Vienna.

BOSTON TEA PARTY: ANNIVERSARY. Dec 16, 1773. Anniversary of Boston patriots' boarding of British vessel at anchor at Boston Harbor. Contents of nearly 350 chests of tea were dumped into the harbor to protest the British monopoly on tea imports. This was one of several events leading to the American Revolution. For info: *The Boston Tea Party*, by Laurie O'Neill (Millbrook, 0-761-30006-6, $23.90 Gr. 3–6).

EID-AL-FITR: CELEBRATING THE FAST. Dec 16. Islamic calendar date: Shawwal 1, 1422. This feast/festival celebrates having completed the Ramadan fasting (which began Nov 16) and usually lasts for several days. Everyone wears new clothes; children receive gifts from parents and relatives; games, folktales, plays, puppet shows, trips to amusement parks; children are allowed to stay up late. Different methods for "anticipating" the visibility of the new moon crescent at Mecca are used by different Muslim groups. US date may vary. For more info: *Id-ul-Fitr*, by Kerena Marchant (Millbrook, 07613-0963-2, $20.90 Gr. K–3).

KAZAKHSTAN: REPUBLIC DAY: 10th ANNIVERSARY. Dec 16. National Day. Commemorates independence from the Soviet Union in 1991.

MEXICO: POSADAS. Dec 16–24. A nine-day annual celebration throughout Mexico. Processions of "pilgrims" knock at doors asking for posada (shelter), commemorating the search by Joseph and Mary for a shelter in which the infant Jesus might be born. Pilgrims are invited inside, and fun and merrymaking ensue with blindfolded guests trying to break a "piñata" (papier mache decorated earthenware utensil filled with gifts and goodies) suspended from the ceiling. Once the piñata is broken, the gifts are distributed and celebration continues.

PHILIPPINES: SIMBANG GABI. Dec 16–25. Nationwide. A nine-day novena of predawn masses, also called "Misa de Gallo." One of the traditional Filipino celebrations of the holiday season.

REENACTMENT OF THE BOSTON TEA PARTY. Dec 16. Congress Street Bridge, Boston, MA. Reenactment of "Boston's most notorious protest, the single most important event leading to the American Revolution." Annually, the Sunday closest to Dec 16. Starts at Old South Meeting House 5:30 PM. Est attendance: 1,000. For info: Boston Tea Party Ship, Congress Street Bridge, Boston, MA 02210. Phone: (617) 338-1773. Fax: (617) 338-1974.

SOUTH AFRICA: RECONCILIATION DAY. Dec 16. National holiday. Celebrates the spirit of reconciliation, national unity and peace amongst all citizens.

TELL SOMEONE THEY'RE DOING A GOOD JOB WEEK. Dec 16–22. Every day this week tell someone "you're doing a good job." For info: Joe Hoppel, Radio Station WCMS, 900 Commonwealth Place, Virginia Beach, VA 23464. Phone: (757) 424-1050. Fax: (804) 424-3479. E-mail: wcms@norfolk.infi.net. Web: www.wcms.com.

BIRTHDAYS TODAY

Bill Brittain, 71, author (*The Wish Giver: Three Tales of Coven Tree*), born Rochester, NY, Dec 16, 1930.

Peter Dickinson, 74, author (*The Lion Tamer's Daughter: And Other Stories*), born Livingston, Zambia, Dec 16, 1927.

DECEMBER 17 — MONDAY

Day 351 — 14 Remaining

AZTEC CALENDAR STONE DISCOVERY: ANNIVERSARY. Dec 17, 1790. One of the wonders of the western hemisphere—the Aztec Calendar or Solar Stone—was found beneath the ground by workmen repairing Mexico City's Central Plaza. The intricately carved stone, 11 feet, 8 inches in diameter and weighing nearly 25 tons, proved to be a highly developed calendar monument to the sun. Believed to have been carved in the year 1479, this extraordinary time-counting basalt tablet originally stood in the Great Temple of the Aztecs. Buried along with other Aztec idols, soon after the Spanish conquest in 1521, it remained hidden until 1790. Its 52-year cycle had regulated many Aztec ceremonies, including human sacrifices to save the world from destruction by the gods.

CLEAN AIR ACT PASSED BY CONGRESS: ANNIVERSARY. Dec 17, 1967. A sweeping set of laws to protect us from air pollution was passed this day. This was the first legislation to place pollution controls on the automobile industry.

FLOYD, WILLIAM: BIRTH ANNIVERSARY. Dec 17, 1734. Signer of the Declaration of Independence, member of Congress, born at Brookhaven, NY. Died at Westernville, NY, Aug 4, 1821.

KING, W.L. MACKENZIE: BIRTH ANNIVERSARY. Dec 17, 1874. Former Canadian prime minister, born at Berlin, Ontario. Served 21 years, the longest term of any prime minister in the English-speaking world. Died at Kingsmere, Canada, July 22, 1950.

DECEMBER 17
HOLIDAY MEMORY CHAIN

December includes several holidays—Chanukah, Christmas, Kwanzaa, Boxing Day and Ramadan (this year)—that are often celebrated by families gathering together to share prayer, gifts, meals and memories. As we grow older, we realize that gifts from the heart are the ones we cherish most. Why not encourage your students to make a family gift that will become a chronicle of their family's life?

Each student will be making a five-to-ten-link paper chain. (Some students will really get into this and can be encouraged to create more.) Offer several colors of construction paper. Students will need permanent markers or crayons. Cut paper into strips that measure 6 1/2 inches long by 1 to 1 1/2 inches wide. Students can scallop or nick edges if they want.

On each strip a student can write a short phrase (or draw a picture) that recalls a particular moment of his or her life or that of a family member. For example, family milestones like: "We got our puppy ____ this year"; "Grandma taught me to how to ____"; "My sister was born on ____"; "Our family moved to ____." Encourage students to remember some of the times when the family laughed together over something silly: "The dog jumped on the kitchen table and ate John's birthday cake."

Each phrase should include just enough description to jar comments of "Oh, yeah—and remember what else happened . . ." or "And after that, we . . ." or "Let's let Susie tell the whole story."

After the individual links have been written, paste or staple them together. This short chain becomes the nucleus for a chain that family members will add links to each year. The chain can be stored with holiday decorations and rehung (and lengthened) the following year.

This is a fun way to get families to share memories with each other. Suggest children ask grandparents to add links right away. It's also a great way to reinforce the importance of oral tradition.

★**PAN AMERICAN AVIATION DAY.** Dec 17. Presidential Proclamation 2446, of Nov 18, 1940, covers all succeeding years (Pub Res No. 105 of Oct 10, 1940).

★**WRIGHT BROTHERS DAY.** Dec 17. Presidential Proclamation always issued for Dec 17 since 1963 (PL88–209 of Dec 17, 1963). Issued twice earlier at Congressional request in 1959 and 1961.

WRIGHT BROTHERS' FIRST POWERED FLIGHT: ANNIVERSARY. Dec 17, 1903. Orville and Wilbur Wright, brothers, bicycle shop operators, inventors and aviation pioneers, after three years of experimentation with kites and gliders, achieved the first documented successful powered and controlled flights of an airplane. The flights, near Kitty Hawk, NC, piloted first by Orville then by Wilbur Wright, were sustained for less than one minute but represented man's first powered airplane flight and the beginning of a new form of transportation. Orville Wright was born at Dayton, OH, Aug 19, 1871, and died there Jan 30, 1948. Wilbur Wright was born at Millville, IN, Apr 16, 1867, and died at Dayton, OH, May 30, 1912. For more info: *The Wright Brothers: How They Invented the Airplane*, by Russell Freedman (Holiday, 0-8234-0875-2, $18.95 Gr. 4–6).

December 2001

S	M	T	W	T	F	S
						1
2	3	4	5	6	7	8
9	10	11	12	13	14	15
16	17	18	19	20	21	22
23	24	25	26	27	28	29
30	31					

BIRTHDAYS TODAY

Ernie Hudson, 56, actor (*Ghostbusters, Ghostbusters II*), born Benton Harbor, MI, Dec 17, 1945.

David Kherdian, 70, author (*The Road from Home: The Story of an Armenian Girl*), born Racine, WI, Dec 17, 1931.

DECEMBER 18 — TUESDAY

Day 352 — 13 Remaining

CAPITOL REEF NATIONAL PARK ESTABLISHED: 30th ANNIVERSARY. Dec 18, 1971. Area of outstanding geological features, colorful canyons, prehistoric Fremont petroglyphs and Mormon historic fruit orchards and buildings in south central Utah, originally proclaimed a national monument Aug 2, 1937, was established as a national park. For more info: www.nps.gov/care/index.htm.

COBB, TY: BIRTH ANNIVERSARY. Dec 18, 1886. Tyrus (Ty) Cobb, Baseball Hall of Fame outfielder, born at Narrows, GA. He played 24 years and got more hits than any other player, until Pete Rose. Inducted into the Hall of Fame in 1936. Died at Atlanta, GA, July 17, 1961. For more info: www.cmgww.com/baseball/cobb/index2.html.

NEW JERSEY RATIFIES CONSTITUTION: ANNIVERSARY. Dec 18, 1787. New Jersey became the third state to ratify the Constitution (following Delaware and Pennsylvania). It did so unanimously.

NIGER: REPUBLIC DAY. Dec 18. National holiday. This West African nation gained autonomy within the French community on this day in 1958.

BIRTHDAYS TODAY

Christina Aguilera, 21, singer, born Staten Island, NY, Dec 18, 1980.

Katie Holmes, 23, actress ("Dawson's Creek"), born Toledo, OH, Dec 18, 1978.

Brad Pitt, 37, actor (*Interview with a Vampire, A River Runs Through It*), born Shawnee, OK, Dec 18, 1964.

Marilyn Sachs, 74, author (the Veronica Ganz series), born The Bronx, NY, Dec 18, 1927.

Steven Spielberg, 54, producer, director (*E.T.: The Extra-Terrestrial, Indiana Jones, Close Encounters of the Third Kind, Jurassic Park*), born Cincinnati, OH, Dec 18, 1947.

Kiefer Sutherland, 35, actor (*Flatliners, A Few Good Men*), born Los Angeles, CA, Dec 18, 1966.

DECEMBER 19 — WEDNESDAY

Day 353 — 12 Remaining

CHRISTMAS GREETINGS FROM SPACE: ANNIVERSARY. Dec 19, 1958. At 3:15 PM, EST, the US Earth satellite *Atlas* transmitted the first radio voice broadcast from space, a 58-word recorded Christmas greeting from President Dwight D. Eisenhower: "to all mankind America's wish for peace on earth and good will toward men everywhere." The satellite had been launched from Cape Canaveral Dec 18.

LA FARGE, OLIVER: 100th BIRTH ANNIVERSARY. Dec 19, 1901. American author and anthropologist, born at New York, NY. La Farge wrote the children's book *Laughing Boy*. He died at Albuquerque, NM, Aug 2, 1963.

WOODSON, CARTER GODWIN: BIRTH ANNIVERSARY. Dec 19, 1875. Historian who introduced black studies to colleges and universities, born at New Canton, VA. His scholarly works included *The Negro in Our History, The Education of the Negro Prior to 1861*. Known as the father of black history, he inaugurated Negro History Week. Woodson was working on a six-volume *Encyclopaedia Africana* when he died at Washington, DC, Apr 3, 1950. For more info: *Carter G. Woodson: The Man Who Put "Black" in American History*, by Jim Haskins and Kathleen Benson (Millbrook, 0-7613-1264-1, $24.90 Gr. 4–6).

BIRTHDAYS TODAY

Eve Bunting, 73, author (*Sixth-Grade Sleepover, Smoky Night*), born Anne Evelyn Bolton, Maghera, Ireland, Dec 19, 1928.

Alyssa Milano, 29, actress ("Who's the Boss," "Melrose Place"), born Brooklyn, NY, Dec 19, 1972.

Warren Sapp, 29, football player, born Plymouth, FL, Dec 19, 1972.

Reggie White, 40, football player, born Chattanooga, TN, Dec 19, 1961.

DECEMBER 20 — THURSDAY

Day 354 — 11 Remaining

AMERICAN POET LAUREATE ESTABLISHMENT: ANNIVERSARY. Dec 20, 1985. A bill empowering the Librarian of Congress to annually name a Poet Laureate/Consultant in Poetry was signed into law by President Ronald Reagan. In return for a $10,000 stipend as Poet Laureate and a salary (about $35,000) as the Consultant in Poetry, the person named will present at least one major work of poetry and will appear at selected national ceremonies. The first Poet Laureate of the US was Robert Penn Warren, appointed to that position by the Librarian of Congress, Feb 26, 1986.

CLINTON IMPEACHMENT PROCEEDINGS: ANNIVERSARY. Dec 20, 1998. President Bill Clinton was impeached by a House of Representatives that was divided along party lines. He was charged with perjury and obstruction of justice stemming from a relationship with a White House intern. He was then tried by the Senate in January 1999. On Feb 12, 1999, he was acquitted on both charges. Clinton was only the second US president to undergo impeachment proceedings. Andrew Johnson was impeached by the House in 1867 but the Senate voted against impeachment and he finished his term of office. See also: "Johnson Impeachment Proceedings: Anniversary" (Feb 24). For more info: *The Impeachment of President Clinton*, by Nathan Aaseng (Lucent, 1-56006-651-2, $18.96 Gr. 6–9).

LOUISIANA PURCHASE DAY. Dec 20, 1803. One of the greatest real estate deals in history, when more than a million square miles of the Louisiana Territory were turned over to the US by France, for a price of about $20 per square mile. It nearly doubled the size of the US, extending the western border to the Rocky Mountains. For more info: *The Louisiana Purchase*, by James A. Corrick (Lucent, 1-56006-637-7, $19.96 Gr. 7–10).

MACAU REVERTS TO CHINESE CONTROL: ANNIVERSARY. Dec 20, 1999. Macau, a tiny province on the southeast coast of China, reverted to Chinese rule on this day. It had been a Portuguese colony since 1557. With the return of Hong Kong in 1997 and the return of Macau, no part of mainland China is occupied by a foreign power.

SACAGAWEA: DEATH ANNIVERSARY. Dec 20, 1812. As a young Shoshone Indian woman, Sacagawea in 1805 (with her two-month-old boy strapped to her back) traveled with the Lewis and Clark Expedition, serving as an interpreter. It is said that the expedition could not have succeeded without her aid. She was born about 1787 and died at Fort Manuel on the Missouri River. Few other women have been so often honored. There are statues, fountains and memorials of her, and her name has been given to a mountain peak. In 2000 the US Mint issued a $1 coin with Sacagawea's picture on it. For more info: *A Picture Book of Sacagawea*, by David A. Adler (Holiday House, 0-823-41485-X, $16.95 All ages); *Girl of the Shining Mountains: Sacagawea's Story*, by Peter Roop and Connie Roop (Hyperion, 0-786-80492-0, $14.99 Gr. 5–8).

SAMUEL SLATER DAY IN MASSACHUSETTS. Dec 20. Proclaimed annually by the governor, this day commemorates Samuel Slater, the founder of the American factory system. He came to America from England and built a cotton mill at Rhode Island in 1790. He directed many New England mills until his death in 1835.

SOUTH CAROLINA: SECESSION ANNIVERSARY. Dec 20, 1860. South Carolina's legislature voted to secede from the US, the first state to do so. Within six weeks, five more states seceded. On Feb 4, 1861, representatives from the six states met at Montgomery, AL to establish a government and on Feb 9, Jefferson Davis was elected president of the Confederate States of America. Eventually, 11 states made up the Confederacy: Alabama, Arkansas, Florida, Georgia, Louisiana, Mississippi, North Carolina, South Carolina, Tennessee, Texas and Virginia .

VIRGINIA COMPANY EXPEDITION TO AMERICA: ANNIVERSARY. Dec 20, 1606. Three small ships, the *Susan Constant*, the *Godspeed* and the *Discovery*, commanded by Captain Christopher Newport, departed London, England, bound for America, where the royally chartered Virginia Company's approximately 120 persons established the first permanent English settlement in what is now the US at Jamestown, VA, May 14, 1607.

BIRTHDAYS TODAY

Michael J. Caduto, 46, author (*Keepers of the Earth, Earth Tales from Around the World*), born Providence, RI, Dec 20, 1955.

Jean Carnahan, 68, US Senator (D, Missouri), appointed to replace her late husband, Mel Carnahan, who won office despite having died during the election, born Washington, DC, Dec 20, 1933.

Lulu Delacre, 44, author (*Arroz Con Leche: Popular Songs and Rhymes from Latin America*), born Rio Piedras, Puerto Rico, Dec 20, 1957.

Uri Geller, 55, psychic, clairvoyant, born Tel Aviv, Israel, Dec 20, 1946.

M.B. Goffstein, 61, author and illustrator (*Fish for Supper*), born St. Paul, MN, Dec 20, 1940.

December 2001

S	M	T	W	T	F	S
						1
2	3	4	5	6	7	8
9	10	11	12	13	14	15
16	17	18	19	20	21	22
23	24	25	26	27	28	29
30	31					

DECEMBER 21 — FRIDAY

Day 355 — 10 Remaining

FIRST CROSSWORD PUZZLE: ANNIVERSARY. Dec 21, 1913. The first crossword puzzle was compiled by Arthur Wynne and published in a supplement to the *New York World*.

HUMBUG DAY. Dec 21. Allows all those preparing for Christmas to vent their frustrations. Twelve "humbugs" allowed. [© 1999 by WH] For info: Tom or Ruth Roy, Wellcat Holidays, 2418 Long Lane, Lebanon, PA 17046. Phone: (717) 279-0184. E-mail: wellcat @supernet.com. Web: www.wellcat.com.

PILGRIM LANDING: ANNIVERSARY. Dec 21, 1620. According to Governor William Bradford's *History of Plymouth Plantation*, "On Munday," [Dec 21, 1620, New Style] the Pilgrims, aboard the *Mayflower*, reached Plymouth, MA, "sounded ye harbor, and founde it fitt for shipping; and marched into ye land, & founde diverse cornfields, and ye best they could find, and ye season & their presente necessitie made them glad to accepte of it. . . . And after wards tooke better view of ye place, and resolved wher to pitch their dwelling; and them and their goods." Plymouth Rock, the legendary place of landing since it first was "identified" in 1769, nearly 150 years after the landing, has been a historic shrine since. The landing anniversary is observed in much of New England as Forefathers' Day.

SPACE MILESTONE: *APOLLO 8* (US). Dec 21, 1968. First moon voyage launched, manned by Colonel Frank Borman, Captain James A. Lovell, Jr and Major William A. Anders. Orbited moon Dec 24, returned to Earth Dec 27. First men to orbit the moon and see the side of the moon away from Earth. For more info: *Project Apollo*, by Diane M. Sipiera amd Paul P. Sipiera (Children's Press, 0-516-20435-1, $21 Gr. K–3).

UNDERDOG DAY. Dec 21. To salute, before the year's end, all of the underdogs and unsung heroes—the Number Two people who contribute so much to the Number One people we read about. (Sherlock Holmes's Dr. Watson and Robinson Crusoe's Friday are examples.) Observed annually on the third Friday in December since its founding in 1976 by the late Peter Moeller, THE Chief Underdog. For info: A. Moeller, Box 71, Clio, MI 48420-1042.

WINTER. Dec 21–Mar 20, 2002. In the Northern Hemisphere winter begins today with the winter solstice, at 2:21 PM, EST. Note that in the Southern Hemisphere today is the beginning of summer. Between the Equator and Arctic Circle the sunrise and sunset points on the horizon are farthest south for the year and daylight length is minimum (ranging from 12 hours, 8 minutes, at the equator to zero at the Arctic Circle). For more info: *The Winter Solstice*, by Ellen Jackson (Millbrook, 0-7613-0297-2, $7.95 Gr. PreK-3).

YALDA. Dec 21. Yalda, the longest night of the year, is celebrated by Iranians. The ceremony has an Indo-Iranian origin, where Light and Good were considered to struggle against Darkness and Evil. With fires burning and lights lit, family and friends gather to stay up through the night helping the sun in its battle against darkness. They recite poetry, tell stories and eat special fruits and nuts until the sun, triumphant, reappears in the morning. For info: Yassaman Djalali, Librarian, West Valley Branch Library, 1243 San Tomas Aquino Rd, San Jose, CA 95117. Phone: (408) 244-4766.

BIRTHDAYS TODAY

Chris Evert Lloyd, 47, broadcaster and former tennis player, born Ft Lauderdale, FL, Dec 21, 1954.

DECEMBER 22 — SATURDAY

Day 356 — 9 Remaining

CAPRICORN, THE GOAT. Dec 22–Jan 19. In the astronomical and astrological zodiac that divides the sun's apparent orbit into 12 segments, the period Dec 22–Jan 19 is identified, traditionally, as the sun-sign of Capricorn, the Goat. The ruling planet is Saturn.

"DING DONG SCHOOL" TV PREMIERE: ANNIVERSARY. Dec 22, 1952. Named by a three-year-old after watching a test broadcast of the opening sequence (a hand ringing a bell), "Ding Dong School" was one of the first children's educational series. Miss Frances (Dr. Frances Horwich, head of Roosevelt College's education department at Chicago) was the host of this weekday show. The show aired until 1956.

FIRST GORILLA BORN IN CAPTIVITY: 45th BIRTH ANNIVERSARY. Dec 22, 1956. "Colo" was born at the Columbus, OH zoo, weighing in at $3^1/_4$ pounds, the first gorilla born in captivity.

MOON PHASE: FIRST QUARTER. Dec 22. Moon enters First Quarter phase at 3:56 PM, EST.

OGLETHORPE, JAMES EDWARD: BIRTH ANNIVERSARY. Dec 22, 1696. English general, author and colonizer of Georgia. Founder of the city of Savannah. Oglethorpe was born at London. He died June 30, 1785, at Cranham Hall, Essex, England.

BIRTHDAYS TODAY

Hector Elizondo, 65, actor (*Pretty Woman*, "Chicago Hope"), born New York, NY, Dec 22, 1936.

Mick Inkpen, 49, author, illustrator (the Kipper series, the Wibbly Pig series) born Romford, England, Dec 22, 1952.

Claudia Alta (Lady Bird) Johnson, 89, former First Lady, widow of Lyndon Johnson, the 36th president of the US, born Karnack, TX, Dec 22, 1912.

Jerry Pinkney, 62, illustrator (*John Henry*), born Philadelphia, PA, Dec 22, 1939.

Diane K. Sawyer, 55, journalist ("60 Minutes," "Prime Time Live"), born Glasgow, KY, Dec 22, 1946.

DECEMBER 23 — SUNDAY

Day 357 — 8 Remaining

FIRST NONSTOP FLIGHT AROUND THE WORLD WITHOUT REFUELING: ANNIVERSARY. Dec 23, 1987. Dick Rutan and Jeana Yeager set a new world record of 216 hours of continuous flight, breaking their own record of 111 hours set July 15, 1986. The aircraft *Voyager* departed from Edwards Air Force Base at California Dec 14, 1987, and landed Dec 23, 1987. The journey covered 24,986 miles at an official speed of 115 miles per hour.

JAPAN: BIRTHDAY OF THE EMPEROR. Dec 23. National Day. Holiday honoring Emperor Akihito, born in 1933.

METRIC CONVERSION ACT: ANNIVERSARY. Dec 23, 1975. The Congress of the US passed Public Law 94–168, known as the Metric Conversion Act of 1975. This act declares that the SI (International System of Units) will be this country's basic system of measurement and establishes the United States Metric Board, which is responsible for the planning, coordination and implementation of the nation's voluntary conversion to SI. (Congress had authorized the metric system as a legal system of measurement in the US by an act passed July 28, 1866. In 1875, the US became one of the original signers of the Treaty of the Metre, which established an international metric system.)

MEXICO: FEAST OF THE RADISHES. Dec 23. Oaxaca. Figurines of people and animals cleverly carved out of radishes are sold during festivities.

TRANSISTOR INVENTED: ANNIVERSARY. Dec 23, 1947. John Bardeen, Walter Brattain and William Shockley of Bell Laboratories shared the Nobel Prize for their invention of the transistor, which led to a revolution in communications and electronics.

WALKER, SARAH BREEDLOVE (MADAME C.J.): BIRTH ANNIVERSARY. Dec 23, 1867. Born at Delta, LA, Madame Walker built a successful hair care business with products for African Americans and was one of the first women in the US to become a millionaire in her own right. She died May 3, 1919, at Irvington, NY. For more info: *Vision of Beauty: The Story of Sarah Breedlove Walker*, by Kathryn Lasky (Candlewick, 0-7636-0253-1, $16.99 Gr. 3–5).

BIRTHDAYS TODAY

Akihito, 68, Emperor of Japan, born Tokyo, Japan, Dec 23, 1933.

Avi, 64, author (*The True Confessions of Charlotte Doyle*), born Avi Wortis, New York, NY, Dec 23, 1937.

Corey Haim, 29, actor (*Murphy's Romance, The Lost Boys*), born Toronto, ON, Canada, Dec 23, 1972.

Martin Kratt, 36, zoologist, cohost with his brother Chris ("Kratts' Creatures"), born Summit, NJ, Dec 23, 1965.

DECEMBER 24 — MONDAY

Day 358 — 7 Remaining

AUSTRIA: "SILENT NIGHT, HOLY NIGHT" CELEBRATIONS. Dec 24. Oberndorf, Hallein and Wagrain, Salzburg, Austria. Commemorating the creation of the Christmas carol here in 1818.

CARSON, CHRISTOPHER "KIT": BIRTH ANNIVERSARY. Dec 24, 1809. American frontiersman, soldier, trapper, guide and Indian agent best known as Kit Carson. Born at Madison County, KY, he died at Fort Lyon, CO, May 23, 1868.

CHRISTMAS EVE. Dec 24. Family gift-giving occasion in many Christian countries.

GRUELLE, JOHNNY: BIRTH ANNIVERSARY. Dec 24, 1880. Author of the Raggedy Ann and Raggedy Andy books, born at Arcola, IL. Died Jan 9, 1938.

LIBYA: INDEPENDENCE DAY: 50th ANNIVERSARY. Dec 24. Libya gained its independence from Italy in 1951.

BIRTHDAYS TODAY

Debra Barracca, 48, author, with husband Sal (*The Adventures of Taxi Dog*), born New York, NY, Dec 24, 1953.

Lynn Munsinger, 50, illustrator (*Tacky the Penguin, Howliday Inn*), born Greenfield, MA, Dec 24, 1951.

Eddie Pope, 28, soccer player, born Greensboro, NC, Dec 24, 1973.

Jeff Sessions, 55, US Senator (R, Alabama), born Hybart, AL, Dec 24, 1946.

DECEMBER 25 — TUESDAY

Day 359 — 6 Remaining

ASARAH B'TEVET. Dec 25. Hebrew calendar date: Tevet 10, 5762. The Fast of the 10th of Tevet begins at first morning light and commemorates the beginning of the Babylonian siege of Jerusalem in the 6th century BC.

BARTON, CLARA: BIRTH ANNIVERSARY. Dec 25, 1821. Clarissa Harlowe Barton, American nurse and philanthropist, founder of the American Red Cross, was born at Oxford, MA. In 1881, she became first president of the American Red Cross (founded May 21, 1881). She died at Glen Echo, MD, Apr 12, 1912.

CHRISTMAS. Dec 25. Christian festival commemorating the birth of Jesus of Nazareth. Most popular of Christian observances, Christmas as a Feast of the Nativity dates from the 4th century. Although Jesus's birth date is not known, the Western church selected Dec 25 for the feast, possibly to counteract the non-Christian festivals of that approximate date. Many customs from non-Christian festivals (Roman Saturnalia, Mithraic sun's birthday, Teutonic yule, Druidic and other winter solstice rites) have been adopted as part of the Christmas celebration (lights, mistletoe, holly and ivy, holiday tree, wassailing and gift giving, for example). Some Orthodox Churches celebrate Christmas Jan 7 based on the "old calendar" (Julian). Theophany (recognition of the divinity of Jesus) is observed Dec 25 and also Jan 6, especially by the Eastern Orthodox Church. For links to sites about Christmas on the web, go to: deil.lang.uiuc.edu/web.pages/holidays/christmas.html.

PAKISTAN: BIRTHDAY OF QAID-I-AZAM. Dec 25. Commemorates the birth in 1876 at Karachi, then part of India, of Mohammed Ali Jinnah, the founder of the Islamic Republic of Pakistan. When Pakistan became independent of India in 1947, he became the first governor general. That year he was given the title Qaid-i-Azam (Great Leader). He died at Karachi, Sept 11, 1948. This day is a holiday in Pakistan.

TAIWAN: CONSTITUTION DAY. Dec 25. National holiday. Commemorates the constitution of 1946.

BIRTHDAYS TODAY

Rickey Henderson, 43, baseball player, born Chicago, IL, Dec 25, 1958.

Mary Elizabeth (Sissy) Spacek, 52, actress (Oscar for *Coal Miner's Daughter; Missing*), born Quitman, TX, Dec 25, 1949.

DECEMBER 26 — WEDNESDAY

Day 360 — 5 Remaining

BAHAMAS: JUNKANOO. Dec 26. Kaleidoscope of sound and spectacle combining a bit of Mardi Gras, mummer's parade and ancient African tribal rituals. Revelers in colorful costumes parade through the streets to sounds of cowbells, goat skin drums and many other homemade instruments. Annually, on Boxing Day.

BOXING DAY. Dec 26. Ordinarily observed on the first day after Christmas. A legal holiday in Canada, the United Kingdom and many other countries. Formerly a day when Christmas gift boxes were expected by a postman, the lamplighter, the trash man and others who render services to the public at large. When Boxing Day falls on a Saturday or Sunday, the Monday or Tuesday immediately following may be proclaimed or observed as a bank or public holiday.

CLERC, LAURENT: BIRTH ANNIVERSARY. Dec 26, 1785. The first deaf teacher in America, Laurent Clerc assisted Thomas Hopkins Gallaudet in establishing the first public school for the deaf, Connecticut Asylum for the Education and Instruction of Deaf and Dumb Persons (now the American School for the Deaf), at Hartford, CT, in 1817. For 41 years Clerc trained new teachers in the use of sign language and in methods of teaching the deaf. Clerc was born at LaBalme, France, and died July 18, 1869.

KIDS AFTER CHRISTMAS. Dec 26–30. Mystic, CT. Everyone pays the youth admission and enjoys a full day of crafts, entertainment and the lore of the sea. Est attendance: 3,000. For info: Mystic Seaport, 75 Greenmanville Ave, Box 6000, Mystic, CT 06355. Phone: (860) 572-5315 or (888) 9SEAPORT. Web: www.mysticseaport.org.

KWANZAA. Dec 26–Jan 1, 2002. American black family observance created in 1966 by Dr. Maulana Karenga in recognition of traditional African harvest festivals. This seven-day festival stresses self-reliance and unity of the black family, with a harvest feast (karamu) on the next to the last day and a day of meditation on the final one. Each day is dedicated to a principle that African Americans should live by— Day 1: Unity; Day 2: Self-determination; Day 3: Collective work and responsibility; Day 4: Cooperative economics; Day 5: Purpose; Day 6: Creativity; Day 7: Faith. Kwanzaa means "first fruit" in Swahili. For more info: *The Children's Book of Kwanzaa: A Guide to Celebrating the Holiday*, by Dolores Johnson (Atheneum, 0-68-980864-X, $16 Gr. 4–6).

MAO TSE-TUNG: BIRTH ANNIVERSARY. Dec 26, 1893. Chinese librarian, teacher, communist revolutionist and "founding father" of the People's Republic of China, born at Hunan Province, China. Died at Beijing, Sept 9, 1976.

NATIONAL WHINER'S DAY™. Dec 26. A day dedicated to whiners, especially those who return Christmas gifts and need lots of attention. People are encouraged to be happy about what they do have, rather than unhappy about what they don't have. The most famous whiner(s) of the year will be announced. Nominations

December 2001

S	M	T	W	T	F	S
						1
2	3	4	5	6	7	8
9	10	11	12	13	14	15
16	17	18	19	20	21	22
23	24	25	26	27	28	29
30	31					

accepted through Dec 15. For more info, please send SASE to: Kevin C. Zaborney, PO Box 64, Fairgrove, MI 48733. Phone: (517) 693-6666. E-mail: holidaymaker@loveslife.com. Web: holidaymaker.loveslife.com

NELSON, THOMAS: BIRTH ANNIVERSARY. Dec 26, 1738. Merchant and signer of the Declaration of Independence, born at Yorktown, VA. Died at Hanover County, VA, Jan 4, 1789.

RADIUM DISCOVERED: ANNIVERSARY. Dec 26, 1898. French scientists Pierre and Marie Curie discovered the element radium, for which they later won the Nobel Prize for Physics.

SAINT STEPHEN'S DAY. Dec 26. One of the seven deacons named by the apostles to distribute alms. Died during 1st century. Feast Day is observed as a public holiday in Austria.

SECOND DAY OF CHRISTMAS. Dec 26. Observed as holiday in many countries.

SHENANDOAH NATIONAL PARK ESTABLISHED: ANNIVERSARY. Dec 26, 1935. Area of Blue Ridge Mountains of Virginia, originally authorized May 22, 1926, was established as a national park. For more info: www.nps.gov/shen/index.html. For more park info: Shenandoah Natl Park, Rte 4, Box 348, Luray, VA 22835.

SLOVENIA: INDEPENDENCE DAY. Dec 26. National holiday. Commemorates the day in 1990 when the results of an election on separation from the Yugoslav Union were announced.

SOUTH AFRICA: DAY OF GOODWILL. Dec 26. National holiday. Replaces Boxing Day.

BIRTHDAYS TODAY

Evan Bayh, 46, US Senator (D, Indiana), born Shirkieville, IN, Dec 26, 1955.

Susan Butcher, 47, sled dog racer, born Cambridge, MA, Dec 26, 1954.

Gray Davis, 59, Governor of California (D), born The Bronx, NY, Dec 26, 1942.

Carlton Fisk, 54, Baseball Hall of Fame player, born Bellows Falls, VT, Dec 26, 1947.

Jean Van Leuween, 64, author (the Oliver & Amanda Pig series, *Going Home*) born Glen Ridge, NJ, Dec 26, 1937.

DECEMBER 27 — THURSDAY

Day 361 — 4 Remaining

CHRISTMAS AT THE TOP MUSEUM. Dec 27–30. Spinning Top Museum, Burlington, WI. Enjoy the traditional, universal toys of tops and top games, well-loved Christmas gifts around the world in the 2-hour museum program: 35 hands-on games and experiments, two videos, view the exhibit of 2,000 items, plus a live show by top collector. Reservations required. For info: Spinning Top Museum, 533 Milwaukee Ave (Hwy 36), Burlington, WI 53105. Phone: (262) 763-3946.

D'AULAIRE, INGRI: BIRTH ANNIVERSARY. Dec 27, 1904. Author, with her husband Edgar (*Norse Gods and Giants*), born at Kongsberg, Norway. Died Oct 24, 1980.

"HOWDY DOODY" TV PREMIERE: ANNIVERSARY. Dec 27, 1947. The first popular children's show was brought to TV by Bob Smith and was one of the first regular NBC shows to be shown in color. The show was set in the circus town of Doodyville, populated by people and puppets. Children sat in the bleachers' "Peanut Gallery" and participated in activities such as songs and stories. Human characters were Buffalo Bob (Bob Smith), the silent clown Clarabell (Bob Keeshan, Bobby Nicholson and Lew Anderson), storekeeper Cornelius Cobb (Nicholson), Chief Thunderthud (Bill LeCornec), Princess Summerfall Winterspring (Judy Tyler and Linda Marsh), Bison Bill (Ted Brown) and wrestler Ugly Sam (Dayton Allen). Puppet costars included Howdy Doody, Phineas T. Bluster, Dilly Dally, Flub-a-Dub, Captain Scuttlebutt, Double Doody and Heidi Doody. The filmed adventures of Gumby were also featured. In the final episode, Clarabell broke his long silence to say, "Goodbye, kids."

PASTEUR, LOUIS: BIRTH ANNIVERSARY. Dec 27, 1822. French chemist-bacteriologist born at Dole, Jura, France. Died at Villeneuve l'Etang, France, Sept 28, 1895. Among his contributions to the germ theory of disease, he was the discoverer of prophylactic inoculation against rabies. He also proved that the spoilage of perishable food products could be prevented by the technique of heat treatment. This process, pasteurization, was named for him.

SAINT JOHN, APOSTLE-EVANGELIST: FEAST DAY. Dec 27. Son of Zebedee, Galilean fisherman, and Salome. Died about AD 100. Roman Rite Feast Day is Dec 27. (Observed May 8 by Byzantine Rite.)

BIRTHDAYS TODAY

Lisa Jakub, 21, actress (*Mrs Doubtfire, A Pig's Tale*), born Toronto, ON, Canada, Dec 27, 1980.

Diane Stanley, 58, author and illustrator (*Peter the Great*), born Abilene, TX, Dec 27, 1943.

DECEMBER 28 — FRIDAY

Day 362 — 3 Remaining

AUSTRALIA: PROCLAMATION DAY. Dec 28. Observed in South Australia.

BRINK, CAROL RYRIE: BIRTH ANNIVERSARY. Dec 28, 1895. Author (*Caddie Woodlawn*), born at Moscow, ID. Died Aug 15, 1981.

HOLY INNOCENTS DAY (CHILDERMAS). Dec 28. Commemoration of the massacre of children at Bethlehem, ordered by King Herod who wanted to destroy, among them, the infant Savior. Early and medieval accounts claimed as many as 144,000 victims, but more recent writers, noting that Bethlehem was a very small town, have revised the estimates of the number of children killed to between six and 20.

IOWA: ADMISSION DAY: ANNIVERSARY. Dec 28. Became 29th state in 1846.

PLEDGE OF ALLEGIANCE RECOGNIZED: ANNIVERSARY. Dec 28, 1945. The US Congress officially recognized the Pledge of Allegiance and urged its frequent recitation in America's schools. The pledge was composed in 1892 by Francis Bellamy, a Baptist minister. At the time, Bellamy was chairman of a committee of state school superintendents of education, and several public schools adopted his pledge as part of the Columbus Day quadricentennial celebration that year. In 1955, the Knights of Columbus persuaded Congress to add the words "under God" to the pledge.

***POOR RICHARD'S ALMANACK*: ANNIVERSARY.** Dec 28, 1732. The *Pennsylvania Gazette* carried the first known advertisement for the first issue of *Poor Richard's Almanack* by Richard Saunders (Benjamin Franklin) for the year 1733. The advertisement promised "many pleasant and witty verses, jests and sayings . . ." America's most famous almanac, *Poor Richard's* was published through the year 1758 and has been imitated many times since. From *The Autobiography of Benjamin Franklin*: "In 1732 I first publish'd my Almanack, under the name of *Richard Saunders*; it was continu'd by me about twenty-five years, commonly call'd *Poor Richard's Almanack.* I endeavor'd to make it both entertaining and useful, and it accordingly came to be in such demand, that I reap'd considerable profit from it, vending annually near ten thousand. And observing that it was generally read, scarce any neighborhood in the province being without it, I consider'd it as a proper vehicle for conveying instruction among the common people, who bought scarcely any other books; I therefore filled all the little spaces that occurr'd between the remarkable days in the calendar with proverbial sentences, chiefly such as inculcated industry and frugality, as the means of procuring wealth, and thereby securing virtue; it being more difficult for a man in want, to act always honestly, as, to use here one of those proverbs, *it is hard for an empty sack to stand upright.*"

WILSON, WOODROW: BIRTH ANNIVERSARY. Dec 28, 1856. The 28th president of the US was born Thomas Woodrow Wilson at Staunton, VA. Twice elected president (1912 and 1916), it was Wilson who said, "The world must be made safe for democracy," as he asked the Congress to declare war on Germany, Apr 2, 1917. His first wife, Ellen, died Aug 6, 1914, and he married Edith Bolling Galt, Dec 18, 1915. He suffered a paralytic stroke Sept 16, 1919, never regaining his health. There were many speculations about who (possibly Mrs Wilson?) was running the government during his illness. His second term of office ended Mar 3, 1921, and he died at Washington, DC, Feb 3, 1924. For info: www.ipl.org/ref/POTUS.

BIRTHDAYS TODAY

Cynthia DeFelice, 50, author (*The Apprenticeship of Lucas Whitaker*), born Philadelphia, PA, Dec 28, 1951.

Elizabeth Fitzgerald Howard, 74, author (*Aunt Flossie's Hats, Chita's Christmas Tree*), born Boston, MA, Dec 28, 1927.

Tim Johnson, 55, US Senator (D, South Dakota), born Canton, SD, Dec 28, 1946.

Patrick Rafter, 29, tennis player, born Mount Isa, Queensland, Australia, Dec 28, 1972.

Todd Richards, 32, Olympic snowboarder, born Worcester, MA, Dec 28, 1969.

December 2001

S	M	T	W	T	F	S
						1
2	3	4	5	6	7	8
9	10	11	12	13	14	15
16	17	18	19	20	21	22
23	24	25	26	27	28	29
30	31					

MacKenzie Rosman, 12, actress ("7th Heaven"), born Charleston, SC, Dec 28, 1989.

Denzel Washington, 47, actor ("St. Elsewhere," *Glory, Malcolm X*), born Mt Vernon, NY, Dec 28, 1954.

DECEMBER 29 — SATURDAY

Day 363 — 2 Remaining

ATWATER, RICHARD: BIRTH ANNIVERSARY. Dec 29, 1892. Author, with his wife Florence, of the Newbery Award winner *Mr Popper's Penguins*. Born at Chicago, IL, he died Aug 21, 1948.

JOHNSON, ANDREW: BIRTH ANNIVERSARY. Dec 29, 1808. The 17th president of the US (Apr 15, 1865–Mar 3, 1869), Andrew Johnson was born at Raleigh, NC. Upon Abraham Lincoln's assassination Johnson became president. He was the only US president to be impeached, and he was acquitted Mar 26, 1868. After his term as president he made several unsuccessful attempts to win public office. Finally he was elected to the US Senate from Tennessee and served in the Senate from Mar 4, 1875, until his death, at Carter's Station, TN, July 31, 1875. For info: www.ipl.org/ref/POTUS.

NEPAL: BIRTHDAY OF HIS MAJESTY THE KING. Dec 29. National holiday of Nepal commemorating birth of the King in 1945. Three-day celebration with huge public rally at Tundikkel, gay pageantry, musical bands and illumination in the towns at night.

TEXAS: ADMISSION DAY: ANNIVERSARY. Dec 29. Became 28th state in 1845.

UNITED NATIONS: INTERNATIONAL DAY FOR BIOLOGICAL DIVERSITY. Dec 29. On Dec 19, 1994, the General Assembly proclaimed this observance for Dec 29, the date of entry into force of the Convention on Biological Diversity (Res 49/119). Designation of the Day had been recommended by the Conference of the Parties to the Convention, held at Nassau Nov 28–Dec 9, 1994. For info: United Nations, Dept of Public Info, New York, NY 10017.

WOUNDED KNEE MASSACRE: ANNIVERSARY. Dec 29, 1890. Anniversary of the massacre of more than 200 Native American men, women and children by the US 7th Cavalry at Wounded Knee Creek, SD. Government efforts to suppress a ceremonial religious practice, the Ghost Dance (which called for a messiah who would restore the bison to the plains, make the white men disappear and bring back the old Native American way of life), had resulted in the death of Sitting Bull Dec 15, 1890, which further inflamed the disgruntled Native Americans and culminated in the slaughter at Wounded Knee Dec 29. For more info: *Wounded Knee, 1890: The End of the Plains Indian Wars*, by Tom Streissguth (Facts on File, 0-8160-3600-4, $19.95, Gr. 7–12).

YMCA ORGANIZED: 150th ANNIVERSARY. Dec 29, 1851. The first US branch of the Young Men's Christian Association was organized at Boston. It was modeled on an organization begun at London in 1844. For more info: www.ymca.net.

BIRTHDAYS TODAY

Molly Garrett Bang, 58, author and illustrator (*The Paper Crane; Ten, Nine, Eight*), born Princeton, NJ, Dec 29, 1943.

Irene Brady, 58, author and illustrator (*Wild Mouse*), born Ontario, OR, Dec 29, 1943.

Ted Danson, 54, actor ("Cheers," *Three Men and a Baby*), born San Diego, CA, Dec 29, 1947.

Jan Greenberg, 59, author (*Chuck Close, Up Close*), born St. Louis, MO, Dec 29, 1942.

DECEMBER 30 — SUNDAY

Day 364 — 1 Remaining

KIPLING, RUDYARD: BIRTH ANNIVERSARY. Dec 30, 1865. English poet, novelist and short story writer, and Nobel prize laureate, Kipling was born at Bombay, India. After working as a journalist at India, he traveled around the world. He married an American and lived at Vermont for several years. Kipling is best known for his children's stories, such as *Jungle Book* and *Just So Stories* and poems such as "The Ballad of East and West" and "If." He died at London, England, Jan 18, 1936.

LUNAR ECLIPSE. Dec 30. Penumbral eclipse of the moon. Moon enters penumbra at 3:25 AM, EST, reaches middle of eclipse at 5:29 AM and leaves penumbra at 7:33 AM. Visible in Greenland, N Europe, Australasia, Asia except SW, Pacific Ocean, the Americas.

MADAGASCAR: NATIONAL HOLIDAY. Dec 30. Anniversary of the change of the name Malagasy Republic to the Democratic Republic of Madagascar in 1975.

MOON PHASE: FULL MOON. Dec 30. Moon enters Full Moon phase at 5:40 AM, EST.

PHILIPPINES: RIZAL DAY. Dec 30. Commemorates martyrdom of Dr. Jose Rizal in 1896.

"THE ROY ROGERS SHOW" TV PREMIERE: 50th ANNIVERSARY. Dec 30, 1951. This very popular TV western starred Roy Rogers and his wife, Dale Evans, as themselves. It also featured Pat Brady as Rogers's sidekick who rode a jeep named Nellybelle, the singing group Sons of the Pioneers, Rogers's horse Trigger, Evans's horse Buttermilk and a German shepherd named Bullet. This half-hour show was especially popular with young viewers.

BIRTHDAYS TODAY

Jane Langton, 79, author (*The Fledgling*), born Boston, MA, Dec 30, 1922.

Matt Lauer, 44, news anchor ("Today"), born New York, NY, Dec 30, 1957.

Mercer Mayer, 58, author and illustrator (*East of the Sun, West of the Moon*), born Little Rock, AR, Dec 30, 1943.

Julianne Moore, 41, actress (*The Lost World: Jurassic Park*), born Fayetteville, NC, Dec 30, 1960.

Tracey Ullman, 42, actress, singer ("The Tracey Ullman Show," *I Love You to Death*), born Buckinghamshire, England, Dec 30, 1959.

Eldrick (Tiger) Woods, 26, golfer, born Cypress, CA, Dec 30, 1975.

DECEMBER 31 — MONDAY

Day 365 — 0 Remaining

FIRST BANK OPENS IN US: ANNIVERSARY. Dec 31, 1781. The first modern bank in the US, the Bank of North America, was organized by Robert Morris and received its charter from the Confederation Congress in 1781. It began operations Jan 7, 1782, at Philadelphia.

LEAP SECOND ADJUSTMENT TIME. Dec 31. One of the times that have been favored for the addition or subtraction of a second from clock time (to coordinate atomic and astronomical time). The determination to adjust is made by the Central Bureau of the International Earth Rotation Service at Paris.

MAKE UP YOUR MIND DAY. Dec 31. A day for all those people who have a hard time making up their minds. Make a decision today and follow through with it! Annually, Dec 31. For info: A.C. Moeller and M.A. Dufour, Box 71, Clio, MI 48420-1042.

MATISSE, HENRI: BIRTH ANNIVERSARY. Dec 31, 1869. Painter, born at Le Cateau, France. Matisse also designed textiles and stained glass windows. Died at Nice, France, Nov 3, 1954. For more info: *Matisse from A to Z*, by Marie Sellier (Peter Bedrick, 0-87226-475-0, $14.95 All ages).

NEW YEAR'S EVE. Dec 31. The last evening of the Gregorian calendar year, traditionally a night for merrymaking to welcome in the new year.

ORANGE BOWL PARADE. Dec 31. Miami, FL. Annual New Year's Eve parade for the past 64 years. Nationally televised, the parade moves 2.2 miles along downtown Miami's Biscayne Boulevard by the bay. Est attendance: 500,000. For info: John Shaffer, Orange Bowl Committee, 601 Brickell Key Dr, Ste 206, Miami, FL 33131. Phone: (305) 371-4600.

PANAMA: ASSUMES CONTROL OF CANAL: ANNIVERSARY. Dec 31, 1999. With the expiration of the Panama Canal Treaty of 1979 at noon, the Republic of Panama assumed full responsibility for the canal and the US Panama Canal Commission ceased to exist.

BIRTHDAYS TODAY

Anthony Hopkins, 64, actor (*Amistad*), born Port Talbot, Wales, Great Britain, Dec 31, 1937.

Val Kilmer, 42, actor (*Batman Forever*), born Los Angeles, CA, Dec 31, 1959.

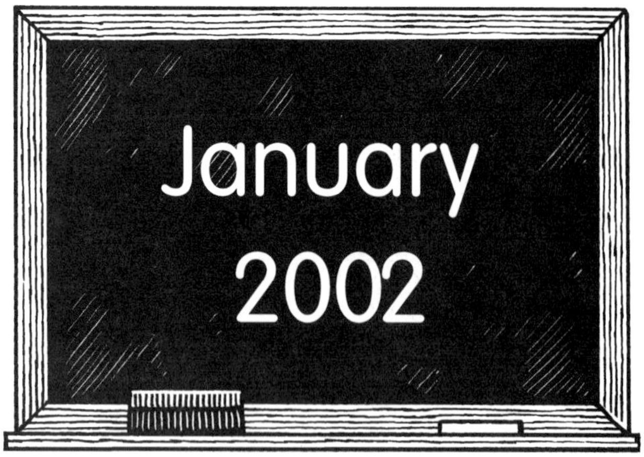

JANUARY 1 — TUESDAY

Day 1 — 364 Remaining

MONDAY, JANUARY ONE, 2002. Jan 1. First day of the first month of the Gregorian calendar year, Anno Domini 2002, a Common Year, and (until July 4th) the 226th year of American independence. New Year's Day is a public holiday in the US and in many other countries. Traditionally, it is a time for personal stocktaking and for making resolutions for the coming year. Financial accounting begins anew for businesses and individuals whose fiscal year is the calendar year. Jan 1 has been observed as the beginning of the year in most English-speaking countries since the British Calendar Act of 1751, prior to which the New Year began Mar 25 (approximating the vernal equinox). Earth begins another orbit of the sun, during which it, and we, will travel some 583,416,000 miles in 365.24219 days. New Year's Day has been called "Everyman's Birthday," and in some countries a year is added to everyone's age Jan 1 rather than on the anniversary of each person's birth.

ACADIA NATIONAL PARK ESTABLISHED: ANNIVERSARY. Jan 1, 1919. Maine's Sieur de Monts National Monument, authorized in 1916, was established as Lafayette National Park in 1919. The name was changed to Acadia National Park by an act of Congress in 1929. For info: www.nps.gov/acad/index.htm.

AUSTRALIA: COMMONWEALTH FORMED: ANNIVERSARY. Jan 1, 1901. The six colonies of Victoria, New South Wales, Queensland, South Australia, Western Australia and Northern Territory were united into one nation. The British Parliament had passed the Commonwealth Constitution Bill in the spring of 1900 and Queen Victoria signed the document Sept 17, 1900.

BEANIE BABIES® INTRODUCED: ANNIVERSARY. Jan 1, 1994. During this month the first nine Beanie Babies were introduced. Since then, more than 135 models of the plush animals were released. For more info: www.ty.com.

BONZA BOTTLER DAY™. Jan 1. (Also Feb 2, Mar 3, Apr 4, May 5, June 6, July 7, Aug 8, Sept 9, Oct 10, Nov 11 and Dec 12.) To celebrate when the number of the day is the same as the number of the month. Bonza Bottler Day™ is an excuse to have a party at least once a month. For info: Gail M. Berger, 109 Matthew Ave, Poca, WV 25159. Phone: (304) 776-7746. E-mail: gberger5@aol.com.

January 2002

S	M	T	W	T	F	S
		1	2	3	4	5
6	7	8	9	10	11	12
13	14	15	16	17	18	19
20	21	22	23	24	25	26
27	28	29	30	31		

BRYCE CANYON NATIONAL PARK ESTABLISHED: ANNIVERSARY. Jan 1, 1928. Utah's Bryce Canyon National Monument, created in 1923, was established as a national park and preserve. For more info: www.nps.gov/brca/index.htm.

CUBA: ANNIVERSARY OF THE REVOLUTION. Jan 1. National holiday celebrating the overthrow of the government of Fulgencio Batista in 1959 by the revolutionary forces of Fidel Castro, which had begun a civil war in 1956.

CUBA: LIBERATION DAY. Jan 1. A national holiday that celebrates the end of Spanish rule in 1899. Cuba, the largest island of the West Indies, was a Spanish possession from its discovery by Columbus (Oct 27, 1492) until 1899. Under US military control 1899–1902 and 1906–09, a republican government took over Jan 28, 1909, and controlled the island until overthrown Jan 1, 1959, by Fidel Castro's revolutionary movement.

CZECH-SLOVAK DIVORCE: ANNIVERSARY. Jan 1, 1993. As Dec 31, 1992, gave way to Jan 1, 1993, the 74-year-old state of Czechoslovakia separated into two nations—the Czech and Slovak Republics. The Slovaks held a celebration through the night in the streets of Bratislava amid fireworks, bell ringing, singing of the new country's national anthem and the raising of the Slovak flag. In the new Czech Republic no official festivities took place, but later in the day the Czechs celebrated with a solemn oath by their parliament. The nation of Czechoslovakia ended peacefully though polls showed that most Slovaks and Czechs would have preferred that Czechoslovakia survive. Before the split Czech Prime Minister Vaclav Klaus and Slovak Prime Minister Vladimir Meciar reached an agreement on dividing everything from army troops and gold reserves to the art on government building walls.

ELLIS ISLAND OPENED: ANNIVERSARY. Jan 1, 1892. Ellis Island was opened on New Year's Day in 1892. Over the years more than 20 million individuals were processed through the immigration station. The island was used as a point of deportation as well; in 1932 alone, 20,000 people were deported from Ellis Island. When the US entered WWII in 1941, Ellis Island became a Coast Guard Station. It closed Nov 12, 1954, and was declared a national park in 1956. After years of disuse it was restored and was reopened as a museum in 1990. For more info: www.nps.gov/stli/serv02.htm.

EURO INTRODUCED: ANNIVERSARY. Jan 1, 1999. The euro, the common currency of 11 members of the European Union, was introduced for use by banks. The value of the currencies of Austria, Belgium, Finland, France, Germany, Ireland, Italy, Luxembourg, the Netherlands, Portugal and Spain are locked in at a permanent conversion rate to the euro. On Jan 1, 2002, euro bills and coins will begin circulating and other currencies will be phased out.

HAITI: INDEPENDENCE DAY. Jan 1. A national holiday commemorating the proclamation of independence in 1804. Haiti, occupying the western third of the island Hispaniola (second largest of the West Indies), was a Spanish colony from the time of its discovery by Columbus in 1492 until 1697, then a French colony until the proclamation of independence in 1804.

JAPANESE ERA NEW YEAR. Jan 1–3. Celebration of the beginning of the year Heisei Fourteen, the 14th year of Emperor Akihito's reign.

KLIBAN, B(ERNARD): BIRTH ANNIVERSARY. Jan 1, 1935. Cartoonist B. Kliban was born at Norwalk, CT. He was known for his satirical drawings of cats engaged in human pursuits, which appeared in the books *Cat* (1975), *Never Eat Anything Bigger than Your Head & Other Drawings* (1976) and *Whack Your Porcupine* (1977). His drawings appeared on T-shirts, greeting cards, calendars, bedsheets and other merchandise, creating a $50 million industry before his death at San Francisco, CA, Aug 12, 1990.

MARCH OF DIMES BIRTH DEFECTS PREVENTION MONTH. Jan 1–31. To heighten awareness of birth defects and how they may be prevented, to inform the public about the work of the March of Dimes and to offer opportunities to new volunteers for service in the prevention of birth defects. For info: March of Dimes Birth Defects Foundation, 1275 Mamaroneck Ave, White Plains, NY 10605. Phone: (914) 997-4600. Web: www.modimes.org.

MEXICO: ZAPATISTA REBELLION: ANNIVERSARY. Jan 1, 1994. Declaring war against the government of President Carlos Salinas de Gortari, the Zapatista National Liberation Army seized four towns in the state of Chiapas in southern Mexico. The rebel group, which took its name from the early 20th-century Mexican revolutionary Emiliano Zapata, issued a declaration stating that they were protesting discrimination against the Indian population of the region and against their severe poverty.

MUMMERS PARADE. Jan 1. Philadelphia, PA. World famous New Year's Day parade of 20,000 spectacularly costumed Mummers in a colorful parade that goes on all day. Est attendance: 200,000. For info: Mummers Parade, 1100 S 2nd St, Philadelphia, PA 19147. Phone: (215) 636-1666. E-mail: mummersmus@aol.com. Web: www.mummers.com.

NATIONAL ENVIRONMENTAL POLICY ACT: ANNIVERSARY. Jan 1, 1970. The National Environmental Policy Act of 1969 established the Council on Environmental Quality and made it federal government policy to protect the environment.

NATIONAL EYE CARE MONTH. Jan 1–31. Sponsored by the American Academy of Ophthalmology, this month promotes awareness of eye health, importance of medical eye care and prevention to avoid eye injuries and disease. A curriculum for middle school students is available at www.eyenet.org/schooleye safety. For info: American Academy of Ophthalmology–NECM, PO Box 7424, San Francisco, CA 94140-7424. Fax: (415) 561-8567. E-mail: PIMR@aao.org. Web: www.eyenet.org. *See* Curriculum Connection.

NATIONAL HOT TEA MONTH. Jan 1–31. To celebrate one of nature's most popular, soothing and relaxing beverages; the only beverage in America commonly served hot or iced, anytime, anywhere, for any occasion. For info: The Tea Council of the USA, 420 Lexington Ave, Ste 825, New York, NY 10170. Phone: (212) 986-6998. Fax: (212) 697-8658.

NATIONAL PERSONAL SELF-DEFENSE AWARENESS MONTH. Jan 1–31. To educate Americans about realistic self-defense options, tactics and techniques in an increasingly aggressive world. Seminars and related events nationally focus on issues of awareness, prevention, risk reduction, confrontation avoidance and physical self-defense techniques to encourage individuals to take a proactive role in their self-defense and in building self-confidence. For info: Natl Self-Defense Institute, Inc, 1521 Alton Rd, Box 131, Miami Beach, FL 33139. Phone: (305) 868-NSDI. Fax: (305) 577-8213.

NEW YEAR'S DAY. Jan 1. Legal holiday in all states and territories of the US and in most other countries. The world's most widely celebrated holiday.

NEW YEAR'S DISHONOR LIST. Jan 1. Since 1976, America's dishonor list of words banished from the Queen's English. Overworked words and phrases (e.g., *uniquely unique, first time ever, safe sex*). Send nominations to the following address: PR Office, Lake Superior State Univ, Sault Ste. Marie, MI 49783. Phone: (906) 635-2315. Fax: (906) 635-2623. Web: www.lssu.edu.

JANUARY 1–31
NATIONAL EYE CARE MONTH

Many children are confused by the terms "nearsighted" and "farsighted." By keeping their definitions straightforward, it's easy to clear up any misunderstandings. People who are nearsighted can only see objects near to them. People who are farsighted can only see objects farther away from their body. (Perhaps the confusion arises from trying to define the terms by what a person can *not* see, rather than by what he or she can see.)

"Sticks and stones may break my bones, but names can never hurt me." We all know this just isn't true. "Four-eyes, four-eyes" is a common, hurtful childhood taunt that proves it. Some children participate in this kind of teasing because since they themselves don't wear glasses, they simply do not understand what glasses do for the person who wears them. And saying glasses help a person see clearly means little to a person with 20/20 vision.

A simple, quick lesson, incorporated as part of the weekly spelling lesson, could be used to introduce the theme of vision month. It will help children understand the frustration of not being able to see clearly. Before the lesson type or clearly print the spelling words on a sheet of paper. Make the letters the type size normally found in a book the children would be reading. Tape the list to the blackboard. Ask the children to copy the list onto their own paper *without leaving their seats.* As long as no one sits really close to the board, chances are no one will be able to accomplish this task. Depending on the age of the students, someone may be brave enough to acknowledge "I can't see them!" Others may wriggle uncomfortably, but remain quiet.

You can make several comments or ask a question or two that will help students realize on their own the purpose of this lesson. Try: "I don't understand the problem, my letters are clearly printed." "Do the words become clearer if I let you move three feet (or one or two rows) closer?" and "I get worried when I can't see something clearly. I have trouble understanding something when I can't see it. And sometimes I'm embarrassed to say I can't see something. Did anyone else feel that way when you first saw my list?" (This may also be a good time to interject comments such as "How would you feel if I had called you names because you were unable to see my list?") From this point, lead into the discussion of vision and eye care. The spelling test was, of course, just a ruse.

Try having the nurse arrange for a visit from an eye care professional. He or she may have diagrams that show how eye shape affects vision. It's possible he or she may have large-sized letters that are printed with a fuzzy outline. That will really let children see the way someone who is near-sighted sees.

The February 2000 issue of *Kids Discover* magazine is devoted to the subject of eyes and vision ($3.50 for a single issue, Gr. 1–7).

OATMEAL MONTH. Jan 1–31. "Celebrate oatmeal, a low-fat, sodium-free whole grain that when eaten daily as a part of a diet that's low in saturated fat and cholesterol may help reduce the risk of heart disease. Delicious recipes, helpful hints and tips from Quaker® Oats, The Oat Expert, will make enjoying the heart health benefits oatmeal has to offer easy, convenient and, above all, delicious." For info: The Oat Expert, 225 W Washington, Ste 1440, Chicago, IL 60606. Phone: (312) 629-1234.

REVERE, PAUL: BIRTH ANNIVERSARY. Jan 1, 1735. American patriot, silversmith and engraver, maker of false teeth, eyeglasses, picture frames and surgical instruments. Best remembered for his famous ride Apr 18, 1775, to warn patriots that the British were coming, celebrated in Longfellow's poem, "The Midnight Ride of Paul Revere." Born at Boston, MA, died there May 10, 1818. For more info: *In Their Own Words: Paul Revere*, by George Sullivan (Scholastic, 0-439-14748-4, $15.95 Gr. 3–6). See also: "Paul Revere's Ride: Anniversary" (Apr 18).

ROSE BOWL GAME: 100th ANNIVERSARY. Jan 1. Pasadena, CA. Football conference champions from Big Ten and Pac-10 meet in the Rose Bowl game. Tournament of Roses has been an annual New Year's Day event since 1890; Rose Bowl football game since 1902. Michigan defeated Stanford 49–0 in what was the first post-season football game. Called the Rose Bowl since 1923, it is preceded each year by the Tournament of Roses Parade. Est attendance: 100,000. For info: Bridget Schinnerer, Program Coord, Rose Bowl Stadium, 1001 Rose Bowl Drive, Pasadena, CA 91103. Phone: (626) 449-4100. Fax: (626) 449-9066. Web: www.tournamentofroses.com.

ROSS, BETSY: 250th BIRTH ANNIVERSARY. Jan 1, 1752. According to legend based largely on her grandson's revelations in 1870, needleworker Betsy Ross created the first stars-and-stripes flag in 1775, under instructions from George Washington. Her sewing and her making of flags were well known, but there is little corroborative evidence of her role in making the first stars-and-stripes. The account is generally accepted, however, in the absence of any documented claims to the contrary. She was born Elizabeth Griscom at Philadelphia, PA, and died there Jan 30, 1836.

RUSSIA: NEW YEAR'S DAY OBSERVANCE. Jan 1–2. National holiday. Modern tradition calls for setting up New Year's trees in homes, halls, clubs, palaces of culture and the hall of the Kremlin Palace. Children's parties with Granddad Frost and his granddaughter, Snow Girl. Games, songs, dancing, special foods, family gatherings and exchanges of gifts and New Year's cards.

SAINT BASIL'S DAY. Jan 1. St. Basil's or St. Vasily's feast day observed by Eastern Orthodox churches. Special traditions for the day include serving St. Basil cakes, each of which contains a coin. Feast day observed Jan 14 by those churches using the Julian calendar.

SOLEMNITY OF MARY, MOTHER OF GOD. Jan 1. Holy Day of Obligation in Roman Catholic Church since calendar reorganization of 1969, replacing the Feast of the Circumcision, which had been recognized for more than 14 centuries.

SUDAN: INDEPENDENCE DAY. Jan 1. National holiday. Sudan was proclaimed a sovereign independent republic Jan 1, 1956, ending its status as an Anglo-Egyptian condominium (since 1899).

TAIWAN: FOUNDATION DAY. Jan 1. National holiday. Commemorates the founding of the Republic of China in 1912.

TOURNAMENT OF ROSES PARADE. Jan 1. Pasadena, CA. 113th annual parade. Rose Parade starting at 8 AM, EST, includes floats, bands and equestrians. Est attendance: 1,000,000. For info: Pasadena Tournament of Roses Assn, 391 S Orange Grove Blvd, Pasadena, CA 91184. Phone: (626) 449-4100. Fax: (626) 449-9066. Web: www.tournamentofroses.com.

UNITED NATIONS: DECADE FOR HUMAN RIGHTS EDUCATION: YEAR EIGHT. Jan 1–Dec 31. On Dec 23, 1994, the General Assembly proclaimed this decade to begin in 1995, and welcomed the Plan of Action for the Decade submitted by the Secretary-General (Res 49/184). The Assembly expressed its conviction that human rights education should constitute a lifelong process, by which people learn respect for the dignity of others. Info from: United Nations, Dept of Public Info, New York, NY 10017.

UNITED NATIONS: DECADE FOR THE ERADICATION OF POVERTY: YEAR SIX. Jan 1–Dec 31. General Assembly, Dec 20, 1995 (Res 50/107 II), proclaimed 1997–2006 (the decade following the International Year for the Eradication of Poverty—1996) to be a time for governments and organizations to pursue implementation of the recommendations of the major UN conferences on this issue, particularly the World Summit for Social Development held in Copenhagen in March 1995. Info from: United Nations, Dept of Public Info, New York, NY 10017.

UNITED NATIONS: INTERNATIONAL DECADE OF THE WORLD'S INDIGENOUS PEOPLE: YEAR NINE. Jan 1–Dec 31. Proclaimed by the General Assembly, Dec 21, 1993 (Res 48/163), this decade (1994–2003) focuses international attention and cooperation on the problems of indigenous people in a range of areas, such as human rights, health, education, development and environment. Governments are encouraged to include representatives of these people in planning and executing goals and activities for the decade. Info from: United Nations, Dept of Public Info, New York, NY 10017.

UNITED NATIONS: INTERNATIONAL DECADE FOR A CULTURE OF PEACE AND NON-VIOLENCE FOR THE CHILDREN OF THE WORLD: YEAR TWO. Jan 1–Dec 31. The General Assembly (Res 53/25) invites religious bodies, educational institutions, artists and the media to support this decade for the benefit of every child of the world. Member states are invited to ensure that the practice of peace and non-violence is taught at all levels in their societies, including in educational institutions.

WAYNE, "MAD ANTHONY": BIRTH ANNIVERSARY. Jan 1, 1745. American Revolutionary War general whose daring, sometimes reckless, conduct earned him the nickname "Mad Anthony" Wayne. His courage and shrewdness as a soldier made him a key figure in the capture of Stony Point, NY (1779), preventing Benedict Arnold's delivery of West Point to the British, and in subduing hostile Indians of the Northwest Territory (1794). He was born at Waynesboro, PA, and died at Presque Isle, PA, Dec 15, 1796.

Z DAY. Jan 1. To give recognition on the first day of the year to all persons and places whose names begin with the letter "Z" and who are always listed or thought of last in any alphabetized list. For info: Tom Zager, 4545 Kirkwood Dr, Sterling Heights, MI 48310.

January 2002

S	M	T	W	T	F	S
		1	2	3	4	5
6	7	8	9	10	11	12
13	14	15	16	17	18	19
20	21	22	23	24	25	26
27	28	29	30	31		

BIRTHDAYS TODAY

Jon Corzine, 55, US Senator (D, New Jersey), born Taylorville, IL, Jan 1, 1947.

Ernest F. Hollings, 80, US Senator (D, South Carolina), born Charleston, SC, Jan 1, 1922.

Gary Johnson, 49, Governor of New Mexico (R), born Minot, ND, Jan 1, 1953.

Tony Knowles, 59, Governor of Alaska (D), born Tulsa, OK, Jan 1, 1943.

JANUARY 2 — WEDNESDAY

Day 2 — 363 Remaining

ASIMOV, ISAAC: BIRTH ANNIVERSARY. Jan 2, 1920. Although Isaac Asimov was one of the world's best-known writers of science fiction, his almost 500 books dealt with subjects as diverse as the Bible, works for preschoolers, college textbooks, mysteries, chemistry, biology, limericks, Shakespeare, Gilbert and Sullivan and modern history. During his prolific career he helped to elevate science fiction from pulp magazines to a more intellectual level. Some of his works include the *Foundation Trilogy, The Robots of Dawn, Robots and Empire, Nemesis, Murder at the A.B.A.* (in which he himself was a character), *The Gods Themselves* and *I, Robot*, in which he posited the famous Three Laws of Robotics. *The Clock We Live On* is a book for children on the origins of calendars. Asimov was born near Smolensk, Russia, and died at New York, NY, Apr 6, 1992.

EARTH AT PERIHELION. Jan 2. At approximately 9 AM, EST, planet Earth will reach Perihelion, that point in its orbit when it is closest to the sun (about 91,400,000 miles). The Earth's mean distance from the sun (mean radius of its orbit) is reached early in the months of April and October. Note that Earth is closest to the sun during Northern Hemisphere winter. See also: "Earth at Aphelion" (July 6).

55-MPH SPEED LIMIT: ANNIVERSARY. Jan 2, 1974. President Richard Nixon signed a bill requiring states to limit highway speeds to a maximum of 55 mph. This measure was meant to conserve energy during the crisis precipitated by the embargo imposed by the Arab oil-producing countries. A plan, used by some states, limited sale of gasoline on odd-numbered days for cars whose plates ended in odd numbers and even-numbered days for even-numbered plates. Some states limited purchases to $2–$3 per auto and lines as long as six miles resulted in some locations. See also: "Arab Oil Embargo Lifted: Anniversary" (Mar 13).

GEORGIA RATIFIES CONSTITUTION: ANNIVERSARY. Jan 2, 1788. By unanimous vote, Georgia became the fourth state to ratify the Constitution.

HAITI: ANCESTORS' DAY. Jan 2. Commemoration of the ancestors. Also known as Hero's Day. Public holiday.

JAPAN: KAKIZOME. Jan 2. Traditional Japanese festival gets under way when the first strokes of the year are made on paper with the traditional brushes.

RUSSIA: PASSPORT PRESENTATION. Jan 2. A ceremony for 16-year-olds, who are recognized as citizens of the country. Always on the first working day of the New Year.

SPACE MILESTONE: *LUNA 1* (USSR). Jan 2, 1959. Launch of robotic moon probe that missed the moon and became the first spacecraft from Earth to orbit the sun.

SPAIN CAPTURES GRANADA: ANNIVERSARY. Jan 2, 1492. Spaniards took the city of Granada from the Moors, ending seven centuries of Muslim rule in Spain.

SWITZERLAND: BERCHTOLDSTAG. Jan 2. Holiday in many cantons. Commemorates Duke Berchtold V, who founded the city of Berne in the 12th century. Now mainly a children's holiday.

TAFT, HELEN HERRON: BIRTH ANNIVERSARY. Jan 2, 1861. Wife of William Howard Taft, 27th president of the US, born at Cincinnati, OH. Died at Washington, DC, May 22, 1943.

WOLFE, JAMES: BIRTH ANNIVERSARY. Jan 2, 1727. English general who commanded the British army's victory over Montcalm's French forces on the Plains of Abraham at Quebec City in 1759. As a result, France surrendered Canada to England. Wolfe was born at Westerham, Kent, England. He died at the Plains of Abraham of battle wounds, Sept 13, 1759.

BIRTHDAYS TODAY

David Cone, 39, baseball player, born Kansas City, MO, Jan 2, 1963.

Dennis Hastert, 60, Speaker of the House of Representatives, born Aurora, IL, Jan 2, 1942.

Richard Riley, 69, former US Secretary of Education, born Greenville, SC, Jan 2, 1933.

JANUARY 3 — THURSDAY

Day 3 — 362 Remaining

ALASKA: ADMISSION DAY: ANNIVERSARY. Jan 3. Alaska, which had been purchased from Russia in 1867, became the 49th state in 1959. The area of Alaska is nearly one-fifth the size of the rest of the US.

BURKINA FASO: ANNIVERSARY OF THE 1966 UPHEAVAL. Jan 3. National holiday. Commemorates the change in government leadership.

CONGRESS ASSEMBLES. Jan 3. The Constitution provides that "the Congress shall assemble at least once in every year. . . ." and the 20th Amendment specifies "and such meeting shall begin at noon on the 3rd day of January, unless they shall by law appoint a different day."

COOLIDGE, GRACE ANNA GOODHUE: BIRTH ANNIVERSARY. Jan 3, 1879. Wife of Calvin Coolidge, 30th president of the US, born at Burlington, VT. Died at Northampton, MA, July 8, 1957.

DRINKING STRAW PATENTED: ANNIVERSARY. Jan 3, 1888. A drinking straw made out of paraffin-covered paper was patented by Marvin Stone of Washington, DC. It replaced natural rye straws.

MOTT, LUCRETIA (COFFIN): BIRTH ANNIVERSARY. Jan 3, 1793. American teacher, minister, antislavery leader and (with Elizabeth Cady Stanton) one of the founders of the women's rights movement in the US. Born at Nantucket, MA, she died near Philadelphia, PA, Nov 11, 1880.

TOLKIEN, J[OHN] R[ONALD] R[EUEL]: BIRTH ANNIVERSARY. Jan 3, 1892. Author of *The Hobbit* (1937) and the trilogy *The Lord of the Rings*. Though best known for his fantasies, Tolkien was also a serious philologist. Born at Bloemfontein, South Africa, he died at Bournemouth, England, Sept 2, 1973.

WIND CAVE NATIONAL PARK ESTABLISHED: ANNIVERSARY. Jan 3, 1903. President Theodore Roosevelt signed a bill on this date establishing South Dakota's Wind Cave a national park and preserve. It was the first national park established for the preservation of a cave. For more info: www.nps.gov/wica/index.htm.

BIRTHDAYS TODAY

Alma Flor Ada, 64, author (*Yours Truly, Goldilocks*), born Camaguey, Cuba, Jan 3, 1938.

Joan Walsh Anglund, 76, author and illustrator (*Crocus in the Snow, Bedtime Book*), born Hinsdale, IL, Jan 3, 1926.

Mel Gibson, 46, actor (*Lethal Weapon*, voice of John Smith in *Pocahontas*), born New York, NY, Jan 3, 1956.

Robert (Bobby) Hull, 63, Hockey Hall of Fame left wing, born Point Anne, Ontario, Canada, Jan 3, 1939.

Alex Linz, 13, actor (*Home Alone 3*), born Santa Barbara, CA, Jan 3, 1989.

Jason Marsden, 27, actor ("Step By Step"), born Providence, RI, Jan 3, 1975.

JANUARY 4 — FRIDAY

Day 4 — 361 Remaining

BRAILLE, LOUIS: BIRTH ANNIVERSARY. Jan 4, 1809. The inventor of a widely used touch system of reading and writing for the blind was born at Coupvray, France. Permanently blinded at the age of three by a leatherworking awl in his father's saddle-making shop, Braille developed a system of writing that used, ironically, an awl-like stylus to punch marks in paper that could be felt and interpreted by the blind. The system was largely ignored until after Braille died in poverty, suffering from tuberculosis, at Paris, Jan 6, 1852. For info: *Louis Braille: The Blind Boy Who Wanted to Read*, by Dennis Fradin (Silver Burdett, 0-614-29054-6, $6.95 Gr. K–5) and *Out of Darkness: The Story of Louis Braille*, by Russell Freedman (Houghton, 0-395-77516-7. $15.95 Gr. 5 & up).

GENERAL TOM THUMB: BIRTH ANNIVERSARY. Jan 4, 1838. Charles Sherwood Stratton, perhaps the most famous midget in history, was born at Bridgeport, CT. His growth almost stopped during his first year, but he eventually reached a height of three feet, four inches and a weight of 70 pounds. "Discovered" by P.T. Barnum in 1842, Stratton, as "General Tom Thumb," became an internationally known entertainer and on tour performed before Queen Victoria and other heads of state. On Feb 10, 1863, he married another midget, Lavinia Warren. Stratton died at Middleborough, MA, July 15, 1883.

GRIMM, JACOB: BIRTH ANNIVERSARY. Jan 4, 1785. Librarian, mythologist and philologist, born at Hanau, Germany. Most remembered for *Grimm's Fairy Tales* (in collaboration with his brother Wilhelm). Died at Berlin, Germany, Sept 20, 1863. See also: "Grimm, Wilhelm Carl: Birth Anniversary" (Feb 24).

MYANMAR: INDEPENDENCE DAY. Jan 4. National Day. The British controlled the country from 1826 until 1948 when it was granted independence. Formerly Burma, the country's name was changed to the Union of Myanmar in 1989 to reflect that the population is made up not just of the Burmese but of many other ethnic groups as well.

NEWTON, SIR ISAAC: BIRTH ANNIVERSARY. Jan 4, 1643. Sir Isaac Newton was the chief figure of the scientific revolution of the 17th century, a physicist and mathematician who laid the foundations of calculus, studied the mechanics of planetary motion and discovered the law of gravitation. Born at Woolsthorpe, England, he died at London, England, Mar 20, 1727. Newton was born before Great Britain adopted the Gregorian calendar. His Julian (Old Style) birth date is Dec 25, 1642. For more info: *Isaac Newton*, by Michael White (Blackbirch, 1-56711-326-5, $19.95 Gr. 4–7).

POLISH-AMERICAN IN THE HOUSE: ANNIVERSARY. Jan 4, 1977. Maryland Democrat Barbara Mikulski took her seat in the US House of Representatives, the first Polish-American ever to do so. An able voice for female as well as working-class Baltimore constituents of the 3rd District, Mikulski went on to be elected to the US Senate.

POP MUSIC CHART INTRODUCED: ANNIVERSARY. Jan 4, 1936. *Billboard* magazine published the first list of best-selling pop records, covering the week that ended Dec 30, 1935. On the list were recordings by the Tommy Dorsey and the Ozzie Nelson orchestras.

TRIVIA DAY. Jan 4. In celebration of those who know all sorts of facts and/or have doctorates in uselessology. For info: Robert L. Birch, Puns Corps, Box 2364, Falls Church, VA 22042-0364. Phone: (703) 533-3668.

UTAH: ADMISSION DAY: ANNIVERSARY. Jan 4. Became the 45th state in 1896.

BIRTHDAYS TODAY

Robert Burleigh, 66, poet (*Hoops*), born Chicago, IL, Jan 4, 1936.

Etienne Delessert, 61, author and illustrator (*How the Mouse Was Hit on the Head With a Stone and So Discovered the World*), born Lausanne, Switzerland, Jan 4, 1941.

Phyllis Reynolds Naylor, 69, author (Newbery for *Shiloh*), born Anderson, IN, Jan 4, 1933.

JANUARY 5 — SATURDAY

Day 5 — 360 Remaining

AILEY, ALVIN: BIRTH ANNIVERSARY. Jan 5, 1931. Born at Rogers, TX, Alvin Ailey began his career as a choreographer in the late 1950s after a successful career as a dancer. He founded the Alvin Ailey American Dance Theater, drawing from classical ballet, jazz, Afro-Caribbean and modern dance idioms to create the 79 ballets of the company's repertoire. He and his work played a central part in establishing a role for blacks in the world of modern dance. Ailey died Dec 1, 1989, at New York, NY.

CARVER, GEORGE WASHINGTON: DEATH ANNIVERSARY. Jan 5, 1943. Black American agricultural scientist, author, inventor and teacher. Born into slavery at Diamond Grove, MO, probably in 1864. His research led to the creation of synthetic products made from peanuts, potatoes and wood. Carver died at Tuskegee, AL. His birthplace became a national monument in 1953. For more info: *George Washington Carver: Nature's Trailblazer*, by Theresa Rogers (Twenty-First Century, 0-8050-2115-9, $14.95 Gr. 5–7).

January 2002

S	M	T	W	T	F	S
		1	2	3	4	5
6	7	8	9	10	11	12
13	14	15	16	17	18	19
20	21	22	23	24	25	26
27	28	29	30	31		

DECATUR, STEPHEN: BIRTH ANNIVERSARY. Jan 5, 1779. American naval officer (whose father and grandfather, both also named Stephen Decatur, were also seafaring men) born at Sinepuxent, MD. In a toast at a dinner in Norfolk in 1815, Decatur spoke his most famous words: "Our country! In her intercourse with foreign nations may she always be in the right; but our country, right or wrong." Mortally wounded in a duel with Commodore James Barron, at Bladensburg, MD, on the morning of Mar 22, 1820, Decatur was carried to his home at Washington where he died a few hours later.

ITALY: EPIPHANY FAIR. Jan 5. Piazza Navona, Rome, Italy. On the eve of Epiphany a fair of toys, sweets and presents takes place among the beautiful Bernini Fountains.

MONDALE, WALTER F.: BIRTHDAY. Jan 5, 1928. The 42nd vice president (1977–81) of the US, born at Ceylon, MN.

MOON PHASE: LAST QUARTER. Jan 5. Moon enters Last Quarter phase at 10:55 PM, EST.

PICCARD, JEANNETTE RIDLON: BIRTH ANNIVERSARY. Jan 5, 1895. First American woman to qualify as a free balloon pilot (1934). One of the first women to be ordained an Episcopal priest (1976). Pilot for record-setting balloon ascent into stratosphere (57,579 ft) from Dearborn, MI, Oct 23, 1934, with her husband, Jean Felix Piccard. She was an identical twin married to an identical twin. Born at Chicago, IL, she died at Minneapolis, MN, May 17, 1981. See also: "Piccard, Jean Felix: Birth Anniversary" (Jan 28) and "Piccard, Auguste: Birth Anniversary" (Jan 28).

TWELFTH NIGHT. Jan 5. Evening before Epiphany. Twelfth Night marks the end of medieval Christmas festivities and the end of Twelfthtide (the 12-day season after Christmas ending with Epiphany). Also called Twelfth Day Eve.

WYOMING INAUGURATES FIRST WOMAN GOVERNOR IN US: ANNIVERSARY. Jan 5, 1925. Nellie Tayloe (Mrs William B.) Ross became the first woman to serve as governor upon her inauguration as governor of Wyoming. She had previously finished out the term of her husband, who had died in office. In 1974 Ella Grasso of Connecticut became the first woman to be elected governor in her own right.

BIRTHDAYS TODAY

Lynne Cherry, 50, author (*The Great Kapok Tree, A River Ran Wild*), born Philadelphia, PA, Jan 5, 1952.

Mike DeWine, 55, US Senator (R, Ohio), born Springfield, OH, Jan 5, 1947.

Warrick Dunn, 27, football player, born Baton Rouge, LA, Jan 5, 1975.

Walter Frederick Mondale, 74, 42nd vice president of the US and candidate for president in 1984, born Ceylon, MN, Jan 5, 1928.

JANUARY 6 — SUNDAY

Day 6 — 359 Remaining

ARMENIAN CHRISTMAS. Jan 6. Christmas is observed in the Armenian Church, the oldest national Christian church.

CARNIVAL SEASON. Jan 6–Feb 12. A secular festival preceding Lent. A time of merrymaking and feasting before the austere days of Lenten fasting and penitence (40 weekdays between Ash Wednesday and Easter Sunday). The word *carnival* probably is derived from the Latin *carnem levare*, meaning "to remove meat." Depending on local custom, the carnival season may start any time between Nov 11 and Shrove Tuesday. Conclusion of the season is much less variable, being the close of Shrove Tuesday in most places. Celebrations vary considerably, but the festival often includes many theatrical aspects (masks, costumes and songs) and has given its name (in the US) to traveling amusement shows that may be seen throughout the year. Observed traditionally in Roman Catholic countries from Epiphany through Shrove Tuesday. For more info: *Carnival*, by Clare Chandler (Millbrook, 0-7613-0373-1, $20.90 Gr. K–3).

EPIPHANY or TWELFTH DAY. Jan 6. Known also as Old Christmas Day and Twelfthtide. On the twelfth day after Christmas, Christians celebrate the visit of the Magi or Wise Men to the baby Jesus. In many countries, this is the day children receive gifts, rather than Christmas day. Epiphany of Our Lord, one of the oldest Christian feasts, is observed in Roman Catholic churches in the US on a Sunday between Jan 2 and 8. Theophany of the Eastern Orthodox Church is observed on this day in churches using the Gregorian calendar and Jan 19 in those churches using the Julian calendar and celebrates the manifestation of the divinity of Jesus at the time of his baptism in the Jordan River by John the Baptist.

ITALY: LA BEFANA. Jan 6. Epiphany festival in which the "Befana," a kindly witch, bestows gifts on children—toys and candy for those who have been good, but a lump of coal or a pebble for those who have been naughty. The festival begins on the night of Jan 5 with much noise and merrymaking (when the Befana is supposed to come down the chimneys on her broom, leaving gifts in children's stockings) and continues with fairs, parades and other activities.

JOAN OF ARC: BIRTH ANNIVERSARY. Jan 6, 1412. Born at the village of Domremy, in the Meuse River valley of France. At this time there was civil war in France, with one faction being aided by the English. As a teenager, Joan led an army to drive the English out of northern France. Captured, she was burned at the stake as a witch and a heretic on May 30, 1431. Her martyrdom inspired the unification of the French people, who drove the English out of France. Joan was made a saint in 1920. For more info: *Joan of Arc*, by Diane Stanley (Morrow, 0-688-14330-X, $15.95 Gr. 4–8). See also: "Saint Joan of Arc: Feast Day" (May 30).

NATIONAL SMITH DAY. Jan 6. The commonest surname in the English-speaking world is Smith. There are an estimated 2,382,500 Smiths in the US. This special day honors the birthday in 1580 of Captain John Smith, the leader of the English colonists who settled at Jamestown, VA, in 1607, thus making him one of the first American Smiths. On this special day, all derivatives, such as Goldsmith, are invited to participate. For info: Adrienne Sioux Koopersmith, 1437 W Rosemont, 1W, Chicago, IL 60660-1319. Phone: (773) 743-5341. Fax: (773) 743-5395. E-mail: kooper@interaccess.com.

NEW MEXICO: ADMISSION DAY: 90th ANNIVERSARY. Jan 6. Became 47th state in 1912.

PAN AM CIRCLES EARTH: 60th ANNIVERSARY. Jan 6, 1942. A Pan American Airways plane arrived in New York to complete the first around-the-world trip by a commercial aircraft.

SANDBURG, CARL: BIRTH ANNIVERSARY. Jan 6, 1878. American poet ("Fog," "Chicago"), biographer of Lincoln, historian and folklorist, born at Galesburg, IL. Died at Flat Rock, NC, July 22, 1967. For more info: *Carl Sandburg: A Biography*, by Milton Meltzer (Millbrook, 0-7613-1364-8, $29.90 Gr. 5–10).

SMITH, JEDEDIAH STRONG: BIRTH ANNIVERSARY. Jan 6, 1799. Mountain man, fur trader and one of the first explorers of the American West, Smith helped develop the Oregon Trail. He was the first American to reach California by land and first to travel by land from San Diego, up the West Coast to the Canadian border. Smith was born at Jericho (now Bainbridge), NY, and was killed by Comanche Indians along the Santa Fe Trail in what is now Kansas, May 27, 1831.

SPACE MILESTONE: *LUNAR EXPLORER* (US). Jan 6, 1998. NASA headed back to the moon for the first time since the *Apollo 17* flight 25 years before. This unmanned probe searches for evidence of frozen water on the moon.

THREE KINGS DAY. Jan 6. Major festival of Christian Church observed in many parts of the world with gifts, feasting, last lighting of Christmas lights and burning of Christmas greens. In many European countries children get their Christmas presents on Three Kings Day. Twelfth and last day of the Feast of the Nativity. Commemorates visit of the Three Wise Men (Kings or Magi) to Bethlehem.

BIRTHDAYS TODAY

Johnny Yong Bosch, 26, actor (*Turbo: A Power Rangers Movie*, "Power Rangers Turbo"), born Topeka, KS, Jan 6, 1976.

Ina R. Friedman, 76, author (*How My Parents Learned to Eat*), born Chester, PA, Jan 6, 1926.

Gabrielle Reece, 32, pro volleyball player, born La Jolla, CA, Jan 6, 1970.

Bob Wise, 54, Governor of West Virginia (D), born Washington, DC, Jan 6, 1948.

JANUARY 7 — MONDAY

Day 7 — 358 Remaining

ENGLAND: PLOUGH MONDAY. Jan 7. Always the Monday after Twelfth Day. Work on the farm is resumed after the festivities of the 12 days of Christmas. On preceding Sunday ploughs may be blessed in churches. Celebrated with dances and plays.

FILLMORE, MILLARD: BIRTH ANNIVERSARY. Jan 7, 1800. The 13th president of the US (July 10, 1850–Mar 3, 1853), Fillmore succeeded to the presidency upon the death of Zachary Taylor, but he did not get the hoped-for nomination from his party in 1852. He ran for president unsuccessfully in 1856 as candidate of the "Know-Nothing Party," whose platform demanded, among other things, that every government employee (federal, state and local) should be a native-born citizen. Fillmore was born at Locke, NY, and died at Buffalo, NY, Mar 8, 1874. For info: www.ipl.org/ref/POTUS.

January 2002

S	M	T	W	T	F	S
		1	2	3	4	5
6	7	8	9	10	11	12
13	14	15	16	17	18	19
20	21	22	23	24	25	26
27	28	29	30	31		

JANUARY 7
TRANSATLANTIC PHONING

The holiday season is winding down. During that time many families telephoned friends and family who live far away. January 7, 1927, was the day transatlantic telephone service was established between New York and London.

Survey your students and list where their families called (and from which cities they received calls) during the past several weeks. Display the world map and let students design their own world calling "tag" that can be fastened on or near the map. One of the interesting things to discuss is the time lag that occurs during some long distance phone calls.

Divide students into small groups. One group could calculate the distance in miles (or kilometers) from your school to the recipient/locale of each call. Another group could investigate time zones and how they affect the hour of day between caller and call recipient. A third group could keep track of relationships: were most calls made to relatives or to family friends?

For an interesting show-and-tell, see if you can locate a telephone with a rotary dial that could be brought to your classroom. Most students are completely baffled by how one should use them to place a call. Antique models have no dial, only a hand crank on the side of the phone box to call the operator who then placed the call.

If students are interested in further pursuing the development of telephone technology, they might want to read *The Telephone*, by Sarah Gearhart (Simon & Schuster, 0-689-82815-2, $17.95 Gr. 4 & up).

FIRST BALLOON FLIGHT ACROSS ENGLISH CHANNEL: ANNIVERSARY. Jan 7, 1785. Dr. John Jeffries, a Boston physician, and Jean-Pierre Blanchard, French aeronaut, crossed the English Channel from Dover, England, to Calais, France, landing in a forest after being forced to throw overboard all ballast, equipment and even most of their clothing to avoid a forced landing in the icy waters of the English Channel. Blanchard's trousers are said to have been the last article thrown overboard.

GERMANY: MUNICH FASCHING CARNIVAL. Jan 7–Feb 12. Munich. From Jan 7 through Shrove Tuesday is Munich's famous carnival season. Costume balls are popular throughout carnival. High points on Fasching Sunday (Feb 10) and Shrove Tuesday (Feb 11) with great carnival outside at the Viktualienmarkt and on Pedestrian Mall.

JAPAN: NANAKUSA. Jan 7. Festival dates back to the 7th century and recalls the seven plants served to the emperor that are believed to have great medicinal value—shepherd's purse, chickweed, parsley, cottonweed, radish, hotoke-no-za and aona.

JAPAN: USOKAE (BULLFINCH EXCHANGE FESTIVAL). Jan 7. Dazaifu, Fukuoka Prefecture. "Good Luck" gilded wood bullfinches, mixed among many plain ones, are sought after by the throngs as priests of the Dazaifu Shrine pass them out in the dim light of a small bonfire.

MONTGOLFIER, JACQUES ETIENNE: BIRTH ANNIVERSARY. Jan 7, 1745. Merchant and inventor born at Vidalon-lez Annonay, Ardèche, France. With his older brother, Joseph Michel, in November 1782, conducted experiments with paper and fabric bags filled with smoke and hot air, which led to invention of the hot-air balloon and humankind's first flight. Died at Serrieres, France, Aug 2, 1799. See also: "First Balloon Flight: Anniversary" (June 5); "Montgolfier, Joseph Michel: Birth Anniversary" and "Aviation History Month" (Nov 1).

OLD CALENDAR ORTHODOX CHRISTMAS. Jan 7. Some Orthodox Churches celebrate Christmas which is the "Old" (Julian) calendar date.

RUSSIA: CHRISTMAS OBSERVANCE. Jan 7. National holiday.

TRANSATLANTIC PHONING: 75th ANNIVERSARY. Jan 7, 1927. Commercial transatlantic telephone service between New York and London was inaugurated. There were 31 calls made the first day. *See* Curriculum Connection.

BIRTHDAYS TODAY

Kay Chorao, 65, author and illustrator (*A Magic Eye for Ida*), born Elkhart, IN, Jan 7, 1937.

Katie Couric, 45, cohost, "Today Show," born Arlington, VA, Jan 7, 1957.

Minfong Ho, 51, author (*Hush!: A Thai Lullaby*), born Rangoon, Burma, Jan 7, 1951.

JANUARY 8 — TUESDAY

Day 8 — 357 Remaining

AT&T DIVESTITURE: 20th ANNIVERSARY. Jan 8, 1982. In the most significant antitrust suit since the breakup of Standard Oil in 1911, American Telephone and Telegraph agreed to give up its 22 local Bell System companies ("Baby Bells"). These companies represented 80 percent of AT&T's assets. This ended the corporation's virtual monopoly of US telephone service.

BATTLE OF NEW ORLEANS: ANNIVERSARY. Jan 8, 1815. British forces suffered crushing losses (more than 2,000 casualties) in an attack on New Orleans, LA. Defending US troops were led by General Andrew Jackson, who became a popular hero as a result of the victory. Neither side knew that the War of 1812 had ended two weeks previously with the signing of the Treaty of Ghent, Dec 24, 1814. Battle of New Orleans Day is observed in Louisiana.

CHOU EN-LAI: DEATH ANNIVERSARY. Jan 8, 1976. Anniversary of the death of Chou En-Lai, premier of the State Council of the People's Republic of China. He was born in 1898 (exact date unknown).

EARTH'S ROTATION PROVED: ANNIVERSARY. Jan 8, 1851. Using a device now known as Foucault's pendulum in his Paris home, physicist Jean Foucault demonstrated that the Earth rotates on its axis.

GREECE: MIDWIFE'S DAY or WOMEN'S DAY. Jan 8. Midwife's Day or Women's Day is celebrated Jan 8 each year to honor midwives and all women. "On this day women stop their housework and spend their time in cafés, while the men do all the housework chores and look after the children." In some villages, men caught outside "will be stripped . . . and drenched with cold water."

MARCO POLO: DEATH ANNIVERSARY. Jan 8, 1324. Merchant famous for his travel to China, where he worked for Kublai Khan. Born around 1254 in Venice, he died there after writing a book about his travels in Asia.

NATIONAL JOYGERM DAY. Jan 8. Myriads of merry mirthmakers harvesting hugs, happiness and humor; validating vision, vigor and vitality; wallowing in the willingness and wish to change their lives from oblivious boredom to beneficent beatitudes. Goal: Rise from muck and mire of misery and lace life with love and laughter. For info: Joygerm Junkie Joan E. White, Founder, Joygerms Unlimited, PO Box 219, Eastwood Station, Syracuse, NY 13206-0219. Phone: (315) 472-2779.

PRESLEY, ELVIS AARON: BIRTH ANNIVERSARY. Jan 8, 1935. Popular American rock singer, born at Tupelo, MS. Although his middle name was spelled incorrectly as "Aron" on his birth certificate, Elvis had it legally changed to "Aaron," which is how it is spelled on his gravestone. Died at Memphis, TN, Aug 16, 1977.

UNIVERSAL LETTER-WRITING WEEK. Jan 8–14. The purpose of this week is for people all over the world to get the new year off to a good start by sending letters and cards to friends and acquaintances not only in their own country but to people throughout the world. For complete information and suggestions about writing good letters, send $4 to cover expense of printing, handling and postage. For info: Dr. Stanley Drake, Pres, Intl Soc of Friendship and Goodwill, 8592 Roswell Rd, Atlanta, GA 30350-1870.

WAR ON POVERTY: ANNIVERSARY. Jan 8, 1964. President Lyndon Johnson declared a War on Poverty in his State of the Union address. He stressed improved education as one of the cornerstones of the program. The following Aug 20, he signed a $947.5 million anti-poverty bill designed to assist more than 30 million citizens.

BIRTHDAYS TODAY

Nancy Bond, 57, author (*A String on the Harp*), born Bethesda, MD, Jan 8, 1945.

Floyd Cooper, 46, author, illustrator (*Coming Home: From the Life of Langston Hughes, Meet Danitra Brown*), born Tulsa, OK, Jan 8, 1956.

Lauren Hewett, 21, actress ("Spellbinder: Land of the Dragon Lord"), born Sydney, Australia, Jan 8, 1981.

Stephen Manes, 53, author (*Be a Perfect Person in Just Three Days*), born Pittsburgh, PA, Jan 8, 1949.

Marjorie Priceman, 44, illustrator (*Zin! Zin! Zin! A Violin; What Zeesie Saw on Delancy Street*), born Long Island, NY, Jan 8, 1958.

Bob Taft, 60, Governor of Ohio (R), born Boston, MA, Jan 8, 1942.

JANUARY 9 — WEDNESDAY

Day 9 — 356 Remaining

AVIATION IN AMERICA: ANNIVERSARY. Jan 9, 1793. A Frenchman, Jean-Pierre Francois Blanchard, made the first manned free-balloon flight in America's history at Philadelphia, PA. The event was watched by President George Washington and many other high government officials. The hydrogen-filled balloon rose to a height of about 5,800 feet, traveled some 15 miles and landed 46 minutes later in New Jersey. Reportedly Blanchard had one passenger on the flight—a little black dog.

CATT, CARRIE LANE CHAPMAN: BIRTH ANNIVERSARY. Jan 9, 1859. American women's rights leader, founder (in 1919) of the National League of Women Voters. Born at Ripon, WI, she died at New Rochelle, NY, Mar 9, 1947.

CONNECTICUT RATIFIES CONSTITUTION: ANNIVERSARY. Jan 9, 1788. By a vote of 128 to 40, Connecticut became the fifth state to ratify the Constitution.

NIXON, RICHARD MILHOUS: BIRTH ANNIVERSARY. Jan 9, 1913. Richard Nixon served as the 36th vice president of the US (under President Dwight D. Eisenhower) Jan 20, 1953, to Jan 20, 1961. He was the 37th president of the US, serving Jan 20, 1969, to Aug 9, 1974, when he resigned the presidency while under threat of impeachment. First US president to resign that office. He was born at Yorba Linda, CA, and died at New York, NY, Apr 22, 1994. For info: www.ipl.org/ref/POTUS.

PANAMA: MARTYRS' DAY. Jan 9. Public holiday.

PHILIPPINES: FEAST OF THE BLACK NAZARENE. Jan 9. Culmination of a nine-day fiesta. Manila's largest procession takes place in the afternoon of Jan 9, in honor of the Black Nazarene, whose shrine is at the Quiapo Church.

BIRTHDAYS TODAY

Clyde Robert Bulla, 88, author (*The Chalk Box Kid*), born King City, MO, Jan 9, 1914.
Sergio Garcia, 22, golfer, born Borriol, Spain, Jan 9, 1980.
Bill Graves, 49, Governor of Kansas (R), born Salina, KS, Jan 9, 1953.
A.J. McLean, 24, singer (Backstreet Boys), born West Palm Beach, FL, Jan 9, 1978.
Joely Richardson, 37, actress (*101 Dalmatians*), born London, England, Jan 9, 1965.

JANUARY 10 — THURSDAY

Day 10 — 355 Remaining

LEAGUE OF NATIONS: ANNIVERSARY. Jan 10, 1920. Through the Treaty of Versailles, the League of Nations came into existence. Fifty nations entered into a covenant designed to avoid war. The US never joined the League of Nations, which was dissolved Apr 18, 1946.

UNITED NATIONS GENERAL ASSEMBLY: ANNIVERSARY. Jan 10, 1946. On the 26th anniversary of the establishment of the unsuccessful League of Nations, delegates from 51 nations met at London, England, for the first meeting of the UN General Assembly.

WOMEN'S SUFFRAGE AMENDMENT INTRODUCED IN CONGRESS: ANNIVERSARY. Jan 10, 1878. Senator A.A. Sargent of California, a close friend of Susan B. Anthony, introduced into the US Senate a women's suffrage amendment known as the Susan B. Anthony Amendment. It wasn't until Aug 26, 1920, 42 years later, that the amendment was signed into law.

BIRTHDAYS TODAY

Lloyd Bloom, 55, illustrator (*Like Jake and Me*), born New York, NY, Jan 10, 1947.
Remy Charlip, 73, author and illustrator (*Hooray for Me!*), born Jan 10, 1929.
Sook Nyul Choi, 65, author (*The Year of Impossible Goodbyes*), born Pyongyang, Korea, Jan 10, 1937.
Glenn Robinson, 29, basketball player, member of 1996 Dream Team, born Gary, IN, Jan 10, 1973.

January 2002

S	M	T	W	T	F	S
		1	2	3	4	5
6	7	8	9	10	11	12
13	14	15	16	17	18	19
20	21	22	23	24	25	26
27	28	29	30	31		

JANUARY 11 — FRIDAY

Day 11 — 354 Remaining

CUCKOO DANCING WEEK. Jan 11–17. To honor the memory of Laurel and Hardy, whose theme, "The Dancing Cuckoos," shall be heard throughout the land as their movies are seen and their antics greeted by laughter by old and new fans of these unique masters of comedy. [Originated by the late William T. Rabe of Sault Ste. Marie, MI.]

"DESIGNATED HITTER" RULE ADOPTED: ANNIVERSARY. Jan 11, 1973. American League adopted the "designated hitter" rule, whereby an additional player is used to bat for the pitcher.

FIRST BLACK SOUTHERN LIEUTENANT GOVERNOR: ANNIVERSARY. Jan 11, 1986. L. Douglas Wilder was sworn in as lieutenant governor of Virginia. He was the first black elected to statewide office in the South since reconstruction. He later served as governor of Virginia.

HOSTOS, EUGENIO MARIA: BIRTH ANNIVERSARY. Jan 11, 1839. Puerto Rican patriot, scholar and author of more than 50 books. Born at Rio Canas, Puerto Rico, he died at Santo Domingo, Dominican Republic, Aug 11, 1903.

LEOPOLD, ALDO: BIRTH ANNIVERSARY. Jan 11, 1886. Naturalist and author who made a profound contribution to the American environmental movement. Best known for his book *A Sand County Almanac.* Born at Burlington, IA, he died Apr 21, 1948, at Sauk County, WI.

MacDONALD, JOHN A.: BIRTH ANNIVERSARY. Jan 11, 1815. Canadian statesman, first prime minister of Canada. Born at Glasgow, Scotland, he died June 6, 1891, at Ottawa, Canada.

NEPAL: NATIONAL UNITY DAY. Jan 11. Celebration paying homage to King Prithvinarayan Shah (1723–75), founder of the present house of rulers of Nepal and creator of the unified Nepal of today.

O'BRIEN, ROBERT C.: BIRTH ANNIVERSARY. Jan 11, 1918. Author (Newbery for *Mrs Frisby and the Rats of NIMH*), born Robert Conly at Brooklyn, NY. Died at Washington, DC, Mar 5, 1973.

US SURGEON GENERAL DECLARES CIGARETTES HAZARDOUS: ANNIVERSARY. Jan 11, 1964. US Surgeon General Luther Terry issued the first government report saying that smoking may be hazardous to one's health.

BIRTHDAYS TODAY

Jean Chretien, 68, 20th prime minister of Canada, born Shawinigan, Quebec, Jan 11, 1934.

JANUARY 12 — SATURDAY

Day 12 — 353 Remaining

"BATMAN" TV PREMIERE: ANNIVERSARY. Jan 12, 1966. ABC's crime-fighting show gained a place in Nielsen's top 10 ratings in its first season. The series was based on the DC Comics characters created by Bob Kane in 1939. Adam West starred as millionaire Bruce Wayne and superhero alter ego, Batman. Burt Ward costarred as Dick Grayson/Robin, the Boy Wonder. A colorful assortment of villains guest-starring each week included: Cesar Romero as the Joker, Eartha Kitt and Julie Newmar as Catwoman, Burgess Meredith as the Penguin and Frank Gorshin as the Riddler. Some other stars making memorable appearances included Liberace, Vincent Price, Milton Berle, Tallulah Bankhead and Ethel Merman. The series played up its comic-strip roots with innovative and sharply skewed camera angles, bright bold colors and wild graphics. "Batman's" memorable theme song, composed by Neal Hefti, can be heard today with some 120 episodes in syndication. Many Batman movies have been made, the first in 1943. The most recent was *Batman & Robin*, released in 1997 and starring George Clooney and Chris O'Donnell.

HANCOCK, JOHN: BIRTH ANNIVERSARY. Jan 12, 1737. American patriot and statesman, first signer of the Declaration of Independence. Born at Braintree, MA, he died at Quincy, MA, Oct 8, 1793. Because his signature was the most conspicuous one on the Declaration, Hancock's name has become part of the American language, referring to any handwritten signature, as in "Put your John Hancock on that!"

HAYES, IRA HAMILTON: 80th BIRTH ANNIVERSARY. Jan 12, 1922. Ira Hayes was one of six US Marines who raised the American flag on Iwo Jima's Mount Suribachi, Feb 23, 1945, following a US assault on the Japanese stronghold. The event was immortalized by AP photographer Joe Rosenthal's famous photo and later by a Marine War Memorial monument at Arlington, VA. Hayes was born on a Pima Indian Reservation at Arizona. He returned home after WWII a much celebrated hero but Hayes was unable to cope with fame. He was found dead of "exposure to freezing weather and over-consumption of alcohol" on the Sacaton Indian Reservation at Arizona, Jan 24, 1955.

LONDON, JACK: BIRTH ANNIVERSARY. Jan 12, 1876. American author of more than 50 books: short stories, novels and travel stories of the sea and of the far north, many marked by brutal realism. His most widely known work is *The Call of the Wild*, the great dog story published in 1903. London was born at San Francisco, CA. He died Nov 22, 1916, near Santa Rosa, CA. For a study guide to *The Call of the Wild*: glencoe.com/sec/literature/litlibrary.

NATIONAL HANDWRITING DAY. Jan 12. Popularly observed on the birthday of John Hancock to encourage more legible handwriting.

PESTALOZZI, JOHANN HEINRICH: BIRTH ANNIVERSARY. Jan 12, 1746. Swiss educational reformer, born at Zurich. His theories laid the groundwork for modern elementary education. He died Feb 17, 1827, at Brugg, Switzerland.

TANZANIA: ZANZIBAR REVOLUTION DAY. Jan 12. National day. Zanzibar became independent in December 1963, under a sultan.

BIRTHDAYS TODAY

Kirstie Alley, 47, actress (*Look Who's Talking*), born Wichita, KS, Jan 12, 1955.

Andrew Lawrence, 14, actor ("Brotherly Love," *Prince for a Day*), born Philadelphia, PA, Jan 12, 1988.

Iza Trapini, 48, author, illustrator (*The Itsy Bitsy Spider, I'm a Little Teapot*), born Warsaw, Poland, Jan 12, 1954.

JANUARY 13 — SUNDAY

Day 13 — 352 Remaining

ALGER, HORATIO, JR: BIRTH ANNIVERSARY. Jan 13, 1834. American clergyman and author of more than 100 popular books for boys (some 20 million copies sold). Honesty, frugality and hard work assured that the heroes of his books would find success, wealth and fame. Born at Revere, MA, he died at Natick, MA, July 18, 1899.

FRISBEE INTRODUCED: ANNIVERSARY. Jan 13, 1957. Legend has it that in the 1920s New England college students tossed pie tins from the Frisbie Baking Company of Bridgeport, CT. The first plastic flying disc was released by the Wham-O Company on this date as the Pluto Platter, for its resemblance to a UFO. In 1958 it was renamed the Frisbee. More than 100 million Frisbees have been sold and there are numerous Frisbee tournaments across America every year. *See* Curriculum Connection.

INTERNATIONAL PRINTING WEEK. Jan 13–19. To develop public awareness of the printing/graphic arts industry. Annually, the week including Ben Franklin's birthday, Jan 17. For info: Kevin P. Keane, Exec Dir, Intl Assn of Printing House Craftsmen, 7042 Brooklyn Blvd, Minneapolis, MN 55429-1370. Phone: (612) 560-1620. Web: www.iaphc.org.

MOON PHASE: NEW MOON. Jan 13. Moon enters New Moon phase at 8:29 AM, EST.

RADIO BROADCASTING: ANNIVERSARY. Jan 13, 1910. Radio pioneer and electron tube inventor Lee De Forest arranged the world's first radio broadcast to the public at New York, NY. He succeeded in broadcasting the voice of Enrico Caruso along with other stars of the Metropolitan Opera to several receiving locations in the city where listeners with earphones marveled at

JANUARY 13
FRISBEE INTRODUCED

Sometimes the simplest toys are the most fun. Many modest, quirky toys have been invented over the years. The Frisbee is one that caught on like wildfire. However, Frisbees aren't the only fad toys that have stood the test of time. Other include the Slinky (see November 26 entry), tiddlywinks, the hula hoop, yo-yos, kites, tops and rubber band jump ropes.

Many people have one or more of these toys in their garage or basement. In recognition of the Frisbee, devote gym period to dusting off some of the old standbys and having new fun with them. Students can decide on their own if they wish to hold formal contests such as who can hula hoop the longest. Or you may want to eliminate competition and emphasize that everyone try all activities for experience. Depending on the climate where you live, outdoor play may not be feasible. If so, Frisbee use may have to be regulated.

Students can ask their parents and grandparents what toys they remember playing with as children. Their findings could be written up (or drawn) and posted on the bulletin board. Many upper elementary students are reading books, such as Laura Ingalls Wilder's *Little House on the Prairie*, that are set in bygone eras. Often, toys are mentioned in these novels. For ideas, see *My Little House Crafts Book: 18 Projects from Laura Ingalls Wilder's Little House Stories*, by Carolyn Strom Collins and Christina Wyss Eriksson (HarperTrophy, 0-06-446204-8, $9.95 Gr. 3 & up). There are other nonfiction books that describe toys from the 19th and early 20th centuries.

Many toys and games can be made easily. Depending upon what supplies are on hand at home, the cost may be little or none. Here's a good opportunity for parents to help their children become resourceful and develop ingenuity. Rubber band jump ropes, for example, are easy to make and can be done so cheaply. The same with kites. Clothespin dolls and homemade paper dolls are other easily-made toys. Checkerboards can be drawn on paper with pennies (one side heads up, the other tails up) or beans used as markers. *Let's Make Toys* by Ivan Bulloch and Diane James (World Book, 0-7166-5604-3, $10 PreK–2), has ideas for the youngest children.

As a fun homework assignment that will foster spending time with family, encourage students to make their own toy or game and play it with a friend or family member. Display their efforts in the classroom.

wireless music from the air. Though only a few were equipped to listen, it was the first broadcast to reach the public and the beginning of a new era in which wireless radio communication became almost universal. See also: "First Scheduled Radio Broadcast: Anniversary" (Nov 2).

SECRET PAL DAY. Jan 13. A day for secret pals to remember and do something special for each other. Annually, the second Sunday in January. For info: Eagles Lodge #4080, PO Box 1319, Hayden Lake, ID 83835. Phone: (208) 772-4901 or (208) 772-0687.

★ **STEPHEN FOSTER MEMORIAL DAY.** Jan 13. Presidential Proclamation 2957 of Dec 13, 1951 (designating Jan 13, 1952), covers all succeeding years. (PL82–225 of Oct 27, 1951.) Observed on the anniversary of Foster's death, Jan 13, 1864, at New York, NY. See also: "Foster, Stephen: Birth Anniversary" (July 4).

SWEDEN: ST. KNUT'S DAY. Jan 13. "The 20th day of Knut" is the traditional end of the Christmas season. In Norway, this day is known as Tyvendedagen, or "20th Day."

SWITZERLAND: MEITLISUNNTIG. Jan 13. On Meitlisunntig, the second Sunday in January, the girls of Meisterschwanden and Fahrwangen, in the Seetal district of Aargau, Switzerland, stage a procession in historical uniforms and a military parade before a female General Staff. According to tradition, the custom dates from the Villmergen War of 1712, when the women of both communes gave vital help that led to victory. Popular festival follows the procession.

TOGO: LIBERATION DAY: ANNIVERSARY. Jan 13. National holiday. Commemorates 1963 uprising.

BIRTHDAYS TODAY

Michael Bond, 76, author (*A Bear Called Paddington, Paddington At Work*), born Newbury, Berkshire, England, Jan 13, 1926.

JANUARY 14 — MONDAY

Day 14 — 351 Remaining

ARNOLD, BENEDICT: BIRTH ANNIVERSARY. Jan 14, 1741. American officer who deserted to the British during the Revolutionary War and whose name has since become synonymous with treachery. Born at Norwich, CT, he died June 14, 1801, at London, England. For more info: *Benedict Arnold and the American Revolution*, by David C. King (Blackbirch, 1-56711-221-8, $19.95 Gr. 5 & up).

JAPAN: COMING-OF-AGE DAY. Jan 14. National holiday for youth of the country who have reached adulthood (20 years of age) during the preceding year. Annually, the second Monday in January.

LOFTING, HUGH: BIRTH ANNIVERSARY. Jan 14, 1886. Author and illustrator, known for the Doctor Dolittle series. In his books the famous Dr. Dolittle has the ability to talk with animals. *The Voyages of Dr. Dolittle* won the Newbery Medal in 1923. Born at Maidenhead, England, Lofting died at Santa Monica, CA, Sept 26, 1947.

NATIONAL CLEAN-OFF-YOUR-DESK DAY. Jan 14. To provide one day early each year for every desk worker to see the top of the desk and prepare for the following year's paperwork. Annually, the second Monday in January. For info: A.C. Moeller, Box 71, Clio, MI 48420-1042.

NATIONAL THANK GOD IT'S MONDAY! DAY. Jan 14. Besides holidays, such as President's Day, being celebrated on Mondays, people everywhere start new jobs, have birthdays, celebrate promotions and begin vacations on Mondays. A day in recognition of this first day of the week. Annually, the second Monday in January. For info: Dorothy Zjawin, 61 W Colfax Ave, Roselle Park, NJ 07204. Phone: (908) 241-6241. Fax: (908) 241-6241.

RATIFICATION DAY. Jan 14, 1784. Anniversary of the act that officially ended the American Revolution and established the US as a sovereign power. On Jan 14, 1784, the Continental Congress, meeting at Annapolis, MD, ratified the Treaty of Paris, thus fulfilling the Declaration of Independence of July 4, 1776.

"THE SIMPSONS" TV PREMIERE: ANNIVERSARY. Jan 14, 1990. FOX TV's hottest animated family, "The Simpsons," premiered as a half-hour weekly sitcom. The originator of Homer, Marge, Bart, Lisa and Maggie is cartoonist Matt Groening.

SPACE MILESTONE: *SOYUZ 4* (USSR). Jan 14, 1969. First docking of two manned spacecraft (with *Soyuz 5*) and first interchange of spaceship personnel in orbit by means of space walks.

WHIPPLE, WILLIAM: BIRTH ANNIVERSARY. Jan 14, 1730. American patriot and signer of the Declaration of Independence. Born at Kittery, ME, he died at Portsmouth, NH, Nov 10, 1785.

BIRTHDAYS TODAY

Shannon Lucid, 59, astronaut, holds the record for longest stay in space by an American, born Shanghai, China, Jan 14, 1943.

JANUARY 15 — TUESDAY

Day 15 — 350 Remaining

"HAPPY DAYS" TV PREMIERE: ANNIVERSARY. Jan 15, 1974. This nostalgic comedy was set in Milwaukee in the 1950s. Teenager Richie Cunningham was played by Ron Howard and his best friends "Potsie" Weber and Ralph Malph by Anson Williams and Don Most. Richie's parents were played by Tom Bosley and Marion Ross and his sister, Joanie, was played by Erin Moran. "The Fonz"—Arthur "Fonzie" Fonzarelli—was played by Henry Winkler. "Happy Days" aired until 1984 and has been in syndication ever since. "Laverne and Shirley" and "Joanie Loves Chachi" were spin-offs of this popular program.

KING, MARTIN LUTHER, JR: BIRTH ANNIVERSARY. Jan 15, 1929. Black civil rights leader, minister, advocate of nonviolence and recipient of the Nobel Peace Prize (1964). Born at Atlanta, GA, he was assassinated at Memphis, TN, Apr 4, 1968. After his death many states and territories observed his birthday as a holiday. In 1983 the Congress approved HR 3706, "A bill to amend Title 5, United States Code, to make the birthday of Mar-

January 2002

S	M	T	W	T	F	S
		1	2	3	4	5
6	7	8	9	10	11	12
13	14	15	16	17	18	19
20	21	22	23	24	25	26
27	28	29	30	31		

tin Luther King, Jr, a legal public holiday." Signed by the president on Nov 2, 1983, it became Public Law 98–144. The law sets the third Monday in January for observance of King's birthday. First observance was Jan 20, 1986. For more info: *Martin Luther King*, by Rosemary Bray (Greenwillow, 0-688-13131-X, $16 Gr. 2–4) and *Dear Dr. King: Letters from Today's Children to Dr. Martin Luther King, Jr*, by Jan Colbert and Ann McMillan Harms (Hyperion, 0-7868-1462-4, $6.99 Gr. 3–8). See also: "King, Martin Luther, Jr: Birthday Observed" (Jan 21).

LIVINGSTON, PHILIP: BIRTH ANNIVERSARY. Jan 15, 1716. Merchant and signer of the Declaration of Independence, born at Albany, NY. Died at York, PA, June 12, 1778.

BIRTHDAYS TODAY

Andrea Martin, 55, actress (*Bogus, Anastasia*), born Portland, ME, Jan 15, 1947.

JANUARY 16 — WEDNESDAY

Day 16 — 349 Remaining

DEAN, DIZZY: BIRTH ANNIVERSARY. Jan 16, 1911. Jay Hanna "Dizzy" Dean, major league pitcher (St. Louis Cardinals) and Baseball Hall of Fame member was born at Lucas, AR. Following his baseball career, Dean established himself as a radio and TV sports announcer and commentator, becoming famous for his innovative delivery. "He slud into third," reported Dizzy, who on another occasion explained that "Me and Paul [baseball player brother Paul "Daffy" Dean] . . . didn't get much education." Died at Reno, NV, July 17, 1974.

EIGHTEENTH (PROHIBITION) AMENDMENT: ANNIVERSARY. Jan 16, 1919. Nebraska became the 36th state to ratify the prohibition amendment on this date, and the 18th Amendment became part of the US Constitution. One year later, Jan 16, 1920, the 18th Amendment took effect and the sale of alcoholic beverages became illegal in the US with the Volstead Act providing for enforcement. This was the first time that an amendment to the Constitution dealt with a social issue. The 21st Amendment, repealing the 18th, went into effect Dec 6, 1933.

EL SALVADOR: NATIONAL DAY OF PEACE. Jan 16. Public holiday. Anniversary of the end of 12 years of civil war with the signing of a peace treaty on Jan 16, 1992.

JAPAN: HARU-NO-YABUIRI. Jan 16. Employees and servants who have been working over the holidays are given a day off.

MALAWI: JOHN CHILEMBWE DAY. Jan 16. National holiday. Commemorates an early martyr for independence who died in 1915.

NATIONAL NOTHING DAY. Jan 16. Anniversary of National Nothing Day, an event created by newspaperman Harold Pullman Coffin and first observed in 1973 "to provide Americans with one national day when they can just sit without celebrating, observing or honoring anything." Since 1975, though many other events have been listed on this day, lighthearted traditional observance of Coffin's idea has continued. Coffin, a native of Reno, NV, died at Capitola, CA, Sept 12, 1981.

PERSIAN GULF WAR BEGINS: ANNIVERSARY. Jan 16, 1991. Allied forces launched a major air offensive against Iraq to begin the Gulf War. The strike was designed to destroy Iraqi air defenses, command, control and communication centers. As Desert Shield became Desert Storm, the world was able to see and hear for the first time an initial engagement of war as CNN broadcasters, stationed at Baghdad, broadcast the attack live.

RELIGIOUS FREEDOM DAY. Jan 16, 1786. The legislature of Virginia adopted a religious freedom statute that protected Virginians against any requirement to attend or support any church and against discrimination. This statute, which had been drafted by Thomas Jefferson and introduced by James Madison, later was the model for the First Amendment to the US Constitution.

★ **RELIGIOUS FREEDOM DAY.** Jan 16. On the day of the adoption in 1786 of a religious freedom statute by the Virginia legislature.

BIRTHDAYS TODAY

Kate McMullan, 55, author (the Dragon Slayers' Academy Series), born St. Louis, MO, Jan 16, 1947.
Martha Weston, 55, author and illustrator (*Bad Baby Brother*), born Asheville, NC, Jan 16, 1947.

JANUARY 17 — THURSDAY

Day 17 — 348 Remaining

BELLAIRS, JOHN: BIRTH ANNIVERSARY. Jan 17, 1938. Author of mystery and horror novels for children, born at Marshall, MI. Some of his best-known books are *The House With a Clock in Its Walls* and *The Figure in the Shadows*, part of a series featuring the orphan Lewis Barnaveldt and his uncle, who is a witch. Another popular series features the character Johnny Dixon (*The Eyes of the Killer Robot*). Bellairs died at Haverhill, MA, Mar 8, 1991. After his death, many of his partial manuscripts were completed and published by writer Brad Strickland.

CORMIER, ROBERT: BIRTH ANNIVERSARY. Jan 17, 1925. Author of 18 critically acclaimed books for young adults, born in Leominster, MA. Among his most significant works are *The Chocolate War, We All Fall Down*, and *Tunes for Bears to Dance To*. He was known for many years to accept telephone calls from his young readers who felt lonely or distraught. In fact, he published his home phone number in his 1977 novel *I Am the Cheese*. He died Nov 2, 2000 at Leominster, MA.

FIRST NUCLEAR-POWERED SUBMARINE VOYAGE: ANNIVERSARY. Jan 17, 1955. The world's first nuclear-powered submarine, the *Nautilus*, now forms part of the *Nautilus* Memorial Submarine Force Library and Museum at the Naval Submarine Base New London at Groton, CT. At 11 AM, EST, her commanding officer, Commander Eugene P. Wilkerson, ordered all lines cast off and sent the historic message: "Under way on nuclear power." Highlights of the *Nautilus*: keel laid by President Harry S Truman June 14, 1952; christened and launched by Mrs Dwight D. Eisenhower Jan 21, 1954; commissioned to the US Navy Sept 30, 1954.

FRANKLIN, BENJAMIN: BIRTH ANNIVERSARY. Jan 17, 1706. "Elder statesman of the American Revolution," oldest signer of both the Declaration of Independence and the Constitution, scientist, diplomat, author, printer, publisher, philosopher, philanthropist and self-made, self-educated man. Author, printer and publisher of *Poor Richard's Almanack* (1733–58). Born at Boston, MA, Franklin died at Philadelphia, PA, Apr 17, 1790. In 1728 Franklin wrote a premature epitaph for himself. It first appeared in print in Ames's 1771 almanac: "The Body of BENJAMIN FRANKLIN/Printer/Like a Covering of an old Book/Its contents torn out/And stript of its Lettering and Gilding,/Lies here, Food for Worms;/But the work shall not be lost,/It will (as he believ'd) appear once more/In a New and more beautiful Edition/Corrected and amended/By the Author." For more info: *The Amazing Life of Benjamin Franklin*, by James Cross Giblin (Scholastic, 0-590-48534-2, $17.95 Gr. 4–6).

JAPAN SUFFERS MAJOR EARTHQUAKE: ANNIVERSARY. Jan 17, 1995. Japan suffered its second most deadly earthquake in the 20th century when a 20-second temblor left 5,500 dead and more than 21,600 people injured. The epicenter was six miles beneath Awaji Island at Osaka Bay. This was just 20 miles west of Kobe, Japan's sixth-largest city and a major port that accounted for 12 percent of the country's exports. Measuring 7.2 on the Richter scale, the quake collapsed or badly damaged more than 30,400 buildings and left 275,000 people homeless. For more info go to the National Earthquake Information Center: wwwneic.cr.usgs.gov.

LEWIS, SHARI: BIRTH ANNIVERSARY. Jan 17, 1934. Puppeteer Shari Lewis, creator of Lamb Chop and Charlie Horse, was born Shari Hurwitz at New York, NY. She died Aug 3, 1998, at Los Angeles, CA.

MEXICO: BLESSING OF THE ANIMALS AT THE CATHEDRAL. Jan 17. Church of San Antonio at Mexico City or Xochimilco provide best sights of chickens, cows and household pets gaily decorated with flowers. (Saint's day for San Antonio Abad, patron saint of domestic animals.)

SOUTHERN CALIFORNIA EARTHQUAKE: ANNIVERSARY. Jan 17, 1994. An earthquake measuring 6.6 on the Richter scale struck the Los Angeles area about 4:20 AM. The epicenter was at Northridge in the San Fernando Valley, about 20 miles northwest of downtown Los Angeles. The death toll was 51, 16 of whom were killed in the collapse of one apartment building. More than 25,000 people were made homeless by the quake. Many buildings were destroyed and others made uninhabitable due to structural damage. A section of the Santa Monica Freeway, part of the Simi Valley Freeway and three major overpasses collapsed. Hundreds of aftershocks occurred in the following several weeks. Costs to repair the damages were estimated at 15–30 billion dollars. For more info go to the National Earthquake Information Center: wwwneic.cr.usgs.gov.

BIRTHDAYS TODAY

Muhammad Ali, 60, former heavyweight champion boxer who changed his name after converting to Islam, born Cassius Marcellus Clay, Jr, Louisville, KY, Jan 17, 1942.

Jim Carrey, 40, actor (*Dumb and Dumber, Ace Ventura, How the Grinch Stole Christmas*), comedian, born Newmarket, ON, Canada, Jan 17, 1962.

Ruth Ann Minner, 67, Governor of Delaware (D), born Milford, DE, Jan 17, 1935.

January 2002

S	M	T	W	T	F	S
		1	2	3	4	5
6	7	8	9	10	11	12
13	14	15	16	17	18	19
20	21	22	23	24	25	26
27	28	29	30	31		

JANUARY 18 — FRIDAY

Day 18 — 347 Remaining

AMERICAN LIBRARY ASSOCIATION MIDWINTER MEETING. Jan 18–23. New Orleans, LA. For info: American Library Assn, 50 E Huron St, Chicago, IL 60611. Phone: (800) 545-2433. Web: www.ala.org.

ARBOR DAY IN FLORIDA. Jan 18. A ceremonial day on the third Friday in January.

FIRST BLACK US CABINET MEMBER: ANNIVERSARY. Jan 18, 1966. Robert Clifton Weaver was sworn in as Secretary of Housing and Urban Development, becoming the first black cabinet member in US history. He was nominated by President Lyndon Johnson. Born Dec 29, 1907 at Washington, DC, Weaver died at New York, NY, July 17, 1997.

LEE-JACKSON DAY IN VIRGINIA. Jan 18. Annually, the Friday preceding the third Monday in January. Honoring Robert E. Lee and Thomas (Stonewall) Jackson.

POOH DAY: A.A. MILNE: BIRTH ANNIVERSARY. Jan 18, 1882. Anniversary of the birth of A(lan) A(lexander) Milne, English author, especially remembered for his children's stories: *Winnie the Pooh* and *The House at Pooh Corner*. Also the author of *Mr Pim Passes By, When We Were Very Young* and *Now We Are Six*. Born at London, England, he died at Hartfield, England, Jan 31, 1956. For more info: www.kirjasto.sci.fi/aamilne.htm

RANSOME, ARTHUR: BIRTH ANNIVERSARY. Jan 18, 1884. Author, born at Leeds, Yorkshire, England. His children's books were based on his travels during his life and featured children whose parents could endulge them in long vacations. His works include *We Didn't Mean to Go to Sea, Secret Water* and *Swallows and Amazons*. He won the Carnegie Medal in 1936 for *The Pigeon Post*. Ransome died June 3, 1967.

ROGET, PETER MARK: BIRTH ANNIVERSARY. Jan 18, 1779. English physician, best known as author of Roget's *Thesaurus of English Words and Phrases*, first published in 1852. Roget was also the inventor of the "log-log" slide rule. Born at London, England, Roget died at West Malvern, Worcestershire, England, Sept 12, 1869.

BIRTHDAYS TODAY

Mark Messier, 41, hockey player, born Edmonton, AB, Canada, Jan 18, 1961.

Alan Schroeder, 41, author of biographies (*Ragtime Tumpie*), born Alameda, CA, Jan 18, 1961.

JANUARY 19 — SATURDAY

Day 19 — 346 Remaining

CÉZANNE, PAUL: BIRTH ANNIVERSARY. Jan 19, 1839. French post-Impressionist painter known for his landscapes, born at Aix-en-Provence, France. He died at Aix, Oct 22, 1906. For more info: *Cézanne from A to Z*, by Marie Sellier (Peter Bedrick, 0-87226-476-9, $14.95 All ages).

CONFEDERATE HEROES DAY. Jan 19. Observed on anniversary of Robert E. Lee's birthday. Official holiday in Texas.

ETHIOPIA: TIMKET. Jan 19. National holiday. Epiphany in the Coptic and Ethiopian Orthodox churches. The festival lasts through Jan 20 or 21. Also a holiday in Eritrea.

LEE, ROBERT E.: BIRTH ANNIVERSARY. Jan 19, 1807. Greatest military leader of the Confederacy, son of Revolutionary War general Henry (Light Horse Harry) Lee. His surrender Apr 9, 1865, to Union General Ulysses S. Grant brought an end to the Civil

JANUARY 19
EDGAR ALLAN POE'S BIRTHDAY

Edgar Allan Poe was born in Boston, Massachusetts, on January 19, 1809. He is known for his tales of horror and suspense and for his poetry. Many young people enjoy a good scare and because Poe's works deliver a fright-filled "punch" in a literary style, they are perfect for classroom use, particularly with junior high and high school students. The gloomy nature of Poe's writing is perfect for capturing student interest on a gray January day.

Have fun with Poe's poems by suggesting groups of students arrange specific poems for choral reading. "The Bells" has several stanzas. Each one presents a different type of bell. It has a marvelous chorus that changes slightly according to which kind of bell the stanza portrays. The bells themselves gradually change from cheery to gloomy. This is also an opportunity to introduce the literary term onomatopoeia.

"The Raven" is probably Poe's most famous poem. Not only is it appropriate for choral reading arrangements, but it also contains some fantastic, unusual vocabulary. Lattice, beguiling, countenance, melancholy, seraphim, and phrases such as "Plutonian shore," are exotic language for many students. Send them on a quest to explain the literary roots of Plutonian shore. The same vocabulary treasures hold true for "The Bells"—euphony and tintinnabulation are two examples.

Read stories such as "The Tell-Tale Heart." Students might want to try their hand at rewriting a portion of them as Reader's Theater or as a play script.

Incorporate music into the curriculum by asking students to chose music they feel best complements the mood of Poe's work. Music that would suit the poem "Annabel Lee" would be vastly different than that used for "The Fall of the House of Usher."

Art projects could include student drawings of how they imagine the houses in Poe's short stories to look.

One final note: Some students feel Poe is going to be boring because he has written works that are deemed classics. However, seventh graders begin nervously biting their nails when Poe's suspense stories are read aloud. That's when you know the story is a success!

War. Born at Westmoreland County, VA, he died at Lexington, VA, Oct 12, 1870. His birthday is observed in Florida, Kentucky, Louisiana, South Carolina and Tennessee. Observed on third Monday in January in Alabama, Arkansas and Mississippi (Jan 21 in 2002).

MINORITY SCIENTISTS SHOWCASE. Jan 19–21. St. Louis, MO. Open new doors to future science careers and interests during Martin Luther King, Jr, weekend with hands-on activities and information available as part of a free program. Meet and talk with African Americans working in science-related fields throughout the St. Louis area. Annually, Martin Luther King, Jr weekend. Est attendance: 2,000. For info: Bev Pfeifer-Harms, St. Louis Science Center, 5050 Oakland Ave, St. Louis, MO 63110. Phone: (314) 289-4419. Fax: (314) 533-8687. E-mail: bpharms@slsc.org. Web: www.slsc.org.

PHILIPPINES: ATI-ATIHAN FESTIVAL. Jan 19–20. Kalibo, Aklan. One of the most colorful celebrations in the Philippines, the Ati-Atihan Festival commemorates the peace pact between the Ati of Panay (pygmies) and the Malays, who were early migrants in the islands. The townspeople blacken their bodies with soot, don colorful and bizarre costumes and sing and dance in the streets. The festival also celebrates the Feast Day of Santo Niño (the infant Jesus). Annually, the third weekend in January.

POE, EDGAR ALLAN: BIRTH ANNIVERSARY. Jan 19, 1809. American poet and story writer, called "America's most famous man of letters." Born at Boston, MA, he was orphaned in dire poverty in 1811 and was raised by Virginia merchant John Allan. A magazine editor of note, he is best remembered for his poetry (especially "The Raven") and for his tales of suspense. Died at Baltimore, MD, Oct 7, 1849. *See* Curriculum Connection.

TIN CAN PATENT: ANNIVERSARY. Jan 19, 1825. Ezra Daggett and Thomas Kensett obtained a patent for a process for storing food in tin cans.

BIRTHDAYS TODAY

Nina Bawden, 77, author (*Carrie's War*), born London, England, Jan 19, 1925.

Jodie Sweetin, 20, actress ("Full House"), born Los Angeles, CA, Jan 19, 1982.

Will Weaver, 52, author (*Farm Team, Striking Out*), born Park Rapids, MN, Jan 19, 1950.

JANUARY 20 — SUNDAY

Day 20 — 345 Remaining

AQUARIUS, THE WATER CARRIER. Jan 20–Feb 19. In the astronomical/astrological zodiac, which divides the sun's apparent orbit into 12 segments, the period Jan 20–Feb 19 is identified, traditionally, as the sun-sign of Aquarius, the Water Carrier. The ruling planet is Uranus or Saturn.

AZERBAIJAN: DAY OF THE MARTYRS. Jan 20. National holiday. Commemorates Azeri civilians killed by Soviets in fight for independence in 1990.

BRAZIL: NOSSO SENHOR DO BONFIM FESTIVAL. Jan 20–30. Salvador, Bahia, Brazil. Our Lord of the Happy Ending Festival is one of Salvador's most colorful religious feasts. Climax comes with people carrying water to pour over church stairs and sidewalks to cleanse them of impurities.

CAMCORDER DEVELOPED: 20th ANNIVERSARY. Jan 20, 1982. Five companies (Hitachi, JVC, Philips, Matsushita and Sony) agreed to cooperate on the construction of a camera with a built-in videocassette recorder.

GUINEA-BISSAU: NATIONAL HEROES DAY. Jan 20. National holiday.

JORDAN: KING'S BIRTHDAY. Jan 30. National holiday. Commemorates the birth of King Abdullah II in 1962.

LEE, RICHARD HENRY: BIRTH ANNIVERSARY. Jan 20, 1732. Signer of the Declaration of Independence. Born at Westmoreland County, VA, he died June 19, 1794, at his birthplace.

US REVOLUTIONARY WAR: CESSATION OF HOSTILITIES: ANNIVERSARY. Jan 20, 1783. The British and US Commissioners signed a preliminary "Cessation of Hostilities," which was ratified by England's King George III Feb 14 and led to the Treaties of Paris and Versailles, Sept 3, 1783, ending the war.

WORLD RELIGION DAY. Jan 20. To proclaim the oneness of religion and the belief that world religion will unify the peoples of the earth. Baha'i-sponsored observance established in 1950. Annually, the third Sunday in January. For info: Office of Public Information, Baha'is of the US, 866 UN Plaza, Ste 120, New York, NY 10017-1822. Phone: (212) 803-2500. Fax: (212) 803-2573. E-mail: usopi-ny@bic.org. Web: www.us.bahai.org.

BIRTHDAYS TODAY

Edwin (Buzz) Aldrin, 72, former astronaut, one of first three men on moon, born Montclair, NJ, Jan 20, 1930.

JANUARY 21 — MONDAY

Day 21 — 344 Remaining

ALLEN, ETHAN: BIRTH ANNIVERSARY. Jan 21, 1738. Revolutionary War hero and leader of the Vermont "Green Mountain Boys." Born at Litchfield, CT, he died at Burlington, VT, Feb 12, 1789.

BRECKINRIDGE, JOHN CABELL: BIRTH ANNIVERSARY. Jan 21, 1821. The 14th vice president of the US (1857–61), serving under President James Buchanan. Born at Lexington, KY, he died there May 17, 1875.

DO SOMETHING: KINDNESS & JUSTICE CHALLENGE. Jan 21–Feb 1. More than two million students perform Acts of Kindness (helping others) and Justice (standing up for what is right) in honor of the Martin Luther King, Jr, national holiday. For two weeks, starting on the Martin Luther King, Jr holiday, K–12 students write down the Acts of Kindness and Justice they perform and post their lists on the Internet. Each school that performs 1,000 or more acts will receive special recognition. A free guide with grade-appropriate curriculum is available for teachers. For info: Do Something, 423 W 55th St, 8th flr, New York, NY 10019. E-mail: mail@dosomething.org. Web: www.dosomething.org.

FIRST CONCORDE FLIGHT: ANNIVERSARY. Jan 21, 1976. The supersonic Concorde airplane was put into service by Britain and France.

JACKSON, THOMAS JONATHAN "STONEWALL": BIRTH ANNIVERSARY. Jan 21, 1824. Confederate general and one of the most famous soldiers of the American Civil War, best known as "Stonewall" Jackson. Born at Clarksburg, VA (now WV), Jackson died of wounds received in battle near Chancellorsville, VA, May 10, 1863.

KING, MARTIN LUTHER, JR: BIRTHDAY OBSERVED. Jan 21. Public Law 98–144 designates the third Monday in January as an annual legal public holiday observing the birth of Martin Luther King, Jr. First observed in 1986. In New Hampshire, this day is designated Civil Rights Day. See also: "King, Martin Luther, Jr: Birth Anniversary" (Jan 15). For links to sites on the Web about Dr. King, go to: deil.lang.uiuc.edu/web.pages/holidays/king.html.

★ **MARTIN LUTHER KING, JR FEDERAL HOLIDAY.** Jan 21. Presidential Proclamation has been issued without request each year for the third Monday in January since 1986.

MOON PHASE: FIRST QUARTER. Jan 21. Moon enters First Quarter phase at 12:46 PM, EST.

BIRTHDAYS TODAY

Hakeem Abdul Olajuwon, 39, basketball player, born Lagos, Nigeria, Jan 21, 1963.

January 2002

S	M	T	W	T	F	S
		1	2	3	4	5
6	7	8	9	10	11	12
13	14	15	16	17	18	19
20	21	22	23	24	25	26
27	28	29	30	31		

JANUARY 22 — TUESDAY

Day 22 — 343 Remaining

ANSWER YOUR CAT'S QUESTION DAY. Jan 22. If you will stop what you are doing and take a look at your cat, you will observe that the cat is looking at you with a serious question. Meditate upon it, then answer the question! Annually, Jan 22. [© 1999 by WH] For info: Tom or Ruth Roy, Wellcat Holidays, 2418 Long Ln, Lebanon, PA 17046. Phone: (717) 279-0184. E-mail: wellcat@supernet.com. Web: www.wellcat.com.

UKRAINE: UKRAINIAN DAY. Jan 22. National holiday. Commemorates 1918 proclamation of the republic.

VINSON, FRED M.: BIRTH ANNIVERSARY. Jan 22, 1890. The 13th Chief Justice of the US Supreme Court, born at Louisa, KY. Served in the House of Representatives, appointed Director of War Mobilization during WWII and Secretary of the Treasury under Harry Truman. Nominated by Truman to succeed Harlan F. Stone as Chief Justice. Died at Washington, DC, Sept 8, 1953.

BIRTHDAYS TODAY

Sheila Gordon, 75, author (*Waiting for the Rain*), born Johannesburg, South Africa, Jan 22, 1927.

Blair Lent, 72, author and illustrator (*Tikki Tikki Tembo*), born Boston, MA, Jan 22, 1930.

Rafe Martin, 56, author (*The Boy Who Lived with the Seals*), born Rochester, NY, Jan 22, 1946.

Beverly Mitchell, 21, actress (*Mother of the Bride*, "7th Heaven"), born Arcadia, CA, Jan 22, 1981.

JANUARY 23 — WEDNESDAY

Day 23 — 342 Remaining

BLACKWELL, ELIZABETH, AWARDED MD: ANNIVERSARY. Jan 23, 1849. Dr. Elizabeth Blackwell became the first woman to receive an MD degree. The native of Bristol, England, was awarded her degree by the Medical Institution of Geneva, NY. For more info: *Elizabeth Blackwell: The First Woman Doctor*, by Ira Peck (Millbrook, 0-7613-1854-2, $21.90 Gr. 4–7).

HEWES, JOSEPH: BIRTH ANNIVERSARY. Jan 23, 1730. Signer of the Declaration of Independence. Born at Princeton, NJ, he died Nov 10, 1779, at Philadelphia, PA.

MANET, ÉDOUARD: BIRTH ANNIVERSARY. Jan 23, 1832. French artist (*Déjeuner dur l'herbe, Olympia*), born at Paris, France. He died at Paris, Apr 30, 1883.

NATIONAL COMPLIMENT DAY. Jan 23. This day is set aside to compliment at least five people. Not only are compliments appreciated by the receiver, they lift the spirit of the giver. Compliments provide a quick and easy way to connect positively with those you come in contact with. Giving compliments forges bonds, dispels loneliness and just plain feels good. Annually, the fourth Wednesday in January. For info: Deborah Hoffman, Positive Results Seminars, 12 Campion Circle, Concord, NH 03303-3410. Phone: (603) 225-0991. E-mail: prseminars@compuserve.com or Katherine Chamberlin, Heart to Heart Seminars, 724 Park Ave, Contoocook, NH 03229-3089. Phone: (603) 746-6227. E-mail: Kathiecham@aol.com.

NATIONAL SCHOOL NURSE DAY. Jan 23. A day to honor and recognize the school nurse, School Nurse Day has been established to foster a better understanding of the role of school nurses in the educational setting. Annually, the fourth Wednesday in January. Brochures available for purchase. For info: Judy Barker, Adm Asst, Natl Assn of School Nurses, Inc, PO Box 1300, Scarborough,

JANUARY 23
SCHOOL NURSE DAY

Many students, particularly elementary children, think of the school nurse as "that person who checks our hair with a tongue depressor." (We all know what she's checking for.) However, school nurses do play an important role in children's lives while they are on school property.

To acknowledge this day, it would be helpful to ask your school nurse to schedule 5-to-10 minute long visits to the classroom, spread out over the course of a few days. During that time she or he can be introduced to the students (an assembly introduction at the beginning of the school year has lost its impact by January). The nurse should briefly describe her/his role in the school: Explain how the school's thermometer works, what first aid measures are available for playground injury and what procedures students should use if they need to take a prescribed medication. Unfortunately, many children do not listen carefully during assemblies on these topics and explanatory papers sent home often get lost or misfiled.

A classroom visit is a perfect time to reinforce the importance of eating a good breakfast and getting exercise to maintain alert minds. Cold season is in full swing during January, so it's a good opportunity for discussing the use of tissues, clean hands and the importance of covering your mouth while sneezing. Depending on district policy and the age of the students, the nurse might want to mention she/he is available if a child is suffering a personal health concern. In this case, the nurse may be the first person a student might feel comfortable approaching, particularly if abuse is an issue.

As part of this day, it would be kind if classes sent short notes of appreciation to their school nurse. Hearing from healthy, happy students is a pleasant change from runny noses and will brighten the nurse's day. Everyone needs a pat on the back from time to time.

ME 04070-1300. Phone: (207) 883-2117. Fax: (207) 883-2683. E-mail: nasnweb@aol.com. *See* Curriculum Connection.

STEWART, POTTER: BIRTH ANNIVERSARY. Jan 23, 1915. Associate Justice of the Supreme Court of the US, nominated by President Eisenhower, Jan 17, 1959. (Oath of office, May 15, 1959.) Born at Jackson, MI, he retired in July 1981 and died Dec 7, 1985, at Putney, VT. Buried at Arlington National Cemetery. For more info: oyez.northwestern.edu/justices/justices.cgi.

TWENTIETH AMENDMENT TO US CONSTITUTION RATIFIED: ANNIVERSARY. Jan 23, 1933. The 20th Amendment was ratified, fixing the date of the presidential inauguration at the current Jan 20 instead of the previous Mar 4. It also specified that were the president-elect to die before taking office, the vice president-elect would succeed to the presidency. In addition, it set Jan 3 as the official opening date of Congress each year.

TWENTY-FOURTH AMENDMENT TO US CONSTITUTION RATIFIED: ANNIVERSARY. Jan 23, 1964. Poll taxes and other taxes were eliminated as a prerequisite for voting in all federal elections by the 24th Amendment.

BIRTHDAYS TODAY

Tom Carper, 55, US Senator (D, Delaware), born Beckley, WV, Jan 23, 1947.

Katherine Holabird, 54, author (the Angelina Ballerina series), born Cambridge, MA, Jan 23, 1948.

JANUARY 24 — THURSDAY

Day 24 — 341 Remaining

BOLIVIA: ALACITIS FAIR. Jan 24–26. La Paz. Traditional annual celebration by Aymara Indians with prayers and offerings to god of prosperity.

CALIFORNIA GOLD DISCOVERY: ANNIVERSARY. Jan 24, 1848. James W. Marshal, an employee of John Sutter, accidentally discovered gold while building a sawmill near Coloma, CA. Efforts to keep the discovery secret failed, and the gold rush got under way in 1849. Had the gold rush not occurred, it might have taken California years to reach the population of 60,000 necessary for statehood, but the 49ers increased the population beyond that figure in one year and in 1850 California became a state.

BIRTHDAYS TODAY

Tatyana M. Ali, 23, actress ("Sesame Street," "The Fresh Prince of Bel Air"), born Long Island, NY, Jan 24, 1979.

Mary Lou Retton, 34, Olympic gold medal gymnast, born Fairmont, WV, Jan 24, 1968.

JANUARY 25 — FRIDAY

Day 25 — 340 Remaining

CURTIS, CHARLES: BIRTH ANNIVERSARY. Jan 25, 1860. The 31st vice president of the US (1929–33). Born at Topeka, KS, he died at Washington, DC, Feb 8, 1936.

FIRST SCHEDULED TRANSCONTINENTAL FLIGHT: ANNIVERSARY. Jan 25, 1959. American Airlines opened the jet age in the US with the first scheduled transcontinental flight on a Boeing 707 nonstop from California to New York.

FIRST WINTER OLYMPICS: ANNIVERSARY. Jan 25, 1924. The First Winter Olympics took place at Chamonix, France, with 16 nations participating. The ski jump, previously unknown, thrilled spectators. The Olympics offered a boost to skiing, which would become much more popular during the next decade.

MACINTOSH COMPUTER RELEASED: ANNIVERSARY. Jan 25, 1984. Apple Computer released its new Macintosh model on this day, which eventually replaced the Apple II. The new computer sold for $2,495.

BIRTHDAYS TODAY

Conrad Burns, 67, US Senator (R, Montana), born Gallatin, MO, Jan 25, 1935.

Chris Chelios, 40, hockey player, born Chicago, IL, Jan 25, 1962.

Debbi Chocolate, 48, author (*A Very Special Kwanzaa, Kente Colors*), born Chicago, IL. Jan 25, 1954.

Christine Lakin, 23, actress ("Step By Step"), born Dallas, TX, Jan 25, 1979.

JANUARY 26 — SATURDAY

Day 26 — 339 Remaining

AUSTRALIA: AUSTRALIA DAY—FIRST BRITISH SETTLEMENT. Jan 26, 1788. A shipload of convicts arrived briefly at Botany Bay (which proved to be unsuitable) and then at Port Jackson (later the site of the city of Sydney). Establishment of an Australian prison colony was to relieve crowding of British prisons. Australia Day, formerly known as Foundation Day or Anniversary Day, has been observed since about 1817 and has been a public holiday since 1838.

COLEMAN, BESSIE: BIRTH ANNIVERSARY. Jan 26, 1893. The first African American to receive a pilot's license, Coleman had to go to France to study flying, since she was denied admission to aviation schools in the US because of her race and sex. She took part in acrobatic air exhibitions where her stunt-flying and figure eights won her many admirers. Born at Atlanta, TX, she died in a plane crash at Jacksonville, FL, Apr 30, 1926. For more info: *Fly, Bessie, Fly*, by Lynn Joseph (Simon & Schuster, 0-689-81339-2, $16 Gr. 1–4).

DENTAL DRILL PATENT: ANNIVERSARY. Jan 26, 1875. George F. Green, of Kalamazoo, MI, patented the electric dental drill.

DODGE, MARY MAPES: BIRTH ANNIVERSARY. Jan 26, 1831. Children's author, known for her book *Hans Brinker or, The Silver Skates*. Born at New York, NY, she died at Ontenora Park, NY, Aug 21, 1905.

DOMINICAN REPUBLIC: NATIONAL HOLIDAY. Jan 26. An official public holiday celebrates the birth anniversary of Juan Pablo Duarte, one of the fathers of the republic.

FRANKLIN PREFERS TURKEY: ANNIVERSARY. Jan 26, 1784. In a letter to his daughter, Benjamin Franklin expressed his unhappiness over the choice of the eagle as the symbol of America. He preferred the turkey. "I wish the bald eagle had not been chosen as the representative of our country; he is a bird of bad moral character; like those among men who live by sharping and robbing; he is generally poor, and often very lousy. The turkey is a much more respectable bird, and withal a true original native of America."

GRANT, JULIA DENT: BIRTH ANNIVERSARY. Jan 26, 1826. Wife of Ulysses Simpson Grant, 18th president of the US. Born at St. Louis, MO, died at Washington, DC, Dec 14, 1902.

INDIA: REPUBLIC DAY. Jan 26. National holiday. Anniversary of Proclamation of the Republic, Basant Panchmi. In 1929, Indian National Congress resolved to work for establishment of a sovereign republic, a goal that was realized Jan 26, 1950, when India became a democratic republic.

MICHIGAN: ADMISSION DAY: ANNIVERSARY. Jan 26. Michigan became 26th state in 1837.

ROCKY MOUNTAIN NATIONAL PARK ESTABLISHED: ANNIVERSARY. Jan 26, 1915. Under President Woodrow Wilson, the area covering more than 1,000 square miles in Colorado became a national park. For more info: www.nps.gov/romo/index.htm.

January 2002

S	M	T	W	T	F	S
		1	2	3	4	5
6	7	8	9	10	11	12
13	14	15	16	17	18	19
20	21	22	23	24	25	26
27	28	29	30	31		

BIRTHDAYS TODAY

Mark Dayton, 55, US Senator (D, Minnesota), born Minneapolis, MN, Jan 26, 1947.

Jules Feiffer, 73, author (*The Man in the Ceiling; Bark, George*), illustrator (*The Phantom Tollbooth*), born Bronx, NY, Jan 26, 1949.

Wayne Gretzky, 41, Hall of Fame hockey player, born Brantford, ON, Canada, Jan 26, 1961.

JANUARY 27 — SUNDAY

Day 27 — 338 Remaining

***APOLLO I*: SPACECRAFT FIRE: 35th ANNIVERSARY.** Jan 27, 1967. Three American astronauts, Virgil I. Grissom, Edward H. White and Roger B. Chaffee, died when fire suddenly broke out at 6:31 PM in *Apollo I* during a launching simulation test, as it stood on the ground at Cape Kennedy, FL, Jan 27, 1967. First launching in the Apollo program had been scheduled for Feb 27, 1967.

CARROLL, LEWIS: BIRTH ANNIVERSARY. Jan 27, 1832. Pseudonym of English mathematician and author, born Charles Lutwidge Dodgson at Cheshire, England. Best known for his children's classic, *Alice's Adventures in Wonderland*. *Alice* was written for Alice Liddell, daughter of a friend, and first published in 1886. *Through the Looking-Glass*, a sequel, and *The Hunting of the Snark* followed. Carroll's books for children proved equally enjoyable to adults, and they overshadowed his serious works on mathematics. He died at Guildford, Surrey, England, Jan 14, 1898. For more info: www.lewiscarroll.org/k12.html.

CATHOLIC SCHOOLS WEEK. Jan 27–Feb 2. Jointly sponsored by the National Catholic Educational Association and the US Catholic Conference. Annually, beginning on the last Sunday in January. For info: Natl Catholic Educational Assn, 1077 30th St NW, Ste 100, Washington, DC 20007-3852. Phone: (202) 337-6232. E-mail: nceaadmin@ncea.org. Web: www.ncea.org.

MOZART, WOLFGANG AMADEUS: BIRTH ANNIVERSARY. Jan 27, 1756. One of the world's greatest music makers. Born at Salzburg, Austria, into a gifted musical family, Mozart began performing at age three and composing at age five. Some of the best known of his more than 600 compositions include the operas *Marriage of Figaro, Don Giovanni, Cosi fan tutte* and *The Magic Flute*, his unfinished Requiem Mass, his C major symphony known as the "Jupiter" and many quartets and piano concertos. He died at Vienna, Dec 5, 1791.

SUPER BOWL XXXVI. Jan 27. New Orleans, LA. The battle between the NFC and AFC champions. Annually, the last Sunday in January. For info: PR Dept, The Natl Football League, 410 Park Ave, New York, NY 10022. Web: www.superbowl.com or www.playfootball.com.

VIETNAM PEACE AGREEMENT SIGNED: ANNIVERSARY. Jan 27, 1973. US and North Vietnam, along with South Vietnam and the Viet Cong, signed an "Agreement on ending the war and restoring peace in Vietnam." Signed at Paris, France, to take effect Jan 28 at 8 AM Saigon time, thus ending US combat role in a war that had involved American personnel stationed in Vietnam since defeated French forces had departed under terms of the Geneva Accords in 1954. This was the longest war in US history with more than one million combat deaths (US: 47,366). However, within weeks of the departure of American troops the war between North and South Vietnam resumed. For the Vietnamese, the war didn't end until Apr 30, 1975, when Saigon fell to Communist forces.

BIRTHDAYS TODAY

Harry Allard, 74, author, with James Marshall (*Miss Nelson Is Missing!*), born Evanston, IL, Jan 27, 1928.

James M. Deem, 52, author (*Bodies from the Bog*), born Wheeling, WV, Jan 27, 1950.

Julie Foudy, 31, soccer player, born San Diego, CA, Jan 27, 1971.

Laura McGee Kvasnosky, 51, author (*Zelda and Ivy*), born Sacramento, CA, Jan 27, 1951.

Julius B. Lester, 63, author (*To Be a Slave, Black Folktales*), born St. Louis, MO, Jan 27, 1939.

Janice VanCleave, 60, author (*Guide to the Best Science Fair Projects; 200 Gooey, Slippery, Slimy, Weird and Fun Experiments; Biology for Every Kid*), born Houston, TX, Jan 27, 1942.

JANUARY 28 — MONDAY

Day 28 — 337 Remaining

***CHALLENGER* SPACE SHUTTLE EXPLOSION: ANNIVERSARY.** Jan 28, 1986. At 11:39 AM, EST, the Space Shuttle *Challenger STS-51L* exploded, 74 seconds into its flight and about 10 miles above the earth. Hundreds of millions around the world watched television replays of the horrifying event that killed seven people, destroyed the billion-dollar craft, suspended all shuttle flights and halted, at least temporarily, much of the US manned space flight program. Killed were teacher Christa McAuliffe (who was to have been the first ordinary citizen in space) and six crew members: Francis R. Scobee, Michael J. Smith, Judith A. Resnik, Ellison S. Onizuka, Ronald E. McNair and Gregory B. Jarvis.

MacKENZIE, ALEXANDER: BIRTH ANNIVERSARY. Jan 28, 1822. The man who became the first Liberal prime minister of Canada (1873–78) was born at Logierait, Perth, Scotland. He died at Toronto, Apr 17, 1892.

MARTÍ, JOSÉ JULIAN: BIRTH ANNIVERSARY. Jan 28, 1853. Cuban author and political activist, born at Havana, Cuba. Martí was exiled to Spain, where he studied law before coming to the US in 1890. He was killed in battle at Dos Rios, Cuba, May 19, 1895.

MOON PHASE: FULL MOON. Jan 28. Moon enters Full Moon phase at 5:50 PM, EST.

PICCARD, AUGUSTE: BIRTH ANNIVERSARY. Jan 28, 1884. Scientist and explorer, born at Basel, Switzerland. Record-setting balloon ascents into stratosphere and ocean depth descents and explorations. Twin brother of Jean Felix Piccard. Died at Lausanne, Switzerland, Mar 24, 1962. See also: "Piccard, Jeannette Ridlon: Birth Anniversary" (Jan 5) and "Piccard, Auguste: Birth Anniversary" (Jan 28).

PICCARD, JEAN FELIX: BIRTH ANNIVERSARY. Jan 28, 1884. Scientist, engineer, explorer, born at Basel, Switzerland. Noted for cosmic-ray research and record-setting balloon ascensions into stratosphere. Reached 57,579 ft in sealed gondola piloted by his wife, Jeannette, in 1934. Twin brother of Auguste Piccard. Died at Minneapolis, MN, Jan 28, 1963. See also: "Piccard, Jeannette Ridlon: Birth Anniversary" (Jan 5) and "Piccard, Auguste: Birth Anniversary" (Jan 28).

TU B'SHVAT. Jan 28. Hebrew calendar date: Shebat 15, 5762. The 15th day of the month of Shebat in the Hebrew calendar year is set aside as Hamishah Asar (New Year of the Trees or Jewish Arbor Day), a time to show respect and appreciation for trees and plants.

BIRTHDAYS TODAY

Nick Carter, 22, singer (Backstreet Boys), born Jamestown, NY, Jan 28, 1980.

Daunte Culpepper, 25, football player, born Ocala, FL, Jan 28, 1977.

Joey Fatone, 25, singer ('N Sync), born Brooklyn, NY, Jan 28, 1977.

Jeanne Shaheen, 55, Governor of New Hampshire (D), born St. Charles, MO, Jan 28, 1947.

Vera B. Williams, 75, author and illustrator (*A Chair for My Mother*), born Hollywood, CA, Jan 28, 1927.

Elijah Wood, 21, actor (*Flipper, Deep Impact*), born Cedar Rapids, IA, Jan 28, 1981.

JANUARY 29 — TUESDAY

Day 29 — 336 Remaining

KANSAS: ADMISSION DAY: ANNIVERSARY. Jan 29. Became the 34th state in 1861.

McKINLEY, WILLIAM: BIRTH ANNIVERSARY. Jan 29, 1843. The 25th president (Mar 4, 1897–Sept 14, 1901) of the US, born at Niles, OH. Died in office, at Buffalo, NY, Sept 14, 1901, as the result of a gunshot wound by an anarchist assassin Sept 6, 1901, while he was attending the Pan-American Exposition. For info: www.ipl.org/ref/POTUS.

NATIONAL PUZZLE DAY. Jan 29. To recognize puzzles and games and their creators. Call or write for free information on the origins and creators of puzzles and games. For info: Carol Handz, Jodi Jill Features, 1705 14th St, Ste 321, Boulder, CO 80302. Phone: (303) 876-9849. Fax: (303) 786-9401. E-mail: jjillone@aol.com.

SCOTLAND: UP HELLY AA. Jan 29. Lerwick, Shetland Islands. Norse galley burned in impressive ceremony symbolizing sacrifice to the sun. Old Viking custom. Annually, the last Tuesday in January. Tourist Information Centre, Market Cross, Lerwick, Shetland, Scotland ZE1 0LU. Phone: (44) (1595) 693434. Fax: (44) (1595) 695807.

BIRTHDAYS TODAY

Christopher Collier, 72, author of historical fiction, with his brother James Lincoln Collier (*My Brother Sam Is Dead*), born New York, NY, Jan 29, 1930.

Dominik Hasek, 37, hockey player, born Pardubice, Czech Republic, Jan 29, 1965.

Andrew Keegan, 23, actor ("Party of Five"), born Shadow Hills, CA, Jan 29, 1979.

Ronald Stacey King, 35, basketball player, born Lawton, OK, Jan 29, 1967.

Bill Peet, 87, author and illustrator (*Whingdingdilly, The Wump World*), born Grandview, IN, Jan 29, 1915.

Jason James Richter, 22, actor (*Free Willy*), born Medford, OR, Jan 29, 1980.

Rosemary Wells, 59, author and illustrator (*Noisy Nora, Benjamin and Tulip*, the Max and Ruby series), born New York, NY, Jan 29, 1943.

Oprah Winfrey, 48, TV talk show hostess (Emmys for "The Oprah Winfrey Show"), actress (*Beloved*), born Kosciusko, MS, Jan 29, 1954.

JANUARY 30 — WEDNESDAY

Day 30 — 335 Remaining

NATIONAL INANE ANSWERING MESSAGE DAY. Jan 30. Annually, the day set aside to change, shorten, replace or delete those ridiculous and/or annoying answering machine messages that waste the time of anyone who must listen to them. [© 1999 by WH]. For info: Thomas and Ruth Roy, Wellcat Holidays, 2418 Long Ln, Lebanon, PA 17046. Phone: (717) 279-0184. E-mail: wellcat@supernet.com. Web: www.wellcat.com.

OSCEOLA: DEATH ANNIVERSARY. Jan 30, 1838. Native American leader during the Second Seminole War (1835–42), he led the fight against the removal of the Florida Seminoles to Indian territory. He was captured under a flag of truce in 1837 and imprisoned at Fort Marion in St. Augustine. He was moved to Fort Moultrie at Charleston Harbor, SC, where he died. He was born near present-day Tuskegee, AL, ca. 1804.

ROOSEVELT, FRANKLIN DELANO: BIRTH ANNIVERSARY. Jan 30, 1882. The 32nd president of the US, Roosevelt was the only president to serve more than two terms, FDR was elected four times. Term of office: Mar 4, 1933–Apr 12, 1945. He supported the Allies in WWII before the US entered the struggle by supplying them with war materials through the Lend-Lease Act; he became deeply involved in broad decision making after the Japanese attack on Pearl Harbor Dec 7, 1941. Born at Hyde Park, NY, he died a few months into his fourth term at Warm Springs, GA, Apr 12, 1945. For info: www.ipl.org/ref/POTUS.

BIRTHDAYS TODAY

Lloyd Alexander, 78, author (*The Black Cauldron*, Newbery for *The High King*), born Philadelphia, PA, Jan 30, 1924.

Richard (Dick) Cheney, 61, 46th vice president of the US, born Lincoln, NE, Jan 30, 1941.

Allan W. Eckert, 71, author (*Incident at Hawk's Hill*), born Buffalo, NY, Jan 30, 1931.

Guy Gilchrist, 45, author, illustrator, cartoonist (*Mudpie, Tiny Dinos*), with his brother Brad Gilchrist, born Winsted, CT, Jan 30, 1957.

Polly Horvath, 45, author (*The Trolls*), born Kalamazoo, MI, Jan 30, 1957.

Tony Johnston, 60, author (*The Magic Maguey*), born Los Angeles, CA, Jan 30, 1942.

Frank O'Bannon, 72, Governor of Indiana (D), born Louisville, KY, Jan 30, 1930.

JANUARY 31 — THURSDAY

Day 31 — 334 Remaining

McDONALD'S INVADES THE SOVIET UNION: ANNIVERSARY. Jan 31, 1990. McDonald's Corporation opened its first fast-food restaurant in the Soviet Union.

MORRIS, ROBERT: BIRTH ANNIVERSARY. Jan 31, 1734. Signer of the Declaration of Independence, the Articles of Confederation and the Constitution. One of only two men to sign all three documents. Born at Liverpool, England, he died May 7, 1806, at Philadelphia, PA.

NAURU: NATIONAL HOLIDAY. Jan 31. Republic of Nauru. Commemorates independence in 1968 from a UN trusteeship administered by Australia, New Zealand and the UK.

ROBINSON, JACKIE: BIRTH ANNIVERSARY. Jan 31, 1919. Jack Roosevelt Robinson, athlete and business executive, first black to enter professional major league baseball (Brooklyn Dodgers, 1947–56). Voted National League's Most Valuable Player in 1949 and elected to the Baseball Hall of Fame in 1962. Born at Cairo, GA, Robinson died at Stamford, CT, Oct 24, 1972.

SPACE MILESTONE: *EXPLORER 1* (US). Jan 31, 1958. The first successful US satellite. Although launched four months later than the Soviet Union's *Sputnik*, *Explorer* reached a higher altitude and detected a zone of intense radiation inside Earth's magnetic field. This was later named the Van Allen radiation belts. More than 65 subsequent *Explorer* satellites were launched through 1984.

SPACE MILESTONE: PROJECT MERCURY TEST (US). Jan 31, 1961. A test of Project Mercury spacecraft accomplished the first US recovery of a large animal from space. Ham, the chimpanzee, successfully performed simple tasks in space.

BIRTHDAYS TODAY

Queen Beatrix, 64, Queen of the Netherlands, born Sostdijk, Netherlands, Jan 31, 1938.

Denise Fleming, 52, author (*In the Small, Small Pond*), born Toledo, OH, Jan 31, 1950.

Gerald McDermott, 61, illustrator and author (Caldecott for *Arrow to the Sun*), born Detroit, MI, Jan 31, 1941.

(Lynn) Nolan Ryan, 55, Baseball Hall of Fame player, born Refugio, TX, Jan 31, 1947.

Justin Timberlake, 21, singer ('N Sync), born Memphis, TN, Jan 31, 1981.

FEBRUARY 1 — FRIDAY

Day 32 — 333 Remaining

★**AMERICAN HEART MONTH.** Feb 1–28. Presidential Proclamation issued each year for February since 1964. (PL88–254 of Dec 30, 1963.)

AMERICAN HEART MONTH. Feb 1–28. Volunteers across the country spend one to four weeks canvassing neighborhoods and providing educational information about heart disease and stroke. For info: Cathy Yarbrough, News Media Relations, American Heart Assn, 7272 Greenville Ave, Dallas, TX 75231. Phone: (800) AHA-USA1. Fax: (214) 369-3685. Web: www.americanheart.org.

BLACK HISTORY MONTH. Feb 1–28. Traditionally the month containing Abraham Lincoln's birthday (Feb 12) and Frederick Douglass's presumed birthday (Feb 14). Observance of a special period to recognize achievements and contributions by African Americans dates from February 1926, when it was launched by Dr. Carter G. Woodson and others. Variously designated Negro History, Black History, Afro-American History, African-American History, Black Heritage and Black Expressions, the observance period was initially one week but since 1976 has been the entire month of February. Each year Black History Month has a theme. Visit the website of the Association for the Study of African-American Life and History for the theme for the current year and information on a theme-related kit you can purchase from the association. The price for the 2001 kit was $50. *Black History Month Resource Book* (2nd ed, Gale, 0-7876-1755-X, $47) includes both programmatic ideas and lists of resources in all media for all ages. For info: Assn for the Study of African-American Life and History, 7961 Eastern Ave, #301, Silver Spring, MD 20910. Phone: (301) 587-5900. Fax: (301) 587-5915. E-mail: asalh@earthlink.net. Web: www.artnoir.com/asalh/.

BLACK MARIA STUDIO: ANNIVERSARY. Feb 1, 1893. The first moving picture studio was completed, built on Thomas Edison's laboratory compound at West Orange, NJ, at a cost of less than $700. The wooden structure of irregular oblong shape was covered with black tar paper. It had a sharply sloping roof hinged at one edge so that half of it could be raised to admit sunlight. Fifty feet in length, it was mounted on a pivot enabling it to be swung around to follow the changing position of the sun. There was a stage draped in black at one end of the single room. Though the structure was officially called a Kinetographic Theater, it was nicknamed the "Black Maria" because it resembled an old-fashioned police wagon. It was described as "hot and cramped" by "Gentleman" Jim Corbett, the pugilistic idol who was the subject of an early movie made in the studio.

FEBRUARY 1–28
BLACK HISTORY MONTH

Learning about the contributions made by African Americans to the arts, sciences and the building of this country is a culturally enriching experience for people of all ages. Too often, however, children think learning any kind of history is boring. A game of history "Go Fish" is an enjoyable learning tool and students can have fun making the card decks.

Cut pieces of poster board into playing card size pieces, 52 cards per deck. Try to have enough poster board to make five complete card decks. (Older students can do this step by themselves.) Have five groups of students go to the learning center. Each student within a group must find the name and accomplishments of at least five people. Some curriculum content areas they can search are: science, art, social studies, literature, athletes (physical education) and music.

Give a blank card deck to each group. Divide each 52-card deck in half. As an art project, students can decorate one side of each card with theme appropriate artwork. On the other side of each of the 26 cards, students should write the name of one person they have discovered and the date he or she was born. On the remaining 26 cards, students can write the achievements of each of those people. Do not write the person's name on this card. Students will remember the people and their contributions better if they think for themselves about the connection. Since each student has found several names, everyone should be busy participating.

Play the game by following standard "Go Fish" rules. Each child asks according to the type of card he or she holds; for example: "Do you have a contribution for George Washington Carver?" Or "Do you have a card for a person who worked with peanuts?" This is a game that students can play when they finish regular class work, or as scheduling permits.

Because this should be a fun activity, each group should make an answer key for their card deck that includes the names of all 26 people and their achievements. Keep several copies with each deck so all players can refer to it when asked. Label each deck and its answer key with a number or name, since there will be variations among the decks according to the names selected by students in the various groups.

There are many new books that will enrich Black History Month. The On My Own Biography series, by the Lerner Publishing Group (call 1-800-328-4929), has several new early reader biographies that feature African Americans. They are entitled: *Jackie Robinson; George Washington Carver; Aunt Clara Brown*; and *Wilma Rudolph*. By various authors, all are suitable for readers Gr. 1–4 and are available in paperback for $5.95 each. *Satchel Paige*, by Lesa Cline-Ransome (Simon & Schuster, 0-689-81151-9, $16 Gr. 1–4), gorgeously illustrated by James Ransome, is a picture-book biography about one of Negro Baseball's legendary pitchers.

Junior high readers should see *Ida B. Wells*, by Dennis Fradin (Clarion, 0-395-89898-6, $18 Gr. 6 & up) for an in-depth read about an extraordinary civil rights activist. *Let It Shine: Stories of Black Women Freedom Fighters*, by Andrea Pinkney (Harcourt, 0-15-201005-X, $20 Gr. 7 & up), is a biographical collection about women who have featured prominently in civil rights issues. *The Black Soldier: 1492 to the Present*, by Catherine Clinton (Clarion, 0-395-67722-X, $17 Gr. 6 & up), contains a wealth of information about people of color who have served in the armed forces.

For other activity ideas, see *A Kid's Guide to African American History*, by Nancy I. Sanders (Chicago Review, 1-55652-417-X, $14.95 Gr. 1–6).

FEBRUARY 1–28
CHILDREN'S DENTAL HEALTH MONTH

February is National Children's Dental Health Month and while the weather outside may be gray and dreary, it's time to stress that teeth should be bright, shiny and, above all, cleaned regularly.

Typical observances of this month include inviting a dental health professional to the school/classroom for tooth care instructions. Many school districts offer presentations along these lines. See if your PTO has anything planned.

Kindergarten and first grade students enjoy having "Lost Tooth" bulletin boards that track the dates each class member loses teeth. At the beginning of the month you might want to have children predict how many teeth will be lost during the month.

While candy is often stressed as the main culprit for tooth decay, there are other foods which can be worse. One example, surprisingly, is potato chips. Saliva turns their starch into a sugar, which stays in the ridges of molars where it begins acting on the enamel. A good book for second through fifth grade students about teeth and tooth decay is *Tooth Decay and Cavities*, by Alvin Silverstein (Orchard, 0-531-16412-8, $6.95).

Laurie Keller has written an amusing and informative book about teeth called *Open Wide: Tooth School Inside* (Holt, 0-8050-6192-4, $16.95 Gr. K–4). All 32 students in the class featured in this book are teeth. They write informal reports (notebook pages similar to the ones featured in Magic School Bus books) about tooth topics. Loads of interesting tooth facts are included and there are plenty of puns and insider tooth jokes.

Science Fair Bunnies, by Kathryn Lasky (Candlewick, 0-7636-0729-0, $15.99 Gr. K–4), is an amusing story of a young bunny whose science fair project about beans fails. The enterprising youngster decides to sacrifice his loose tooth and those of two classmates (by not leaving them for the tooth fairy) in the name of science. He does a project to see how teeth discolor when left in tea, Jell-O and grape juice for an extended period of time.

CAR INSURANCE FIRST ISSUED: ANNIVERSARY. Feb 1, 1898. Travelers Insurance Company issued the first car insurance against accidents with horses.

EASY-BAKE® OVEN DEBUTS: ANNIVERSARY. Feb 1, 1964. This toy was officially introduced this month at the American Toy Fair. Later Easy-Bake brand snack mixes to be used with the ovens were introduced. More than 16 million ovens and more than 100 million mix sets have been sold.

FIRST SESSION OF THE SUPREME COURT: ANNIVERSARY. Feb 1, 1790. The Supreme Court of the United States met for the first time at New York City with Chief Justice John Jay presiding.

FREEDOM DAY: ANNIVERSARY. Feb 1. Anniversary of President Abraham Lincoln's approval, Feb 1, 1865, of the 13th Amendment to the US Constitution (abolishing slavery): "1. Neither slavery nor involuntary servitude, except as a punishment for crime whereof the party shall have been duly convicted, shall exist within the United States or any place subject to their jurisdiction. 2. Congress shall have power to enforce this article by appropriate legislation." The amendment had been proposed by the Congress Jan 31, 1865; ratification was completed Dec 18, 1865.

February 2002

S	M	T	W	T	F	S
					1	2
3	4	5	6	7	8	9
10	11	12	13	14	15	16
17	18	19	20	21	22	23
24	25	26	27	28		

G.I. JOE INTRODUCED: ANNIVERSARY. Feb 1, 1964. This toy action figure was introduced by Hasbro and sold for $2.49. It was the first mass-market doll intended for boys and was a great success.

GREENSBORO SIT-IN: ANNIVERSARY. Feb 1, 1960. Commercial discrimination against blacks and other minorities provoked a nonviolent protest. At Greensboro, NC, four students from the Agricultural and Technical College at Greensboro (Ezell Blair, Jr, Franklin McCain, Joseph McNeill and David Richmond) sat down at a Woolworths store lunch counter and ordered coffee. Refused service, they remained all day. The following days similar sit-ins took place at the Woolworths lunch counter. Before the week was over they were joined by a few white students. The protest spread rapidly, especially in southern states. More than 1,600 persons were arrested before the year was over for participating in sit-ins. Civil rights for all became a cause for thousands of students and activists. In response, equal accommodation regardless of race became the rule at lunch counters, hotels and business establishments in thousands of places.

HUGHES, LANGSTON: 100th BIRTH ANNIVERSARY. Feb 1, 1902. African American poet and author, born at Joplin, MO. Among his works are the poetry collection *Montage of a Dream Deferred*, plays, a novel and short stories. Hughes died May 22, 1967, at New York, NY. For more info: *Langston Hughes: Great American Poet*, by Patricia and Fredrick McKissack (Enslow, 0-8949-00315-2 Gr. K–3).

LIBRARY LOVERS' MONTH. Feb 1–28. A monthlong celebration of school, public and private libraries of all types. This is a time for everyone, especially library support groups, to recognize the value of libraries and to work to ensure that the nation's libraries will continue to serve. For info: Stephanie Stokes, Friends and Foundations of California Libraries, 1980 Washington, No 107, San Francisco, CA 94109-2930. Phone: (415) 749-0130. Fax: (415) 749-0735. E-mail: librarylovers@calibraries.org. Web: www.calibraries.org/librarylovers.

★**NATIONAL AFRICAN AMERICAN HISTORY MONTH.** Feb 1–28.

NATIONAL CHERRY MONTH. Feb 1–28. To publicize the colorful red tart cherry. Recipes, posters and table tents available. For info: Jane Baker, Mktg Dir, Cherry Marketing Institute, PO Box 30285, Lansing, MI 48909-7785. Phone: (517) 669-4264. Fax: (517) 669-3354. E-mail: jbaker@cherrymkt.org. Web: www.cherrymkt.org.

NATIONAL CHILDREN'S DENTAL HEALTH MONTH. Feb 1–28. To increase dental awareness and stress the importance of regular dental care. For info: American Dental Assn, 211 E Chicago Ave, Chicago, IL 60611. To purchase materials, phone in US: (800) 947-4746. Web: www.ada.org. *See* Curriculum Connection.

NATIONAL EDUCATION GOALS: ANNIVERSARY. Feb 1, 1990. In September 1989, President Bush and 50 governors met at a historic Education Summit to draft goals for American K–12 schools for the year 2000. In February 1990, the National Education Goals were announced by the president and adopted by the governors. In July 1990, the National Education Goals Panel was formed to assess and report state and national progress toward the goals. For more info: www.negp.gov.

FEBRUARY 1–28
WILD BIRD FEEDING MONTH

During Wild Bird Feeding Month treat your students to the joy of watching birds and appreciating their contributions to our world. There are many varieties of bird feeders that can be made using household supplies. An inexpensive pan, with holes punched in the bottom for drainage, can be suspended with wire from a tree limb. A quick trip to the library will yield a number of how-to books with instructions for making simple feeders. (February is also Library Lover's Month. Make sure your students develop a lifelong love affair with the public library in your town!)

Bird seed can be purchased in bulk fairly cheaply. Solicit funds (with a student written grant proposal) from your school's PTO. Ask local dealers if they will give the school an educator's discount. Keep a log of the birds that visit your feeder. Note which ones eat from the feeder and which ones prefer to eat seed that has fallen to the ground.

Being able to identify a bird is satisfying for children. They love recognizing and naming cardinals and bluejays rather than saying "that bird." Look for Carol Lerner's *Backyard Birds of Summer* (Morrow, 0-688-13600-1, $16 Gr. K–3) and *Backyard Birds of Winter* (0-688-12819-X, $16 Gr. K–3). Also, Peterson's Field Guides now have paperback guides for children about backyard birds and songbirds. These books contain a lot of information and helpful birding tips.

If a child can identity a bird by its call, it's even more satisfying. There are many CDs and cassettes available for birdcall identification. Check your library and interlibrary loan possibilities. Start with a few of the birds most frequently seen in your area. Birdsongs are a lovely way to augment and complement your music curriculum. *Songbirds: The Language of Song*, by Sylvia A. Johnson (Carolrhoda, 1-57505-483-3, $23.93 Gr. 2–7), is a fantastic book that explains how birds learn to sing, why they do, and the physical mechanics that enable them to sing.

Some areas have raptor recovery centers. If one is near your school, you might want to call and ask if they are willing to do presentations to school groups. Many children, particularly if they live in a urban area, have no idea of the size of owls and hawks. There is usually a program fee or donation request for school presentations.

NATIONAL SIGN UP FOR SUMMER CAMP MONTH. Feb 1–28. Every year more than nine million children continue a national tradition by attending day or resident camps. Building self-confidence, learning new skills and making memories that last a lifetime are just a few examples of what makes camp special and why camp does children a world of good. To find the right program, parents begin looking at summer camps during this month—and sign their children up while there are still vacancies. For info: Public Relations, American Camping Assn, 5000 State Rd 67N, Martinsville, IN 46151. Phone: (765) 342-8456. E-mail: jmccormick@aca-camps.org. Web: www.ACAcamps.org.

NATIONAL WILD BIRD FEEDING MONTH. Feb 1–28. To recognize that February is one of the most difficult winter months in much of the US for birds to survive in the wild and to encourage people to provide food, water and shelter to supplement the wild birds' natural diet of weed seeds and harmful insects. For info: Sue Wells, Exec Dir, Natl Bird-Feeding Soc, PO Box 23, Northbrook, IL 60065-0023. Phone: (847) 272-0135. E-mail: feedbirds@aol.com. *See* Curriculum Connection.

NORTH CAROLINA SWEETPOTATO MONTH. Feb 1–28. To educate the public about the nutritional benefits and versatility of sweet potatoes. North Carolina farmers want America to know that sweet potatoes aren't just for turkeys anymore. Available year-round, sweet potatoes are loaded with beta carotene and vitamin C. They can be boiled, baked, microwaved, grilled, broiled, fried, mashed, sauteed, candied or served raw. North Carolina produces more sweet potatoes than any other state. For info: Sue Johnson-Langdon, North Carolina SweetPotato Commission, 1327 N Brightleaf Blvd, Ste H, Smithfield, NC 27577. Phone: (919) 989-7323. Fax: (919) 989-3015. E-mail: ncsweetsue@aol.com. Web: www.ncsweetpotatoes.com.

RETURN SHOPPING CARTS TO THE SUPERMARKET MONTH. Feb 1–28. A monthlong opportunity to return stolen shopping carts, milk crates, bread trays and ice cream baskets to supermarkets and to avoid the increased food prices that these thefts cause. Annually, the month of February. Sponsor: Illinois Food Retailers Association. For info: Anthony A. Dinolfo, Grocer-"Retired," 163 Fairfield Dr, New Lenox, IL 60451-3523. Phone: (815) 463-9136.

ROBINSON CRUSOE DAY. Feb 1. Anniversary of the rescue, Feb 1, 1709, of Alexander Selkirk, Scottish sailor who had been put ashore (in September 1704) on the uninhabited island, Juan Fernandez, at his own request after a quarrel with his captain. His adventures formed the basis for Daniel Defoe's book *Robinson Crusoe*. A day to be adventurous and self-reliant.

ST. LAURENT, LOUIS STEPHEN: BIRTH ANNIVERSARY. Feb 1, 1882. Canadian lawyer and prime minister, born at Compton, Quebec. Died at Quebec City, July 25, 1973.

BIRTHDAYS TODAY

Michael B. Enzi, 58, US Senator (R, Wyoming), born Bremerton, WA, Feb 1, 1944.

Jerry Spinelli, 61, author (*Wringer*, Newbery for *Maniac Magee*), born Norristown, PA, Feb 1, 1941.

Boris Yeltsin, 71, former Russian president, born Sverdlovsk, Russia, Feb 1, 1931.

FEBRUARY 2 — SATURDAY

Day 33 — 332 Remaining

BABE VOTED INTO BASEBALL HALL OF FAME: ANNIVERSARY. Feb 2, 1936. The five charter members of the brand-new Baseball Hall of Fame at Cooperstown, NY, were announced. Of 226 ballots cast, Ty Cobb was named on 222, Babe Ruth on 215, Honus Wagner on 215, Christy Mathewson on 205 and Walter Johnson on 189. A total of 170 votes were necessary to be elected to the Hall of Fame.

BAN ON AFRICAN NATIONAL CONGRESS LIFTED: ANNIVERSARY. Feb 2, 1990. The 30-year ban on the African National Congress was lifted by South African President F.W. de Klerk. De Klerk also vowed to free Nelson Mandela and lift restrictions on 33 other opposition groups.

BONZA BOTTLER DAY™. Feb 2. To celebrate when the number of the day is the same as the number of the month. Bonza Bottler Day™ is an excuse to have a party at least once a month. For info: Gail M. Berger, 109 Matthew Ave, Poca, WV 25159. Phone: (304) 776-7746. E-mail: gberger5@aol.com.

CALIFORNIA KIWIFRUIT DAY. Feb 2. National campaign to educate Americans about the nutritional benefits of kiwifruit, the most nutrient-dense fruit (they provide twice the vitamin C of oranges), ways to enjoy kiwifruit and kiwifruit's colorful history.

Annually, Feb 2. For info: Katie Mauro, Porter Novelli, 444 Market St, Ste 3000, San Francisco, CA 94111. Fax: (415) 733-1770.

CANDLEMAS DAY or PRESENTATION OF THE LORD. Feb 2. Observed in Roman Catholic and Eastern Orthodox churches. Commemorates presentation of Jesus in the temple and the purification of Mary 40 days after his birth. Candles have been blessed since the 11th century. Formerly called the Feast of Purification of the Blessed Virgin Mary. Old Scottish couplet proclaims: "If Candlemas is fair and clear/There'll be two winters in the year."

GROUNDHOG DAY. Feb 2. Old belief that if the sun shines on Candlemas Day, or if the groundhog sees his shadow when he emerges on this day, six weeks of winter will ensue. For links to websites about Groundhog Day, go to deil.lang.uiuc.edu/web.pages/holidays/groundhog.html.

GROUNDHOG DAY IN PUNXSUTAWNEY, PENNSYLVANIA. Feb 2. Widely observed traditional annual Candlemas Day event at which "Punxsutawney Phil, king of the weather prophets," is the object of a search. Tradition is said to have been established by early German settlers. The official trek (which began in 1887) is followed by a weather prediction for the next six weeks. Phil made his dramatic film debut with Bill Murray in *Groundhog Day*.

LAURA INGALLS WILDER GINGERBREAD SOCIABLE. Feb 2. Pomona, CA. The 35th annual event commemorates the birthday (Feb 7, 1867) of the renowned author of the Little House books. The library has on permanent display the handwritten manuscript of *Little Town on the Prairie* and other Wilder memorabilia. Entertainment by fiddlers, craft displays, apple cider and gingerbread. Annually, the first Saturday in February. Est attendance: 300. For info: Marguerite F. Raybould, Friends of the Pomona Public Library, 625 S Garey Ave, Pomona, CA 91766. Phone: (909) 620-2017. Fax: (909) 620-3713.

MEXICO: DIA DE LA CANDELARIA. Feb 2. All Mexico celebrates Candlemas Day with dances, processions and bullfights.

***THE RECORD OF A SNEEZE* : ANNIVERSARY.** Feb 2, 1893. One day after Thomas Edison's "Black Maria" studio was completed at West Orange, NJ, a studio cameraman took the first "close-up" in film history. *The Record of a Sneeze*, starring Edison's assistant Fred P. Ott, was also the first motion picture to receive a copyright (1894). See also: "Black Maria Studio: Anniversary" (Feb 1).

TREATY OF GUADALUPE HIDALGO: ANNIVERSARY. Feb 2, 1848. The war between Mexico and the US formally ended with the signing of the Treaty of Guadalupe Hidalgo, signed in the village for which it was named. The treaty provided for Mexico's cession to the US of the territory that became the states of California, Nevada, Utah, most of Arizona and parts of New Mexico, Colorado and Wyoming, in exchange for $15 million from the US. In addition, Mexico relinquished all rights to Texas north of the Rio Grande. The Senate ratified the treaty Mar 10, 1848.

WALTON, GEORGE: DEATH ANNIVERSARY. Feb 2, 1804. Signer of the Declaration of Independence. Born at Prince Edward County, VA, 1749 (exact date unknown). Died at Augusta, GA.

February 2002

S	M	T	W	T	F	S
					1	2
3	4	5	6	7	8	9
10	11	12	13	14	15	16
17	18	19	20	21	22	23
24	25	26	27	28		

BIRTHDAYS TODAY

Judith Viorst, 71, author (*The Tenth Good Thing About Barney; Alexander and the Terrible, Horrible, No-Good, Very Bad Day*), born Newark, NJ, Feb 2, 1931.

FEBRUARY 3 — SUNDAY

Day 34 — 331 Remaining

AFRICAN AMERICAN READ-IN. Feb 3–4. Schools, libraries and community organizations are urged to make literacy a significant part of Black History Month by hosting Read-Ins in their communities. Report your results by submitting the 2002 African American Read-In Chain Report Card. This 13th national Read-In is sponsored by the Black Caucus of the National Council of Teachers of English. Annually, the first Sunday in February for communities and the first Monday in February for schools. For a Read-In Chain Packet: Dr. Sandra E. Gibbs, NCTE Special Programs, 1111 W Kenyon Rd, Urbana, IL 61801-1096. Phone: (217) 328-3870. E-mail: sgibbs@ncte.org. Web: www.ncte.org.

ENDANGERED SPECIES ACT: ANNIVERSARY. Feb 3, 1973. President Richard Nixon signed the Endangered Species Act into law. *See* Curriculum Connection.

FIFTEENTH AMENDMENT TO US CONSTITUTION RATIFIED: ANNIVERSARY. Feb 3, 1870. The 15th Amendment granted that the right of citizens to vote shall not be denied on account of race, color or previous condition of servitude.

HALFWAY POINT OF WINTER. Feb 3. On this date at 2:19 PM, EST, 44 days, 23 hours and 58 minutes of winter will have elapsed and the equivalent remain before Mar 20, 2002, which is the spring equinox and the beginning of spring.

INCOME TAX BIRTHDAY: SIXTEENTH AMENDMENT TO US CONSTITUTION: RATIFICATION ANNIVERSARY. Feb 3, 1913. The 16th Amendment granted Congress the authority to levy taxes on income. (Church bells did not ring throughout the land and no dancing in the streets was reported.)

JAPAN: BEAN-THROWING FESTIVAL (SETSUBUN). Feb 3. Setsubun marks the last day of winter according to the lunar calendar. Throngs at temple grounds throw beans to drive away imaginary devils.

MOZAMBIQUE: HEROES' DAY. Feb 3. National holiday. Commemorates all heroic citizens, especially Eduardo Mondlane, assassinated on this date in 1969.

NORTH AMERICA'S COLDEST RECORDED TEMPERATURE: 55th ANNIVERSARY. Feb 3, 1947. At Snag, in Canada's Yukon Territory, a temperature of 81 degrees below zero (Fahrenheit) was recorded on this date, a record low for all of North America.

SPACE MILESTONE: *CHALLENGER STS-10* (US). Feb 3, 1984. Shuttle *Challenger* launched from Kennedy Space Center, FL, with a crew of five (Vance Brand, Robert Gibson, Ronald McNair, Bruce McCandless and Robert Stewart). On Feb 7 two astronauts became the first to fly freely in space (propelled by their backpack jets), untethered to any craft. Landed at Cape Canaveral, FL, Feb 11.

SWITZERLAND: HOMSTROM. Feb 3. Scuol. Burning of straw men on poles as a symbol of winter's imminent departure. Annually, the first Sunday in February.

VIETNAM: ANNIVERSARY OF THE FOUNDING OF THE COMMUNIST PARTY. Feb 3. National holiday. Vietnamese Communist Party founded in 1930.

FEBRUARY 3

ENDANGERED SPECIES ACT

On February 3, 1973, the Endangered Species Act was signed. Encourage students to realize the causes that have led to the very real possibility that animals are in danger of extinction. Then, make the idea of threatened species immediately relevant to your students by extending the theme to include animals and plants threatened in your own community or state.

Housing subdivisions and industrial complexes are being built at an astounding rate. In many cases, their construction encroaches on undeveloped lands that often include forests, fields, and wetlands. Environmentalists and conservationists are concerned about the threat to many species of animals and plants. Loss of habitat has led to a number of species' inclusion on lists of threatened or endangered species. What's happening in your state? Exploring this question should lead to many project ideas. Here are a few prompts.

Supplement the geography curriculum by dividing the state into its natural geographical regions. Point out the importance of including population densities within each geographical province. State geological surveys can supply information, and often maps. Have groups of students research the animal and plant life that are typically found in those areas today. The important thrust of this project is to make children aware of how to access valuable primary source materials that concern their state. Find out if your state has a plan to protect and/or encourage the maintenance of open space as part of construction plans. An example is "Illinois Tomorrow," a program that encourages municipalities to work together and plan ways to preserve open space and rebuild urban areas. Your state governor's office or the United States Fish and Wildlife Service can steer students toward appropriate sources and agencies that will have information for your state.

A social studies project would focus on past usages of the state's lands. Depending on where you live, choose an increment of years appropriate to your area. Again, students should focus on human population density and its influence on the land and animal and plant life in the area.

Math projects have many possibilities. For example: several pie charts showing the percentages of animals, people, and undeveloped lands for different time periods. A line graph that reflects human population increases could be plotted on the same graph with animal population densities. See *Tiger Math: Learning to Graph from a Baby Tiger*, by Ann Whitehead Nagda and Cindy Bickel (Henry Holt, 0-8050-6248-3, $16 Gr. 2–5).

Discover if any animals and plants have been listed as endangered or protected species in your state. Examples include: gila monsters, snowy owls, certain species of stickleback fish, and lady slippers. In some regions, protecting endangered species has caused major conflicts between environmentalists and industry, particularly when restrictions involve loss of jobs. For a state-by-state list of endangered animals, go to the US Fish and Wildlife Service's website at endangered.fws.gov.

One book you may find useful is *The Environmental Movement*, by Laurence Pringle (HarperCollins, 0-688-1562-22 $16.95 Gr. 5 & up). Students will gain insight into many of the environmental issues suggested above. The end of the book includes a number of addresses for environmental and government agencies, plus a suggested reading list. For younger readers see *There's Still Time*, by Mark Galan (National Geographic, 0-7922-7092-4, $15 Gr. 4–7.).

BIRTHDAYS TODAY

Joan Lowery Nixon, 75, author (the Orphan Train series), born Los Angeles, CA, Feb 3, 1927.

Paul S. Sarbanes, 69, US Senator (D, Maryland), born Salisbury, MD, Feb 3, 1933.

Maura Tierney, 37, actress (*Liar, Liar*), born Boston, MA, Feb 3, 1965.

FEBRUARY 4 — MONDAY

Day 35 — 330 Remaining

ANGOLA: BEGINNING OF THE ARMED STRUGGLE DAY. Feb 4. National holiday. Commemorates the beginning of the war of independence against the Portuguese in 1961.

APACHE WARS BEGAN: ANNIVERSARY. Feb 4, 1861. The period of conflict known as the Apache Wars began at Apache Pass, AZ, when Army Lieutenant George Bascom arrested Apache Chief Cochise for raiding a ranch. Cochise escaped and declared war. The wars lasted 25 years under the leadership of Cochise and, later, Geronimo.

BOY SCOUTS OF AMERICA ANNIVERSARY WEEK. Feb 4–10. Commemorating the founding of the organization Feb 8, 1910. Annually, the week including the founding day, Feb 8. For info: Boy Scouts of America, 1325 W Walnut Hill Ln, Irving, TX 75015-2079. Phone: (214) 580-2263. Web: www.bsa.scouting.org.

LINDBERGH, CHARLES AUGUSTUS: 100th BIRTH ANNIVERSARY. Feb 4, 1902. American aviator Charles "Lucky Lindy" Lindbergh was the first to fly solo and nonstop over the Atlantic Ocean, New York to Paris, May 20–21, 1927. Born at Detroit, MI, he died at Kipahula, Maui, HI, Aug 27, 1974. For more info: *Flight: The Journey of Charles Lindbergh*, by Robert Burleigh (Philomel Books, 0-3992-2272-3, $16.99 Gr. K–3) and *Charles A. Lindbergh: A Human Hero*, by James Giblin (Clarion, 0-395-63389-3, $18 Gr. 4–7) and www.pbs.org/wgbh/amex/lindbergh. See also: "Lindbergh Flight: Anniversary" (May 20).

MOON PHASE: LAST QUARTER. Feb 4. Moon enters Last Quarter phase at 8:33 AM, EST.

NATIONAL SCHOOL COUNSELING WEEK. Feb 4–8. Promotes counseling in the school and community. For info: American School Counselor Assn, 801 N Fairfax St, Ste 310, Alexandria, VA 22314. Phone: (800) 306-4722. Fax: (703) 683-1619. E-mail: asca@erols.com. Web: www.schoolcounselor.org.

QUAYLE, J. DANFORTH: BIRTHDAY. Feb 4, 1947. The 44th vice president (1989–93) of the US, born at Indianapolis, IN.

SRI LANKA: INDEPENDENCE DAY. Feb 4. Democratic Socialist Republic of Sri Lanka observes National Day. On Feb 4, 1948, Ceylon (as it was then known) obtained independence from Great Britain. The name Sri Lanka was adopted in 1972.

BIRTHDAYS TODAY

Russell Hoban, 77, author of books illustrated by his wife Lillian (*Bedtime for Frances*), born Lansdale, PA, Feb 4, 1925.

Rosa Lee Parks, 89, civil rights leader who refused to give up her seat on the bus, born Tuskegee, AL, Feb 4, 1913.

FEBRUARY 5 — TUESDAY

Day 36 — 329 Remaining

FAMILY-LEAVE BILL: ANNIVERSARY. Feb 5, 1993. President Bill Clinton signed legislation requiring companies with 50 or more employees (and all government agencies) to allow employees to take up to 12 weeks unpaid leave in a 12-month period to deal with the birth or adoption of a child or to care for a relative with a serious health problem. The bill became effective Aug 5, 1993.

MEXICO: CONSTITUTION DAY: 85th ANNIVERSARY. Feb 5. The present constitution, embracing major social reforms, was adopted in 1917. National holiday.

WEATHERMAN'S [WEATHERPERSON'S] DAY. Feb 5. Commemorates the birth of one of America's first weathermen, John Jeffries, a Boston physician who kept detailed records of weather conditions, 1774–1816. Born at Boston, Feb 5, 1744, and died there Sept 16, 1819. See also: "First Balloon Flight Across English Channel: Anniversary" (Jan 7).

WITHERSPOON, JOHN: BIRTH ANNIVERSARY. Feb 5, 1723. Clergyman, signer of the Declaration of Independence and reputed coiner of the word *Americanism* (in 1781). Born near Edinburgh, Scotland. Died at Princeton, NJ, Nov 15, 1794.

BIRTHDAYS TODAY

Henry Louis (Hank) Aaron, 68, baseball executive, Baseball Hall of Fame outfielder, all-time home run leader, born Mobile, AL, Feb 5, 1934.

Roberto Alomar, 34, baseball player, born Ponce, Puerto Rico, Feb 5, 1968.

Patricia Lauber, 78, author (the Let's Read and Find Out science series, *Volcano: The Eruption and Healing of Mount St. Helens*), born New York, NY, Feb 5, 1924.

David Wiesner, 45, author and illustrator (Caldecott for *Tuesday*), born Bridgewater, NJ, Feb 5, 1957.

FEBRUARY 6 — WEDNESDAY

Day 37 — 328 Remaining

ACCESSION OF QUEEN ELIZABETH II: 50th ANNIVERSARY. Feb 6, 1952. Princess Elizabeth Alexandra Mary succeeded to the British throne (becoming Elizabeth II, Queen of the United Kingdom of Great Britain and Northern Ireland and Head of the Commonwealth) upon the death of her father, King George VI, Feb 6, 1952. Her coronation took place June 2, 1953, at Westminster Abbey at London. For info: www.royal.gov.uk/family/hmqueen.htm.

BURR, AARON: BIRTH ANNIVERSARY. Feb 6, 1756. Third vice president of the US (Mar 4, 1801–Mar 3, 1805). While vice president, Burr challenged political enemy Alexander Hamilton to a duel and mortally wounded him July 11, 1804, at Weehawken, NJ. Indicted for the challenge and for murder, he returned to Washington to complete his term of office (during which he presided over the impeachment trial of Supreme Court Justice Samuel Chase). In 1807 Burr was arrested, tried for treason (in an alleged scheme to invade Mexico and set up a new nation in the West) and acquitted. Born at Newark, NJ, he died at Staten Island, NY, Sept 14, 1836.

February 2002

S	M	T	W	T	F	S
					1	2
3	4	5	6	7	8	9
10	11	12	13	14	15	16
17	18	19	20	21	22	23
24	25	26	27	28		

MASSACHUSETTS RATIFIES CONSTITUTION: ANNIVERSARY. Feb 6, 1788. By a vote of 187 to 168, Massachusetts became the sixth state to ratify the Constitution.

NEW ZEALAND: WAITANGI DAY. Feb 6. National Day. Commemorates signing of the Treaty of Waitangi in 1840 (at Waitangi, Chatham Islands, New Zealand). The treaty, between the native Maori and the European peoples, provided for development of New Zealand under the British Crown.

100 BILLIONTH CRAYOLA CRAYON® PRODUCED: ANNIVERSARY. Feb 6, 1996. On this date, the 100 billionth crayola was produced by Binney & Smith, Inc, in New York. The first box of eight crayons was introduced in 1903 in the popular yellow and green box. Since 1903, crayons have come in boxes of 24, 48, 64 and 96. The word *crayola* means oily chalk.

REAGAN, RONALD W: BIRTHDAY. Feb 6, 1911. The 40th president (Jan 20, 1981–Jan 20, 1989) of the US, born at Tampico, IL. Former motion picture actor and governor of California (1967–74); he was the oldest and first divorced person to become president. For info: www.ipl.org/ref/POTUS.

RUTH, "BABE": BIRTH ANNIVERSARY. Feb 6, 1895. One of baseball's greatest heroes, George Herman "Babe" Ruth was born at Baltimore, MD. The left-handed pitcher—"the Sultan of Swat"—hit 714 home runs in 22 major league seasons of play and played in 10 World Series. Died at New York, NY, Aug 16, 1948.

BIRTHDAYS TODAY

Tom Brokaw, 62, TV journalist, born Yankton, SD, Feb 6, 1940.

Ronald Reagan, 91, 40th president of the US, born Tampico, IL, Feb 6, 1911.

FEBRUARY 7 — THURSDAY

Day 38 — 327 Remaining

BALLET INTRODUCED TO THE US: 175th ANNIVERSARY. Feb 7, 1827. Renowned French danseuse Madame Francisquy Hutin introduced ballet to the US with a performance of *The Deserter*, staged at the Bowery Theater, New York, NY. A minor scandal erupted when the ladies in the lower boxes left the theater upon viewing the light and scanty attire of Madame Hutin and her troupe.

DICKENS, CHARLES: BIRTH ANNIVERSARY. Feb 7, 1812. English social critic and novelist, born at Portsmouth, England. Among his most successful books: *Oliver Twist, The Posthumous Papers of the Pickwick Club, David Copperfield* and *A Christmas Carol.* Died at Gad's Hill, England, June 9, 1870, and was buried at Westminster Abbey. For more info: *Charles Dickens: The Man Who Had Great Expectations*, by Diane Stanley and Peter Vennema (Morrow, 0-688-09111-3, $14.93 Gr. 4–8).

ELEVENTH AMENDMENT TO US CONSTITUTION (SOVEREIGNTY OF THE STATES): RATIFICATION ANNIVERSARY. Feb 7, 1795. The 11th Amendment to the Constitution was ratified, curbing the powers of the federal judiciary in relation to the states. The amendment reaffirmed the sovereignty of the states by prohibiting suits against them.

FLORIDA STATE FAIR. Feb 7–18 (tentative). Florida State Fair Grounds, Tampa, FL. The fair features the best arts, crafts, competitive exhibits, equestrian shows, livestock, entertainment and food found in Florida. Also not to be missed is "Cracker Country," where cultural and architectural history has been preserved. Annually, in February. Est attendance: 500,000. For info: Sherry Powell, Mktg & Advertising Mgr, Florida State Fair, PO Box 11766, Tampa, FL 33680. Phone: (813) 621-7821 or (813) 622-PARK. Web: www.fl-ag.com/statefair.

GIPSON, FRED: BIRTH ANNIVERSARY. Feb 7, 1908. Born near Mason, TX. Gipson is known for such works as *Old Yeller, Savage Sam* and *Little Arliss*. In 1959, he won the William Allen White Children's Book Award and the First Sequoyah Award. Gipson died at Mason County, TX, Aug 17, 1973.

GRENADA: INDEPENDENCE DAY. Feb 7. National Day. Commemorates independence from Great Britain in 1974.

NATIONAL GIRLS AND WOMEN IN SPORTS DAY. Feb 7. Celebrates and honors all girls and women participating in sports. Recognizes the passage of Title IX in 1972, the law that guarantees gender equity in federally funded school programs, including athletics. Sponsored by Girls Inc, the Girl Scouts, the National Association for Girls and Women in Sports, the Women's Sports Foundation and the YWCA. For info: Women's Sports Foundation, Eisenhower Park, East Meadow, NY 11554. Phone: (516) 542-4700.

SPACE MILESTONE: *STARDUST* (US). Feb 7, 1999. *Stardust* began its 3 billion-mile journey to collect comet dust on this date. The unmanned mission will meet up with Comet Wild-2 in January 2004 and the comet samples will reach Earth in January 2006. This is the first US mission devoted solely to a comet. NASA plans three more over a four-year period.

WILDER, LAURA INGALLS: BIRTH ANNIVERSARY. Feb 7, 1867. Author of *The Little House on the Prairie* and its sequels. Born at Pepin, WI, Wilder died Feb 10, 1957, at Mansfield, MO. For more info, go to the Little House on the Prairie home page at www.vvv.com/~jenslegg/index.htm.

BIRTHDAYS TODAY

Garth Brooks, 40, singer, born Tulsa, OK, Feb 7, 1962.
Juwan Howard, 29, basketball player, born Chicago, IL, Feb 7, 1973.
Herb Kohl, 67, US Senator (D, Wisconsin), born Milwaukee, WI, Feb 7, 1935.
Pete Postlethwaite, 57, actor (*The Lost World: Jurassic Park*), born London, England, Feb 7, 1945.

FEBRUARY 8 — FRIDAY

Day 39 — 326 Remaining

BOY SCOUTS OF AMERICA FOUNDED: ANNIVERSARY. Feb 8, 1910. The Boy Scouts of America was founded at Washington, DC, by William Boyce, based on the work of Sir Robert Baden-Powell with the British Boy Scout Association. For more info: www.bsa.scouting.org.

JAPAN: HA-RI-KU-YO (NEEDLE MASS). Feb 8. Ha-Ri-Ku-Yo, a Needle Mass, may be observed on either Feb 8 or Dec 8. Girls do no needlework; instead they gather old and broken needles, which they dedicate to the Awashima Shrine at Wakayama. Girls pray to Awashima Myozin (their protecting deity) that their needlework, symbolic of love and marriage, will be good. Participation in the Needle Mass hopefully leads to a happy marriage.

JAPAN: SNOW FESTIVAL. Feb 8–12. Sapporo, Hokkaido. Huge, elaborate snow and ice sculptures are erected on the Odori-Koen Promenade.

100th DAY OF SCHOOL. Feb 8. Use your own school calendar to compute this date for your students. This day can help you teach lower elementary students the concept of 100. For activities that will facilitate this, visit users.aol.com/a100thday/ideas.html. The following books will also be helpful: *100 Days of School*, by Trudy Harris (Millbrook, 0-7613-1271-4, $21.90 Gr. K–2); *The 100th Day of School*, by Angela Shelf Medearis (Scholastic, 0-590-25944-X, $3.99 Gr. K–2) and *100th Day of School Activities*, by Hope Blecher-Sass (Teacher Created Materials, 1-57690-199-8, $2.95). Also see the November 1999 issue of *Book Links* for "Celebrating the One Hundredth Day of School."

OPERA DEBUT IN THE COLONIES: ANNIVERSARY. Feb 8, 1735. The first opera produced in the colonies was performed at the Courtroom, at Charleston, SC. The opera was *Flora; or the Hob in the Well*, written by Colley Cibber.

SHERMAN, WILLIAM TECUMSEH: BIRTH ANNIVERSARY. Feb 8, 1820. Born at Lancaster, OH, General Sherman is especially remembered for his devastating march through Georgia during the Civil War and his statement "War is hell." Died at New York, NY, Feb 14, 1891.

SLOVENIA: PRESEREN DAY. Feb 8. National holiday. Commemorates France Preseren, Slovenia's national poet, who died on this day in 1849.

SPACE MILESTONE: *ARABSAT-1*. Feb 8, 1985. League of Arab States communications satellite launched into geosynchronous orbit from Kourou, French Guiana, by European Space Agency.

VERNE, JULES: BIRTH ANNIVERSARY. Feb 8, 1828. French writer, sometimes called "the father of science fiction," born at Nantes, France. Author of *Around the World in Eighty Days, Twenty Thousand Leagues Under the Sea* and many other novels. Died at Amiens, France, Mar 24, 1905.

WINTER OLYMPICS OPENING CEREMONY. Feb 8. Salt Lake City, UT. More than 3,500 athletes from 80 nations will compete in 16 sports at the XIX Winter Olympics. Closing ceremonies are on Feb 24. For info: Salt Lake Olympic Committee, PO

Box 45002, Salt Lake City, UT 84145-0002. Phone: (801) 212-2002. Web: www.slc2002.org.

BIRTHDAYS TODAY

Ted Koppel, 62, TV journalist ("Nightline"), born Lancashire, England, Feb 8, 1940.

Alonzo Mourning, 32, basketball player, born Chesapeake, VA, Feb 8, 1970.

Anne Rockwell, 68, author (*Apples and Pumpkins, Things That Go, Sweet Potato Pie*), born Memphis, TN, Feb 8, 1934.

FEBRUARY 9 — SATURDAY

Day 40 — 325 Remaining

BRAZIL: CARNIVAL. Feb 9–12. Especially in Rio de Janeiro, this carnival is one of the great folk festivals, and the big annual event in the life of Brazilians. Begins on Saturday night before Ash Wednesday and continues through Shrove Tuesday.

HARRISON, WILLIAM HENRY: BIRTH ANNIVERSARY. Feb 9, 1773. Ninth president of the US (Mar 4–Apr 4, 1841). His term of office was the shortest in our nation's history—32 days. He was the first president to die in office (of pneumonia contracted during inaugural ceremonies). Born at Berkeley, VA, he died at Washington, DC, Apr 4, 1841. His grandson Benjamin Harrison was the 23rd president of the US. For info: www.ipl.org/ref/POTUS.

BIRTHDAYS TODAY

David Gallagher, 17, actor ("7th Heaven"), born College Point, NY, Feb 9, 1985.

Joe Pesci, 59, actor (*Home Alone, Home Alone 2*), born Newark, NJ, Feb 9, 1943.

FEBRUARY 10 — SUNDAY

Day 41 — 324 Remaining

FASCHING SUNDAY. Feb 10. Germany and Austria. The last Sunday before Lent.

FRENCH AND INDIAN WAR ENDS: ANNIVERSARY. Feb 10, 1763. The Treaty of Paris was signed, ending the French and Indian War in North America. Known in Europe as the Seven Years War, this conflict ranged from North America to India, with many European nations involved. In North America French expansion in the Ohio River Valley in the 1750s led to conflict with Great Britain. Some Indians fought alongside the French; a young George Washington fought for the British. As a result of the signing of the Treaty of Paris, France lost all claims to Canada and had to cede Louisiana to Spain. Fifteen years later French bitterness over the loss of its North American colonies to Britain contributed to France's supporting the colonists in the American Revolution. For info: *Struggle for a Continent: The French and Indian Wars*, by Betsy Maestro (HarperCollins, 0-688-1345103, $15.89 Gr. 3–6).

ITALY: CARNIVAL WEEK. Feb 10–16. Milan. Carnival week is held according to local tradition, with shows and festive events for children on Tuesday and Thursday. Parades of floats, figures in the costume of local folk characters Meneghin and Cecca, parties and more traditional events are held on Saturday. Annually, the Sunday–Saturday of Ash Wednesday week.

February 2002

S	M	T	W	T	F	S
					1	2
3	4	5	6	7	8	9
10	11	12	13	14	15	16
17	18	19	20	21	22	23
24	25	26	27	28		

FEBRUARY 10–16
CHILD PASSENGER SAFETY AWARENESS WEEK—DANGEROUS DIALING

More and more people have cell phones in their cars. Unquestionably, the presence of cell phones can be a plus. They can be used for 911 emergencies or to report other drivers who may be driving dangerously. They are also a lifeline for travelers whose cars experience mechanical difficulty. But they can also be a very real danger to anyone riding in a car.

You have probably noticed people chatting on the phone while driving their car. Perhaps you have "dialed out" while driving. Each year many people are injured, and some killed, in automobile accidents caused by someone who is not focused on the task at hand—driving. The few seconds it takes to pick up a car phone, or the quick glance needed to punch in a phone number, are all it takes for a car to drift into another lane, swerve out of control and cause an accident.

About 94 million people own mobile phones. A report issued by the National Highway Traffic Safety Administration found in a 1997 survey that 85 percent of cell phone users talk on the phone while driving. In most cases, that means only one hand is on the wheel. Safety administrators think that 25 percent of all auto crashes may be the result of drivers who are distracted. In addition to cell phone use, drivers' attention is diverted by eating, drinking, changing cassettes or CDs, looking in the mirror, etc. In 1997, the New England Journal of Medicine reported a study that indicated that talking on the phone while driving increases the risk of an accident by as much as four times.

This week is set aside to foster awareness of making automobile travel safer for children. Car seats are a necessity. But making children aware of activities that cause driver distraction may give them something to think about as they near the age of obtaining their own driver's license. This is the perfect week to encourage a poster campaign against driving while distracted.

Let children decide on a schoolwide theme, perhaps something such as: We Take Our Lives Seriously; or Keep Both Hands on the Wheel. Display the posters in the hallways of your school for a day or two. But more importantly, arrange with the public library, your town's municipal building or area merchants to let you display the posters in prominent locations in their facility. Adults need to see them and think about the issue of child safety. Most parents would never knowingly place their child in jeopardy. But, we can all do with an occasional reminder.

For information about safe cell phone usage and other child passenger safety issues, contact the National Highway Traffic Safety Administration at www.nhtsa.gov. You might also wish to contact Advocates for Cell Phone Safety, 407 S Sixth St, Dept P, Perkasie, PA 18944. Enclose a self-addressed, stamped envelope if you are requesting information.

MALTA: FEAST OF ST. PAUL'S SHIPWRECK. Feb 10. Valletta. Holy day of obligation. Commemorates shipwreck of St. Paul on the north coast of Malta in AD 60.

★ **NATIONAL CHILD PASSENGER SAFETY AWARENESS WEEK.** Feb 10–16. Always the week in February containing Valentine's Day. For info: Office of Occupant Protection, Natl Highway Safety Administration, 400 Seventh St SW, Washington, DC 20590. Phone: (202) 366-9550. *See* Curriculum Connection.

SHROVETIDE. Feb 10–12. The three days before Ash Wednesday: Shrove Sunday, Monday and Tuesday—a time for confession and for festivity before the beginning of Lent.

TWENTY-FIFTH AMENDMENT TO US CONSTITUTION RATIFIED (PRESIDENTIAL SUCCESSION, DISABILITY): 35th ANNIVERSARY. Feb 10, 1967. Procedures for presidential succession were further clarified by the 25th Amendment, along with provisions for continuity of power in the event of a disability or illness of the president.

BIRTHDAYS TODAY

Lucy Cousins, 38, author, illustrator (the Maisy books, *ZaZa's Baby Brother, Kay Cat and Beaky Boo*), born Reading, England, Feb 10, 1964.

Frank Keating, 58, Governor of Oklahoma (R), born St. Louis, MO, Feb 10, 1944.

E.L. Konigsburg, 72, author (Newbery for *The View From Saturday, From the Mixed-up Files of Mrs Basil E. Frankweiler*), born Elaine Lobl, New York, NY, Feb 10, 1930.

Mark Teague, 39, author (*The Secret Shortcut*), illustrator (the Poppleton series, *Flying Dragon Room*), born La Mesa, CA, Feb 10, 1963.

Tina Thompson, 27, basketball player, born Los Angeles, CA, Feb 10, 1975.

FEBRUARY 11 — MONDAY

Day 42 — 323 Remaining

CAMEROON: YOUTH DAY. Feb 11. Public holiday.

CARNIVAL. Feb 11–12. Period of festivities, feasts, foolishness and gaiety immediately before Lent begins on Ash Wednesday. Ordinarily Carnival includes only Fasching (the Feast of Fools), being the Monday and Tuesday immediately preceding Ash Wednesday. The period of Carnival may also be extended to include longer periods in some areas.

DENMARK: STREET URCHINS' CARNIVAL. Feb 11. Observed on Shrove Monday.

EDISON, THOMAS ALVA: BIRTH ANNIVERSARY. Feb 11, 1847. American inventive genius and holder of more than 1,200 patents (including the incandescent electric lamp, phonograph, electric dynamo and key parts of many now-familiar devices such as the movie camera, telephone transmitter, etc). Edison said, "Genius is 1 percent inspiration and 99 percent perspiration." His birthday is now widely observed as Inventor's Day. Born at Milan, OH, and died at Menlo Park, NJ, Oct 18, 1931. For more info: *Thomas Edison*, by Anna Sproule (Blackbirch, 1-56711-331-1, $19.95 Gr. 5–7).

FASCHING. Feb 11–12. In Germany and Austria, Fasching, also called Fasnacht, Fasnet or Feast of Fools, is a Shrovetide festival with processions of masked figures, both beautiful and grotesque. Always the two days (Rose Monday and Shrove Tuesday) between Fasching Sunday and Ash Wednesday.

FULLER, MELVILLE WESTON: BIRTH ANNIVERSARY. Feb 11, 1833. Eighth chief justice of the US Supreme Court. Born at Augusta, ME, he died at Sorrento, ME, July 4, 1910.

ICELAND: BUN DAY. Feb 11. Children invade homes in the morning with colorful sticks and receive gifts of whipped cream buns (on the Monday before Shrove Tuesday).

IRAN: NATIONAL DAY. Feb 11. National holiday. Commemorates the founding of the republic in 1979.

JAPAN: NATIONAL FOUNDATION DAY. Feb 11. Marks the founding of the Japanese nation. In 1872 the government officially set Feb 11, 660 BC, as the date of accession to the throne of the Emperor Jimmu (said to be Japan's first emperor) and designated the day a national holiday by the name of Empire Day. The holiday was abolished after WWII, but was revived as National Foundation Day in 1966. Ceremonies are held with Their Imperial Majesties the Emperor and Empress, the Prime Minister and other dignitaries attending.

MANDELA, NELSON: PRISON RELEASE: ANNIVERSARY. Feb 11, 1990. After serving more than 27½ years of a life sentence (convicted, with eight others, of sabotage and conspiracy to overthrow the government), South Africa's Nelson Mandela, 71 years old, walked away from the Victor Verster prison farm at Paarl, South Africa, a free man. He had survived the governmental system of apartheid. Mandela greeted a cheering throng of well-wishers, along with hundreds of millions of television viewers worldwide, with demands for an intensification of the struggle for equality for blacks, who make up nearly 75 percent of South Africa's population. For more info: www.anc.org.za /people/mandela.html or *Nelson Mandela*, by Reggie Finlayson (Lerner, 0-8225-4936-0, $25.26 Gr. 4–7).

SHROVE MONDAY. Feb 11. The Monday before Ash Wednesday. In Germany and Austria, this is called Rose Monday.

SPACE MILESTONE: *ENDEAVOUR* MAPPING MISSION (US). Feb 11, 2000. This manned flight spent 11 days in space creating a 3-D map of more than 70 percent of the Earth's surface. It will be the most accurate and complete topographic map of the Earth ever produced.

SPACE MILESTONE: *OSUMI* (JAPAN). Feb 11, 1970. First Japanese satellite launched. Japan became fourth nation to send a satellite into space.

TRINIDAD: CARNIVAL. Feb 11–12. Port of Spain. Called by islanders "the mother of all carnivals," a special tradition that brings together people from all over the world in an incredible colorful setting that includes the world's most celebrated calypsonians, steel band players, costume designers and masqueraders. Annually, the two days before Ash Wednesday. For info: Natl Carnival Commission, Tourism and Industrial Development Co, Administration Bldg, Queen Park Savannah, Port of Spain, Trinidad and Tobago, West Indies. Phone: (809) 623-1932. Fax: (809) 623-3848.

VATICAN CITY: INDEPENDENCE ANNIVERSARY. Feb 11, 1929. The Lateran Treaty, signed by Pietro Cardinal Gasparri and Benito Mussolini, guaranteed the independence of the State of Vatican City and recognized the sovereignty of the Holy See over it. Area is about 109 acres.

BIRTHDAYS TODAY

Brandy, 23, singer, actress ("Cinderella," "Moesha"), born Brandy Norwood at Macomb, MS, Feb 11, 1979.

Jeb Bush, 49, Governor of Florida (R), born Midland, TX, Feb 11, 1953.
Matthew Lawrence, 22, actor ("Brotherly Love," "Boy Meets World"), born Abington, PA, Feb 11, 1980.
Mike Leavitt, 51, Governor of Utah (R), born Cedar City, UT, Feb 11, 1951.
Jane Yolen, 63, author (*Owl Moon*), born New York, NY, Feb 11, 1939.

FEBRUARY 12 — TUESDAY

Day 43 — 322 Remaining

ADAMS, LOUISA CATHERINE JOHNSON: BIRTH ANNIVERSARY. Feb 12, 1775. Wife of John Quincy Adams, sixth president of the US. Born at London, England, she died at Washington, DC, May 14, 1852.

CHINESE NEW YEAR. Feb 12. Traditional Chinese lunar year begins at sunset on the day of second New Moon following the winter solstice. The New Year can begin any time from Jan 10 through Feb 19. Begins year 4700 of the ancient Chinese calendar, designated as the Year of the Horse. Generally celebrated until the Lantern Festival 15 days later, but merchants usually reopen their stores and places of business on the fifth day of the first lunar month (Feb 16, 2002). See also: "China: Lantern Festival" (Feb 26). This holiday is celebrated as Tet in Vietnam. For more info: *Celebrating Chinese New Year*, by Diane Hoyt-Goldsmith (Holiday House, 0-8234-1393-4, $16.95 Gr. 3–5) or *Chinese New Year*, by Sarah Moyse (Millbrook, 0-7613-0374-X, $20.90 Gr. K–3).

DARWIN, CHARLES ROBERT: BIRTH ANNIVERSARY. Feb 12, 1809. Author and naturalist, born at Shrewsbury, England. Best remembered for his books *On the Origin of Species by Means of Natural Selection, or the Preservation of Favoured Races in the Struggle for Life* and *The Descent of Man and Selection in Relation to Sex.* Died at Down, Kent, England, Apr 19, 1882. For more info: *Charles Darwin: Revolutionary Biologist*, by J. Edward Evans (Lerner, 0-8225-4914-X, $21.50 Gr. 6–9).

ICELAND: BURSTING DAY. Feb 12. Shrove Tuesday feasts with salted mutton and thick pea soup.

KOSCIUSKO, THADDEUS: BIRTH ANNIVERSARY. Feb 12, 1746. Polish patriot and American Revolutionary War figure. Born at Lithuania, he died at Solothurn, Switzerland, Oct 15, 1817. The governor of Massachusetts proclaims the first Sunday in February as Kosciusko Day (Feb 3 in 2002).

LINCOLN, ABRAHAM: BIRTH ANNIVERSARY. Feb 12, 1809. The 16th president of the US (Mar 4, 1861–Apr 15, 1865) and the first to be assassinated (on Good Friday, Apr 14, 1865, at Ford's Theatre at Washington, DC). His presidency encompassed the tragic Civil War. Especially remembered are his Emancipation Proclamation (Jan 1, 1863) and his Gettysburg Address (Nov 19, 1863). Born at Hardin County, KY, he died at Washington, DC, Apr 15, 1865. Lincoln's birthday is observed as part of President's Day in most states, but is a legal holiday in Florida, Illinois and Kentucky and an optional bank holiday in Iowa, Maryland, Michigan, Pennsylvania, Washington and West Virginia. See also: "Presidents' Day," (Feb 21). For more info: *Lincoln: A Photobiography*, by Russell Freedman (Houghton Mifflin, 0-89-919380-3, $17 Gr. 4–6) and *Lincoln: In His Own Words*, edited by Milton Meltzer (Harcourt Brace, 0-15-245437-3, $22.95 Gr. 6–8). For links to Lincoln sites on the Web, go to www.ipl.org/ref/POTUS or deil.lang.uiuc.edu/web.pages/holidays/lincoln.html.

February 2002

S	M	T	W	T	F	S
					1	2
3	4	5	6	7	8	9
10	11	12	13	14	15	16
17	18	19	20	21	22	23
24	25	26	27	28		

LOST PENNY DAY. Feb 12. Today is set aside to put all of those pennies stashed in candy dishes, bowls and jars back in circulation. Take those pennies and give them to a shelter or agency that assists the homeless or your local Humane Society. Annually, on President Abraham Lincoln's birthday, the man depicted on the copper penny. [©1995] For info: Adrienne Sioux Koopersmith, 1437 W Rosemont, #1W, Chicago, IL 60660-1319. Phone: (773) 743-5341. Fax: (773) 743-5395. E-mail: adrienne@21stcentury.net.

MARDI GRAS. Feb 12. Celebrated especially at New Orleans, LA, Mobile, AL, and certain Mississippi and Florida cities. Last feast before Lent. Although Mardi Gras (Fat Tuesday, literally) is properly limited to Shrove Tuesday, it has come to be popularly applied to the preceding two weeks of celebration.

MOON PHASE: NEW MOON. Feb 12. Moon enters New Moon phase at 2:41 AM, EST.

MYANMAR: UNION DAY. Feb 12. National holiday. Commemorates the formation of the Union of Burma on this date in 1947. Later the country's name was changed to Myanmar.

NAACP FOUNDED: ANNIVERSARY. Feb 12, 1909. The National Association for the Advancement of Colored People was founded by W.E.B. Dubois and Ida Wells-Barnett, among others, to wage a militant campaign against lynching and other forms of racial oppression. Its legal wing brought many lawsuits that successfully challenged segregation in the 1950s and 60s. For more info: www.naacp.org. The Feb 2001 issue of *Cobblestone* magazine is devoted to the NAACP.

★**NATIONAL CONSUMER PROTECTION WEEK.** Feb 12–17 (tentative).

SAFETYPUP'S® BIRTHDAY. Feb 12. This year Safetypup®, created by the National Child Safety Council, joyously celebrates his birthday by bringing safety awareness/education messages to children in a positive, nonthreatening manner. Safetypup® has achieved a wonderful balance of safety sense, caution and child-like enthusiasm about life and helping kids "Stay Safe and Sound." For info: Barbara Handley Huggett, Dir, NCSC, Research and Development, Box 1368, Jackson, MI 49204-1368. Phone: (517) 764-6070.

SHROVE TUESDAY. Feb 12. Always the day before Ash Wednesday. Sometimes called Pancake Tuesday. A legal holiday in certain counties in Florida.

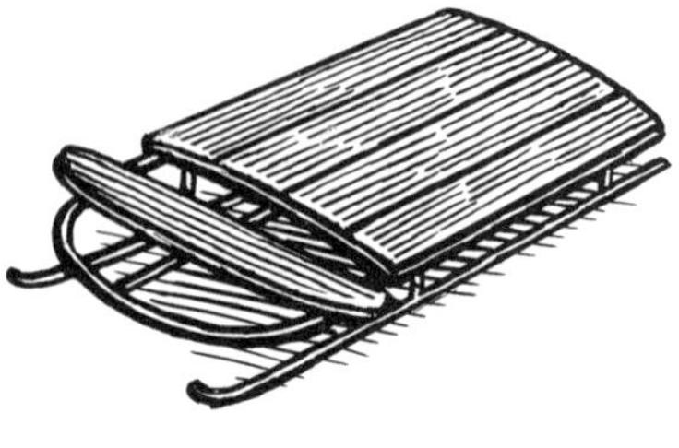

BIRTHDAYS TODAY

Ann Atwood, 89, author and illustrator (*Haiku: The Mood of Earth*), born California, Feb 12, 1913.
Judy Blume, 64, author (*Blubber, Superfudge*), born Elizabeth, NJ, Feb 12, 1938.

Joanna Kerns, 49, actress ("Growing Pains"), born San Francisco, CA, Feb 12, 1953.

Josephine Poole, 69, author (*Joan of Arc*), born London, England, Feb 12, 1933.

Christina Ricci, 22, actress (*Casper, Addams Family Values*), born Santa Monica, CA, Feb 12, 1980.

David Small, 57, illustrator (*The Library*, Caldecott for *So You Want to be President?*), author (*George Washington's Cows, Imogene's Antlers*), born Detroit, MI, Feb 12, 1945.

Arlen Specter, 72, US Senator (R, Pennsylvania), born Wichita, KS, Feb 12, 1930.

Jacqueline Woodson, 38, author (*I Hadn't Meant to Tell You This*, Coretta Scott King Award for *Miracle's Boys*), born Columbus, OH, Feb 12, 1964.

FEBRUARY 13 — WEDNESDAY

Day 44 — 321 Remaining

ASH WEDNESDAY. Feb 13. Marks the beginning of Lent. Forty weekdays and six Sundays (Saturday considered a weekday) remain until Easter Sunday. Named for use of ashes in ceremonial penance.

FIRST MAGAZINE PUBLISHED IN AMERICA: ANNIVERSARY. Feb 13, 1741. Andrew Bradford published *The American Magazine* just three days ahead of Benjamin Franklin's *General Magazine*.

GET A DIFFERENT NAME DAY. Feb 13. If you dislike your name, or merely find it boring, today is the day to adopt the moniker of your choice. [© 1999 by WPL] For info: Thomas or Ruth Roy, Wellness Permission League, 2418 Long Ln, Lebanon, PA 17046. Phone: (230) 332-4886. Fax: (230) 332-4886. E-mail: wellcat@supernet.com. Web: www.wellcat.com.

LENT BEGINS. Feb 13–Mar 30. Most Christian churches observe period of fasting and penitence (40 weekdays and six Sundays—Saturday considered a weekday) beginning on Ash Wednesday and ending on the Saturday before Easter.

TRUMAN, BESS (ELIZABETH) VIRGINIA WALLACE: BIRTH ANNIVERSARY. Feb 13, 1885. Wife of Harry S Truman, 33rd president of the US. Born at Independence, MO, and died there Oct 18, 1982.

WOOD, GRANT: BIRTH ANNIVERSARY. Feb 13, 1892. American artist, especially noted for his powerful realism and satirical paintings of the American scene, was born near Anamosa, IA. He was a printer, sculptor, woodworker and high school and college teacher. Among his best-remembered works are *American Gothic, Fall Plowing* and *Stone City*. Died at Iowa City, IA, Feb 12, 1942.

BIRTHDAYS TODAY

Janet Taylor Lisle, 55, author (*Afternoon of the Elves*), born Englewood, NJ, Feb 13, 1947.

Ouida Sebestyen, 78, author (*Words by Heart*), born Vernon, TX, Feb 13, 1924.

William Sleator, 57, author (*The Boy Who Reversed Himself*), born Havre de Grace, MD, Feb 13, 1945.

Simms Taback, 70, author and illustrator (Caldecott for *Joseph Had a Little Overcoat;* Caldecott honor for *There Was an Old Lady Who Swallowed a Fly*), born New York, NY, Feb 13, 1932.

Chuck Yeager, 79, pilot who broke the sound barrier, born Myra, WV, Feb 13, 1923.

FEBRUARY 14 — THURSDAY

Day 45 — 320 Remaining

ARIZONA: ADMISSION DAY: 90th ANNIVERSARY. Feb 14. Arizona became the 48th state in 1912.

BELGIUM: CAT FESTIVAL. Feb 14. Traditional cultural observance. Annually, on the second day of Lent.

CHILDREN'S LITERATURE CONFERENCE. Feb 14–16. Hyatt Regency, Columbus, OH. For info: Roy Wilson, Ohio State Univ. Phone: (614) 292-7902. E-mail: wilson.418@osu.edu.

ENIAC COMPUTER INTRODUCED: ANNIVERSARY. Feb 14, 1946. J. Presper Eckert and John W. Mauchly demonstrated the Electronic Numerical Integrator and Computer (ENIAC) for the first time at the University of Pennsylvania. The huge computer occupied a 1,500-square-foot room and contained nearly 18,000 vacuum tubes. The Army commissioned the computer to speed the calculation of firing tables for artillery. By the time the computer was ready, World War II was over. However, ENIAC prepared the way for future generations of computers.

FERRIS WHEEL DAY. Feb 14, 1859. Anniversary of the birth of George Washington Gale Ferris, American engineer and inventor, at Galesburg, IL. Among his many accomplishments as a civil engineer, Ferris is best remembered as the inventor of the Ferris wheel, which he developed for the World's Columbian Exposition at Chicago, IL, in 1893. Built on the Midway Plaisance, the 250-feet-in-diameter Ferris wheel (with 36 coaches, each capable of carrying 40 passengers), proved one of the greatest attractions of the fair. It was America's answer to the Eiffel Tower of the Paris International Exposition of 1889. Ferris died at Pittsburgh, PA, Nov 22, 1896.

FIRST PRESIDENTIAL PHOTOGRAPH: ANNIVERSARY. Feb 14, 1849. President James Polk became the first US president to be photographed while in office. The photographer was Mathew B. Brady, who would become famous for his photography during the American Civil War.

OREGON: ADMISSION DAY: ANNIVERSARY. Feb 14. Became 33rd state in 1859.

RACE RELATIONS DAY. Feb 14. A day designated by some churches to recognize the importance of interracial relations. Formerly was observed on Abraham Lincoln's birthday or on the Sunday preceding it. Since 1970 observance has generally been Feb 14.

READ TO YOUR CHILD DAY. Feb 14. Motto: "Show your kids you love them: Read to them." To encourage parents, teachers and other caregivers to engage in the wonderfully beneficial and delightfully fun practice of reading to children. A packet of materials is available, including ideas for campaigns to promote literacy, plus reproducible flyers on classroom reading, family reading at home and sharing books with babies. Flyers describe the benefits of read-aloud sessions, give tips for oral reading and list books people can read for more information. Annually, on Valentine's Day. For packet send business-sized, stamped, self-addressed envelope plus two first-class stamps tucked inside (to cover photocopy expenses) to Dee Anderson, 1023 25 St, #1, Moline, IL 61265.

VALENTINE'S DAY. Feb 14. St. Valentine's Day celebrates the feasts of two Christian martyrs of this name. One, a priest and physician, was beheaded at Rome, Italy, Feb 14, AD 269, during the reign of Emperor Claudius II. Another Valentine, the Bishop of Terni, is said to have been beheaded, also at Rome, Feb 14 (possibly in a later year). Both history and legend are vague and contradictory about details of the Valentines and some say that Feb 14 was selected for the celebration of Christian martyrs as a diversion from the ancient pagan observance of Lupercalia. An old legend has it that birds choose their mates on Valentine's Day. Now it is one of the most widely observed unofficial holidays. It is an occasion for the exchange of gifts (usually books, flowers or sweets) and greeting cards with affectionate or humorous messages. For more info: *Heart, Cupids, and Roses: The Story of Valentine Symbols*, by Edna Barth (Clarion, 0-618-06789-2, $16 Gr. 3–6) or *Let's Celebrate Valentine's Day*, by Peter Roop (Millbrook, 07613-0972-1, $19.90 Gr. PreK–3). For links to Valentine's Day sites on the Web go to: deil.lang.uiuc.edu/web.pages/holidays/valentine.html.

BIRTHDAYS TODAY

Drew Bledsoe, 30, football player, born Ellensburg, WA, Feb 14, 1972.

Odds Bodkin, 49, storyteller, author (*The Crane Wife*), born New York, NY, Feb 14, 1953.

Judd Gregg, 55, US Senator (R, New Hampshire), born Nashua, NH, Feb 14, 1947.

February 2002

S	M	T	W	T	F	S
					1	2
3	4	5	6	7	8	9
10	11	12	13	14	15	16
17	18	19	20	21	22	23
24	25	26	27	28		

Jamake Highwater, 60, author (*Anpao: An American Indian Odyssey*), born Glacier County, MT, Feb 14, 1942.

Steve McNair, 29, football player, born Mount Olive, MS, Feb 14, 1973.

Phyllis Root, 53, author (*What Baby Wants*), born Fort Wayne, IN, Feb 14, 1949.

Donna Shalala, 61, former US Secretary of Health and Human Services (Clinton administration), born Cleveland, OH, Feb 14, 1941.

Paul O. Zelinsky, 49, illustrator (Caldecott for *Rapunzel*; *Rumpelstiltskin*), born Evanston, IL, Feb 14, 1953.

FEBRUARY 15 — FRIDAY

Day 46 — 319 Remaining

CANADA: MAPLE LEAF FLAG ADOPTED: ANNIVERSARY. Feb 15, 1965. The new Canadian national flag was raised in Ottawa, Canada's capital, on this day. The red-and-white flag with a red maple leaf in the center replaced the Red Ensign flag, which had the British Union Jack in the upper left-hand corner. Commemorated as National Flag of Canada Day.

CLARK, ABRAHAM: BIRTH ANNIVERSARY. Feb 15, 1726. Signer of the Declaration of Independence, farmer and lawyer. Born at Elizabethtown, NJ, and died there Sept 15, 1794.

GALILEI, GALILEO: BIRTH ANNIVERSARY. Feb 15, 1564. Physicist and astronomer who helped overthrow medieval concepts of the world, born at Pisa, Italy. He proved the theory that all bodies, large and small, descend at equal speed and gathered evidence to support Copernicus's theory that the Earth and other planets revolve around the sun. Galileo died at Florence, Italy, Jan 8, 1642. For more info: *Starry Messenger*, by Peter Sis (Farrar, Straus, 0-374-37191-1, $16 Gr. 2–6).

THE NATIONAL CONFERENCE ON EDUCATION. Feb 15–17. San Diego, CA. 134th annual conference. For info: American Assn of School Administrators, 1801 N Moore St, Arlington, VA 22209. Phone: (703) 528-0700. Web: www.aasa.org.

RIVER OF WORDS ENVIRONMENTAL POETRY AND ART CONTEST. Feb 15. Deadline for submissions for this annual poetry and art contest on the theme of watersheds. Open to students K–12. Co-sponsored by the International Rivers Network and the Library of Congress Center for the Book. Teacher's Guide and teacher training workshops available. For entry form, contact the following: River of Words Project, 1847 Berkeley Way, Berkeley, CA 94703. Phone: (510) 848-1155. Fax: (510) 848-1008. E-mail: row@irn.org. Web: www.irn.org/row.

SUTTER, JOHN AUGUSTUS: BIRTH ANNIVERSARY. Feb 15, 1803. Born at Kandern, Germany, Sutter established the first white settlement on the site of Sacramento, CA, in 1839, and owned a large tract of land there, which he named New Helvetia. The first great gold strike in the US was on his property, at Sutter's Mill, Jan 24, 1848. His land was soon overrun by gold seekers who, he claimed, slaughtered his cattle and stole or destroyed his property. Sutter was bankrupt by 1852. Died at Washington, DC, June 18, 1880.

BIRTHDAYS TODAY

Norman Bridwell, 74, author and illustrator (*Clifford, the Big Red Dog*), born Kokomo, IN, Feb 15, 1928.

Jan Spivey Gilchrist, 53, illustrator, author (*Nathaniel Talking*, *Lift Ev'ry Voice and Sing*), born Chicago, IL, Feb 15, 1949.

Matt Groening, 48, cartoonist ("The Simpsons"), born Portland, OR, Feb 15, 1954.

Doris Orgel, 73, author (*The Devil in Vienna*), born Vienna, Austria, Feb 15, 1929.

FEBRUARY 16 — SATURDAY

Day 47 — 318 Remaining

HEART 2 HEART DAY. Feb 16. Confide something to your diary—start young and you'll write a whole book before you know it! Annually, two days after Valentine's Day. For info: Fine Print Publishing Co, PO Box 916401, Longwood, FL 32791-6401. Phone: (407) 814-7777. Fax: (407) 814-7677.

LITHUANIA: INDEPENDENCE DAY. Feb 16. National Day. The anniversary of Lithuania's declaration of independence in 1918 is observed as the Baltic state's Independence Day. In 1940, Lithuania became a part of the Soviet Union under an agreement between Joseph Stalin and Adolf Hitler. On Mar 11, 1990, Lithuania declared its independence from the Soviet Union, the first of the Soviet republics to do so. After demanding independence, Lithuania set up a border police force and aided young men in efforts to avoid the Soviet military draft, prompting then Soviet leader Mikhail Gorbachev to send tanks into the capital of Vilnius and impose oil and gas embargoes. In the wake of the failed coup attempt in Moscow, Aug 19, 1991, Lithuanian independence finally was recognized.

WILSON, HENRY: BIRTH ANNIVERSARY. Feb 16, 1812. The 18th vice president of the US (1873–75). Born at Farmington, NH, died at Washington, DC, Nov 22, 1875.

BIRTHDAYS TODAY

Jerome Bettis, 30, football player, born Detroit, MI, Feb 16, 1972.
LeVar Burton, 45, actor, host ("Reading Rainbow"), born Landsthul, Germany, Feb 16, 1957.

FEBRUARY 17 — SUNDAY

Day 48 — 317 Remaining

BROTHERHOOD/SISTERHOOD WEEK. Feb 17–23. A kick-off period for programs emphasizing a commitment to brotherhood/sisterhood. The National Program Office develops educational materials for use during this period that can be used year- round. Annually, the third full week in February. Sponsor: The National Conference for Community and Justice (founded as the National Conference of Christians and Jews). For info: Natl Conference for Community and Justice, 475 Park Ave South, 19th fl, New York, NY 10016-6901. Phone: (212) 545-1300. Web: www.nccj.org.

GERONIMO: DEATH ANNIVERSARY. Feb 17, 1909. American Indian of the Chiricahua (Apache) tribe was born about 1829 in Arizona. He was the leader of a small band of warriors whose devastating raids in Arizona, New Mexico and Mexico caused the US Army to send 5,000 men to recapture him after his first escape. He was confined at Fort Sill, OK, where he died after dictating, for publication, the story of his life.

HOMES FOR BIRDS WEEK. Feb 17–23. A week to encourage people to clean out, fix up and put up homes for wild birds. Annually, the third week in February. For info: John F. Gardner, Pres, Wild Bird Marketplace, 1891 Santa Barbara Dr, Ste 106, Lancaster, PA 17601. Phone: (717) 581-5310. Fax: (717) 581-5312. E-mail: jfg@wildbird.com. Web: www.wm-bird.com.

LUXEMBOURG: BÜRGSONNDEG. Feb 17. Young people build a huge bonfire on a hill to celebrate the victorious sun, marking the end of winter. A tradition dating to pre-Christian times. The Sunday after Ash Wednesday.

NATIONAL ENGINEERS WEEK. Feb 17–23. This annual observance, cosponsored by 74 national engineering societies and 61 major national corporations, will feature classroom programs in elementary and secondary schools throughout the US, shopping mall exhibits, engineering workplace tours and other events. For more info: Natl Engineers Week Headquarters, 1420 King St, Alexandria, VA 22314. Phone: (703) 684-2852. E-mail: eweek@nspe.org. Web: www.eweek.org.

NATIONAL PTA FOUNDERS' DAY: ANNIVERSARY. Feb 17, 1897. Celebrates the PTA's founding by Phoebe Apperson Hearst and Alice McLellan Birney. For info: Natl PTA, 330 N Wabash, Ste 2100, Chicago, IL 60611. Phone: (312) 670-6782. Fax: (312) 670-6783. E-mail: info@pta.org. Web: www.pta.org.

BIRTHDAYS TODAY

Vanessa Atler, 20, gymnast, born Valencia, CA, Feb 17, 1982.
Joseph Gordon-Levitt, 21, actor ("3rd Rock from the Sun," *Halloween H20*), born Los Angeles, CA, Feb 17, 1981.
Michael Jeffrey Jordan, 39, former basketball player, former minor league baseball player, born Brooklyn, NY, Feb 17, 1963.
Robert Newton Peck, 74, author (the Soup series, *A Day No Pigs Would Die*), born Vermont, Feb 17, 1928.
Chaim Potok, 73, author (*Zebra and Other Stories*), born Brooklyn, NY, Feb 17, 1929.
Craig Thomas, 69, US Senator (R, Wyoming), born Cody, WY, Feb 17, 1933.

FEBRUARY 18 — MONDAY

Day 49 — 316 Remaining

COW MILKED WHILE FLYING IN AN AIRPLANE: ANNIVERSARY. Feb 18, 1930. Elm Farm Ollie became the first cow to fly in an airplane. During the flight, which was attended by reporters, she was milked and the milk was sealed in paper containers and parachuted over St. Louis, MO.

DAVIS, JEFFERSON: INAUGURATION ANNIVERSARY. Feb 18, 1861. In the years before the Civil War, Jefferson Davis was the acknowledged leader of the Southern bloc in the US Senate and a champion of states' rights, but he had little to do with the secessionist movement until after his home state of Mississippi joined the Confederacy Jan 9, 1861. Davis withdrew from the Senate that same day. He was unanimously chosen as president of the Confederacy's provisional government and inaugurated at Montgomery, AL, Feb 18. Within the next year he was elected to a six-year term by popular vote and was inaugurated a second time Feb 22, 1862, at Richmond, VA.

GAMBIA: INDEPENDENCE DAY. Feb 18, 1965. National holiday. Independence from Britain granted. Referendum in April 1970 established Gambia as a republic within the Commonwealth.

PLANET PLUTO DISCOVERY: ANNIVERSARY. Feb 18, 1930. Pluto, the ninth planet, was discovered by astronomer Clyde Tombaugh at the Lowell Observatory at Flagstaff, AZ. It was given the name of the Roman god of the underworld. Some astronomers do not believe that Pluto is a planet. For more info: *Uranus, Neptune, and Pluto*, by Robin Kerrod (Lerner, 0-8225-3908-X, $21.27 Gr. 4–6) or go to Nine Planets: Multimedia Tour of the Solar System at www.seds.org/billa/tnp.

PRESIDENTS' DAY. Feb 18. Presidents' Day observes the birthdays of George Washington (Feb 22) and Abraham Lincoln (Feb 12). With the adoption of the Monday Holiday Law (which moved the observance of George Washington's birthday from Feb 22 each year to the third Monday in February), some of the specific significance of the event was lost and added impetus was given to the popular description of that holiday as Presidents' Day. Present usage often regards Presidents' Day as a day to honor all former presidents of the US. While the federal holiday still is George

Washington's birthday, many states now declare Presidents' Day to be a holiday. Annually, the third Monday in February.

WASHINGTON, GEORGE: BIRTHDAY OBSERVANCE (LEGAL HOLIDAY). Feb 18. Legal public holiday (Public Law 90–363 sets Washington's birthday observance on the third Monday in February each year—applicable to federal employees and to the District of Columbia). Observed on this day in all states. See also: "Washington, George: Birth Anniversary" (Feb 22). For links to websites about this holiday and George Washington, go to: deil.lang.uiuc.edu/web.pages/holidays/washington.html.

BIRTHDAYS TODAY

Barbara Joosse, 53, author (*Mama, Do You Love Me?; Ghost Trap: A Wild Willie Mystery*), born Grafton, WI, Feb 18, 1949.

John William Warner, 75, US Senator (R, Virginia), born Washington, DC, Feb 18, 1927.

FEBRUARY 19 — TUESDAY

Day 50 — 315 Remaining

COPERNICUS, NICOLAUS: BIRTH ANNIVERSARY. Feb 19, 1473. Polish astronomer and priest who revolutionized scientific thought with what came to be called the Copernican theory, that placed the sun instead of the Earth at the center of our planetary system. Born at Torun, Poland, died at East Prussia, May 24, 1543.

JAPANESE INTERNMENT: 60th ANNIVERSARY. Feb 19, 1942. As a result of President Franklin Roosevelt's Executive Order 9066, some 110,000 Japanese-Americans living in coastal Pacific areas were placed in concentration camps in remote areas of Arizona, Arkansas, inland California, Colorado, Idaho, Utah and Wyoming. The interned Japanese-Americans (two-thirds were US citizens) lost an estimated $400 million in property. They were allowed to return to their homes Jan 2, 1945. For more info: *Life in a Japanese American Internment Camp*, by Diane Yancey (Lucent, 1-56006-345-9, $17.96 Gr. 6–12).

BIRTHDAYS TODAY

Jeff Daniels, 47, actor (*101 Dalmatians, Fly Away Home*), born Chelsea, MI, Feb 19, 1955.

Jill Krementz, 62, author and photographer (*A Very Young Dancer*, the How It Feels series), born New York, NY, Feb 19, 1940.

FEBRUARY 20 — WEDNESDAY

Day 51 — 314 Remaining

ADAMS, ANSEL: 100th BIRTH ANNIVERSARY. Feb 20, 1902. American photographer, known for his photographs of Yosemite National Park, born at San Francisco, CA. Adams died at Monterey, CA, Apr 22, 1984. For info: *Eye on the World: A Story About Ansel Adams*, by Julie Dunlap (Carolrhoda, 0-876-14966-2, $5.95 Gr. K–3).

DOUGLASS, FREDERICK: DEATH ANNIVERSARY. Feb 20, 1895. American journalist, orator and antislavery leader. Born at Tuckahoe, MD, probably in February 1817. Died at Anacostia Heights, Washington, DC. His original name before his escape from slavery was Frederick Augustus Washington Bailey. For more info: *Frederick Douglass in His Own Words*, edited by Milton Meltzer (Harcourt, 0-15-229492-9, $22 Gr. 7 and up) or *Frederick Douglass: Leader Against Slavery*, by Patricia and Fredrick McKissack (Enslow, 0-8949-0306-3, $14.95 Gr. K–3). See also: "Douglass Escapes to Freedom: Anniversary" (Sept 3).

MOON PHASE: FIRST QUARTER. Feb 20. Moon enters First Quarter phase at 7:02 AM, EST.

NORTHERN HEMISPHERE HOODIE-HOO DAY. Feb 20. At high noon (local time) citizens are asked to go outdoors and yell "Hoodie-Hoo" to chase away winter and make ready for spring, one month away. [© 1999 by WH] For info: Tom or Ruth Roy, Wellcat Holidays, 2418 Long Ln, Lebanon, PA 17046. Phone: (230) 332-4886. E-mail: wellcat@supernet.com. Web: www.wellcat.com.

PISCES, THE FISH. Feb 20–Mar 20. In the astronomical/astrological zodiac, which divides the sun's apparent orbit into 12 segments, the period Feb 20–Mar 20 is identified, traditionally, as the sun sign of Pisces, the Fish. The ruling planet is Neptune.

SPACE MILESTONE: *FRIENDSHIP 7* (US): FIRST AMERICAN TO ORBIT EARTH: 40th ANNIVERSARY. Feb 20, 1962. John Herschel Glenn, Jr, became the first American, and the third man, to orbit Earth. Aboard the capsule *Friendship 7*, he made three orbits of Earth. Spacecraft was *Mercury-Atlas 6*. In 1998 the 77-year-old Glenn went into space once again on the space shuttle *Discovery* to study the effects of aging.

SPACE MILESTONE: *MIR* SPACE STATION (USSR): ANNIVERSARY. Feb 20, 1986. A "third-generation" orbiting space station, *Mir* (Peace), was launched without crew from the Baikonur space center at Leninsk, Kazakhstan. It is 40 feet long, weighs 47 tons and has six docking ports. Russian and American crews used the station for 15 years. Russia planned to take *Mir* out of service in Mar 2001.

STUDENT VOLUNTEER DAY. Feb 20. To honor students who give of themselves and of their personal time to improve the lives of others and their communities. Annually, Feb 20. Est attendance: 250. For info: Susquehanna Univ, Center for Service Learning and Volunteer Programs, 514 University Ave, Selinsgrove, PA 17870-1001. Phone: (570) 372-4139. Fax: (570) 372-2745. E-mail: woodsd@susqu.edu.

BIRTHDAYS TODAY

Charles Barkley, 39, former basketball player, born Leeds, AL, Feb 20, 1963.

Rosemary Harris, 79, author (*The Moon in the Cloud*), born London, England, Feb 20, 1923.

February 2002

S	M	T	W	T	F	S
					1	2
3	4	5	6	7	8	9
10	11	12	13	14	15	16
17	18	19	20	21	22	23
24	25	26	27	28		

Brian Littrell, 27, singer (Backstreet Boys), born Lexington, KY, Feb 20, 1975.

Mitch McConnell, 60, US Senator (R, Kentucky), born Colbert County, AL, Feb 20, 1942.

FEBRUARY 21 — THURSDAY

Day 52 — 313 Remaining

BANGLADESH: MARTYRS' DAY. Feb 21. National mourning day or Shaheed Day in memory of martyrs of the Bengali Language Movement in 1952.

BATTLE OF VERDUN: ANNIVERSARY. Feb 21–Dec 18, 1916. The German High Command launched an offensive on the Western Front at Verdun, France, which became WWI's single longest battle. An estimated one million men were killed, decimating both the German and French armies.

FIRST WOMAN TO GRADUATE FROM DENTAL SCHOOL: ANNIVERSARY. Feb 21, 1866. Lucy Hobbs became the first woman to graduate from a dental school at Cincinnati, OH.

WASHINGTON MONUMENT DEDICATED: ANNIVERSARY. Feb 21, 1885. Monument to the first president was dedicated at Washington, DC. For more info: www.nps.gov/wash/index.htm.

YAWM ARAFAT: THE STANDING AT ARAFAT. Feb 21. Islamic calendar date: Dhu-Hijjah 9, 1422. The day when people on the Hajj (pilgrimage to Mecca) assemble for "the Standing" at the plain of Arafat at Mina, Saudi Arabia, near Mecca. This gathering is a foreshadowing of the Day of Judgment. Different methods for "anticipating" the visibility of the new moon crescent at Mecca are used by different Muslim groups. US date may vary.

BIRTHDAYS TODAY

Jim Aylesworth, 59, author (*The Gingerbread Man*), born Jacksonville, FL, Feb 21, 1943.

Charlotte Church, 16, singer (*Voice of an Angel*), born Wales, Feb 21, 1986.

Patricia Hermes, 66, author (*When Snow Lay Soft on the Mountain*), born Brooklyn, NY, Feb 21, 1936.

Jennifer Love Hewitt, 23, actress (*I Know What You Did Last Summer*, "Party of Five"), born Waco, TX, Feb 21, 1979.

Victor Martinez, 48, author (National Book Award for *Parrot in the Oven: Mi Vida*), born Fresno, CA, Feb 21, 1954.

Olympia J. Snowe, 55, US Senator (R, Maine), born Augusta, ME, Feb 21, 1947.

FEBRUARY 22 — FRIDAY

Day 53 — 312 Remaining

BADEN-POWELL, ROBERT: BIRTH ANNIVERSARY. Feb 22, 1857. British army officer who founded the Boy Scouts and Girl Guides. Born at London, England, he died at Kenya, Africa, Jan 8, 1941.

EID-AL-ADHA: FEAST OF THE SACRIFICE. Feb 22. Islamic calendar date: Dhu-Hijja 10, 1422. Commemorates Abraham's willingness to sacrifice his son Ishmael in obedience to God. It is part of the Hajj (pilgrimage to Mecca). The day begins with the sacrifice of an animal in remembrance of the Angel Gabriel's substitution of a lamb as Abraham's offering. One-third of the meat is given to the poor and the rest is shared with friends and family. Celebrated with gifts and general merrymaking, the festival usually continues for several days. It is celebrated as Tabaski in Benin, Burkina Faso, Guinea, Guinea-Bissau, Ivory Coast, Mali, Niger and Senegal and as Kurban Bayram in Turkey and Bosnia. Different methods for "anticipating" the visibility of the moon crescent at Mecca are used by different Muslim groups. US date may vary.

MONTGOMERY BOYCOTT ARRESTS: ANNIVERSARY. Feb 22, 1956. On Feb 20 white city leaders of Montgomery, AL, issued an ultimatum to black organizers of the three-month-old Montgomery bus boycott. They said if the boycott ended immediately there would be "no retaliation whatsoever." If it did not end, it was made clear they would begin arresting black leaders. Two days later, 80 well-known boycotters, including Rosa Parks, Martin Luther King, Jr, and E.D. Nixon, marched to the sheriff's office in the county courthouse, where they gave themselves up for arrest. They were booked, fingerprinted and photographed. The next day the story was carried by newspapers all over the world.

SAINT LUCIA: INDEPENDENCE DAY. Feb 22. National holiday. Commemorates independence from Britain in 1979.

WADLOW, ROBERT PERSHING: BIRTH ANNIVERSARY. Feb 22, 1918. Tallest man in recorded history, born at Alton, IL. Though only 9 lbs at birth, by age 10 Wadlow already stood more than 6 feet tall and weighed 210 lbs. When Wadlow died at age 22, he was a remarkable 8 feet 11.1 inches tall, 490 lbs. His gentle, friendly manner in the face of constant public attention earned him the name "Gentle Giant." Wadlow died July 15, 1940, at Manistee, MI, of complications resulting from a foot infection.

WASHINGTON, GEORGE: BIRTH ANNIVERSARY. Feb 22, 1732. First president of the US ("First in war, first in peace and first in the hearts of his countrymen" in the words of Henry "Light-Horse Harry" Lee). Born at Westmoreland County, VA, Feb 22, 1732 (New Style). When he was born the colonies were still using the Julian (Old Style) calendar and the year began in March, so the date on the calendar when he was born was Feb 11, 1731. He died at Mount Vernon, VA, Dec 14, 1799. See also: "Washington, George: Birthday Observance (Legal Holiday)" (Feb 18 in 2002). For info: www.ipl.org/ref/POTUS.

WOOLWORTHS FIRST OPENED: ANNIVERSARY. Feb 22, 1879. The first chain store, Woolworths, opened at Utica, NY. In 1997, the closing of the chain was announced.

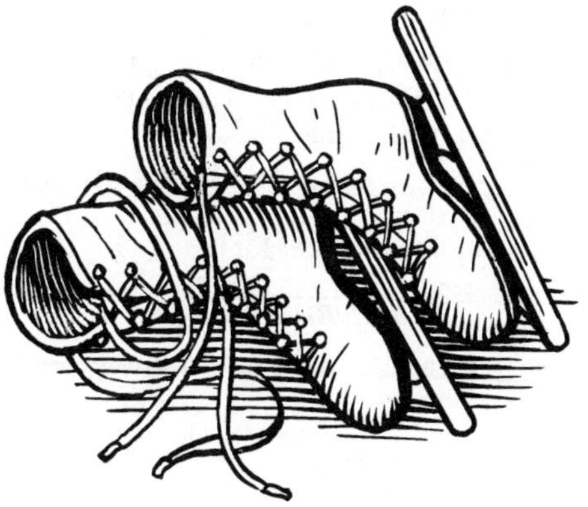

BIRTHDAYS TODAY

Drew Barrymore, 27, actress (*E.T.: The Extra Terrestrial; The Wedding Singer*), born Los Angeles, CA, Feb 22, 1975.

Michael Te Pei Chang, 30, tennis player, born Hoboken, NJ, Feb 22, 1972.

Lisa Fernandez, 31, softball player, born Long Beach, CA, Feb 22, 1971.

William Frist, 50, US Senator (R, Tennessee), born Nashville, TN, Feb 22, 1952.

Edward Moore (Ted) Kennedy, 70, US Senator (D, Massachusetts), born Boston, MA, Feb 22, 1932.

Jayson Williams, 34, basketball player, born Ritter, SC, Feb 22, 1968.

FEBRUARY 23 — SATURDAY

Day 54 — 311 Remaining

BRUNEI DARUSSALAM: NATIONAL DAY. Feb 23. National holiday.

DU BOIS, W.E.B.: BIRTH ANNIVERSARY. Feb 23, 1868. William Edward Burghardt Du Bois, American educator and leader of the movement for black equality. Born at Great Barrington, MA, he died at Accra, Ghana, Aug 27, 1963. "The cost of liberty," he wrote in 1909, "is less than the price of repression." The Feb 2000 issue of *Cobblestone* magazine is devoted to Du Bois.

FIRST CLONING OF AN ADULT ANIMAL: 5th ANNIVERSARY. Feb 23, 1997. Researchers in Scotland announced the first cloning of an adult animal, a lamb they named Dolly with a genetic makeup identical to that of her mother. This led to worldwide speculation about the possibility of human cloning. On Mar 4, President Clinton imposed a ban on the federal funding of human cloning research.

GUYANA: ANNIVERSARY OF REPUBLIC. Feb 23, 1970. National holiday.

HANDEL, GEORGE FREDERICK: BIRTH ANNIVERSARY. Feb 23, 1685. Born at Halle, Saxony, Germany, Handel and Bach, born the same year, were perhaps the greatest masters of Baroque music. Handel's most frequently performed work is the oratorio *Messiah*, which was first heard in 1742. He died at London, England, Apr 14, 1759. See also: "Bach, Johann Sebastian: Birth Anniversary" (Mar 21).

IWO JIMA DAY: ANNIVERSARY. Feb 23, 1945. The American flag was raised on the Pacific island of Iwo Jima by US marines after the World War II battle.

TAYLOR, GEORGE: DEATH ANNIVERSARY. Feb 23, 1781. Signer of the Declaration of Independence. Born 1716 at British Isles (exact date unknown). Died at Easton, PA.

BIRTHDAYS TODAY

Laura Geringer, 54, author (the Myth Men series), born New York, NY, Feb 23, 1948.

Patricia Richardson, 50, actress ("Home Improvement"), born Bethesda, MD, Feb 23, 1952.

Rodney Slater, 47, former US Secretary of Transportation (Clinton administration), born Tutwyler, MS, Feb 23, 1955.

February 2002

S	M	T	W	T	F	S
					1	2
3	4	5	6	7	8	9
10	11	12	13	14	15	16
17	18	19	20	21	22	23
24	25	26	27	28		

Walter Wick, 49, illustrator, photographer (the I Spy series, *A Drop of Water*), born Hartford, CT, Feb 23, 1953.

FEBRUARY 24 — SUNDAY

Day 55 — 310 Remaining

ESTONIA: INDEPENDENCE DAY. Feb 24. National holiday. Commemorates declaration of independence from the Soviet Union in 1918. However, independence was brief; Estonia was to be part of the Soviet Union until 1991.

GREGORIAN CALENDAR DAY: ANNIVERSARY. Feb 24, 1582. Pope Gregory XIII, enlisting the expertise of distinguished astronomers and mathematicians, issued a bull correcting the Julian calendar that was then 10 days in error. The new calendar named for him, the Gregorian calendar, became effective Oct 4, 1582, in most Catholic countries, in 1752 in Britain and the American colonies, in 1918 in Russia and in 1923 in Greece. It is the most widely used calendar in the world today. See also: "Calendar Adjustment Day: Anniversary" (Sept 2) and "Gregorian Calendar Adjustment: Anniversary" (Oct 4).

GRIMM, WILHELM CARL: BIRTH ANNIVERSARY. Feb 24, 1786. Mythologist and author, born at Hanau, Germany. Best remembered for *Grimm's Fairy Tales*, in collaboration with his brother, Jacob. Died at Berlin, Germany, Dec 16, 1859. See also: "Grimm, Jacob: Birth Anniversary" (Jan 4).

JOHNSON IMPEACHMENT PROCEEDINGS: ANNIVERSARY. Feb 24, 1867. In a showdown over Reconstruction policy following the Civil War, the House of Representatives voted to impeach President Andrew Johnson. During the two years following the end of the war, the Republican-controlled Congress had sought to severely punish the South. Congress passed the Reconstruction Act that divided the South into five military districts headed by officers who were to take their orders from General Grant, the head of the army, instead of from President Johnson. In addition, Congress passed the Tenure of Office Act, which required Senate approval before Johnson could remove any official whose appointment was originally approved by the Senate. Johnson vetoed this act but the veto was overridden by Congress. To test the constitutionality of the act, Johnson dismissed Secretary of War Edwin Stanton, triggering the impeachment vote. On Mar 5, 1868, the Senate convened as a court to hear the charges against President Johnson. The Senate vote of 35–19 fell one vote short of the two-thirds majority necessary for impeachment. For more info: www.law.umkc.edu/faculty/projects/ftrials/ftrials.htm.

WAGNER, HONUS: BIRTH ANNIVERSARY. Feb 24, 1874. American baseball great, born John Peter Wagner at Carnegie, PA. Nicknamed the "Flying Dutchman," Wagner was among the first five players elected to the Baseball Hall of Fame in 1936. Died at Carnegie, Dec 6, 1955.

WINTER OLYMPICS CLOSING CEREMONY. Feb 24. Salt Lake City, UT. More than 3.5 billion people around the world watched on TV as 3,500 athletes from 80 nations competed at the XIX Winter Olympics. Opening ceremonies were on Feb 8. For info: Salt Lake Olympic Committee, PO Box 45002, Salt Lake City, UT 84145-0002. Phone: (801) 212-2002. Web: www.slc2002.org.

BIRTHDAYS TODAY

Beth Broderick, 43, actress ("Sabrina, the Teenage Witch"), born Long Beach, CA, Feb 24, 1959.

Lleyton Hewitt, 21, tennis player, born Adelaide, Australia, Feb 24, 1981.

Steven Jobs, 47, co-founder of Apple computer company, born Los Altos, CA, Feb 24, 1955.

Joseph I. Lieberman, 60, US Senator (D, Connecticut), born Stamford, CT, Feb 24, 1942.

Uri Orlev, 71, author (*Lydia, Queen of Palestine; The Man from the Other Side*), born Warsaw, Poland, Feb 24, 1931.

George Ryan, 68, Governor of Illinois (R), born Maquoketa, IA, Feb 24, 1934.

Don Siegelman, 56, Governor of Alabama (D), born Mobile, AL, Feb 24, 1946.

FEBRUARY 25 — MONDAY

Day 56 — 309 Remaining

CLAY BECOMES HEAVYWEIGHT CHAMP: ANNIVERSARY. Feb 25, 1964. Twenty-two-year-old Cassius Clay (later Muhammad Ali) became world heavyweight boxing champion by defeating Sonny Liston. At the height of his athletic career Ali was well known for both his fighting ability and personal style. His most famous saying was, "I am the greatest!" In 1967 he was convicted of violating the Selective Service Act and was stripped of his title for refusing to be inducted into the armed services during the Vietnam War. Ali cited religious convictions as his reason for refusal. In 1971 the Supreme Court reversed the conviction. Ali is the only fighter to win the heavyweight title three separate times. He defended that title nine times.

KUWAIT: NATIONAL DAY. Feb 25. National holiday.

NATIONAL BANK CHARTERED BY CONGRESS: ANNIVERSARY. Feb 25, 1791. The First Bank of the US at Philadelphia, PA, was chartered. Proposed as a national (or central) bank by Alexander Hamilton, it lost its charter in 1811. The Second Bank of the US received a charter in 1816, which expired in 1836. Since that time, the US has had no central bank. Central banking functions are carried out by the Federal Reserve System, established in 1913.

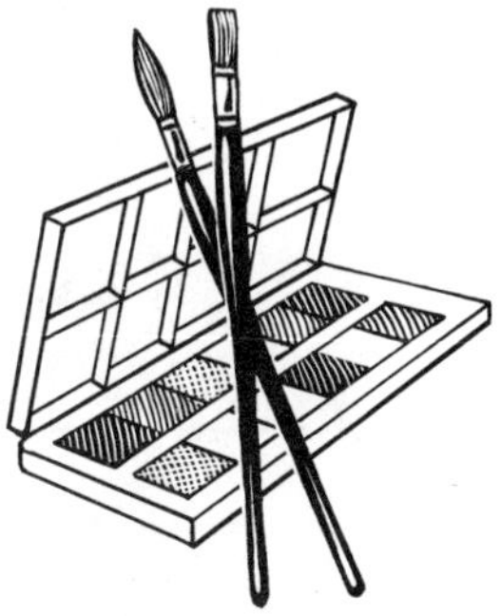

RENOIR, PIERRE AUGUSTE: BIRTH ANNIVERSARY. Feb 25, 1841. Impressionist painter, born at Limoges, France. Renoir's paintings are known for their joy and sensuousness as well as their use of light. In his later years he was crippled by arthritis and would paint with the brush strapped to his hand. He died at Cagnes-sur-Mer, Provence, France, Dec 17, 1919.

TA'ANIT ESTHER (FAST OF ESTHER). Feb 25. Hebrew calendar date: Adar 13, 5762. Commemorates Queen Esther's fast, in the 6th century BC, to save the Jews of ancient Persia. Ordinarily observed Adar 13, the Fast of Esther is observed on the previous Thursday (Adar 11) when Adar 13 is a Sabbath.

BIRTHDAYS TODAY

Cynthia Voigt, 60, author (Newbery for *Homecoming; Dicey's Song*), born Boston, MA, Feb 25, 1942.

FEBRUARY 26 — TUESDAY

Day 57 — 308 Remaining

CHINA: LANTERN FESTIVAL. Feb 26. Traditional Chinese festival falls on 15th day of first month of Chinese lunar calendar year. Lantern processions mark end of the Chinese New Year holiday season. See also: "Chinese New Year" (Feb 12).

CODY, WILLIAM FREDERIC "BUFFALO BILL": BIRTH ANNIVERSARY. Feb 26, 1846. American frontiersman who claimed to have killed more than 4,000 buffalos, born at Scott County, IA. Subject of many heroic yarns, Cody became successful as a showman, taking his Wild West Show across the US and to Europe. Died Jan 10, 1917, at Denver, CO.

FEDERAL COMMUNICATIONS COMMISSION CREATED: ANNIVERSARY. Feb 26, 1934. President Franklin D. Roosevelt ordered the creation of a Communications Commission, which became the FCC. It was created by Congress June 19, 1934, to oversee communication by radio, wire or cable. TV and satellite communication later became part of its charge.

GRAND CANYON NATIONAL PARK ESTABLISHED: ANNIVERSARY. Feb 26, 1919. By an act of Congress, Grand Canyon National Park was established. An immense gorge cut through the high plateaus of northwest Arizona by the raging Colorado River and covering 1,218,375 acres, Grand Canyon National Park is considered one of the most spectacular natural phenomena in the world. For more info: www.nps.gov/grca.

KUWAIT: LIBERATION DAY. Feb 26. National holiday. Commemorates the liberation of Kuwait City from Iraqi troops on this day in 1991.

NATIONAL ASSOCIATION OF INDEPENDENT SCHOOLS ANNUAL CONFERENCE. Feb 26–Mar 1. San Francisco, CA. For info: Natl Assn of Independent Schools, 1620 L St NW, Ste 1100, Washington, DC 20036. Phone: (202) 973-9700. E-mail: confpreview@nais-schools.org. Web: www.nais.org.

PURIM. Feb 26. Hebrew calendar date: Adar 14, 5762. Feasts, gifts, charity and the reading of the Book of Esther mark this joyous commemoration of Queen Esther's intervention, in the 6th century BC, to save the Jews of ancient Persia. Haman's plot to exterminate the Jews was thwarted, and he was hanged on the very day he had set for the execution of the Jews.

STRAUSS, LEVI: BIRTH ANNIVERSARY. Feb 26, 1829. Bavarian immigrant Levi Strauss created the world's first pair of jeans—Levi's 501 jeans—for California's gold miners in 1850. Born at Buttenheim, Bavaria, Germany, he died in 1902.

TAIWAN: LANTERN FESTIVAL AND TOURISM DAY. Feb 26. Fifteenth day of the First Moon of the lunar calendar marks end of New Year holiday season. Lantern processions and contests.

BIRTHDAYS TODAY

Sarah Ezer, 21, actress ("The Adventures of Shirley Holmes: Detective"), born Vancouver, BC, Canada, Feb 26, 1981.

Marshall Faulk, 29, football player, born New Orleans, LA, Feb 26, 1973.

Sharon Bell Mathis, 65, author (*The Hundred Penny Box*), born Atlantic City, NJ, Feb 26, 1937.

Jenny Thompson, 29, Olympic swimmer, born Dover, NH, Feb 26, 1973.

Bernard Wolf, 72, author (*HIV Positive*), born New York, NY, Feb 26, 1930.

FEBRUARY 27 — WEDNESDAY

Day 58 — 307 Remaining

DOMINICAN REPUBLIC: INDEPENDENCE DAY. Feb 27. National Day. Independence gained in 1844 with the withdrawal of Haitians, who had controlled the area for 22 years.

KUWAIT LIBERATED AND 100-HOUR WAR ENDS: ANNIVERSARY. Feb 27, 1991. Allied troops entered Kuwait City, Kuwait, four days after launching a ground offensive. President George Bush declared Kuwait to be liberated and ceased all offensive military operations in the Gulf War. The end of military operations at midnight EST came 100 hours after the beginning of the land attack.

LONGFELLOW, HENRY WADSWORTH: BIRTH ANNIVERSARY. Feb 27, 1807. American poet and writer, born at Portland, ME. He is best remembered for his classic narrative poems, such as *The Song of Hiawatha, Paul Revere's Ride* and *The Wreck of the Hesperus*. Died at Cambridge, MA, Mar 24, 1882. For more info: *Henry Wadsworth Longfellow: America's Beloved Poet*, by Bonnie Lukes (Morgan Reynolds, 1-883846-31-5, $19.95 Gr. 6–12).

MOON PHASE: FULL MOON. Feb 27. Moon enters Full Moon phase at 4:17 AM, EST.

NO BRAINER DAY. Feb 27. This is a day where you can slack off, play hookey or find the easy way out. If you are going to do anything at all, make it a no-brainer, something you can do without any serious thought. A drop in heart attacks is found on days like this—just what the doctor ordered. You have the rest of the year for a hectic schedule. For info: Adrienne Sioux Koopersmith, 1437 W Rosemont, 1W, Chicago, IL 60660-1319. Phone: (773) 743-5341. Fax: (773) 743-5395. E-mail: kooper@interaccess.com.

PERIGEAN SPRING TIDES. Feb 27. Spring tides, the highest possible tides, occur when New Moon or Full Moon takes place within 24 hours of the moment the Moon is nearest Earth (perigee) in its monthly orbit, at 4 AM, EST. The word *spring* refers not to the season but comes from the German word *springen*, "to rise up."

TWENTY-SECOND AMENDMENT TO US CONSTITUTION (TWO-TERM LIMIT): RATIFICATION ANNIVERSARY. Feb 27, 1950. After the four successive presidential terms of Franklin Roosevelt, the 22nd Amendment limited the tenure of presidential office to two terms.

BIRTHDAYS TODAY

Uri Shulevitz, 67, author and illustrator (*The Treasure*), born Warsaw, Poland, Feb 27, 1935.

FEBRUARY 28 — THURSDAY

Day 59 — 306 Remaining

TAIWAN: TWO-TWENTY-EIGHT DAY. Feb 28. National holiday. Commemorates the thousands of Taiwanese killed in 1947 following the transfer of control from the Japanese to the Nationalists.

TENNIEL, JOHN: BIRTH ANNIVERSARY. Feb 28, 1820. Illustrator and cartoonist, born at London, England. Best remembered for his illustrations for Lewis Carroll's *Alice's Adventures in Wonderland*. Died at London, Feb 25, 1914.

BIRTHDAYS TODAY

Eric Lindros, 29, hockey player, born London, ON, Canada, Feb 28, 1973.

Donna Jo Napoli, 54, author (*The Prince of the Pond, Stones in Water*), born Miami, FL, Feb 28, 1948.

Dean Smith, 71, basketball coach, born Emporia, KS, Feb 28, 1931.

MARCH 1 — FRIDAY

Day 60 — 305 Remaining

★**AMERICAN RED CROSS MONTH.** Mar 1–31. Presidential Proclamation for Red Cross Month issued each year for March since 1943. Issued as American Red Cross Month since 1987.

THE ARRIVAL OF MARTIN PINZON: ANNIVERSARY. Mar 1, 1493. Martin Alonzo Pinzon (1440–1493), Spanish shipbuilder and navigator (and co-owner of the *Niña* and the *Pinta*), accompanied Christopher Columbus on his first voyage, as commander of the *Pinta*. Storms separated the ships on their return voyage, and the *Pinta* first touched land at Bayona, Spain, where Pinzon gave Europe its first news of the discovery of the New World before Columbus's landing at Palos. Pinzon's brother, Vicente Yanez Pinzon, was commander of the third caravel of the expedition, the *Niña*.

ARTICLES OF CONFEDERATION RATIFIED: ANNIVERSARY. Mar 1, 1781. This compact made among the original 13 states had been adopted by the Continental Congress Nov 15, 1777, and submitted to the states for ratification Nov 17, 1777. Maryland was the last state to approve, Feb 27, 1781, but Congress named Mar 1, 1781, as the day of formal ratification. The Articles of Confederation remained the supreme law of the nation until Mar 4, 1789, when Congress first met under the Constitution.

BOSNIA AND HERZEGOVINA: INDEPENDENCE DAY. Mar 1. Commemorates independence in 1991.

HEMOPHILIA MONTH. Mar 1–31. For info: Natl Hemophilia Foundation, 116 W 32nd St, 11th Floor, New York, NY 10001. Phone: (800) 42H-ANDI. Web: www.hemophilia.org.

★**IRISH-AMERICAN HERITAGE MONTH.** Mar 1–31. Presidential Proclamation called for by House Joint Resolution 401 (PL 103–379).

JAPAN: OMIZUTORI (WATER-DRAWING FESTIVAL). Mar 1–14. Todaiji, Nara. At midnight, a solemn rite is performed in the flickering light of pine torches. People rush for sparks from the torches, which are believed to have magic power against evil. Most spectacular on the night of Mar 12. The ceremony of drawing water is observed at 2 AM Mar 13, to the accompaniment of ancient Japanese music.

KOREA: SAMILJOL or INDEPENDENCE MOVEMENT DAY. Mar 1. Koreans observe the anniversary of the independence movement against Japanese colonial rule in 1919.

MARCH 1
NATIONAL PIG DAY

It's time to PIG OUT! There's something about pigs that makes us smile. Try saying Porky Pig, Wilbur, Babe and Arnold Ziffle (remember him from"Green Acres"?); you'll probably be smiling before you're finished. Kick off a National Pig Day celebration with the following quiz. See how many students can fill in the blanks correctly. (You may have to leave some out for very young children.) Students can have fun making their own quiz for a different animal.

As sloppy as a ____.	___ barrel politics
A ___ in a poke.	___-back ride
A greedy ___ .	___-headed
And ___ may fly.	___ wild.

Casting pearls before ______.
You can't turn a ____'s ear into a silk purse.

Regardless of the reasons, pigs are attention grabbers and worth sneaking into the curriculum. You might want to consider a short pig unit. The wide variety of pig books makes it possible to use a whole language approach. There are even several pig math books.

Middle and junior high school educators may be leery about incorporating a pig novel into a literature group. Don't be. Any initial resistance to animal fantasy quickly wears off when the plot and characters are well-developed, especially in a novel such as *Charlotte's Web.* Charlotte and Wilbur's friendship is one of the most endearing (and enduring) tales in children's literature. Unfortunately, by the time most children reach middle school, *Charlotte's Web* has dropped out of sight. That's a shame. Middle school and junior high years are the time when children begin struggling with who they are. They are ultraconscious about friends and the meaning of friendship.

In reading class, dust off copies of *Charlotte's Web,* by E.B. White (HarperCollins, 0-06-440055-7, $5.95), and let the children read it [again]. Middle school students are the perfect age for recognizing emotional nuances and appreciating White's clever use of language, two things many of them probably missed if they read the book as a primary student. Pose provocative questions about friendship and its responsibilities and group discussions will take off. Also, because children already know the story line and are comfortable with the characters, you can dig into the novel and use it to teach literary elements like setting, characterization, plot, irony and theme.

Two books that will leave younger students chuckling are: *Swine Divine,* by Jan Carr (Holiday House, 0-8234-1434-5, $15.95 Gr. K–4), and *Swine Lake,* by James Marshall (HarperCollins, 0-06-205171-7, $15.95 Gr. 1 & up). Both are filled with puns that would be great to stimulate similar creative writing projects. *When Pigasso Met Mootisse,* by Nina Laden (Chronicle Books, 0-8118-1121-2, $15.95 Gr. K–4), is a clever way to introduce modern art.

Pigs will also fit nicely into the science curriculum. For farm animal units get a copy of *Life on a Pig Farm,* by Judy Wolfman (Carolrhoda, 1-57505-237-7, $16.95 Gr. 2–7). It has great pictures. For a geological unit starring pigs see Tomi Ungerer's *The Mellops Go Spelunking* (Roberts Rinehart, 1-57098-228-7, $5.95 Gr. K–4) for a light-hearted exploration of a cave. Other Mellops adventures include the *The Mellops Strike Oil.*

There are loads of pig books out there. Your librarian can suggest ways to find them.

And in case you're stuck on quiz answers, here are some clues: pig, sow, pork, piggy, swine and hog.

MARCH 1–31
WOMEN'S HISTORY MONTH

Why not fly during Women's History Month? Called aviatrixes in the early days of aviation, female pilots evinced the same bravery and capability shown by their male counterparts. There were more than 1,000 women who flew warplanes during World War II. See www.wasp-wwii.org for more information about the many women who qualified to fly military transport planes in the United States.

Many children have heard of Amelia Earhart. She was the second pilot to fly solo across the Atlantic Ocean. (Charles Lindbergh was the first.) The disappearance of her plane in 1937, while flying over the Pacific Ocean, has stymied and intrigued thousands of people. Students could become Flight Investigators and research the route she took. Use a map to chart her course. Recent search investigations have proposed several likely conclusions about the site of her plane's crash. Different students might present the pros and cons for each conclusion. Patricia Lauber's *Lost Star: The Story of Amelia Earhart* (Scholastic, 0-590-41159-4, $4.50 Gr. 4–7) will engage upper elementary and middle school readers, and Pam Muñoz Ryan's picture book *Amelia and Eleanor Go For a Ride* (Scholastic, 0-590-96075-X, $16.95 Gr. 1–4) provides an interesting historical moment for younger readers.

Bessie Coleman, the first black aviatrix, was denied the opportunity to become a pilot in the United States. She had her sights firmly fixed on becoming a pilot and went to France to accomplish her goal. Upon her return, she gained further note as a stunt pilot. *Fly, Bessie, Fly!*, by Lynn Joseph (Simon & Schuster, 0-689-81339-2, $16 Gr. K–3); *Nobody Owns the Sky*, by Reeve Lindbergh (Candlewick, 0-7636-0361-9, $5.99 Gr. K–3); and *Up in the Air*, by Philip S. Hart (Lerner, 0-87614-978-6, $6.95, Gr. 4–7), are three marvelous biographies about Bessie Coleman that readers will enjoy.

Sally Ride was the first American woman to travel in space. In 1983, she was a member of the crew on the space shuttle *Challenger*. (The first woman in space was Russia's Valentina Tereshkova, whose rocket ship orbited the earth 45 times in 1963.) Sally Ride's autobiography *To Space and Back*, (Morrow, 0-688-09112-1, $12.95 Gr. 3–7), gives readers a glimpse into the struggles and joys of being an astronaut. Ride is also the author of several other books about space.

For a more recent look at women pilots, junior high students might enjoy researching the struggle women have had to become commercial airline pilots.

MENTAL RETARDATION AWARENESS MONTH. Mar 1–31. To educate the public about the needs of this nation's more than seven million citizens with mental retardation and about ways to prevent retardation. The Arc is a national organization on mental retardation, formerly the Association for Retarded Citizens. For info: Liz Moore, The Arc, 500 E Border St, Ste 300, Arlington, TX 76010. Phone: (817) 261-6003. Fax: (817) 277-3491. Web: www.thearc.org.

MUSIC IN OUR SCHOOLS MONTH. Mar 1–31. To increase public awareness of the importance of music education as part of a balanced curriculum. Additional information and awareness items are available from MENC. For info: Deidre Healy, Mgr Special Programs, MENC: Music Educators Natl Conference, 1806 Robert Fulton Dr, Reston, VA 20191. Phone: (800) 336-3768. Web: www.menc.org.

March 2002

S	M	T	W	T	F	S
					1	2
3	4	5	6	7	8	9
10	11	12	13	14	15	16
17	18	19	20	21	22	23
24	25	26	27	28	29	30
31						

NATIONAL CRAFT MONTH. Mar 1–31. Promoting the fun and creativity of hobbies and crafts. For info: Hobby Industry Assn, Natl Craft Month, Richartz and Fliss, 400 Morris Ave, Denville, NJ 07834. Phone: (973) 627-8180. Fax: (973) 672-8410. Web: www.i-craft.com. Info also available from: Assn of Crafts and Creative Industries, 1100-H Brandywine Blvd, PO Box 2188, Zanesville, OH 43702-2188. Phone: (614) 452-4541.

NATIONAL FROZEN FOOD MONTH. Mar 1–31. Promotes a national awareness of the economical and nutritional benefits of frozen foods. Annually, the month of March. For info: Julie Henderson, VP Communications, Natl Frozen Food Assn, 4755 Linglestown Rd, Ste 300, Harrisburg, PA 17112. Phone: (717) 657-8601. Fax: (717) 657-9862. E-mail: nffm@nffa.org. Web: www.nffa.org.

NATIONAL MIDDLE LEVEL EDUCATION MONTH. Mar 1–31. To encourage middle level schools to schedule local events focusing on the educational needs of early adolescents. For info: Dir of Middle Level Services, Natl Assn of Secondary School Principals, 1904 Association Dr, Reston, VA 20190. Phone: (703) 860-7263. Web: www.nassp.org.

NATIONAL NUTRITION MONTH®. Mar 1–31. To educate consumers about the importance of good nutrition by providing the latest practical information on how simple it can be to eat healthfully. For info: The American Dietetic Assn, Natl Center for Nutrition and Dietetics, 216 W Jackson Blvd, Chicago, IL 60606-6995. Phone: (312) 899-0040. Fax: (312) 899-4739. E-mail: nnm@eatright.org. Web: www.eatright.org.

NATIONAL PIG DAY. Mar 1. To accord to the pig its rightful, though generally unrecognized, place as one of man's most intelligent and useful domesticated animals. Annually, Mar 1. For more info send SASE to: Ellen Stanley, 7006 Miami, Lubbock, TX 79413. *See* Curriculum Connection.

NATIONAL TALK WITH YOUR TEEN ABOUT SEX MONTH. Mar 1–31. The importance of frank talk with teenagers about sex is emphasized. Parents are encouraged to provide their teenage children with current, accurate information and open lines for communication, as well as support their self-esteem, reduce misinformation and guide teenagers toward making responsible decisions regarding sex. Annually, the month of March. For info send SASE to: Teresa Langston, Dir, Parenting Without Pressure (PWOP), 1330 Boyer St, Longwood, FL 32750-6311. Phone: (407) 767-2524.

NATIONAL UMBRELLA MONTH. Mar 1–31. In honor of one of the most versatile and underrated inventions of the human race, this month is dedicated to the purchase, use of and conversation about umbrellas. Annually, the month of March. For info: Thomas Edward Knibb, 8819 Adventure Ave, Walkersville, MD 21793-7828. Phone: (301) 898-3009.

NATIONAL WOMEN'S HISTORY MONTH. Mar 1–31. A time for reexamining and celebrating the wide range of women's contributions and achievements that are too often overlooked in the telling of US history. A theme kit on Women's History Month for grades 5–12 is available each year from the National Women's History Project. For info: Natl Women's History Project, 7738 Bell Rd, Dept P, Windsor, CA 95492. Phone: (707) 838-6000. Fax: (707) 838-0478. E-mail: nwhp@aol.com. Web: www.nwhp.org.

NEBRASKA: ADMISSION DAY: ANNIVERSARY. Mar 1. Nebraska became the 37th state in 1867.

NEWSCURRENTS STUDENT EDITORIAL CARTOON CONTEST DEADLINE. Mar 1. Students in grades K–12 can win US Savings Bonds and get their work published in a national book by entering the annual Newscurrents Student Editorial Cartoon Contest. Participants must submit original cartoons on any subject of nationwide interest by this date. Complete rules available. For info: Jeff Robbins, Knowledge Unlimited, PO Box 52, Madison, WI 53701. Phone: (800) 356-2303. Fax: (800) 618-1570. E-mail: jrobbins@ku.com. Web: www.knowledgeunlimited.com.

OHIO: ADMISSION DAY: ANNIVERSARY. Mar 1. Ohio became the 17th state in 1803.

OPTIMISM MONTH. Mar 1–31. To encourage people to boost their optimism. Research proves optimists achieve more health, prosperity and happiness than pessimists. Use this monthlong celebration to practice optimism and turn optimism into a delightful, permanent habit. Free "Tip Sheets" available. For info: Dr. Michael Mercer & Dr. Maryann Troiani, The Mercer Group, Inc, 25597 Drake Rd, Barrington, IL 60010. Phone: (847) 382-0690. For media interviews, Victoria Sterling. Phone: (847) 382-6420.

PARAGUAY: NATIONAL HEROES' DAY. Mar 1. National holiday. Honors all who have died for the country.

PEACE CORPS FOUNDED: ANNIVERSARY. Mar 1, 1961. Official establishment of the Peace Corps by President John F. Kennedy's signing of executive order. The Peace Corps has sent more than 150,000 volunteers to 132 developing countries to help people help themselves. The volunteers assist in projects such as health, education, water sanitation, agriculture, nutrition and forestry. For info: Peace Corps, 1990 K St, Washington, DC 20526. Phone: (800) 424-8580 or (202) 606-3010. Fax: (202) 606-3110. Web: www.peacecorps.gov.

PLAY-THE-RECORDER MONTH. Mar 1–31. American Recorder Society members all over the continent will celebrate the organization's annual Play-the-Recorder Month by performing in public places such as libraries, bookstores, museums and shopping malls. Some will offer workshops on playing the recorder or demonstrations in schools. Founded in 1939, the ARS is the membership organization for all recorder players, including amateurs to leading professionals. Annually, the month of March. For info: American Recorder Soc, PO Box 631, Littleton, CO 80160-0631. Phone: (303) 347-1120. E-mail: recorder@compuserve.com. Web: ourworld.compuserve.com/homepages/recorder.

RED CROSS MONTH. Mar 1–31. To make the public aware of American Red Cross service in the community. There are some 1,300 Red Cross offices nationwide; each local office plans its own activities. For info on activities in your area, contact your local Red Cross office. For info: American Red Cross Natl HQ, Office of Public Inquiry, 1621 N Kent St, Arlington, VA 22209. Phone: (703) 248-4222. E-mail: info@usa.redcross.org. Web: www.redcross.org.

RETURN THE BORROWED BOOKS WEEK. Mar 1–7. To remind you to make room for those precious old volumes that will be returned to you, by cleaning out all that worthless trash that your friends are waiting for. Annually, the first seven days of March. For info: Inter-Global Soc for Prevention of Cruelty to Cartoonists, Al Kaelin, Secy, 3119 Chadwick Dr, Los Angeles, CA 90032. Phone: (323) 221-7909.

SILLY PUTTY® DEBUTS: ANNIVERSARY. Mar 1, 1950. Sometime this month, Silly Putty was launched in Connecticut by Peter Hodgson. It had been discovered six years earlier by an engineer at General Electric who was trying to develop a synthetic rubber. He combined boric acid and silicone oil and got bouncing putty. No one at GE could figure out anything practical to do with it. Hodgson bought a batch of the stuff, put it in plastic eggs and it went on to become a very popular toy. More than 300 million eggs have been sold. Silly Putty even went to the moon in 1968 with the *Apollo* 8 astronauts. In the late 1970s, Silly Putty was bought by Binney & Smith Inc, the company that makes Crayola crayons. For more info: www.sillyputty.com.

SLAYTON, DONALD "DEKE" K.: BIRTH ANNIVERSARY. Mar 1, 1924. "Deke" Slayton, longtime chief of flight operations at the Johnson Space Center, was born at Sparta, WI. Slayton was a member of Mercury Seven, the original group of young military aviators chosen to inaugurate America's sojourn into space. Unfortunately, a heart problem prevented him from participating in any of the Mercury flights. When in 1971 the heart condition mysteriously went away, Slayton flew on the last Apollo Mission. The July 1975 flight, involving a docking with a Soviet Soyuz spacecraft, symbolized a momentary thaw in relations between the two nations. During his years as chief of flight operations, Slayton directed astronaut training and selected the crews for nearly all missions. He died June 13, 1993, at League City, TX.

SWITZERLAND: CHALANDRA MARZ. Mar 1. Engadine. Springtime traditional event when costumed young people, ringing bells and cracking whips, drive away the demons of winter.

WALES: SAINT DAVID'S DAY. Mar 1. Celebrates patron saint of Wales. Welsh tradition calls for the wearing of a leek on this day.

★**WOMEN'S HISTORY MONTH.** Mar 1–31. *See* Curriculum Connection.

WORLD DAY OF PRAYER. Mar 1. An ecumenical event that reinforces bonds between peoples of the world as they join in a global circle of prayer. Annually, the first Friday in March. Sponsor: International Committee for World Day of Prayer. Church Women United is the National World Day of Prayer Committee for the US. For info: Mary Cline Detrick, Dir for Ecumenical Celebrations, Church Women United, 475 Riverside Dr, 5th Floor, New York, NY 10115. Phone: (212) 870-2347 or (800) 298-5551. Fax: (212) 870-2338.

YELLOWSTONE NATIONAL PARK ESTABLISHED: ANNIVERSARY. Mar 1, 1872. The first area in the world to be designated a national park, most of Yellowstone is in Wyoming, with small sections in Montana and Idaho. It was established by an act of Congress. For more info: www.nps.gov/yell.

YOUTH ART MONTH. Mar 1–31. To emphasize the value and importance of participation in art activities and education for all children and youth. For info: Council for Art Education, Inc, 128 Main St, PO Box 479, Hanson, MA 02341. Phone: (781) 293-4100. Fax: (781) 294-0808.

BIRTHDAYS TODAY

Barbara Helen Berger, 57, author (*A Lot of Otters*), born Lancaster, CA, Mar 1, 1945.

John B. Breaux, 58, US Senator (D, Louisiana), born Crowley, LA, Mar 1, 1944.

Stephen Davis, 28, football player, born Spartanburg, SC, Mar 1, 1974.

Mark-Paul Gosselaar, 28, actor ("Saved by the Bell," "She Cried No"), born Panorama City, CA, Mar 1, 1974.

Yolanda Griffith, 32, basketball player, born Chicago, IL, Mar 1, 1970.

Ron Howard, 48, actor ("Happy Days," "Andy Griffith Show"), producer, director (*Parenthood, Far and Away*), born Duncan, OK, Mar 1, 1954.

Alan Thicke, 55, actor ("Growing Pains"), born Kirkland Lake, ON, Canada, Mar 1, 1947.

MARCH 2 — SATURDAY

Day 61 — 304 Remaining

ETHIOPIA: ADWA DAY. Mar 2, 1896. Ethiopian forces under Menelik II inflicted a crushing defeat on the invading Italians at Adwa.

GEISEL, THEODOR "DR. SEUSS": BIRTH ANNIVERSARY. Mar 2, 1904. Theodor Seuss Geisel, the creator of *The Cat in the Hat* and *How the Grinch Stole Christmas*, was born at Springfield, MA. Known to children and parents as Dr. Seuss, his books have sold more than 200 million copies and have been translated into 20 languages. His career began with *And to Think That I Saw It on Mulberry Street*, which was turned down by 27 publishing houses before being published by Vanguard Press. His books included many messages, from environmental consciousness in *The Lorax* to the dangers of pacifism in *Horton Hatches the Egg* and *Yertle the Turtle*'s thinly veiled references to Hitler as the title character. He was awarded a Pulitzer Prize in 1984 "for his contribution over nearly half a century to the education and enjoyment of America's children and their parents." He died Sept 24, 1991, at La Jolla, CA.

HIGHWAY NUMBERS INTRODUCED: ANNIVERSARY. Mar 2, 1925. A joint board of state and federal highway officials created the first system of interstate highway numbering in the US. Standardized road signs identifying the routes were also introduced. Later the system would be improved with the use of odd and even numbers that distinguish between north-south and east-west routes, respectively.

HOUSTON, SAM: BIRTH ANNIVERSARY. Mar 2, 1793. American soldier and politician, born at Rockbridge County, VA, is remembered for his role in Texas history. Houston was a congressman (1823–27) and governor (1827–29) of Tennessee. He resigned his office as governor in 1829 and rejoined the Cherokee Indians (with whom he had lived for several years as a teenage runaway), who accepted him as a member of their tribe. Houston went to Texas in 1832 and became commander of the Texan army in the War for Texan Independence, which was secured when Houston routed the much larger Mexican forces led by Santa Ana, Apr 21, 1836, at the Battle of San Jacinto. After Texas's admission to the Union, Houston served as US senator and later as governor of the state. He was deposed in 1861 when he refused to swear allegiance to the Confederacy. Houston, the only person to have been elected governor of two different states, failed to serve his full term of office in either. The city of Houston, TX, was named for him. He died July 26, 1863, at Huntsville, TX.

MOUNT RAINIER NATIONAL PARK ESTABLISHED: ANNIVERSARY. Mar 2, 1899. Located in the Cascade Range in north-central Washington state, this is the fourth oldest park in the national park system. For more info: www.nps.gov/mora.

March 2002

S	M	T	W	T	F	S
					1	2
3	4	5	6	7	8	9
10	11	12	13	14	15	16
17	18	19	20	21	22	23
24	25	26	27	28	29	30
31						

READ ACROSS AMERICA DAY. Mar 2. A national reading campaign that advocates that all children read a book the evening of Mar 2. Celebrated on Dr. Seuss's birthday. For info: Natl Education Assn, 1201 16th St NW, Washington, DC, 20036. Phone: (202) 822-7830. Fax: (888) 747-READ. Web: www.nea.org/readacross.

SPACE MILESTONE: *PIONEER 10* (US): 30th ANNIVERSARY. Mar 2, 1972. This unmanned probe began a journey on which it passed and photographed Jupiter and its moons, 620 million miles from Earth, in December 1973. It crossed the orbit of Pluto, and then in 1983 become the first known Earth object to leave our solar system. On Sept 22, 1987 *Pioneer 10* reached another space milestone at 4:19 PM, when it reached a distance 50 times farther from the sun than the sun is from Earth.

SPACE MILESTONE: *SOYUZ 28* (USSR). Mar 2, 1978. Cosmonauts Alexi Gubarev and Vladimir Remek linked with *Salyut 6* space station Mar 3, visiting crew of *Soyuz 26*. Returned to Earth Mar 10. Remek, from Czechoslovakia, was the first person in space from a country other than the US or USSR. Launched Mar 2, 1978.

TEXAS INDEPENDENCE DAY. Mar 2, 1836. Texas adopted Declaration of Independence from Mexico.

BIRTHDAYS TODAY

Leo Dillon, 69, illustrator, with his wife Diane Dillon (Caldecotts for *Why Mosquitoes Buzz in People's Ears, Ashanti to Zulu: African Traditions*), born Brooklyn, NY, Mar 2, 1933.

Russell D. Feingold, 49, US Senator (D, Wisconsin), born Janesville, WI, Mar 2, 1953.

Anne Isaacs, 53, author (*Swamp Angel, Treehouse Tales*), born Buffalo, NY, Mar 2, 1949.

MARCH 3 — SUNDAY

Day 62 — 303 Remaining

BONZA BOTTLER DAY™. Mar 3. To celebrate when the number of the day is the same as the number of the month. Bonza Bottler Day™ is an excuse to have a party at least once a month. For info: Gail M. Berger, 109 Matthew Ave, Poca, WV 25159. Phone: (304) 776-7746. E-mail: gberger5@aol.com.

BULGARIA: LIBERATION DAY. Mar 3. Grateful tribute to the Russian, Romanian and Finnish soldiers and Bulgarian volunteers who, in the Russo-Turkish War, 1877–78, liberated Bulgaria from five centuries of Ottoman rule.

CONSERVE WATER/DETECT-A-LEAK WEEK. Mar 3–9. To help everyone learn why it is important to conserve our water and how to help accomplish this goal. Annually, the first full week in March. For info: American Leak Detection, 888 Research Dr, Ste 100, Palm Springs, CA 92262. Phone: (800) 755-6697. Fax: (760) 320-1288. E-mail: sbangs@leakbusters.com. Web: www.leakbusters.com.

FLORIDA: ADMISSION DAY: ANNIVERSARY. Mar 3. Became 27th state in 1845.

I WANT YOU TO BE HAPPY DAY. Mar 3. A day dedicated to reminding people to be thoughtful of others by showing love and care and concern, even if things are not going well for them. For info: Harriette W. Grimes, Grandmother, PO Box 545, Winter Garden, FL 34777-0545. Phone: (407) 656-3830. Fax: (407) 656-2790.

JAPAN: HINAMATSURI (DOLL FESTIVAL). Mar 3. This special festival for girls is observed throughout Japan. Annually, Mar 3.

MALAWI: MARTYR'S DAY. Mar 3. Public holiday in Malawi.

MISSOURI COMPROMISE: ANNIVERSARY. Mar 3, 1820. In Feb, 1819, a bill was introduced into Congress that would admit Missouri to the Union as a state that prohibited slavery. At the time there were 11 free states and 10 slave states. Southern congressmen feared this would upset the balance of power between North and South. As a compromise, on this date Missouri was admitted as a slave state but slavery was forever prohibited in the northern part of the Louisiana Purchase. In 1854, this act was repealed when Kansas and Nebraska were allowed to decide on slave or free status by popular vote.

NATIONAL ANTHEM DAY. Mar 3, 1931. The bill designating "The Star-Spangled Banner" as our national anthem was adopted by the US Senate and went to President Herbert Hoover for signature. The president signed it the same day.

SAVE YOUR VISION WEEK. Mar 3–9. To remind Americans that vision is one of the most vital of all human needs and its protection is of great significance to the health and welfare of every individual. Annually, the first full week in March. For info: American Optometric Assn, 243 N Lindbergh Blvd, St. Louis, MO 63141. Phone: (314) 991-4100. Fax: (314) 991-4101. E-mail: optinfo@aol.com. Web: www.aoanet.org.

★ **SAVE YOUR VISION WEEK.** Mar 3–9. Presidential Proclamation issued for the first full week of March since 1964, except 1971 and 1982 when issued for the second week of March. (PL88–1942, of Dec 30, 1963.)

***TIME* MAGAZINE FIRST PUBLISHED: ANNIVERSARY.** Mar 3, 1923. The first issue of *Time* bore this date. The magazine was founded by Henry Luce and Briton Hadden. In 1996 *Time for Kids* was launched. For more info: www.timeforkids.com.

BIRTHDAYS TODAY

Jessica Biel, 20, actress ("7th Heaven"), born Ely, MN, Mar 3, 1982.
Jacqueline (Jackie) Joyner-Kersee, 40, Olympic gold medal heptathlete, born East St. Louis, IL, Mar 3, 1962.
Patricia MacLachlan, 64, author (Newbery for *Sarah, Plain and Tall*), born Cheyenne, WY, Mar 3, 1938.

MARCH 4 — MONDAY

Day 63 — 302 Remaining

ADAMS, JOHN QUINCY: RETURN TO CONGRESS ANNIVERSARY. Mar 4, 1830. John Quincy Adams returned to the House of Representatives to represent the district of Plymouth, MA. He was the first former president to do so and served for eight consecutive terms.

CONGRESS: ANNIVERSARY OF FIRST MEETING UNDER CONSTITUTION. Mar 4, 1789. The first Congress met at New York, NY. A quorum was obtained in the House on Apr 1, in the Senate Apr 5 and the first Congress was formally organized Apr 6. Electoral votes were counted, and George Washington was declared president (69 votes) and John Adams vice president (34 votes).

GROVER CLEVELAND'S SECOND PRESIDENTIAL INAUGURATION: ANNIVERSARY. Mar 4, 1893. Grover Cleveland was inaugurated for a second but nonconsecutive term as president. In 1885 he had become 22nd president of the US and in 1893 the 24th. Originally a source of some controversy, the Congressional Directory for some time listed him only as the 22nd president. The directory now lists him as both the 22nd and 24th presidents, though some historians continue to argue that one person cannot be both. Benjamin Harrison served during the

MARCH 4–8
NEWSPAPER IN EDUCATION WEEK

This week is devoted to bringing newspapers into children's lives. It's a great opportunity to focus attention on print as an important informational medium.

Each day during the week focus on a different section of the newspaper. The Home/Family section (which may be called Living, or something else, in your paper), which often contains the comics, is a good attention grabber for Monday morning. Survey students for which features within this section they read most frequently. You can use the same survey-style response to rank their favorite comic strips. Have students chart the results as a bar graph for math.

On Tuesday, you might choose to feature the first section and focus on headline styles. It's also a good opportunity to learn percentage and area. Do this by measuring the page and then comparing the relative area occupied by featured stories with that occupied by advertisements.

Devote Wednesday to sports. Before doing so, poll the class to determine what their favorite sports are. Rank them numerically. When looking at the sports section, see if the coverage given various sports reflects the interest of the class. If it doesn't, as a language arts activity (and a lesson on consumer input) students could sum up their findings in a letter to the sports editor of the newspaper and ask what determines how much page space a particular sport is given.

On Thursday, take a look at the Business and Classified Advertising sections. Explain what the stock report figures mean and why they interest so many adults. Note what kind of want ads the paper carries. Students could have fun writing their own mock ads that would feature old toys or sporting equipment they wish they could sell. By Thursday, the class has had time to look at several sections in depth. Have them find out which sections contain the most advertisements for consumer goods and how the ads change to reflect the nature of the section.

Hopefully, during the week students have taken note of the main stories. On Friday, focus on the editorial pages to see how quickly, if at all, people have responded to the breaking news of the earlier days. Each student should try writing a letter to the editor about a subject that concerned him or her. Many editorial pages have Web addresses, so you won't need stamps and envelopes. But students should use a writing process that includes revision before e-mailing a letter. Read one or two columns by featured editorial writers and discuss how their views complement or disagree with those of the students.

If you are willing to give producing your own classroom newspaper a try, get a copy of *Creating a Classroom Newspaper*, by Kathleen Buss and Leslie McClain-Ruelle. It is published by the International Reading Association and offers a great deal of practical advice. The price is $16.95 for nonmembers of the IRA; the publication number is 274-448. To order, call 302-731-1600 or visit the IRA on-line bookstore at bookstore.reading.org.

Also talk about other places people get the news. In addition to radio and television, you might visit the CNN website (www.cnn.com) for the day's news. Also look at a newsmagazine such as *Time for Kids*, which has versions for grades K–1, 2–3 and 4–6 and Spanish editions as well. Its website is www.timeforkids.com.

intervening term, defeating Cleveland in electoral votes, though not in the popular vote.

GUAM: DISCOVERY DAY or MAGELLAN DAY. Mar 4. Commemorates discovery of Guam in 1521. Annually, the first Monday in March.

HOT SPRINGS NATIONAL PARK ESTABLISHED: ANNIVERSARY. Mar 4, 1921. To protect the Hot Springs of Arkansas the government set aside Hot Springs Reservation on Apr 20, 1832. In 1921 the area became a national park. For more info: www.nps.gov/hots/index.htm.

NATIONAL SCHOOL BREAKFAST WEEK. Mar 4–8. To focus on the importance of a nutritious breakfast served in the schools, giving children a good start to their day. Annually, the first full week in March (weekdays). For info: American School Food Service Assn, 1600 Duke St, 7th Floor, Alexandria, VA 22314-3436. Phone: (703) 739-3900. E-mail: asfsa@asfsa.org. Web: www.asfsa.org.

NEWSPAPER IN EDUCATION WEEK. Mar 4–8. A weeklong celebration using newspapers in the classroom as living textbooks. Each year, more than 700 newspapers in the US and Canada participate in this event. Annually, the first full week in March (weekdays). For info: Mgr Education Programs, Newspaper Assn of America Foundation, 1921 Gallows Rd, Ste 600, Vienna, VA 22182-3900. Phone: (703) 902-1730. E-mail: abboj@naa.org. Web: www.naa.org. *See* Curriculum Connection.

OLD INAUGURATION DAY. Mar 4. Anniversary of the date set for beginning the US presidential term of office, 1789–1933. Although the Continental Congress had set the first Wednesday of March 1789 as the date for the new government to convene, a quorum was not present to count the electoral votes until Apr 6. Though George Washington's term of office began Mar 4, he did not take the oath of office until Apr 30, 1789. All subsequent presidential terms (except successions following the death of an incumbent), until Franklin D. Roosevelt's second term, began Mar 4. The 20th Amendment (ratified Jan 23, 1933) provided that "the terms of the President and Vice President shall end at noon on the 20th day of January . . . and the terms of their successors shall then begin."

PENNSYLVANIA DEEDED TO WILLIAM PENN: ANNIVERSARY. Mar 4, 1681. To satisfy a debt of £16,000, King Charles II of England granted a royal charter, deed and governorship of Pennsylvania to William Penn.

***PEOPLE* MAGAZINE: ANNIVERSARY.** Mar 4, 1974. This popular magazine highlighting celebrities was officially launched with the Mar 4, 1974, issue featuring a cover photo of Mia Farrow.

PULASKI, CASIMIR: BIRTH ANNIVERSARY. Mar 4, 1747. American Revolutionary War hero, General Kazimierz (Casimir) Pulaski, born at Winiary, Mazovia, Poland, the son of a count. He was a patriot and military leader in Poland's fight against Russia of 1770–71 and went into exile at the partition of Poland in 1772. He went to America in 1777 to join the Revolution, fighting with General Washington at Brandywine and also serving at Germantown and Valley Forge. He organized the Pulaski Legion to wage guerrilla warfare against the British. Mortally wounded in a heroic charge at the siege of Savannah, GA, he died aboard the warship *Wasp* Oct 11, 1779. Pulaski Day is celebrated Oct 11 in Nebraska schools and in Massachusetts and on the first Monday of March in Illinois and Indiana (Mar 4 in 2002). It is a day of special school observance in Wisconsin on Mar 4.

March 2002

S	M	T	W	T	F	S
					1	2
3	4	5	6	7	8	9
10	11	12	13	14	15	16
17	18	19	20	21	22	23
24	25	26	27	28	29	30
31						

ROCKNE, KNUTE: BIRTH ANNIVERSARY. Mar 4, 1888. Legendary Notre Dame football coach, born at Voss, Norway. Known for such sayings as "Win one for the Gipper," he died at Cottonwood Falls, KS, Mar 31, 1931.

SPACE MILESTONE: *OGO 5* (US). Mar 4, 1968. Orbiting Geophysical Observatory (OGO) collected data on sun's influence on Earth. Launched Mar 4, 1968. Six OGOs were launched in all.

TELEVISION ACADEMY HALL OF FAME: FIRST INDUCTEES ANNOUNCED: ANNIVERSARY. Mar 4, 1984. The Television Academy of Arts and Sciences announced the formation of the Television Academy Hall of Fame at Burbank, CA. The first inductees were Lucille Ball, Milton Berle, Paddy Chayefsky, Norman Lear, Edward R. Murrow, William S. Paley and David Sarnoff. For more info: www.emmys.org.

VERMONT: ADMISSION DAY: ANNIVERSARY. Mar 4. Vermont became the 14th state in 1791.

BIRTHDAYS TODAY

David A. Carter, 45, author, illustrator (*Jingle Bugs, Alpha Bugs, How Many Bugs in a Box?*), born Salt Lake City, UT, Mar 4, 1957.

Peyton Manning, 26, football player, born New Orleans, LA, Mar 4, 1976.

Rick Perry, 52, Governor of Texas (R), born Haskell, TX, Mar 4, 1950.

Dav Pilkey, 36, author and illustrator (The Dumb Bunnies series, The Captain Underpants series,*The Paperboy*), also known as Sue Denim, born Cleveland, OH, Mar 4, 1966.

Peggy Rathmann, 49, author and illustrator (Caldecott for *Officer Buckle and Gloria*), born St. Paul, MN, Mar 4, 1953.

MARCH 5 — TUESDAY

Day 64 — 301 Remaining

BOSTON MASSACRE: ANNIVERSARY. Mar 5, 1770. A skirmish between British troops and a crowd at Boston, MA, became widely publicized and contributed to the unpopularity of the British regime in America before the American Revolution. Five men were killed and six more were injured by British troops commanded by Captain Thomas Preston.

CHANNEL ISLANDS NATIONAL PARK ESTABLISHED: ANNIVERSARY. Mar 5, 1980. California's Channel Islands Monument, authorized in 1938 by President Franklin D. Roosevelt, consisted of the islands of Anacapa and Santa Barbara. In 1980 President Jimmy Carter signed a bill establishing the Channel Islands National Park consisting of the islands Anacapa, San Miguel, Santa Barbara, Santa Cruz and Santa Rosa. For more info: www.nps.gov/chis.index.htm.

CRISPUS ATTUCKS DAY: DEATH ANNIVERSARY. Mar 5, 1770. Honors Crispus Attucks, possibly a runaway slave, who was the first to die in the Boston Massacre.

MERCATOR, GERHARDUS: BIRTH ANNIVERSARY. Mar 5, 1512. Cartographer-geographer Mercator was born at Rupelmonde, Belgium. His Mercator projection for maps provided an accurate ratio of latitude to longitude and is still used today. He also introduced the term "atlas" for a collection of maps. He died at Duisberg, Germany, Dec 2, 1594.

MOON PHASE: LAST QUARTER. Mar 5. Moon enters Last Quarter phase at 8:24 PM, EST.

PYLE, HOWARD: BIRTH ANNIVERSARY. Mar 5, 1853. Illustrator and author, known for the children's books *Bearskin* and *The Merry Adventures of Robin Hood*. Born at Wilmington, DE, Pyle died at Florence, Italy, Nov 9, 1911.

SAINT PIRAN'S DAY. Mar 5. Celebrates the birthday of St. Piran, the patron saint of Cornish tinners. Cornish worldwide celebrate this day. For info: The Cornish American Heritage Soc, 2405 N Brookfield Rd, Brookfield, WI 53045. Phone: (414) 786-9358. E-mail: jjolliff@post.its.mcw.edu.

TOWN MEETING DAY IN VERMONT. Mar 5. The first Tuesday in March is an official state holiday in Vermont. Nearly every town elects officers, approves budget items and deals with a multitude of other items in a daylong public meeting of the voters.

BIRTHDAYS TODAY

Merrion Frances (Mem) Fox, 56, author (*Possum Magic, Koala Lou*), born Australia, Mar 5, 1946.

John Kitzhaber, 55, Governor of Oregon (D), born Colfax, WA, Mar 5, 1947.

Jake Lloyd, 13, actor (*Star Wars: The Phantom Menace*), born Fort Collins, CO, Mar 5, 1989.

MARCH 6 — WEDNESDAY

Day 65 — 300 Remaining

BROWNING, ELIZABETH BARRETT: BIRTH ANNIVERSARY. Mar 6, 1806. English poet, author of *Sonnets from the Portuguese*, wife of poet Robert Browning and subject of the play *The Barretts of Wimpole Street*, was born near Durham, England. She died at Florence, Italy, June 29, 1861.

FALL OF THE ALAMO: ANNIVERSARY. Mar 6, 1836. Anniversary of the fall of the Texan fort, the Alamo, in what is now San Antonio, TX. The siege, led by Mexican general Santa Ana, began Feb 23 and reached its climax Mar 6, when the last of the defenders was slain. Texans, under General Sam Houston, rallied with the war cry "Remember the Alamo" and, at the Battle of San Jacinto, Apr 21, defeated and captured Santa Ana, who signed a treaty recognizing Texas's independence. For more info: www.thealamo.org.

GHANA: INDEPENDENCE DAY: 45th ANNIVERSARY. Mar 6. National holiday. Received independence from Great Britain in 1957.

MICHELANGELO: BIRTH ANNIVERSARY. Mar 6, 1475. Michelangelo Buonarroti, a prolific Renaissance painter, sculptor, architect and poet who had a profound effect on Western art, born at Caprese, Italy. Michelangelo's fresco painting on the ceiling of the Sistine Chapel at the Vatican in Rome and his statues *David* and *The Pieta* are among his best-known achievements. Appointed architect of St. Peter's in 1542, a post he held until his death Feb 18, 1564, at Rome. For more info: *Michelangelo*, by Gabriella Di Cagno (Peter Bedrick, 0-87226-319-3, $22.50 Gr. 4–7) or *Michelangelo* by Diane Stanley (HarperCollins, 0-688-15086-1, $15.98 Gr. 5–8).

BIRTHDAYS TODAY

Christopher Samuel Bond, 63, US Senator (R, Missouri), born St. Louis, MO, Mar 6, 1939.

Alan Greenspan, 76, economist, Chairman of the Federal Reserve Board, born New York, NY, Mar 6, 1926.

Thatcher Hurd, 53, author, illustrator (*Zoom City, Blackberry Ramble*), born Burlington, VT, Mar 6, 1949.

Shaquille Rashan O'Neal, 30, basketball player, born Newark, NJ, Mar 6, 1972.

Chris Raschka, 43, author, illustrator (Caldecott honor for *Yo! Yes?; Charlie Parker Played Be-Bop*), born Huntington, PA, Mar 6, 1959.

MARCH 7 — THURSDAY

Day 66 — 299 Remaining

BURBANK, LUTHER: BIRTH ANNIVERSARY. Mar 7, 1849. American naturalist and author, creator and developer of many new varieties of flowers, fruits, vegetables and trees. Luther Burbank's birthday is observed by some as Bird and Arbor Day. Born at Lancaster, MA, he died at Santa Rosa, CA, Apr 11, 1926.

HOPKINS, STEPHEN: BIRTH ANNIVERSARY. Mar 7, 1707. Colonial governor (Rhode Island) and signer of the Declaration of Independence. Born at Providence, RI, and died there July 13, 1785.

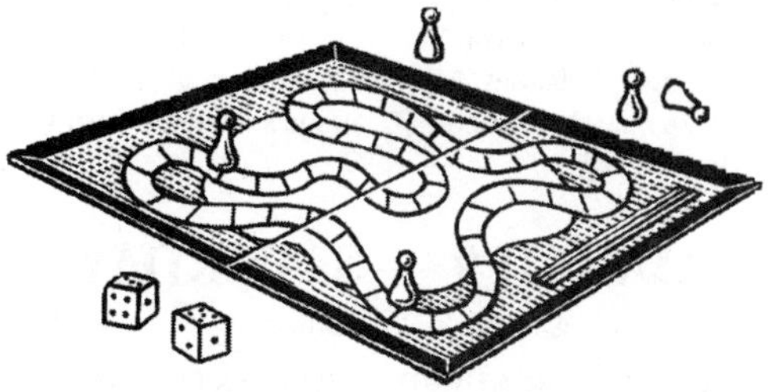

MONOPOLY INVENTED: ANNIVERSARY. Mar 7, 1933. While unemployed during the Depression, Charles Darrow devised this game. He sold it himself for two years; Monopoly was mass marketed by Parker Brothers beginning in 1935. Darrow died a millionaire in 1967.

BIRTHDAYS TODAY

Michael Eisner, 60, Disney executive, born Mount Kisco, NY, Mar 7, 1942.

MARCH 8 — FRIDAY

Day 67 — 298 Remaining

FIRST US INCOME TAX: ANNIVERSARY. Mar 8, 1913. The Internal Revenue Service began to levy and collect income taxes.

GRAHAME, KENNETH: BIRTH ANNIVERSARY. Mar 8, 1859. Scottish author, born at Edinburgh. His children's book, *The Wind in the Willows*, has as its main characters a mole, a rat, a badger and a toad. He died July 6, 1932, at Pangbourne, Berkshire.

INTERNATIONAL (WORKING) WOMEN'S DAY. Mar 8. A day to honor women, especially working women. Said to commemorate an 1857 march and demonstration at New York, NY, by female garment and textile workers. Believed to have been first proclaimed for this date at an international conference of women held at Helsinki, Finland, in 1910, "that henceforth Mar 8 should be declared International Women's Day." The 50th anniversary observance, at Peking, China, in 1960, cited Clara Zetkin (1857–1933) as "initiator of Women's Day on Mar 8." This is perhaps the most widely observed holiday of recent origin and is unusual among holidays originating in the US in having been widely adopted and observed in other nations, including socialist countries. In Russia it is a national holiday, and flowers or gifts are presented to women workers.

RUSSIA: INTERNATIONAL WOMEN'S DAY. Mar 8. National holiday.

SYRIAN ARAB REPUBLIC: REVOLUTION DAY. Mar 8. Official public holiday commemorating assumption of power by Revolutionary National Council in 1963.

UNITED NATIONS: INTERNATIONAL WOMEN'S DAY. Mar 8. An international day observed by the organizations of the United Nations system. For more info, visit the UN's website for children at www.un.org/Pubs/CyberSchoolBus/.

VAN BUREN, HANNAH HOES: BIRTH ANNIVERSARY. Mar 8, 1783. Wife of Martin Van Buren, 8th president of the US. Born at Kinderhook, NY, she died at Albany, NY, Feb 5, 1819.

BIRTHDAYS TODAY

George Allen, 50, US Senator (R, Virginia), born Whittier, CA, Mar 8, 1952.

Freddie Prinze Jr, 26, actor ("Family Matters," *I Know What You Did Last Summer*), born Albuquerque, NM, Mar 8, 1976.

Robert Sabuda, 37, illustrator (*The Christmas Alphabet, The Paper Dragon*), born Pinckney, MI, Mar 8, 1965.

James Van Der Beek, 25, actor ("Dawson's Creek"), born Cheshire, CT, Mar 8, 1977.

MARCH 9 — SATURDAY

Day 68 — 297 Remaining

ASSOCIATION FOR SUPERVISION AND CURRICULUM DEVELOPMENT CONFERENCE. Mar 9–11. San Antonio, TX. For info: Assn for Supervision and Curriculum Development, 1703 N Beauregard St, Alexandria, VA 22311-1714. Phone: (703) 578-9600. Fax: (703) 575-5400. Web: www.ascd.org.

BARBIE DEBUTS: ANNIVERSARY. Mar 9, 1959. The popular doll debuted in stores. More than 800 million dolls have been sold. For more info: www.barbie.com.

BELIZE: BARON BLISS DAY. Mar 9. Official public holiday. Celebrated in honor of Sir Henry Edward Ernest Victor Bliss, a great benefactor of Belize.

GRANT COMMISSIONED COMMANDER OF ALL UNION ARMIES: ANNIVERSARY. Mar 9, 1864. In Washington, DC, Ulysses S. Grant accepted his commission as Lieutenant General, becoming the commander of all the Union armies.

PANIC DAY. Mar 9. Run around all day in a panic, telling others you can't handle it anymore. [© 1999 by WH] For info: Tom or Ruth Roy, Wellcat Holidays, 2418 Long Ln, Lebanon, PA 17046. Phone: (230) 332-4886. E-mail: wellcat@supernet.com. Web: www.wellcat.com.

VESPUCCI, AMERIGO: BIRTH ANNIVERSARY. Mar 9, 1451. Italian navigator, merchant and explorer for whom the Americas were named. Born at Florence, Italy. He participated in at least two expeditions between 1499 and 1502 which took him to the coast of South America, where he discovered the Amazon and Plata rivers. Vespucci's expeditions were of great importance because he believed that he had discovered a new continent, not just a new route to the Orient. Neither Vespucci nor his exploits achieved the fame of Columbus, but the New World was to be named for Amerigo Vespucci, by an obscure German geographer and mapmaker, Martin Waldseemuller. Ironically, in his work as an outfitter of ships, Vespucci had been personally acquainted with Christopher Columbus. Vespucci died at Seville, Spain, Feb 22, 1512. See also: "Waldseemuller, Martin: Remembrance Day" (Apr 25).

March 2002

S	M	T	W	T	F	S
					1	2
3	4	5	6	7	8	9
10	11	12	13	14	15	16
17	18	19	20	21	22	23
24	25	26	27	28	29	30
31						

BIRTHDAYS TODAY

Margot Apple, 56, illustrator (*Sheep in a Jeep*), born Detroit, MI, Mar 9, 1946.

Emmanuel Lewis, 31, actor ("Webster"), born Brooklyn, NY, Mar 9, 1971.

MARCH 10 — SUNDAY

Day 69 — 296 Remaining

CHILDREN'S LITERATURE FESTIVAL. Mar 10–12. Central Missouri State University, Warrensburg, MO. Designed for teachers to introduce them to authors of children's and young adult literature. Est attendance: 7,000. For info: Children's Literature Festival, Central Missouri State Univ, Warrensburg, MO 64093. Phone: (660) 543-4306. Fax: (660) 543-8001. Web: library.cmsu.edu.

GIRL SCOUT WEEK. Mar 10–17. To observe the anniversary of the founding of the Girl Scouts of the USA, the largest voluntary organization for girls and women in the world, which began Mar 12, 1912. Special observances include: Girl Scout Sabbath, Mar 16, Girl Scout Sunday, Mar 17, when Girl Scouts gather to attend religious services together, and Girl Scout Birthday, Mar 12. For info: Media Services, Girl Scouts of the USA, 420 Fifth Ave, New York, NY 10018. Phone: (212) 852-8000. Fax: (212) 852-6514. Web: www.gsusa.org.

SALVATION ARMY IN THE US: ANNIVERSARY. Mar 10, 1880. Commissioner George Scott Railton and seven women officers landed at New York to officially begin the work of the Salvation Army in the US. For more info: www.salvationarmyusa.org.

TELEPHONE INVENTION: ANNIVERSARY. Mar 10, 1876. Alexander Graham Bell transmitted the first telephone message to his assistant in the next room: "Mr Watson, come here, I want you," at Cambridge, MA. See also: "Bell, Alexander Graham: Birth Anniversary" (Mar 3).

TUBMAN, HARRIET: DEATH ANNIVERSARY. Mar 10, 1913. American abolitionist, Underground Railroad leader, born a slave at Bucktown, Dorchester County, MD, about 1820 or 1821. She escaped from a Maryland plantation in 1849 and later helped more than 300 slaves reach freedom. Died at Auburn, NY. For more info: *Minty: A Story of Young Harriet Tubman*, by Alan Schroeder (Dial, 0-8037-1889-6, $16.99 Gr. K–3). For more info on the Undergound Railroad, visit www.undergroundrailroad.com or www.nationalgeographic.com/features/99/railroad.

US PAPER MONEY ISSUED: ANNIVERSARY. Mar 10, 1862. The first paper money was issued in the US on this date. The denominations were $5 (Hamilton), $10 (Lincoln) and $20 (Liberty). They were not legal tender when first issued but became so by an act on Mar 17, 1862.

YOUNG INVENTORS AWARENESS WEEK. Mar 10–17 (tentative). Inventors IPO sponsors a national inventors week in March. They help local schools across the country to organize an inventors week, where school children can invent, build and display their ideas. A percentage of the company's profits are donated to help sponsor the events. For info: Dan Stalfire, Inventors IPO, 1108 Harvest Glen Dr., Plano, TX 75023. Phone: 972-423-2195. Fax: 972-578-7965. E-mail: dan@im-images.com. Web: www.inventorsipo.com.

BIRTHDAYS TODAY

Kim Campbell, 55, first woman prime minister of Canada (1993), born Vancouver Island, BC, Canada, Mar 10, 1947.

MARCH 11 — MONDAY

Day 70 — 295 Remaining

BUREAU OF INDIAN AFFAIRS ESTABLISHED: ANNIVERSARY. Mar 11, 1824. The US War Department created the Bureau of Indian Affairs.

CAMP FIRE BOYS AND GIRLS BIRTHDAY WEEK. Mar 11–17. To celebrate the anniversary of Camp Fire Boys and Girls (founded in 1910 as Camp Fire Girls). For info: Camp Fire Boys and Girls, 4601 Madison Ave, Kansas City, MO 64112. Phone: (816) 756-1950. Fax: (816) 756-0258. E-mail: info@campfire.org. Web: www.campfire.org.

FLU PANDEMIC OF 1918 HITS US: ANNIVERSARY. Mar 11, 1918. The first cases of the "Spanish" influenza were reported in the US when 107 soldiers became sick at Fort Riley, KS. By the end of 1920 nearly 25 percent of the US population had had it. As many as 500,000 civilians died from the virus, exceeding the number of US troops killed abroad in WWI. Worldwide, more than 1 percent of the global population, or 22 million people, had died by 1920. The origin of the virus was never determined absolutely, though it was probably somewhere in Asia. The name "Spanish" influenza came from the relatively high number of cases in that country early in the epidemic. Due to the panic, cancellation of public events was common and many public service workers wore masks on the job. Emergency tent hospitals were set up in some locations due to overcrowding.

GAG, WANDA: BIRTH ANNIVERSARY. Mar 11, 1893. Author and illustrator (*Millions of Cats*), born at New Ulm, MN. Died at Milford, NJ, June 27, 1946. For more info: homepage.fcgnetworks .net/tortakales/illustrators/Gag.html.

INTERNATIONAL BRAIN AWARENESS WEEK. Mar 11–17. For info: Dana Alliance for Brain Initiatives, 745 Fifth Ave, Ste 700, New York, NY 10151. E-mail: dabiinfo@dana.org. Web: www .dana.org.

JOHNNY APPLESEED DAY (JOHN CHAPMAN DEATH ANNIVERSARY). Mar 11, 1845. Anniversary of the death of John Chapman, better known as Johnny Appleseed, believed to have been born at Leominster, MA, Sept 26, 1774. The planter of orchards and friend of wild animals was regarded by the Indians as a great medicine man. He died at Allen County, IN. See also: "Appleseed, Johnny: Birth Anniversary" (Sept 26).

KEATS, EZRA JACK: BIRTH ANNIVERSARY. Mar 11, 1916. Author and illustrator (Caldecott for *The Snowy Day*), born at Brooklyn, NY. Died May 6, 1983, at New York, NY.

PAINE, ROBERT TREAT: BIRTH ANNIVERSARY. Mar 11, 1731. Jurist and signer of the Declaration of Independence. Born at Boston, MA, died there May 11, 1814.

UNITED KINGDOM: COMMONWEALTH DAY. Mar 11. Replaces Empire Day observance recognized until 1958. Observed on second Monday in March. Also observed in the British Virgin Islands, Gibraltar and Newfoundland, Canada.

BIRTHDAYS TODAY

Roy Barnes, 54, Governor of Georgia (D), born Mableton, GA, Mar 11, 1948.

Curtis Brown, Jr, 46, astronaut, commander of the 1998 shuttle *Discovery*, born Elizabethtown, NC, Mar 11, 1956.

Jonathan London, 55, author (the Froggy series), born Brooklyn, NY, Mar 11, 1947.

Gale Norton, 48, US Secretary of the Interior (George W. Bush administration), born Witchita, KS, Mar 11, 1954.

Antonin Scalia, 66, Associate Justice of the US Supreme Court, born Trenton, NJ, Mar 11, 1936.

MARCH 12 — TUESDAY

Day 71 — 294 Remaining

BOYCOTT, CHARLES CUNNINGHAM: BIRTH ANNIVERSARY. Mar 12, 1832. Charles Cunningham Boycott, born at Norfolk, England, has been immortalized by having his name become part of the English language. In County Mayo, Ireland, the Tenants' "Land League" in 1880 asked Boycott, an estate agent, to reduce rents (because of poor harvest and dire economic conditions). Boycott responded by serving eviction notices on the tenants, who retaliated by refusing to have any dealings with him. Charles Stewart Parnell, then president of the National Land League and agrarian agitator, retaliated against Boycott by formulating and implementing the method of economic and social ostracism that came to be called a "boycott." Boycott died at Suffolk, England, June 19, 1897.

GIRL SCOUTS OF THE USA FOUNDING: 90th ANNIVERSARY. Mar 12, 1912. Juliet Low founded the Girl Scouts of the USA at Savannah, GA. For more info: www.gsusa.org.

GREAT BLIZZARD OF '88: ANNIVERSARY. Mar 12, 1888. One of the most devastating blizzards to hit the northeastern US began in the early hours of Monday, Mar 12, 1888. A snowfall of 40–50 inches, accompanied by gale-force winds, left drifts as high as 30–40 feet. More than 400 people died in the storm (200 at New York City alone). For more info: *Blizzard: The Storm That Changed America*, by Jim Murphy (Scholastic, 0-59-067309-2, $18.95 Gr. 3–7).

LESOTHO: MOSHOESHOE'S DAY. Mar 12. National holiday. Commemorates the great leader, Chief Moshoeshoe I, who unified the Basotho people, beginning in 1820.

MAURITIUS: INDEPENDENCE DAY. Mar 12. National holiday commemorates attainment of independent nationhood (within the British Commonwealth) by this island state in the western Indian Ocean on this day in 1968.

NATIONAL BRAIN BEE. Mar 12. Baltimore, MD. A Q&A competition about the human brain for high school students. Students are quizzed about intelligence, memory, emotions, sensations, movement, stress, aging, sleep and brain disorders. Thirty cities throughout North America conduct local brain bees during January and February, the winners of which are invited to Nationals at the University of Maryland in Baltimore during Brain Awareness Week. The competitors are recognized by the National Institutes of Health and Wellness on Capitol Hill in Washington. Thousands of dollars in scholarships are awarded. For info: Norbert Myslinski, Natl Brain Bee, 666 W Baltimore St, Baltimore, MD 21201. Phone: (410) 706-7258. Fax: (410) 706-0193. E-mail: nrm001@dental.umaryland.edu. Web: www.sfn.org/BAW/bee.

PIERCE, JANE MEANS APPLETON: BIRTH ANNIVERSARY. Mar 12, 1806. Wife of Franklin Pierce, 14th president of the US. Born at Hampton, NH, she died at Concord, NH, Dec 2, 1863.

PUBLIC LIBRARY ASSOCIATION CONFERENCE. Mar 12–16. Phoenix, AZ. For info: Public Library Assn/ALA, 50 E Huron St, Chicago, IL 60611. Phone: (800) 545-2433. Web: www.ala.org/pla.

SUN YAT-SEN: DEATH ANNIVERSARY. Mar 12, 1925. The heroic leader of China's 1911 revolution is remembered on the anniversary of his death at Peking, China. Observed as Arbor Day in Taiwan.

BIRTHDAYS TODAY

Kent Conrad, 54, US Senator (D, North Dakota), born Bismarck, ND, Mar 12, 1948.

Virginia Hamilton, 66, author (*The People Could Fly, M.C. Higgins the Great*), born Yellow Springs, OH, Mar 12, 1936 (some sources say 1933).

Naomi Shihab Nye, 50, author (*Habibi, This Same Sky*), born St. Louis, MO, Mar 12, 1952.

Darryl Strawberry, 40, baseball player, born Los Angeles, CA, Mar 12, 1962.

MARCH 13 — WEDNESDAY

Day 72 — 293 Remaining

ARAB OIL EMBARGO LIFTED: ANNIVERSARY. Mar 13, 1974. The oil-producing Arab countries agreed to lift their five-month embargo on petroleum sales to the US. During the embargo prices went up 300 percent and a ban was imposed on Sunday gasoline sales. The embargo was in retaliation for US support of Israel during the October 1973 Middle-East War.

DEAF HISTORY MONTH. Mar 13–Apr 15. Observance of three of the most important anniversaries for deaf Americans: Apr 15, 1817, establishment of the first public school for the deaf in America, later known as The American School for the Deaf; Apr 8, 1864, charter signed by President Lincoln authorizing the board of directors of the Columbia Institution (now Gallaudet University) to grant college degrees to deaf students; Mar 13, 1988, the victory of the Deaf President Now movement at Gallaudet. For info: FOLDA, Inc, 2930 Craiglawn Rd, Silver Spring, MD 20904-1816. Phone: (301) 572-5168. Fax: (301) 572-4134. E-mail: alhagemeyer@juno.com. Web: www.LibraryDeaf.com. *See* Curriculum Connection.

EARMUFFS PATENTED: ANNIVERSARY. Mar 13, 1887. Chester Greenwood of Maine received a patent for earmuffs.

FILLMORE, ABIGAIL POWERS: BIRTH ANNIVERSARY. Mar 13, 1798. First wife of Millard Fillmore, 13th president of the US. Born at Stillwater, NY. It is said that the White House was without any books until Abigail Fillmore, formerly a teacher, made a room on the second floor into a library. Within a year, Congress appropriated $250 for the president to spend on books for the White House. Died at Washington, DC, Mar 30, 1853.

MOON PHASE: NEW MOON. Mar 13. Moon enters New Moon phase at 9:02 PM, EST.

NATIONAL OPEN AN UMBRELLA INDOORS DAY. Mar 13. The purpose of this day is for people to open umbrellas indoors and note whether they have any bad luck. For interviews, call 24 hours in advance. Annually, Mar 13. For info: Thomas Edward Knibb, 8819 Adventure Ave, Walkersville, MD 21793-7828. Phone: (301) 898-3009. E-mail: tomknibb@juno.com.

March 2002

S	M	T	W	T	F	S
					1	2
3	4	5	6	7	8	9
10	11	12	13	14	15	16
17	18	19	20	21	22	23
24	25	26	27	28	29	30
31						

MARCH 13–APRIL 15
DEAF HISTORY MONTH

Baby boomers are getting older. And with age come joys (grandparenting) and woes (bifocals). Many children will have older family members and friends who may be experiencing some hearing loss. This can be frustrating for all concerned.

Older children can understand the phrase "enunciate clearly." Lessons on sound wavelengths are really helpful at the middle school and junior high levels. As part of the science curriculum, you might study sound waves and how they move. Also, let students research what sound ranges a person is likely to lose first. (High frequencies such as birdcalls, a high-pitched child's voice and the beginning consonant sounds of "s," "t," or "p.")

Older children can also think about how hearing loss may distort a person's perception of a conversation. For example, a question such as "Do you like the speeches?" might be answered with "Yes, I like peaches." Both parties may chuckle when the confusion is sorted out. But it's sad if neither party realizes the problem is hearing related. The off base response may be mistakenly interpreted as a sign of senility.

Try incorporating a lesson in rhyme for younger children. This can be combined with Poetry Month (April), or used as a preparation before it. Start by choosing a simple word, such as cat. Talk about the difficulty people with a hearing loss might have in hearing this word. Discuss how mishearing the first letter easily creates a completely different word. List words that are formed by changing only the first letter of "cat."

In small groups, or pairs, do the same exercise with words of two or more syllables, which the students have chosen. Students should write the initial word at the top of each sheet of paper and list the rhyming words below. When reading the lists aloud, you can define the word rhyme and ask if anyone can think of a kind of writer who would welcome lists like the ones the students have just completed. In addition to gaining a better understanding (and hopefully, more tolerance) of the stress of hearing loss, the class will have generated its own Classroom Rhyming Dictionary, which can be bound and distributed for use during Poetry Month. Think of several catchy titles for the new book and let students vote on which one they want to use.

For an historical focus, you might want to discuss Ludwig van Beethoven (1770–1827) and play some of the music he wrote. He began going deaf in his early thirties and continued to compose music after becoming completely deaf several years later. You might also feature music performed by Evelyn Glennie, a present day percussionist who happens to be hearing impaired.

Children's books on deafness include *Deafness*, by Elaine Landau (Twenty-First Century, 0-8050-2993-1, $22.40 Gr. 4–7) and *Everything You Need to Know about Deafness*, by Carol Basinger (Rosen, 0-8239-3165-X, $17.95 Gr. 7 & up).

PLANET URANUS DISCOVERY: ANNIVERSARY. Mar 13, 1781. German-born English astronomer Sir William Herschel discovered the seventh planet from the sun, Uranus. For more info: *Uranus, Neptune, and Pluto*, by Robin Kerrod (Lerner, 0-8225-3908-X, $21.27 Gr. 4–6) or go to Nine Planets: Multimedia Tour of the Solar System at www.seds.org/billa/tnp.

PRIESTLY, JOSEPH: BIRTH ANNIVERSARY. Mar 13, 1733. English clergyman and scientist, discoverer of oxygen, born at Fieldhead, England. He and his family narrowly escaped an angry mob attacking their home because of his religious and political views. They moved to the US in 1794. Died at Northumberland, PA, Feb 6, 1804.

SAINT AUBIN, HELEN "CALLAGHAN": BIRTH ANNIVERSARY. Mar 13, 1929. Helen Candaele St. Aubin, known as Helen Callaghan during her baseball days, was born at Vancouver, British Columbia, Canada. Saint Aubin and her sister, Margaret Maxwell, were recruited for the All-American Girls Professional Baseball League, which flourished in the 1940s when many major league players were off fighting WWII. She first played at age 15 for the Minneapolis Millerettes, an expansion team that moved to Indiana and became the Fort Wayne Daisies. For the 1945 season the left-handed outfielder led the league with a .299 average and 24 extra base hits. In 1946 she stole 114 bases in 111 games. Her son Kelly Candaele's documentary on the women's baseball league inspired the film *A League of Their Own*. Saint Aubin, who was known as the "Ted Williams of women's baseball," died Dec 8, 1992, at Santa Barbara, CA.

BIRTHDAYS TODAY

Diane Dillon, 69, illustrator, with her husband Leo Dillon (Caldecotts for *Why Mosquitoes Buzz in People's Ears, Ashanti to Zulu: African Traditions*), born Glendale, CA, Mar 13, 1933.

John Hoeven, 45, Governor of North Dakota (R), born Bismarck, ND, Mar 13, 1957.

Ellen Raskin, 74, author (Newbery for *The Westing Game*), born Milwaukee, WI, Mar 13, 1928 (some sources say 1925).

MARCH 14 — THURSDAY

Day 73 — 292 Remaining

DE ANGELI, MARGUERITE: BIRTH ANNIVERSARY. Mar 14, 1889. Author and illustrator, born at Lampeer, MI. She won the Newbery Medal in 1950 for her classic *The Door in the Wall*. Her first book was *Ted & Nina Go to the Grocery Store* in 1935. She died at Detroit, MI, June 16, 1987. For more info: www.deangeli.lapeer.org.

EINSTEIN, ALBERT: BIRTH ANNIVERSARY. Mar 14, 1879. Theoretical physicist best known for his theory of relativity. Born at Ulm, Germany, he won the Nobel Prize in 1921. Died at Princeton, NJ, Apr 18, 1955. For more info: *Einstein, Visionary Scientist*, by John B. Severance (Clarion, 0-395-93100-2, $15 Gr. 5–8).

JONES, CASEY: BIRTH ANNIVERSARY. Mar 14, 1864. Railroad engineer and hero of ballad, whose real name was John Luther Jones. Born near Cayce, KY, he died in a railroad wreck near Vaughn, MS, Apr 30, 1900.

MARSHALL, THOMAS RILEY: BIRTH ANNIVERSARY. Mar 14, 1854. The 28th vice president of the US (1913–21). Born at North Manchester, IN, he died at Washington, DC, June 1, 1925.

MOTH-ER DAY. Mar 14. A day set aside to honor moth collectors and specialists. Celebrated in museums or libraries with moth collections. For info: Bob Birch, Puns Corps Grand Punscorpion, Box 2364, Falls Church, VA 22042-0364. Phone: (703) 533-3668.

TAYLOR, LUCY HOBBS: BIRTH ANNIVERSARY. Mar 14, 1833. Lucy Beaman Hobbs, first woman in America to receive a degree in dentistry (Ohio College of Dental Surgery, 1866) and to be admitted to membership in a state dental association. Born at Franklin County, NY. In 1867 she married James M. Taylor, who also became a dentist (after she instructed him in the essentials). Active women's rights advocate. Died at Lawrence, KS, Oct 3, 1910.

BIRTHDAYS TODAY

Michael Caine, 69, actor (*The Muppet Christmas Carol*), born Bermondsey, London, England, Mar 14, 1933.

Jordan Taylor Hanson, 19, singer (Hanson), born Jenks, OK, Mar 14, 1983.

MARCH 15 — FRIDAY

Day 74 — 291 Remaining

BE KIND TO ANIMALS KIDS CONTEST DEADLINE. Mar 15. Application deadline for this contest. The national winner will receive a $5,000 scholarship. For info: American Humane Assn, 63 Inverness Dr East, Englewood, CO 80112. Phone: (303) 792-9900. Web: www.americanhumane.org.

BELARUS: CONSTITUTION DAY. Mar 15. National holiday. Commemorates the constitution adopted on 1994.

IDES OF MARCH. Mar 15. On the Roman calendar, days were not numbered sequentially through a month. Instead, each month had three division days: kalends, nones and ides. Days were then numbered around these divisions: e.g., III Kalends or IV Nones. The ides occurred on the 15th of the month (or on the 13th in months with fewer than 31 days). Julius Caesar was assassinated on this day in 44 BC. This system continued to be used in Europe through the Middle Ages. When Shakespeare wrote "Beware the ides of March" in his play *Julius Caesar*, his audience understood what this meant.

ISLAMIC NEW YEAR. Mar 15. Islamic calendar date: Muharram 1, 1423. The first day of the first month of the Islamic calendar. Different methods for "anticipating" the visibility of the new moon crescent at Mecca are used by different groups. US date may vary.

JACKSON, ANDREW: BIRTH ANNIVERSARY. Mar 15, 1767. Seventh president of the US (Mar 4, 1829–Mar 3, 1837) was born in a log cabin at Waxhaw, SC. Jackson was the first president since George Washington who had not attended college. He was a military hero in the War of 1812. His presidency reflected his democratic and egalitarian values. Died at Nashville, TN, June 8, 1845. His birthday is observed as a holiday in Tennessee. For info: www.ipl.org/ref/POTUS.

LIBERIA: J.J. ROBERTS DAY. Mar 15. National holiday. Commemorates the birth in 1809 of the country's first president.

MAINE: ADMISSION DAY: ANNIVERSARY. Mar 15. Became 23rd state in 1820. Prior to this date, Maine had been part of Massachusetts.

WASHINGTON'S ADDRESS TO CONTINENTAL ARMY OFFICERS: ANNIVERSARY. Mar 15, 1783. George Washington addressed a meeting at Newburgh, NY, of Continental Army officers who were dissatisfied and rebellious for want of back pay, food, clothing and pensions. General Washington called for patience, opening his speech with the words: "I have grown grey in your service. . . ." Congress later acted to satisfy most of the demands.

"THE WONDER YEARS" TV PREMIERE: ANNIVERSARY. Mar 15, 1988. A coming-of-age tale set in suburbia in the 1960s and 1970s. This drama/comedy starred Fred Savage as Kevin Arnold, Josh Saviano as his best friend Paul and Danica McKellar as girlfriend Winnie. Kevin's dad was played by Dan Lauria, his homemaker mom by Alley Mills, his hippie sister by Olivia D'Abo and his bully brother by Jason Hervey. Narrator Daniel Stern was the voice of the grown-up Kevin. Though the series ended in 1993, it remains popular in reruns.

BIRTHDAYS TODAY

Ruth Bader Ginsburg, 69, Associate Justice of the US Supreme Court, born Brooklyn, NY, Mar 15, 1933.
Don Sundquist, 66, Governor of Tennessee (R), born Moline, IL, Mar 15, 1936.
Ruth White, 60, author (*Belle Prater's Boy*), born Whitewood, VA, Mar 15, 1942.

MARCH 16 — SATURDAY

Day 75 — 290 Remaining

BLACK PRESS DAY: 175th ANNIVERSARY OF THE FIRST BLACK NEWSPAPER. Mar 16, 1827. Anniversary of the founding of the first black newspaper in the US, *Freedom's Journal*, on Varick Street at New York, NY.

CLYMER, GEORGE: BIRTH ANNIVERSARY. Mar 16, 1739. Signer of the Declaration of Independence and of the US Constitution. Born at Philadelphia, PA, and died there Jan 24, 1813.

GODDARD DAY. Mar 16, 1926. Commemorates first liquid-fuel-powered rocket flight, devised by Robert Hutchings Goddard (1882–1945) at Auburn, MA.

"THE GUMBY SHOW" TV PREMIERE: 45th ANNIVERSARY. Mar 16, 1957. This kids' show was a spin-off from "Howdy Doody," where the character of Gumby was first introduced in 1956. Gumby and his horse Pokey were clay figures whose adventures were filmed using the process of "claymation." "The Gumby Show," created by Art Clokey, was first hosted by Bobby Nicholson and later by Pinky Lee. It was syndicated in 1966 and again in 1988. In 1995 *Gumby: The Movie* was released.

MADISON, JAMES: BIRTH ANNIVERSARY. Mar 16, 1751. Fourth president of the US (Mar 4, 1809–Mar 3, 1817), born at Port Conway, VA. He was president when British forces invaded Washington, DC, requiring Madison and other high officials to flee while the British burned the Capitol, the president's residence and most other public buildings (Aug 24–25, 1814). Died at Montpelier, VA, June 28, 1836. For more info: *The Great Little Madison*, by Jean Fritz (Putnam, 0-399-21768-1, $15.99, Gr. 7–9) or www.ipl.org/ref/POTUS.

NIXON, THELMA CATHERINE PATRICIA RYAN: 90th BIRTH ANNIVERSARY. Mar 16, 1912. Wife of Richard Milhous Nixon, 37th president of the US. Born at Ely, NV, she died at Park Ridge, NJ, June 22, 1993.

SAVE THE FLORIDA PANTHER DAY. Mar 16. A ceremonial day on the third Saturday in March.

March 2002

S	M	T	W	T	F	S
					1	2
3	4	5	6	7	8	9
10	11	12	13	14	15	16
17	18	19	20	21	22	23
24	25	26	27	28	29	30
31						

US MILITARY ACADEMY FOUNDED: 200th ANNIVERSARY. Mar 16, 1802. President Thomas Jefferson signed legislation establishing the United States Military Academy to train officers for the army. The Academy opened on July 4, 1802. The college is located at West Point, NY, on the site of the oldest continuously occupied military post in America. Women were admitted to West Point in 1976. The Academy's motto is "Duty, Honor, Country." For more info: www.usma.edu.

BIRTHDAYS TODAY

Mary Chalmers, 75, author and illustrator (*Come for a Walk With Me*), born Camden, NJ, Mar 16, 1927.
Sid Fleischman, 82, author (Newbery for *The Whipping Boy*), born Albert Sidney Fleischman, Brooklyn, NY, Mar 16, 1920.
William Mayne, 74, author (*Lady Muck*), born Kingston-upon-Hull, England, Mar 16, 1928.

MARCH 17 — SUNDAY

Day 76 — 289 Remaining

CAMP FIRE BOYS AND GIRLS BIRTHDAY SUNDAY. Mar 17. A day when Camp Fire Boys and Girls commemorate the organization's founding and worship together and participate in the services of their churches or temples. For info: Camp Fire Boys and Girls, 4601 Madison Ave, Kansas City, MO 64112. Phone: (816) 756-1950. Fax: (816) 756-0258. E-mail: info@campfire.org. Web: www.campfire.org.

CAMP FIRE BOYS AND GIRLS: ANNIVERSARY. Mar 17. To commemorate the anniversary of the founding of Camp Fire Boys and Girls and the service given to children and youth across the nation. Founded in 1910 as Camp Fire Girls. For info: Camp Fire Boys and Girls, 4601 Madison Ave, Kansas City, MO 64112. Phone: (816) 756-1950. Fax: (816) 756-0258. E-mail: info@campfire.org. Web: www.campfire.org.

EVACUATION DAY IN MASSACHUSETTS. Mar 17. Proclaimed annually by the governor, Evacuation Day commemorates the anniversary of the evacuation from Boston of British troops in 1776.

IRELAND: NATIONAL DAY. Mar 17. St. Patrick's Day is observed in the Republic of Ireland as a legal national holiday.

NATIONAL AGRICULTURE WEEK. Mar 17–23. To honor America's providers of food and fiber and to educate the general public about the US agricultural system. Annually, the week that includes the first day of spring. For info: Agriculture Council of America, 11020 King St, Ste 205, Overland Park, KS 66210. Phone: (913) 491-1895. Fax: (913) 491-6502. E-mail: info@agday.org. Web: www.agday.org.

★**NATIONAL POISON PREVENTION WEEK.** Mar 17–23. Presidential Proclamation issued each year for the third week of March since 1962. (PL87–319 of Sept 26, 1961.)

NATIONAL POISON PREVENTION WEEK. Mar 17–23. To aid in encouraging the American people to learn of the dangers of accidental poisoning and to take preventive measures against it. Annually, the third full week in March. For info: Ken Giles, Secy, Poison Prevention Week Council, Box 1543, Washington, DC 20013. E-mail: kgiles@cpsc.gov. Web: www.cpsc.gov.

NORTHERN IRELAND: SAINT PATRICK'S DAY HOLIDAY. Mar 17. National Holiday.

PASSION WEEK. Mar 17–23. The week beginning on the fifth Sunday in Lent; the week before Holy Week.

PASSIONTIDE. Mar 17–30. The last two weeks of Lent (Passion Week and Holy Week), beginning with the fifth Sunday of Lent

(Passion Sunday) and continuing through the day before Easter (Holy Saturday).

RUSTIN, BAYARD: BIRTH ANNIVERSARY. Mar 17, 1910. Black pacifist and civil rights leader, Bayard Rustin was an organizer and participant in many of the great social protest marches—for jobs, freedom and nuclear disarmament. He was arrested and imprisoned more than 20 times for his civil rights and pacifist activities. Born at West Chester, PA, Rustin died at New York, NY, Aug 24, 1987.

SAINT PATRICK'S DAY. Mar 17. Commemorates the patron saint of Ireland, Bishop Patrick (AD 389–461) who, about AD 432, left his home in the Severn Valley, England, and introduced Christianity into Ireland. Feast Day in the Roman Catholic Church. A national holiday in Ireland and Northern Ireland. For links to websites about St. Patrick's Day, go to: deil.lang.uiuc.edu/web.pages/holidays/stpatrick.html.

SAINT PATRICK'S DAY PARADE. Mar 17. Fifth Avenue, New York, NY. Held since 1762, the parade of 125,000 begins the two-mile march at 11:30 AM and lasts about six hours. Starts on 42nd Street and 5th Avenue and ends at 86th Street and First Avenue. Est attendance: 1,000,000. For info: NY CVB, 810 Seventh Ave, New York, NY 10019. Phone: (800) NYC-VISIT or (212) 484-1222.

SOUTH AFRICAN WHITES VOTE TO END MINORITY RULE: 10th ANNIVERSARY. Mar 17, 1992. A referendum proposing ending white minority rule through negotiations was supported by a whites-only ballot. The vote of 1,924,186 (68.6 percent) whites in support of President F.W. de Klerk's reform policies was greater than expected.

TANEY, ROGER B.: 225th BIRTH ANNIVERSARY. Mar 17, 1777. Fifth Chief Justice of the Supreme Court, born at Calvert County, MD. Served as Attorney General under President Andrew Jackson. Nominated as Secretary of the Treasury, he became the first presidential nominee to be rejected by the Senate because of his strong stance against the Bank of the United States as a central bank. A year later, he was nominated to the Supreme Court as an associate justice by Jackson, but his nomination was stalled until the death of Chief Justice John Marshall July 6, 1835. Taney was nominated to fill Marshall's place on the bench and after much resistance he was sworn in as Chief Justice in March 1836. His tenure on the Supreme Court is most remembered for the Dred Scott decision. He died at Washington, DC, Oct 12, 1864.

BIRTHDAYS TODAY

Keith Baker, 49, author (*Big Fat Hen, Hide and Snake*), born LaGrande, OR, Mar 17, 1953.

Patrick Duffy, 53, actor ("Step By Step"), born Townsend, MT, Mar 17, 1949.

Penelope Lively, 69, author (*Moon Tiger*), born Cairo, Egypt, Mar 17, 1933.

MARCH 18 — MONDAY

Day 77 — 288 Remaining

ARUBA: FLAG DAY. Mar 18. Aruba national holiday. Display of flags, national music and folkloric events.

AUSTRALIA: CANBERRA DAY. Mar 18. Australian Capital Territory. Public holiday the third Monday in March.

CALHOUN, JOHN CALDWELL: BIRTH ANNIVERSARY. Mar 18, 1782. American statesman and first vice president of the US to resign that office (Dec 28, 1832). Born at Abbeville District, SC, he died at Washington, DC, Mar 31, 1850.

CLEVELAND, GROVER: BIRTH ANNIVERSARY. Mar 18, 1837. The 22nd (Mar 4, 1885–Mar 3, 1889) and 24th (Mar 4, 1893–Mar 3, 1897) president of the US was born Stephen Grover Cleveland at Caldwell, NJ. He ran for president for the intervening term and received a plurality of votes cast but failed to win electoral college victory for that term. Only president to serve two nonconsecutive terms. Also the only president to be married in the White House. He married 21-year-old Frances Folsom, his ward. Their daughter, Esther, was the first child of a president to be born in the White House. Died at Princeton, NJ, June 24, 1908. For info: www.ipl.org/ref/POTUS.

CYPRUS: GREEN MONDAY. Mar 18. Green, or Clean, Monday is the first Monday of Lent on the Orthodox calendar. Lunch in the fields, with bread, olives and uncooked vegetables and no meat or dairy products.

JORDAN'S BACK!: ANNIVERSARY. Mar 18, 1995. Michael Jordan, considered one of the National Basketball Association's greatest all-time players, made history again when he announced that he was returning to professional play after a 17-month break. The 32-year-old star had retired just before the start of the 1993–94 season, following the murder of his father, James Jordan. Jordan, who averaged 32.3 points a game during regular season play, had led the Chicago Bulls to three successive NBA titles. While retired, he tried a baseball career, playing for the Chicago White Sox minor league team. After returning to the Bulls, he led them to three more NBA titles. He announced his retirement again Jan 13, 1999, after the six-month NBA lockout was resolved.

NATIONAL ENERGY EDUCATION WEEK. Mar 18–22. To make energy education part of the school curriculum. The week ending on the second to the last Friday in March. For info: Natl Energy Education Development Project, PO Box 2518, Reston, VA 20195. Phone: (800) 875-5029.

ORTHODOX LENT. Mar 18–Apr 27. Great Lent or Easter Lent, observed by Eastern Orthodox Churches, lasts until Holy Week begins on Orthodox Palm Sunday (Apr 28).

SPACE MILESTONE: *VOSKHOD 2* (USSR). Mar 18, 1965. Colonel Leonov stepped out of the capsule for 20 minutes in a special space suit, the first man to leave a spaceship. It was two months prior to the first US space walk. See also "Space Milestone: *Gemini 4* (US)" (June 3).

BIRTHDAYS TODAY

Bonnie Blair, 38, former Olympic gold medal speed skater, born Cornwall, NY, Mar 18, 1964.

Douglas Florian, 52, poet, illustrator (*Beast Feast, Insectlopedia, Mammalabilia*), born New York, NY, Mar 18, 1950.

Queen Latifah, 32, singer, actress ("Living Single"), born Dana Owens, East Orange, NJ, Mar 18, 1970.

MARCH 19 — TUESDAY

Day 78 — 287 Remaining

BRADFORD, WILLIAM: BIRTH ANNIVERSARY. Mar 19, 1589. Pilgrim father, governor of Plymouth Colony, born at Yorkshire, England, and baptized Mar 19, 1589. Sailed from Southampton, England, on the *Mayflower* in 1620. Died at Plymouth, MA, May 9, 1657. For more info: *William Bradford: Rock of Plymouth*, by Kieran Doherty (Twenty-First Century, 0-7613-1304-4, $22.90 Gr. 6–10).

EARP, WYATT: BIRTH ANNIVERSARY. Mar 19, 1848. Born at Monmouth, IL, and died Jan 13, 1929, at Los Angeles, CA. A legendary figure of the Old West, Earp worked as a railroad hand, saloonkeeper, gambler, lawman, gunslinger, miner and real estate investor at various times. Best known for his involvement in the gunfight at the OK Corral Oct 26, 1881, at Tombstone, AZ.

IRAN: NATIONAL DAY OF OIL. Mar 19. National holiday. Commemorates nationalization of oil fields in 1963.

McKEAN, THOMAS: BIRTH ANNIVERSARY. Mar 19, 1734. Signer of the Declaration of Independence. Born at Chester County, PA, he died June 24, 1817.

SWALLOWS RETURN TO SAN JUAN CAPISTRANO. Mar 19. Traditional date (St. Joseph's Day), since 1776, for swallows to return to old mission of San Juan Capistrano, CA.

US STANDARD TIME ACT: ANNIVERSARY. Mar 19, 1918. Anniversary of passage by the Congress of the Standard Time Act, which authorized the Interstate Commerce Commission to establish standard time zones for the US. The act also established Daylight Saving Time, to save fuel and to promote other economies in a country at war. Daylight Saving Time first went into operation on Easter Sunday, Mar 31, 1918. The Uniform Time Act of 1966, as amended in 1986, by Public Law 99–359, now governs standard time in the US. See also: "US: Daylight Saving Time Begins" (Apr 7).

WARREN, EARL: BIRTH ANNIVERSARY. Mar 19, 1891. American jurist, 14th Chief Justice of the US Supreme Court. Born at Los Angeles, CA, died at Washington, DC, July 9, 1974.

BIRTHDAYS TODAY

Glenn Close, 55, actress (*101 Dalmatians*), born Greenwich, CT, Mar 19, 1947.

March 2002

S	M	T	W	T	F	S
					1	2
3	4	5	6	7	8	9
10	11	12	13	14	15	16
17	18	19	20	21	22	23
24	25	26	27	28	29	30
31						

Hazel Dodge, 43, author (*The Ancient Life: Life in Classical Athens & Rome*), born Feltham, England, Mar 19, 1959.

Bruce Willis, 47, actor (*Die Hard*, voice in *Look Who's Talking 2*), born Penn's Grove, NJ, Mar 19, 1955.

MARCH 20 — WEDNESDAY

Day 79 — 286 Remaining

ANONYMOUS GIVING WEEK. Mar 20–26. A time to celebrate the true spirit of giving. Experience the joy in random acts of kindness. Leave a legacy of anonymous contribution. Perfect for a one-time or all-week adventure designed to share time, talent and treasure. Annually, beginning on the first day of spring. For info: Janna Krammer, Legacy Institute, 42805 Blackhawk Rd, Harris, MN 55032. Phone: (612) 674-0227. Fax: (612) 674-0228. E-mail: info@legacyinstitute.com.

CHILDREN'S BOOK FESTIVAL. Mar 20–22 (tentative). Hattiesburg, MS. This three-day spring festival brings together children's authors and illustrators for workshops, question–and–answer sessions and storytelling. For info: Kalicia Henderson, Children's Book Festival, USM Continuing Education, Box 5055B, Hattiesburg, MS 39406. Phone: (601) 266-4186. Web: ocean.st.usm.edu/~mhamilto/.

JAPAN: VERNAL EQUINOX DAY. Mar 20. A national holiday in Japan. When Mar 20 falls on a weekend, it is celebrated on the nearest weekday.

LEGOLAND OPENS: ANNIVERSARY. Mar 20, 1999. The Legoland theme park for children ages 2–12 opened on this day at Carlsbad, CA. It is the third Legoland park; the others are in Denmark and England. More than 30 million Lego pieces went into the construction of 40 rides and attractions. Since its beginnings in the 1950s, the Danish maker has manufactured more than 189 billion Lego blocks. Legos were introduced in the US in 1962. For info: Legoland, One Lego Dr, Carlsbad, CA 92008. Phone: (760) 918-LEGO. Web: www.lego.com.

NATIONAL AGRICULTURE DAY. Mar 20. A day to honor America's providers of food and fiber and to educate the general public about the US agricultural system. Week of celebration: Mar 17–23. Annually, the first day of spring. For info: Agriculture Council of America, 11020 King St, Ste 205, Overland Park, KS 66210. Phone: (913) 491-1895. Fax: (913) 491-6502. E-mail: aca@nama.org. Web: www.agday.org.

SPRING. Mar 20–June 21. In the Northern Hemisphere spring begins today with the vernal equinox, at 2:16 PM, EST. Note that in the Southern Hemisphere today is the beginning of autumn. Sun rises due east and sets due west everywhere on Earth (except near poles) and the daylight length (interval between sunrise and sunset) is virtually the same everywhere today: 12 hours, 8 minutes.

TUNISIA: INDEPENDENCE DAY. Mar 20. Commemorates treaty in 1956 by which France recognized Tunisian autonomy.

WARMEST US WINTER ON RECORD: ANNIVERSARY. Mar 20, 2000. The warmest winter in US history ended on this date. The National Climatic Data Center later declared the winter of 1999–2000 the warmest US winter in the 103 years that the Federal Government had been keeping record of climatic conditions.

BIRTHDAYS TODAY

Mitsumasa Anno, 76, author and illustrator (*Topsy-Turvies, Anno's Alphabet*), born Tsuwano, Japan, Mar 20, 1926.

Ellen Conford, 60, author (*Hail, Hail Camp Timberwood*), born New York, NY, Mar 20, 1942.

Lois Lowry, 65, author (Newbery for *Number the Stars, The Giver*), born Honolulu, HI, Mar 20, 1937.

Bill Martin, Jr, 86, author (*Brown Bear, Brown Bear, What Did You See?; Knots on a Counting Rope; Chicka Chicka Boom Boom*), born Hiawatha, KS, Mar 20, 1916.

Patrick James (Pat) Riley, 57, basketball coach and former player, born Schenectady, NY, Mar 20, 1945.

Fred Rogers, 74, producer, TV personality ("Mr Rogers' Neighborhood"), born Latrobe, PA, Mar 20, 1928.

Louis Sachar, 48, author (Newbery and National Book Award for *Holes*), born East Meadow, NY, Mar 20, 1954.

MARCH 21 — THURSDAY

Day 80 — 285 Remaining

ABSOLUTELY INCREDIBLE KID DAY. Mar 21. Camp Fire Boys and Girls, one of the nation's oldest and largest youth development organizations, holds this annual event to encourage adults to write a letter to a child in their life to tell children how special they are and how much they mean to them. Annually, the third Thursday in March. For info: Camp Fire Boys and Girls, 4601 Madison Ave, Kansas City, MO 64112. Phone: (816) 756-1950. Fax: (816) 756-0258. E-mail: kidday@yahoo.com. Web: www.campfire.org/.

ARIES, THE RAM. Mar 21–Apr 19. In the astronomical/astrological zodiac, which divides the sun's apparent orbit into 12 segments, the period Mar 21–Apr 19 is identified, traditionally, as the sun sign of Aries, the Ram. The ruling planet is Mars.

BACH, JOHANN SEBASTIAN: BIRTH ANNIVERSARY. Mar 21, 1685. Organist and composer, one of the most influential composers in musical history. Born at Eisenach, Germany, he died at Leipzig, Germany, July 28, 1750. For more info: *Sebastian: A Book about Bach*, by Jeanette Winter (Harcourt, 0-15-200629-X, $16 Gr. 2–4).

FIRST ROUND-THE-WORLD BALLOON FLIGHT: ANNIVERSARY. Mar 21, 1999. Swiss psychiatrist Bertrand Piccard and British copilot Brian Jones landed in the Egyptian desert on this date, having flown 29,056 miles nonstop around the world in a hot-air balloon, the *Breitling Orbiter 3*. Leaving from Chateau d'Oex in the Swiss Alps on Mar 1, the trip took 19 days, 21 hours and 55 minutes. Piccard is the grandson of balloonist Auguste Piccard, who was the first to ascend into the stratosphere in a balloon. See also: "Piccard, Auguste: Birth Anniversary" (Jan 28).

IRANIAN NEW YEAR: NORUZ. Mar 21. National celebration for all Iranians, this is the traditional Persian New Year. (In Iran spring comes Mar 21.) It is a celebration of nature's rebirth. Every household spreads a special cover with symbols for the seven good angels on it. These symbols are sprouts, wheat germ, apples, hyacinth, fruit of the jujube, garlic and sumac heralding life, rebirth, health, happiness, prosperity, joy and beauty. A fish bowl is also customary, representing the end of the astrological year, and wild rue is burned to drive away evil and bring about a happy New Year. This pre-Islamic holiday, a legacy of Zoroastrianism, is also celebrated as Navruz, Nau-Roz or Noo Roz in Afghanistan, Albania, Azerbaijan, Kazakhstan, Kyrgyzstan, Tajikistan and Turkmenistan. For info: Mahvash Tafreshi, Librarian, Farmingdale Public Library, 116 Merritts Rd, Farmingdale, NY 11735. Phone: (516) 249-9090. Fax: (516) 694-9697 or Yassaman Djalali, Librarian, West Valley Branch Library, 1243 San Tomas Aquino Rd, San Jose, CA 95117. Phone: (408) 244-4766.

LEWIS, FRANCIS: BIRTH ANNIVERSARY. Mar 21, 1713. Signer of the Declaration of Independence, born at Wales. Died Dec 31, 1802, at Long Island, NY.

MEXICO: BENITO JUAREZ' BIRTH ANNIVERSARY. Mar 21. A full-blooded Zapotec Indian, Benito Pablo Juarez was born at Oaxaca, Mexico in 1806, and learned Spanish at age 12. Juarez became judge of the civil court in Oaxaca in 1842, a member of congress in 1846 and governor in 1847. In 1858, following a rebellion against the constitution, he became president. He died at Mexico City, July 18, 1872. A symbol of liberation and of Mexican resistance to foreign intervention, his birthday is a public holiday in Mexico.

MOON PHASE: FIRST QUARTER. Mar 21. Moon enters First Quarter phase at 9:28 PM, EST.

NAMIBIA: INDEPENDENCE DAY. Mar 21. National Day. Commemorates independence from South Africa in 1990.

NAW-RUZ. Mar 21. Baha'i New Year's Day. Astronomically fixed to commence the year. One of the nine days of the year when Baha'is suspend work. For info: Baha'is of the US, Office of Public Info, 866 UN Plaza, Ste 120, New York, NY 10017-1822. Phone: (212) 803-2500. Fax: (212) 803-2573. E-mail: usopi-ny@bic.org. Web: www.us.bahai.org.

POCAHONTAS (REBECCA ROLFE): DEATH ANNIVERSARY. Mar 21, 1617. Pocahontas, daughter of Powhatan, born about 1595, near Jamestown, VA, leader of the Indian union of Algonkin nations, helped to foster good will between the colonists of the Jamestown settlement and her people. Pocahontas converted to Christianity, was baptized with the name Rebecca and married John Rolfe Apr 5, 1614. In 1616, she accompanied Rolfe on a trip to his native England, where she was regarded as an overseas "ambassador." Pocahontas's stay in England drew so much attention to the Virginia Company's Jamestown settlement that lotteries were held to help support the colony. Shortly before she was scheduled to return to Jamestown, Pocahontas died at Gravesend, Kent, England, of either smallpox or pneumonia. For more info: *Pocahontas: An American Princess*, by Joyce Milton (Penguin Putnam, 0-448-42298-0, $13.89 Gr. 2–3).

SINGLE PARENTS DAY. Mar 21. Dedicated to recognizing and heightening awareness of Americans to the issues related to single-parent households. In 1984, Congress established Mar 21 as Single Parents Day. Each year the Coalition for Single Parents gives out the Single Parent of the Year Award. 2000 recipients: Candace Carpenter, CEO of ivillage.com and Kimi Gray, National Public Housing Advocate. For info: Janice S. Moglen, PO Box 61014, Denver, CO 80206. Phone: (303) 899-4971. Fax: (303) 832-1667. E-mail: daymar21@privatei.com.

SOUTH AFRICA: HUMAN RIGHTS DAY. Mar 21. National holiday. Commemorates the massacre in 1960 at Sharpeville and all those who lost their lives in the struggle for equal rights as citizens of South Africa.

UNITED NATIONS: INTERNATIONAL DAY FOR THE ELIMINATION OF RACIAL DISCRIMINATION. Mar 21. Initiated by the United Nations General Assembly in 1966 to be observed annually Mar 21, the anniversary of the killing of 69 African demonstrators at Sharpeville, South Africa, in 1960, as a day to remember "the victims of Sharpeville and those countless others in different parts of the world who have fallen victim to racial injustice" and to promote efforts to eradicate racial discrimination worldwide. Info from: United Nations, Dept of Public Info, New York, NY 10017.

BIRTHDAYS TODAY

Matthew Broderick, 40, actor (*Inspector Gadget*), born New York, NY, Mar 21, 1962.

Peter Catalanotto, 43, author and illustrator (*Dylan's Day Out*), born Long Island, NY, Mar 21, 1959.

Lisa Desimini, 38, author and illustrator (*My House*), born Brooklyn, NY, Mar 21, 1964.
Michael Foreman, 64, author and illustrator (*Seal Surfer*), born Pakefield, Suffolk, England, Mar 21, 1938.
Margaret Mahy, 66, author (*The Rattlebang Picnic*), born Whakatane, New Zealand, Mar 21, 1936.
Rosie O'Donnell, 40, talk show host, actress (*A League of Their Own, The Flintstones*), born Commack, NY, Mar 21, 1962.
David Wisniewski, 49, illustrator and author (Caldecott for *Golem*), born Middlesex, England, Mar 21, 1953.

MARCH 22 — FRIDAY

Day 81 — 284 Remaining

CALDECOTT, RANDOLPH: BIRTH ANNIVERSARY. Mar 22, 1846. Illustrator who brought greater beauty to children's books, born at Chester, England. He died at St. Augustine, FL, Feb 12, 1886. The Caldecott Medal given annually by the American Library Association for the most distinguished American picture book for children is named in his honor. For info: *Randolph Caldecott: The Children's Illustrator*, by Marguerite Lewis (Highsmith, 0-913853-22-4, $10.95 Gr. 2–7).

EQUAL RIGHTS AMENDMENT SENT TO STATES FOR RATIFICATION: 30th ANNIVERSARY. Mar 22, 1972. The Senate passed the 27th Amendment, prohibiting discrimination on the basis of sex, sending it to the states for ratification. Hawaii led the way as the first state to ratify and by the end of the year 22 states had ratified it. On Oct 6, 1978, the deadline for ratification was extended to June 30, 1982, by Congress. The amendment still lacked three of the required 38 states for ratification. This was the first extension granted since Congress set seven years as the limit for ratification. The amendment failed to achieve ratification as the deadline came and passed and no additional states ratified the measure.

FIRST WOMEN'S COLLEGIATE BASKETBALL GAME: ANNIVERSARY. Mar 22, 1893. The first women's collegiate basketball game was played at Smith College at Northampton, MA. Senda Berenson, then Smith's director of physical education and "mother of women's basketball," supervised the game, in which Smith's sophomore team beat the freshman team 5–4. For info: Dir of Media Relations, Smith College, Office of College Relations, Northampton, MA 01063. Phone: (413) 585-2190. Fax: (413) 585-2174. E-mail: lfenlason@colrel.smith.edu. Web: www.smith.edu.

INTERNATIONAL GOOF-OFF DAY. Mar 22. A day of relaxation and a time to be oneself; a day for some good-humored fun and some good-natured silliness. Everyone needs one special day each year to goof off. For info: Monica A. Dufour, 471 S Vanburen Circle, Davison, MI 48423-8535. Phone: (810) 658-3147.

LASER PATENTED: ANNIVERSARY. Mar 22, 1960. The first patent for a laser (Light Amplification by Stimulated Emission of Radiation) was granted to Arthur Schawlow and Charles Townes.

NATIONAL ART EDUCATION ASSOCIATION ANNUAL CONVENTION. Mar 22–26. Miami Beach, FL. For info: Natl Art Education Assn, 1916 Association Dr, Reston, VA 20191-1590. Phone: (703) 860-8000. Web: www.naea-reston.org.

March 2002

S	M	T	W	T	F	S
					1	2
3	4	5	6	7	8	9
10	11	12	13	14	15	16
17	18	19	20	21	22	23
24	25	26	27	28	29	30
31						

NO HOMEWORK DAY. Mar 22. Teachers don't give students homework on this day. Annually, the last Friday in March except when this falls during spring break.

PUERTO RICO: EMANCIPATION DAY. Mar 22. Holiday commemorating the end of slavery in 1873.

SHABBAT ACROSS AMERICA. Mar 22. More than 600 participating synagogues (Conservative, Orthodox, Reform and Reconstructionist) encourage Jews to observe the Sabbath on this Friday night. This will also be observed in Canada as Shabbat Across Canada. For info: Natl Jewish Outreach Program, 485 5th Ave, New York, NY 10017-6104. Phone: (888) SHABBAT or (212) 986-7450. Web: www.njop.org/saapage/saa2.htm.

SPACE MILESTONE: RECORD TIME IN SPACE. Mar 22, 1995. A Russian cosmonaut returned to Earth after setting a record of 439 days in space aboard *Mir*. Previous records include three Soviet cosmonauts who spent 237 days in space at *Salyut 7* space station in 1984, a Soviet cosmonaut who spent 326 days aboard *Mir* in 1987 and two Soviets who spent 366 days aboard *Mir* in 1988. The longest stay in space by any US astronaut was Shannon Lucid's 188-day stay on *Mir* in 1996. This also set a record for women in space.

UNITED NATIONS: WORLD DAY FOR WATER. Mar 22. The General Assembly declared this observance (Res 47/193) to promote public awareness of how water resource development contributes to economic productivity and social well-being.

BIRTHDAYS TODAY

Shawn Bradley, 30, basketball player, born Landstuhl, West Germany, Mar 22, 1972.
Robert Quinlan (Bob) Costas, 50, sportscaster, born New York, NY, Mar 22, 1952.
Orrin Grant Hatch, 68, US Senator (R, Utah), born Pittsburgh, PA, Mar 22, 1934.
Cristen Powell, 23, race car driver, born Portland, OR, Mar 22, 1979.
William Shatner, 71, actor (Captain Kirk of "Star Trek"; "TJ Hooker"), author (Tek novels), born Montreal, QC, Canada, Mar 22, 1931.
Elvis Stojko, 30, figure skater, born Newmarket, ON, Canada, Mar 22, 1972.

MARCH 23 — SATURDAY

Day 82 — 283 Remaining

COLFAX, SCHUYLER: BIRTH ANNIVERSARY. Mar 23, 1823. The 17th vice president of the US (1869–73). Born at New York, NY. Died Jan 13, 1885, at Mankato, MN.

LIBERTY DAY: ANNIVERSARY. Mar 23, 1775. Anniversary of Patrick Henry's speech for arming the Virginia militia at St. John's Church, Richmond, VA. "I know not what course others may take, but as for me, give me liberty or give me death."

NEAR MISS DAY. Mar 23, 1989. A mountain-sized asteroid passed within 500,000 miles of Earth, a very close call according to NASA. Impact would have equaled the strength of 40,000 hydrogen bombs, created a crater the size of the District of Columbia and devastated everything for 100 miles in all directions.

NEW ZEALAND: OTAGO AND SOUTHLAND PROVINCIAL ANNIVERSARY. Mar 23. In addition to the statutory public holidays of New Zealand, there is in each provincial district a holiday for the provincial anniversary. This is observed in Otago and Southland.

PAKISTAN: REPUBLIC DAY. Mar 23. National holiday. The All-India-Muslim League adopted a resolution calling for a Muslim homeland in 1940. On the same day in 1956 Pakistan declared itself a republic.

UNITED NATIONS: WORLD METEOROLOGICAL DAY. Mar 23. An international day observed by meteorological services throughout the world and by the organizations of the UN system. For info: United Nations, Dept of Public Info, New York, NY 10017.

BIRTHDAYS TODAY

Eleanor Cameron, 90, author (*The Court of the Stone Children*), born Winnipeg, MB, Canada, Mar 23, 1912.

Mike Easley, 52, Governor of North Carolina (D), born Nash County, NC, Mar 23, 1950.

Tom Glavine, 36, baseball player, born Concord, MA, Mar 23, 1966.

Jason Kidd, 29, basketball player, born San Francisco, CA, Mar 23, 1973.

Moses Eugene Malone, 48, former basketball player, born Petersburg, VA, Mar 23, 1954.

MARCH 24 — SUNDAY

Day 83 — 282 Remaining

EXXON VALDEZ OIL SPILL: ANNIVERSARY. Mar 24, 1989. The tanker *Exxon Valdez* ran aground at Prince William Sound, leaking 11 million gallons of oil into one of nature's richest habitats. For more info: *The Exxon Valdez*, by Victoria Sherrow (Enslow, 0-7660-1058-9, $18.85 Gr. 4–8).

HOLY WEEK. Mar 24–30. Christian observance dating from the fourth century, known also as Great Week. The seven days beginning on the sixth and final Sunday in Lent (Palm Sunday), consisting of: Palm Sunday, Monday of Holy Week, Tuesday of Holy Week, Spy Wednesday (or Wednesday of Holy Week), Maundy Thursday, Good Friday and Holy Saturday (or Great Sabbath or Easter Even). A time of solemn devotion to and memorializing of the suffering (passion), death and burial of Christ. Formerly a time of strict fasting.

HOUDINI, HARRY: BIRTH ANNIVERSARY. Mar 24, 1874. Magician and escape artist, born at Budapest, Hungary. Lecturer, athlete, author, expert on history of magic, exposer of fraudulent mediums and motion picture actor. Was best known for his ability to escape from locked restraints (handcuffs, straitjackets, coffins, boxes and milk cans). He died at Detroit, MI, Oct 31, 1926. Anniversary of his death (Halloween) has been the occasion for meetings of magicians and attempts at communication by mediums. For more info: *Spellbinder: The Life of Harry Houdini*, by Tom Lalicki (Holiday, 0-8234-1499-X, $18.95 Gr. 3–7).

PALM SUNDAY. Mar 24. Commemorates Christ's last entry into Jerusalem, when His way was covered with palms by the multitudes. Beginning of Holy (or Great) Week in Western Christian churches.

PHILIPPINE INDEPENDENCE: ANNIVERSARY. Mar 24, 1934. President Franklin Roosevelt signed a bill granting independence to the Philippines. The bill, which took effect July 4, 1946, brought to a close almost half a century of US control of the islands.

POWELL, JOHN WESLEY: BIRTH ANNIVERSARY. Mar 24, 1834. American geologist and explorer, born at Mount Morris, NY. Powell is best known for his explorations of the Grand Canyon by boat on the Colorado River. He died at Haven, ME, Sept 23, 1902. For more info: *Exploring the Earth with John Wesley Powell*, by Michael Elsohn Ross (Carolrhoda, 1-5750-5254-7, $19.94 Gr. 5–6).

RHODE ISLAND VOTERS REJECT CONSTITUTION: ANNIVERSARY. Mar 24, 1788. In a popular referendum, Rhode Island rejected the new Constitution by a vote of 2,708 to 237. The state later (May 29, 1790) ratified the Constitution and ratified the Bill of Rights, June 7, 1790.

TB BACILLUS DISCOVERED: ANNIVERSARY. Mar 24, 1882. The tuberculosis bacillus was discovered by German scientist Robert Koch.

UNITED KINGDOM: SUMMER TIME. Mar 24–Oct 27. "Summer Time" (one hour in advance of Standard Time), similar to daylight-saving time, is observed from 0100 hours on the day after the fourth Saturday in March until 0100 hours on the day after the fourth Saturday in October.

BIRTHDAYS TODAY

Dr. Roger Bannister, 73, distance runner, broke the 4-minute-mile record in 1954, born Harrow, Middlesex, England, Mar 24, 1929.

MARCH 25 — MONDAY

Day 84 — 281 Remaining

ASHURA: TENTH DAY. Mar 25. Islamic calendar date: Muharram 10, 1423. Commemorates death of Muhammad's grandson and the Battle of Karbala. A time of fasting, reflection and meditation. Jews of Medina fasted on the tenth day in remembrance of their salvation from Pharoah. Different methods for "anticipating" the visibility of the new moon crescent at Mecca are used by different groups. US date may vary.

BORGLUM, GUTZON: BIRTH ANNIVERSARY. Mar 25, 1871. American sculptor who created the huge sculpture of four American presidents (Washington, Jefferson, Lincoln and Theodore Roosevelt) at Mount Rushmore National Memorial in the Black Hills of South Dakota. Born John Gutzon de la Mothe Borglum at Bear Lake, ID, the son of Mormon pioneers, he worked the last 14 years of his life on the Mount Rushmore sculpture. He died at Chicago, IL, Mar 6, 1941.

FEAST OF ANNUNCIATION. Mar 25. Celebrated in the Roman Catholic Church in commemoration of the message of the Angel Gabriel to Mary that she was to be the Mother of Christ.

GREECE: INDEPENDENCE DAY. Mar 25. National holiday. Celebrates the beginning of the Greek revolt for independence from the Ottoman Empire in 1821. Greece attained independence in 1829.

★ **GREEK INDEPENDENCE DAY: A NATIONAL DAY OF CELEBRATION OF GREEK AND AMERICAN DEMOCRACY.** Mar 25.

MARYLAND DAY. Mar 25. Commemorates arrival of Lord Baltimore's first settlers in Maryland in 1634.

NATIONAL SLEEP AWARENESS WEEK. Mar 25–31. All Americans are urged to recognize the dangers of untreated sleep disorders and the importance of proper sleep to their health, safety and productivity. "8ZZZs, please!" For info: Natl Sleep Foundation, 1522 K St NW, Ste 500, Washington, DC 20005. Phone: (888) NSF-SLEEP. Web: www.sleepfoundation.org.

NATO ATTACKS YUGOSLAVIA: ANNIVERSARY. Mar 25, 1999. After many weeks of unsuccessful negotiations with Yugoslav leader Slobodan Milosevic over the treatment of ethnic Albanians in the Kosovo Province by Serb forces, NATO forces began bombing Serbia and Kosovo. In retaliation, hundreds of thousands of Kosovo Albanians were driven from their homes into Albania, Macedonia and Montenegro. Peace talks began in June 1999.

PECAN DAY: ANNIVERSARY. Mar 25, 1775. Anniversary of the planting by George Washington of pecan trees (some of which still survive) at Mount Vernon. The trees were a gift to Washington from Thomas Jefferson, who had planted a few pecan trees from the southern US at Monticello, VA. The pecan, native to southern North America, is sometimes called "America's own nut." First cultivated by American Indians, it has been transplanted to other continents but has failed to achieve wide use or popularity outside the US.

SEWARD'S DAY: ANNIVERSARY OF THE ACQUISITION OF ALASKA. Mar 25. Observed in Alaska near anniversary of its acquisition from Russia in 1867. The treaty of purchase was signed between the Russians and the Americans Mar 30, 1867, and ratified by the Senate May 28, 1867. The territory was formally transferred Oct 18, 1867. Annually, the last Monday in March.

TRIANGLE SHIRTWAIST FIRE: ANNIVERSARY. Mar 25, 1911. At about 4:30 PM, fire broke out at the Triangle Shirtwaist Company at New York, NY, minutes before the seamstresses were to go home. Some workers were fatally burned while others leaped to their deaths from the windows of the 10-story building. The fire lasted only 18 minutes but left 146 workers dead, most of them young immigrant women. It was found that some of the deaths were a direct result of workers being trapped on the ninth floor by a locked door. Labor law forbade locking factory doors while employees were at work, and owners of the company were indicted on charges of first- and second-degree manslaughter. The tragic fire became a turning point in labor history, bringing about reforms in health and safety laws. For more info: *The Triangle Shirtwaist Company Fire of 1911*, by Gina DeAngelis (Chelsea House, 0-7910-5267-2, $19.95 Gr. 7–12).

BIRTHDAYS TODAY

John Ensign, 44, US Senator (R, Nevada), born Roseville, CA, Mar 25, 1958.

Cammi Granato, 31, Olympic ice hockey player, born Maywood, IL, Mar 25, 1971.

March 2002

S	M	T	W	T	F	S
					1	2
3	4	5	6	7	8	9
10	11	12	13	14	15	16
17	18	19	20	21	22	23
24	25	26	27	28	29	30
31						

Elton John, 55, singer, songwriter, born Reginald Kenneth Dwight, Pinner, England, Mar 25, 1947.

Avery Johnson, 37, basketball player, born New Orleans, LA, Mar 25, 1965.

MARCH 26 — TUESDAY

Day 85 — 280 Remaining

AMERICAN DIABETES ALERT. Mar 26. A one-day "wake-up call" for those eight million Americans who have diabetes and don't even know it. During the Alert, local ADA affiliates use the diabetes risk test—a simple paper-and-pencil quiz—to communicate the risk factors and symptoms of the disease. For more info: call 1-800-DIABETES (342-2383). Annually, the fourth Tuesday in March.

BANGLADESH: INDEPENDENCE DAY. Mar 26. Commemorates East Pakistan's independence in 1971 as the state of Bangladesh. Celebrated with parades, youth festivals and symposia.

CAMP DAVID ACCORD SIGNED: ANNIVERSARY. Mar 26, 1979. Israeli Prime Minister Menachem Begin and Egyptian President Anwar Sadat signed the Camp David peace treaty, ending 30 years of war between their two countries. The agreement was fostered by President Jimmy Carter.

FROST, ROBERT LEE: BIRTH ANNIVERSARY. Mar 26, 1874. American poet who tried his hand at farming, teaching, shoemaking and editing before winning acclaim as a poet. Pulitzer Prize winner. Born at San Francisco, CA, he died at Boston, MA, Jan 29, 1963.

MacDONALD, BETTY: BIRTH ANNIVERSARY. Mar 26, 1908. Born Anne Elizabeth Bard at Boulder, CO. She was the author of the Mrs. Piggle-Wiggle series, books featuring a character parents turned to when their children's behavior was out of control. Mrs. Piggle-Wiggle was famous for her "Won't-Pick-Up-the-Toys Cure" and her "Answer-Backers Cure." Titles in the series include *Mrs. Piggle-Wiggle* and *Hello, Mrs. Piggle-Wiggle*. MacDonald died at Carmel Valley, CA, Feb 7, 1958.

MAKE UP YOUR OWN HOLIDAY DAY. Mar 26. This day is a day you may name for whatever you wish. Reach for the stars! Make up a holiday! Annually, Mar 26. [© 1999 by WH] For info: Thomas and Ruth Roy, Wellcat Holidays, 2418 Long Ln, Lebanon, PA 17046. Phone: (230) 332-4886. E-mail: wellcat@supernet.com. Web: www.wellcat.com.

PRINCE JONAH KUHIO KALANIANOLE DAY. Mar 26. Hawaii. Commemorates the man who, as Hawaii's delegate to the US Congress, introduced the first bill for statehood in 1919. Not until 1959 did Hawaii become a state.

SOVIET COSMONAUT RETURNS TO NEW COUNTRY: 10th ANNIVERSARY. Mar 26, 1992. After spending 313 days in space in the Soviet *Mir* space station, cosmonaut Serge Krikalev returned to Earth and to what was for him a new country. He left Earth May 18, 1991, a citizen of the Soviet Union, but during his stay aboard the space station, the Soviet Union crumbled and became the Commonwealth of Independent States. Originally scheduled to return in October 1991, Krikalev's return was delayed by five months due to his country's disintegration and the ensuing monetary problems.

BIRTHDAYS TODAY

Marcus Allen, 42, football player, born San Diego, CA, Mar 26, 1960.

Thomas A. (T.A.) Barron, 50, author (*The Lost Years of Merlin, The Fires of Merlin, The Ancient One*), born in Colorado, Mar 26, 1952.

Lincoln Chafee, 49, US Senator (R, Rhode Island), born Warwick, RI, Mar 26, 1953.

Elaine Lan Chao, 49, US Secretary of Labor (George W. Bush administration), born Taipei, Taiwan, Mar 26, 1953.

Sandra Day O'Connor, 72, Associate Justice of the US Supreme Court, born El Paso, TX, Mar 26, 1930.

John Houston Stockton, 40, basketball player, born Spokane, WA, Mar 26, 1962.

MARCH 27 — WEDNESDAY

Day 86 — 279 Remaining

EARTHQUAKE STRIKES ALASKA: ANNIVERSARY. Mar 27, 1964. The strongest earthquake in North American history (8.4 on the Richter scale) struck Alaska, east of Anchorage. 117 people were killed. This was the second worst earthquake of the twentieth century in terms of magnitude. For more info go to the National Earthquake Information Center: wwwneic.cr.usgs.gov. *See* Curriculum Connection.

FUNKY WINKERBEAN: ANNIVERSARY. Mar 27, 1972. Anniversary of the nationally syndicated comic strip. For info: Tom Batiuk, Creator, 2750 Substation Rd, Medina, OH 44256. Phone: (330) 722-8755.

MYANMAR: RESISTANCE DAY. Mar 27. National holiday. Commemorates the day in 1945 when Burma (later Myanmar) joined the Allies in World War II.

NATIONAL SCIENCE TEACHERS ASSOCIATION NATIONAL CONVENTION. Mar 27–30. San Diego, CA. For info: Natl Science Teachers Assn, 1840 Wilson Blvd, Arlington, VA 22201-3000. Phone: (703) 243-7100. Web: www.nsta.org.

PASSOVER BEGINS AT SUNDOWN. Mar 27. See "Pesach" (Mar 28).

ROENTGEN, WILHELM KONRAD: BIRTH ANNIVERSARY. Mar 27, 1845. German scientist who discovered x-rays (1895) and won a Nobel Prize in 1901. Born at Lennep, Prussia, he died at Munich, Germany, Feb 10, 1923. See also: "X-Ray Discovery Day: Anniversary" (Nov 8).

BIRTHDAYS TODAY

Mariah Carey, 32, singer, born New York, NY, Mar 27, 1970.

Randall Cunningham, 39, football player, born Santa Barbara, CA, Mar 27, 1963.

Dick King-Smith, 80, author (*Babe: the Gallant Pig, A Mouse Called Wolf, The Cuckoo Child*), born Bitton, Gloucestershire, England, Mar 27, 1922.

Patricia Wrede, 49, author (*Dealing with Dragons, Talking to Dragons*), born Chicago, IL, Mar 27, 1953.

MARCH 27
EARTHQUAKE!

On this day in 1964 the worst earthquake in recent US history occurred. Thousands of earthquakes take place every day all over the world, but most of them are too minor to be sensed without technical equipment like a seismograph. However, in the last decade, major earthquakes in southern California, Japan and Turkey have shown how dangerous quakes can be.

Ask your students where the worst earthquakes in the United States have occurred and they will probably say California. Actually, Alaska has been the site of some of the world's worst earthquakes in terms of magnitude. The US Geological Survey's National Earthquake Information Center has loads of information about quakes. Go to wwwneic.cr.usgs.gov and click on General Earthquake Information.

Looking at lists of the worst earthquakes of the past century and of the decade, your students might notice that the quakes with the highest scores on the Richter scale don't necessarily cause the largest number of deaths. Brainstorm about why more people died in the Mexico City earthquake than in the worst earthquake of the twentieth century in Chile (see May 22). Discuss such things as population density and the quality of building construction. Compare the San Francisco earthquake of 1989 (see Oct 17) and the one in Turkey in 1999 (see Aug 17). Though their Richter scales were 7.1 and 7.4, respectively, the death tolls were 67 in San Francisco and 15,000 in Turkey. These are both densely populated areas. Why the difference in the number of people killed?

With older students, discuss the Richter scale and the fact that it is not arithmetic but logarithmic. That means an earthquake of 8 on the Richter scale is not twice as strong as one that is 4 on the scale but is several hundreds time stronger. The National Earthquake Information Center site has information explaining this.

Discuss earthquake safety with your students; even if you don't live in an area that is prone to earthquakes, your students may vacation in such a place. For more information, go to the Red Cross site at www.crossnet.org/disaster/safety/earth.html. This Website is also available in Spanish.

Books: *Earthquakes,* by Seymour Simon (Morrow, 0-6880-9633-6, $14.95 PreK–3); *Quakes!* by Catherine McMorrow (Random House, 0-679-96945-4, $11.99 Gr. 1–5); *Earthquakes,* by Sally M. Walker (Carolrhoda, 0-8761-4888-7, $21.27 Gr. 4–7) or *Earthquakes and Volcanoes,* by Lin Sutherland (Readers Digest, 1-5758-4380-3, $18.99 Gr. 4–7).

MARCH 28 — THURSDAY

Day 87 — 278 Remaining

CZECH REPUBLIC: TEACHERS' DAY. Mar 28. Celebrates birth on this day of Jan Amos Komensky (Comenius), Moravian educational reformer (1592–1671).

★ **EDUCATION AND SHARING DAY.** Mar 28.

"GREATEST SHOW ON EARTH" FORMED: ANNIVERSARY. Mar 28, 1881. P.T. Barnum and James A. Bailey merged their circuses to form the "Greatest Show on Earth." For more info: www.ringling.com/history.

INDIA: HOLI. Mar 28. In this spring Hindu festival people run through the streets sprinkling each other with colored water and tossing brightly hued powders. This is observed by Hindus without regard to caste. Huge bonfires are built on the eve of Holi. Because there is no universally accepted Hindu calendar, this holiday may be celebrated on a different date in some parts of India but it always falls in February or March.

LIBYA: BRITISH BASES EVACUATION DAY. Mar 28. National holiday. Commemorates the day in 1970 when British bases in Libya were closed.

MAUNDY THURSDAY or HOLY THURSDAY. Mar 28. The Thursday before Easter, originally "dies mandate," celebrates Christ's injunction to love one another, "Mandatus novum do vobis. . . ." ("A new commandment I give to you. . . .")

MOON PHASE: FULL MOON. Mar 28. Moon enters Full Moon phase at 1:25 PM, EST.

PERIGEAN SPRING TIDES. Mar 28. Spring tides, the highest possible tides, which occur when New Moon or Full Moon takes place within 24 hours of the moment the Moon is nearest Earth (perigee) in its monthly orbit at 1 PM, EST. The word *spring* refers not to the season but comes from the German word *springen*, "to rise up."

PESACH or PASSOVER. Mar 28–Apr 4. Hebrew calendar dates: Nisan 15–22, 5762. Mar 28, the first day of Passover, begins an eight-day celebration of the delivery of the Jews from slavery in Egypt. Unleavened bread (matzoh) is eaten at this time.

SPACE MILESTONE: *NOAA 8* (US). Mar 28, 1983. Search and Rescue Satellite (SARSAT) launched from Vandenburg Air Force Base, CA, to aid in locating ships and aircraft in distress. *Kosmos 1383*, launched July 1, 1982, by the USSR, in a cooperative rescue effort, is credited with saving more than 20 lives.

THREE MILE ISLAND NUCLEAR POWER PLANT ACCIDENT: ANNIVERSARY. Mar 28, 1979. A series of accidents beginning at 4 AM, EST, at Three Mile Island on the Susquehanna River about 10 miles southeast of Harrisburg, PA, was responsible for extensive reevaluation of the safety of existing nuclear power generating operations. Equipment and other failures reportedly brought Three Mile Island close to a meltdown of the uranium core, threatening extensive radiation contamination. For more info: www.pbs.org/wgbh/amex/world.

BIRTHDAYS TODAY

Byrd Baylor, 78, author (*I'm In Charge of Celebrations*), born San Antonio, TX, Mar 28, 1924.

Frank Hughes Murkowski, 69, US Senator (R, Alaska), born Seattle, WA, Mar 28, 1933.

MARCH 29 — FRIDAY

Day 88 — 277 Remaining

"AMERICA'S SUBWAY" DAY: ANNIVERSARY. Mar 29, 1976. The Washington (DC) Metropolitan Area Transit Authority ran its first Metrorail passenger train 26 years ago. The Metro system consisted of only five stations and 4.6 miles on the Red Line Route. In 1999 two more stations and three miles of track were added to the system. Metro now consists of 78 stations and 98 miles of service. Passengers make more than 500,000 trips each weekday in the nation's capital and the greater Washington area. Many of these are made by tourists from across the country and around the world — hence the moniker "America's Subway." For info: Cheryl Johnson, Washington Metropolitan Area Transit Authority, 600 Fifth St NW, Washington, DC 20001. Phone: (202) 962-1051. Fax: (202) 962-2897.

CANADA: BRITISH NORTH AMERICA ACT: ANNIVERSARY. Mar 29, 1867. This act of the British Parliament established the Dominion of Canada, uniting Ontario, Quebec, Nova Scotia and New Brunswick. Union was proclaimed July 1, 1867. The remaining colonies in Canada were still ruled directly by Great Britain until Manitoba joined the Dominion in 1870, British Columbia in 1871, Prince Edward Island in 1873, Alberta and Saskatchewan in 1905 and Newfoundland in 1949. See also: "Canada: Canada Day" (July 1).

CENTRAL AFRICAN REPUBLIC: BOGANDA DAY. Mar 29. National holiday. Commemorates the death in 1959 of the first president, Barthelemy Boganda.

GOOD FRIDAY. Mar 29. Observed in commemoration of the crucifixion. Oldest Christian celebration. Possible corruption of "God's Friday." Observed in some manner by most Christian sects and as a public holiday or part holiday in Delaware, Florida, Hawaii, Illinois, Indiana, Kentucky, New Jersey, North Carolina, Pennsylvania and Tennessee.

HOOVER, LOU HENRY: BIRTH ANNIVERSARY. Mar 29, 1875. Wife of Herbert Clark Hoover, 31st president of the US. Born at Waterloo, IA, she died at Palo Alto, CA, Jan 7, 1944.

MADAGASCAR: COMMEMORATION DAY: 55th ANNIVERSARY. Mar 29. Commemoration Day for the victims of the rebellion in 1947 against French colonization.

TAIWAN: YOUTH DAY. Mar 29.

TEXAS LOVE THE CHILDREN DAY. Mar 29. A day recognizing every child's right and need to be loved. Promoting the hope that one day all children will live in loving, safe environments and will be given proper health care and equal learning opportunities. Precedes the start of National Child Abuse Prevention Month (April). For info: Patty Murphy, 7713 Chasewood Dr, North Richland Hills, TX 76180. Phone: (817) 498-5840. E-mail: MURPH0@flash.net.

TWENTY-THIRD AMENDMENT TO US CONSTITUTION RATIFIED: ANNIVERSARY. Mar 29, 1961. District of Columbia residents were given the right to vote in presidential elections under the 23rd Amendment.

TYLER, JOHN: BIRTH ANNIVERSARY. Mar 29, 1790. The 10th president of the US (Apr 6, 1841–Mar 3, 1845). Born at Greenway, VA, Tyler succeeded to the presidency upon the death of William Henry Harrison. Tyler's first wife died while he was president, and he remarried before the end of his term of office, becoming the first president to marry while in office. Fifteen children were born of the two marriages. In 1861 he was elected to the Congress of the Confederate States but died at Richmond, VA, Jan 18, 1862, before being seated. His death received no official tribute from the US government. For info: www.ipl.org/ref/POTUS.

March 2002

S	M	T	W	T	F	S
					1	2
3	4	5	6	7	8	9
10	11	12	13	14	15	16
17	18	19	20	21	22	23
24	25	26	27	28	29	30
31						

YOUNG, DENTON TRUE (CY): BIRTH ANNIVERSARY. Mar 29, 1867. Baseball Hall of Fame pitcher, born at Gilmore, OH. Young is baseball's all-time winningest pitcher, having accumulated 511 victories in his 22-year career. The Cy Young Award is given each year in his honor to major league's best pitcher. Inducted into the Hall of Fame in 1937. Died at Peoli, OH, Nov 4, 1955.

BIRTHDAYS TODAY

Lucy Lawless, 34, actress ("Xena"), born Mount Albert, Auckland, New Zealand, Mar 29, 1968.

MARCH 30 — SATURDAY

Day 89 — 276 Remaining

ANESTHETIC FIRST USED IN SURGERY: ANNIVERSARY. Mar 30, 1842. Dr. Crawford W. Long, having seen the use of nitrous oxide and sulfuric ether at "laughing gas" parties, observed that individuals under their influences felt no pain. On this date, he removed a tumor from the neck of a man who was under the influence of ether.

DOCTORS' DAY. Mar 30. Traditional annual observance since 1933 to honor America's physicians on anniversary of occasion when Dr. Crawford W. Long became the first physician to use ether as an anesthetic agent in a surgical technique, Mar 30, 1842. The red carnation has been designated the official flower of Doctors' Day.

EASTER EVEN. Mar 30. The Saturday before Easter. Last day of Holy Week and of Lent.

PENCIL PATENTED: ANNIVERSARY. Mar 30, 1858. First pencil with the eraser top was patented by Hyman Lipman.

SEWELL, ANNA: BIRTH ANNIVERSARY. Mar 30, 1820. Born at Yarmouth, England, Anna Sewell is best known for her book *Black Beauty*. Published in 1877, her tale centers around the abuses and injustices to horses she saw while growing up. She died at Old Catton, Norfolk, England, Apr 25, 1878.

TRINIDAD AND TOBAGO: SPIRITUAL BAPTIST LIBERATION SHOUTER DAY. Mar 30. Public Holiday. For info: Information Dept, Tourism Div, Tourism and Industrial Development Co, 10-14 Phillips St, Port of Spain, Trinidad, West Indies.

VAN GOGH, VINCENT: BIRTH ANNIVERSARY. Mar 30, 1853. Dutch post-Impressionist painter, especially known for his bold and powerful use of color (*Sunflowers, The Starry Night*). Born at Groot Zundert, Netherlands, he died at Auvers-sur-Oise, France, July 29, 1890. For more info: *Vincent Van Gogh*, by Enrica Crispino (Peter Bedrick, 0-87226-525-0, $22.50 Gr. 4–7).

BIRTHDAYS TODAY

Robert C. Smith, 61, US Senator (R, New Hampshire), born Tuftonboro, NH, Mar 30, 1941.

MARCH 31 — SUNDAY

Day 90 — 275 Remaining

CHAVEZ, CESAR ESTRADA: 75th BIRTH ANNIVERSARY. Mar 31, 1927. Labor leader who organized migrant farm workers in support of better working conditions. Chavez initiated the National Farm Workers Association in 1962, attracting attention to the migrant farm workers' plight by organizing boycotts of products including grapes and lettuce. He was born at Yuma, AZ, and died Apr 23, 1993, at San Luis, AZ. His birthday is a holiday in California. For more info: *Cesar Chávez: Leader for Migrant Farm Workers*, by Doreen Gonzales (Enslow, 0-89490-760-3, $19.95 Gr. 5–8).

CHESNUT, MARY BOYKIN MILLER: BIRTH ANNIVERSARY. Mar 31, 1823. Born at Pleasant Hill, SC, and died Nov 22, 1886, at Camden, SC. During the Civil War Chesnut accompanied her husband, a Confederate staff officer, on military missions. She kept a journal of her experiences and observations, which was published posthumously as *A Diary from Dixie*, a perceptive portrait of Confederate military and political leaders and an insightful view of Southern life during the Civil War.

EASTER SUNDAY. Mar 31. Commemorates the Resurrection of Christ. Most joyous festival of the Christian year. The date of Easter, a movable feast, is derived from the lunar calendar: the first Sunday following the first ecclesiastical full moon on or after

MARCH 31
HAYDN'S BIRTHDAY

Franz Joseph Haydn was born on March 31, 1732, in Rohrau, Austria. He was a lifelong music lover. As a young boy, he sang soprano in the choir at Saint Stephen's Cathedral in Vienna. Later, he worked as a music teacher. He studied with Nicola Porpora, an Italian composer.

In 1760, Haydn was hired by the Hungarian Esterhazy princes. Haydn served as their resident composer for 30 years, providing the music for their church services and for their entertainment. During his career, Haydn composed hundreds of works that included vocal music, orchestral pieces, two dozen operas and chamber music. Haydn died on May 31, 1809.

While working for Prince Nikolaus, Haydn and the other court musicians resided at Esterhaza, the family's royal retreat. The musicians were not allowed to bring their family members. This caused familial strife as the days, weeks and months wore on, keeping the musicians away from their homes. The musicians reported their grievances to Haydn, who spoke with Prince Nikolaus. Nikolaus turned a deaf ear to the musicians' requests to go home. In response, Haydn wrote his Symphony no. 45, named *The Farewell Symphony*. In this piece, the musicians leave the stage one at a time, each blowing out a candle as he departs. At the symphony's end, the stage is left dark and deserted. Supposedly, the tone of the music and the empty stage conveyed the desired message to Prince Nikolaus. He ordered the court to pack up and return home.

Anna Celenza has written an amusing and informative children's picture book that explains the background of Haydn's life and the story behind *The Farewell Symphony*. Her book, *The Farewell Symphony* (Charlesbridge, 1-5709-1406-0, $19.95 Gr. K & up), comes with a CD that contains the symphony and another of Haydn's works.

Celebrate Haydn's birthday by sharing his symphony and his story with your students. It's a lot more interesting than singing Happy Birthday.

Mar 21—always between Mar 22 and Apr 25. The Council of Nicaea (AD 325) prescribed that Easter be celebrated on the Sunday after Passover, as that feast's date had been established in Jesus' time. Orthodox Christians continue to use the Julian calendar, so that Easter can sometimes be as much as five weeks apart in the Western and Eastern churches. Easter in 2003 will be Apr 20; in 2004 will be Apr 11; in 2005 will be Mar 27. Many other dates in the Christian year are derived from the date of Easter. See also: "Orthodox Easter Sunday or Pascha." For links to Easter websites, go to: deil.lang.uiuc.edu/web.pages/holidays/easter .html.

EIFFEL TOWER: ANNIVERSARY. Mar 31, 1889. Built for the Paris Exhibition of 1889, the tower was named for its architect, Alexandre Gustave Eiffel, and is one of the world's best-known landmarks.

EUROPE: SUMMER DAYLIGHT SAVING TIME. Mar 31–Oct 27. Many European countries observe daylight-saving (summer) time from 2 AM on the last Sunday in March until 3 AM on the last Sunday in October.

GORE, ALBERT, JR.: BIRTHDAY. Mar 31, 1948. The 45th vice president (1993–2001) of the US, born at Washington, DC.

HAYDN, FRANZ JOSEPH: BIRTH ANNIVERSARY. Mar 31, 1732. Composer of symphonies, oratorios and Masses, born at Rohrau, Austria. Haydn was a friend of Mozart and Beethoven. He died May 31, 1809, at Vienna, Austria. *See* Curriculum Connection.

JOHNSON, JOHN (JACK) ARTHUR: BIRTH ANNIVERSARY. Mar 31, 1878. In 1908 Jack Johnson became the first African American to win the heavyweight boxing championship when he defeated Tommy Burns at Sydney, Australia. Unable to accept a black's triumph, the boxing world tried to find a white challenger. Jim Jeffries, former heavyweight title holder, was badgered out of retirement. On July 4, 1919, at Reno, NV, the "battle of the century" proved to be a farce when Johnson handily defeated Jeffries. Race riots swept the US and plans to exhibit the film of the fight were canceled. Johnson was born at Galveston, TX, and died in an automobile accident June 10, 1946, at Raleigh, NC. He was inducted into the Boxing Hall of Fame in 1990. The film *The Great White Hope* is based on his life.

NASA AMES SPACE SETTLEMENT CONTEST. Mar 31. Deadline for annual contest for 6th–12th graders to design an orbital space settlement. For info: Al Globus, MS T27A-1, NASA Ames Research Center, Moffett Field, CA 94035. Web: lifesci3.arc .nasa.gov/SpaceSettlement/Contest.

US AIR FORCE ACADEMY ESTABLISHED: ANNIVERSARY. Mar 31, 1954. The US Air Force Academy was established at Colorado Springs, CO, to train officers for the Air Force. Women were first admitted in 1976. For more info: www.usafa.edu.

US VIRGIN ISLANDS: TRANSFER DAY: 85th ANNIVERSARY. Mar 31. Commemorates transfer resulting from purchase of the Virgin Islands by the US from Denmark, Mar 31, 1917, for $25 million.

BIRTHDAYS TODAY

William Daniels, 75, actor ("Boy Meets World"), born Brooklyn, NY, Mar 31, 1927.

Angus King, Jr, 58, Governor of Maine (I), born Alexandria, VA, Mar 31, 1944.

Patrick J. Leahy, 62, US Senator (D, Vermont), born Montpelier, VT, Mar 31, 1940.

Rhea Perlman, 54, actress (*Matilda*), born Brooklyn, NY, Mar 31, 1948.

Steve Smith, 33, basketball player, born Highland Park, MI, Mar 31, 1969.

APRIL 1 — MONDAY

Day 91 — 274 Remaining

ALCOHOL AWARENESS MONTH. Apr 1–30. To help raise awareness among community prevention leaders and citizens about the problem of underage drinking. Concentrates on community grassroots activities. For info: Public Info Dept, Natl Council on Alcoholism and Drug Dependence, Inc, 12 W 21st St, New York, NY 10010. Phone: (212) 206-6770. Fax: (212) 645-1690. Web: www.ncadd.org.

APRIL FOOLS' or ALL FOOLS' DAY. Apr 1. April Fool's Day seems to have begun in France in 1564. Apr 1 used to be New Year's Day but the New Year was changed to Jan 1 that year. People who insisted on celebrating the "old" New Year became known as April fools. The general concept of a feast of fools, however, is an old one. The Romans had such a day and medieval monasteries had days when the abbot or bishop was replaced for a day by a common monk, who would order his superiors to do the most menial or ridiculous tasks. "The joke of the day is to deceive persons by sending them upon frivolous and nonsensical errands; to pretend they are wanted when they are not, or, in fact, any way to betray them into some supposed ludicrous situation, so as to enable you to call them 'An April Fool.'"–Brady's *Clavis Calendaria*, 1812. For links to April Fools' Day sites on the Web, go to: deil.lang.uiuc.edu/web.pages/holidays/aprilfool.html.

BULGARIA: SAINT LASARUS DAY. Apr 1. Ancient Slavic holiday of young girls, in honor of the goddess of spring and love.

CANADA: NUNAVUT INDEPENDENCE: ANNIVERSARY. Apr 1, 1999. Nunavut became Canada's third independent territory. This self-governing territory with an Inuit majority was created from the eastern half of the Northwest Territories. In 1992 Canada's Inuit people accepted a federal land-claim package granting them control over the new territory.

★**CANCER CONTROL MONTH.** Apr 1–30.

EASTER MONDAY. Apr 1. Holiday or bank holiday in many places, including England, Northern Ireland, Wales, Canada and North Carolina in the US.

EGG SALAD WEEK. Apr 1–7. Dedicated to the many delicious uses for all of the Easter eggs that have been cooked, colored, hidden and found. Annually, the full week after Easter. For info: Linda Braun, Consumer Serv Dir, American Egg Board, 1460 Renaissance Dr, Park Ridge, IL 60068. E-mail: aebnet@aol.com. Web: www.aeb.org.

EXCHANGE CLUB CHILD ABUSE PREVENTION MONTH. Apr 1–30. Nationwide effort to raise awareness of child abuse and how to prevent it. For info: The Natl Exchange Club, Foundation for Prevention of Child Abuse, 3050 Central Ave, Toledo, OH 43606-1700. Phone: (419) 535-3232 or (800) 760-3413. Fax: (419) 535-1989. E-mail: info@preventchildabuse.com. Web: www.preventchildabuse.com.

GOLDEN RULE WEEK. Apr 1–7. The purpose of this week is to remind everyone of the importance of the Golden Rule in making this a better world in which we all may live. For a copy of the Golden Rule of 10 religions, send $4 to cover printing and postage. For info: Dr. S. J. Drake, Pres, Intl Society of Friendship and Goodwill, 8592 Roswell Rd, Ste 434, Atlanta, GA 30350-1870.

HARVEY, WILLIAM: BIRTH ANNIVERSARY. Apr 1, 1578. Physician, born at Folkestone, England. The first to discover the mechanics of the circulation of the blood. Died at Roehampton, England, June 3, 1657.

APRIL 1–30
HUMOR MONTH

There's nothing like a good story. And if it's a humorous one—why then, it makes our hearts lighter. Tall tales have a larger-than-life quality that can't help but bring a smile to our faces. The exaggerations found in tall tales cross over into the outlandish and that makes them all the more appealing. Why not feature tall-tale read alouds in your classroom this month? There are a number of picture books that students from kindergarten through high school will enjoy. Junior high and high school students may groan at first, but they'll secretly be entertained. And collections of tall tales from lands other than the United States are becoming more widely available.

It's easy to find tall tales that will blend right into curriculum content areas. American history is chock full of figures who have become larger than life. *The Narrow Escapes of Davy Crockett*, by Ariane Dewey, (out of print, but available in library collections, Gr 3–5), and *Pecos Bill*, by Steven Kellogg (Morrow, 0-68-805871-X, $17 Gr 1–3), chronicle the adventures of two well-known American folk legends. *Will Rogers: Larger than Life*, by Debbie Dadey (Walker, 0-8027-8681-2, $16.95 All ages), features the adventures of one of America's best-loved humorists. For a tall tale about a woman, see Anne Isaacs' *Swamp Angel* (Penguin, 0-14-055908-6, $6.99 All ages).

Heat Wave, by Helen Ketteman (Walker, 0-8027-7577-2, $6.95 All ages), and *Chinook*, by Michael O. Tunnell (out of print, but available in library collections, All ages), are two way-out tales that will complement weather units.

Collections that contain selections suitable for reading aloud include: *McBroom's Wonderful One Acre Farm*, by Sid Fleischman (Morrow, 0-688-15595-2, $4.95 Gr. 3 & up); Mary Pope Osborne's *American Tall Tales* (Knopf, 0-679-80089-1, $22 Gr. 3 & up); and *Cut From the Same Cloth: American Women of Myth, Legend, and Tall Tale*, by Robert San Souci (Putnam, 0-698-11811-1, $6.99 Gr. 3 & up). After reading aloud several tall tales, discuss what elements they have in common. Most tall tales, while over-the-top, are not mean-spirited in nature.

Have fun writing tall tales as a small group exercise—it spreads the humor. You might suggest students try creating tall tales that feature prominent early settlers of your area, well-known regional landmarks, imaginary crops of the area or local industry.

There are many more tall-tale books available in your public library. For a list of humor books, consult *The Literature of Delight: A Critical Guide to Humorous Books for Children*, by Kimberly Olson Fakih (Bowker, 0-8352-3027-9, $40).

INTERNATIONAL AMATEUR RADIO MONTH. Apr 1–30. To disseminate information about the important part amateur radio operators or "hams" throughout the world are playing in promoting friendship, peace and good will. To obtain complete information about becoming an International Good Will Ambassador as well as a list of amateur radio operators in many countries, send $4 to cover expense of printing, handling and postage. Annually, the month of April. For info: Dr. Stanley Drake, Pres, Intl Soc of Friendship and Good Will, 8592 Roswell Rd, Ste 434, Atlanta, GA 30350-1870.

KEEP AMERICA BEAUTIFUL MONTH. Apr 1–30. To educate Americans about their personal responsibility for litter prevention, proper waste disposal and environmental improvement through various community projects. Annually, the month of April. For info: Dir of Communications, Keep America Beautiful, Inc, Washington Square, 1010 Washington Blvd, Stamford, CT 06901. Phone: (203) 323-8987. Fax: (203) 325-9199. E-mail: keepamerbe@aol.com.

MATHEMATICS EDUCATION MONTH. Apr 1–30. An opportunity for students, teachers, parents and the community as a whole to focus on the importance of mathematics and the changes taking place in mathematics education. For info: Communications Mgr, Natl Council of Teachers of Mathematics, 1906 Association Dr, Reston, VA 20191-1593. Phone: (703) 620-9840. Fax: (703) 476-2970. E-mail: infocentral@nctm.org. Web: www.nctm.org.

MONTH OF THE YOUNG CHILD®. Apr 1–30. Michigan. To promote awareness of the importance of young children and their specific needs in today's society. Many communities celebrate with special events for children and families. For info: Michigan Assn for the Education of Young Children, Beacon Pl, Ste 1-D, 4572 S Hagadorn Road, East Lansing, MI 48823-5385. Phone: (800) 336-6424 or (517) 336-9700. Fax: (517) 336-9790. E-mail: moyc@miaeyc.com. Web: www.miaeyc.com.

NATIONAL AUTISM AWARENESS MONTH. Apr 1–30. A month filled with events such as poster contests, a state proclamation by the governor and family activities on autism. This is a national celebration. Annually, the month of April. For info: Coord of Mktg & PR, COSAC, 1450 Parkside Ave, Ste 22, Ewing, NJ 08638. Phone: (609) 883-8100. Fax: (609) 883-5509. E-mail: njautism@aol.com. Web: www.njautism.org/homepage.

★**NATIONAL CHILD ABUSE PREVENTION MONTH.** Apr 1–30.

NATIONAL HUMOR MONTH. Apr 1–30. Focuses on the joy and therapeutic value of laughter and how it can reduce stress, improve job performance and enrich the quality of life. For info: send SASE (55¢) to: Larry Wilde, Dir, The Carmel Institute of Humor, 25470 Canada Dr, Carmel, CA 93923-8926. E-mail: larrywilde@aol.com. *See* Curriculum Connection.

NATIONAL KNUCKLES DOWN MONTH. Apr 1–30. To recognize and revive the American tradition of playing and collecting marbles and keep it rolling along. Please send self-addressed, stamped envelope with inquiries. For info: Cathy C. Runyan-Svacina, The Marble Lady, 7812 NW Hampton Rd, Kansas City, MO 64152. Phone: (816) 587-8687. Fax: Same as phone.

April 2002

S	M	T	W	T	F	S
	1	2	3	4	5	6
7	8	9	10	11	12	13
14	15	16	17	18	19	20
21	22	23	24	25	26	27
28	29	30				

NATIONAL POETRY MONTH. Apr 1–30. Annual observance to pay tribute to the great legacy and ongoing achievement of American poets and the vital place of poetry in American culture. In a proclamation issued in honor of the first observance, President Bill Clinton called it "a welcome opportunity to celebrate not only the unsurpassed body of literature produced by our poets in the past, but also the vitality and diversity of voices reflected in the works of today's American poets . . . Their creativity and wealth of language enrich our culture and inspire a new generation of Americans to learn the power of reading and writing at its best." Spearheaded by the Academy of American Poets, this is the largest and most extensive celebration of poetry in American history. For info: Academy of American Poets, 584 Broadway, Ste 1208, New York, NY 10012-3250. Phone: (212) 274-0343. Web: www.poets.org/npm/index.cfm.

NATIONAL YOUTH SPORTS SAFETY MONTH. Apr 1–30. Bringing public attention to the prevalent problem of injuries in youth sports. This event promotes safety in sports activities and is supported by more than 60 national sports and medical organizations. For info: Michelle Glassman, Exec Dir, Natl Youth Sports Safety Fdtn, 333 Longwood Ave, Ste 202, Boston, MA 02115. Phone: (617) 277-1171. Fax: (617) 277-2278. E-mail: NYSSF@aol.com. Web: www.nyssf.org.

PREVENTION OF ANIMAL CRUELTY MONTH. Apr 1–30. The ASPCA sponsors this crucial month, which is designed to prevent cruelty to animals by focusing on public awareness, advocacy and public education campaigns. For info: ASPCA Public Affairs Dept, 424 E 92nd St, New York, NY 10128. Phone: (212) 876-7700. E-mail: press@aspca.org. Web: www.aspca.org.

SCHOOL LIBRARY MEDIA MONTH. Apr 1–30. Celebrates the work of school library media specialists in our nation's elementary and secondary schools. For info: American Assn of School Librarians, American Library Assn, 50 E Huron St, Chicago, IL 60611. Phone: (800) 545-2433. E-mail: AASL@ala.org. Web: www.ala.org/aasl.

SOUTH AFRICA: FAMILY DAY. Apr 1. National holiday. Annually, Easter Monday.

TAIWAN: BIRTHDAY OF KUAN YIN, GODDESS OF MERCY. Apr 1. Nineteenth day of Second Moon of the lunar calendar, celebrated at Taipei's Lungshan (Dragon Mountain) and other temples.

US HOUSE OF REPRESENTATIVES ACHIEVES A QUORUM: ANNIVERSARY. Apr 1, 1789. First session of Congress was held Mar 4, 1789, but not enough representatives arrived to achieve a quorum until Apr 1.

WHITE HOUSE EASTER EGG ROLL. Apr 1. Traditionally held on the south lawn of the executive mansion on Easter Monday. Custom is said to have started at the Capitol grounds about 1810. It was transferred to the White House Lawn in the 1870s.

ZAM! ZOO AND AQUARIUM MONTH. Apr 1–30. A national celebration to focus public attention on the role of zoos and aquariums in wildlife education and conservation. Held at 184 AZA member institutions in the US and Canada. Sponsor: American Zoo and Aquarium Association. For information, contact your local zoo or aquarium. For info: American Zoo and Aquarium Assn, 8403 Colesville Rd, Ste 710, Silver Spring, MD 20910-3314. Phone: (301) 562-0777. Web: www.aza.org.

BIRTHDAYS TODAY

Anne McCaffrey, 76, author (*The Dragonriders of Pern*), born Cambridge, MA, Apr 1, 1926.
Karen Wallace, 51, author (*Imagine You Are a Crocodile*), born Ottawa, ON, Canada, Apr 1, 1951.

APRIL 2 — TUESDAY

Day 92 — 273 Remaining

ANDERSEN, HANS CHRISTIAN: BIRTH ANNIVERSARY. Apr 2, 1805. Author chiefly remembered for his more than 150 fairy tales, many of which are regarded as classics of children's literature. Among his tales are "The Princess and the Pea," "The Snow Queen" and "The Ugly Duckling." Andersen was born at Odense, Denmark, and died at Copenhagen, Denmark, Aug 4, 1875.

BARTHOLDI, FREDERIC AUGUSTE: BIRTH ANNIVERSARY. Apr 2, 1834. French sculptor who created *Liberty Enlightening the World* (better known as the Statue of Liberty), which stands in New York Harbor. Also remembered for the *Lion of Belfort* at Belfort, France. Born at Colman, Alsace, France, he died at Paris, France, Oct 4, 1904.

FIRST WHITE HOUSE EASTER EGG ROLL: 125th ANNIVERSARY. Apr 2, 1877. The first White House Easter Egg Roll took place during the administration of Rutherford B. Hayes. The traditional event was discontinued by President Franklin D. Roosevelt in 1942 and reinstated Apr 6, 1953, by President Dwight D. Eisenhower.

INTERNATIONAL CHILDREN'S BOOK DAY. Apr 2. Commemorates the international aspects of children's literature and observes Hans Christian Andersen's birthday. Sponsor: International Board on Books for Young People, Nonnenweg 12, Postfach, CH-4003 Basel, Switzerland. For info: USBBY Secretariat, c/o Intl Reading Assn, Box 8139, Newark, DE 19714-8139.

NATIONAL CATHOLIC EDUCATIONAL ASSOCIATION CONVENTION AND EXPOSITION. Apr 2–5. Atlantic City, NJ. Annual meeting for NCEA members and anyone working in, or interested in, the welfare of Catholic education. Theme: Catholic Educators: Navigators of Promise. Est attendance: 11,000. For info: Nancy Brewer, Conv Dir, Natl Catholic Educational Assn, 1077 30th St NW, Ste 100, Washington, DC 20007. Phone: (202) 337-6232. Fax: (202) 333-6706. E-mail: convasst@ncea.org. Web: www.ncea.org.

NICKELODEON CHANNEL TV PREMIERE: ANNIVERSARY. Apr 2, 1979. Nickelodeon, the cable TV network for kids owned by MTV Networks, premiered. In 1985, Nick at Nite began offering classic TV programs in the evening hours. For more info: teachers.nick.com.

PASCUA FLORIDA DAY. Apr 2. Also known as Florida State Day, this holiday commemorates the sighting of Florida by Ponce de León in 1513. He named the land Pascua Florida because of its discovery at Easter, the "Feast of the Flowers." Florida also commemorates Pascua Florida Week, Mar 27–Apr 2. When April 2 falls on a weekend, the governor may declare the preceding Friday or the following Monday as State Day.

PONCE DE LEÓN DISCOVERS FLORIDA: ANNIVERSARY. Apr 2, 1513. Juan Ponce de León discovered Florida, landing at the site that became the city of St. Augustine. He claimed the land for the king of Spain.

US MINT: ANNIVERSARY. Apr 2, 1792. The first US Mint was established at Philadelphia, PA, as authorized by an act of Congress. For more info: www.usmint.gov/kids.

BIRTHDAYS TODAY

Ruth Heller, 78, science author and illustrator (the How to Hide . . . series), born Winnipeg, MB, Canada, Apr 2, 1924.
Dave Ross, 53, author (*A Book of Kisses*), born Scotia, NY, Apr 2, 1949.
Doug Wechsler, 51, author (*Bizarre Bugs*), born New York, NY, Apr 2, 1951.

APRIL 3 — WEDNESDAY

Day 93 — 272 Remaining

"BETWEEN THE LIONS" PREMIERE: ANNIVERSARY. Apr 3, 2000. This animated PBS show is designed to help children ages 4–7 learn to read. The lions Theo, Cleo, Lionel and Leona run a magical library. For info: www.pbs.org/wgbh/lions.

BLACKS RULED ELIGIBLE TO VOTE: ANNIVERSARY. Apr 3, 1944. The US Supreme Court, in an 8–1 ruling, declared that blacks could not be barred from voting in the Texas Democratic primaries. The high court repudiated the contention that political parties are private associations and held that discrimination against blacks violated the 15th Amendment.

BOSTON PUBLIC LIBRARY: ANNIVERSARY. Apr 3, 1848. The Massachusetts legislature passed legislation enabling Boston to levy a tax for a public library. This created the funding model for public libraries in the US. The Boston Public Library opened its doors in 1854. For more info: www.bpl.org.

COUNCIL FOR EXCEPTIONAL CHILDREN ANNUAL CONVENTION. Apr 3–7. New York, NY. For info: Council for Exceptional Children, 1920 Association Dr, Reston, VA 20191-1589. Phone: (888) CEC-SPED or (703) 620-3660. Fax: (703) 264-9494. Web: www.cec.sped.org.

IRVING, WASHINGTON: BIRTH ANNIVERSARY. Apr 3, 1783. American author, attorney and one-time US Minister to Spain, Irving was born at New York, NY. Creator of *Rip Van Winkle* and *The Legend of Sleepy Hollow*, he was also the author of many historical and biographical works, including *A History of the Life and Voyages of Christopher Columbus* and *Life of Washington*. Died at Tarrytown, NY, Nov 28, 1859.

ISLE ROYALE NATIONAL PARK ESTABLISHED: ANNIVERSARY. Apr 3, 1940. Isle Royale is the largest of a group of more than 200 islands that make up this national park preserve. To preserve upper Michigan's flora and fauna, Congress authorized a national park in 1931 and it was established in 1940. For more info: www.nps.gov/isro/index.htm.

ITALY: BOLOGNA INTERNATIONAL CHILDREN'S BOOK FAIR. Apr 3–6 (tentative). Bologna Exhibition Centre, Bologna, Italy. Publishers from 79 countries exhibit their books to the trade. Est attendance: 25,000. For info: Bologna Children's Book Fair, Piazza Costituzione, Italy. Phone: 51-282-361. Fax: 51-282-333. E-mail: dir.com@bolognafiere.it. Web: www.bologna fiere.it/BookFair.

MARSHALL PLAN: ANNIVERSARY. Apr 3, 1948. Suggested by Secretary of State George C. Marshall in a speech at Harvard, June 5, 1947, the legislation for the European Recovery Program, popularly known as the Marshall Plan, was signed by President Truman on Apr 3, 1948. After distributing more than $12 billion in war-torn Europe, the program ended in 1952.

WOMAN PRESIDES OVER US SUPREME COURT: ANNIVERSARY. Apr 3, 1995. Supreme Court Justice Sandra Day O'Connor became the first woman to preside over the US high court when she sat in for Chief Justice William H. Rehnquist and second in seniority Justice John Paul Stevens when both were out of town.

BIRTHDAYS TODAY

Amanda Bynes, 16, actress ("All That," "The Amanda Show"), born Thousand Oaks, CA, Apr 3, 1986.

Jane Goodall, 68, biologist, author (*The Chimpanzee Family Book*), born London, England, Apr 3, 1934.

Eddie Murphy, 41, comedian, actor (*Doctor Dolittle*), born Brooklyn, NY, Apr 3, 1961.

Picabo Street, 31, Olympic skier, born Triumph, ID, Apr 3, 1971.

APRIL 4 — THURSDAY

Day 94 — 271 Remaining

BONZA BOTTLER DAY™. Apr 4. To celebrate when the number of the day is the same as the number of the month. Bonza Bottler Day™ is an excuse to have a party at least once a month. For info: Gail M. Berger, 109 Matthew Ave, Poca, WV 25159. Phone: (304) 776-7746. E-mail: gberger5@aol.com.

DIX, DOROTHEA LYNDE: 200th BIRTH ANNIVERSARY. Apr 4, 1802. American social reformer and author, born at Hampden, ME. She left home at age 10, was teaching at age 14 and founded a home for girls at Boston while still in her teens. In spite of frail health, she was a vigorous crusader for humane conditions in insane asylums, jails and almshouses and for the establishment of state-supported institutions to serve those needs. Named superintendent of women nurses during the Civil War. Died at Trenton, NJ, July 17, 1887.

FLAG ACT OF 1818: ANNIVERSARY. Apr 4, 1818. Congress approved the first flag of the US.

KING, MARTIN LUTHER, JR: ASSASSINATION ANNIVERSARY. Apr 4, 1968. The Reverend Dr. Martin Luther King, Jr, was shot at Memphis, TN. James Earl Ray was serving a 99-year sentence for the crime at the time of his death in 1998. See also: "King, Martin Luther, Jr: Birth Anniversary" (Jan 15).

KING OPPOSES VIETNAM WAR: 35th ANNIVERSARY. Apr 4, 1967. Speaking before the Overseas Press Club at New York City, Reverend Dr. Martin Luther King, Jr, announced his opposition to the Vietnam War. That same day at the Riverside Church, King suggested that those who saw the war as dishonorable and unjust should avoid military service. He proposed that the US take new initiatives to conclude the war.

MOON PHASE: LAST QUARTER. Apr 4. Moon enters Last Quarter phase at 10:29 AM, EST.

April 2002

S	M	T	W	T	F	S
	1	2	3	4	5	6
7	8	9	10	11	12	13
14	15	16	17	18	19	20
21	22	23	24	25	26	27
28	29	30				

NATIONAL READING A ROAD MAP WEEK. Apr 4–10. To promote map reading as an enjoyable pastime and as a survival skill for present and future drivers and all armchair travelers. Motto: Happiness is knowing how to read a road map. For info: RosaLind Schilder, 309 Florence Ave, #225N, Jenkintown, PA 19046. E-mail: mikenroz18@aol.com.

NORTH ATLANTIC TREATY RATIFIED: ANNIVERSARY. Apr 4, 1949. The North Atlantic Treaty Organization was created by this treaty, which was signed by 12 nations, including the US. (Other countries joined later.) The NATO member nations are united for common defense.

SALTER ELECTED FIRST WOMAN MAYOR IN US: ANNIVERSARY. Apr 4, 1887. The first woman elected mayor in the US was Susanna Medora Salter, who was elected mayor of Argonia, KS. Her name had been submitted for election without her knowledge by the Woman's Christian Temperance Union, and she did not know she was a candidate until she went to the polls to vote. She received a two-thirds majority vote and served one year for the salary of $1.

SENEGAL: INDEPENDENCE DAY. Apr 4. National holiday. Commemorates independence from France in 1960.

THANK YOU SCHOOL LIBRARIAN DAY. Apr 4. Recognizes the unique contribution made by school librarians who are resource people extraordinaire, supporting the myriad educational needs of faculty, staff, students and parents *all year long*! Three cheers to all the public, private and parochial school infomaniacs whose true love of reading and lifelong learning make them great role models for kids of all ages. To help celebrate, take your school librarian to lunch, donate a book in his/her honor to the library, tell your librarian what a difference he/she has made in your life. Sponsor: "Carpe Libris" (Seize the Book), a loosely knit group of underappreciated librarians. For info: Judyth Lessee, Organizer, Carpe Libris, PO Box 40503, Tucson, AZ 85717-0503. Phone: (520) 318-2954. E-mail: rinophyl@rtd.com.

VIRGINIA HAMILTON CONFERENCE. Apr 4–5 (tentative). Kent State Univ, Kent, OH. Eighteenth annual conference on multicultural literature for children and young adults. For info: College of Continuing Studies, Kent State University, PO Box 5190, Kent, OH 44242-0001. Phone: (800) 672-KSU2. E-mail: amanna@slis.kent.edu. Web: dept.kent.edu/virginiahamiltonconf.

VITAMIN C ISOLATED: 70th ANNIVERSARY. Apr 4, 1932. Vitamin C was first isolated by C.C. King at the University of Pittsburgh.

BIRTHDAYS TODAY

Maya Angelou, 74, poet, author (*My Painted House, My Friendly Chicken, and Me; Life Doesn't Frighten Me*), born St Louis, MO, Apr 4, 1928.

Richard G. Lugar, 70, US Senator (R, Indiana), born Indianapolis, IN, Apr 4, 1932.

Johanna Reiss, 70, author (*The Upstairs Room*), born Winterswijk, Netherlands, Apr 4, 1932.

APRIL 5 — FRIDAY

Day 95 — 270 Remaining

CHINA: QING MING FESTIVAL. Apr 5. This Confucian festival was traditionally celebrated on the fourth or fifth day of the third month but is now on a fixed date in China. It is observed by the maintenance of ancestral graves, the presentation of food, wine and flowers as offerings and the burning of paper money at gravesides to help ancestors in the afterworld. People also picnic and gather for family meals. Also observed in Korea and Taiwan.

LISTER, JOSEPH: 175th BIRTH ANNIVERSARY. Apr 5, 1827. English physician who was the founder of aseptic surgery, born at Upton, Essex, England. Died at Walmer, England, Feb 10, 1912.

NATIONAL GEOGRAPHY BEE, STATE LEVEL. Apr 5. Site is different in each state—many are in state capital. Winners of school-level competitions who scored in the top 100 in their state on a written test compete in the State Geography Bees. The winner of each state bee will go to Washington, DC, for the national level in May. Est attendance: 450. For info: Natl Geography Bee, Natl Geographic Soc, 1145 17th St NW, Washington, DC 20036. Phone: (202) 857-7001. Web: www.nationalgeographic.com.

RESNIK, JUDITH A.: BIRTH ANNIVERSARY. Apr 5, 1949. Dr. Judith A. Resnik, the second American woman in space (1984), was born at Akron, OH. The 36-year-old electrical engineer was the mission specialist on the Space Shuttle *Challenger*. She perished with all others aboard when *Challenger* exploded Jan 28, 1986. See also: "*Challenger* Space Shuttle Explosion: Anniversary" (Jan 28).

STUDENT GOVERNMENT DAY IN MASSACHUSETTS. Apr 5. Proclaimed annually by the governor for the first Friday in April.

TAIWAN: NATIONAL TOMB-SWEEPING DAY. Apr 5. National holiday since 1972. According to Chinese custom, the tombs of ancestors are swept "clear and bright" and rites honoring ancestors are held. Tomb-Sweeping Day is observed Apr 5, except in leap years, when it falls Apr 4.

WASHINGTON, BOOKER TALLAFERRO: BIRTH ANNIVERSARY. Apr 5, 1856. Black educator and leader, born at Franklin County, VA. "No race can prosper," he wrote in *Up from Slavery*, "till it learns that there is as much dignity in tilling a field as in writing a poem." Died at Tuskegee, AL, Nov 14, 1915. For more info: *The Story of Booker T. Washington*, by Patricia and Fredrick McKissack (Children's Press, 0-5160-4758-2, $20.50 Gr. 3–7).

BIRTHDAYS TODAY

Richard Peck, 68, author (Newbery for *A Year Down Yonder*, Newbery honor for *A Long Way from Chicago*), born Decatur, IL, Apr 5, 1934.

Colin Powell, 65, US Secretary of State, former Chairman US Joint Chiefs of Staff, born New York, NY, Apr 5, 1937.

APRIL 6 — SATURDAY

Day 96 — 269 Remaining

"BARNEY & FRIENDS" TV PREMIERE: 10th ANNIVERSARY. Apr 6, 1992. Although most adults find it saccharine, this PBS show is enormously popular with preschoolers. Purple dinosaur Barney, his dinosaur pals Baby Bop and B.J. and a multiethnic group of children sing, play games and learn simple lessons about getting along with one another. "Bedtime with Barney" was a 1994 prime-time special. For more info: www.pbs.org/barney.

FIRST MODERN OLYMPICS: ANNIVERSARY. Apr 6, 1896. The first modern Olympics formally opened at Athens, Greece, after a 1,500-year hiatus. For more info: www.museum.olympic.org.

NATIONAL ASSOCIATION OF ELEMENTARY SCHOOL PRINCIPALS ANNUAL CONFERENCE. Apr 6–9. San Antonio, TX. For info: Natl Assn of Elementary School Principals, 1615 Duke St, Alexandria, VA 22314. Phone: (703) 684-3345 or (800) 38-NAESP. Fax: (800) 39N-AESP. E-mail: naesp@naesp.org. Web: www.naesp.org.

NATIONAL SCHOOL BOARDS ASSOCIATION ANNUAL CONFERENCE. Apr 6–9. New Orleans, LA. For info: Natl School Boards Assn, 1680 Duke St, Alexandria, VA 22314. Phone: (703) 838-6722. Fax: (703) 683-7590. E-mail: info@nsba.org. Web: www.nsba.org.

NORTH POLE DISCOVERED: ANNIVERSARY. Apr 6, 1909. Robert E. Peary reached the North Pole after several failed attempts. The team consisted of Peary, leader of the expedition, Matthew A. Henson, a black man who had served with Peary since 1886 as ship's cook, carpenter and blacksmith, and then as Peary's co-explorer and valuable assistant and four Eskimo guides—Coquesh, Ootah, Eginwah and Seegloo. They sailed July 17, 1908, on the ship *Roosevelt*, wintering on Ellesmere Island. After a grueling trek with dwindling food supplies, Henson and two of the Eskimos were first to reach the Pole. An exhausted Peary arrived 45 minutes later and confirmed their location. Dr. Frederick A. Cook, surgeon on an earlier expedition with Peary, claimed to have reached the Pole first, but that could not be substantiated and the National Geographic Society credited the Peary expedition.

TEFLON INVENTED: ANNIVERSARY. Apr 6, 1938. Polytetrafluoroethylene resin was invented by Roy J. Plunkett while he was employed by E.I. Du Pont de Nemours & Co. Commonly known as Teflon, it revolutionized the cookware industry. This substance or something similar coated three-quarters of the pots and pans in America at the time of Plunkett's death in 1994.

THAILAND: CHAKRI DAY. Apr 6. Commemorates foundation of present dynasty by King Rama I (1782–1809), who also established Bangkok as capital.

US ENTERS WORLD WAR I: 85TH ANNIVERSARY. Apr 6, 1917. After Congress approved a declaration of war against Germany, the US entered WWI, which had begun in 1914.

US SENATE ACHIEVES A QUORUM: ANNIVERSARY. Apr 6, 1789. The US Senate was formally organized after achieving a quorum.

YMCA HEALTHY KIDS DAY. Apr 6 (tentative). To promote the health of children nationwide. Contact your local YMCA for events in your area. Annually, on a Saturday in April. For info: YMCA of the USA, 101 N Wacker Dr, Chicago, IL 60606. Phone: (312) 269-1198 or (312) 977-9063. Web: www.ymca.net.

BIRTHDAYS TODAY

Alice Bach, 60, author (*The Meat in the Sandwich*), born New York, NY, Apr 6, 1942.

Graeme Base, 44, author and illustrator (*The Worst Band in the Universe*), born Amersham, England, Apr 6, 1958.

Candace Cameron Bure, 26, actress ("Full House"), born Panorama City, CA, Apr 6, 1976.

APRIL 7 — SUNDAY

Day 97 — 268 Remaining

CHECK YOUR BATTERIES DAY. Apr 7. A day set aside for checking the batteries in your smoke detector, carbon monoxide detector, HVAC thermostat, audio/visual remote controls and other electronic devices. This could save your life! Annually, the first Sunday in April.

DAYLIGHT SAVING TIME BEGINS. Apr 7–Oct 27. Daylight Saving Time begins at 2 AM. The Uniform Time Act of 1966 (as amended in 1986 by Public Law 99–359), administered by the US Dept of Transportation, provides that Standard Time in each zone be advanced one hour from 2 AM on the first Sunday in April until 2 AM on the last Sunday in October (except where state legislatures provide exemption, as in Hawaii and parts of Arizona and Indiana). Many use the popular rule "spring forward, fall back," to remember which way to turn their clocks.

KING, WILLIAM RUFUS DEVANE: BIRTH ANNIVERSARY. Apr 7, 1786. The 13th vice president of the US who died on the 46th day after taking the Oath of Office, of tuberculosis, at Cahaba, AL, Apr 18, 1853. The Oath of Office had been administered to King Mar 4, 1853, at Havana, Cuba, as authorized by a special act of Congress (the only presidential or vice presidential oath to be administered outside the US). Born at Sampson County, NY, King was the only vice president of the US who had served in both the House of Representatives and the Senate.

METRIC SYSTEM: ANNIVERSARY. Apr 7, 1795. The metric system was adopted at France, where it had been developed.

NATIONAL BLUE RIBBON WEEK. Apr 7–13. Wear a blue ribbon to show your concern about and objection to child abuse. Nationwide public awareness effort. Annually, the first full week in April. For info: The Natl Exchange Club, 3050 Central Ave, Toledo, OH 43606-1700. Phone: (419) 535-3232 or (800) 924-2643. Fax: (419) 535-1989. E-mail: nechq@aol.com. Web: www.nationalexchangeclub.com.

NATIONAL PUBLIC HEALTH WEEK. Apr 7–13. Annually, the first full week in April. For info: American Public Health Assn, 1015 15th St NW, Washington, DC 20005. Phone: (202) 789-5600.

NATIONAL WEEK OF THE OCEAN. Apr 7–13. A week focusing on humanity's interdependence with the ocean, asking each of us to appreciate, protect and use the ocean wisely. Annually, the second full week in April. For info: *The Oceans Atlas*, by Anita Ganeri (DK, 1-56458-475-5, $19.95 Gr. 3–8). For info: Pres/Cofounder, Cynthia Hancock, Natl Week of the Ocean, Inc, PO Box 179, Ft Lauderdale, FL 33302. Phone: (954) 462-5573.

NO HOUSEWORK DAY. Apr 7. No trash. No dishes. No making of beds or washing of laundry. And no guilt. Give it a rest. [© 1999 by WH] For info: Tom or Ruth Roy, Wellcat Holidays, 2418 Long Ln, Lebanon, PA 17046. Phone: (230) 332-4886. E-mail: wellcat@supernet.com. Web: www.wellcat.com.

April 2002

S	M	T	W	T	F	S
	1	2	3	4	5	6
7	8	9	10	11	12	13
14	15	16	17	18	19	20
21	22	23	24	25	26	27
28	29	30				

RWANDA: GENOCIDE'S REMEMBRANCE DAY. Apr 7. National holiday. Memorial to the massacres of 1994.

UNITED NATIONS: WORLD HEALTH DAY. Apr 7. A United Nations observance commemorating the establishment of the World Health Organization in 1948. For more information, visit the UN's website for children at www.un.org/Pubs/CyberSchoolBus/.

WEEK OF THE YOUNG CHILD. Apr 7–13. To focus on the importance of quality early childhood education. For info: Pat Spahr, Dir of Info Development, Natl Assn for the Educ of Young Children, 1509 16th St NW, Washington, DC 20036. Phone: (800) 424-2460. Fax: (202) 328-1846. E-mail: naeyc@naeyc.org. Web: www.naeyc.org.

WORLD HEALTH ORGANIZATION: ANNIVERSARY. Apr 7, 1948. This agency of the UN was founded to coordinate international health systems. It is headquartered at Geneva. Among its achievements is the elimination of smallpox.

WORLD HEALTH DAY. Apr 7. A complete planning kit available. For info: American Assn for World Health, World Health Day, 1825 K St NW, Ste 1208, Washington, DC 20006. Phone: (202) 466-5883. Fax: (202) 466-5896. E-mail: aawhstaff@aol.com. Web: www.aawhworldhealth.org.

BIRTHDAYS TODAY

Alan R. Carter, 55, author (*Up Country*), born Eau Claire, WI, Apr 7, 1947.

Jackie Chan, 48, actor, martial arts star, born Hong Kong, Apr 7, 1954.

APRIL 8 — MONDAY

Day 98 — 267 Remaining

BIRTHDAY OF THE BUDDHA: BIRTH ANNIVERSARY. Apr 8. Among Buddhist holidays, this is the most important as it commemorates the birthday of the Buddha. It is known as the Day of Vesak. The founder of Buddhism had the given name Siddhartha, the family name Gautama and the clan name Shaka. He is commonly called the Buddha, meaning in Sanskrit "the enlightened one." He is thought to have lived in India from c. 563 BC to 483 BC. Because it is often observed on the lunar calendar, this holiday can occur in April or May. It is a holiday in Indonesia, Korea, Thailand and Singapore.

BLACK SENATE PAGE APPOINTED: ANNIVERSARY. Apr 8, 1965. Sixteen-year-old Lawrence Bradford of New York City was the first black page appointed to the US Senate.

HOME RUN RECORD SET BY HANK AARON: ANNIVERSARY. Apr 8, 1974. Henry ("Hammerin' Hank") Aaron hit the 715th home run of his career, breaking the record set by Babe Ruth in 1935. Playing for the Atlanta Braves, Aaron broke the record at Atlanta in a game against the Los Angeles Dodgers. He finished his career in 1976 with a total of 755 home runs. This record remains unbroken. At the time of his retirement, Aaron also held records for first in RBIs, second in at-bats and runs scored and third in base hits.

JAPAN: FLOWER FESTIVAL (HANA MATSURI). Apr 8. Commemorates Buddha's birthday. Ceremonies in all temples.

MORRIS, LEWIS: BIRTH ANNIVERSARY. Apr 8, 1726. Signer of the Declaration of Independence, born at Westchester County, NY. Died Jan 22, 1798, at the Morrisania manor at NY.

SEVENTEENTH AMENDMENT TO US CONSTITUTION RATIFIED: ANNIVERSARY. Apr 8, 1913. Prior to the 17th Amendment, members of the Senate were elected by each state's respective legislature. The advent and popularity of primary elections during the last decade of the 19th century and the early 20th century and a string of senatorial scandals, most notably a scandal involving William Lorimer, an Illinois political boss in 1909, forced the Senate to end its resistance to a constitutional amendment requiring direct popular election of senators.

VOYAGEURS NATIONAL PARK ESTABLISHED: ANNIVERSARY. Apr 8, 1975. Minnesota's Voyageurs land was preserved by Congress on Jan 8, 1971. Four years later, it became the 36th US national park. For more info: www.nps.gov/voya/index.htm.

WHITE, RYAN: DEATH ANNIVERSARY. Apr 8, 1990. This young man, born Dec 6, 1971, at Kokomo, IN, put the face of a child on AIDS and helped promote greater understanding of the disease. Ryan, a hemophiliac, contracted AIDS from a blood transfusion. Banned from the public school system in Central Indiana in 1984 at the age of 10, he moved with his mother and sister to Cicero, IN, where he was accepted by students and faculty alike. Ryan once stated that he only wanted to be treated as a normal teenager, but that was not to be as media attention made him a celebrity. A few days after attending the Academy Awards in 1990, 18-year-old Ryan was hospitalized and lost his valiant fight, at Indianapolis, IN. His funeral was attended by many celebrities.

WILLIAMS, WILLIAM: BIRTH ANNIVERSARY. Apr 8, 1731. Signer of the Declaration of Independence, born at Lebanon, CT. Died there Aug 2, 1811.

BIRTHDAYS TODAY

Kofi Annan, 64, UN Secretary General, born Kumasi, Ghana, Apr 8, 1938.

Susan Bonners, 55, author and illustrator (*A Penguin Year*), born Chicago, IL, Apr 8, 1947.

Ruth Chew, 82, author and illustrator (*The Wednesday Witch*), born Minneapolis, MN, Apr 8, 1920.

Elizabeth (Betty) Ford, 84, former First Lady, wife of Gerald Ford, 38th president of the US, born Chicago, IL, Apr 8, 1918.

Trina Schart Hyman, 63, illustrator (Caldecott for *Saint George and the Dragon*, Caldecott Honors for *Hershel and the Hanukkah Goblins, Little Red Riding Hood, A Child's Calendar*), born Philadelphia, PA, Apr 8, 1939.

Taran Noah Smith, 18, actor ("Home Improvement"), born San Francisco, CA, Apr 8, 1984.

APRIL 9 — TUESDAY

Day 99 — 266 Remaining

AMERICAN ALLIANCE FOR HEALTH, PHYSICAL EDUCATION, RECREATION AND DANCE ANNUAL MEETING. Apr 9–13. San Diego, CA. For info: American Alliance for Health, Physical Education, Recreation & Dance, 1900 Association Dr, Reston, VA 20191-1599. Phone: (800) 213-7193 or (703) 476-3400. Web: www.aahperd.org.

BLACK PAGE APPOINTED TO US HOUSE OF REPRESENTATIVES: ANNIVERSARY. Apr 9, 1965. Fifteen-year-old Frank Mitchell of Springfield, IL, was the first black appointed a page to the US House of Representatives.

CHILDREN'S DAY IN FLORIDA. Apr 9. A legal holiday on the second Tuesday in April.

CIVIL RIGHTS BILL OF 1866: ANNIVERSARY. Apr 9, 1866. The Civil Rights Bill of 1866, passed by Congress over the veto of President Andrew Johnson, granted blacks the rights and privileges of American citizenship and formed the basis for the Fourteenth Amendment to the US Constitution.

CIVIL WAR ENDING: ANNIVERSARY. Apr 9, 1865. At 1:30 PM, General Robert E. Lee, commander of the Army of Northern Virginia, surrendered to General Ulysses S. Grant, commander-in-chief of the Union Army, ending four years of civil war. The meeting took place in the house of Wilmer McLean at the village of Appomattox Court House, VA. Confederate soldiers were permitted to keep their horses and go free to their homes, while Confederate officers were allowed to retain their swords and side arms as well. Grant wrote the terms of surrender. Formal surrender took place at the Courthouse Apr 12. Death toll for the Civil War is estimated at 500,000 men.

ECKERT, J(OHN) PRESPER, JR: BIRTH ANNIVERSARY. Apr 9, 1919. Coinventor with John W. Mauchly of ENIAC (Electronic Numerical Integrator and Computer), which was first demonstrated at the Moore School of Electrical Engineering at the University of Pennsylvania at Philadelphia Feb 14, 1946. This is generally considered the birth of the computer age. Originally designed to process artillery calculations for the Army, ENIAC was also used in the Manhattan Project. Eckert and Mauchly formed Electronic Control Company, which later became Unisys Corporation. Eckert was born at Philadelphia and died at Bryn Mawr, PA, June 3, 1995.

HOLOCAUST DAY (YOM HASHOAH). Apr 9. Hebrew calendar date: Nisan 27, 5762. A day established by Israel's Knesset as a memorial to the Jewish dead of WWII. Anniversary in Jewish calendar of Nisan 27, 5705 (corresponding to Apr 10, 1945, in the Gregorian calendar), the day on which Allied troops liberated the first Nazi concentration camp, Buchenwald, north of Weimar, Germany, where about 56,000 prisoners, many of them Jewish, perished.

KRUMGOLD, JOSEPH: BIRTH ANNIVERSARY. Apr 9, 1908. Author (Newbery for *Onion John* and . . . *And Now Miguel*), born at Jersey City, NJ. Died July 10, 1980.

PHILIPPINES: BATAAN DAY: 60th ANNIVERSARY. Apr 9, 1942. Araw Ng Kagitingan, national observance to commemorate the fall of Bataan. The infamous "Death March" is reenacted at the Mount Samat Shrine, the Dambana ng Kagitingan.

ROBESON, PAUL BUSTILL: BIRTH ANNIVERSARY. Apr 9, 1898. Paul Robeson, born at Princeton, NJ, was an All-American football player at Rutgers University and received his law degree from Columbia University in 1923. After being seen by Eugene O'Neill in an amateur stage production, he was offered a part in

O'Neill's play, *The Emperor Jones*. His performance in that play with the Provincetown Players established him as an actor. Without ever having taken a voice lesson, he also became a popular singer. His stage credits include *Show Boat, Porgy and Bess, The Hairy Ape* and *Othello*, which enjoyed the longest Broadway run of a Shakespearean play. In 1950 he was denied a passport by the US for refusing to sign an affidavit stating whether he was or ever had been a member of the Communist Party. The action was overturned by the Supreme Court in 1958. His film credits include *Emperor Jones, Show Boat* and *Song of Freedom*. Robeson died at Philadelphia, PA, Jan 23, 1976. For more info: *Paul Robeson: A Voice to Remember*, by Patricia and Fredrick McKissack (Enslow, 0-8949-0310-1, $14.95 Gr. K–3).

TESOL ANNUAL CONFERENCE. Apr 9–13. Salt Lake City, UT. Annual meeting of Teachers of English to Speakers of Other Languages. For info: TESOL, 700 S Washington St, Ste 200, Alexandria, VA 22314. Phone: (703) 836-0774. E-mail: conv@tesol.edu. Web: www.tesol.edu.

TUNISIA: MARTYRS' DAY. Apr 9.

WINSTON CHURCHILL DAY. Apr 9. Anniversary of enactment of legislation in 1963 that made the late British statesman an honorary citizen of the US.

BIRTHDAYS TODAY

Margaret Peterson Haddix, 38, author (*Running Out of Time, Among the Hidden*), born Washington Court House, OH, Apr 9, 1964.

Jacques Villeneuve, 31, auto racer, born St. Jean d'Iberville, QC, Canada, Apr 9, 1971.

APRIL 10 — WEDNESDAY

Day 100 — 265 Remaining

COMMODORE PERRY DAY. Apr 10, 1794. Matthew Calbraith Perry, commodore in the US Navy, negotiator of first treaty between US and Japan (Mar 31, 1854). Born at South Kingston, RI, he died Mar 4, 1858, at New York, NY.

PULITZER, JOSEPH: BIRTH ANNIVERSARY. Apr 10, 1847. American journalist and newspaper publisher, founder of the Pulitzer Prizes, born at Budapest, Hungary. Died at Charleston, SC, Oct 29, 1911. Pulitzer Prizes have been awarded annually since 1917.

ROBERT GRAY BECOMES FIRST AMERICAN TO CIRCUMNAVIGATE THE EARTH: ANNIVERSARY. Apr 10, 1790. When Robert Gray docked the *Columbia* at Boston Harbor, he became the first American to circumnavigate the earth. He sailed from Boston, MA, in September 1787, to trade with Indians of the Pacific Northwest. From there he sailed to China and then continued around the world. His 42,000-mile journey opened trade between New England and the Pacific Northwest and helped the US establish claims to the Oregon Territory.

SAFETY PIN PATENTED: ANNIVERSARY. Apr 10, 1849. Walter Hunt of New York patented the first safety pin.

April 2002

S	M	T	W	T	F	S
	1	2	3	4	5	6
7	8	9	10	11	12	13
14	15	16	17	18	19	20
21	22	23	24	25	26	27
28	29	30				

SALVATION ARMY FOUNDER'S DAY. Apr 10, 1829. Birth anniversary of William Booth, a Methodist minister who began an evangelical ministry in the East End of London in 1865 and established mission stations to feed and house the poor. In 1878 he changed the name of the organization to the Salvation Army. Booth was born at Nottingham, England, he died at London, Aug 20, 1912.

BIRTHDAYS TODAY

David A. Adler, 55, author (Cam Jansen mystery series), born New York, NY, Apr 10, 1947.

Haley Joel Osment, 14, actor (*The Sixth Sense, Bogus*), born Los Angeles, CA, Apr 10, 1988.

Martin Waddell, 61, author (*Can't You Sleep, Little Bear?; Owl Babies*), born Belfast, Northern Ireland, Apr 10, 1941.

APRIL 11 — THURSDAY

Day 101 — 264 Remaining

CIVIL RIGHTS ACT OF 1968: ANNIVERSARY. Apr 11, 1968. Exactly one week after the assassination of Martin Luther King, Jr, the Civil Rights Act of 1968 (protecting civil rights workers, expanding the rights of Native Americans and providing antidiscrimination measures in housing) was signed into law by President Lyndon B. Johnson, who said: " . . . the proudest moments of my presidency have been times such as this when I have signed into law the promises of a century."

EVERETT, EDWARD: BIRTH ANNIVERSARY. Apr 11, 1794. American statesman and orator, born at Dorcester, MA. It was Edward Everett who delivered the main address at the dedication of Gettysburg National Cemetery, Nov 19, 1863. President Abraham Lincoln also spoke at the dedication, and his brief speech (less than two minutes) has been called one of the most eloquent in the English language. Once a candidate for vice president of the US (1860), Everett died at Boston, MA, Jan 15, 1865.

HUGHES, CHARLES EVANS: BIRTH ANNIVERSARY. Apr 11, 1862. The 11th chief justice of the US Supreme Court. Born at Glens Falls, NY, he died at Osterville, MA, Aug 27, 1948. For more info: oyez.northwestern.edu/justices/justices.cgi.

LIBERATION OF BUCHENWALD CONCENTRATION CAMP: ANNIVERSARY. Apr 11, 1945. Buchenwald, north of Weimar, Germany, was entered by Allied troops. It was the first of the Nazi concentration camps to be liberated. It had been established in 1937 and about 56,000 people died there. For more info: www.ushmm.org/outreach.

★**NATIONAL D.A.R.E. DAY.** Apr 11. The Drug Abuse Resistance Education (D.A.R.E.) program helps children in grades K–12 learn the skills they need to avoid involvement in drugs, gangs and violence.

SPACE MILESTONE: *APOLLO 13* (US). Apr 11, 1970. Astronauts Lovell, Haise and Swigert were endangered when an oxygen tank ruptured. The planned moon landing was cancelled. Details of the accident were made public and the world shared concern for the crew who splashed down successfully in the Pacific Apr 17. The film *Apollo 13*, starring Tom Hanks, accurately told this story.

UGANDA: LIBERATION DAY. Apr 11. Republic of Uganda celebrates anniversary of overthrow of Idi Amin's dictatorship in 1979.

BIRTHDAYS TODAY

Josh Server, 23, actor (Nickelodeon's "All That"), born Highland Park, IL, Apr 11, 1979.

APRIL 12 — FRIDAY

Day 102 — 263 Remaining

ANNIVERSARY OF THE BIG WIND. Apr 12, 1934. The highest-velocity natural wind ever recorded occurred in the morning at the Mount Washington, NH, Observatory. Three weather observers, Wendell Stephenson, Alexander McKenzie and Salvatore Pagliuca, observed and recorded the phenomenon in which gusts reached 231 miles per hour—"the strongest natural wind ever recorded on the earth's surface."

CLAY, HENRY: 225th BIRTH ANNIVERSARY. Apr 12, 1777. Statesman, born at Hanover County, VA. Was the Speaker of the House of Representatives and later became the leader of the new Whig party. He was defeated for the presidency three times. Clay died at Washington, DC, June 29, 1852.

MOON PHASE: NEW MOON. Apr 12. Moon enters New Moon phase at 3:21 PM, EDT.

POLIO VACCINE: ANNIVERSARY. Apr 12, 1955. Anniversary of announcement that the polio vaccine developed by American physician Dr. Jonas E. Salk was "safe, potent and effective." Incidence of the dreaded infantile paralysis, or poliomyelitis, declined by 95 percent following introduction of preventive vaccines. The first mass innoculation of children against polio began in Pittsburgh, Feb 23, 1954.

ROOSEVELT, FRANKLIN DELANO: DEATH ANNIVERSARY. Apr 12, 1945. With the end of WWII only months away, the nation and the world were stunned by the sudden death of the president shortly into his fourth term of office. Roosevelt, the 32nd president of the US (Mar 4, 1933–Apr 12, 1945), was the only president to serve more than two terms—he was elected to four consecutive terms. He died at Warm Springs, GA.

SPACE MILESTONE: *COLUMBIA STS 1* (US) FIRST SHUTTLE FLIGHT: ANNIVERSARY. Apr 12, 1981. First flight of Shuttle *Columbia.* Two astronauts (John Young and Robert Crippen), on first manned US space mission since *Apollo-Soyuz* in July 1976, spent 54 hours in space (36 orbits of Earth) before landing at Edwards Air Force Base, CA, Apr 14.

SPACE MILESTONE: *VOSTOK I*, FIRST MAN IN SPACE: ANNIVERSARY. Apr 12, 1961. Yuri Gagarin became the first man in space when he made a 108-minute voyage, orbiting Earth in a 10,395-lb vehicle, *Vostok I*, launched by the USSR.

SPOTLIGHT ON BOOKS. Apr 12–13 (tentative). Alexandria, MN. Program designed for parents, teachers, librarians and community leaders who want to promote the satisfaction of reading. Honors authors of children and young adult literature that represent cultural diversity in their books. Sponsors: Bemidji State University and Northern Lights Library Network. For info: Dir, Northern Lights Library Network, PO Box 845, Alexandria, MN 56308. Phone: (320) 762-1032. E-mail: nloffice@northernlights.lib.mn.us.

TRUANCY LAW: ANNIVERSARY. Apr 12, 1853. The first truancy law was enacted at New York. A $50 fine was charged against parents whose children between the ages of five and 15 were absent from school.

BIRTHDAYS TODAY

Nicholas Brendon, 31, actor ("Buffy the Vampire Slayer"), born Los Angeles, CA, Apr 12, 1971.

Beverly Cleary, 86, author (Ramona series for children; winner of the Newbery Medal for *Dear Mr Henshaw*), born McMinnville, OR, Apr 12, 1916.

Gary Soto, 50, poet, author (*Neighborhood Odes, Too Many Tamales*), born Fresno, CA, Apr 12, 1952.

APRIL 13 — SATURDAY

Day 103 — 262 Remaining

BUTTS, ALFRED M.: BIRTH ANNIVERSARY. Apr 13, 1899. Alfred Butts was a jobless architect in the Depression when he invented the board game Scrabble. The game was just a fad for Butts's friends until a Macy's executive saw the game being played at a resort in 1952, and the world's largest store began carrying it. Manufacturing of the game was turned over to Selchow & Righter when 35 workers were producing 6,000 sets a week. Butts received three cents per set for years. He said, "One-third went to taxes. I gave one-third away, and the other third enabled me to have an enjoyable life." Butts was born at Poughkeepsie, NY. He died Apr 4, 1993, at Rhinebeck, NY.

HENRY, MARGUERITE: 100th BIRTH ANNIVERSARY. Apr 13, 1902. Born at Milwaukee, WI, Henry received the Newbery Medal in 1949 for her book *The King of the Wind.* She also authored *Misty of Chincoteague, Brighty of Grand Canyon* and other books about horses. Henry died at Rancho Santa Fe, CA, Nov 26, 1997.

INDIA: BAISAKHI. Apr 13. Sikh holiday that commemorates the founding of the brotherhood of Khalsa in 1699. A large fair is held at the Golden Temple at Amritsar, the central shrine of Sikhism.

JEFFERSON, THOMAS: BIRTH ANNIVERSARY. Apr 13, 1743. Third president of the US (Mar 4, 1801–Mar 3, 1809), born at Shadwell, VA. He had previously served as vice president under John Adams. Jefferson, who died at Charlottesville, VA, July 4, 1826, wrote his own epitaph: "Here was buried Thomas Jefferson, author of the Declaration of American Independence, of the statute of Virginia for religious freedom, and father of the University of Virginia." A holiday in Alabama and Oklahoma. For info: www.ipl.org/ref/POTUS.

★**JEFFERSON, THOMAS: BIRTH ANNIVERSARY.** Apr 13. Presidential Proclamation 2276, of Mar 21, 1938, covers all succeeding years. (Pub Res No. 60 of Aug 16, 1937.)

***SILENT SPRING* PUBLICATION: 40th ANNIVERSARY.** Apr 13, 1962. Rachel Carson's *Silent Spring* warned humankind that for the first time in history every person is subjected to contact with dangerous chemicals from conception until death. Carson painted a vivid picture of how chemicals—used in many ways but particularly in pesticides—have upset the balance of nature, undermining the survival of countless species. This enormously popular and influential book was a soft-spoken battle cry to protect our natural surroundings. Its publication signaled the beginning of the environmental movement.

SRI LANKA: SINHALA AND TAMIL NEW YEAR. April 13–14. This New Year festival includes traditional games, the wearing of new clothes in auspicious colors and special foods. Public holiday.

THAILAND: SONGKRAN FESTIVAL. Apr 13–15. Public holiday. Thai water festival. To welcome the new year the image of Buddha is bathed with holy or fragrant water and lustral water is sprinkled on celebrants. Joyous event, especially observed at Thai Buddhist temples.

YO-YO DAYS. Apr 13–14 (tentative). Spinning Top Museum, Burlington, WI. Seventh annual yo-yo convention, Wisconsin State Yo-Yo Contest, classes, demonstrations, collections of yo-yos on exhibit and yo-yo shows for all generations. For info: Spinning Top Museum, 533 Milwaukee Ave (Hwy 36), Burlington, WI 53105. Phone: (262) 763-3946.

BIRTHDAYS TODAY

Jonathan Brandis, 26, actor (*Outside Providence, Ladybugs*), born Danbury, CT, Apr 13, 1976.

Ben Nighthorse Campbell, 69, US Senator (R, Colorado), born Auburn, CA, Apr 13, 1933.

Erik Christian Haugaard, 79, author (*The Rider and His Horse*), born Frederiksberg, Denmark, Apr 13, 1923.

Lee Bennett Hopkins, 64, poet (*Blast Off!: Poems about Space*), born Scranton, PA, Apr 13, 1938.

APRIL 14 — SUNDAY

Day 104 — 261 Remaining

FIRST AMERICAN ABOLITION SOCIETY FOUNDED: ANNIVERSARY. Apr 14, 1775. The first abolition organization formed in the US was The Society for the Relief of Free Negroes Unlawfully Held in Bondage, founded at Philadelphia, PA.

FIRST DICTIONARY OF AMERICAN ENGLISH PUBLISHED: ANNIVERSARY. Apr 14, 1828. Noah Webster published his *American Dictionary of the English Language*.

HONDURAS: DIA DE LAS AMERICAS. Apr 14. Honduras. Pan-American Day, a national holiday.

★**JEWISH HERITAGE WEEK.** Apr 14–21.

LINCOLN, ABRAHAM: ASSASSINATION ANNIVERSARY. Apr 14, 1865. President Abraham Lincoln was shot while watching a performance of *Our American Cousin* at Ford's Theatre, Washington, DC. He died the following day. Assassin was John Wilkes Booth, a young actor.

MOMENT OF LAUGHTER DAY. Apr 14. Laughter is a potent and powerful way to deal with the difficulties of modern living. Since the physical, emotional and spiritual benefits of laughter are widely accepted, this day is set aside for everyone to take the necessary time to experience the power of laughter. For info: Izzy Gesell, Head Honcho of Wide Angle Humor, PO Box 962, Northampton, MA 01061. Phone: (413) 586-2634. Fax: (413) 585-0407. E-mail: izzy@izzyg.com. Web: www.izzyg.com.

April 2002

S	M	T	W	T	F	S
	1	2	3	4	5	6
7	8	9	10	11	12	13
14	15	16	17	18	19	20
21	22	23	24	25	26	27
28	29	30				

NATIONAL LIBRARY WEEK. Apr 14–20. A nationwide observance sponsored by the American Library Association. Celebrates libraries and librarians, the pleasures and importance of reading and invites library use and support. For programming ideas, see: *Library Celebrations*, by Cyndy Dingwall (Highsmith, 1-5795-0027-7, $16.95). Call the American Library Association at 1-800-545-2433 for a catalog of NLW materials. For info: American Library Assn, Public Info Office, 50 E Huron St, Chicago, IL 60611. Phone: (312) 280-5044. Fax: (312) 944-8520. E-mail: pio@ala.org. Web: www.ala.org.

★**NATIONAL ORGAN AND TISSUE DONOR AWARENESS WEEK.** April 14–20.

NATIONAL ORGAN AND TISSUE DONOR AWARENESS WEEK. Apr 14–20. To encourage Americans to consider organ and tissue donation and to sign donor cards when getting a driver's license. For info: Natl Kidney Foundation, 30 E 33rd St, New York, NY 10016. Phone: (800) 622-9010 or (212) 889-2210. Web: www.kidney.org or www.organdonor.gov.

★**PAN AMERICAN DAY.** Apr 14. Presidential Proclamation 1912, of May 28, 1930, covers every Apr 14 (required by Governing Board of Pan American Union). Proclamation issued each year since 1948.

★**PAN AMERICAN WEEK.** Apr 14–20. Presidential Proclamation customarily issued as "Pan American Day and Pan American Week." Always issued for the week including Apr 14, except in 1965, from 1946 through 1948, 1955 through 1977, and 1979.

PAN-AMERICAN DAY IN FLORIDA. Apr 14. A holiday to be observed in the public schools of Florida honoring the republics of Latin America. If Apr 14 should fall on a day that is not a school day, then Pan-American Day should be observed on the preceding school day, Apr 12 in 2002.

SULLIVAN, ANNE: BIRTH ANNIVERSARY. Apr 14, 1866. Anne Sullivan, born at Feeding Hills, MA, became well known for "working miracles" with Helen Keller, who was blind and deaf. Nearly blind herself, Sullivan used a manual alphabet communicated by the sense of touch to teach Keller to read, write and speak and then to help her go on to higher education. Anne Sullivan died Oct 20, 1936, at Forest Hills, NY.

BIRTHDAYS TODAY

Cynthia Cooper, 39, basketball player, born Chicago, IL, Apr 14, 1963.

Sarah Michelle Gellar, 25, actress ("Buffy the Vampire Slayer"), born New York, NY, Apr 14, 1977.

Gregory Alan (Greg) Maddux, 36, baseball player, born San Angelo, TX, Apr 14, 1966.

Pete Rose, 61, former baseball manager and player, born Cincinnati, OH, Apr 14, 1941.

APRIL 15 — MONDAY

Day 105 — 260 Remaining

ASTRONOMY WEEK. Apr 15–21. To take astronomy to the people. Astronomy Week is observed during the calendar week in which Astronomy Day falls, beginning on Monday and continuing through Sunday. See also: "Astronomy Day" (Apr 20).

FIRST MCDONALD'S OPENS: ANNIVERSARY. Apr 15, 1955. The first franchised McDonald's was opened at Des Plaines, IL, by Ray Kroc, who had gotten the idea from a hamburger joint at San Bernardino, CA, run by the McDonald brothers. By the mid-1990s, there were more than 15,000 McDonald's in 70 countries.

FIRST SCHOOL FOR DEAF FOUNDED: ANNIVERSARY. Apr 15, 1817. Thomas Hopkins Gallaudet and Laurent Clerc founded the first US public school for the deaf, Connecticut Asylum for the Education and Instruction of Deaf and Dumb Persons (now the American School for the Deaf), at Hartford, CT.

INCOME TAX PAY DAY. Apr 15. A day all Americans need to know—the day by which taxpayers are supposed to make their accounting of the previous year and pay their share of the cost of government. The US Internal Revenue Service provides free forms.

★**NATIONAL PARK WEEK.** Apr 15–21.

NATIONAL WILDLIFE WEEK. Apr 15–21. In 1938, the National Wildlife Federation created National Wildlife Week, a celebration to alert the public to the needs of wildlife and NWF's efforts to preserve wildlife and their habitats. NWF educates students, families, and adults about wildlife conservation issues and encourages them to become environmental stewards. For info: National Wildlife Federation, 8925 Leesburg Pike, Vienna, VA 22184. Phone: (703) 790-4000. E-mail: wildlife@nwf.org. Web: www.nwf.org.

PATRIOT'S DAY IN MASSACHUSETTS AND MAINE. Apr 15. Commemorates Battles of Lexington and Concord, 1775. Annually, the third Monday in April.

SINKING OF THE *TITANIC*: 90th ANNIVERSARY. Apr 15, 1912. The "unsinkable" luxury liner *Titanic* on its maiden voyage from Southampton, England, to New York, NY, struck an iceberg just before midnight Apr 14, and sank at 2:27 AM, Apr 15. The *Titanic* had 2,224 persons aboard. Of these, more than 1,500 were lost. About 700 people were rescued from the icy waters off Newfoundland by the liner *Carpathia*, which reached the scene about two hours after the *Titanic* went down. The sunken *Titanic* was located and photographed in September 1985. In July 1986, an expedition aboard the *Atlantis II* descended to the deck of the *Titanic* in a submersible craft, *Alvin*, and guided a robot named Jason, Jr, in a search of the ship. Two memorial bronze plaques were left on the deck of the ship.

YOUNG PEOPLES' POETRY WEEK. Apr 15–21. Annually, during National Poetry Month. An annual event, sponsored by The Children's Book Council, that highlights poetry for children and young adults and encourages everyone to celebrate poetry—read it, enjoy it, write it—in their homes, childcare centers, classrooms, libraries and bookstores. The CBC is coordinating its promotional efforts with the Academy of American Poets, the sponsor of National Poetry Month in April, and The Center for the Book in the Library of Congress. For info: Children's Book Council, 568 Broadway, Ste 404, New York, NY 10012. Phone: (212) 966-1990. Fax: (212) 966-2073. E-mail: staff@cbcbooks.org. Web: www.cbcbooks.org.

BIRTHDAYS TODAY

Evelyn Ashford, 45, Olympic gold medal track athlete, born Shreveport, LA, Apr 15, 1957.

Jacqueline Briggs Martin, 57, author (*Snowflake Bentley*), born Lewiston, ME, Apr 15, 1945.

Emma Thompson, 43, actress (*Junior*), born Paddington, England, Apr 15, 1959.

APRIL 16 — TUESDAY

Day 106 — 259 Remaining

DENMARK: QUEEN MARGRETHE'S BIRTHDAY. Apr 16. Thousands of children gather to cheer the queen at Amalienborg Palace and the Royal Guard wears scarlet gala uniforms.

DIEGO, JOSE de: BIRTH ANNIVERSARY. Apr 16, 1866. Puerto Rican patriot and political leader, Jose de Diego was born at Aguadilla, Puerto Rico. His birthday is a holiday in Puerto Rico. He died July 16, 1918, at New York, NY.

ISRAEL: YOM HA'ZIKKARON (REMEMBRANCE DAY). Apr 16. Hebrew date: Iyar 4, 5762. Honors the more than 20,000 Israeli soldiers killed in battle since the start of the nation's war for independence in 1947. Always the day before Israeli Independence Day.

MASIH, IQBAL: DEATH ANNIVERSARY. Apr 16, 1995. Twelve-year-old Iqbal Masih, born at Pakistan in 1982, who reportedly had received death threats after speaking out against Pakistan's child labor practices, was shot to death, at Muridke Village, Punjab Province. Masih, who was sold into labor as a carpet weaver at the age of four, spent the next six years of his life shackled to a loom. He began speaking out against child labor after escaping from servitude at the age of ten. In November of 1994 he spoke at an international labor conference in Sweden, and he received a $15,000 Reebok Youth in Action Award a month later. There were reports after the shooting that Masih's death was arranged by a "carpet mafia." For more info: *Iqbal Masih and the Crusaders against Child Slavery*, by Susan Kuklin (Holt, 0-8050-5459-6, $16.95 Gr. 6–12).

WILLIAMS, GARTH: BIRTH ANNIVERSARY. Apr 16, 1912. One of the most beloved and prolific children's illustrators of all time. Born in New York City, NY, he tried to become a cartoonist, but instead found success as the illustrator of E.B. White's *Stuart Little*, published in 1945. He soon turned to illustrating full time, creating illustrations for all nine of Laura Ingalls Wilder's "Little House" books, as well as White's *Charlotte's Web* and George Selden's *The Cricket in Times Square*. He also illustrated books by Margaret Wise Brown, Randall Jarrell and Russell Hoban, among others. In 1958, he became a subject of controversy with his publication of *The Rabbit's Wedding*, a book that he both wrote and illustrated, that told the story of a marriage between a black rabbit and a white rabbit. He died on May 8, 1996, at his home in Marfil, Guanajuato, Mexico.

WRIGHT, WILBUR: BIRTH ANNIVERSARY. Apr 16, 1867. Aviation pioneer (with his brother Orville), born at Millville, IN. Died at Dayton, OH, May 30, 1912.

BIRTHDAYS TODAY

Kareem Abdul-Jabbar, 55, Basketball Hall of Fame center, born Lewis Ferdinand Alcindor, Jr, New York, NY, Apr 16, 1947.

Anthony Principi, 56, US Secretary of Veteran's Affairs (George W. Bush administration), born New York, NY, Apr 16, 1946.

Eleanor E. Tate, 54, author (*The Secret of Gumbo Grove*), born Canton, MO, Apr 16, 1948.

APRIL 17 — WEDNESDAY

Day 107 — 258 Remaining

AMERICAN SAMOA: FLAG DAY. Apr 17. National holiday commemorating first raising of American flag in what was formerly Eastern Samoa in 1900. Public holiday with singing, dancing, costumes and parades.

FAMILIES LAUGHING THROUGH STORIES WEEK. Apr 17–23 (tentative). Free through its website, or for a fee for mailed packets, Teachable Moments Publishing distributes educational information to family-oriented and storytelling agencies and organizations, teaching them how to encourage instruction that will enhance the telling of humorous family stories. This activity not only promotes the art of storytelling, but also leaves lasting, laughing memories for family participants. For info: Shirley Trout, Teachable Moments, PO Box 359, Waverly, NE 68462. Phone: (402) 786-3100. Fax: (402) 788-2131. E-mail: strout@teachable moments.com. Web: www.teachablemoments.com.

ISRAEL: YOM HA'ATZMA'UT (INDEPENDENCE DAY). Apr 17. Hebrew calendar date: Iyar 5, 5762. Celebrates proclamation of independence from British mandatory rule by Palestinian Jews and establishment of the state of Israel and the provisional government May 14, 1948 (Hebrew calendar date: Iyar 5, 5708). Dates in the Hebrew calendar vary from their Gregorian equivalents from year to year, so, while Iyar 5 in 1948 was May 14, in 2002 it is Apr 17.

NEW JERSEY DAY. Apr 17. The governor issues annually a proclamation designating April 17 as New Jersey Day, commemorating the anniversary of the beginning of unified government in the state.

SPACE MILESTONE: *COLUMBIA NEUROLAB* (US). Apr 17, 1998. Seven astronauts and scientists were launched with 2,000 animals (crickets, mice, snails and fish) to study the nervous system in space.

SYRIAN ARAB REPUBLIC: INDEPENDENCE DAY. Apr 17. Official holiday. Proclaimed independence from France in 1946.

VERRAZANO DAY: ANNIVERSARY. Apr 17, 1524. Celebrates discovery of New York harbor by Giovanni Verrazano, Florentine navigator, 1485–1527.

BIRTHDAYS TODAY

Jane Kurtz, 50, author (*Pulling the Lion's Tale*), born Portland, OR, Apr 17, 1952.

April 2002

S	M	T	W	T	F	S
	1	2	3	4	5	6
7	8	9	10	11	12	13
14	15	16	17	18	19	20
21	22	23	24	25	26	27
28	29	30				

APRIL 18 — THURSDAY

Day 108 — 257 Remaining

CANADA: CONSTITUTION ACT OF 1982: 20th ANNIVERSARY. Apr 18, 1982. Replacing the British North America Act of 1867, the Canadian Constitution Act of 1982 provides Canada with a new set of fundamental laws and civil rights. Signed by Queen Elizabeth II, at Parliament Hill, Ottawa, Canada, it went into effect at 12:01 AM, Sunday, Apr 19, 1982.

THE HOUSE THAT RUTH BUILT: ANNIVERSARY. Apr 18, 1923. More than 74,000 fans attended Opening Day festivities as the New York Yankees inaugurated their new stadium. Babe Ruth christened it with a game-winning three-run homer into the right-field bleachers. In his coverage of the game for the *New York Evening Telegram* sportswriter Fred Lieb described Yankee Stadium as "The House That Ruth Built," and the name stuck.

NATIONAL TEACH CHILDREN TO SAVE DAY. Apr 18. Contact your local bank for materials for grades K–12. For info: American Bankers Assn Education Foundation, 1120 Connecticut Ave NW, Washington, DC 20036. Phone: (202) 663-5000. Web: www.aba.com.

PAUL REVERE'S RIDE: ANNIVERSARY. Apr 18, 1775. The "Midnight Ride" of Paul Revere and William Dawes started at about 10 PM, to warn American patriots between Boston, MA, and Concord, MA, of the approaching British. For more info: *The Midnight Ride of Paul Revere*, by Henry Wadsworth Longfellow (National Geographic, 0-7922-7674-4, $16.95 Gr. K–3).

PET OWNERS INDEPENDENCE DAY. Apr 18. Dog and cat owners take day off from work and the pets go to work in their place, since most pets are jobless, sleep all day and do not even take out the trash. [© 1999 by WH] For info: Tom or Ruth Roy, Wellcat Holidays, 2418 Long Ln, Lebanon, PA 17046. Phone: (230) 332-4886. E-mail: wellcat@supernet.com. Web: www.wellcat .com.

SAN FRANCISCO 1906 EARTHQUAKE: ANNIVERSARY. Apr 18, 1906. The business section of San Francisco, approximately 10,000 acres, was destroyed by earthquake. The first quake registered at 5:13 AM, followed by fire. Nearly 4,000 lives were lost during the quake.

"THIRD WORLD" DAY: ANNIVERSARY. Apr 18, 1955. Anniversary of the first use of the phrase "third world," which was used by Indonesia's President Sukarno in his opening speech at the Bandung Conference. Representatives of nearly 30 African and Asian countries (2,000 attendees) heard Sukarno praise the American war of independence, "the first successful anticolonial war in history." More than half the world's population, he said, was represented at this "first intercontinental conference of the so-called colored peoples, in the history of mankind." The phrase and the idea of a "third world" rapidly gained currency, generally signifying the aggregate of nonaligned peoples and nations—the nonwhite and underdeveloped portion of the world.

ZIMBABWE: INDEPENDENCE DAY. Apr 18. National holiday commemorates the recognition by Great Britain of Zimbabwean independence in 1980. Prior to this, the country had been the British colony of Southern Rhodesia.

BIRTHDAYS TODAY

Melissa Joan Hart, 26, actress ("Sabrina, the Teenage Witch"), born Long Island, NY, Apr 18, 1976.

Rick Moranis, 49, actor (*Honey, I Shrunk the Kids; Honey, We Shrunk Ourselves*), born Toronto, ON, Canada, Apr 18, 1953.

APRIL 19 — FRIDAY

Day 109 — 256 Remaining

BATTLE OF LEXINGTON AND CONCORD: ANNIVERSARY. Apr 19, 1775. Massachusetts. Start of the American Revolution as the British fired the "shot heard 'round the world."

GARFIELD, LUCRETIA RUDOLPH: BIRTH ANNIVERSARY. Apr 19, 1832. Wife of James Abram Garfield, the 20th president of the US, born at Hiram, OH. Died at Pasadena, CA, Mar 14, 1918.

NATIONAL YOUTH SERVICE DAY. Apr 19–20. An annual public education and recruitment campaign, highlighting the efforts of young people to become involved in volunteering and promoting the benefits of youth service to the American people. More than two million people participate. For info: Youth Service America, 1101 15th St NW, Ste 200, Washington, DC 20005. Phone: (202) 296-2992. Web: www.ysa.org.

OKLAHOMA CITY BOMBING: ANNIVERSARY. Apr 19, 1995. A car bomb exploded outside the Alfred P. Murrah Federal Building at Oklahoma City, OK, at 9:02 AM, killing 168 people, 19 of them children at a day-care center; a nurse died of head injuries sustained while helping in rescue efforts. The bomb, estimated to have weighed 5,000 pounds, had been placed in a rented truck. The blast ripped off the north face of the nine-story building, leaving a 20-foot-wide crater and debris two stories high. Cost of the damage was estimated at $500 million. Structurally unsound and increasingly dangerous, the bombed building was razed May 23. Timothy J. McVeigh, a decorated Gulf War army vet who is alleged to have been deeply angered by the Bureau of Alcohol, Tobacco and Firearms attack on the Branch Davidian compound at Waco, TX, exactly two years before, was convicted of the bombing. Terry L. Nicholls, an army buddy of McVeigh, was convicted of lesser charges. For more info: *The Oklahoma City Bombing*, by Victoria Sherrow (Enslow, 0-7660-1061-9, $18.95 Gr. 4–8).

PATRIOT'S DAY IN FLORIDA. Apr 19. A ceremonial day commemorating the first blood shed in the American Revolution at Lexington and Concord in 1775.

SHERMAN, ROGER: BIRTH ANNIVERSARY. Apr 19, 1721. American statesman, member of the Continental Congress (1774–81 and 1783–84), signer of the Declaration of Independence and of the Constitution, was born at Newton, MA. He also calculated astronomical and calendar information for an almanac. Sherman died at New Haven, CT, July 23, 1793.

SIERRA LEONE: NATIONAL HOLIDAY. Apr 19. Sierra Leone became a republic in 1971.

SPACE MILESTONE: *SALYUT* (USSR): ANNIVERSARY. Apr 19, 1971. The Soviet Union launched *Salyut*, the first manned orbiting space laboratory. It was replaced in 1986 by *Mir*, a manned space station and laboratory.

BIRTHDAYS TODAY

Tim Curry, 56, actor (*Muppet Treasure Island, Home Alone 2*), born Cheshire, England, Apr 19, 1946.

APRIL 20 — SATURDAY

Day 110 — 255 Remaining

ASTRONOMY DAY. Apr 20. To take astronomy to the people. International Astronomy Day is observed on a Saturday near the first quarter moon between mid-April and mid-May. Cosponsored by 15 astronomical organizations. See also: "Astronomy Week" (Apr 15). For info: Gary E. Tomlinson, Coord, Astronomy Day Headquarters, c/o Chaffee Planetarium, 272 Pearl NW, Grand Rapids, MI 49504. Phone: (616) 456-3532. E-mail: gtomlinson@triton.net. Web: www.astroleague.org.

EGYPT: SHAM EL-NESSIM. Apr 20 (tentative date). Sporting Holiday. This feast has been celebrated by all Egyptians since pharaonic time; people go out and spend the day in parks and along the Nile's banks. For info: Egyptian Tourist Authority, 645 N Michigan Ave, Ste 829, Chicago, IL 60611. Phone: (312) 280-4666.

HITLER, ADOLF: BIRTH ANNIVERSARY. Apr 20, 1889. German dictator, frustrated artist, obsessed with superiority of the "Aryan race" and the evil of Marxism (which he saw as a Jewish plot). Hitler was born at Braunau am Inn, Austria. Turning to politics, despite a five-year prison sentence (writing *Mein Kampf* during the nine months he served), his rise was predictable and a German plebiscite vested sole executive power in Führer Adolf Hitler Aug 19, 1934. Facing certain defeat by the Allied Forces, he shot himself Apr 30, 1945, while his mistress, Eva Braun, took poison in a Berlin bunker where they had been hiding for more than three months.

MOON PHASE: FIRST QUARTER. Apr 20. Moon enters First Quarter phase at 8:48 AM, EDT.

TAURUS, THE BULL. Apr 20–May 20. In the astronomical/astrological zodiac that divides the sun's apparent orbit into 12 segments, the period Apr 20–May 20 is identified, traditionally, as the sun sign of Taurus, the Bull. The ruling planet is Venus.

BIRTHDAYS TODAY

Mary Hoffman, 57, author (*Amazing Grace*), born Eastleigh, Hampshire, England, Apr 20, 1945.

Joey Lawrence, 26, actor ("Brotherly Love," "Blossom"), born Strawbridge, PA, Apr 20, 1976.

Pat Roberts, 66, US Senator (R, Kansas), born Topeka, KS, Apr 20, 1936.

John Paul Stevens, 82, Associate Justice of the US Supreme Court, born Chicago, IL, Apr 20, 1920.

APRIL 21 — SUNDAY

Day 111 — 254 Remaining

BRAZIL: TIRADENTES DAY. Apr 21. National holiday commemorating execution of national hero, dentist Jose da Silva Xavier, nicknamed Tiradentes (tooth-puller), a conspirator in revolt against the Portuguese in 1789.

FROEBEL, FRIEDRICH: BIRTH ANNIVERSARY. Apr 21, 1782. German educator and author Friedrich Froebel, who believed that play is an important part of a child's education, was born at Oberwiessbach, Thuringia. Froebel invented the kindergarten, founding the first one at Blankenburg, Germany, in 1837. Froebel also invented a series of toys which he intended to stimulate learning. (The American architect Frank Lloyd Wright as a child received these toys [maplewood blocks] from his mother and spoke throughout his life of their value.) Froebel's ideas about the role of directed play, toys and music in children's education had a profound influence in England and the US, where the nursery school became a further extension of his ideas. Froebel died at Marienthal, Germany, June 21, 1852.

GRANGE WEEK. Apr 21–27. State and local recognition for Grange's contribution to rural/urban America. Celebrated at National Headquarters at Washington, DC, and in all states with local, county and state Granges. Begun in 1867, the National Grange is the oldest US rural community service, family-oriented organization with a special interest in agriculture. Annually, the last full week in April. For info: Kermit W. Richardson, Natl Master, The Natl Grange, 1616 H St NW, Washington, DC 20006. Phone: (202) 628-3507 or (888) 4-GRANGE. Fax: (202) 347-1091. Web: www.grange.org.

GREECE: DUMB WEEK. Apr 21–27. The week preceding Holy Week on the Orthodox calendar is known as Dumb Week, as no services are held in churches throughout this period except on Friday, eve of the Saturday of Lazarus.

INDONESIA: KARTINI DAY. Apr 21. Republic of Indonesia. Honors Raden Adjeng Kartini, pioneer in the emancipation of the women of Indonesia.

ITALY: BIRTHDAY OF ROME. Apr 21. Celebration of the founding of Rome, traditionally thought to be in 753 BC.

KINDERGARTEN DAY. Apr 21. A day to recognize the importance of play, games and "creative self-activity" in children's education and to note the history of the kindergarten. Observed on the anniversary of the birth of Friedrich Froebel (Apr 21, 1782) who established the first kindergarten in 1837. German immigrants brought Froebel's ideas to the US in the 1840s. The first kindergarten in a public school in the US was started in 1873, at St. Louis, MO.

NATIONAL COIN WEEK. Apr 21–27. To promote the history and lore of numismatics and the hobby of coin collecting. For info: James Taylor, Dir of Educ, American Numismatic Assn, 818 N Cascade Ave, Colorado Springs, CO 80903. Phone: (719) 632-2646 or (800) 367-9723. Fax: (719) 634-4085. E-mail: anaedu@money.org. Web: www.money.org.

NATIONAL PTA EARTH WEEK. Apr 21–27. In 1990, the National PTA recognized the importance of the environment to the health and safety of our children and designated the week in which Earth Day falls (Apr 22) as Earth Week. During Earth Week, PTA members and others work to improve the environment in their homes, schools and communities. For info: Natl PTA Environmental Awareness Program, 330 N Wabash Ave, Ste 2100, Chicago, IL 60611-3690. Phone: (312) 670-6782. Fax: (312) 670-6783. E-mail: info@pta.org. Web: www.pta.org.

NATIONAL VOLUNTEER WEEK. Apr 21–27. National Volunteer Week honors those who reach out to others through volunteer community service and calls attention to the need for more community services for individuals, groups and families to help solve serious social problems that affect our communities. For info: Customer Information Center, Points of Light Foundation, 1737 H St NW, Washington, DC 20006. Phone: (202) 223-9186. Fax: (202) 223-9256. E-mail: volnet@aol.com. Web: www.pointsoflight.org.

★ **NATIONAL VOLUNTEER WEEK.** Apr 21–27.

April 2002

S	M	T	W	T	F	S
	1	2	3	4	5	6
7	8	9	10	11	12	13
14	15	16	17	18	19	20
21	22	23	24	25	26	27
28	29	30				

NATIONAL YWCA WEEK. Apr 21–27. To promote the YWCA of the USA nationally. Annually, the last full week in April. For info: YWCA of the USA, Empire State Bldg, Ste 301, 350 Fifth Ave, New York, NY 10118. Phone: (212) 273-7800. Web: www.ywca.org.

READING IS FUN WEEK. Apr 21–27. To highlight the importance and fun of reading. Annually, the last full week of April. For info: Rachael Walker, Reading Is Fundamental, Inc, 600 Maryland Ave SW, Rm 600, Washington, DC 20024-2569. Phone: (202) 287-3371. Fax: (202) 287-3196. Web: www.rif.org.

SAN JACINTO DAY. Apr 21. Texas. Commemorates Battle of San Jacinto in which Texas won independence from Mexico. A 570-foot monument, dedicated on the 101st anniversary of the battle, marks the site on the banks of the San Jacinto River, about 20 miles from the present city of Houston, TX, where General Sam Houston's Texans decisively defeated the Mexican forces led by Santa Ana in the final battle between Texas and Mexico.

SKY AWARENESS WEEK. Apr 21–27. A celebration of the sky and an opportunity to appreciate its natural beauty, to understand sky and weather processes and to work together to protect the sky as a natural resource (it's the only one we have). Events are held at schools, nature centers, etc, all across the US. For info: Mike Mogil, How The Weatherworks, 301 Creek Valley Ln, Rockville, MD 20850-5604. Phone: (301) 990-9324 or (301) 527-9339. Fax: (630) 563-1782. E-mail: skyweek@weatherworks.com. Web: www.weatherworks.com.

BIRTHDAYS TODAY

Queen Elizabeth II, 76, Queen of the United Kingdom, born London, England, Apr 21, 1926.
Charles Grodin, 67, actor (*Beethoven, Beethoven's 2nd*), born Pittsburgh, PA, Apr 21, 1935.
Barbara Park, 55, author (the Junie B. Jones series), born Mt Holly, NJ, Apr 21, 1947.

APRIL 22 — MONDAY

Day 112 — 253 Remaining

BRAZIL: DISCOVERY OF BRAZIL DAY. Apr 22. Commemorates discovery by Pedro Alvarez Cabral in 1500.

CANADA: NEWFOUNDLAND: SAINT GEORGE'S DAY. Apr 22. Holiday observed in Newfoundland on Monday nearest Feast Day (Apr 23) of Saint George.

COINS STAMPED "IN GOD WE TRUST": ANNIVERSARY. Apr 22, 1864. By Act of Congress, the phrase "In God We Trust" began to be stamped on all US coins.

CONFEDERATE MEMORIAL DAY IN ALABAMA. Apr 22. State holiday on the fourth Monday in April.

EARTH DAY. Apr 22. Earth Day, first observed Apr 22, 1970, with the message "Give Earth a Chance" and attention to reclaiming the purity of the air, water and living environment. Earth Day 1990 was a global event with more than 200 million participating in 142 countries. Annually, Apr 22. Note: Earth Day activities are held by many groups on various dates, often on the weekend closest to Apr 22. The vernal equinox (i.e., the first day of spring) has been chosen by some for this observance. For info: Earth Day Network, PO Box 9827, San Diego, CA 92169. Phone: (619) 272-0347. Fax: (619) 272-2933. E-mail: cdchase@znet.com. Web: www.sdearthtimes.com/edn.

FIRST SOLO TRIP TO NORTH POLE: ANNIVERSARY. Apr 22, 1994. Norwegian explorer Borge Ousland became the first person to make the trip to the North Pole alone. The trip took 52 days, during which he pulled a 265-pound sled. Departing from Cape Atkticheskiy at Siberia Mar 2, he averaged about 18½ miles per day over the 630-mile journey. Ousland had traveled to the Pole on skis with Erling Kagge in 1990.

105
x 3
315

NATIONAL COUNCIL OF TEACHERS OF MATHEMATICS ANNUAL MEETING. Apr 22–24. Las Vegas, NV. For info: Natl Council of Teachers of Mathematics, 1906 Association Dr, Reston, VA 20191-1593. Phone: (703) 620-9840. Fax: (703) 476-2970. E-mail: infocentral@nctm.org. Web: www.nctm.org.

NATIONAL PLAYGROUND SAFETY WEEK. Apr 22–26. An opportunity for families, community parks, schools and child-care facilities to focus on preventing public playground-related injuries. Sponsored by the National Program for Playground Safety (NPPS), this event helps educate the public about the more than 200,000 children (that's one child every 2 ½ minutes) that require emergency room treatment for playground-related injuries each year. For info: Natl Program for Playground Safety, School of HPELS, UNI, Cedar Falls, IA 50614-0618. Phone: (800) 554-PLAY. Fax: (319) 273-7308. Web: www.uni.edu/playground.

NATIONAL TV-TURNOFF WEEK. Apr 22–28 (tentative). For the ninth annual event, more than 7 million Americans will go without TV for 7 days. For info: TV-Turnoff Network, 1611 Connecticut Ave NW, Ste 3A, Washington, DC 20009. Phone: (800) 939-6737 or (202) 518-5556. Web: www.tvturnoff.org.

OKLAHOMA DAY. Apr 22. Oklahoma.

OKLAHOMA LAND RUSH: ANNIVERSARY. Apr 22, 1889. At noon a gun shot signaled the start of the Oklahoma land rush as thousands of settlers rushed into the territory to claim land. Under pressure from cattlemen, the federal government opened 1,900,000 acres of central Oklahoma that had been bought from the Creek and Seminole tribes.

BIRTHDAYS TODAY

Eileen Christelow, 59, author (*Five Little Monkeys Jumping on the Bed, Don't Wake Up Mama!*), born Washington, DC, Apr 22, 1943.

Paula Fox, 79, author (Newbery for *The Slave Dancer*), born New York, NY, Apr 22, 1923.

S.E. Hinton, 53, author (*The Outsiders, Tex*), born New York, NY, Apr 22, 1949.

APRIL 23 — TUESDAY

Day 113 — 252 Remaining

BERMUDA: PEPPERCORN CEREMONY. Apr 23. St. George. Commemorates the payment of one peppercorn in 1816 to the governor of Bermuda for rental of Old State House by the Masonic Lodge.

BUCHANAN, JAMES: BIRTH ANNIVERSARY. Apr 23, 1791. The 15th president of the US, born near Mercersburg, PA, was the only president who never married. He served one term in office, Mar 4, 1857–Mar 3, 1861, and died at Lancaster, PA, June 1, 1868. For info: www.ipl.org/ref/POTUS.

FIRST MOVIE THEATER OPENS: ANNIVERSARY. Apr 23, 1896. The first movie theater opened in Koster and Bial's Music Hall at New York City. Up until this time, people viewed movies individually by looking into a Kinetoscope, a box-like "peep show." The first Kinetoscope parlor opened at New York in 1894. But in 1896 Thomas Edison introduced the Vitascope which projected films on a screen. This was the first time in the US that an audience sat in a theater and viewed a movie together.

FIRST PUBLIC SCHOOL IN AMERICA: ANNIVERSARY. Apr 23, 1635. The Boston Latin School opened and is America's oldest public school. This is the Gregorian calendar date; the school was actually founded Apr 13 on the Julian calendar. For more info: bls.org.

PEARSON, LESTER B.: BIRTH ANNIVERSARY. Apr 23, 1897. The 14th prime minister of Canada, born at Toronto, Canada. He was Canada's chief delegate at the San Francisco conference where the UN charter was drawn up and later served as president of the General Assembly. He wrote the proposal that resulted in the formation of the North Atlantic Treaty Organization (NATO). He was awarded the Nobel Peace Prize. Died at Rockcliffe, Canada, Dec 27, 1972. For more info: www.uwc.ca/pearson/library/lester/lester.htm.

PHYSICISTS DISCOVER TOP QUARK: ANNIVERSARY. Apr 23, 1994. Physicists at the Department of Energy's Fermi National Accelerator Laboratory found evidence for the existence of the subatomic particle called the top quark, the last undiscovered quark of the six predicted to exist by current scientific theory. The discovery provides strong support for the quark theory of the structure of matter. Quarks are subatomic particles that make up protons and neutrons found in the nuclei of atoms. The five other quark types that had already been proven to exist are the up quark, down quark, strange quark, charm quark and bottom quark. Further experimentation over many months confirmed the discovery, and it was publicly announced Mar 2, 1995.

SAINT GEORGE FEAST DAY. Apr 23. Martyr and patron saint of England, who died Apr 23, AD 303. Hero of the George and the dragon legend. The story says that his faith helped him slay a vicious dragon that demanded daily sacrifice after the king's daughter became the intended victim.

SHAKESPEARE, WILLIAM: BIRTH AND DEATH ANNIVERSARY. Apr 23. England's most famous and most revered poet and playwright. He was born at Stratford-on-Avon, England, Apr 23, 1564 (Old Style), baptized there three days later and died there on his birthday, Apr 23, 1616 (Old Style). Author of at least 36 plays and 154 sonnets, Shakespeare created the most influential and lasting body of work in the English language, an extraordinary exploration of human nature. His epitaph: "Good frend for Jesus sake forbeare, To digg the dust enclosed heare. Blese be ye man that spares thes stones, And curst be he that moves my bones." For more info: *Bard of Avon: The Story of William Shakespeare*, by Diane Stanley and Peter Vennema (Morrow, 0-688-09109-1, $15.93 Gr. K–3).

SPAIN: BOOK DAY AND LOVER'S DAY. Apr 23. Barcelona. Saint George's Day and the anniversary of the death of Spanish writer Miguel de Cervantes have been observed with special ceremonies in the Palacio de la Disputacion and throughout the city since 1714. Book stands are set up in the plazas and on street corners. This is Spain's equivalent of Valentine's Day. Women give books to men; men give roses to women.

TURKEY: NATIONAL SOVEREIGNTY AND CHILDREN'S DAY. Apr 23. Commemorates Grand National Assembly's inauguration in 1923.

UNITED NATIONS: WORLD BOOK AND COPYRIGHT DAY. Apr 23. Observed throughout the United Nations system.

BIRTHDAYS TODAY

Gabriel Damon, 26, actor (*Newsies*), born Reno, NV, Apr 23, 1976.
Barry Watson, 28, actor ("7th Heaven"), born Traverse City, MI, Apr 23, 1974.

APRIL 24 — WEDNESDAY

Day 114 — 251 Remaining

ARMENIA: ARMENIAN MARTYRS DAY. Apr 24. Commemorates the massacre of Armenians under the Ottoman Turks in 1915 and when deportations from Turkey began. Also called Armenian Genocide Memorial Day. Adolf Hitler, in a speech at Obersalzberg Aug 22, 1939, is reported to have said, "Who today remembers the Armenian extermination?" in an apparent justification of the Nazi's use of genocide.

IBM PERSONAL COMPUTER INTRODUCED: ANNIVERSARY. Apr 24, 1981. Although IBM was one of the pioneers in making mainframe and other large computers, this was the company's first foray into the desktop computer market. Eventually, more IBM-compatible computers were manufactured by IBM's competitors than by IBM itself.

IRELAND: EASTER RISING. Apr 24, 1916. Irish nationalists seized key buildings in Dublin and proclaimed an Irish republic. The rebellion collapsed, however, and it wasn't until 1922 that the Irish Free State, the predecessor of the Republic of Ireland, was established.

LIBRARY OF CONGRESS: ANNIVERSARY. Apr 24, 1800. Congress approved an act providing "for the purchase of such books as may be necessary for the use of Congress . . . and for fitting up a suitable apartment for containing them." Thus began one of the world's greatest libraries. Originally housed in the Capitol, it moved to its own quarters in 1897. For more information about the library, visit its website at lcweb.loc.gov.

NESS, EVALINE: BIRTH ANNIVERSARY. Apr 24, 1911. Author and illustrator (Caldecott for *Sam, Bangs & Moonshine*), born at Union City, OH. Died Aug 12, 1986.

BIRTHDAYS TODAY

A. Paul Cellucci, 54, Governor of Massachusetts (R), born Hudson, MA, Apr 24, 1948.
Jim Geringer, 58, Governor of Wyoming (R), born Wheatland, WY, Apr 24, 1944.
Larry (Chipper) Jones, 30, baseball player, born DeLand, FL, Apr 24, 1972.

APRIL 25 — THURSDAY

Day 115 — 250 Remaining

ANZAC DAY: ANNIVERSARY. Apr 25. Australia, New Zealand and Samoa. Memorial day and veterans' observance, especially to mark WWI Anzac landing at Gallipoli, Turkey, in 1915 (ANZAC: Australia and New Zealand Army Corps).

EGYPT: SINAI DAY. Apr 25. National holiday celebrating the liberation of Sinai in 1982 after the peace treaty between Egypt and Israel. For info: Egyptian Tourist Authority, 645 N Michigan Ave, Ste 829, Chicago, IL 60611. Phone: (312) 280-4666. Fax: (312) 280-4788.

April 2002

S	M	T	W	T	F	S
	1	2	3	4	5	6
7	8	9	10	11	12	13
14	15	16	17	18	19	20
21	22	23	24	25	26	27
28	29	30				

FIRST LICENSE PLATES: ANNIVERSARY. Apr 25, 1901. New York began requiring license plates on automobiles, the first state to do so.

ICELAND: "FIRST DAY OF SUMMER." Apr 25. A national public holiday, *Sumardagurinn fyrsti*, with general festivities, processions and much street dancing, especially at Reykjavik, greets the coming of summer. Flags are flown on this day. Annually, the Thursday between April 19 and 25.

ITALY: LIBERATION DAY. Apr 25. National holiday. Commemorates the liberation of Italy from German troops in 1945.

LOVELACE, MAUD HART: BIRTH ANNIVERSARY. Apr 25, 1892. Author of the Betsy-Tacy books, born at Mankato, MN. Died at California, Mar 11, 1980.

MARCONI, GUGLIELMO: BIRTH ANNIVERSARY. Apr 25, 1874. Inventor of wireless telegraphy (1895) born at Bologna, Italy. Died at Rome, Italy, July 20, 1937.

NATIONAL PLAYGROUND SAFETY DAY. Apr 25. An opportunity for families, community parks, schools and childcare facilities to focus on preventing public playground-related injuries. Sponsored by the National Program for Playground Safety (NPPS), this event helps educate the public about the more than 200,000 children (that's one child every 2 ½ minutes) that require emergency room treatment for playground-related injuries each year. Annually, the last Thursday in April. For info: Natl Program for Playground Safety, School of HPELS, UNI, Cedar Falls, IA 50614-0618. Phone: (800) 554-PLAY. Fax: (319) 273-7308. Web: www.uni.edu/playground.

PORTUGAL: LIBERTY DAY. Apr 25. Public holiday. Anniversary of the 1974 revolution.

SPACE MILESTONE: HUBBLE SPACE TELESCOPE DEPLOYED (US). Apr 25, 1990. Deployed by *Discovery*, this telescope is the largest on-orbit observatory to date and is capable of imaging objects up to 14 billion light-years away. The resolution of images was expected to be seven to 10 times greater than images from Earth-based telescope's, since the Hubble Space Telescope is not hampered by Earth's atmospheric distortion. Launched Apr 12, 1990, from Kennedy Space Center, FL. Unfortunately, the telescope's lenses were defective so that the anticipated high quality of imaging was not possible. In 1993, however, the world watched as a shuttle crew successfully retrieved the Hubble from orbit, executed the needed repair and replacement work and released it into orbit once more. In December 1999, the space shuttle *Discovery* was launched to do major repairs on the telescope.

SWAZILAND: NATIONAL FLAG DAY. Apr 25. National holiday.

TAKE OUR DAUGHTERS TO WORK DAY. Apr 25. A national public education campaign sponsored by the Ms Foundation for Women in which girls aged nine–15 go to work with adult hosts—parents, grandparents, cousins, aunts, uncles, friends. Take Our Daughters to Work Day has succeeded in mobilizing parents, educators, employers and other caring adults to take action to redress the inequalities in girls' lives and focus national attention on the concerns, hopes and dreams of girls. Annually, the fourth Thursday in April. For info: Lauren Wechsler, Natl Media Mgr, Take Our Daughters to Work Day, Ms Foundation for Women, 120 Wall St, 33rd Floor, New York, NY 10005. Phone: (800) 676-7780 or (212) 742-2300. Fax: (212) 742-1531. E-mail: todtwcom@ms.foundation.org. Web: www.ms.foundation.org.

THEODORE ROOSEVELT NATIONAL PARK ESTABLISHED: ANNIVERSARY. Apr 25, 1947. Located in North Dakota, the Theodore Roosevelt National Park includes two sections of the Badlands on the Missouri River as well as Theodore Roosevelt's Elkhorn Ranch. For more info: www.nps.gov/thro/index.htm.

WALDSEEMULLER, MARTIN: REMEMBRANCE DAY. Apr 25, 1507. Little is known about the obscure scholar now called the "godfather of America," the German geographer and mapmaker Martin Waldseemuller, who gave America its name. In a book titled *Cosmographiae Introductio*, published Apr 25, 1507, Waldseemuller wrote: "Inasmuch as both Europe and Asia received their names from women, I see no reason why any one should justly object to calling this part Amerige, i.e., the land of Amerigo, or America, after Amerigo, its discoverer, a man of great ability." Believing it was the Italian navigator and merchant Amerigo Vespucci who had discovered the new continent, Waldseemuller sought to honor Vespucci by placing his name on his map of the world, published in 1507. First applied only to the South American continent, it soon was used for both the American continents. Waldseemuller did not learn about the voyage of Christopher Columbus until several years later. Of the thousand copies of his map that were printed, only one is known to have survived. Waldseemuller probably was born at Radolfzell, Germany, about 1470. He died at St. Die, France, about 1517–20. See also: "Vespucci, Amerigo: Birth Anniversary" (Mar 9).

BIRTHDAYS TODAY

Tim Duncan, 26, basketball player, born St. Croix, US Virgin Islands, Apr 25, 1976.

Jon Kyl, 60, US Senator (R, Arizona), born Oakland, NE, Apr 25, 1942.

George Ella Lyon, 53, author (*Come a Tide, Dreamplace*), born Harlan, KY, Apr 25, 1949.

APRIL 26 — FRIDAY

Day 116 — 249 Remaining

AUDUBON, JOHN JAMES: BIRTH ANNIVERSARY. Apr 26, 1785. American artist and naturalist, best known for his *Birds of America*, born at Haiti. Died Jan 27, 1851, at New York, NY. For more info: *Capturing Nature: The Writings and Art of John James Audubon*, edited by Peter and Connie Roop (Walker, 0-8027-8205-1, $17.85 Gr. 4–6).

CHERNOBYL NUCLEAR REACTOR DISASTER: ANNIVERSARY. Apr 26, 1986. At 1:23 AM, local time, an explosion occurred at the Chernobyl atomic power station at Pripyat in the Ukraine. The resulting fire burned for days, sending radioactive material into the atmosphere. More than 100,000 persons were evacuated from a 300-square-mile area around the plant. Three months later 31 people were reported to have died and thousands exposed to dangerous levels of radiation. Estimates projected an additional 1,000 cancer cases in nations downwind of the radioactive discharge. The plant was encased in a concrete tomb in an effort to prevent the still-hot reactor from overheating again and to minimize further release of radiation.

CONFEDERATE MEMORIAL DAY IN FLORIDA AND GEORGIA. Apr 26. See also: Confederate Memorial Day entries for Apr 29, May 10 and June 3.

CONNECTICUT STORYTELLING FESTIVAL. Apr 26–28. Connecticut College, New London, CT. Annual festival features performances for families and adults, plus workshops and story-sharing by Connecticut and nationally renowned storytellers.

APRIL 26
NATIONAL ARBOR DAY

There's nothing like a walk in the forest on a cool, crisp day, or listening to the leaves rustle in the wind as you snuggle in bed. Unless it's leaning against a tree trunk and savoring the shade on a hot summer day. And what about climbing up into a tree and feeling as though you are on top of the world? Then again, there's nothing like the thrill of building a tree house (and using it for a clubhouse with your friends). And, of course, the marvelous crackles when you jump into a pile of leaves.

Celebrate Arbor Day by enjoying the trees in your life. Let students work in small groups. They could share some of their experiences with trees at various times of the year. For example: pussy willow "fuzzies"; maple tree "helicopters"; oak trees and acorn "fingertip hats"; sycamore tree "itchy balls"; or maybe evergreens and pine cones.

As a science project, list and describe the trees found in your school's neighborhood. Students could collect a fallen leaf and press it, or they could draw the leaf. Paste the leaf (or drawing) on a sheet of paper and write facts about the tree beneath it. Bind the pages into a classroom "Trees Around Our School" book.

If you really like to plan ahead, make this a project introduced in September and have students keep a monthly journal about a particular tree and how it changes each month. Their observations can be in a factual or poetic vein. Have them press a leaf from the tree. By the time Arbor Day rolls around, they each have a booklet that can be assembled on Arbor Day. Each student will have a neat end-of-the-year science journal and a writing project as well.

You might want to approach the PTO or school administration and find out if they have plans for an Arbor Day planting at your school. Participate in that by researching the kind of tree being planted. If no project is planned, suggest planting a tree.

For a social studies project, let students contact the municipal building via letters or phone calls. Have them discover which department handles trees and if that department has a list of the oldest trees in your community. If possible, get pictures. Students can do research and write each tree's perspective of the social changes it has "seen" during its lifetime.

Writing projects could include writing a poem or prose piece about a student's favorite tree. *Old Elm Speaks*, by Kristine O'Connell George (Clarion, 0-395-87611-7, $15 Gr. K–5), and *My Favorite Tree: Terrific Trees of North America*, by Diane Iverson (Dawn, 1-8832-2093-9, $9.95 Gr. K–7), are wonderful for stimulating ideas.

There are lots of fun art projects your students can do with leaves. Make leaf prints by dipping a leaf in paint. For a twist, have students print the leaf with the stem pointing toward the top edge of the paper. Then, have them add crayon or marker lines to incorporate the leaf into an article of clothing.

There are many books worth having in your classroom for an Arbor Day celebration. *Tree Trunk Traffic*, by Bianca Lavies (Penguin, 0-14-054837-8, $4.99 Gr. K–4), has great photos of creatures that live in a 70-year-old maple tree. *A Log's Life*, by Wendy Pfeffer (Simon & Schuster, 0-689-80636-1, $16 Gr. K–4), is a beautiful paper collage presentation of the life cycle of a tree and the life it supports as the tree grows, falls and then decays. *A Tree is Growing*, by Arthur Dorros (Scholastic, 0-590-45300-9, $15.95 Gr. 3–7), chronicles the growing stages of an oak tree. Although this focuses on the oak, there are gorgeous line drawings of many other leaves.

Annually, the last full weekend in April. Est attendance: 300. For info: Annie Burnham, Adm, Connecticut Storytelling Center, Connecticut College Box 5295, 270 Mohegan Ave, New London, CT 06320. Phone: (860) 439-2764. Fax: (860) 439-2895. E-mail: csc@conncoll.edu.

DENMARK: COMMON PRAYER DAY. Apr 26. Public holiday. The fourth Friday after Easter, known as "Store Bededag," is a day for prayer and festivity.

MOON PHASE: FULL MOON. Apr 26. Moon enters Full Moon phase at 11:00 PM, EDT.

NATIONAL ARBOR DAY. Apr 26. The Committee for National Arbor Day has as its goal the observance of Arbor Day in all states on the same day, the last Friday in April. This unified Arbor Day date would provide our citizenry with the opportunity to learn about the importance of trees to our way of life. This date is a good planting date for many states throughout the country. National Arbor Day has been observed in 1970, 1972, 1988, 1990, 1991 and 1993 by presidential proclamation. More than half the states now observe Arbor Day on the proposed April Friday. Sponsors include: International Society of Arboriculture, Society of Municipal Arborists, American Association of Nurserymen, National Arborist Association, National Recreation and Park Association and the Arborists Association of New Jersey. For info: Committee for Natl Arbor Day, 63 Fitzrandolph Rd, West Orange, NJ 07052. Phone: (201) 731-0840. Fax: (201) 731-6020. *See* Curriculum Connection.

RICHTER SCALE DAY. Apr 26. A day to recognize the importance of Charles Francis Richter's research and his work in development of the earthquake magnitude scale that is known as the Richter scale. Richter, an American author, physicist and seismologist, was born Apr 26, 1900, near Hamilton, OH. An Earthquake Awareness Week was observed in recognition of his work. Richter died at Pasadena, CA, Sept 30, 1985.

SOUTH AFRICAN MULTIRACIAL ELECTIONS: ANNIVERSARY. Apr 26–29, 1994. For the first time in the history of South Africa, the nation's approximately 18 million blacks voted in multiparty elections. This event marked the definitive end of apartheid, the system of racial separation that had kept blacks and other minorities out of the political process. The election resulted in Nelson Mandela of the African National Congress being elected president and F.W. de Klerk (incumbent president) of the National Party vice president.

TANZANIA: UNION DAY. Apr 26. Celebrates union between mainland Tanzania (formerly Tanganyika) and the islands of Zanzibar and Pemba, in 1964.

BIRTHDAYS TODAY

Patricia Reilly Giff, 67, author (*Lily's Crossing*), born Brooklyn, NY, Apr 26, 1935.

April 2002

S	M	T	W	T	F	S
	1	2	3	4	5	6
7	8	9	10	11	12	13
14	15	16	17	18	19	20
21	22	23	24	25	26	27
28	29	30				

APRIL 27 — SATURDAY

Day 117 — 248 Remaining

BABE RUTH DAY: 55th ANNIVERSARY. Apr 27, 1947. Babe Ruth Day was celebrated in every ballpark in organized baseball in the US as well as Japan. Mortally ill with throat cancer, Ruth appeared at Yankee Stadium to thank his former club for the honor.

BEMELMANS, LUDWIG: BIRTH ANNIVERSARY. Apr 27, 1898. Author, illustrator and artist, born at Austria. Ludwig Bemelmans created the Madeline series, including *Mad About Madeline: The Complete Series*. In 1998, a Madeline film was released. Bemelmans died at New York, NY, Oct 1, 1962. For more info: *Bemelmans: The Life & Art of Madeline's Creator*, by John Bemelmans Marciano (Viking, 0-670-88460-X, $40).

GRANT, ULYSSES SIMPSON: BIRTH ANNIVERSARY. Apr 27, 1822. The 18th president of the US (Mar 4, 1869–Mar 3, 1877), born Hiram Ulysses Grant at Point Pleasant, OH. He graduated from the US Military Academy in 1843. President Lincoln promoted Grant to lieutenant general in command of all the Union armies Mar 9, 1864. On Apr 9, 1865, Grant received General Robert E. Lee's surrender, at Appomattox Court House, VA, which he announced to the Secretary of War as follows: "General Lee surrendered the Army of Northern Virginia this afternoon on terms proposed by myself. The accompanying additional correspondence will show the conditions fully." Nicknamed "Unconditional Surrender Grant," he died at Mount McGregor, NY, July 23, 1885, just four days after completing his memoirs. He was buried at Riverside Park, New York, NY, where Grant's Tomb was dedicated in 1897. For info: www.ipl.org/ref/POTUS.

LANTZ, WALTER: BIRTH ANNIVERSARY. Apr 27, 1900. Originator of Universal Studios' animated opening sequence for their first major musical film, *The King of Jazz*. Walter Lantz is best remembered as the creator of Woody Woodpecker, the bird with the wacky laugh and the taunting ways. Lantz received a lifetime achievement Academy Award for his animation in 1979. He was born at New Rochelle, NY, and died Mar 22, 1994, at Burbank, CA.

MAGELLAN, FERDINAND: DEATH ANNIVERSARY. Apr 27, 1521. Portuguese explorer Ferdinand Magellan was probably born near Oporto, Portugal, about 1480, but neither the place nor the date is certain. Usually thought of as the first man to circumnavigate the earth, he died before completing the voyage; thus his co-leader, Basque navigator Juan Sebastian de Elcano, became the world's first circumnavigator. The westward, 'round-the-world expedition began Sept 20, 1519, with five ships and about 250 men. Magellan was killed by natives of the Philippine island of Mactan.

MORSE, SAMUEL FINLEY BREESE: BIRTH ANNIVERSARY. Apr 27, 1791. American artist and inventor, after whom the Morse code is named, was born at Charlestown, MA, and died at New York, NY, Apr 2, 1872. Graduating from Yale University in 1810, he went to the Royal Academy of London to study painting. After returning to America he achieved success as a portraitist. Morse conceived the idea of an electromagnetic telegraph while on shipboard, returning from art instruction in Europe in 1832, and he proceeded to develop his idea. With financial assistance approved by Congress, the first telegraph line in the US was constructed, between Washington, DC, and Baltimore, MD. The first message tapped out by Morse from the Supreme Court Chamber at the US Capitol building May 24, 1844, was: "What hath God wrought?"

SCHOOL PRINCIPALS' RECOGNITION DAY IN MASSACHUSETTS. Apr 27. Proclaimed annually by the governor.

SIERRA LEONE: INDEPENDENCE DAY. Apr 27. National Day. Commemorates independence from Britain in 1961.

SLOVENIA: INSURRECTION DAY. Apr 27. National holiday. Commemorates the founding of the resistance against Axis troops in 1941.

SOUTH AFRICA: FREEDOM DAY. Apr 27. National holiday. Commemorates the day in 1994 when, for the first time, all South Africans had the opportunity to vote.

TOGO: INDEPENDENCE DAY. Apr 27. National holiday. Gained independence from France in 1960.

YUGOSLAVIA: NATIONAL DAY: ANNIVERSARY. Apr 27.

BIRTHDAYS TODAY

John Burningham, 66, author (*Hey! Get Off Our Train; Cloudland*), born Farnham, Surrey, England, Apr 27, 1936.

Coretta Scott King, 75, lecturer, writer, widow of Dr. Martin Luther King, Jr, born Marion, AL, Apr 27, 1927.

Nancy Shaw, 56, author (*Sheep in a Jeep, Sheep in a Shop*), born Pittsburgh, PA, Apr 27, 1946.

APRIL 28 — SUNDAY

Day 118 — 247 Remaining

AFGHANISTAN: ISLAMIC STATE'S VICTORY DAY. Apr 28. National holiday. Commemorates the Mujaheddin capture of Kabul in 1992.

BIOLOGICAL CLOCK GENE DISCOVERED: ANNIVERSARY. Apr 28, 1994. Northwestern University announced that the so-called biological clock, that gene governing the daily cycle of waking and sleeping called the circadian rhythm, had been found in mice. Never before pinpointed in a mammal, the biological clock gene was found on mouse chromosome #5.

INTERNATIONAL READING ASSOCIATION ANNUAL CONVENTION. Apr 28–May 3. San Francisco, CA. 47th annual convention. For info: Intl Reading Assn, 800 Barksdale Rd, PO Box 8139, Newark, DE 19714-8139. Phone: (302) 731-1600. E-mail: conferences@reading.org. Web: www.reading.org.

MARYLAND RATIFIES CONSTITUTION: ANNIVERSARY. Apr 28, 1788. Maryland became the seventh state to ratify the Constitution, by a vote of 63 to 11.

MONROE, JAMES: BIRTH ANNIVERSARY. Apr 28, 1758. The fifth president of the US was born at Westmoreland County, VA, and served two terms in that office (Mar 4, 1817–Mar 3, 1825). Monrovia, the capital city of Liberia, is named after him, as is the Monroe Doctrine, which he enunciated at Washington, DC, Dec 2, 1823. Last of three presidents to die on US Independence Day, Monroe died at New York, NY, July 4, 1831. For info: www.ipl.org/ref/POTUS.

MOTHER, FATHER DEAF DAY. Apr 28. A day to honor deaf parents and recognize the gifts of culture and language they give to their hearing children. Annually, the last Sunday of April. Sponsored by Children of Deaf Adults International, Inc (CODA). For info: Trudy Schafer-Jeffers, CODA, PO Box 30715, Santa Barbara, CA, 93130-0715. Phone: (617) 789-3862 (TTY or Voice). Fax: (301) 572-4134.

MUTINY ON THE *BOUNTY*: ANNIVERSARY. Apr 28, 1789. The most famous of all naval mutinies occurred on board HMS *Bounty*. Captain of the *Bounty* was Lieutenant William Bligh, a mean-tempered disciplinarian. The ship, with a load of breadfruit tree plants from Tahiti, was bound for Jamaica. Fletcher Christian, leader of the mutiny, put Bligh and 18 of his loyal followers adrift in a 23-foot open boat. Miraculously Bligh and all of his supporters survived a 47-day voyage of more than 3,600 miles, before landing on the island of Timor, June 14, 1789. In the meantime, Christian had put all of the remaining crew (excepting eight men and himself) ashore at Tahiti where he picked up 18 Tahitians (six men and 12 women) and set sail again. Landing at Pitcairn Island in 1790 (probably uninhabited at the time), they burned the *Bounty* and remained undiscovered for 18 years, when an American whaler, the *Topaz*, called at the island (1808) and found only one member of the mutinous crew surviving. However, the little colony had thrived and, when counted by the British in 1856, numbered 194 persons.

NATIONAL PUPPETRY DAY. Apr 28. A day to celebrate the lively art of puppetry through performances, seminars, lectures and parades. Sponsored by Puppeteers of America, Inc. For info: Heather Loewenstein, 1820 McGee, Kansas City, MO 69108. E-mail: hlstoney@worldnet.att.net. Web: www.puppeteers.org.

ORTHODOX PALM SUNDAY. Apr 28. Celebration of Christ's entry into Jerusalem, when his way was covered with palms by the multitudes. Beginning of Holy Week in the Orthodox Church.

BIRTHDAYS TODAY

Lois Duncan, 68, author (*The Circus Comes Home, I Know What You Did Last Summer*), born Philadelphia, PA, Apr 28, 1934.

Amy Hest, 52, author (*In the Rain with Baby Duck, When Jessie Came Across the Sea*), born New York, NY, Apr 28, 1950.

Virginia Kroll, 54, author (*Beginnings: How Families Came to Be; Masai and I; Jaha and Jamil Went Down the Hill*), born Buffalo, NY, Apr 28, 1948.

Harper Lee, 76, author (*To Kill A Mockingbird*), 1961 Pulitzer Prize for fiction, born Monroeville, AL, Apr 28, 1926.

Jay Leno, 52, TV talk show host ("Tonight Show"), comedian, born New Rochelle, NY, Apr 28, 1950.

Catherine Reef, 51, writer of history and biography (*John Steinbeck*), born New York, NY, Apr 28, 1951.

Nate Richert, 24, actor ("Sabrina, the Teenage Witch"), born St. Paul, MN, Apr 28, 1978.

APRIL 29 — MONDAY

Day 119 — 246 Remaining

CONFEDERATE MEMORIAL DAY IN MISSISSIPPI. Apr 29. Annually, last Monday in April. Observed on other days in other states.

ELLINGTON, "DUKE" (EDWARD KENNEDY): BIRTH ANNIVERSARY. Apr 29, 1899. "Duke" Ellington, one of the most influential individuals in jazz history, was born at Washington, DC. By 1923 he was leading a small group of musicians at the Kentucky Club at New York City who became the core of his big band. Ellington is credited with being one of the founders of big band jazz. He used his band as an instrument for composition and orchestration to create big band pieces, film scores, operas, ballets, Broadway shows and religious music. Ellington was responsible for more than 1,000 musical pieces. He drew together instruments from different sections of the orchestra to develop unique and haunting sounds such as that of his famous "Mood Indigo." "Duke" Ellington died May 24, 1974, at New York City. For more info: *Duke Ellington: The Piano Prince and His Orchestra*, by Andrea Davis Pinkney (Hyperion, 0-7868-2150-7, $16.49 Gr. K–3).

ELLSWORTH, OLIVER: BIRTH ANNIVERSARY. Apr 29, 1745. Third chief justice of the US Supreme Court, born at Windsor, CT. Died there on Nov 26, 1807.

HIROHITO MICHI-NO-MIYA, EMPEROR: BIRTH ANNIVERSARY. Apr 29, 1901. Former Emperor of Japan, born at Tokyo. Hirohito's death Jan 27, 1989, ended the reign of the world's longest ruling monarch. He became the 124th in a line of monarchs when he ascended to the Chrysanthemum Throne in 1926. Hirohito presided over perhaps the most eventful years in the 2,500 years of recorded Japanese history, including the attempted military conquest of Asia, the attack on the US that brought that country into WWII, leading to Japan's ultimate defeat after the US dropped atomic bombs on Hiroshima and Nagasaki and the amazing economic restoration following the war that led Japan to a preeminent position of economic strength. Although he opposed initiating hostilities with the US, he signed a declaration of war, allowing Japan's militarist Prime Minister, Hideki Tojo, to begin the fateful campaign. During the war's final days he overruled Tojo and advocated surrender. Hirohito broadcast a taped message to the Japanese people to stop fighting and "endure the unendurable." This radio message was the first time the emperor's voice had ever been heard outside the imperial household and inner circle of government. After the war, Hirohito was allowed to remain on his throne. He denounced his divinity in 1946, bestowed upon him by Japanese law, and became a "symbol of the state" in Japan's new parliamentary democracy. Hirohito turned his energies to his real passion, marine biology, becoming a recognized world authority in the field.

JAPAN: GREENERY DAY. Apr 29. National holiday.

TAIWAN: CHENG CHENG KUNG LANDING DAY. Apr 29. Commemorates landing in Taiwan in 1661 of Ming Dynasty loyalist Cheng Cheng Kung (Koxinga), who ousted Dutch colonists who had occupied Taiwan for 37 years. Main ceremonies held at Tainan, in south Taiwan, where Dutch had their headquarters and where Cheng is buried. Cheng's birthday is also joyously celebrated, but according to the lunar calendar—on the 14th day of the seventh moon, Aug 22, 2002.

ZIPPER PATENTED: ANNIVERSARY. Apr 29, 1913. Gideon Sundbach of Hoboken, NJ, received a patent for the zipper.

BIRTHDAYS TODAY

Andre Kirk Agassi, 32, tennis player, born Las Vegas, NV, Apr 29, 1970.

Kate Mulgrew, 47, actress ("Star Trek: Voyager"), born Dubuque, IA, Apr 29, 1955.

Jill Paton Walsh, 65, author (*Fireweed*), born London, England, Apr 29, 1937.

Debbie Stabenow, 52, US Senator (D, Michigan), born Clare, MI, Apr 29, 1950.

April 2002

S	M	T	W	T	F	S
	1	2	3	4	5	6
7	8	9	10	11	12	13
14	15	16	17	18	19	20
21	22	23	24	25	26	27
28	29	30				

APRIL 30 — TUESDAY

Day 120 — 245 Remaining

DÍA DE LOS NIÑOS/DÍA DE LOS LIBROS. Apr 30. A celebration of children and bilingual literacy. Cosponsored by REFORMA: The National Association to Promote Library Services to the Spanish Speaking and MANA: A National Latina Organization. Annually, Apr 30. For info: Natl Assn for Bilingual Education, 1220 L St NW, Ste 605, Washington, DC 20005-4018. Phone: (202) 898-1829. Web: www.nabe.org.

FIRST PRESIDENTIAL TELECAST: ANNIVERSARY. Apr 30, 1939. Franklin D. Roosevelt was the first president to appear on television in a telecast from the New York World's Fair. However, since scheduled programming had yet to begin, he was beamed to only 200 TV sets in a 40-mile radius. See also: "Regular TV Broadcasts Begin: Anniversary" (July 1).

HARRISON, MARY SCOTT LORD DIMMICK: BIRTH ANNIVERSARY. Apr 30, 1858. Second wife of Benjamin Harrison, 23rd president of the US, born at Honesdale, PA. Died at New York, NY, Jan 5, 1948.

INTERNATIONAL SCHOOL SPIRIT SEASON. Apr 30–Sept 30. To recognize everyone who has helped to make school spirit better and to provide time to plan improved spirit ideas for the coming school year. For info: Jim Hawkins, Chairman, Pepsters, Committee for More School Spirit, PO Box 122652, San Diego, CA 92112. Phone: (619) 280-0999.

LAG B'OMER. Apr 30. Hebrew calendar date: Iyar 18, 5762. Literally, the 33rd day of the omer (harvest time), the 33rd day after the beginning of Passover. Traditionally a joyous day for weddings, picnics and outdoor activities.

LOUISIANA: ADMISSION DAY: ANNIVERSARY. Apr 30. Became 18th state in 1812.

NATIONAL HONESTY DAY (WITH HONEST ABE AWARDS). Apr 30. To celebrate honesty and those who are honest and honorable in their dealings with others. Nominations accepted for most honest people and companies. Winners to be awarded "Honest Abe" awards and given "Abies" on National Honesty Day. Annually, Apr 30. For info: M. Hirsh Goldberg, Author of *The Book of Lies*, 3103 Szold Dr, Baltimore, MD 21208. Phone: (410) 486-4150.

NETHERLANDS: QUEEN'S BIRTHDAY. Apr 30. A public holiday in celebration of the Queen's birthday and the Dutch National Day. The whole country parties as young and old participate in festivities such as markets, theater, music and games.

ORGANIZATION OF AMERICAN STATES FOUNDED: ANNIVERSARY. Apr 30, 1948. This regional alliance was founded by 21 nations of the Americas at Bogota, Colombia. Its purpose is to further economic development and integration among nations of the Western hemisphere, to promote representative democracy and to help overcome poverty. The Pan-American Union, with offices at Washington, DC, serves as the General Secretariat for the OAS. For more info: www.oas.org.

SPANK OUT DAY USA. Apr 30. A day on which all caretakers of children—parents, teachers and daycare workers—are asked not to use corporal punishment as discipline and to become aquainted with positive, effective disciplinary alternatives. For info: Nadine Block, EPOCH-USA, 155 W Main St, Ste 100-B, Columbus, OH 43215. Phone: (614) 221-8829. E-mail: nblock@infinet.com. Web: www.stophitting.com.

SWEDEN: FEAST OF VALBORG. Apr 30. An evening celebration in which Sweden "sings in the spring" by listening to traditional hymns to the spring, often around community bonfires. Also known as Walpurgis Night, the Feast of Valborg occurs annually, Apr 30.

THEATER IN NORTH AMERICA FIRST PERFORMANCE: ANNIVERSARY. Apr 30, 1598. On the banks of the Rio Grande, near present day El Paso, TX, the first North American theatrical performance was acted. The play was a Spanish comedia featuring an expedition of soldiers. On July 10 of the same year, the same group produced *Moros y Los Cristianos* (Moors and Christians), an anonymous play.

VIETNAM: LIBERATION DAY. Apr 30. National holiday. Commemorates the fall of Saigon in 1975, ending the Vietnam War.

WASHINGTON, GEORGE: PRESIDENTIAL INAUGURATION ANNIVERSARY. Apr 30, 1789. George Washington was inaugurated as the first president of the US under the new Constitution at New York, NY. Robert R. Livingston administered the oath of office to Washington on the balcony of Federal Hall, at the corner of Wall and Broad Streets.

BIRTHDAYS TODAY

Dorothy Hinshaw Patent, 62, author (*Bold and Bright Black-and-White Animals*), born Rochester, MN, Apr 30, 1940.

Isiah Thomas, 41, Basketball Hall of Famer, coach, born Chicago, IL, Apr 30, 1961.

MAY 1 — WEDNESDAY

Day 121 — 244 Remaining

★**ASIAN PACIFIC AMERICAN HERITAGE MONTH.** May 1–31. Presidential Proclamation issued honoring Asian Pacific Americans each year since 1979. Public Law 102-450 of Oct 28, 1992, designated the observance for the month of May each year.

FREEDOM SHRINE MONTH. May 1–31. To bring America's heritage of freedom to public attention through presentations or rededications of Freedom Shrine displays of historic American documents by Exchange Clubs. For info: The Natl Exchange Club, 3050 Central Ave, Toledo, OH 43606-1700. Phone: (419) 535-3232 or (800) 924-2643. Fax: (419) 535-1989. E-mail: nechq@aol.com. Web: www.nationalexchangeclub.com.

"FREEDOM RIDERS": ANNIVERSARY. May 1, 1961. Militant students joined James Farmer of the Congress of Racial Equality (CORE) to conduct "freedom rides" on public transportation from Washington, DC, across the deep South to New Orleans. The trips were intended to test Supreme Court decisions and Interstate Commerce Commission regulations prohibiting discrimination in interstate travel. In several places riders were brutally beaten by local people and policemen. The rides were patterned after a similar challenge to segregation, the 1947 Journey of Reconciliation, which tested the US Supreme Court's June 3, 1946, ban against segregation in interstate bus travel. For more info: *Freedom Rides: Journey for Justice*, by James Haskins (Hyperion, 0-7868-0048-8, $14.95 Gr. 6–8).

GET CAUGHT READING MONTH. May 1–31. Celebrities appear in ads appealing to young people to remind them of the joys of reading. For info: Assn of American Publishers, 71 Fifth Ave, New York, NY 10003. Phone: (212) 255-0200. Web: www.publishers.org.

GREAT BRITAIN FORMED: ANNIVERSARY. May 1, 1707. A union between England and Scotland resulted in the formation of Great Britain. (Wales had been part of England since the 1500s.) Today's United Kingdom consists of Great Britain and Northern Ireland.

May 2002

S	M	T	W	T	F	S
			1	2	3	4
5	6	7	8	9	10	11
12	13	14	15	16	17	18
19	20	21	22	23	24	25
26	27	28	29	30	31	

KEEP MASSACHUSETTS BEAUTIFUL MONTH. May 1–31. Proclaimed annually by the governor.

LABOR DAY. May 1. In 76 countries, May 1 is observed as a workers' holiday. When it falls on a Saturday or Sunday, the following Monday is observed as a holiday. Bermuda, Canada and the US are the only countries that observe Labor Day in September.

★**LAW DAY.** May 1. Presidential Proclamation issued each year for May 1 since 1958 at request. (PL87–20 of Apr 7, 1961.)

LAW ENFORCEMENT APPRECIATION MONTH IN FLORIDA. May 1–31. A ceremonial observance. May 15 is designated Law Enforcement Memorial Day.

LEI DAY. May 1. Hawaii. On this special day—the Hawaiian version of May Day—leis are made, worn, given, displayed and entered in lei-making contests. One of the most popular Lei Day celebrations takes place in Honolulu at Kapiolani Park at Waikiki. Includes the state's largest lei contest, the crowning of the Lei Day Queen, Hawaiian music, hula and flowers galore.

★**LOYALTY DAY.** May 1. Presidential Proclamation issued annually for May 1 since 1959 at request. (PL85–529 of July 18, 1958.) Note that an earlier proclamation was issued in 1955.

MARSHALL ISLANDS: CONSTITUTION DAY. May 1. National holiday.

MAY DAY. May 1. The first day of May has been observed as a holiday since ancient times. Spring festivals, maypoles and May baskets are still common, but the political importance of May Day has grown since the 1880s, when it became a workers' day. Now widely observed as a workers' holiday or as Labor Day. In most European countries, when May Day falls on Saturday or Sunday, the Monday following is observed as a holiday, with bank and store closings, parades and other festivities.

MOTHER GOOSE DAY. May 1. To re-appreciate the old nursery rhymes. Motto is "Either alone or in sharing, read childhood nursery favorites and feel the warmth of Mother Goose's embrace." Annually, May 1. For info: Gloria T. Delamar, Founder, Mother Goose Soc, 7303 Sharpless Rd, Melrose Park, PA 19027. Phone: (215) 782-1059. E-mail: Mother.Goose.Society@juno.com. Web: www.gbalc.org/MotherGooseSociety.

NATIONAL ALLERGY/ASTHMA AWARENESS MONTH. May 1–31. Kit of materials available for $15 from this nonprofit organization. For info: Frederick S. Mayer, Pres, Pharmacist Planning Services, Inc, c/o Allergy Council of America (ACA), 101 Lucas Valley Rd, #210, San Rafael, CA 94903. Phone: (415) 479-8628. Fax: (415) 479-8608. E-mail: ppsi@aol.com. Web: www.ppsinc.org.

NATIONAL BARBECUE MONTH. May 1–31. To encourage people to start enjoying barbecuing early in the season when Daylight Saving Time lengthens the day. Annually, the month of May. Sponsor: Barbecue Industry Association. For info: NBM, DHM Group, Inc, PO Box 767, Dept CC, Holmdel, NJ 07733-0767. Fax: (732) 946-3343.

NATIONAL BIKE MONTH. May 1–31. 45th annual celebration of bicycling for recreation and transportation. Local activities sponsored by bicycling organizations, environmental groups, PTAs, police departments, health organizations and civic groups. About five million participants nationwide. Annually, the month of May. For info: Donald Tighe, Program Dir, League of American Bicyclists, 1612 K St, Ste 401, Washington, DC 20006. Phone: (202) 822-1333. Fax: (202) 822-1334. E-mail: DWTLAW@aol.com. Web: www.bikeleague.org.

NATIONAL BOOK MONTH. May 1–31. When the world demands more and more of our time, National Book Month invites everyone in America to take time out to treat themselves to a unique pleasure: reading a good book. Readers participate in National Book Month annually through literary events held at schools, bookstores, libraries, community centers and arts organizations. The organization also sponsors the annual National Book Awards, which include an award for a children's book. For info: Natl Book Foundation, 260 Fifth Ave, Rm 904, New York, NY 10001. Phone: (212) 685-0261. Fax: (212) 235-6570. E-mail: NatBkFdn@mindspring.com. Web: www.nationalbook.org.

NATIONAL EGG MONTH. May 1–31. Dedicated to the versatility, convenience, economy and good nutrition of "the incredible edible egg." Annually, the month of May. For info: Linda Braun, Consumer Serv Dir, American Egg Board, 1460 Renaissance Dr, Park Ridge, IL 60068. E-mail: aeb@aeb.org. Web: www.aeb.org.

NATIONAL HAMBURGER MONTH. May 1–31. Sponsored by White Castle, the original fast-food hamburger chain, founded in 1921, to pay tribute to one of America's favorite foods. With or without condiments, on or off a bun or bread, hamburgers have grown in popularity since the early 1920s and are now an American meal mainstay. For info: White Castle System, Inc, Mktg Dept, 555 W Goodale St, Columbus, OH 43215-1171. Phone: (614) 228-5781. Fax: (614) 228-8841. Web: www.whitecastle.com.

NATIONAL HEPATITIS AWARENESS MONTH. May 1–31. For info: Hepatitis Foundation Intl, 30 Sunrise Terrace, Cedar Grove, NJ 07009. Phone: (800) 891-0707. E-mail: hfi@intac.com. Web: www.hepfi.org.

NATIONAL MENTAL HEALTH MONTH. May 1–31. For info: Natl Mental Health Assn, 1021 Prince St, Alexandria, VA 22314-2971. Phone: (800) 969-6642 or (703) 684-7722. E-mail: nmhainfo@aol.com. Web: www.nmha.org.

NATIONAL MOVING MONTH. May 1–31. Recognizing America's mobile roots and kicking off the busiest moving season of the year. Each year more than 21 million Americans move between Memorial Day and Labor Day, with the average American moving every seven years. During this month moving experts will be educating Americans on how to plan a successful move, to pack efficiently and handle the uncertainties and questions that moving children may have. For info: Allied Van Lines, PO Box 9569, Downers Grove, IL 60515. Phone: (630) 241-2538. Fax: (630) 241-4343. Web: www.alliedvan.com.

NATIONAL SALAD MONTH. May 1–31. Americans celebrate salads and their role in today's healthy lifestyle. Annually, the month of May. For info: The Assn for Dressings and Sauces, 5775 Peachtree-Dunwoody Rd, Ste 500-G, Atlanta, GA 30342. Phone: (404) 252-3663. Fax: (404) 252-0774. E-mail: ads@assnhq.com. Web: www.dressings-sauces.org.

NATIONAL SALSA MONTH. May 1–31. Recognizing salsa as America's favorite condiment, used more often than even ketchup as a topping, dip, marinade and to spice up countless recipes. National Salsa Month celebrates more than 50 years of picante sauce, a salsa created in 1947, and celebrates Cinco de Mayo, a Mexican holiday now recognized across North America. For info: Mary Uhlig, VP, Dublin & Assoc, 111 Soledad, Ste 1600, San Antonio, TX 78205. Phone: (210) 227-0221. Fax: (210) 226-7097. Web: www.pacefoods.com.

NATIONAL TEACHING AND JOY MONTH. May 1–31. A month of celebrating the joy of great teaching and great learning. Thank a teacher for creating an atmosphere of joy. Notice those students who demonstrate a love of learning. Call or write someone who helped you learn an important life skill. For info: Dr. Jim Scott, Jackson Community College, 2111 Emmons Rd, Jackson, MI 49201. Phone: (517) 796-8488. Fax: (517) 796-8631. E-mail: jim_scott@jackson.cc.mi.us and Bob Sornson, Dir of Special Education, Northville Public Schools, Northville, MI.

★**OLDER AMERICANS MONTH.** May 1–31. Presidential Proclamation; from 1963 through 1973 this was called "Senior Citizens Month." In May 1974 it became Older Americans Month. In 1980 the title included Senior Citizens Day, which was observed May 8, 1980. Always has been issued since 1963.

PEN-FRIENDS WEEK INTERNATIONAL. May 1–7. To encourage everyone to have one or more pen-friends not only in their own country but in other countries. For complete information on how to become a good pen-friend and information about how to write good letters, send $4 to cover expense of printing, handling and postage. Annually, May 1–7. For info: Dr. Stanley J. Drake, Pres, Intl Soc of Friendship and Good Will, 8592 Roswell Rd, Ste 434, Atlanta, GA 30350-1870.

PHILADELPHIA INTERNATIONAL CHILDREN'S FESTIVAL. May 1–5 (tentative). Philadelphia, PA. 18th annual festival of theater and film. In addition to eight theater pieces from around the world, there will be free outdoor performances by musicians, singers and jugglers and craft activities. Est attendance: 20,000. For info: The Annenberg School, University of Pennsylvania, 3620 Walnut St, Philadelphia, PA 19104. Phone: (215) 898-3900.

PROJECT ACES DAY. May 1. Fourteenth annual celebration of fitness when All Children Exercise Simultaneously. "The World's Largest Exercise Class" takes place the first Wednesday in May as schools in all 50 states and 50 different countries hold fitness classes, assemblies and other fitness education events involving millions of children, parents and teachers. Conducted in cooperation with the President's Council of Physical Fitness and Sports during National Physical Fitness and Sports Month. For info send SASE to: Dept C, Youth Fitness Coalition, PO Box 6452, Jersey City, NJ 07306-0452. Phone: (201) 433-8993. E-mail: yfcprojectaces@excite.com. Web: www.projectaces.com.

RUSSIA: INTERNATIONAL LABOR DAY. May 1–2. Public holiday in Russian Federation. "Official May Day demonstrations of working people."

SAVE THE RHINO DAY. May 1. May day! May day! Rhinos still in danger! Help save the world's remaining rhinos on the verge of extinction! Get involved with local, national and international conservation efforts to stop the senseless slaughter of these gentle pachyderms. Call your local zoo or write Really, Rhinos! for a $5 information packet. For info: Judyth Lessee, Founder, Really, Rhinos!, PO Box 40503, Tucson, AZ 85717-0503. Phone: (520) 327-9048. E-mail: rinophyl@rtd.com.

SCHOOL PRINCIPALS' DAY. May 1. A day of recognition for all elementary, middle and high school principals for their leadership and dedication to providing the best education possible for their students. Annually, May 1. For info: Janet Dellaria, 202 Bennett St, Geneva, IL 60134. Phone: (630) 232-0425.

VEGETARIAN RESOURCE GROUP'S ESSAY CONTEST FOR KIDS. May 1. Children ages 18 and under are encouraged to submit a two–three-page essay on topics related to vegetarianism. Essays accepted up to May 1. Winners announced Sept 15 and will receive a $50 savings bond. For info: The Vegetarian Resource Group, PO Box 1463, Baltimore, MD 21203. Phone: (410) 366-8343. Fax: (410) 366-8804. E-mail: vrg@vrg.org. Web: www.vrg.org.

WILLIAMS, ARCHIE: BIRTH ANNIVERSARY. May 1, 1915. Archie Williams, along with Jesse Owens and others, debunked Hitler's theory of the superiority of Aryan athletes at the 1936 Berlin Olympics. As a black member of the US team, Williams won a gold medal by running the 400-meter in 46.5 seconds (.4 second slower than his own record of earlier that year). Williams, who was born at Oakland, CA, earned a degree in mechanical engineering from the University of California–Berkeley in 1939 but had to dig ditches for a time because they weren't hiring black engineers. In time Williams became an airplane pilot and for 22 years he trained Tuskegee Institute pilots including the black air corps of WWII. He joined the Army Air Corps in 1942. When asked during a 1981 interview about his treatment by the Nazis during the 1936 Olympics, he replied, "Well, over there at least we didn't have to ride in the back of the bus." Archie Williams died June 24, 1993, at Fairfax, CA.

BIRTHDAYS TODAY

Daniel Kirk, 50, author, illustrator (*Bigger, Breakfast at the Liberty Diner*), born Elyria, OH, May 1, 1952.
Curtis Martin, 29, football player, born Pittsburgh, PA, May 1, 1973.
Elizabeth Marie Pope, 85, author (*The Perilous Gard*), born Washington, DC, May 1, 1917.

MAY 2 — THURSDAY

Day 122 — 243 Remaining

KING JAMES BIBLE PUBLISHED: ANNIVERSARY. May 2, 1611. King James I had appointed a committee of learned men to produce a new translation of the Bible in English which was published this day. This version, popularly called the King James Version, is known in England as the Authorized Version.

LEONARDO DA VINCI: DEATH ANNIVERSARY. May 2, 1519. Italian artist, scientist and inventor. Painter of the famed *Last Supper*, perhaps the first painting of the High Renaissance, and of the *Mona Lisa*. Inventor of the first parachute. Born at Vinci, Italy, in 1452 (exact date unknown), he died at Amboise, France. For more info: *Leonardo Da Vinci*, by Diane Stanley (Morrow, 0-688-10438-X, $15.93 Gr. K–3) or www.mos.org/sln/Leonardo/LeoHomePage.html.

★ **NATIONAL DAY OF PRAYER.** May 2. Presidential Proclamation always issued for the first Thursday in May since 1981. (PL100–307 of May 5, 1988.) From 1957 to 1981, a day in October was designated, except in 1972 and 1975 through 1977.

ROBERT'S RULES DAY. May 2, 1837. Anniversary of the birth of Henry M. Robert (General, US Army), author of *Robert's Rules of Order*, a standard parliamentary guide. Born at Robertville, SC, he died at Hornell, NY, May 11, 1923.

May 2002

S	M	T	W	T	F	S
			1	2	3	4
5	6	7	8	9	10	11
12	13	14	15	16	17	18
19	20	21	22	23	24	25
26	27	28	29	30	31	

SPACE DAY. May 2 (tentative). Previous Space Days have included a live broadcast over the Web in which astronauts and scientists answered questions from kids worldwide; a live satellite broadcast about space exploration, and local events in schools and communities. The Space Day website contains lesson plans for teachers and games and puzzles for kids. For info: www.spaceday.com.

SPOCK, BENJAMIN: BIRTH ANNIVERSARY. May 2, 1903. Pediatrician and author, born at New Haven, CT. His book on child-rearing, *Common Sense Book of Baby and Child Care* later called *Baby and Child Care*, has sold more than 30 million copies. In 1955 he became professor of child development at Western Reserve University at Cleveland, OH. He resigned from this position in 1967 to devote his time to the pacifism movement. Spock died at San Diego, CA, Mar 15, 1998.

WHALE AWARENESS DAY IN MASSACHUSETTS. May 2. Proclaimed annually by the governor for the first Thursday in May.

BIRTHDAYS TODAY

Scott McCallum, 52, Governor of Wisconsin (R), born Fond du Lac, WI, May 2, 1950.
Jenna Von Oy, 25, actress (voice on "Pepper Ann," "Blossom"), born Newtown, CT, May 2, 1977.

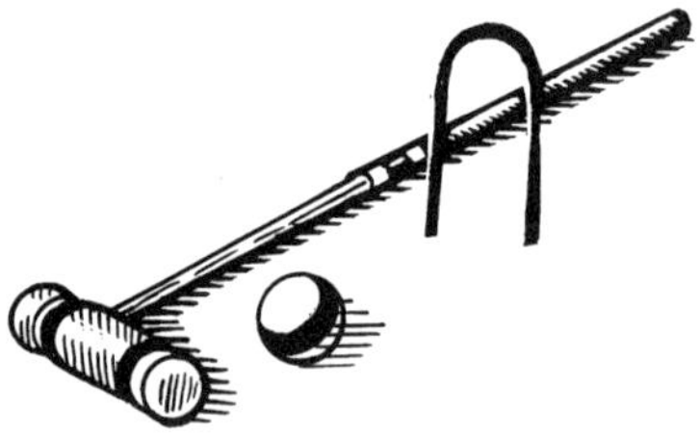

MAY 3 — FRIDAY

Day 123 — 242 Remaining

"CBS EVENING NEWS" TV PREMIERE: ANNIVERSARY. May 3, 1948. This news program began as a 15-minute telecast with Douglas Edwards as anchor. Walter Cronkite succeeded him in 1962 and expanded the show to 30 minutes; Eric Sevareid served as commentator. Dan Rather anchored the newscasts upon Cronkite's retirement in 1981. At one point, to boost sagging ratings, Connie Chung was added to the newscast as Rather's coanchor, but she left in 1995 in a well-publicized dispute. Rather remains solo, and, as Cronkite would say, "And that's the way it is. . ."

INTERNATIONAL TUBA DAY. May 3. To recognize tubists in musical organizations around the world who have to go through the hassle of handling a tuba in order to make beautiful music. Annually, the first Friday in May. Est attendance: 300. For info: Dr. Sy Brandon, Music Dept, Millersville Univ, PO Box 1002, Millersville, PA 17551-0302. Phone: (717) 872-3439. Fax: (717) 871-2304. E-mail: sbrandon@marander.millersv.edu.

JAPAN: CONSTITUTION MEMORIAL DAY. May 3. National holiday commemorating constitution of 1947.

MEXICO: DAY OF THE HOLY CROSS. May 3. Celebrated especially by construction workers and miners, a festive day during which anyone who is building must give a party for the workers. A flower-decorated cross is placed on every piece of new construction in the country.

NATIONAL PUBLIC RADIO FIRST BROADCAST: ANNIVERSARY. May 3, 1971. National noncommercial radio network, financed by Corporation for Public Broadcasting, began programming.

POLAND: CONSTITUTION DAY (SWIETO TRZECIEGO MAJO). May 3. National Day. Celebrates ratification of Poland's first constitution, 1791.

UNITED NATIONS: WORLD PRESS FREEDOM DAY. May 3. A day to recognize that a free, pluralistic and independent press is an essential component of any democratic society and to promote press freedom in the world.

BIRTHDAYS TODAY

Michael Cadnum, 53, author (*Heat, The Book of the Lion*), born Orange, CA, May 3, 1949.

Mavis Jukes, 55, author (*Like Jake and Me*), born Nyack, NY, May 3, 1947.

Pete Seeger, 83, folksinger, author (*Abiyoyo*), born New York, NY, May 3, 1919.

Ron Wyden, 53, US Senator (D, Oregon), born Wichita, KS, May 3, 1949.

MAY 4 — SATURDAY

Day 124 — 241 Remaining

CHINA: YOUTH DAY. May 4. Annual public holiday "recalls the demonstration on May 4, 1919, by thousands of patriotic students in Beijing's Tiananmen Square to protest imperialist aggression in China."

CURAÇAO: MEMORIAL DAY. May 4. Victims of WWII are honored on this day. Military ceremonies at the War Monument. Not an official public holiday.

DISCOVERY OF JAMAICA BY CHRISTOPHER COLUMBUS: ANNIVERSARY. May 4, 1494. Christopher Columbus discovered Jamaica. The Arawak Indians were its first inhabitants.

FEMINIST BOOKSTORE WEEK. May 4–12. Visit your favorite feminist bookstore for author signings and other special events. Annually, the weekend before Mother's Day through Mother's Day. For info: Feminist Bookstore News, PO Box 882554, San Francisco, CA 94188. Phone: (415) 642-9993. Fax: (415) 642-9995. E-mail: carol@FemBkNews.com.

JAPAN: GOLDEN WEEK HOLIDAY. May 4. National holiday.

MALTA: CARNIVAL. May 4–5. Valletta. Festival dates from 1535 when Knights of St. John introduced Carnival at Malta. Dancing, bands, decorated trucks and grotesque masks. Annually, the first weekend after May 1.

MANN, HORACE: BIRTH ANNIVERSARY. May 4, 1796. American educator, author, public servant, known as the "father of public education in the US," was born at Franklin, MA. Founder of Westfield (MA) State College, president of Antioch College and editor of the influential *Common School Journal*. Mann died at Yellow Springs, OH, Aug 2, 1859.

MOON PHASE: LAST QUARTER. May 4. Moon enters Last Quarter phase at 3:16 AM, EDT.

NATIONAL WEATHER OBSERVER'S DAY. May 4. For those people, amateurs and professionals alike, who love to follow the everyday phenomenon known as weather. Annually, May 4. For info: Alan W. Brue, 1317 London Way, Litha Springs, GA 30122. E-mail: afn05660@afn.org. *See* Curriculum Connection.

SCHOOL-TO-WORK LAUNCHED: ANNIVERSARY. May 4, 1994. President Clinton signed the School-to-Work Opportuni-

MAY 4
NATIONAL WEATHER OBSERVER'S DAY

Today is a good day to go outdoors and take a serious look at the weather. There are a number of ways to incorporate observing the weather into various areas of school curricula. Since the actual date is a Saturday, classroom activities will have to take place on the day before. A short weekend assignment for Saturday can be one that includes family or friends from outside the classroom.

On Friday, go outside for five to ten minutes, depending on the age of the students. Emphasize how accurately scientists must make observations. Have students list as many words as they can to describe the weather. Ask them to notice air temperature relative to that of the classroom. Bring a thermometer with you and take the actual temperature. Take it twice: once in the sun and again in the shade. Notice cloud patterns, if any, and the color of the sky. Is there any wind? If so, describe it. If it's raining, students may need to look out the window. Have a small can or bottle handy to collect raindrops for a specific period of time.

These observations can be carried out for a second time, as a homework assignment on Saturday. Now, the students will be experts, so they can be the teachers who direct family members and friends in carrying out the exercise. On Monday, let each student make a quick list of descriptive words found in his or her weekend observations. Share them in class during language arts as a mini lesson on word choice and writing to create vivid images.

Some weather words—contrail, rainbow, and dog days, for example— are unusual. Another way to incorporate them into language arts is by letting children write a short paragraph to define what they think one of the words may mean. Later, let them use the dictionary to look up the technical definition. Some children may wish to write a short poem based on their weather observations. Others may wish to draw a picture that shows their favorite kind of weather.

In math, older students can create math problems using the temperature recordings they have observed. Convert Fahrenheit temperatures to Celsius. Create a subtraction or addition problem to discover how many degrees warmer or colder the outside air is compared to the classroom's temperature and the temperature recorded in the sun versus that from the shade.

A longer lesson might introduce line graphs. To do this, students would have to use newspaper archives or the Internet. Let them compare and graph recorded temperatures for January 4th, February 4th, March 4th, April 4th and May 4th. List the five months on the horizontal X axis and a suitable temperature range on the Y axis. How much has the temperature changed during the five months?

Measure how much rain you collected in the can. Calculate the volume of the can and the volume of raindrops collected and the rate at which they fell. Then calculate how much rain (at the same rate) would fall in 10 hours, 24 hours, etc.

Some useful books include: *Weather Sky*, by Bruce McMillan (Farrar, Straus and Giroux, 0-374-38261-1, $16.95 Gr. 3–7); *I Call It Sky*, by Will C. Howell (Walker, 0-8027-8677-4, $15.95 Gr. K–3); *Hurricanes: Earth's Mightiest Storms*, by Patricia Lauber (Scholastic, 0-590-47406-5, $16.95 Gr. 3 & up); *Tornadoes*, by Seymour Simon (Morrow, 0-688-14846-5, $16 Gr. 2–7); *Weather Forecasting*, by Gail Gibbons (Simon & Schuster, 0-689-71683-4, $5.99 Gr. K–3); and *Weather Words and What They Mean*, also by Gibbons (Holiday House, 0-8234-0952-X, $6.95 Gr. K–3).

ties Act. It provides seed money to states and local partnerships to develop school-to-work systems of education reform, worker preparation and economic development to prepare youth for the high-wage, high-skill careers of the global economy. For info: Natl School-to-Work Learning & Information Center, 400 Virginia Ave, Rm 150, Washington, DC 20024. Phone: (800) 251-7236. Fax: (202) 401-6211. E-mail: stw-lc@ed.gov. Web: stw.ed.gov/general/general.htm.

SPACE MILESTONE: *ATLANTIS* (US). May 4, 1989. First American planetary expedition in 11 years. Space shuttle *Atlantis* was launched, its major objective to deploy the *Magellan* spacecraft on its way to Venus to map the planet's surface. The shuttle was on its 65th orbit when it landed May 8, mission accomplished.

TYLER, JULIA GARDINER: BIRTH ANNIVERSARY. May 4, 1820. Second wife of John Tyler, 10th president of the US, born at Gardiners Island, NY. Died at Richmond, VA, July 10, 1889.

BIRTHDAYS TODAY

Lance Bass, 23, musician ('N Sync), born Laurel, MS, May 4, 1979.

Ben Grieve, 26, baseball player, 1998 American League Rookie of the Year, born Arlington, TX, May 4, 1976.

Dawn Staley, 32, basketball player, born Philadelphia, PA, May 4, 1970.

Don Wood, 57, illustrator (*King Bidgood's in the Bathtub*), born Atwater, CA, May 4, 1945.

MAY 5 — SUNDAY

Day 125 — 240 Remaining

BASEBALL'S FIRST PERFECT GAME: ANNIVERSARY. May 5, 1904. Denton T. "Cy" Young pitched baseball's first perfect game, not allowing a single opposing player to reach first base. Young's outstanding performance led the Boston Americans in a 3–0 victory over Philadelphia in the American League. The Cy Young Award for pitching was named in his honor.

BE KIND TO ANIMALS WEEK®. May 5–11. To promote kindness and humane care toward animals. Annually, the first full week of May. Features "Be Kind to Animals Kid Contest." For info: Joyce Briggs, American Humane Assn, 63 Inverness Dr E, Englewood, CO 80112. Phone: (800) 227-4645 or (303) 792-9900. Fax: (303) 792-5333. E-mail: joyceb@americanhumane.org. Web: www.americanhumane.org.

BLY, NELLIE: BIRTH ANNIVERSARY. May 5, 1867. Born at Cochran's Mills, PA, Nellie Bly was the pseudonym used by pioneering American journalist Elizabeth Cochrane Seaman. Like her namesake in a Stephen Foster song, Nellie Bly was a social reformer and human rights advocate. As a journalist, she is best known for her exposé of conditions in what were then known as "insane asylums," where she posed as an "inmate." As an adventurer, she is best known for her 1889–90 tour around-the-world in 72 days, in which she bettered the time of Jules Verne's fictional character Phileas Fogg by eight days. She died at New York, NY, Jan 27, 1922. For more info: www.pbs.org/wgbh/amex/world.

BONZA BOTTLER DAY™. May 5. To celebrate when the number of the day is the same as the number of the month. Bonza Bottler Day™ is an excuse to have a party at least once a month.

May 2002

S	M	T	W	T	F	S
			1	2	3	4
5	6	7	8	9	10	11
12	13	14	15	16	17	18
19	20	21	22	23	24	25
26	27	28	29	30	31	

For info: Gail M. Berger, 109 Matthew Ave, Poca, WV 25159. Phone: (304) 776-7746. E-mail: gberger5@aol.com.

ETHIOPIA: PATRIOTS VICTORY DAY. May 5. National holiday. Commemorates the 1941 liberation of Addis Ababa.

HALFWAY POINT OF SPRING. May 5. On this date at 11:50 AM, EDT, 46 days, 21 hours and 34 minutes of spring will have elapsed, and the equivalent will remain before June 21, which is the summer solstice and the beginning of summer.

JAPAN: CHILDREN'S DAY. May 5. National holiday. Observed on the fifth day of the fifth month each year. For more info: *Japanese Children's Day and the Oban Festival*, by Dianne M. MacMillan (Enslow, 0-8949-0818-9, $18.95 Gr. PreK–3).

KOREA: CHILDREN'S DAY. May 5. A time for families to take their children on excursions. Parks and children's centers throughout the country are packed with excited and colorfully dressed children. A national holiday since 1975.

LIONNI, LEO: BIRTH ANNIVERSARY. May 5, 1910. Author and illustrator, born at Amsterdam, Netherlands. Lionni wrote his first children's book *Little Blue and Little Yellow* in 1959. He wrote and illustrated more than 30 children's books including *Frederick* and *Swimmy*. He died at Chianti, Italy, Oct 11, 1999.

MEXICO: CINCO DE MAYO. May 5. Mexican national holiday recognizing the anniversary of the Battle of Puebla, May 5, 1862, in which Mexican troops under General Ignacio Zaragoza, outnumbered three to one, defeated invading French forces of Napoleon III. Anniversary is observed by Mexicans everywhere with parades, festivals, dances and speeches.

NATIONAL FAMILY WEEK. May 5–11. Traditionally the first Sunday and the first full week in May are observed as National Family Week in many Christian churches.

NATIONAL PET WEEK. May 5–11. To promote public awareness of veterinary medical service for animal health and care. Annually, the first full week in May. For info: The American Veterinary Medical Assn, 1931 N Meacham Rd, Schaumburg, IL 60173. Phone: (847) 925-8070. Fax: (847) 925-1329. Web: www.avma.org.

NATIONAL PTA TEACHER APPRECIATION WEEK. May 5–11. PTAs across the country conduct activities to strengthen respect and support for teachers and the teaching profession. Annually, the first full week in May. For info: Natl PTA, 330 N Wabash Ave, Ste 2100, Chicago, IL 60611. Phone: (312) 670-6782. Fax: (312) 670-6783. E-mail: info@pta.org. Web: www.pta.org/programs/tchappwk.htm.

NATIONAL TOURISM WEEK. May 5–11. To promote and enhance awareness of travel and tourism's importance to the economic, social and cultural well-being of the US. Annually, beginning the first Sunday in May. For info: Travel Industry Assn of America, 1100 New York Ave NW, Ste 450, Washington, DC 20005-3934. Phone: (202) 408-8422. E-mail: ckeefe@tia.org. Web: www.tia.org.

NETHERLANDS: LIBERATION DAY. May 5. National holiday. Marks liberation of the Netherlands from Nazi Germany in 1945.

ORTHODOX EASTER SUNDAY OR PASCHA. May 5. Observed by Eastern Orthodox Churches. See also: "Easter Sunday" (Mar 31).

RURAL LIFE SUNDAY OR SOIL STEWARDSHIP SUNDAY. May 5. With an increase in ecological and environmental concerns, Rural Life Sunday emphasizes the concept that Earth belongs to God, who has granted humanity the use of it, along with the responsibility of caring for it wisely. Rural Life Sunday was first observed in 1929. The day is observed annually by churches of many Christian denominations and includes pulpit exchanges by rural and urban pastors. Under the auspices of the National Association of Soil and Water Conservation Districts, the week beginning with Rural Life Sunday is now widely observed as Soil Stewardship Week, with the Sunday itself alternatively termed Soil Stewardship Sunday. Traditionally, Rural Life Sunday is Rogation Sunday, the Sunday preceding Ascension Day.

SPACE MILESTONE: *FREEDOM 7* (US): ANNIVERSARY. May 5, 1961. First US astronaut in space, second man in space, Alan Shepard, Jr, projected 115 miles into space in suborbital flight reaching a speed of more than 5,000 mph. This was the first piloted Mercury mission.

THAILAND: CORONATION DAY. May 5. Thailand.

BIRTHDAYS TODAY

Danielle Fishel, 21, actress ("Boy Meets World"), born Mesa, AZ, May 5, 1981.

MAY 6 — MONDAY

Day 126 — 239 Remaining

★ **NATIONAL CHARTER SCHOOLS WEEK.** May 6–10 (tentative). President Clinton declared this for the first time in 2000. It may be just a one-time declaration.

PEARY, ROBERT E.: BIRTH ANNIVERSARY. May 6, 1856. Born at Cresson, PA. Peary served as a cartographic draftsman in the US Coast and Geodetic Survey for two years, then joined the US Navy's Corps of Civil Engineers in 1881. He first worked as an explorer in tropical climates as he served as subchief of the Inter-Ocean Canal Survey in Nicaragua. After reading of the inland ice of Greenland, Peary became attracted to the Arctic. He organized and led eight Arctic expeditions and is credited with the verification of Greenland's island formation, proving that the polar ice cap extended beyond 82° north latitude, and the discovery of the Melville meteorite on Melville Bay, in addition to his famous discovery of the North Pole, Apr 6, 1909. Peary died Feb 20, 1920, at Washington, DC.

PENN, JOHN: BIRTH ANNIVERSARY. May 6, 1740. Signer of the Declaration of Independence, born at Caroline County, VA. Died Sept 14, 1788.

PUBLIC SERVICE RECOGNITION WEEK. May 6–12. Take this opportunity to thank the "Unsung Heroes and Heroines" of the public work force who perform a range of vital services. Public employees are scientists and police officers, teachers and doctors, astronauts and zoologists, engineers and food inspectors, forest rangers and claims representatives, researchers and foreign service agents. Free resource materials to promote the celebration available. Annually, the first Monday–Sunday in May. For info: Nick Nolan, Exec Dir, Public Employees Roundtable, PO Box 44801, Washington, DC 20026-4801. Phone: (202) 401-4344. E-mail: permail@patriot.net. Web: www.theroundtable.org.

SWITZERLAND: PACING THE BOUNDS. May 6. Liestal. Citizens set off at 8 AM and march along boundaries to the beating of drums and firing of pistols and muskets. Occasion for fetes. Annually, the Monday before Ascension Day.

BIRTHDAYS TODAY

Tony Blair, 49, British prime minister, born Edinburgh, Scotland, May 6, 1953.

George Clooney, 41, actor ("ER," *Batman and Robin*), born Augusta, KY, May 6, 1961.

Kristine O'Connell George, 48, author (*The Great Frog Race: And Other Poems*), born Denver, CO, May 6, 1954.

Ted Lewin, 67, author and illustrator (*The Storytellers*), born Buffalo, NY, May 6, 1935.

Willie Mays, 71, Baseball Hall of Fame outfielder, born Westfield, AL, May 6, 1931.

Barbara McClintock, 47, author and illustrator (*The Fantastic Drawings of Danielle*), born Flemington, NJ, May 6, 1955.

Richard C. Shelby, 68, US Senator (D, Alabama), born Birmingham, AL, May 6, 1934.

MAY 7 — TUESDAY

Day 127 — 238 Remaining

BARRIER AWARENESS DAY IN KENTUCKY. May 7.

BEAUFORT SCALE DAY: (FRANCIS BEAUFORT BIRTH ANNIVERSARY). May 7, 1774. A day to honor the British naval officer, Sir Francis Beaufort, who devised in 1805 a scale of wind force from 0 (calm) to 12 (hurricane) that was based on observation, not requiring any special instruments. The scale was adopted for international use in 1874 and has since been enlarged and refined. Beaufort was born at Flower Hill, Meath, Ireland, and died at Brighton, England, Dec 17, 1857.

BEETHOVEN'S *NINTH SYMPHONY* PREMIERE: ANNIVERSARY. May 7, 1824. Beethoven's *Ninth Symphony in D Minor* was performed for the first time at Vienna, Austria. Known as the *Choral* because of his use of voices in symphonic form for the first time, the Ninth was his musical interpretation of Schiller's *Ode to Joy*. Beethoven was completely deaf when he composed it, and it was said a soloist had to tug on his sleeve when the performance was over to get him to turn around and see the enthusiastic response he could not hear.

BROWNING, ROBERT: BIRTH ANNIVERSARY. May 7, 1812. English poet and husband of poet Elizabeth Barrett Browning, born at Camberwell, near London. Known for his dramatic monologues. Died at Venice, Italy, Dec 12, 1889.

CHILDHOOD DEPRESSION AWARENESS DAY. May 7. Also known as Green Ribbon Day. Annually, the first Tuesday in the first full week in May. For info: Natl Mental Heath Assn, 1021 Prince St, Alexandria, VA 22314-2971. Phone: (800) 969-6642 or (703) 684-7722. Web: www.nmha.org.

DIEN BIEN PHU FALLS: ANNIVERSARY. May 7, 1954. Vietnam's victory over France at Dien Bien Phu ended the Indochina War. This battle is considered one of the greatest victories won by a former colony over a colonial power.

EL SALVADOR: DAY OF THE SOLDIER. May 7. National holiday. Commemorates the founding of the armed forces in 1824.

GERMANY'S FIRST SURRENDER: ANNIVERSARY. May 7, 1945. Russian, American, British and French ranking officers crowded into a second-floor recreation room of a small redbrick schoolhouse (which served as Eisenhower's headquarters) at Reims, Germany. Representing Germany, Field Marshall Alfred Jodl signed an unconditional surrender of all German fighting forces. After a signing that took almost 40 minutes, Jodl was ushered into Eisenhower's presence. The American general asked the German if he fully understood what he had signed and informed Jodl that he would be held personally responsible for any deviation from the terms of the surrender, including the requirement that German commanders sign a formal surrender to the USSR at a time and place determined by that government.

NATIONAL TEACHER DAY. May 7. To pay tribute to American educators, sponsored by the National Education Association, Teacher Day falls during the National PTA's Teacher Appreciation Week. Local communities and organizations are encouraged to use this opportunity to honor those who influence and inspire the next generation through their work. Annually, the Tuesday of the first full week in May. For info: Natl Education Assn (NEA), 1201 16th St NW, Washington, DC 20036. Phone: (202) 833-4000. Web: www.nea.org.

TCHAIKOVSKY, PETER ILICH: BIRTH ANNIVERSARY. May 7, 1840. Ranked among the outstanding composers of all time, Peter Ilich Tchaikovsky was born at Vatkinsk, Russia. His musical talent was not encouraged and he embarked upon a career in law, not studying music seriously until 1861. Among his famous works are the three-act ballet *Sleeping Beauty*, two-act ballet *The Nutcracker* and the symphony *Pathetique*. Mystery surrounds Tchaikovsky's death. It was believed he'd caught cholera from contaminated water, but 20th-century scholars believe he probably committed suicide to avoid his homosexuality being revealed. He died at St. Petersburg, Nov 6, 1893.

BIRTHDAYS TODAY

Pete V. Domenici, 70, US Senator (R, New Mexico), born Albuquerque, NM, May 7, 1932.

Nonny Hogrogian, 70, author and illustrator (Caldecott for *One Fine Day*), born New York, NY, May 7, 1932.

May 2002

S	M	T	W	T	F	S
			1	2	3	4
5	6	7	8	9	10	11
12	13	14	15	16	17	18
19	20	21	22	23	24	25
26	27	28	29	30	31	

MAY 8 — WEDNESDAY

Day 128 — 237 Remaining

CZECH REPUBLIC: LIBERATION DAY. May 8. Commemorates the liberation of Czechoslovakia from the Germans in 1945.

THE DAY OF THE TEACHER (EL DIA DEL MAESTRO). May 8. California honors its teachers every year on the Day of the Teacher. Patterned after "El Dia Del Maestro" celebrated in Mexico, the Day of the Teacher was originated by the Association of Mexican-American Educators and the California Teachers Association and designated by the California legislature. A tribute to all teachers and their lasting influence on children's lives. Annually, the second Wednesday of May. For info: California Teachers Assn, PO Box 921, Burlingame, CA 94010. Phone: (650) 697-1400. Fax: (650) 697-0786. Web: www.cta.org.

DUNANT, JEAN HENRI: BIRTH ANNIVERSARY. May 8, 1828. Author and philanthropist, founder of the Red Cross Society, was born at Geneva, Switzerland. Nobel prize winner in 1901. Died at Heiden, Switzerland, Oct 30, 1910.

FRANCE: ARMISTICE DAY. May 8. Commemorates the surrender of Germany to Allied forces and the cessation of hostilities in 1945.

GERMANY'S SECOND SURRENDER: ANNIVERSARY. May 8, 1945. Stalin refused to recognize the document of unconditional surrender signed at Reims the previous day, so a second signing was held at Berlin. The event was turned into an elaborate formal ceremony by the Soviets who had lost some 20 million lives during the war. As in the Reims document, the end of hostilities was set for 12:01 AM local time on May 9.

LAVOISIER, ANTOINE LAURENT: EXECUTION ANNIVERSARY. May 8, 1794. French chemist and the "father of modern chemistry." Especially noted for having first explained the real nature of combustion and for showing that matter is not destroyed in chemical reactions. Born at Paris, France, Aug 26, 1743, Lavoisier was guillotined at the Place de la Revolution for his former position as a tax collector. The Revolutionary Tribunal is reported to have responded to a plea to spare his life with the statement: "We need no more scientists in France."

NO SOCKS DAY. May 8. If we give up wearing socks for one day, it will mean a little less laundry, thereby contributing to the betterment of the environment. Besides, we will all feel a bit freer, at least for one day. Annually, May 8. [© 1999 by WH] For info: Thomas and Ruth Roy, Wellcat Holidays, 2418 Long Ln, Lebanon, PA 17046. Phone: (230) 332-4886. E-mail: wellcat@supernet.com. Web: www.wellcat.com.

SLOVAKIA: LIBERATION DAY. May 8. Commemorates the liberation of Czechoslovakia from the Germans in 1945.

TRUMAN, HARRY S: BIRTH ANNIVERSARY. May 8, 1884. The 33rd president of the US, succeeded to that office upon the death of Franklin D. Roosevelt, Apr 12, 1945, and served until Jan 20, 1953. Born at Lamar, MO, Truman was the last of nine US presidents who did not attend college. Affectionately nicknamed "Give 'em Hell Harry" by admirers. Truman died at Kansas City, MO, Dec 26, 1972. His birthday is a holiday in Missouri. For info: www.ipl.org/ref/POTUS.

V-E DAY: ANNIVERSARY. May 8, 1945. Victory in Europe Day commemorates the unconditional surrender of Germany to Allied Forces. The surrender document was signed by German representatives at General Dwight D. Eisenhower's headquarters at Reims to become effective, and hostilities to end, at one minute past midnight on May 9, 1945, which was 9:01 PM, EDT, on May 8 in the US. President Harry S Truman on May 8 declared May 9,

1945, to be "V-E Day," but it later came to be observed on May 8 in the US. A separate German surrender to the USSR was signed at Karlshorst, near Berlin, May 8. See also: "Russia: Victory Day: Anniversary" (May 9).

WORLD RED CROSS DAY. May 8. A day for commemorating the birth of Jean Henry Dunant, the Swiss founder of the International Red Cross Movement in 1863, and for recognizing the humanitarian work of the Red Cross around the world. For info on activities in your area, contact your local Red Cross chapter. For info: Darren Irby, Media Associate, American Red Cross Natl Headquarters, 1621 N Kent St, Arlington, VA 22209. Phone: (703) 248-4219. Fax: (703) 248-4256.

BIRTHDAYS TODAY

Peter Benchley, 62, author (*Jaws*), born New York, NY, May 8, 1940.

Peter Connolly, 67, author (*The Ancient City: Life in Classical Athens & Rome*), born Surrey, England, May 8, 1935.

Milton Meltzer, 87, author (*Langston Hughes: A Biography; Brother, Can You Spare a Dime: The Great Depression*), born Worcester, MA, May 8, 1915.

MAY 9 — THURSDAY

Day 129 — 236 Remaining

ASCENSION DAY. May 9. Commemorates Christ's ascension into heaven. Observed since AD 68. Ascension Day is the 40th day after the Resurrection, counting Easter as the first day.

BARRIE, J.M.: BIRTH ANNIVERSARY. May 9, 1860. Author, born at Kirriemuir, Scotland. Wrote the popular children's tale *Peter Pan*, which first became a movie in 1924. Barrie died at London, England, June 19, 1937.

BROWN, JOHN: BIRTH ANNIVERSARY. May 9, 1800. Abolitionist leader, born at Torrington, CT, and hanged Dec 2, 1859, at Charles Town, WV. Leader of attack on Harpers Ferry, Oct 16, 1859, which was intended to give impetus to movement for escape and freedom for slaves. His aim was frustrated and in fact resulted in increased polarization and sectional animosity. Legendary martyr of the abolitionist movement. For more info: *Fiery Vision: The Life and Death of John Brown*, by Clinton Cox (Scholastic, 0-590-47574-6, $15.95 Gr. 5–8).

DU BOIS, WILLIAM PENE: BIRTH ANNIVERSARY. May 9, 1916. Illustrator and author of children's books, born at Nutley, NJ. Du Bois was the recipient of the Newbery Medal in 1948 for his book, *The Twenty-One Balloons*. He died at Nice, France, Feb 5, 1993.

ESTES, ELEANOR: BIRTH ANNIVERSARY. May 9, 1906. Author, born at West Haven, CT. Known for her book *The Hundred Dresses*, Estes won a Newbery Medal in 1952 for her children's book *Ginger Pye*. Died at Hamden, CT, July 15, 1988.

EUROPEAN UNION: ANNIVERSARY OBSERVANCE. May 9, 1950. Member countries of the European Union commemorate the announcement by French statesman Robert Schuman of the "Schuman Plan" for establishing a single authority for production of coal, iron and steel in France and Germany. This organization was a forerunner of the European Economic Community, founded in 1957, which later became the European Union.

THE READ IN. May 9. A daylong reading project for students in grades K–12. During the 9th annual Read In, students will chat together online with 22 of the best children's and young adult literature authors. This day is a culmination of several weeks of online participation by teachers and students during which they share information about their schools and communities. Annually, the second Thursday in May. For info: Jane Coffey, Program Dir, The Read In Foundation, 6043 Channel Dr, Riverbank, CA 95367. Phone: (209) 869-0713. E-mail: Thereadin@aol.com. Web: www.readin.org.

RUSSIA: VICTORY DAY: ANNIVERSARY. May 9. National holiday observed annually to commemorate the 1945 Allied Forces defeat of Nazi Germany in WWII and to honor the 20 million Soviet people who died in that war. Hostilities ceased and the German surrender became effective at one minute after midnight May 9, 1945. See also: "V-E Day: Anniversary" (May 9).

"VAST WASTELAND" SPEECH: ANNIVERSARY. May 9, 1961. Speaking before the bigwigs of network TV at the annual convention of the National Association of Broadcasters, Newton Minow, the new chairman of the Federal Communications Commission, exhorted those executives to sit through an entire day of their own programming. He suggested that they "will observe a vast wasteland." Further, he urged them to try for "imagination in programming, not sterility; creativity, not imitation; experimentation, not conformity; excellence, not mediocrity."

BIRTHDAYS TODAY

Richard Adams, 82, author (*Watership Down*), born Newbury, England, May 9, 1920.

John D. Ashcroft, 60, US Attorney General (George W. Bush administration), former US Senator (D, Missouri), born Chicago, IL, May 9, 1942

Candice Bergen, 56, actress ("Murphy Brown"), daughter of ventriloquist Edgar Bergen, born Beverly Hills, CA, May 9, 1946.

Tony Gwynn, 42, baseball player, born Los Angeles, CA, May 9, 1960.

MAY 10 — FRIDAY

Day 130 — 235 Remaining

CONFEDERATE MEMORIAL DAY IN SOUTH CAROLINA. May 10. See also Apr 26, Apr 29 and June 3 for Confederate Memorial Day observances in other southern states.

GOLDEN SPIKE DRIVING: ANNIVERSARY. May 10, 1869. Anniversary of the meeting of Union Pacific and Central Pacific railways, at Promontory Point, UT. On that day a golden spike was driven by Leland Stanford, president of the Central Pacific, to celebrate the linkage. The golden spike was promptly removed for preservation. Long called the final link in the ocean-to-ocean railroad, this event cannot be accurately described as completing the transcontinental railroad, but it did complete continuous rail tracks between Omaha and Sacramento. See also: "Transcontinental US Railway Completion: Anniversary" (Aug 15).

ISRAEL: YOM YERUSHALAYIM (JERUSALEM DAY): 35th ANNIVERSARY. May 10. Hebrew calendar date: Iyar 28, 5762. Commemorates the liberation of the old city, June 7, 1967.

JEFFERSON DAVIS CAPTURED: ANNIVERSARY. May 10, 1865. Confederate President Jefferson Davis, his wife and cabinet officials were captured at Irwinville, GA, by the 4th Michigan Cavalry. The prisoners were taken to Nashville, TN, and later sent to Richmond, VA.

ROSS, GEORGE: BIRTH ANNIVERSARY. May 10, 1730. Lawyer and signer of the Declaration of Independence, born at New Castle, DE. Died at Philadelphia, PA, July 14, 1779.

SINGAPORE: VESAK DAY. May 10. Public holiday. Monks commemorate their Lord Buddha's entry into Nirvana by chanting holy sutras and freeing captive birds.

TRUST YOUR INTUITION DAY. May 10. Today is the day we pay homage to the wonderful gift of sixth sense, "gut" feelings or that still small voice that is sometimes the only clue we have to go on in this ever-changing world. [©1994] For info: Adrienne Sioux Koopersmith, 1437 W Rosemont, #1W, Chicago, IL 60660-1319. Phone: (773) 743-5341. Fax: (773) 743-5395. E-mail: adrienet@earthlink.net.

BIRTHDAYS TODAY

Caroline B. Cooney, 55, author (*The Face on the Milk Carton, Driver's Ed, Whatever Happened to Janie?*), born Geneva, NY, May 10, 1947.

Christopher Paul Curtis, 48, author (Newbery for *Bud, Not Buddy;* Newbery Honor for *The Watsons Go to Birmingham—1963*), born Flint, MI, May 10, 1954.

Bruce McMillan, 55, author and illustrator (*Jelly Beans for Sale*), born Boston, MA, May 10, 1947.

Rick Santorum, 44, US Senator (R, Pennsylvania), born Winchester, VA, May 10, 1949.

Kenan Thompson, 24, actor ("All That," "Kenan & Kel"), born Atlanta, GA, May 10, 1978.

MAY 11 — SATURDAY

Day 131 — 234 Remaining

EAT WHAT YOU WANT DAY. May 11. Here's a day you may actually enjoy yourself. Ignore all those on-again/off-again warnings. [© 1999 by WH] For info: Tom and Ruth Roy, Wellcat Holidays, 2418 Long Ln, Lebanon, PA 17046. Phone: (230) 332-4886. E-mail: wellcat@supernet.com. Web: www.wellcat.com.

FAIRBANKS, CHARLES WARREN: 150th BIRTH ANNIVERSARY. May 11, 1852. The 26th vice president of the US (1905–09) born at Unionville Center, OH. Died at Indianapolis, IN, June 4, 1918.

GLACIER NATIONAL PARK ESTABLISHED: ANNIVERSARY. May 11, 1910. This national park is located in northwest Montana, on the Canadian border. In 1932 Glacier and Waterton Lakes National Park in Alberta were joined together by the governments of the US and Canada as Waterton-Glacier International Peace Park. For more info: www.nps.gov/glac.

GRAHAM, MARTHA: BIRTH ANNIVERSARY. May 11, 1894. Martha Graham was born at Allegheny, PA, and became one of the giants of the modern dance movement in the US. She began her dance career at the comparatively late age of 22 and joined the Greenwich Village Follies in 1923. Her new ideas began to surface in the late '20s and '30s, and by the mid-1930s she was incorporating the rituals of the southwestern American Indians in her work. She is credited with bringing a new psychological depth to modern dance by exploring primal emotions and ancient rituals in her work. She performed until the age of 75, and premiered in her 180th ballet, *The Maple Leaf Rag*, in the fall of 1990. Died Apr 1, 1991, at New York, NY. For more info: *Martha Graham: A Dancer's Life*, by Russell Freedman (Clarion, 0-395-74655-8, $18 Gr. 7–12).

May 2002

S	M	T	W	T	F	S
			1	2	3	4
5	6	7	8	9	10	11
12	13	14	15	16	17	18
19	20	21	22	23	24	25
26	27	28	29	30	31	

HART, JOHN: DEATH ANNIVERSARY. May 11, 1779. Signer of the Declaration of Independence, farmer and legislator, born about 1711 (exact date unknown), at Stonington, CT, died at Hopewell, NJ.

JAPAN: CORMORANT FISHING FESTIVAL. May 11–Oct 15. Cormorant fishing on the Nagara River, Gifu. "This ancient method of catching Ayu, a troutlike fish, with trained cormorants, takes place nightly under the light of blazing torches."

MINNESOTA: ADMISSION DAY: ANNIVERSARY. May 11. Became 32nd state in 1858.

NETHERLANDS: NATIONAL WINDMILL DAY. May 11. About 950 windmills still survive and some 300 still are used occasionally and have been designated national monuments by the government. As many windmills as possible are in operation on National Windmill Day for the benefit of tourists. Annually, the second Saturday in May.

BIRTHDAYS TODAY

Sheila Burnford, 84, author (*The Incredible Journey*), born Scotland, May 11, 1918.

James Jeffords, 68, US Senator (R, Vermont), born Rutland, VT, May 11, 1934.

Austin O'Brien, 21, actor ("The Baby-Sitters Club," *My Girl 2*), born Eugene, OR, May 11, 1981.

Natasha Richardson, 39, actress (*The Parent Trap*), born London, England, May 11, 1963.

Peter Sis, 53, illustrator and author (*The Starry Messenger*), born Prague, Czechoslovakia, May 11, 1949.

Zilpha Keatley Snyder, 75, author (*The Witches of Worm, The Headless Cupid*), born Lemoore, CA, May 11, 1927.

MAY 12 — SUNDAY

Day 132 — 233 Remaining

GIRLS INCORPORATED WEEK. May 12–18. To focus national and local attention on the goals of Girls Incorporated as an organization for the rights and needs of girls. Begins the second Sunday in May. For info: Girls Inc, 120 Wall St, 3rd Fl, New York, NY 10005. Phone: (212) 509-2000. Web: www.girlsinc.org.

ITALY: WEDDING OF THE SEA. May 12. Venice. The feast of the Ascension is the occasion of the ceremony recalling the "Wedding of the Sea" performed by Venice's Doge, who cast his ring into the sea from the ceremonial ship known as the *Bucintoro*, to symbolize eternal dominion. Annually, on the Sunday following Ascension.

LEAR, EDWARD: BIRTH ANNIVERSARY. May 12, 1812. English artist and author, remembered for his children's book *The Owl and the Pussycat*. Born at Highgate, England, Lear died at San Remo, Italy, Jan 29, 1888.

LIMERICK DAY. May 12. Observed on the birthday of one of its champions, Edward Lear, who was born in 1812. The limerick, which dates from the early 18th century, has been described as the "only fixed verse form indigenous to the English language." It gained its greatest popularity following the publication of Edward Lear's *Book of Nonsense* (and its sequels). Write a limerick today! Example: There was a young poet named Lear/Who said, it is just as I fear/Five lines are enough/For this kind of stuff/Make a limerick each day of the year.

MOON PHASE: NEW MOON. May 12. Moon enters New Moon phase at 6:45 AM, EDT.

★**MOTHER'S DAY.** May 12. Presidential Proclamation always issued for the second Sunday in May. (Pub Res No. 2 of May 8, 1914.)

MOTHER'S DAY. May 12. Observed first in 1907 at the request of Anna Jarvis of Philadelphia, PA, who asked her church to hold service in memory of all mothers on the anniversary of her mother's death. Annually, the second Sunday in May. For links to Mother's Day sites on the Web, go to: deil.lang.uiuc.edu/web .pages/holidays/mother.html.

NATIONAL ALCOHOL AND OTHER DRUG-RELATED BIRTH DEFECTS WEEK. May 12–18. For info: Natl Council on Alcoholism and Drug Dependence, 12 W 21st St, New York, NY 10010. Phone: (212) 206-6770.

NATIONAL FAMILY MONTH®. May 12–June 16. A monthlong national observance to celebrate and promote strong, supportive families. Sponsored by KidsPeace®, a private, not-for-profit organization that has been helping kids overcome crisis since 1982. Annually, Mother's Day through Father's Day. For info: Paula Knouse, KidsPeace, 5300 Kidspeace Dr, Orefield, PA 18069. Phone: (610) 799-8325. Web: www.kidspeace.org.

NATIONAL HISTORIC PRESERVATION WEEK. May 12–18. To draw public attention to historic preservation including neighborhoods, districts, landmark buildings, open space and maritime heritage. Annually, the second full week in May. For info: Diana Onorio, Natl Trust for Historic Preservation, 1785 Massachusetts Ave NW, Washington, DC 20036. Phone: (202) 588-6141. Fax: (202) 588-6299. E-mail: pr@nthp.org. Web: www.national trust.org.

NATIONAL POLICE WEEK. May 12–18. See also: "Peace Officer Memorial Day" (May 15). For info: American Police Hall of Fame and Museum, 3801 Biscayne Blvd, Miami, FL 33137. Phone: (305) 573-0070.

★**NATIONAL TRANSPORTATION WEEK.** May 12–18. Presidential Proclamation issued for week including third Friday in May since 1960. (PL 86–475 of May 20, 1960, first requested; PL87–449 of May 14, 1962, requested an annual proclamation.)

NIGHTINGALE, FLORENCE: BIRTH ANNIVERSARY. May 12, 1820. English nurse and public health activist who contributed perhaps more than any other single person to the development of modern nursing procedures and the dignity of nursing as a profession. During the Crimean War, she supervised nursing care in the British hospital at Scutari, Turkey, where she reduced the death rate dramatically. Returning to England, she reorganized the army medical service. She was the founder of the Nightingale training school for nurses and author of *Notes on Nursing*. Born at Florence, Italy, she died at London, England, Aug 13, 1910.

★**POLICE WEEK.** May 12–18. Presidential Proclamation 3537 of May 4, 1963, covers all succeeding years. (PL87–726 of Oct 1, 1962.) Always the week including May 15 since 1962.

BIRTHDAYS TODAY

Jennifer Armstrong, 41, author (*Steal Away, Shipwreck at the Bottom of the World*), born Waltham, MA, May 12, 1961.
Yogi Berra, 77, former baseball manager and Baseball Hall of Fame catcher, born Lawrence Peter Berra, St. Louis, MO, May 12, 1925.
Tony Hawk, 33, skateboarder, born Carlsbad, CA, May 12, 1969.
Farley Mowat, 81, author (*Owls in the Family*), born Belleville, ON, Canada, May 12, 1921.

MAY 13 — MONDAY

Day 133 — 232 Remaining

NATIONAL ETIQUETTE WEEK. May 13–19. A national recognition of proper etiquette in all areas of American life (business, social, dining, international, wedding, computer, etc.). A self-assessment on the current status of civility in the US. Annually, the second week in May starting on Monday. For info: Sandra Morisset, Protocol Training Services, PO Box 4981, New York, NY 10185. Phone: (212) 802-9098.

RABI'I: THE MONTH OF THE MIGRATION. May 13. Begins on Islamic calendar date Rabi'I 1, 1423. The month of the migration or Hegira of the Prophet Muhammad from Mecca to Medina in AD 622, the event that was used as the starting year of the Islamic era. Different methods for "anticipating" the visibility of the new moon crescent at Mecca are used by different Muslim groups. US date may vary.

SEATTLE INTERNATIONAL CHILDREN'S FESTIVAL. May 13–18. Seattle, WA. The largest performing arts festival for families in the US. Artists from Europe, Asia, Africa, Australia and the Americas present theater, dance, music, puppets and acrobatics. Est attendance: 51,000. For info: Seattle Intl Children's Festival, 305 Harrison, Seattle, WA 98109-3944. Phone: (206) 684-7338. E-mail: kidsfest@seattleinternational.org. Web: www .seattleinternational.org.

SPACE MILESTONE: *ENDEAVOUR* (US): 10th ANNIVERSARY. May 13, 1992. Three astronauts from the shuttle *Endeavour* simultaneously walked in space for the first time.

BIRTHDAYS TODAY

Francine Pascal, 64, author (the Sweet Valley High series), born New York, NY, May 13, 1938.
Dennis Keith (Worm) Rodman, 41, former basketball player, born Trenton, NJ, May 13, 1961.
Stevie Wonder, 51, singer, musician (16 Grammy Awards; "I Just Called to Say I Love You"), born Steveland Morris Hardaway, Saginaw, MI, May 13, 1951.

MAY 14 — TUESDAY

Day 134 — 231 Remaining

CARLSBAD CAVERNS NATIONAL PARK ESTABLISHED: ANNIVERSARY. May 14, 1930. Located in southwestern New Mexico, Carlsbad Caverns was proclaimed a national monument, Oct 25, 1923, and later established as national park and preserve. For more info: www.nps.gov/carl/index.htm.

FAHRENHEIT, GABRIEL DANIEL: BIRTH ANNIVERSARY. May 14, 1686. German physicist whose name is attached to one of the major temperature measurement scales. He introduced the use of mercury in thermometers and greatly improved their accuracy. Born at Danzig, Germany, he died at Amsterdam, Holland, Sept 16, 1736.

FIRST FEMALE HOUSE PAGE APPOINTMENT: ANNIVERSARY. May 14, 1973. The House of Representatives received formal approval of the appointment of female pages in 1972. In the 93rd Congress, Felda Looper was appointed as the first female page with a regular term. Gene Cox had served as a female page for three hours 34 years earlier.

JAMESTOWN, VIRGINIA: FOUNDING ANNIVERSARY. May 14, 1607. The first permanent English settlement in what is now the US took place at Jamestown, VA (named for England's King James I), on this date. Captains John Smith and Christopher Newport were among the leaders of the group of royally chartered Virginia Company settlers who had traveled from Plymouth, England, in three small ships: *Susan Constant, Godspeed* and *Discovery*.

LEWIS AND CLARK EXPEDITION: ANNIVERSARY. May 14, 1804. Charged by President Thomas Jefferson with finding a route to the Pacific, Meriwether Lewis and Captain William Clark left St. Louis, MO, May 14, 1804. They arrived at the Pacific coast of Oregon in November 1805 and returned to St. Louis, Sept 23, 1806. For more info: *In Their Own Words: Lewis and Clark*, by George Sullivan (Scholastic, 0-439-14749-2, $15.95 Gr. 3–6) and www.pbs.org/lewisandclark.

MILLION MOM MARCH: ANNIVERSARY. May 14, 2000. Women rallied in Washington, DC, and 60 other cities to urge Congress to "get serious about common sense gun legislation." For info: Million Mom March, PO Box 762, Washington, DC 20044-0762. Phone: (888) 989-MOMS. Web: www.millionmommarch.com.

NORWAY: MIDNIGHT SUN AT NORTH CAPE. May 14–July 30. In the "Land of the Midnight Sun," this is the first day of the season with around-the-clock sunshine. At North Cape and parts of Russia, Alaska, Canada and Greenland surrounding the Arctic Ocean, the sun never dips below the horizon from May 14 to July 30, but the night is bright long before and after these dates. At the equator, on the other hand, the length of day and night never varies.

SELDEN, GEORGE: BIRTH ANNIVERSARY. May 14, 1929. Born at Hartford, CT, author of beloved classic novels about animal characters from his native town. *The Cricket in Times Square* describes the adventures of a Connecticut cricket who, by chance, travels to the Times Square Subway Station in New York. Sequels include *Chester Cricket's New Home, Harry Cat's Pet Puppy,* and *Tucker's Countryside*. He died at New York, NY, Dec 5, 1989.

May 2002

S	M	T	W	T	F	S
			1	2	3	4
5	6	7	8	9	10	11
12	13	14	15	16	17	18
19	20	21	22	23	24	25
26	27	28	29	30	31	

SMALLPOX VACCINE DISCOVERED: ANNIVERSARY. May 14, 1796. In the 18th century, smallpox was a widespread and often fatal disease. Edward Jenner, a physician in rural England, heard reports of dairy farmers who apparently became immune to smallpox as a result of exposure to cowpox, a related but milder disease. After two decades of studying the phenomenon, Jenner injected cowpox into a healthy eight-year-old boy, who subsequently developed cowpox. Six weeks later, Jenner inoculated the boy with smallpox. He remained healthy. Jenner called this new procedure *vaccination*, from *vaccinia*, another term for cowpox. Within 18 months, 12,000 people in England had been vaccinated and the number of smallpox deaths dropped by two-thirds.

SPACE MILESTONE: *SKYLAB* (US). May 14, 1973. The US launched *Skylab*, its first manned orbiting laboratory.

"THE STARS AND STRIPES FOREVER" DAY: ANNIVERSARY. May 14, 1897. Anniversary of the first public performance of John Philip Sousa's march, "The Stars and Stripes Forever," at Philadelphia, PA. The occasion was the unveiling of a statue of George Washington. President William McKinley was present.

WAAC: 60th ANNIVERSARY. May 14, 1942. During WWII women became eligible to enlist for noncombat duties in the Women's Auxiliary Army Corps (WAAC) by an act of Congress. Women also served as Women Appointed for Voluntary Emergency Service (WAVES), Women's Auxiliary Ferrying Squadron (WAFS) and Coast Guard or Semper Paratus Always Ready Service (SPARS), the Women's Reserve of the Marine Corps.

BIRTHDAYS TODAY

Byron L. Dorgan, 60, US Senator (D, North Dakota), born Dickinson, ND, May 14, 1942.

George Lucas, 58, filmmaker (*The Empire Strikes Back, Star Wars*), born Modesto, CA, May 14, 1944.

Atanasio (Tony) Perez, 60, Baseball Hall of Fame player and former manager, born Camaguey, Cuba, May 14, 1942.

Valerie Still, 41, basketball player, born Lexington, KY, May 14, 1961.

MAY 15 — WEDNESDAY

Day 135 — 230 Remaining

BAUM, L(YMAN) FRANK: BIRTH ANNIVERSARY. May 15, 1856. The American newspaperman who wrote the Wizard of Oz stories was born at Chittenango, NY. Although *The Wonderful Wizard of Oz* is the most famous, Baum also wrote many other books for children, including more than a dozen about Oz. He died at Hollywood, CA, May 6, 1919.

FIRST FLIGHT ATTENDANT: ANNIVERSARY. May 15, 1930. Ellen Church became the first airline stewardess (today's flight attendant), flying on a United Airlines flight from San Francisco to Cheyenne, WY.

GASOLINE RATIONING: 60th ANNIVERSARY. May 15, 1942. Seventeen eastern states initiated gasoline rationing as part of the war effort. By Sept 25, rationing was nationwide. A limit of three gallons a week for nonessential purposes was set and a 35 mph speed limit was imposed.

JAPAN: AOI MATSURI (HOLLYHOCK FESTIVAL). May 15. Kyoto. The festival features a pageant reproducing imperial processions of ancient times that paid homage to the shrine of Shimogamo and Kamigamo.

MEXICO: SAN ISIDRO DAY. May 15. Day of San Isidro Labrador celebrated widely in farming regions to honor St. Isidore, the Plowman. Livestock is gaily decorated with flowers. Celebrations usually begin about May 13 and continue for about a week.

NYLON STOCKINGS: ANNIVERSARY. May 15, 1940. Nylon hose went on sale at stores throughout the country. Competing producers bought their nylon yarn from E.J. du Pont de Nemours. W.H. Carothers of Du Pont developed nylon, called "Polymer 66," in 1935. It was the first totally man-made fiber and over time substituted for other materials and came to have widespread application.

PARAGUAY: INDEPENDENCE DAY. May 15. Commemorates independence from Spain, attained 1811.

★**PEACE OFFICER MEMORIAL DAY.** May 15. Presidential Proclamation 3537, of May 4, 1963, covers all succeeding years. (PL87–726 of Oct 1, 1962.) Always May 15 of each year since 1963; however, first issued in 1962 for May 14.

PEACE OFFICER MEMORIAL DAY. May 15. An event honored by some 21,000 police departments nationwide. Memorial ceremonies at 10 AM in American Police Hall of Fame and Museum, Miami, FL. See also: "National Police Week" (May 12–18). Sponsor: National Association of Chiefs of Police. Est attendance: 1,000. For info: American Police Hall of Fame and Museum, 3801 Biscayne Blvd, Miami, FL 33137. Phone: (305) 573-0070. Web: www.aphf.org.

PITTSBURGH INTERNATIONAL CHILDREN'S FESTIVAL. May 15–19. Pittsburgh, PA. Festival featuring performers from around the world. Kids can explore the world through theater, music, dance, circus and puppetry. 17th annual festival. Est attendance: 100,000. For info: Pittsburgh International Children's Theater, 182 Allegheny Center Mall, Pittsburgh, PA 15212-5334. Phone: (412) 321-5520.

UNITED NATIONS: INTERNATIONAL DAY OF FAMILIES. May 15. The general assembly (Res 47/237) Sept 20, 1993, voted this as an annual observance beginning in 1994.

WILSON, ELLEN LOUISE AXSON: BIRTH ANNIVERSARY. May 15, 1860. First wife of Woodrow Wilson, 28th president of the US, born at Savannah, GA. She died at Washington, DC, Aug 6, 1914.

BIRTHDAYS TODAY

Madeleine Albright, 65, former US Secretary of State (Clinton administration), born Prague, Czechoslovakia, May 15, 1937.
David Almond, 51, author (*Skellig,*, Michael L. Printz Award for *Kit's Wilderness*), born Newcastle-upon-Tyne, England, May 15, 1951.
George Brett, 49, Baseball Hall of Fame player, born Glen Dale, WV, May 15, 1953.
Nancy Garden, 64, author (*Dove and Sword, Annie on My Mind*), born Boston, MA, May 15, 1938.
Norma Fox Mazer, 71, author (*A Figure of Speech*), born New York, NY, May 15, 1931.
Leigh Ann Orsi, 21, actress ("Home Improvement," *Pet Shop*), born Los Angeles, CA, May 15, 1981.
Emmitt Smith, 33, football player, born Escambia, FL, May 15, 1969.
Paul Zindel, 66, author (*The Pigman*), born Staten Island, NY, May 15, 1936.

MAY 16 — THURSDAY

Day 136 — 229 Remaining

BIOGRAPHERS DAY. May 16, 1763. Anniversary of the meeting, at London, England, of James Boswell and Samuel Johnson, beginning history's most famous biographer-biographee relationship. Boswell's *Journal of a Tour to the Hebrides* (1785) and his *Life of Samuel Johnson* (1791) are regarded as models of biographical writing. Thus, this day is recommended as one on which to start reading or writing a biography.

FIRST ACADEMY AWARDS: ANNIVERSARY. May 16, 1929. About 270 people attended a dinner at the Hollywood Roosevelt Hotel at which the first Academy Awards were given in 12 categories for films made in 1927–1928. The silent film *Wings* won Best Picture. A committee of only 20 members selected the winners that year. By the third year, the entire membership of the Academy voted. For links to Academy Awards sites on the web, go to: deil.lang.uiuc.edu/web.pages/holidays/oscars.html.

GWINNETT, BUTTON: 225th DEATH ANNIVERSARY. May 16, 1777. Signer of the Declaration of Independence, born at Down Hatherley, Gloucestershire, England, about 1735 (exact date unknown). Died following a duel at St. Catherine's Island, off of Savannah, GA.

MORTON, LEVI PARSONS: BIRTH ANNIVERSARY. May 16, 1824. The 22nd vice president of the US (1889–93) born at Shoreham, VT. Died at Rhinebeck, NY, May 16, 1920.

REY, MARGARET: BIRTH ANNIVERSARY. May 16, 1906. Children's author, born at Hamburg, Germany. Together with her illustrator husband, H.A. Rey, she produced the Curious George series. Rey died at Cambridge, MA, Dec 21, 1996.

BIRTHDAYS TODAY

Caroline Arnold, 58, author (*Trapped in Tar*), born Minneapolis, MN, May 16, 1944.
David Boreanaz, 31, actor ("Buffy the Vampire Slayer"), born Philadelphia, PA, May 16, 1971.
Bruce Coville, 52, author (*Aliens Ate My Homework*), born Syracuse, NY, May 16, 1950.
Tracey Gold, 33, actress ("Growing Pains"), born New York, NY, May 16, 1969.
Gabriela Sabatini, 32, tennis player, born Buenos Aires, Argentina, May 16, 1970.
Joan Benoit Samuelson, 45, Olympic gold medal runner, born Cape Elizabeth, ME, May 16, 1957.

MAY 17 — FRIDAY

Day 137 — 228 Remaining

BROWN v BOARD OF EDUCATION DECISION: ANNIVERSARY. May 17, 1954. The US Supreme Court ruled unanimously that segregation of public schools "solely on the basis of race" denied black children "equal educational opportunity" even though "physical facilities and other 'tangible' factors may have been equal. Separate educational facilities are inherently unequal." The case was argued before the Court by Thurgood Marshall, who would go on to become the first black appointed to the Supreme Court. For more info: www.yale.edu/ynhti/pubs/A5/wolff.html.

JENNER, EDWARD: BIRTH ANNIVERSARY. May 17, 1749. English physician, born at Berkeley, England. He was the first to establish a scientific basis for vaccination with his work on smallpox. Jenner died at Berkeley, England, Jan 26, 1823.

NEW YORK STOCK EXCHANGE ESTABLISHED: ANNIVERSARY. May 17, 1792. Some two dozen merchants and brokers agreed to establish what is now known as the New York Stock Exchange. In fair weather they operated under a buttonwood tree on Wall Street, at New York, NY. In bad weather they moved to the shelter of a coffeehouse to conduct their business. For more info: www.nyse.com.

NORWAY: CONSTITUTION DAY OR INDEPENDENCE DAY. May 17. National holiday. The constitution was signed in 1814. Parades and children's festivities.

MAY 17
DINOSAUR NAMED SUE FIRST EXHIBITED

The name *Tyrannosaurus rex* sends shivers of fear and delight up our spines. This "tyrant king" of the dinosaur world has filled the dreams (and toy boxes) of many young dinosaur lovers. *T. rex* lived during the last half of the Cretaceous Period (138 to 65 million years ago). In the past, scientists believed this large creature, whose head was nearly 12 feet above the ground, was primarily a scavenger and thought its tiny front legs and 40-foot-long body were not suited for a predator. Now, scientists believe *T. rex's* powerful hind legs allowed it to chase and capture prey. The use of the short front limbs is still under discussion. Perhaps studying the *T. rex* skeleton on exhibit in Chicago's Field Museum will help answer some of the many questions about this incredible animal.

On May 17, 2000, people crowded into Chicago's Field Museum to visit the stunning new exhibit of the 65-million-year-old *Tyrannosaurus rex*, now fondly referred to as Sue. The most complete *T. rex* skeleton ever discovered towers above the heads of those lucky enough to see her "in person." But living too far away from Illinois is not a valid excuse for not visiting her. Your students can meet Sue in books and on a wonderful website.

The Field Museum's website on Sue has an image gallery that contains clear and informative photographs, close-up shots of her body parts, and details of the skeleton's preservation and preparation process. There are also sections of the site that provide answers to frequently asked questions and information about the fossil's discovery and history. Encourage your students to visit www.fmnh.org/sue/default.htm.

Books that offer a wealth of information about Sue, for a wide range of students, are readily available. Young listeners will be enchanted by *The Field Mouse and a Dinosaur Named Sue*, by Jan Wahl (Scholastic, 0-439-09984-6, $12.95 Gr. PreK–2). Told from the mouse's point of view, this book will keep young listeners on the edge of their seats as the tiny mouse watches all the excitement and disruption of its home (under one of Sue's bones). Independent readers will find the early reader *A Dinosaur Named Sue*, by Fay Robinson (Scholastic, 0-439-09983-8, $3.99 Gr. 2–5), and the heavily-illustrated *A Dinosaur Named Sue: The Story of the Colossal Fossil*, by Pat Relf (Scholastic, 0-439-09985-4, $15.95 Gr. 3–6), interesting and informative. Young adult and adult readers will enjoy *Tyrannosaurus Sue*, by Steve Fiffer (W. H. Freeman, 0-7167-4017-6, $24.95). This book offers an in-depth account of the process of discovering, buying and exhibiting the skeleton.

May 2002

S	M	T	W	T	F	S
			1	2	3	4
5	6	7	8	9	10	11
12	13	14	15	16	17	18
19	20	21	22	23	24	25
26	27	28	29	30	31	

SCIENCE OLYMPIAD. May 17–18. University of Delaware, Newark, DE. A fun day for grades K–3 involves children in non-competitive hands-on science experiences at the school or district level. For grades 4–6, teams compete at the district or regional level. For grades 6–9 and 9–12, competition takes place at the state and national level as well. For info: Science Olympiad, 5955 Little Pine Lane, Rochester, MI 48306. Phone: (248) 651-4013. Fax: (248) 651-7835. Web: www.macomb.k12.mi.us/ims/cr/science/so/nsoly.

SHAVUOT or FEAST OF WEEKS. May 17. Jewish Pentecost holy day. Hebrew date, Sivan 6, 5762. Celebrates giving of Torah (the Law) to Moses on Mount Sinai.

SUE EXHIBITED: ANNIVERSARY. May 17, 2000. Sue, the largest and most complete *Tyrannosaurus rex* ever discovered, went on exhibition this day at the Field Museum in Chicago. Sue's skeleton was discovered in South Dakota in 1990. It is 90 percent complete and is 41 feet long and 13 feet tall at the hips. The meat-eating dinosaur is 67 million years old and would have weighed 7 tons when it was alive. Sue is named after Susan Hendrickson, the fossil hunter who discovered the dinosaur. The Field Museum spent more than $8 million to purchase Sue in 1997. A life-size cast of Sue will be exhibited at Disney World. For info: Field Museum, Roosevelt Road at Lake Shore Drive, Chicago, IL 60605-2496. Phone: (312) 322-8859. Web: www.fmnh.org/Sue. *See* Curriculum Connection.

TEACHER'S DAY IN FLORIDA. May 17. A ceremonial day on the third Friday in May.

UNITED NATIONS: WORLD TELECOMMUNICATION DAY. May 17. A day to draw attention to the necessity and importance of further development of telecommunications in the global community. For more information, visit the UN's website for children at www.un.org/Pubs/CyberSchoolBus/.

BIRTHDAYS TODAY

Eloise Greenfield, 73, author (*Night on Neighborhood Street*), born Parmalee, NC, May 17, 1929.

Mia Hamm, 30, soccer player, born Selma, AL, May 17, 1972.

Ben Nelson, 61, US Senator (D, Nebraska), born McCook, NE, May 17, 1941.

Gary Paulsen, 63, author (*The Hatchet*), born Minneapolis, MN, May 17, 1939.

Bob Saget, 46, actor ("Full House"), host ("America's Funniest Home Videos"), born Philadelphia, PA, May 17, 1956.

MAY 18 — SATURDAY

Day 138 — 227 Remaining

★**ARMED FORCES DAY.** May 18. Presidential Proclamation 5983, of May 17, 1989, covers the third Saturday in May in all succeeding years. Originally proclaimed as "Army Day" for Apr 6, beginning in 1936 (S.Con.Res. 30 of Apr 2, 1936). S.Con.Res. 5 of Mar 16, 1937, requested annual Apr 6 issuance, which was done through 1949. Always the third Saturday in May since 1950. Traditionally issued once by each Administration.

FONTEYN, MARGOT: BIRTH ANNIVERSARY. May 18, 1919. Born Margaret Hookman at Reigate, Surrey, England, Margot Fonteyn was a famed ballet dancer during the '30s and '40s. She died at Panama City, Panama, Feb 21, 1991.

HAITI: FLAG AND UNIVERSITY DAY. May 18. Public holiday.

HOBAN, LILLIAN: BIRTH ANNIVERSARY. May 18, 1925. Illustrator (*Best Friends for Frances, Bread and Jam for Frances*); author (*Joe and Betsy the Dinosaur, Arthur's Loose Tooth*), born

Philadelphia, PA, May 18, 1925. Died at New York, NY, July 17, 1998.

INTERNATIONAL MUSEUM DAY. May 18. To pay tribute to museums of the world. "Museums are an important means of cultural exchange, enrichment of cultures and development of mutual understanding, cooperation and peace among people." Annually, May 18. Sponsor: International Council of Museums, Paris, France. For info: AAM/ICOM, 1575 Eye St NW, 4th Fl, Washington, DC 20005. Phone: (202) 289-9115. Fax: (202) 289-6578.

MOUNT SAINT HELENS ERUPTION: ANNIVERSARY. May 18, 1980. A major eruption of Mount St. Helens volcano, in southwestern Washington, blew steam and ash more than 11 miles into the sky. This was the first major eruption of Mount St. Helens since 1857, though Mar 26, 1980, there had been a warning eruption of smaller magnitude. For more info visit Volcano World: volcano.und.nodak.edu.

NATIONAL SAFE BOATING WEEK. May 18–24. Brings boating safety to the public's attention, decreases the number of boating fatalities and makes the waterways safer for all boaters. Sponsor: US Coast Guard. For info: Jo Calkin, Commandant (G-OPB-2), US Coast Guard, 2100 Second St SW, Washington, DC 20593. Phone: (800) 368-5647.

★**NATIONAL SAFE BOATING WEEK.** May 18–24. Presidential Proclamation during May since 1995. From 1958 through 1977, issued for a week including July 4 (PL85–445 of June 4, 1958). From 1981 through 1994, issued for the first week in June (PL96–376 of Oct 3, 1980). From 1995, issued for a seven-day period ending on the Friday before Memorial Day. Not issued from 1978 through 1980.

POPE JOHN PAUL II: BIRTHDAY. May 18, 1920. Karol Wojtyla, 264th pope of the Roman Catholic Church, born at Wadowice, Poland. Elected pope Oct 16, 1978. He was the first non-Italian to be elected pope in 456 years (since the election of Pope Adrian VI, in 1522) and the first Polish pope.

TURKMENISTAN: REVIVAL AND UNITY DAY. May 18. National holiday. Commemorates the 1992 constitution.

URUGUAY: BATTLE OF LAS PIEDRAS DAY. May 18. National holiday. Commemorates an 1811 battle fought for independence from Spain.

VISIT YOUR RELATIVES DAY. May 18. A day to renew family ties and joys by visiting often-thought-of-seldom-seen relatives. Annually, May 18. For info: A.C. Moeller, Box 71, Clio, MI 48420-1042.

BIRTHDAYS TODAY

Karyn Bye, 31, Olympic ice hockey player, born River Falls, WI, May 18, 1971.

Debra (Debbie) Dadey, 43, author, with Marcia Thornton Jones (The Bailey School Kids series), born Morganfield, KY, May 18, 1959.

Irene Hunt, 95, author (*Across Five Aprils*), born Newton, IL, May 18, 1907.

Reginald Martinez (Reggie) Jackson, 56, Baseball Hall of Fame outfielder, born Wyncote, PA, May 18, 1946.

MAY 19 — SUNDAY

Day 139 — 226 Remaining

BOYS' CLUBS FOUNDED: ANNIVERSARY. May 19, 1906. The Federated Boys' Clubs, which later became the Boys' and Girls' Clubs of America, was founded. For more info: www.bgca.org.

MALCOLM X: BIRTH ANNIVERSARY. May 19, 1925. Black nationalist and civil rights activist Malcolm X was born Malcolm Little at Omaha, NE. While serving a prison term he resolved to transform his life. On his release in 1952 he changed his name to Malcolm X and worked for the Nation of Islam until he was suspended by Black Muslim leader Elijah Muhammed Dec 4, 1963. Malcolm X later made the pilgrimage to Mecca and became an orthodox Muslim. He was assassinated as he spoke to a meeting at the Audubon Ballroom at New York, NY, Feb 21, 1965. For more info: *Malcolm X: By Any Means Necessary*, by Walter Dean Myers (Scholastic, 0-590-46484-1, $10.75 Gr. 6–9) or *Malcolm X: A Fire Burning Brightly*, by Walter Dean Myers (HarperCollins, 0-06-027708-4, $15.95 Gr. 3–6).

MOON PHASE: FIRST QUARTER. May 19. Moon enters First Quarter phase at 3:42 PM, EDT.

NATIONAL EMERGENCY MEDICAL SERVICES (EMS) WEEK. May 19–25. Honoring EMS providers nationwide who provide lifesaving care in a multitude of circumstances. Also a time for the public to learn about injury prevention, safety awareness and emergency preparedness. Annually, the third week in May. For info: American College of Emergency Physicians, PO Box 619911, Dallas, TX 75261-9911. Phone: (800) 798-1822. E-mail: emsweek@acep.org. Web: www.acep.org.

PENTECOST. May 19. The Christian feast of Pentecost commemorates descent of the Holy Spirit unto the Apostles, 50 days after Easter. Observed on the seventh Sunday after Easter. Recognized since the third century. See also: "Whitsunday" (May 19).

★**SMALL BUSINESS WEEK.** May 19–25 (tentative). To honor the 22 million small businesses in the US. Originally, the first full week in June; now in May. For info: Small Business Administration, Info Services, 409 3rd St SW, 7th Floor, Washington, DC 20416. Phone: (202) 205-6606 or (202) 205-6531. Web: www.sba.gov.

TURKEY: YOUTH AND SPORTS DAY. May 19. Public holiday commemorating the beginning of a national movement for independence in 1919, led by Mustafa Kemal Ataturk.

TWENTY-SEVENTH AMENDMENT RATIFIED: 10th ANNIVERSARY. May 19, 1992. The 27th amendment to the Constitution was ratified, prohibiting Congress from giving itself immediate pay raises.

VIETNAM: HO CHI MINH'S BIRTHDAY. May 19. National holiday. Leader of wars against France and America; born May 19, 1890. Died Sept 2, 1969.

WHITSUNDAY. May 19. Whitsunday, the seventh Sunday after Easter, is a popular time for baptism. "White Sunday" is named for the white garments formerly worn by the candidates for baptism and occurs at the Christian feast of Pentecost. See also: "Pentecost" (May 19).

★**WORLD TRADE WEEK.** May 19–25. Presidential Proclamation has been issued each year since 1948 for the third week of May with three exceptions: 1949, 1955 and 1966.

BIRTHDAYS TODAY

Arthur Dorros, 52, author (*Abuela, La Isla*), born Washington, DC, May 19, 1950.

Sarah Ellis, 50, author (*Back of Beyond: Stories of the Supernatural*), born Vancouver, BC, Canada, May 19, 1952.
Tom Feelings, 69, author (*Soul Looks Back in Wonder; The Middle Passage: White Ships, Black Cargo*), born Brooklyn, NY, May 19, 1933.
Kevin Garnett, 26, basketball player, born Mauldin, SC, May 19, 1976.
Eric Lloyd, 16, actor (*Dunston Checks In, The Santa Clause*), born Glendale, CA, May 19, 1986.

MAY 20 — MONDAY

Day 140 — 225 Remaining

BUCKLE UP AMERICA! WEEK. May 21–27. An observance to remind Americans of the importance of wearing seat belts. For info: Office of Occupant Protection, Natl Highway Safety Administration, 400 Seventh St SW, Washington, DC 20590. Phone: (202) 366-9550.

CAMEROON: NATIONAL HOLIDAY. May 20. Republic of Cameroon. Commemorates declaration of the United Republic of Cameroon May 20, 1972. Prior to this, the country had been a federal republic with two states, Eastern Cameroon and Western Cameroon.

CANADA: VICTORIA DAY. May 20. Commemorates the birth of Queen Victoria, May 24, 1819. Observed annually on the first Monday preceding May 25.

COUNCIL OF NICAEA I: ANNIVERSARY. May 20–Aug 25, 325. The first ecumenical council of Christian Church, called by Constantine I, first Christian emperor of the Roman Empire. Nearly 300 bishops are said to have attended this first of 21 ecumenical councils (latest, Vatican II, began Sept 11, 1962), which was held at Nicaea, in Asia Minor (today's Turkey). The council condemned Arianism (which denied the divinity of Christ), formulated the Nicene Creed and fixed the day of Easter—always on a Sunday.

ELIZA DOOLITTLE DAY. May 20. To honor Miss Doolittle (heroine of Bernard Shaw's *Pygmalion*) for demonstrating the importance and the advantage of speaking one's native language properly. For info: H.M. Chase, Doolittle Day Committee, 2460 Devonshire Rd, Ann Arbor, MI 48104-2706.

HOMESTEAD ACT: ANNIVERSARY. May 20, 1862. President Lincoln signed the Homestead Act, opening millions of acres of government-owned land in the West to settlers or "homesteaders," who had to reside on the land and cultivate it for five years.

LINDBERGH FLIGHT: 75th ANNIVERSARY. May 20–21, 1927. Anniversary of the first solo trans-Atlantic flight. Captain Charles Augustus Lindbergh, 25-year-old aviator, departed from muddy Roosevelt Field, Long Island, NY, alone at 7:52 AM, May 20, 1927, in a Ryan monoplane named *Spirit of St. Louis*. He landed at Le Bourget airfield, Paris, at 10:24 PM Paris time (5:24 PM, NY time), May 21, winning a $25,000 prize offered by Raymond Orteig for the first nonstop flight between New York City and Paris, France (3,600 miles). The "flying fool" as he had been dubbed by some doubters became "Lucky Lindy," an instant world hero. See also: "Lindbergh, Charles Augustus: Birth Anniversary" (Feb 4).

May 2002

S	M	T	W	T	F	S
			1	2	3	4
5	6	7	8	9	10	11
12	13	14	15	16	17	18
19	20	21	22	23	24	25
26	27	28	29	30	31	

MADISON, DOLLY (DOROTHEA) DANDRIDGE PAYNE TODD: BIRTH ANNIVERSARY. May 20, 1768. Wife of James Madison, 4th president of the US, born at Guilford County, NC. Died at Washington, DC, July 12, 1849.

NATIONAL BACKYARD GAMES WEEK. May 20–27. Observance to celebrate the unofficial start of summer by fostering social interaction and family togetherness through backyard games. Get outside and be both physically and mentally stimulated, playing classic games of the past while discovering and creating new ways to be active and interact with neighbors and friends. For info: Frank Beres, Patch Products, PO Box 268, Beloit, WI 53511. Phone: (608) 362-6896. Fax: (608) 362-8178. E-mail: patch@patchproducts.com. Web: www.patchproducts.com.

NATIONAL EDUCATIONAL BOSSES WEEK. May 20–24. A special week to honor bosses in the field of education such as principals and school superintendents. Annually, the third week in May. For info: Natl Assn of Educational Office Personnel, PO Box 12619, Wichita, KS 67277. Fax: (316) 942-7100.

WEIGHTS AND MEASURES DAY: ANNIVERSARY. May 20. Anniversary of international treaty, signed May 20, 1875, providing for the establishment of an International Bureau of Weights and Measures. The bureau was founded on international territory at Sevres, France.

WHITMONDAY. May 20. The day after Whitsunday is observed as a public holiday in many European countries.

BIRTHDAYS TODAY

Caralyn Buehner, 39, author (*The Escape of Marvin the Ape; It's a Spoon, Not a Shovel*), born St. George, UT, May 20, 1963.
Michael Crapo, 51, US Senator (R, Idaho), born Idaho Falls, May 20, 1951.
Mary Pope Osborne, 53, author (the Magic Tree House series, *One World, Many Religions*), born Fort Sill, OK, May 20, 1949.
David Wells, 39, baseball player, born Torrance, CA, May 20, 1963.

MAY 21 — TUESDAY

Day 141 — 224 Remaining

AMERICAN RED CROSS: FOUNDING ANNIVERSARY. May 21, 1881. Commemorates the founding of the American Red Cross by Clara Barton, its first president. The Red Cross had been founded in Switzerland in 1864 by representatives from 16 European nations. The organization is a voluntary, not-for-profit organization governed and directed by volunteers and provides disaster relief at home and abroad. 1.1 million volunteers are involved in community services such as collecting and distributing donated blood and blood products, teaching health and safety classes and acting as a medium for emergency communication between Americans and their armed forces.

CANADA: CALGARY INTERNATIONAL CHILDREN'S FESTIVAL. May 21–25. Calgary, AB. One of the largest children's festivals in North America, this event boasts the best in international theater, music, puppetry, dance, storytelling, mime, spectacle and more. For info: Calgary Intl Children's Festival, 205 8 Ave SE, Calgary, AB Canada T2G. Phone: (403) 294-7414. E-mail: admin@calgarychildfest.org. Web: www.calgarychildfest.org.

FITZGERALD, JOHN D.: DEATH ANNIVERSARY. May 21, 1988. Born in either 1906 or 1907 in Price, UT, the author of eight semi-autobiographical novels about growing up in a small Mormon community. *The Great Brain* chronicles the exploits of his older brother Tom, a twelve-year-old swindler with a "money-loving heart." John, who narrates the stories, both admires and is dis-

MAY 21
GEOGRAPHY BEE

Today is the day the finals in the National Geography Bee are being held in Washington, D.C. Why not hold your own classroom Geography Bee? You can have several variations on this theme; a straightforward Bee, similar to the National Bee, is one possibility. However, several variations will allow you to incorporate more students and are likely to be more fun.

Team play fosters cooperative learning skills. Divide students into groups of three or four. Instruct each team to choose a name for itself. Students can respond as a team to questions that pertain to geographical connections to the curriculum. Consultation among team members would be allowed and the spokesperson for each team could rotate to a different team member each round. Have a selection of reference books like almanacs and an encyclopedia on hand to formulate questions and answers.

A variation would be to assign a geographical feature as a specialty to each team. For example: team specialties could be rivers, mountain ranges, states, etc. Ask teams to generate the questions which will be posed to opposing teams. The asking team must be able to supply the correct answer. See which team can answer the most questions correctly.

A few truly motivated (or competitive) students may wish to offer a classroom challenge to another classroom. Structure the rules of this version to resemble those on "Who Wants to Be A Millionaire". Choose a student to be Regis. Students from each class can be the "phone" resources à la the TV show.

You can play a game of Geography: Near and Farther with upper elementary, middle and junior high students. Start by thinking of a geographical location or a state. Let students play a version of Twenty Questions to find the answer. Restrict questioning so the responses can be only with the words "near" or "farther." For example: If you live in New York, and your mystery location is California, questions might be, "Is it nearer than Nebraska?" "Is it farther than Mississippi?" The student who guesses the correct location gets to think of the next location and be the "teacher." This one is fun as a quick game while waiting in line, etc.

For very young primary students, hold a local Geography Bee. After explaining the term, think of well-known local "hot spots" and provide clues to help students recognize them. They could be places inside the school building, local lakes or rivers, even playground equipment. The goal is quick student recognition, so make your clues strong ones.

gusted by his brother's antics. Sequels include *The Great Brain at the Academy* and *Me and My Little Brain*. Fitzgerald died at Titus, FL, May 21, 1988.

GEMINI, THE TWINS. May 21–June 20. In the astronomical/astrological zodiac, which divides the sun's apparent orbit into 12 segments, the period May 21–June 20 is traditionally identified as the sun sign period of Gemini, the Twins. The ruling planet is Mercury.

NATIONAL BIKE TO WORK DAY. May 21. At the state or local level, Bike to Work events are conducted by small and large businesses, city governments, bicycle clubs and environmental groups. About two million participants nationwide. Annually, the third Tuesday in May. For info: Donald Tighe, Program Dir, League of American Bicyclists, 1612 K St NW, Ste 401, Washington, DC 20006. Phone: (202) 822-1333. Fax: (202) 822-1334. E-mail: bikeleague@aol.com. Web: www.bikeleague.org.

NATIONAL GEOGRAPHY BEE: NATIONAL FINALS. May 21–22. National Geographic Society Headquarters, Washington, DC. The first- place winner from each state-level competition, Apr 6, advances to the national level. Alex Trebek of "Jeopardy!" fame moderates the finals which are televised on PBS stations. Students compete for scholarships and prizes totaling more than $50,000. Est attendance: 400. For info: Natl Geography Bee, Natl Geographic Soc, 1145 17th St NW, Washington, DC 20036. Phone: (202) 857-7001. Web: www.nationalgeographic.com. *See* Curriculum Connection.

BIRTHDAYS TODAY

Judge Reinhold, 46, actor (*The Santa Clause*), born Wilmington, DE, May 21, 1956.

Ricky Williams, 25, football player, born San Diego, CA, May 21, 1977.

MAY 22 — WEDNESDAY

Day 142 — 223 Remaining

CRATER LAKE NATIONAL PARK ESTABLISHED: 100th ANNIVERSARY. May 22, 1902. One of the world's deepest lakes, Crater Lake was first discovered in 1853. In 1885 William Gladstone Steele saw the Oregon lake and made it his personal goal to establish the lake and surrounding areas as a national park. His goal was attained 17 years later. For more info: www.nps.gov/crla/index.htm.

LOBEL, ARNOLD: BIRTH ANNIVERSARY. May 22, 1933. Illustrator and author (the Frog and Toad series, Caldecott for *Fables*), born at Los Angeles, CA. Died Dec 4, 1987, at New York, NY.

"MISTER ROGERS' NEIGHBORHOOD" TV PREMIERE: 35th ANNIVERSARY. May 22, 1967. Presbyterian minister Fred Rogers hosted this long-running PBS children's program. Puppets and human characters interacted in the neighborhood of make-believe. Rogers played the voices of many of the puppets and educated young viewers on a variety of important subjects. The human cast members included: Betty Aberlin, Joe Negri, David Newell, Don Brockett, Francois Clemmons, Audrey Roth, Elsie Neal and Yoshi Ito. In 2001 the last episode was filmed. Amost 1,000 half-hour episodes of the program have aired.

NATIONAL MARITIME DAY. May 22. Anniversary of departure for first steamship crossing of the Atlantic from Savannah, GA, to Liverpool, England, by the steamship *Savannah* in 1819.

★ **NATIONAL MARITIME DAY.** May 22. Presidential Proclamation always issued for May 22 since 1933. (Pub Res No. 7 of May 20, 1933.)

SRI LANKA: NATIONAL HEROES DAY. May 22. Commemorates the struggle of the leaders of the National Independence Movement to liberate the country from colonial rule. Public holiday.

WORST EARTHQUAKE OF THE 20TH CENTURY: ANNIVERSARY. May 22, 1960. An earthquake of a magnitude 9.5 struck southern Chile, killing 2,000 people and leaving 2,000,000 homeless. The earthquake also caused damage in Hawaii, Japan and the Philippines. While 20th-century earthquakes in Mexico City, Japan and Turkey resulted in far more deaths, this earthquake in Chile was of the highest magnitude on the Richter scale. For more info: wwwneic.cr.usgs.gov/neis/eqlists/10maps_world.html.

YEMEN: NATIONAL DAY. May 22. Public holiday. Commemorates the reunification of Yemen in 1990.

BIRTHDAYS TODAY

Ann Cusack, 41, actress (*A League of Their Own*, "The Jeff Foxworthy Show"), born Evanston, IL, May 22, 1961.

MAY 23 — THURSDAY

Day 143 — 222 Remaining

BROWN, MARGARET WISE: BIRTH ANNIVERSARY. May 23, 1910. Children's author, born at Brooklyn, NY. Brown wrote *Goodnight Moon* and *The Runaway Bunny*. She died at Nice, France, Nov 13, 1952.

DEBORAH SAMSON DAY IN MASSACHUSETTS. May 23. Proclaimed annually by the governor to commemorate Deborah Samson, a Massachusetts schoolteacher who outfitted herself in men's clothing and fought in the American Revolution.

MESMER, FRIEDRICH ANTON: BIRTH ANNIVERSARY. May 23, 1734. German physician after whom Mesmerism was named. Magnetism and hypnotism were used by him in treating disease. Born at Iznang, Swabia, Germany, he died Mar 5, 1815, at Meersburg, Swabia, Germany.

NEW YORK PUBLIC LIBRARY: ANNIVERSARY. May 23, 1895. New York's then-governor Samuel J. Tilden was the driving force that resulted in the combining of the private Astor and Lenox libraries with a $2 million endowment and 15,000 volumes from the Tilden Trust to become the New York Public Library. For more info: www.nypl.org.

O'DELL, SCOTT: BIRTH ANNIVERSARY. May 23, 1898. Born at Los Angeles, CA. Scott O'Dell won the Newbery Medal in 1961 for his book *Island of the Blue Dolphins*. He published more than 26 children's books, including *The Black Pearl*. In 1972, O'Dell was awarded the Hans Christian Andersen International Award for lifetime achievement. He died at Santa Monica, CA, Oct 15, 1989. For a study guide to *Island of the Blue Dolphins*: glencoe.com/sec/literature/litlibrary.

SOUTH CAROLINA RATIFIES CONSTITUTION: ANNIVERSARY. May 23, 1788. By a vote of 149 to 73, South Carolina became the eighth state to ratify the Constitution.

May 2002

S	M	T	W	T	F	S
			1	2	3	4
5	6	7	8	9	10	11
12	13	14	15	16	17	18
19	20	21	22	23	24	25
26	27	28	29	30	31	

SWEDEN: LINNAEUS DAY. May 23. Stenbrohult. Commemorates the birth in 1707, of Carolus Linnaeus (Carl von Linne), Swedish naturalist who died at Uppsala, Sweden, Jan 10, 1778.

BIRTHDAYS TODAY

Susan Cooper, 67, author (Newbery for *The Grey King*), born Buckinghamshire, England, May 23, 1935.

Jewel, 28, singer, born Jewel Kilcher, Payson, UT, May 23, 1974.

MAY 24 — FRIDAY

Day 144 — 221 Remaining

BASEBALL FIRST PLAYED UNDER LIGHTS: ANNIVERSARY. May 24, 1935. The Cincinnati Reds defeated the Philadelphia Phillies by a score of 2–1, as more than 20,000 fans enjoyed the first night baseball game in the major leagues. The game was played at Crosley Field, Cincinnati, OH.

BELIZE: COMMONWEALTH DAY. May 24. Public holiday.

BROOKLYN BRIDGE OPENED: ANNIVERSARY. May 24, 1883. Nearly 14 years in construction, the $16 million Brooklyn Bridge over the East River connecting Manhattan and Brooklyn opened. Designed by John A. Roebling, the steel suspension bridge has a span of 1,595 feet. For more info: *The Brooklyn Bridge*, by Elaine Pascoe (Blackbirch, 1-56711-173-4, $17.95 Gr. 4–6).

BULGARIA: ENLIGHTENMENT AND CULTURE DAY. May 24. National holiday celebrated by schoolchildren, students, people of science and art.

ECUADOR: BATTLE OF PICHINCHA DAY. May 24. National holiday. Commemorates the 1822 battle that marked the final defeat of Spain in Ecuador.

ERITREA: INDEPENDENCE DAY. May 24. National Day. Gained independence from Ethiopia in 1993 after 30-year civil war.

LEUTZE, EMANUEL: BIRTH ANNIVERSARY. May 24, 1816. Itinerant painter, born at Wurttemberg, Germany, who came to the US when he was nine years old and began painting by age 15. He painted some of the most famous of American works, such as *Washington Crossing the Delaware* (which is in the Metropolitan Museum of Art in New York), *Washington Rallying the Troops at Monmouth* and *Columbus Before the Queen*. Died July 18, 1868, at Washington, DC.

MORSE OPENS FIRST US TELEGRAPH LINE: ANNIVERSARY. May 24, 1844. The first US telegraph line was formally opened between Baltimore, MD, and Washington, DC. Samuel F.B. Morse sent the first officially telegraphed words "What hath God wrought?" from the Capitol building to Baltimore. Earlier messages had been sent along the historic line during testing, and one, sent May 1, contained the news that Henry Clay had been nominated as president by the Whig party, from a meeting in Baltimore. This message reached Washington one hour prior to a train carrying the same news.

BIRTHDAYS TODAY

Diane DeGroat, 55, illustrator and author (*Happy Birthday to You, You Belong in the Zoo*), born Newton, NJ, May 24, 1947.

John Rowland, 45, Governor of Connecticut (R), born Waterbury, CT, May 24, 1957.

MAY 25 — SATURDAY

Day 145 — 220 Remaining

AFRICAN FREEDOM DAY. May 25. Public holiday in Chad, Zambia, Zimbabwe and some other African states. Members of the Organization for African Unity (formed May 25, 1963) commemorate their independence from colonial rule with sports contests, political rallies and tribal dances.

ARGENTINA: NATIONAL HOLIDAY. May 25. Commemoration of the declaration of independence of Argentina in 1810.

ARTHUR: ANNIVERSARY. May 25, 1976. Celebrate the anniversary of the first publication of Arthur—the star of one of the most successful children's books series and the Emmy Award-winning television show. Created by children's author and illustrator Marc Brown, the Arthur series of 75 books has sold more than 30 million copies. The Children's Museum of Manhattan hosted the Arthur's World Exhibit from May–September 2001. Teachers, librarians and parents are invited to join in the festivities by creating their own birthday bash featuring lots of fun reading and writing-related activities. For ideas and materials: Web: www.pbskids.org.arthur.

CONSTITUTIONAL CONVENTION: ANNIVERSARY. May 25, 1787. At Philadelphia, PA, the delegates from seven states, forming a quorum, opened the Constitutional Convention, which had been proposed by the Annapolis Convention, Sept 11–14, 1786. Among those who were in attendance: George Washington, Benjamin Franklin, James Madison, Alexander Hamilton and Elbridge Gerry.

JORDAN: INDEPENDENCE DAY. May 25. National holiday. Commemorates treaty in 1946, proclaiming autonomy (from Britain) and establishing monarchy.

MAWLID AL NABI: THE BIRTHDAY OF THE PROPHET MUHAMMAD. May 25. Mawlid al-Nabi (Birth of the Prophet Muhammad) is observed on Muslim calendar date Rabi al-Awal 12, 1423. Different methods for calculating the visibility of the new moon crescent at Mecca are used by different Muslim groups.

NATIONAL MISSING CHILDREN'S DAY. May 25. To promote awareness of the problem of missing children, to offer a forum for change and to offer safety information for children in school and communities. Annually, May 25. For info: Child Find of America, Inc, PO Box 277, New Paltz, NY 12561-0277. Phone: (914) 255-1848. Natl toll-free hotline phone numbers: (800) I-AM-LOST or (800) A-WAY-OUT.

NATIONAL TAP DANCE DAY. May 25. To celebrate this unique American art form that represents a fusion of African and European cultures and to transmit tap to succeeding generations through documentation and archival and performance support. Held on the anniversary of the birth of Bill "Bojangles" Robinson to honor his outstanding contribution to the art of tap dancing on stage and in films through the unification of diverse stylistic and racial elements.

POETRY DAY IN FLORIDA. May 25. In 1947 the Legislature decreed this day to be Poetry Day in all the public schools of Florida.

ROBINSON, BILL "BOJANGLES": BIRTH ANNIVERSARY. May 25, 1878. Born at Richmond, VA, the grandson of a slave, Robinson is considered one of the greatest tap dancers. He is best known for a routine in which he tap-danced up and down a staircase with Shirley Temple. He taught Gene Kelly, Sammy Davis, Jr, and others. He died at New York, NY, Nov 25, 1949.

BIRTHDAYS TODAY

Martha Alexander, 82, author and illustrator (*Nobody Asked Me If I Wanted a Baby Sister*), born Augusta, GA, May 25, 1920.
Ann McGovern, 72, author (*Too Much Noise*), born New York, NY, May 25, 1930.
Gordon Smith, 50, US Senator (R, Oregon), born Pendleton, OR, May 25, 1952.
Sheryl Swoopes, 31, basketball player, US Olympic Basketball Team, born Brownfield, TX, May 25, 1971.
Joyce Carol Thomas, 64, author (*Marked by Fire, Brown Honey in Broomwheat Tea*), born Ponca City, OK, May 25, 1938.

MAY 26 — SUNDAY

Day 146 — 219 Remaining

AUSTRALIA: SORRY DAY. May 26. A day to express sorrow for the forced removal of Aboriginal children from their families. For info: www.acn.net.au/articles/sorry.

GEORGIA: INDEPENDENCE RESTORATION DAY. May 26. National Day. Commemorates independence from the Soviet Union in 1991.

ITALY: PALIO DEI BALESTRIERI. May 26. Gubbio. The last Sunday in May is set aside for a medieval crossbow contest between Gubbio and Sansepolcro; medieval costumes, arms.

LUNAR ECLIPSE. May 26. Penumbral eclipse of the Moon. Moon enters penumbra 6:12 AM, EDT, middle of eclipse 8:03 AM, Moon leaves penumbra 9:53 AM. The beginning of the penumbral phase is visible in most of North America except the northeast, Central America, western South America, extreme northeast Russia, eastern Asia, Australia, most of Antarctica, the Pacific Ocean and the southeast Indian Ocean; the end visible in southwestern Alaska, Asia except the extreme north, Australia, the eastern Indian Ocean and most of the Pacific Ocean except the extreme eastern part.

MOON PHASE: FULL MOON. May 26. Moon enters Full Moon phase at 7:51 AM, EDT.

TRINITY SUNDAY. May 26. Christian Holy Day on the Sunday after Pentecost commemorates the Holy Trinity, the three divine persons—Father, Son and Holy Spirit—in one God. See also: "Pentecost" (May 19).

BIRTHDAYS TODAY

Brent Musburger, 63, sportscaster, born Portland, OR, May 26, 1939.
Paul E. Patton, 65, Governor of Kentucky (D), born Fallsburg, KY, May 26, 1937.
Sally Kristen Ride, 51, one of the first seven women in the US astronaut program and the first American woman in space, born Encino, CA, May 26, 1951.

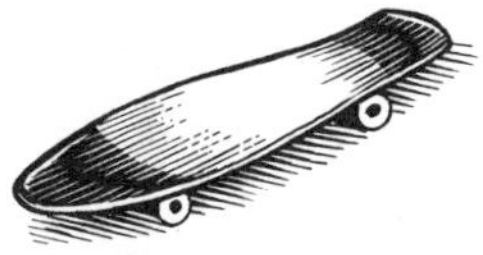

MAY 27 — MONDAY

Day 147 — 218 Remaining

BLOOMER, AMELIA JENKS: BIRTH ANNIVERSARY. May 27, 1818. American social reformer and women's rights advocate, born at Homer, NY. Her name is remembered especially because of her work for more sensible dress for women and her recommendation of a costume that had been introduced about 1849 by Elizabeth Smith Miller but came to be known as the "Bloomer Costume" or "Bloomers." Amelia Bloomer died at Council Bluffs, IA, Dec 30, 1894. For more info: *You Forgot Your Skirt, Amelia Bloomer*, by Shana Corey (Scholastic, 0-439-07819-9, $16.95 Gr. K–3).

CARSON, RACHEL (LOUISE): 95th BIRTH ANNIVERSARY. May 27, 1907. American scientist and author, born at Springdale, PA. She was the author of *The Sea Around Us* and *Silent Spring* (1962), a book that provoked widespread controversy over the use of pesticides and contributed to the beginning of the environmental movement. She died Apr 14, 1964, at Silver Spring, MD. For more info: *Rachel Carson: A Wonder of Nature*, by Catherine Reef (Twenty-First Century, 0-941477-38-X, $14.95 Gr. 2–5).

CELLOPHANE TAPE PATENTED: ANNIVERSARY. May 27, 1930. Richard Gurley Drew received a patent for his adhesive tape, later manufactured by 3M as Scotch tape.

DUNCAN, ISADORA: BIRTH ANNIVERSARY. May 27, 1878. American-born interpretive dancer who revolutionized the entire concept of dance. Bare-footed, freedom-loving, liberated woman and rebel against tradition, she experienced worldwide professional success and profound personal tragedy (her two children drowned, her marriage failed and she met a bizarre death when the long scarf she was wearing caught in a wheel of the open car in which she was riding, strangling her). Born at San Francisco, CA, she died at Nice, France, Sept 14, 1927.

GOLDEN GATE BRIDGE OPENED: 65th ANNIVERSARY. May 27, 1937. More than 200,000 people crossed San Francisco's Golden Gate Bridge on its first day.

HICKOCK, WILD BILL: BIRTH ANNIVERSARY. May 27, 1837. American frontiersman, legendary marksman, lawman, army scout and gambler, he was born at Troy Grove, IL, and died Aug 2, 1876, at Deadwood, SD. Hickock's end came when he was shot dead at a poker table by a drunk in the Number Ten saloon.

HUMPHREY, HUBERT HORATIO: BIRTH ANNIVERSARY. May 27, 1911. Born at Wallace, SD, he served as 38th vice president of the US and ran for president in 1968 but lost narrowly to Richard Nixon. Humphrey died at Waverly, MN, Jan 13, 1978.

MEMORIAL DAY. May 27. Legal public holiday. Also known as Decoration Day because of the tradition of decorating the graves of servicemen. An occasion for honoring those who have died in battle. Observance dates from Civil War years in US: first documented observance at Waterloo, NY, May 5, 1865. See also: "Confederate Memorial Day" (Apr 26, Apr 29, May 10 and June 3).

★ **MEMORIAL DAY, PRAYER FOR PEACE.** May 27. Presidential Proclamation issued each year since 1948. PL81–512 of May 11, 1950, asks President to proclaim annually this day as a day of prayer for permanent peace. PL90–363 of June 28, 1968, requires that beginning in 1971 it will be observed the last Monday in May. Often titled "Prayer for Peace Memorial Day," and traditionally requests the flying of the flag at half-staff "for the customary forenoon period."

May 2002

S	M	T	W	T	F	S
			1	2	3	4
5	6	7	8	9	10	11
12	13	14	15	16	17	18
19	20	21	22	23	24	25
26	27	28	29	30	31	

BIRTHDAYS TODAY

Christopher J. Dodd, 58, US Senator (D, Connecticut), born Willimantic, CT, May 27, 1944.

Antonio Freeman, 30, football player, born Baltimore, MD, May 27, 1972.

Lynn Sweat, 68, illustrator (the Amelia Bedelia books), born Alexandria, LA, May 27, 1934.

Frank Thomas, 34, baseball player, born Columbus, GA, May 27, 1968.

MAY 28 — TUESDAY

Day 148 — 217 Remaining

AZERBAIJAN: DAY OF THE REPUBLIC. May 28. Public holiday. Commemorates the declaration of the Azerbaijan Democratic Republic in 1918.

FLEMING, IAN: BIRTH ANNIVERSARY. May 28, 1908. Author of *Chitty Chitty Bang Bang*, which was made into a popular movie for children, as well as the James Bond series of books. Born at London, England, he died at Canterbury, England, Aug 12, 1964.

SIERRA CLUB FOUNDED: ANNIVERSARY. May 28, 1892. Founded by famed naturalist John Muir, the Sierra Club promotes conservation of the natural environment by influencing public policy. It has been especially important in the founding of and protection of our national parks. For info: Sierra Club, 85 Second St, 2nd Floor, San Francisco, CA 94105-3441. Phone: (415) 977-5500. Web: www.sierraclub.org.

THORPE, JAMES FRANCIS (JIM): BIRTH ANNIVERSARY. May 28, 1888. This distinguished Native American athlete was the winner of pentathlon and decathlon events at the 1912 Olympic Games and a professional baseball and football player. Born near Prague, OK, he died at Lomita, CA, Mar 28, 1953.

BIRTHDAYS TODAY

Glen Rice, 35, basketball player, born Flint, MI, May 28, 1967.

MAY 29 — WEDNESDAY

Day 149 — 216 Remaining

AMNESTY ISSUED FOR SOUTHERN REBELS: ANNIVERSARY. May 29, 1865. President Andrew Johnson issued a proclamation giving a general amnesty to all who participated in the rebellion against the US. High-ranking members of the Confederate government and military and those who owned more than $20,000 worth of property were excepted and had to apply individually to the President for a pardon. Once an oath of allegiance was taken, all former property rights, except those in slaves, were returned to the former owners.

CONSTANTINOPLE FELL TO THE TURKS: ANNIVERSARY. May 29, 1453. The city of Constantinople was captured by the Turks, who renamed it Istanbul (although the name wasn't officially changed until 1930). This conquest marked the end of the Byzantine Empire; the city became the capital of the Ottoman Empire.

MAY 29
MOUNT EVEREST SUMMIT REACHED

On May 29, 1953, Edmund Hillary, a New Zealander, and his Sherpa guide, Tensing Norgay, became the first people to reach the summit of Mount Everest, the world's highest mountain. Hearing about braving icy temperatures and crossing treacherous crevasses fascinates children greatly. Learning about Hillary's adventure is exciting and informative. And readers will want to follow up with additional books about more recent summit adventures.

For geography, students could make a list of the world's 10 highest mountains. Locate them on a map and calculate the distance your school is from each mountain. More in-depth research could include locating satellite images of the appropriate mountain ranges and pinpointing each mountain's location in the range. Students could look for photographs that show the specific routes used while attempting to reach each summit. For a height comparison, graph the elevation of your town against that of each mountain. How many times would you have to "stack" up your town to reach the height of the world's top 10 mountains?

For science, students could find information about the specific dangers on Mount Everest; for example, how oxygen levels change at higher elevations and how low oxygen levels affect the human body. The "Nova" website has information on this topic at www.pbs.org/nova/everest. Also visit www.nationalgeographic.com/everest/index.html. Nighttime wind velocity is high on top of Mount Everest. How does it compare with that of Mount Washington, in New Hampshire? With those of thunderstorms and hurricanes? Researching terms such as glacier, crevasse and icefall will help to illustrate the dangers involved in mountain climbing.

In language arts, students could try to put themselves in the shoes of Hillary and Norgay once they had reached the summit. Have the class write a short paragraph to answer: How would you feel if you were standing on the top of the world? or What things in your life make you feel as if you are standing on top of the world?

Several recently published books elaborate on Hillary's historic achievement. *Triumph on Everest*, by Broughton Coburn (National Geographic, 0-7922-7114-9, $17.95 Gr. 4 & up), is a photobiography of Hillary's life. *Mystery on Everest*, by Audrey Salkeld (National Geographic, 0-7922-7222-6, $17.95 Gr. 4 & up), is the riveting story of George Mallory, who died in 1924 while attempting to reach Mount Everest's summit. Middle school and junior high readers will enjoy *Within Reach: My Everest Story*, by Mark Pfetzer & Jack Galvin (Penguin, 0-14-130497-9, $6.99 Gr. 5 & up), the autobiography of the teenager who ascended Mount Everest. High school readers will devour *Into Thin Air*, by Jon Krakauer (Doubleday, 0-385-49208-1, $7.99 Adult), and will want to look at www.mteverest.net.

HENRY, PATRICK: BIRTH ANNIVERSARY. May 29, 1736. American revolutionary leader and orator, born at Studley, VA, and died near Brookneal, VA, June 6, 1799. Especially remembered for his speech (Mar 23, 1775) for arming the Virginia militia, at St. John's Church, Richmond, VA, when he declared: "I know not what course others may take, but as for me, give me liberty or give me death."

KENNEDY, JOHN FITZGERALD: 85th BIRTH ANNIVERSARY. May 29, 1917. The 35th president of the US, born at Brookline, MA. Kennedy was the youngest man ever elected to the presidency, the first Roman Catholic and the first president to have served in the US Navy. He was assassinated while riding in an open automobile, at Dallas, TX, Nov 22, 1963. (Accused assassin Lee Harvey Oswald was killed at the Dallas police station by a gunman, Jack Ruby, two days later.) He was the fourth US president to be killed by an assassin, and the second to be buried at Arlington National Cemetery (the first was William Howard Taft). For more info: www.ipl.org/ref/POTUS or www.cs.umb.edu/jfklibrary/index.htm.

MOUNT EVEREST SUMMIT REACHED: ANNIVERSARY. May 29, 1953. New Zealand explorer Sir Edmund Hillary and Tensing Norgay, a Sherpa guide, became the first team to reach the summit of Mount Everest, the world's highest mountain. *See* Curriculum Connection.

NATIONAL SPELLING BEE FINALS. May 29–30. Washington, DC. Newspapers and other sponsors across the country send 245–255 youngsters to the finals at Washington, DC. Annually, Wednesday and Thursday of Memorial Day week. Est attendance: 1,000. For info: Dir, Natl Spelling Bee, Scripps-Howard, PO Box 5380, Cincinnati, OH 45201. Phone: (513) 977-3040.

RHODE ISLAND RATIFIES CONSTITUTION: ANNIVERSARY. May 29. Became the 13th state to ratify the Constitution in 1790.

VIRGINIA PLAN PROPOSED: ANNIVERSARY. May 29, 1787. Just five days after the Constitutional Convention met at Philadelphia, PA, the "Virginia Plan" was proposed. It called for establishment of a government consisting of a legislature with two houses, an executive (chosen by the legislature) and a judicial branch.

WISCONSIN: ADMISSION DAY: ANNIVERSARY. May 29, 1848. Became 30th state in 1848.

BIRTHDAYS TODAY

Andrew Clements, 53, author (*Frindle, Big Al*), born Camden, NJ, May 29, 1949.

Brock Cole, 64, author and illustrator (*Buttons, The Facts Speak for Themselves, The Goats*), born Charlotte, MI, May 29, 1938.

Rupert Everett, 43, actor (*Inspector Gadget*), born Norfolk, England, May 29, 1959.

Blake Foster, 17, actor (*Turbo: A Power Rangers Movie*, "Power Rangers Turbo"), born Northridge, CA, May 29, 1985.

MAY 30 — THURSDAY

Day 150 — 215 Remaining

CROATIA: NATIONAL DAY. May 30. Public holiday commemorating statehood in 1990.

FIRST AMERICAN DAILY NEWSPAPER PUBLISHED: ANNIVERSARY. May 30, 1783. *The Pennsylvania Evening Post* became the first daily newspaper published in the US. The paper was published at Philadelphia, PA, by Benjamin Towne.

LINCOLN MEMORIAL DEDICATION: 80th ANNIVERSARY. May 30, 1922. The memorial is made of marble from Colorado and Tennessee and limestone from Indiana. It stands in West Potomac Park at Washington, DC. The outside columns are Doric, the inside, Ionic. The Memorial was designed by architect Henry Bacon and its cornerstone was laid in 1915. A skylight lets light into the interiors where the compelling statue "Seated Lincoln," by sculptor Daniel Chester French, is situated. For more info: www.nps.gov/linc/index.htm.

SAINT JOAN OF ARC: FEAST DAY. May 30. French heroine and martyr, known as the Maid of Orleans, led the French against the English invading army. She was captured, found guilty of heresy and burned at the stake in 1431 (at age 19). Her innocence was declared in 1456 and she was canonized in 1920.

SPACE MILESTONE: *MARINER 9* (US): ANNIVERSARY. May 30, 1971. Unmanned spacecraft was launched, entering Martian orbit the following Nov 13. The craft relayed temperature and gravitational fields and sent back spectacular photographs of both the surface of Mars and of her two moons. It was the first spacecraft to orbit another planet.

TRINIDAD: INDIAN ARRIVAL DAY. May 30. Port of Spain. Public holiday. About 40 percent of Trinidad's population is descended from immigrants who were brought from India by the British in the 1840s.

BIRTHDAYS TODAY

Blake Bashoff, 21, actor (*The New Swiss Family Robinson*), born Philadelphia, PA, May 30, 1981.

Omri Katz, 26, actor ("Eerie, Indiana"), born Los Angeles, CA, May 30, 1976.

Trey Parker, 30, director, creator ("South Park"), born Auburn, AL, May 30, 1972.

Manuel (Manny) Ramirez, 30, baseball player, born Santo Domingo, Dominican Republic, May 30, 1972.

MAY 31 — FRIDAY

Day 151 — 214 Remaining

COPYRIGHT LAW PASSED: ANNIVERSARY. May 31, 1790. President George Washington signed the first US copyright law. It gave protection for 14 years to books written by US citizens. In 1891, the law was extended to cover books by foreign authors as well.

JOHNSTOWN FLOOD: ANNIVERSARY. May 31, 1889. Heavy rains caused the Connemaugh River Dam to burst. At nearby Johnstown, PA, the resulting flood killed more than 2,300 persons and destroyed the homes of thousands more. Nearly 800 unidentified drowning victims were buried in a common grave at Johnstown's Grandview Cemetery. So devastating was the flood and so widespread the sorrow for its victims that "Johnstown Flood" entered the language as a phrase to describe a disastrous event. The valley city of Johnstown, in the Allegheny Mountains, has been damaged repeatedly by floods. Floods in 1936 (25 deaths) and 1977 (85 deaths) were the next most destructive.

WHITMAN, WALT: BIRTH ANNIVERSARY. May 31, 1819. Poet and journalist, born at West Hills, Long Island, NY. Whitman's best known work, *Leaves of Grass* (1855), is a classic of American poetry. His poems celebrated all of modern life, including subjects that were considered taboo at the time. He died Mar 26, 1892, at Camden, NJ.

WORLD CUP KOREA/JAPAN. May 31–June 30. The 17th World Cup competition in soccer (known as football in most of the world) will begin in Seoul, Korea, on May 31, 2002, with the world championship team being crowned in Yokohama, Japan, on June 30. Thirty-two teams will compete with half the matches played in Korea and half in Japan. For info: Federation Internationale de Football Assn, FIFA House, Hitzigweg 11, PO Box 85, 8030 Zurich, Switzerland. Phone: 41-1384 9595. Fax: 41-1384 9696. Web: www.fifa.com.

WORLD NO-TOBACCO DAY. May 31. Intended to discourage tobacco users from consuming tobacco and to encourage governments, communities, groups and individuals to become aware of the challenge and to take action. Annually, May 31. For info: World No-Tobacco Day, American Assn for World Health, 1825 K St NW, Ste 1208, Washington, DC 20006. Phone: (202) 466-5883. Fax: (202) 466-5896. E-mail: aawhstaff@aol.com. Web: www.aawhworldhealth.org.

BIRTHDAYS TODAY

Clint Eastwood, 72, actor, director (Oscar for *Unforgiven*), born San Francisco, CA, May 31, 1930.

Kenny Lofton, 35, baseball player, born East Chicago, IN, May 31, 1967.

Harry Mazer, 77, author (*The Wild Kid*), born New York, NY, May 31, 1925.

JUNE 1 — SATURDAY

Day 152 — 213 Remaining

ATLANTIC, CARIBBEAN AND GULF HURRICANE SEASON. June 1–Nov 30. For info: US Dept of Commerce, Natl Oceanic and Atmospheric Admin, Rockville, MD 20852. Web: www.nws.noaa.gov.

CANCER FROM THE SUN MONTH. June 1–30. To promote education and awareness of the dangers of skin cancer from too much exposure to the sun. Kit of materials available for $15 from this nonprofit organization. For info: Frederick Mayer, Pres, Pharmacy Council on Dermatology (PCD), 101 Lucas Valley Rd, #210, San Rafael, CA 94903. Phone: (415) 479-8628. Fax: (415) 479-8608. E-mail: ppsi@aol.com. Web: www.ppsinc.org.

CHILDREN'S AWARENESS MONTH. June 1–30. A monthlong celebration of being aware of America's children in our everyday lives and communities while lovingly remembering all of America's children who we have lost through violence and violent deaths in our nation. These could have been our child or grandchild. We choose to remember the living during the month of June. For info: Judith Natale, CEO & Founder, Natl Children & Family Awareness of America, Administrative Headquarters, 3060 Rt 405 Hwy, Muncy, PA 17756-8808. Phone: (888) MAA-DESK. E-mail: MaaJudith@aol.com.

CHINA: INTERNATIONAL CHILDREN'S DAY. June 1. Shanghai.

CNN DEBUTED: ANNIVERSARY. June 1, 1980. The Cable News Network, TV's first all-news service, went on the air.

FIREWORKS SAFETY MONTH. June 1–July 4. Activities during this month are designed to warn and educate parents and children about the dangers of playing with fireworks. Prevent Blindness America will offer suggestions for safer ways to celebrate the Fourth of July. Materials that can easily be posted or distributed to the community will be provided. For info: Prevent Blindness America®, 500 E Remington Rd, Schaumburg, IL 60173. Phone: (800) 331-2020. Fax: (847) 843-8458. Web: www.preventblindness.org.

INTERNATIONAL VOLUNTEERS WEEK. June 1–7. To honor men and women throughout the world who serve as volunteers, rendering valuable service without compensation to the communities in which they live and to honor nonprofit organizations dedicated to making the world a better place in which to live. For complete info, send $4 to cover expense of printing, handling and postage. Annually, the first seven days of June. For info: Dr. Stanley Drake, Pres, Intl Soc of Friendship and Good Will, 8592 Roswell Rd, Ste 434, Atlanta, GA 30350-1870.

JUNE IS TURKEY LOVERS' MONTH. June 1–30. A monthlong campaign to promote awareness and increase turkey consumption at a nonholiday time. Annually, the month of June. For info: Natl Turkey Federation, 1225 New York Ave NW, Ste 400, Washington, DC 20005. Phone: (202) 898-0100. Fax: (202) 898-0203. E-mail: info@turkeyfed.org. Web: www.eatturkey.com.

KENTUCKY: ADMISSION DAY: ANNIVERSARY. June 1. Became 15th state in 1792.

KENYA: MADARAKA DAY. June 1. Madaraka Day (Self-Rule Day) is observed as a national public holiday.

MARQUETTE, JACQUES: BIRTH ANNIVERSARY. June 1, 1637. Father Jacques Marquette (Père Marquette), Jesuit missionary-explorer of the Great Lakes region. Born at Laon, France, he died at Ludington, MI, May 18, 1675.

NATIONAL ACCORDION AWARENESS MONTH. June 1–30. To increase public awareness of this multicultural instrument and its influence and popularity in today's music. For info: All Things Accordion, PO Box 475136, San Francisco, CA 94147-5136. Phone: (415) 440-0800. E-mail: bellows@ladyofspain.com.

NATIONAL BLESS-A-CHILD MONTH. June 1–30. Grassroots community activities to increase public awareness of the challenges facing at-risk children and promote volunteer as well as community involvement in their lives. For info: Donna Strout, Operation Blessing Intl, 977 Centerville Turnpike, Virginia Beach, VA 23463. Phone: (757) 226-2443. Fax: (757) 226-6183. E-mail: donna.strout@OB.ORG.

NATIONAL CANDY MONTH. June 1–30. Sponsored by *Confectioner Magazine* and manufacturers, wholesalers and retailers to promote candy as a fun food and enhance consumer awareness of products available in the US. Consumer celebrations include chocolate festivals, contests and information on candy making, decorating with candy and the history of chocolate and chewing and bubble gum. For info: Lisbeth Echeandia, Confectioner Magazine, PO Box 388, Savoy, TX 75479. Phone: (800) 826-8586. E-mail: confectioner@texoma.net.

NATIONAL FROZEN YOGURT MONTH. June 1–30. To inform the public of the benefits and colorful history of frozen yogurt, one of America's new favorite desserts. Annually, the month of June. For info: Stacy Duckett, TCBY, 1200 TCBY Tower, 425 W Capitol Ave, Little Rock, AR 72201. Phone: (501) 688-8229.

NATIONAL ROSE MONTH. June 1–30. To recognize American-grown roses, our national floral emblem. America's favorite flower is grown in all 50 states and more than 1.2 billion fresh cut roses are sold at retail each year. The year 2002 has been designated the Year of the Rose. For info: Mktg Dir, Roses Inc, Box 99, Haslett, MI 48840. Phone: (517) 339-9544. Web: www.rosesinc.org.

NATIONAL SAFETY MONTH. June 1–30. For info: Laura Wilkinson, Natl Safety Council, 1121 Spring Lake Dr, Itasca, IL 60143-3201. Phone: (800) 621-7615. E-mail: wilkinsonl@nsc.org. Web: www.nsc.org.

SAMOA: NATIONAL DAY. June 1. Holiday in the country formerly known as Western Samoa.

STAND FOR CHILDREN DAY. June 1. Stand for Children is a national organization that encourages individuals to improve children's lives. Its mission is to identify, train and connect local children's activists engaging in advocacy, awareness-raising and service initiatives as part of Children's Action Teams. Annually, June 1. On this day each year a special issue, such as quality child care, is highlighted. For more info: *Stand for Children*, by Marian

Wright Edelman (Hyperion, 0-7868-0365-7, $15.95 Gr. 5–8). For info: Children's Defense Fund, Stand for Children, 1834 Connecticut Ave NW, Washington, DC 20009. Phone: (800) 663-4032. Fax: (202) 234-0217. E-mail: tellstand@stand.org. Web: www.stand.org.

TENNESSEE: ADMISSION DAY: ANNIVERSARY. June 1. Became 16th state in 1796. Observed as a holiday in Tennessee.

BIRTHDAYS TODAY

Alexi Lalas, 32, soccer player, born Detroit, MI, June 1, 1970.

JUNE 2 — SUNDAY

Day 153 — 212 Remaining

BHUTAN: CORONATION DAY. June 2. National holiday. Anniversary of the coronation of the 4th king in 1974.

BULGARIA: HRISTO BOTEV DAY. June 2. Poet and national hero Hristro Botev fell fighting Turks, 1876.

CORPUS CHRISTI (US OBSERVANCE). June 2. A movable Roman Catholic celebration commemorating the institution of the Holy Eucharist. The solemnity has been observed on the Thursday following Trinity Sunday since 1246, except in the US, where it is observed on the Sunday following Trinity Sunday.

ITALY: REPUBLIC DAY. June 2. National holiday. Commemorates referendum in 1946 in which republic status was selected instead of return to monarchy.

JAPAN: DAY OF THE RICE GOD. June 2. Chiyoda. Annual rice-transplanting festival observed on first Sunday in June. Centuries-old rural folk ritual revived in 1930s and celebrated with colorful costumes, parades, music, dancing and prayers to the Shinto rice god Wbai-sama.

MOON PHASE: LAST QUARTER. June 2. Moon enters Last Quarter phase at 8:05 PM, EDT.

TEACHER'S DAY IN MASSACHUSETTS. June 2. Proclaimed annually by the governor for the first Sunday in June.

UNITED KINGDOM: CORONATION DAY. June 2. Commemorates the crowning of Queen Elizabeth II in 1953.

YELL "FUDGE" AT THE COBRAS IN NORTH AMERICA DAY. June 2. Anywhere north of the Panama Canal. In order to keep poisonous cobra snakes out of North America, all citizens are asked to go outdoors at noon, local time, and yell "Fudge." Fudge makes cobras gag and the mere mention of it makes them skedaddle. Annually, June 2. [© 1999 by WH] For info: Thomas or Ruth Roy, Wellcat Holidays, 2418 Long Lane, Lebanon, PA 17046. Phone: (230) 332-4886. E-mail: wellcat@supernet.com. Web: www.wellcat.com.

BIRTHDAYS TODAY

Dana Carvey, 47, comedian, actor (*Wayne's World*, "Saturday Night Live"), born Missoula, MT, June 2, 1955.

Paul Galdone, 88, author (*The Little Red Hen*), born Budapest, June 2, 1914.

Norton Juster, 73, author (*The Phantom Tollbooth*), born Brooklyn, NY, June 2, 1929.

June 2002

S	M	T	W	T	F	S
						1
2	3	4	5	6	7	8
9	10	11	12	13	14	15
16	17	18	19	20	21	22
23	24	25	26	27	28	29
30						

Jerry Mathers, 54, actor ("Leave It to Beaver"), born Sioux City, IA, June 2, 1948.

Helen Oxenbury, 64, author, illustrator (the Tom & Pippo series, *Clap Hands, Tickle Tickle*), born Suffolk, England, June 2, 1938.

JUNE 3 — MONDAY

Day 154 — 211 Remaining

CHIMBORAZO DAY. June 3. To bring the shape of the earth into focus by publicizing the fact that Mount Chimborazo, Ecuador, near the equator, pokes farther out into space than any other mountain on earth, including Mount Everest. (The distance from sea level at the equator to the center of the earth is 13 miles greater than the radius to sea level at the north pole. This means that New Orleans is about six miles further from the center of the earth than is Lake Itasca at the headwaters of the Mississippi, so the Mississippi flows uphill.) For info: Robert L. Birch, Puns Corps, Box 2364, Falls Church, VA 22042-0364. Phone: (703) 533-3668.

CONFEDERATE MEMORIAL DAY/JEFFERSON DAVIS DAY IN KENTUCKY. June 3. Commemorated on the birthday of Jefferson Davis.

DAVIS, JEFFERSON: BIRTH ANNIVERSARY. June 3, 1808. American statesman, US senator, only president of the Confederate States of America. Imprisoned May 10, 1865–May 13, 1867, but never brought to trial, deprived of rights of citizenship after the Civil War. Davis was born at Todd County, KY, and died at New Orleans, LA, Dec 6, 1889. His citizenship was restored, posthumously, Oct 17, 1978, when President Carter signed an Amnesty Bill. This bill, he said, "officially completes the long process of reconciliation that has reunited our people following the tragic conflict between the states." Davis's birth anniversary is observed in Florida, Kentucky and South Carolina on this day, in Alabama on the first Monday in June and in Mississippi on the last Monday in May. Davis's birth anniversary is observed as Confederate Memorial Day in Kentucky and Tennessee.

DREW, CHARLES RICHARD: BIRTH ANNIVERSARY. June 3, 1904. African American physician who discovered how to store blood plasma and who organized the blood bank system in the US and UK during WWII. Born at Washington, DC, he was killed in an automobile accident near Burlington, NC, Apr 1, 1950. For more info: *Charles Drew: A Life-Saving Doctor*, by Miles Shapiro (Raintree, 0-8172-4403-4, $18.98 Gr. 5–12).

FIRST WOMAN RABBI IN US: 30th ANNIVERSARY. June 3, 1972. Sally Jan Priesand was ordained the first woman rabbi in the US. She became assistant rabbi at the Stephen Wise Free Synagogue, New York City, Aug 1, 1972.

HOBART, GARRET AUGUSTUS: BIRTH ANNIVERSARY. June 3, 1844. The 24th vice president of the US (1897–99), born at Long Branch, NJ. Died at Paterson, NJ, Nov 21, 1899.

SPACE MILESTONE: *GEMINI 4* (US). June 3, 1965. James McDivitt and Edward White made 66 orbits of Earth. White took the first space walk by an American and maneuvered 20 minutes outside the capsule.

BIRTHDAYS TODAY

Margaret Cosgrove, 76, author and illustrator (*Wonders of the Tree World*), born Sylvania, OH, June 3, 1926.

Anita Lobel, 68, author and illustrator (*Away From Home; One Lighthouse, One Moon*), born Krakow, Poland, June 3, 1934.

JUNE 4 — TUESDAY

Day 155 — 210 Remaining

CHINA: TIANANMEN SQUARE MASSACRE: ANNIVERSARY. June 4, 1989. After almost a month and a half of student demonstrations for democracy, the Chinese government ordered its troops to open fire on the unarmed protestors at Tiananmen Square at Beijing. The demonstrations began Apr 18 as several thousand students marched to mourn the death of Hu Yaobang, a pro-reform leader within the Chinese government. A ban was imposed on such demonstrations; Apr 22, 100,000 gathered in Tiananmen Square in defiance of the ban. On May 13, 2,000 of the students began a hunger strike and May 20, the government imposed martial law and began to bring in troops. On June 2, the demonstrators turned back an advance of unarmed troops in the first clash with the People's Army. Under the cover of darkness, early June 4, troops opened fire on the assembled crowds and armored personnel carriers rolled into the square crushing many of the students as they lay sleeping in their tents. Although the government claimed that few died in the attack, estimates range from several hundred to several thousand casualties. In the following months thousands of demonstrators were rounded up and jailed.

FINLAND: FLAG DAY. June 4. Finland's armed forces honor the birth anniversary of Carl Gustaf Mannerheim, born in 1867.

GHANA: REVOLUTION DAY. June 4. National holiday.

TONGA: EMANCIPATION DAY. June 4. National holiday. Commemorates independence from Britain in 1970.

UNITED NATIONS: INTERNATIONAL DAY OF INNOCENT CHILDREN VICTIMS OF AGGRESSION. June 4. On Aug 19, 1982, the General Assembly decided to commemorate June 4 of each year as the International Day of Innocent Children Victims of Aggression.

BIRTHDAYS TODAY

Andrea Jaeger, 37, former tennis player, born Chicago, IL, June 4, 1965.

Scott Wolf, 34, actor ("Party of Five"), born Boston, MA, June 4, 1968.

JUNE 5 — WEDNESDAY

Day 156 — 209 Remaining

APPLE II COMPUTER RELEASED: 25th ANNIVERSARY. June 5, 1977. The Apple II computer, with 4K of memory, went on sale for $1,298. Its predecessor, the Apple I, was sold largely to electronic hobbyists the previous year. Apple released the Macintosh computer Jan 24, 1984.

DENMARK: CONSTITUTION DAY. June 5. National holiday. Commemorates Denmark's becoming a constitutional monarchy in 1849.

FIRST BALLOON FLIGHT: ANNIVERSARY. June 5, 1783. The first public demonstration of a hot-air balloon flight took place at Annonay, France, where the coinventor brothers, Joseph and Jacques Montgolfier, succeeded in launching their unmanned 33-foot-diameter *globe aerostatique*. It rose an estimated 1,500 feet and traveled, windborne, about 7,500 feet before landing after the 10-minute flight—the first sustained flight of any object achieved by man. The first manned flight was three months later. See also: "First Manned Flight: Anniversary" (Oct 15).

IRAN: FIFTEENTH OF KHORDAD. June 5. National holiday. Commemorates the deaths of clerics in 1963 in a clash with the shah's forces.

SCARRY, RICHARD McCLURE: BIRTH ANNIVERSARY. June 5, 1919. Author and illustrator of children's books was born at Boston, MA. Two widely known books of the more than 250 Scarry authored are *Richard Scarry's Best Word Book Ever* (1965) and *Richard Scarry's Please & Thank You* (1973). The pages are crowded with small animal characters who live like humans. More than 100 million copies of his books sold worldwide. Died Apr 30, 1994, at Gstaad, Switzerland.

UNITED NATIONS: WORLD ENVIRONMENT DAY. June 5. Observed annually on the anniversary of the opening of the UN Conference on the Human Environment held in Stockholm in 1972, which led to establishment of UN Environment Programme, based in Nairobi. The General Assembly has urged marking the day with activities reaffirming concern for the preservation and enhancement of the environment. For more info, visit the UN's website for children at www.un.org/Pubs/CyberSchool Bus/.

BIRTHDAYS TODAY

Allan Ahlberg, 64, author (*The Jolly Postman*), born Croydon, England, June 5, 1938.

Joe Clark, 63, Canada's 16th prime minister, 1979–80, born High River, AB, Canada, June 5, 1939.

Mark Wahlberg, 31, singer (Marky Mark), host ("AIXN"), born Dorchester, MA, June 5, 1971.

JUNE 6 — THURSDAY

Day 157 — 208 Remaining

AARDEMA, VERNA: BIRTH ANNIVERSARY. June 6, 1911. Author (*Why Mosquitoes Buzz in People's Ears*), born at New Era, MI. Died May 11, 2000. *See* Curriculum Connection.

BONZA BOTTLER DAY™. June 6. To celebrate when the number of the day is the same as the number of the month. Bonza Bottler Day™ is an excuse to have a party at least once a month. For info: Gail M. Berger, 109 Matthew Ave, Poca, WV 25159. Phone: (304) 776-7746. E-mail: gberger5@aol.com.

D-DAY: ANNIVERSARY. June 6, 1944. In the early-morning hours Allied forces landed in Normandy on the north coast of France.

In an operation that took months of planning, a fleet of 2,727 ships of every description converged from British ports from Wales to the North Sea. Operation *Overlord* involved 2,000,000 tons of war materials, including more than 50,000 tanks, armored cars, jeeps, trucks and half-tracks. The US alone sent 1,700,000 fighting men. The Germans believed the invasion would not take place under the adverse weather conditions of this early June day. But as the sun came up the village of Saint Mère Eglise was liberated by American parachutists and by nightfall the landing of 155,000 Allies attested to the success of D-Day. The long-awaited second front of WWII had at last materialized.

HALE, NATHAN: BIRTH ANNIVERSARY. June 6, 1755. American patriot Nathan Hale was born at Coventry, CT. During the battles for New York in the American Revolution, he volunteered to seek military intelligence behind enemy lines and was captured on the night of Sept 21, 1776. In an audience before General William Howe, Hale admitted he was an American officer and was ordered hanged the following morning. Although some question them, his dying words, "I only regret that I have but one life to lose for my country," have become a symbol of American patriotism. He was hanged Sept 22, 1776, at Manhattan, NY.

KOREA: MEMORIAL DAY. June 6. Nation pays tribute to the war dead and memorial services are held at the National Cemetery at Seoul. Legally recognized Korean holiday.

SPACE MILESTONE: *SOYUZ 11* (USSR): ANNIVERSARY. June 6, 1971. Launched with cosmonauts G.T. Dobrovolsky, V.N. Volkov and V.I. Patsayev, who died during the return landing June 30, 1971, after a 24-day space flight. *Soyuz 11* had docked at *Salyut* orbital space station June 7–29; the cosmonauts entered the space station for the first time and conducted scientific experiments. First humans to die in space.

SUSAN B. ANTHONY FINED FOR VOTING: ANNIVERSARY. June 6, 1872. Seeking to test for women the citizenship and voting rights extended to black males under the 14th and 15th Amendments, Susan B. Anthony led a group of women who registered and voted at a Rochester, NY, election. She was arrested, tried and sentenced to pay a fine. She refused to do so and was allowed to go free by a judge who feared she would appeal to a higher court.

SWEDEN: FLAG DAY. June 6. Commemorates the day upon which Gustavus I (Gustavus Vasa) ascended the throne of Sweden in 1523.

BIRTHDAYS TODAY

Dalai Lama, 67, Tibet's spiritual leader and Nobel Peace Prize winner, born Taktser, China, June 6, 1935.

Marian Wright Edelman, 63, president of Children's Defense Fund, civil rights activist, born Bennettsville, SC, June 6, 1939.

Staci Keanan, 27, actress ("Step By Step"), born Devon, PA, June 6, 1975.

Cynthia Rylant, 48, author (Newbery for *Missing May*), born Hopewell, VA, June 6, 1954.

Peter Spier, 75, illustrator and author (Caldecott for *Noah's Ark*), born Amsterdam, Netherlands, June 6, 1927.

June 2002

S	M	T	W	T	F	S
						1
2	3	4	5	6	7	8
9	10	11	12	13	14	15
16	17	18	19	20	21	22
23	24	25	26	27	28	29
30						

JUNE 6
VERNA AARDEMA'S BIRTHDAY

Children and adults have been enchanted by Verna Aardema's many folktales and stories, which are appropriate and fun for all ages. Well-known for retelling African tales, Aardema wrote more than 25 books before she died in May 2000.

Why Mosquitos Buzz in People's Ears, one of her best known (and widely loved) tales, received the 1976 Caldecott Medal for the abstract illustrations by Leo and Diane Dillon and was the first Caldecott Medal awarded to an African American illustrator. The story, considering the topic, has one of the most logical and satisfying ends a folktale could have.

Bringing the Rain to Kapiti Plain (Nandi tale) is a delightful cumulative tale about a drought. As each animal, including a shepherd boy, does its own part trying to end the drought, they begin a chain of events that restores lush greenery to the parched land. Young listeners will love chiming in for the text repetitions. It would also make a great felt-board story with animal cutouts. In addition to reading this story just because it's a great book, you can use it to complement weather or geography units.

Koi and the Kola Nuts (Liberian tale) underscores the use of the magic number "3" in folktales. The lush illustrations perfectly depict the jungle areas where Koi attempts to complete the three impossible tasks set out for him by a demanding king. The tale concludes with a succinctly stated moral that reflects the Golden Rule (Do Unto Others. . .), which is found in many cultures.

Anansi Does the Impossible (Ashanti tale) adds to the collection of spider tales that fascinate readers. The tricky Anansi always manages to cleverly attain his goals. Compare the adventures in Aardema's Anansi story with those in *A Story, A Story*, by Gail Haley (Simon & Schuster, 0-689-71201-4, $5.99 All ages). Again, these stories stand on their own, but if you wish to use them to complement units on spiders or make art projects that feature spiders, go ahead. One way to hold the spider theme and honor Aardema would be to cut out a bulletin board size shape of the African continent, superimpose a spider's web on it and then connect each of Aardema's African tales to its appropriate geographical location with pictures and or book reviews written by students.

To learn more about the African cultures that produced these folktales, consult *From Afar to Zulu: A Dictionary of African Cultures*, by Jim Haskins and Joann Biondi (Walker, 0-8027-8290-6, $10.95 Gr. 4–7) or *Peoples of the World: Africans South of the Sahara*, by Joyce Moss and George Wilson (Gale, 0-8103-7942-2, $55 Gr. 7 & up).

Aardema wrote many more books your students will love. All are readily available in school and public libraries (bookstores, too).

JUNE 7 — FRIDAY

Day 158 — 207 Remaining

APGAR, VIRGINIA: BIRTH ANNIVERSARY. June 7, 1909. Dr. Apgar developed the simple assessment method that permits doctors and nurses to evaluate newborns while they are still in the delivery room to identify those in need of immediate medical care. The Apgar score was first published in 1953 and the Perinatal Section of the American Academy of Pediatrics is named for Dr. Apgar. Born at Westfield, NJ, Apgar died Aug 7, 1974, at New York, NY.

BAHAMAS: LABOR DAY. June 7. Public holiday. First Friday in June celebrated with parades, displays and picnics.

BROOKS, GWENDOLYN: BIRTH ANNIVERSARY. June 7, 1917. Born in Topeka, KS, she was a poet who wrote about the struggles of African Americans, particularly women. Some of her most significant works include the poetry collections *Family Pictures* and *Blacks*, and the children's book *The Tiger Who Wore White Gloves*. In 1950, she became the first black writer to win the Pulitzer Prize, for her work "Annie Allen." She died at Chicago, IL, Dec 3, 2000.

GAUGUIN, PAUL: BIRTH ANNIVERSARY. June 7, 1848. French painter, born at Paris. He became a painter in middle age and renounced his life at Paris and moved to Tahiti. He is remembered for his broad, flat tones and use of color. He died on the island of Hiva Oa in the Marquesas, May 8, 1903.

VCR INTRODUCED: ANNIVERSARY. June 7, 1975. The Sony Corporation released its videocassette recorder, the Betamax, which sold for $995. Eventually, another VCR format, VHS, proved more successful and Sony stopped making the Betamax.

BIRTHDAYS TODAY

Louise Erdrich, 48, author (*The Birchbark House, Tracks*), born Little Falls, MN, June 7, 1954.

Nikki Giovanni, 59, author (*Spin a Soft Black Song*), born Knoxville, TN, June 7, 1943.

Allen Iverson, 27, basketball player, born Hampton, VA, June 7, 1975.

Anna Kournikova, 21, tennis player, born Moscow, Russia, June 7, 1981.

Mike Modano, 32, hockey player, born Livonia, MI, June 7, 1970.

Larisa Oleynik, 21, actress ("The Secret World of Alex Mack"), born San Francisco, CA, June 7, 1981.

JUNE 8 — SATURDAY

Day 159 — 206 Remaining

BILL OF RIGHTS PROPOSED: ANNIVERSARY. June 8, 1789. The Bill of Rights, which led to the first 10 amendments to the US Constitution, was first proposed by James Madison.

COCHISE: DEATH ANNIVERSARY. June 8, 1874. Born around 1810 in the Chiricahua Mountains of Arizona, Cochise became a fierce and courageous leader of the Apache. After his arrest in 1861, he escaped and launched the Apache Wars, which lasted for 25 years. He died 13 years later near his stronghold in southeastern Arizona.

INTERNATIONAL YOUNG EAGLES DAY. June 8. The Young Eagles Program offers youth 8–17 an opportunity to fly in a private airplane with a qualified pilot. On the second Saturday in June each year local chapters celebrate International Young Eagles Day with special exhibits and unreserved flights. For info: Young Eagles Program, Experimental Aircraft Assn Aviation Foundation, PO Box 2683, Oshkosh, WI 54903-2683. Phone: (877) 806-8902. Web: www.youngeagles.org.

McKINLEY, IDA SAXTON: BIRTH ANNIVERSARY. June 8, 1847. Wife of William McKinley, 25th president of the US, born at Canton, OH. Died at Canton, May 26, 1907.

TAKE A KID FISHING WEEKEND. June 8–9 (tentative). St. Paul, MN. Resident adults may fish without a license on these days when fishing with a child under age 16. For info: Jack Skrypek, Fisheries Chief, DNR, Box 12, 500 Lafayette Rd, St. Paul, MN 55155. Phone: (612) 296-0792 or (612) 296-3325. Fax: (612) 297-4916. Web: www.dnr.state.mn.us.

UNITED KINGDOM: TROOPING THE COLOUR—QUEEN'S OFFICIAL BIRTHDAY PARADE. June 8 (tentative). National holiday in the United Kingdom. Horse Guards Parade, Whitehall, London. Colorful ceremony with music and pageantry during which Her Majesty The Queen takes the salute. Starts at 11 AM. When requesting info, send stamped, self-addressed envelope. [Final date not set at press time.] Trooping the Colour is always on a Saturday in June; the Queen's real birthday is Apr 21. Est attendance: 10,000. For info: The Ticket Office, HQ Household Division, 1 Chelsea Barracks, London, England SW1H 8RF. Phone: (44) (207) 414-2479.

WHITE, BYRON RAYMOND: 85th BIRTHDAY. June 8, 1917. Retired associate justice of the Supreme Court of the US, nominated by President Kennedy Apr 3, 1962. (Oath of office, Apr 16, 1962.) Justice White was born at Fort Collins, CO. For more info: oyez.northwestern.edu/justices/justices.cgi.

WRIGHT, FRANK LLOYD: BIRTH ANNIVERSARY. June 8, 1867. American architect, born at Richland Center, WI. In his autobiography Wright wrote: "No house should ever be *on* any hill or on anything. It should be *of* the hill, belonging to it, so hill and house could live together each the happier for the other." Wright died at Phoenix, AZ, Apr 9, 1959.

WYTHE, GEORGE: DEATH ANNIVERSARY. June 8, 1806. Signer of the Declaration of Independence. Born at Elizabeth County, VA, about 1726 (exact date unknown). Died at Richmond, VA.

BIRTHDAYS TODAY

Tim Berners-Lee, 47, inventor of the World Wide Web, born London, England, June 8, 1955.

Barbara Pierce Bush, 77, former First Lady, wife of George H.W. Bush, 41st president of the US, born Rye, NY, June 8, 1925.

Lindsay Davenport, 26, tennis player, born Palos Verdes, CA, June 8, 1976.

Judy Sierra, 57, author (*Nursery Tales Around the World, Counting Crocodiles*), born Washington, DC, June 8, 1945.

JUNE 9 — SUNDAY

Day 160 — 205 Remaining

CHILDREN'S DAY IN MASSACHUSETTS. June 9. Annually, the second Sunday in June. The governor proclaims this day each year.

CHILDREN'S SUNDAY. June 9. Traditionally the second Sunday in June is observed as Children's Sunday in many Christian churches.

DONALD DUCK: BIRTHDAY. June 9, 1934. Donald Duck was "born," introduced in the Disney short, *Orphans' Benefit*.

JORDAN: ACCESSION DAY. June 9. National holiday. Commemorates the accession to the throne of King Abdullah II in 1999.

★ **NATIONAL FLAG WEEK.** June 9–15. Presidential Proclamation issued each year since 1966 for the week including June 14. (PL89–443 of June 9, 1966.) In addition, the president often calls upon the American people to participate in public ceremonies in which the Pledge of Allegiance is recited. For info: www.usflag.org.

RACE UNITY DAY. June 9. Baha'i-sponsored observance promoting racial harmony and understanding and the essential unity of humanity. Annually, the second Sunday in June. For info: Office of Public Information, Baha'is of the US, 866 UN Plaza, Ste 120,

New York, NY 10017-1822. Phone: (212) 803-2500. Fax: (212) 803-2573. E-mail: usopi-ny@bic.org. Web: www.us.bahai.org.

BIRTHDAYS TODAY

Michael J. Fox, 41, actor ("Family Ties," *Back to the Future* films), born Edmonton, AB, Canada, June 9, 1961.

JUNE 10 — MONDAY

Day 161 — 204 Remaining

BALLPOINT PEN PATENTED: ANNIVERSARY. June 10, 1943. Hungarian Laszlo Biro patented the ballpoint pen, which he had been developing since the 1930s. He was living at Argentina, where he had gone to escape the Nazis. In many languages, the word for ballpoint pen is "biro."

CONGO (BRAZZAVILLE): DAY OF NATIONAL RECONCILIATION. June 10. National holiday in Congo (Brazzaville).

JORDAN: GREAT ARAB REVOLT AND ARMY DAY. June 10. Commemorates the beginning of the Great Arab Revolt in 1916. National holiday.

MOON PHASE: NEW MOON. June 10. Moon enters New Moon phase at 7:46 PM, EDT.

★**NATIONAL LITTLE LEAGUE BASEBALL WEEK.** June 10–16. Presidential Proclamation 3296, of June 4, 1959, covers all succeeding years. Always the week beginning with the second Monday in June. (H.Con.Res. 17 of June 1, 1959.)

PORTUGAL: DAY OF PORTUGAL. June 10. National holiday. Anniversary of the death in 1580 of Portugal's national poet, Luis Vas de Camoes (Camoens), born in 1524 (exact date unknown) at either Lisbon or possibly Coimbra. Died at Lisbon, Portugal.

QUEEN ELIZABETH II'S OFFICIAL BIRTHDAY. June 10. A holiday in Australia, Belize, Cayman Islands, Fiji and Papua New Guinea on the second Monday in June. In New Zealand and Tuvalu it is commemorated on the first Monday in June. Queen Elizabeth's real birthday is Apr 21.

SOLAR ECLIPSE. June 10. Annular eclipse of the sun. Eclipse begins at 4:51 PM, EDT, reaches greatest eclipse at 7:48 PM, and ends at 10:36 PM. Visible in eastern Asia, Japan, Indonesia, northern Australia, Pacific Ocean, northern Mexico, USA, Canada except the extreme northeastern part.

BIRTHDAYS TODAY

John Edwards, 49, US Senator (D, North Carolina), born Seneca, SC, June 10, 1953.
Charlotte Herman, 65, author (*The House on Walenska Street, Millie Cooper 3B*), born Chicago, IL, June 10, 1937.
Tara Lipinski, 20, figure skater, born Philadelphia, PA, June 10, 1982.
Maurice Sendak, 74, author, illustrator (*Chicken Soup with Rice*, Caldecott for *Where the Wild Things Are*), born Brooklyn, NY, June 10, 1928.
Leelee Sobieski, 20, actress (*Deep Impact*), born Liliane Sobieski, New York, NY, June 10, 1982.

June 2002

S	M	T	W	T	F	S
						1
2	3	4	5	6	7	8
9	10	11	12	13	14	15
16	17	18	19	20	21	22
23	24	25	26	27	28	29
30						

JUNE 11 — TUESDAY

Day 162 — 203 Remaining

COUSTEAU, JACQUES: BIRTH ANNIVERSARY. June 11, 1910. French undersea explorer, writer and filmmaker, born at St. Andre-de-Cubzac, France. He invented the Aqualung, which allowed him and his colleagues to produce more than 80 documentary films about undersea life, two of which won Oscars. This scientist and explorer was awarded the French Legion of Honor for his work in the Resistance in WWII. He died at Paris, France, June 25, 1997. For more info: *Jacques Cousteau*, by Lesley A. Dutemple (Lerner, 0-8225-4979-4, $25.26 Gr. 6–10).

KING KAMEHAMEHA I DAY. June 11. Designated state holiday in Hawaii honors memory of Hawaiian monarch (1737–1819). Governor appoints state commission to plan annual celebration.

LIBYA: AMERICAN BASES EVACUATION DAY. June 11. National holiday. Commemorates the closing of an American military base in 1970.

MOUNT PINATUBO ERUPTS IN PHILIPPINES: ANNIVERSARY. June 11, 1991. Long-dormant volcano Mount Pinatubo erupted with a violent explosion, spewing ash and gases that could be seen for more than 60 miles, into the air. The surrounding areas were covered with ash and mud created by rainstorms. US military bases Clark and Subic Bay were also damaged. On July 6, 1992, Ellsworth Dutton of the National Oceanic and Atmospheric Administration's Climate Monitoring and Diagnostics Laboratory announced that a layer of sulfuric acid droplets released into the Earth's atmosphere by the eruption had cooled the planet's average temperature by about 1 degree Fahrenheit. The greatest difference was noted in the Northern Hemisphere with a drop of 1.5 degrees. Although the temperature drop was temporary, the climate trend made determining the effect of greenhouse warming on the Earth more difficult. For more info visit Volcano World: volcano.und.nodak.edu.

RANKIN, JEANNETTE: BIRTH ANNIVERSARY. June 11, 1880. First woman elected to the US Congress, a reformer, feminist and pacifist, was born at Missoula, MT. She was the only member of Congress to vote against a declaration of war against Japan in December 1941. Died May 18, 1973, at Carmel, CA.

BIRTHDAYS TODAY

Parris Glendening, 60, Governor of Maryland (D), born The Bronx, NY, June 11, 1942.
Joe Montana, 46, former sportscaster and football player, born New Eagle, PA, June 11, 1956.
Robert Munsch, 57, author (*Love You Forever, The Paper Bag Princess*), born Pittsburgh, PA, June 11, 1945.
Gene Wilder, 69, actor (*Willy Wonka & the Chocolate Factory*), born Milwaukee, WI, June 11, 1933.

JUNE 12 — WEDNESDAY

Day 163 — 202 Remaining

BIG BEND NATIONAL PARK ESTABLISHED: ANNIVERSARY. June 12, 1944. Area on the "big bend" of the Rio Grande River in western Texas along the Mexican border, authorized June 20, 1935, was established as a national park. For more info: www.nps.gov/bibe/index.htm.

BUSH, GEORGE H.W.: BIRTHDAY. June 12, 1924. The 41st president (Jan 20, 1989–Jan 20, 1993) of the US, born at Milton, MA. Bush had served as the 43rd vice president under Ronald Reagan. For info: www.ipl.org/ref/POTUS.

FRANK, ANNE: BIRTH ANNIVERSARY. June 12, 1929. Born at Frankfurt, Germany. Anne Frank moved with her family to Amsterdam to escape the Nazis but after Holland was invaded by Germany, they had to go into hiding. In 1942, Anne began to keep a diary. She died at Bergen-Belsen concentration camp in 1945. After the war, her father published her diary, on which a stage play and movie were later based. See also: "Diary of Anne Frank: The Last Entry: Anniversary" (Aug 1). For more info: *Anne Frank: A Hidden Life*, by Mirjam Pressler (Dutton, 0-52546330-5, $15.99 Gr. 5–12) or www.annefrank.com.

***LOVING v VIRGINIA* : 35th ANNIVERSARY.** June 12, 1967. The US Supreme Court decision in *Loving v Virginia* swept away all 16 remaining state laws prohibiting interracial marriages.

NATIONAL BASEBALL HALL OF FAME: ANNIVERSARY. June 12, 1939. The National Baseball Hall of Fame and Museum, Inc, was dedicated at Cooperstown, NY. More than 200 individuals have been honored for their contributions to the game of baseball by induction into the Baseball Hall of Fame. The first players chosen for membership (1936) were Ty Cobb, Honus Wagner, Babe Ruth, Christy Mathewson and Walter Johnson. Relics and memorabilia from the history of baseball are housed at this shrine of America's national sport.

PHILIPPINES: INDEPENDENCE DAY. June 12. National holiday. Declared independence from Spain in 1898.

RUSSIA: INDEPENDENCE DAY. June 12. National holiday. Commemorates the election in 1991 of the first popularly elected leader (Yeltsin) in the 1,000-year history of the Russian state.

BIRTHDAYS TODAY

Spencer Abraham, 50, US Secretary of Energy (George W. Bush administration), former US Senator (R, MI), born Lansing, MI, June 12, 1952.

George Herbert Walker Bush, 78, 41st president of the US, born Milton, MA, June 12, 1924.

Helen Lester, 66, author (*Hooway for Wodney Wat*), born Evanston, IL, June 12, 1936.

Hillary McKay, 43, author (*The Amber Cat*), born the Midlands, England, June 12, 1959.

JUNE 13 — THURSDAY

Day 164 — 201 Remaining

AMERICAN LIBRARY ASSOCIATION ANNUAL CONFERENCE. June 13–19. Atlanta, GA. Est attendance: 20,000. For info: Public Information Office, American Library Assn, 50 E Huron St, Chicago, IL 60611. Phone: (312) 280-5044. Fax: (312) 944-8520. E-mail: pio@ala.org. Web: www.ala.org.

GOODMAN, BENNY: DEATH ANNIVERSARY. June 13, 1986. Jazz clarinetist and bandleader, born Benjamin David Goodman on May 9, 1909 at Chicago, IL. His band was the first to play jazz at New York's Carnegie Hall. He died June 13, 1986, at New York, NY. *See* Curriculum Connection.

***MIRANDA* DECISION: ANNIVERSARY.** June 13, 1966. The US Supreme Court rendered a 5–4 decision in the case of *Miranda v*

JUNE 13
BENNY GOODMAN: DEATH ANNIVERSARY

The musical world mourned on June 13, 1986, when Benny Goodman died in his sleep. Goodman, a wildly popular clarinetist, strongly influenced the direction of American music, and earned him the nickname "King of Swing."

Benjamin David Goodman, born on May 9, 1909, was one of twelve children. His father was a tailor who had fled Russia because of anti-Semitism. Benny grew up in Chicago. He began seriously studying the clarinet when he was 10 years old. Lessons in the local synagogue were followed by lessons at Chicago's Hull House, an organization which provided services for underprivileged children. When Benny was 14 years old, his father died, and Benny supplemented the family income by playing his clarinet in a Chicago dance hall. He quickly made a name for himself on the local music scene, and by the time he was 17, left to establish a career in New York.

A brilliant soloist, Goodman also led small combos and big bands which were popular in ballroom performances and as radio broadcasts. Goodman was a trailblazer, too. He was the first bandleader to feature black musicians playing with white musicians. Two famous jazz players—pianist Teddy Wilson and vibraphonist Lionel Hampton— were introduced by Benny Goodman.

In 1935, Goodman decided to showcase music arranged by Fletcher Henderson, a bandleader whose arrangements had a bold, "hot" sound. The songs were real crowd pleasers and when Goodman played them in Los Angeles' Palomar Ballroom, he essentially ushered in the era of swing music.

Swing has become very popular again and young people have taken the music and dances to heart. Get your students' blood circulating with a dose of "Jumpin' at the Woodside" or "Sing, Sing, Sing." Goodman's recordings are widely available, so check at your public library.

Often physical education classes feature a dance unit. If you find a couple of teens who are into swing dancing and get them to give a few lessons, you'll find kids look forward to the chance to "strut their stuff."

Once Upon a Time in Chicago: The Story of Benny Goodman, by Jonah Winter (Hyperion, 0-7868-0462-9, $14.99 All ages), is a wonderful picture-book biography of Goodman's rise to fame from modest beginnings. A CD collection entitled *The Best of Benny Goodman* features 10 of Goodman's well-known hits, including the songs mentioned above.

Feet will tap of their own accord if you invite Goodman and his soaring clarinet into your room. Try it and see.

Arizona, holding that the Fifth Amendment of the Constitution "required warnings before valid statements could be taken by police." The decision has been described as "providing basic legal protections to persons who might otherwise not be aware of their rights." Ernesto Miranda, the 23-year-old whose name became nationally known, was retried after the Miranda Decision, convicted and sent back to prison. Miranda was stabbed to death in a card game dispute at Phoenix, AZ, in 1976. A suspect in the killing was released by police after he had been read his "Miranda rights." Police procedures now routinely require the reading of a prisoner's constitutional rights ("Miranda") before questioning.

ORTHODOX ASCENSION DAY. June 13. Observed by Eastern Orthodox Churches.

SCOTT, WINFIELD: BIRTH ANNIVERSARY. June 13, 1786. American army general, negotiator of peace treaties with the Indians and twice nominated for president (1848 and 1852). Leader of brilliant military campaign in Mexican War in 1847. Scott was born at Petersburg, VA, and died at West Point, NY, May 29, 1866.

BIRTHDAYS TODAY

Tim Allen, 49, comedian, actor ("Home Improvement"), born Denver, CO, June 13, 1953.

Jennifer Gillom, 38, basketball player, born Abbeville, MS, June 13, 1964.

Ashley Olsen, 15, actress ("Full House," "Two of a Kind"), born Los Angeles, CA, June 13, 1987.

Mary-Kate Olsen, 15, actress ("Full House," "Two of a Kind"), born Los Angeles, CA, June 13, 1987.

JUNE 14 — FRIDAY

Day 165 — 200 Remaining

ARMY ESTABLISHED BY CONGRESS: ANNIVERSARY. June 14, 1775. Anniversary of Resolution of the Continental Congress establishing the army as the first US military service.

BARTLETT, JOHN: BIRTH ANNIVERSARY. June 14, 1820. American editor and compiler of Bartlett's *Familiar Quotations* [1855] was born at Plymouth, MA. Though he had little formal education, he created one of the most-used reference works of the English language. No quotation of his own is among the more than 22,000 listed today, but in the preface to the first edition he wrote that the object of this work was to show "the obligation our language owes to various authors for numerous phrases and familiar quotations which have become 'household words.' " Bartlett died at Cambridge, MA, Dec 3, 1905. His book remains in print today in the 16th edition.

FIRST NONSTOP TRANSATLANTIC FLIGHT: ANNIVERSARY. June 14–15, 1919. Captain John Alcock and Lieutenant Arthur W. Brown flew a Vickers Vimy bomber 1,900 miles nonstop from St. Johns, Newfoundland, to Clifden, County Galway, Ireland. In spite of their crash landing in an Irish peat bog, their flight inspired public interest in aviation. See also: "Lindbergh Flight: Anniversary" (May 20).

★ **FLAG DAY.** June 14. Presidential Proclamation issued each year for June 14. Proclamation 1335, of May 30, 1916, covers all succeeding years. Has been issued annually since 1941. (PL81–203 of Aug 3, 1949.) Customarily issued as "Flag Day and National Flag Week," as in 1986; the president usually mentions "a time to honor America," Flag Day to Independence Day (89 Stat. 211). See also: "National Flag Day USA: Pause for the Pledge" (this date).

June 2002

S	M	T	W	T	F	S
						1
2	3	4	5	6	7	8
9	10	11	12	13	14	15
16	17	18	19	20	21	22
23	24	25	26	27	28	29
30						

FLAG DAY: 225th ANNIVERSARY OF THE STARS AND STRIPES. June 14, 1777. John Adams introduced the following resolution before the Continental Congress, meeting at Philadelphia, PA: "Resolved, That the flag of the thirteen United States shall be thirteen stripes, alternate red and white; that the union be thirteen stars, white on a blue field, representing a new constellation." Legal holiday in Pennsylvania. For more info: www.flagday.org.

HOORAY FOR YEAR-ROUND SCHOOL DAY. June 14. To promote the benefits of a year-round school calendar which makes learning a continuous process and better suits the demanding educational needs of today's world. Annually, the second Friday in June. For more info, send 9½" SASE to: Hooray for Year-Round School Day, Horace Mann Choice School, 3530-38th Ave, Rock Island, IL 61201.

JAPAN: RICE PLANTING FESTIVAL. June 14. Osaka. Ceremonial transplanting of rice seedlings in paddy field at Sumiyashi Shrine, Osaka.

MALAWI: FREEDOM DAY. June 14. National holiday. Commemorates free elections of 1994.

NATIONAL FLAG DAY USA: PAUSE FOR THE PLEDGE. June 14. Held simultaneously across the country at 7 PM, EDT. Public law 99–54 recognizes the Pause for the Pledge as part of National Flag Day ceremonies. The concept of the Pause for the Pledge of Allegiance was conceived as a way for all citizens to share a patriotic moment. National ceremony at Fort McHenry National Monument and Historic Shrine.

STOWE, HARRIET BEECHER: BIRTH ANNIVERSARY. June 14, 1811. American writer Harriet Beecher Stowe, daughter of the Reverend Lyman Beecher and sister of Henry Ward Beecher. Author of *Uncle Tom's Cabin*, an antislavery novel that provoked a storm of protest and resulted in fame for its author. Two characters in the novel attained such importance that their names became part of the English language—the Negro slave, Uncle Tom, and the villainous slaveowner, Simon Legree. The reaction to *Uncle Tom's Cabin* and its profound political impact are without parallel in American literature. It is said that during the Civil War, when Harriet Beecher Stowe was introduced to President Abraham Lincoln, his words to her were, "So you're the little woman who wrote the book that made this great war." Stowe was born at Litchfield, CT, and died at Hartford, CT, July 1, 1896. For more info: *Harriet Beecher Stowe and the Beecher Preachers*, by Jean Fritz (Putnam, 0-399-22666-4, $15.99 Gr. 7–9).

UNIVAC COMPUTER: ANNIVERSARY. June 14, 1951. Univac 1, the world's first commercial computer, designed for the US

Bureau of the Census, was unveiled, demonstrated and dedicated at Philadelphia, PA. Though this milestone of the computer age was the first commercial electronic computer, it had been preceded by ENIAC (Electronic Numeric Integrator and Computer), completed under the supervision of J. Presper Eckert, Jr, and John W. Mauchly, at the University of Pennsylvania, in 1946.

WARREN G. HARDING BECOMES FIRST PRESIDENT TO BROADCAST ON RADIO: 80th ANNIVERSARY. June 14, 1922. Warren G. Harding became the first president to broadcast a message over the radio. The event was the dedication of the Francis Scott Key Memorial at Baltimore, MD. The first official government message was broadcast Dec 6, 1923.

BIRTHDAYS TODAY

Bruce Degen, 57, author and illustrator (*Jamberry*), born Brooklyn, NY, June 14, 1945.

Stephanie Maria (Steffi) Graf, 33, tennis player, born Bruhl, West Germany, June 14, 1969.

James Gurney, 44, author and illustrator (*Dinotopia*), born Glendale, CA, June 14, 1958.

Laurence Yep, 54, author (*Dragon's Gate, The Rainbow People*), born San Francisco, CA, June 14, 1948.

JUNE 15 — SATURDAY

Day 166 — 199 Remaining

ARKANSAS: ADMISSION DAY: ANNIVERSARY. June 15. Became the 25th state in 1836.

CHINA: DRAGON BOAT FESTIVAL. June 15. An important Chinese observance, the Dragon Boat Festival commemorates a hero of ancient China, poet Qu Yuan, who drowned himself in protest against injustice and corruption. It is said that rice dumplings were cast into the water to lure fish away from the body of the martyr, and this is remembered by the eating of zhong zi, glutenous rice dumplings filled with meat and wrapped in bamboo leaves. Dragon boat races are held on rivers. The Dragon Boat Festival is observed in many countries by their Chinese populations. Also called Fifth Month Festival or Summer Festival. Annually, the fifth day of the fifth lunar month.

JACKSON, RACHEL DONELSON ROBARDS: BIRTH ANNIVERSARY. June 15, 1767. Wife of Andrew Jackson, 7th president of the US, born at Halifax County, NC. Died at Nashville, TN, Dec 22, 1828.

KOREA: TANO DAY. June 15. Fifth day of fifth lunar month. Summer food offered at the household shrine of the ancestors. Also known as Swing Day, since girls, dressed in their prettiest clothes, often compete in swinging matches. The Tano Festival usually lasts from the third through eighth day of the fifth lunar month: June 13–18.

MAGNA CARTA DAY: ANNIVERSARY. June 15. Anniversary of King John's sealing, in 1215, of the Magna Carta "in the meadow called Ronimed between Windsor and Staines on the fifteenth day of June in the seventeenth year of our reign." This document is regarded as the first charter of English liberties and one of the most important documents in the history of political and human freedom. Four original copies of the 1215 charter survive. The Apr 2000 issue of *Calliope* magazine is devoted to the Magna Carta.

NATIVE AMERICANS GAIN CITIZENSHIP: ANNIVERSARY. June 15, 1924. The US Congress passed a law on this day recognizing the citizenship of Native Americans.

TWELFTH AMENDMENT TO US CONSTITUTION RATIFIED: ANNIVERSARY. June 15, 1804. The 12th Amendment to the Constitution was ratified. It changed the method of electing the president and vice president after a tie in the electoral college during the election of 1800. Rather than each elector voting for two candidates with the candidate receiving the most votes elected president and the second-place candidate elected vice president, each elector was now required to designate his choice for president and vice president, respectively.

WORLD JUGGLING DAY. June 15. Juggling clubs all over the world hold local festivals to demonstrate, teach and celebrate their art. For info: Intl Jugglers' Assn, PO Box 218, Montague, MA 01351. Phone: (413) 367-2401. Fax: (413) 367-0259. E-mail: IJugglersA@aol.com. Web: www.juggle.org/wjd/.

BIRTHDAYS TODAY

Courteney Cox Arquette, 38, actress ("Friends," "Family Ties"), born Birmingham, AL, June 15, 1964.

Wade Boggs, 44, baseball player, born Omaha, NE, June 15, 1958.

Christopher Castile, 22, actor ("Step By Step," *Beethoven*), born Los Alamitos, CA, June 15, 1980.

Brian Jacques, 63, author (the Redwall series), born Liverpool, England, June 15, 1939.

Justin Leonard, 30, golfer, born Dallas, TX, June 15, 1972.

Betty Ren Wright, 75, author (*The Dollhouse Murders*), born Wakefield, MI, June 15, 1927.

JUNE 16 — SUNDAY

Day 167 — 198 Remaining

★**FATHER'S DAY.** June 16. Presidential Proclamation issued for third Sunday in June in 1966 and annually since 1971. (PL92–278 of Apr 24, 1972.)

FATHER'S DAY. June 16. Recognition of the third Sunday in June as Father's Day occurred first at the request of Mrs John B. Dodd of Spokane, WA, June 19, 1910. It was proclaimed for that date by the mayor of Spokane and recognized by the governor of Washington. The idea was publicly supported by President Calvin Coolidge in 1924, but not presidentially proclaimed until 1966. It was assured of annual recognition by Public Law 92–278 of April 1972.

SOUTH AFRICA: YOUTH DAY. June 16. National holiday. Commemorates a student uprising in 1976 in Soweto against "Bantu Education" and the enforced teaching of the Afrikaans language.

SPACE MILESTONE: FIRST WOMAN IN SPACE, *VOSTOK 6* (USSR). June 16, 1963. Valentina Tereshkova, 26, former cotton-mill worker, born on a collective farm near Yaroslavl, USSR, became the first woman in space when her spacecraft, *Vostok 6*, took off from the Tyuratam launch site. She manually controlled *Vostok 6* during the 70.8-hour flight through 48 orbits of Earth and landed by parachute (separate from her cabin) June 19, 1963. In November 1963 she married cosmonaut Andrian Nikolayev, who had piloted *Vostok 3* through 64 earth orbits, Aug 11–15, 1962. Their child Yelena (1964) was the first born to space-traveler parents.

BIRTHDAYS TODAY

Lincoln Almond, 66, Governor of Rhode Island (R), born Central Falls, RI, June 16, 1936.

Kalli Dakos, 52, author, poet (*Mrs. Cole on an Onion Roll; If You're Not Here, Please Raise Your Hand*), born Ottawa, ON, Canada, June 16, 1950.

Cobi Jones, 32, soccer player, played in 1994 World's Cup, born Westlake Village, CA, June 16, 1970.

Kerry Wood, 25, baseball player, born Irving, TX, June 16, 1977.

JUNE 17 — MONDAY

Day 168 — 197 Remaining

BRANSCUM, ROBBIE: BIRTH ANNIVERSARY. June 17, 1937. Author best known for *The Adventures of Johnny May* and *Cameo Rose*. She won the Friends of American Writers Award in 1977 and the Edgar Allan Poe Award in 1983. Born near Big Flat, AR, Branscum died at Harrisonburg, VA, May 24, 1997.

BUNKER HILL DAY IN MASSACHUSETTS. June 17. Legal holiday in the county in commemoration of the Battle of Bunker Hill that took place in 1775. Proclaimed annually by the governor.

HOOPER, WILLIAM: BIRTH ANNIVERSARY. June 17, 1742. Signer of the Declaration of Independence, born at Boston, MA. Died Oct 14, 1790, at Hillsboro, NC.

ICELAND: INDEPENDENCE DAY. June 17. Anniversary of founding of republic in 1944 and independence from Denmark is major festival, especially in Reykjavik. Parades, competitions, street dancing.

MOON PHASE: FIRST QUARTER. June 17. Moon enters First Quarter phase at 8:29 PM, EDT.

SOUTH AFRICA REPEALS LAST APARTHEID LAW: ANNIVERSARY. June 17, 1991. The Parliament of South Africa repealed the Population Registration Act, removing the law that was the foundation of apartheid. The law, first enacted in 1950, required the classification by race of all South Africans at birth. It established four compulsory racial categories: white, mixed race, Asian and black. Although this marked the removal of the last of the apartheid laws, blacks in South Africa still could not vote.

UNITED NATIONS: WORLD DAY TO COMBAT DESERTIFICATION AND DROUGHT. June 17. Proclaimed by the General Assembly Dec 19, 1994 (Res 49/115). States were invited to devote the World Day to promoting public awareness of the need for international cooperation to combat desertification and the effects of drought and on the implementation of the UN Convention to Combat Desertification. For info: United Nations, Dept of Public Info, New York, NY 10017.

US VIRGIN ISLANDS: ORGANIC ACT DAY: ANNIVERSARY. June 17. Commemorates the enactment by the US Congress, July 22, 1954, of the Revised Organic Act, under which the government of the Virgin Islands is organized. Observed annually on the third Monday in June.

June 2002

S	M	T	W	T	F	S
						1
2	3	4	5	6	7	8
9	10	11	12	13	14	15
16	17	18	19	20	21	22
23	24	25	26	27	28	29
30						

BIRTHDAYS TODAY

Leslie Baker, 53, author and illustrator (*The Third-Story Cat*), born Baltimore, MD, June 17, 1949.

Liza Ketchum, 56, author (*Orphan Journey Home, The Gold Rush*), born Albany, NY, June 17, 1946.

Roderick R. (Rod) Paige, 69, US Secretary of Education (George W. Bush administration), born Monticello, MS, June 17, 1933.

Venus Williams, 22, tennis player, born Lynwood, CA, June 17, 1980.

JUNE 18 — TUESDAY

Day 169 — 196 Remaining

FIRST AMERICAN WOMAN IN SPACE: ANNIVERSARY. June 18, 1983. Dr. Sally Ride, 32-year-old physicist and pilot, functioned as a "mission specialist" and became the first American woman in space when she began a six-day mission aboard the space shuttle *Challenger*. The "near-perfect" mission was launched from Cape Canaveral, FL, and landed, June 24, 1983, at Edwards Air Force Base, CA.

NATIONAL SPLURGE DAY. June 18. Today is the day to go out and do something indulgent. Have fun! [©1994] For info: Adrienne Sioux Koopersmith, 1437 W Rosemont, #1W, Chicago, IL 60660-1319. Phone: (773) 743-5341. Fax: (773) 743-5395. E-mail: adrienet@earthlink.net.

SEYCHELLES: CONSTITUTION DAY. June 18. National holiday commemorating 1993 constitution.

SPACE MILESTONE: *CHALLENGER STS-7* (US). June 18, 1983. Shuttle *Challenger*, launched from Kennedy Space Center, FL, with crew of five, including Sally K. Ride (first American woman in space), Robert Crippen, Norman Thagard, John Fabian and Frederick Houck. Landed at Edwards Air Force Base, CA, June 24, after a near-perfect six-day mission.

WAR OF 1812: DECLARATION ANNIVERSARY. June 18, 1812. After much debate in Congress between "hawks" such as Henry Clay and John Calhoun, and "doves" such as John Randolph, Congress issued a declaration of war on Great Britain. The action was prompted primarily by Britain's violation of America's rights on the high seas and British incitement of Indian warfare on the frontier. War was seen by some as a way to acquire Florida and Canada. The hostilities ended with the signing of the Treaty of Ghent, Dec 24, 1814, at Ghent, Belgium.

BIRTHDAYS TODAY

Pam Conrad, 55, author (*Prairie Songs*), born New York, NY, June 18, 1947.

Pat Hutchins, 60, author and illustrator (*Changes, Changes; The Wind Blew*), born Yorkshire, England, June 18, 1942.

Angela Johnson, 41, author (*Heaven*), born Tuskegee, AL, June 18, 1961.

Paul McCartney, 60, singer, songwriter (The Beatles), born Liverpool, England, June 18, 1942.

John D. Rockefeller IV, 65, US Senator (D, West Virginia), born New York, NY, June 18, 1937.

Chris Van Allsburg, 53, illustrator and author (Caldecotts for *The Polar Express, Jumanji*), born Grand Rapids, MI, June 18, 1949.

JUNE 19 — WEDNESDAY

Day 170 — 195 Remaining

EMANCIPATION DAY IN TEXAS. June 19, 1865. In honor of the emancipation of the slaves in Texas.

FORTAS, ABE: BIRTH ANNIVERSARY. June 19, 1910. Abe Fortas was born at Memphis, TN. He was appointed to the Supreme Court by President Lyndon Johnson in 1965. Prior to his appointment he was known as a civil libertarian, having argued cases for government employees and other individuals accused by Senator Joe McCarthy of having communist affiliations. He argued the 1963 landmark Supreme Court case of *Gideon v Wainwright*, which established the right of indigent defendants to free legal aid in criminal prosecutions. In 1968, he was nominated by Johnson to succeed Chief Justice Earl Warren, but his nomination was withdrawn after much conservative opposition in the Senate. In 1969 Fortas became the first Supreme Court Justice to be forced to resign after revelations about questionable financial dealings were made public. He died Apr 5, 1982, at Washington, DC.

GARFIELD: BIRTHDAY. June 19, 1978. America's favorite lasagna-loving cat celebrates his birthday. *Garfield*, a modern classic comic strip created by Jim Davis, first appeared in 1978, and has brought laughter to millions. For info: Paws, Inc, Kim Campbell, 5440 E Co Rd 450 N, Albany, IN 47320. Web: www.garfield.com.

GEHRIG, LOU: BIRTH ANNIVERSARY. June 19, 1903. Henry Louis Gehrig, Baseball Hall of Fame first baseman, born Ludwig Heinrich Gehrig, at New York, NY. Gehrig, known as the "Iron Horse," played in 2,130 consecutive games, a record not surpassed until Cal Ripken did in 1995. He played 17 years with the Yankees, hit .340 and slugged 493 home runs, 23 of them grand slams. Gehrig retired in 1939 and was diagnosed with the degenerative muscle disease amyotrophic lateral sclerosis, later known as Lou Gehrig's disease. Died at New York, NY, June 2, 1941.

JUNETEENTH. June 19. Celebrated in Texas to commemorate the day when Union General Granger proclaimed the slaves of Texas free. This is also a ceremonial holiday in Florida, commemorating the day slaves in Florida were notified of the Emancipation Proclamation. Juneteenth has become a day for commemoration by African Americans in many parts of the US.

URUGUAY: ARTIGAS DAY. June 19. National holiday. Commemorates the father of Uruguayan independence, General José Gervasio Artigas, born on this day in 1764.

BIRTHDAYS TODAY

Andrew Lauer, 37, actor (*I'll Be Home for Christmas*), born Santa Monica, CA, June 19, 1965.

Brian McBride, 30, soccer player, born Arlington Heights, IL, June 19, 1972.

JUNE 20 — THURSDAY

Day 171 — 194 Remaining

ARGENTINA: FLAG DAY. June 20. National holiday.

CHESNUTT, CHARLES W.: BIRTH ANNIVERSARY. June 20, 1858. Born at Cleveland, OH, Chesnutt was considered by many as the first important black novelist. His collections of short stories included *The Conjure Woman* (1899) and *The Wife of His Youth and Other Stories of the Color Line* (1899). *The Colonel's Dream* (1905) dealt with the struggles of the freed slave. His work has been compared to later writers such as William Faulkner, Richard Wright and James Baldwin. He died Nov 15, 1932, at Cleveland.

CHICAGO BULLS WIN THIRD CONSECUTIVE NBA CHAMPIONSHIP: ANNIVERSARY. June 20, 1993. With a four-games-to-two victory over the Phoenix Suns in the National Basketball Association (NBA) finals the Chicago Bulls earned their third straight NBA title. The Bulls became the first team to win three in a row since 1966, when the Boston Celtics won their eighth in a row. In 1996 they won the NBA title for a fourth time, in 1997 for a fifth and in 1998 for a sixth, for another three-in-a-row sweep.

WEST VIRGINIA: ADMISSION DAY: ANNIVERSARY. June 20. Became 35th state in 1863. Observed as a holiday in West Virginia. The state of West Virginia is a product of the Civil War. Originally part of Virginia, West Virginia became a separate state when Virginia seceded from the Union.

BIRTHDAYS TODAY

John Goodman, 50, actor (*Arachnophobia, The Flintstones*), born Afton, MO, June 20, 1952.

Annette Curtis Klause, 49, author (*Blood and Chocolate*), born Bristol, England, June 20, 1953.

JUNE 21 — FRIDAY

Day 172 — 193 Remaining

CANCER, THE CRAB. June 21–July 22. In the astronomical/astrological zodiac, which divides the sun's apparent orbit into 12 segments, the period June 21–July 22 is identified, traditionally, as the sun sign of Cancer, the Crab. The ruling planet is the moon.

NEW HAMPSHIRE RATIFIES CONSTITUTION: ANNIVERSARY. June 21, 1788. By a vote of 57 to 47, New Hampshire became the ninth state to ratify the Constitution.

SUMMER. June 21–Sept 23. In the Northern Hemisphere summer begins today with the summer solstice, at 9:24 AM, EDT. Note that in the Southern Hemisphere today is the beginning of winter. Anywhere between the Equator and Arctic Circle, the sun rises and sets farthest north on the horizon for the year and length of daylight is maximum (12 hours, 8 minutes at equator, increasing to 24 hours at Arctic Circle).

TOMPKINS, DANIEL D.: BIRTH ANNIVERSARY. June 21, 1774. Sixth vice president of the US (1817–25), born at Fox Meadows, NY. Died at Staten Island, NY, June 11, 1825.

WASHINGTON, MARTHA DANDRIDGE CUSTIS: BIRTH ANNIVERSARY. June 21, 1731. Wife of George Washington, first president of the US, born at New Kent County, VA. Died at Mount Vernon, VA, May 22, 1802.

BIRTHDAYS TODAY

Berkeley Breathed, 45, cartoonist ("Bloom County"), born Croatia, June 21, 1957.
Robert Kraus, 77, author (*Leo the Late Bloomer*), born Milwaukee, WI, June 21, 1925.
Togo D. West, 60, former US Secretary of Veterans Affairs (Clinton administration), born Winston-Salem, NC, June 21, 1942.
Prince William, 20, son of Prince Charles and Princess Diana, born London, England, June 21, 1982.

JUNE 22 — SATURDAY

Day 173 — 192 Remaining

CROATIA: ANTIFASCIST STRUGGLE COMMEMORATION DAY. June 22. National holiday. Anniversary of uprising against German invaders in 1941.

NATIONAL PTA CONVENTION. June 22–25. San Antonio, TX. Each year, the National PTA Convention and Exhibition serves as an important meeting ground where child advocates convene to work, learn and share. Attending the convention can put you in touch with the information, ideas and materials you need to help make your dreams for children happen! National PTA, 330 N. Wabash Ave., Suite 2100, Chicago IL, 60611. Phone: (800) 307-4PTA (4782). E-mail: info@pta.org. Web: www.pta.org.

SWITZERLAND: MORAT BATTLE ANNIVERSARY. June 22, 1476. The little, walled town of Morat played a decisive part in Swiss history. There, the Confederates were victorious over Charles the Bold of Burgundy, laying the basis for French-speaking areas to become Swiss. Now an annual children's festival.

US DEPARTMENT OF JUSTICE: ANNIVERSARY. June 22, 1870. Established by an act of Congress, the Department of Justice is headed by the attorney general. Prior to 1870, the attorney general (whose office had been created Sept 24, 1789) had been a member of the president's cabinet but had not been the head of a department.

BIRTHDAYS TODAY

Dianne Feinstein, 69, US Senator (D, California), born San Francisco, CA, June 22, 1933.
Lindsay Ridgeway, 17, actress ("Boy Meets World"), born Loma Linda, CA, June 22, 1985.
Kurt Warner, 31, football player, born Burlington, IA, June 22, 1971.

JUNE 23 — SUNDAY

Day 174 — 191 Remaining

AMERICA'S KIDS DAY. June 23. A day set aside to reach out and teach our children in America the value of life, liberty and the pursuit of happiness. A time to help our kids learn about the great nation that they live in and help by demonstrating what it means to be an American. A time to teach them the historical value of their heritage as America's kids. "America . . . They're not heavy . . . They're our children." Annually, the fourth Sunday in June. For info: Judith Natale, CEO & Founder, Natl Children & Family Awareness of America, Administrative Headquarters, 3060 Rt 405 Hwy, Muncy, PA 17756-8808. Phone: (888) MAA-DESK. E-mail: ChildAware@aol.com or MaaJudith@aol.com.

DENMARK: MIDSUMMER EVE. June 23. Celebrated all over the country with bonfires and merrymaking.

ESTONIA: VICTORY DAY. June 23. National holiday. Commemorates a battle against the Germans in 1919, during the War of Independence.

FIRST TYPEWRITER: ANNIVERSARY. June 23, 1868. First US typewriter was patented by Luther Sholes.

HELEN KELLER DEAF-BLINDNESS AWARENESS WEEK. June 23–29. A Presidential Proclamation in 1984. A week to observe the birth anniversary of Helen Keller who was born June 27, 1880. Annually, the full week that includes Helen Keller's birthday. For info: Library for Deaf Action, 2930 Craiglawn Rd, Silver Spring, MD 20904-1816. Phone: (301) 572-5168 (TTY). Fax: (301) 572-4134. E-mail: alhagemeyer@juno.com. Web: www.LibraryDeaf.com.

JOHN CARVER DAY IN MASSACHUSETTS. June 23. Proclaimed annually by the governor on the fourth Sunday in June to commemorate the first governor of the Plymouth Colony, John Carver, who served from 1620 to 1621.

LAURA INGALLS WILDER PAGEANT. June 28–July 14 (weekends). De Smet, SD. An outdoor pageant on the natural prairie stage depicting "Medley of Memories," historically based on Laura Ingalls Wilder's life. Est attendance: 10,000. For info: The Laura Ingalls Wilder Pageant, PO Box 154, De Smet, SD 57231. Phone: (605) 692-2108 or (800) 880-3383.

LUXEMBOURG: NATIONAL HOLIDAY. June 23. Commemorating birth of His Royal Highness Grand Duke Jean in 1921. Luxembourg's independence is also celebrated.

MIDSUMMER DAY/EVE CELEBRATIONS. June 23. Celebrates the beginning of summer with maypoles, music, dancing and bonfires. Observed mainly in northern Europe, including Finland, Latvia and Sweden. Day of observance is sometimes St.

June 2002

S	M	T	W	T	F	S
						1
2	3	4	5	6	7	8
9	10	11	12	13	14	15
16	17	18	19	20	21	22
23	24	25	26	27	28	29
30						

John's Day (June 24), with celebration on St. John's Eve (June 23) as well, or June 19. Time approximates the summer solstice. See also: "Summer" (June 21).

ORTHODOX PENTECOST. June 23. Observed by Eastern Orthodox churches.

TAIWAN: BIRTHDAY OF CHENG HUANG. June 23. Thirteenth day of fifth moon. Celebrated with a procession of actors on stilts doing dragon and lion dances.

BIRTHDAYS TODAY

Theodore Taylor, 81, author (*The Cay*), born Statesville, NC, June 23, 1921.

Clarence Thomas, 54, Associate Justice of the Supreme Court, born Pinpoint, GA, June 23, 1948.

JUNE 24 — MONDAY

Day 175 — 190 Remaining

BERLIN AIRLIFT: ANNIVERSARY. June 24, 1948. In the early days of the Cold War the Soviet Union challenged the West's right of access to Berlin. The Soviets created a blockade and an airlift to supply some 2,250,000 people at West Berlin resulted. The airlift lasted a total of 321 days and brought into Berlin 1,592,787 tons of supplies. Joseph Stalin finally backed down and the blockade ended May 12, 1949.

CANADA: NEWFOUNDLAND DISCOVERY DAY. June 24. Commemorates the discovery of Newfoundland by John Cabot in 1497. Observed on the Monday nearest June 24.

CANADA: QUEBEC FÊTE NATIONALE. June 24. Saint Jean Baptiste Day.

CIARDI, JOHN: BIRTH ANNIVERSARY. June 24, 1916. Poet for adults and children (*You Read to Me, I'll Read to You*), born at Boston, MA. Died Mar 30, 1986, at Edison, NJ.

LATVIA: JOHN'S DAY (MIDSUMMER NIGHT DAY). June 24. The festival of Jani, which commemorates the summer solstice and the name day of (Janis) John, is one of Latvia's most ancient as well as joyous rituals. This festival is traditionally celebrated in the countryside, as it emphasizes fertility and the beginning of summer. Festivities begin June 23. For info: Embassy of Latvia, 4325 17th St NW, Washington, DC 20011. Phone: (202) 726-8213.

LUNAR ECLIPSE. June 24. Penumbral eclipse of the moon. Moon enters penumbra at 4:18 PM, EDT, reaches middle of eclipse at 5:27 PM and leaves penumbra at 6:35 PM. The beginning of penumbral phase visible in Australia, Indonesia, southern and western Asia, Europe except the extreme north, Africa, extreme eastern South America, Antarctica, the Indian Ocean, the eastern North Atlantic Ocean, the South Atlantic Ocean and the southwestern Pacific Ocean; the end visible in Africa, Europe except the extreme north, most of South America except the northwest, Antarctica, western Australia, southwest Asia, the Indian Ocean, the eastern North Atlantic Ocean, the South Atlantic Ocean and the southeastern South Pacific Ocean.

MOON PHASE: FULL MOON. June 24. Moon enters Full Moon phase at 5:42 PM, EDT.

SCOTLAND: BANNOCKBURN DAY. June 24. Anniversary of the Battle of Bannockburn in 1314 when Robert the Bruce defeated the English, winning Scottish independence.

THORNTON, MATTHEW: DEATH ANNIVERSARY. June 24, 1803. Signer of the Declaration of Independence. Born at Ireland about 1714, he died at Newburyport, MA.

VENEZUELA: BATTLE OF CARABOBO DAY. June 24. National holiday. Commemorates a victory in 1821 that assured independence from Spain.

BIRTHDAYS TODAY

Leonard Everett Fisher, 78, illustrator and author (*Great Wall of China*), born New York, NY, June 24, 1924.

Kathryn Lasky, 58, author (*Sugaring Time*), born Indianapolis, IN, June 24, 1944.

Jean Marzollo, 60, author (*Happy Birthday, Martin Luther King*), born Manchester, CT, June 24, 1942.

George Pataki, 57, Governor of New York (R), born Peekskill, NY, June 24, 1945.

Predrag (Preki) Radosavljevic, 39, soccer player, born Belgrade, Yugoslavia, June 24, 1963.

JUNE 25 — TUESDAY

Day 176 — 189 Remaining

BATTLE OF LITTLE BIGHORN: ANNIVERSARY. June 25, 1876. Lieutenant Colonel George Armstrong Custer, leading military forces of more than 200 men, attacked an encampment of Sioux Indians led by Chiefs Sitting Bull and Crazy Horse near Little Bighorn River, MT. Custer and all men in his immediate command were killed in the brief battle (about two hours) of Little Bighorn. For more info: *It Is a Good Day to Die: Indian Eyewitnesses Tell the Story of the Battle of Little Bighorn*, by Herman Viola (Crown, 0-517-70913-9, $19.99 Gr. 5–8).

CBS SENDS FIRST COLOR TV BROADCAST OVER THE AIR: ANNIVERSARY. June 25, 1951. Columbia Broadcasting System broadcast the first color television program. The four-hour program was carried by stations in New York City, Baltimore, Philadelphia, Boston and Washington, DC, although no color sets were owned by the public. At the time CBS, itself, owned fewer than 40 color receivers.

CIVIL WAR IN YUGOSLAVIA: ANNIVERSARY. June 25, 1991. In an Eastern Europe freed from the iron rule of communism and the USSR, separatist and nationalist tensions suppressed for decades rose to a violent boiling point. The republics of Croatia and Slovenia declared their independence, sparking a fractious and bitter war that spread throughout what was formerly Yugoslavia. Ethnic rivalries between Serbians and Croatians began the military conflicts that spread to Slovenia, and in 1992 fighting began in Bosnia-Herzegovina between Serbians and ethnic Muslims. Although the new republics were recognized by the UN and sanctions passed to stop the fighting, it raged on through 1995 despite the efforts of UN peacekeeping forces.

KIM CAMPBELL SWORN IN AS CANADIAN PRIME MINISTER: ANNIVERSARY. June 25, 1993. After winning the June 13 election to the leadership of the ruling Progressive-Conservative Party, Kim Campbell became Canada's 19th prime minister and its first woman prime minister. However, in the general election held Oct 25, 1993, the Liberal Party routed the Progressive-Conservatives in the worst defeat for a governing political party in Canada's 126-year history, reducing the former government's seats in the House of Commons from 154 to 2. Campbell was among those who lost their seats.

KOREAN WAR BEGAN: ANNIVERSARY. June 25, 1950. Forces from northern Korea invaded southern Korea, beginning a civil war. US ground forces entered the conflict June 30. An armistice was signed at Panmunjom July 27, 1953, formally dividing the country in two—North Korea and South Korea. For more info:

korea50.army.mil/teachers.html. The Fall 1999 issue of *Cobblestone* (for students ages 9–14) is devoted to the Korean War.

LAST GREAT BUFFALO HUNT: ANNIVERSARY. June 25–27, 1882. By 1882 most of the estimated 60–75 million buffalo had been killed by white hide hunters, the meat left to rot. Buffalo numbered only about 50,000 when "The Last Great Buffalo Hunt" took place on Indian reservation lands near Hettinger, ND. Some 2,000 Teton Sioux Indians in full hunting regalia killed about 5,000 buffalo. The occasion is also referred to as "The Last Stand of the American Buffalo" as within 16 months the last of the free-ranging buffalo were gone. For more info: *Buffalo Hunt*, by Russell Freedman (Holiday House, 0-8234-0702-0, $19.95 Gr. 3–7). For info: Wendy Hehn, Dir Community Promotions, Box 1323, Hettinger, ND 58639. Phone: (701) 567-2531. Fax: (701) 567-2690. E-mail: adamsdv@hettinger.ctctel.com. Web: www.hettingernd.com.

MONTSERRAT: VOLCANO ERUPTS: ANNIVERSARY. June 25, 1997. After lying dormant for 400 years, the Soufriere Hills volcano began to come to life in July 1995. It erupted in 1997, covering Plymouth, Montserrat's capital city, and two-thirds of the rest of the lush Caribbean island with a heavy layer of ash. Two-thirds of the population relocated to other islands or to Great Britain. For more info visit Volcano World: volcano.und.nodak.edu.

MOZAMBIQUE: INDEPENDENCE DAY. June 25. National holiday. Commemorates independence from Portugal in 1975.

SLOVENIA: NATIONAL DAY. June 25. Public holiday. Commemorates independence from the former Yugoslavia in 1991.

SUPREME COURT BANS SCHOOL PRAYER: 40th ANNIVERSARY. June 25, 1962. The US Supreme Court ruled that a prayer read aloud in public schools violated the 1st Amendment's separation of church and state. The court again struck down a law pertaining to the First Amendment when it disallowed an Alabama law that permitted a daily one-minute period of silent meditation or prayer in public schools June 1, 1985. (Vote 6–3.)

TWO YUGOSLAV REPUBLICS DECLARE INDEPENDENCE: ANNIVERSARY. June 25, 1991. The republics of Slovenia and Croatia formally declared independence from Yugoslavia. The two northwestern republics did not, however, secede outright.

VIRGINIA RATIFIES CONSTITUTION: ANNIVERSARY. June 25. Became the 10th state to ratify the Constitution in 1788.

BIRTHDAYS TODAY

Eric Carle, 73, author (*The Very Hungry Caterpillar, The Very Busy Spider, The Grouchy Ladybug*), born Syracuse, NY, June 25, 1929.

Dikembe Mutombo, 36, basketball player, born Kinshasa, Zaire, June 25, 1966.

June 2002

S	M	T	W	T	F	S
						1
2	3	4	5	6	7	8
9	10	11	12	13	14	15
16	17	18	19	20	21	22
23	24	25	26	27	28	29
30						

JUNE 26 — WEDNESDAY

Day 177 — 188 Remaining

BAR CODE INTRODUCED: ANNIVERSARY. June 26, 1974. A committee formed in 1970 by US grocers and food manufacturers recommended in 1973 a Universal Product Code (i.e., a bar code) for supermarket items that would allow electronic scanning of prices. On this day in 1974 a pack of Wrigley's gum was swiped across the first checkout scanner at a supermarket at Troy, OH. Today bar codes are used to keep track of everything from freight cars to cattle.

BORDEN, SIR ROBERT LAIRD: BIRTH ANNIVERSARY. June 26, 1854. Canadian statesman and prime minister, born at Grand Pre, Nova Scotia. Died at Ottawa, June 10, 1937.

BUCK, PEARL: BIRTH ANNIVERSARY. June 26, 1892. Author (*The Big Wave*), noted authority on China and humanitarian. Nobel Prize winner. Born at Hillsboro, WV. Died Mar 6, 1973, at Danby, VT.

CN TOWER: OPENING ANNIVERSARY. June 26, 1976. Birthday of the world's tallest building and freestanding structure, the CN Tower, 1,815 feet, 5 inches high, at Toronto, Ontario, Canada. For info: CN Tower, 301 Front St W, Toronto, ON, Canada M5V 2T6. Phone: (416) 360-8500. Fax: (416) 601-4713.

FARLEY, WALTER: BIRTH ANNIVERSARY. June 26, 1922. Children's author, born at New York, NY. He wrote the tale of the famous horse, *The Black Stallion* and later wrote the prequel, *The Young Black Stallion* with his son in 1989. Farley died at Sarasota, FL, Oct 16, 1989.

FLAG AMENDMENT DEFEATED: ANNIVERSARY. June 26, 1990. The Senate rejected a proposed constitutional amendment that would have permitted states to prosecute those who destroyed or desecrated American flags. Similar legislation continues to be considered by Congress.

MADAGASCAR: INDEPENDENCE DAY. June 26. National holiday. Commemorates independence from France in 1960.

MIDDLETON, ARTHUR: BIRTH ANNIVERSARY. June 26, 1742. American Revolutionary leader and signer of the Declaration of Independence, born near Charleston, SC. Died at Goose Creek, SC, Jan 1, 1787.

PIZARRO, FRANCISCO: DEATH ANNIVERSARY. June 26, 1541. Spanish conqueror of Peru, born at Extremadura, Spain, ca. 1471. Pizarro died at Lima, Peru.

SAINT LAWRENCE SEAWAY DEDICATION: ANNIVERSARY. June 26, 1959. President Dwight D. Eisenhower and Queen Elizabeth II jointly dedicated the St. Lawrence Seaway in formal ceremonies held at St. Lambert, Quebec, Canada. A project undertaken jointly by Canada and the US, the waterway (which provides access between the Atlantic Ocean and the Great Lakes) had been opened to traffic Apr 25, 1959.

UNITED NATIONS CHARTER SIGNED: ANNIVERSARY. June 26, 1945. The UN Charter was signed at San Francisco by 50 nations.

UNITED NATIONS: INTERNATIONAL DAY AGAINST DRUG ABUSE AND ILLICIT TRAFFICKING. June 26. Following a recommendation of the 1987 International Conference on Drug Abuse and Illicit Trafficking, the United Nations General Assembly (Res 42/112), expressed its determination to strengthen action and cooperation for an international society free of drug abuse and proclaimed June 26 as an annual observance to raise public awareness. For info: UN, Dept of Public Info, Public Inquiries Unit, RM GA-57, New York, NY 10017. Phone: (212) 963-4475. Fax: (212) 963-0071. E-mail: inquiries@un.org.

ZAHARIAS, MILDRED "BABE" DIDRIKSON: BIRTH ANNIVERSARY. June 26, 1914. Born Mildred Ella Didrikson at Port Arthur, TX, the great athlete was nicknamed "Babe" after legendary baseball player Babe Ruth. She was named to the women's All-America basketball team when she was 16. At the 1932 Olympic Games, she won two gold medals and also set world records in the javelin throw and the 80-meter high hurdles; only a technicality prevented her from obtaining the gold in the high jump. Didrikson married professional wrestler George Zaharias in 1938, six years after she began playing golf casually. In 1946 Babe won the US Women's Amateur tournament, and in 1947 she won 17 straight golf championships and became the first American winner of the British Ladies' Amateur Tournament. Turning professional in 1948, she won the US Women's Open in 1950 and 1954, the same year she won the All-American Open. Babe also excelled in softball, baseball, swimming, figure skating, billiards—even football. In a 1950 Associated Press poll she was named the woman athlete of the first half of the 20th century. She died of cancer, Sept 27, 1956, at Galveston, TX. For more info: *Babe Didrikson Zaharias: The Making of a Champion*, by Russell Freedman. (Clarion, 0-395-63367-2, $18 Gr. 5 & up).

BIRTHDAYS TODAY

Robert Burch, 77, author (*Christmas with Ida Early*), born Inman, GA, June 26, 1925.

Derek Jeter, 28, baseball player, born Pequannock, NJ, June 26, 1974.

Chris O'Donnell, 32, actor (*Batman & Robin*), born Winnetka, IL, June 26, 1970.

Jason Schwartzman, 22, actor (*Rushmore*), born Los Angeles, CA, June 26,1980.

Nancy Willard, 66, author (Newbery for *A Visit to William Blake's Inn: Poems for Innocent and Experienced Travelers*), born Ann Arbor, MI, June 26, 1936.

Charlotte Zolotow, 87, author (*Mr. Rabbit and the Lovely Present, William's Doll, The Unfriendly Book*), born Norfolk, VA, June 26, 1915.

JUNE 27 — THURSDAY

Day 178 — 187 Remaining

DJIBOUTI: INDEPENDENCE DAY: 25th ANNIVERSARY. June 27. National day. Commemorates independence from France in 1977.

FAST OF TAMMUZ. June 27. Jewish holiday. Hebrew calendar date: Tammuz 17, 5762. Shiva Asar B'Tammuz begins at first light of day and commemorates the first-century Roman siege that breached the walls of Jerusalem. Begins a three-week time of mourning.

HAPPY BIRTHDAY TO "HAPPY BIRTHDAY TO YOU." June 27, 1859. The melody of probably the most often sung song in the world, "Happy Birthday to You," was composed by Mildred J. Hill, a schoolteacher, born at Louisville, KY on this date. Her younger sister, Patty Smith Hill, was the author of the lyrics which were first published in 1893 as "Good Morning to All," a classroom greeting published in the book *Song Stories for the Sunday School*. The lyrics were amended in 1924 to include a stanza beginning "Happy Birthday to You." Now it is sung somewhere in the world every minute of the day. Although the authors are believed to have earned very little from the song, reportedly it later generated about $1 million a year for its copyright owner. The song is expected to enter public domain upon expiration of copyright in 2010. Mildred Hill died at Chicago, IL, June 5, 1916 without knowing that her melody would become the world's most popular song. Patty Hill, born Mar 27, 1868, at Louisville, KY, died at New York, NY, May 25, 1946.

KELLER, HELEN: BIRTH ANNIVERSARY. June 27, 1880. Born at Tuscumbia, AL, Helen Keller was left deaf and blind by a disease she contracted at 18 months of age. With the help of her teacher, Anne Sullivan, she graduated from college and had a career as an author and lecturer. She died June 1, 1968, at Westport, CT. For more info: *A Girl Named Helen Keller*, by Margo Lundell (Scholastic, 0-590-47963-6, $3.99 Gr. 1–3) or *Helen Keller*, by Johanna Hurwitz (Random House, 0-679-87705-3, $3.99 Gr. 2–4) or *Helen Keller*, by Lois Nicholson (Chelsea House, 0-7910-2086-X, $19.95 Gr. 4 & up).

BIRTHDAYS TODAY

Bruce Babbitt, 64, former US Secretary of Interior (Clinton administration), born Los Angeles, CA, June 27, 1938.

Lucille Clifton, 66, author (*Everett Anderson's Goodbye*), born Depew, NY, June 27, 1936.

James Lincoln Collier, 74, author of historical fiction, with his brother Christopher Collier (*My Brother Sam Is Dead*), born New York, NY, June 27, 1928.

Captain Kangaroo (Bob Keeshan), 75, TV personality, born Lynbrook, NY, June 27, 1927.

JUNE 28 — FRIDAY

Day 179 — 186 Remaining

BISCAYNE NATIONAL PARK ESTABLISHED: ANNIVERSARY. June 28, 1980. Including the coral reefs and waters of Biscayne Bay and the area of the Atlantic Ocean which surrounds the northernmost Florida Keys, Biscayne National Monument was authorized Oct 18, 1968. It became a national park in 1980. For more info: www.nps.gov/bisc/index.htm.

FORBES, ESTHER: BIRTH ANNIVERSARY. June 28, 1891. Author and illustrator, born at Westborough, MA. She won the Pulitzer Prize for history in 1943 for her book *Paul Revere and the World He Lived In*. Her children's book, *Johnny Tremain*, was awarded the 1944 Newbery Medal. Forbes died at Worcester, MA, Aug 12, 1967. For a study guide to *Johnny Tremain*: glencoe.com /sec/literature/litlibrary.

MONDAY HOLIDAY LAW: ANNIVERSARY. June 28, 1968. President Lyndon B. Johnson approved Public Law 90–363, which amended section 6103(a) of title 5, United States Code, establishing Monday observance of Washington's Birthday, Memorial Day, Labor Day, Columbus Day and Veterans Day. The new holiday law took effect Jan 1, 1971. Veterans Day observance subsequently reverted to its former observance date, Nov 11. See individual holidays for more details.

TREATY OF VERSAILLES: ANNIVERSARY. June 28, 1919. The signing of the Treaty of Versailles at Versailles, France formally ended World War I.

BIRTHDAYS TODAY

John Elway, 42, former football player, born Port Angeles, WA, June 28, 1960.

Mark Grace, 38, baseball player, born Winston-Salem, NC, June 28, 1964.

Bette Greene, 68, author (*Philip Hall Likes Me, I Reckon Maybe*), born Memphis, TN, June 28, 1934.

Carl Levin, 68, US Senator (D, Michigan), born Detroit, MI, June 28, 1934.

JUNE 29 — SATURDAY

Day 180 — 185 Remaining

KEPES, JULIET A.: BIRTH ANNIVERSARY. June 29, 1919. Author and illustrator (Caldecott for *Five Little Monkeys*), born at London, England. Died Mar 11, 1999, at Cambridge, MA.

LATHROP, JULIA C.: BIRTH ANNIVERSARY. June 29, 1858. A pioneer in the battle to establish child-labor laws, Julia C. Lathrop was the first woman member of the Illinois State Board of Charities and in 1900 was instrumental in establishing the first juvenile court in the US. In 1912, President Taft named Lathrop chief of the newly created Children's Bureau, then part of the US Department of Commerce and Labor. In 1925 she became a member of the Child Welfare Committee of the League of Nations. Born at Rockford, IL, she died there, Apr 15, 1932.

MESA VERDE NATIONAL PARK ESTABLISHED: ANNIVERSARY. June 29, 1906. Area of southwest Colorado established as a national park. For more info: www.nps.gov/meve/index.htm.

PETER AND PAUL DAY. June 29. Feast day for Saint Peter and Saint Paul. Commemorates dual martyrdom of Christian apostles Peter (by crucifixion) and Paul (by beheading) during persecution by Roman Emperor Nero. Observed since third century.

SAINT-EXUPERY, ANTOINE DE: BIRTH ANNIVERSARY. June 29, 1900. French aviator and children's author, born at Lyons, France. Saint-Exupery is best known for *The Little Prince*. Other books include *Wind, Sand and Stars* and *Night Flight*. Saint-Exupery died at sea, July 31, 1944.

SPACE MILESTONE: *ATLANTIS* DOCKS WITH *MIR*. June 29, 1995. An American space shuttle docked with a Russian space station for the first time, creating the biggest craft ever assembled in space. This linkup was the first step toward the creation of an International Space Station.

BIRTHDAYS TODAY

Theo Fleury, 34, hockey player, born Oxbow, SK, Canada, June 29, 1968.

Ann Veneman, 53, US Secretary of Agriculture (George W. Bush administration), born Sacramento, CA, June 6, 1949.

JUNE 30 — SUNDAY

Day 181 — 184 Remaining

CHARLES BLONDIN'S CONQUEST OF NIAGARA FALLS: ANNIVERSARY. June 30, 1859. Charles Blondin, a French acrobat and aerialist (whose real name was Jean François Gravelet), in view of a crowd estimated at more than 25,000 persons, walked across Niagara Falls on a tightrope. The walk required only about five minutes. On separate occasions he crossed blindfolded, pushing a wheelbarrow, carrying a man on his back and even on stilts. Blondin was born Feb 28, 1824, at St. Omer, France, and died at London, England, Feb 19, 1897.

CONGO (KINSHASA): INDEPENDENCE DAY. June 30. National holiday. The Democratic Republic of Congo was previously known as Zaire. Commemorates independence from Belgium in 1960.

GUATEMALA: ARMED FORCES DAY. June 30. Guatemala observes public holiday.

LAST HURRAH FOR BRITISH HONG KONG: 5th ANNIVERSARY. June 30, 1997. The crested flag of the British Crown Colony was officially lowered at midnight and replaced by a new flag (marked by the bauhinia flower) representing China's sovereignty over Hong Kong and the official transfer of power. Though Britain owned Hong Kong in perpetuity, the land areas surrounding the city were leased from China and the lease expired July 1, 1997. Rather than renegotiate a new lease, Britain ceded its claim to Hong Kong.

LEAP SECOND ADJUSTMENT TIME. June 30. June 30 is one of the times that has been favored for the addition or subtraction of a second from our clock time (to coordinate atomic and astronomical time). The determination to adjust is made by the Central Bureau of the International Earth Rotation Service, at Paris, France.

MONROE, ELIZABETH KORTRIGHT: BIRTH ANNIVERSARY. June 30, 1768. Wife of James Monroe, fifth president of the US, born at New York, NY. Died at their Oak Hill estate at Loudon County, VA, Sept 23, 1830.

NATIONAL EDUCATION ASSOCIATION MEETING. June 30–July 5. Dallas, TX. Delegates from the local and state level debate issues and set NEA policy at the Representative Assembly. Est attendance: 10,000. For info: Natl Education Assn, 1201 16th St NW, Washington, DC 20036-3290. Phone: (202) 822-7769. Web: www.nea.org.

NOW FOUNDED: ANNIVERSARY. June 30, 1966. The National Organization for Women was founded at Washington, DC, by people attending the Third National Conference on the Commission on the Status of Women. NOW's purpose is to take action to take women into full partnership in the mainstream of American society, exercising all privileges and responsibilities in equal partnership with men. For info: Natl Organization for Women, 733 15th St NW, Washington, DC 20005. Phone: (202) 628-8NOW. Web: www.now.org.

ORTHODOX FESTIVAL OF ALL SAINTS. June 30. Observed by Eastern Orthodox churches on the Sunday following Orthodox Pentecost (June 23 in 2002). Marks the end of the 18-week Triodion cycle.

TWENTY-SIXTH AMENDMENT RATIFIED: ANNIVERSARY. June 30, 1971. The 26th Amendment to the Constitution granted the right to vote in all federal, state and local elections to all persons 18 years or older. On the date of ratification the US gained an additional 11 million voters. Up until this time, the minimum voting age was set by the states; in most states it was 21.

WHEELER, WILLIAM ALMON: BIRTH ANNIVERSARY. June 30, 1819. The 19th vice president of the US (1877–81), born at Malone, NY. Died there, June 4, 1887.

BIRTHDAYS TODAY

Dr. Robert Ballard, 60, explorer, oceanographer, author (*Exploring the Titanic, Ghost Liners*), born Witchita, KS, June 30, 1942.

Mollie Hunter, 80, author (*A Sound of Chariots*), born Longniddry, Scotland, June 30, 1922.

David McPhail, 62, author and illustrator (*Pigs Ahoy!*), born Newburyport, MA, June 30, 1940.

Mitchell (Mitch) Richmond, 37, basketball player, born Ft Lauderdale, FL, June 30, 1965.

JULY 1 — MONDAY

Day 182 — 183 Remaining

BATTLE OF GETTYSBURG: ANNIVERSARY. July 1, 1863. After the Southern success at Chancellorsville, VA, Confederate General Robert E. Lee led his forces on an invasion of the North, initially targeting Harrisburg, PA. As Union forces moved to counter the invasion, the battle lines were eventually formed at Gettysburg, PA, in one of the Civil War's most crucial battles, beginning July 1, 1863. On the climactic third day of the battle (July 3), Lee ordered an attack on the center of the Union line, later to be known as Pickett's Charge. The 15,000 rebels were repulsed, ending the Battle of Gettysburg. After the defeat, Lee's forces retreated back to Virginia, listing more than one-third of the troops as casualties in the failed invasion. Union General George Meade initially failed to pursue the retreating rebels, allowing Lee's army to escape across the rain-swollen Potomac River. This battle had the highest casualties of any in the Civil War.

BOTSWANA: SIR SERETSE KHAMA DAY. July 1. National holiday. Commemorates birth in 1921 of first president.

BRITISH VIRGIN ISLANDS: TERRITORY DAY. July 1. National holiday.

BURUNDI: INDEPENDENCE DAY: 40th ANNIVERSARY. July 1. National holiday. Anniversary of establishment of independence in 1962. Had been under Belgian administration as part of Ruanda-Urundi.

CANADA: CANADA DAY. July 1. National holiday. Canada's national day, formerly known as Dominion Day. Observed on following day when July 1 is a Sunday. Commemorates the confederation of Upper and Lower Canada and some of the Maritime Provinces into the Dominion of Canada in 1867.

CARIBBEAN OR CARICOM DAY. July 1. The anniversary of the treaty establishing the Caribbean Community (also called the Treaty of Chaguaramas), signed by the prime ministers of Barbados, Guyana, Jamaica and Trinidad and Tobago, July 4, 1973. Observed as a public holiday in Guyana and St. Vincent. Annually, the first Monday in July.

July 2002

S	M	T	W	T	F	S
	1	2	3	4	5	6
7	8	9	10	11	12	13
14	15	16	17	18	19	20
21	22	23	24	25	26	27
28	29	30	31			

DIANA, PRINCESS OF WALES: BIRTH ANNIVERSARY. July 1, 1961. Former wife of Charles, Prince of Wales, and mother of Prince William and Prince Harry. Born Lady Diana Spencer at Sandringham, England, she died in an automobile accident at Paris, France, Aug 31, 1997.

DORSEY, THOMAS A.: BIRTH ANNIVERSARY. July 1, 1899. Thomas A. Dorsey, the father of gospel music, was born at Villa Rica, GA. Originally a blues composer, Dorsey eventually combined blues and sacred music to develop gospel music. It was Dorsey's composition "Take My Hand, Precious Lord" that Reverend Dr. Martin Luther King, Jr, had asked to have performed just moments before his assassination. Dorsey, who composed more than 1,000 gospel songs and hundreds of blues songs in his lifetime, died Jan 23, 1993, at Chicago, IL.

FIRST ADHESIVE US POSTAGE STAMPS ISSUED: ANNIVERSARY. July 1, 1847. The first adhesive US postage stamps were issued by the US Postal Service.

FIRST US ZOO: ANNIVERSARY. July 1, 1874. The Philadelphia Zoological Society, the first US zoo, opened. Three thousand visitors traveled by foot, horse and carriage, and steamboat to visit the exhibits. Price of admission was 25 cents for adults and 10 cents for children. There were 1,000 animals in the zoo on opening day. For more info: www.phillyzoo.org.

GHANA: REPUBLIC DAY. July 1. National holiday. Commemorates the inauguration of the Republic in 1960.

NATIONAL BAKED BEAN MONTH. July 1–31. To pay tribute to one of America's favorite and most healthful and nutritious foods, baked beans, made with dry or canned beans. For info: Therese Schueneman, Bean Education & Awareness Network, 303 E Wacker Dr, Ste 440, Chicago, IL 60601. Phone: (312) 861-5200. Fax: (312) 861-5252. Web: www.americanbean.org.

NATIONAL HOT DOG MONTH. July 1–31. Celebrates one of America's favorite hand–held foods with fun facts and new topping ideas. More than 16 billion hot dogs per year are sold in the US. For info: Natl Hot Dog & Sausage Council, 1700 N Moore St, Ste 1600, Arlington, VA 22209. Phone: (703) 841-2400. Web: www.hot-dog.org.

NATIONAL JULY BELONGS TO BLUEBERRIES MONTH. July 1–31. To make the public aware that this is the peak month for fresh blueberries. For info: North American Blueberry Council, 4995 Golden Foothill Parkway, Ste #2, El Dorado Hills, CA 95762.

NATIONAL RECREATION AND PARKS MONTH. July 1–31. To showcase and invite community participation in quality leisure activities for all segments of the population. For info: Natl Recreation and Park Assn, 22377 Belmont Ridge Rd, Ashburn, VA 20148. Phone: (703) 858-0784. Fax: (703) 858-0794. E-mail: info@nrpa.org. Web: www.activeparks.org.

NICK AT NITE TV PREMIERE: ANNIVERSARY. July 1, 1985. The first broadcast of Nick at Nite, the creation of the kids' network Nickelodeon. Owned and operated by MTV Networks, Nick at Nite presents many of the old classic television series, such as "Happy Days," "The Brady Bunch" and "My Three Sons." For more info visit www.nick-at-nite.com.

REGULAR TV BROADCASTS BEGIN: ANNIVERSARY. July 1, 1941. The Federal Communications Commission allowed 18 television stations to begin broadcasting this day. However, only two were ready: the New York stations owned by NBC and CBS.

RWANDA: INDEPENDENCE DAY: 40th ANNIVERSARY. July 1. National holiday. Commemorates independence from Belgium in 1962.

SPACE MILESTONE: *KOSMOS 1383* (USSR): 20th ANNIVERSARY. July 1, 1982. First search and rescue satellite—equipped to hear distress calls from aircraft and ships—launched in cooperative project with the US and France.

WALKMAN DEBUTS: ANNIVERSARY. July 1, 1979. This month Sony introduced the Walkman under the name Soundabout, selling for $200. It had been released in Japan six months earlier. More than 185 million have been sold.

ZAMBIA: HEROES DAY. July 1. First Monday in July is Zambian national holiday—memorial day for Zambians who died in the struggle for independence. Political rallies stress solidarity.

ZIP CODES INAUGURATED: ANNIVERSARY. July 1, 1963. The US Postal Service introduced the five-digit zip code on this day. Some large cities had had two-digit zone codes prior to this date. For example, a neighborhood in New York with a zone code of 16 now had a zip code of 10016.

BIRTHDAYS TODAY

Diane Hoyt-Goldsmith, 52, author (*Buffalo Days*), born Peoria, IL, July 1, 1950.

Carl Lewis, 41, Olympic gold medal sprinter and long jumper, born Birmingham, AL, July 1, 1961.

Emily Arnold McCully, 63, author and illustrator (Caldecott for *Mirette on the High Wire*), born Galesburg, IL, July 1, 1939.

JULY 2 — TUESDAY

Day 183 — 182 Remaining

CIVIL RIGHTS ACT OF 1964: ANNIVERSARY. July 2, 1964. President Lyndon Johnson signed the Voting Rights Act of 1964 into law, prohibiting discrimination on the basis of race in public accommodations, in publicly owned or operated facilities, in employment and union membership and in the registration of voters. The bill included Title VI, which allowed for the cutoff of federal funding in areas where discrimination persisted.

CONSTITUTION OF THE US TAKES EFFECT: ANNIVERSARY. July 2, 1788. Cyrus Griffin of Virginia, the president of the Congress, announced that the Constitution had been ratified by the required nine states (the ninth being New Hampshire, June 21, 1788), and a committee was appointed to make preparations for the change of government.

DECLARATION OF INDEPENDENCE RESOLUTION: ANNIVERSARY. July 2, 1776. Anniversary of adoption by the Continental Congress, Philadelphia, PA, of a resolution introduced June 7, 1776, by Richard Henry Lee of Virginia: "Resolved, That these United Colonies are, and of right ought to be, free and independent States, that they are absolved from all allegiance to the British Crown, and that all political connection between them and the State of Great Britain is, and ought to be, totally dissolved. That it is expedient forthwith to take the most effectual measures for forming foreign Alliances. That a plan of confederation be prepared and transmitted to the respective Colonies for their consideration and approbation." This resolution prepared the way for adoption, July 4, 1776, of the Declaration of Independence. See also: "Declaration of Independence: Approval and Signing Anniversary" (July 4).

HALFWAY POINT OF 2002. July 2. At noon on July 2, 2002, 182½ days of the year will have elapsed and 182½ will remain before Jan 1, 2003.

MARSHALL, THURGOOD: BIRTH ANNIVERSARY. July 2, 1908. Thurgood Marshall, the first African American on the US Supreme Court, was born at Baltimore, MD. For more than 20 years, he served as director-counsel of the NAACP Legal Defense and Educational Fund. He experienced his greatest legal victory May 17, 1954, when the Supreme Court decision on *Brown v Board of Education* declared an end to the "separate but equal" system of racial segregation in public schools in 21 states. Marshall argued 32 cases before the Supreme Court, winning 29 of them, before becoming a member of the high court himself. Nominated by President Lyndon Johnson, he began his 24-year career on the high court Oct 2, 1967, becoming a voice of dissent in an increasingly conservative court. Marshall announced his retirement June 27, 1991, and he died Jan 24, 1993, at Washington, DC.

MOON PHASE: LAST QUARTER. July 2. Moon enters Last Quarter phase at 1:19 PM, EDT.

VESEY, DENMARK: DEATH ANNIVERSARY. July 2, 1822. Planner of what would have been the biggest slave revolt in US history, Denmark Vesey was executed at Charleston, SC. He had been born around 1767, probably in the West Indies, where he was sold at around age 14 to Joseph Vesey, captain of a slave ship. He purchased his freedom in 1800. In 1818 Vesey and others began to plot an uprising; he held secret meetings, collected disguises and firearms and chose a date in June 1822. But authorities were warned, and police and the military were out in full force. Over the next two months 130 blacks were taken into custody; 35, including Vesey, were hanged and 31 were exiled. As a result of the plot Southern legislatures passed more rigorous slave codes.

ZAMBIA: UNITY DAY. July 2. Memorial day for Zambians who died in the struggle for independence. Political rallies stressing solidarity throughout country. Annually, the first Tuesday in July.

BIRTHDAYS TODAY

Jose Canseco, Jr, 38, baseball player, born Havana, Cuba, July 2, 1964.

Vicente Fox Quesada, 60, president of Mexico, born Mexico City, Mexico, July 2, 1942.

Jack Gantos, 51, author (the Rotten Ralph series, *Joey Pigza Swallowed the Key*), born Mount Pleasant, PA, July 2, 1951.

Rita Golden Gelman, 65, author (*More Spaghetti, I Say!*), born Bridgeport, CT, July 2, 1937.

Jean Craighead George, 83, author (Newbery for *Julie of the Wolves*), born Washington, DC, July 2, 1919.

Lindsay Lohan, 16, actress (*The Parent Trap*), born New York, NY, July 2, 1986.

Chris Lynch, 40, author (*Slot Machine*), born Boston, MA, July 2, 1962.

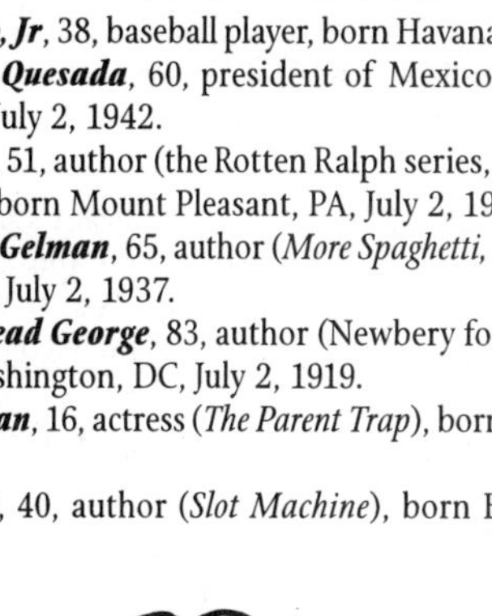

JULY 3 — WEDNESDAY

Day 184 — 181 Remaining

AIR CONDITIONING APPRECIATION DAYS. July 3–Aug 15. Northern Hemisphere. During Dog Days, the hottest time of the year in the Northern Hemisphere, to acknowledge the contribution of air conditioning to a better way of life. Annually, July 3–Aug 15. For info: Air-Conditioning and Refrig Institute, 4301 N Fairfax Dr, Ste 425, Arlington, VA 22203. Phone: (703) 524-8800. Fax: (703) 528-3816. E-mail: ari@ari.org. Web: www.ari.org.

BELARUS: INDEPENDENCE DAY. July 3. National holiday. A former republic of the Soviet Union, it became independent in 1991.

BENNETT, RICHARD BEDFORD: BIRTH ANNIVERSARY. July 3, 1870. Former Canadian prime minister, born at Hopewell Hill, New Brunswick, Canada. Died at Mickelham, England, June 26, 1947.

CANADA: NEWFOUNDLAND MEMORIAL DAY. July 3.

DOG DAYS. July 3–Aug 15. Hottest days of the year in Northern Hemisphere. Usually about 40 days, but variously reckoned at 30–54 days. Popularly believed to be an evil time "when the sea boiled, wine turned sour, dogs grew mad, and all creatures became languid, causing to man burning fevers, hysterics and phrensies" (from Brady's *Clavis Calendarium*, 1813). Originally the days when Sirius, the Dog Star, rose just before or at about the same time as sunrise (no longer true owing to precession of the equinoxes). Ancients sacrificed a brown dog at beginning of Dog Days to appease the rage of Sirius, believing that star was the cause of the hot, sultry weather.

HUNTINGTON, SAMUEL: BIRTH ANNIVERSARY. July 3, 1731. President of the Continental Congress, Governor of Connecticut, signer of the Declaration of Independence, born at Windham, CT, died at Norwich, CT, Jan 5, 1796.

IDAHO: ADMISSION DAY: ANNIVERSARY. July 3. Became 43rd state in 1890.

NATIONAL TOM SAWYER DAYS (WITH FENCE PAINTING CONTEST). July 3–6 (tentative). Hannibal, MO. Frog jumping, mud volleyball, Tom and Becky Contest, parade, Tomboy Sawyer Contest, 10K run, arts & crafts show and fireworks launched from the banks of the Mississippi River. Highlight is the National Fence Painting Contest. Sponsor: Hannibal Jaycees. Est attendance: 100,000. For info: Hannibal Visitors Bureau, 505 N 3rd St, Hannibal, MO 63401. Phone: (573) 221-2477.

STAY OUT OF THE SUN DAY. July 3. For health's sake, give your skin a break today. [© 1999 by WH] For info: Tom and Ruth Roy, Wellcat Holidays, 2418 Long Ln, Lebanon, PA 17046. Phone: (230) 332-4886. E-mail: wellcat@supernet.com. Web: www.wellcat.com.

VIRGIN ISLANDS: DANISH WEST INDIES EMANCIPATION DAY. July 3, 1848. Commemorates freeing of slaves in the Danish West Indies. Ceremony at Frederiksted, St. Croix, where actual proclamation was first read by Governor-General Peter Von Scholten.

July 2002

S	M	T	W	T	F	S
	1	2	3	4	5	6
7	8	9	10	11	12	13
14	15	16	17	18	19	20
21	22	23	24	25	26	27
28	29	30	31			

BIRTHDAYS TODAY

Moises Alou, 36, baseball player, born Atlanta, GA, July 3, 1966.

Franny Billingsley, 48, author (*Well Wished*), born Chicago, IL, July 3, 1954.

Tom Cruise, 40, actor (*Rain Man; Mission: Impossible*), born Syracuse, NY, July 3, 1962.

Teemu Selanne, 32, hockey player, born Helsinki, Finland, July 3, 1970.

JULY 4 — THURSDAY

Day 185 — 180 Remaining

"AMERICA THE BEAUTIFUL" PUBLISHED: ANNIVERSARY. July 4, 1895. The poem "America the Beautiful" by Katherine Lee Bates, a Wellesley College professor, was first published in the *Congregationalist*, a church publication. Later it was set to music. For more info: *Purple Mountain Majesties: The Story of Katherine Lee Bates and "America the Beautiful"*, by Barbara Younger (Dutton, 0-525-45653-8, $15.99 Gr. 3–5). In *America the Beautiful* 16 landscape paintings by Neil Waldman help bring the lyrics alive for children (0-689-31861-8, Atheneum, $16 All ages).

COOLIDGE, CALVIN: BIRTH ANNIVERSARY. July 4, 1872. The 30th president of the US was born John Calvin Coolidge at Plymouth, VT. He succeeded to the presidency Aug 3, 1923, following the death of Warren G. Harding. Coolidge was elected president once, in 1924, but did "not choose to run for president in 1928." Nicknamed Silent Cal, he is reported to have said, "If you don't say anything, you won't be called on to repeat it." Coolidge died at Northampton, MA, Jan 5, 1933. For info: www.ipl.org/ref/POTUS.

DECLARATION OF INDEPENDENCE APPROVAL AND SIGNING: ANNIVERSARY. July 4, 1776. The Declaration of Independence was approved by the Continental Congress: "Signed by Order and in Behalf of the Congress, John Hancock, President, Attest, Charles Thomson, Secretary." The official signing occurred Aug 2, 1776. For more info: *Give Me Liberty! The Story of the Declaration of Independence*, by Russell Freedman (Holiday House, 0-8234-1448-5, $24.95 Gr. 5–8) or go to Ben's Guide to US Government for Kids: bensguide.gpo.gov. See also: "Declaration of Independence: Official Signing: Anniversary" (Aug 2).

FOSTER, STEPHEN: BIRTH ANNIVERSARY. July 4, 1826. Stephen Collins Foster, one of America's most famous and best-loved songwriters, was born at Lawrenceville, PA. Among his nearly 200 songs: "Oh! Susanna," "Camptown Races," "Old Folks at Home" ("Swanee River"), "Jeanie with the Light Brown Hair,"

"Old Black Joe" and "Beautiful Dreamer." Foster died in poverty at Bellevue Hospital at New York, NY, Jan 13, 1864. The anniversary of his death has been observed as Stephen Foster Memorial Day by Presidential Proclamation since 1952.

INDEPENDENCE DAY (FOURTH OF JULY). July 4, 1776. The US commemorates adoption of the Declaration of Independence by the Continental Congress. The nation's birthday. Legal holiday in all states and territories. For links to websites about the Fourth of July, go to: deil.lang.uiuc.edu/web.pages/holidays/fourth.html.

PHILIPPINES: FIL-AMERICAN FRIENDSHIP DAY. July 4. Formerly National Independence Day, when the Philippines were a colony of the US, now celebrated as Fil-American Friendship Day.

SPACE MILESTONE: *MARS PATHFINDER* (US): 5th ANNIVERSARY. July 4, 1997. Unmanned spacecraft landed on Mars after a seven-month flight. Carried *Sojourner*, a roving robotic explorer that sent back photographs of the landscape. One of its missions was to find if life ever existed on Mars. See also: "Space Milestone: *Mars Global Surveyor*" (Sept 11). For more info: *The Adventures of Sojourner: The Mission to Mars that Thrilled the World*, by Susi Trautmann Wunsch (Firefly, 0-9650493-5-3, $22.95 Gr. 4–7).

SPACE MILESTONE: *NOZOMI* (JAPAN). July 4, 1998. Japan launched this mission to Mars, making it the third country (after the US and Russia) to try an interplanetary space mission. *Nozomi*, which means "Hope," will orbit 84 miles above Mars and beam images back to Earth.

BIRTHDAYS TODAY

Harvey Grant, 37, basketball player, born Augusta, GA, July 4, 1965.
Horace Grant, 37, basketball player, born Augusta, GA, July 4, 1965.

JULY 5 — FRIDAY

Day 186 — 179 Remaining

ALGERIA: INDEPENDENCE DAY: 40th ANNIVERSARY. July 5. National holiday. Commemorates the day in 1962 when Algeria gained independence from France, after more than 100 years as a colony.

BARNUM, PHINEAS TAYLOR: BIRTH ANNIVERSARY. July 5, 1810. Promoter of the bizarre and unusual. Barnum's American Museum opened in 1842, promoting unusual acts including the Feejee Mermaid, Chang and Eng (the original Siamese Twins) and General Tom Thumb. In 1850 he began his promotion of Jenny Lind, "The Swedish Nightingale," and parlayed her singing talents into a major financial success. Barnum also cultivated a keen interest in politics. As a founder of the newspaper *Herald of Freedom*, his outspoken editorials resulted not only in lawsuits but also in at least one jail sentence. In 1852 he declined the Democratic nomination for governor of Connecticut but did serve two terms in the Connecticut legislature beginning in 1865. He was defeated in a bid for US Congress in 1866 but served as mayor of Bridgeport, CT, from 1875 to 1876. In 1871 "The Greatest Show on Earth" opened at Brooklyn, NY; Barnum merged with his rival J.A. Bailey in 1881 to form the Barnum and Bailey Circus. P.T. Barnum was born at Bethel, CT, and died at Bridgeport, CT, Apr 7, 1891.

CAPE VERDE: NATIONAL DAY. July 5. Commemorates independence from Portugal in 1975.

MICHIGAN STORYTELLERS FESTIVAL. July 5–7. Flint, MI. Storytelling performances, workshops and swaps come together for family fun and professional support at this 22nd annual event. Annually, the weekend after July 4th. Est attendance: 1,500. For info: Cynthia Stilley, Flint Public Library, 1026 E Kearsley, Flint, MI 48502. Phone: (810) 232-7111. Fax: (810) 232-8360. E-mail: cstilley@flint.lib.mi.us.

SLOVAKIA: SAINT CYRIL AND METHODIUS DAY. July 5. This day is dedicated to the Greek priests and scholars from Thessaloniki, who were invited by Prince Rastislav of Great Moravia to introduce Christianity and the first Slavic alphabet to the pagan people of the kingdom in AD 863.

VENEZUELA: INDEPENDENCE DAY. July 5. National holiday. Commemorates Proclamation of Independence from Spain in 1811. Independence achieved in 1821.

BIRTHDAYS TODAY

Janice Del Negro, 47, author (*Lucy Dove*), born The Bronx, NY, July 5, 1955.
Meredith Ann Pierce, 44, fantasy author (*The Darkangel*), born Seattle, WA, July 5, 1958.

JULY 6 — SATURDAY

Day 187 — 178 Remaining

BUSH, GEORGE W.: BIRTHDAY. July 6, 1946. The 43d president of the US, born at New Haven, CT.

COMOROS: INDEPENDENCE DAY: ANNIVERSARY. July 6. Federal and Islamic Republic of Comoros commemorates Declaration of Independence from France in 1975.

CZECH REPUBLIC: COMMEMORATION DAY OF BURNING OF JOHN HUS. July 6. In honor of Bohemian religious reformer John Hus, who was condemned as a heretic and burned at the stake on this date in 1415.

EARTH AT APHELION. July 6. At approximately midnight, EDT, planet Earth will reach aphelion, that point in its orbit when it is farthest from the sun (about 94,510,000 miles). The Earth's mean distance from the sun (mean radius of its orbit) is reached early in the months of April and October. Note that Earth is farthest from the sun during Northern Hemisphere summer. See also: "Earth at Perihelion" (Jan 2).

FIRST SUCCESSFUL ANTIRABIES INOCULATION: ANNIVERSARY. July 6, 1885. Louis Pasteur gave the first successful antirabies inoculation to a boy who had been bitten by an infected dog.

GERMANY: CAPITAL RETURNS TO BERLIN: ANNIVERSARY. July 6, 1999. The monthlong process of moving the German government from Bonn to Berlin began, eight years after Parliament had voted to return to its prewar seat. Berlin officially became the capital of Germany on Sept 1, 1999, and Parliament reconvened at the newly restored Reichstag on Sept 7, 1999.

LITHUANIA: DAY OF STATEHOOD. July 6. National holiday. Commemorates the 1252 crowning of Mindaugas, who united Lithuania.

LUXEMBOURG: ETTELBRUCK REMEMBRANCE DAY. July 6. In honor of US General George Patton, Jr, liberator of the Grand-Duchy of Luxembourg in 1945, who is buried at the American Military Cemetery at Hamm, Germany, among 5,100 soldiers of his famous Third Army.

MAJOR LEAGUE BASEBALL HOLDS FIRST ALL-STAR GAME: ANNIVERSARY. July 6, 1933. The first midsummer All-Star Game was held at Comiskey Park, Chicago, IL. Babe Ruth led the American League with a home run, as they defeated the National League 4–2. Prior to the summer of 1933, All-Star contests consisted of pre- and postseason exhibitions that often found teams made up of a few stars playing beside journeymen and even minor leaguers.

MALAWI: REPUBLIC DAY. July 6. National holiday. Commemorates independence of the former Nyasaland from Britain in 1964 and Malawi's becoming a republic in 1966.

UNITED NATIONS: INTERNATIONAL DAY OF COOPERATIVES. July 6. On Dec 16, 1992, the General Assembly proclaimed this observance for the first Saturday of July 1995 (Res 47/60). On Dec 23, 1994, recognizing that cooperatives are becoming an indispensable factor of economic and social development, the Assembly invited governments, international organizations, specialized agencies and national and international cooperative organizations to observe this day annually (Res 49/155). For info: United Nations, Dept of Public Info, New York, NY 10017.

BIRTHDAYS TODAY

George W. Bush, 56, 43d president of the US, former Governor of Texas (R), born New Haven, CT, July 6, 1946.

Tamera Mowry, 24, actress ("Sister, Sister"), born West Germany, July 6, 1978.

Tia Mowry, 24, actress ("Sister, Sister"), born West Germany, July 6, 1978.

Nancy Davis Reagan, 81, former First Lady, wife of Ronald Reagan, 40th president of the US, born New York, NY, July 6, 1921.

July 2002

S	M	T	W	T	F	S
	1	2	3	4	5	6
7	8	9	10	11	12	13
14	15	16	17	18	19	20
21	22	23	24	25	26	27
28	29	30	31			

JULY 7 — SUNDAY

Day 188 — 177 Remaining

BONZA BOTTLER DAY™. July 7. To celebrate when the number of the day is the same as the number of the month. Bonza Bottler Day™ is an excuse to have a party at least once a month. For info: Gail M. Berger, 109 Matthew Ave, Poca, WV 25159. Phone: (304) 776-7746. E-mail: gberger5@aol.com.

FATHER-DAUGHTER TAKE A WALK TOGETHER DAY. July 7. A special time in the summer for fathers and daughters of all ages to spend time together in the beautiful weather. Annually, July 7. For info: Janet Dellaria, 202 N Bennett St, Geneva, IL 60134. Phone: (630) 232-0425

HAWAII ANNEXED BY US: ANNIVERSARY. July 7, 1898. President William McKinley signed a resolution annexing Hawaii. No change in government took place until 1900, when Congress passed an act making Hawaii an "incorporated" territory of the US. This act remained in effect until Hawaii became a state in 1959.

JAPAN: TANABATA (STAR FESTIVAL). July 7. As an offering to the stars, children set up bamboo branches to which colorful strips of paper bearing poems are tied.

PAIGE, LEROY ROBERT (SATCHEL): BIRTH ANNIVERSARY. July 7, 1906. Baseball Hall of Fame pitcher, born at Mobile, AL. Paige was the greatest attraction in the Negro Leagues and was also, at age 42, the first black pitcher in the American League. Inducted into the Hall of Fame in 1971. Died at Kansas City, MO, June 8, 1982. For more info: *Satchel Paige*, by Lesa Cline-Ransome (S&S, 0-689-81151-9, $16 Gr. 2–4).

SOLOMON ISLANDS: INDEPENDENCE DAY. July 7. National holiday. Commemorates independence from Britain in 1978.

TANZANIA: SABA SABA DAY. July 7. Tanzania's mainland ruling party, TANU, was formed in 1954.

BIRTHDAYS TODAY

Michelle Kwan, 22, figure skater, born Torrance, CA, July 7, 1980.

Lisa Leslie, 30, basketball player, US Olympic Basketball Team, born Gardena, CA, July 7, 1972.

Joe Sakic, 33, hockey player, born Burnaby, BC, Canada, July 7, 1969.

Harriet Ziefert, 61, author (*My Tooth Is Loose, Where's Nicky?*), born Maplewood, NJ, July 7, 1941.

JULY 8 — MONDAY

Day 189 — 176 Remaining

DECLARATION OF INDEPENDENCE FIRST PUBLIC READING: ANNIVERSARY. July 8, 1776. Colonel John Nixon read the Declaration of Independence to the assembled residents at Philadelphia's Independence Square.

ROCKEFELLER, NELSON ALDRICH: BIRTH ANNIVERSARY. July 8, 1908. The 41st vice president of the US (1974–77), born at Bar Harbor, ME. Rockefeller was nominated for vice president by President Ford when Ford assumed the presidency after the resignation of Richard Nixon. Rockefeller was the second person to have become vice president without being elected (Gerald Ford was the first). Rockefeller also served as governor of New York. He died Jan 26, 1979, at New York, NY.

BIRTHDAYS TODAY

Raffi Cavoukian, 54, children's singer and songwriter, born Cairo, Egypt, July 8, 1948.

James Cross Giblin, 69, author (*Chimney Sweep*), born Cleveland, OH, July 8, 1933.

Phil Gramm, 60, US Senator (R, Texas), born Fort Benning, GA, July 8, 1942.

JULY 9 — TUESDAY

Day 190 — 175 Remaining

ARGENTINA: INDEPENDENCE DAY. July 9. Anniversary of establishment of independent republic, with the declaration of independence from Spain in 1816.

FOURTEENTH AMENDMENT TO US CONSTITUTION RATIFIED: ANNIVERSARY. July 9, 1868. The 14th Amendment defined US citizenship and provided that no State shall have the right to abridge the rights of any citizen without due process and equal protection under the law. Coming three years after the Civil War, the 14th Amendment also included provisions for barring individuals who assisted in any rebellion or insurrection against the US from holding public office and releasing federal and state governments from any financial liability incurred in the assistance of rebellion or insurrection against the US.

MOROCCO: YOUTH DAY. July 9. National holiday. On the birthday in 1929 of the former King Hassan II, who died in 1999.

BIRTHDAYS TODAY

Nancy Farmer, 61, author (*A Girl Named Disaster; The Ear, the Eye and the Arm*), born Phoenix, AZ, July 9, 1941.

Trent Green, 32, football player, born St. Louis, MO, July 9, 1970.

Tom Hanks, 46, actor (*Big, Sleepless in Seattle*; Oscars for *Philadelphia, Forrest Gump*), born Concord, CA, July 9, 1956.

Donald Rumsfeld, 70, US Secretary of Defense (Ford and George W. Bush administrations), born Evanston, IL, July 9, 1932.

Fred Savage, 26, actor ("The Wonder Years," *The Princess Bride*), born Highland Park, IL, July 9, 1976.

JULY 10 — WEDNESDAY

Day 191 — 174 Remaining

ASHE, ARTHUR: BIRTH ANNIVERSARY. July 10, 1943. Born at Richmond, VA, Arthur Ashe became a legend for his list of firsts as a black tennis player. He was chosen for the US Davis Cup team in 1963 and became captain in 1980. He won the US men's singles championship and US Open in 1968 and in 1975 the men's singles at Wimbledon. Ashe won a total of 33 career titles. In 1985 he was inducted into the International Tennis Hall of Fame. A social activist, Ashe worked to eliminate racism and stereotyping. He helped create inner-city tennis programs for youth and wrote the three-volume *A Hard Road to Glory: A History of the African-American Athlete*. Aware that *USA Today* intended to publish an article revealing that he was infected with the AIDS virus, Ashe announced Apr 8, 1992, that he probably contracted HIV through a transfusion during bypass surgery in 1983. He began a $5 million fund-raising effort on behalf of the Arthur Ashe Foundation for the Defeat of AIDS and during his last year campaigned for public awareness of the AIDS epidemic. He died at New York, NY, Feb 6, 1993.

BAHAMAS: INDEPENDENCE DAY. July 10. Public holiday. At 12:01 AM in 1973, the Bahamas gained their independence after 250 years as a British Crown Colony.

BORIS YELTSIN INAUGURATED AS RUSSIAN PRESIDENT: ANNIVERSARY. July 10, 1991. Boris Yeltsin took the oath of office as the first popularly elected president in Russia's 1,000-year history. He defeated the Communist Party candidate resoundingly, establishing himself as a powerful political counterpoint to Mikhail Gorbachev, the president of the Soviet Union, of which Russia was the largest republic. Yeltsin had been dismissed from the Politburo in 1987 and resigned from the Communist Party in 1989. His popularity forced Gorbachev to make concessions to the republics in the new union treaty forming the Confederation of Independent States. Suffering from poor health, Yeltsin resigned as president at the end of 1999.

CLERIHEW DAY. July 10. A day recognized in remembrance of Edmund Clerihew Bentley, journalist and author of the celebrated detective thriller *Trent's Last Case* (1912), but perhaps best known for his invention of a popular humorous verse form, the clerihew, consisting of two rhymed couplets of unequal length:/Edmund's middle name was Clerihew/A name possessed by very few,/But verses by Mr Bentley/Succeeded eminently./ Bentley was born at London, July 10, 1875, and died there, Mar 30, 1956.

DALLAS, GEORGE MIFFLIN: BIRTH ANNIVERSARY. July 10, 1792. The 11th vice president of the US (1845–49), born at Philadelphia, PA. Died there, Dec 31, 1864.

DON'T STEP ON A BEE DAY. July 10. Eleven-year-old Michael Roy of the Wellness Permission League reminds kids and grownups that now is the time of year when going barefoot can mean getting stung by a bee. If you get stung tell Mom. [© 1999 by WH] For info: Michael Roy, Wellcat Holidays, 2418 Long Ln, Lebanon, PA 17046. Phone: (230) 332-4886. E-mail: wellcat@supernet.com. Web: www.wellcat.com.

MOON PHASE: NEW MOON. July 10. Moon enters New Moon phase at 6:26 AM, EDT.

O'HARA, MARY: BIRTH ANNIVERSARY. July 10, 1885. Born at Cape May, NJ, Mary O'Hara Alsop wrote the children's horse tale *My Friend Flicka*. She died at Chevy Chase, MD, Oct 15, 1980.

SPACE MILESTONE: *TELSTAR* (US): 40th ANNIVERSARY. July 10, 1962. First privately owned satellite (American Telephone and Telegraph Company) and first satellite to relay live TV pictures across the Atlantic was launched.

US LIFTS SANCTIONS AGAINST SOUTH AFRICA: ANNIVERSARY. July 10, 1991. President George Bush lifted US trade and investment sanctions against South Africa. The sanctions had been imposed through the Comprehensive Anti-Apartheid Act of 1986, which Congress had passed to punish South Africa for policies of racial separation.

WYOMING: ADMISSION DAY: ANNIVERSARY. July 10. Became 44th state in 1890.

BIRTHDAYS TODAY

Candice F. Ransom, 50, author (*The Big Green Pocketbook*), born Washington, DC, July 10, 1952.

JULY 11 — THURSDAY

Day 192 — 173 Remaining

ADAMS, JOHN QUINCY: BIRTH ANNIVERSARY. July 11, 1767. Sixth president of the US and the son of the second president, John Quincy Adams was born at Braintree, MA. After his single term as president, he served 17 years as a member of Congress from Plymouth, MA. He died Feb 23, 1848, at the House of Representatives (in the same room in which he had taken the presidential Oath of Office Mar 4, 1825). For info: www.ipl.org/ref/POTUS.

DAY OF THE FIVE BILLION: 15th ANNIVERSARY. July 11, 1987. An eight-pound baby boy, Matej Gaspar, born at 1:35 AM, EST, at Zagreb, Yugoslavia, was proclaimed the five billionth inhabitant of Earth. The United Nations Fund for Population Activities, hoping to draw attention to population growth, proclaimed July 11 as "Day of the Five Billion," noting that 150 babies are born each minute. See also: "Day of the Six Billion: Anniversary" (Oct 12).

MONGOLIA: NAADAM NATIONAL HOLIDAY. July 11. Public holiday. Commemorates overthrow of the feudal monarch in 1921.

SMITH, JAMES: DEATH ANNIVERSARY. July 11, 1806. Signer of the Declaration of Independence, born at Ireland about 1719 (exact date unknown). Died at York, PA.

SPACE MILESTONE: *SKYLAB* (US): FALLS TO EARTH. July 11, 1979. The 82-ton spacecraft launched May 14, 1973, re-entered Earth's atmosphere. Expectation was that 20–25 tons probably would survive to hit Earth, including one piece of about 5,000 pounds. This generated intense international public interest in where it would fall. The chance that some person would be hit by a piece of *Skylab* was calculated at one in 152. Targets were drawn and *Skylab* parties were held but *Skylab* broke up and fell to Earth in a shower of pieces over the Indian Ocean and Australia, with no known casualties.

UNITED NATIONS: WORLD POPULATION DAY. July 11. In June 1989, the Governing Council of the United Nations Development Programme recommended that July 11 be observed by the international community as World Population Day. An outgrowth of the Day of Five Billion (July 11, 1987), the Day seeks to focus public attention on the urgency and importance of population issues, particularly in the context of overall development plans and programs and the need to create solutions to these problems. For info: United Nations, Dept of Public Info, Public Inquiries Unit, RM GA-57, New York, NY 10017. Phone: (212) 963-4475. Fax: (212) 963-0071. E-mail: inquiries@un.org.

WHITE, E.B.: BIRTH ANNIVERSARY. July 11, 1899. Author of books for adults and children (*Charlotte's Web, Trumpet of the Swan, Stuart Little*) and *New Yorker* editor. Born at Mount Vernon, NY, White died at North Brooklyn, ME, Oct 1, 1985.

BIRTHDAYS TODAY

Helen Cresswell, 68, author (*The Night Watchmen*), born Nottinghamshire, England, July 11, 1934.
Mike Foster, 72, Governor of Louisiana (R), born Shreveport, LA, July 11, 1930.
Jane Gardam, 74, author (*A Long Way from Verona*), born Coatham, England, July 11, 1928.
Patricia Polacco, 58, author (*Chicken Sunday, Pink and Say*), born Lansing, MI, July 11, 1944.
James Stevenson, 73, author and illustrator (*I Meant to Tell You*), born New York, NY, July 11, 1929.

JULY 12 — FRIDAY

Day 193 — 172 Remaining

ETCH-A-SKETCH INTRODUCED: ANNIVERSARY. July 12, 1960. In 1958 a French garage mechanic named Arthur Granjean developed a drawing toy he called The Magic Screen. In 1959 he exhibited his toy at a toy fair at Nuremberg, West Germany, where it was seen by a representative of the Ohio Art Company, a toy company at Bryan, OH. The rights were purchased and the product was renamed and released in 1960. More than 100 million have been sold.

KIRIBATI: INDEPENDENCE DAY. July 12. Republic of Kiribati attained independence from Britain in 1979. Formerly known as the Gilbert Islands.

NORTHERN IRELAND: ORANGEMEN'S DAY. July 12. National holiday commemorates Battle of Boyne, July 1 (Old Style), 1690, in which the forces of King William III of England, Prince of Orange, defeated those of James II, at Boyne River in Ireland. Ordinarily observed July 12. If July 12 is a Saturday or a Sunday the holiday observance is on the following Monday.

SAO TOME AND PRINCIPE: NATIONAL DAY. July 12. National holiday observed. Commemorates independence from Portugal in 1975.

SPYRI, JOHANNA: BIRTH ANNIVERSARY. July 12, 1827. Children's author, born at Hirzel, Switzerland. Her book *Heidi* is the story of an orphan girl who goes to live with her grandfather in the mountains. *Heidi* was made into a movie in 1920. Spyri wrote several other books, including *Heidi Grows Up* and *Heidi's Children*. She died at Zurich, Switzerland, July 7, 1901.

THOREAU, HENRY DAVID: BIRTH ANNIVERSARY. July 12, 1817. American author and philosopher, born at Concord, MA. Died there May 6, 1862. In *Walden* he wrote, "I frequently tramped eight or ten miles through the deepest snow to keep an appointment with a beechtree, or a yellow birch, or an old acquaintance among the pines." For more info: *Into the Deep Forest with Henry David Thoreau*, by Jim Murphy (Clarion, 0-395-60522-9, $14.95 Gr. 5–8).

BIRTHDAYS TODAY

Bill Cosby, 64, comedian, actor (Emmys for "I Spy," "The Cosby Show"), born Philadelphia, PA, July 12, 1938.

July 2002

S	M	T	W	T	F	S
	1	2	3	4	5	6
7	8	9	10	11	12	13
14	15	16	17	18	19	20
21	22	23	24	25	26	27
28	29	30	31			

Kristi Yamaguchi, 31, Olympic gold medal figure skater, born Hayward, CA, July 12, 1971.

JULY 13 — SATURDAY

Day 194 — 171 Remaining

JAPAN: BON FESTIVAL (FEAST OF LANTERNS). July 13–15. Religious rites throughout Japan in memory of the dead, who, according to Buddhist belief, revisit Earth during this period. Lanterns are lighted for the souls. Spectacular bonfires in the shape of the character *dai* are burned on hillsides on the last day of the Bon or O-Bon Festival, bidding farewell to the spirits of the dead.

JULY 13
WORLD CUP SOCCER

World Cup soccer was first inaugurated on July 13, 1930, with 14 nations participating. This year's finalists completed a grueling year-long series of games to win their places in the final games in June. The closing match has been played (Japan and Korea hosted the World Cup), the new world champion enthroned, and those who don't understand soccer have been, well, left out.

Soccer is the most popular sport in the world and, at last, the United States is catching on. More and more children are participating in American Youth Soccer Organizations and club soccer teams are popping up everywhere. Lighten up summer school days by giving soccer a chance.

In many countries, soccer is called football. One of the ways you and your students might find soccer interesting is by comparing it to American football. Fans of both sports should be able to give the basic information about roster size and position. Specifics such as field size, ball size and particular equipment needs will require short research exercises, which are good opportunities to stretch catalog and Internet searching skills. Don't forget to compare length of games and time periods. Enterprising students might want to make some Venn diagrams to illustrate similarities and differences.

Graph information on the number of countries that have professional soccer teams versus those who have teams that play American-style football.

In gym, set up a line of traffic cones for dribbling a soccer ball. Give each child two or three timed runs. Encourage them to better their own times rather than beat someone else. If you can get two hula hoops, or similarly sized open circles, experiment with accuracy. Hang them so that they are about the height of a student's head above the ground. Is it easier to throw a football through the hoop or kick a soccer ball through it?

If you feel like rabble-rousing (stress it's all in fun), suggest high school students survey, measure, and compare the amount of running done by a soccer player with that of a football player. Both sports require intense conditioning but in different areas.

Matt Christopher, a popular author of children's novels that feature sports, has written several books that center around soccer. High school students will enjoy *Go for the Goal*, by soccer star Mia Hamm (HarperCollins, 0-06-093159-0, $12) and Joe McGinniss's *Miracle of Castel di Sangro* (Broadway Books, 0-7679-0599-7, $14.95). McGinniss's book is about a hard-luck Italian soccer team that makes it into premier league. It's enormously popular with high school boys who wouldn't normally be caught dead reading.

NORTHWEST ORDINANCE: ANNIVERSARY. July 13, 1787. The Northwest Ordinance, providing for government of the territory north of the Ohio River, became law. The ordinance guaranteed freedom of worship and the right to trial by jury, and it prohibited slavery.

WORLD CUP INAUGURATED: ANNIVERSARY. July 13, 1930. The first World Cup soccer competition was held at Montevideo, Uruguay, with 14 countries participating. The host country had the winning team. *See* Curriculum Connection.

BIRTHDAYS TODAY

Marcia Brown, 84, illustrator and author (Caldecott Awards for *Shadow, Once a Mouse, Cinderella*), born Rochester, NY, July 13, 1918.

Ashley Bryan, 79, author and illustrator (*Lion and the Ostrich: And Other African Folk Tales*), born The Bronx, NY, July 13, 1923.

Harrison Ford, 60, actor (*The Fugitive*; the *Star Wars* and *Indiana Jones* films), born Chicago, IL, July 13, 1942.

Patrick Stewart, 62, actor ("Star Trek: The Next Generation," *Excalibur, LA Story*), born Mirfield, England, July 13, 1940.

JULY 14 — SUNDAY

Day 195 — 170 Remaining

AMERICAN FEDERATION OF TEACHERS CONVENTION. July 14–19. Hilton Hotel, Las Vegas, NV. For info: American Federation of Teachers, 555 New Jersey Ave NW, Washington, DC 20001. Phone: (202) 879-4587. Web: www.aft.org.

★ **CAPTIVE NATIONS WEEK.** July 14–20. Presidential proclamation issued each year since 1959 for the third week of July. (PL86–90 of July 17, 1959.)

CHILDREN'S PARTY AT GREEN ANIMALS. July 14. Green Animals Topiary Garden, Portsmouth, RI. Annual party for children and adults at Green Animals, a delightful topiary garden and children's toy museum. Party includes pony rides, merry-go-round, games, clowns, refreshments, hot dogs, hamburgers and more. Annually, July 14. Est attendance: 800. For info: The Preservation Soc of Newport County, 424 Bellevue Ave, Newport, RI 02840. Phone: (401) 847-1000. Fax: (401) 847-1361. Web: www.NewportMansions.org.

FORD, GERALD R.: BIRTHDAY. July 14, 1913. The 38th president (1974–77) of the US. He was born Leslie King at Omaha, NE. He was named the 41st vice president in 1973 on the resignation of Spiro Agnew and became president on Aug 9, 1974, after the resignation of Richard M. Nixon. He was the only nonelected vice president and president of the US. For info: www.ipl.org/ref/POTUS.

FRANCE: BASTILLE DAY OR FÊTE NATIONAL. July 14. Public holiday commemorating the fall of the Bastille at the beginning of the French Revolution in 1789. Also celebrated or observed in many other countries. For more info: www.premier-ministre.gouv.fr/GB/HIST/FETNAT.HTM.

GARFIELD, LEON: BIRTH ANNIVERSARY. July 14, 1921. Author of children's books (*Smith*), born at Brighton, England. Died at London, England, June 2, 1996.

GUTHRIE, WOODY: 90th BIRTH ANNIVERSARY. July 14, 1912. Singer famous for the song "This Land Is Your Land." Guthrie wrote more than 1,000 folk songs, ballads and children's songs. Born at Okemah, OK, Guthrie died at New York, NY, Oct 3, 1967. For more info: *This Land Is Your Land*, by Woody Guthrie (Little, Brown, 0-31-639215-4, $15.95 Gr. K–3).

PARISH, PEGGY: BIRTH ANNIVERSARY. July 14, 1927. Author of the Amelia Bedelia series about the maid who takes things too literally. Titles include *Amelia Bedelia and the Surprise Shower, Thank You Amelia Bedelia,* and *Play Ball, Amelia Bedelia!* Parish was born at Manning, SC, and died there on Nov 19, 1988.

SCHWAN'S USA CUP. July 14–20 (tentative). Blaine, MN. The 18th annual youth soccer tournament for boys and girls will include teams from 25 countries. For info: Schwan's USA Cup, Natl Sports Center, 1700 105th Ave NE, Blaine, MN 55449-4500. Phone: (612) 785-5656. E-mail: registrar@usacup.com. Web: www.usacup.com.

SINGER, ISAAC BASHEVIS: BIRTH ANNIVERSARY. July 14, 1904. Author who wrote in Yiddish and won the Nobel Prize for literature in 1978. His books for children include *The Fearsome Inn, When Shlemiel Went to Warsaw and Other Stories* and *Zlateh the Goat and Other Stories.* Born at Radzymin, Poland, I.B. Singer died at Surfside, FL, July 24, 1991.

BIRTHDAYS TODAY

Gerald Rudolph Ford, 89, 38th president of the US, born Leslie King, Omaha, NE, July 14, 1913.

Matthew Fox, 36, actor ("Party of Five"), born Crowheart, WY, July 14, 1966.

Laura Joffe Numeroff, 49, author (*If You Give a Mouse a Cookie*), born Brooklyn, NY, July 14, 1953.

Harriette Gillem Robinet, 71, author (*Forty Acres and Maybe a Mule*), born Washington, DC, July 14, 1931.

JULY 15 — MONDAY

Day 196 — 169 Remaining

BATTLE OF THE MARNE: ANNIVERSARY. July 15, 1918. General Erich Ludendorff launched Germany's fifth, and last, offensive to break through the Château-Thierry salient during WWI. This all-out effort involved three armies branching out from Rheims to cross the Marne River. The Germans were successful in crossing the Marne near Chateau-Thierry before American, British and Italian divisions stopped their progress. On July 18 General Foch, Commander-in-Chief of the Allied troops, launched a massive counteroffensive that resulted in a German retreat that continued for four months until they sued for peace in November.

MAXWELL, GAVIN: BIRTH ANNIVERSARY. July 15, 1914. Born at Elrig, Scotland. Children's author and illustrator, known for *Ring of Bright Water* and *The Rocks Remain.* Maxwell died at Inverness, Scotland, Sept 6, 1969.

MOORE, CLEMENT CLARKE: BIRTH ANNIVERSARY. July 15, 1779. American author and teacher, best remembered for his popular verse, "A Visit from Saint Nicholas" ("'Twas the Night Before Christmas"), which was first published anonymously and without Moore's knowledge in a newspaper, Dec 23, 1823. Moore was born at New York, NY, and died at Newport, RI, July 10, 1863.

REMBRANDT: BIRTH ANNIVERSARY. July 15, 1606. Dutch painter and etcher, born at Leiden, Holland. Known for *The Night Watch* and many portraits and self-portraits, he died at Amsterdam, Holland, Oct 4, 1669. For more info: *Rembrandt and 17th Century Holland,* by Claudio Pescio (Peter Bedrick, 0-87226-317-7, $22.50 Gr. 4–7).

SAINT FRANCES XAVIER CABRINI: BIRTH ANNIVERSARY. July 15, 1850. First American saint, founder of schools, orphanages, convents and hospitals, born at Lombardy, Italy. Died of malaria at Chicago, IL, Dec 22, 1917. Canonized July 7, 1946.

SAINT SWITHIN'S DAY. July 15. Swithun (Swithin), Bishop of Winchester (AD 852–862), died July 2, 862. Little is known of his life, but his relics were transferred into Winchester Cathedral July 15, 971, a day on which there was a heavy rainfall. According to old English belief, it will rain for 40 days thereafter when it rains on this day. "St. Swithin's Day, if thou dost rain, for 40 days it will remain; St. Swithin's Day, if thou be fair, for 40 days, –will rain nea mair."

BIRTHDAYS TODAY

Marcia Thornton Jones, 44, author, with Debbie Dadey (the Bailey School Kids series), born Joliet, IL, July 15, 1958.

Jesse Ventura, 51, Governor of Minnesota (I), born Minneapolis, MN, July 15, 1951.

George V. Voinovich, 66, US Senator (R, Ohio), born Cleveland, OH, July 15, 1936.

JULY 16 — TUESDAY

Day 197 — 168 Remaining

AMUNDSEN, ROALD: BIRTH ANNIVERSARY. July 16, 1872. Norwegian explorer, born near Oslo, Roald Amundsen was the first man to sail from the Atlantic to the Pacific Ocean via the Northwest Passage (1903–05). He discovered the South Pole (Dec 14, 1911) and flew over the North Pole in a dirigible in 1926. He flew, with five companions, from Norway, June 18, 1928, in a daring effort to rescue survivors of an Italian Arctic expedition. No trace of the rescue party or the airplane was ever located. See also: "South Pole Discovery: Anniversary" (Dec 14).

ATOMIC BOMB TESTED: ANNIVERSARY. July 16, 1945. In the New Mexican desert at Alamogordo Air Base, 125 miles southeast of Albuquerque, the experimental atomic bomb was set off at 5:30 AM. Dubbed "Fat Boy" by its creator, the plutonium bomb vaporized the steel scaffolding holding it as the immense fireball rose 8,000 feet in a fraction of a second—ultimately creating a mushroom cloud to a height of 41,000 feet. At ground zero the bomb emitted heat three times the temperature of the interior of the sun. All plant and animal life for a mile around ceased to exist. When informed by President Truman at Potsdam of the successful experiment, Winston Churchill responded, "It's the Second Coming in wrath!"

July 2002

S	M	T	W	T	F	S
	1	2	3	4	5	6
7	8	9	10	11	12	13
14	15	16	17	18	19	20
21	22	23	24	25	26	27
28	29	30	31			

COMET CRASHES INTO JUPITER: ANNIVERSARY. July 16, 1994. The first fragment of the comet Shoemaker-Levy crashed into the planet Jupiter, beginning a series of spectacular collisions, each unleashing more energy than the combined effect of an explosion of all our world's nuclear arsenal. Video imagery from earthbound telescopes as well as the Hubble telescope provided vivid records of the explosions and their aftereffects. In 1993 the comet had shattered into a series of about a dozen large chunks that resembled "pearls on a string" after its orbit brought it within the gravitational effects of our solar system's largest planet. For more info: *Discovering Jupiter: The Amazing Collision in Space*, by Melvin Berger (Scholastic, 0-5904-8824-4, $4.95 Gr. K–3).

DISTRICT OF COLUMBIA: ESTABLISHING LEGISLATION ANNIVERSARY. July 16, 1790. George Washington signed legislation that selected the District of Columbia as the permanent capital of the US. Boundaries of the district were established in 1792. Plans called for the government to remain housed at Philadelphia, PA, until 1800, when the new national capital would be ready for occupancy.

SPACE MILESTONE: *APOLLO 11* (US): MAN SENT TO THE MOON. July 16, 1969. This launch resulted in man's first moon landing, the first landing on any extraterrestrial body. See also: "Space Milestone: Moon Day" (July 20).

WELLS, IDA B.: BIRTH ANNIVERSARY. July 16, 1862. African American journalist and anti-lynching crusader Ida B. Wells was born the daughter of slaves at Holly Springs, MS, and grew up as Jim Crow and lynching were becoming prevalent. Wells argued that lynchings occurred not to defend white women but because of whites' fear of economic competition from blacks. She traveled extensively, founding anti-lynching societies and black women's clubs. Wells's *Red Record* (1895) was one of the first accounts of lynchings in the South. She died Mar 25, 1931, at Chicago, IL. For more info: *Ida B. Wells: Mother of the Civil Rights Movement*, by Dennis Brindell Fradin and Judith Bloom Fradin (Clarion, 0-395-89898-6, $18 Gr. 5 & up) or *Ida B. Wells-Barnett: A Voice Against Violence*, by Patricia and Fredrick McKissack (Enslow, 0-8949-0301-2, $14.95 Gr. K–3).

BIRTHDAYS TODAY

Arnold Adoff, 67, poet (*Black Is Brown Is Tan*), born The Bronx, NY, July 16, 1935.

Richard Egielski, 50, author (*The Gingerbread Boy*), born New York, NY, July 16, 1952.

Alexis Herman, 55, former Secretary of Labor (Clinton administration), born Mobile, AL, July 16, 1947.

Barry Sanders, 34, former football player, born Wichita, KS, July 16, 1968.

Eve Titus, 80, author (Basil of Baker Street, the Anatole series), born New York, NY, July 16, 1922.

JULY 17 — WEDNESDAY

Day 198 — 167 Remaining

DISNEYLAND OPENED: ANNIVERSARY. July 17, 1955. Disneyland, America's first theme park, opened at Anaheim, CA.

GERRY, ELBRIDGE: BIRTH ANNIVERSARY. July 17, 1744. Fifth vice president of the US (1813–14), born at Marblehead, MA. Died at Washington, DC, Nov 23, 1814. His name became part of the language (gerrymander) after he signed a redistricting bill while governor of Massachusetts in 1812.

IRAQ: NATIONAL DAY. July 17. National holiday commemorating the 1968 revolution.

KOREA: CONSTITUTION DAY. July 17. Legal national holiday. Commemorates the proclamation of the constitution of the republic of Korea in 1948. Ceremonies at Seoul's capitol plaza and all major cities.

MOON PHASE: FIRST QUARTER. July 17. Moon enters First Quarter phase at 12:47 AM, EDT.

PUERTO RICO: MUÑOZ-RIVERA DAY. July 17. Public holiday on the anniversary of the birth of Luis Muñoz-Rivera. The Puerto Rican patriot, poet and journalist was born at Barranquitas, Puerto Rico, in 1859. He died at Santurce, a suburb of San Juan, Puerto Rico, Nov 15, 1916.

SPACE MILESTONE: *APOLLO-SOYUZ* LINKUP (US, USSR). July 17, 1975. After three years of planning, negotiation and preparation, the first US–USSR joint space project reached fruition with the linkup in space of *Apollo 18* (crew: T. Stafford, V. Brand, D. Slayton; landed in Pacific Ocean July 24, during 136th orbit) and *Soyuz 19* (crew: A.A. Leonov, V.N. Kubasov; landed July 21, after 96 orbits). *Apollo 18* and *Soyuz 19* were linked for 47 hours (July 17–19) while joint experiments and transfer of personnel and materials back and forth between craft took place. Launch date was July 15, 1975.

SPACE MILESTONE: *SOYUZ T-12* (USSR). July 17, 1984. Cosmonaut Svetlana Savitskaya became the first woman to walk in space (July 25) and the first woman to make more than one space voyage. With cosmonauts V. Dzhanibekov and I. Volk. Docked at *Salyut 7* July 18 and returned to Earth July 29.

BIRTHDAYS TODAY

Chris Crutcher, 56, author (*Staying Fat for Sarah Byrnes, Athletic Shorts*), born Cascade, ID, July 17, 1946.

Karla Kuskin, 70, author and illustrator (*The Philharmonic Gets Dressed, City Dog*), born New York, NY, July 17, 1932.

JULY 18 — THURSDAY

Day 199 — 166 Remaining

DELAWARE STATE FAIR. July 18–27. Harrington, DE. Fireworks, country, gospel and pop talent, rodeos, demolition derby, amusement rides and harness racing. Plenty of food and entertainment. Est attendance: 216,000. For info: Delaware State Fair, PO Box 28, Harrington, DE 19952. Phone: (302) 398-3269. Fax: (302) 398-5030. Web: www.delawarestatefair.com.

PRESIDENTIAL SUCCESSION ACT: 55th ANNIVERSARY. July 18, 1947. President Harry S Truman signed an Executive Order determining the line of succession should the president be temporarily incapacitated or die in office. The speaker of the house and president pro tem of the senate are next in succession after the vice president. This line of succession became the 25th Amendment to the Constitution, which was ratified Feb 10, 1967.

RUTLEDGE, JOHN: DEATH ANNIVERSARY. July 18, 1800. American statesman, associate justice on the Supreme Court, born at Charleston, SC, in September 1739. Nominated second Chief Justice of the Supreme Court to succeed John Jay and served as Acting Chief Justice until his confirmation was denied because of his opposition to the Jay Treaty. He died at Charleston, SC.

URUGUAY: CONSTITUTION DAY. July 18. National holiday. Commemorates the country's first constitution, adopted on this day in 1830.

BIRTHDAYS TODAY

Felicia Bond, 48, illustrator (*If You Give a Mouse a Cookie, Tumble Bumble*), born Yokohama, Japan, July 18, 1954.

John Glenn, 81, astronaut, first American to orbit Earth, former US Senator (D, Ohio), born Cambridge, OH, July 18, 1921.

Anfernee (Penny) Hardaway, 30, basketball player, born Memphis, TN, July 18, 1972.

Nelson Mandela, 84, former president of South Africa, born Transkei, South Africa, July 18, 1918.

Jerry Stanley, 61, author (*Hurry Freedom!; Children of the Dust Bowl*), born Highland Park, MI, July 18, 1941.

JULY 19 — FRIDAY

Day 200 — 165 Remaining

DEGAS, EDGAR: BIRTH ANNIVERSARY. July 19, 1834. French Impressionist painter, especially noted for his paintings of ballet dancers and horse races, was born at Paris, France. He died at Paris, Sept 26, 1917. For more info: *Edgar Degas*, by Mike Venezia (Children's Press, 0-516-21593-0 Gr. 2–4).

MERRIAM, EVE: BIRTH ANNIVERSARY. July 19, 1916. Poet, known for her children's books *You Be Good and I'll Be Night* and *A Gaggle of Geese*. Born at Philadelphia, PA, Merriam died Apr 11, 1992.

July 2002

S	M	T	W	T	F	S
	1	2	3	4	5	6
7	8	9	10	11	12	13
14	15	16	17	18	19	20
21	22	23	24	25	26	27
28	29	30	31			

NEWBERY, JOHN: BIRTH ANNIVERSARY. July 19, 1713. The first bookseller and publisher to make a specialty of children's books. Born at Waltham St. Lawrence, England, he died Dec 22, 1767, at London, England. The American Library Association awards the Newbery Medal annually for the most distinguished contribution to American literature for children.

NICARAGUA: NATIONAL LIBERATION DAY. July 19. Following the National Day of Joy (July 17—anniversary of date in 1979 when dictator Anastasio Somoza Debayle fled Nicaragua) is annual July 19 observance of National Liberation Day, anniversary of day the National Liberation Army claimed victory over the Somoza dictatorship.

NORTH DAKOTA STATE FAIR. July 19–27. Minot, ND. For nine days the State Fair features the best in big-name entertainment, farm and home exhibits, displays, the Midway and NPRA rodeo. Est attendance: 250,000. For info: North Dakota State Fair, Box 1796, Minot, ND 58702. Phone: (701) 857-7620. Fax: (701) 857-7622. E-mail: ndsf@minot.com.

WOMEN'S RIGHTS CONVENTION AT SENECA FALLS: ANNIVERSARY. July 19, 1848. A convention concerning the rights of women, called by Lucretia Mott and Elizabeth Cady Stanton, was held at Seneca Falls, NY, July 19–20, 1848. The issues discussed included voting, property rights and divorce. The convention drafted a "Declaration of Sentiments" that paraphrased the Declaration of Independence, addressing man instead of King George, and called for women's "immediate admission to all the rights and privileges which belong to them as citizens of the United States." This convention was the beginning of an organized women's rights movement in the US. The most controversial issue was Stanton's demand for women's right to vote.

BIRTHDAYS TODAY

Teresa Edwards, 38, basketball player, born Cairo, GA, July 19, 1964.

Chris Kratt, 33, biologist, cohost with his brother Martin ("Kratts' Creatures"), born Summit, NJ, July 19, 1969.

JULY 20 — SATURDAY

Day 201 — 164 Remaining

COLOMBIA: INDEPENDENCE DAY. July 20. National holiday. Commemorates the beginning of the independence movement with an uprising against Spanish officials in 1810 at Bogota. Colombia gained independence from Spain in 1819 when Simon Bolivar decisively defeated the Spanish.

FIRST SPECIAL OLYMPICS: ANNIVERSARY. July 20, 1968. One thousand mentally retarded athletes from the US and Canada competed in the first Special Olympics at Soldier Field, Chicago, IL. Today more than one million athletes from 146 countries compete in local, national and international games.

JAPAN: MARINE DAY. July 20. National holiday.

PROVENSEN, MARTIN: BIRTH ANNIVERSARY. July 20, 1916. Author and illustrator, with his wife Alice (Caldecott for *The Glorious Flight: Across the Channel with Louis Bleriot*), born at Chicago, IL. Died Mar 27, 1987, at New York, NY.

SPACE MILESTONE: MOON DAY. July 20, 1969. Anniversary of man's first landing on moon. Two US astronauts (Neil Alden Armstrong and Edwin Eugene Aldrin, Jr) landed lunar module *Eagle* at 4:17 PM, EDT, and remained on lunar surface 21 hours, 36 minutes and 16 seconds. The landing was made from the *Apollo XI*'s orbiting command and service module, code named *Columbia*, whose pilot, Michael Collins, remained aboard. Armstrong was first to set foot on the moon. Armstrong and Aldrin were outside the spacecraft, walking on the moon's surface, approximately

2¼ hours. The astronauts returned to Earth July 24, bringing photograph and rock samples. For more info: *One Giant Leap: The Story of Neil Armstrong*, by Don Brown (Houghton, 0-395-88401-2, $16 Gr. 2–4).

BIRTHDAYS TODAY

Mark Buehner, 43, illustrator (*Harvey Potter's Balloon Farm, The Adventures of Taxi Dog, The Escape of Marvin the Ape*), born Salt Lake City, UT, July 20, 1959.

Larry E. Craig, 57, US Senator (R, Idaho), born Council, ID, July 20, 1945.

John Daley, 17, actor ("Freaks and Geeks"), born Wheeling, IL, July 20, 1985.

Peter Forsberg, 29, hockey player, born Ornskoldvik, Sweden, July 20, 1973.

Charles Johnson, Jr, 31, baseball player, born Ft Pierce, FL, July 20, 1971.

Barbara Ann Mikulski, 66, US Senator (D, Maryland), born Baltimore, MD, July 20, 1936.

JULY 21 — SUNDAY

Day 202 — 163 Remaining

BELGIUM: NATIONAL HOLIDAY. July 21. Marks accession of first Belgian king, Leopold I, in 1831 after independence from the Netherlands.

CLEVELAND, FRANCES FOLSOM: BIRTH ANNIVERSARY. July 21, 1864. Wife of Grover Cleveland, 22nd and 24th president of the US, born at Buffalo, NY. She was the youngest First Lady at age 22, and the first to marry a president in the White House. Died at Princeton, NJ, Oct 29, 1947.

GUAM: LIBERATION DAY. July 21. US forces returned to Guam in 1944.

NATIONAL ICE CREAM DAY. July 21. To promote America's favorite dessert, ice cream, on "Sundae Sunday." Annually, the third Sunday in July.

BIRTHDAYS TODAY

Brandi Chastain, 34, soccer player (US Soccer Team), born San Jose, CA, July 21, 1968.

Hatty Jones, 14, actress (*Madeline*), born London, England, July 21, 1988.

Janet Reno, 64, former US Attorney General (Clinton administration), born Miami, FL, July 21, 1938.

Paul D. Wellstone, 58, US Senator (D, Minnesota), born Washington, DC, July 21, 1944.

Robin Williams, 50, actor (*Patch Adams, Hook, Mrs Doubtfire*), born Chicago, IL, July 21, 1952.

JULY 22 — MONDAY

Day 203 — 162 Remaining

BIANCO, MARGERY WILLIAMS: BIRTH ANNIVERSARY. July 22, 1881. Author of children's books (*The Velveteen Rabbit*, written under the name Margery Williams). Born at London, England, she died at New York, NY, Sept 4, 1944.

PIED PIPER OF HAMELIN: ANNIVERSARY—MAYBE. July 22, 1376. According to legend, the German town of Hamelin, plagued with rats, bargained with a piper who promised to, and did, pipe the rats out of town and into the Weser River. Refused payment for his work, the piper then piped the children out of town and into a hole in a hill, never to be seen again. More recent historians suggest that the event occurred in 1284 when young men of Hamelin left the city on colonizing adventures. *See* Curriculum Connection.

SPOONER'S DAY *(WILLIAM SPOONER BIRTH ANNIVERSARY).* July 22. A day named for the Reverend William Archibald Spooner (born at London, England, July 22, 1844), whose frequent slips of the tongue led to coinage of the term *spoonerism* to describe them. A day to remember the scholarly man whose accidental transpositions gave us blushing crow (for crushing blow),

JULY 22
PIED PIPER OF HAMELIN: MYTH OR REALITY?

The Pied Piper legend of Hamelin, Germany, became widely known after Robert Browning wrote a poem recounting the story of the strange man whose music spirited away the town's children.

As legend has it, the town of Hamelin was infested by rats. Desperate to rid themselves of the rats, the mayor agreed to pay a wandering piper a certain sum of money if he got rid of them. After the piper's music lured the rats away to a watery death in the Weser River, the mayor reneged on the deal. In response, the piper played another tune which lured the town's children into following him out of town. They followed him into a cave inside Koppen Hill and were never seen again.

It appears that the story's roots may lie partially in truth. In the 1280s, the Bishop of Olmütz sent an agent to Hamelin to recruit the youth to settle the area of Moravia. A second explanation suggests the children may have been taken as part of the Children's Crusades. A third possibility, although rather far-fetched, reports that the children were kidnapped by robbers. Whether the story is fact or fiction is irrelevant. It's a great tale with a grim moral about what happens to people who make promises and don't keep them.

Older children will enjoy reading Browning's poem. Younger children will enjoy picture-book versions of the poem/story. Two out-of-print versions to look for in your library include one illustrated by Donna Diamond and a retelling by Barbara Bartos-Hoppner. Kate Greenaway's illustrated version (Dover, 0-486-29619-9, $7.95 All ages) is available in stores as is a retelling by Robert Holden (Houghton Mifflin, 0-395-89918-4, $15 All ages). The illustrations in Holden's book are by Drahos Zak. These odd, quirky drawings will appeal to kids with an offbeat sense of humor and older students as well. It would be fun to compare several versions and let the children decide how different illustrations set the story's tone.

A fun writing exercise would be to do your own version of the Pied Piper of ______ and fill in your town's name. Create your own problem and select a piece of music that the students think would entice them to follow it.

tons of soil (for sons of toil), queer old dean (for dear old queen), swell foop (for fell swoop) and half-warmed fish (for half-formed wish). Warden of New College, Oxford, 1903–24, Spooner died at Oxford, England, Aug 29, 1930.

US GIRLS' JUNIOR (GOLF) CHAMPIONSHIP. July 22–27. Echo Lake Country Club, Westfield, NJ. For info: US Golf Assn, Golf House, Championship Dept, Far Hills, NJ 07931. Phone: (908) 234-2300. Fax: (908) 234-9687. E-mail: usga@ix.netcom .com. Web: www.usga.org.

VIRGIN ISLANDS: HURRICANE SUPPLICATION DAY. July 22. Legal holiday. Population attends churches to pray for protection from hurricanes. Annually, the fourth Monday in July.

BIRTHDAYS TODAY

Tim Brown, 36, football player, born Dallas, TX, July 22, 1966.

Kay Bailey Hutchison, 59, US Senator (R, Texas), born Galveston, TX, July 22, 1943.

JULY 23 — TUESDAY

Day 204 — 161 Remaining

ALL-AMERICAN SOAP BOX DERBY. July 23–28. Akron, OH. Boys and girls, ages 9–16, build their own cars and race them down Derby Downs. This is the 65th annual race. Est attendance: 20,000. For info: Intl Soap Box Derby, PO Box 7225, Derby Downs, Akron, OH 44306. Phone: (330) 733-9723. E-mail: 2077607@mci mail.com. Web: aasbd.org.

EGYPT, ARAB REPUBLIC OF: 50th ANNIVERSARY NATIONAL DAY. July 23, 1952. Anniversary of the Revolution in 1952, which was launched by army officers and changed Egypt from a monarchy to a republic.

FIRST US SWIMMING SCHOOL: 175th OPENING ANNIVERSARY. July 23, 1827. The first swimming school in the US opened at Boston, MA. Its pupils included John Quincy Adams and James Audubon.

LEO, THE LION. July 23–Aug 22. In the astronomical/astrological zodiac, which divides the sun's apparent orbit into 12 segments, the period July 23–Aug 22 is identified, traditionally, as the sun sign of Leo, the Lion. The ruling planet is the sun.

SPACE MILESTONE: *COLUMBIA*: FIRST FEMALE COMMANDER. July 23, 1999. Colonel Eileen Collins led a shuttle mission to deploy a $1.5 billion X-ray telescope, the Chandra Observatory, into space. It is a sister satellite to the Hubble Space Telescope. It is named after Nobel Prize winner Subrahmanyar Chandrasekhar.

SPACE MILESTONE: *SOYUZ 37* (USSR). July 23, 1980. Cosmonauts Viktor Gorbatko and, the first non-Caucasian in space, Lieutenant Colonel Pham Tuan (Vietnam), docked at *Salyut 6* July 24. Returned to Earth July 31.

July 2002

S	M	T	W	T	F	S
	1	2	3	4	5	6
7	8	9	10	11	12	13
14	15	16	17	18	19	20
21	22	23	24	25	26	27
28	29	30	31			

BIRTHDAYS TODAY

Anthony M. Kennedy, 66, Supreme Court Justice, born Sacramento, CA, July 23, 1936.

Gary Payton, 34, basketball player, born Oakland, CA, July 23, 1968.

Robert Quackenbush, 73, author (the Miss Mallard series), born Hollywood, CA, July 23, 1929.

JULY 24 — WEDNESDAY

Day 205 — 160 Remaining

BOLIVAR, SIMON: BIRTH ANNIVERSARY. July 24, 1783. "The Liberator," born at Caracas, Venezuela. Commemorated in Venezuela and other Latin American countries. Died Dec 17, 1830, at Santa Marta, Colombia. Bolivia is named after him.

EARHART, AMELIA: BIRTH ANNIVERSARY. July 24, 1897. Aviator born at Atchison, KS. First woman to cross the Atlantic solo and fly solo across the Pacific from Hawaii to California. Lost in the Pacific Ocean on flight from New Guinea to Howland Island, July 2, 1937.

MOON PHASE: FULL MOON. July 24. Moon enters Full Moon phase at 5:07 AM, EDT.

PIONEER DAY: ANNIVERSARY. July 24. Utah. Commemorates the first settlement in the Salt Lake Valley in 1847 by Brigham Young.

WHOLE LANGUAGE UMBRELLA CONFERENCE. July 24–27 (tentative). This conference presents children's authors speaking about their books. For info: Natl Council of Teachers of English, 1111 W Kenyon Rd, Urbana, IL 61801-1096. Phone: (800) 369-6283 or (217) 328-3870. Web: www.ncte.org/wlu.

BIRTHDAYS TODAY

Barry Bonds, 38, baseball player, born Riverside, CA, July 24, 1964.

Karl Malone, 39, basketball player, born Summerfield, LA, July 24, 1963.

Albert Marrin, 66, author of military history (*Commander in Chief Abraham Lincoln and the Civil War*), born New York, NY, July 24, 1936.

Anna Paquin, 20, actress (*Fly Away Home*), born Wellington, New Zealand, July 24, 1982.

Mara Wilson, 15, actress (*Mrs Doubtfire, Matilda*), born Burbank, CA, July 24, 1987.

JULY 25 — THURSDAY

Day 206 — 159 Remaining

COSTA RICA: GUANACASTE DAY. July 25. National holiday. Commemorates the transfer of the region of Guanacaste from Nicaragua to Costa Rica which was confirmed by a referendum on this day in 1825.

HARRISON, ANNA SYMMES: BIRTH ANNIVERSARY. July 25, 1775. Wife of William Henry Harrison, ninth president of the US, born at Morristown, NJ. Died at North Bend, IN, Feb 25, 1864.

PUERTO RICO: CONSTITUTION DAY: 50th ANNIVERSARY. July 25. Also called Commonwealth Day or Occupation Day. Commemorates proclamation of constitution in 1952.

TEST-TUBE BABY: BIRTHDAY. July 25, 1978. Anniversary of the birth of Louise Brown at Oldham, England. First documented birth of a baby conceived outside the body of a woman. Parents: Gilbert John and Lesley Brown, of Bristol, England. Physicians: Patrick Christopher Steptoe and Robert Geoffrey Edwards.

TUNISIA: REPUBLIC DAY: 45th ANNIVERSARY. July 25. National holiday. Commemorates the proclamation of the republic in 1957.

BIRTHDAYS TODAY

Ron Barrett, 65, illustrator (*Cloudy with a Chance of Meatballs*), born The Bronx, NY, July 25, 1937.

Clyde Watson, 55, author (*Applebet: An ABC*), born New York, NY, July 25, 1947.

JULY 26 — FRIDAY

Day 207 — 158 Remaining

AMERICANS WITH DISABILITIES ACT SIGNED: ANNIVERSARY. July 26, 1990. President Bush signed the Americans with Disabilities Act, which went into effect two years later. It required that public facilities be made accessible to the disabled.

CATLIN, GEORGE: BIRTH ANNIVERSARY. July 26, 1796. American artist known for his paintings of Native American life, born at Wilkes-Barre, PA. He toured the West, painting more than 500 portraits. He died Dec 23, 1872, at Jersey City, NJ.

CLINTON, GEORGE: BIRTH ANNIVERSARY. July 26, 1739. Fourth vice president of the US (1805–12), born at Little Britain, NY. Died at Washington, DC, Apr 20, 1812.

CUBA: NATIONAL HOLIDAY: ANNIVERSARY OF REVOLUTION. July 26. Anniversary of 1953 beginning of Fidel Castro's revolutionary "26th of July Movement."

CURAÇAO: CURAÇAO DAY. July 26. "Although not officially recognized by the government as a holiday, various social entities commemorate the fact that on this day Alonso de Ojeda, a companion of Christopher Columbus, discovered the Island of Curaçao in 1499, sailing into Santa Ana Bay, the entrance of the harbor of Willemstad."

IOWA STORYTELLING FESTIVAL. July 26–27. City Park, Clear Lake, IA. This annual storytelling event is held in a scenic lakeside setting. Friday evening "Stories After Dark." Two performances Saturday plus story exchange for novice tellers. Annually, the last Friday and Saturday in July. Est attendance: 800. For info: Jean Casey, Dir, Clear Lake Public Library, 200 N 4th St, Clear Lake, IA 50428. Phone: (515) 357-6133. Fax: (515) 357-4645.

LIBERIA: INDEPENDENCE DAY. July 26. National holiday. Became republic in 1847, under aegis of the US Societies for Repatriating Former Slaves in Africa.

MALDIVES: INDEPENDENCE DAY. July 26. National holiday. Commemorates the independence of this group of 200 islands in the Indian Ocean from Britain in 1965.

NEW YORK RATIFIES CONSTITUTION: ANNIVERSARY. July 26. Became 11th state to ratify the Constitution in 1788.

US ARMY FIRST DESEGREGATED: ANNIVERSARY. July 26, 1944. During WWII the US Army ordered desegregation of its training camp facilities. Later the same year black platoons were assigned to white companies in a tentative step toward integration of the battlefield. However, it was not until after the War—July 26, 1948—that President Harry Truman signed an order officially integrating the armed forces.

US DEPARTMENT OF DEFENSE CREATED: 55th ANNIVERSARY. July 26, 1947. President Truman signed legislation unifying the War Department (Army) and the Navy in the Department of Defense. The Air Force was made independent of the Army at the same time. Truman nominated James Forrestal to be the first Secretary of Defense. The legislation also provided for the National Security Council, the Central Intelligence Agency and the Joint Chiefs of Staff.

BIRTHDAYS TODAY

Jan Berenstain, 79, author and illustrator, with her husband Stan (the Berenstain Bears series), born Philadelphia, PA, July 26, 1923.

JULY 27 — SATURDAY

Day 208 — 157 Remaining

AIDS NAMED: 20th ANNIVERSARY. July 27, 1982. The Centers for Disease Control adopted Acquired Immune Deficiency Syndrome as the official name for a new disease that was first described in a CDC newsletter on June 5, 1981. The virus that causes AIDS was identified in 1983 and in May 1985 was named Human Immunodeficiency Virus (HIV) by the International Committee on the Taxonomy of Viruses. The first death from this disease in the developed world occurred in 1959. More than 420,000 Americans have died of AIDS. Worldwide, more than 22 million people have died of AIDS.

BARBOSA, JOSÉ CELSO: BIRTH ANNIVERSARY. July 27, 1857. Puerto Rican physician and patriot, born at Bayamon, Puerto Rico. His birthday is a holiday in Puerto Rico. He died at San Juan, Puerto Rico, Sept 21, 1921.

INSULIN FIRST ISOLATED: ANNIVERSARY. July 27, 1921. Dr. Frederick Banting and his assistant at the University of Toronto Medical School, Charles Best, gave insulin to a dog whose pancreas had been removed. In 1922 insulin was first administered to a diabetic, a 14-year-old boy.

KOREAN WAR ARMISTICE: ANNIVERSARY. July 27, 1953. Armistice agreement ending war that had lasted three years and 32 days was signed at Panmunjom, Korea (July 26, US time), by US and North Korean delegates. Both sides claimed victory at conclusion of two years, 17 days of truce negotiations. For more info: korea50.army.mil/teachers.html. The Fall 1999 issue of *Cobblestone* (for ages 9–14) was devoted to the Korean War.

MONTANA STATE FAIR. July 27–Aug 3. Great Falls, MT. Horse racing, petting zoo, carnival, discount days, nightly entertainment and plenty of food. Est attendance: 200,000. For info: Kelly Michel, State Fair, Box 1888, Great Falls, MT 59403. Phone: (406) 727-8900. Fax: (406) 452-8955.

US DEPARTMENT OF STATE FOUNDED: ANNIVERSARY. July 27, 1789. The first presidential cabinet department, called the Department of Foreign Affairs, was established by the Congress. Later the name was changed to Department of State.

BIRTHDAYS TODAY

Christina Björk, 64, author (*Linnea in Monet's Garden*), born Stockholm, Sweden, July 27, 1938.
Donald Evans, 56, US Secretary of Commerce (George W. Bush administration), born Houston, TX, July 27, 1946.
Paul Janeczko, 57, poet (*Home on the Range: Cowboy Poetry*), born Passaic, NJ, July 27, 1945.
Alex Rodriguez, 27, baseball player, born New York, NY, July 27, 1975.

JULY 28 — SUNDAY

Day 209 — 156 Remaining

HEYWARD, THOMAS: BIRTH ANNIVERSARY. July 28, 1746. American Revolutionary soldier, signer of the Declaration of Independence. Died Mar 6, 1809.

ONASSIS, JACQUELINE LEE BOUVIER KENNEDY: BIRTH ANNIVERSARY. July 28, 1929. Editor, widow of John Fitzgerald Kennedy (35th president of the US), born at Southampton, NY. Later married (Oct 20, 1968) Greek shipping magnate Aristotle Socrates Onassis, who died Mar 15, 1975. The widely admired and respected former First Lady died May 19, 1994, at New York, NY.

★ **PARENTS' DAY.** July 28. To pay tribute to the millions of men and women whose devotion as parents strengthens our society and forms the foundation for a bright future for America. Public Law 103-362.

PERU: INDEPENDENCE DAY. July 28. San Martin declared independence in 1821. After the final defeat of Spanish troops by Simon Bolivar in 1824, Spanish rule ended.

POTTER, (HELEN) BEATRIX: BIRTH ANNIVERSARY. July 28, 1866. Author and illustrator of the Peter Rabbit stories for children, born at London, England. Died at Sawrey, Lancashire, Dec 22, 1943. For more info: *Beatrix Potter*, by Alexandra Wallner (Holiday House, 0-8234-1181-8, $15.95 Gr. K–2) or the Peter Rabbit Homepage at www.peterrabbit.co.uk.

WORLD WAR I BEGINS: ANNIVERSARY. July 28, 1914. Archduke Francis Ferdinand of Austria-Hungary and his wife were assassinated at Sarajevo, Bosnia, by a Serbian nationalist, touching off the conflict that became WWI. Austria-Hungary declared war on Serbia July 28, the formal beginning of the war. Within weeks, Germany entered the war on the side of Austria-Hungary and Russia, France and Great Britain on the side of Serbia.

BIRTHDAYS TODAY

Natalie Babbitt, 70, author and illustrator (*Tuck Everlasting*), born Dayton, OH, July 28, 1932.
Jim Davis, 57, creator ("Garfield"), born Marion, IN, July 28, 1945.
Judy Martz, 59, Governor of Montana (R), born Big Timber, MT, July 28, 1943.

July 2002

S	M	T	W	T	F	S
	1	2	3	4	5	6
7	8	9	10	11	12	13
14	15	16	17	18	19	20
21	22	23	24	25	26	27
28	29	30	31			

JULY 29 — MONDAY

Day 210 — 155 Remaining

NASA ESTABLISHED: ANNIVERSARY. July 29, 1958. President Eisenhower signed a bill creating the National Aeronautics and Space Administration to direct US space policy. For more info: www.nasa.gov.

ROOSEVELT, ALICE HATHAWAY LEE: BIRTH ANNIVERSARY. July 29, 1861. First wife of Theodore Roosevelt, 26th President of the US, whom she married in 1880. Born at Chestnut Hill, MA, she died at New York, NY, Feb 14, 1884.

BIRTHDAYS TODAY

Debbie Black, 36, basketball player, born Philadelphia, PA, July 29, 1966.
Sharon Creech, 57, author (Newbery for *Walk Two Moons*), born Cleveland, OH, July 29, 1945.
Elizabeth Hanford Dole, 66, former president of American Red Cross, former US Secretary of Transportation and US Secretary of Labor, born Salisbury, NC, July 29, 1936.
Peter Jennings, 64, journalist (anchorman for "ABC Evening News"), born Toronto, ON, Canada, July 29, 1938.
Kathleen Krull, 50, author of nonfiction (*Wilma Unlimited: How Wilma Rudolph Became the World's Fastest Woman*), born Ft Leonard Wood, MO, July 29, 1952.
Ronnie Musgrove, 46, Governor of Mississippi (R), born David Ronald Musgrove, Panola County, MS, July 29, 1956.
Connie Porter, 43, author (*Meet Addy, Addy Learns a Lesson*), born Lackawanna, NY, July 29, 1959.

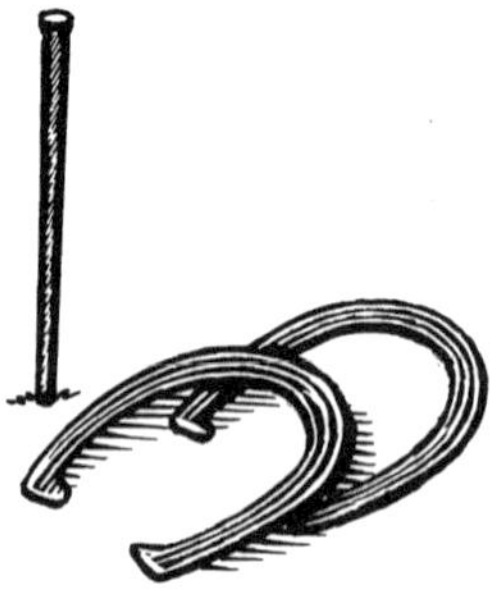

JULY 30 — TUESDAY

Day 211 — 154 Remaining

PAPERBACK BOOKS INTRODUCED: ANNIVERSARY. July 30, 1935. Although books bound in soft covers were first introduced in 1841 at Leipzig, Germany, by Christian Bernhard Tauchnitz, the modern paperback revolution dates to the publication of the first Penguin paperback by Sir Allen Lane at London in 1935. Penguin Number 1 was *Ariel the Life of Shelley* by Andre Maurois.

SOUTH DAKOTA STATE FAIR. July 30–Aug 5. Huron, SD. Grandstand entertainment nightly, 10 free stages with multiple shows daily, hundreds of commercial exhibits and thousands of livestock exhibits. One of the largest agricultural fairs in the US. Est attendance: 250,000. For info: Craig Atkins, Mgr, South Dakota State Fair, PO Box 1275, Huron, SD 57350-1275. Phone: (605) 353-7340. Fax: (605) 353-7348. E-mail: statefair@state.sd.us.

VANUATU: INDEPENDENCE DAY. July 30. Vanuatu became an independent republic in 1980, breaking ties with France and the UK, and observes its national holiday.

BIRTHDAYS TODAY

Irene Ng, 28, actress ("Mystery Files of Shelby Woo"), born Malaysia, July 30, 1974.

Marcus Pfister, 42, author, illustrator (*The Rainbow Fish, Dazzle the Dinosaur*), born Bern, Switzerland, July 30, 1960.

Arnold Schwarzenegger, 55, bodybuilder, actor (*The Terminator, Twins, True Lies*), born Graz, Austria, July 30, 1947.

JULY 31 — WEDNESDAY

Day 212 — 153 Remaining

CHINCOTEAGUE PONY PENNING. July 31–Aug 1. Chincoteague Island, VA. To round up the 150 wild ponies living on Assateague Island and swim them across the inlet to Chincoteague, where about 50–60 of them are sold. Annually, the last Wednesday and Thursday of July. Marguerite Henry's *Misty of Chincoteague* is an account of this event. Est attendance: 50,000. For info: Jacklyn Russell, Chamber of Commerce, Box 258, Chincoteague, VA 23336. Phone: (757) 336-6161. Fax: (757) 336-1242. E-mail: pony@shore.intercom.net. Web: www.chincoteague.com/ponya.html.

US PATENT OFFICE OPENS: ANNIVERSARY. July 31, 1790. The first US Patent Office opened its doors and the first US patent was issued to Samuel Hopkins of Vermont for a new method of making pearlash and potash. The patent was signed by George Washington and Thomas Jefferson.

BIRTHDAYS TODAY

Lynne Reid Banks, 73, author (*The Indian in the Cupboard*), born London, England, July 31, 1929.

Dean Cain, 36, actor ("Lois & Clark"), born Mt Clemens, MI, July 31, 1966.

J.K. Rowling, 37, author (the Harry Potter series), born Joanne Rowling, Bristol, England, July 31, 1965.

THE NATIONAL EDUCATION GOALS

1. By the year 2000, all children in America will start school ready to learn.
2. By the year 2000, the high school graduation rate will increase to at least 90 percent.
3. By the year 2000, American students will leave grades four, eight, and twelve having demonstrated competency in challenging subject matter including English, mathematics, science, foreign languages, civics and government, economics, art, history, and geography; and every school in America will insure that all students learn to use their minds well, so they may be prepared for responsible citizenship, further learning, and productive employment in our nations modern economy.
4. By the year 2000, the nation's teaching force will have access to programs for the continued improvement of their professional skills and the opportunity to acquire the knowledge and skills needed to instruct and prepare all American students for the next century.
5. By the year 2000, U.S. students will be first in the world in science and mathematics achievement.
6. By the year 2000, every adult American will be literate and will possess the knowledge and skills necessary to compete in a global economy and exercise the rights and responsibilities of citizenship.
7. By the year 2000, every school in America will be free of drugs, violence, and the unauthorized presence of firearms and alcohol and will offer a disciplined environment conducive to learning.
8. By the year 2000, every school will promote partnerships that will increase parental involvement and participation in promoting the social, emotional, and academic growth of children.

In September, 1989, President George Bush and the governors of the 50 states convened a historic Education Summit and agreed to set education goals for the nation. In February, 1990, the National Education Goals were announced by President Bush and adopted by governors. The National Education Goals Panel was created by President Bush and the 50 governors in July, 1990, to measure progress towards the goals. The Panel is an independent executive branch agency charged with a variety of responsibilities to support systemwide education reform. In March, 1994, President Clinton signed the "Goals 2000: Educate America Act" which codified the eight National Education Goals.

The Panel had issued many reports in the last ten years. For the most current information:

National Education Goals Panel
1255 22nd St NW, Ste 502
Washington, DC 20037
Phone: (202) 724-0015
Fax: (202) 632-0957
Web: www.negp.gov

CALENDAR INFORMATION FOR THE YEAR 2001

Time shown is Eastern Standard Time. All dates are given in terms of the Gregorian calendar.
(Based in part on information prepared by the Nautical Almanac Office, US Naval Observatory.)

ERAS	YEAR	BEGINS
Jewish*	5762	Sept 18
Chinese (Year of the Snake)	4699	Jan 24
Japanese (Heisei)	13	Jan 1
Indian (Saka)	1923	Mar 20
Islamic (Hegira)**	1422	Mar 26

*Year begins at sunset. **Year begins at moon crescent.

RELIGIOUS CALENDARS—2001

Christian Holy Days

Epiphany	Jan 6
Shrove Tuesday	Feb 27
Ash Wednesday	Feb 28
Lent	Feb 28–Apr 14
Palm Sunday	Apr 8
Good Friday	Apr 13
Easter Day	Apr 15
Ascension Day	May 24
Whit Sunday (Pentecost)	June 3
Trinity Sunday	June 10
First Sunday in Advent	Dec 2
Christmas Day (Tuesday)	Dec 25

Eastern Orthodox Church Observances

Great Lent begins	Feb 26
Pascha (Easter)	Apr 15
Ascension	May 24
Pentecost	June 3

Jewish Holy Days

Purim	Mar 9
Passover (1st day)	Apr 8
Shavuot	May 28
Tisha B'av	July 29
Rosh Hashanah (New Year)	Sept 18–19
Yom Kippur	Sept 27
Succoth	Oct 2–10
Chanukah	Dec 10–17

Islamic Holy Days

Islamic New Year (1422)	Mar 26
First Day of Ramadan (1422)	Nov 16
Eid-Al-Fitr (1422)	Dec 16

CIVIL CALENDAR—USA—2001

New Year's Day	Jan 1
Martin Luther King's Birthday (obsvd)	Jan 15
Lincoln's Birthday	Feb 12
Washington's Birthday (obsvd)/Presidents' Day	Feb 19
Memorial Day (obsvd)	May 28
Independence Day	July 4
Labor Day	Sept 3
Columbus Day (obsvd)	Oct 8
General Election Day	Nov 6
Veterans Day	Nov 11
Thanksgiving Day	Nov 22

Other Days Widely Observed in US—2001

Groundhog Day (Candlemas)	Feb 2
St. Valentine's Day	Feb 14
St. Patrick's Day	Mar 17
Mother's Day	May 13
Flag Day	June 14
Father's Day	June 17
National Grandparents Day	Sept 9
Hallowe'en	Oct 31

CIVIL CALENDAR—CANADA—2001

Victoria Day	May 21
Canada Day	July 2
Labor Day	Sept 3
Thanksgiving Day	Oct 8
Remembrance Day	Nov 11
Boxing Day	Dec 26

CIVIL CALENDAR—MEXICO—2001

New Year's Day	Jan 1
Constitution Day	Feb 5
Benito Juarez Birthday	Mar 21
Labor Day	May 1
Battle of Puebla Day (Cinco de Mayo)	May 5
Independence Day*	Sept 16
Dia de La Raza	Oct 12
Mexican Revolution Day	Nov 20
Guadalupe Day	Dec 12

*Celebration begins Sept 15 at 11:00 p.m.

ECLIPSES—2001

Total eclipse of the Moon	Jan 9
Total eclipse of the Sun	June 21
Partial eclipse of the Moon	July 5
Annular eclipse of the Sun	Dec 14
Penumbral clipse of the Moon	Dec 30

SEASONS—2001

Spring (Vernal Equinox)	Mar 20, 8:31 am, est
Summer (Summer Solstice)	June 21, 3:38 am, edt
Autumn (Autumnal Equinox)	Sept 22, 7:04 pm, edt
Winter (Winter Solstice)	Dec 21, 2:21 pm, est

DAYLIGHT SAVING TIME SCHEDULE—2001

Sunday, Apr 1, 2:00 am–Sunday, Oct 28, 2:00 am—in all time zones.

CALENDAR INFORMATION FOR THE YEAR 2002

Time shown is Eastern Standard Time. All dates are given in terms of the Gregorian calendar.
(Based in part on information prepared by the Nautical Almanac Office, US Naval Observatory.)

ERAS	YEAR	BEGINS
Jewish*	5763	Sept 6
Chinese (Year of the Horse)	4700	Feb 12
Japanese (Heisei)	14	Jan 1
Indian (Saka)	1924	Mar 21
Islamic (Hegira)**	1423	Mar 15

*Year begins at sunset. **Year begins at moon crescent.

RELIGIOUS CALENDARS—2002

Christian Holy Days

Epiphany . . . Jan 6
Shrove Tuesday . . . Feb 12
Ash Wednesday . . . Feb 13
Lent . . . Feb 13–Mar 30
Palm Sunday . . . Mar 24
Good Friday . . . Mar 29
Easter Day . . . Mar 31
Ascension Day . . . May 9
Whit Sunday (Pentecost) . . . May 19
Trinity Sunday . . . May 26
First Sunday in Advent . . . Dec 1
Christmas Day (Wednesday) . . . Dec 25

Eastern Orthodox Church Observances

Great Lent begins . . . Mar 18
Pascha (Easter) . . . May 5
Ascension . . . June 13
Pentecost . . . June 23

Jewish Holy Days

Purim . . . Feb 26
Passover (1st day) . . . Mar 28
Shavuot . . . May 17
Tisha B'av . . . July 18
Rosh Hashanah (New Year) . . . Sept 7–8
Yom Kippur . . . Sept 16
Succoth . . . Sept 21–29
Chanukah . . . Nov 30–Dec 7

Islamic Holy Days

Islamic New Year (1423) . . . Mar 15
First Day of Ramadan (1423) . . . Nov 6
Eid-Al-Fitr (1423) . . . Dec 5

CIVIL CALENDAR—USA—2002

New Year's Day . . . Jan 1
Martin Luther King's Birthday (obsvd) . . . Jan 21
Lincoln's Birthday . . . Feb 12
Washington's Birthday (obsvd)/Presidents' Day . . . Feb 18
Memorial Day (obsvd) . . . May 27
Independence Day . . . July 4
Labor Day . . . Sept 2
Columbus Day (obsvd) . . . Oct 14
General Election Day . . . Nov 5
Veterans Day . . . Nov 11
Thanksgiving Day . . . Nov 28

Other Days Widely Observed in US—2002

Groundhog Day (Candlemas) . . . Feb 2
St. Valentine's Day . . . Feb 14
St. Patrick's Day . . . Mar 17
Mother's Day . . . May 12
Flag Day . . . June 14
Father's Day . . . June 16
National Grandparents Day . . . Sept 8
Hallowe'en . . . Oct 31

CIVIL CALENDAR—CANADA—2002

Victoria Day . . . May 20
Canada Day . . . July 1
Labor Day . . . Sept 2
Thanksgiving Day . . . Oct 14
Remembrance Day . . . Nov 11
Boxing Day . . . Dec 26

CIVIL CALENDAR—MEXICO—2002

New Year's Day . . . Jan 1
Constitution Day . . . Feb 5
Benito Juarez Birthday . . . Mar 21
Labor Day . . . May 1
Battle of Puebla Day (Cinco de Mayo) . . . May 5
Independence Day* . . . Sept 16
Dia de La Raza . . . Oct 12
Mexican Revolution Day . . . Nov 20
Guadalupe Day . . . Dec 12

*Celebration begins Sept 15 at 11:00 P.M.

ECLIPSES—2002

Penumbral eclipse of the Moon . . . May 26
Annular eclipse of the Sun . . . June 10
Penumbral eclipse of the Moon . . . June 24
Penumbral eclipse of the Moon . . . Nov 19
Total eclipse of the Sun . . . Dec 4

SEASONS—2002

Spring (Vernal Equinox) . . . Mar 20, 2:16 PM, EST
Summer (Summer Solstice) . . . June 21, 9:24 AM, EDT
Autumn (Autumnal Equinox) . . . Sept 23, 12:56 AM, EDT
Winter (Winter Solstice) . . . Dec 21, 8:15 PM, EST

DAYLIGHT SAVING TIME SCHEDULE—2002

Sunday, Apr 7, 2:00 AM–Sunday, Oct 27, 2:00 AM—in all time zones.

Perpetual Calendar, 1753–2100

A perpetual calendar lets you find the day of the week for any date in any year. Since January 1 may fall on any of the seven days of the week, and may be a leap or non-leap year, 14 different calendars are possible. The number next to each year corresponds to one of the 14 calendars. Calendar 2 will be used in 2001; calendar 3 will be used in 2002.

Year	No.	Year	No.	Year	No.	Year	No.	Year	No.	Year	No.	Year	No.	Year	No.	Year	No.
1753	2	1792	8	1831	7	1870	7	1909	6	1948	12	1987	5	2026	5	2065	5
1754	3	1793	3	1832	8	1871	1	1910	7	1949	7	1988	13	2027	6	2066	6
1755	4	1794	4	1833	3	1872	9	1911	1	1950	1	1989	1	2028	14	2067	7
1756	12	1795	5	1834	4	1873	4	1912	9	1951	2	1990	2	2029	2	2068	8
1757	7	1796	13	1835	5	1874	5	1913	4	1952	10	1991	3	2030	3	2069	3
1758	1	1797	1	1836	13	1875	6	1914	5	1953	5	1992	11	2031	4	2070	4
1759	2	1798	2	1837	1	1876	14	1915	6	1954	6	1993	6	2032	12	2071	5
1760	10	1799	3	1838	2	1877	2	1916	14	1955	7	1994	7	2033	7	2072	13
1761	5	1800	4	1839	3	1878	3	1917	2	1956	8	1995	1	2034	1	2073	1
1762	6	1801	5	1840	11	1879	4	1918	3	1957	3	1996	9	2035	2	2074	2
1763	7	1802	6	1841	6	1880	12	1919	4	1958	4	1997	4	2036	10	2075	3
1764	8	1803	7	1842	7	1881	7	1920	12	1959	5	1998	5	2037	5	2076	11
1765	3	1804	8	1843	1	1882	1	1921	7	1960	13	1999	6	2038	6	2077	6
1766	4	1805	3	1844	9	1883	2	1922	1	1961	1	2000	14	2039	7	2078	7
1767	5	1806	4	1845	4	1884	10	1923	2	1962	2	2001	2	2040	8	2079	1
1768	13	1807	5	1846	5	1885	5	1924	10	1963	3	2002	3	2041	3	2080	9
1769	1	1808	13	1847	6	1886	6	1925	5	1964	11	2003	4	2042	4	2081	4
1770	2	1809	1	1848	14	1887	7	1926	6	1965	6	2004	12	2043	5	2082	5
1771	3	1810	2	1849	2	1888	8	1927	7	1966	7	2005	7	2044	13	2083	6
1772	11	1811	3	1850	3	1889	3	1928	8	1967	1	2006	1	2045	1	2084	14
1773	6	1812	11	1851	4	1890	4	1929	3	1968	9	2007	2	2046	2	2085	2
1774	7	1813	6	1852	12	1891	5	1930	4	1969	4	2008	10	2047	3	2086	3
1775	1	1814	7	1853	7	1892	13	1931	5	1970	5	2009	5	2048	11	2087	4
1776	9	1815	1	1854	1	1893	1	1932	13	1971	6	2010	6	2049	6	2088	12
1777	4	1816	9	1855	2	1894	2	1933	1	1972	14	2011	7	2050	7	2089	7
1778	5	1817	4	1856	10	1895	3	1934	2	1973	2	2012	8	2051	1	2090	1
1779	6	1818	5	1857	5	1896	11	1935	3	1974	3	2013	3	2052	9	2091	2
1780	14	1819	6	1858	6	1897	6	1936	11	1975	4	2014	4	2053	4	2092	10
1781	2	1820	14	1859	7	1898	7	1937	6	1976	12	2015	5	2054	5	2093	5
1782	3	1821	2	1860	8	1899	1	1938	7	1977	7	2016	13	2055	6	2094	6
1783	4	1822	3	1861	3	1900	2	1939	1	1978	1	2017	1	2056	14	2095	7
1784	12	1823	4	1862	4	1901	3	1940	9	1979	2	2018	2	2057	2	2096	8
1785	7	1824	12	1863	5	1902	4	1941	4	1980	10	2019	3	2058	3	2097	3
1786	1	1825	7	1864	13	1903	5	1942	5	1981	5	2020	11	2059	4	2098	4
1787	2	1826	1	1865	1	1904	13	1943	6	1982	6	2021	6	2060	12	2099	5
1788	10	1827	2	1866	2	1905	1	1944	14	1983	7	2022	7	2061	7	2100	6
1789	5	1828	10	1867	3	1906	2	1945	2	1984	8	2023	1	2062	1		
1790	6	1829	5	1868	11	1907	3	1946	3	1985	3	2024	9	2063	2		
1791	7	1830	6	1869	6	1908	11	1947	4	1986	4	2025	4	2064	10		

1

JAN

S	M	T	W	T	F	S
1	2	3	4	5	6	7
8	9	10	11	12	13	14
15	16	17	18	19	20	21
22	23	24	25	26	27	28
29	30	31				

APR

S	M	T	W	T	F	S
						1
2	3	4	5	6	7	8
9	10	11	12	13	14	15
16	17	18	19	20	21	22
23	24	25	26	27	28	29
30						

JULY

S	M	T	W	T	F	S
						1
2	3	4	5	6	7	8
9	10	11	12	13	14	15
16	17	18	19	20	21	22
23	24	25	26	27	28	29
30	31					

OCT

S	M	T	W	T	F	S
1	2	3	4	5	6	7
8	9	10	11	12	13	14
15	16	17	18	19	20	21
22	23	24	25	26	27	28
29	30	31				

FEB

S	M	T	W	T	F	S
			1	2	3	4
5	6	7	8	9	10	11
12	13	14	15	16	17	18
19	20	21	22	23	24	25
26	27	28				

MAY

S	M	T	W	T	F	S
	1	2	3	4	5	6
7	8	9	10	11	12	13
14	15	16	17	18	19	20
21	22	23	24	25	26	27
28	29	30	31			

AUG

S	M	T	W	T	F	S
		1	2	3	4	5
6	7	8	9	10	11	12
13	14	15	16	17	18	19
20	21	22	23	24	25	26
27	28	29	30	31		

NOV

S	M	T	W	T	F	S
			1	2	3	4
5	6	7	8	9	10	11
12	13	14	15	16	17	18
19	20	21	22	23	24	25
26	27	28	29	30		

MAR

S	M	T	W	T	F	S
			1	2	3	4
5	6	7	8	9	10	11
12	13	14	15	16	17	18
19	20	21	22	23	24	25
26	27	28	29	30	31	

JUNE

S	M	T	W	T	F	S
				1	2	3
4	5	6	7	8	9	10
11	12	13	14	15	16	17
18	19	20	21	22	23	24
25	26	27	28	29	30	

SEPT

S	M	T	W	T	F	S
					1	2
3	4	5	6	7	8	9
10	11	12	13	14	15	16
17	18	19	20	21	22	23
24	25	26	27	28	29	30

DEC

S	M	T	W	T	F	S
					1	2
3	4	5	6	7	8	9
10	11	12	13	14	15	16
17	18	19	20	21	22	23
24	25	26	27	28	29	30
31						

2

2001

JAN

S	M	T	W	T	F	S
	1	2	3	4	5	6
7	8	9	10	11	12	13
14	15	16	17	18	19	20
21	22	23	24	25	26	27
28	29	30	31			

APR

S	M	T	W	T	F	S
1	2	3	4	5	6	7
8	9	10	11	12	13	14
15	16	17	18	19	20	21
22	23	24	25	26	27	28
29	30					

JULY

S	M	T	W	T	F	S
1	2	3	4	5	6	7
8	9	10	11	12	13	14
15	16	17	18	19	20	21
22	23	24	25	26	27	28
29	30	31				

OCT

S	M	T	W	T	F	S
	1	2	3	4	5	6
7	8	9	10	11	12	13
14	15	16	17	18	19	20
21	22	23	24	25	26	27
28	29	30	31			

FEB

S	M	T	W	T	F	S
				1	2	3
4	5	6	7	8	9	10
11	12	13	14	15	16	17
18	19	20	21	22	23	24
25	26	27	28			

MAY

S	M	T	W	T	F	S
		1	2	3	4	5
6	7	8	9	10	11	12
13	14	15	16	17	18	19
20	21	22	23	24	25	26
27	28	29	30	31		

AUG

S	M	T	W	T	F	S
			1	2	3	4
5	6	7	8	9	10	11
12	13	14	15	16	17	18
19	20	21	22	23	24	25
26	27	28	29	30	31	

NOV

S	M	T	W	T	F	S
				1	2	3
4	5	6	7	8	9	10
11	12	13	14	15	16	17
18	19	20	21	22	23	24
25	26	27	28	29	30	

MAR

S	M	T	W	T	F	S
				1	2	3
4	5	6	7	8	9	10
11	12	13	14	15	16	17
18	19	20	21	22	23	24
25	26	27	28	29	30	31

JUNE

S	M	T	W	T	F	S
					1	2
3	4	5	6	7	8	9
10	11	12	13	14	15	16
17	18	19	20	21	22	23
24	25	26	27	28	29	30

SEPT

S	M	T	W	T	F	S
						1
2	3	4	5	6	7	8
9	10	11	12	13	14	15
16	17	18	19	20	21	22
23	24	25	26	27	28	29
30						

DEC

S	M	T	W	T	F	S
						1
2	3	4	5	6	7	8
9	10	11	12	13	14	15
16	17	18	19	20	21	22
23	24	25	26	27	28	29
30	31					

3

2002

JAN

S	M	T	W	T	F	S
		1	2	3	4	5
6	7	8	9	10	11	12
13	14	15	16	17	18	19
20	21	22	23	24	25	26
27	28	29	30	31		

APR

S	M	T	W	T	F	S
	1	2	3	4	5	6
7	8	9	10	11	12	13
14	15	16	17	18	19	20
21	22	23	24	25	26	27
28	29	30				

JULY

S	M	T	W	T	F	S
	1	2	3	4	5	6
7	8	9	10	11	12	13
14	15	16	17	18	19	20
21	22	23	24	25	26	27
28	29	30	31			

OCT

S	M	T	W	T	F	S
		1	2	3	4	5
6	7	8	9	10	11	12
13	14	15	16	17	18	19
20	21	22	23	24	25	26
27	28	29	30	31		

FEB

S	M	T	W	T	F	S
					1	2
3	4	5	6	7	8	9
10	11	12	13	14	15	16
17	18	19	20	21	22	23
24	25	26	27	28		

MAY

S	M	T	W	T	F	S
			1	2	3	4
5	6	7	8	9	10	11
12	13	14	15	16	17	18
19	20	21	22	23	24	25
26	27	28	29	30	31	

AUG

S	M	T	W	T	F	S
				1	2	3
4	5	6	7	8	9	10
11	12	13	14	15	16	17
18	19	20	21	22	23	24
25	26	27	28	29	30	31

NOV

S	M	T	W	T	F	S
					1	2
3	4	5	6	7	8	9
10	11	12	13	14	15	16
17	18	19	20	21	22	23
24	25	26	27	28	29	30

MAR

S	M	T	W	T	F	S
					1	2
3	4	5	6	7	8	9
10	11	12	13	14	15	16
17	18	19	20	21	22	23
24	25	26	27	28	29	30
31						

JUNE

S	M	T	W	T	F	S
						1
2	3	4	5	6	7	8
9	10	11	12	13	14	15
16	17	18	19	20	21	22
23	24	25	26	27	28	29
30						

SEPT

S	M	T	W	T	F	S
1	2	3	4	5	6	7
8	9	10	11	12	13	14
15	16	17	18	19	20	21
22	23	24	25	26	27	28
29	30					

DEC

S	M	T	W	T	F	S
1	2	3	4	5	6	7
8	9	10	11	12	13	14
15	16	17	18	19	20	21
22	23	24	25	26	27	28
29	30	31				

4

2003

JAN

S	M	T	W	T	F	S
			1	2	3	4
5	6	7	8	9	10	11
12	13	14	15	16	17	18
19	20	21	22	23	24	25
26	27	28	29	30	31	

APR

S	M	T	W	T	F	S
		1	2	3	4	5
6	7	8	9	10	11	12
13	14	15	16	17	18	19
20	21	22	23	24	25	26
27	28	29	30			

JULY

S	M	T	W	T	F	S
		1	2	3	4	5
6	7	8	9	10	11	12
13	14	15	16	17	18	19
20	21	22	23	24	25	26
27	28	29	30	31		

OCT

S	M	T	W	T	F	S
			1	2	3	4
5	6	7	8	9	10	11
12	13	14	15	16	17	18
19	20	21	22	23	24	25
26	27	28	29	30	31	

FEB

S	M	T	W	T	F	S
						1
2	3	4	5	6	7	8
9	10	11	12	13	14	15
16	17	18	19	20	21	22
23	24	25	26	27	28	

MAY

S	M	T	W	T	F	S
				1	2	3
4	5	6	7	8	9	10
11	12	13	14	15	16	17
18	19	20	21	22	23	24
25	26	27	28	29	30	31

AUG

S	M	T	W	T	F	S
					1	2
3	4	5	6	7	8	9
10	11	12	13	14	15	16
17	18	19	20	21	22	23
24	25	26	27	28	29	30
31						

NOV

S	M	T	W	T	F	S
						1
2	3	4	5	6	7	8
9	10	11	12	13	14	15
16	17	18	19	20	21	22
23	24	25	26	27	28	29
30						

MAR

S	M	T	W	T	F	S
						1
2	3	4	5	6	7	8
9	10	11	12	13	14	15
16	17	18	19	20	21	22
23	24	25	26	27	28	29
30	31					

JUNE

S	M	T	W	T	F	S
1	2	3	4	5	6	7
8	9	10	11	12	13	14
15	16	17	18	19	20	21
22	23	24	25	26	27	28
29	30					

SEPT

S	M	T	W	T	F	S
	1	2	3	4	5	6
7	8	9	10	11	12	13
14	15	16	17	18	19	20
21	22	23	24	25	26	27
28	29	30				

DEC

S	M	T	W	T	F	S
	1	2	3	4	5	6
7	8	9	10	11	12	13
14	15	16	17	18	19	20
21	22	23	24	25	26	27
28	29	30	31			

5

JAN

S	M	T	W	T	F	S
				1	2	3
4	5	6	7	8	9	10
11	12	13	14	15	16	17
18	19	20	21	22	23	24
25	26	27	28	29	30	31

APR

S	M	T	W	T	F	S
			1	2	3	4
5	6	7	8	9	10	11
12	13	14	15	16	17	18
19	20	21	22	23	24	25
26	27	28	29	30		

JULY

S	M	T	W	T	F	S
			1	2	3	4
5	6	7	8	9	10	11
12	13	14	15	16	17	18
19	20	21	22	23	24	25
26	27	28	29	30	31	

OCT

S	M	T	W	T	F	S
				1	2	3
4	5	6	7	8	9	10
11	12	13	14	15	16	17
18	19	20	21	22	23	24
25	26	27	28	29	30	31

FEB

S	M	T	W	T	F	S
1	2	3	4	5	6	7
8	9	10	11	12	13	14
15	16	17	18	19	20	21
22	23	24	25	26	27	28

MAY

S	M	T	W	T	F	S
					1	2
3	4	5	6	7	8	9
10	11	12	13	14	15	16
17	18	19	20	21	22	23
24	25	26	27	28	29	30
31						

AUG

S	M	T	W	T	F	S
						1
2	3	4	5	6	7	8
9	10	11	12	13	14	15
16	17	18	19	20	21	22
23	24	25	26	27	28	29
30	31					

NOV

S	M	T	W	T	F	S
1	2	3	4	5	6	7
8	9	10	11	12	13	14
15	16	17	18	19	20	21
22	23	24	25	26	27	28
29	30					

MAR

S	M	T	W	T	F	S
1	2	3	4	5	6	7
8	9	10	11	12	13	14
15	16	17	18	19	20	21
22	23	24	25	26	27	28
29	30	31				

JUNE

S	M	T	W	T	F	S
	1	2	3	4	5	6
7	8	9	10	11	12	13
14	15	16	17	18	19	20
21	22	23	24	25	26	27
28	29	30				

SEPT

S	M	T	W	T	F	S
		1	2	3	4	5
6	7	8	9	10	11	12
13	14	15	16	17	18	19
20	21	22	23	24	25	26
27	28	29	30			

DEC

S	M	T	W	T	F	S
		1	2	3	4	5
6	7	8	9	10	11	12
13	14	15	16	17	18	19
20	21	22	23	24	25	26
27	28	29	30	31		

6

JAN

S	M	T	W	T	F	S
					1	2
3	4	5	6	7	8	9
10	11	12	13	14	15	16
17	18	19	20	21	22	23
24	25	26	27	28	29	30
31						

APR

S	M	T	W	T	F	S
				1	2	3
4	5	6	7	8	9	10
11	12	13	14	15	16	17
18	19	20	21	22	23	24
25	26	27	28	29	30	

JULY

S	M	T	W	T	F	S
				1	2	3
4	5	6	7	8	9	10
11	12	13	14	15	16	17
18	19	20	21	22	23	24
25	26	27	28	29	30	31

OCT

S	M	T	W	T	F	S
					1	2
3	4	5	6	7	8	9
10	11	12	13	14	15	16
17	18	19	20	21	22	23
24	25	26	27	28	29	30
31						

FEB

S	M	T	W	T	F	S
	1	2	3	4	5	6
7	8	9	10	11	12	13
14	15	16	17	18	19	20
21	22	23	24	25	26	27
28						

MAY

S	M	T	W	T	F	S
						1
2	3	4	5	6	7	8
9	10	11	12	13	14	15
16	17	18	19	20	21	22
23	24	25	26	27	28	29
30	31					

AUG

S	M	T	W	T	F	S
1	2	3	4	5	6	7
8	9	10	11	12	13	14
15	16	17	18	19	20	21
22	23	24	25	26	27	28
29	30	31				

NOV

S	M	T	W	T	F	S
	1	2	3	4	5	6
7	8	9	10	11	12	13
14	15	16	17	18	19	20
21	22	23	24	25	26	27
28	29	30				

MAR

S	M	T	W	T	F	S
	1	2	3	4	5	6
7	8	9	10	11	12	13
14	15	16	17	18	19	20
21	22	23	24	25	26	27
28	29	30	31			

JUNE

S	M	T	W	T	F	S
		1	2	3	4	5
6	7	8	9	10	11	12
13	14	15	16	17	18	19
20	21	22	23	24	25	26
27	28	29	30			

SEPT

S	M	T	W	T	F	S
			1	2	3	4
5	6	7	8	9	10	11
12	13	14	15	16	17	18
19	20	21	22	23	24	25
26	27	28	29	30		

DEC

S	M	T	W	T	F	S
			1	2	3	4
5	6	7	8	9	10	11
12	13	14	15	16	17	18
19	20	21	22	23	24	25
26	27	28	29	30	31	

7

JAN

S	M	T	W	T	F	S
						1
2	3	4	5	6	7	8
9	10	11	12	13	14	15
16	17	18	19	20	21	22
23	24	25	26	27	28	29
30	31					

APR

S	M	T	W	T	F	S
					1	2
3	4	5	6	7	8	9
10	11	12	13	14	15	16
17	18	19	20	21	22	23
24	25	26	27	28	29	30

JULY

S	M	T	W	T	F	S
					1	2
3	4	5	6	7	8	9
10	11	12	13	14	15	16
17	18	19	20	21	22	23
24	25	26	27	28	29	30
31						

OCT

S	M	T	W	T	F	S
						1
2	3	4	5	6	7	8
9	10	11	12	13	14	15
16	17	18	19	20	21	22
23	24	25	26	27	28	29
30	31					

FEB

S	M	T	W	T	F	S
		1	2	3	4	5
6	7	8	9	10	11	12
13	14	15	16	17	18	19
20	21	22	23	24	25	26
27	28					

MAY

S	M	T	W	T	F	S
1	2	3	4	5	6	7
8	9	10	11	12	13	14
15	16	17	18	19	20	21
22	23	24	25	26	27	28
29	30	31				

AUG

S	M	T	W	T	F	S
	1	2	3	4	5	6
7	8	9	10	11	12	13
14	15	16	17	18	19	20
21	22	23	24	25	26	27
28	29	30	31			

NOV

S	M	T	W	T	F	S
		1	2	3	4	5
6	7	8	9	10	11	12
13	14	15	16	17	18	19
20	21	22	23	24	25	26
27	28	29	30			

MAR

S	M	T	W	T	F	S
		1	2	3	4	5
6	7	8	9	10	11	12
13	14	15	16	17	18	19
20	21	22	23	24	25	26
27	28	29	30	31		

JUNE

S	M	T	W	T	F	S
			1	2	3	4
5	6	7	8	9	10	11
12	13	14	15	16	17	18
19	20	21	22	23	24	25
26	27	28	29	30		

SEPT

S	M	T	W	T	F	S
				1	2	3
4	5	6	7	8	9	10
11	12	13	14	15	16	17
18	19	20	21	22	23	24
25	26	27	28	29	30	

DEC

S	M	T	W	T	F	S
				1	2	3
4	5	6	7	8	9	10
11	12	13	14	15	16	17
18	19	20	21	22	23	24
25	26	27	28	29	30	31

8

JAN

S	M	T	W	T	F	S
1	2	3	4	5	6	7
8	9	10	11	12	13	14
15	16	17	18	19	20	21
22	23	24	25	26	27	28
29	30	31				

APR

S	M	T	W	T	F	S
1	2	3	4	5	6	7
8	9	10	11	12	13	14
15	16	17	18	19	20	21
22	23	24	25	26	27	28
29	30					

JULY

S	M	T	W	T	F	S
1	2	3	4	5	6	7
8	9	10	11	12	13	14
15	16	17	18	19	20	21
22	23	24	25	26	27	28
29	30	31				

OCT

S	M	T	W	T	F	S
	1	2	3	4	5	6
7	8	9	10	11	12	13
14	15	16	17	18	19	20
21	22	23	24	25	26	27
28	29	30	31			

FEB

S	M	T	W	T	F	S
			1	2	3	4
5	6	7	8	9	10	11
12	13	14	15	16	17	18
19	20	21	22	23	24	25
26	27	28	29			

MAY

S	M	T	W	T	F	S
		1	2	3	4	5
6	7	8	9	10	11	12
13	14	15	16	17	18	19
20	21	22	23	24	25	26
27	28	29	30	31		

AUG

S	M	T	W	T	F	S
			1	2	3	4
5	6	7	8	9	10	11
12	13	14	15	16	17	18
19	20	21	22	23	24	25
26	27	28	29	30	31	

NOV

S	M	T	W	T	F	S
				1	2	3
4	5	6	7	8	9	10
11	12	13	14	15	16	17
18	19	20	21	22	23	24
25	26	27	28	29	30	

MAR

S	M	T	W	T	F	S
				1	2	3
4	5	6	7	8	9	10
11	12	13	14	15	16	17
18	19	20	21	22	23	24
25	26	27	28	29	30	31

JUNE

S	M	T	W	T	F	S
					1	2
3	4	5	6	7	8	9
10	11	12	13	14	15	16
17	18	19	20	21	22	23
24	25	26	27	28	29	30

SEPT

S	M	T	W	T	F	S
						1
2	3	4	5	6	7	8
9	10	11	12	13	14	15
16	17	18	19	20	21	22
23	24	25	26	27	28	29
30						

DEC

S	M	T	W	T	F	S
						1
2	3	4	5	6	7	8
9	10	11	12	13	14	15
16	17	18	19	20	21	22
23	24	25	26	27	28	29
30	31					

9

JAN

S	M	T	W	T	F	S
	1	2	3	4	5	6
7	8	9	10	11	12	13
14	15	16	17	18	19	20
21	22	23	24	25	26	27
28	29	30	31			

APR

S	M	T	W	T	F	S
	1	2	3	4	5	6
7	8	9	10	11	12	13
14	15	16	17	18	19	20
21	22	23	24	25	26	27
28	29	30				

JULY

S	M	T	W	T	F	S
	1	2	3	4	5	6
7	8	9	10	11	12	13
14	15	16	17	18	19	20
21	22	23	24	25	26	27
28	29	30	31			

OCT

S	M	T	W	T	F	S
		1	2	3	4	5
6	7	8	9	10	11	12
13	14	15	16	17	18	19
20	21	22	23	24	25	26
27	28	29	30	31		

FEB

S	M	T	W	T	F	S
				1	2	3
4	5	6	7	8	9	10
11	12	13	14	15	16	17
18	19	20	21	22	23	24
25	26	27	28	29		

MAY

S	M	T	W	T	F	S
			1	2	3	4
5	6	7	8	9	10	11
12	13	14	15	16	17	18
19	20	21	22	23	24	25
26	27	28	29	30	31	

AUG

S	M	T	W	T	F	S
				1	2	3
4	5	6	7	8	9	10
11	12	13	14	15	16	17
18	19	20	21	22	23	24
25	26	27	28	29	30	31

NOV

S	M	T	W	T	F	S
					1	2
3	4	5	6	7	8	9
10	11	12	13	14	15	16
17	18	19	20	21	22	23
24	25	26	27	28	29	30

MAR

S	M	T	W	T	F	S
					1	2
3	4	5	6	7	8	9
10	11	12	13	14	15	16
17	18	19	20	21	22	23
24	25	26	27	28	29	30
31						

JUNE

S	M	T	W	T	F	S
						1
2	3	4	5	6	7	8
9	10	11	12	13	14	15
16	17	18	19	20	21	22
23	24	25	26	27	28	29
30						

SEPT

S	M	T	W	T	F	S
1	2	3	4	5	6	7
8	9	10	11	12	13	14
15	16	17	18	19	20	21
22	23	24	25	26	27	28
29	30					

DEC

S	M	T	W	T	F	S
1	2	3	4	5	6	7
8	9	10	11	12	13	14
15	16	17	18	19	20	21
22	23	24	25	26	27	28
29	30	31				

10

JAN

S	M	T	W	T	F	S
		1	2	3	4	5
6	7	8	9	10	11	12
13	14	15	16	17	18	19
20	21	22	23	24	25	26
27	28	29	30	31		

APR

S	M	T	W	T	F	S
		1	2	3	4	5
6	7	8	9	10	11	12
13	14	15	16	17	18	19
20	21	22	23	24	25	26
27	28	29	30			

JULY

S	M	T	W	T	F	S
		1	2	3	4	5
6	7	8	9	10	11	12
13	14	15	16	17	18	19
20	21	22	23	24	25	26
27	28	29	30	31		

OCT

S	M	T	W	T	F	S
			1	2	3	4
5	6	7	8	9	10	11
12	13	14	15	16	17	18
19	20	21	22	23	24	25
26	27	28	29	30	31	

FEB

S	M	T	W	T	F	S
					1	2
3	4	5	6	7	8	9
10	11	12	13	14	15	16
17	18	19	20	21	22	23
24	25	26	27	28	29	

MAY

S	M	T	W	T	F	S
				1	2	3
4	5	6	7	8	9	10
11	12	13	14	15	16	17
18	19	20	21	22	23	24
25	26	27	28	29	30	31

AUG

S	M	T	W	T	F	S
					1	2
3	4	5	6	7	8	9
10	11	12	13	14	15	16
17	18	19	20	21	22	23
24	25	26	27	28	29	30
31						

NOV

S	M	T	W	T	F	S
						1
2	3	4	5	6	7	8
9	10	11	12	13	14	15
16	17	18	19	20	21	22
23	24	25	26	27	28	29
30						

MAR

S	M	T	W	T	F	S
						1
2	3	4	5	6	7	8
9	10	11	12	13	14	15
16	17	18	19	20	21	22
23	24	25	26	27	28	29
30	31					

JUNE

S	M	T	W	T	F	S
1	2	3	4	5	6	7
8	9	10	11	12	13	14
15	16	17	18	19	20	21
22	23	24	25	26	27	28
29	30					

SEPT

S	M	T	W	T	F	S
	1	2	3	4	5	6
7	8	9	10	11	12	13
14	15	16	17	18	19	20
21	22	23	24	25	26	27
28	29	30				

DEC

S	M	T	W	T	F	S
	1	2	3	4	5	6
7	8	9	10	11	12	13
14	15	16	17	18	19	20
21	22	23	24	25	26	27
28	29	30	31			

11

JAN	S	M	T	W	T	F	S
				1	2	3	4
	5	6	7	8	9	10	11
	12	13	14	15	16	17	18
	19	20	21	22	23	24	25
	26	27	28	29	30	31	

APR	S	M	T	W	T	F	S
				1	2	3	4
	5	6	7	8	9	10	11
	12	13	14	15	16	17	18
	19	20	21	22	23	24	25
	26	27	28	29	30		

JULY	S	M	T	W	T	F	S
				1	2	3	4
	5	6	7	8	9	10	11
	12	13	14	15	16	17	18
	19	20	21	22	23	24	25
	26	27	28	29	30	31	

OCT	S	M	T	W	T	F	S
					1	2	3
	4	5	6	7	8	9	10
	11	12	13	14	15	16	17
	18	19	20	21	22	23	24
	25	26	27	28	29	30	31

FEB	S	M	T	W	T	F	S
							1
	2	3	4	5	6	7	8
	9	10	11	12	13	14	15
	16	17	18	19	20	21	22
	23	24	25	26	27	28	29

MAY	S	M	T	W	T	F	S
						1	2
	3	4	5	6	7	8	9
	10	11	12	13	14	15	16
	17	18	19	20	21	22	23
	24	25	26	27	28	29	30
	31						

AUG	S	M	T	W	T	F	S
							1
	2	3	4	5	6	7	8
	9	10	11	12	13	14	15
	16	17	18	19	20	21	22
	23	24	25	26	27	28	29
	30	31					

NOV	S	M	T	W	T	F	S
	1	2	3	4	5	6	7
	8	9	10	11	12	13	14
	15	16	17	18	19	20	21
	22	23	24	25	26	27	28
	29	30					

MAR	S	M	T	W	T	F	S
	1	2	3	4	5	6	7
	8	9	10	11	12	13	14
	15	16	17	18	19	20	21
	22	23	24	25	26	27	28
	29	30	31				

JUNE	S	M	T	W	T	F	S
		1	2	3	4	5	6
	7	8	9	10	11	12	13
	14	15	16	17	18	19	20
	21	22	23	24	25	26	27
	28	29	30				

SEPT	S	M	T	W	T	F	S
			1	2	3	4	5
	6	7	8	9	10	11	12
	13	14	15	16	17	18	19
	20	21	22	23	24	25	26
	27	28	29	30			

DEC	S	M	T	W	T	F	S
			1	2	3	4	5
	6	7	8	9	10	11	12
	13	14	15	16	17	18	19
	20	21	22	23	24	25	26
	27	28	29	30	31		

12

JAN	S	M	T	W	T	F	S
					1	2	3
	4	5	6	7	8	9	10
	11	12	13	14	15	16	17
	18	19	20	21	22	23	24
	25	26	27	28	29	30	31

APR	S	M	T	W	T	F	S
					1	2	3
	4	5	6	7	8	9	10
	11	12	13	14	15	16	17
	18	19	20	21	22	23	24
	25	26	27	28	29	30	

JULY	S	M	T	W	T	F	S
					1	2	3
	4	5	6	7	8	9	10
	11	12	13	14	15	16	17
	18	19	20	21	22	23	24
	25	26	27	28	29	30	31

OCT	S	M	T	W	T	F	S
						1	2
	3	4	5	6	7	8	9
	10	11	12	13	14	15	16
	17	18	19	20	21	22	23
	24	25	26	27	28	29	30
	31						

FEB	S	M	T	W	T	F	S
	1	2	3	4	5	6	7
	8	9	10	11	12	13	14
	15	16	17	18	19	20	21
	22	23	24	25	26	27	28
	29						

MAY	S	M	T	W	T	F	S
							1
	2	3	4	5	6	7	8
	9	10	11	12	13	14	15
	16	17	18	19	20	21	22
	23	24	25	26	27	28	29
	30	31					

AUG	S	M	T	W	T	F	S
	1	2	3	4	5	6	7
	8	9	10	11	12	13	14
	15	16	17	18	19	20	21
	22	23	24	25	26	27	28
	29	30	31				

NOV	S	M	T	W	T	F	S
		1	2	3	4	5	6
	7	8	9	10	11	12	13
	14	15	16	17	18	19	20
	21	22	23	24	25	26	27
	28	29	30				

MAR	S	M	T	W	T	F	S
		1	2	3	4	5	6
	7	8	9	10	11	12	13
	14	15	16	17	18	19	20
	21	22	23	24	25	26	27
	28	29	30	31			

JUNE	S	M	T	W	T	F	S
			1	2	3	4	5
	6	7	8	9	10	11	12
	13	14	15	16	17	18	19
	20	21	22	23	24	25	26
	27	28	29	30			

SEPT	S	M	T	W	T	F	S
				1	2	3	4
	5	6	7	8	9	10	11
	12	13	14	15	16	17	18
	19	20	21	22	23	24	25
	26	27	28	29	30		

DEC	S	M	T	W	T	F	S
				1	2	3	4
	5	6	7	8	9	10	11
	12	13	14	15	16	17	18
	19	20	21	22	23	24	25
	26	27	28	29	30	31	

13

JAN	S	M	T	W	T	F	S
						1	2
	3	4	5	6	7	8	9
	10	11	12	13	14	15	16
	17	18	19	20	21	22	23
	24	25	26	27	28	29	30
	31						

APR	S	M	T	W	T	F	S
						1	2
	3	4	5	6	7	8	9
	10	11	12	13	14	15	16
	17	18	19	20	21	22	23
	24	25	26	27	28	29	30

JULY	S	M	T	W	T	F	S
						1	2
	3	4	5	6	7	8	9
	10	11	12	13	14	15	16
	17	18	19	20	21	22	23
	24	25	26	27	28	29	30
	31						

OCT	S	M	T	W	T	F	S
							1
	2	3	4	5	6	7	8
	9	10	11	12	13	14	15
	16	17	18	19	20	21	22
	23	24	25	26	27	28	29
	30	31					

FEB	S	M	T	W	T	F	S
		1	2	3	4	5	6
	7	8	9	10	11	12	13
	14	15	16	17	18	19	20
	21	22	23	24	25	26	27
	28	29					

MAY	S	M	T	W	T	F	S
	1	2	3	4	5	6	7
	8	9	10	11	12	13	14
	15	16	17	18	19	20	21
	22	23	24	25	26	27	28
	29	30	31				

AUG	S	M	T	W	T	F	S
		1	2	3	4	5	6
	7	8	9	10	11	12	13
	14	15	16	17	18	19	20
	21	22	23	24	25	26	27
	28	29	30	31			

NOV	S	M	T	W	T	F	S
			1	2	3	4	5
	6	7	8	9	10	11	12
	13	14	15	16	17	18	19
	20	21	22	23	24	25	26
	27	28	29	30			

MAR	S	M	T	W	T	F	S
			1	2	3	4	5
	6	7	8	9	10	11	12
	13	14	15	16	17	18	19
	20	21	22	23	24	25	26
	27	28	29	30	31		

JUNE	S	M	T	W	T	F	S
				1	2	3	4
	5	6	7	8	9	10	11
	12	13	14	15	16	17	18
	19	20	21	22	23	24	25
	26	27	28	29	30		

SEPT	S	M	T	W	T	F	S
					1	2	3
	4	5	6	7	8	9	10
	11	12	13	14	15	16	17
	18	19	20	21	22	23	24
	25	26	27	28	29	30	

DEC	S	M	T	W	T	F	S
					1	2	3
	4	5	6	7	8	9	10
	11	12	13	14	15	16	17
	18	19	20	21	22	23	24
	25	26	27	28	29	30	31

14

2000

JAN	S	M	T	W	T	F	S
							1
	2	3	4	5	6	7	8
	9	10	11	12	13	14	15
	16	17	18	19	20	21	22
	23	24	25	26	27	28	29
	30	31					

APR	S	M	T	W	T	F	S
							1
	2	3	4	5	6	7	8
	9	10	11	12	13	14	15
	16	17	18	19	20	21	22
	23	24	25	26	27	28	29
	30						

JULY	S	M	T	W	T	F	S
							1
	2	3	4	5	6	7	8
	9	10	11	12	13	14	15
	16	17	18	19	20	21	22
	23	24	25	26	27	28	29
	30	31					

OCT	S	M	T	W	T	F	S
	1	2	3	4	5	6	7
	8	9	10	11	12	13	14
	15	16	17	18	19	20	21
	22	23	24	25	26	27	28
	29	30	31				

FEB	S	M	T	W	T	F	S
			1	2	3	4	5
	6	7	8	9	10	11	12
	13	14	15	16	17	18	19
	20	21	22	23	24	25	26
	27	28	29				

MAY	S	M	T	W	T	F	S
		1	2	3	4	5	6
	7	8	9	10	11	12	13
	14	15	16	17	18	19	20
	21	22	23	24	25	26	27
	28	29	30	31			

AUG	S	M	T	W	T	F	S
			1	2	3	4	5
	6	7	8	9	10	11	12
	13	14	15	16	17	18	19
	20	21	22	23	24	25	26
	27	28	29	30	31		

NOV	S	M	T	W	T	F	S
				1	2	3	4
	5	6	7	8	9	10	11
	12	13	14	15	16	17	18
	19	20	21	22	23	24	25
	26	27	28	29	30		

MAR	S	M	T	W	T	F	S
				1	2	3	4
	5	6	7	8	9	10	11
	12	13	14	15	16	17	18
	19	20	21	22	23	24	25
	26	27	28	29	30	31	

JUNE	S	M	T	W	T	F	S
					1	2	3
	4	5	6	7	8	9	10
	11	12	13	14	15	16	17
	18	19	20	21	22	23	24
	25	26	27	28	29	30	

SEPT	S	M	T	W	T	F	S
						1	2
	3	4	5	6	7	8	9
	10	11	12	13	14	15	16
	17	18	19	20	21	22	23
	24	25	26	27	28	29	30

DEC	S	M	T	W	T	F	S
						1	2
	3	4	5	6	7	8	9
	10	11	12	13	14	15	16
	17	18	19	20	21	22	23
	24	25	26	27	28	29	30
	31						

SELECTED SPECIAL YEARS: 1965–2005

Intl Cooperation Year: 1965
Intl Book Year: 1972
World Population Year: 1974
Intl Women's Year: 1975
Intl Year of the Child: 1979
Intl Year for Disabled Persons: 1981
World Communications Year: 1983
Intl Youth Year: 1985
Intl Year of Peace: 1986
Intl Year of Shelter for the Homeless: 1987
Year of the Reader: 1987
Year of the Young Reader: 1989
Intl Literacy Year: 1990
US Decade of the Brain: 1990-99
Intl Space Year: 1992
Intl Year for World's Indigenous Peoples: 1993
Intl Year of the Family: 1994
Year for Tolerance: 1995
Intl Year for Eradication of Poverty: 1996
Intl Year of the Ocean: 1998
Intl Year of Older Persons: 1999
Intl Year for the Culture of Peace: 2000
Intl Year of Thanksgiving: 2000
Intl Year of Volunteers: 2001
Intl Year of Dialogue Among Civilizations: 2001
Intl Year of Mobilization Against Racism: 2001
Intl Year of Mountains: 2002
Intl Year of Ecotourism: 2002
Intl Year of Microcredit: 2005

CHINESE CALENDAR

The Chinese lunar year is divided into 12 months of 29 or 30 days. The calendar is adjusted to the length of the solar year by the addition of extra months at regular intervals. The years are arranged in major cycles of 60 years. Each successive year is named after one of 12 animals. These 12-year cycles are continuously repeated.

1996 . . . . Rat
1997 . . . . Ox
1998 . . . . Tiger
1999 . . . . Hare
2000 . . . . Dragon
2001 . . . . Snake
2002 . . . . Horse
2003 . . . . Sheep (Goat)
2004 . . . . Monkey
2005 . . . . Rooster
2006 . . . . Dog
2007 . . . . Pig

LOOKING FORWARD

2001 • 21st Century and Third Millennium of the Christian Era
2002 • Winter Olympics (Salt Lake City)
• Soccer's World Cup (Japan/Korea)
• Euro currency in circulation
2003 • Ohio Statehood Bicentennial
• Wright Brothers' first flight, 100th anniversary
2004 • First successful newspaper in America, 300th anniversary
• US presidential election
• Summer Olympics (Athens, Greece)
2006 • Benjamin Franklin's birth, 300th anniversary
• Woodrow Wilson's birth, 150th anniversary
• Winter Olympics (Turin, Italy)
2007 • Oklahoma Statehood Centennial
• Jamestown Colony, 400th anniversary
• Sputnik launched by USSR, 50th anniversary
• William H. Taft's birth, 150th anniversary
2008 • James Monroe's birth, 250th anniversary
• Andrew Johnson's birth, 200th anniversary
• Theodore Roosevelt's birth, 150th anniversary
• Lyndon Johnson's birth, 100th anniversary
• US presidential election
2009 • Abraham Lincoln's birth, 200th anniversary
2010 • US population projected to be 298,000,000
• 23rd Decennial Census of the US
2011 • Ronald Reagan's birth, 100th anniversary
2012 • Arizona Statehood Centennial
• Louisiana Statehood Bicentennial
• New Mexico Statehood Centennial
• US presidential election
2013 • Richard Nixon's birth, 100th anniversary
• Gerald Ford's birth, 100th anniversary
2015 • US population projected to be 310,000,000
2016 • Indiana Statehood Bicentennial
• US presidential election
2017 • Mississippi Statehood Bicentennial
• John Q. Adams's birth, 250th anniversary
• Andrew Jackson's birth, 250th anniversary
• John F. Kennedy's birth, 100th anniversary
2018 • Illinois Statehood Bicentennial
2019 • Alabama Statehood Bicentennial
• Apollo 11 astronauts walk on moon, 50th anniversary
2020 • US population projected to be 323,000,000
• 24th Decennial Census of the US
• Maine State Bicentennial
• US presidential election
2050 • US population projected to be 394,000,000
• World population of 9 billion predicted
2061 • Halley's comet returns

SOME FACTS ABOUT THE STATES

State	Capital	Popular name	Area (sq. mi.)	State bird	State flower	State tree	Admitted to the Union	Order of Admission
Alabama	Montgomery	Cotton or Yellowhammer State; or Heart of Dixie	51,609	Yellowhammer	Camellia	Southern pine (Longleaf pine)	1819	22
Alaska	Juneau	Last Frontier	591,004	Willow ptarmigan	Forget-me-not	Sitka spruce	1959	49
Arizona	Phoenix	Grand Canyon State	114,000	Cactus wren	Saguaro (giant cactus)	Palo Verde	1912	48
Arkansas	Little Rock	The Natural State	53,187	Mockingbird	Apple blossom	Pine	1836	25
California	Sacramento	Golden State	158,706	California valley quail	Golden poppy	California redwood	1850	31
Colorado	Denver	Centennial State	104,091	Lark bunting	Rocky Mountain columbine	Blue spruce	1876	38
Connecticut	Hartford	Constitution State	5,018	Robin	Mountain laurel	White oak	1788	5
Delaware	Dover	First State	2,044	Blue hen chicken	Peach blossom	American holly	1787	1
Florida	Tallahassee	Sunshine State	58,664	Mockingbird	Orange blossom	Cabbage (sabal) palm	1845	27
Georgia	Atlanta	Empire State of the South	58,910	Brown thrasher	Cherokee rose	Live oak	1788	4
Hawaii	Honolulu	Aloha State	6,471	Nene (Hawaiian goose)	Hibiscus	Kukui	1959	50
Idaho	Boise	Gem State	83,564	Mountain bluebird	Syringa (mock orange)	Western white pine	1890	43
Illinois	Springfield	Prairie State	56,345	Cardinal	Native violet	White oak	1818	21
Indiana	Indianapolis	Hoosier State	36,185	Cardinal	Peony	Tulip tree or yellow poplar	1816	19
Iowa	Des Moines	Hawkeye State	56,275	Eastern goldfinch	Wild rose	Oak	1846	29
Kansas	Topeka	Sunflower State	82,277	Western meadowlark	Sunflower	Cottonwood	1861	34
Kentucky	Frankfort	Bluegrass State	40,409	Kentucky cardinal	Goldenrod	Kentucky coffeetree	1792	15
Louisiana	Baton Rouge	Pelican State	47,752	Pelican	Magnolia	Bald cypress	1812	18
Maine	Augusta	Pine Tree State	33,265	Chickadee	White pine cone and tassel	White pine	1820	23
Maryland	Annapolis	Old Line State	10,577	Baltimore oriole	Black-eyed Susan	White oak	1788	7
Massachusetts	Boston	Bay State	8,284	Chickadee	Mayflower	American elm	1788	6
Michigan	Lansing	Wolverine State	58,527	Robin	Apple blossom	White pine	1837	26
Minnesota	St. Paul	North Star State	84,402	Common loon	Pink and white lady's-slipper	Norway, or red, pine	1858	32
Mississippi	Jackson	Magnolia State	47,689	Mockingbird	Magnolia	Magnolia	1817	20
Missouri	Jefferson City	Show Me State	69,697	Bluebird	Hawthorn	Flowering dogwood	1821	24
Montana	Helena	Treasure State	147,046	Western meadowlark	Bitterroot	Ponderosa pine	1889	41
Nebraska	Lincoln	Cornhusker State	77,355	Western meadowlark	Goldenrod	Cottonwood	1867	37
Nevada	Carson City	Silver State	110,540	Mountain bluebird	Sagebrush	Single-leaf piñon	1864	36
New Hampshire	Concord	Granite State	9,304	Purple finch	Purple lilac	White birch	1788	9
New Jersey	Trenton	Garden State	7,787	Eastern goldfinch	Purple violet	Red oak	1787	3
New Mexico	Santa Fe	Land of Enchantment	121,593	Roadrunner	Yucca flower	Piñon, or nut pine	1912	47
New York	Albany	Empire State	49,108	Bluebird	Rose	Sugar maple	1788	11
North Carolina	Raleigh	Tar Heel State or Old North State	52,669	Cardinal	Dogwood	Pine	1789	12
North Dakota	Bismarck	Peace Garden State	70,702	Western meadowlark	Wild prairie rose	American elm	1889	39

State	Capital	Popular name	Area (sq. mi.)	State bird	State flower	State tree	Admitted to the Union	Order of Admission
Ohio	Columbus	Buckeye State	41,330	Cardinal	Scarlet carnation	Buckeye	1803	17
Oklahoma	Oklahoma City	Sooner State	69,956	Scissortail flycatcher	Mistletoe	Redbud	1907	46
Oregon	Salem	Beaver State	97,073	Western meadowlark	Oregon grape	Douglas fir	1859	33
Pennsylvania	Harrisburg	Keystone State	45,308	Ruffed grouse	Mountain laurel	Hemlock	1787	2
Rhode Island	Providence	Ocean State	1,212	Rhode Island Red	Violet	Red maple	1790	13
South Carolina	Columbia	Palmetto State	31,113	Carolina wren	Carolina jessamine	Palmetto	1788	8
South Dakota	Pierre	Sunshine State	77,116	Ring-necked pheasant	American pasqueflower	Black Hills spruce	1889	40
Tennessee	Nashville	Volunteer State	42,114	Mockingbird	Iris	Tulip poplar	1796	16
Texas	Austin	Lone Star State	266,807	Mockingbird	Bluebonnet	Pecan	1845	28
Utah	Salt Lake City	Beehive State	84,899	Sea Gull	Sego lily	Blue spruce	1896	45
Vermont	Montpelier	Green Mountain State	9,614	Hermit thrush	Red clover	Sugar maple	1791	14
Virginia	Richmond	Old Dominion	40,767	Cardinal	Dogwood	Dogwood	1788	10
Washington	Olympia	Evergreen State	68,139	Willow goldfinch	Coast rhododendron	Western hemlock	1889	42
West Virginia	Charleston	Mountain State	24,231	Cardinal	Rhododendron	Sugar maple	1863	35
Wisconsin	Madison	Badger State	56,153	Robin	Wood violet	Sugar maple	1848	30
Wyoming	Cheyenne	Equality State	97,809	Meadowlark	Indian paintbrush	Cottonwood	1890	44

STATE & TERRITORY ABBREVIATIONS: UNITED STATES

Alabama . . . . . AL
Alaska . . . . . AK
Arizona . . . . . AZ
Arkansas . . . . . AR
American Samoa . . . . . AS
California . . . . . CA
Colorado . . . . . CO
Connecticut . . . . . CT
Delaware . . . . . DE
District of Columbia . . . . . DC
Florida . . . . . FL
Georgia . . . . . GA
Guam . . . . . GU
Hawaii . . . . . HI
Idaho . . . . . ID
Illinois IL
Indiana . . . . . IN
Iowa . . . . . IA
Kansas . . . . . KS
Kentucky . . . . . KY
Louisiana . . . . . LA
Maine . . . . . ME
Maryland . . . . . MD
Massachusetts . . . . . MA
Michigan . . . . . MI
Minnesota . . . . . MN
Mississippi . . . . . MS
Missouri . . . . . MO
Montana . . . . . MT
Nebraska . . . . . NE
Nevada . . . . . NV
New Hampshire . . . . . NH
New Jersey . . . . . NJ
New Mexico . . . . . NM
New York . . . . . NY
North Carolina . . . . . NC
North Dakota . . . . . ND
Ohio . . . . . OH
Oklahoma . . . . . OK
Oregon . . . . . OR
Pennsylvania . . . . . PA
Puerto Rico . . . . . PR
Rhode Island . . . . . RI
South Carolina . . . . . SC
South Dakota . . . . . SD
Tennessee . . . . . TN
Texas . . . . . TX
Utah . . . . . UT
Vermont . . . . . VT
Virginia . . . . . VA
Virgin Islands VI
Washington . . . . . WA
West Virginia . . . . . WV
Wisconsin . . . . . WI
Wyoming . . . . . WY

PROVINCE & TERRITORY ABBREVIATIONS: CANADA

Alberta . . . . . AB
British Columbia . . . . . BC
Manitoba . . . . . MB
New Brunswick . . . . . NB
Newfoundland . . . . . NF
Nova Scotia . . . . . NS
Ontario . . . . . ON
Prince Edward Island . . . . . PE
Quebec . . . . . QC
Saskatchewan . . . . . SK
Yukon Territory . . . . . YT
Northwest Territories . . . . . NT

SOME FACTS ABOUT CANADA

Province/Territory	Capital	Population*	Flower	Land/Fresh Water (sq. mi.)	Total Area
Alberta	Edmonton	2,774,512	Wild rose	400,423/10,437	410,860
British Columbia	Victoria	3,835,748	Pacific dogwood	578,230/11,227	589,458
Manitoba	Winnipeg	1,141,727	Prairie crocus	340,834/63,129	403,964
New Brunswick	Fredericton	761,873	Purple violet	44,797/835	45,633
Newfoundland	St. John's	571,192	Pitcher plant	230,219/21,147	251,367
Northwest Territories	Yellowknife	66,164	Mountain avens	2,017,306/82,829	2,100,136
Nova Scotia	Halifax	941,235	Mayflower	32,835/1,647	34,482
Ontario	Toronto	11,209,474	White trillium	553,788/110,229	664,012
Prince Edward Island	Charlottetown	137,316	Lady's-slipper	3,515/0	3,515
Quebec	Quebec City	7,366,883	White garden lily	843,109/114,269	957,379
Saskatchewan	Regina	1,020,138	Red lily	354,365/51,347	405,712
Yukon Territory	Whitehorse	31,107	Fireweed	297,050/2,784	299,835

*1996

SOME FACTS ABOUT THE PRESIDENTS

	Name	Birthdate, Place	Party	Tenure	Died	First Lady	Vice President
1.	George Washington	2/22/1732, Westmoreland Cnty, VA	Federalist	1789–1797	12/14/1799	Martha Dandridge Custis	John Adams
2.	John Adams	10/30/1735, Braintree (Quincy), MA	Federalist	1797–1801	7/4/1826	Abigail Smith	Thomas Jefferson
3.	Thomas Jefferson	4/13/1743, Shadwell, VA	Democratic-Republican	1801–1809	7/4/1826	Martha Wayles Skelton	Aaron Burr, 1801–05 George Clinton, 1805–09
4.	James Madison	3/16/1751, Port Conway, VA	Democratic-Republican	1809–1817	6/28/1836	Dolley Payne Todd	George Clinton, 1809–12 Elbridge Gerry, 1813–14(?)
5.	James Monroe	4/28/1758, Westmoreland Cnty, VA	Democratic-Republican	1817–1825	7/4/1831	Elizabeth Kortright	Daniel D. Tompkins
6.	John Q. Adams	7/11/1767, Braintree (Quincy), MA	Democratic-Republican	1825–1829	2/23/1848	Louisa Catherine Johnson	John C. Calhoun
7.	Andrew Jackson	3/15/1767, Waxhaw Settlement, SC	Democrat	1829–1837	6/8/1845	Mrs. Rachel Donelson Robards	John C. Calhoun, 1829–32 Martin Van Buren, 1833–37
8.	Martin Van Buren	12/5/1782, Kinderhook, NY	Democrat	1837–1841	7/24/1862	Hannah Hoes	Richard M. Johnson
9.	William H. Harrison	2/9/1773, Charles City Cnty, VA	Whig	1841	4/4/1841†	Anna Symmes	John Tyler
10.	John Tyler	3/29/1790, Charles City Cnty, VA	Whig	1841–1845	1/18/1862	Letitia Christian Julia Gardiner	
11.	James K. Polk	11/2/1795, near Pineville, NC	Democrat	1845–1849	6/15/1849	Sarah Childress	George M. Dallas
12.	Zachary Taylor	11/24/1784, Barboursville, VA	Whig	1849–1850	7/9/1850†	Margaret Mackall Smith	Millard Fillmore
13.	Millard Fillmore	1/7/1800, Locke, NY	Whig	1850–1853	3/8/1874	Abigail Powers Mrs. Caroline Carmichael McIntosh	
14.	Franklin Pierce	11/23/1804, Hillsboro, NH	Democrat	1853–1857	10/8/1869	Jane Means Appleton	William R. D. King
15.	James Buchanan	4/23/1791, near Mercersburg, PA	Democrat	1857–1861	6/1/1868		John C. Breckinridge

16.	Abraham Lincoln	2/12/1809, near Hodgenville, KY	Republican	1861–1865	4/15/1865*	Mary Todd	Hannibal Hamlin, 1861–65 Andrew Johnson, 1865
17.	Andrew Johnson	12/29/1808, Raleigh, NC	Democrat	1865–1869	7/31/1875	Eliza McCardle	
18.	Ulysses S. Grant	4/27/1822, Point Pleasant, OH	Republican	1869–1877	7/23/1885	Julia Boggs Dent	Schuyler Colfax, 1869–73 Henry Wilson, 1873–75
19.	Rutherford B. Hayes	10/4/1822, Delaware, OH	Republican	1877–1881	1/17/1893	Lucy Ware Webb	William A. Wheeler
20.	James A. Garfield	11/19/1831, Orange, OH	Republican	1881	9/19/1881*	Lucretia Rudolph	Chester A. Arthur
21.	Chester A. Arthur	10/5/1829, Fairfield, VT	Republican	1881–1885	11/18/1886	Ellen Lewis Herndon	
22.	Grover Cleveland	3/18/1837, Caldwell, NJ	Democrat	1885–1889	6/24/1908	Frances Folsom	Thomas A. Hendricks, 1885
23.	Benjamin Harrison	8/20/1833, North Bend, OH	Republican	1889–1893	3/13/1901	Caroline Lavinia Scott Mrs. Mary Dimmick	Levi P. Morton
24.	Grover Cleveland	3/18/1837, Caldwell, NJ	Democrat	1893–1897	6/24/1908	Frances Folsom	Adlai Stevenson, 1893–97
25.	William McKinley	1/29/1843, Niles, OH	Republican	1897–1901	9/14/1901*	Ida Saxton	Garret A. Hobart, 1897–99 Theodore Roosevelt, 1901
26.	Theodore Roosevelt	10/27/1858, New York, NY	Republican	1901–1909	1/6/1919	Alice Hathaway Lee Edith Kermit Carow	Charles W. Fairbanks
27.	William H. Taft	9/15/1857, Cincinnati, OH	Republican	1909–1913	3/8/1930	Helen Herron	James S. Sherman
28.	Woodrow Wilson	12/28/1856, Staunton, VA	Democrat	1913–1921	2/3/1924	Ellen Louise Axson Edith Bolling Galt	Thomas R. Marshall
29.	Warren G. Harding	11/2/1865, near Corsica, OH	Republican	1921–1923	8/2/1923†	Florence Kling DeWolfe	Calvin Coolidge
30.	Calvin Coolidge	7/4/1872, Plymouth Notch, VT	Republican	1923–1929	1/5/1933	Grace Anna Goodhue	Charles G. Dawes
31.	Herbert C. Hoover	8/10/1874, West Branch, IA	Republican	1929–1933	10/20/1964	Lou Henry	Charles Curtis
32.	Franklin D. Roosevelt	1/30/1882, Hyde Park, NY	Democrat	1933–1945	4/12/1945†	Eleanor Roosevelt	John N. Garner, 1933–41 Henry A. Wallace, 1941–45 Harry S. Truman, 1945
33.	Harry S. Truman	5/8/1884, Lamar, MO	Democrat	1945–1953	12/26/1972	Elizabeth Virginia (Bess) Wallace	Alben W. Barkley
34.	Dwight D. Eisenhower	10/14/1890, Denison, TX	Republican	1953–1961	3/28/1969	Mamie Geneva Doud	Richard M. Nixon
35.	John F. Kennedy	5/29/1917, Brookline, MA	Democrat	1961–1963	11/22/1963*	Jacqueline Lee Bouvier	Lyndon B. Johnson
36.	Lyndon B. Johnson	8/27/1908, near Stonewall, TX	Democrat	1963–1969	1/22/1973	Claudia Alta (Lady Bird) Taylor	Hubert H. Humphrey
37.	Richard M. Nixon	1/9/1913, Yorba Linda, CA	Republican	1969–1974**	4/22/1994	Thelma Catherine (Pat) Ryan	Spiro T. Agnew, 1969–73 Gerald R. Ford, 1973–74
38.	Gerald R. Ford	7/14/1913, Omaha, NE	Republican	1974–1977		Elizabeth (Betty) Bloomer	Nelson A. Rockefeller
39.	James E. Carter, Jr	10/1/1924, Plains, GA	Democrat	1977–1981		Rosalynn Smith	Walter F. Mondale
40.	Ronald W. Reagan	2/6/1911, Tampico, IL	Republican	1981–1989		Nancy Davis	George H. W. Bush
41.	George H. W. Bush	6/12/1924, Milton, MA	Republican	1989–1993		Barbara Pierce	J. Danforth Quayle
42.	William J. Clinton	8/19/1946, Hope, AR	Democrat	1993–2001		Hillary Rodham	Albert Gore, Jr.
43.	George W. Bush	7/6/1946, New Haven, CT	Republican	2001–		Laura Welch	Richard Cheney

*assassinated while in office
**resigned Aug 9, 1974
† died while in office—nonviolently

Sources: *World Book*, 1991 Edition; *Encyclopedia Americana*, 1990 Edition; *Collier's Encyclopedia*, 1994 Edition

2001 AMERICAN LIBRARY ASSOCIATION AWARDS FOR CHILDREN'S BOOKS

NEWBERY MEDAL

For most distinguished contribution to American literature for children published in 2000:

Richard Peck, author, *A Year Down Yonder* (Dial Books for Young Readers, 0-8037-2518-3, $16.99 Ages 12 & up)

Honor Books

Joan Bauer, author, *Hope Was Here* (G. P. Putnam's Sons, 0-399-23142-0, $16.99 Gr. 8 & up)

Sharon Creech, author, *The Wanderer* (HarperCollins, 0-06-027730-0, $15.95 Gr. 5–9)

Kate DiCamillo, author, *Because of Winn-Dixie* (Candlewick Press, 0-7636-0776-2, $15.99 Ages 8–12)

Jack Gantos, author, *Joey Pigza Loses Control* (Farrar, Straus and Giroux, 0-374-39989-1, $16 Ages 9–12)

CALDECOTT MEDAL

For most distinguished American picture book for children published in 2000:

David Small, illustrator, *So You Want to Be President?*, written by Judith St. George (Philomel Books, 0-399-23407-1, $17.99 Ages 7–12)

Honor Books

Christopher Bing, illustrator, *Casey At the Bat*, written by Ernest Lawrence Thayer (Handprint Books, 1-929-76609-9, $17.95, Gr. 3 & up)

Betsy Lewin, illustrator, *Click Clack Moo: Cows That Type*, written by Doreen Cronin (Simon & Schuster, 0-689-83213-3, $15 Ages 5–7)

Ian Falconer, author and illustrator, *Olivia* (Simon & Schuster, 0-689-82953-1, $16 Ages 3–7)

CORETTA SCOTT KING AWARD

For outstanding books by African American authors:

Jacqueline Woodson, author, *Miracle's Boys* (G. P. Putnam's Sons, 0-399-23113-7, $15.99 Gr. 6–10)

Honor Book

Andrea Davis Pinkney, author, *Let It Shine! Stories of Black Women Freedom Fighters*, illustrated by Stephen Alcorn (Harcourt/Gulliver Books, 0-15-201005-X, $20 Gr. 4–7)

For outstanding books by African American illustrators:

Bryan Collier, author and illustrator, *Uptown* (Henry Holt, 0-8050-5721-8, $15.95 Ages 5–8)

Honor Books:

Bryan Collier, author and illustrator, *Freedom River* (Hyperion, 0-7868-0350-9, $14.99 Ages 7–10)

E. B. Lewis, illustrator, *Virgie Goes to School with Us Boys*, written by Elizabeth Fitzgerald Howard (Simon & Schuster, 0-689-80076-2, $16 Ages 5–9)

R. Gregory Christie, illustrator, *Only Passing Through: The Story of Sojourner Truth*, written by Anne Rockwell (Random House, 0-679-89186-2, $16.95 Ages 9–12)

MICHAEL L. PRINTZ AWARD

For excellence in writing literature for young adults:

David Almond, author, *Kit's Wilderness* (Delacorte Press, 0-385-32665-3, $15.95 Gr. 5–9)

Honor Books

Carolyn Coman, author, *Many Stones* (Front Street Press, 1-886910-55-3, $15.95 Gr. 8 & up)

Carol Plum-Ucci, author, *The Body of Christopher Creed* (Harcourt, 0-15-202388-7, $17 Gr. 8 & up)

Louise Rennison, author, *Angus, Thongs, and Full-Frontal Snogging* (HarperCollins, 0-06-028871-X, $15.89 Ages 12 & up)

ROBERT F. SIBERT AWARD

For most distinguished informational book for children published in 2000:

Marc Aronson, author, *Sir Walter Ralegh and the Quest for El Dorado* (Clarion Books, 0-395-84827-X, $20 Gr. 7 & up)

Honor Books

Joan Dash, author, *The Longitude Prize*, illustrated by Dusan Petricic (Farrar, Straus and Giroux, 0-374-34636-4, $16 Gr. 6 & up)

Jim Murphy, author, *Blizzard!* (Scholastic Press, 0-590-67309-2, $18.95, Gr. 5 & up)

Sophie Webb, author, *My Season with Penguins: An Antarctic Journal* (Houghton Mifflin, 0-395-92291-7, $15 Gr. 4–8)

Judd Winick, author and illustrator, *Pedro and Me: Friendship, Loss, and What I Learned* (Henry Holt, 0-8050-6403-6, $15 Gr. 9 & up)

MARGARET A. EDWARDS AWARD

For lifetime achievement in writing books for young adults:

Robert Lipsyte, recipient

LAURA INGALLS WILDER MEDAL

For an author or illustrator whose books, published in the United States, have made, over a period of years, a substantial and lasting contribution to literature for children:

Milton Meltzer, recipient

MILDRED L. BATCHELDER AWARD

For the best children's book first published in a foreign language in a foreign country and subsequently translated into English for publication in the US:

Scholastic Press/Arthur A. Levine, publisher, *Samir and Yonatan*, written by Daniella Carmi, translated by Yael Lotan (0-439-13504-4, $15.95 Gr. 4–8)

Honor Book

David R. Godine, publisher, *Ultimate Game*, written by Christian Lehmann, translated by William Rodarmor (1-56792-107-8, $16.95, Gr. 9 & up)

ANDREW CARNEGIE MEDAL FOR EXCELLENCE IN CHILDREN'S VIDEO

Paul R. Gagne, *Antarctic Antics* (Weston Woods, Gr. K–3)

MAY HILL ARBUTHNOT LECTURE AWARD

Philip Pullman, recipient

RESOURCES

PROFESSIONAL READING

Financial Tips for Teachers, by Alan Jay Weiss and Larry Strauss. 7th edition. Lowell House, 0-7373-0302-6, $13.95.

Unbelievably Good Deals That You Absolutely Can't Get Unless You're a Teacher, by Barry Harrington and Beth Christensen. 2nd edition. Contemporary Books, 0-8092-2877-7, $12.95.

BIBLIOGRAPHIES

Exploring Science in the Library: Resources and Activities for Young People, edited by Maria Sosa and Tracy Gath. American Library Association, 0-8389-0768-7, $32.

Hands-on supplemental activities for science instruction in the library with an annotated bibliography of science trade books.

Literature Connection to American History, K-6: Resources to Enhance and Entice, by Lynda G. Adamson. Libraries Unlimited, 1-56308-502-X, $33.50.

A similar volume by Adamson covers books appropriate for grades 7-12.

Great Books for African American Children, by Pamela Toussaint. Plume, 0-45-228044-3, $12.95.

Once Upon a Heroine: 450 Books for Girls to Love, by Alison Cooper-Mullin and Jennifer Marmaduke Coye. Contemporary Books, 0-8092-3020-8, $16.95.

ACTIVITY BOOKS

Library Celebrations, by Cyndy Dingwall. Highsmith, 1-5795-0027-7, $16.95.

Creative programs for Children's Book Week, National Library Week, author visits and other events that celebrate books and libraries.

HOLIDAY BOOKS

The Latino Holiday Book: From Cinco de Mayo to Dia de los Muertos: The Celebrations and Traditions of Hispanic-Americans, by Valerie Menard. Marlowe, 1-5692-4646-7, $15.95.

Halloween Program Sourcebook, edited by Sue Ellen Thompson. Omnigraphics, 0-7808-0388-4, $48.

Thanksgiving Program Sourcebook, edited by Sue Ellen Thompson. Omnigraphics, 0-7808-0403-1, $48.

PERIODICALS

These publications suggest books or websites related to specific themes for grades K–8.

Book Links: Connecting Books, Libraries, and Classrooms. 6/year at $25.95. American Library Association, 50 E Huron St, Chicago, IL 60611. Web: www.ala.org/BookLinks.

Web Feet K–8: Subject Guide to Web Sites & Additional Resources. 12/year at $165. Rock Hill Communications, 14 Rock Hill Rd, Bala Cynwyd, PA 19004. Web: www.webfeetguides.com.

WEBSITES

Ben's Guide to US Government for Kids: bensguide.gpo.gov

Information about the branches of government, the election process and more for grades K–2, 3–5, 6–8 and 9–12. Also links to other government websites for children.

US Government site: www.firstgov.gov

Serves as an index to hundreds of government websites.

CIA World Factbook: www.odci.gov/cia/publications/factbook/index.html.

Detailed information about every country of the world.

United Nations Infonation: www.un.org/Pubs/CyberSchoolBus/infonation/e_infonation.htm.

Statistical information on 185 nations.

Fifty States and Capitals: www.50states.com

Information on US states and territories, plus many relevant links.

Consumer Information Center: www.pueblo.gsa.gov.

Many helpful government pamphlets available online.

Libraries: sunsite.berkeley.edu/Libweb.

Links to the catalogs of more than 2,000 libraries in 70 countries can be found here.

The American Memory Project at the Library of Congress: memory.loc.gov/ammem/amhome.html.

Thousands of photographs and the text of documents and pamphlets suitable for upper elementary and middle school students.

Ask ERIC: www.askeric.org.

The Virtual Library section of this site contains lesson plans, links to the companion study guides to TV series and access to the journal literature and research reports in the ERIC (Education Resources Information Center) system.

Oyate Native American site: www.oyate.org.

This site features evaluations of books and other materials for children that provide honest portrayals of Native Americans.

Center for the Study of Books in Spanish for Children and Adolescents site: www.csusm.edu/cwis/campus_centers/csb.

Evaluations of more than 5,000 books in Spanish for youth.

Literature Study Guides: glencoe.com/sec/literature/litlibrary

Study guides for more than 50 novels for middle schoolers and up.

PBS site: www.pbs.org.

This site has information on kids' favorite TV shows, such as "Arthur" and "Clifford." "Reading Rainbow" is also found here. Bill Nye, the Science Guy, has his own website at nyelabs.kcts.org.

CBC site: www.cbc4kids.ca

This site from the Canadian Broadcasting Corporation has stuff for kids on both sides of the border.

How Stuff Works site: www.howstuffworks.com

Simple explanations of how airplanes fly or refrigerator work.

MathStories: www.mathstories.com

More than 4,000 math word problems for grades 1–8.

Author sites.

Many children's authors and illustrators have websites. Dav Pilkey, Virginia Hamilton and Jan Brett, for example, have interesting ones. For links to these sites, go to the Children's Literature Web Guide at www.acs.ucalgary.ca/~dkbrown/authors.html or Kay Vandergrift's Learning about the Author and Illustrator Pages at www.scils.rutgers.edu/special.kay/author.html. For scheduled chats with authors, go to Scholastic's Authors Online site: teacher.scholastic.com/authorsandbooks/authors/index.htm.

Corporate websites.

These sites sometimes have useful information for teachers. For example, look at www.crayola.com.

STATE GOVERNORS/US SENATORS/US SUPREME COURT

GOVERNORS

Name(Party, State)

Don Siegelman (D, AL)
Tony Knowles (D, AK)
Jane Dee Hull (R, AZ)
Mike Huckabee (R, AR)
Gray Davis (D, CA)
Bill Owens (R, CO)
John Rowland (R, CT)
Ruth Ann Minner (D, DE)
Jeb Bush (R, FL)
Roy Barnes (D, GA)
Ben Cayetano (D, HI)
Dirk Kempthorne (R, ID)
George Ryan (R, IL)
Frank O'Bannon (D, IN)
Tom Vilsack (D, IA)
Bill Graves (R, KS)
Paul E. Patton (D, KY)
Mike Foster (R, LA)
Angus King, Jr (I, ME)
Parris Glendening (D, MD)
Paul Celluci (R, MA)
John Engler (R, MI)
Jesse Ventura (I, MN)
Ronnie Musgrove (D, MS)
Bob Holden (D, MO)
Judy Martz (R, MT)
Mike Johanns (R, NE)
Kenny Guinn (R, NV)
Jeanne Shaheen (D, NH)
Donald T. DiFrancesco (R, NJ)*
Gary Johnson (R, NM)
George Pataki (R, NY)
Mike Easley (D, NC)
John Hoeven (R, ND)
Bob Taft (R, OH)
Frank Keating (R, OK)
John Kitzhaber (D, OR)
Thomas J. Ridge (R, PA)
Lincoln Almond (R, RI)
Jim Hodges (D, SC)
William Janklow (R, SD)
Don Sundquist (R, TN)
Rick Perry (R, TX)
Mike Leavitt (R, UT)
Howard Dean (D, VT)
James Gilmore (R, VA)*
Gary Locke (D, WA)
Bob Wise (D, WV)
Scott McCallum (R, WI)
Jim Geringer (R, WY)

*Denotes governorship or senate seat up for reelection at press time.

SENATORS

Name (Party, State)

Jeff Sessions (R, AL)
Richard C. Shelby (R, AL)
Ted Stevens (R, AK)
Frank H. Murkowski (R, AK)
Jon Kyl (R, AZ)
John McCain (R, AZ)
Blanche Lambert Lincoln (D, AR)
Tim Hutchinson (R, AR)
Dianne Feinstein (D, CA)
Barbara Boxer (D, CA)
Wayne Allard (R, CO)
Ben Nighthorse Campbell (R, CO)
Christopher J. Dodd (D, CT)
Joseph I. Lieberman (D, CT)
Thomas Carper (D, DE)
Joseph R. Biden, Jr (D, DE)
Robert Graham (D, FL)
Bill Nelson (D, FL)
Max Cleland (D, GA)
Zell Miller (D, GA)
Daniel K. Inouye (D, HI)
Daniel K. Akaka (D, HI)
Larry E. Craig (R, ID)
Michael Crapo (R, ID)
Richard J. Durbin (D, IL)
Peter Fitzgerald (R, IL)
Richard G. Lugar (R, IN)
Evan Bayh (D, IN)
Charles E. Grassley (R, IA)
Tom Harkin (D, IA)
Sam Brownback (R, KS)
Pat Roberts (R, KS)
Jim Bunning (R, KY)
Mitch McConnell (R, KY)
Mary L. Landrieu (D, LA)
John B. Breaux (D, LA)
Susan M. Collins (R, ME)
Olympia J. Snowe (R, ME)
Paul S. Sarbanes (D, MD)
Barbara A. Mikulski (D, MD)
Edward M. Kennedy (D, MA)
John F. Kerry (D, MA)
Debbie Stabenow (D, MI)
Carl Levin (D, MI)
Mark Dayton (D, MN)
Paul D. Wellstone (D, MN)
Thad Cochran (R, MS)
Trent Lott (R, MS)
Jean Carnahan (D, MO)
Christopher S. Bond (R, MO)
Max S. Baucus (D, MT)
Conrad Burns (R, MT)
Chuck Hagel (R, NE)
Ben Nelson (D, NE)
Harry M. Reid (D, NV)
John Ensign (R, NV)
Robert C. Smith (R, NH)
Judd Gregg (R, NH)
Robert G. Torricelli (D, NJ)
Jon Corzine (D, NJ)
Pete V. Domenici (R, NM)
Jeff Bingaman (D, NM)
Hillary Rodham Clinton (D, NY)
Charles E. Schumer (D, NY)
Jesse A. Helms (R, NC)
John Edwards (D, NC)
Kent Conrad (D, ND)
Byron L. Dorgan (D, ND)
George Voinovich (R, OH)
Mike DeWine (R, OH)
James M. Inhofe (R, OK)
Don Nickles (R, OK)
Gordon Smith (R, OR)
Ron Wyden (D, OR)
Arlen Specter (R, PA)
Rick Santorum (R, PA)
Jack Reed (D, RI)
Lincoln Chafee (R, RI)
Strom Thurmond (R, SC)
Ernest F. Hollings (D, SC)
Tim Johnson (D, SD)
Thomas A. Daschle (D, SD)
William Frist (R, TN)
Fred D. Thompson (R, TN)
Phil Gramm (R, TX)
Kay Bailey Hutchison (R, TX)
Orrin G. Hatch (R, UT)
Robert F. Bennett (R, UT)
Patrick J. Leahy (D, VT)
James M. Jeffords (R, VT)
John W. Warner (R, VA)
George Allen (R, VA)
Maria Cantwell (D, WA)
Patty Murray (D, WA)
Robert C. Byrd (D, WV)
John D. Rockefeller IV (D, WV)
Herbert H. Kohl (D, WI)
Russell D. Feingold (D, WI)
Michael B. Enzi (R, WY)
Craig Thomas (R, WY)

SUPREME COURT JUSTICES

Name (Appointed by, Year)

William H. Rehnquist, Chief Justice (Reagan, 1986)
John P. Stevens (Ford, 1975)
Sandra Day O'Connor (Reagan, 1981)
Antonin Scalia (Reagan, 1986)
Anthony M. Kennedy (Reagan, 1988)
David H. Souter (G.H.W. Bush, 1990)
Clarence Thomas (G.H.W. Bush, 1991)
Ruth Bader Ginsburg (Clinton, 1993)
Stephen G. Breyer (Clinton, 1994)

ALPHABETICAL INDEX

Events are generally listed under key words; events that can be attended are also listed under the states or countries where they are to be held. Many broad categories have been created, including African American, Agriculture, Animals, Aviation, Books, Civil Rights, Civil War, Computer, Constitution, Disabled, Earthquakes, Education, Employment, Environment, Ethnic Observances, Fire, Food and Beverages, Health and Welfare, Human Relations, Library/Librarians, Literature, Music, Native American, Parades, Poetry, Reading, Revolution (American), Safety, Science/Technology, Space Milestones, Storytelling, Television, Time, United Nations, United States, World War I, World War II, Women, names of sports, etc. The index indicates only the initial date for each event. See the chronology for inclusive dates of events lasting more than one day.

Aardema, Verna: Birth Anniv, June 6
Aaron, Hank: Birth, Feb 5
Aaron, Hank: Home Run Record: Anniv, Apr 8
Abbott and Costello Show TV Premiere: Anniv, Dec 5
Abdul-Jabbar, Kareem: Birth, Apr 16
Abolition Soc Founded, First American: Anniv, Apr 14
Abraham, Spencer: Birth, June 12
Absolutely Incredible Kid Day, Mar 21
Academy Awards, First: Anniv, May 16
Acadia Natl Park Established: Anniv, Jan 1
Accession of Queen Elizabeth II: Anniv, Feb 6
According to Hoyle Day, Aug 29
Accordion Awareness Month, Natl, June 1
Ackerman, Diane: Birth, Oct 7
Ada, Alma Flor: Birth, Jan 3
Adams, Abigail: Birth Anniv, Nov 22
Adams, Ansel: Birth Anniv, Feb 20
Adams, John: Birth Anniv, Oct 30
Adams, John Quincy: Birth Anniv, July 11
Adams, John Quincy: Returns to Congress, Mar 4
Adams, Louisa Catherine Johnson: Birth Anniv, Feb 12
Adams, Richard: Birth, May 9
Adams, Samuel: Birth Anniv, Sept 27
Addams Family TV Premiere: Anniv, Sept 18
Addams, Jane: Birth Anniv, Sept 6
Adler, David A.: Birth, Apr 10
Adoff, Arnold: Birth, July 16
Adopt-a-Shelter Dog Month, Oct 1
Adoption Month, Natl (Pres Proc), Nov 1
Adoption Week, Natl, Nov 18
Advent, First Sunday of, Dec 2
Affleck, Ben: Birth, Aug 15
Afghanistan,
  Independence Day, **Aug 19**
  Islamic State's Victory Day, **Apr 28**
AFL Founded: Anniv, Dec 8
AFL-CIO Founded: Anniv, Dec 5
African Freedom Day, May 25
African Natl Congress Ban Lifted, Feb 2
African American. See also King, Martin Luther, Jr.,
  African American History Month, Natl (Pres Proc), **Feb 1**
  African American Read-In, **Feb 3**
  Amistad Seized: Anniv, **Aug 29**
  Banneker, Benjamin: Birth Anniv, **Nov 9**
  Black History Month, **Feb 1**
  Black Page Appointed US House: Anniv, **Apr 9**
  Black Poetry Day, **Oct 17**
  Black Press Day: Anniv of First Black Newspaper in US, **Mar 16**
  Black Senate Page Appointed: Anniv, **Apr 8**
  Blacks Ruled Eligible to Vote: Anniv, **Apr 3**
  Brown, Jesse Leroy: Birth Anniv, **Oct 13**
  Bud Billiken Parade (Chicago, IL), **Aug 11**
  Carver, George Washington: Death Anniv, **Jan 5**
  Civil Rights Act of 1964: Anniv, **July 2**
  Civil Rights Act of 1968: Anniv, **Apr 11**
  Civil Rights Bill of 1866: Anniv, **Apr 9**
  Coleman, Bessie: Birth Anniv, **Jan 26**
  Crispus Attucks Day, **Mar 5**
  Desegregated, US Army First: Anniv, **July 26**
  Douglass, Frederick: Death Anniv, **Feb 20**
  Drew, Charles: Birth Anniv, **June 3**
  Du Bois, W.E.B.: Birth Anniv, **Feb 23**
  Emancipation of 500: Anniv, **Aug 1**
  Escape to Freedom (F. Douglass): Anniv, **Sept 3**
  First American Abolition Soc Founded: Anniv, **Apr 14**
  First Black Governor Elected: Anniv, **Nov 7**
  First Black Plays in NBA Game: Anniv, **Oct 31**
  First Black Serves in US House Reps: Anniv, **Dec 12**
  First Black Southern Lt Governor: Anniv, **Jan 11**
  First Black US Cabinet Member: Anniv, **Jan 18**
  First Natl Convention for Blacks: Anniv, **Sept 15**
  Forten, James: Birth Anniv, **Sept 2**
  Foster, Andrew "Rube": Birth Anniv, **Sept 17**
  Frederick Douglass Speaks: Anniv, **Aug 11**
  Freedom Riders: Anniv, **May 1**
  Haley, Alex Palmer: Birth Anniv, **Aug 11**
  Historically Black Colleges and Universities Week, Natl (Pres Proc), **Sept 16**
  Hughes, Langston: Birth Anniv, **Feb 1**
  John Brown's Raid: Anniv, **Oct 16**
  Johnson, John (Jack) Arthur: Birth Anniv, **Mar 31**
  Juneteenth, **June 19**
  King Wins Nobel Peace Prize: Anniv, **Oct 14**
  King, Martin Luther, Jr: Birth Anniv, **Jan 15**
  Kwanzaa Fest, **Dec 26**
  Little Rock Nine: Anniv, **Sept 23**
  Loving v Virginia: Anniv, **June 12**
  Malcolm X: Birth Anniv, **May 19**
  Meredith (James) Enrolls at Ole Miss: Anniv, **Sept 30**
  Million Man March: Anniv, **Oct 16**
  Minority Enterprise Development Week (Pres Proc), **Sept 23**
  Minority Scientists Showcase (St. Louis, MO), **Jan 19**
  Montgomery Boycott Arrests: Anniv, **Feb 22**
  Montgomery Bus Boycott Begins: Anniv, **Dec 5**
  NAACP Founded: Anniv, **Feb 12**
  Ralph Bunche Awarded Nobel Peace Prize: Anniv, **Dec 10**
  Robinson Named First Black Manager: Anniv, **Oct 3**
  Robinson, Roscoe, Jr.: Birth Anniv, **Oct 11**
  Rosa Parks Day, **Dec 1**
  Stokes Becomes First Black Mayor in US: Anniv, **Nov 13**
  Truth, Sojourner: Death Anniv, **Nov 26**
  Tubman, Harriet: Death Anniv, **Mar 10**
  Vesey, Denmark: Death Anniv, **July 2**
  Washington, Booker T.: Birth Anniv, **Apr 5**
  Wells, Ida B.: Birth Anniv, **July 16**
  Wheatley, Phillis: Death Anniv, **Dec 5**
Agassi, Andre: Birth, Apr 29
Agnew, Spiro: Birth Anniv, Nov 9
Agriculture,
  Agriculture Day, Natl, **Mar 20**
  Agriculture Week, Natl, **Mar 17**
  Alabama State Fair, South (Montgomery, AL), **Oct 5**
  Alaska State Fair (Palmer, AK), **Aug 24**
  Arizona State Fair (Phoenix, AZ), **Oct 21**
  Arkansas State Fair (Little Rock, AR), **Oct 5**
  Big E (West Springfield, MA), **Sept 14**
  California State Fair (Sacramento, CA), **Aug 17**
  Colorado State Fair (Pueblo, CO), **Aug 17**
  Delaware State Fair (Harrington, DE), **July 18**
  Farm Animals Awareness Week, Natl, **Sept 16**
  Farm Safety Week, Natl (Pres Proc), **Sept 16**
  Farm-City Week, Natl (Pres Proc), **Nov 16**
  FFA Convention, Natl (Louisville, KY), **Oct 24**
  Florida State Fair (Tampa, FL), **Feb 7**
  Georgia National Fair (Perry, GA), **Oct 5**
  Grange Week, **Apr 21**
  Illinois State Fair (Springfield, IL), **Aug 10**
  Indiana State Fair (Indianapolis, IN), **Aug 8**
  Iowa State Fair (Des Moines, IA), **Aug 9**
  Kansas State Fair (Hutchinson, KS), **Sept 7**
  Kentucky State Fair (Louisville, KY), **Aug 16**
  Louisiana, State Fair of (Shreveport, LA), **Oct 19**
  Maryland State Fair (Timonium, MD), **Aug 24**
  Michigan State Fair (Detroit, MI), **Aug 21**
  Minnesota State Fair (St. Paul, MN), **Aug 23**
  Mississippi State Fair (Jackson, MS), **Oct 3**
  Missouri State Fair (Sedalia, MO), **Aug 9**
  Montana State Fair (Great Falls, MT), **July 27**
  MontanaFair (Billings, MT), **Aug 11**
  Nebraska State Fair (Lincoln, NE), **Aug 24**
  Nevada State Fair (Reno, NV), **Aug 22**
  New Mexico State Fair (Albuquerque, NM), **Sept 7**
  New York State Fair (Syracuse, NY), **Aug 23**
  North Dakota State Fair (Minot, ND), **July 19**
  Ohio State Fair (Columbus, OH), **Aug 3**
  Oklahoma, State Fair of (Oklahoma City, OK), **Sept 14**
  Oregon State Fair (Salem, OR), **Aug 23**
  Rural Life Sunday, **May 5**
  South Carolina State Fair (Columbia, SC), **Oct 4**
  South Dakota State Fair (Huron, SD), **July 30**
  Sussex County Farm & Horse Show/New Jersey State Fair (Augusta, NJ), **Aug 3**
  Texas, State Fair of (Dallas, TX), **Sept 28**
  Utah State Fair (Salt Lake City, UT), **Sept 6**
  Vermont State Fair (Rutland, VT), **Aug 31**

Virginia on Strawberry Hill, State Fair of (Richmond, VA), **Sept 27**
Wisconsin State Fair (Milwaukee, WI), **Aug 3**
Wyoming State Fair (Douglas, WY), **Aug 11**
Aguilera, Christina: Birth, Dec 18
Ahlberg, Allan: Birth, June 5
Ahlberg, Janet: Birth, Oct 21
Aichinger, Helga: Birth, Nov 29
AIDS Day, World (UN), Dec 1
AIDS Day, World (US observance), Dec 1
AIDS Named: Anniv, July 27
AIDS: White, Ryan, Apr 8
Aiken, Joan: Birth, Sept 4
Aikman, Troy: Birth, Nov 21
Ailey, Alvin: Birth Anniv, Jan 5
Air Conditioning Appreciation Days, July 3
Akaka, Daniel: Birth, Sept 11
Akihito: Birth, Dec 23
Alabama,
Admission Day, **Dec 14**
American Indian Heritage Day, **Oct 8**
Battle of Mobile Bay: Anniv, **Aug 5**
Confederate Memorial Day, **Apr 22**
South Alabama State Fair (Montgomery), **Oct 5**
Alamo: Anniv of the Fall, Mar 6
Alaska,
Admission Day, **Jan 3**
Alaska Day, **Oct 18**
Alaska Day Celebration (Sitka), **Oct 14**
Earthquake Strikes Alaska: Anniv, **Mar 27**
Gates of the Arctic Natl Park: Anniv, **Dec 2**
Glacier Bay Natl Park: Anniv, **Dec 2**
Katami Natl Park: Anniv, **Dec 2**
Kenai Fjords Natl Park: Anniv, **Dec 2**
Kobuk Valley Natl Park: Anniv, **Dec 2**
Lake Clark Natl Park: Anniv, **Dec 2**
Seward's Day, **Mar 25**
State Fair (Palmer), **Aug 24**
Wrangell-Saint Elias Natl Park: Anniv, **Dec 2**
Albania: Independence Day, Nov 28
Alborough, Jez: Birth, Nov 13
Albright, Madeleine: Birth, May 15
Alcohol and Other Drug-Related Birth Defects Week, Natl, May 12
Alcohol Awareness Month, Natl, Apr 1
Alcott, Louisa May: Birth Anniv, Nov 29
Aldrin, Buzz: Birth, Jan 20
Alexander, Lloyd: Birth, Jan 30
Alexander, Martha: Birth, May 25
Alger, Horatio, Jr: Birth Anniv, Jan 13
Algeria,
Independence Day, **July 5**
Revolution Anniv, **Nov 1**
Ali, Muhammad: Birth, Jan 17
Ali, Muhammad: Clay Becomes Heavyweight Champ, Feb 25
Ali, Tatyana M.: Birth, Jan 24
Alice in Wonderland Published: Anniv, Nov 26
Aliki: Birth, Sept 3
All Fools' Day, Apr 1
All Hallows, Nov 1
All Hallows Eve, Oct 31
All Saints' Day, Nov 1
All Souls' Day, Nov 2
All-Star Game, Major League Baseball First, July 6
Allard, Harry: Birth, Jan 27
Allard, Wayne: Birth, Dec 2
Allen, Ethan: Birth Anniv, Jan 21
Allen, George: Birth, Mar 8
Allen, Marcus: Birth, Mar 26
Allen, Tim: Birth, June 13
Allergy/Asthma Awareness Month, Natl, May 1
Alley, Kirstie: Birth, Jan 12
Almanack, Poor Richard's: Anniv, Dec 28
Almond, David: Birth, May 15
Almond, Lincoln: Birth, June 16
Alomar, Roberto: Birth, Feb 5
Alou, Moises: Birth, July 3
Alphabet Day (Korea), Oct 9
Alvin Show TV Premiere: Anniv, Oct 4
Ambrus, Victor: Birth, Aug 19
America Goes Back to School (Pres Proc), Sept 3
America Recycles Day (Pres Proc), Nov 15
America the Beautiful Published, July 4
America's First Department Store (Salt Lake City, UT), Oct 16
America's Kids Day, June 23
America's Subway Day: Anniv, Mar 29
America, God Bless, 1st Performed: Anniv, Nov 11
American Assn of School Administrators: Natl Conference on Education, Feb 15
American Assn of School Librarians Conference (Indianapolis, IN), Nov 14
American Council on Teaching of Foreign Languages Annual Conference (Washington, DC), Nov 16
American Education Week, Nov 11
American Education Week (Pres Proc), Nov 11
American Family Day in Arizona, Aug 5
American Federation of Labor Founded: Anniv, Dec 8
American Federation of Teachers Conv (Las Vegas, NV), July 14
American History Essay Contest, Aug 1
American Indian Heritage Day (AL), Oct 8
American Indian Heritage Month, Natl (Pres Proc), Nov 1
American Library Assn Annual Conference (Atlanta, GA), June 13
American Library Assn Midwinter Mtg (New Orleans, LA), Jan 18
American Red Cross: Founding Anniv, May 21
American Samoa: White Sunday, Oct 14
American Teddy Bear Day, Natl, Nov 14
Americans with Disabilities Act: Anniv, July 26
Amistad Seized: Anniv, Aug 29
Amundsen, Roald: Birth Anniv, July 16
Ancestor Appreciation Day, Sept 27
Ancona, George: Birth, Dec 4
Andersen, Hans Christian: Birth Anniv, Apr 2
Anderson, Laurie Halse: Birth, Oct 23
Andorra: National Holiday, Sept 8
Andrews, Julie: Birth, Oct 1
Andy Griffith Show TV Premiere: Anniv, Oct 3
Anesthetic First Used in Surgery: Anniv, Mar 30
Angel Day, Be an, Aug 22
Angelou, Maya: Birth, Apr 4
Anglund, Joan Walsh: Birth, Jan 3
Angola,
Beginning of the Armed Struggle, **Feb 4**
Independence Day, **Nov 11**
Animals. See also Horses,
Adopt-a-Shelter Dog Month, **Oct 1**
Answer Your Cat's Question Day, **Jan 22**
Be Kind to Animals Kids Contest Deadline, **Mar 15**
Be Kind to Animals Week, **May 5**
Cat Fest (Belgium), **Feb 14**
Cow Milked While Flying: Anniv, **Feb 18**
Dog Week, Natl, **Sept 23**
Elephant Appreciation Day, **Sept 22**
Farm Animals Awareness Week, Natl, **Sept 16**
First US Zoo: Anniv (Philadelphia, PA), **July 1**
Gorilla Born in Captivity, First: Anniv, **Dec 22**
Keiko Returns to Iceland: Anniv, **Sept 10**
Last Great Buffalo Hunt: Anniv, **June 25**
Moth-er Day, **Mar 14**
Mule Day, **Oct 26**
Pet Owners Independence Day, **Apr 18**
Pet Week, Natl, **May 5**
Pig Day, Natl, **Mar 1**
Pony Penning, Chincoteague (Chincoteague Island, VA), **July 31**
Prevention of Animal Cruelty Month, **Apr 1**
Save the Rhino Day, **May 1**
Whale Awareness Day in MA, **May 2**
ZAM! Zoo and Aquarium Month, **Apr 1**
Annan, Kofi: Birth, Apr 8
Anno, Mitsumasa: Birth, Mar 20
Annunciation, Feast of, Mar 25
Anonymous Giving Week, Mar 20
Antarctica Made a Scientific Preserve: Anniv, Dec 1
Anthem Day, Natl, Mar 3
Anthony, Susan B.: Fined for Voting: Anniv, June 6
Antietam, Battle of: Anniv, Sept 17
Antigua,
National Holiday, **Nov 1**
August Monday, **Aug 6**
Apache Wars Began: Anniv, Feb 4
Apartheid Law, South Africa Repeals Last: Anniv, June 17
Apgar, Virginia: Birth Anniv, June 7
Aphelion, Earth at, July 6
Apollo I: Spacecraft Fire: Anniv, Jan 27
Appert, Nicolas: Birth Anniv, Oct 23
Apple II Computer Released: Anniv, June 5
Apple, Margot: Birth, Mar 9
Appleseed, Johnny: Birth Anniv, Sept 26
Appleseed: Johnny Appleseed Day, Mar 11
April Fools' Day, Apr 1
Aquarius Begins, Jan 20
Arab Oil Embargo Lifted: Anniv, Mar 13
Arab-Israeli War (Yom Kippur War), Oct 6
Arafat, Yasser: Birth, Aug 4
Arbor Day in Florida, Jan 18
Arbor Day, Natl (Proposed), Apr 26
Arches Natl Park Established: Anniv, Nov 12
Area Codes Introduced: Anniv, Nov 10
Argentina,
Death Anniversary of San Martin, **Aug 17**
Flag Day, **June 20**
Independence Day, **July 9**
National Holiday, **May 25**
Aries Begins, Mar 21
Arizona,
Admission Day, **Feb 14**
American Family Day, **Aug 5**
Apache Wars Began: Anniv, **Feb 4**
Arizona State Fair (Phoenix), **Oct 21**
Children's Fest of Fun (Tempe), **Dec 8**
Grand Canyon Natl Park: Anniv, **Feb 26**
Petrified Forest Natl Park: Anniv, **Dec 9**
Public Library Assn Conference (Phoenix), **Mar 12**
Arkansas,
Admission Day: Anniv, **June 15**
Hot Springs Natl Park: Anniv, **Mar 4**
State Fair and Livestock Show (Little Rock), **Oct 5**
Armed Forces Day (Egypt), Oct 6
Armed Forces Day (Pres Proc), May 18
Armenia,
Armenian Christmas, **Jan 6**
Armenian Martyrs Day, **Apr 24**
National Day, **Sept 21**
Armistice Day, Nov 11
Armstrong, BJ: Birth, Sept 9
Armstrong, Jennifer: Birth, May 12
Armstrong, Lance: Birth, Sept 18
Armstrong, Neil Alden: Birth, Aug 5
Armstrong, William H.: Birth Anniv, Sept 14
Army Established: Anniv, June 14
Army First Desegregated, US: Anniv, July 26
Arnold, Benedict: Birth Anniv, Jan 14
Arnold, Caroline: Birth, May 16
Arnosky, Jim: Birth, Sept 1
Arquette, Courteney Cox: Birth, June 15
Art Education Assn Annual Convention, Natl (Miami Beach, FL), Mar 22

Arthur TV Premiere: Anniv, Oct 7
Arthur, Chester A.: Birth Anniv, Oct 5
Arthur, Ellen: Birth Anniv, Aug 30
Arthur: Anniv, May 25
Articles of Confederation: Ratification Anniv, Mar 1
Arts and Crafts: Craft Month, Natl, Mar 1
Arts, Fine and Performing; Art Shows,
Mazza Collection Institute (Findlay, OH), **Nov 10**
Theater in North America, First Performance: Anniv, **Apr 30**
Youth Art Month, **Mar 1**
Aruba: Flag Day, Mar 18
Asarah B'Tevet, Dec 25
Ascension Day, May 9
Asch, Frank: Birth, Aug 6
Ash Wednesday, Feb 13
Ashabranner, Brent: Birth, Nov 3
Ashcroft, John D.: Birth, May 9
Ashe, Arthur: Birth Anniv, July 10
Ashford, Evelyn: Birth, Apr 15
Ashura: Tenth Day (Islamic), Mar 25
Asian Pacific American Heritage Month (Pres Proc), May 1
Asimov, Isaac: Birth Anniv, Jan 2
Assn of Independent Schools Conference, Natl (San Francisco, CA), Feb 26
Assumption of the Virgin Mary, Aug 15
Astrology,
Aquarius, **Jan 20**
Aries, **Mar 21**
Cancer, **June 21**
Capricorn, **Dec 22**
Gemini, **May 21**
Leo, **July 23**
Libra, **Sept 23**
Pisces, **Feb 20**
Sagittarius, **Nov 23**
Scorpio, **Oct 23**
Taurus, **Apr 20**
Virgo, **Aug 23**
Astronomy Day, Apr 20
Astronomy Week, Apr 15
AT&T Divestiture: Anniv, Jan 8
Atchison, David R.: Birth Anniv, Aug 11
Atlantic Charter Signing: Anniv, Aug 14
Atler, Vanessa: Birth, Feb 17
Atomic Bomb Dropped on Hiroshima: Anniv, Aug 6
Atomic Bomb Dropped on Nagasaki: Anniv, Aug 9
Atomic Bomb Tested: Anniv, July 16
Atomic Plant Begun, Oak Ridge: Anniv, Aug 1
Attucks, Crispus: Day, Mar 5
Atwater, Richard: Birth Anniv, Dec 29
Atwood, Ann: Birth, Feb 12
Audubon, John J.: Birth Anniv, Apr 26
Austin, Stephen F.: Birth Anniv, Nov 3
Austin, Tracy: Birth, Dec 12
Australia,
Anzac Day, **Apr 25**
Australia Day, **Jan 26**
Canberra Day, **Mar 18**
Commonwealth Formed: Anniv, **Jan 1**
Picnic Day, **Aug 6**
Proclamation Day, **Dec 28**
Queen Elizabeth II's Official Birthday, **June 10**
Recreation Day, **Nov 5**
Sorry Day, **May 26**
Austria,
National Day, **Oct 26**
Silent Night, Holy Night Celebrations, **Dec 24**
Authors' Day, Natl, Nov 1
Autism Awareness Month, Natl, Apr 1
Automobile Speed Reduction: Anniv, Nov 25
Automobiles (including shows, races, etc),
Buckle Up America! Week, **May 20**
55 mph Speed Limit: Anniv, **Jan 2**
Gasoline Rationing: Anniv, **May 15**
Soap Box Derby, All-American (Akron, OH), **July 23**
Autumn Begins, Sept 22
Autumn, Halfway Point of, Nov 6
Avi: Birth, Dec 23
Aviation; Air Shows; Airplane Fly-ins,
Aviation Day, Natl (Pres Proc), **Aug 19**
Aviation History Month, **Nov 1**
Aviation in America: Anniv, **Jan 9**
Balloon Crossing of Atlantic: Anniv, **Aug 17**
Berlin Airlift: Anniv, **June 24**
Civil Aviation Day, Intl, **Dec 7**
Coleman, Bessie: Birth Anniv, **Jan 26**
First Balloon Flight Across English Channel: Anniv, **Jan 7**
First Balloon Flight: Anniv, **June 5**
First Concorde Flight: Anniv, **Jan 21**
First Flight Attendant: Anniv, **May 15**
First Man-Powered Flight: Anniv, **Aug 23**
First Manned Flight (Balloon): Anniv, **Oct 15**
First Nonstop Flight of World/No Refueling: Anniv, **Dec 23**
First Nonstop Transatlantic Flight: Anniv, **June 14**
First Round-the-World Balloon Flight: Anniv, **Mar 21**
Lindbergh Flight: Anniv, **May 20**
Lindbergh, Charles A.: Birth Anniv, **Feb 4**
Montgolfier, Jacques: Birth Anniv, **Jan 7**
Pan American Aviation Day (Pres Proc), **Dec 17**
Solo Transatlantic Balloon Crossing: Anniv, **Sept 14**
Sound Barrier Broken: Anniv, **Oct 14**
US Air Force Established: Birth, **Sept 18**
Wright Brothers Day (Pres Proc), **Dec 17**
Wright Brothers' First Powered Flight: Anniv, **Dec 17**
Young Eagles Day, Intl, **June 8**
Aylesworth, Jim: Birth, Feb 21
Azarian, Mary: Birth, Dec 8
Azerbaijan,
Day of the Martyrs, **Jan 20**
Day of the Republic, **May 28**
Aztec Calendar Stone Discovery: Anniv, Dec 17
Azzi, Jennifer: Birth, Aug 31
Babbitt, Bruce: Birth, June 27
Babbitt, Natalie: Birth, July 28
Baby Safety Month, Sept 1
Bach, Alice: Birth, Apr 6
Bach, Johann Sebastian: Birth Anniv, Mar 21
Back to School Head Lice Prevention Campaign, Sept 1
Back-to-School Month, Natl, Aug 1
Backyard Games Week, Natl, May 20
Backyard Natl Children's Film Fest, Nov 2
Baden-Powell, Robert: Birth Anniv, Feb 22
Badlands Natl Park: Anniv, Nov 10
Bagnold, Enid: Birth Anniv, Oct 27
Baha'i,
Baha'i New Year's Day: Naw-Ruz, **Mar 21**
Race Unity Day, **June 9**
World Religion Day, **Jan 20**
Bahamas,
Discovery Day, **Oct 12**
Emancipation Day, **Aug 6**
Independence Day, **July 10**
Junkanoo, **Dec 26**
Labor Day, **June 7**
Bahrain: Independence Day, Dec 16
Baisakhi (India), Apr 13
Baiul, Oksana: Birth, Nov 16
Baked Bean Month, Natl, July 1
Baker, Jeannie: Birth, Nov 2
Baker, Keith: Birth, Mar 17
Baker, Leslie: Birth, June 17
Baker, Vin: Birth, Nov 23
Balboa: Pacific Ocean Discovered: Anniv, Sept 25
Ballard, Dr. Robert: Birth, June 30
Ballet Introduced to the US: Anniv, Feb 7
Balloons, Hot-Air,
Aviation in America: Anniv, **Jan 9**
Balloon Crossing of Atlantic: Anniv, **Aug 17**
First Balloon Flight Across English Channel: Anniv, **Jan 7**
First Balloon Flight: Anniv, **June 5**
First Manned Flight: Anniv, **Oct 15**
First Round-the-World Balloon Flight: Anniv, **Mar 21**
Solo Transatlantic Balloon Crossing: Anniv, **Sept 14**
Ballpoint Pen Patented: Anniv, June 10
Bang, Molly Garrett: Birth, Dec 29
Bangladesh,
Independence Day, **Mar 26**
Martyrs' Day, **Feb 21**
Solidarity Day, **Nov 7**
Victory Day, **Dec 16**
Bank Opens in US, First: Anniv, Dec 31
Banks, Lynne Reid: Birth, July 31
Banks, Tyra: Birth, Dec 4
Banned Books Week, Sept 22
Banneker, Benjamin: Birth Anniv, Nov 9
Bannister, Dr. Roger: Birth, Mar 24
Bar Code Introduced: Anniv, June 26
Barbados: Independence Day, Nov 30
Barbecue Month, Natl, May 1
Barber, Red: First Baseball Games Televised: Anniv, Aug 26
Barbie Debuts: Anniv, Mar 9
Barbosa, Jose Celso: Birth Anniv, July 27
Barbuda. See Antigua, Aug 6
Barbuda: See Antigua, Nov 1
Barkley, Alben: Birth Anniv, Nov 24
Barkley, Charles: Birth, Feb 20
Barnes, Roy: Birth, Mar 11
Barney & Friends TV Premiere: Anniv, Apr 6
Barnum, Phineas Taylor: Birth Anniv, July 5
Baron Bliss Day (Belize), Mar 9
Barracca, Debra: Birth, Dec 24
Barracca, Sal: Birth, Nov 10
Barrett, Brendon Ryan: Birth, Aug 5
Barrett, Ron: Birth, July 25
Barrie, J.M.: Birth Anniv, May 9
Barrier Awareness Day in Kentucky, May 7
Barron, T.A.: Birth, Mar 26
Barry, John: Death Anniv, Sept 13
Barrymore, Drew: Birth, Feb 22
Bartholdi, Frederic A.: Birth Anniv, Apr 2
Bartlett, John: Birth Anniv, June 14
Barton, Clara: American Red Cross Founding Anniv, May 21
Barton, Clara: Birth Anniv, Dec 25
Base, Graeme: Birth, Apr 6
Baseball. See also Softball,
Babe Sets Home Run Record: Anniv, **Sept 30**
Baseball First Played Under Lights: Anniv, **May 24**
Baseball Hall of Fame, Natl: Anniv, **June 12**
Baseball's First Perfect Game: Anniv, **May 5**
Cobb, Ty: Birth Anniv, **Dec 18**
Designated Hitter Rule Adopted: Anniv, **Jan 11**
First Baseball Games Televised: Anniv, **Aug 26**
Gehrig, Lou: Birth Anniv, **June 19**
Home Run Record: Anniv, **Apr 8**
House That Ruth Built: Anniv, **Apr 18**
Little League Baseball Week, Natl (Pres Proc), **June 10**
Little League World Series (Williamsport, PA), **Aug 17**
Major League Baseball First All-Star Game: Anniv, **July 6**
Major League's First Doubleheader: Anniv, **Sept 25**
Maris Hits 61st Home Run: Anniv, **Oct 1**
McGwire Hits 62nd Home Run: Anniv, **Sept 8**
Robinson Named First Black Manager: Anniv, **Oct 3**

Bashoff, Blake: Birth, May 30
Basinger, Kim: Birth, Dec 8
Basketball,
Basketball Created: Anniv, **Dec 1**
Chicago Bulls Third Straight Title: Anniv, **June 20**
First Black Plays in NBA Game: Anniv, **Oct 31**
First Women's Collegiate Basketball Game: Anniv, **Mar 22**
Hall of Fame Enshrinement Ceremonies (Springfield, MA), **Oct 5**
Jordan's Back! Anniv, **Mar 18**
Bass, Lance: Birth, May 4
Bastille Day (France), July 14
Batman TV Premiere: Anniv, Jan 12
Battle of Brandywine: Anniv, Sept 11
Battle of Britain Day (England), Sept 15
Battle of Britain Week (England), Sept 9
Battle of Lexington and Concord, Apr 19
Battle of Little Bighorn: Anniv, June 25
Baucus, Max: Birth, Dec 11
Bauer, Marion Dane: Birth, Nov 20
Baum, L. Frank: Birth Anniv, May 15
Bawden, Nina: Birth, Jan 19
Bayh, Evan: Birth, Dec 26
Baylor, Byrd: Birth, Mar 28
Be an Angel Day, Aug 22
Be Kind to Animals Kids Contest Deadline, Mar 15
Be Kind to Animals Week, May 5
Be Kind to Humankind Week, Aug 25
Be Late for Something Day, Sept 5
Bean Month, Natl Baked, July 1
Bean Throwing Fest (Japan), Feb 3
Beanie Babies Introduced: Anniv, Jan 1
Beatrix, Queen: Birth, Jan 31
Beatty, Patricia: Birth, Aug 26
Beaufort Scale Day, May 7
Becker, Boris: Birth, Nov 22
Beddows, Eric: Birth, Nov 29
Beethoven's Ninth Symphony Premiere: Anniv, May 7
Beethoven, Ludwig van: Birth Anniv, Dec 16
Beggar's Night, Oct 31
Behn, Harry: Birth Anniv, Sept 24
Belarus,
Constitution Day, **Mar 15**
Independence Day, **July 3**
Belgium,
Cat Fest, **Feb 14**
National Holiday, **July 21**
Wedding of the Giants, **Aug 26**
Belize,
Baron Bliss Day, **Mar 9**
Columbus Day, **Oct 12**
Commonwealth Day, **May 24**
Garifuna Day, **Nov 19**
Independence Day, **Sept 21**
Saint George's Caye Day, **Sept 10**
Bellairs, John: Birth Anniv, Jan 17
Belle, Albert: Birth, Aug 25
Bemelmans, Ludwig: Birth Anniv, Apr 27
Ben-Gurion, David: Birth Anniv, Oct 16
Benchley, Peter: Birth, May 8
Benin, People's Republic of: National Day, Aug 1
Bennett, Richard Bedford: Birth Anniv, July 3
Bennett, Robert F.: Birth, Sept 18
Bennington Battle Day, Aug 16
Bentley, Edmund Clerihew: Clerihew Day, July 10
Berenstain, Jan: Birth, July 26
Berenstain, Stan: Birth, Sept 29
Berg, Bjorn: Birth, Sept 17
Bergen, Candice: Birth, May 9
Berger, Barbara Helen: Birth, Mar 1
Berlin Airlift: Anniv, June 24
Berlin Wall Erected: Anniv, Aug 13
Berlin Wall Opened: Anniv, Nov 9
Bermuda: Peppercorn Ceremony, Apr 23
Berners-Lee, Tim: Birth, June 8
Bernstein, Leonard: Birth Anniv, Aug 25
Berra, Yogi: Birth, May 12
Bettis, Jerome: Birth, Feb 16
Between the Lions Premiere: Anniv, Apr 3
Bhutan,
Coronation Day, **June 2**
National Day, **Aug 8**
Bialik, Mayim: Birth, Dec 12
Bianco, Margery Williams: Birth Anniv, July 22
Bible Week, Natl, Nov 18
Bichette, Dante: Birth, Nov 18
Bicycle,
Bike Month, Natl, **May 1**
Bike to Work Day, Natl, **May 21**
Biden, Joseph Robinette, Jr: Birth, Nov 20
Biel, Jessica: Birth, Mar 3
Bierhorst, John: Birth, Sept 2
Big Bend Natl Park: Anniv, June 12
Big Wind: Anniv, Apr 12
Biggio, Craig: Birth, Dec 14
Bill of Rights Day (Pres Proc), Dec 15
Bill of Rights Proposed: Anniv, June 8
Bill of Rights: Anniv, Dec 15
Bill of Rights: Anniv of First State Ratification, Nov 20
Billingsley, Franny: Birth, July 3
Bingaman, Jeff: Birth, Oct 3
Biographers Day, May 16
Biological Clock Gene Discovered: Anniv, Apr 28
Bird, Larry: Birth, Dec 7
Birds,
Homes for Birds Week, **Feb 17**
Swallows Return to San Juan Capistrano, **Mar 19**
Wild Bird Feeding Month, Natl, **Feb 1**
Birdseye, Clarence: Birth Anniv, Dec 9
Birth Defects Prevention Month, March of Dimes, Jan 1
Biscayne Natl Park: Anniv, June 28
Bjork, Christina: Birth, July 27
Black Friday, Nov 23
Black Maria Studio: Anniv, Feb 1
Black Nazarene, Feast of the (Philippines), Jan 9
Black Poetry Day, Oct 17
Black Press Day: Anniv of the First Black Newspaper, Mar 16
Black, Debbie: Birth, July 29
Blackmun, Harry A.: Birth Anniv, Nov 12
Blackwell, Elizabeth, Awarded MD: Anniv, Jan 23
Blair, Bonnie: Birth, Mar 18
Blair, Tony: Birth, May 6
Blake, Jeff: Birth, Dec 4
Bledsoe, Drew: Birth, Feb 14
Bless-A-Child Month, Natl, June 1
Blessing of Animals at the Cathedral (Mexico), Jan 17
Blizzard of '88, Great: Anniv, Mar 12
Block, Francesca Lia: Birth, Dec 3
Blondin, Charles: Conquest of Niagara Falls: Anniv, June 30
Bloom, Lloyd: Birth, Jan 10
Bloomer, Amelia Jenks: Birth Anniv, May 27
Blos, Joan W.: Birth, Dec 9
Blue Moon, Nov 30
Blue Ribbon Week, Natl (Child Abuse), Apr 7
Blueberries Month, Natl July Belongs to, July 1
Bluford, Guion S., Jr: Birth, Nov 22
Blumberg, Rhoda: Birth, Dec 14
Blume, Judy: Birth, Feb 12
Bly, Nellie: Around the World in 72 Days: Anniv, Nov 14
Bly, Nellie: Birth Anniv, May 5
Boats, Ships, Things That Float,
First American to Circumnavigate Earth: Anniv, **Apr 10**
Fulton Sails Steamboat: Anniv, **Aug 17**
Halifax, Nova Scotia, Destroyed: Anniv, **Dec 6**
Historical Regatta (Italy), **Sept 2**
Safe Boating Week, Natl, **May 18**
Safe Boating Week, Natl (Pres Proc), **May 18**
Bodkin, Odds: Birth, Feb 14
Boer War: Anniv, Oct 12
Boggs, Wade: Birth, June 15
Boitano, Brian: Birth, Oct 22
Bolivar, Simon: Birth Anniv, July 24
Bolivia,
Alacitis Fair, **Jan 24**
Independence Day, **Aug 6**
Bologna Intl Children's Book Fair (Italy), Apr 3
Bombing, Oklahoma City: Anniv, Apr 19
Bon Fest (Feast of Lanterns) (Japan), July 13
Bonaparte, Napoleon: Birth Anniv, Aug 15
Bond, Christopher Samuel: Birth, Mar 6
Bond, Felicia: Birth, July 18
Bond, Michael: Birth, Jan 13
Bond, Nancy: Birth, Jan 8
Bonds, Barry: Birth, July 24
Bonners, Susan: Birth, Apr 8
Bonsall, Brian: Birth, Dec 3
Bonza Bottler Day, Jan 1
Bonza Bottler Day, Feb 2
Bonza Bottler Day, Mar 3
Bonza Bottler Day, Apr 4
Bonza Bottler Day, May 5
Bonza Bottler Day, June 6
Bonza Bottler Day, July 7
Bonza Bottler Day, Aug 8
Bonza Bottler Day, Sept 9
Bonza Bottler Day, Oct 10
Bonza Bottler Day, Nov 11
Bonza Bottler Day, Dec 12
Books. See also Library/Librarians,
African American Read-In, **Feb 3**
Arthur: Anniv, **May 25**
Authors' Day, Natl, **Nov 1**
Banned Books Week, **Sept 22**
Bible Week, Natl, **Nov 18**
Biographers Day, **May 16**
Bologna Intl Children's Book Fair (Italy), **Apr 3**
Book Day (Spain), **Apr 23**
Book It! Reading Incentive Program, **Oct 1**
Book Month, Natl, **May 1**
Chicago Latino Book & Family Fest (IL), **Dec 8**
Children's Book Day, Intl, **Apr 2**
Children's Book Week, Natl, **Nov 12**
Children's Literature Fest (Warrensburg, MO), **Mar 10**
Copyright Law Passed: Anniv, **May 31**
David McCord Children's Literature Fest (Framingham, MA), **Nov 1**
Dia de los Ninos/Dia de los Libros, **Apr 30**
Dictionary Day, **Oct 16**
Fest of Books for Young People (Iowa City, IA), **Nov 3**
First Dictionary of American English Published: Anniv, **Apr 14**
Get Caught Reading Month, **May 1**
Guadalajara Intl Book Fair, **Nov 24**
Jewish Book Month, **Nov 10**
Los Angeles Latino Book & Family Fest (Los Angeles, CA), **Oct 13**
Mazza Collection Institute (Findlay, OH), **Nov 10**
Paperback Books Introduced: Anniv, **July 30**
Read Across America Day, **Mar 2**
Read In, **May 9**
Read to Your Child Day, **Feb 14**
Reading Is Fun Week, **Apr 21**
Return the Borrowed Books Week, **Mar 1**
San Bernardino Latino Book & Family Fest (CA), **Dec 1**
Southern Fest of Books (Nashville, TN), **Oct 12**
Spotlight On Books (Alexandria, MN), **Apr 12**

Teen Read Week, **Oct 14**
World Book and Copyright Day (UN), **Apr 23**
Young Reader's Day, Natl, **Nov 14**
Boone, Daniel: Birth Anniv, Nov 2
Borden, Sir Robert Laird: Birth Anniv, June 26
Boreanaz, David: Birth, May 16
Borglum, Gutzon: Birth Anniv, Mar 25
Bosch, Johnny Yong: Birth, Jan 6
Bosnia and Herzegovina,
Independence Day, **Mar 1**
National Day, **Nov 25**
Boston Massacre: Anniv, Mar 5
Boston Public Library: Anniv, Apr 3
Boston Tea Party, Reenactment of (Boston, MA), Dec 16
Boston Tea Party: Anniv, Dec 16
Botswana,
Independence Day, **Sept 30**
Sir Seretse Khama Day, **July 1**
Bounty, Mutiny on the: Anniv, Apr 28
Bowman, Jessica: Birth, Nov 26
Boxer, Barbara: Birth, Nov 11
Boxing: Clay Becomes Heavyweight Champ: Anniv, Feb 25
Boxing Day (United Kingdom), Dec 26
Boy Scouts of America Anniv Week, Feb 4
Boy Scouts of America Founded: Anniv, Feb 8
Boy Scouts: Baden-Powell, Robert: Birth Anniv, Feb 22
Boycott, Charles C.: Birth Anniv, Mar 12
Boys' Clubs Founded: Anniv, May 19
Bradbury, Ray: Birth, Aug 22
Bradford, William: Birth Anniv, Mar 19
Bradley, Shawn: Birth, Mar 22
Brady Bunch TV Premiere, The: Anniv, Sept 26
Brady, Irene: Birth, Dec 29
Brady, Mathew: First Presidential Photograph: Anniv, Feb 14
Braille, Louis: Birth Anniv, Jan 4
Brain Awareness Week, Intl, Mar 11
Brain Bee, Natl, Mar 12
Brandeis, Louis D.: Birth Anniv, Nov 13
Brandis, Jonathan: Birth, Apr 13
Brandy: Birth, Feb 11
Branscum, Robbie: Birth Anniv, June 17
Braxton, Carter: Birth Anniv, Sept 10
Brazil,
Carnival, **Feb 9**
Discovery of Brazil Day, **Apr 22**
Independence Day, **Sept 7**
Independence Week, **Sept 1**
Nosso Senhor Do Bonfim Fest, **Jan 20**
Republic Day, **Nov 15**
Tiradentes Day, **Apr 21**
Breathed, Berke: Birth, June 21
Breaux, John B.: Birth, Mar 1
Breckinridge, John Cabell: Birth Anniv, Jan 21
Brendon, Nicholas: Birth, Apr 12
Brett, George: Birth, May 15
Brett, Jan: Birth, Dec 1
Breyer, Stephen G.: Birth, Aug 15
Bridwell, Norman: Birth, Feb 15
Brink, Carol Ryrie: Birth Anniv, Dec 28
British North America Act: Anniv, Mar 29
British Virgin Islands: Territory Day, July 1
Brittain, Bill: Birth, Dec 16
Broderick, Beth: Birth, Feb 24
Broderick, Matthew: Birth, Mar 21
Brokaw, Tom: Birth, Feb 6
Brooklyn Bridge Opened: Anniv, May 24
Brooks, Bruce: Birth, Sept 23
Brooks, Garth: Birth, Feb 7
Brooks, Gwendolyn: Birth Anniv, June 7
Brotherhood/Sisterhood Week, Feb 17
Brower, Jordan: Birth, Oct 14
Brown, Curtis, Jr: Birth, Mar 11
Brown, Jesse Leroy: Birth Anniv, Oct 13
Brown, John: Birth Anniv, May 9
Brown, John: Raid Anniv, Oct 16
Brown, Louise: First Test Tube Baby Birth, July 25
Brown, Marc: Birth, Nov 25
Brown, Marcia: Birth, July 13
Brown, Margaret Wise: Birth Anniv, May 23
Brown, Tim: Birth, July 22
Brownback, Sam: Birth, Sept 12
Browne, Anthony: Birth, Sept 11
Browning, Elizabeth Barrett: Birth Anniv, Mar 6
Browning, Robert: Birth Anniv, May 7
Bruchac, Joseph: Birth, Oct 16
Brunei: National Day, Feb 23
Brunhoff, Jean de: Birth Anniv, Dec 9
Bryan, Ashley: Birth, July 13
Bryan, Zachery Ty: Birth, Oct 9
Bryant, Kobe: Birth, Aug 23
Bryce Canyon Natl Park: Anniv, Jan 1
Buchanan, James: Birth Anniv, Apr 23
Buck, Pearl: Birth Anniv, June 26
Buckle Up America! Week, May 20
Buddha: Birth Anniv, Apr 8
Buehner, Caralyn: Birth, May 20
Buehner, Mark: Birth, July 20
Buffalo Bill (William F. Cody): Birth Anniv, Feb 26
Buffalo Hunt, Last Great: Anniv, June 25
Bulgaria,
Enlightenment and Culture Day, **May 24**
Hristo Botev Day, **June 2**
Liberation Day, **Mar 3**
Saint Lasarus Day, **Apr 1**
Unification Day, **Sept 6**
Bulla, Clyde Robert: Birth, Jan 9
Bullett, Vicky: Birth, Oct 4
Bullfinch Exchange Fest (Japan), Jan 7
Bun Day (Iceland), Feb 11
Bunche, Ralph: Awarded Nobel Peace Prize: Anniv, Dec 10
Bunche, Ralph: Birth Anniv, Aug 7
Bunker Hill Day (MA), June 17
Bunning, Jim: Birth, Oct 23
Bunting, Eve: Birth, Dec 19
Buonarroti Simoni, Michelangelo: Birth Anniv, Mar 6
Burbank, Luther: Birth Anniv, Mar 7
Burch, Robert: Birth, June 26
Bure, Candace Cameron: Birth, Apr 6
Bureau of Indian Affairs Established, Mar 11
Burger, Warren E.: Birth Anniv, Sept 17
Burk, Martha (Calamity Jane): Death Anniv, Aug 1
Burkina Faso,
Anniv of the 1966 Upheaval, **Jan 3**
National Day, **Dec 11**
Republic Day, **Aug 5**
Revolution Day, **Aug 4**
Burleigh, Robert: Birth, Jan 4
Burnett, Frances Hodgson: Birth Anniv, Nov 24
Burnford, Sheila: Birth, May 11
Burningham, John: Birth, Apr 27
Burns, Conrad: Birth, Jan 25
Burns, Steven: Birth, Oct 9
Burr, Aaron: Birth Anniv, Feb 6
Burrise, Nakia: Birth, Oct 21
Burroughs, Edgar Rice: Birth Anniv, Sept 1
Bursting Day (Iceland), Feb 12
Burton, LeVar: Birth, Feb 16
Burton, Tim: Birth, Aug 25
Burton, Virginia Lee: Birth Anniv, Aug 30
Burundi,
Assassination of the Hero of the Nation Day, **Oct 13**
Independence Day, **July 1**
Bush, Barbara Pierce: Birth, June 8
Bush, George H.W.: Birthday, June 12
Bush, George W.: Birth, July 6
Bush, George W.: See Supreme Court Rules for Bush: Anniv, Dec 12
Bush, Jeb: Birth, Feb 11
Bush, Laura: Birth, Nov 4
Business Week, Small (Pres Proc), May 19
Business: AT&T Divestiture: Anniv, Jan 8
Butcher, Susan: Birth, Dec 26
Butts, Alfred M.: Birth Anniv, Apr 13
Buy Nothing Day, Nov 23
Byars, Betsy: Birth, Aug 7
Bye, Karyn: Birth, May 18
Bynes, Amanda: Birth, Apr 3
Byrd, Robert C.: Birth, Nov 20
Cabbage Patch Dolls Debuted: Anniv, Oct 7
Cabrillo Day (CA), Sept 28
Cadnum, Michael: Birth, May 3
Caduto, Michael J.: Birth, Dec 20
Cain, Dean: Birth, July 31
Caine, Michael: Birth, Mar 14
Calamity Jane (Martha Burk): Death Anniv, Aug 1
Caldecott, Randolph: Birth Anniv, Mar 22
Calderon, Sila Maria: Birth, Sept 23
Calendar Adjustment Day: Anniv, Sept 2
Calendar Day, Gregorian, Feb 24
Calendar Stone, Aztec, Discovery: Anniv, Dec 17
Calhoun, John C.: Birth Anniv, Mar 18
Calhoun, Mary: Birth, Aug 3
California,
Admission Day, **Sept 9**
American Alliance for Health, Phys Ed, Recreation & Dance, Annual Meeting (San Diego), **Apr 9**
Assn of Independent Schools Conference, Natl (San Francisco), **Feb 26**
Cabrillo Day, **Sept 28**
California Gold Discovery: Anniv, **Jan 24**
California State Fair (Sacramento), **Aug 17**
Cesar Chavez Day, **Mar 31**
Channel Islands Natl Park: Anniv, **Mar 5**
Conference on Education, Natl (San Diego), **Feb 15**
Disneyland Opened: Anniv, **July 17**
Golden Gate Bridge Opened: Anniv, **May 27**
Lassen Volcanic Natl Park: Anniv, **Aug 9**
Laura Ingalls Wilder Gingerbread Sociable (Pomona), **Feb 2**
Los Angeles Founded: Anniv, **Sept 4**
Los Angeles Latino Book & Family Fest (Los Angeles), **Oct 13**
Pasadena Doo Dah Parade (Pasadena), **Nov 25**
Reading Assn, Intl, Annual Conv (San Francisco), **Apr 28**
Redwood Natl Park: Anniv, **Oct 2**
Rose Bowl Game (Pasadena), **Jan 1**
San Bernardino Latino Book & Family Fest, **Dec 1**
Science Teachers Assn Conv, Natl (San Diego), **Mar 27**
Sequoia and Kings Canyon Natl Parks: Anniv, **Sept 25**
Southern California Earthquake: Anniv, **Jan 17**
Swallows Return to San Juan Capistrano, **Mar 19**
Tournament of Roses Parade (Pasadena), **Jan 1**
Yosemite Natl Park: Anniv, **Oct 1**
Call, Brandon: Birth, Oct 17
Calmenson, Stephanie: Birth, Nov 28
Cambodia,
Constitutional Declaration Day, **Sept 24**
Independence Day, **Nov 9**
Peace Treaty Day, **Oct 23**
Camcorder Developed: Anniv, Jan 20
Cameron, Ann: Birth, Oct 21
Cameron, Eleanor: Birth, Mar 23
Cameron, Kirk: Birth, Oct 12
Cameroon,
National Holiday, **May 20**
Volcanic Eruption: Anniv, **Aug 22**
Youth Day, **Feb 11**
Camp David Accord Signed: Anniv, Mar 26
Camp Fire Birthday Sunday, Mar 17
Camp Fire Birthday Week, Mar 11

Camp Fire Founders Day, Mar 17
Camp Week, Natl Sign Up for Summer, Feb 1
Campaign for Healthier Babies, Oct 1
Campanella, Roy: Birth Anniv, Nov 19
Campbell, Ben Nighthorse: Birth, Apr 13
Campbell, Kim: Birth, Mar 10
Canada,
- Boxing Day, **Dec 26**
- British North America Act: Anniv, **Mar 29**
- Calgary Intl Children's Fest, **May 21**
- Campbell, Kim, 19th Prime Minister: Anniv, **June 25**
- Canada Day, **July 1**
- Children's Literature New England Institute (Toronto), **Aug 1**
- Civic Holiday, **Aug 6**
- CN Tower: Anniv, **June 26**
- Constitution Act: Anniv, **Apr 18**
- Geographic Education, Natl Council for (Vancouver, BC), **Aug 1**
- Halifax, Nova Scotia, Destroyed: Anniv, **Dec 6**
- Klondike Eldorado Gold Discovery: Anniv, **Aug 31**
- Labor Day, **Sept 3**
- Maple Leaf Flag Adopted: Anniv, **Feb 15**
- Newfoundland Discovery Day, **June 24**
- Newfoundland Memorial Day, **July 3**
- Newfoundland Saint George's Day, **Apr 22**
- North America's Coldest Recorded Temperature: Anniv, **Feb 3**
- Nunavut Independence: Anniv, **Apr 1**
- Quebec Fete Nationale, **June 24**
- Remembrance Day, **Nov 11**
- Riel, Louis: Hanging Anniv, **Nov 16**
- Thanksgiving Day, **Oct 8**
- Victoria Day, **May 20**
- Yukon Discovery Day, **Aug 13**

Canadian Pacific Railway: Transcontinental Completion Anniv, Nov 7
Cancer (Zodiac) Begins, June 21
Cancer Control Month (Pres Proc), Apr 1
Cancer in the Sun Month, June 1
Candlemas Day (Presentation of the Lord), Feb 2
Candy Month, Natl, June 1
Cannon, Janell: Birth, Nov 3
Canseco, Jose, Jr: Birth, July 2
Cantwell, Maria: Birth, Oct 13
Cape Verde: National Day, July 5
Capitol Cornerstone Laid, US: Anniv, Sept 18
Capitol Reef Natl Park: Anniv, Dec 18
Capricorn Begins, Dec 22
Captain Kangaroo TV Premiere: Anniv, Oct 3
Captain Kangaroo: Birth, June 27
Captive Nations Week (Pres Proc), July 14
Carey, Mariah: Birth, Mar 27
Caribbean or Caricom Day, July 1
Caricom or Caribbean Day, July 1
Carle, Eric: Birth, June 25
Carlsbad Caverns Natl Park: Anniv, May 14
Carlson, Nancy: Birth, Oct 10
Carlstrom, Nancy White: Birth, Aug 4
Carnahan, Jean: Birth, Dec 20
Carnegie, Andrew: Birth Anniv, Nov 25
Carnival, Feb 11
Carnival (Malta), May 4
Carnival (Port of Spain, Trinidad and Tobago), Feb 11
Carnival Season, Jan 6
Carnival Week (Milan, Italy), Feb 10
Carper, Tom: Birth, Jan 23
Carrey, Jim: Birth, Jan 17
Carroll, Charles: Birth Anniv, Sept 19
Carroll, Lewis: Birth Anniv, Jan 27
Carson, Christopher "Kit": Birth Anniv, Dec 24
Carson, Rachel: Birth Anniv, May 27
Carson, Rachel: Silent Spring Publication: Anniv, Apr 13
Carter, Aaron: Birth, Dec 7
Carter, Alan R.: Birth, Apr 7
Carter, Cris: Birth, Nov 25
Carter, David A.: Birth, Mar 4
Carter, Jimmy: Birthday, Oct 1
Carter, Nick: Birth, Jan 28
Carter, Robert III: Emancipation of 500: Anniv, Aug 1
Carter, Rosalynn (Eleanor) Smith: Birth, Aug 18
Cartier, Jacques: Death Anniv, Sept 1
Cartoons: Garfield Birthday, June 19
Carver, George Washington: Death Anniv, Jan 5
Carvey, Dana: Birth, June 2
Case, Steve: Birth, Aug 21
Caseley, Judith: Birth, Oct 17
Castile, Christopher: Birth, June 15
Castro, Fidel: Birth, Aug 13
Cat Fest (Belgium), Feb 14
Catalanotto, Peter: Birth, Mar 21
Catholic Educational Assn Conv/Expo, Natl (Atlantic City, NJ), Apr 2
Catholic Schools Week, Jan 27
Catlin, George: Birth Anniv, July 26
Catt, Carrie Lane Chapman: Birth Anniv, Jan 9
Cavoukian, Raffi: Birth, July 8
Caxton, William: Birth Anniv, Aug 13
Cayetano, Ben: Birth, Nov 14
CBS Evening News TV Premiere: Anniv, May 3
CD Player Debuts: Anniv, Oct 1
Cellophane Tape Patented: Anniv, May 27
Cellucci, A. Paul: Birth, Apr 24
Central African Republic,
- Boganda Day, **Mar 29**
- Independence Day, **Aug 13**
- National Day, **Dec 3**

Cezanne, Paul: Birth Anniv, Jan 19
Chad,
- African Freedom Day, **May 25**
- Independence Day, **Aug 11**
- Republic Day, **Nov 28**

Chafee, Lincoln: Birth, Mar 26
Challenger Space Shuttle Explosion: Anniv, Jan 28
Chalmers, Mary: Birth, Mar 16
Chamberlain, Wilt: Birth Anniv, Aug 21
Chan, Jackie: Birth, Apr 7
Chang, Michael Te Pei: Birth, Feb 22
Channel Islands Natl Park: Anniv, Mar 5
Chanukah, Dec 10
Chao, Elaine: Birth, Mar 26
Chapman, John: Death Anniv: Johnny Appleseed Day, Mar 11
Character Counts Week, Natl (Pres Proc), Oct 14
Charles, Prince: Birth, Nov 14
Charlip, Remy: Birth, Jan 10
Charter Schools Week, Natl (Pres Proc), May 6
Chase, Chevy: Birth, Oct 8
Chasez, JC: Birth, Aug 8
Chastain, Brandi: Birth, July 21
Chauvin Day, Aug 15
Chavez, Cesar Estrada: Birth Anniv, Mar 31
Check Your Batteries Day, Apr 7
Chelios, Chris: Birth, Jan 25
Chemistry Week, Natl, Nov 4
Cheney, Dick: Birth, Jan 30
Cheney, Lynne: Birth, Aug 14
Cheng Cheng Kung: Birth Anniv (Taiwan), Sept 1
Cheng Huang: Birth Anniv Celebration (Taiwan), June 23
Chernobyl Nuclear Reactor Disaster: Anniv, Apr 26
Cherokee Strip Day (OK), Sept 16
Cherry Month, Natl, Feb 1
Cherry, Lynne: Birth, Jan 5
Chesnut, Mary Boykin Miller: Birth Anniv, Mar 31
Chesnutt, Charles W.: Birth Anniv, June 20
Chess, Victoria: Birth, Nov 16
Chew, Ruth: Birth, Apr 8
Chiang Kai-Shek Day (Taiwan), Oct 31
Chicago Bulls Third Straight Title: Anniv, June 20
Chicago Fire, Great: Anniv, Oct 8
Chicago Intl Children's Film Fest, Oct 11
Chief Joseph Surrender: Anniv, Oct 5
Child Health Day (Pres Proc), Oct 1
Child Health Month, Oct 1
Child Passenger Safety Awareness Week, Natl (Pres Proc), Feb 10
Child Safety Council, Natl: Founding Anniv, Nov 9
Childermas, Dec 28
Childhood Depression Awareness Day, May 7
Childhood Injury Prevention Week, Natl, Sept 1
Children,
- Absolutely Incredible Kid Day, **Mar 21**
- Adoption Month, Natl (Pres Proc), **Nov 1**
- Alcohol and Other Drug-Related Birth Defects Week, Natl, **May 12**
- America's Kids Day, **June 23**
- Australia: Sorry Day, **May 26**
- Baby Safety Month, **Sept 1**
- Child Abuse Prevention Month, Natl (Pres Proc), **Apr 1**
- Children's Awareness Month, **June 1**
- Children's Book Day, Intl, **Apr 2**
- Children's Book Week, Natl, **Nov 12**
- Children's Day (Japan), **May 5**
- Children's Day (Korea), **May 5**
- Children's Day, Intl (China), **June 1**
- Children's Day, Natl (Pres Proc), **Oct 14**
- Children's Day, Universal (UN), **Nov 20**
- Children's Day/Natl Sovereignty (Turkey), **Apr 23**
- Children's Film Fest, Intl (Oulu, Finland), **Nov 19**
- Children's Party at Green Animals (Newport, RI), **July 14**
- Dr. Seuss (Geisel): Birth Anniv, **Mar 2**
- Exchange Club Child Abuse Prevention Month, **Apr 1**
- Family Month, Natl, **May 12**
- Firepup's Birthday, **Oct 1**
- Innocent Children Victims of Aggression, Intl Day of, **June 4**
- Japan: Shichi-Go-San, **Nov 15**
- Knuckles Down Month, Natl, **Apr 1**
- Library Card Sign-up Month, **Sept 1**
- Little League Baseball Week, Natl (Pres Proc), **June 10**
- Little League Baseball World Series (Williamsport, PA), **Aug 17**
- Merlin's Snug Hugs for Kids, **Nov 1**
- Safe Toys and Gifts Month, **Dec 1**
- Stand for Children Day, **June 1**
- UN: Decade for a Culture of Peace and Non-Violence for the Children of the World, Intl, **Jan 1**
- Universal Children's Week, **Oct 1**
- Video Games Day, **Sept 12**
- Young Child, Week of the, **Apr 7**
- Youth Day (Cameroon), **Feb 11**
- Youth Day (Zambia), **Aug 6**
- YWCA Week, Natl, **Apr 21**

Children's Book Festival (Hattiesburg, MS), Mar 20
Children's Day (Woodstock, VT), Aug 25
Children's Day in Florida, Apr 9
Children's Day in MA, June 9
Children's Day of Broadcasting, Intl, Dec 9
Children's Eye Health and Safety Month, Sept 1
Children's Fest of Fun (Tempe, AZ), Dec 8
Children's Fest, Intl (Vienna, VA), Sept 15
Children's Good Manners Month, Sept 1
Children's Literature Conference (Columbus, OH), Feb 14
Children's Literature Fest (Keene, NH), Oct 27

Children's Literature Fest (Warrensburg, MO), Mar 10
Children's Literature New England Institute (Toronto, Canada), Aug 1
Children's Memorial Day, Natl, Dec 9
Children's Sunday, June 9
Children's Vision and Learning Month, Aug 1
Childress, Alice: Birth, Oct 12
Chile,
Independence Day, **Sept 18**
National Month, **Sept 1**
Worst Earthquake of the 20th Century: Anniv, **May 22**
Chimborazo Day, June 3
China, People's Republic of,
Double 10th Day, **Oct 10**
Dragon Boat Fest, **June 15**
Fest of Hungry Ghosts, **Sept 2**
International Children's Day, **June 1**
Lantern Fest, **Feb 26**
Mid-Autumn Fest, **Oct 1**
National Day, **Oct 1**
Qing Ming Fest, **Apr 5**
Sun Yat-Sen Birth Anniv, **Nov 12**
Tiananmen Square Massacre: Anniv, **June 4**
Youth Day, **May 4**
Chinese Nationalists Move to Formosa: Anniv, Dec 8
Chinese New Year, Feb 12
Chirac, Jacques Rene: Birth, Nov 29
Chlumsky, Anna: Birth, Dec 3
Chocolate, Debbi: Birth, Jan 25
Choi, Sook Nyul: Birth, Jan 10
Chorao, Kay: Birth, Jan 7
Chou En-Lai: Death Anniv, Jan 8
Chretien, Jean: Birth, Jan 11
Christelow, Eileen: Birth, Apr 22
Christmas,
Armenian Christmas, **Jan 6**
Black Friday, **Nov 23**
Christmas, **Dec 25**
Christmas at the Top Museum (Burlington, WI), **Dec 27**
Christmas Eve, **Dec 24**
Christmas Greetings from Space: Anniv, **Dec 19**
Christmas Tree/Rockefeller Center (New York, NY), **Nov 28**
Humbug Day, **Dec 21**
Navidades (Puerto Rico), **Dec 15**
Netherlands: Sinterklaas, **Dec 5**
Old Calendar Orthodox Christmas, **Jan 7**
Russia: Christmas Day, **Jan 7**
Saint Nicholas Day, **Dec 6**
Shopping Reminder Day, **Nov 25**
Silent Night, Holy Night Celebrations (Austria), **Dec 24**
Whiner's Day, Natl, **Dec 26**
Christopher, Matt: Birth Anniv, Aug 16
Chung Yeung Fest (Hong Kong), Oct 25
Church, Charlotte: Birth, Feb 21
Churchill, Winston: Day, Apr 9
Ciardi, John: Birth Anniv, June 24
Cigarettes Reported Hazardous: Anniv, Jan 11
Cinco de Mayo (Mexico), May 5
Circle K Service Week, Intl, Nov 4
Circus: Greatest Show on Earth: Anniv, Mar 28
Citizenship Day (Pres Proc), Sept 17
Civil Aviation Day, Intl, Dec 7
Civil Rights,
Brown v Board of Education: Anniv, **May 17**
Civil Rights Act of 1964: Anniv, **July 2**
Civil Rights Act of 1968: Anniv, **Apr 11**
Civil Rights Bill of 1866: Anniv, **Apr 9**
Civil Rights Week (MA), **Dec 8**
Freedom Riders: Anniv, **May 1**
Greensboro Sit-in: Anniv, **Feb 1**
King Wins Nobel Peace Prize: Anniv, **Oct 14**
Little Rock Nine: Anniv, **Sept 23**
March on Washington: Anniv, **Aug 28**
Marshall, Thurgood: Birth Anniv, **July 2**
Meredith (James) Enrolls at Ole Miss: Anniv, **Sept 30**
Montgomery Boycott Arrests: Anniv, **Feb 22**
Montgomery Bus Boycott: Anniv, **Dec 5**
Rosa Parks Day, **Dec 1**
Rustin, Bayard: Birth Anniv, **Mar 17**
24th Amendment (Eliminated Poll Taxes), **Jan 23**
Voting Rights Act Signed: Anniv, **Aug 6**
Civil War, American,
Amnesty Issued for Southern Rebels: Anniv, **May 29**
Battle of Antietam: Anniv, **Sept 17**
Battle of Gettysburg: Anniv, **July 1**
Battle of Mobile Bay: Anniv, **Aug 5**
Civil War Ending: Anniv, **Apr 9**
Davis, Jefferson: Inauguration: Anniv, **Feb 18**
Fort Sumter Shelled by North: Anniv, **Aug 17**
Grant Commissioned Commander: Anniv, **Mar 9**
Grant Put in Charge of Mississippi: Anniv, **Oct 16**
Jefferson Davis Captured: Anniv, **May 10**
Johnson Impeachment Proceedings: Anniv, **Feb 24**
Lincoln Approves 13th Amendment (Freedom Day), **Feb 1**
Lincoln Assassination Anniv, **Apr 14**
Lincoln's Gettysburg Address: Anniv, **Nov 19**
SC: Secession Anniv, **Dec 20**
Sherman Enters Atlanta: Anniv, **Sept 2**
Clark, Abraham: Birth Anniv, Feb 15
Clark, Barney: Artificial Heart Transplant: Anniv, Dec 2
Clark, Joe: Birth, June 5
Clay (Muhammad Ali) Becomes Heavyweight Champ: Anniv, Feb 25
Clay, Cassius, Jr (Muhammad Ali): Birth, Jan 17
Clay, Henry: Birth Anniv, Apr 12
Clean Air Act Passed by Congress: Anniv, Dec 17
Clean-Off-Your-Desk Day, Natl, Jan 14
Cleary, Beverly: Birth, Apr 12
Cleland, Max: Birth, Aug 24
Clemens, Roger: Birth, Aug 4
Clemens, Samuel (Mark Twain): Birth Anniv, Nov 30
Clemente, Roberto: Birth Anniv, Aug 18
Clements, Andrew: Birth, May 29
Clerc, Laurent: Birth Anniv, Dec 26
Clerc-Gallaudet Week, Dec 2
Clerihew Day (Edmund Bentley Clerihew Birth Anniv), July 10
Cleveland, Esther: First White House Presidential Baby, Aug 30
Cleveland, Frances: Birth Anniv, July 21
Cleveland, Grover: Birth Anniv, Mar 18
Cleveland, Grover: Second Pres Inauguration: Anniv, Mar 4
Clifton, Lucille: Birth, June 27
Climo, Shirley: Birth, Nov 25
Clinton, George: Birth Anniv, July 26
Clinton, Hillary Rodham: Birth, Oct 26
Clinton, William Jefferson: Birth, Aug 19
Clinton, William: Impeachment Proceedings: Anniv, Dec 20
Cloning of an Adult Animal, First: Anniv, Feb 23
Clooney, George: Birth, May 6
Close, Glenn: Birth, Mar 19
Clymer, George: Birth Anniv, Mar 16
CN Tower: Anniv, June 26
CNN Debuted: Anniv, June 1
Coast Guard Day, Aug 4
Cobb, Ty: Birth Anniv, Dec 18
Cochise: Death Anniv, June 8
Cochran, Jacqueline: Death Anniv, Aug 9
Cochran, Thad: Birth, Dec 7
Cody, William F. "Buffalo Bill": Birth Anniv, Feb 26
Cohen, William S.: Birth, Aug 28
Coin Week, Natl, Apr 21
Coins Stamped "In God We Trust": Anniv, Apr 22
Cold War: Treaty Signed to Mark End: Anniv, Nov 19
Cole, Babette: Birth, Sept 10
Cole, Brock: Birth, May 29
Cole, Joanna: Birth, Aug 11
Coleman, Bessie: Birth Anniv, Jan 26
Colfax, Schuyler: Birth Anniv, Mar 23
Collier, Christopher: Birth, Jan 29
Collier, James Lincoln: Birth, June 27
Collins, Eileen: Birth, Nov 19
Collins, Stephen: Birth, Oct 1
Collins, Susan M.: Birth, Dec 7
Colombia,
Battle of Boyaca, **Aug 7**
Cartagena Independence Day, **Nov 11**
Independence Day, **July 20**
Colonies Become US: Anniv, Sept 9
Color TV Broadcast, First: Anniv, June 25
Colorado,
Admission Day, **Aug 1**
Colorado Day, **Aug 6**
Mesa Verde Natl Park: Anniv, **June 29**
Rocky Mountain Natl Park: Anniv, **Jan 26**
State Fair (Pueblo), **Aug 17**
Columbus, Christopher,
Columbus Day (Observed), **Oct 8**
Columbus Day (Traditional), **Oct 12**
Columbus Day, Natl (Pres Proc), **Oct 8**
Columbus Sails for New World: Anniv, **Aug 3**
Discovery of Jamaica By: Anniv, **May 4**
Coman, Carolyn: Birth, Oct 28
Commodore Perry Day, Apr 10
Common Prayer Day (Denmark), Apr 26
Commonwealth Day (United Kingdom), Mar 11
Commonwealth Day, Belize, May 24
Communication Week, World, Nov 1
Communications: UN World Telecommunication Day, May 17
Communist Party Suspended, Soviet: Anniv, Aug 29
Community Education Day, Natl, Nov 13
Comoros: Independence Day, July 6
Compliment Day, Natl, Jan 23
Computer,
Apple II Computer Released: Anniv, **June 5**
Computer Learning Month, **Oct 1**
Eckert, J. Presper, Jr: Birth Anniv, **Apr 9**
ENIAC Introduced: Anniv, **Feb 14**
IBM PC Introduced: Anniv, **Apr 24**
Internet Created: Anniv, **Oct 29**
Macintosh Computer Released: Anniv, **Jan 25**
Microsoft Releases Windows: Anniv, **Nov 10**
Mouse Developed: Anniv, **Dec 9**
Shareware Day, Intl, **Dec 9**
Technology + Learning Conference (Atlanta, GA), **Nov 7**
World Wide Web: Anniv, **Aug 1**
Concorde Flight, First: Anniv, Jan 21
Cone, David: Birth, Jan 2
Cone, Molly: Birth, Oct 3
Confederate Heroes Day, Jan 19
Confederate Memorial Day (FL, GA), Apr 26
Confederate Memorial Day (MS), Apr 29
Confederate Memorial Day (SC), May 10
Confederate Memorial Day (AL), Apr 22
Confederate Memorial Day/Jefferson Davis Day (KY), June 3
Confederation, Articles of: Ratification Anniv, Mar 1
Conference on Education, Natl (San Diego, CA), Feb 15
Conford, Ellen: Birth, Mar 20
Confucius: Birthday and Teachers' Day (Taiwan), Sept 28

Confucius: Birthday Observance (Hong Kong), Oct 13
Congo (Brazzaville),
Day of National Reconciliation, **June 10**
National Holiday, **Aug 15**
Congo (Kinshasa): Independence Day, June 30
Congress (House of Reps) First Quorum: Anniv, Apr 1
Congress Assembles (US), Jan 3
Congress First Meets in Washington: Anniv, Nov 21
Congress: First Meeting Anniv, Mar 4
Connecticut,
Connecticut Storytelling Fest (New London), **Apr 26**
Kid'rific (Hartford), **Sept 8**
Kids After Christmas (Mystic), **Dec 26**
Ratification Day, **Jan 9**
Connery, Sean: Birth, Aug 25
Connolly, Peter: Birth, May 8
Conrad, Kent: Birth, Mar 12
Conrad, Pam: Birth, June 18
Conserve Water/Detect-a-Leak Week, Mar 3
Constantinople Fell to the Turks: Anniv, May 29
Constitution, US,
11th Amendment Ratified (States' Sov): Anniv, **Feb 7**
12th Amendment Ratified, **June 15**
13th Amendment Ratified: Anniv, **Dec 6**
14th Amendment Ratified, **July 9**
15th Amendment Ratified, **Feb 3**
16th Amendment Ratified (Income Tax), **Feb 3**
17th Amendment Ratified: Anniv, **Apr 8**
18th Amendment (Prohibition): Anniv, **Jan 16**
19th Amendment Ratified, **Aug 18**
20th Amendment (Inaugural, Congress opening dates), **Jan 23**
21st Amendment Ratified, **Dec 5**
22nd Amendment (Two Term Limit): Ratified, **Feb 27**
23rd Amendment Ratified, **Mar 29**
24th Amendment (Eliminated Poll Taxes), **Jan 23**
25th Amendment (Pres Succession, Disability), **Feb 10**
26th Amendment Ratified, **June 30**
27th Amendment Ratified: Anniv, **May 19**
Bill of Rights: Anniv of First State Ratification, **Nov 20**
Constitution Center Groundbreaking, Natl: Anniv, **Sept 17**
Constitution of the US: Anniv, **Sept 17**
Constitution Week (Pres Proc), **Sept 17**
Constitution Week, Natl, **Sept 16**
Constitutional Convention: Anniv, **May 25**
Equal Rights Amendment Sent to States for Ratification, **Mar 22**
Great Debate (Constitutional Convention): Anniv, **Aug 6**
Presidential Succession Act: Anniv, **July 18**
Religious Freedom Day, **Jan 16**
Takes Effect: Anniv, **July 2**
Veep Day, **Aug 9**
Women's Suffrage Amendment Introduced: Anniv, **Jan 10**
Consumer Protection Week, Natl (Pres Proc), Feb 12
Continental Congress Assembly, First: Anniv, Sept 5
Cook, James: Birth Anniv, Oct 27
Cook, Rachel Leigh: Birth, Oct 4
Cooksey, Danny: Birth, Nov 2
Coolidge, Calvin: Birth Anniv, July 4
Coolidge, Grace Anna Goodhue: Birth Anniv, Jan 3
Cooney, Barbara: Birth Anniv, Aug 6
Cooney, Caroline B.: Birth, May 10
Cooney, Joan Ganz: Birth, Nov 30
Cooper, Cynthia: Birth, Apr 14
Cooper, Floyd: Birth, Jan 8
Cooper, James Fenimore: Birth Anniv, Sept 15
Cooper, Justin: Birth, Nov 17
Cooper, Susan: Birth, May 23
Cooperatives, UN Intl Day of, July 6
Copernicus, Nicolaus: Birth Anniv, Feb 19
Copland, Aaron: Birth Anniv, Nov 14
Copperfield, David: Birth, Sept 16
Copyright Law Passed: Anniv, May 31
Cormier, Robert: Birth Anniv, Jan 17
Corpus Christi (US): Observance, June 2
Cortes Conquers Mexico: Anniv, Nov 8
Corzine, Jon: Birth, Jan 1
Cosby Show TV Premiere, The: Anniv, Sept 20
Cosby, Bill: Birth, July 12
Cosgrove, Margaret: Birth, June 3
Costa Rica,
Independence Day, **Sept 15**
Feast of Our Lady of the Angels, **Aug 2**
Guanacaste Day, **July 25**
Costas, Bob: Birth, Mar 22
Cote D'Ivoire,
Death of the First President, **Dec 7**
National Day, **Aug 7**
Council for Exceptional Children Annual Convention (New York, NY), Apr 3
Council of Nicaea I: Anniv, May 20
Couric, Katie: Birth, Jan 7
Cousins, Lucy: Birth, Feb 10
Cousteau, Jacques: Birth Anniv, June 11
Coville, Bruce: Birth, May 16
Cow Milked While Flying: Anniv, Feb 18
Cowboys, Frontier, Old West,
Burk, Martha (Calamity Jane): Death Anniv, **Aug 1**
Oakley, Annie: Birth Anniv, **Aug 13**
Cowley, Joy: Birth, Aug 7
Craig, Helen: Birth, Aug 30
Craig, Larry E.: Birth, July 20
Crapo, Michael: Birth, May 20
Crater Lake Natl Park: Anniv, May 22
Creech, Sharon: Birth, July 29
Cresswell, Helen: Birth, July 11
Crews, Donald: Birth, Aug 30
Crispus Attucks Day, Mar 5
Croatia,
Antifascist Struggle Commemoration Day, **June 22**
Homeland Thanksgiving Day, **Aug 5**
National Day, **May 30**
Crockett, Davy: Birth Anniv, Aug 17
Crossword Puzzle, First: Anniv, Dec 21
Cruise, Tom: Birth, July 3
Crutcher, Chris: Birth, July 17
Cuba,
Anniv of the Revolution, **Jan 1**
Beginning of Independence Wars Day, **Oct 10**
Liberation Day: Anniv, **Jan 1**
National Day, **July 26**
Cuckoo Dancing Week, Jan 11
Culkin, Macaulay: Birth, Aug 26
Culpepper, Daunte: Birth, Jan 28
Cummings, Pat: Birth, Nov 9
Cunningham, Randall: Birth, Mar 27
Cuomo, Andrew: Birth, Dec 6
Curacao,
Curacao Day, **July 26**
Kingdom Day and Antillean Flag Day, **Dec 15**
Memorial Day, **May 4**
Curie, Marie Sklodowska: Birth Anniv, Nov 7
Curry, Tim: Birth, Apr 19
Curtis, Charles: Birth Anniv, Jan 25
Curtis, Christopher Paul: Birth, May 10
Curtis, Jamie Lee: Birth, Nov 22
Cusack, Ann: Birth, May 22
Cushman, Karen: Birth, Oct 4
Custer Battlefield Becomes Little Bighorn Battlefield, Nov 26
Custer, George: Battle of Little Bighorn: Anniv, June 25
Custodial Workers Day, Natl, Oct 2
Cyprus,
Green Monday, **Mar 18**
Independence Day, **Oct 1**
Czech Republic,
Commemoration Day, **July 6**
Foundation of the Republic, **Oct 28**
Independence Day, **Oct 28**
Liberation Day, **May 8**
Teachers' Day, **Mar 28**
Czechoslovakia,
Czech-Slovak Divorce: Anniv, **Jan 1**
Czechoslovakia Ends Communist Rule: Anniv, **Nov 29**
D'Aulaire, Edgar Parin: Birth Anniv, Sept 30
D'Aulaire, Ingri: Birth Anniv, Dec 27
D-Day: Anniv, June 6
D.A.R.E. Day, Natl (Pres Proc), Apr 11
D.A.R.E. Launched: Anniv, Sept 1
Dadey, Debbie: Birth, May 18
Daguerre, Louis: Birth Anniv, Nov 18
Dahl, Roald: Birth Anniv, Sept 13
Dakides, Tara: Birth, Aug 20
Dakos, Kalli: Birth, June 16
Dalai Lama: Birth, June 6
Daley, John: Birth, July 20
Daley, William: Birth, Aug 9
Dallas, George: Birth Anniv, July 10
Damon, Gabriel: Birth, Apr 23
Damon, Matt: Birth, Oct 8
Damus, Mike: Birth, Sept 30
Dance,
Ailey, Alvin: Birth Anniv, **Jan 5**
Ballet Introduced to US: Anniv, **Feb 7**
Duncan, Isadora: Birth Anniv, **May 27**
Graham, Martha: Birth Anniv, **May 11**
Robinson, Bill "Bojangles": Birth Anniv, **May 25**
Tap Dance Day, Natl, **May 25**
Dance, American Alliance for Health, Physical Education, Recreation, Annual Meeting, Apr 9
Daniels, Jeff: Birth, Feb 19
Daniels, William: Birth, Mar 31
Danson, Ted: Birth, Dec 29
Danziger, Paula: Birth, Aug 18
Dare, Virginia: Birth Anniv, Aug 18
Darwin, Charles Robert: Birth Anniv, Feb 12
Daschle, Thomas Andrew: Birth, Dec 9
Daughters To Work Day, Take Our, Apr 25
Davenport, Lindsay: Birth, June 8
David McCord Children's Literature Fest, Nov 1
Davis, Gray: Birth, Dec 26
Davis, Jefferson: Birth Anniv, June 3
Davis, Jefferson: Captured: Anniv, May 10
Davis, Jefferson: Inauguration: Anniv, Feb 18
Davis, Jim: Birth, July 28
Davis, Stephen: Birth, Mar 1
Davis, Terrell: Birth, Oct 28
Davy Crockett TV Premiere: Anniv, Dec 15
Dawes, Charles G.: Birth Anniv, Aug 27
Day for Tolerance, Intl, Nov 16
Day of Concern about Young People and Gun Violence, Natl (Pres Proc), Oct 21
Day of National Concern about Young People and Gun Violence, Oct 21
Day of the Race: See Columbus Day, Oct 12
Day of the Six Billion: Anniv, Oct 12
Day, Alexandra: Birth, Sept 7
Daylight Saving Time Begins, US, Apr 7
Daylight Saving Time Ends, US, Oct 28
Dayton, Mark: Birth, Jan 26
de Angeli, Marguerite: Birth Anniv, Mar 14
De Forest, Lee: Birth Anniv, Aug 26
de Trevino, Elizabeth Borton: Birth, Sept 2
Deaf Awareness Week, Sept 23
Deaf Day, Mother, Father, Apr 28
Deaf History Month, Mar 13
Deaf, First School for: Anniv, Apr 15

Dean, Dizzy: Birth Anniv, Jan 16
Dean, Howard: Birth, Nov 17
Debate, Great (over Constitution): Anniv, Aug 6
Deborah Samson Day (MA), May 23
Debussy, Claude: Birth Anniv, Aug 22
Decatur, Stephen: Birth Anniv, Jan 5
Decisions: Make Up Your Mind Day, Dec 31
Declaration of Independence,
Approval and Initial Signing: Anniv, **July 4**
First Public Reading: Anniv, **July 8**
Official Signing Anniv, **Aug 2**
Resolution Anniv, **July 2**
DeClements, Barthe: Birth, Oct 8
Decoration Day (Memorial Day), May 27
Deem, James M.: Birth, Jan 27
Deepavali, Nov 14
DeFelice, Cynthia: Birth, Dec 28
Defenders Day, Sept 12
Degas, Edgar: Birth Anniv, July 19
Degen, Bruce: Birth, June 14
DeGroat, Diane: Birth, May 24
Del Negro, Janice: Birth, July 5
Delacre, Lulu: Birth, Dec 20
Delaware,
Delaware State Fair (Harrington), **July 18**
Ratification Day, **Dec 7**
Delessert, Etienne: Birth, Jan 4
Demi: Birth, Sept 2
Denmark,
Common Prayer Day, **Apr 26**
Constitution Day, **June 5**
Midsummer Eve, **June 23**
Queen Margrethe's Birthday, **Apr 16**
Street Urchins' Carnival, **Feb 11**
Dental Drill Patent: Anniv, Jan 26
Dental Health Month, Natl Children's, Feb 1
Dental Hygiene Month, Natl, Oct 1
Dental School, First Woman to Graduate: Anniv, Feb 21
DePaola, Tomie: Birth, Sept 15
Des'ree: Birth, Nov 30
Desegregated, US Army First: Anniv, July 26
Desert Shield: Anniv, Aug 7
Desert Storm: Kuwait Liberated: Anniv, Feb 27
Desert Storm: Persian Gulf War Begins: Anniv, Jan 16
Designated Hitter Rule Adopted: Anniv, Jan 11
Desimini, Lisa: Birth, Mar 21
Desk Day, Natl Clean-Off-Your, Jan 14
Development Information Day, World (UN), Oct 24
Devers, Gail: Birth, Nov 19
Devil's Night, Oct 30
DeVito, Danny: Birth, Nov 17
Dewey, Jennifer Owings: Birth, Oct 2
Dewey, John: Birth Anniv, Oct 20
Dewey, Melvil: Birth Anniv, Dec 10
DeWine, Mike: Birth, Jan 5
Dia de la Raza (Mexico), Oct 12
Dia de la Raza: See Columbus Day, Oct 12
Dia de los Ninos/Dia de los Libros, Apr 30
Diabetes Alert, American, Mar 26
Diana, Princess of Wales: Birth Anniv, July 1
DiCaprio, Leonardo: Birth, Nov 11
Dickens, Charles: Birth Anniv, Feb 7
Dickinson, Emily: Birth Anniv, Dec 10
Dickinson, Peter: Birth, Dec 16
Dictionary Day, Oct 16
Didrikson, Babe: See under Zaharias, June 26
Diefenbaker, John: Birth Anniv, Sept 18
Diego, Jose De: Birth Anniv, Apr 16
Dien Bien Phu Falls: Anniv, May 7
DiFrancesco, Donald T.: Birth, Nov 20
Dillon, Barbara: Birth, Sept 2
Dillon, Diane: Birth, Mar 13
Dillon, Leo: Birth, Mar 2
DiMaggio, Joe: Birth Anniv, Nov 25
Ding Dong School TV Premiere: Anniv, Dec 22
Dinosaur Month, Intl, Oct 1
Dinosaur, Month of the, Oct 1
Dinosaur: Sue Exhibited: Anniv, May 17
Dinosaur: Jobaria Exhibited: Anniv, Nov 13
Disabled,
Americans with Disabilities Act: Anniv, **July 26**
Barrier Awareness Day in Kentucky, **May 7**
Clerc-Gallaudet Week, **Dec 2**
Deaf Awareness Week, **Sept 23**
Deaf History Month, **Mar 13**
Disability Day in Kentucky, **Aug 2**
Disability Employment Awareness Month, Natl (Pres Proc), **Oct 1**
Disabled Persons, Intl Day of, **Dec 3**
First School for Deaf: Anniv, **Apr 15**
Helen Keller Deaf-Blindness Awareness Week, **June 23**
Mother, Father Deaf Day, **Apr 28**
Disarmament Week, Oct 24
Discovery Young Scientist Challenge (Washington, DC), Oct 20
Dishonor List, New Year's, Jan 1
Disney World Opened: Anniv, Oct 1
Disney, Walt: Birth Anniv, Dec 5
Disneyland Opened: Anniv, July 17
Diversity Awareness Month, Oct 1
Diwali, Nov 14
Dix, Dorothea L.: Birth Anniv, Apr 4
Djibouti: Independence Day, June 27
Do Something: Kindness & Justice Challenge, Jan 21
Doctors' Day, Mar 30
Dodd, Christopher J.: Birth, May 27
Dodge, Hazel: Birth, Mar 19
Dodge, Mary Mapes: Birth Anniv, Jan 26
Dodgson, Charles Lutwidge: See Carroll, Lewis, Jan 27
Dog Days, July 3
Dog Week, Natl, Sept 23
Dole, Elizabeth Hanford: Birth, July 29
Doll Fest (Japan), Mar 3
Domenici, Pete V.: Birth, May 7
Domestic Violence Awareness Month, Oct 1
Domestic Violence Awareness Month, Natl (Pres Proc), Oct 1
Dominica: National Day, Nov 3
Dominican Republic,
Independence Day, **Feb 27**
National Holiday, **Jan 26**
Restoration of the Republic, **Aug 16**
Don't Step on a Bee Day, July 10
Donald Duck: Birth, June 9
Doolittle, Eliza: Day, May 20
Dorgan, Byron L.: Birth, May 14
Dorough, Howie: Birth, Aug 22
Dorros, Arthur: Birth, May 19
Dorsey, Thomas A.: Birth Anniv, July 1
Double 10th Day (China), Oct 10
Douglas, William O.: Birth Anniv, Oct 16
Douglass, Frederick,
Death Anniv, **Feb 20**
Escape to Freedom: Anniv, **Sept 3**
Frederick Douglass Speaks: Anniv, **Aug 11**
Dragon Boat Fest (China), June 15
Dragonwagon, Crescent: Birth, Nov 25
Drew, Charles: Birth Anniv, June 3
Drinking Straw Patented: Anniv, Jan 3
Drug Abuse/Illicit Trafficking, Intl Day Against (UN), June 26
Drum Month, Intl, Nov 1
Du Bois, W.E.B.: Birth Anniv, Feb 23
Du Bois, William Pene: Birth Anniv, May 9
Duffy, Patrick: Birth, Mar 17
Duke, Patty: Birth, Dec 14
Dumb Week (Greece), Apr 21
Dunant, Jean Henri: Birth Anniv, May 8
Duncan, Isadora: Birth Anniv, May 27
Duncan, Lois: Birth, Apr 28
Duncan, Tim: Birth, Apr 25
Dunn, Shannon: Birth, Nov 26
Dunn, Warrick: Birth, Jan 5
Durbin, Richard J.: Birth, Nov 21
Duvoisin, Roger: Birth Anniv, Aug 28
Dygard, Thomas J.: Birth, Aug 10
Eager, Edward: Death Anniv, Oct 23
Earhart, Amelia: Birth Anniv, July 24
Earmuffs Patented: Anniv, Mar 13
Earp, Wyatt: Birth Anniv, Mar 19
Earth at Aphelion, July 6
Earth at Perihelion, Jan 2
Earth Day (Environment), Apr 22
Earth's Rotation Proved: Anniv, Jan 8
Earth, First Picture of, From Space: Anniv, Aug 7
Earthquake,
Earthquake Strikes Alaska: Anniv, **Mar 27**
Japan Suffers Major Quake: Anniv, **Jan 17**
Mexico City Earthquake: Anniv, **Sept 19**
Missouri Earthquakes: Anniv, **Dec 6**
San Francisco 1906 Earthquake: Anniv, **Apr 18**
San Francisco 1989 Earthquake: Anniv, **Oct 17**
Southern California: Anniv, **Jan 17**
Turkish Earthquake: Anniv, **Aug 17**
Worst Earthquake of the 20th Century: Anniv, **May 22**
Easley, Mike: Birth, Mar 23
East Coast Blackout: Anniv, Nov 9
Easter,
Easter Even, **Mar 30**
Easter Monday, **Apr 1**
Easter Sunday, **Mar 31**
Easter Sundays Through the Year 2005, **Mar 31**
Holy Week, **Mar 24**
Orthodox Easter Sunday, **May 5**
Passion Week, **Mar 17**
Passiontide, **Mar 17**
White House Easter Egg Roll, **Apr 1**
White House Easter Egg Roll: Anniv, **Apr 2**
Easter Rising (Ireland), Apr 24
Eastman, P.D.: Birth, Nov 25
Eastwood, Clint: Birth, May 31
Easy-Bake Oven: Anniv, Feb 1
Eat What You Want Day, May 11
Eckert, Allan W.: Birth, Jan 30
Eckert, J. Presper, Jr: Birth Anniv, Apr 9
Eclipses,
Annular Solar Eclipse, **June 10**
Annular Solar Eclipse, **Dec 14**
Penumbral Lunar Eclipse, **June 24**
Penumbral Lunar Eclipse, **May 26**
Penumbral Lunar Eclipse, **Dec 30**
Ecuador,
Battle of Pichincha Day, **May 24**
Chimborazo Day, **June 3**
Day of Quito, **Dec 6**
Independence Day, **Aug 10**
Edelman, Marian Wright: Birth, June 6
Edens, Cooper: Birth, Sept 25
Ederle, Gertrude: Birth Anniv, Oct 23
Ederle, Gertrude: Swims English Channel: Anniv, Aug 6
Edison, Thomas: Birth Anniv, Feb 11
Edison, Thomas: Black Maria Studio: Anniv, Feb 1
Edison, Thomas: Incandescent Lamp Demonstrated: Anniv, Oct 21
Edison, Thomas: Record of a Sneeze: Anniv, Feb 2
Edmund Fitzgerald Sinking: Anniv, Nov 10
Education, Learning, Schools,
America Goes Back to School (Pres Proc), **Sept 3**
American Education Week, **Nov 11**
American Education Week (Pres Proc), **Nov 11**
American Federation of Teachers Conv (Las Vegas, NV), **July 14**
Art Education Assn Annual Convention (Miami Beach, FL), **Mar 22**

Assn of Independent Schools Conference, Natl (San Francisco, CA), **Feb 26**
Back-to-School Month, Natl, **Aug 1**
Banned Books Week, **Sept 22**
Catholic Educational Assn Conv/Expo, Natl (Atlantic City, NJ), **Apr 2**
Catholic Schools Week, **Jan 27**
Charter Schools Week, Natl (Pres Proc), **May 6**
Chemistry Week, Natl, **Nov 4**
Children's Vision and Learning Month, **Aug 1**
Community Education Assn Conference, Natl (Reno, NV), **Nov 17**
Community Education Day, Natl, **Nov 13**
Computer Learning Month, **Oct 1**
Conference on Education, Natl (San Diego, CA), **Feb 15**
Council for Exceptional Children (New York, NY), **Apr 3**
Day of the Teacher (El Dia Del Maestro), **May 8**
Education and Sharing Day (Pres Proc), **Mar 28**
Education Assn Meeting, Natl (Dallas, TX), **June 30**
Education Goals, Natl: Anniv, **Feb 1**
Education of Young Children, Natl Assn for the, Conference (New York, NY), **Nov 20**
Educational Bosses Week, Natl, **May 20**
Educational Communications and Technology, Assn for, Conference (Atlanta, GA), **Nov 7**
Educational Support Personnel Day, Natl, **Nov 14**
Elementary School Principals, Natl Assn of, Annual Conf (San Antonio, TX), **Apr 6**
Family Sexuality Education Month, Natl, **Oct 1**
Froebel, Friedrich: Birth Anniv, **Apr 21**
Geographic Education, Natl Council for, Meeting, **Aug 1**
Geography Awareness Week, Natl, **Nov 11**
Geography Bee Finals, Natl (Washington, DC), **May 21**
Geography Bee, School Level, Natl, **Nov 30**
Geography Bee, State Level, Natl, **Apr 5**
Gifted Children Conv, Natl Assn (Cincinnati, OH), **Nov 7**
Historically Black Colleges and Universities Week (Pres Proc), **Sept 16**
Hooray for Year-Round School Day, **June 14**
Kindergarten Day, **Apr 21**
Library Card Sign-up Month, **Sept 1**
Library Week, Natl, **Apr 14**
Literacy Day, Intl (UN), **Sept 8**
Mathematics Education Month, **Apr 1**
Mathematics, Natl Council of Teachers of, Annual Meeting (Las Vegas, NV), **Apr 22**
Metric Week, Natl, **Oct 7**
Middle Level Education Month, Natl, **Mar 1**
Middle School Assn, Natl, Annual Conf (Washington, DC), **Nov 1**
Museum Day, Intl, **May 18**
Music in Our Schools Month, **Mar 1**
Newspaper in Education Week, **Mar 4**
No Homework Day, **Mar 22**
One Hundredth Day of School, **Feb 8**
Project ACES Day, **May 1**
PTA Founders' Day, Natl, **Feb 17**
PTA Teacher Appreciation Week, Natl, **May 5**
Public School, First in America: Anniv, **Apr 23**
Read to Your Child Day, **Feb 14**
Reading Is Fun Week, **Apr 21**
School Boards Assn Annual Conference, Natl (New Orleans, LA), **Apr 6**
School Breakfast Week, Natl, **Mar 4**
School Bus Safety Week, Natl, **Oct 21**
School Celebration, Natl, **Oct 12**
School Counseling Week, Natl, **Feb 4**
School for Deaf Founded, First: Anniv, **Apr 15**
School Library Media Month, **Apr 1**
School Lunch Week, Natl, **Oct 15**
School Nurse Day, Natl, **Jan 23**
School Principals' Recognition Day, **Apr 27**
School Spirit Season, Intl, **Apr 30**
School Success Month, Natl, **Sept 1**
School-to-Work Launched: Anniv, **May 4**
SchoolTech Expo and Conference (Chicago, IL), **Oct 18**
Science Teachers Assn Conv, Natl (San Diego, CA), **Mar 27**
Snow Day for Southern Students, **Dec 3**
Social Studies, Natl Council for the, Annual Mtg (Washington, DC), **Nov 16**
Spelling Bee Finals, Natl, **May 29**
Student Day, Natl, **Sept 20**
Student Volunteer Day, **Feb 20**
Substitute Teacher Appreciation Week, **Sept 9**
Sullivan, Anne: Birth Anniv, **Apr 14**
Teacher Day, Natl, **May 7**
Teacher's Day (FL), **May 17**
Teacher's Day (MA), **June 2**
Teachers of English, Natl Council of, Annual Conf (Baltimore, MD), **Nov 15**
Teachers' Day (Czech Republic), **Mar 28**
Teaching and Joy Month, Natl, **May 1**
Texas PTA Conv (Dallas, TX), **Nov 16**
Thank You, School Librarian Day, **Apr 4**
Truancy Law: Anniv, **Apr 12**
Young Child, Week of the, **Apr 7**
Edwards, John: Birth, June 10
Edwards, Julie Andrews: Birth, Oct 1
Edwards, Teresa: Birth, July 19
Egg Month, Natl, May 1
Egg Roll, White House Easter Egg Roll: Anniv, Apr 2
Egg Salad Week, Apr 1
Egielski, Richard: Birth, July 16
Egypt,
Armed Forces Day, **Oct 6**
Camp David Accord Signed: Anniv, **Mar 26**
National Day, **July 23**
Sham El-Nesim, **Apr 20**
Sinai Day, **Apr 25**
Ehlert, Lois: Birth, Nov 9
Eid-al-Adha: Feast of the Sacrifice (Islamic), Feb 22
Eiffel Tower: Anniv (Paris, France), Mar 31
Eiffel, Alexandre Gustave: Birth Anniv, Dec 15
Einstein, Albert: Atomic Bomb Letter Anniv, Aug 2
Einstein, Albert: Birth Anniv, Mar 14
Eisenberg, Hallie Kate: Birth, Aug 2
Eisenhower, Dwight David: Birth Anniv, Oct 14
Eisenhower, Mamie Doud: Birth Anniv, Nov 14
Eisner, Michael: Birth, Mar 7
El Salvador,
Day of the First Shout for Independence, **Nov 5**
Day of the Soldier, **May 7**
Independence Day, **Sept 15**
Natl Day of Peace, **Jan 16**
Election Day, Nov 6
Electric Lighting, First: Anniv, Sept 4
Electricity: Incandescent Lamp Demonstrated: Anniv, Oct 21
Elementary School Principals, Natl Assn of, Annual Conference (San Antonio, TX), Apr 6
Elephant Appreciation Day, Sept 22
Elephant Round-Up at Surin (Thailand), Nov 17
Eliot, John: Birth Anniv, Aug 5
Elizabeth I: Birth Anniv, Sept 7
Elizabeth II, Accession of Queen: Anniv, Feb 6
Elizabeth II, Queen: Birth, Apr 21
Elizondo, Hector: Birth, Dec 22
Ellerbee, Linda: Birth, Aug 15
Ellington, Duke: Birth Anniv, Apr 29
Ellis Island Opened: Anniv, Jan 1
Ellis, Sarah: Birth, May 19
Ellsworth, Oliver: Birth Anniv, Apr 29
Elway, John: Birth, June 28
Emancipation Day (Texas), June 19
Emancipation of 500: Anniv, Aug 1
Emancipation Proclamation: Anniv, Sept 22
Emberley, Ed: Birth, Oct 19
Emergency Medical Services Week, Natl, May 19
Emmett, Daniel D.: Birth Anniv, Oct 29
Employment (employers, occupations, professions),
AFL-CIO Founded: Anniv, **Dec 5**
Agriculture Day, Natl, **Mar 20**
Agriculture Week, Natl, **Mar 17**
Air Conditioning Appreciation Days, **July 3**
Bike to Work Day, Natl, **May 21**
Clean-Off-Your-Desk Day, Natl, **Jan 14**
Custodial Workers Day, Natl, **Oct 2**
Dental Hygiene Month, Natl, **Oct 1**
Educational Bosses Week, Natl, **May 20**
Emergency Medical Services Week, Natl, **May 19**
Engineers Week, Natl, **Feb 17**
Get Organized Week, **Oct 7**
Labor Day, **Sept 3**
New York Stock Exchange: Anniv, **May 17**
Peace Officer Memorial Day, Natl, **May 15**
Police Week, Natl, **May 12**
Printing Week, Intl, **Jan 13**
Public Service Recognition Week, **May 6**
Shop/Office Workers' Holiday (Iceland), **Aug 6**
Small Business Week (Pres Proc), **May 19**
Take Our Daughters to Work Day, **Apr 25**
Tell Someone They're Doing a Good Job Week, **Dec 16**
Tourism Week, Natl, **May 5**
Triangle Shirtwaist Fire: Anniv, **Mar 25**
Weather Observer's Day, Natl, **May 4**
Weatherman's Day, **Feb 5**
Working Women's Day, Intl, **Mar 8**
Endangered Species Act: Anniv, Feb 3
Energy Education Week, Natl, Mar 18
Engdahl, Sylvia Louise: Birth, Nov 24
Engineers Week, Natl, Feb 17
England,
Accession of Queen Elizabeth II: Anniv, **Feb 6**
Battle of Britain Day, **Sept 15**
Battle of Britain Week, **Sept 9**
Great Britain Formed: Anniv, **May 1**
Great Fire of London: Anniv, **Sept 2**
Guy Fawkes Day, **Nov 5**
Last Hurrah for British Hong Kong, **June 30**
Plough Monday, **Jan 7**
Saint George: Feast Day, **Apr 23**
Scotland Yard: First Appearance Anniv, **Sept 29**
Engler, John: Birth, Oct 12
English Colony in North America, First: Anniv, Aug 5
ENIAC Computer Introduced: Anniv, Feb 14
Ensign, John: Birth, Mar 25
Environmental,
America Recycles Day (Pres Proc), **Nov 15**
Arbor Day, Natl (Proposed), **Apr 26**
Bike to Work Day, Natl, **May 21**
Biological Diversity, Intl Day of, **Dec 29**
Chernobyl Reactor Disaster: Anniv, **Apr 26**
Clean Air Act Passed by Congress: Anniv, **Dec 17**
Conserve Water/Detect-a-Leak Week, **Mar 3**
Disaster Reduction, Natural, Intl Day For (UN), **Oct 10**
Earth Day, **Apr 22**
Endangered Species Act: Anniv, **Feb 3**
Environment Day, World (UN), **June 5**
Environmental Policy Act, Natl: Anniv, **Jan 1**

Exxon Valdez Oil Spill: Anniv, **Mar 24**
Keep America Beautiful Month, Natl, **Apr 1**
Preservation of the Ozone Layer, UN Intl Day for, **Sept 16**
President's Environmental Youth Award Natl Competition, **Aug 1**
PTA Earth Week, Natl, **Apr 21**
Public Lands Day, **Sept 8**
Rainforest Week, Natl, **Oct 14**
Recreation and Parks Month, Natl, **July 1**
River of Words Poetry and Art Contest, **Feb 15**
Rural Life Sunday, **May 5**
Save the Rhino Day, **May 1**
Sierra Club Founded: Anniv, **May 28**
Silent Spring Publication: Anniv, **Apr 13**
Sky Awareness Week, **Apr 21**
Water Pollution Control Act: Anniv, **Oct 18**
Water, World Day for (UN), **Mar 22**
Week of the Ocean, Natl, **Apr 7**
World Day to Combat Desertification and Drought, **June 17**
Enzi, Michael B.: Birth, Feb 1
Epiphany (Twelfth Day), Jan 6
Equatorial Guinea,
Armed Forces Day, **Aug 3**
Constitution Day, **Aug 15**
Independence Day, **Oct 12**
Equinox, Autumn, Sept 22
Equinox, Spring, Mar 20
Erdrich, Louise: Birth, June 7
Erie Canal: Anniv, Oct 26
Erikson, Leif: Day (Iceland), Oct 9
Erikson, Leif: Day (Pres Proc), Oct 9
Eritrea: Independence Day, May 24
Estes, Eleanor: Birth Anniv, May 9
Estonia,
Baltic States' Independence Recognized: Anniv, **Sept 6**
Day of National Rebirth, **Nov 16**
Independence Day, **Feb 24**
Victory Day, **June 23**
Etch-A-Sketch Introduced: Anniv, July 12
Ethiopia,
Adwa Day, **Mar 2**
Cross Day, **Sept 27**
New Year's Day, **Sept 11**
Patriots Victory Day, **May 5**
Timket, **Jan 19**
Ethnic Observances. See also nationality names,
Asian Pacific American Heritage Month (Pres Proc), **May 1**
German-American Day (Pres Proc), **Oct 6**
Hispanic Heritage Month (Pres Proc), **Sept 15**
Irish-American Heritage Month (Pres Proc), **Mar 1**
Midsummer Day/Eve Celebrations, **June 23**
Polish American Heritage Month, **Oct 1**
Polish-American in the House (Mikulski): Anniv, **Jan 4**
Swedish Language and Culture Day Camp (Cambridge, MN), **Aug 27**
Etiquette Week, Natl, May 13
Euro Introduced: Anniv, Jan 1
Europe: Summer Daylight-Saving Time, Mar 31
European Union: Schuman Plan Anniv, May 9
Evacuation Day (MA), Mar 17
Evans, Donald: Birth, July 27
Everett, Edward: Birth Anniv, Apr 11
Everett, Rupert: Birth, May 29
Everglades Natl Park: Anniv, Dec 6
Evert Lloyd, Chris: Birth, Dec 21
Ewing, Patrick: Birth, Aug 5
Exchange Club Child Abuse Prevention Month, Apr 1
Exchange Club: Freedom Shrine Month, May 1
Explosion: Halifax, Nova Scotia, Destroyed: Anniv, Dec 6
Exxon Valdez Oil Spill: Anniv, Mar 24
Eye Care Month, Natl, Jan 1
Ezer, Sarah: Birth, Feb 26
Fahrenheit, Gabriel D.: Birth Anniv, May 14
Fairbanks, Charles W.: Birth Anniv, May 11
Fall of the Alamo: Anniv, Mar 6
Families Laughing Through Stories Week, Apr 17
Family,
Adoption Week, Natl, **Nov 18**
Ancestor Appreciation Day, **Sept 27**
Children's Good Manners Month, **Sept 1**
Domestic Violence Awareness Month, **Oct 1**
Exchange Club Child Abuse Prevention Month, **Apr 1**
Families Laughing Through Stories Week, **Apr 17**
Families, UN Intl Day of, **May 15**
Family Day in Nevada, **Nov 23**
Family Health Month, **Oct 1**
Family Literacy Day, Natl, **Nov 1**
Family Month, Natl, **May 12**
Family Sexuality Education Month, Natl, **Oct 1**
Family Week, Natl, **May 5**
Family Week, Natl (Pres Proc), **Nov 18**
Family-Leave Bill: Anniv, **Feb 5**
Father's Day, **June 16**
Father's Day (Pres Proc), **June 16**
Father-Daughter Take a Walk Together Day, **July 7**
Frugal Fun Day, Intl, **Oct 6**
Love the Children Day, **Mar 29**
Loving v Virginia: Anniv, **June 12**
Mother's Day, **May 12**
Moving Month, Natl, **May 1**
Parents' Day (Pres Proc), **July 28**
Read to Your Child Day, **Feb 14**
School Success Month, Natl, **Sept 1**
Single Parents Day, **Mar 21**
Take Our Daughters to Work Day, **Apr 25**
Talk With Your Teen About Sex Month, Natl, **Mar 1**
Universal Children's Week, **Oct 1**
Visit Your Relatives Day, **May 18**
Farber, Norma: Birth Anniv, Aug 6
Farley, Walter: Birth Anniv, June 26
Farm Safety Week, Natl (Pres Proc), Sept 16
Farm-City Week, Natl (Pres Proc), Nov 16
Farmer, Nancy: Birth, July 9
Farragut, David: Battle of Mobile Bay: Anniv, Aug 5
Fasching (Germany, Austria), Feb 11
Fasching Sunday (Germany, Austria), Feb 10
Fast of Esther: Ta'anit Esther, Feb 25
Fast of Gedalya, Sept 20
Fat Albert and the Cosby Kids TV Premiere: Anniv, Sept 9
Father's Day, June 16
Father's Day (Pres Proc), June 16
Father-Daughter Take a Walk Together Day, July 7
Fatone, Joey: Birth, Jan 28
Faulk, Marshall: Birth, Feb 26
Favre, Brett: Birth, Oct 10
Fawkes, Guy: Day (England), Nov 5
FDR: See First Presidential Telecast: Anniv, Apr 30
Feast of Lanterns (Bon Fest) (Japan), July 13
Feast of St. Paul's Shipwreck (Valletta, Malta), Feb 10
Feast of the Immaculate Conception, Dec 8
Federal Communications Commission Created: Anniv, Feb 26
Federal Lands Cleanup Day (Pres Proc), Sept 8
Federov, Sergei: Birth, Dec 13
Feelings, Tom: Birth, May 19
Feiffer, Jules: Birth, Jan 26
Feingold, Russell D.: Birth, Mar 2
Feinstein, Dianne: Birth, June 22
Feminist Bookstore Week, May 4
Fence Painting Contest: Natl Tom Sawyer (Hannibal, MO), July 3
Fenner, Carol: Birth, Sept 30
Fermi, Enrico: Birth Anniv, Sept 29
Fernandez, Lisa: Birth, Feb 22
Ferrigno, Lou: Birth, Nov 9
Ferris Wheel Day, Feb 14
FFA Convention, Natl (Louisville, KY), Oct 24
Field, Sally: Birth, Nov 6
Fiji: Independence Day, Oct 8
Fillmore, Abigail P.: Birth Anniv, Mar 13
Fillmore, Caroline: Birth Anniv, Oct 21
Fillmore, Millard: Birth Anniv, Jan 7
Film,
Academy Awards, First: Anniv, **May 16**
Backyard Natl Children's Film Fest, **Nov 2**
Black Maria Studio: Anniv, **Feb 1**
Chicago Intl Children's Film Fest, **Oct 11**
Children's Film Fest, Intl (Oulu, Finland), **Nov 19**
Donald Duck: Birth, **June 9**
First Movie Theater Opens, **Apr 23**
Record of a Sneeze: Anniv, **Feb 2**
Wizard of Oz First Released: Anniv, **Aug 25**
Fine, Anne: Birth, Dec 7
Finland,
Children's Film Fest, Intl (Oulu), **Nov 19**
Flag Day, **June 4**
Independence Day: Anniv, **Dec 6**
Fire,
Apollo Spacecraft Fire: Anniv, **Jan 27**
Fire Prevention Week, **Oct 7**
Fire Prevention Week (Pres Proc), **Oct 7**
Firepup's Birthday, **Oct 1**
Great Chicago Fire: Anniv, **Oct 8**
Great Fire of London: Anniv, **Sept 2**
Peshtigo (WI) Forest Fire: Anniv, **Oct 8**
Triangle Shirtwaist Fire: Anniv, **Mar 25**
Fireworks Safety Month, June 1
First American to Orbit Earth: Anniv, Feb 20
First Automatic Toll Collection Machine: Anniv, Nov 19
First Black Southern Lt Governor: Anniv, Jan 11
First Car Insurance: Anniv, Feb 1
First Commercial Oil Well: Anniv, Aug 27
First Dictionary of American English Published: Anniv, Apr 14
First Flight Attendant: Anniv, May 15
First License Plates: Anniv, Apr 25
First McDonald's Opens: Anniv, Apr 15
First Movie Theater Opens: Anniv, Apr 23
First Presidential Telecast: Anniv, Apr 30
First Scheduled Radio Broadcast: Anniv, Nov 2
First Session of the Supreme Court, Feb 1
First Televised Presidential Debate: Anniv, Sept 26
First Typewriter: Anniv, June 23
First US Census: Anniv, Aug 1
First US Income Tax: Anniv, Mar 8
First Winter Olympics: Anniv, Jan 25
First Woman Supreme Court Justice: Anniv, Sept 25
Fiscal Year, US Federal, Oct 1
Fishel, Danielle: Birth, May 5
Fisher, Leonard Everett: Birth, June 24
Fishing,
Hunting and Fishing Day, Natl (Pres Proc), **Sept 22**
Take a Kid Fishing Weekend (St. Paul, MN), **June 8**
ZAM! Zoo and Aquarium Month, **Apr 1**
Fisk, Carlton: Birth, Dec 26
Fitch, Sheree: Birth, Dec 3
Fitr, Eid-al-: (Islamic) Celebrating the Fast, Dec 16
Fitzgerald, John D.: Death Anniv, May 21
Fitzgerald, Peter: Birth, Oct 20
Fitzhugh, Louise: Birth Anniv, Oct 5
5-A-Day Week, Natl, Sept 9

Five Billion, Day of the: Anniv, July 11
Flag Act of 1818: Anniv, Apr 4
Flag Day (Pres Proc), June 14
Flag Day USA, Pause for Pledge, Natl, June 14
Flag Day: Anniv of the Stars and Stripes, June 14
Flag of Canada Day, Natl, Feb 15
Flag Week, Natl (Pres Proc), June 9
Fleischman, Paul: Birth, Sept 5
Fleischman, Sid: Birth, Mar 16
Fleming, Alexander: Birth Anniv, Aug 6
Fleming, Denise: Birth, Jan 31
Fleming, Ian: Birth Anniv, May 28
Fleury, Theo: Birth, June 29
Flintstones TV Premiere: Anniv, Sept 30
Flood, Johnstown: Anniv, May 31
Florian, Douglas: Birth, Mar 18
Florida,
- Admission Day, **Mar 3**
- Arbor Day, **Jan 18**
- Art Education Assn Annual Convention, Natl (Miami Beach), **Mar 22**
- Biscayne Natl Park: Anniv, **June 28**
- Children's Day, **Apr 9**
- Confederate Memorial Day, **Apr 26**
- Disney World Opened: Anniv, **Oct 1**
- Everglades Natl Park: Anniv, **Dec 6**
- Grandmother's Day, **Oct 14**
- Juneteenth, **June 19**
- Law Enforcement Appreciation Month, **May 1**
- Orange Bowl Parade (Miami), **Dec 31**
- Pan-American Day, **Apr 14**
- Pascua Florida Day, **Apr 2**
- Patriot's Day, **Apr 19**
- Poetry Day, **May 25**
- Ponce de Leon Discovers Florida: Anniv, **Apr 2**
- Retired Teacher's Day, **Nov 19**
- Save the Florida Panther Day, **Mar 16**
- State Day, **Apr 2**
- State Fair (Tampa), **Feb 7**
- Teacher's Day, **May 17**

Flowers, Flower Shows,
- Flower Fest (Hana Matsuri, Japan), **Apr 8**
- Lei Day (Hawaii), **May 1**
- Poinsettia Day, **Dec 12**
- Rose Month, Natl, **June 1**
- Tournament of Roses Parade (Pasadena, CA), **Jan 1**

Floyd, William: Birth Anniv, Dec 17
Flu Pandemic of 1918 Hits US: Anniv, Mar 11
Fonteyn, Margot: Birth Anniv, May 18
Food and Beverage-Related Events and Observances,
- Appert, Nicholas: Birth Anniv, **Oct 23**
- Baked Bean Month, Natl, **July 1**
- Barbecue Month, Natl, **May 1**
- Blueberries Month, Natl July Belongs to, **July 1**
- Bun Day (Iceland), **Feb 11**
- California Kiwifruit Day, **Feb 2**
- Candy Month, Natl, **June 1**
- Cherry Month, Natl, **Feb 1**
- Eat What You Want Day, **May 11**
- Egg Month, Natl, **May 1**
- Egg Salad Week, **Apr 1**
- First McDonald's Opens: Anniv, **Apr 15**
- Food Day, World (UN), **Oct 16**
- Frozen Food Month, Natl, **Mar 1**
- Frozen Yogurt Month, Natl, **June 1**
- Hamburger Month, Natl, **May 1**
- Honey Month, Natl, **Sept 1**
- Hot Dog Month, Natl, **July 1**
- Hot Tea Month, Natl, **Jan 1**
- Ice Cream Cone: Birth, **Sept 22**
- Ice Cream Day, Natl, **July 21**
- June Is Turkey Lovers' Month, **June 1**
- Mustard Day, Natl, **Aug 4**
- North Carolina SweetPotato Month, **Feb 1**
- Oatmeal Month, **Jan 1**
- Pasta Month, Natl, **Oct 1**
- Peanut Butter Lover's Month, **Nov 1**
- Pecan Day, **Mar 25**
- Popcorn Poppin' Month, Natl, **Oct 1**
- Return Shopping Carts to the Supermarket Month, **Feb 1**
- Rice God, Day of the (Chiyoda, Japan), **June 2**
- Rice Planting Fest (Osaka, Japan), **June 14**
- Salad Month, Natl, **May 1**
- Salsa Month, Natl, **May 1**
- Sandwich Day, **Nov 3**
- School Breakfast Week, Natl, **Mar 4**
- Split Pea Soup Week, Natl, **Nov 4**
- Vegetarian Awareness Month, **Oct 1**
- Vegetarian Day, World, **Oct 1**
- Vegetarian Resource Group's Essay Contest for Kids, **May 1**
- World Food Day, **Oct 16**

Football,
- Football League, Natl, Formed: Anniv, **Sept 17**
- Rose Bowl Game (Pasadena, CA), **Jan 1**
- Super Bowl (New Orleans, LA), **Jan 27**

Forbes, Esther: Birth Anniv, June 28
Ford, Betty: Birth, Apr 8
Ford, Gerald R.: Birth, July 14
Ford, Gerald: Veep Day, Aug 9
Ford, Gerald: Vice President Sworn In: Anniv, Dec 6
Ford, Harrison: Birth, July 13
Foreign Languages, American Council on Teaching, Annual Conference (Washington, DC), Nov 16
Foreman, Michael: Birth, Mar 21
Forest Products Week, Natl (Pres Proc), Oct 21
Forsberg, Peter: Birth, July 20
Fort Sumter Shelled by North: Anniv, Aug 17
Fortas, Abe: Birth Anniv, June 19
Forten, James: Birth Anniv, Sept 2
Foster, Andrew "Rube": Birth Anniv, Sept 17
Foster, Blake: Birth, May 29
Foster, Jodie: Birth, Nov 19
Foster, Mike: Birth, July 11
Foster, Stephen: Birth Anniv, July 4
Foster, Stephen: Memorial Day (Pres Proc), Jan 13
Foucault, Jean: Earth's Rotation Proved: Anniv, Jan 8
Foudy, Julie: Birth, Jan 27
Foundation Day, Natl (Japan), Feb 11
Fox, Matthew: Birth, July 14
Fox, Mem: Birth, Mar 5
Fox, Michael J.: Birth, June 9
Fox, Paula: Birth, Apr 22
Fox, Vicente: Birth, July 2
Foxx, Jimmie: Birth Anniv, Oct 22
Fraggle Rock TV Premiere: Anniv, Sept 12
France,
- Armistice Day, **May 8**
- Bastille Day, **July 14**
- Eiffel Tower: Anniv (Paris), **Mar 31**

Frank, Anne, Diary: Last Entry: Anniv, Aug 1
Frank, Anne: Birth Anniv, June 12
Frank, Jason David: Birth, Sept 4
Franklin Prefers Turkey: Anniv, Jan 26
Franklin, Benjamin: Birth Anniv, Jan 17
Franklin, Benjamin: Poor Richard's Almanack: Anniv, Dec 28
Fraser, Brendan: Birth, Dec 3
Freedman, Russell: Birth, Oct 11
Freedom Day: Anniv, Feb 1
Freedom Riders: Anniv, May 1
Freedom Shrine Month, May 1
Freeman, Antonio: Birth, May 27
Freeman, Don: Birth Anniv, Aug 11
French and Indian War Ends: Anniv, Feb 10
French West Indies: Concordia Day (St. Martin), Nov 11
Friedle, Will: Birth, Aug 11
Friedman, Ina R.: Birth, Jan 6
Friendship: Secret Pal Day, Jan 13
Frisbee Introduced: Anniv, Jan 13
Frist, William: Birth, Feb 22
Fritz, Jean: Birth, Nov 16
Froebel, Friedrich: Birth Anniv, Apr 21
Frost, Robert Lee: Birth Anniv, Mar 26
Frozen Food Month, Natl, Mar 1
Frozen Yogurt Month, Natl, June 1
Frugal Fun Day, Intl, Oct 6
Fuller, Melville Weston: Birth Anniv, Feb 11
Fulton, Robert: Sails Steamboat: Anniv, Aug 17
Funky Winkerbean: Anniv, Mar 27
G.I. Joe Introduced: Anniv, Feb 1
Gabon: National Day, Aug 17
Gag, Wanda: Birth Anniv, Mar 11
Galdone, Paul: Birth, June 2
Galeota, Michael: Birth, Aug 28
Galilei, Galileo: Birth Anniv, Feb 15
Gallagher, David: Birth, Feb 9
Gallaudet, Thomas Hopkins: Birth Anniv, Dec 10
Galveston, TX Hurricane: Anniv, Sept 8
Gambia: Independence Day, Feb 18
Game and Puzzle Week, Natl, Nov 18
Games: JCC Maccabi Youth Games, Aug 19
Gandhi, Mohandas: Birth Anniv, Oct 2
Gannett, Ruth Stiles: Birth, Aug 12
Gantos, Jack: Birth, July 2
Garcia, Sergio: Birth, Jan 9
Gardam, Jane: Birth, July 11
Garden, Nancy: Birth, May 15
Gardiner, John Reynolds: Birth, Dec 6
Gardner, Randy: Birth, Dec 2
Garfield, James A.: Birth Anniv, Nov 19
Garfield, Leon: Birth Anniv, July 14
Garfield, Lucretia R.: Birth Anniv, Apr 19
Garfield: Birthday, June 19
Garner, Alan: Birth, Oct 17
Garner, John Nance: Birth Anniv, Nov 22
Garnett, Kevin: Birth, May 19
Gates of the Arctic Natl Park: Anniv, Dec 2
Gates, Bill: Birth, Oct 28
Gauguin, Paul: Birth Anniv, June 7
Gedalya, Fast of, Sept 20
Gehrig, Lou: Birth Anniv, June 19
Geiger, Matt: Birth, Sept 10
Geisel, Theodor "Dr. Seuss": Birth Anniv, Mar 2
Geisert, Arthur: Birth, Sept 20
Gellar, Sarah Michelle: Birth, Apr 14
Geller, Uri: Birth, Dec 20
Gelman, Rita Golden: Birth, July 2
Gemini Begins, May 21
General Motors: Founding Anniv, Sept 16
Geographic Education, Natl Council for, Meeting, Aug 1
Geography Awareness Week, Natl, Nov 11
Geography Bee Finals, Natl (Washington, DC), May 21
Geography Bee, School Level, Natl, Nov 30
Geography Bee, State Level, Natl, Apr 5
George, Eddie: Birth, Sept 24
George, Jean Craighead: Birth, July 2
George, Kristine O'Connell: Birth, May 6
Georgia,
- American Library Assn Annual Conference (Atlanta), **June 13**
- Confederate Memorial Day, **Apr 26**
- Educational Communications and Technology, Assn for, Conference (Atlanta), **Nov 7**
- Georgia National Fair (Perry), **Oct 5**
- Jefferson Davis Captured: Anniv, **May 10**
- Oglethorpe, James: Birth Anniv, **Dec 22**
- Ratification Day, **Jan 2**
- Sherman Enters Atlanta: Anniv, **Sept 2**
- Technology + Learning Conference (Atlanta), **Nov 7**

Georgia (Europe): Independence Restoration Day, May 26
Geringer, Jim: Birth, Apr 24
Geringer, Laura: Birth, Feb 23
German,
German-American Day (Pres Proc), **Oct 6**
Germany,
Berlin Airlift: Anniv, **June 24**
Berlin Wall Opened: Anniv, **Nov 9**
Buss und Bettag, **Nov 21**
Capital Returns to Berlin: Anniv, **July 6**
Day of Remembrance for Victims of Nazism, **Jan 27**
Kristallnacht: Anniv, **Nov 9**
Munich Fasching Carnival, **Jan 7**
Reunification Anniv, **Oct 3**
Volkstrauertag, **Nov 18**
Geronimo: Death Anniv, Feb 17
Gerry, Elbridge: Birth Anniv, July 17
Gershwin, George: Birth Anniv, Sept 26
Gershwin, Ira: Birth Anniv, Dec 6
Gerstein, Mordicai: Birth, Nov 24
Get a Different Name Day, Feb 13
Get Caught Reading Month, May 1
Get Organized Week, Oct 7
Gettysburg Address, Lincoln's: Anniv, Nov 19
Ghana,
Independence Day, **Mar 6**
Republic Day, **July 1**
Revolution Day, **June 4**
Ghosts, Fest of Hungry (China), Sept 2
Gibbons, Gail: Birth, Aug 1
Giblin, James Cross: Birth, July 8
Gibson, Mel: Birth, Jan 3
Giff, Patricia Reilly: Birth, Apr 26
Gilchrist, Brad: Birth, Oct 25
Gilchrist, Guy: Birth, Jan 30
Gilchrist, Jan Spivey: Birth, Feb 15
Gillom, Jennifer: Birth, June 13
Gilmore, James: Birth, Oct 6
Ginsburg, Ruth Bader: Birth, Mar 15
Ginza Holiday: Japanese Cultural Fest (Chicago, IL), Aug 17
Giovanni, Nikki: Birth, June 7
Gipson, Fred: Birth Anniv, Feb 7
Girl Scout Week, Mar 10
Girl Scouts Founding: Anniv, Mar 12
Girls and Women in Sports Day, Natl, Feb 7
Girls Incorporated Week, May 12
Glacier Bay Natl Park: Anniv, Dec 2
Glacier Natl Park: Anniv, May 11
Glavine, Tom: Birth, Mar 23
Glendening, Parris: Birth, June 11
Glenn, John: Birth, July 18
Glickman, Dan: Birth, Nov 24
Goble, Paul: Birth, Sept 17
God Bless America First Performed: Anniv, Nov 11
Goddard Day, Mar 16
Goddard, Robert H.: Birth Anniv, Oct 5
Godden, Rumer: Birth Anniv, Dec 10
Goffstein, M.B.: Birth, Dec 20
Gold Discovery, California: Anniv, Jan 24
Gold Discovery, Klondike Eldorado: Anniv, Aug 31
Gold Star Mother's Day (Pres Proc), Sept 30
Gold, Tracey: Birth, May 16
Goldberg, Whoopi: Birth, Nov 13
Goldblum, Jeff: Birth, Oct 22
Golden Gate Bridge Opened: Anniv, May 27
Golden Rule Week, Apr 1
Golden Spike Driving: Anniv, May 10
Golf,
US Girls' Junior Chmpshp (Westfield, NJ), **July 22**
Zaharias, Mildred Babe Didrikson: Birth Anniv, **June 26**
Good Friday, Mar 29
Good Morning America TV Premiere: Anniv, Nov 6
Goodall, Jane: Birth, Apr 3
Goode, Diane: Birth, Sept 14
Gooden, Dwight: Birth, Nov 16
Goodman, Benny: Death Anniv, June 13
Goodman, John: Birth, June 20
Goof-Off Day, Intl, Mar 22
Gordon, Jeff: Birth, Aug 4
Gordon, Sheila: Birth, Jan 22
Gordon-Levitt, Joseph: Birth, Feb 17
Gore, Albert, Jr.: Birthday, Mar 31
Gorilla Born in Captivity, First: Anniv, Dec 22
Gosselaar, Mark-Paul: Birth, Mar 1
Gould, Benjamin: Birth, Oct 25
Grace, Mark: Birth, June 28
Graf, Steffi: Birth, June 14
Graham, Martha: Birth Anniv, May 11
Graham, Robert: Birth, Nov 9
Grahame, Kenneth: Birth Anniv, Mar 8
Gramm, Phil: Birth, July 8
Granato, Cammi: Birth, Mar 25
Grand Canyon Natl Park: Anniv, Feb 26
Grandma Moses Day, Sept 7
Grandmother's Day in Florida, Oct 14
Grandparents Day, Natl (Pres Proc), Sept 9
Grange Week, Apr 21
Grant, Harvey: Birth, July 4
Grant, Horace: Birth, July 4
Grant, Julia Dent: Birth Anniv, Jan 26
Grant, Ulysses S.,
Birth Anniv, **Apr 27**
Commissioned Commander: Anniv, **Mar 9**
Put in Charge of Mississippi: Anniv, **Oct 16**
Grassley, Charles Ernest: Birth, Sept 17
Graves, Bill: Birth, Jan 9
Gray, Elizabeth: See Vining, Elizabeth: Birth Anniv, Oct 6
Gray, Robert, Circumnavigates the Earth: Anniv, Apr 10
Great (Holy) Week, Mar 24
Great American Smokeout, Nov 15
Great American Smokeout Day, Natl (Pres Proc), Nov 15
Great Britain Formed: Anniv, May 1
Greatest Show on Earth Formed: Anniv, Mar 28
Greece,
Dumb Week, **Apr 21**
Independence Day, **Mar 25**
Midwife's Day or Women's Day, **Jan 8**
Ochi Day, **Oct 28**
Greek Independence Day (Pres Proc), Mar 25
Green Monday (Cyprus), Mar 18
Green, Trent: Birth, July 9
Greenberg, Jan: Birth, Dec 29
Greene, Bette: Birth, June 28
Greene, Rhonda Gowler: Birth, Oct 29
Greenfield, Eloise: Birth, May 17
Greensboro Sit-in: Anniv, Feb 1
Greenspan, Alan: Birth, Mar 6
Greenwich Mean Time Begins: Anniv, Sept 25
Gregg, Judd: Birth, Feb 14
Gregorian Calendar Adjustment: Anniv, Oct 4
Gregorian Calendar Day, Feb 24
Grenada,
Emancipation Day, **Aug 6**
Independence Day, **Feb 7**
Grenadines and Saint Vincent: Independence Day, Oct 27
Gretzky, Wayne: Birth, Jan 26
Grieve, Ben: Birth, May 4
Griffey, George (Ken), Jr: Birth, Nov 21
Griffith, Andy, Show TV Premiere: Anniv, Oct 3
Griffith, Yolanda: Birth, Mar 1
Grimes, Nikki: Birth, Oct 20
Grimm, Jacob: Birth Anniv, Jan 4
Grimm, Wilhelm: Birth Anniv, Feb 24
Grodin, Charles: Birth, Apr 21
Groening, Matt: Birth, Feb 15
Grouch Day, Natl, Oct 15
Groundhog Day, Feb 2
Groundhog Day (Punxsutawney, PA), Feb 2
Gruelle, Johnny: Birth Anniv, Dec 24
Guadalajara Intl Book Fair, Nov 24
Guadalupe Hidalgo, Treaty of: Anniv, Feb 2
Guadalupe Mountains Natl Park: Anniv, Sept 30
Guadalupe, Day of Our Lady of, Dec 12
Guam,
Discovery Day, **Mar 4**
Lady of Camarin Day, **Dec 8**
Liberation Day, **July 21**
Magellan Day, **Mar 4**
Guatemala,
Armed Forces Day, **June 30**
Independence Day, **Sept 15**
Kite Fest of Santiago Sacatepequez, **Nov 1**
Revolution Day, **Oct 20**
Guinea-Bissau,
Colonization Martyr's Day, **Aug 3**
Independence Day, **Sept 24**
Natl Heroes Day, **Jan 20**
Re-Adjustment Movement's Day, **Nov 14**
Guinea: Independence Day, Oct 2
Gumbel, Bryant: Birth, Sept 29
Gumby Show TV Premiere: Anniv, Mar 16
Gun Violence, Day of National Concern about Young People and, Oct 21
Gurney, James: Birth, June 14
Guthrie, Woody: Birth, July 14
Gutman, Dan: Birth, Oct 19
Guy, Rosa: Birth, Sept 1
Guyana: National Day, Feb 23
Gwinnett, Button: Death Anniv, May 16
Gwynn, Tony: Birth, May 9
Habitat Day, World (UN), Oct 1
Haddix, Margaret Peterson: Birth, Apr 9
Hagel, Chuck: Birth, Oct 4
Hague, Michael: Birth, Sept 8
Hahn, Mary Downing: Birth, Dec 9
Haim, Corey: Birth, Dec 23
Haiti,
Ancestors' Day, **Jan 2**
Discovery Day: Anniv, **Dec 5**
Flag and University Day, **May 18**
Independence Day, **Jan 1**
Halcyon Days, Dec 14
Hale, Nathan: Birth Anniv, June 6
Haleakala Natl Park: Anniv, Sept 30
Haley, Alex Palmer: Birth Anniv, Aug 11
Haley, Gail E.: Birth, Nov 4
Halfway Point of 2002, July 2
Halfway Point of Autumn, Nov 6
Halfway Point of Spring, May 5
Halfway Point of Summer, Aug 6
Halfway Point of Winter, Feb 3
Hall, Donald: Birth, Sept 29
Hall, Lynn: Birth, Nov 9
Halley, Edmund: Birth Anniv, Nov 8
Halloween,
Devil's Night, **Oct 30**
Hallowe'en or All Hallow's Eve, **Oct 31**
Magic Day, Natl, **Oct 31**
Trick or Treat or Beggar's Night, **Oct 31**
UNICEF Day, Natl (Pres Proc), **Oct 31**
Unmasking Halloween Dangers, **Oct 1**
Hamburger Month, Natl, May 1
Hamilton, Scott: Birth, Aug 28
Hamilton, Virginia: Birth, Mar 12
Hamlin, Hannibal: Birth Anniv, Aug 27
Hamm, Mia: Birth, May 17
Hammon, Jupiter: Birth Anniv, Oct 17
Hancock, John: Birth Anniv, Jan 12
Handel, George Frederick: Birth Anniv, Feb 23
Handford, Martin: Birth, Sept 27
Handwriting Day, Natl, Jan 12
Hangul (Korea), Oct 9
Hanks, Tom: Birth, July 9
Hannukah, Dec 10
Hansen, Joyce: Birth, Oct 18
Hanson, (Clarke) Isaac: Birth, Nov 17
Hanson, Jordan Taylor: Birth, Mar 14
Hanson, Zachary Walker: Birth, Oct 22

Happy Birthday to "Happy Birthday to You", June 27
Happy Day, I Want You to Be, Mar 3
Happy Days TV Premiere: Anniv, Jan 15
Hardaway, Penny: Birth, July 18
Hardaway, Tim: Birth, Sept 1
Harding, Florence: Birth Anniv, Aug 15
Harding, Warren G.: Birth Anniv, Nov 2
Harding, Warren G.: First Radio Broadcast, June 14
Harkin, Thomas R.: Birth, Nov 19
Harris, Ed: Birth, Nov 28
Harris, Joel Chandler: Birth Anniv, Dec 9
Harris, Rosemary: Birth, Feb 20
Harrison, Anna: Birth Anniv, July 25
Harrison, Benjamin: Birth Anniv, Aug 20
Harrison, Caroline L.S.: Birth Anniv, Oct 1
Harrison, Mary: Birth Anniv, Apr 30
Harrison, William Henry: Birth Anniv, Feb 9
Harry (Prince), son of Charles and Diana: Birth, Sept 15
Hart, John: Death Anniv, May 11
Hart, Melissa Joan: Birth, Apr 18
Haru-No-Yabuiri (Japan), Jan 16
Harvest Moon, Oct 2
Harvey, William: Birth Anniv, Apr 1
Hasek, Dominik: Birth, Jan 29
Haskins, James: Birth, Sept 19
Hastert, Dennis: Birth, Jan 2
Hatch, Orrin Grant: Birth, Mar 22
Hatcher, Teri: Birth, Dec 8
Haugaard, Erik Christian: Birth, Apr 13
Hawaii,
Haleakala Natl Park: Anniv, **Sept 30**
Hawaii Annexed by US: Anniv, **July 7**
Hawaii Statehood: Anniv, **Aug 21**
King Kamehameha I Day, **June 11**
Lei Day, **May 1**
Prince Jonah Kuhio Kalanianole Day, **Mar 26**
Hawk, Tony: Birth, May 12
Hawke, Ethan: Birth, Nov 6
Haydn, Franz Joseph: Birth Anniv, Mar 31
Hayes, Ira Hamilton: Birth Anniv, Jan 12
Hayes, Lucy: Birth Anniv, Aug 28
Hayes, Rutherford B.: Birth Anniv, Oct 4
Health and Welfare,
Adoption Week, Natl, **Nov 18**
AIDS Day, World (UN), **Dec 1**
AIDS Day, World (US observance), **Dec 1**
AIDS Named: Anniv, **July 27**
Alcohol and Other Drug-Related Birth Defects Week, Natl, **May 12**
Alcohol Awareness Month, Natl, **Apr 1**
Allergy/Asthma Awareness Month, Natl, **May 1**
American Red Cross: Founding Anniv, **May 21**
Anesthetic First Used in Surgery: Anniv, **Mar 30**
Artificial Heart Transplant: Anniv, **Dec 2**
Autism Awareness Month, Natl, **Apr 1**
Back to School Head Lice Prevention Campaign, **Sept 1**
Campaign for Healthier Babies, **Oct 1**
Cancer Control Month (Pres Proc), **Apr 1**
Cancer in the Sun Month, **June 1**
Child Health Day (Pres Proc), **Oct 1**
Child Health Month, **Oct 1**
Children's Dental Health Month, Natl, **Feb 1**
Children's Eye Health and Safety Month, **Sept 1**
Children's Vision and Learning Month, **Aug 1**
Cigarettes Reported Hazardous: Anniv, **Jan 11**
Crime Prevention Month, Natl, **Oct 1**
Dental Hygiene Month, Natl, **Oct 1**
Diabetes Alert, American, **Mar 26**
Doctors' Day, **Mar 30**
Emergency Medical Services Week, Natl, **May 19**
Eye Care Month, Natl, **Jan 1**
Family Health Month, **Oct 1**
Family Sexuality Education Month, Natl, **Oct 1**
5-A-Day Week, Natl, **Sept 9**
Flu Pandemic of 1918 Hits US: Anniv, **Mar 11**
Goof-Off Day, Intl, **Mar 22**
Great American Smokeout, **Nov 15**
Great American Smokeout Day, Natl (Pres Proc), **Nov 15**
Health Education Week, Natl, **Oct 15**
Healthy Skin Month, Natl, **Nov 1**
Heart Month, American, **Feb 1**
Heart Month, American (Pres Proc), **Feb 1**
Helen Keller Deaf-Blindness Awareness Week, **June 23**
Hemophilia Month, **Mar 1**
Hepatitis Awareness Month, **May 1**
Hug-A-Week for the Hearing Impaired, **Dec 1**
Insulin First Isolated: Anniv, **July 27**
KidsDay, Natl, **Sept 15**
Lister, Joseph: Birth Anniv, **Apr 5**
March of Dimes Birth Defects Prevention Month, **Jan 1**
Mental Health Month, Natl, **May 1**
Mental Retardation Awareness Month, **Mar 1**
Mother, Father Deaf Day, **Apr 28**
Nutrition Month, Natl, **Mar 1**
Organ and Tissue Awareness Week, Natl (Pres Proc), **Apr 14**
Organ and Tissue Donor Awareness Week, Natl, **Apr 14**
Orthodontic Health Month, Natl, **Oct 1**
Pan American Health Day (Pres Proc), **Dec 2**
Pediatric Cancer Awareness Month, **Oct 1**
Poison Prevention Week, Natl, **Mar 17**
Polio Vaccine: Anniv, **Apr 12**
Population Day, World (UN), **July 11**
Project ACES Day, **May 1**
Public Health Week, Natl, **Apr 7**
Red Cross Month, **Mar 1**
Red Cross Month, American (Pres Proc), **Mar 1**
Safe Boating Week, Natl, **May 18**
Save Your Vision Week, **Mar 3**
Save Your Vision Week (Pres Proc), **Mar 3**
School Breakfast Week, Natl, **Mar 4**
School Counseling Week, Natl, **Feb 4**
School Lunch Week, Natl, **Oct 15**
Sleep Awareness Week, Natl, **Mar 25**
Social Security Act: Anniv, **Aug 14**
Speech-Lang-Hearing Conv, American (New Orleans, LA), **Nov 15**
Stay Out of the Sun Day, **July 3**
Stop the Violence Day, Natl, **Nov 22**
Stuttering Awareness Day, Intl, **Oct 22**
Successful Antirabies Inoculation, First: Anniv, **July 6**
TB Bacillus Discovered: Anniv, **Mar 24**
Test Tube Baby: Birth, **July 25**
Vegetarian Awareness Month, **Oct 1**
Vitamin C Isolated: Anniv, **Apr 4**
Volunteer Week, Natl, **Apr 21**
Volunteers Week, Intl, **June 1**
Walk Our Children to School Day, Natl, **Oct 2**
White Cane Safety Day (Pres Proc), **Oct 15**
White, Ryan: (AIDS) Death Anniv, **Apr 8**
World AIDS Day (Pres Proc), **Dec 1**
World Food Day (UN), **Oct 16**
World Health Day, **Apr 7**
World Health Day (UN), **Apr 7**
World No-Tobacco Day, **May 31**
World Red Cross Day, **May 8**
YMCA Healthy Kids Day, **Apr 6**
Health, Physical Education, Recreation and Dance, American Alliance for, Annual Meeting, Apr 9
Hearne, Betsy: Birth, Oct 6
Heart 2 Heart Day, Feb 16
Heart Month, American (Pres Proc), Feb 1
Heller, Ruth: Birth, Apr 2
Hello Day, World, Nov 21
Helms, Jesse: Birth, Oct 18
Hemophilia Month, Mar 1
Henderson, Meredith: Birth, Nov 24
Henderson, Rickey: Birth, Dec 25
Hendricks, Thomas A.: Birth Anniv, Sept 17
Henkes, Kevin: Birth, Nov 27
Henry, Marguerite: Birth Anniv, Apr 13
Henry, Patrick: Birth Anniv, May 29
Henson, Jim: Birth Anniv, Sept 24
Henson, Matthew A.: Birth Anniv, Aug 8
Hepatitis Awareness Month, May 1
Herman, Alexis: Birth, July 16
Herman, Charlotte: Birth, June 10
Hermes, Patricia: Birth, Feb 21
Hernandez, Orlando: Birth, Oct 11
Hesse, Karen: Birth, Aug 29
Hest, Amy: Birth, Apr 28
Hewes, Joseph: Birth Anniv, Jan 23
Hewett, Lauren: Birth, Jan 8
Hewitt, Jennifer Love: Birth, Feb 21
Hewitt, Lleyton: Birth, Feb 24
Heyward, Thomas: Birth Anniv, July 28
Hickock, Wild Bill: Birth Anniv, May 27
Hicks, Catherine: Birth, Aug 6
Highwater, Jamake: Birth, Feb 14
Highway Numbers Introduced: Anniv, Mar 2
Hill, Eric: Birth, Sept 7
Hill, Grant: Birth, Oct 5
Hinamatsuri (Japan), Mar 3
Hingis, Martina: Birth, Sept 30
Hinton, S.E.: Birth, Apr 22
Hirohito Michi-no-Miya, Emperor: Birth Anniv, Apr 29
Hiroshima Day, Aug 6
Hispanic,
Chicago Latino Book & Family Fest (IL), **Dec 8**
Cinco de Mayo (Mexico), **May 5**
Day of the Teacher (El Dia Del Maestro), **May 8**
Hispanic Heritage Month, Natl (Pres Proc), **Sept 15**
Los Angeles Latino Book & Family Fest (Los Angeles, CA), **Oct 13**
San Bernardino Latino Book & Family Fest (CA), **Dec 1**
Historic Preservation Week, Natl, May 12
Historically Black Colleges and Universities Week, Natl (Pres Proc), Sept 16
History Day, Natl, Sept 1
History Month, Black, Feb 1
Hitler, Adolf: Birth Anniv, Apr 20
Ho, Minfong: Birth, Jan 7
Hoban, Lillian: Birth Anniv, May 18
Hoban, Russell: Birth, Feb 4
Hobart, Garret A.: Birth Anniv, June 3
Hobbs, Lucy: First Woman to Graduate Dental School: Anniv, Feb 21
Hobbs, Will: Birth, Aug 22
Hoberman, Mary Ann: Birth, Aug 12
Hockey Mask Invented: Anniv, Nov 1
Hodges, Jim: Birth, Nov 19
Hoeven, John: Birth, Mar 13
Hoff, Syd: Birth, Sept 4
Hoffman, Mary: Birth, Apr 20
Hogan, Hulk: Birth, Aug 11
Hogrogian, Nonny: Birth, May 7
Holabird, Katherine: Birth, Jan 23
Holden, Bob: Birth, Aug 24
Holdsclaw, Chamique: Birth, Aug 9
Holi, Mar 28
Holiday Day, Make Up Your Own, Mar 26
Holiday, First US by Presidential Proclamation: Anniv, Nov 26
Holling, Holling C.: Birth Anniv, Aug 2
Hollings, Ernest F.: Birth, Jan 1
Hollyhock Fest (Kyoto, Japan), May 15
Holmes, Katie: Birth, Dec 18

Holocaust Day (Israel), Apr 9
Holt, Kimberly Willis: Birth, Sept 9
Holy Innocents Day, Dec 28
Holy See: National Holiday, Oct 22
Holy Thursday, Mar 28
Holy Week, Mar 24
Home Improvement TV Premiere: Anniv, Sept 17
Home Run Record: Anniv, Apr 8
Homestead Act: Anniv, May 20
Honduras,
Dia De Las Americas, **Apr 14**
Francisco Morazan Holiday, **Oct 3**
Hurricane Mitch: Anniv, **Oct 27**
Independence Day, **Sept 15**
Honest Abe Awards: Natl Honesty Day, Apr 30
Honesty Day, Natl, Apr 30
Honey Month, Natl, Sept 1
Hong Kong,
Birthday of Confucius (Observance), **Oct 13**
Chung Yeung Fest, **Oct 25**
Last Hurrah for British, **June 30**
Liberation Day, **Aug 27**
Hood, John B.: Sherman Enters Atlanta: Anniv, Sept 2
Hoodie-Hoo Day, Northern Hemisphere, Feb 20
Hooper, William: Birth Anniv, June 17
Hooray for Year-Round School Day, June 14
Hoover, Herbert Clark: Birth Anniv, Aug 10
Hoover, Lou H.: Birth Anniv, Mar 29
Hopkins, Anthony: Birth, Dec 31
Hopkins, Lee Bennett: Birth, Apr 13
Hopkins, Stephen: Birth Anniv, Mar 7
Hopkinson, Francis: Birth Anniv, Sept 21
Horses,
Chincoteague Pony Penning (Chincoteague Island, VA), **July 31**
Iron Horse Outraced by Horse: Anniv, **Sept 18**
Kentucky State Fair (Louisville, KY), **Aug 16**
Horvath, Polly: Birth, Jan 30
Hostos, Eugenio Maria: Birth Anniv, Jan 11
Hot Dog Month, Natl, July 1
Hot Springs Natl Park: Anniv, Mar 4
Houdini, Harry: Birth Anniv, Mar 24
House of Representatives, First Black Serves in: Anniv, Dec 12
House of Representatives, US: First Quorum Anniv, Apr 1
Housework Day, No, Apr 7
Houston, Sam: Birth Anniv, Mar 2
Houston, Whitney: Birth, Aug 9
Howard, Elizabeth Fitzgerald: Birth, Dec 28
Howard, Juwan: Birth, Feb 7
Howard, Ron: Birth, Mar 1
Howdy Doody TV Premiere: Anniv, Dec 27
Howe, James: Birth, Aug 2
Hoyle, Edmund: Death Anniv, Aug 29
Hoyt-Goldsmith, Diane: Birth, July 1
Hubble Space Telescope Deployed: Space Milestone, Apr 25
Huckabee, Mike: Birth, Aug 24
Hudson, Ernie: Birth, Dec 17
Hug-A-Week for the Hearing Impaired, Dec 1
Hughes, Charles E.: Birth Anniv, Apr 11
Hughes, Langston: Birth Anniv, Feb 1
Hull, Bobby: Birth, Jan 3
Hull, Brett: Birth, Aug 9
Hull, Jane Dee: Birth, Aug 8
Human Relations,
Amateur Radio Month, Intl, **Apr 1**
American Red Cross: Founding Anniv, **May 21**
Be an Angel Day, **Aug 22**
Be Kind to Humankind Week, **Aug 25**
Black History Month, **Feb 1**
Brotherhood/Sisterhood Week, **Feb 17**
Circle K Service Week, Intl, **Nov 4**
Communication Week, World, **Nov 1**
Diversity Awareness Month, **Oct 1**
Emancipation Proclamation: Anniv, **Sept 22**
Etiquette Week, Natl, **May 13**
Helen Keller Deaf-Blindness Awareness Week, **June 23**
Honesty Day, Natl, **Apr 30**
Human Rights Day (Pres Proc), **Dec 10**
Human Rights Day (UN), **Dec 10**
Human Rights Month, Universal, **Dec 1**
Human Rights Week (Pres Proc), **Dec 10**
I Want You to Be Happy Day, **Mar 3**
Joygerm Day, Natl, **Jan 8**
League of Nations: Anniv, **Jan 10**
Lost Penny Day, **Feb 12**
Loving v Virginia: Anniv, **June 12**
Make a Difference Day, **Oct 27**
Peace Corps Founded: Anniv, **Mar 1**
Pen-Friends Week Intl, **May 1**
Pet Peeve Week, Natl, **Oct 8**
Poverty, Intl Day for Eradication, **Oct 17**
Race Relations Day, **Feb 14**
Ralph Bunche Awarded Nobel Peace Prize: Anniv, **Dec 10**
Random Acts of Kindness Week, **Nov 11**
Red Cross Day, World, **May 8**
Salvation Army Founder's Day, **Apr 10**
Salvation Army in US: Anniv, **Mar 10**
Smile Week, Natl, **Aug 6**
Stop the Violence Day, Natl, **Nov 22**
UN Decade for Eradication of Poverty, **Jan 1**
UN Decade for Human Rights Education, **Jan 1**
Volunteer Week, Natl, **Apr 21**
Volunteers Week, Intl, **June 1**
World Day of Prayer, **Mar 1**
World Hello Day, **Nov 21**
Humbug Day, Dec 21
Humor, Comedy,
Humor Month, Natl, **Apr 1**
Moment of Laughter Day, **Apr 14**
Humphrey, Hubert: Birth Anniv, May 27
Hungary,
Anniv of 1956 Revolution, **Oct 23**
Hungary Declared Independent: Anniv, **Oct 23**
St. Stephen's Day, **Aug 20**
Hunt, Bonnie: Birth, Sept 22
Hunt, Charlotte: See Demi: Birth, Sept 2
Hunt, Irene: Birth, May 18
Hunter's Moon, Nov 1
Hunter, Mollie: Birth, June 30
Hunting and Fishing Day, Natl (Pres Proc), Sept 22
Huntington, Samuel: Birth Anniv, July 3
Hurd, Thatcher: Birth, Mar 6
Hurricane,
Atlantic, Caribbean and Gulf Hurricane Season, **June 1**
Galveston, TX: Anniv, **Sept 8**
Hurricane Hugo Hits American Coast: Anniv, **Sept 21**
Hurricane Mitch: Anniv, **Oct 27**
Hurricane Supplication Day (Virgin Islands), **July 22**
Hurricane Thanksgiving Day (Virgin Islands), **Oct 15**
Hurwitz, Johanna: Birth, Oct 9
Hus, John: Commemoration Day (Czech), July 6
Hussein: King of Jordan: Birth Anniv, Nov 14
Hutchins, Hazel: Birth, Aug 9
Hutchins, Pat: Birth, June 18
Hutchinson, Tim: Birth, Aug 11
Hutchison, Kay Bailey: Birth, July 22
Hyman, Trina Schart: Birth, Apr 8
I Love Lucy TV Premiere: Anniv, Oct 15
I Want You to Be Happy Day, Mar 3
IBM PC Introduced: Anniv, Apr 24
Ice Cream Cone: Birth, Sept 22
Ice Cream Day, Natl, July 21
Iceland,
August Holiday, **Aug 6**
Bun Day, **Feb 11**
Bursting Day, **Feb 12**
First Day of Summer, **Apr 25**
Independence Day, **June 17**
Leif Erikson Day, **Oct 9**
Shop and Office Workers' Holiday, **Aug 6**
Idaho,
Admission Day, **July 3**
Ides of March, Mar 15
Illinois,
Admission Day, **Dec 3**
Bud Billiken Parade (Chicago), **Aug 11**
Chicago Intl Children's Film Fest, **Oct 11**
Chicago Latino Book & Family Fest, **Dec 8**
Ginza Holiday: Japanese Cultural Fest (Chicago), **Aug 17**
Illinois State Fair (Springfield), **Aug 10**
SchoolTech Expo and Conference (Chicago), **Oct 18**
Immaculate Conception, Feast Of, Dec 8
Immigration: Ellis Island Opened: Anniv, Jan 1
Impeachment Proceedings, Clinton: Anniv, Dec 20
Impeachment Proceedings: Johnson: Anniv, Feb 24
Inane Answering Message Day, Natl, Jan 30
Inauguration Day, Old, Mar 4
Incandescent Lamp Demonstrated: Anniv, Oct 21
Income Tax Birthday, Feb 3
Income Tax Pay Day, Apr 15
Independence Day (Russia), June 12
Independence Day, US (Fourth of July), July 4
Independent Schools Conference, Natl Assn of (San Francisco, CA), Feb 26
India,
Baisakhi, **Apr 13**
Children's Day, **Nov 14**
Deepavali (Diwali), **Nov 14**
Gandhi, Mohandas: Birth Anniv, **Oct 2**
Holi, **Mar 28**
Independence Day, **Aug 15**
Republic Day: Anniv, **Jan 26**
Indiana,
Admission Day, **Dec 11**
American Assn of School Librarians Conf (Indianapolis), **Nov 14**
State Fair (Indianapolis), **Aug 8**
Indigenous People, UN Intl Decade of World's, Jan 1
Indonesia,
Independence Day, **Aug 17**
Kartini Day, **Apr 21**
Inhofe, James M.: Birth, Nov 17
Inkpen, Mick: Birth, Dec 22
Inouye, Daniel Ken: Birth, Sept 7
Insulin First Isolated: Anniv, July 27
Internet Created: Anniv, Oct 29
Inventors' Month, Natl, Aug 1
Iowa,
Admission Day, **Dec 28**
Fest of Books for Young People (Iowa City), **Nov 3**
Iowa Storytelling Fest (Clear Lake), **July 26**
State Fair, Iowa (Des Moines), **Aug 9**
Iran,
Day of Oil, Natl, **Mar 19**
Fifteenth of Khordad, **June 5**
National Day, **Feb 11**
New Year, **Mar 21**
Yalda, **Dec 21**
Iraq,
Desert Shield: Anniv, **Aug 7**
Kuwait Liberated: Anniv, **Feb 27**
National Day, **July 17**
Persian Gulf War Begins: Anniv, **Jan 16**
Ireland,
Easter Rising, **Apr 24**
National Day, **Mar 17**
Irish Famine Begins: Anniv, Sept 9

Irish-American Heritage Month (Pres Proc), Mar 1
Irving, Washington: Birth Anniv, Apr 3
Isaacs, Anne: Birth, Mar 2
Isle Royale Natl Park: Anniv, Apr 3
Ismail, Raghib: Birth, Nov 18
Isra al Mi'raj: Ascent of Prophet Muhammad, Oct 14
Israel,
Camp David Accord Signed: Anniv, **Mar 26**
Hashoah/Holocaust Day, **Apr 9**
Yom Ha'atzma'ut (Independence Day), **Apr 17**
Yom Ha'Zikkaron (Remembrance Day), **Apr 16**
Yom Yerushalayim (Jerusalem Day), **May 10**
Italy,
Bologna Intl Children's Book Fair, **Apr 3**
Carnival Week (Milan), **Feb 10**
Epiphany Fair, **Jan 5**
Historical Regatta, **Sept 2**
La Befana, **Jan 6**
Liberation Day, **Apr 25**
Palio Dei Balestrieri (crossbow), **May 26**
Republic Day, **June 2**
Vesuvius Day, **Aug 24**
Victory Day, **Nov 4**
Wedding of the Sea (Venice), **May 12**
Iverson, Allen: Birth, June 7
Iwo Jima Day, Feb 23
Jackson, Andrew: Birth Anniv, Mar 15
Jackson, Jermaine: Birth, Dec 11
Jackson, Jesse: Birth, Oct 8
Jackson, Michael: Birth, Aug 29
Jackson, Phil: Birth, Sept 17
Jackson, Rachel D.: Birth Anniv, June 15
Jackson, Reggie: Birth, May 18
Jackson, Thomas J. "Stonewall": Birth Anniv, Jan 21
Jacques, Brian: Birth, June 15
Jaeger, Andrea: Birth, June 4
Jakub, Lisa: Birth, Dec 27
Jamaica,
Discovery By Columbus: Anniv, **May 4**
Independence Achieved: Anniv, **Aug 6**
Independence Day Observed, **Aug 6**
Natl Heroes Day, **Oct 15**
James, Edgerrin: Birth, Aug 1
James, Jesse: Birth Anniv, Sept 5
Jamestown, VA: Founding Anniv, May 14
Janeczko, Paul: Birth, July 27
Janklow, William: Birth, Sept 13
Japan,
Atomic Bomb Dropped on Hiroshima: Anniv, **Aug 6**
Atomic Bomb Dropped on Nagasaki: Anniv, **Aug 9**
Autumnal Equinox Day, **Sept 22**
Bean Throwing Fest (Setsubun), **Feb 3**
Birthday of the Emperor, **Dec 23**
Bon Fest (Feast of Lanterns), **July 13**
Children's Day, **May 5**
Coming-of-Age Day, **Jan 14**
Constitution Memorial Day, **May 3**
Cormorant Fishing Fest, **May 11**
Culture Day, **Nov 3**
Day of the Rice God (Chiyoda), **June 2**
Doll Fest (Hinamatsuri), **Mar 3**
Flower Fest (Hana Matsuri), **Apr 8**
Foundation Day, Natl, **Feb 11**
Golden Week Holiday, **May 4**
Greenery Day, **Apr 29**
Ha-Ri-Ku-Yo (Needle Mass), **Feb 8**
Haru-No-Yabuiri, **Jan 16**
Health-Sports Day, **Oct 8**
Hiroshima Day, **Aug 6**
Hollyhock Fest (Kyoto), **May 15**
Japanese Era New Year, **Jan 1**
Kakizome, **Jan 2**
Labor Thanksgiving Day, **Nov 23**
Marine Day, **July 20**
Nanakusa, **Jan 7**
Newspaper Week, **Oct 1**
Old People's Day, **Sept 15**
Rice Planting Fest (Osaka), **June 14**
Shichi-Go-San, **Nov 15**
Snow Fest, **Feb 8**
Suffers Major Earthquake: Anniv, **Jan 17**
Tanabata (Star Fest), **July 7**
Usokae (Bullfinch Exchange Fest), **Jan 7**
Vernal Equinox Day, **Mar 20**
Water-Drawing Fest, **Mar 1**
World Cup, **May 31**
Japanese,
Ginza Holiday (Chicago, IL), **Aug 17**
Japanese Internment (WWII): Anniv, Feb 19
Jason XIII Project, Sept 4
Jay, John: Birth Anniv, Dec 12
JCC Maccabi Youth Games, Aug 19
Jefferson, Martha: Birth Anniv, Oct 19
Jefferson, Thomas: Birth Anniv, Apr 13
Jefferson, Thomas: Birth Anniv (Pres Proc), Apr 13
Jeffords, James: Birth, May 11
Jeffries, John: Weatherman's Day, Feb 5
Jemison, Mae: Birth, Oct 17
Jenner, Edward: Birth Anniv, May 17
Jennings, Peter: Birth, July 29
Jeter, Derek: Birth, June 26
Jetsons TV Premiere: Anniv, Sept 23
Jewel: Birth, May 23
Jewish Heritage Week (Pres Proc), Apr 14
Jewish Observances,
Asarah B'Tevet, **Dec 25**
Chanukah, **Dec 10**
Fast of Gedalya, **Sept 20**
Fast of Tammuz, **June 27**
Israel Yom Ha'atzma'ut (Independence Day), **Apr 17**
Israel Yom Yerushalayim, **May 10**
Jewish Book Month, **Nov 10**
Kristallnacht: Anniv, **Nov 9**
Lag B'Omer, **Apr 30**
Liberation of Buchenwald: Anniv, **Apr 11**
Passover Begins, **Mar 27**
Pesach (Passover), **Mar 28**
Purim, **Feb 26**
Rosh Hashanah (New Year), **Sept 18**
Rosh Hashanah Begins, **Sept 17**
Shabbat Across America, **Mar 22**
Shavuot, **May 17**
Shemini Atzeret, **Oct 9**
Simchat Torah, **Oct 10**
Sukkot Begins, **Oct 1**
Sukkot/Succoth/Feast of Tabernacles, **Oct 2**
Ta'anit Esther (Fast of Esther), **Feb 25**
Tu B'Shvat, **Jan 28**
Yom Hashoah/Holocaust Day (Israel), **Apr 9**
Yom Kippur, **Sept 27**
Yom Kippur Begins, **Sept 26**
Jinnah: see Pakistan: Birth of Qaid-i-Azam, Dec 25
Joan of Arc: Birth Anniv, Jan 6
Jobaria Exhibited: Anniv, Nov 13
Jobs, Steven: Birth, Feb 24
Johanns, Mike: Birth, Aug 18
John Carver Day (MA), June 23
John, Elton: Birth, Mar 25
Johnny Appleseed Day, Mar 11
Johnson, Andrew, Impeachment Proceedings: Anniv, Feb 24
Johnson, Andrew: Birth Anniv, Dec 29
Johnson, Angela: Birth, June 18
Johnson, Ashley: Birth, Aug 9
Johnson, Avery: Birth, Mar 25
Johnson, Charles: Birth, July 20
Johnson, Crockett: Birth Anniv, Oct 20
Johnson, Eliza M.: Birth Anniv, Oct 4
Johnson, Gary: Birth, Jan 1
Johnson, John (Jack): Birth Anniv, Mar 31
Johnson, Keyshawn: Birth, Nov 22
Johnson, Lady Bird: Birth, Dec 22
Johnson, Lyndon B.: Birth Anniv, Aug 27
Johnson, Lyndon B.: Monday Holiday Law: Anniv, June 28
Johnson, Magic: Birth, Aug 14
Johnson, Randy: Birth, Sept 10
Johnson, Richard M.: Birth Anniv, Oct 17
Johnson, Shannon: Birth, Aug 18
Johnson, Tim: Birth, Dec 28
Johnston, Tony: Birth, Jan 30
Johnstown Flood: Anniv, May 31
Jones, Casey: Birth Anniv, Mar 14
Jones, Chipper: Birth, Apr 24
Jones, Cobi: Birth, June 16
Jones, Diana Wynne: Birth, Aug 16
Jones, Eddie: Birth, Oct 20
Jones, Hatty: Birth, July 21
Jones, Marcia Thornton: Birth, July 15
Jones, Marion: Birth, Oct 12
Joosse, Barbara: Birth, Feb 18
Jordan,
Accession Day, **June 9**
Great Arab Revolt and Army Day, **June 10**
Independence Day, **May 25**
King Hussein: Birth Anniv, **Nov 14**
King's Birthday, **Jan 20**
Jordan, Michael: Birth, Feb 17
Jordan's Back! Anniv, Mar 18
Joseph, Chief, Surrender: Anniv, Oct 5
Joseph, Chief: Death Anniv, Sept 21
Journalism,
Around the World in 72 Days: Anniv, **Nov 14**
First American Daily Newspaper Published: Anniv, **May 30**
First American Newspaper: Anniv, **Sept 25**
First Magazine Published in America: Anniv, **Feb 13**
Japan: Newspaper Week, **Oct 1**
Newscurrents Student Editorial Cartoon Contest, **Mar 1**
Newspaper Carrier Day, **Sept 4**
Newspaper in Education Week, **Mar 4**
People Magazine: Anniv, **Mar 4**
UN: World Press Freedom Day, **May 3**
Joyce, William: Birth, Dec 11
Joygerm Day, Natl, Jan 8
Joyner-Kersee, Jackie: Birth, Mar 3
Juarez, Benito: Birth Anniv, Mar 21
Juggling Day, World, June 15
Jukes, Mavis: Birth, May 3
June Is Turkey Lovers' Month, June 1
Juneteenth, June 19
Junkanoo (Bahamas), Dec 26
Jupiter, Comet Crashes into: Anniv, July 16
Juster, Norton: Birth, June 2
Justice, US Dept of: Anniv, June 22
Kamehameha Day (HI), June 11
Kansas,
Admission Day, **Jan 29**
Literature Fest (Lawrence), **Oct 16**
Salter Elected First Woman Mayor in US: Anniv, **Apr 4**
State Fair (Hutchinson), **Sept 7**
Kariya, Paul: Birth, Oct 16
Katami Natl Park: Anniv, Dec 2
Katz, Omri: Birth, May 30
Kazakhstan,
Constitution Day, **Aug 31**
Independence Day, **Oct 25**
Republic Day, **Dec 16**
Keanan, Staci: Birth, June 6
Keane, Bil: Birth, Oct 5
Keating, Frank: Birth, Feb 10
Keats, Ezra Jack: Birth Anniv, Mar 11
Keegan, Andrew: Birth, Jan 29
Keep America Beautiful Month, Natl, Apr 1
Keep Massachusetts Beautiful Month, May 1
Keeshan, Bob (Captain Kangaroo): Birth, June 27
Kehret, Peg: Birth, Nov 11
Keiko Returns to Iceland: Anniv, Sept 10
Keller, Helen: Birth Anniv, June 27
Kellogg, Steven: Birth, Oct 26
Kelly, Walt: Birth Anniv, Aug 25
Kemp, Shawn: Birth, Nov 26
Kempthorne, Dirk: Birth, Oct 29
Kenai Fjords Natl Park: Anniv, Dec 2

Kennedy, Anthony M.: Birth, July 23
Kennedy, Edward Moore: Birth, Feb 22
Kennedy, Jacqueline: See Onassis, July 28
Kennedy, John Fitzgerald,
Birth Anniv, **May 29**
First Televised Presidential Debate: Anniv, **Sept 26**
John F. Kennedy Day in Massachusetts, **Nov 25**
Kennedy, Robert F: Birth Anniv, Nov 20
Kentucky,
Admission Day, **June 1**
Barrier Awareness Day, **May 7**
Confederate Memorial Day/Jefferson Davis Day, **June 3**
Corn Island Storytelling Fest (Louisville), **Sept 13**
Disability Day, **Aug 2**
FFA Convention, Natl (Louisville), **Oct 24**
Grandmother's Day, **Oct 14**
State Fair (Louisville), **Aug 16**
Kenya,
Jamhuri Day, **Dec 12**
Kenyatta Day, **Oct 20**
Madaraka Day, **June 1**
Kepes, Juliet A.: Birth Anniv, June 29
Kerns, Joanna: Birth, Feb 12
Kerr, Steve: Birth, Sept 27
Kerry, John F.: Birth, Dec 11
Ketchum, Liza: Birth, June 17
Key, Francis Scott: Birth Anniv, Aug 1
Key, Francis Scott: Star-Spangled Banner Inspired: Anniv, Sept 13
Kherdian, David: Birth, Dec 17
Kid'rific (Hartford, CT), Sept 8
Kidd, Jason: Birth, Mar 23
Kids After Christmas (Mystic, CT), Dec 26
Kids Love a Mystery Month, Oct 1
Kids' Day, Kiwanis, Natl, Sept 22
Kids' Goals Education Week, Nov 5
KidsDay, Natl, Sept 15
Kilmer, Val: Birth, Dec 31
Kimmel, Eric A.: Birth, Oct 30
Kindergarten Day, Apr 21
Kindness & Justice Challenge, Do Something:, Jan 21
Kindness Week, Random Acts of, Nov 11
King James Bible Published: Anniv, May 2
King, Angus, Jr: Birth, Mar 31
King, Coretta Scott: Birth, Apr 27
King, Martin Luther, Jr,
Assassination Anniv, **Apr 4**
Birth Anniv, **Jan 15**
Birthday Observed, **Jan 21**
King Opposes Vietnam War: Anniv, **Apr 4**
King Wins Nobel Peace Prize: Anniv, **Oct 14**
March on Washington: Anniv, **Aug 28**
Martin Luther King, Jr Federal Holiday (Pres Proc), **Jan 21**
King, Ronald Stacey: Birth, Jan 29
King, Stephen: Birth, Sept 21
King, W.L. MacKenzie: Birth Anniv, Dec 17
King, William R.: Birth Anniv, Apr 7
King-Smith, Dick: Birth, Mar 27
Kipling, Rudyard: Birth Anniv, Dec 30
Kiribati: Independence Day, July 12
Kirk, Daniel: Birth, May 1
Kirkpatrick, Chris: Birth, Oct 17
Kirsten, Samantha and Molly Debut: Anniv, Sept 15
Kite Fest of Santiago Sacatepequez (Guatemala), Nov 1
Kitzhaber, John: Birth, Mar 5
Kiwanis Kids' Day, Natl, Sept 22
Kiwifruit Day, California, Feb 2
Klause, Annette Curtis: Birth, June 20
Kleven, Elisa: Birth, Oct 14
Kliban, B(ernard): Birth Anniv, Jan 1
Kline, Suzy: Birth, Aug 27
Klondike Eldorado Gold Discovery: Anniv, Aug 31
Knight, Hilary: Birth, Nov 1
Knowles, Tony: Birth, Jan 1
Knuckles Down Month, Natl, Apr 1
Kobuk Valley Natl Park: Anniv, Dec 2
Kohl, Herb: Birth, Feb 7
Konigsburg, E.L.: Birth, Feb 10
Koppel, Ted: Birth, Feb 8
Korea,
Alphabet Day (Hangul), **Oct 9**
Children's Day, **May 5**
Chusok, **Oct 1**
Constitution Day, **July 17**
Korea, North and South, End War: Anniv, **Dec 13**
Korean War Armistice: Anniv, **July 27**
Korean War Began: Anniv, **June 25**
Liberation Day, **Aug 15**
Memorial Day, **June 6**
National Day, **Sept 9**
National Foundation Day, **Oct 3**
Samiljol (Independence Movement Day), **Mar 1**
Tano Day, **June 15**
World Cup, **May 31**
Korman, Gordon: Birth, Oct 23
Kosciusko, Thaddeus: Birth Anniv, Feb 12
Kournikova, Anna: Birth, June 7
Krakatoa Eruption: Anniv, Aug 26
Kratt, Chris: Birth, July 19
Kratt, Martin: Birth, Dec 23
Kraus, Robert: Birth, June 21
Krementz, Jill: Birth, Feb 19
Kristallnacht: Anniv, Nov 9
Kroll, Virginia: Birth, Apr 28
Krull, Kathleen: Birth, July 29
Krumgold, Joseph: Birth Anniv, Apr 9
Kukla, Fran and Ollie TV Premiere: Anniv, Nov 29
Kurban Bayram: See Eid-al-Adha, Feb 22
Kurtz, Jane: Birth, Apr 17
Kuskin, Karla: Birth, July 17
Kuwait,
Kuwait Liberated: Anniv, **Feb 27**
Liberation Day, **Feb 26**
National Day, **Feb 25**
Kvasnosky, Laura McGee: Birth, Jan 27
Kwan, Michelle: Birth, July 7
Kwanzaa, Dec 26
Kyl, Jon: Birth, Apr 25
Kyrgyzstan: Independence Day, Aug 31
L'Enfant, Pierre C.: Birth Anniv, Aug 2
L'Engle, Madeleine: Birth, Nov 29
La Befana (Italy), Jan 6
La Farge, Oliver: Birth Anniv, Dec 19
Labor Day, May 1
Labor. See also Employment,
AFL Founded: Anniv, **Dec 8**
AFL-CIO Founded: Anniv, **Dec 5**
Day of the Holy Cross, **May 3**
Labor Day, **Sept 3**
Labor Day (Bahamas), **June 7**
Laettner, Christian: Birth, Aug 17
Lafayette, Marquis de: Birth Anniv, Sept 6
Lag B'Omer, Apr 30
Lailat ul Qadr: (Islamic) Night of Power, Dec 6
Lake Clark Natl Park: Anniv, Dec 2
Lakin, Christine: Birth, Jan 25
Lalas, Alexi: Birth, June 1
Landrieu, Mary L.: Birth, Nov 23
Lands Day, Public, Sept 8
Langton, Jane: Birth, Dec 30
Lantz, Walter: Birth Anniv, Apr 27
Lao People's Dem Repub: Natl Holiday, Dec 2
Larson, Gary: Birth, Aug 14
Laser Patented: Anniv, Mar 22
Lasky, Kathryn: Birth, June 24
Lassen Volcanic Natl Park: Anniv, Aug 9
Lassie TV Premiere: Anniv, Sept 12
Late for Something Day, Be, Sept 5
Lathrop, Julia C.: Birth Anniv, June 29
Latino Book & Family Fest (Chicago, IL), Dec 8
Latino Book & Family Fest (Los Angeles, CA), Oct 13
Latino Book & Family Fest (San Bernardino, CA), Dec 1
Latvia,
Baltic States' Independence Recognized: Anniv, **Sept 6**
Independence Day, **Nov 18**
John's Day (Midsummer Night Day), **June 24**
Lauber, Patricia: Birth, Feb 5
Lauer, Andrew: Birth, June 19
Lauer, Matt: Birth, Dec 30
Laura Ingalls Wilder Fest (Mansfield, MO), Sept 15
Laura Ingalls Wilder Fest (Pepin, WI), Sept 15
Laura Ingalls Wilder Pageant (De Smet, SD), June 23
Laurel and Hardy: Cuckoo Dancing Week, Jan 11
Laurier, Sir Wilfred: Birth Anniv, Nov 20
Lavoisier, Antoine: Execution Anniv, May 8
Law Day (Pres Proc), May 1
Law Enforcement Appreciation Month in Florida, May 1
Lawless, Lucy: Birth, Mar 29
Lawrence (of Arabia), T.E.: Birth Anniv, Aug 16
Lawrence, Andrew: Birth, Jan 12
Lawrence, Jacob: Birth Anniv, Sept 7
Lawrence, Joey: Birth, Apr 20
Lawrence, Matthew: Birth, Feb 11
Lawson, Robert: Birth Anniv, Oct 4
Le Guin, Ursula K.: Birth, Oct 21
Leaf, Munro: Birth Anniv, Dec 4
League of Nations: Anniv, Jan 10
Leahy, Patrick J.: Birth, Mar 31
Leap Second Adjustment Time, June 30
Leap Second Adjustment Time, Dec 31
Lear, Edward: Birth Anniv, May 12
Leave It to Beaver TV Premiere: Anniv, Oct 4
Leavitt, Mike: Birth, Feb 11
Lebanon: Independence Day, Nov 22
Lee, Francis Lightfoot: Birth Anniv, Oct 14
Lee, Harper: Birth, Apr 28
Lee, Richard Henry: Birth Anniv, Jan 20
Lee, Robert E.,
Birth Anniv, **Jan 19**
Lee-Jackson Day, **Jan 18**
Legoland Opens: Anniv, Mar 20
Lei Day (Hawaii), May 1
Lemieux, Mario: Birth, Oct 5
Leno, Jay: Birth, Apr 28
Lenski, Lois: Birth Anniv, Oct 14
Lent Begins, Feb 13
Lent, Blair: Birth, Jan 22
Lent, Orthodox, Mar 18
Leo Begins, July 23
Leonard, Justin: Birth, June 15
Leonardo Da Vinci: Death Anniv, May 2
Leopold, Aldo: Birth Anniv, Jan 11
Leslie, Lisa: Birth, July 7
Lesotho,
Moshoeshoe's Day, **Mar 12**
National Day, **Oct 4**
Lester, Helen: Birth, June 12
Lester, Julius B.: Birth, Jan 27
Letter-Writing Week, Universal, Jan 8
Leutze, Emanuel: Birth Anniv, May 24
Levin, Carl: Birth, June 28
Levine, Gail Carson: Birth, Sept 17
Lewin, Ted: Birth, May 6
Lewis and Clark Expedition: Anniv, May 14
Lewis, C.S.: Birth Anniv, Nov 29
Lewis, Carl: Birth, July 1
Lewis, Emmanuel: Birth, Mar 9
Lewis, Francis: Birth Anniv, Mar 21
Lewis, Meriwether: Birth Anniv, Aug 18
Lewis, Shari: Birth Anniv, Jan 17
Liberia,
Flag Day, **Aug 24**
J.J. Roberts Day, **Mar 15**
National Day, **July 26**
Thanksgiving Day, **Nov 1**

Liberty Day, Mar 23
Libra Begins, Sept 23
Library/Librarians,
American Assn of School Librarians Conference (Indianapolis, IN), **Nov 14**
American Library Assn Annual Conference (Atlanta, GA), **June 13**
American Library Assn Midwinter Mtg (New Orleans, LA), **Jan 18**
Boston Public Library: Anniv, **Apr 3**
Intl Federation of Library Assns Conference (Boston, MA), **Aug 16**
Library Card Sign-up Month, **Sept 1**
Library Lovers' Month, **Feb 1**
Library of Congress: Anniv, **Apr 24**
Library Week, Natl, **Apr 14**
New York Public Library: Anniv, **May 23**
Novello Fest of Reading (Charlotte, NC), **Oct 12**
Public Library Assn Conference (Phoenix, AZ), **Mar 12**
School Library Day, Intl, **Oct 15**
School Library Media Month, **Apr 1**
Teen Read Week, **Oct 14**
Thank You, School Librarian Day, **Apr 4**
Libya,
American Bases Evacuation Day, **June 11**
British Bases Evacuation Day, **Mar 28**
Independence Day, **Dec 24**
Revolution Day, **Sept 1**
Lieberman, Joseph I.: Birth, Feb 24
Liechtenstein: National Day, Aug 15
Limerick Day, May 12
Lincoln, Abraham,
Assassination Anniv, **Apr 14**
Birth Anniv, **Feb 12**
Emancipation Proclamation: Anniv, **Sept 22**
Gettysburg Address: Anniv, **Nov 19**
Lincoln Memorial Dedication: Anniv, **May 30**
Lincoln, Blanche Lambert: Birth, Sept 30
Lincoln, Mary Todd: Birth Anniv, Dec 13
Lindbergh, Charles A.: Birth Anniv, Feb 4
Lindbergh Flight: Anniv, May 20
Lindgren, Astrid: Birth, Nov 14
Lindros, Eric: Birth, Feb 28
Linz, Alex: Birth, Jan 3
Lionni, Leo: Birth Anniv, May 5
Lions Club Intl Peace Poster Contest, Oct 1
Lipinski, Tara: Birth, June 10
Lipnicki, Jonathan: Birth, Oct 22
Lisle, Janet Taylor: Birth, Feb 13
Lister, Joseph: Birth Anniv, Apr 5
Liszt, Franz: Birth Anniv, Oct 22
Literacy Day, Intl (UN), Sept 8
Literature,
Alice in Wonderland Published: Anniv, **Nov 26**
American Poet Laureate Establishment: Anniv, **Dec 20**
Asimov, Isaac: Birth Anniv, **Jan 2**
Authors' Day, Natl, **Nov 1**
Black Poetry Day, **Oct 17**
Children's Book Day, Intl, **Apr 2**
Children's Book Fest (Hattiesburg, MS), **Mar 20**
Children's Book Week, Natl, **Nov 12**
Children's Literature Conference (Columbus, OH), **Feb 14**
Children's Literature New England Institute (Toronto, Canada), **Aug 1**
Children's Literature Fest (Warrensburg, MO), **Mar 10**
David McCord Children's Literature Fest (Framingham, MA), **Nov 1**
Eliza Doolittle Day, **May 20**
Fest of Books for Young People (Iowa City, IA), **Nov 3**
First Magazine Published in America: Anniv, **Feb 13**
Kids Love a Mystery Month, **Oct 1**
Laura Ingalls Wilder Fest (Mansfield, MO), **Sept 15**
Laura Ingalls Wilder Gingerbread Sociable (Pomona, CA), **Feb 2**
Literature Fest (Lawrence, KS), **Oct 16**
Poetry Month, Natl, **Apr 1**
Silent Spring Publication: Anniv, **Apr 13**
Texas Book Fest (Austin), **Nov 2**
Virginia Hamilton Conf (Kent, OH), **Apr 4**
White, E.B.: Birth Anniv, **July 11**
Whitman, Walt: Birth Anniv, **May 31**
Whole Language Umbrella Conference, **July 24**
Young Peoples' Poetry Week, **Apr 15**
Lithgow, John: Birth, Oct 19
Lithuania,
Baltic States' Independence Recognized: Anniv, **Sept 6**
Day of Statehood, **July 6**
Independence Day, **Feb 16**
Little House on the Prairie TV Premiere: Anniv, Sept 11
Little League Baseball Week, Natl (Pres Proc), June 10
Little League Baseball World Series (Williamsport, PA), Aug 17
Little Rock Nine: Anniv, Sept 23
Littrell, Brian: Birth, Feb 20
Lively, Penelope: Birth, Mar 17
Livingston, Myra Cohn: Birth, Aug 17
Livingston, Philip: Birth Anniv, Jan 15
Livingston, Robert: Birth Anniv, Nov 27
LL Cool J: Birth, Aug 16
Lloyd, Eric: Birth, May 19
Lloyd, Jake: Birth, Mar 5
Lobel, Anita: Birth, June 3
Lobel, Arnold: Birth Anniv, May 22
Lobo, Rebecca: Birth, Oct 6
Lodge, Bernard: Birth, Oct 19
Lofting, Hugh: Birth Anniv, Jan 14
Lofton, Kenny: Birth, May 31
Lohan, Lindsay: Birth, July 2
London, Jack: Birth Anniv, Jan 12
London, Jonathan: Birth, Mar 11
Lone Ranger TV Premiere: Anniv, Sept 15
Longfellow, Henry Wadsworth: Birth Anniv, Feb 27
Lopez, Mario: Birth, Oct 10
Los Angeles (CA) Founded: Anniv, Sept 4
Lost Penny Day, Feb 12
Lott, Trent: Birth, Oct 9
Louisiana,
Admission Day, **Apr 30**
American Library Assn Midwinter Mtg (New Orleans), **Jan 18**
American Speech-Lang-Hearing Assn Conv (New Orleans), **Nov 15**
Louisiana Purchase Day, **Dec 20**
School Boards Assn Annual Conference, Natl (New Orleans), **Apr 6**
State Fair of Louisiana (Shreveport), **Oct 19**
Super Bowl (New Orleans), **Jan 27**
Love the Children Day, Mar 29
Lovelace, Maud Hart: Birth Anniv, Apr 25
Lover's Day, Book Day and (Spain), Apr 23
Loving v Virginia: Anniv, June 12
Low, Juliet: Birth Anniv, Oct 31
Lowry, Lois: Birth, Mar 20
Loyalty Day (Pres Proc), May 1
Lucas, George: Birth, May 14
Lucid, Shannon: Birth, Jan 14
Lugar, Richard G.: Birth, Apr 4
Luxembourg,
Burgsonndeg, **Feb 17**
Ettelbruck Remembrance Day, **July 6**
Liberation Ceremony, **Sept 9**
National Holiday, **June 23**
Lynch, Chris: Birth, July 2
Lynch, Thomas: Birth Anniv, Aug 5
Lyon, George Ella: Birth, Apr 25
Lyons, Mary: Birth, Nov 28
MacArthur Returns to the Philippines: Anniv, Oct 20
Macau Reverts to Chinese Control: Anniv, Dec 20
Macaulay, David: Birth, Dec 2
Macchio, Ralph: Birth, Nov 4
MacDonald, Betty: Birth Anniv, Mar 26
MacDonald, John A.: Birth Anniv, Jan 11
Macedonia, Former Yugoslav Republic of: National Day, Aug 2
Macintosh Computer Released: Anniv, Jan 25
MacKenzie, Alexander: Birth Anniv, Jan 28
MacLachlan, Patricia: Birth, Mar 3
MacMurray, Fred: Birth Anniv, Aug 30
Madagascar,
Commemoration Day, **Mar 29**
Independence Day, **June 26**
National Holiday, **Dec 30**
Maddux, Greg: Birth, Apr 14
Madison, Dolly: Birth Anniv, May 20
Madison, James: Birth Anniv, Mar 16
Magazine, First Published in America: Anniv, Feb 13
Magellan, Ferdinand: Death Anniv, Apr 27
Magic Day, Natl, Oct 31
Magna Carta Day, June 15
Mahy, Margaret: Birth, Mar 21
Mail-Order Catalog: Anniv, Aug 18
Mail: World Post Day (UN), Oct 9
Maine,
Acadia Natl Park: Anniv, **Jan 1**
Admission Day, **Mar 15**
Patriot's Day, **Apr 15**
Make a Difference Day, Oct 27
Make Up Your Mind Day, Dec 31
Make Up Your Own Holiday Day, Mar 26
Malawi,
Freedom Day, **June 14**
John Chilembwe Day, **Jan 16**
Martyr's Day, **Mar 3**
Republic Day, **July 6**
Malaysia:Freedom Day, Aug 31
Malcolm X: Birth Anniv, May 19
Maldives: National Day, July 26
Mali: Independence Day, Sept 22
Malone, Karl: Birth, July 24
Malone, Moses: Birth, Mar 23
Malta,
Carnival, **May 4**
Feast of St. Paul's Shipwreck (Valletta), **Feb 10**
Independence Day, **Sept 21**
Republic Day, **Dec 13**
Man-Powered Flight, First: Anniv, Aug 23
Mandel, Howie: Birth, Nov 29
Mandela, Nelson: Arrest Anniv, Aug 4
Mandela, Nelson: Birth, July 18
Mandela, Nelson: Prison Release Anniv, Feb 11
Manes, Stephen: Birth, Jan 8
Manet, Edouard: Birth Anniv, Jan 23
Mankiller, Wilma: Birth, Nov 18
Mann, Horace: Birth Anniv, May 4
Manning, Peyton: Birth, Mar 4
Mantle, Mickey: Birth Anniv, Oct 20
Mao Tse-Tung: Birth Anniv, Dec 26
Maps: Natl Reading a Road Map Week, Apr 4
Maradona, Diego: Birth, Oct 30
Marathon, Days of: Anniv, Sept 2
Marbles: Natl Knuckles Down Month, Apr 1
Marcellino, Fred: Birth, Oct 25
March of Dimes Birth Defects Prevention Month, Jan 1
Marco Polo: Death Anniv, Jan 8
Marconi, Guglielmo: Birth Anniv, Apr 25
Mardi Gras, Feb 12
Marine Corps Birthday, Nov 10
Marine War Memorial: Hayes, Ira: Birth Anniv, Jan 12
Maris Hits 61st Home Run: Anniv, Oct 1
Maris, Roger: Birth Anniv, Sept 10
Maritime Day, Natl, May 22
Maritime Day, Natl (Pres Proc), May 22
Marquette, Jacques: Birth Anniv, June 1
Marrin, Albert: Birth, July 24
Marsalis, Wynton: Birth, Oct 18

Marsden, Jason: Birth, Jan 3
Marshall Islands: National Day, May 1
Marshall Plan: Anniv, Apr 3
Marshall, James: Birth Anniv, Oct 10
Marshall, John: Birth Anniv, Sept 24
Marshall, Thomas Riley: Birth Anniv, Mar 14
Marshall, Thurgood: Birth Anniv, July 2
Marti, Jose Julian: Birth Anniv, Jan 28
Martin, Andrea: Birth, Jan 15
Martin, Ann: Birth, Aug 12
Martin, Bill, Jr: Birth, Mar 20
Martin, Curtis: Birth, May 1
Martin, Jacqueline Briggs: Birth, Apr 15
Martin, Rafe: Birth, Jan 22
Martinez, Mel: Birth, Oct 23
Martinez, Pedro: Birth, Oct 25
Martinez, Victor: Birth, Feb 21
Martinmas, Nov 11
Martyrs' Day (Bangladesh), Feb 21
Martyrs' Day (Panama), Jan 9
Martz, Judy: Birth, July 28
Maryland,
Defenders Day, **Sept 12**
Maryland Day, **Mar 25**
Ratification Day, **Apr 28**
State Fair (Timonium), **Aug 24**
Teachers of English, Natl Council of, Annual Conf (Baltimore), **Nov 15**
Marzollo, Jean: Birth, June 24
Masih, Iqbal: Death Anniv, Apr 16
Massachusetts,
Basketball Hall of Fame Enshrinement (Springfield), **Oct 5**
Big E (West Springfield), **Sept 14**
Boston Public Library: Anniv, **Apr 3**
Bunker Hill Day, **June 17**
Children's Day, **June 9**
Civil Rights Week, **Dec 8**
David McCord Children's Literature Fest (Framingham), **Nov 1**
Deborah Samson Day, **May 23**
Evacuation Day, **Mar 17**
First Women's Collegiate Basketball Game: Anniv, **Mar 22**
Intl Federation of Library Assns Annual Conference (Boston), **Aug 16**
John Carver Day, **June 23**
John F. Kennedy Day, **Nov 25**
Keep Massachusetts Beautiful Month, **May 1**
Native American Day, **Sept 21**
Patriot's Day, **Apr 15**
Ratification Day, **Feb 6**
Reenactment of Boston Tea Party (Boston), **Dec 16**
Samuel Slater Day, **Dec 20**
School Principals' Recognition Day, **Apr 27**
State Constitution Day, **Oct 25**
Student Government Day, **Apr 5**
Teacher's Day, **June 2**
Whale Awareness Day, **May 2**
MATHCOUNTS, Nov 1
Mathematics Education Month, Apr 1
Mathematics, Natl Council of Teachers of, Annual Mtg (Las Vegas, NV), Apr 22
Mathers, Jerry: Birth, June 2
Mathis, Sharon Bell: Birth, Feb 26
Matisse, Henri: Birth Anniv, Dec 31
Maundy Thursday (Holy Thursday), Mar 28
Mauritania: Independence Day, Nov 28
Mauritius: Independence Day, Mar 12
Mawlid al Nabi: Birthday of Prophet Muhammad, May 25
Maxwell, Gavin: Birth Anniv, July 15
May Day, May 1
Mayer, Mercer: Birth, Dec 30
Mayflower Day, Sept 16
Mayne, William: Birth, Mar 16
Mays, Willie: Birth, May 6
Mazer, Harry: Birth, May 31
Mazer, Norma Fox: Birth, May 15
Mazowiecki, Tadeusz: Poland: Solidarity Founded, Aug 31
Mazza Collection Institute (Findlay, OH), Nov 10
McArdle, Andrea: Birth, Nov 4
McAuliffe, Christa: Birth Anniv, Sept 2
McBride, Brian: Birth, June 19
McCaffrey, Anne: Birth, Apr 1
McCain, John Sidney, III: Birth, Aug 29
McCallum, Scott: Birth, May 2
McCarthy, Andrew: Birth, Nov 29
McCartney, Paul: Birth, June 18
McClintock, Barbara: Birth, May 6
McCloskey, Robert: Birth, Sept 15
McConnell, Mitch: Birth, Feb 20
McCully, Emily Arnold: Birth, July 1
McDermott, Gerald: Birth, Jan 31
McDonald's Invades the Soviet Union: Anniv, Jan 31
McGovern, Ann: Birth, May 25
McGraw, Eloise Jarvis: Birth Anniv, Dec 9
McGuffey, William H.: Birth Anniv, Sept 23
McGwire Hits 62nd Home Run: Anniv, Sept 8
McGwire Hits 70th Home Run: Anniv, Sept 27
McGwire, Mark: Birth, Oct 1
McKay, Hillary: Birth, June 12
McKean, Thomas: Birth Anniv, Mar 19
McKinley, Ida Saxton: Birth Anniv, June 8
McKinley, Robin: Birth, Nov 16
McKinley, William: Birth Anniv, Jan 29
McKissack, Fredrick: Birth, Aug 12
McKissack, Patricia: Birth, Aug 9
McLean, A.J.: Birth, Jan 9
McMillan, Bruce: Birth, May 10
McMullan, Kate: Birth, Jan 16
McNabb, Donovan: Birth, Nov 25
McNair, Steve: Birth, Feb 14
McPhail, David: Birth, June 30
Meddaugh, Susan: Birth, Oct 4
Medical School for Women Opened: Anniv, Nov 1
Meltzer, Milton: Birth, May 8
Memorial Day (Observed), May 27
Memorial Day (Pres Proc), May 27
Memorial Day, Confederate (FL, GA), Apr 26
Mental Health Month, Natl, May 1
Mental Retardation Awareness Month, Mar 1
Mercator, Gerhardus: Birth Anniv, Mar 5
Meredith (James) Enrolls at Ole Miss: Anniv, Sept 30
Merlin's Snug Hug for Kids, Nov 1
Merriam, Eve: Birth Anniv, July 19
Mesa Verde Natl Park: Anniv, June 29
Mesmer, Friedrich: Birth Anniv, May 23
Messier, Mark: Birth, Jan 18
Meteor Showers, Perseid, Aug 9
Meteorological Day, World (UN), Mar 23
Metric Conversion Act: Anniv, Dec 23
Metric System Developed: Anniv, Apr 7
Metric Week, Natl, Oct 7
Mexican-American: Day of the Teacher (El Dia Del Maestro), May 8
Mexico,
Aztec Calendar Stone Discovery: Anniv, **Dec 17**
Benito Juarez: Birth Anniv, **Mar 21**
Blessing of Animals at the Cathedral, **Jan 17**
Cinco de Mayo, **May 5**
Constitution Day, **Feb 5**
Cortes Conquers Mexico: Anniv, **Nov 8**
Day of the Dead, **Nov 1**
Day of the Holy Cross, **May 3**
Dia de la Candelaria, **Feb 2**
Dia de la Raza, **Oct 12**
Feast of the Radishes (Oaxaca), **Dec 23**
Guadalajara Intl Book Fair, **Nov 24**
Guadalupe Day, **Dec 12**
Independence Day, **Sept 16**
Mexico City Earthquake: Anniv, **Sept 19**
Posadas, **Dec 16**
President's State of the Union Address, **Sept 1**
Revolution Day, **Nov 20**
San Isidro Day, **May 15**
Treaty of Guadalupe Hidalgo (with US): Anniv, **Feb 2**
Zapatista Rebellion: Anniv, **Jan 1**
Mfume, Kweisi: Birth, Oct 24
Michigan,
Admission Day, **Jan 26**
Isle Royale Natl Park: Anniv, **Apr 3**
Michigan Storytellers Fest (Flint), **July 5**
Michigan Thanksgiving Parade (Detroit), **Nov 22**
Month of the Young Child, **Apr 1**
State Fair (Detroit), **Aug 21**
Michaelmas, Sept 29
Michelangelo: Birth Anniv, Mar 6
Michelson, Albert: First US Scientist Receives Nobel: Anniv, Dec 10
Mickey Mouse Club TV Premiere: Anniv, Oct 3
Mickey Mouse's Birthday, Nov 18
Micronesia, Federated States of: Independence Day, Nov 3
Microsoft Releases Windows: Anniv, Nov 10
Middle Level Education Month, Natl, Mar 1
Middle School Assn, Natl, Annual Conf (Washington, DC), Nov 1
Middleton, Arthur: Birth Anniv, June 26
Midori: Birth, Oct 25
Midsummer Day/Eve Celebrations, June 23
Midwife's Day (Greece), Jan 8
Mighty Mouse Playhouse TV Premiere: Anniv, Dec 10
Mikulski, Barbara Ann: Birth, July 20
Mikulski, Barbara: Polish-American in the House: Anniv, Jan 4
Milano, Alyssa: Birth, Dec 19
Miles, Miska: Birth Anniv, Nov 14
Miller, Jeremy: Birth, Oct 21
Miller, Reggie: Birth, Aug 24
Million Man March: Anniv, Oct 16
Million Mom March: Anniv, May 14
Milne, A.A.: Birth Anniv (Pooh Day), Jan 18
Minarik, Else Holmelund: Birth, Sept 13
Mind Day, Make Up Your, Dec 31
Mineta, Norman: Birth, Nov 12
Minner, Ruth Ann: Birth, Jan 17
Minnesota,
Admission Day, **May 11**
Schwan's USA Cup (Blaine), **July 14**
Spotlight On Books (Alexandria), **Apr 12**
State Fair (St. Paul), **Aug 23**
Take a Kid Fishing Weekend (St. Paul), **June 8**
Voyageurs Natl Park: Anniv, **Apr 8**
Minority Enterprise Development Week (Pres Proc), Sept 23
Minow, Newton: Vast Wasteland Speech: Anniv, May 9
Mint, US: Anniv, Apr 2
Miranda Decision: Anniv, June 13
Mischief Night, Nov 4
Missing Children's Day, Natl, May 25
Mississippi,
Admission Day, **Dec 10**
Children's Book Fest (Hattiesburg), **Mar 20**
Confederate Memorial Day, **Apr 29**
Meredith (James) Enrolls at Ole Miss: Anniv, **Sept 30**
State Fair (Jackson), **Oct 3**
Missouri,
Admission Day, **Aug 10**
Children's Literature Fest (Warrensburg), **Mar 10**
Earthquakes: Anniv, **Dec 6**
Laura Ingalls Wilder Fest (Mansfield), **Sept 15**
Minority Scientists Showcase (St. Louis), **Jan 19**
Missouri Day, **Oct 17**

Sesame Street, Can You Tell Me How to Get to (St. Louis), **Dec 8**
State Fair (Sedalia), **Aug 9**
Tom Sawyer Days, Natl (Hannibal), **July 3**
Missouri Compromise: Anniv, Mar 3
Mister Rogers' Neighborhood TV Premiere: Anniv, May 22
Mitchell, Beverly: Birth, Jan 22
Mitchell, Kel: Birth, Aug 25
Mitchell, Maria: Birth Anniv, Aug 1
Moceanu, Dominique: Birth, Sept 30
Modano, Mike: Birth, June 7
Mohr, Nicholasa: Birth, Nov 1
Moldova,
Independence Day, **Aug 27**
National Language Day, **Aug 31**
Molitor, Paul: Birth, Aug 22
Mom Is a Student Day, My, Oct 15
Moment of Laughter Day, Apr 14
Monaco:National Holiday, Nov 19
Mondale, Walter F.: Birthday, Jan 5
Monday Holiday Law: Anniv, June 28
Monet, Claude: Birth Anniv, Nov 14
Money, Paper, Issued: Anniv, Mar 10
Mongolia
National Holiday, **July 11**
Republic Day, **Nov 26**
Monica: Birth, Oct 24
Monkey Trial: John T. Scopes Birth Anniv, Aug 3
Monopoly Invented: Anniv, Mar 7
Monroe Doctrine: Anniv, Dec 2
Monroe, Elizabeth K.: Birth Anniv, June 30
Monroe, James: Birth Anniv, Apr 28
Montana,
Admission Day, **Nov 8**
Battle of Little Bighorn: Anniv, **June 25**
MontanaFair (Billings), **Aug 11**
State Fair (Great Falls), **July 27**
Montana, Joe: Birth, June 11
Montessori, Maria: Birth Anniv, Aug 31
Montgolfier, Jacques: Birth Anniv, Jan 7
Montgolfier, Joseph M.: Birth Anniv, Aug 26
Montgomery Boycott Arrests: Anniv, Feb 22
Montgomery Bus Boycott Begins: Anniv, Dec 5
Montgomery, Lucy Maud: Birth Anniv, Nov 30
Month of the Dinosaur, Oct 1
Month of the Young Adolescent, Oct 1
Montross, Eric Scott: Birth, Sept 23
Montserrat: Volcano Erupts: Anniv, June 25
Moon Day (First Moon Landing), July 20
Moon Fest, Oct 1
Moon, Harvest, Oct 2
Moon, Hunter's, Nov 1
Moon, Warren: Birth, Nov 18
Moore, Clement: Birth Anniv, July 15
Moore, Julianne: Birth, Dec 30
Moranis, Rick: Birth, Apr 18
Morazan, Francisco: Holiday (Honduras), Oct 3
Morocco: Youth Day, July 9
Morris, Ann: Birth, Oct 1
Morris, Lewis: Birth Anniv, Apr 8
Morris, Robert: Birth Anniv, Jan 31
Morse, Samuel F.: Birth Anniv, Apr 27
Morse, Samuel: Opens First US Telegraph Line: Anniv, May 24
Morton, Levi P.: Birth Anniv, May 16
Moser, Barry: Birth, Oct 15
Moses, Edwin: Birth, Aug 31
Moses, Grandma Day, Sept 7
Moshoeshoe's Day (Lesotho), Mar 12
Moss, Randy: Birth, Nov 13
Most, Bernard: Birth, Sept 2
Moth-er Day, Mar 14
Mother Goose Day, May 1
Mother Teresa: Birth Anniv, Aug 27
Mother's Day, May 12
Mother's Day (Pres Proc), May 12
Mother, Father Deaf Day, Apr 28
Mott, Lucretia: Birth Anniv, Jan 3
Mount Everest Summit Reached: Anniv, May 29
Mount Rainier Natl Park: Anniv, Mar 2
Mount Rushmore Completion: Anniv, Oct 31
Mount Saint Helens Eruption: Anniv, May 18
Mourning, Alonzo: Birth, Feb 8
Moving Month, Natl, May 1
Mowat, Farley: Birth, May 12
Mowry, Tamera: Birth, July 6
Mowry, Tia: Birth, July 6
Moya, Carlos: Birth, Aug 27
Mozambique,
Armed Forces Day, **Sept 24**
Heroes' Day, **Feb 3**
Independence Day, **June 25**
Mozart, Wolfgang Amadeus: Birth Anniv, Jan 27
Muhammad: Isra al Mi'raj: Ascent of Prophet, Oct 14
Muhammad: Mawlid al Nabi: Birth of Muhammad, May 25
Muharram: See Islamic New Year, Mar 15
Mule Day, Oct 26
Mulgrew, Kate: Birth, Apr 29
Mull, Martin: Birth, Aug 18
Muniz, Frankie: Birth, Dec 5
Munoz-Rivera, Luis: Birth Anniv, July 17
Munro, Roxie: Birth, Sept 5
Munsch, Robert: Birth, June 11
Munsinger, Lynn: Birth, Dec 24
Muppet Show TV Premiere, The: Anniv, Sept 13
Muppets: Henson, Jim: Birth Anniv, Sept 24
Murkowski, Frank Hughes: Birth, Mar 28
Murphy, Eddie: Birth, Apr 3
Murphy, Jim: Birth, Sept 25
Murray, Bill: Birth, Sept 21
Murray, Patty: Birth, Oct 11
Musburger, Brent: Birth, May 26
Museum Day, Intl, May 18
Musgrove, Ronnie: Birth, July 29
Musial, Stan: Birth, Nov 21
Music,
Aberdeen Intl Youth Fest (Aberdeen, Scotland), **Aug 1**
Accordion Awareness Week, Natl, **June 1**
America the Beautiful Published, **July 4**
Beethoven's Ninth Symphony Premiere: Anniv, **May 7**
Calgary Intl Children's Fest, **May 21**
Drum Month, Intl, **Nov 1**
God Bless America 1st Performed: Anniv, **Nov 11**
Happy Birthday to "Happy Birthday to You", **June 27**
Music in Our Schools Month, **Mar 1**
Opera Debuts in the Colonies: Anniv, **Feb 8**
Piano Month, Natl, **Sept 1**
Pop Music Chart Introduced: Anniv, **Jan 4**
Saxophone Day, **Nov 6**
Stars and Stripes Forever Day, **May 14**
Tuba Day, Intl, **May 3**
Muslim Observances,
Ashura: Tenth Day, **Mar 25**
Eid-al-Adha: Feast of the Sacrifice, **Feb 22**
Eid-al-Fitr: Celebrating the Fast, **Dec 16**
Isra al Mi'raj: Ascent of Prophet Muhammad, **Oct 14**
Lailat ul Qadr: The Night of Power, **Dec 6**
Mawlid al Nabi: Birthday of Prophet Muhammad, **May 25**
Muharram (New Year), **Mar 15**
Rabi'I: Month of the Migration, **May 13**
Ramadan: Islamic Month of Fasting, **Nov 16**
Yawm Arafat: The Standing at Arafat, **Feb 21**
Mustard Day, Natl, Aug 4
Muster, Thomas: Birth, Oct 2
Mutiny on the Bounty: Anniv, Apr 28
Mutombo, Dikembe: Birth, June 25
My Mom Is a Student Day, Oct 15
Myanmar,
Independence Day, **Jan 4**
Resistance Day, **Mar 27**
Union Day, **Feb 12**
Myers, Walter Dean: Birth, Aug 12
NAACP Founded: Anniv, Feb 12
NAFTA Signed: Anniv, Dec 8
Naismith, James: Birth Anniv, Nov 6
Name Day, Get a Different, Feb 13
Namibia,
Heroes' Day, **Aug 26**
Independence Day, **Mar 21**
Nanakusa (Japan), Jan 7
Napoli, Donna Jo: Birth, Feb 28
NASA Ames Space Settlement Contest, Mar 31
National Bank, Chartered by Congress: Anniv, Feb 25
National Park Week (Pres Proc), Apr 15
Native-American,
American Indian Heritage Day (AL), **Oct 8**
American Indian Heritage Month, Natl (Pres Proc), **Nov 1**
Apache Wars Began: Anniv, **Feb 4**
Battle of Little Bighorn: Anniv, **June 25**
Bureau of Indian Affairs Established, **Mar 11**
Chief Joseph Surrender: Anniv, **Oct 5**
Cochise: Death Anniv, **June 8**
Crow Reservation Opened for Settlement: Anniv, **Oct 15**
Custer Battlefield Becomes Little Bighorn, **Nov 26**
Hayes, Ira Hamilton: Birth Anniv, **Jan 12**
Joseph, Chief: Death Anniv, **Sept 21**
Last Great Buffalo Hunt: Anniv, **June 25**
Minority Enterprise Development Week (Pres Proc), **Sept 23**
Native American Day (MA), **Sept 21**
Native Americans Day in South Dakota, **Oct 8**
Native Americans Gain Citizenship: Anniv, **June 15**
Osceola: Death Anniv, **Jan 30**
Philip, King: Assassination: Anniv, **Aug 12**
Pocahontas: Death Anniv, **Mar 21**
Red Cloud: Death Anniv, **Dec 10**
Sitting Bull: Death Anniv, **Dec 15**
Tecumseh: Death Anniv, **Oct 5**
Wounded Knee Massacre: Anniv, **Dec 29**
NATO Attacks Yugoslavia: Anniv, Mar 25
Nauru: National Day, Jan 31
Nautilus: First Nuclear-Powered Submarine Voyage: Anniv, Jan 17
Navy Day, Oct 27
Navy: Sea Cadet Month, Sept 1
Naylor, Phyllis Reynolds: Birth, Jan 4
Nebraska,
Admission Day, **Mar 1**
Nebraska State Fair (Lincoln), **Aug 24**
Near Miss Day, Mar 23
Nehru, Jawaharlal: Birth Anniv, Nov 14
Neither Snow Nor Rain Day, Sept 7
Nelson, Ben: Birth, May 17
Nelson, Bill: Birth, Sept 29
Nelson, Thomas: Birth Anniv, Dec 26
Nepal,
King's Birthday National Holiday, **Dec 29**
National Unity Day, **Jan 11**
Neptune Discovery: Anniv, Sept 23
Nesbit, E. (Edith): Birth Anniv, Aug 15
Ness, Evaline: Birth Anniv, Apr 24
Netherlands,
Liberation Day, **May 5**
National Windmill Day, **May 11**
Prinsjesdag (Parliament opening), **Sept 18**
Queen's Birthday, **Apr 30**
Sinterklaas, **Dec 5**
Neufeld, John: Birth, Dec 14
Nevada,
Admission Day, **Oct 31**

American Federation of Teachers Conv (Las Vegas), **July 14**
Community Education Assn Conference, Natl (Reno), **Nov 17**
Family Day, **Nov 23**
State Fair (Reno), **Aug 22**
Teachers of Mathematics, Natl Council of, Annual Mtg (Las Vegas), **Apr 22**
Nevis: Independence Day, Sept 19
New Hampshire,
Children's Literature Fest (Keene), **Oct 27**
Ratification Day, **June 21**
New Jersey,
Catholic Educational Assn Conv/Expo, Natl (Atlantic City), **Apr 2**
New Jersey Day, **Apr 17**
Ratification Day, **Dec 18**
Sussex County Farm & Horse Show/New Jersey State Fair (Augusta), **Aug 3**
US Girls' Junior (Golf) Chmpshp (Westfield), **July 22**
New Mexico,
Admission Day, **Jan 6**
Carlsbad Caverns Natl Park: Anniv, **May 14**
State Fair (Albuquerque), **Sept 7**
New Orleans, Battle of: Anniv, Jan 8
New Year,
Chinese New Year, **Feb 12**
Ethiopia: New Year's Day, **Sept 11**
Iranian New Year (Persian), **Mar 21**
Japanese Era New Year, **Jan 1**
Muharram (Islamic New Year), **Mar 15**
Naw-Ruz (Baha'i New Year's Day), **Mar 21**
New Year's Day, **Jan 1**
New Year's Day (Gregorian), **Jan 1**
New Year's Day Observance (Russia), **Jan 1**
New Year's Dishonor List, **Jan 1**
New Year's Eve, **Dec 31**
Rosh Hashanah (Jewish), **Sept 18**
Sri Lanka: Sinhala and Tamil New Year, **Apr 13**
New York,
Brooklyn Bridge Opened: Anniv, **May 24**
Christmas Tree/Rockefeller Center (New York), **Nov 28**
Council for Exceptional Children Annual Convention (New York), **Apr 3**
Education of Young Children, Natl Assn for the, Conference (New York), **Nov 20**
Great Blizzard of '88: Anniv, **Mar 12**
Macy's Thanksgiving Day Parade (New York), **Nov 22**
New York City Subway: Anniv, **Oct 27**
New York Public Library: Anniv, **May 23**
Ratification Day, **July 26**
Saint Patrick's Day Parade (New York), **Mar 17**
State Fair (Syracuse), **Aug 23**
New York Stock Exchange Established: Anniv, May 17
New Zealand,
Anzac Day, **Apr 25**
Labor Day, **Oct 22**
New Zealand First Sighted by Europeans, **Dec 13**
Otago/Southland Provincial Anniv, **Mar 23**
Waitangi Day, **Feb 6**
Newbery, John: Birth Anniv, July 19
Newscurrents Student Editorial Cartoon Contest, Mar 1
Newspaper in Education Week, Mar 4
Newspaper Week (Japan), Oct 1
Newspaper, First American: Anniv, Sept 25
Newton, Sir Isaac: Birth Anniv, Jan 4
Nez Perce: Chief Joseph Surrender: Anniv, Oct 5
Ng, Irene: Birth, July 30
Niagara Falls, Charles Blondin's Conquest of: Anniv, June 30
Nicaragua,
Independence Day, **Sept 15**
National Liberation Day, **July 19**
Nick at Nite: Anniv, July 1
Nickelodeon Channel TV Premiere: Anniv, Apr 2
Nickles, Don: Birth, Dec 6
Nielsen, Arthur Charles: Birth Anniv, Sept 5
Niger,
Independence Day, **Aug 3**
Republic Day, **Dec 18**
Nigeria: Independence Day, Oct 1
Night Out, Natl, Aug 7
Nightingale, Florence: Birth Anniv, May 12
911 Day, Sept 11
Nixon, Joan Lowery: Birth, Feb 3
Nixon, Pat: Birth Anniv, Mar 16
Nixon, Richard M.,
Birth Anniv, **Jan 9**
First Televised Presidential Debate: Anniv, **Sept 26**
Resigns: Anniv, **Aug 9**
No Brainer Day, Feb 27
No Homework Day, Mar 22
No Housework Day, Apr 7
No Socks Day, May 8
No-Tobacco Day, World, May 31
Nobel Prize Ceremonies (Oslo, Norway/Stockholm, Sweden), Dec 10
Nobel Prize, First US Scientist Receives: Anniv, Dec 10
Nobel, Alfred: Birth Anniv, Oct 21
Nomo, Hideo: Birth, Aug 31
North Atlantic Treaty Ratified: Anniv, Apr 4
North Carolina,
Greensboro Sit-in: Anniv, **Feb 1**
North Carolina SweetPotato Month, **Feb 1**
Novello Festival of Reading (Charlotte), **Oct 12**
Ratification Day, **Nov 21**
North Cascades Natl Park: Anniv, Oct 2
North Dakota,
Admission Day, **Nov 2**
State Fair (Minot), **July 19**
Theodore Roosevelt Natl Park: Anniv, **Apr 25**
North Pole Discovered: Anniv, Apr 6
North Pole, Solo Trip to: Anniv, Apr 22
North, Sterling: Birth Anniv, Nov 4
Northern Hemisphere Hoodie-Hoo Day, Feb 20
Northern Ireland,
Orangemen's Day, **July 12**
Saint Patrick's Day, **Mar 17**
Northern Pacific Railroad Completed: Anniv, Sept 8
Northwest Ordinance: Anniv, July 13
Norton, Gale: Birth, Mar 11
Norton, Mary: Birth Anniv, Dec 10
Noruz, Mar 21
Norway,
Constitution or Independence Day, **May 17**
Midnight Sun at North Cape, **May 14**
Nobel Prize Awards Ceremony (Oslo), **Dec 10**
St. Knut's Day, **Jan 13**
Nothing Day, Natl, Jan 16
NOW Founded: Anniv, June 30
Nuclear Chain Reaction, First Self-Sustaining: Anniv, Dec 2
Nuclear Power Plant Accident, Three Mile Island: Anniv, Mar 28
Nuclear-Free World, First Step Toward a: Anniv, Dec 8
Nuclear-Powered Submarine Voyage, First: Anniv, Jan 17
Numeroff, Laura Joffe: Birth, July 14
Nunavut Independence: Anniv, Apr 1
Nutrition Month, Natl, Mar 1
Nutt Day, Emma M., Sept 1
Nye, Bill: Birth, Nov 27
Nye, Naomi Shihab: Birth, Mar 12
Nylon Stockings: Anniv, May 15
O'Bannon, Frank: Birth, Jan 30
O'Brien, Austin: Birth, May 11
O'Brien, Robert C.: Birth Anniv, Jan 11
O'Connor, Sandra Day: Birth, Mar 26
O'Connor, Sandra Day: First Woman Supreme Court Justice: Anniv, Sept 25
O'Dell, Scott: Birth Anniv, May 23
O'Donnell, Chris: Birth, June 26
O'Donnell, Rosie: Birth, Mar 21
O'Hara, Mary: Birth Anniv, July 10
O'Higgins, Bernardo: Birth Anniv, Aug 20
O'Keeffe, Georgia: Birth Anniv, Nov 15
O'Neal, Shaquille: Birth, Mar 6
O'Neal, Tatum: Birth, Nov 5
O'Neill, Paul: Birth, Dec 4
Oakley, Annie: Birth Anniv, Aug 13
Oatmeal Month, Jan 1
Ocean, Natl Week of the, Apr 7
October War (Yom Kippur War), Oct 6
Odie's Birthday, Aug 8
Oglethorpe, James: Birth Anniv, Dec 22
Ohio,
Admission Day, **Mar 1**
Children's Literature Conference (Columbus), **Feb 14**
Gifted Children Conv, Natl Assn (Cincinnati), **Nov 7**
Mazza Collection Institute (Findlay), **Nov 10**
Soap Box Derby, All-American (Akron), **July 23**
State Fair (Columbus), **Aug 3**
Stokes Becomes First Black Mayor in US: Anniv, **Nov 13**
Storyteller of the Year Contest, Natl (Millersport), **Sept 1**
Virginia Hamilton Conf (Kent), **Apr 4**
Oil Embargo Lifted, Arab: Anniv, Mar 13
Oil: 55 mph Speed Limit: Anniv, Jan 2
Oil: First Commercial Oil Well: Anniv, Aug 27
Oklahoma,
Admission Day, **Nov 16**
Cherokee Strip Day, **Sept 16**
Land Rush Begins, **Apr 22**
Oklahoma Day, **Apr 22**
State Fair (Oklahoma City), **Sept 14**
Oklahoma City Bombing: Anniv, Apr 19
Olajuwon, Hakeem: Birth, Jan 21
Old Inauguration Day, Mar 4
Older Americans Month (Pres Proc), May 1
Oleynik, Larisa: Birth, June 7
Olsen, Ashley: Birth, June 13
Olsen, Mary-Kate: Birth, June 13
Olympics,
First Modern Olympics Began: Anniv, **Apr 6**
First Special Olympics: Anniv, **July 20**
First Winter Olympics: Anniv, **Jan 25**
Winter Olympics Closing Ceremony (Salt Lake City, UT), **Feb 24**
Winter Olympics Opening Ceremony (Salt Lake City, UT), **Feb 8**
Oman: National Holiday, Nov 18
Onassis, Jacqueline Kennedy: Birth Anniv, July 28
100 Billionth Crayon Produced: Anniv, Feb 6
One Hundredth Day of School, Feb 8
Open An Umbrella Indoors Day, Natl, Mar 13
Opera Debuts in the Colonies: Anniv, Feb 8
Optimism Month, Mar 1
Orangemen's Day (Northern Ireland), July 12
Oregon,
Admission Day, **Feb 14**
Crater Lake Natl Park: Anniv, **May 22**
State Fair (Salem), **Aug 23**
Organ and Tissue Donor Awareness Week, Natl, Apr 14
Organ and Tissue Donor Awareness Week, Natl (Pres Proc), Apr 14
Organic Act Day (US Virgin Islands), June 17
Organization of American States Founded: Anniv, Apr 30
Orgel, Doris: Birth, Feb 15
Orlev, Uri: Birth, Feb 24

Orsi, Leigh Ann: Birth, May 15
Orthodontic Health Month, Natl, Oct 1
Orthodox Ascension Day, June 13
Orthodox Christmas, Old Calendar, Jan 7
Orthodox Easter Sunday, May 5
Orthodox Festival of All Saints, June 30
Orthodox Lent, Mar 18
Orthodox Palm Sunday, Apr 28
Orthodox Pentecost, June 23
Osborne, Mary Pope: Birth, May 20
Osceola: Death Anniv, Jan 30
Osment, Haley Joel: Birth, Apr 10
Osmond, Donny: Birth, Dec 9
Overseas Chinese Day (Taiwan), Oct 21
Owens, Bill: Birth, Oct 22
Owens, Jesse: Birth Anniv, Sept 12
Oxenbury, Helen: Birth, June 2
Paca, William: Birth Anniv, Oct 31
Pacific Ocean Discovered: Anniv, Sept 25
Pacing the Bounds (Liestal, Switzerland), May 6
Paige, Rod: Birth, June 17
Paige, Satchel: Birth Anniv, July 7
Paine, Robert Treat: Birth Anniv, Mar 11
Pak, Se Ri: Birth, Sept 28
Pakistan,
Birthday of Qaid-i-Azam, **Dec 25**
Founder's Death Anniv (Qaid-i-Azam), **Sept 11**
Republic Day, **Mar 23**
Palm Sunday, Mar 24
Palm Sunday, Orthodox, Apr 28
Paltrow, Gwyneth: Birth, Sept 28
Pan Am Circles Earth: Anniv, Jan 6
Pan American Aviation Day (Pres Proc), Dec 17
Pan American Day (Pres Proc), Apr 14
Pan American Health Day (Pres Proc), Dec 2
Pan American Week (Pres Proc), Apr 14
Pan-American Day in Florida, Apr 14
Panama,
Assumes Control of Canal: Anniv, **Dec 31**
First Shout of Independence, **Nov 10**
Flag Day, **Nov 4**
Independence Day, **Nov 3**
Independence from Spain Day, **Nov 28**
Martyrs' Day, **Jan 9**
Panic Day, Mar 9
Paper Money Issued: Anniv, Mar 10
Paperback Books Introduced: Anniv, July 30
Papua New Guinea: Independence Day, Sept 16
Paquin, Anna: Birth, July 24
Parades,
Bud Billiken Parade (Chicago, IL), **Aug 11**
Macy's Thanksgiving Day Parade (New York, NY), **Nov 22**
Michigan Thanksgiving Parade (Detroit, MI), **Nov 22**
Mummers Parade (Philadelphia, PA), **Jan 1**
Orange Bowl Parade (Miami, FL), **Dec 31**
Pasadena Doo Dah Parade (Pasadena, CA), **Nov 25**
Saint Patrick's Day Parade (New York, NY), **Mar 17**
Tournament of Roses Parade (Pasadena, CA), **Jan 1**
Paraguay,
Boqueron Day, **Sept 29**
Independence Day, **May 15**
National Heroes' Day, **Mar 1**
Parents' Day (Pres Proc), July 28
Paris, Treaty of, Ends American Rev, Sept 3
Parish, Peggy: Birth, July 14
Park, Barbara: Birth, Apr 21
Parker, Charlie: Birth Anniv, Aug 29
Parker, Steve: Birth, Dec 7
Parker, Trey: Birth, May 30
Parks Month, Natl Recreation and, July 1
Parks, Rosa Lee: Birth, Feb 4
Parks, Rosa: Day, Dec 1
Partridge Family TV Premiere: Anniv, Sept 25
Partridge, Elizabeth: Birth, Oct 1
Pascal, Francine: Birth, May 13
Pascua Florida Day, Apr 2
Passion Week, Mar 17
Passiontide, Mar 17
Passover, Mar 28
Passover Begins, Mar 27
Passport Presentation (Russia), Jan 2
Pasta Month, Natl, Oct 1
Pasteur, Louis: Birth Anniv, Dec 27
Pasteur, Louis: First Successful Antirabies Inoculation, July 6
Pataki, George: Birth, June 24
Patent Office Opens, US: Anniv, July 31
Patent, Dorothy Hinshaw: Birth, Apr 30
Paterson, Katherine: Birth, Oct 31
Patinkin, Mandy: Birth, Nov 30
Paton Walsh, Jill: Birth, Apr 29
Patriot's Day (MA, ME), Apr 15
Patriot's Day in Florida, Apr 19
Patton, Paul E.: Birth, May 26
Pauley, Jane: Birth, Oct 31
Paulsen, Gary: Birth, May 17
Pause for Pledge (Natl Flag Day USA), June 14
Payton, Gary: Birth, July 23
Peace,
Disarmament Week, **Oct 24**
Lions Club Intl Peace Poster Contest, **Oct 1**
Peace Corps Founded: Anniv, **Mar 1**
Peace Officer Memorial Day (Pres Proc), **May 15**
Peace Officer Memorial Day, Natl, **May 15**
UN Intl Day of Peace, **Sept 18**
UN: Decade for a Culture of Peace and Non-Violence for the Children of the World, Intl, **Jan 1**
World Hello Day, **Nov 21**
Peanut Butter Lover's Month, Nov 1
Peanuts Debuts: Anniv, Oct 2
Pearl Harbor Day, Dec 7
Pearl Harbor Remembrance Day, Natl (Pres Proc), Dec 7
Pearson, Lester B.: Birth Anniv, Apr 23
Peary, Robert E.: Birth Anniv, May 6
Peary, Robert E.: North Pole Discovered: Anniv, Apr 6
Pecan Day, Mar 25
Peck, Richard: Birth, Apr 5
Peck, Robert Newton: Birth, Feb 17
Pediatric Cancer Awareness Month, Oct 1
Peet, Bill: Birth, Jan 29
Pele: Birth, Oct 23
Pen-Friends Week Intl, May 1
Pencil Patented: Anniv, Mar 30
Penichiero, Ticha: Birth, Sept 18
Penn, John: Birth Anniv, May 6
Penn, William: Birth Anniv, Oct 14
Penn, William: Pennsylvania Deeded to: Anniv, Mar 4
Pennsylvania,
Battle of Gettysburg: Anniv, **July 1**
First American Abolition Soc Founded: Anniv, **Apr 14**
First Natl Convention for Blacks: Anniv, **Sept 15**
First US Zoo: Anniv (Philadelphia), **July 1**
Groundhog Day in Punxsutawney, PA (Punxsutawney), **Feb 2**
Highlights Foundation Writer's Workshop (Honesdale), **Sept 12**
Johnstown Flood: Anniv, **May 31**
Little League Baseball World Series (Williamsport), **Aug 17**
Mummers Parade (Philadelphia), **Jan 1**
Northern Appalachian Story Fest (Mansfield), **Sept 14**
Pennsylvania Deeded to William Penn: Anniv, **Mar 4**
Philadelphia Intl Children's Fest, **May 1**
Pittsburgh Intl Children's Fest, **May 15**
Ratification Day, **Dec 12**
Pentecost, May 19
People Magazine: Anniv, Mar 4
Peppercorn Ceremony (Bermuda), Apr 23
Perez, Tony: Birth, May 14
Perigean Spring Tides, Feb 27
Perigean Spring Tides, Mar 28
Perigean Spring Tides, Aug 18
Perigean Spring Tides, Sept 17
Perihelion, Earth at, Jan 2
Perlman, Rhea: Birth, Mar 31
Perry, Matthew: Commodore Perry Day, Apr 10
Perry, Oliver H.: Birth Anniv, Aug 23
Perry, Rick: Birth, Mar 4
Perseid Meteor Showers, Aug 9
Persian Gulf War,
Desert Shield: Anniv, **Aug 7**
Kuwait Liberated: Anniv, **Feb 27**
Persian Gulf War Begins: Anniv, **Jan 16**
Personal Self-Defense Awareness Month, Natl, Jan 1
Peru,
Day of National Honor, **Oct 9**
Day of the Navy, **Oct 8**
Independence Day, **July 28**
Saint Rose of Lima Day, **Aug 30**
Pesach (Passover), Mar 28
Pesach Begins, Mar 27
Pesci, Joe: Birth, Feb 9
Peshtigo Forest Fire: Anniv, Oct 8
Pestalozzi, Johann Heinrich: Birth Anniv, Jan 12
Pet Owners Independence Day, Apr 18
Pet Peeve Week, Natl, Oct 8
Pet Week, Natl, May 5
Peter and Paul Day, June 29
Peterson, Roger Tory: Birth Anniv, Aug 28
Petrified Forest Natl Park: Anniv, Dec 9
Pfister, Marcus: Birth, July 30
Philadelphia Intl Children's Fest, May 1
Philip, King: Assassination Anniv, Aug 12
Philippines,
Ati-Atihan Fest, **Jan 19**
Bataan Day: Anniv, **Apr 9**
Bonifacio Day, **Nov 30**
Feast of the Black Nazarene, **Jan 9**
Fil-American Friendship Day, **July 4**
Independence Day, **June 12**
Mount Pinatubo Erupts in Philippines: Anniv, **June 11**
Natl Heroes' Day, **Aug 26**
Philippine Independence: Anniv, **Mar 24**
Rizal Day, **Dec 30**
Simbang Gabi, **Dec 16**
Phillips, Stone: Birth, Dec 2
Photography: First Presidential Photograph: Anniv, Feb 14
Physical Education, Recreation and Dance, American Alliance for Health, Annual Meeting, Apr 9
Piaget, Jean: Birth Anniv, Aug 9
Piano Month, Natl, Sept 1
Piazza, Mike: Birth, Sept 4
Picasso, Pablo: Birth Anniv, Oct 25
Piccard, Auguste: Birth Anniv, Jan 28
Piccard, Jean Felix: Birth Anniv, Jan 28
Piccard, Jeannette Ridlon: Birth Anniv, Jan 5
Pickett's Charge: Battle of Gettysburg: Anniv, July 1
Pickett, Bill: Birth Anniv., Dec 5
Pied Piper of Hamelin: Anniv, July 22
Pierce, Franklin: Birth Anniv, Nov 23
Pierce, Jane: Birth Anniv, Mar 12
Pierce, Meredith Ann: Birth, July 5
Pierce, Tamora: Birth, Dec 13
Pig Day, Natl, Mar 1
Pilgrim Landing: Anniv, Dec 21
Pilkey, Dav: Birth, Mar 4
Pinkney, Andrea Davis: Birth, Sept 25
Pinkney, J. Brian: Birth, Aug 28
Pinkney, Jerry: Birth, Dec 22
Pinkwater, Daniel: Birth, Nov 15
Pinzon, Martin: Arrival Anniv, Mar 1

Piper, Watty: Birth Anniv, Sept 15
Pippen, Scottie: Birth, Sept 25
Pisces Begins, Feb 20
Pitcher, Molly: Birth Anniv, Oct 13
Pitt, Brad: Birth, Dec 18
Pittsburgh Intl Children's Fest, May 15
Pizarro, Francisco: Death Anniv, June 26
Planet Neptune Discovery: Anniv, Sept 23
Planet Pluto Discovery: Anniv, Feb 18
Planet Uranus Discovery: Anniv, Mar 13
Play Presented in North American Colonies, First: Anniv, Aug 27
Play-Doh Day, Natl, Sept 16
Play-the-Recorder Month, Mar 1
Playground Safety Day, Natl, Apr 25
Playground Safety Week, Natl, Apr 22
Pledge Across America: Natl School Celebration, Oct 12
Pledge of Allegiance Recognized: Anniv, Dec 28
Pledge of Allegiance, Pause for (Natl Flag Day USA), June 14
Plough Monday (England), Jan 7
Pluto Discovery, Planet: Anniv, Feb 18
Pocahontas: Death Anniv, Mar 21
Poe, Edgar Allan: Birth Anniv, Jan 19
Poetry,
  American Poet Laureate Establishment: Anniv, **Dec 20**
  Limerick Day, **May 12**
  Poetry Day in Florida, **May 25**
  Poetry Month, Natl, **Apr 1**
  Wheatley, Phillis: Death Anniv, **Dec 5**
  Young Peoples' Poetry Week, **Apr 15**
Poinsett, Joel Roberts: Death Anniv, Dec 12
Poinsettia Day, Dec 12
Poison Prevention Week, Natl, Mar 17
Poison Prevention Week, Natl (Pres Proc), Mar 17
Pokemon Debuts: Anniv, Sept 28
Polacco, Patricia: Birth, July 11
Poland,
  Constitution Day, **May 3**
  Independence Day, **Nov 11**
  Solidarity Founded Anniv, **Aug 31**
Police Week (Pres Proc), May 12
Police Week, Natl, May 12
Police: Peace Officer Memorial Day (Pres Proc), May 15
Police: Peace Officer Memorial Day, Natl, May 15
Polio Vaccine: Anniv, Apr 12
Polish American Heritage Month, Oct 1
Polish-American in the House (Mikulski): Anniv, Jan 4
Polk, James: Birth Anniv, Nov 2
Polk, James: First Presidential Photograph: Anniv, Feb 14
Polk, Sarah Childress: Birth Anniv, Sept 4
Ponce de Leon Discovers Florida: Anniv, Apr 2
Pony Penning, Chincoteague (Chincoteague Island, VA), July 31
Pooh Day (A.A. Milne Birth Anniv), Jan 18
Poole, Josephine: Birth, Feb 12
Poor Richard's Almanack: Anniv, Dec 28
Pop Music Chart Introduced: Anniv, Jan 4
Popcorn Poppin' Month, Natl, Oct 1
Pope John Paul I: Birth Anniv, Oct 17
Pope John Paul II: Birth, May 18
Pope John XXIII: Birth Anniv, Nov 25
Pope Paul VI: Birth Anniv, Sept 26
Pope, Eddie: Birth, Dec 24
Pope, Elizabeth Marie: Birth, May 1
Population Day, World (UN), July 11
Population: Day of Five Billion: Anniv, July 11
Population: Day of the Six Billion: Anniv, Oct 12
Porter, Connie: Birth, July 29
Portugal,
  Day of Portugal, **June 10**
  Independence Day, **Dec 1**
  Liberty Day, **Apr 25**
  Republic Day, **Oct 5**
Post Day, World (UN), Oct 9
Post, Emily: Birth Anniv, Oct 30
Postlethwaite, Pete: Birth, Feb 7
Postmaster General Established, US: Anniv, Sept 22
Potok, Chaim: Birth, Feb 17
Potter, Beatrix: Birth Anniv, July 28
Poverty, Intl Day for Eradication, Oct 17
Poverty, UN Decade for the Eradication of, Jan 1
Poverty, War on: Anniv, Jan 8
Powell, Colin: Birth, Apr 5
Powell, Cristen: Birth, Mar 22
Powell, John Wesley: Birth Anniv, Mar 24
Powell, Lewis F., Jr: Birth Anniv, Sept 19
Pratt, Kyla: Birth, Aug 12
Prayer,
  National Day of Prayer (Pres Proc), **May 2**
  Supreme Court Bans School Prayer: Anniv, **June 25**
  World Day of Prayer, **Mar 1**
Prelutsky, Jack: Birth, Sept 8
Presentation of the Lord (Candlemas Day), Feb 2
Preservation Week, Natl Historic, May 12
President First Occupies White House: Anniv, Nov 1
President's Environmental Youth Award Natl Competition, Aug 1
Presidential Inauguration Anniv, George Washington, Apr 30
Presidential Inauguration, G. Cleveland's Second: Anniv, Mar 4
Presidential Photograph, First: Anniv, Feb 14
Presidents' Day, Feb 18
Presley, Elvis: Birth Anniv, Jan 8
Prevention of Animal Cruelty Month, Apr 1
Priceman, Marjorie: Birth, Jan 8
Priesand, Sally: First Woman Rabbi in US: Anniv, June 3
Priestly, Joseph: Birth Anniv, Mar 13
Prime Meridian Set: Anniv, Nov 1
Prince Harry (son of Charles and Diana): Birth, Sept 15
Prince Jonah Kuhio Kalanianole Day (HI), Mar 26
Prince William: Birth, June 21
Principi, Anthony: Birth, Apr 16
Pringle, Laurence: Birth, Nov 26
Printing Week, Intl, Jan 13
Prinze, Freddie Jr: Birth, Mar 8
Procrastination: Be Late for Something Day, Sept 5
Prohibition (18th) Amendment: Anniv, Jan 16
Prohibition Repealed: 21st Amendment Ratified, Dec 5
Project ACES Day, May 1
Provensen, Alice: Birth, Aug 14
Provensen, Martin: Birth Anniv, July 20
PTA Convention, National (San Antonio, TX), June 22
PTA Convention, Texas (Dallas, TX), Nov 16
PTA Earth Week, Natl, Apr 21
PTA Founders' Day, Natl, Feb 17
PTA Teacher Appreciation Week, Natl, May 5
Public Health Week, Natl, Apr 7
Public Lands Day, Sept 8
Public Library Assn Conference (Phoenix, AZ), Mar 12
Public Radio, Natl: Anniv, May 3
Public School, First in America: Anniv, Apr 23
Public Service Recognition Week, May 6
Public Television Debuts: Anniv, Nov 3
Puerto Rico,
  Barbosa, Jose Celso: Birth Anniv, **July 27**
  Constitution Day, **July 25**
  Diego, Jose de: Birth Anniv, **Apr 16**
  Discovery Day, **Nov 19**
  Emancipation Day, **Mar 22**
  Hostos, Eugenio Maria: Birth Anniv, **Jan 11**
  Munoz-Rivera Day, **July 17**
  Navidades, **Dec 15**
  US Virgin Islands-Puerto Rico Friendship Day, **Oct 8**
Pulaski, General Casimir: Memorial Day (Pres Proc), Oct 11
Pulaski, Casimir: Birth Anniv, Mar 4
Pulitzer, Joseph: Birth Anniv, Apr 10
Pullman, Philip: Birth, Oct 19
Puppetry Day, Natl, Apr 28
Purim, Feb 26
Purple Heart: Anniv, Aug 7
Putin, Vladimir: Birth, Oct 7
Puzzle Day, Natl, Jan 29
Puzzle Week, Natl Game and, Nov 18
Pyle, Howard: Birth Anniv, Mar 5
Qatar: Independence Day, Sept 3
Qing Ming Fest, Apr 5
Quackenbush, Robert: Birth, July 23
Quark, Physicists Discover Top: Anniv, Apr 23
Quayle, Dan: Birthday, Feb 4
Queen Elizabeth II's Official Birthday, June 10
Queen's Official Birthday/Trooping Colours (United Kingdom), June 8
Queen Latifah: Birth, Mar 18
Quinn, Kenny: Birth, Aug 24
Rabbi, First Woman Rabbi in US: Anniv, June 3
Rabi'l: Month of the Migration, May 13
Race Relations Day, Feb 14
Race Unity Day, June 9
Racial Discrimination, Intl Day for Elimination of (UN), Mar 21
Racism/Racial Discrimination, Third Decade to Combat (UN), Dec 10
Radio,
  Amateur Radio Month, Intl, **Apr 1**
  Children's Day of Broadcasting, Intl, **Dec 9**
  Federal Communications Commission Created: Anniv, **Feb 26**
  First Scheduled Radio Broadcast: Anniv, **Nov 2**
  Public Radio, Natl: Anniv, **May 3**
  Radio Broadcast by a President, First, **June 14**
  Radio Broadcasting: Anniv, **Jan 13**
  Radio Commercials: Anniv, **Aug 28**
  Transistor Invented: Anniv, **Dec 23**
Radishes, Feast of (Oaxaca, Mexico), Dec 23
Radium Discovered: Anniv, Dec 26
Radke, Brad: Birth, Oct 27
Radosavljevic, Preki: Birth, June 24
Raffi: Birth, July 8
Rafter, Patrick: Birth, Dec 28
Railroad,
  Canadian Pacific Railway: Transcontinental Completion Anniv, **Nov 7**
  Golden Spike Driving: Anniv, **May 10**
  Iron Horse Outraced by Horse: Anniv, **Sept 18**
  New York City Subway: Anniv, **Oct 27**
  Northern Pacific Railroad Completed: Anniv, **Sept 8**
  Transcontinental US Railway Completion: Anniv, **Aug 15**
Rainey, Joseph: First Black in US House of Reps: Anniv, Dec 12
Rainforest Week, World, Oct 14
Raleigh, Sir Walter: Death Anniv, Oct 29
Ramadan: Islamic Month of Fasting, Nov 16
Ramirez, Manny: Birth, May 30
Ramis, Harold: Birth, Nov 21
Randolph, Peyton: Death Anniv, Oct 22
Random Acts of Kindness Week, Nov 11
Rankin, Jeannette: Birth Anniv, June 11
Ransom, Candice F.: Birth, July 10
Ransome, Arthur: Birth Anniv, Jan 18

Ransome, James: Birth, Sept 25
Raschka, Chris: Birth, Mar 6
Rashad, Ahmad: Birth, Nov 19
Raskin, Ellen: Birth, Mar 13
Rather, Dan: Birth, Oct 31
Rathmann, Peggy: Birth, Mar 4
Ratification Day, Jan 14
Rawlings, Marjorie Kinnan: Birth Anniv, Aug 8
Rawls, Wilson: Birth Anniv, Sept 24
Read, George: Birth Anniv, Sept 18
Reading. See also Books; Literature,
African American Read-In, **Feb 3**
Banned Books Week, **Sept 22**
Book It! Reading Incentive Program, **Oct 1**
Children's Book Week, Natl, **Nov 12**
Children's Literature Conference (Columbus, OH), **Feb 14**
Family Literacy Day, Natl, **Nov 1**
Get Caught Reading Month, **May 1**
Mother Goose Day, **May 1**
Read Across America Day, **Mar 2**
Read In, **May 9**
Read to Your Child Day, **Feb 14**
Reader's Day, Natl Young, **Nov 14**
Reading Assn, Intl, Annual Conv (San Francisco, CA), **Apr 28**
Reading Is Fun Week, **Apr 21**
Teen Read Week, **Oct 14**
Young Reader's Day, Natl, **Nov 14**
Reagan, Nancy: Birth, July 6
Reagan, Ronald: Birthday, Feb 6
Recreation and Dance, American Alliance for Health, Physical Education, Annual Meeting, Apr 9
Recreation and Parks Month, Natl, July 1
Red Cloud: Death Anniv, Dec 10
Red Cross Day, World, May 8
Red Cross Month, Mar 1
Red Cross Month, American (Pres Proc), Mar 1
Redwood Natl Park: Anniv, Oct 2
Reece, Gabrielle: Birth, Jan 6
Reed, Jack: Birth, Nov 12
Reed, Walter: Birth Anniv, Sept 13
Reeder, Carolyn: Birth, Nov 16
Reef, Catherine: Birth, Apr 28
Reeve, Christopher: Birth, Sept 25
Reformation Day, Oct 31
Regular TV Broadcasts Begin: Anniv, July 1
Rehnquist, William Hubbs: Birth, Oct 1
Reid, Harry: Birth, Dec 2
Reinhard, Johan: Birth, Dec 13
Reinhold, Judge: Birth, May 21
Reiss, Johanna: Birth, Apr 4
Religious Freedom Day, Jan 16
Religious Freedom Day (Pres Proc), Jan 16
Rembrandt: Birth Anniv, July 15
Remembrance Day (Canada), Nov 11
Reno, Janet: Birth, July 21
Renoir, Pierre: Birth Anniv, Feb 25
Republican Symbol: Anniv, Nov 7
Resnik, Judith A.: Birth Anniv, Apr 5
Retired Teacher's Day in Florida, Nov 19
Retrocession Day (Taiwan), Oct 25
Retton, Mary Lou: Birth, Jan 24
Return Shopping Carts to the Supermarket Month, Feb 1
Return the Borrowed Books Week, Mar 1
Reunification of Germany: Anniv, Oct 3
Revere, Paul: Birth Anniv, Jan 1
Revere, Paul: Ride Anniv, Apr 18
Revolution, American,
Battle of Brandywine: Anniv, **Sept 11**
Battle of Lexington and Concord, **Apr 19**
Bennington Battle Day, **Aug 16**
Boston Tea Party: Anniv, **Dec 16**
Cessation of Hostilities: Anniv, **Jan 20**
Evacuation Day (MA), **Mar 17**
Hale, Nathan: Birth Anniv, **June 6**
Henry, Patrick: Birth Anniv, **May 29**
Independence Day (US), **July 4**
Liberty Day, **Mar 23**
Middleton, Arthur: Birth Anniv, **June 26**
Paris, Treaty of: Signing Anniv, **Sept 3**
Paul Revere's Ride: Anniv, **Apr 18**
Shays Rebellion: Anniv, **Aug 29**
Yorktown Day, **Oct 19**
Yorktown Day (Yorktown, VA), **Oct 19**
Revolution, Russian: Anniv, Nov 7
Rey, H.A.: Birth Anniv, Sept 16
Rey, Margaret: Birth Anniv, May 16
Rhino Day, Save the, May 1
Rhode Island,
Children's Party at Green Animals (Newport), **July 14**
Ratification Day, **May 29**
Voters Reject Constitution: Anniv, **Mar 24**
Ricci, Christina: Birth, Feb 12
Rice, Condoleezza: Birth, Nov 14
Rice, Glen: Birth, May 28
Rice, Jerry: Birth, Oct 13
Richard, Adrienne: Birth, Oct 31
Richard, Rocket: Birth Anniv, Aug 4
Richards, Todd: Birth, Dec 28
Richardson, Joely: Birth, Jan 9
Richardson, Kevin: Birth, Oct 3
Richardson, Natasha: Birth, May 11
Richardson, Patricia: Birth, Feb 23
Richert, Nate: Birth, Apr 28
Richmond, Mitch: Birth, June 30
Richter Scale Day, Apr 26
Richter, Conrad: Birth Anniv, Oct 13
Richter, Jason James: Birth, Jan 29
Ride, Sally Kristen: Birth, May 26
Ridge, Thomas J.: Birth, Aug 26
Ridgeway, Lindsay: Birth, June 22
Riel, Louis: Hanging Anniv, Nov 16
Riley, Pat: Birth, Mar 20
Riley, Richard: Birth, Jan 2
Rimes, LeAnn: Birth, Aug 28
Rinaldi, Ann: Birth, Aug 27
Ringgold, Faith: Birth, Oct 8
Ripken, Cal, Jr: Birth, Aug 24
River of Words Environmental Poetry and Art Contest, Feb 15
Rivera, Mariano: Birth, Nov 29
Road Map Week, Natl Reading a, Apr 4
Robert's Rules Day, May 2
Roberts, Pat: Birth, Apr 20
Robeson, Paul: Birth Anniv, Apr 9
Robinet, Harriette Gillem: Birth, July 14
Robinson Crusoe Day, Feb 1
Robinson Named First Black Manager: Anniv, Oct 3
Robinson, Bill "Bojangles": Birth Anniv, May 25
Robinson, David: Birth, Aug 6
Robinson, Glenn: Birth, Jan 10
Robinson, Jackie: Birth Anniv, Jan 31
Robinson, Roscoe, Jr: Birth Anniv, Oct 11
Rockefeller, John D., IV: Birth, June 18
Rockefeller, Nelson Aldrich: Birth Anniv, July 8
Rockne, Knute: Birth Anniv, Mar 4
Rockwell, Anne: Birth, Feb 8
Rocky and His Friends TV Premiere: Anniv, Nov 19
Rocky Mountain Natl Park: Anniv, Jan 26
Rodman, Dennis: Birth, May 13
Rodney, Caesar: Birth Anniv, Oct 7
Rodriguez, Alex: Birth, July 27
Rodriguez, Ivan: Birth, Nov 30
Roentgen, Wilhelm K.: Birth Anniv, Mar 27
Rogers, Fred: Birth, Mar 20
Rogers, Roy: Birth Anniv, Nov 5
Roget, Peter Mark: Birth Anniv, Jan 18
Rohmann, Eric: Birth, Oct 26
Roker, Al: Birth, Aug 20
Roller Skating Month, Natl, Oct 1
Roman Catholic: New Catechism: Anniv, Nov 16
Romania: National Day, Dec 1
Rome: Birthday (Italy), Apr 21
Ronaldo: Birth, Sept 22
Roosevelt, Alice: Birth Anniv, July 29
Roosevelt, Anna Eleanor: Birth Anniv, Oct 11
Roosevelt, Edith Kermit Carow: Birth Anniv, Aug 6
Roosevelt, Franklin Delano,
Birth Anniv, **Jan 30**
Death Anniv, **Apr 12**
Elected to Fourth Term: Anniv, **Nov 7**
Roosevelt, Theodore: Birth Anniv, Oct 27
Root, Phyllis: Birth, Feb 14
Roots: Alex Palmer Haley: Birth Anniv, Aug 11
Rose Bowl Game (Pasadena, CA), Jan 1
Rose Month, Natl, June 1
Rose, Pete: Birth, Apr 14
Roseanne: Birth, Nov 3
Rosh Hashanah, Sept 18
Rosh Hashanah Begins, Sept 17
Rosman, MacKenzie: Birth, Dec 28
Ross, Betsy: Birth Anniv, Jan 1
Ross, Dave: Birth, Apr 2
Ross, George: Birth Anniv, May 10
Ross, Nellie Tayloe: Wyoming Inaugurates First US Woman Gov: Anniv, Jan 5
Rowland, John: Birth, May 24
Rowling, J.K.: Birth, July 31
Roy Rogers Show TV Premiere: Anniv, Dec 30
Roy, Patrick: Birth, Oct 5
Rubens, Paul: Birth, Aug 27
Rugrats TV Premiere: Anniv, Aug 11
Rumsfeld, Donald: Birth, July 9
Rural Life Sunday, May 5
Russia,
Baltic States' Independence Recognized: Anniv, **Sept 6**
Boris Yeltsin Inaugurated: Anniv, **July 10**
Christmas Day, **Jan 7**
Constitution Day, **Dec 12**
Great October Socialist Revolution: Anniv, **Nov 7**
Independence Day, **June 12**
Intl Labor Day, **May 1**
McDonald's Invades the Soviet Union: Anniv, **Jan 31**
New Year's Day Observance, **Jan 1**
October Revolution, **Nov 7**
Passport Presentation, **Jan 2**
Soviet Communist Party Suspended: Anniv, **Aug 29**
Soviet Cosmonaut Returns to New Country: Anniv, **Mar 26**
Soviet Union Dissolved: Anniv, **Dec 8**
Victory Day, **May 9**
Women's Day, Intl, **Mar 8**
Rustin, Bayard: Birth Anniv, Mar 17
Ruth, George Herman,
Babe Ruth Day: Anniv, **Apr 27**
Babe Sets Home Run Record: Anniv, **Sept 30**
Birth Anniv, **Feb 6**
House That Ruth Built: Anniv, **Apr 18**
Voted into Hall of Fame: Anniv, **Feb 2**
Rutherford, Ernest: Birth Anniv, Aug 30
Rutledge, Edward: Birth Anniv, Nov 23
Rutledge, John: Death Anniv, July 18
Rwanda,
Genocide's Remembrance Day, **Apr 7**
Independence Day, **July 1**
Republic Day, **Sept 25**
Ryan, George: Birth, Feb 24
Ryan, Meg: Birth, Nov 19
Ryan, Nolan: Birth, Jan 31
Rylant, Cynthia: Birth, June 6
Sabatini, Gabriela: Birth, May 16
Sabin, Albert Bruce: Birth Anniv, Aug 26
Sabuda, Robert: Birth, Mar 8
Sacagawea: Death Anniv, Dec 20
Sachar, Louis: Birth, Mar 20
Sachs, Marilyn: Birth, Dec 18
Sadie Hawkins Day, Nov 3
Safe Schools Week, America's, Oct 14
Safe Toys and Gifts Month, Dec 1
Safety Pin Patented: Anniv, Apr 10

Safety. See also Crime,
America's Safe Schools Week, **Oct 14**
Automobile Speed Reduction: Anniv, **Nov 25**
Baby Safety Month, **Sept 1**
Buckle Up America! Week, **May 20**
Check Your Batteries Day, **Apr 7**
Child Passenger Safety Awareness Week, Natl (Pres Proc), **Feb 10**
Child Safety Council, Natl: Founding Anniv, **Nov 9**
Childhood Injury Prevention Week, Natl, **Sept 1**
Children's Eye Health and Safety Month, **Sept 1**
Crime Prevention Month, Natl, **Oct 1**
Day of National Concern about Young People and Gun Violence, **Oct 21**
Emergency Medical Services Week, Natl, **May 19**
Farm Safety Week, Natl (Pres Proc), **Sept 16**
Fire Prevention Week, **Oct 7**
Fire Prevention Week (Pres Proc), **Oct 7**
Firepup's Birthday, **Oct 1**
Fireworks Safety Month, **June 1**
Missing Children's Day, Natl, **May 25**
Night Out, Natl, **Aug 7**
911 Day, **Sept 11**
Personal Self-Defense Awareness Month, Natl, **Jan 1**
Playground Safety Day, Natl, **Apr 25**
Playground Safety Week, Natl, **Apr 22**
Poison Prevention Week, Natl, **Mar 17**
Poison Prevention Week, Natl (Pres Proc), **Mar 17**
Safe Boating Week, Natl, **May 18**
Safe Toys and Gifts Month, **Dec 1**
Safety Month, Natl, **June 1**
Safetypup's Birthday, **Feb 12**
Unmasking Halloween Dangers, **Oct 1**
Walk Our Children to School Day, Natl, **Oct 2**
Youth Sports Safety Month, Natl, **Apr 1**
Saget, Bob: Birth, May 17
Sagittarius Begins, Nov 23
Saint Andrew's Day, Nov 30
Saint Aubin, Helen "Callaghan": Birth Anniv, Mar 13
Saint Augustine, Feast of, Aug 28
Saint Basil's Day, Jan 1
Saint Christopher: Independence Day, Sept 19
Saint Clare of Assisi: Feast Day, Aug 11
Saint David's Day (Wales), Mar 1
Saint Eustatius, West Indies: Statia and America Day, Nov 16
Saint Frances Xavier Cabrini: Birth Anniv, July 15
Saint Francis of Assisi: Feast Day, Oct 4
Saint George's Day (Newfoundland, Canada), Apr 22
Saint George: Feast Day (England), Apr 23
Saint Januarius: Feast Day, Sept 19
Saint Jerome, Feast of, Sept 30
Saint Joan of Arc: Feast Day, May 30
Saint John, Apostle-Evangelist: Feast Day, Dec 27
Saint Jude's Day, Oct 28
Saint Lasarus Day (Bulgaria), Apr 1
Saint Lawrence Seaway: Dedication Anniv, June 26
Saint Lucia: Independence Day, Feb 22
Saint Luke: Feast Day, Oct 18
Saint Nicholas Day, Dec 6
Saint Patrick's Day, Mar 17
Saint Patrick's Day (Northern Ireland), Mar 17
Saint Patrick's Day Parade (New York, NY), Mar 17
Saint Piran's Day, Mar 5
Saint Stephen's Day, Dec 26
Saint Swithin's Day, July 15
Saint Valentine's Day, Feb 14
Saint Vincent and the Grenadines: Independence Day, Oct 27
Saint Vincent De Paul: Feast Day, Sept 27
Saint-Exupery, Antoine de: Birth Anniv, June 29
Sakic, Joe: Birth, July 7
Salaam, Rashaan: Birth, Oct 8
Salad Month, Natl, May 1
Salk, Jonas: Birth Anniv, Oct 28
Salsa Month, Natl, May 1
Salter, Susanna, Elected 1st Woman Mayor in US: Anniv, Apr 4
Salvation Army Founder's Day, Apr 10
Salvation Army in US: Anniv, Mar 10
Samoa,
Anzac Day, **Apr 25**
Natl Day, **June 1**
White Sunday, **Oct 14**
Samoa, American: Flag Day, Apr 17
Sampras, Pete: Birth, Aug 12
Samuelson, Joan Benoit: Birth, May 16
San Francisco 1906 Earthquake: Anniv, Apr 18
San Francisco 1989 Earthquake: Anniv, Oct 17
San Isidro Day (Mexico), May 15
San Jacinto Day (TX), Apr 21
San Marino: National Day, Sept 3
San Souci, Robert D.: Birth, Oct 10
Sandburg, Carl: Birth Anniv, Jan 6
Sanders, Barry: Birth, July 16
Sanders, Deion: Birth, Aug 9
Sanders, Summer: Birth, Oct 13
Sanderson, Ruth: Birth, Nov 24
Sandler, Adam: Birth, Sept 9
Sandwich Day: John Montague Birth Anniv, Nov 3
Santa Lucia Day (Sweden), Dec 13
Santorum, Rick: Birth, May 10
Sao Tome and Principe: National Day, July 12
Sapp, Warren: Birth, Dec 19
Sarbanes, Paul S.: Birth, Feb 3
Saudi Arabia: Kingdom Unification, Sept 23
Savage, Ben: Birth, Sept 13
Savage, Fred: Birth, July 9
Save the Florida Panther Day, Mar 16
Save the Rhino Day, May 1
Save Your Vision Week, Mar 3
Save Your Vision Week (Pres Proc), Mar 3
Sawyer, Diane K.: Birth, Dec 22
Sax, Adolphe: Birth Anniv (Saxophone Day), Nov 6
Saxophone Day, Nov 6
Say, Allen: Birth, Aug 28
Scalia, Antonin: Birth, Mar 11
Scarry, Richard M.: Birth Anniv, June 5
Schaefer, Jack: Birth Anniv, Nov 19
Schenk de Regniers, Beatrice: Birth Anniv, Aug 16
Schilling, Curt: Birth, Nov 14
Schmidt, Mike: Birth, Sept 27
School Boards Assn Annual Conference, Natl (New Orleans, LA), Apr 6
School Breakfast Week, Natl, Mar 4
School Bus Safety Week, Natl, Oct 21
School Celebration, Natl, Oct 12
School Counseling Week, Natl, Feb 4
School Library Day, Intl, Oct 15
School Library Media Month, Apr 1
School Lunch Week, Natl, Oct 15
School Lunch Week, Natl (Pres Proc), Oct 14
School Nurse Day, Natl, Jan 23
School Principals' Day, May 1
School Principals' Recognition Day (MA), Apr 27
School Spirit Season, Intl, Apr 30
School-to-Work Launched: Anniv, May 4
SchoolTech Expo and Conference, Oct 18
Schroder, Gerhard: Birth, Sept 27
Schroeder, Alan: Birth, Jan 18
Schulz, Charles: Birth Anniv, Nov 26
Schuman Plan Anniv: European Union, May 9
Schuman, William Howard: Birth Anniv, Aug 4
Schumann, Clara: Birth Anniv, Sept 13
Schumer, Charles E.: Birth, Nov 23
Schwan's USA Cup (Blaine, MN), July 14
Schwartzman, Jason: Birth, June 26
Schwarzenegger, Arnold: Birth, July 30
Science and Technology,
Biological Clock Gene Discovered: Anniv, **Apr 28**
Biological Diversity, Intl Day of, **Dec 29**
Brain Awareness Week, Intl, **Mar 11**
Brain Bee, Natl, **Mar 12**
Camcorder Developed: Anniv, **Jan 20**
Cellophane Tape Patented: Anniv, **May 27**
Chemistry Week, Natl, **Nov 4**
Cloning of an Adult Animal, First: Anniv, **Feb 23**
Dinosaur Month, Intl, **Oct 1**
Discovery Young Scientist Challenge (Washington, DC), **Oct 20**
Earth's Rotation Proved: Anniv, **Jan 8**
Energy Education Week, Natl, **Mar 18**
First Self-Sustaining Nuclear Chain Reaction: Anniv, **Dec 2**
First US Scientist Receives Nobel: Anniv, **Dec 10**
Jason XIII Project, **Sept 4**
Laser Patented: Anniv, **Mar 22**
Metric System Developed: Anniv, **Apr 7**
Minority Scientists Showcase (St. Louis, MO), **Jan 19**
Month of the Dinosaur, **Oct 1**
Physicists Discover Top Quark: Anniv, **Apr 23**
Radium Discovered: Anniv, **Dec 26**
Science Olympiad, **May 17**
Science Teachers Assn Conv, Natl (San Diego, CA), **Mar 27**
Sky Awareness Week, **Apr 21**
Vitamin C Isolated: Anniv, **Apr 4**
West Point Bicentennial Engineering Design Contest, **Nov 11**
X-Ray Discovery Day: Anniv, **Nov 8**
Science Fiction: Asimov, Isaac: Birth Anniv, Jan 2
Scieszka, Jon: Birth, Sept 8
Scolari, Peter: Birth, Sept 12
Scopes, John T.: Birth Anniv, Aug 3
Scorpio Begins, Oct 23
Scotland,
Aberdeen Intl Youth Fest (Aberdeen), **Aug 1**
Bannockburn Day, **June 24**
Up Helly AA, **Jan 29**
Scotland Yard: First Appearance Anniv, Sept 29
Scott, Chad: Birth, Sept 6
Scott, Winfield: Birth Anniv, June 13
Scout Week, Girl, Mar 10
Scrabble inventor: Butts, Alfred M.: Birth Anniv, Apr 13
Sea Cadet Month, Sept 1
Seattle Intl Children's Fest, May 13
Sebestyen, Ouida: Birth, Feb 13
Second Day of Christmas, Dec 26
Secret Pal Day, Jan 13
Seeger, Pete: Birth, May 3
Segar, E.C.: Birth Anniv, Dec 8
Selanne, Teemu: Birth, July 3
Selden, George: Birth Anniv, May 14
Seles, Monica: Birth, Dec 2
Senate Quorum, First: Anniv, Apr 6
Senate: Black Page Appointed: Anniv, Apr 8
Sendak, Maurice: Birth, June 10
Senegal: Independence Day, Apr 4
Senior Citizens,
Older Americans Month (Pres Proc), **May 1**
Older Persons, Intl Day for, **Oct 1**
Sequoia and Kings Canyon Natl Parks: Anniv, Sept 25
Server, Josh: Birth, Apr 11

Sesame Street TV Premiere: Anniv, Nov 10
Sesame Street, Can You Tell Me How to Get to (St. Louis, MO), Dec 8
Sessions, Jeff: Birth, Dec 24
Seton, Elizabeth Ann: Birth Anniv, Aug 28
Setsubun (Japan), Feb 3
Seurat, Georges: Birth Anniv, Dec 2
Seuss, Dr.: Geisel, Theodor: Birth Anniv, Mar 2
Sewall, Marcia: Birth, Nov 5
Seward's Day (AK), Mar 25
Sewell, Anna: Birth Anniv, Mar 30
Sex Month, Natl Talk With Your Teen About, Mar 1
Sexuality Education Month, Natl Family, Oct 1
Seychelles: Constitution Day, June 18
Shabbat Across America, Mar 22
Shaheen, Jeanne: Birth, Jan 28
Shakespeare, William: Birth and Death Anniv, Apr 23
Shalala, Donna: Birth, Feb 14
Shamu: Birthday, Sept 26
Shannon, David: Birth, Oct 5
Shareware Day, Intl, Dec 9
Shatner, William: Birth, Mar 22
Shavuot, May 17
Shaw, Nancy: Birth, Apr 27
Shays Rebellion: Anniv, Aug 29
Shelby, Richard C.: Birth, May 6
Shelley, Mary Wollstonecraft: Birth Anniv, Aug 30
Shemini Atzeret, Oct 9
Shenandoah Natl Park: Anniv, Dec 26
Shepard, Alan: Birth Anniv, Nov 18
Sherman Enters Atlanta: Anniv, Sept 2
Sherman, James S.: Birth Anniv, Oct 24
Sherman, Roger: Birth Anniv, Apr 19
Sherman, William Tecumseh: Birth Anniv, Feb 8
Shopping Carts to the Supermarket Month, Return, Feb 1
Shopping Reminder Day, Nov 25
Shriver, Maria: Birth, Nov 6
Shrove Monday, Feb 11
Shrove Tuesday, Feb 12
Shrovetide, Feb 10
Shulevitz, Uri: Birth, Feb 27
Siegelman, Don: Birth, Feb 24
Sierra Club Founded: Anniv, May 28
Sierra Leone,
  Independence Day, **Apr 27**
  National Holiday, **Apr 19**
Sierra, Judy: Birth, June 8
Sikh: Baisakhi (India), Apr 13
Silent Spring Publication: Anniv, Apr 13
Silly Putty Debuts: Anniv, Mar 1
Silverstein, Shel: Birth Anniv, Oct 18
Silverstone, Alicia: Birth, Oct 4
Simchat Torah, Oct 10
Simon, Paul: Birth, Oct 13
Simon, Seymour: Birth, Aug 9
Simpsons TV Premiere: Anniv, Jan 14
Sinai Day (Egypt), Apr 25
Sinbad: Birth, Nov 10
Singapore,
  National Day, **Aug 9**
  Vesak Day, **May 10**
Singer, Isaac Bashevis: Birth Anniv, July 14
Single Parents Day, Mar 21
Singletary, Mike: Birth, Oct 9
Sis, Peter: Birth, May 11
Sisters' Day, Aug 5
Sitting Bull: Death Anniv, Dec 15
Skating: Natl Roller Skating Month, Oct 1
Sky Awareness Week, Apr 21
Skylab Falls to Earth, July 11
Slater, Rodney: Birth, Feb 23
Slater, Samuel, Day (MA), Dec 20
Slavery: First American Abolition Soc Founded: Anniv, Apr 14
Slayton, Donald "Deke" K.: Birth Anniv, Mar 1
Sleator, William: Birth, Feb 13
Sleep Awareness Week, Natl, Mar 25
Slinky Introduced: Anniv, Nov 26
Slobodkina, Esphyr: Birth, Sept 22
Slovakia,
  Czech-Slovak Divorce: Anniv, **Jan 1**
  Liberation Day, **May 8**
  National Day, **Sept 1**
  Natl Uprising Day, **Aug 29**
  St. Cyril and Methodius Day, **July 5**
Slovenia,
  Independence Day, **Dec 26**
  Insurrection Day, **Apr 27**
  Preseren Day, **Feb 8**
  National Day, **June 25**
Small Business Week (Pres Proc), May 19
Small, David: Birth, Feb 12
Smallpox Vaccine Discovered: Anniv, May 14
Smile Week, Natl, Aug 6
Smith Day, Natl, Jan 6
Smith, Akili: Birth, Aug 21
Smith, Betty: Birth Anniv, Dec 15
Smith, Dean: Birth, Feb 28
Smith, Emmitt: Birth, May 15
Smith, Gordon: Birth, May 25
Smith, James: Death Anniv, July 11
Smith, Jedediah Strong: Birth Anniv, Jan 6
Smith, Kate: God Bless America 1st Perf: Anniv, Nov 11
Smith, Lane: Birth, Aug 25
Smith, Robert C.: Birth, Mar 30
Smith, Samantha: Death Anniv, Aug 25
Smith, Steve: Birth, Mar 31
Smith, Taran Noah: Birth, Apr 8
Smith, Will: Birth, Sept 25
Smithsonian Institution Founded: Anniv, Aug 10
Smits, Rik: Birth, Aug 23
Smokeout, Great American, Nov 15
Snow Day for Southern Students, Dec 3
Snow Fest (Japan), Feb 8
Snowe, Olympia J.: Birth, Feb 21
Snyder, Zilpha Keatley: Birth, May 11
Soap Box Derby, All-American (Akron, OH), July 23
Sobieski, Leelee: Birth, June 10
Sobol, Donald: Birth, Oct 4
Soccer,
  Schwan's USA Cup (Blaine, MN), **July 14**
  World Cup, **May 31**
  World Cup Inaugurated: Anniv, **July 13**
Social Security Act: Anniv, Aug 14
Social Studies, Natl Council for the, Annual Mtg (Washington, DC), Nov 16
Soil Stewardship Sunday: See Rural Life Sunday, May 5
Solemnity of Mary, Jan 1
Solomon Islands: Independence Day, July 7
Solstice, Summer, June 21
Solstice, Winter, Dec 21
Somalia: National Day, Oct 21
Sorbo, Kevin: Birth, Sept 24
Sorenstam, Annika: Birth, Oct 9
Sosa, Sammy: Birth, Nov 12
Soto, Gary: Birth, Apr 12
Sound Barrier Broken: Anniv, Oct 14
Sousa, John P.: Birth Anniv, Nov 6
Sousa: Stars and Stripes Forever Day, May 14
Souter, David H.: Birth, Sept 17
South Africa,
  African Natl Congress Ban Lifted: Anniv, **Feb 2**
  Boer War: Anniv, **Oct 12**
  Day of Goodwill, **Dec 26**
  Family Day, **Apr 1**
  Freedom Day, **Apr 27**
  Heritage Day, **Sept 24**
  Human Rights Day, **Mar 21**
  Multiracial Elections: Anniv, **Apr 26**
  National Women's Day, **Aug 9**
  New Constitution: Anniv, **Nov 18**
  Reconciliation Day, **Dec 16**
  Repeals Last Apartheid Law: Anniv, **June 17**
  US Sanctions Lifted: Anniv, **July 10**
  Whites Vote to End Minority Rule: Anniv, **Mar 17**
  Youth Day, **June 16**
South Carolina,
  Confederate Memorial Day, **May 10**
  Fort Sumter Shelled by North: Anniv, **Aug 17**
  Ratification Day, **May 23**
  Secession Anniv, **Dec 20**
  State Fair (Columbia), **Oct 4**
South Dakota,
  Admission Day, **Nov 2**
  Badlands Natl Park: Anniv, **Nov 10**
  Laura Ingalls Wilder Pageant (De Smet), **June 23**
  Native Americans Day, **Oct 8**
  State Fair (Huron), **July 30**
  Wind Cave Natl Park: Anniv, **Jan 3**
South Pole Discovery: Anniv, Dec 14
Southern Fest of Books (Nashville, TN), Oct 12
Space (excluding Space Milestones),
  Apollo I: Spacecraft Fire: Anniv, **Jan 27**
  Astronomy Day, **Apr 20**
  Astronomy Week, **Apr 15**
  Challenger Space Shuttle Explosion: Anniv, **Jan 28**
  Christmas Greetings from Space: Anniv, **Dec 19**
  Comet Crashes into Jupiter: Anniv, **July 16**
  First American Woman in Space: Anniv, **June 18**
  First Man in Space: Anniv, **Apr 12**
  First Picture of Earth: Anniv, **Aug 7**
  First Woman in Space: Anniv, **June 16**
  First Woman to Walk in Space, **July 17**
  NASA Ames Space Settlement Contest, **Mar 31**
  NASA Established, **July 29**
  Near Miss Day, **Mar 23**
  Soviet Cosmonaut Returns to New Country: Anniv, **Mar 26**
Space Day, May 2
Space Milestones,
  Year 1 (1957),
    Sputnik 1, **Oct 4**
    Sputnik 2, **Nov 3**
  Year 2 (1958),
    Explorer 1, **Jan 31**
  Year 3 (1959),
    Luna 1, **Jan 2**
    Luna 2, **Sept 12**
  Year 4 (1960),
    Echo 1, **Aug 12**
    Sputnik 5, **Aug 19**
  Year 5 (1961),
    Project Mercury Test, **Jan 31**
    Vostok 1, **Apr 12**
    Freedom 7, **May 5**
  Year 6 (1962),
    Friendship 7, **Feb 20**
    Telstar, **July 10**
  Year 7 (1963),
    Vostok 6, **June 16**
  Year 9 (1965),
    Voskhod 2, **Mar 18**
    Gemini 4, **June 3**
    Pegasus 1, **Sept 17**
    Venera 3, **Nov 16**
  Year 10 (1966),
    Gemini 12, **Nov 11**
  Year 12 (1968),
    OGO 5, **Mar 4**
    Apollo 8, **Dec 21**
  Year 13 (1969),
    Soyuz 4, **Jan 14**
    Apollo 11, **July 16**
    Moon Day, **July 20**
  Year 14 (1970) ,
    Osumi, **Feb 11**

Apollo 13, **Apr 11**
Space Rescue Agreement, **Oct 28**
Luna 17, **Nov 10**
Year 15 (1971),
Salyut, **Apr 19**
Mariner 9, **May 30**
Soyuz 11, **June 6**
Year 16 (1972),
Pioneer 10, **Mar 2**
Year 17 (1973),
Skylab, **May 14**
Year 19 (1975),
Apollo-Soyuz Linkup, **July 17**
Year 21 (1977),
Voyager 2, **Aug 20**
Voyager 1, **Sept 5**
Year 22 (1978),
Soyuz 28, **Mar 2**
Year 23 (1979),
Skylab Falls to Earth, **July 11**
Year 24 (1980),
Soyuz 37, **July 23**
Year 25 (1981),
Columbia STS-1, **Apr 12**
Year 26 (1982),
Kosmos 1383, **July 1**
Year 27 (1983),
NOAA 8, **Mar 28**
Challenger STS-7, **June 18**
Year 28 (1984),
Challenger STS-10, **Feb 3**
Soyuz T-12, **July 17**
Discovery, **Aug 30**
Year 29 (1985),
Arabsat-1, **Feb 8**
Year 30 (1986),
Mir Space Station, **Feb 20**
Year 32 (1988),
Discovery, **Sept 29**
Year 33 (1989),
Atlantis, **May 4**
Year 34 (1990),
Hubble Space Telescope, **Apr 25**
Year 36 (1992),
Endeavour, **May 13**
Year 39 (1995),
Atlantis Docks with Mir, **June 29**
Record Time, **Mar 22**
Galileo, **Dec 7**
Year 41 (1997),
Mars Pathfinder, **July 4**
Mars Global Surveyor, **Sept 11**
Cassini, **Oct 15**
Year 42 (1998),
Lunar Explorer, **Jan 6**
Columbia Neurolab, **Apr 17**
Nozomi, **July 4**
Discovery: Oldest Man in Space, **Oct 29**
International Space Station Launch, **Dec 4**
Mars Climate Orbiter, **Dec 11**
Year 43 (1999),
Stardust, **Feb 7**
Columbia: First Female Commander, **July 23**
Year 44 (2000),
Endeavour Mapping Mission, **Feb 11**
100th Space Shuttle Flight, **Oct 11**
ISS Inhabited, **Nov 2**
Spacek, Sissy: Birth, Dec 25
Spain,
Book Day and Lover's Day, **Apr 23**
Constitution Day, **Dec 6**
National Holiday, **Oct 12**
Spain Captures Granada: Anniv, **Jan 2**
Spanish Flu: Pandemic of 1918 Hits US: Anniv, Mar 11
Spanish-American War: Treaty of Paris Signed: Anniv, Dec 10
Spank Out Day USA, Apr 30
Speare, Elizabeth George: Birth Anniv, Nov 21
Spears, Britney: Birth, Dec 2
Special Olympics, First: Anniv, July 20
Specter, Arlen: Birth, Feb 12
Speech-Lang-Hearing Assn Conv, American (New Orleans, LA), Nov 15
Spelling Bee Finals, Natl, May 29
Spielberg, Steven: Birth, Dec 18
Spier, Peter: Birth, June 6
Spinelli, Jerry: Birth, Feb 1
Split Pea Soup Week, Natl, Nov 4
Splurge Day, Natl, June 18
Spock, Benjamin: Birth Anniv, May 2
Spooner's Day, July 22
Spooner, William: Birth Anniv, July 22
Sports: Sham El-Nesim (Egypt), Apr 20
Spotlight On Books (Alexandria, MN), Apr 12
Sprewell, Latrell: Birth, Sept 8
Spring Begins, Mar 20
Spring, Halfway Point, May 5
Springfield, Adam: Birth, Nov 2
Spyri, Johanna: Birth Anniv, July 12
Sri Lanka,
Independence Day, **Feb 4**
Natl Heroes Day, **May 22**
Sinhala and Tamil New Year, **Apr 13**
St. Laurent, Louis Stephen: Birth Anniv, Feb 1
Stabenow, Debbie: Birth, Apr 29
Stackhouse, Jerry: Birth, Nov 5
Staley, Dawn: Birth, May 4
Stamos, John: Birth, Aug 19
Stamps,
Postage Stamps, First Adhesive US: Anniv, **July 1**
Stamp Collecting Month, Natl, **Oct 1**
Stand for Children Day, June 1
Standard Time Act, US: Anniv, Mar 19
Stanley, Diane: Birth, Dec 27
Stanley, Jerry: Birth, July 18
Stanton, Elizabeth: Birth Anniv, Nov 12
Staples, Suzanne Fisher: Birth, Aug 27
Star Fest (Tanabata) (Japan), July 7
Star Trek TV Premiere: Anniv, Sept 8
Star-Spangled Banner Inspired: Anniv, Sept 13
Stars and Stripes Forever Day, May 14
State Constitution Day (MA), Oct 25
State Dept Founded, US: Anniv, July 27
State Fairs. See Agriculture
Statue of Liberty: Dedication Anniv, Oct 28
Stay Out of the Sun Day, July 3
Steig, William: Birth, Nov 14
Steptoe, John: Birth, Sept 14
Stevens, John Paul: Birth, Apr 20
Stevens, Ted: Birth, Nov 18
Stevenson, Adlai: Birth, Oct 23
Stevenson, Alexandra: Birth, Dec 15
Stevenson, James: Birth, July 11
Stevenson, Robert L.: Birth Anniv, Nov 13
Stewart, Kordell: Birth, Oct 16
Stewart, Patrick: Birth, July 13
Stewart, Potter: Birth Anniv, Jan 23
Stewart, Sarah: Birth, Aug 27
Still, Valerie: Birth, May 14
Stine, R.L.: Birth, Oct 8
Stinson, Andrea: Birth, Nov 25
Stock Exchange, NY, Established: Anniv, May 17
Stock Market Crash (1929): Anniv, Oct 29
Stockings, Nylon: Anniv, May 15
Stockton, John Houston: Birth, Mar 26
Stockton, Richard: Birth Anniv, Oct 1
Stojko, Elvis: Birth, Mar 22
Stokes, Carl: Becomes First Black Mayor in US: Anniv, Nov 13
Stone, Harlan Fiske: Birth Anniv, Oct 11
Stone, Lucy: Birth Anniv, Aug 13
Stone, Thomas: Death Anniv, Oct 5
Stookey, Paul: Birth, Nov 30
Stop the Violence Day, Natl, Nov 22
Story, Joseph: Birth Anniv, Sept 18
Storytelling,
Calgary Intl Children's Fest (Canada), **May 21**
Connecticut Storytelling Fest (New London, CT), **Apr 26**
Corn Island Storytelling Fest (Louisville, KY), **Sept 13**
Iowa Storytelling Fest (Clear Lake, IA), **July 26**
Michigan Storytellers Fest (Flint, MI), **July 5**
Northern Appalachian Story Fest (Mansfield, PA), **Sept 14**
Storyteller of the Year Contest, Natl (Millersport, OH), **Sept 1**
Storytelling Fest, Natl (Jonesborough, TN), **Oct 5**
Stoudamire, Damon: Birth, Sept 3
Stowe, Harriet Beecher: Birth Anniv, June 14
Stratemeyer, Edward L.: Birth Anniv, Oct 4
Strauss, Levi: Birth Anniv, Feb 26
Strawberry, Darryl: Birth, Mar 12
Street, Picabo: Birth, Apr 3
Strong, Rider: Birth, Dec 11
Strug, Kerri: Birth, Nov 19
Student Day, Natl, Sept 20
Student Government Day (MA), Apr 5
Student Volunteer Day, Feb 20
Stuttering Awareness Day, Intl, Oct 22
Submarine: Anniv of First Nuclear-Powered Voyage, Jan 17
Substitute Teacher Appreciation Week, Sept 9
Subway, New York City: Subway Anniv, Oct 27
Succoth, Oct 2
Sudan: Independence Day, Jan 1
Sue Exhibited: Anniv, May 17
Sukkot, Oct 2
Sukkot Begins, Oct 1
Sullivan, Anne: Birth Anniv, Apr 14
Summer Begins, June 21
Summer Daylight-Saving Time (Europe), Mar 31
Summer Time (United Kingdom), Mar 24
Summer, Halfway Point, Aug 6
Summers, Lawrence: Birth, Nov 30
Sun Yat-Sen: Birth Anniv, Nov 12
Sun Yat-Sen: Death Anniv, Mar 12
Sundquist, Don: Birth, Mar 15
Super Bowl (New Orleans, LA), Jan 27
Super Mario Brothers Released: Anniv, Oct 1
Supervision and Curriculum Development, Assn for, Convention (San Antonio, TX), Mar 9
Supreme Court Bans School Prayer: Anniv, June 25
Supreme Court Rules for Bush: Anniv, Dec 12
Supreme Court Term Begins, Oct 1
Supreme Court, First Session of: Anniv, Feb 1
Supreme Court: Brown v Board of Education: Anniv, May 17
Supreme Court: Woman Presides Over: Anniv, Apr 3
Suriname: Independence Day, Nov 25
Sutcliffe, Rosemary: Birth Anniv, Dec 14
Sutherland, Catherine: Birth, Oct 24
Sutherland, Kiefer: Birth, Dec 18
Sutter, John A.: Birth Anniv, Feb 15
Swallows Return to San Juan Capistrano, Mar 19
Swaziland,
Flag Day, Natl, **Apr 25**
Independence Day, **Sept 6**
Sweat, Lynn: Birth, May 27
Sweden,
All Saints' Day, **Nov 3**
Feast of Valborg, **Apr 30**
Flag Day, **June 6**
Gustavus Adolphus Day, **Nov 6**
Linnaeus Day (Stenbrohult), **May 23**
Nobel Prize Awards Ceremony (Stockholm), **Dec 10**
Saint Martin's Day, **Nov 11**

Santa Lucia Day, **Dec 13**
St. Knut's Day, **Jan 13**
Swedish Language and Culture Day Camp (Cambridge, MN), Aug 27
Sweetin, Jodie: Birth, Jan 19
Swimming and Diving,
First Woman Swims English Channel: Anniv, **Aug 6**
Swimming School Opens, First US, **July 23**
Switzerland,
Berchtoldstag, **Jan 2**
Chalandra Marz, **Mar 1**
Homstrom (Scuol), **Feb 3**
Meitlisunntig, **Jan 13**
Morat Battle: Anniv, **June 22**
National Day, **Aug 1**
Pacing the Bounds (Liestal), **May 6**
Swoopes, Sheryl: Birth, May 25
Symone, Raven: Birth, Dec 10
Syria,
Independence Day, **Apr 17**
Revolution Day, **Mar 8**
Ta'anit Esther (Fast of Esther), Feb 25
Taback, Simms: Birth, Feb 13
Tabaski: See Eid-al-Adha, Feb 22
Tabernacles, Feast of: First Day, Oct 2
Taft, Bob: Birth, Jan 8
Taft, Helen Herron: Birth Anniv, Jan 2
Taft, William H.: Birth Anniv, Sept 15
Taiwan,
Birthday of Cheng Huang, **June 23**
Birthday of Kuan Yin, Goddess of Mercy, **Apr 1**
Cheng Cheng Kung Landing Day, **Apr 29**
Cheng Cheng Kung: Birth Anniv, **Sept 1**
Chiang Kai-Shek Day, **Oct 31**
Confucius's Birthday and Teachers' Day, **Sept 28**
Constitution Day, **Dec 25**
Foundation Day, **Jan 1**
Lantern Fest and Tourism Day, **Feb 26**
Overseas Chinese Day, **Oct 21**
Retrocession Day, **Oct 25**
Tomb-Sweeping Day, Natl, **Apr 5**
Two-Twenty-Eight Day, **Feb 28**
Youth Day, **Mar 29**
Tajikistan: Independence Day, Sept 9
Take Charge of Your TV Week, Sept 24
Take Our Daughters to Work Day, Apr 25
Talk With Your Teen About Sex Month, Natl, Mar 1
Tallarico, Tony: Birth, Sept 20
Tammuz, Fast of, June 27
Taney, Roger B.: Birth Anniv, Mar 17
Tanzania,
Farmers' Day, **Aug 8**
Independence and Republic Day, **Dec 9**
Saba Saba Day, **July 7**
Union Day, **Apr 26**
Zanzibar Revolution Day, **Jan 12**
Tap Dance Day, Natl, May 25
Tate, Eleanor E.: Birth, Apr 16
Taurus Begins, Apr 20
Tax, Income, Pay Day, Apr 15
Taylor, George: Death Anniv, Feb 23
Taylor, Lucy Hobbs: Birth Anniv, Mar 14
Taylor, Margaret S.: Birth Anniv, Sept 21
Taylor, Mildred: Birth, Sept 13
Taylor, Sydney: Birth Anniv, Oct 31
Taylor, Theodore: Birth, June 23
Taylor, Zachary: Birth Anniv, Nov 24
TB Bacillus Discovered: Anniv, Mar 24
Tchaikovsky, Peter Ilich: Birth Anniv, May 7
Tea Month, Natl Hot, Jan 1
Teach Children to Save Day, Natl, Apr 18
Teacher Appreciation Week, Natl PTA, May 5
Teacher Day, Natl, May 7
Teacher's Day (MA), June 2
Teacher's Day in Florida, May 17
Teacher, Day of the (El Dia Del Maestro), May 8
Teachers of English, Natl Council of, Annual Convention (Baltimore, MD), Nov 15
Teachers of Mathematics, Natl Council of, Annual Mtg (Las Vegas, NV), Apr 22
Teachers' Day, Confucius's Birthday and (Taiwan), Sept 28
Teaching and Joy Month, Natl, May 1
Teague, Mark: Birth, Feb 10
Technology + Learning Conference (Atlanta, GA), Nov 7
Tecumseh: Death Anniv, Oct 5
Teddy Bear Day, Natl American, Nov 14
Teddy Bear: Anniv, Nov 18
Teen Read Week, Oct 14
Teflon Invented: Anniv, Apr 6
Telecommunication Day, World (UN), May 17
Telegraph Line, Morse Opens First US: Anniv, May 24
Telephone Operator, First: Emma M. Nutt Day, Sept 1
Telephone: Anniv, Mar 10
Television,
Abbott and Costello Show TV Premiere: Anniv, **Dec 5**
Addams Family Premiere: Anniv, **Sept 18**
Alvin Show Premiere: Anniv, **Oct 4**
Andy Griffith Show Premiere: Anniv, **Oct 3**
Arthur Premiere: Anniv, **Oct 7**
Barney & Friends Premiere: Anniv, **Apr 6**
Batman Premiere: Anniv, **Jan 12**
Between the Lions Premiere: Anniv, **Apr 3**
Brady Bunch Premiere: Anniv, **Sept 26**
Captain Kangaroo Premiere: Anniv, **Oct 3**
CBS Evening News Premiere: Anniv, **May 3**
Children's Day of Broadcasting, Intl, **Dec 9**
CNN Debuted: Anniv, **June 1**
Cosby Show Premiere: Anniv, **Sept 20**
Davy Crockett Premiere: Anniv, **Dec 15**
Ding Dong School Premiere: Anniv, **Dec 22**
Fat Albert and the Cosby Kids Premiere: Anniv, **Sept 9**
First Baseball Games Televised: Anniv, **Aug 26**
First Color TV Broadcast: Anniv, **June 25**
First Presidential Telecast: Anniv, **Apr 30**
First Televised Presidential Debate: Anniv, **Sept 26**
Flintstones TV Premiere: Anniv, **Sept 30**
Fraggle Rock Premiere: Anniv, **Sept 12**
Good Morning America Premiere: Anniv, **Nov 6**
Gumby Show Premiere: Anniv, **Mar 16**
Happy Days Premiere: Anniv, **Jan 15**
Home Improvement Premiere: Anniv, **Sept 17**
Howdy Doody Premiere: Anniv, **Dec 27**
I Love Lucy Premiere: Anniv, **Oct 15**
Jetsons Premiere: Anniv, **Sept 23**
Kukla, Fran and Ollie Premiere: Anniv, **Nov 29**
Lassie Premiere: Anniv, **Sept 12**
Leave It to Beaver Premiere: Anniv, **Oct 4**
Little House on the Prairie Premiere: Anniv, **Sept 11**
Lone Ranger Premiere: Anniv, **Sept 15**
Mickey Mouse Club Premiere: Anniv, **Oct 3**
Mighty Mouse Playhouse Premiere: Anniv, **Dec 10**
Mister Rogers' Neighborhood Premiere: Anniv, **May 22**
Muppet Show Premiere: Anniv, **Sept 13**
Nick at Nite: Anniv, **July 1**
Nickelodeon Channel Premiere: Anniv, **Apr 2**
Nielsen, Arthur Charles: Birth Anniv, **Sept 5**
Partridge Family Premiere: Anniv, **Sept 25**
Pokeman Debuts: Anniv, **Sept 28**
Public Television Debits: Anniv, **Nov 3**
Regular TV Broadcasts Begin: Anniv, **July 1**
Rocky and His Friends Premiere: Anniv, **Nov 19**
Roy Rogers Show Premiere: Anniv, **Dec 30**
Rugrats Premiere: Anniv, **Aug 11**
Sesame Street Premiere: Anniv, **Nov 10**
Sesame Street, Can You Tell Me How to Get to (St. Louis, MO), **Dec 8**
Simpsons Premiere: Anniv, **Jan 14**
Star Trek Premiere: Anniv, **Sept 8**
Take Charge of Your TV Week, **Sept 24**
Television Academy Hall of Fame First Inductees, **Mar 4**
TV-Turnoff Week, Natl, **Apr 22**
Vast Wasteland Speech: Anniv, **May 9**
Walt Disney Premiere: Anniv, **Oct 27**
Wishbone Premiere: Anniv, **Oct 9**
Wonder Years Premiere: Anniv, **Mar 15**
World Television Day, **Nov 21**
Tell Someone They're Doing a Good Job Week, Dec 16
Temperature, North America's Coldest Recorded: Anniv, Feb 3
Tennessee,
Admission Day, **June 1**
Oak Ridge Atomic Plant Begun: Anniv, **Aug 1**
Southern Fest of Books (Nashville), **Oct 12**
Storytelling Fest, Natl (Jonesborough), **Oct 5**
State Fair (Nashville), **Sept 7**
Tenniel, John: Birth Anniv, Feb 28
Teresa, Mother: Birth Anniv, Aug 27
TESOL Annual Conference (Salt Lake City, UT), Apr 9
Test Tube Baby Birth, July 25
Testaverde, Vinny: Birth, Nov 13
Tet: See Chinese New Year, Feb 12
Texas,
Admission Day, **Dec 29**
Alamo, Fall of the, **Mar 6**
Big Bend Natl Park: Anniv, **June 12**
Education Assn Meeting, Natl (Dallas), **June 30**
Elementary School Principals, Natl Assn of, Annual Conf (San Antonio), **Apr 6**
Emancipation Day, **June 19**
Galveston Hurricane: Anniv, **Sept 8**
Guadalupe Mountains Natl Park: Anniv, **Sept 30**
Independence Day, **Mar 2**
Juneteenth, **June 19**
PTA Convention, Natl (San Antonio), **June 22**
San Jacinto Day, **Apr 21**
State Fair (Dallas), **Sept 28**
Supervision and Curriculum Development, Assn for, Conference (San Antonio), **Mar 9**
Texas Book Fest (Austin), **Nov 2**
Texas PTA Conv (Dallas), **Nov 16**
Thailand,
Birth of the Queen, **Aug 12**
Chakri Day, **Apr 6**
Chulalongkorn Day, **Oct 23**
Constitution Day, **Dec 10**
Coronation Day, **May 5**
Elephant Round-Up at Surin, **Nov 17**
King's Birthday and National Day, **Dec 5**
Songkran Fest, **Apr 13**
Thank God It's Monday! Day, Natl, Jan 14
Thank You, School Librarian Day, Apr 4
Thanksgiving Day, Nov 22
Thanksgiving Day (Canada), Oct 8
Thanksgiving Day (Pres Proc), Nov 22
Thanksgiving Day Parade, Macy's (New York, NY), Nov 22
Thanksgiving Parade, Michigan (Detroit, MI), Nov 22
Theater,
Calgary Intl Children's Fest (Canada), **May 21**
First Play Presented in North American Colonies: Anniv, **Aug 27**
Laura Ingalls Wilder Pageant (De Smet, SD), **June 23**
Philadelphia Intl Children's Fest, **May 1**
Pittsburgh Intl Children's Fest (PA), **May 15**

Seattle Intl Children's Fest, **May 13**
Theater in North America, First Performance: Anniv, **Apr 30**
Theodore Roosevelt Natl Park: Anniv, Apr 25
Thicke, Alan: Birth, Mar 1
Third World Day: Anniv, Apr 18
Thomas, Clarence: Birth, June 23
Thomas, Craig: Birth, Feb 17
Thomas, Frank: Birth, May 27
Thomas, Isiah: Birth, Apr 30
Thomas, Jonathan Taylor: Birth, Sept 8
Thomas, Joyce Carol: Birth, May 25
Thomas, Marlo: Birth, Nov 21
Thompson, Emma: Birth, Apr 15
Thompson, Fred: Birth, Aug 19
Thompson, Jenny: Birth, Feb 26
Thompson, Kay: Birth Anniv, Nov 9
Thompson, Kenan: Birth, May 10
Thompson, Tina: Birth, Feb 10
Thompson, Tommy G.: Birth, Nov 19
Thoreau, Henry David: Birth Anniv, July 12
Thornton, Matthew: Death Anniv, June 24
Thorpe, James: Birth Anniv, May 28
Three Kings Day, Jan 6
Three Mile Island Nuclear Power Plant Accident: Anniv, Mar 28
Thumb, Tom: Birth Anniv, Jan 4
Thurber, James: Birth Anniv, Dec 8
Thurmond, Strom: Birth, Dec 5
Tiananmen Square Massacre: Anniv, June 4
Tides, Perigean Spring, Feb 27
Tides, Perigean Spring, Mar 28
Tides, Perigean Spring, Sept 17
Tides, Perigean Spring, Aug 18
Tierney, Maura: Birth, Feb 3
Timberlake, Justin: Birth, Jan 31
Time,
Daylight Saving Time Begins, US, **Apr 7**
Daylight Saving Time Ends, US, **Oct 28**
Leap Second Adjustment Time, **June 30**
Leap Second Adjustment Time, **Dec 31**
Prime Meridian Set: Anniv, **Nov 1**
Summer Daylight-Saving Time (Europe), **Mar 31**
Summer Time (United Kingdom), **Mar 24**
Time Zone Plan, US Uniform: Anniv, **Nov 18**
US Standard Time Act: Anniv, **Mar 19**
Time Magazine First Published: Anniv, Mar 3
Tin Can Patent: Anniv, Jan 19
Titanic, Sinking of the: Anniv, Apr 15
Titus, Eve: Birth, July 16
Tobacco: World No-Tobacco Day, May 31
Tobago,
Carnival (Port of Spain), **Feb 11**
Emancipation Day, **Aug 1**
Independence Day, **Aug 31**
Spiritual Baptist Liberation Shouter Day, **Mar 30**
Togo,
Independence Day, **Apr 27**
Liberation Day, **Jan 13**
Tolkien, J.R.R.: Birth Anniv, Jan 3
Toll Collection Machine, First Automatic: Anniv, Nov 19
Tom Sawyer Days, Natl (Hannibal, MO), July 3
Tomb-Sweeping Day, Natl (Taiwan), Apr 5
Tompkins, Daniel D.: Birth Anniv, June 21
Tonga: Emancipation Day, June 4
Torricelli, Robert G.: Birth, Aug 26
Tourism Week, Natl, May 5
Tournament of Roses Parade (Pasadena, CA), Jan 1
Town Meeting Day (VT), Mar 5
Town Watch: Natl Night Out, Aug 7
Towne, Benjamin: First American Daily Newspaper: Anniv, May 30
Trachtenberg, Michelle: Birth, Oct 11
Trade Week, World (Pres Proc), May 19
Transatlantic Flight, First Nonstop: Anniv, June 14
Transatlantic Phoning: Anniv, Jan 7
Transcontinental Flight, First Scheduled: Anniv, Jan 25
Transfer Day (US Virgin Islands), Mar 31
Transistor Invented: Anniv, Dec 23
Transportation Week, Natl (Pres Proc), May 12
Trapini, Iza: Birth, Jan 12
Travers, Mary: Birth, Nov 7
Travers, P.L.: Birth Anniv, Aug 9
Treasury Dept, US: Anniv, Sept 2
Treaty of Guadalupe Hidalgo: Anniv, Feb 2
Triangle Shirtwaist Fire: Anniv, Mar 25
Trick or Treat Night, Oct 31
Trinidad,
Carnival (Port of Spain), **Feb 11**
Emancipation Day, **Aug 1**
Independence Day, **Aug 31**
Indian Arrival Day (Port of Spain), **May 30**
Spiritual Baptist Liberation Shouter Day, **Mar 30**
Trinity Sunday, May 26
Tripp, Valerie: Birth, Sept 12
Trivia Day, Jan 4
Truancy Law: Anniv, Apr 12
Truman, Bess (Elizabeth): Birth Anniv, Feb 13
Truman, Harry S: Birth Anniv, May 8
Trust Your Intuition Day, May 10
Truth, Sojourner: Death Anniv, Nov 26
Tu B'Shvat, Jan 28
Tuba Day, Intl, May 3
Tubman, Harriet: Death Anniv, Mar 10
Tudor, Tasha: Burgess, Starling: Birth, Aug 28
Tunis, John: Birth Anniv, Dec 7
Tunisia,
Independence Day, **Mar 20**
Martyrs' Day, **Apr 9**
Republic Day, **July 25**
Women's Day, **Aug 13**
Turkey,
Earthquake: Anniv, **Aug 17**
National Sovereignty/Children's Day, **Apr 23**
Republic Day, **Oct 29**
Victory Day, **Aug 30**
Youth and Sports Day, **May 19**
Turkey Lovers' Month, June Is, June 1
Turkmenistan,
Independence Day, **Oct 27**
Neutrality Day, **Dec 12**
Revival and Unity Day, **May 18**
Turner, Megan Whalen: Birth, Nov 21
Turner, Ted: Birth, Nov 19
Tut, King: Tomb Discovery Anniv, Nov 4
Tuttle, Merlin: Birth, Aug 24
Tutu, Desmond: Birth, Oct 7
Tuvalu: National Holiday, Oct 1
Twain, Mark (Samuel Clemens): Birth Anniv, Nov 30
Twelfth Day (Epiphany), Jan 6
Twelfth Night, Jan 5
Tyler, John: Birth Anniv, Mar 29
Tyler, Julia G.: Birth Anniv, May 4
Tyler, Letitia Christian: Birth Anniv, Nov 12
Uchida, Yoshiko: Birth Anniv, Nov 24
Uganda,
Independence Day, **Oct 9**
Liberation Day, **Apr 11**
Ukraine,
Chernobyl Reactor Disaster: Anniv, **Apr 26**
Independence Day, **Aug 24**
October Revolution, **Nov 7**
Ukrainian Day, **Jan 22**
Ullman, Tracey: Birth, Dec 30
Umbrella Month, Natl, Mar 1
Underdog Day, Dec 21
UNESCO: Anniv, Nov 4
UNICEF Anniv [UN], Dec 11
Union of Soviet Socialist Republics,
Saint Petersburg Name Restored: Anniv, **Sept 6**
Soviet Union Dissolved: Anniv, **Dec 8**
United Arab Emirates: Natl Day (Independence), Dec 2
United Kingdom,
Boxing Day, **Dec 26**
Commonwealth Day, **Mar 11**
Coronation Day, **June 2**
Holocaust Memorial Day, **Jan 27**
Summer Time, **Mar 24**
Trooping Colours/Queen's Official Birthday, **June 8**
United Nations,
Biological Diversity, Intl Day of, **Dec 29**
Charter Signed: Anniv, **June 26**
Cooperatives, Intl Day of, **July 6**
Day for Tolerance, Intl, **Nov 16**
Decade for a Culture of Peace and Non-Violence for the Children of the World, Intl, **Jan 1**
Disabled Persons, Intl Day of, **Dec 3**
Disarmament Week, **Oct 24**
Drug Abuse/Illicit Trafficking, Intl Day Against, **June 26**
Eradication of Poverty, Decade for the, **Jan 1**
Families, Intl Day of, **May 15**
General Assembly Opening Day, **Sept 18**
Human Rights Day, **Dec 10**
Human Rights Education, Decade for, **Jan 1**
Indigenous People, Intl Decade of World's, **Jan 1**
Innocent Children Victims of Aggression, Intl Day of, **June 4**
Intl Civil Aviation Day, **Dec 7**
Intl Day of Peace, **Sept 18**
Intl Day of the World's Indigenous People, **Aug 9**
Intl Year of Volunteers, **Aug 1**
Literacy Day, Intl, **Sept 8**
Natural Disaster Reduction, Intl Day for, **Oct 10**
Older Persons, Intl Day for, **Oct 1**
Poverty, Intl Day for Eradication, **Oct 17**
Preservation of the Ozone Layer, Intl Day for, **Sept 16**
Racial Discrimination, Intl Day for Elimination of, **Mar 21**
Racism/Racial Discrimination, Third Decade to Combat, **Dec 10**
Telecommunication Day, World, **May 17**
UNESCO: Anniv, **Nov 4**
UNICEF Anniv, **Dec 11**
UNICEF Day, Natl (Pres Proc), **Oct 31**
United Nations Day, **Oct 24**
United Nations Day (Pres Proc), **Oct 24**
United Nations General Assembly: Anniv, **Jan 10**
Universal Children's Day, **Nov 20**
Volunteer Day for Economic/Social Dvmt, Intl, **Dec 5**
Water, World Day for, **Mar 22**
Women's Day, Intl, **Mar 8**
World AIDS Day, **Dec 1**
World AIDS Day (US observance), **Dec 1**
World Book and Copyright Day, **Apr 23**
World Day to Combat Desertification and Drought, **June 17**
World Development Information Day, **Oct 24**
World Environment Day, **June 5**
World Food Day, **Oct 16**
World Habitat Day, **Oct 1**
World Health Day, **Apr 7**
World Health Organization: Anniv, **Apr 7**
World Meteorological Day, **Mar 23**
World Population Day, **July 11**
World Post Day, **Oct 9**
World Press Freedom Day, **May 3**
World Television Day, **Nov 21**
Year of Dialogue Among Civilizations, **Aug 1**
United States (government and history),
Air Force Established: Birth, **Sept 18**
Army Established: Anniv, **June 14**
Blacks Ruled Eligible to Vote: Anniv, **Apr 3**

Bureau of Indian Affairs Established, **Mar 11**
Capitol Cornerstone Laid: Anniv, **Sept 18**
Civil Rights Act of 1964: Anniv, **July 2**
Clinton Impeachment Proceedings: Anniv, **Dec 20**
Coins Stamped "In God We Trust": Anniv, **Apr 22**
Colonies Become US: Anniv, **Sept 9**
Congress Assembles, **Jan 3**
Congress First Meets in Washington: Anniv, **Nov 21**
Congress: First Meeting Anniv, **Mar 4**
Constitution of the US: Anniv, **Sept 17**
Department of Defense Created: Anniv, **July 26**
Dept of Justice: Anniv, **June 22**
Dept of State Founded: Anniv, **July 27**
Family-Leave Bill: Anniv, **Feb 5**
Federal Communications Commission Created: Anniv, **Feb 26**
Female House Page, First: Anniv, **May 14**
55 mph Speed Limit: Anniv, **Jan 2**
First Census: Anniv, **Aug 1**
First US Income Tax: Anniv, **Mar 8**
Flag Amendment Defeated: Anniv, **June 26**
Independence Day, **July 4**
Japanese Internment: Anniv, **Feb 19**
Johnson Impeachment Proceedings: Anniv, **Feb 24**
Library of Congress: Anniv, **Apr 24**
NAFTA Signed: Anniv, **Dec 8**
Nuclear-Free World, First Step Toward a: Anniv, **Dec 8**
Paper Money Issued: Anniv, **Mar 10**
Peace Corps Founded: Anniv, **Mar 1**
Persian Gulf War Begins: Anniv, **Jan 16**
Philippine Independence: Anniv, **Mar 24**
Postmaster General Established: Anniv, **Sept 22**
President First Occupies White House: Anniv, **Nov 1**
Presidential Succession Act: Anniv, **July 18**
Ratification Day, **Jan 14**
Sanctions Against South Africa Lifted: Anniv, **July 10**
Senate Quorum: Anniv, **Apr 6**
Standard Time Act: Anniv, **Mar 19**
Supreme Court Bans School Prayer: Anniv, **June 25**
Treasury Department: Anniv, **Sept 2**
Treaty of Guadalupe Hidalgo (with Mexico): Anniv, **Feb 2**
27th Amendment Ratified: Anniv, **May 19**
Uniform Time Zone Plan: Anniv, **Nov 18**
US Capital Established at NYC: Anniv, **Sept 13**
US Enters WWI: Anniv, **Apr 6**
US Mint: Anniv, **Apr 2**
Vietnam Peace Agreement Signed: Anniv, **Jan 27**
WAAC: Anniv, **May 14**
War Department: Establishment Anniv, **Aug 7**
War of 1812: Declaration Anniv, **June 18**
War on Poverty: Anniv, **Jan 8**
Water Pollution Control Act: Anniv, **Oct 18**
What Do You Love About America Day, **Nov 21**
White House Easter Egg Roll: Anniv, **Apr 2**
UNIVAC Computer: Anniv, June 14
Universal Human Rights Month, Dec 1
Universal Letter-Writing Week, Jan 8
Unmasking Halloween Dangers, Oct 1
Up Helly AA (Scotland), Jan 29
Uranus (planet) Discovery: Anniv, Mar 13
Uruguay,
Artigas Day, **June 19**
Battle of Las Piedras Day, **May 18**
Constitution Day, **July 18**
Independence Day, **Aug 25**
US Air Force Academy Established: Anniv, Mar 31
US House, Black Page Appointed: Anniv, Apr 9
US Military Academy Founded: Anniv, Mar 16
US Naval Academy Founded: Anniv, Oct 10
US Navy: Authorization Anniv, Oct 13
US Virgin Islands,
Danish West Indies Emancipation Day, **July 3**
Hurricane Supplication Day, **July 22**
Hurricane Thanksgiving Day, **Oct 15**
Liberty Day, **Nov 1**
Organic Act Day, **June 17**
Puerto Rico Friendship Day, **Oct 8**
Transfer Day, **Mar 31**
Virgin Islands Natl Park: Anniv, **Aug 2**
Utah,
Admission Day, **Jan 4**
America's First Department Store (Salt Lake City), **Oct 16**
Arches Natl Park: Anniv, **Nov 12**
Bryce Canyon Natl Park: Anniv, **Jan 1**
Capitol Reef Natl Park: Anniv, **Dec 18**
Pioneer Day, **July 24**
State Fair (Salt Lake City), **Sept 6**
TESOL Annual Conference (Salt Lake City), **Apr 9**
Winter Olympics Closing Ceremony (Salt Lake City), **Feb 24**
Winter Olympics Opening Ceremony (Salt Lake City), **Feb 8**
Zion Natl Park: Anniv, **Nov 19**
Uzbekistan,
Constitution Day, **Dec 10**
Independence Day, **Sept 1**
V-E Day, May 8
V-J Day (Announcement), Aug 14
V-J Day (Ratification), Sept 2
Valderrama, Carlos: Birth, Sept 2
Valentine's Day, Feb 14
Valenzuela, Fernando: Birth, Nov 1
Van Allsburg, Chris: Birth, June 18
Van Buren, Hannah Hoes: Birth Anniv, Mar 8
Van Buren, Martin: Birth Anniv, Dec 5
Van Der Beek, James: Birth, Mar 8
Van Dyke, Dick: Birth, Dec 13
Van Exel, Nick: Birth, Nov 27
Van Gogh, Vincent: Birth Anniv, Mar 30
Van Horn, Keith: Birth, Oct 23
Van Laan, Nancy: Birth, Nov 18
Van Leuween, Jean: Birth, Dec 26
VanCleave, Janice: Birth, Jan 27
Vanuatu: Independence Day, July 30
Vatican City: Independence Anniv, Feb 11
Vatican Council II: Anniv, Oct 11
VCR Introduced: Anniv, June 7
Veep Day, Aug 9
Vegetarian Awareness Month, Oct 1
Vegetarian Day, World, Oct 1
Vegetarian Resource Group's Essay Contest for Kids, May 1
VelJohnson, Reginald: Birth, Aug 16
Veneman, Ann: Birth, June 29
Venezuela,
Battle of Carabobo Day, **June 24**
Independence Day, **July 5**
Ventura, Jesse: Birth, July 15
Vermont,
Admission Day, **Mar 4**
Children's Day (Woodstock), **Aug 25**
State Fair (Rutland), **Aug 31**
Town Meeting Day, **Mar 5**
Verne, Jules: Birth Anniv, Feb 8
Verrazano Day, Apr 17
Vesey, Denmark: Death Anniv, July 2
Vespucci, Amerigo: Birth Anniv, Mar 9
Vesuvius Day, Aug 24
Veterans Day, Nov 12
Veterans Day, Nov 11
Veterans Day (Pres Proc), Nov 11
Victoria Day (Canada), May 20
Victory in Europe Day, May 8
Video Games Day, Sept 12
Vietnam,
Anniversary of the Founding of the Communist Party, **Feb 3**
Ho Chi Minh's Birthday, **May 19**
Independence Day, **Sept 2**
Liberation Day, **Apr 30**
Tet: See Chinese New Year, **Feb 12**
Vietnam War,
Dien Bien Phu Falls: Anniv, **May 7**
King Opposes Vietnam War: Anniv, **Apr 4**
Vietnam Conflict Begins [with French]: Anniv, **Aug 22**
Vietnam Peace Agreement Signed: Anniv, **Jan 27**
Viking: Up Helly AA (Scotland), Jan 29
Villeneuve, Jacques: Birth, Apr 9
Vilsack, Tom: Birth, Dec 13
Vining, Elizabeth Gray: Birth Anniv, Oct 6
Vinson, Fred M.: Birth Anniv, Jan 22
Violence Day, Natl Stop the, Nov 22
Violence, YWCA Week Without, Oct 21
Viorst, Judith: Birth, Feb 2
Virginia,
Children's Fest, Intl (Vienna), **Sept 15**
Chincoteague Pony Penning (Chincoteague Island), **July 31**
Lee-Jackson Day, **Jan 18**
Ratification Day, **June 25**
Shenandoah Natl Park: Anniv, **Dec 26**
State Fair on Strawberry Hill (Richmond), **Sept 27**
Virginia Children's Fest (Norfolk), **Oct 27**
Yorktown Day (Yorktown), **Oct 19**
Yorktown Victory Day, **Oct 8**
Virginia Company Expedition to America: Anniv, Dec 20
Virginia Hamilton Conference (Kent, OH), Apr 4
Virginia Plan Proposed: Anniv, May 29
Virgo Begins, Aug 23
Visit Your Relatives Day, May 18
Vitamin C Isolated: Anniv, Apr 4
Voigt, Cynthia: Birth, Feb 25
Voinovich, George V.: Birth, July 15
Volcanoes: Montserrat: Volcano Erupts: Anniv, June 25
Volcanoes: Cameroon: Eruption: Anniv, Aug 22
Volcanoes: Mount Pinatubo Erupts in Philippines: Anniv, June 11
Volcanoes: Mount Saint Helens Eruption: Anniv, May 18
Volcanoes: Vesuvius Day, Aug 24
Volunteer Day for Economic/Social Dvmt, Intl (UN), Dec 5
Volunteer Day, Student, Feb 20
Volunteer Week, Natl, Apr 21
Volunteer Week, Natl (Pres Proc), Apr 21
Volunteers Week, Intl, June 1
Volunteers: Make a Difference Day, Oct 27
Volunteers: UN: Year of Volunteers, Intl, Aug 1
Von Oy, Jenna: Birth, May 2
von Steuben, Baron Friedrich: Birth Anniv, Sept 17
Vonnegut, Kurt, Jr: Birth, Nov 11
Vote: Blacks Ruled Eligible to Vote: Anniv, Apr 3
Voting Age Changed (26th Amendment): Anniv, June 30
Voting Rights Act Signed: Anniv, Aug 6
Voyageurs Natl Park: Anniv, Apr 8
Waber, Bernard: Birth, Sept 27
Waddell, Martin: Birth, Apr 10
Wadlow, Robert Pershing: Birth Anniv, Feb 22
Wagner, Honus: Birth Anniv, Feb 24
Wahlberg, Mark: Birth, June 5
Waitangi Day (New Zealand), Feb 6
Waite, Morrison R.: Birth Anniv, Nov 29
Waldseemuller, Martin: Remembrance Day, Apr 25
Wales: Saint David's Day, Mar 1

Walesa, Lech: Birth, **Sept 29**
Walesa, Lech: Solidarity Founded Anniv, **Aug 31**
Walk Our Children to School Day, Natl, **Oct 2**
Walk Our Children to School Week, Natl, **Oct 1**
Walker, Antoine: Birth, **Aug 12**
Walker, Larry: Birth, **Dec 1**
Walker, Madame C.J.: Birth Anniv, **Dec 23**
Walkman Debuts: Anniv, **July 1**
Wallace, Henry A.: Birth Anniv, **Oct 7**
Wallace, Karen: Birth, **Apr 1**
Wallenberg, Raoul: Birth Anniv, **Aug 5**
Waller, Tisha: Birth, **Dec 1**
Walt Disney TV Premiere: Anniv, **Oct 27**
Walter, Mildred Pitts: Birth, **Sept 9**
Walters, Barbara: Birth, **Sept 25**
Walton, George: Death Anniv, **Feb 2**
Wang, Garrett: Birth, **Dec 15**
War of 1812: Declaration Anniv, **June 18**
War on Poverty: Anniv, **Jan 8**
Warner Weather Quotation: Anniv, **Aug 24**
Warner, John William: Birth, **Feb 18**
Warner, Kurt: Birth, **June 22**
Warren, Earl: Birth Anniv, **Mar 19**
Washington,
- Admission Day, **Nov 11**
- Mount Rainier Natl Park: Anniv, **Mar 2**
- North Cascades Natl Park: Anniv, **Oct 2**
- Seattle Intl Children's Fest, **May 13**

Washington, Booker T.: Birth Anniv, **Apr 5**
Washington, Denzel: Birth, **Dec 28**
Washington, District of Columbia,
- American Council on Teaching of Foreign Languages, **Nov 16**
- Discovery Young Scientist Challenge, **Oct 20**
- District Establishing Legislation: Anniv, **July 16**
- Geography Bee Finals, Natl, **May 21**
- Invasion Anniv, **Aug 24**
- Middle School Assn, Natl, Annual Conf, **Nov 1**
- Social Studies, Natl Council for the, Annual Mtg, **Nov 16**
- Spelling Bee Finals, Natl, **May 29**
- Washington Monument Dedicated: Anniv, **Feb 21**
- Youth of the Year, Natl, **Sept 26**

Washington, George,
- Address to Continental Army Officers: Anniv, **Mar 15**
- Birth Anniv, **Feb 22**
- Birthday Observance (Legal Holiday), **Feb 18**
- Presidential Inauguration Anniv, **Apr 30**
- White House Cornerstone Laid: Anniv, **Oct 13**

Washington, Martha: Birth Anniv, **June 21**
Water-Drawing Fest (Japan), **Mar 1**
Waterton-Glacier Intl Peace Park: Anniv, **May 11**
Watson, Barry: Birth, **Apr 23**
Watson, Clyde: Birth, **July 25**
Wayne, "Mad Anthony": Birth Anniv, **Jan 1**
Weather,
- Meteorological Day, World (UN), **Mar 23**
- North America's Coldest Recorded Temperature: Anniv, **Feb 3**
- Warmest US Winter on Record, **Mar 20**
- Warner Quotation: Anniv, **Aug 24**
- Weather Observer's Day, Natl, **May 4**
- Weatherman's Day, **Feb 5**

Weatherspoon, Teresa: Birth, **Dec 8**
Weaver, Robert C.: First Black US Cabinet Member: Anniv, **Jan 18**
Weaver, Will: Birth, **Jan 19**
Webster, Noah: Birth Anniv, **Oct 16**
Webster-Ashburton Treaty Signed: Anniv, **Aug 9**
Wechsler, Doug: Birth, **Apr 2**
Wedding of the Giants (Belgium), **Aug 26**
Wedding of the Sea (Venice, Italy), **May 12**
Week of the Ocean, Natl, **Apr 7**
Wegman, William: Birth, **Dec 2**
Weights and Measures Day, **May 20**
Weizmann, Chaim: Birth Anniv, **Nov 27**
Welfare. See Health and Welfare
Wells, David: Birth, **May 20**
Wells, Ida B.: Birth Anniv, **July 16**
Wells, Rosemary: Birth, **Jan 29**
Wellstone, Paul D.: Birth, **July 21**
West Point Bicentennial Engineering Design Contest, **Nov 11**
West Virginia,
- Admission Day, **June 20**

West, Togo D.: Birth, **June 21**
Weston, Martha: Birth, **Jan 16**
Whale Awareness Day (MA), **May 2**
What Do You Love About America Day, **Nov 21**
Wheatley, Phillis: Death Anniv, **Dec 5**
Wheeler, William A.: Birth Anniv, **June 30**
Whelan, Gloria: Birth, **Nov 23**
Whiner's Day, Natl, **Dec 26**
Whipple, William: Birth Anniv, **Jan 14**
White Cane Safety Day (Pres Proc), **Oct 15**
White House Cornerstone Laid: Anniv, **Oct 13**
White House Easter Egg Roll, **Apr 1**
White Sunday (American Samoa), **Oct 14**
White Sunday (Samoa), **Oct 14**
White, Byron R.: Birth, **June 8**
White, E.B.: Birth Anniv, **July 11**
White, Edward Douglass: Birth Anniv, **Nov 3**
White, Jaleel: Birth, **Nov 27**
White, Reggie: Birth, **Dec 19**
White, Ruth: Birth, **Mar 15**
White, Ryan: Death Anniv, **Apr 8**
Whitman, Christine T.: Birth, **Sept 26**
Whitman, Walt: Birth Anniv, **May 31**
Whitmonday, **May 20**
Whitsunday, **May 19**
Whole Language Umbrella Conference, **July 24**
Wick, Walter: Birth, **Feb 23**
Wiesner, David: Birth, **Feb 5**
Wiggin, Kate Douglas: Birth Anniv, **Sept 28**
Wilder, Gene: Birth, **June 11**
Wilder, L. Douglas: First Black Governor Elected: Anniv, **Nov 7**
Wilder, Laura Ingalls Gingerbread Sociable (Pomona, CA), **Feb 2**
Wilder, Laura Ingalls: Birth Anniv, **Feb 7**
Wildlife Week, Natl, **Apr 15**
Wilkins, Roy: Birth Anniv, **Aug 30**
Willard, Frances E. C.: Birth Anniv, **Sept 28**
Willard, Nancy: Birth, **June 26**
William the Conqueror: Death Anniv, **Sept 9**
William, Prince: Birth, **June 21**
Williams, Archie: Birth Anniv, **May 1**
Williams, Garth: Birth Anniv, **Apr 16**
Williams, Jayson: Birth, **Feb 22**
Williams, Margery: See Bianco, Margery Williams: Birth Anniv, **July 22**
Williams, Natalie: Birth, **Nov 30**
Williams, Ricky: Birth, **May 21**
Williams, Robin: Birth, **July 21**
Williams, Serena: Birth, **Sept 26**
Williams, Ted: Birth, **Aug 30**
Williams, Venus: Birth, **June 17**
Williams, Vera B.: Birth, **Jan 28**
Williams, William: Birth Anniv, **Apr 8**
Willis, Bruce: Birth, **Mar 19**
Wilson, Edith: Birth Anniv, **Oct 15**
Wilson, Ellen L.: Birth Anniv, **May 15**
Wilson, Henry: Birth Anniv, **Feb 16**
Wilson, James: Birth Anniv, **Sept 14**
Wilson, Mara: Birth, **July 24**
Wilson, Woodrow: Birth Anniv, **Dec 28**
Wind Cave Natl Park: Anniv, **Jan 3**
Windmill Day, Natl (Netherlands), **May 11**
Winfrey, Oprah: Birth, **Jan 29**
Winkerbean, Funky: Anniv, **Mar 27**
Winkler, Henry: Birth, **Oct 30**
Winslet, Kate: Birth, **Oct 5**
Winter Begins, **Dec 21**
Winter Solstice: Yalda (Iran), **Dec 21**
Winter, Halfway Point, **Feb 3**
Winter, Jeanette: Birth, **Oct 6**
Winthrop, Elizabeth: Birth, **Sept 14**
Wisconsin,
- Admission Day, **May 29**
- Christmas at the Top Museum (Burlington), **Dec 27**
- Laura Ingalls Wilder Festival (Pepin), **Sept 15**
- State Fair (Milwaukee), **Aug 3**
- Yo-Yo Days (Burlington), **Apr 13**

Wise, Bob: Birth, **Jan 6**
Wishbone TV Premiere: Anniv, **Oct 9**
Wisniewski, David: Birth, **Mar 21**
Witherspoon, John: Birth Anniv, **Feb 5**
Witt, Katarina: Birth, **Dec 3**
Wizard of Oz First Released: Anniv, **Aug 25**
Wojciechowska, Maia: Birth, **Aug 7**
Wojtyla: Pope John Paul II: Birth, **May 18**
Wolcott, Oliver: Birth Anniv, **Nov 20**
Wolf, Bernard: Birth, **Feb 26**
Wolf, Scott: Birth, **June 4**
Wolfe, James: Birth Anniv, **Jan 2**
Women,
- Around the World in 72 Days: Anniv, **Nov 14**
- Blackwell, Elizabeth, Awarded MD: Anniv, **Jan 23**
- Bloomer, Amelia Jenks: Birth Anniv, **May 27**
- Campbell, Kim, First Woman Prime Minister, **June 25**
- Catt, Carrie Chapman: Birth Anniv, **Jan 9**
- English Channel, First Woman Swims: Anniv, **Aug 6**
- Equal Rights Amendment Sent to States for Ratification: Anniv, **Mar 22**
- Female House Page, First: Anniv, **May 14**
- First American Woman in Space: Anniv, **June 18**
- First US Woman Governor Inaugurated, **Jan 5**
- First Woman in Space: Space Milestone, **June 16**
- First Woman Rabbi in US: Anniv, **June 3**
- First Woman Supreme Court Justice: Anniv, **Sept 25**
- First Woman to Graduate Dental School: Anniv, **Feb 21**
- First Woman to Walk in Space, **July 17**
- First Women's Collegiate Basketball Game: Anniv, **Mar 22**
- Girls and Women in Sports Day, Natl, **Feb 7**
- Medical School for Women Opened: Anniv, **Nov 1**
- Meitlisunntig (Switzerland), **Jan 13**
- Mott, Lucretia: Birth Anniv, **Jan 3**
- 19th Amendment Ratified, **Aug 18**
- NOW Founded: Anniv, **June 30**
- Pocahontas: Death Anniv, **Mar 21**
- Russia: Women's Day, Intl, **Mar 8**
- Salter Elected First Woman Mayor in US: Anniv, **Apr 4**
- Stanton, Elizabeth: Birth Anniv, **Nov 12**
- Stone, Lucy: Birth Anniv, **Aug 13**
- Susan B. Anthony Fined for Voting: Anniv, **June 6**
- Take Our Daughters to Work Day, **Apr 25**
- Truth, Sojourner: Death Anniv, **Nov 26**
- WAAC: Anniv, **May 14**
- Willard, Frances E.C.: Birth Anniv, **Sept 28**
- Woman Presides Over US Supreme Court: Anniv, **Apr 3**
- Women's Day, Intl (UN), **Mar 8**
- Women's Equality Day, **Aug 26**
- Women's Equality Day (Pres Proc), **Aug 26**
- Women's History Month (Pres Proc), **Mar 1**
- Women's History Month, Natl, **Mar 1**

Women's Rights Convention Held (Seneca Falls): Anniv, **July 19**
Women's Suffrage Amendment Introduced: Anniv, **Jan 10**
Working Women's Day, Intl, **Mar 8**
YWCA Week, Natl, **Apr 21**
Wonder Years Premiere: Anniv, Mar 15
Wonder, Stevie: Birth, May 13
Wood, Don: Birth, May 4
Wood, Elijah: Birth, Jan 28
Wood, Grant: Birth Anniv, Feb 13
Wood, Kerry: Birth, June 16
Woodard, Alfre: Birth, Nov 8
Woods, Tiger: Birth, Dec 30
Woodson, Carter Godwin: Birth Anniv, Dec 19
Woodson, Jacqueline: Birth, Feb 12
Woolworths Opened: Anniv, Feb 22
Working Women's Day, Intl, Mar 8
World AIDS Day (Pres Proc), Dec 1
World Communion Sunday, Oct 7
World Cup Inaugurated: Anniv, July 13
World Cup Korea/Japan, May 31
World Day of Prayer, Mar 1
World Food Day, Oct 16
World Health Organization: Anniv, Apr 7
World Juggling Day, June 15
World Peace Day, Nov 17
World Religion Day, Jan 20
World Television Day, Nov 21
World Trade Week (Pres Proc), May 19
World War I,
Anzac Day, **Apr 25**
Armistice: Anniv, **Nov 11**
Battle of the Marne: Anniv, **July 15**
Battle of Verdun, **Feb 21**
Begins: Anniv, **July 28**
Treaty of Versailles: Anniv, **June 28**
US Enters: Anniv, **Apr 6**
World War II,
Atomic Bomb Dropped on Hiroshima: Anniv, **Aug 6**
Atomic Bomb Dropped on Nagasaki: Anniv, **Aug 9**
Atomic Bomb Tested: Anniv, **July 16**
Battle of the Bulge: Anniv, **Dec 16**
D-Day: Anniv, **June 6**
Diary of Anne Frank: Last Entry: Anniv, **Aug 1**
Gasoline Rationing: Anniv, **May 15**
Germany's First Surrender: Anniv, **May 7**
Germany's Second Surrender: Anniv, **May 8**
Italy Surrenders: Anniv, **Sept 3**
Iwo Jima Day, **Feb 23**
Japan's Unconditional Surrender: Anniv, **Aug 10**
Japanese Internment: Anniv, **Feb 19**
Kristallnacht: Anniv, **Nov 9**
Liberation of Buchenwald: Anniv, **Apr 11**
MacArthur Returns to the Philippines: Anniv, **Oct 20**
Oak Ridge Atomic Plant Begun: Anniv, **Aug 1**
Paris Liberated: Anniv, **Aug 25**
Pearl Harbor Day, **Dec 7**
Pearl Harbor Remembrance Day, Natl (Pres Proc), **Dec 7**
Raising Flag on Iwo Jima: Hayes, Ira: Birth Anniv, **Jan 12**
Roosevelt, Franklin D.: Death Anniv, **Apr 12**
Russia: Victory Day, **May 9**
V-E Day, **May 8**
V-J Day (Announcement), **Aug 14**
V-J Day (Ratification), **Sept 2**
WAAC: Anniv, **May 14**
World Wide Web: Anniv, Aug 1
Wounded Knee Massacre: Anniv, Dec 29
Wozniak, Stephen: Birth, Aug 11
Wrangell-Saint Elias Natl Park: Anniv, Dec 2
Wrede, Patricia: Birth, Mar 27
Wright Brothers Day (Pres Proc), Dec 17
Wright Brothers' First Powered Flight: Anniv, Dec 17
Wright, Betty Ren: Birth, June 15
Wright, Frank Lloyd: Birth Anniv, June 8
Wright, Orville: Birth Anniv, Aug 19
Wright, Richard: Birth Anniv, Sept 4
Wright, Wilbur: Birth Anniv, Apr 16
Writing: Heart 2 Heart Day, Feb 16
Wyden, Ron: Birth, May 3
Wyoming,
Admission Day, **July 10**
First US Woman Governor Inaugurated, **Jan 5**
State Fair (Douglas), **Aug 11**
Yellowstone Natl Park: Anniv, **Mar 1**
Wythe, George: Death Anniv, June 8
X-Ray Discovery Day: Anniv, Nov 8
Yalda (Iran), Dec 21
Yamaguchi, Kristi: Birth, July 12
Yankee Stadium Opens, Apr 18
Yankovic, Al: Birth, Oct 23
Yawm Arafat (Islamic): The Standing at Arafat, Feb 21
Yeager, Chuck: Birth, Feb 13
Yell "Fudge" at the Cobras in North America Day, June 2
Yellowstone Natl Park: Anniv, Mar 1
Yeltsin, Boris, Inaugurated Russian President: Anniv, July 10
Yeltsin, Boris: Birth, Feb 1
Yemen: Natl Day, May 22
Yep, Laurence: Birth, June 14
YMCA Healthy Kids Day, Apr 6
YMCA Organized: Anniv, Dec 29
Yo-Yo Days (Burlington, WI), Apr 13
Yolen, Jane: Birth, Feb 11
Yom Hashoah (Israel), Apr 9
Yom Kippur, Sept 27
Yom Kippur Begins, Sept 26
Yom Kippur War, Oct 6
Yorinks, Arthur: Birth, Aug 21
Yorktown Day, Oct 19
Yorktown Day (Yorktown, VA), Oct 19
Yorktown Victory Day (VA), Oct 8
Yosemite Natl Park Established: Anniv, Oct 1
Young Adolescent, Month of the, Oct 1
Young Child, Month of the (MI), Apr 1
Young Eagles Day, Intl, June 8
Young Inventors Awareness Week, Mar 10
Young Peoples' Poetry Week, Apr 15
Young, Cy: Birth Anniv, Mar 29
Young, Ed: Birth, Nov 28
Young, Steve: Birth, Oct 11
Yount, Robin: Birth, Sept 16
Youth Appreciation Week, Nov 12
Youth Art Month, Mar 1
Youth Day, Mar 29
Youth Day (Cameroon), Feb 11
Youth Day (China), May 4
Youth of the Year, Natl (Washington, DC), Sept 26
Youth Service Day, Natl, Apr 19
Youth Sports Safety Month, Natl, Apr 1
Youth: Sea Cadet Month, Sept 1
Yugoslavia,
Civil War: Anniv, **June 25**
National Day, **Apr 27**
NATO Attacks: Anniv, **Mar 25**
Slovenia and Croatia Independence: Anniv, **June 25**
YWCA Week Without Violence, Oct 21
YWCA Week, Natl, Apr 21
Z Day, Jan 1
Zaharias, Mildred Babe Didrikson: Birth Anniv, June 26
Zaire. See Congo (Kinshasa)
ZAM! Zoo and Aquarium Month, Apr 1
Zambia,
African Freedom Day, **May 25**
Heroes Day, **July 1**
Independence Day, **Oct 22**
Unity Day, **July 2**
Youth Day, **Aug 6**
Zegers, Kevin: Birth, Sept 19
Zelinsky, Paul O.: Birth, Feb 14
Zemach, Margot: Birth Anniv, Nov 30
Ziefert, Harriet: Birth, July 7
Zimbabwe,
African Freedom Day, **May 25**
Heroes' Day, **Aug 11**
Independence Day, **Apr 18**
Zindel, Paul: Birth, May 15
Zion Natl Park: Anniv, Nov 19
Zion, Gene: Birth Anniv, Oct 5
Zip Codes Inaugurated: Anniv, July 1
Zipper Patented: Anniv, Apr 29
Zolotin, Adam: Birth, Nov 29
Zolotow, Charlotte: Birth, June 26